THE MEDIEVAL WO1

This groundbreaking collection brings the Middle Ages to life, and conveys the distinctiveness of this diverse, constantly changing period. From the contributions of thirty-eight scholars, one medieval world merges from many disparate worlds, stretching from Connacht to Constantinople and from Tynemouth to Timbuktu. This remarkable set of reconstructions presents the reader with the future of the medieval past, offering fresh appraisals of the evidence and of modern historical writing.

Chapters are thematically linked in four sections:

- identities in the medieval world
- beliefs, social values and symbolic order
- power and power structures
- elites, organisations and groups

This volume is packed full of original scholarship and is set to become essential reading for anyone studying medieval history.

Contributors: Stuart Airlie, Mario Ascheri, Agostino Paravicini Bagliani, Dominique Barthélemy, Nora Berend, Peter Biller, Paul Binski, Alain Bourear, Maria João Branco, Elizabeth A.R. Brown, James Brundage, Philippe Buc, Charles Burnett, James Burns, David d'Avray, Paul Fouracre, Sarah Hamilton, Caroline Humfress, Timothy Insoll, Peter Jackson, Ruth Karras, Gàbor Klaniczay, Cristina La Rocca, Jacques Le Goff, C.H. Lawrence, Peter Linehan, Máire Ní Mhaonaigh, Yoshiki Morimoto, Janet L. Nelson, David Nirenberg, Linda Paterson, Timothy Reuter, Susan Reynolds, Magnus Ryan, Jonathan Shepard, Pauline Stafford, Christopher Tyerman, and Jack Watt.

The editors: Peter Linehan is Fellow and Dean of St John's College, Cambridge, and Janet L. Nelson is Professor of Medieval History at King's College, London.

THE MEDIEVAL WORLD

Edited by
Peter Linehan and Janet L. Nelson

Routledge
Taylor & Francis Group

LONDON AND NEW YORK

First published 2001
by Routledge
2 Park Square, Milton Park, Abingdon, Oxon, OX14 4RN

Simultaneously published in the USA and Canada
by Routledge
270 Madison Ave, New York, NY 10016

First published in paperback 2003

Reprinted 2004, 2005, 2006

Transferred to Digital Printing 2007

Routledge is an imprint of the Taylor & Francis Group, an informa business

Typeset in Garamond by Keystroke, Jacaranda Lodge, Wolverhampton
Printed and bound in Great Britain by TJI Digital, Padstow, Cornwall

British Library Cataloguing in Publication Data
A catalogue record for this book is available from the British Library

Library of Congress Cataloging in Publication Data
has been applied for

ISBN 10 : 0–415–30234–X (paperback)
ISBN 10 : 0–415–18151–8

ISBN 13 : 978–0–415–30234–0 (paperback)
ISBN 13 : 978–0–415–18151–8

This book is dedicated to their long-suffering families in partial expiation for its editors' repeated failure to get home in time for supper

CONTENTS

— Contents —

ILLUSTRATIONS

CONTRIBUTORS

Stuart Airlie is Senior Lecturer in Medieval History at the University of Glasgow. He has written widely on earlier medieval politics and society, and a major study of these themes is forthcoming. The history of film is another of his interests.

Mario Ascheri is Professor of Legal History at the University of Siena. His many published works include *Siena nel Renascimiento* (1985) and *I libri del leoni: la nobiltà di Siena in età medicea 1557–1737* (1996).

Dominique Barthélemy counts as many serfs among his ancestors as he does knights. A student of Georges Duby, he teaches at the University of Paris IV and the École Pratique des Hautes Études where he occupies the chair of the History of Feudal France.

Nora Berend is Assistant Lecturer in Medieval History at Cambridge University and a Fellow of St Catharine's College. Her book *At the Gate of Christendom: Jews, Muslims and 'pagans' in medieval Hungary* was published in 2001 by Cambridge University Press.

Peter Biller is Professor of History at the University of York. He has published more or less across the whole range of medieval religion, from theology to heresy, and from sexual ethics to healing. His *The Measure of Multitude: population in medieval thought* was published by Oxford University Press in 2000, and *The Waldenses: between a religious order and a church 1170–1530* by Variorum in 2001.

Paul Binski has taught at Yale and Manchester Universities and is now University Lecturer and Head of the Department of History of Art at Cambridge University and a Fellow of Gonville and Caius College. His *Westminster Abbey and the Plantagenets. Kingship and the representation of power 1200–1400* was published in 1995.

Alain Boureau is Directeur d'études at the École des Hautes Études en Sciences Sociales, Paris. The most recent of his published works is *Théologie, science et censure au XIIIe siecle: le cas de Jean Peckham* (1999) and, in English translation, *The Lord's First Night. The myth of the droit de cuissage* (1998).

Maria João Branco is Assistant Professor of Medieval History at the Universidade Aberta, Lisbon and Director of the Centre of Portuguese Language of the Istituto

Camões, University of Oxford. Her earlier works having included studies of female monasticism and the irregular behaviour of churchmen, she is currently researching the subject of royal power and ecclesiastics in thirteenth-century Portugal.

Elizabeth A. R. Brown is Professor Emerita at Brooklyn College and the Graduate School, City University of New York. She has published major papers on many aspects of the cultural, political and legal history of the later medieval and early modern periods – a chronological distinction the utility of which her work has little time for. Two collections of her papers, *Politics and Institutions in Capetian France* and *The Monarchy of Capetian France and Royal Ceremonial* appeared in 1991.

James Brundage is Ahmanson-Murphy Distinguished Professor of History and Law at the University of Kansas. His publications include nine books and more than two hundred articles and reviews, many of which deal with the history of medieval sex law. He is currently at work on studies of professional canon lawyers and the history of legal ethics.

Philippe Buc studied in Paris and now teaches at Stanford University, USA. He is the author of *L'Ambiguïté du livre: prince, pouvoir et peuple dans les commentaires de la Bible au Moyen Age* (1994), and has published widely on the cultural history of Late Antiquity and the Middle Ages. His *The Dangers of Ritual* is forthcoming from Princeton University Press.

Charles Burnett is Professor of the History of Arabic/Islamic Influence in Europe in the Middle Ages at the Warburg Institute, University of London. He is the author of *Magic and Divination in the Middle Ages* (1996), *The Introduction of Arabic Learning into England* (1997), and several editions of Medieval Latin and Arabic texts.

James Burns is Professor Emeritus of the History of Political Thought in the University of London. He edited *The Cambridge History of Medieval Political Thought* and his publications include *Lordship, Kingship and Empire: the idea of monarchy 1400–1525* (1992).

David d'Avray is Professor of Medieval History at University College London. His publications on medieval religious and cultural history include *The Preaching of the Friars* (1985) and *Death and the Prince: memorial preaching before 1350* (1994).

Paul Fouracre is Reader in Medieval History at Goldsmiths' College, University of London. He is co-author of *Late Merovingian France: history and hagiography, 640–720* (1996) and has co-edited *The Settlement of Disputes in Early Medieval Europe* (1986) and *Property and Power in the Early Middle Ages* (1995). His *The Age of Charles Martel* was published in 2000.

Sarah Hamilton is Lecturer in Medieval History at the University of Exeter. Her *The Practice of Penance* is due to be published in 2001.

Caroline Humfress is Assistant Professor in Rhetoric and Law in the Department of Rhetoric, University of California, Berkeley. The author of various articles on postclassical Roman law and early medieval political thought, she has published (with P. Garnsey) *The Evolution of the Late Antique World* (2001). Her *Orthodoxy and the Courts in Late Antiquity* is due for publication by Oxford University Press in 2001.

Timothy Insoll is Lecturer in Archaeology at the University of Manchester. He has directed archaeological excavations in Timbuktu and Gao and conducted fieldwork in Eritrea, India, Uganda, Turkey and the UK. He is the author of *Islam, Archaeology and History: the Gao region, Mali* (1996) and *The Archaeology of Islam* (1999), and editor of *Case Studies in Archaeology and World Religions* (1999).

Peter Jackson is Professor of Medieval History at Keele University. He was editor of *The Cambridge History of Islam*, vol. VI (1986), and joint editor of *The Mission of Friar William of Rubruck* (1990). His most recent publication is *The Delhi Sultanate* (1999). He is also the author of various articles on the Mongols, the Crusades, and the eastern Islamic world.

Ruth Mazo Karras teaches in the Department of History at the University of Minnesota, USA. She has published widely on gender and sexuality in the Middle Ages and is the author of *Common Women: prostitution and sexuality in medieval England* (1996).

Gábor Klaniczay is Rector of the Collegium Budapest Institute of Advanced Study and author of *The Uses of Supernatural Power: the transformation of popular religion in medieval and early modern Europe* (1990) and of many other studies of the culture of Eastern and Central as well as of Western Europe in the medieval and early modern periods.

Cristina La Rocca teaches medieval history at the University of Padua. She is the author of *Pacifico di Verona* (1995) and of many studies on the history and archaeology of towns and on legal and gender history in early medieval Italy.

C. H. Lawrence is Professor Emeritus of Medieval History at Bedford College, University of London and author of *Medieval Monasticism: forms of religious life in Western Europe in the Middle Ages* (1984), *The Friars: the impact of the early mendicant movement on Western society* (1994), and many studies of the medieval Church.

Jacques Le Goff was for many years Directeur d'études at the École des Hautes Études en Sciences Sociales, Paris. The most recent of his formidable list of publications, which began with *Marchands et banquiers du Moyen Age* (1956), and many of which have appeared in English translation, is *Saint François d'Assise* (1999).

Peter Linehan is Dean of St John's College Cambridge and Corresponding Member of the Real Academia de la Historia (Madrid). Beginning with *The Spanish Church and the Papacy in the Thirteenth Century* (1971), he has published numerous works on the history of medieval Spain and Portugal in particular. A third volume of his collected papers is due to appear in 2002.

Yoshiki Morimoto teaches at the Institute of Comparative Studies in International Cultures and Societies at Kurum University, Japan. Having studied in Belgium, he has written extensively on early medieval European economic and social history.

Janet L. Nelson is Professor of Medieval History at King's College, University of London. She is the author of *Charles the Bald* (1992) and of three volumes of collected papers: *Politics and Ritual in Early Medieval Europe* (1986), *The Frankish World* (1996), and *Rulers and Ruling Families in Early Medieval Europe* (1999). She has co-edited: (with Frans Theuws) *Rituals of Power: from late Antiquity to the early Middle Ages* (2000) and serves on the editorial board of *Past & Present* and the editorial collective of *History Workshop Journal*.

Máire Ní Mhaonaigh is University Lecturer in the Department of Anglo-Saxon, Norse, and Celtic, University of Cambridge, and a Fellow of St John's College. She is the author of a number of articles on literary and historical topics, and has recently co-edited (with Howard B. Clarke and Raghnall Ó Floinn), *Ireland and Scandinavia in the Early Viking Age* (Dublin 1998).

David Nirenberg is Charlotte Bloomberg Professor of the Humanities in the Department of History at the Johns Hopkins University, Baltimore. He is the author of *Communities of Violence: persecution of minorities in the Middle Ages* (1996). His research focuses on social and cultural relations between Christians, Jews, and Muslims in medieval Europe and the Mediterranean.

Agostino Paravicini Bagliani is Professor of Medieval History at the University of Lausanne. The most recent of his numerous publications on the history of the medieval papacy, the study of medicine and natural science, and the role of ritual, are *La Cour des papes au XIII siècle* (1995) and *Il trono di Pietro: l'universalità del papato da Alessandro III a Bonifacio VIII* (1996). An English translation of his *Il corpo del Papa* (1994) was published by Chicago University Press in 2000, entitled *The Pope's Body*.

Linda Paterson is Professor of Medieval French at the University of Warwick. A noted authority on Occitan literature and pioneer of interdisciplinary studies on French culture and society in the central medieval period, she is the author of *The World of the Troubadours* (1997).

Timothy Reuter was formerly Professor of Medieval History at the University of Southampton. His published works have ranged widely across the field of medieval social and political history, with particular emphasis on Germany. His *Germany in the Early Middle Ages* was published in 1992. Volumes edited by him include *The Medieval Nobility* (1978) and volume III of *The New Cambridge Medieval History* (2000).

Susan Reynolds is a Senior Research Fellow at the Institute of Historical Research, University of London. Her interests have included medieval urban history as well as, more recently, political and ideological themes. She is the author of *Kingdoms and Communities in Western Europe* (second edn 1997) and *Fiefs and Vassals: the medieval evidence reconsidered* (1994).

Magnus Ryan is Lecturer in Late Medieval Studies at the Warburg Institute, University of London. His publications include articles on Roman, canon, and feudal law in the later Middle Ages, and on medieval political theory.

Jonathan Shepard, until 1999 University Lecturer in Russian and Byzantine History at the University of Cambridge and a Fellow of Peterhouse, is now living quietly on the South Coast. He is co-author (with Simon Franklin) of *The Emergence of the Rus 750–1200* (1996), published in a Russian-language edition in St Petersburg in 2000.

Pauline Stafford is Professor of Medieval History at the University of Liverpool, and author of, most recently, *Unification and Conquest: a political and social history of England in the tenth and eleventh centuries* (1989), and *Queen Emma and Queen Edith: queenship and women's power in eleventh-century England* (1997).

Christopher Tyerman is Lecturer in Medieval History at Hertford College Oxford and Head of History at Harrow School. His books include *England and the Crusades* (1988), *Who's Who in Early Medieval England 1066–1272* (1996), and *The Invention of the Crusades* (1998). He is at present working on a book on the Crusades for Penguin.

J. A. Watt is Professor Emeritus of Medieval History at the University of Newcastle upon Tyne. He has published widely on the subjects of the history of canon law, medieval political thought, and the history of medieval Ireland. The second edition of his *The Church in Medieval Ireland* appeared in 1998.

ABBREVIATIONS

BHL   *Bibliotheca hagiographica latina antiquae et mediae aetatis*

CCSL   *Corpus Christianorum series Latina*

CSEL   *Corpus scriptorum ecclesiasticorum latinorum*

FRB   *Fontes rerum Bohemicarum*

MGH   Monumenta Germaniae Historica

PL   J. P. Migne, *Patrologia Latina*, 217 vols.

SC   Sources chrétiennes, Paris: Éds du Cerf

SRA   Scriptores rerum Austriacarum

CHAPTER ONE

INTRODUCTION

Peter Linehan and Janet L. Nelson

Not *another* book on the Middle Ages, the reader may well protest at the outset of the twenty-first century – rather as medievalists' (not to mention others') young children do towards the end of a long day on being confronted with ('it's a promise') the very last Romanesque monument until after breakfast tomorrow.

But, as most children know, unlike breakfast, tomorrow never comes. And as the smartest of them sooner rather than later work out for themselves, that is because there's always *another* tomorrow, with the future of that peculiar past forever reaching forward and with something time-consuming and really interesting forever waiting around the next corner.

Which is precisely why we are offering you this volume. For this is the medievalist's impression too. This is the medievalist's sense of the way ahead. It was in that spirit that sometime in 1996 we embarked on the making of this volume.

What we had in mind then, in those heady far-off days, was a volume which, as we indicated in our prospectus to potential contributors, would supply something of what we had found lacking in 'the experience we have of teaching the subject and of trying to convey something of its distinctive flavour'.

We knew that the *New Cambridge Medieval History* was under way. More than that, in 1996 we were both involved in and committed to it. We still are. But whenever that noble undertaking eventually reaches port there will still be need for an account of the Middle Ages which because it occupies less space on the shelf sharpens the appetite for more. And this, we hope, is that.

We have not aimed for completeness of coverage, therefore. We will fall easy prey to critics whose measure requires treatment of Bohemia in all its aspects, the importance of fishing, developments in Poland, and the distribution of snakes in Iceland, for example.

Putting together this book has proved to be a learning experience in more ways than one. We already knew, of course, that Europe (and its neighbours) during the Middle Ages saw change, and displayed variety – yet just how profound and subtle were the changes and just how rich the variety only began to become clear to us as the contributors' work came in. Now, we hope, readers of this book will share our sense of wonder. Though we had known it in theory, we had not quite appreciated before in such concrete terms the dependence of historians' interpretations of the

1

past on their own particular experiences of time and place. While not all contributors have been concerned with tracing interpretative shifts over the past two centuries, a good many have thought it necessary to discuss methodological problems. Historiographical debates murmur, brew, sometimes even boil over. This book is not an assemblage of information, nor a survey of knowledge: rather it is a set of reconstructions, and of views from multiple perspectives. The balance of our coverage reflects, to a considerable extent, current concerns and recent critical debates. In each of the four sections into which the book is divided, contributors address, in more or less explicit terms, questions of approach and methodology. Many partial worlds emerge as one medieval world.

The coexistence of multiple identities as a defining feature of the Middle Ages is the theme of Part I. East and West within Europe were already distinct cultures in the Roman Empire, and Christianity overlaid that difference without ever transcending it (Shepard). Selves were defined by reference to Others within Christendom, therefore, but also to Others outside it. Unsurprisingly, difference was perceived most clearly at the edges of the Christian world: where Christians and non-Christians shared boundaries, as in Spain and Hungary (Linehan, Nirenberg, Berend) or where Mongol attacks in the thirteenth century inspired embassies that were also quite literally missions (Jackson). We wanted to highlight the unsatisfactory nature of conventional differentation of Europe into East and West (Burnett). Then there was the uneasy and equivocal situation of non-Christians *within* Western society to be accounted for (Tyerman, Watt). Last but not least in this section (though this is a theme that recurs elsewhere as well), we wanted to convey a sense of our contemporary awareness of the Middle Ages as Other – a perception which has marked, and also allowed, the modernity of modern culture, and nowhere more clearly, over the past century, than in film (Airlie).

The contributions to Part II examine from various angles and for various periods the medieval symbolic universe, changing cultural patterns, and the relations between Christian belief and practice. Ritual is explored in contexts where ecclesiastical and secular, clerical and lay, interact and mutually influence each other, as in the representation of kingship and the imposition of penance (Buc, Hamilton). Chivalry is critically analysed as a code of conduct, and also as a modern construct (Barthélemy). The central and later Middle Ages emerge as an important period in the elaboration of marriage doctrine, and in the imagery of the crucifixion in art (d'Avray, Binski). Heresy offers both a window on this world and a peephole on modern assumptions and prejudices about the Middle Ages (Biller). Attitudes to the body are shown not only to have changed but to have varied regionally, in ways that can be correlated with the evolving theories of theologians as well as medics (Paravicini Bagliani). Literary depictions of, and social experience of, gender relations (Paterson, Karras) changed in ways shaped in part by the emergence of ecclesiastical government and canon law (Brundage).

Part III surveys and dissects power-relations at varied places and times throughout the medieval period, within Latin Europe and beyond it. Theoderic's regime in Italy shows a barbarian kingdom absorbed and replicated in microcosm in the Roman Empire, urban life being adapted to new material circumstances (La Rocca). Exposure of the structures of power underpinning the relatively large states of the earlier

Middle Ages allows cultural adaptation and innovation to show up strongly, while comparison with Ireland clarifies the distinctiveness both of certain features of the Irish political scene and of large-scale states elsewhere in the earlier medieval West (Fouracre, Ní Mhaonaigh). Assemblies were to remain, throughout the medieval period from the Carolingians onwards, the key institution of government, yet their workings did not eclipse the power of royal women, and they throve alongside, not against the grain of, royal authority: there were, and distinctively, such things as medieval states (Reuter, Stafford, Reynolds). In the central medieval period, with the growth of papal government, the institutional Church functioned as a polity (Burns) and certain principles were (more or less) immutable (Ryan). Yet leading churchmen in the various parts of Europe contributed, often in paradoxical ways, to the development of royal government, as the case of Portugal shows (Branco), while power in Italy operated pre-eminently in towns and through urban institutions (Ascheri). As ever, variety is the name of the medieval game. Comparison with an African state in the same period, and somewhat later, highlights both governmental exploitation of similar economic resources, and distinctive features of Islamic sub-Saharan states (Insoll).

The fourth and last part moves definitively to the sub-state level and to the roles of groups, elite and otherwise. In late Antiquity, professional lawyers eased the transition from pre- to post-Christian (Humfress). By the ninth century, great landlords (ecclesiastical ones are uniquely well-documented) and their provosts and bailiffs dominated the countryside, though their management did not exclude peasant initiatives there, but rather stimulated them (Morimoto). Monasticism, in all its many and varied guises, functioned as a key economic and social institution throughout the medieval period, and here again continuities are much in evidence (Nelson). Yet in the central Middle Ages, monastic communities conspired with the papacy to create and sustain papal government, with papally conferred privilege the hallmark of that collusion (Boureau). Education, another privilege to which the establishment held the key, was not uniformly benevolent in its effects, and among the ranks of the lower clergy not even marginally effective (Le Goff; Lawrence). The resilient elites of Central and Eastern Europe show another adaptive response to economic and social change towards the end of the medieval period and into the early modern one, as western models were borrowed and tailored without loss of distinctive indigenous traits (Klaniczay). The artificiality of conventional periodisation is clear: the Middle Ages were not wholly different from the period that came after (Brown). This section thus picks up the themes of variety within some forms of over-arching culture, and of continuity across the late medieval–early modern divide.

Of course, there are gaps, not all of them of our own making. We particularly regret the under-representation of economic history, and of German history and German historians. On the other hand, we are delighted to have been able to inveigle so many French and Italian colleagues into what has emerged as a genuinely international enterprise. Every one of the four sections has been strengthened by that dimension. The recurrent preoccupations of our contributors with symbolic representations, with gender, with boundaries and frontiers, with cultural identities and distinctions, show our book to be a child of our time. It is also a book for our time.

We should like to thank, above all, our contributors whose enthusiasm ensured the success of this project, and the quality of whose work has made the book a historiographical landmark: it is they who, from new vantage-points, have presented the medieval world anew. Our thanks go likewise to those at Routledge, especially Vicky Peters and Ruth Jeavons, whose support and confidence sustained our editorial resolve; also to Susan Mansfield for cheerfully undertaking the labour of retyping a chapter in the office of St John's College Cambridge, the need to ask her to do so confirming that the Middle Ages of medievalists is forever with us. Chapters 11, 12, 19, 34, 35 and 36 were translated from French originals by Jinty Nelson, and chapter 26 from the Italian by Peter Linehan with the kind assistance of Magnus Ryan.

Co-editing can sometimes wreck a friendship, but in this case the experience has further cemented a longstanding one, formed when, nearly forty years ago, the Editors of this volume learned about medieval history at the feet of Walter Ullmann. We would like to think that Walter might have relished at least part of this book. Of the hefty chapters on law, political ideas, and ritual, he would surely have approved. Of those on material culture and the fact that there is more about gender here than about Gregory VII he would have had something to say too, though probably not much that would have been useful to the blurb-writers. Be that as it may, however, differently and together we honour his memory.

PART I

---◆---

IDENTITIES: SELVES AND OTHERS

INTRODUCTION

The word 'medieval', derived from 'the Middle Ages', that is, the period between Classical Antiquity and the Renaissance, only really has any meaning (how much is debatable) with reference to Europe. But what is Europe? The contributions in Part I address that question, directly or indirectly, from many different angles. First and foremost, European culture was based on that of Rome which in many ways incorporated that of Greece. The existence of the Roman Empire between the first century BC and the fifth century AD ensured that classical forms and norms were spread and rooted throughout much of geographical Europe. In, say, 400, urban civilisation, with its aqueducts, theatres, forums, temples, looked similar whether you were in Bordeaux or Brindisi, Tarragona or Thessaloniki. Roman citizens using the same law could make contracts that were standard in form, and equally valid, in London and Lyons, Nantes and Naples. Latin was the language of the military and of the educated in Cologne or Corinth, Seville or Syracuse. Surveyors and engineers worked to the same rule-books in Galicia and Calabria. Over all these aspects of social life brooded the Roman state, with its tax system, its armies, its vast public works.

Yet this neat picture of homogeneity is only part of the story. Regional differences remained fundamental, rooted as they were in geography and ecology. The economic integration of city and countryside, and the pervasive impact of human action on the landscape, were nowhere clearer than in the Po valley, the region that since the later sixth century, thanks to the arrival then of Lombards from the Danube area, has been called Lombardy. Settlement patterns there would change little between Roman times and the twentieth century. Contrast, though, the region's political centrality to the Roman Empire, especially *c.*400 when the imperial capital was Milan, with its political fragmentation in the Middle Ages; and then again, contrast that fragmentation with the region's economic centrality from the twelfth to the fifteenth century. Many other regions never displayed the standard, symmetrical, land divisions of the Po valley, or boasted its bustling commercial cities: Galicia and Brittany retained their own distinct Celtic languages and legal customs into modern times, the Tyrol and the Tuscan Appennines kept their distinctive forms of land-use. Beneath its smooth surface, the Roman Empire, especially towards its more mountainous spines and peripheral edges, was lumpily diverse. In the Middle Ages, with the superstructure of the imperial regime removed, that regional diversity became fascinatingly obvious, not least in the emergence from Latin of distinct Romance languages such as Occitan, Catalan and Provençal. Now, in the early twenty-first century, Europeans worry about the fading of local customs and centuries- (perhaps millennia-) old forms of land-use, and struggle to preserve (and reinvent) regional traditions.

Such differences at the level of whole provinces, say the divisions between Spain and France and Italy, crystallised in new political formations in the fifth and sixth centuries, with the establishment of kingdoms. Even though Charlemagne (as every continental school-boy and -girl knows) was crowned emperor on Christmas Day 800 and so revived a Roman Empire, this was a mere ghost of the old, and never worked as an institutionalised unified state. For the most part, the medieval state was the kingdom: a new, distinctively medieval, unit of political power, with a new ideological basis in the bond between king and people and the territorial specificity of its own cult-sites and ritual centres. While it is certainly true that most modern European states have been busily fabricating 'medieval' traditions for themselves since at least the nineteenth century, not all traditions claiming medieval roots are bogus: in England, the legal system, for instance, and in France, the notion of national unity, are, in truth, medieval creations.

On the other hand, medieval kingdoms were untidy states. They claimed no monopoly on political power within their boundaries (though they did have clear boundaries), but instead accommodated multiple levels of relatively autonomous power – such as aristocratic territorial lordships, or regional elites whose collective ascendancy was institutionalised in assemblies – and discrete cells of power in the forms of towns privileged with rights of self-government. Power in medieval societies, in short, was layered and split, in ways that made them, functionally and conceptually, very different from the Roman Empire. For that matter, medieval layers and splits are distinct from modern ones, and hence not captured (hard as some historians have tried) by modern concepts of devolution and subsidiarity.

Within the Roman Empire, there was another kind of difference, on a much vaster scale than that between regions and provinces: the division between East and West. The formation of the empire had gummed Greek-speaking and Latin-speaking areas together, but could not make them cohere. The legacy of Hellenistic monarchy, that is, of Alexander the Great and his heirs, which predated Rome's conquest of Greece and the eastern Mediterranean lands, and made its own amalgam of near-eastern and Greek cultures, proved remarkably durable. Empire penetrated the depths of political life in Greece, Asia Minor, the Levant, and Egypt as it never did in the landmass of Rome's western provinces with their very different traditions of aristocratic 'liberty'. Bi-lingualism in Greek and Latin was official in the Roman Empire – laws were issued in both languages, for instance – but in social practice people mostly used one or the other – or one of any number of other regional languages. Elites in Asia Minor or Egypt used Greek, in Spain and Gaul, Latin. The administrative division of the empire between East and West in the fourth and fifth centuries coincided with the period of political strain and eventual division in the West brought about by the immigration of 'barbarians' (as Roman writers called the Goths, Franks, Vandals, and others) and the formation of 'barbarian' kingdoms. After 476, there was no longer a western emperor at all. The establishment of a kingdom involved some degree of violent expropriation of the indigenous provincial populations but a much larger degree of cooperation and entente between indigenous elites and incoming ones. For example, the creation of a kingdom covering most of Gaul by Clovis, king of the Franks, and his followers in the decades around 500 could not have been achieved without such indigenous collaboration. Paradoxically, though, Clovis made sure of the approval of the emperor in far-off Constantinople: the idea of empire persisted even when, and where, no eastern cavalry would ever appear over the horizon.

There never was any neat coincidence between the Roman Empire and Europe: on the one hand, much of the European continent was beyond the bounds of the empire; on the other, the empire stretched, eastwards and southwards, into large swathes of Asia and Africa. What happened in the centuries between *c*.400 and *c*.1500 was that Europe took shape, filled its spaces, acquired an identity of sorts. The result was a world with clear debts to Rome, but just as clearly, very different from it. To weigh up the contrasts and the continuities – and to observe the contrasts emerging as more important than the continuities – the most direct way is to consider religious change over the long run. First, Christianity grew up within the Roman Empire, to become its official religion in the fourth century. An emperor's act of state could not magic cultural integration into being. Over many centuries, however, Christianisation pervaded the forms and norms of the old empire and spread far beyond: it was not Roman-imperial but medieval missionaries who took Christianity to the lands beyond the Rhine: (using modern terminology) to Scotland in the seventh century, Germany in the eighth, Denmark and Sweden and Norway in the ninth and tenth, Poland, Czechia and Hungary in the tenth and eleventh. Even that picture of a process is too tidy: there is always an exception, in this case Ireland, never part of the Roman Empire but converted in Roman times by multiple individual efforts, a spin-off from contacts established through trading, including slave-trading. Thus Irish missionaries played a part in many of those earlier-medieval enterprises which by *c*.1000 had brought most of western, northern and central Europe into Christendom.

In *c*.1000, that Christendom was one. At the same time, it was, for all practical purposes, divided. Divided, first, in the sense that there were, even among those kingdoms and people converted by Latin-using missionaries, multiple local and regional churches with distinct cultic traditions which, given the importance of ritual in religion, mattered a great deal to their practitioners. There were also distinct structures of church government within the various kingdoms, and in these churches-within-kingdoms, churchmen unsurprisingly operated with the support of kings and aristocrats. Although the pope was recognised as the successor to St Peter and custodian of Peter's relics in Rome, papal authority was precisely of this cultic kind. Many pilgrims journeyed to Rome, yet seldom did earlier-medieval Christians appeal to the pope for judgment. Bishops and archbishops in their own church councils ran ecclesiastical government on provincial lines.

Christendom was divided, too, on grander lines. Rome was only one of five patriarchal sees: the other four, reflecting the eastern Mediterranean origins of Christianity itself, were located in the eastern Roman Empire, in Constantinople – that was naturally the most important, being the imperial capital – and in Antioch, Jerusalem and Alexandria. By *c*.1000, Constantinople (for reasons to be outlined presently) was left as the only politically significant eastern player: its patriarch confronted the pope in Rome as one ecclesiastical leader to another. 'Confronted', however, only in a figurative sense: for one thing, there was seldom any issue that divided them, for another, patriarch and pope never actually met, since in the three centuries before 1000, there was relatively little ecclesiastical (or any other) coming and going between western and eastern Christian worlds, and occasional embassies could take care of such contacts as there were. As within the West, cultic differences had insensibly come into being, and grown, between East and West. The eastern emperors had never given up their universal claims. Though they grudgingly acknowledged western emperors from Charlemagne on, they never recognised them

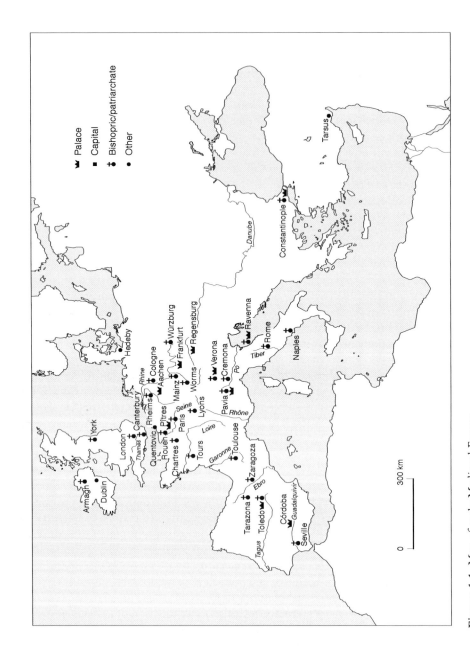

Figure 1.1 Map of early Medieval Europe.

as Roman: instead the Greek-speaker with his capital in Constantinople was the sole *basileus Romaion*, emperor of the Romans. ('Byzantium', 'the Byzantine Empire', are modern historians' terms which no *basileus* would ever have used.) Charlemagne's grandsons, in the ninth century, were powerful enough as kings to have political ambitions in central Europe. Here they inevitably competed ('clashed' would overstate the case) with Constantinople's ambitions to extend its cultural and diplomatic influence. Missionaries, from the barbarian successor-states to the Frankish empire on the one hand, Byzantium on the other, vied to convert Bulgars, Moravians, and Russians. Geography had much to do with outcomes. By *c.*1000, the dividing-lines of European Christendom between East and West had been fixed where they remain today: with Poland, Czechia and Hungary, and, further south, Croatia, in the Latin Church, Bulgaria, Russia, and Serbia in the Greek one. Yet *c.*1000, a German bishop, hearing of Greek clergy's conversion of the Russian prince, rejoiced that he was now with 'us', meaning Christians. In both East and West, there was still a sense of Christendom as one.

That sense, at least on the part of churchmen, was fostered from the seventh century onwards by the rise of Islam. Within four generations of Muḥammad's death in 632, Muslim armies had conquered much of what had been the Asiatic and African provinces of the Roman Empire – Syria, Palestine, Egypt, and North Africa including what are now Libya, Algeria and Morocco – and finally, in 711–14 virtually the whole of the Iberian peninsula. Constantinople lost all its eastern provinces except Anatolia which nevertheless suffered repeated raids. In the Mediterranean itself, Arab fleets conquered Cyprus and later Crete (825) and Sicily (827). Churchmen in both East and West, when they mentioned these disasters, attributed them to divine punishment for Christians' sins and called for repentance. Yet for the most part, regarding those they called 'Saracens' or 'Hagarenes', churchmen said little and, as far as religion went, understood less. Within regions under Muslim rule, Christians suffered no persecution unless they courted martyrdom. Church leaders in Córdoba and Carthage, Damascus and Jerusalem advocated a policy of peaceful coexistence. Christian potentates, especially in the West, did not differentiate on grounds of religion between those rulers with whom they entertained diplomatic contacts: Charlemagne received envoys from 'the kings of the Irish' and 'the king of the Persians', the latter's being more welcome because their master was far more prestigious and sent far richer gifts. By *c.*1000, the emirate at Córdoba had declared itself an independent caliphate and its power was at its zenith. The envoy of Otto I of Germany to Córdoba was mightily impressed, in 953, by the caliph's wealth and military power, and thought his regime might have something to offer by way of a role-model to a German kingdom racked by intra-dynastic disputes and regional rebellion.

In the eleventh and twelfth centuries, this relatively comfortable world of live-and-let-live changed dramatically and permanently, as Latin Christendom went on the march. The motors of change were demographic and economic growth. Western aristocracies and peasantries alike were producing larger numbers of surviving offspring. These could not be contained within the old structures of settlement and landowning. Adjustments that over centuries had been gradual and obscure now tipped into explosive change. New lands were brought into cultivation and new villages and towns proliferated with the encouragement of lords; output increased, as did the volume of exchanges between countryside and towns. By *c*.1200, significant sectors of the economy were effectively monetised. Aristocratic youths competed for the lands, heiresses, the profits of war. Colonising efforts led and manned by ambitious and aggressive nobles also involved the mobilisation of peasant enterprise. Western Europe began to expand on frontier after frontier: in the British Isles as Anglo-Saxon, then Anglo-Norman, war-lords and settlers moved into the Celtic lands; in Spain as Leonese–Castilian and Aragonese, with plenty of French freebooters in support, took first treasure, then territory, from the now-fragmented states of Muslim al-Andalus; in southern Italy and Sicily, as Norman mercenaries-turned-colonists carved out for themselves a kingdom in the sun; in Palestine with the establishment, mostly by French and Flemish and (again) Norman nobles, of a Latin Christian kingdom and satellite principalities in the wake of the First Crusade (1099), then with the creation by Italian merchants of commercial enclaves in the coastal towns of Syria and Palestine and also in the great ports of Byzantium; and in central and northern Europe, as German nobles and their followers imposed their lordship over Slavs and others in the Baltic lands. It was not all aggression and expropriation: on some of these frontiers, especially in central Europe, there was peaceful settlement on newly cultivated lands and in newly founded towns. But one story of Europe in the central Middle Ages is of militarism, colonialism, and racism. Some of its main aspects are the themes of chapters in Part I.

The Europe that expanded was Latin, not Greek: indeed Latin Europe's expansion was at the expense of, among others, the Greeks. Relations that, with ups and downs, had been relatively smooth in the earlier Middle Ages now became rough; and a breach over ritual differences and ecclesiastical politics in 1054 that seemed reparable in the twelfth century was made irreparable after the conquest and plundering of Constantinople in 1204 by westerners on the Fourth Crusade. In the Eastern Mediterranean, crusading, primarily directed against Muslims, always involved Eastern Christian victims as well. In western Europe, Jews were victims of savage pogroms at the time of the First Crusade (1096). A European identity was formed at the expense of minorities: to identify and organise was also to exclude. There was a clear link between crusading and the persecution of the Jews. In Spain, where Muslims, Christians and Jews had co-existed, and even in a few cases co-operated intellectually by the fruitful exchange of their various readings of classical philosophy and cosmological lore, the spirit of live-and-let-live came under increasing pressure. By the mid-thirteenth century, the policing of the frontiers of Latin Christian belief and cultic practice had been assigned to professional inquisitors, and heretics as well as infidels were on the run. Some Europeans, and these included traders as well as missionaries and scholars, were becoming aware of cultures far to the East, beyond Byzantium and beyond Islam. The forms and tempo of external contact varied in different regions. Hungary's self-identification came in the fourteenth century, by reference to the pagan Cumans. By the later Middle Ages, Europe had become Europe by negation: by asserting what it was not, and by proscribing assorted Others.

One European identity, or perhaps one set of identities, forms much of the substance of the stories in Part I. These stories, articulated in the late twentieth century, are well-suited to the mood of post-colonial times. There are other possible stories, though, and other more positive images of medieval Europe emerge in this book. In terms of recent historians' writing, the Latin Christian Church stands in the centre of contested territory: persecutor or emancipator, instrument of oppression or enabling agency? Marxist historiography contributed much to the demonising of a feudal Church, aligned with the powers that were, manipulating and exploiting the ignorant. Yet it was Antonio Gramsci who identified Saints Francis and Dominic and their followers the friars as prototypes of organic intellectuals, by which he meant that they identified with and articulated the interests of the poor and unprivileged. The Church itself was both the site and the agent of social change. As a collectivity of believers, it represented demand for cultic and symbolic adaptation to new circumstances. As an institution, it responded to such demand. The Church was the beneficiary of demographic and economic growth: new land, new recruits, and new money made possible new church foundations and new and larger church schools producing trained personnel. The availability of new capital and new cadres made possible institutional consolidation. A centralised ecclesiastical goverment presupposed widely supported means and ends. The means were supplied by the income from Christendom-wide taxation to which the crusades gave the first big spur. The ends were provided by the needs of increasing numbers of churches (with a small 'c'), and also of lay individuals and communities, for authoritative intervention in their disputes over power and resources. In the earlier Middle Ages, such disputes had generally been resolved locally, by consensus or by violence. In the central Middle Ages, a larger and more differentiated world required new agencies of organisation and conciliation. No secular regime could supply these on the scale required. The popes of the central Middle Ages capitalised on a unique set of circumstances, responded to demand, found qualified agents and supporters. Thus was created the first great European government, the high-medieval papacy – perceived by contemporaries (who were anything but naive) not just as the venal instrument of vested interests, but as a utility, and a force for good. This book faithfully represents the complexity of the medieval Church as a distinctively European phenomenon – as the conduit of authority which legitimated the power exercised by Europe's secular rulers, and as the institution which, while proclaiming the belief that there was no tomorrow, nevertheless proceeded as though it was all destined to go on forever.

The placing of Part I's final chapter is deliberate. Identities, medieval and modern, are constructs of selves and others at the same time. Thus, how modern people see the Middle Ages tells us as much about ourselves as about them. Many modern writers of fiction, in a number of genres, have used a blend of historical knowledge and imagination to represent times and places that are more or less evocatively medieval, and more or less historical, from Middle-Earth to Camelot. Umberto Eco's *The Name of the Rose* enjoyed huge success among those sometimes called the chattering classes, world-wide. The audience for Ellis Peters' detective stories is different but no less addicted to medieval reconstructions. Film, as a visual medium, is an even better gauger of variety in modern images of the medieval. Where the medieval world is concerned, serious students of history and consumers of fictions and images are not separate categories of people, as most of us well know. As we reflect on the way in which medieval people shaped their identities, we perceive at the same time the instability of the historians' images – and their self-reflections. In its versions of the Middle Ages, film also shows us ourselves.

COURTS IN EAST AND WEST

—•—

Jonathan Shepard

In most pre-industrial societies formidable practical obstacles face those aspiring to paramount authority over other persons well beyond their own immediate district or kin-group. They rely heavily on face-to-face dealings in order to gain active cooperation from the heads of other powerful families or groupings. Notions of abstract authority which can be delegated by the ruler to his agents are not, without benefit of widespread literacy and urban culture, readily grasped by those due to be drawn into their ambit. A court, in the sense of an entourage of notables revolving around an overlord, of variegated and fluctuating composition but observing ritual deference towards him, is a means of concretising and enhancing his authority. On the one hand, the overlord can hope to reinforce his personal ties with individuals and, on the other, some conception of an order transcending bilateral, essentially personal relationships may be propagated. In this way courts serve to bring focus and cohesion to polities whose paramount rulers rely on the essentially voluntary cooperation of the magnates and others who matter at grass-roots.

It would not be hard to draw a stark contrast between, on the one hand, the courts of rulers in the early medieval West, where a king often dealt with his magnates as, in effect, first among equals and, on the other, the court of the Eastern emperor, glorifying his autocratic rule. Few major Western rulers could afford to remain fixed to a single seat of governance; more often they perambulated between pockets of disposable resources or active allegiance. 'Frontiers' were seldom clear-cut or coterminous with linguistic or other such cultural boundaries and the concept of 'natural barriers' had little force at a time when any form of long-distance communication was hazardous and costly. At the same time, notions at grass-roots of wider regional, let alone 'national' or 'ethnic', identities beyond membership of one's kin-group or immediate locality were indistinct and confined mainly to pious bookmen. The Byzantine *basileus*, in contrast, resided in a city whose monuments bespoke world-class dominion. Through the ceremonial performed at his court the message went out that his rule was God-willed and world-wide, being that of the 'empire of the Romans'. It offered the best hope for mankind's future, in that emperors since Constantine the Great had been charged with the task of converting individuals and peoples to Christianity.

This contrast between East and West is not wholly illusory, but it is important to remember that the concept of the ruler as converter of peoples, guardian of the Church and even, in some sense, high priest, was not exclusive to Byzantium. If the idea of the ruler as a 'new Constantine' was most developed and vigorously reiterated in Byzantium (Magdalino 1994; Dagron 1996), it had abiding resonance for polities in the West. The Byzantine court's image of divinely ordained hierarchy posed a kind of standing reminder as to what ambitious potentates might yet achieve. Of course, their standpoints varied markedly from that of the *basileus*. But when individual rulers turned their attention from primarily martial feats to means of underpinning the *status quo*, the image of imperial order – *taxis* – projected from the Bosporus had its appeal. Fundamental tasks of maintaining order and defeating rebellion could appear recognisably similar to the rulers of extensive realms in East and West (Shepard 1998: 170).

For both sets of dynasts Christian governance was a matter of upholding grand ideas among 'small worlds' and a miscellany of peripheries: in so far as courts generated a kind of magnetic field towards which many disparate elements were drawn, they brought aspirations of rulership closer to realisation. It is probably no accident that some of the most substantial data about the Early Byzantine court relates to the sixth century, when the empire came under pressure on several fronts more or less simultaneously and was riven internally by bitter religious disputes. Justinian's multiple commitments led him to allow for a 'soft frontier' in the Balkans, relying on a sort of archipelago of strongholds, often small and cheaply constructed, to fly the imperial flag amid Slavs, Antes and other aliens newly infesting the Balkans. Outposts were established to the north of the Danube and massive lines of walls were built on the Crimea and on the east coast of the Black Sea (Obolensky 1994: 3–4, 6–10, 24–8; Evans 1996: 222–3; Patoura 1997: 79–80, 84–5; Kislinger 1998: 54–8). But neither these measures nor the high-quality defence works raised on the Persian frontier could forestall sudden enemy incursions or the appearance of northern 'barbarians' before the capital itself, Constantinople. Thus in 540 Antioch fell to a surprise attack by the Persians and in 558 or 559 a horde of nomads ranged up to the walls of Constantinople and inspired terror in the citizens (Agathias, *Histories*, V.11).[1]

Such conspicuous insecurity made the crafting of an image of order, splendour and majesty all the more important to Justinian's regime. The palace complex, set amid newly built or refurbished sanctuaries, became the visual confirmation of the claim which decree after decree made for the emperor in its preamble: that Justinian was restoring 'order' to the level attained in antiquity, while also providing for his subjects' spiritual welfare, being uniquely answerable for this to God (Maas 1986: 24–5). Some thirty-three churches were built in Constantinople, far in excess of what was needed for strictly pastoral purposes (Mango 1985: 52). They served to house relics and to attract the attention of the saints, 'for when the emperor is pious, divinity walks not far from human affairs, but is given to mingling with men and to delight in associating with them' (Procopius, *Buildings*, I.1.27). The church of Holy Wisdom (Haghia Sophia), 'extraordinary to those who see it, quite unbelievable to those who merely hear of it' (Procopius, *Buildings*, I.4.24), lay within easy walking and processing distance of the palace, in effect making up the palace complex, together with the Hippodrome. Whether or not Justinian, upon entering Haghia Sophia, actually exclaimed, 'Solomon, I have outdone you!' (Moorhead 1994: 58; Koder 1994, I: 140–2; Evans 1996: 258; Rousseau 1998: 121–30), this saying linked him personally with the building in Byzantine popular tradition. And if we believe Procopius, the emperor and empress deliberately made their palace – which he equates with the court – a social hub: 'in earlier reigns few visited the palace, and then with difficulty', but

> these two . . . compelled everyone to dance attendance upon them like slaves. Almost any day one could see the law-courts virtually deserted but at the emperor's court an insolent crowd, elbowing and shoving. . . . Those who were apparently close friends of the imperial couple stood there through the whole day and often much of the night, getting no sleep or food at the normal times, till they were worn out completely: this was all that their apparent good fortune brought them.
>
> (Procopius, *Secret History*, XXX. 30–1)

Procopius' allegations can never be taken at face value (Cameron 1985: 49–66, 253–60), but they are in key with Justinian's general tendency to reserve decision-making for himself and to stockpile resources in Constantinople, the city outside which he seldom set foot. Greater numbers of persons frequenting the palace increased the risk of unseemly disarray, while also opening up new opportunities for displays of majesty. It was during Justinian's reign that court ceremonial was codified to a greater extent than had been thought possible or necessary before, by Peter the Patrician (Cameron 1979b: 7–8; Antonopoulos 1990: 14–15, 157–60, 196–216). And it is no accident that Justinian took steps to formalise his control over the manufacture and wearing of jewellery of the sort used to adorn the costume of emperors and courtiers. Ornaments comprising pearls, emeralds and 'hyacinths' (sapphires) were only to be worked up 'inside my court by palace craftsmen' (*Corpus iuris civilis*, XI.11.1; Hill 1983: 144–5; Stout 1994: 83, 95–6). While claiming the exclusive right to distribute gold, he sought to monopolise supplies of another vital medium of court life and diplomacy: silk. There can be little doubt that he actively promoted sericulture in Constantinople or that he sought to concentrate the manufacture of fine silks inside his palace complex. Silk worms' eggs were acquired from India, Central Asia or perhaps from further east along the Silk Routes: it is likely that more than one démarche in quest of them is mentioned in our sources (Procopius, *Wars*, I.20.9–12; VIII.17.1–8; Theophanes of Byzantium, in Photius (1959, I: 77–8); Evans 1996: 234–5; Muthesius 1996: 120–2, 270–4).

Procopius' caricature of Justinian's court implies that many of those attending were supposed to be enjoying 'good fortune', and in fact turned up voluntarily. The long reach of the image of the imperial court is registered by the famous mosaics in Ravenna's San Vitale: Justinian and Theodora are making presentations before the enthroned Christ. The imperial pair stand out by virtue of their nimbuses, purple vestments and bejewelled imperial headgear. But they do not have exclusive access to the divine: each stands flanked by representatives of high society (Deichmann 1976, II.2: 185–6; 1958, III: *Tafeln* IX and X, figs. 358–65; Stout 1994: 83, 85 and

Figure 2.1 St Sophia, Constantinople. Justinian's Church of the Holy Wisdom, constructed 532–7. The inscription in the dome and the four medallions in the choir, as well as the pulpit, the tribune on either side of the apse, the railings and the chandeliers are all post-1453 embellishments. Photo courtesy of Dumbarton Oaks, Washington, DC.

figs. 5.8, 5.9, p. 84). It is very probable that the mosaics were commissioned by Ravenna's bishop, Maximian, newly arrived after a spell at Constantinople and eager to flaunt his connections with both God and emperor. He is standing to the right of the emperor, cross in hand, his name inscribed above his head (Deichmann 1969, I: 242–3, 254–5; Deichmann 1976, II.2: 186–7; Deichmann 1958, III: *Tafel* X, figs. 359, 370). Maximian had particular grounds for impressing the emperor's majesty upon the citizens of Ravenna, seeing that they had at first obstructed his entry to his see. Thus the mosaics themselves refract the allure which the court exerted on those living on the periphery, presenting an image of exclusiveness but also demonstrating the possibility of admission for those who, like Maximian, served the emperor well.

Around AD 566, some twenty years after the mosaics of San Vitale were executed, another provincial, a native of North Africa, composed the fullest surviving tableau of early Byzantine palace ceremonial. Corippus' poem in praise of Justin II focuses on the person of Justinian's nephew and successor and on his special relationship with the palace, 'born in *imperium* and reared in the midst of the palace among the loyal bands and troops of servants' (Corippus 1976: 79, 114), banqueting with his wife off the world's finest wines but then retiring 'to govern so many far-flung peoples' (Corippus 1976: 65, 105). A particular set of events is recounted, the funeral of Justinian and the inauguration rites of the new emperor. In reality these events were fraught with political tension and involved constitutional innovations on Justin's part (Corippus 1976: 5), but they are represented in the court poem as smooth and inevitable: Justin, 'our lord and common benefactor, is the great spring of the court, the spring that enriches all' (Corippus 1976: 35, 86), and his munificence is likened to that of the mother-swallow, which leans over her brood and 'distributes the pious food so as to nourish them all' (Corippus 1976: 81, 115).

The court is thus presented by Corippus as a tranquil environment from which control is rightfully exercised, and patronage dispensed, across the entire world. Extensive coverage is given to Justin's reception of an embassy from the khagan of the Avars. Correct handling of 'barbarians' was a specifically imperial attribute, demonstrated in setpiece receptions: the outsiders were subjected to the court's house-rules, prostrating themselves before the emperor. A speech put into Justin's mouth lays claim to the high moral ground – 'God is the strength and glory of our empire' (Corippus 1976: 21, 107) – but his guards embody the brute force also at his disposal: the envoys upon crossing the threshold beheld 'the tall men standing there. . . . They shuddered at the sight of the lances, and cruel axes and saw the other wonders of the noble procession. And they believed that the Roman palace was another heaven' (Corippus 1976: 68, 107). An imperial spin could be put on the presence of other emissaries at court, giving the impression that it was the consequence of acts of submission on the part of their leaders, and that these potentates were prepared to 'serve' the emperor, furnishing him with military manpower. 'See', said Justin to the Avar envoys, 'Scaldor [another barbarian potentate] is ready to serve in our palace and sends us legates and countless gifts' (Corippus 1976: 72, 109–10, 193). Such manifestations could lead one set of barbarians to suspect that another was willing to cooperate with, if not 'serve', the emperor. This could intimidate them, in turn, into agreeing to cooperation or 'service' with the emperor.

Extant pieces of jewellery and precious fabrics illustrate the imperial court's high standing in far-flung places. For example, early Merovingian jewellers seem to have turned out close imitations of bejewelled collars and other neck ornaments of the style used in the imperial court, and these, in turn, may have set the style for the multipart necklaces with pendants found in southern Scandinavian women's graves (Vierck 1981: 81–3, 88, 90–4; *Abb.* 16, p. 89; *Abb.* 17, p. 91; *Tafel* 9, p. 111; Campbell 1992: 91–3 and n. 99 on 100). And it is not impossible that there were some direct contacts between Scandinavian elite groups and the imperial court: Heruli warriors served in the armies of Justinian (Teall 1965: 299–300, 309–13; Vierck 1981: 67–8, 96; Pohl 1997: 90–1). Later in the sixth century, or early in the seventh, statuettes of a Byzantine ruler were being turned out from a terracotta mould now in a museum in Samarkand; the mould had been copied from a figurine which may have been sent as an imperial gift to a West Turkish leader. The Byzantine ruler wears a high diadem with pendilia hanging almost to the shoulder and has the imperial sash (*loros*) draped over one shoulder, while his left hand holds a cross-topped orb (Haussig 1979: 190–1 and fig. 3).

In the later sixth century the Byzantine emperor could still plausibly lay claim to be a 'world-class' ruler, in terms of territorial power and material resources, and the triumphalism of imperial propaganda gain some confirmation from events, not least the wide-ranging religious missions which Justinian sponsored (Engelhardt 1974: 80–90, 100–3, 178–86). But there can be little doubt that Justinian was consciously 'punching above his weight' or that there is a direct connection between his frequent resort to diplomacy and the greater elaboration of court ceremonial which characterised his regime. When Justinian revived triumphs and other ceremonies in celebration of victory, he was signalling real feats of arms in Italy and North Africa. But he was also conjuring up for himself and his successors an aura of God-given order, exemplified by his court. This served to dignify the constant rounds of negotiation, compromise and accommodation with Lombard, Gepid and other barbarian potentates which, he well foresaw, were becoming unavoidable (Obolensky 1994: 24–7; Chrysos 1985: 43–5; Pohl 1997: 82–95, 101–3, 131–3). In the palace and the city, at least, the emperor could show mastery of his environment down to the finest detail and demonstrate the uniqueness of his access to God (Cameron 1979b: 17–18: Olster 1996: 98–101). His court vouchsafed to those fortunate enough to attend a glimpse of the way things ought to be. The ceremonies became, literally, affirmations of faith. The celebration of the liturgy and the acclamations, solemn entrances and processions were variants of the same basic theme of supplication of superhuman power. If Corippus in the 560s was still declaiming in fairly general terms that God was the 'strength and glory of our empire' (Corippus 1976: 71, 109), the devotion of emperor and people soon afterwards began to focus on more specific pledges of divine aid in the form of relics, most notably, in the early seventh century, the Robe and Girdle of the Mother of God which protected the city of Constantinople from barbarian assaults (Cameron 1978: 95–105; Cameron 1979a: 44–8). The burgeoning cults of relics and icons and the elaboration of a liturgical court culture in the 'navel of the world' – as a seventh-century work called Constantinople (Olster 1996:101) – were variant responses to the new sense of insecurity which beset Constantinopolitans and provincials alike.

The court of the emperor was already being projected as a version of heaven by the later sixth century and from around that time we first find archangels being depicted in imperial garb, notably in the church of San Apollinare in Classe, near Ravenna (Deichmann 1976, II.2: 245–6, 262–4; Deichmann 1958, III: figs. 370, 402–3). But it was in the Middle Byzantine era that notions of the intermingling between the emperor's court and God's gained richest visual expression. For example an ivory depicts Leo VI and the archangel Gabriel, each holding an orb and wearing the imperial sash, against a background clearly evocative of Haghia Sophia in Constantinople; the Mother of God is also depicted there, adding a jewel to Leo's crown (Corrigan 1978: figs. 1 and 2 on 408, 410–13; Maguire 1997: 249–50). The plainest assertion of the utility of ceremonial to the imperial regime comes from this time, when external pressures on Byzantium were starting to ease but the prevailing *mentalité* was still that of a beleaguered citadel. Writing in the mid-tenth century, Constantine VII Porphyrogenitus maintains that ceremonial, when well-staged, makes imperial authority appear more elegant and 'better-ordered': 'on account of this it is wonderful both to the nations [i.e. foreigners] and to our own people' (*DC*, preface, I, 4; ed. Vogt, I, 1). Thus, he seems to imply, the image of order and orchestrated deference before the emperor could help to bring about the reality desired and he himself believes that this is all in accordance with God's will. The cycle of ceremonies is interwoven with liturgical offices and amounts to an incessant act of collective intercession before Him. The majority of the happenings prescribed in Constantine's *Book of Ceremonies* take place in or around the palace complex – a regular cycle of liturgies, numerous processions and feasts; and celebrations, as appropriate, of births, weddings and victories. A copy of Constantine's treatise is to be placed in the heart of the palace to serve as a 'clear and freshly polished mirror' of what is proper for the emperor and 'the senatorial order' (*DC*, preface, I, 4–5; ed. Vogt, I, 2; Cameron 1987: 122–3, 130–1). But there were occasions when an emperor might need to forsake the palace, and Constantine's treatise on imperial campaigning offers a snapshot of what was deemed essential for the keeping up of appearances outside the palace. The stocking up with coins and valuables to be distributed as gifts is of prime concern and Constantine specifies the types of silken garments and other precious cloths to be brought along: the highest quality silks were 'for distinguished refugees and for sending to distinguished and powerful foreigners'; somewhat inferior garments were destined for senior commanders but these were still embroidered with 'eagles and imperial symbols', whereas those of lower quality still were not (Constantine VII 1990: 110–11). As in the time of Justin II, the emperor needed to show himself to be the 'spring that enriches all', and, while foreign notables received the best silks, they could also, through sporting 'imperial silks', be regarded as acknowledging a relationship of dependency *vis-à-vis* the emperor: many of the vestments corresponded with the costume of a particular category of imperial title-holder.

If Michael Psellus could write in the mid-eleventh century of 'these two things sustaining the hegemony of the Romans, I mean, titles and money' (Michael Psellus 1926, I: 132), it was the ceremonial life of the court which breathed life into the titles and gave extra worth to the stipends accompanying them. Ultimately, nothing could substitute for the gold largesse dispensed by the emperor but he could trade on the ambition of many, whether living beneath or beyond his dominion, to receive it and to flaunt their associations with him by means of their silks and other accoutrements. If well-to-do, they could represent this in pictorial form, as Maximian had done in sixth-century Ravenna and as local notables seem to have done in Cappadocia in the 960s, when they commissioned a church wall-painting of Nicephorus II Phocas and the other members of his family then holding top offices. They may also have wanted to thank the Phocases for some gift or privilege (Thierry 1985: 478, 481–2; Oikonomides 1996: 23–6). Likewise grateful monks of the monastery of Nea Moni on Chios commemorated the gifts received from Constantine IX Monomachus with mosaics of biblical scenes closely connected with the liturgy of the court (Mouriki 1985; Maguire 1992: 209–13 and figs. 8–12). At a lowlier yet more exotic level, well-to-do Khazars together with Turks from the Ferghana valley in Central Asia were sufficiently eager to join the imperial bodyguard to make down-payments so as to buy themselves a place. Their numbers by the end of the ninth century were such that Leo VI thought it worthwhile to specify the amount of these payments and of the honorarium which these guardsmen should receive (*DC*, II.49, 50, I, 693, 697–8). The borderline between the Byzantine emperor's 'real' and 'pretended' authority was as indistinct as that between his notional dominions and the regions where he exercised direct rule, implanting garrisons and levying taxes. There was no knowing the range of his potential contacts and the presence at court of the Ferghana guardsmen, of Pechenegs and other nomads from the western Eurasian steppes and, from the tenth century, of Scandinavians, served to corroborate threats such as those hurled at Liudprand of Cremona and his lord, Otto of Saxony, in 968: 'With money, which gives us power, we shall stir up all the nations against him and shatter him, like a potter's vessel' (Liudpr., *Leg*. 53; cf. Jeremiah 19.11).

Ritual, yet far from meaningless, participation in a kind of 'Commonwealth' was not peculiar to the celebrants of medieval Byzantium. There functioned on nineteenth-century Bali what has been described as a 'theatre state' where the members of local elites converged on a central point to participate in rituals revolving round the figure of the king, who acted on behalf of the supreme god, Shiva (Geertz 1980: 106). The rituals involved processions and acts of worship, consecration and feasting, staged in and around the palace complex. The latter has been described as a 'stretch of sanctified space', while the court as a whole made up 'the exemplary centre' (Geertz 1980: 109). The message of the rituals was essentially static, that the existing hierarchy was god-willed and an individual should accept his inherited place in it (Geertz 1980: 120). Yet while the pageantry and junketings served ostensibly to glorify the ruler and worship the gods, they were in fact the arena for intensive rivalries and fluctuating alliances among the lesser lords. Successful jockeying for position in a ceremony could raise one's standing significantly. The king presided over these goings-on and although the need to appear above the fray constrained his ability to intervene actively in disputes, standing at the apex of the collective acts of devotion and celebration invested him with power of a sort. The Great Imperturbable was custodian of a generally sought-after order, which all were committed to jointly celebrating and upholding (Geertz 1980: 130–1). Bali's 'theatre state' offers some analogies with the ideal order which the Byzantine court encapsulated and proclaimed. Constantine VII expressly states that the rhythm of the

Figure 2.2 The Virgin adds a pearl of wisdom to Leo VI's crown. Ivory (Constantinople) 886–912 (reverse). Inscription in Greek paraphrasing Ps. 44.5: 'Strive, prosper and reign, Lord Leo.' Staatliche Museen zu Berlin – Preußischer Kulturbesitz Museum für Spätantike und Byzantinische Kunst.

ceremonial should 'reproduce the harmony and movement of the Universe which the Creator brings' (*DC*, preface, I, 5; ed. Vogt, I, 2). The yearning to participate in the ceremonies apparently ran through various sectors of Byzantine society and one of the aims of the treatises on ceremonial was to forestall unseemly disputes over precedence (Oikonomides 1972: 82–3, 128–9, 232–5; *DC*, preface, I, 4; ed. Vogt, I, 1; McCormick 1985: 5; Kazhdan and McCormick 1997: 196–7). This dynamic of tension finely contained would have been familiar to the denizens of the Balinese *negara*. And its basic principles were not entirely alien to the more pretentious elites of the early medieval West.

This is not to deny that the values and customs of the essentially warrior elites of the West differed substantively from Byzantium's, or that they usually found ritual expression in forms distinct from those of the *basileus'* palace. For example, feasting was normally the occasion for celebrating fellowship and camaraderie rather than exalting the lord or ruler as sublimely apart (Leyser 1994b: 201–4; Nelson 1996: 123). One of the ways in which Charlemagne consorted with his 'nobles and friends' and others was by swimming with them, sometimes hundreds at a time, a pastime offering little scope for sumptuous vestments (Einhard, *Life of Charlemagne*, 22). Einhard emphasises that for most of the time Charlemagne's clothing 'differed hardly at all from that of the common people', and that he 'loathed foreign garments, no matter how beautiful they might be' (*Life of Charlemagne*, 23). This may well be a dig at the bejewelled apparel of Byzantine rulers and their courtiers. Liudprand likewise praises the well-shorn Western ruler who wears 'a garment quite different from a woman's dress' and a 'hat' in contrast to the effeminate tunics with long sleeves reaching down to the ankles and 'bonnets' of Byzantine emperors and their envoys (Liudpr., *Leg.* 37, 40). Even the Frankish prescriptions for palace life and conduct whose aspirations come closest to those of the Byzantine court presuppose a rather differently structured society. Dhuoda hoped that her son would be a 'useful servitor' 'with companions in arms in the royal and imperial court or elsewhere' (Dhuoda 1998: 104–5; Nelson 1992: 41, 49). Later in the ninth century Hincmar of Rheims' *Government of the Palace* paid much attention to assemblies and the consultation of 'magnates' and counsellors as well as to kin-groups and regional diversity (Hincmar 1980: 66–7, 82–97; Nelson 1992: 45–8). Such concerns would have seemed demeaning or superfluous to the *basileus*: they smacked of collectivism and recognised too overtly the disparate nature of the communities which made up a realm.

Nevertheless there are underlying analogies between Eastern and Western establishments which go beyond the level of the banal. The *basileus* and Frankish and Saxon potentates were alike aspiring to forms of hegemony over extensive regions where the means of directly imposing their will were slight. They needed perforce to implicate within their regimes men of note, standing or substance from the periphery, and the court offered an obvious meeting-point. Such was the case whether its prevailing ethos was autocratic or collaborative. And for this purpose ritual as a means of creating a sense of unique occasion was often of the essence (Leyser 1982, 1994; Reuter 1993; Koutrakou 1994; Nelson 1994, 1996). It was precisely *because* their respective versions of hegemony were ill-defined and inclined to be brittle that relations between Eastern and Western emperors could take a sudden turn towards mutual denunciation: they were all living in glass houses. The recriminations which a few jibes at their respective pretensions could unleash are exemplified by the celebrated exchange between Basil I and Emperor Louis II (*MGH*, *Epp.* VII: 386–94; Wickham 1998: 253–4). What is less well appreciated, because seldom fully articulated, is a sense of affinity between the courts of East and West, overriding their indubitable rivalries. Yet that it existed and was not merely a matter of rhetorical topoi is overwhelmingly likely. Eastern emperors such as Michael II and Theophilus presupposed sympathetic interest in their quelling of internal disorder and victories over the Muslims on the part of Western rulers, and in 841–2 Theophilus was proposing to marry his daughter to the then youthful Louis II (Shepard 1995: 45–7; Shepard 1998: 170; Wickham 1998: 246, 250–2).

The closeness with which Western potentates followed goings-on in the Great Palace occasionally emerges from non-narrative sources. For example, in November 813 Pope Leo III wrote to Charlemagne, relaying a tale he had heard from one of 'some Greek men' newly arrived from the east (*MGH, Epp.* V: 99). Reportedly, the wife of a former emperor and her lover had seized power in the palace, but the reigning emperor, Leo V, had managed to slip back into Constantinople, challenge the usurper to single combat in the Hippodrome and put him to death, together with his scheming paramour. Pope Leo added that some divergent details had been furnished by another informant (*MGH, Epp.* V: 99–100; Sansterre 1996: 373–8; Wickham 1998: 245–6). He refrained from choosing between the two versions, forwarding them on the assumption that, as Chris Wickham put it, 'the Frankish ruler wanted to know it all' (1998: 246). The tale relayed by Pope Leo is notable both for the almost wholly fictitious nature of its contents and for its assumption of the reader's acquaintance with the inauguration ritual and landmarks of the Eastern capital (*MGH, Epp.* V, 99–100). Charlemagne's curiosity will have been the keener for the fact that his imperial title had gained Byzantine recognition just a year earlier, when Eastern envoys acclaimed him 'in their own manner, that is in the Greek tongue, calling him emperor and *basileus*' (*Annales Regni Francorum* 1895: 136). But a more abiding interest is suggested by his possession of a square table on which was depicted 'the city of Constantinople' (Einhard, *Life of Charlemagne*, 33). The only other earthly city engraved on the silver tables listed in his will was Rome.

Charlemagne's interest in the Eastern seat of empire did not begin with his assumption of 'the name of emperor', nor was it unique. It is worth glancing at three instances when he and later rulers explicitly referred to the Eastern court and capital in mounting showpieces of their own authority. Firstly, it is now clear that the fortified 'city of Charles' which Charlemagne had built on newly conquered Saxon land in 776–7 is identifiable as Paderborn (Hauck 1986: 516–18, 528). The complex, comprising a royal hall juxtaposed to a 'great church' (*ecclesia magna*) of the Saviour, seems to have been an evocation of Haghia Sophia's proximity to the palace of the *basileus*, while the naming of the town after Charlemagne recalled the naming of Constantinople after the archetypal converter of peoples, Constantine the Great (Hauck 1986: fig. 1a on 514, 515, 531–2 and n. 86; cf. Collins 1998: 50, 140). What Constantine had achieved in the East, Charlemagne would match through imposing Christianity on the Saxons *en masse*, and building the palace complex at Paderborn made his aspirations manifest.[2]

The second episode occurred in 876, when Charles the Bald appeared before an assembly of bishops and other notables, 'clad in the Greek fashion' in a *dalmatica* 'reaching to the ankles' and a 'girdle hanging down to his feet' (*Annales de Saint-Bertin* 1964: 205; *Annales Fuldenses* 1960: 100–1). His assumption of Byzantine or Byzantinising garb was partly directed at a number of recalcitrant churchmen attending the assembly; but it fits in with other gestures at Ponthion serving to display his right to lordship over many peoples, not least the baptism of a group of Northmen and the acclamations of the pregnant empress by 'everyone . . . , each standing in position according to his rank' (*Annales de Saint-Bertin* 1964: 205, 206; Nelson 1991: 191, n. 6, 195, n. 21; Nelson 1992: 243–4). Above all, Charles was trying to bolster his legitimacy as emperor in the face of hostility from Louis the

German, whose son, Carloman, he had just deflected from the imperial crown. Expressing East Frankish resentment, the *Annals of Fulda* draw a direct connection between Charles' donning of 'new and unusual garb' and his pretensions to be called 'emperor and Augustus of all the kings on this side of the sea'. He reportedly boasted that 'he would assemble so great a host from different places that the horses would drink the Rhine dry' (*Annales Fuldenses* 1960: 100–1). In such a situation the ensemble of ceremonies was designed to 'speak' to persons from as many regions as possible.

Our final instance is provided by Otto III's deportment south of the Alps. Combining anxiety for personal salvation with advanced education and a certain ruthlessness, this short-lived emperor has attracted much speculation as to his aims (Leyser 1973: 117–19; Sansterre 1989; Görich 1993: 187–209, 261–74; Althoff 1996: 1–36, 114–25, 142–52, 171–81, 190–207). What is beyond doubt is Otto's belief in a God-given right to hegemony over numerous peoples and a high-minded sense of his duties. His court was the means of encapsulating that belief and projecting it outwards to distant subjects. He could thereby concretise his 'renewal' of 'the Roman empire'. It was, significantly, a feature of Otto's court that a Saxon chronicler picked out in order to illustrate his claim that Otto had tried to revive 'the ancient customs of the Romans': Otto sometimes sat alone at a separate table, elevated above his fellow diners (Thietmar 1935: 185).[3] To dine apart or with a few guests at a separate raised table was also the *basileus'* practice at certain banquets and this was most probably the model of Otto's dining ritual (Oikonomides 1972: 28 and n. 34, 164, n. 136, 274 and n. 34; Leyser 1994a: 164; Leyser 1994b: 202 and n. 79). Presumably he himself took it to originate from ancient Rome. The Byzantine court thus served as a kind of template of impeccably imperial ways which Otto sought to adopt for his own purposes. Gerbert's claims that 'Ours, ours is the Roman empire' and that 'you [Otto] surpass the Greeks in *imperium* and reign over the Romans by hereditary right' (Havet 1889: 237) echoed Otto's own aspirations. Otto's choice of the Palatine Hill as abode for his court for quite lengthy spells from 998 until his death is particularly suggestive: this had been the site of the Caesars' palaces from the reign of Augustus onwards (Brühl 1954: 17–18, 26–30). But only the Eastern emperor had maintained a court continuously since Antiquity, and only he could offer Otto a working model of imperial 'Roman' customs. It is no accident that those few protocols incorporated in the twelfth-century *Treatise on the Emperor's Court Ceremonies* which seem to date from Otto's time relate to the ceremonial bestowal of titles, including that of *patricius*, a procedure practised at the contemporary Byzantine court (Schramm 1969, III: 352–3; *DC*, I.57 (48), I, 244–55; ed. Vogt, II, 51–60; Bloch 1984: 87–9; Ladner 1988: 26–7). Faced with a medley of elites in Venice, Rome and other parts of Italy and in need of their cooperation, Otto tried to draw them into his charmed circle, simultaneously showing off his God-given right freely to choose his agents and installing northerners in Italian offices and the papal Curia.

All three of the above-mentioned initiatives were ephemeral, and one should note that they were taken either in Italy or soon after their authors' visiting the peninsula. But it is worth noting what these three rulers had in common: each had recently tried to extend or markedly to enhance his dominion and each faced likely rebellion.

The court on the Bosporus had the merit of being at once extraneous (and thus not specific to any particular grouping among the ruler's subjects) and yet of some repute, in that its origins were supposed to lie in the imperial Roman past: Liudprand of Cremona supposed – mistakenly – that the institution of the 'purple-born' (*porphyrogeniti*) went back to the days of Constantine the Great (Liudpr., *Ant.* I.6–7; III.31). And as Otto III, for one, was well aware, the *basileus*' own hegemony rested heavily on the more or less voluntary cooperation of elites living in the empire's peripheral regions and beyond – in effect, on consensus. In that sense his court offered an 'exemplary centre' to virtually any potentate aspiring to preside over a Christian order and the effects of its magnetic field were probably wider-ranging and more manifold than the few recorded cases of overt imitation might suggest. These cases make up the colourful extremes of a broad spectrum of responses which ranged from regarding the 'Greeks' as a foil against which to define one's own distinctive garb and customs to the selective adaptation of particular symbols or ceremonies and a sense, albeit incompletely expressed, of shared values and aspirations.

To make these assertions is to assume a rather high degree of awareness of the Eastern court on the part of Western elites. Such an assumption might seem questionable in view of the hazards and expense of travel. However, one form of journey was probably commoner than has generally been supposed: embassies (Barnwell 1997: 134–9). To societies where the personal qualities of a leader counted for much and where individual sworn agreements underpinned order, formal exchanges of gifts and greetings between potentates aspiring to legitimacy were no less important. It was therefore probably a frequent practice to renew treaties and other agreements upon the death of one of the main parties to them (Barnwell 1997: 137; Chrysos 1992: 32). This alone would have generated a fair number of embassies. Moreover, the reception and sending of embassies was practised with particular vigour by the Eastern emperors, who showed a consistent penchant for initiating exchanges and visits to their capital (Chrysos 1992: 31–3; Shepard 1992: 51–3). The formal receptions of foreign 'friends' to the sound of organs were happenings at which the *basileus* outdazzled and outplayed virtually any other potentate's efforts and sometimes envoys were received serially, one by one (*DC* II.15, II, 569; Maliaras 1991: 142–56, 188). Visiting envoys were encouraged to attend other ceremonies, too: Liudprand was urged to watch the Easter dispensing of pay and in effect became a participant there himself, receiving gold from the emperor (Liudpr., *Leg.* 9; McCormick 1985: 9). Thus the workings of imperial diplomacy served to draw representatives of foreign potentates to the exemplary centre on the Bosporus and this did something to maintain awareness of it in their home courts.

It was, however, the embassies sent by the *basileus* to the courts of others which had most impact. If it was mainly the hand-picked associates of a foreign potentate who beheld the emperor in full glory, the latter's envoys could reach a wider audience. Imperial embassies varied greatly in size and composition according to circumstances, and messengers were probably sufficient for minor exchanges concerning mundane matters such as the return of runaway slaves (*Povest' Vremennykh Let* 1950, I: 36; Lounghis 1980: 299–302, 371–3). But even they may sometimes have seized the chance for showing off the wealth and power of their master and a grander class of embassy was certainly sent to Muslim overlords such as the 'Abbāsid caliphs and

Figure 2.3 Otto III (983–1002) with clerical and secular attendants. From the tenth-century Gospel Book of Otto III. Bildarchiv Preussischer Kulturbesitz.

the rulers of Egypt (Soucek 1997; Grabar 1997: 117–21; Shepard 2000: 387–9). It is most probable that similar embassies headed westwards. Liudprand of Cremona denounced not merely the Byzantine envoys' 'brooches, long flowing hair and tunics reaching down to their ankles', but also the fact that they wore them all the time, 'when they ride or walk or sit at table with us'; further, and most disgraceful 'to all of our men', the Byzantine envoys alone were allowed to kiss Otto I and his son with covered heads (*Leg.* 37). Liudprand's complaint that Byzantine envoys in the West were allowed 'to keep to their own ways' whereas he, at Constantinople, was expected to conform highlights a key feature of Byzantine grand embassies: they were in effect miniature versions of the court on location (above, p.20), the head or heads of the embassy being invested with a certain imperial dignity. The 'sacred' letters which they brought were objects of value and striking appearance in themselves (Dölger 1976: 14–17), and they were probably read out and bestowed in a variant of the rites of delivery and reception of letters current within the empire (Mullett 1992: 204–6, 216; Soucek 1997: 408–9; Leyser 1994b: 213 and n. 129). The grand embassies were equipped with some of the court's most characteristic furnishings, silks and other precious fabrics, gold and silver vessels and other valuable containers (Grabar 1997: 118–20; Soucek 1997: 405–10); a wide range of artefacts was carried for possible presentation even by essentially functional missions (*DC* II.44, I, 661–2). Not merely did they publicise the skills of the emperor's craftsmen: they also mirrored the diversity of *objets d'art* on display at court, offering observers a glimpse of what might be in store for them there. The hierarchical significance of the vestments was probably expounded in words akin to the ones addressed to Liudprand: 'those who are unique in the grace of their virtue should also be unique in the beauty of their clothing' (Liudpr., *Leg.* 54). The heads of grand embassies, themselves holding at least the title of *patricius*, were leading quite sizable companies, perhaps fifty or more persons strong (McCormick 1994: 26–7 and 44, n. 46), and presumably stationing themselves according to rank at receptions. Such companies could be conceived of as performing a chant so attractive that Charlemagne had part of it translated into Latin (Notker the Stammerer, *Deeds of Emperor Charlemagne*, II.7; McCormick 1995: 374–5).

Through the medium of embassies the Eastern court cast a more pervasive penumbra than its proceedings at Constantinople alone might suggest. The very infrequency of the really grand embassies probably heightened their impact, in that the rarity of the luxuries brought in their train heightened their desirability. The visible hierarchy of clothing was more or less self-explanatory, and at least some members of grand embassies were well-qualified to expound the symbolic significance of 'their own ways' and of the gifts they brought. The best-known intellectuals to be recorded as on embassies are those sent to the *basileus'* rival in Baghdad, for example, John the Grammarian, Photius and Leo Choerosphactes (Magdalino 1998: 195–205). But it has been pointed out that some, at least, of the churchmen sent to Frankish courts in the ninth century were capable exponents of theology (McCormick 1994: 30). Communications which intellectuals on missions to more or less neophyte or pagan rulers reportedly delivered are imbued with imperial ideology (Zástěrová 1983: 690–701; Dagron 1996: 68–9; Simeonova 1998: 124–52), and Photius' precepts on the duties and conduct of a Christian ruler in his letter to Khan Boris of Bulgaria have aptly been termed 'a vision of the court of God' (Mayr-Harting 1994: 24). There is no reason to suppose that ambassadors were any less forthcoming in expatiating upon their empire or Christian rulership in general during their sometimes protracted stays at Western courts.

Thus 'text', in written form or enunciated,[4] may often have been available to supplement the 'image' of felicitous hierarchy which Byzantine grand embassies presented. They could, while travelling, impress the majesty and wealth of the *basileus* upon 'barbarian' notables who lacked the means or inclination to pay a visit to Byzantium and who might have only loose ties with their local potentate. These were offered a fresh yardstick against which to appraise and perhaps belittle that potentate. Thus the grander sort of embassy presented a challenge, as well as an opportunity (and even an education) to the rulers whom it was formally visiting. Indirectly it could subvert, as well as offering rulers the chance to borrow such features of the court as appeared to cater for structural problems occurring within their own regimes.

One recurring dilemma of rulership in the early medieval West was how to provide for the succession to full authority of one's son or other chosen heir. It was in this sphere that a ruler might well feel dissatisfied with his own family's customs, nobles' predilections or churchmen's rites, particularly if he was an *arriviste* or had laid claim to markedly heightened status. Such a problem was faced by the Ostrogoth king Theoderic, who in any case lacked a son (Heather 1995: 165–71). Charlemagne adapted certain salient features of Byzantine ceremonial when he saw to the crowning of Louis the Pious as his co-emperor before an assembly of the empire's magnates in 813 (Wendling 1985: 220–3, 228–9; Classen 1985: 100–1). The Eastern court was of interest in relation to matters of succession for another newcomer to the imperial title by dint of military *virtus*, Otto of Saxony. We have already noted the interest which Liudprand showed in the Byzantine notion of the 'purple-born' (above, p. 26), and a generation later Gerbert of Aurillac and Archbishop Egbert of Trier assumed one another's familiarity with the Byzantine practice of co-emperorship (Gerbert 1993, I: 52–3; Ohnsorge 1958: 271–2). It was partly because of such familiarity among the members of Western elites that Otto I determined to secure a purple-born princess for his son and heir, Otto II, in the later 960s. This is the characteristic of the sought-after bride which Liudprand underscores in his account of his embassy of 968 (*Leg.* 15–16). Besides desiring general prestige from a marriage bond with the Eastern *Augustus*, Liudprand and his master may tacitly have shared the Byzantine sense that conceptions and births vouchsafed to those reigning within the palace were a mark of divine favour: the offspring represented God's blessing and held out the prospect of further favours to come (Treitinger 1938: 109–10; Dagron 1994: 109 and n. 22, 130–2, 140–2). This quality, denoting special fitness to reign, attached to the purple-born for the rest of their lives, investing them with a form of sacrality. It was most probably the same attribute which appealed to another *arriviste* intent on enhancing the status of his son and thereby ensuring his succession. In 988 Hugh Capet caused Gerbert to write to the Eastern emperor requesting 'a daughter of the holy empire' – presumably a *porphyrogenita* – as bride for his son, Robert (Gerbert 1993, I: 268–71; Leyser 1982b: 115–16). For *nouveaux* regimes a bond with a princess supposed to be the outcome of a kind of divine visitation brought unique validation: embodying, as she did, elements of ritual and God-willed rulership in her very person, she could literally transfuse legitimate ascendancy into the veins of the next generation. Such qualities were not lost on another ambitious potentate still in need of legitimation in the late 980s, Vladimir Sviatoslavich, prince of the Rusý. At that time he made himself sufficiently useful or menacing to the empire to gain the hand of a *porphyrogenita*, Anna (Franklin and Shepard 1996: 162–4).

The ascendancy of Otto I, as of Hugh Capet and Vladimir, was due above all to the successful exercise of military *virtus*, dispensation of benefits and winning of widespread confidence (Leyser 1994a: 148–9, 164). To dynasts eager to mark out their regime as God-willed and secure for their heirs, a marriage-tie with the celebrated exemplary centre held out the prospect of, as it were, instant legitimacy, in a form at once alien yet reputable. It is a mark of their need of such a talisman that Otto and, most probably, Vladimir were ready to use force – by launching assaults on, respectively, the Byzantine cities of Bari and Cherson. Otto had, in the end, to settle for less than a *porphyrogenita* as bride for his son, and reportedly his acceptance of Theophano, 'not the desired virgin', evoked ridicule from the Italians and anger among the Germans (Thietmar 1935: 57; Wolf 1991: 385–6; Leyser 1994a: 156–7). An almost contemporary source sympathetic to the regime refers to Theophano as a 'distinguished royal bride' 'from the palace of the Augustus' (*Vita Mahthildis Antiquior* 1852: 581). This was an attempt to put a brave face on things, special pleading in an awkward situation through emphasis on Theophano's associations with the palace. But it also testifies to the aura of antique and rightful dominion which the rhythms of the *basileus'* court still generated at the end of the tenth century, in a fashion reminiscent of the Balinese *negara*'s. So long as sacral kingship with its attendant ritual was integral to the regimes of aspiring overlords in the West, the Eastern court was not merely a useful source of gifts and greetings. It offered them and their notables a graphic model of how to go through the motions of deference: as in the entrances and processions prescribed in the *Book of Ceremonies*, everyone might be induced to act in unison, 'each standing in position according to his rank' (*Annales de Saint-Bertin* 1964: 205; above, p. 24). The image was no less haunting for being almost unattainable.

NOTES

1   The drastic, often unforeseeable, fluctuations in the strategic and financial position of the empire under Justinian were particularly well brought out by Teall 1965: 303–4, 314–15, 319–21.

2   Charlemagne's choice of name may well have been swayed by his awareness of Orosius' account of the refounding of the ancient Byzantium as 'the city of Constantine' (Hauck 1986: 518, 529–31). But the naming of the new base and its layout probably had broader connotations that were not the product of a written text alone. It is noteworthy that the church at Aachen dedicated to Mary in which Charlemagne was acclaimed emperor in 812 was, with its central plan forming an octagon, clearly designed to evoke Eastern imperial architecture, as exemplified by San Vitale in Ravenna (Falkenstein 1991: 282–8).

3   A comparable attitude was struck by the expansionist King Leovigild of Spain (568–86): his hegemonial pretensions were expressed by such reportedly unprecedented gestures as seating himself 'among his own (*inter suos*) upon a throne, clad in a royal vestment' (Isidore of Seville 1894: 288; Linehan 1993: 22 and n.2).

4   The larger embassies may well have contained interpreters of written and spoken Greek. There is anyway evidence of the presence at Carolingian courts and ecclesiastical centres of individual Greeks (Berschin 1988: 117–18, 132–3; McCormick 1994: 18–20, 29). They could have acted as interpreters and also translators.

ABBREVIATIONS

DC	Constantine VII, *De cerimoniis aulae byzantinae*, ed. I.I. Reiske, vols 1–2 (Corpus Scriptorum Historiae Byzantinae) (Bon: Weber, 1829–30)
ed. Vogt	Constantine VII, *Le livre des cérémonies*, ed. A. Vogt, vols 1–2 (Paris: Les Belles Lettres, 1935–9)
Liudpr., *Ant.*	Liudprand, *Antapodosis*, in *Opera*, ed. J. Becker (MGH, Scriptores rerum Germanicarum in usum scholarum) (Hanover/Leipzig 1915)
Liudpr., *Leg.*	Liudprand, *Legatio*, in *Opera*, ed. J. Becker (MGH, Scriptores rerum Germanicarum in usum scholarum) (Hanover/Leipzig 1915)
MGH, Epp.	Monumenta Germaniae Historica, Epistulae
MGH, SS	Monumenta Germaniae Historica, Scriptores

REFERENCES

Althoff, G. (1996) *Otto III.*, Darmstadt: Wissenschaftliche Buchgesellschaft.

Annales Fuldenses (1960) ed. R. Rau *et al.* (Ausgewählte Quellen zur deutschen Geschichte des Mittelalters 7, Quellen zur karolingischen Reichsgeschichte 3), Berlin.

Annales Regni Francorum (1895) ed. F. Kurze (MGH, Scriptores rerum Germanicarum in usum scholarum), Hanover.

Annales de Saint-Bertin (1964), ed. F. Grat, J. Vielliard and S. Clémencet, Paris: Librairie C. Klincksieck.

Antonopoulos, P. (1990) *Petros Patrikios. ho Byzantinos diplomates, axiomatouchos kai syngrapheas*, Athens: Historikes Ekdoseis S. D. Vasilopoulos.

Barnwell, P.S. (1997) 'War and peace: historiography and seventh-century embassies', *Early Medieval Europe* 6: 127–39.

Berschin, W. (1988) *Greek Letters and the Latin Middle Ages from Jerome to Nicholas of Cusa*, tr. J.C. Frakes, Washington, DC: Catholic University of America Press.

Bloch, H. (1984) 'Der Autor der "Graphia aureae urbis Romae"', *Deutsches Archiv für Erforschung des Mittelalters* 40: 55–175.

Brühl, C. (1954) 'Die Kaiserpfalz bei St Peter und die Pfalz Ottos III. auf dem Palatin', *Quellen und Forschungen aus italienischen Archiven und Bibliotheken* 34: 1–30.

Cameron, Averil (1978) 'The Theotokos in sixth-century Constantinople', *Journal of Theological Studies* 29: 79–108.

—— (1979a) 'The Virgin's Robe: an episode in the history of early seventh-century Constantinople', *Byzantion* 49: 42–56.

—— (1979b) 'Images of authority: elites and icons in late sixth-century Byzantium', *Past and Present*, no. 84: 3–35.

—— (1985) *Procopius and the Sixth Century*, London: Duckworth.

—— (1987) 'The construction of court ritual: the Byzantine *Book of Ceremonies*', in D. Cannadine and S. Price (eds), *Rituals of Royalty. Power and Ceremonial in Traditional Societies*, Cambridge: Cambridge University Press, 106–36.

Campbell, J. (1992) 'The impact of the Sutton Hoo discovery on the study of Anglo-Saxon history', in C.B. Kendall and P.S. Wells (eds) *Voyage to the Other World. The Legacy of Sutton Hoo* (Medieval Studies at Minnesota 5), Minneapolis: University of Minnesota Press, 79–101.

Chrysos, E. (1985) 'Zur Reichsideologie und Westpolitik Justinians. Der Friedenplan des Jahres 540', in V. Vavřínek (ed.), *From Late Antiquity to Early Byzantium*, Prague: Academia, 40–8.

—— (1992) 'Byzantine diplomacy, A.D. 300–800: means and ends', in J. Shepard and S. Franklin (eds), *Byzantine Diplomacy*, Aldershot: Variorum, 25–39.

Classen, P. (1985) *Karl der Grosse, das Papsttum und Byzanz*, ed. H. Fuhrmann and C. Märtl (Beiträge zur Geschichte und Quellenkunde des Mittelalters 9), Sigmaringen: Thorbecke.

Collins, R. (1998) *Charlemagne*, Basingstoke: Macmillan.

Constantine VII (1990) *Three Treatises on Imperial Military Expeditions*, ed. and tr. J.F. Haldon (Corpus fontium historiae byzantinae 28. Series Vindoboniensis), Vienna.

Corippus (1976) *In laudem Iustini Augusti minoris libri IV*, ed. and tr. Averil Cameron, London: Athlone Press.

Corrigan, K. (1978) 'The ivory scepter of Leo VI: a statement of post-Iconoclastic imperial ideology', *Art Bulletin* 60: 407–16.

Dagron, G. (1994) 'Nés dans la pourpre', *Travaux et Mémoires* 12: 105–42.

—— (1996) *Empereur et prêtre: étude sur le 'césaropapisme' byzantin*, Paris: Gallimard.

Deichmann, F.W. (1958–89, I–III) *Ravenna: Hauptstadt des spätantiken Abendlandes*, Wiesbaden: Steier.

Dhuoda (1998) *Handbook for her Warrior Son. Liber Manualis,* ed. and tr. M. Thiébaux, Cambridge: Cambridge University Press.

Dölger, F. (1976) 'Die Kaiserurkunde der Byzantiner als Ausdruck ihrer politischen Anschauungen', repr. in Dölger's *Byzanz und die europäische Staatenwelt*, Darmstadt: Wissenschaftliche Buchgesellschaft, 9–33.

Engelhardt, I. (1974) *Mission und Politik in Byzanz. Ein Beitrag zur Strukturanalyse Byzantinischer Mission zur Zeit Justins und Justinians* (Miscellanea Byzantina Monacensia 19), Munich: Institut für Byzantinistik und neugriechische Philologie der Universität.

Evans, J.A.S. (1996) *The Age of Justinian. The Circumstances of Imperial Power*, London/New York: Routledge.

Falkenstein, L. (1991) 'Charlemagne et Aix-la-Chapelle', *Byzantion* 61: 231–89.

Franklin, S. and Shepard, J. (1996) *The Emergence of Rus 750–1200*, London: Longmans.

Geertz, C. (1980) *Negara. The Theatre State in Nineteenth-Century Bali*, Princeton: Princeton University Press.

Gerbert of Aurillac (1993, I–II) *Correspondance*, ed. and tr. P. Riché and J.P. Callu, Paris: Les Belles Lettres.

Görich, K. (1993) *Otto III. Romanus Saxonicus et Italicus. Kaiserliche Rompolitik und sächsische Historiographie*, Sigmaringen: Thorbecke.

Grabar, O. (1997) 'The shared culture of objects', in H. Maguire (ed.), *Byzantine Court Culture from 829 to 1204*, Washington, DC: Dumbarton Oaks Research Library and Collection, 115–29.

Hauck, K. (1986) 'Karl als neuer Konstantin 777. Die archäologischen Entdeckungen in Paderborn in historischer Sicht', *Frühmittelalterliche Studien* 20: 513–40.

Haussig, H.W. (1979) 'La missione cristiana nell' Asia centrale e orientale nei secoli VI e VII e le sue tracce archeologiche e letterarie', *XXVI Corso di Cultura sull' Arte Ravennnate e Byzantina*, Ravenna: Edizioni del Girasole 171–95.

Havet, J. (ed.) (1889) *Lettres de Gerbert (983–997)*, Paris: A. Picard.

Heather, P. (1995) 'Theoderic, king of the Goths', *Early Medieval History* 4: 145–73.

Herrin, J. (1991) 'Byzance: le palais et la Ville', *Byzantion* 61: 213–30.

Hill, B.T. (1983) 'Constantinopolis', in T. Hackens and R. Winkes (eds), *Gold Jewelry. Craft, Style and Meaning from Mycenae to Constantinopolis*, Louvain-la-Neuve, Institut supérieur d'archéologie et d'histoire de l'art: Collège Erasme, 141–60.

Hincmar of Rheims (1980) *De ordine palatii*, ed. T. Gross and R. Schieffer (MGH, Fontes iuris Germanici antiqui in usum scholarum 3) ed. T. Mommsen, Hanover.

Isidore of Seville (1894) *Historia Gothorum*, MGH, Auctores Antiquissimi XI, 267–95.

Kazhdan, A. and McCormick, M. (1997) 'The social world of the Byzantine court', in H. Maguire (ed.), *Byzantine Court Culture from 829 to 1204*, Washington, DC: Dumbarton Oaks Research Library and Collection, 167–97.

Kislinger, E. (1998) 'Ein Angriff zu viel. Zur Verteidigung der Thermopylen in justinianischer Zeit', *Byzantinische Zeitschrift* 91: 49–58.

Koder, J. (1994, I) 'Justinians Sieg über Salomon', in M. Vasilaki *et al.* (eds), *Thymiama ste mneme tes Laskarinas Boura*, Athens: Mouseio Benake,135–42.

Koutrakou, N.-C. (1994) *La propagande impériale byzantine. Persuasion et réaction (VIII–X siècles)*, Athens: Université nationale d'Athènes, Faculté des Lettres. Bibliothèque 'Sophie N. Saripolou'.

Ladner, G. (1988) *L'immagine dell' imperatore Ottone III* (Unione Internazionale degli Istituti di Archeologia, Storia e Storia dell' Arte in Roma. Conferenze 5), Rome.

Leyser, K. (1982a) 'Ottonian government', repr. in Leyser's *Medieval Germany and its Neighbours*, London: Hambledon Press, 69–101.

—— (1982b) 'The tenth century in Byzantine–Western relations', repr. in Leyser's *Medieval Germany and its Neighbours*, London: Hambledon Press, 103–37.

—— (1994a) '*Theophanu Divina Gratia Imperatrix Augusta*: Western and Eastern emperorship in the later tenth century', repr. in Leyser's *Communications and Power in Medieval Europe*, ed. T. Reuter, London: Hambledon Press, 143–64.

—— (1994b) 'Ritual, ceremony and gesture: Ottonian Germany', repr. in Leyser's *Communications and Power in Medieval Europe*, ed. T. Reuter, London: Hambledon Press, 189–213.

Linehan, P. (1993) *History and the Historians of Medieval Spain*, Oxford: Clarendon Press.

Lounghis, T.C. (1980) *Les ambassades byzantines en Occident depuis la fondation des états barbares jusqu' aux Croisades*, Athens: T. C. Lounghis.

Maas, M. (1986) 'Roman history and Christian ideology in Justinianic reform legislation', *Dumbarton Oaks Papers* 40: 17–31.

Magdalino, P. (ed.) (1994) *New Constantines: the Rhythm of Imperial Renewal in Byzantium, 4th – 13th centuries*, Aldershot: Variorum.

—— (1998), 'The road to Baghdad', in L. Brubaker (ed.), *Byzantium in the Ninth Century: dead or alive?*, Aldershot: Ashgate, 195–213.

Maguire, H. (1992) 'The mosaics of Nea Moni: an imperial reading', *Dumbarton Oaks Papers* 46: 205–14.

—— (1997) 'The heavenly court', in H. Maguire (ed.), *Byzantine Court Culture from 829 to 1204*, Washington, DC: Dumbarton Oaks Research Library and Collection, 247–58.

Maliaras, N. (1991) *Die Orgel im byzantinischen Hofzeremoniell des 9. und des 10. Jahrhunderts. Eine Quellenuntersuchung* (Miscellanea Byzantina Monacensia 33), Munich: Institüt für Byzantinistik und neugrieschiche Philologie der Universität.

Mango, C. (1985) *Le développement urbain de Constantinople (IV–VII siècles)* (Travaux et mémoires du Centre de recherche d'histoire et civilisation de Byzance. Monographes 2), Paris: Diffusion de Boccard.

Mayr-Harting, H. (1994) *Two Conversions to Christianity: the Bulgarians and the Anglo-Saxons* (The Stenton Lectures 27), Reading: University of Reading.

McCormick, M. (1985) 'Analyzing imperial ceremonies', *Jahrbuch der österreichischen Byzantinistik* 35: 1–20.

—— (1994) 'Diplomacy and the Carolingian encounter with Byzantium down to the accession of Charles the Bald', in B. McGinn and W. Otten (eds), *Eriugena: East and West* (Notre Dame Conferences in Medieval Studies 5), Notre Dame, 15–48.

—— (1995) 'Byzantium and the West, 700–900', in R. McKitterick (ed.), *New Cambridge Medieval History*, II, Cambridge: Cambridge University Press, 349–80.

Michael Psellus (1926–8, I–II) *Chronographia*, ed. E. Renauld, Paris: Les Belles Lettres.

Moorhead, J. (1994) *Justinian*, London: Longmans.

Mouriki, D. (1985, I–II) *The Mosaics of Nea Moni on Chios*, tr. R. Burgi, Athens: Commercial Bank of Greece.

Mullett, M. (1992) 'The language of diplomacy', in J. Shepard and S. Franklin (eds), *Byzantine Diplomacy*, Aldershot: Variorum, 203–16.

Muthesius, A. (1996) *Studies in Byzantine and Islamic Silk Weaving*, London: Pindar Press.

Nelson, J. (tr.) (1991) *The Annals of St-Bertin*, Manchester: Manchester University Press.

—— (1992) *Charles the Bald*, London: Longmans.

—— (1994) 'Kingship and empire in the Carolingian world', in R. McKitterick (ed.), *Carolingian Culture: Emulation and Innovation*, Cambridge: Cambridge University Press, 52–87.

Nelson, J. (1996) 'The Lord's Anointed and the people's choice: Carolingian royal ritual', repr. in Nelson's *The Frankish World 750–900*, London: Hambledon Press, 99–131.

Obolensky, D. (1994) 'The principles and methods of Byzantine diplomacy', repr. in Obolensky's *Byzantium and the Slavs*, New York: St Vladimir's Seminary Press, 1–22.

—— (1994) 'The Empire and its northern neighbours 565–1018', repr. in Obolensky's *Byzantium and the Slavs*, New York: St Vladimir's Seminary Press, 23–73.

Ohnsorge, W. (1958) 'Das Mitkaisertum in der abendländischen Geschichte des früheren Mittelalters', repr. in Ohnsorge's *Abendland und Byzanz*, Darmstadt: Wissenschaftliche Buchgesellschaft, 261–87.

Oikonomides, N. (1972) *Les listes de préséance byzantines des IX et X siècles*, Paris: Centre national de la recherche scientifique.

—— (1996) 'The significance of some imperial monumental portraits of the X and XI centuries', *Zograf* 25: 23–6.

Olster, D. (1996) 'From periphery to center: the transformation of late Roman self-definition in the seventh century', in R.W. Mathisen and H.S. Sivan (eds), *Shifting Frontiers in Late Antiquity*, Aldershot: Ashgate, 93–101.

Patoura, S. (1997) 'Une nouvelle considération sur la politique de Justinien envers les peuples du Danube', *Byzantinoslavica* 57: 78–86.

Photius (1959–91, I–IX), *Bibliothèque*, ed. and tr. R. Henry, Paris: Les Belles Lettres.

Pohl, W. (1997) 'The Empire and the Lombards: treaties and negotiations in the sixth century', in W. Pohl (ed.), *Kingdoms of the Empire. The Integration of Barbarians in Late Antiquity*, Leiden: Brill, 75–133.

Povest' Vremennykh Let (1950, I–II) ed. V.P. Adrianova-Peretts and D.S. Likhachev, Moscow-Leningrad: Izdatel'stvo Akademii Nauk SSSR.

Reuter, T. (1993) 'The origins of the German *Sonderweg?* The Empire and its rulers in the High Middle Ages', in A. Duggan (ed.), *Kings and Kingship in Medieval Europe*, London: King's College London Centre for Late Antique and Medieval Studies, 179–211.

Rousseau, P. (1998) 'Procopius's *Buildings* and Justinian's pride', *Byzantion*, 68: 121–30.

Sansterre, J.-M. (1989) 'Otton III et les saints ascètes de son temps', *Rivista di storia della chiesa in Italia*, 43: 377–412.

—— (1996) 'Les informations parvenues en Occident sur l'avènement de l'empereur Léon V et le siège de Constantinople par les Bulgares en 813', *Byzantion* 66: 373–80.

Schramm, P. (1968–71, I–IV) *Kaiser, Könige und Päpste. Gesammelte Aufsätze zur Geschichte des Mittelalters*, Stuttgart: Anton Hiersemann.

Shepard, J. (1992) 'Byzantine diplomacy, A.D. 800–1204: means and ends', in J. Shepard and S. Franklin (eds), *Byzantine Diplomacy*, Aldershot: Variorum, 41–71.

—— (1995) 'The Rhos guests of Louis the Pious: whence and wherefore?', *Early Medieval Europe* 4: 41–60.

—— (1998) 'Byzantine relations with the outside world in the ninth century: an introduction', in L. Brubaker (ed.), *Byzantium in the Ninth Century: Dead or Alive?*, Aldershot: Ashgate, 167–80.

—— (2000) 'Messages, ordres et ambassades: diplomatie centrale et frontalière à Byzance (IX–XI siècles)', in A. Dierkens, J.-L. Kupper and J.-M. Sansterre (eds), *Voyages et voyageurs à Byzance et en Occident du VI au XI siècle*, Geneva: Librairie Droz S.A., 375–96.

Simeonova, L. (1998) *Diplomacy of the Letter and the Cross. Photios, Bulgaria and the Papacy, 860s–880s*, Amsterdam: Adolf Hakkert.

Soucek, P. (1997) 'Byzantium and the Islamic world', in H.C. Evans and W.D. Wixom (eds), *The Glory of Byzantium. Art and Culture of the Middle Byzantine Era A.D. 843–1261*, New York: Metropolitan Museum of Art, 403–11.

Stout, A.M. (1994) 'Jewelry as a symbol of status in the Roman Empire', in J. L. Sebesta and L. Bonfante (eds) *The World of Roman Costume*, Madison, Wisconsin: University of Wisconsin Press, 77–100.

Teall, J. L. (1965) 'The barbarians in Justinian's armies', *Speculum* 40: 294–322.

Thierry, N. (1985) 'Un portrait de Jean Tzimiskès en Cappadoce', *Travaux et Mémoires* 9: 477–84.

Thietmar of Merseburg (1935) *Chronicon*, ed. R. Holtzmann (MGH Scriptores rerum Germanicarum, nova series 9), Berlin.

Treitinger, O. (1938) *Die oströmische Kaiser- und Reichsidee nach ihrer Gestaltung im höfischen Zeremoniell vom oströmischen Staats- und Reichsgedanken*, Jena: Verlag der Frummannschen Buchhandlung.

Vasilaki, M. *et al.* (eds) (1994, I–II) *Thymiama ste mneme tes Laskarinas Boura*, Athens: Mouseio Benake.

Vierck, H. (1981) '*Imitatio imperii* und *interpretatio Germanica* vor der Wikingerzeit', in R. Zeitler (ed.), *Les pays du nord et Byzance (Scandinavie et Byzance). Actes du colloque nordique et international de byzantinologie* (Acta Universitatis Upsaliensis. *Figura* nov. series 19), Uppsala: Uppsala universitet, 64–113.

Vita Mahthildis Antiquior (1852) ed. G.H. Pertz (MGH, Scriptores 10), Hanover, 575–82.

von Euw, A. and Schreiner, P. (eds) (1991, I–II) *Kaiserin Theophanu. Begegnung des Ostens und Westens um die Wende des ersten Jahrtausends*, Cologne: Schnutgen-Museum.

Wendling, W. (1985) 'Die Erhebung Ludwigs des Frommen zum Mitkaiser im Jahre 813 und ihre Bedeutung für die Verfassungsgeschichte des Frankenreiches', *Frühmittelalterliche Studien* 19: 201–38.

Wickham, C. (1998) 'Ninth-century Byzantium through Western eyes', in L. Brubaker (ed.), *Byzantium in the Ninth Century: DEAD OR ALIVE?*, Aldershot: Ashgate, 245–56.

Wolf, G. (1991, II) 'Wer war Theophanu?', in A. von Euw and P. Schreiner (eds), *Kaiserin Theophanu. Begegnung des Ostens und Westens um die Wende des ersten Jahrtausends*, Cologne: Schnutgen-Museum, 385–96.

Zástêrová, B. (1983) 'Un témoignage inaperçu relatif à la diffusion de l'idéologie politique byzantine dans le milieu slave, au 9 siècle', *Okeanos* = *Harvard Ukrainian Studies* 7: 691–701.

CHAPTER THREE

AT THE SPANISH FRONTIER[1]

Peter Linehan

What with priests and mullahs on either side of it and men and even women crossing and recrossing more or less unhindered, it always was its own sort of frontier. It had been so almost since whenever it was within a few years of the 'Arab' (actually mostly Berber) invasion of 711 that the myth of the origins of the Spanish Reconquest had begun to take shape, with at its core the symbolic breaching by don Oppas of both the physical and the confessional lines which separated the peninsula's new alien masters from the Christian remnants of the old order holed up in their cave at Covadonga. Oppas, the collaborationist bishop whose failed attempt to persuade don Pelayo and his band to surrender on terms to the invaders, as he himself and so many of the Visigothic old guard had done already, set the scene for the annihilation of 180,000 or so 'Arabs', was medieval Spain's very first, and also perhaps its only wholly uncomplicated frontiersman (Gil Fernández *et al.* 1985: 126).

Don Pelayo, that Asturian hybrid of Moses and Asterix, and don Oppas, the hero and villain respectively of the dramatic encounter which stands at the beginning of the story of the history of medieval Spain, are inseparable from the scene of that encounter. For Spanish nationalists Covadonga is the cradle of the national epic. From here, high up in the mountains of the north, for them there began that fight-back which would end in 1492 with the reconquest of Granada – or what nationalists of another allegiance prefer to call its conquest, or incorporation. Now provided with cafés, car parks, votive candles, just about adequate lavatories and all the other paraphernalia appropriate to such shrines, Covadonga is also the original location of a frontier, a frontier which, according to that same view of the Spanish Middle Ages, is as precisely definable as the process of reconquest itself, a frontier only a few feet wide in the mid-710s (if history is to be believed as well as the historians), but a frontier which for those for whom history is a black and white affair marked for almost eight hundred years a dividing line between Christian and Muslim Spain, and so between Christendom itself and Islam in the West.

Others, scholars in the United States in the main, have thought it helpful to subject the medieval Spanish peninsula to the analysis advanced by F. J. Turner in his celebrated paper on the role of the frontier in American society ('doubtless the most influential paper ever presented before a congress of historians'), according to which what had determined the course of the history of the United States until

Turner set pen to paper was, first, the 'safety valve' provided by the availability of free land on the Western frontier, and then, when that supply was exhausted, the consequences for the hinterland of the removal of that mechanism (Turner 1921: 1–38; Lewis 1958: 475; Bishko 1963: 47–9). In fact, although for adventurers from northern Europe, for whom all the inhabitants they encountered (Christians, Jews and Muslims alike) were equally foreign, the Spanish frontier may indeed have borne some resemblance to Turner's Wild West (Defourneaux 1949: 125–230; David 1936), for the inhabitants of its hinterland the unremitting tale of those almost eight sometimes hard-fought centuries was one of varying shades of grey. Where it bordered on Africa, Europe's frontier was significantly different from its eastern counterpart.[2] Here the 'other' was unnervingly close. Indeed, here the 'other' was both behind you and all around. There were D. Oppas look-alikes to be encountered (or suspected) at every village oven. There may even have been Moorish sympathisers in the recesses of the cave at Covadonga.

Unrecognisable as the precursor of Webb's 'sharp edge of sovereignty' (Webb 1953: 2; cf. Truyol y Serra 1957; Bazzana 1997), therefore, medieval Spain's frontier was probably permeable from the outset. It was certainly accustomed to two-way traffic forever after. In the 850s Alvarus, a Christian monk of Córdoba – a city which by then had been under Islamic domination for almost a century and a half – travelled north to Pamplona and in a library in the foothills of the Pyrenees 'suddenly' chanced on a highly tendentious potted history of the life of the Prophet. It was almost as if this was the first that he had ever heard of him (Gil 1973: ii.483). Then, in the 950s, the Christian king of León journeyed in the other direction. This was Sancho the Fat. So fat was he, this warrior king, that he could hardly walk, let alone ride. So, he sent to Córdoba for a cure and, having been rendered a mere shadow of his former self, surrendered various frontier fortresses as the price of his therapy.

Or such was the story related in the Leonese chronicle of Sampiro in the eleventh century and canonised in Spain's first national history, Alfonso X's *Estoria de España*, in the thirteenth (Pérez de Urbel 1952: 336; Menéndez Pidal 1977: 408). And it is all very much in accordance with the recent observation of a student of the period that 'the Umayyads saw in the Christians on their borders and their struggles with them simply a protracted border problem, without any implicit religious or ideological content or promise for themselves' (Wasserstein 1985: 22). From Arabic sources, however, we learn that in fact not only had Sancho travelled to Córdoba himself but he had gone there accompanied both by his uncle, the ruler of Navarre García Sánchez, and by his grandmother Queen Toda, and that on their arrival all of them did obeisance to the Caliph 'Abd al-Raḥmān III, who thereafter dispatched a Jewish physician and diplomat of noted prowess to minister to the corpulent monarch after he had taken refuge across a different frontier, in the Christian kingdom of Pamplona (García de Valdeavellano 1968: ii. 139; Rodríguez Fernández 1987: 31–7). In the guise of medicine man, Abū Yūsuf Ḥasdai ben Shaprūt represented the third active element within the medieval peninsula. The Jew as enemy of the Catholic cause and the Moors' fifth-columnist in 711, was a later development. In that guise, the guise in which he was to have to endure a long and sombre future, it is not until the 1230s that we can say that the Jew-as-subversive was securely established

(Linehan 1993: 75). But long before the 1230s, on the Spanish sector of the frontier between Christianity and Islam the Jewish presence further complicated an already complex social situation – just as it does today for analogising prospectors operating in that area of the historical past.

And all the time there were manuscripts moving noiselessly to and fro – manuscripts of music and mathematics whose annotations and ultimate location bear witness to their having made the round trip between Catalonia and al-Andalus for correction and updating in ninth-century Europe's intellectual capital. And then, later on, Europe's most inquisitive scholars located the West's intellectual frontier on the Ebro and the Tagus and made Toledo and other centres so many conduits for the transmission of ancient Greek learning to the medieval West (Díaz y Díaz 1969; d'Alverny 1982).

And five hundred years after Eulogius's journey, the Christian king of Navarre sought safe conducts from the Christian king of Aragón for a number of his subjects undertaking pilgrimage to the Holy Land. But not to Jerusalem. For these pilgrim subjects of Charles II of Navarre, who was a Frenchman, were Muslims bound for *their* Holy Land, for Mecca. 'One cannot but be surprised to find Peter the Ceremonious – one of the victors, after all, of the battle of Río Salado [1340] – granting a passport for the *ḥajj*', Harvey remarks (Boswell 1977: 292, 446; Harvey 1990: 142). Indeed one cannot, and not least because the practice had been expressly forbidden by canon law since the General Council of Vienne in 1311–12 had directed Christian rulers 'in no way to tolerate' the passage of 'Saracens' to that 'place where there was once buried a certain Saracen whom other Saracens hold to be a saint' (Tanner 1990: 380).

Such casual disregard for the normal indecencies of Holy War certainly came as a surprise to crusaders arriving from parts of Europe where frontiers had something rather more hard and fast about them. The culture shock which Europeans experienced, both on the Spanish frontier and in the Latin kingdom, when they found the local Christians and Moors sipping what appeared to be, and indeed may have been, orange juice together, resounds down the centuries. The Saracens were the descendants of Hagar, Abraham's concubine, Eusebius and Bede had concurred in asserting – though later students of the subject were not so sure. 'Why, for example', Southern inquires on their behalf, 'were these people called Saracens if they were descended not from Sarah but from Hagar?' 'This is the kind of question that scholarly writers liked to investigate' (Southern 1962: 17). But it was not one that preoccupied Pope Clement IV, for example, for all that he was scholarly. It was not with etymologies that he was concerned. What Clement IV was concerned with in 1265 was the marked reluctance of Christian kings to eliminate the spawn of that 'menstruating woman' for once and for all; that and reports of the debate which Jaume I of Aragón had recently staged between Christian and Jewish champions at Barcelona (Jordan 1893–1945: no. 15; Chazan 1992: 93): Spain's failure, in short, to have done with the frontier forever.

Yet in 1234, as the Christian Castilians were gathering their forces, with a view indeed to having done with that frontier – and just two years after he had promulgated a code of canon law incorporating decrees designed to reduce the old enemy to submission – Pope Clement's predecessor but three, Gregory IX, had licensed the archbishop of Toledo, no less, to establish commercial relations between his frontier strongholds and the Moors of Granada (Rodríguez Molina 1997: 264). There had been no interruption of the age-old practice of trading across the line. Indeed there was still altogether too much of it. Pope Gregory had excluded only arms and horses from the terms of his permission to the archbishop. This was slack of him. Eleven years earlier *his* predecessor, Honorius III, had been horrified to learn that among the commodities being traded by the Christian noblemen of Aragón were their Christian noblewomen (Canellas López 1989: no. 918).

Little wonder then that two and three hundred years on, new generations of visitors from beyond the Pyrenees wondered whether there was a frontier there at all. 'By their fruits ye shall know them', the Dutchman Henry Cock observed in 1585 when, while travelling through parts of Aragón supposedly reconquered in the early twelfth century, in the up-country village of Asco he found both pork and wine proscribed (Morel Fatio and Rodríguez Villa 1876: 180). It was the old, old story. A century earlier, during the reign of Enrique IV, the Constable of Castile had been observed at early mass 'all got up as a Moor, and very nice too',[3] while at his master's court both French and Bohemian visitors had encountered the Christian monarch guarded by Moorish warriors from Granada (not to mention negroes), clothed and worshipping 'in the heathen manner', and seated on the ground with his queen to receive them (MacKay 1976: 29). In F. J. Turner's terms, this was the equivalent of inhabited wigwams on nineteenth-century Fifth Avenue.

By 1585 almost ninety years had elapsed since the conquest of Granada and the supposed removal of the frontier between Christianity and Islam by which Spain had been polluted (Pope Clement's word) since 711. But never mind the frontier. Was Christianity itself even engaged yet with Auden's 'fragment'

> nipped off from hot
> Africa, soldered so crudely to inventive Europe?

This was not a frontier between the Cross and the Crescent, it was a public bath. In the togetherness of various municipal bath houses across that sector of the peninsula which was under Christian domination, cleanliness and godliness continued (almost) to co-exist, with sexual segregation rigidly enforced, and Christians, Muslims and Jews bathing on different days, but with all of them sharing the same water. In 1292 (the year after the demise of the Latin kingdom of Jerusalem), Sancho IV of Castile spent his Christmas in a Jewish household in Córdoba. Here at least (in the bath-house, that is), 'some degree of acculturation clearly took place', it has reasonably been suggested (Powers 1979: 665; Gaibrois de Ballesteros 1922–8: ii. 189).

But not always. According to one account, after the Castilians had lost the critical battle of Sagrajas in 1086 King Alfonso VI was assured by his 'wise men' that the reason for this reverse was that his soldiers had been washing too often. 'So the king had the baths of his kingdom destroyed and by various exertions made his soldiers sweat.' Thus the thirteenth-century chronicler Bishop Lucas of Túy writing either at León or in that rainy corner of Galicia where the perennial problem has always been condensation and damp walls rather than sweaty bodies (Schottus 1608: 102; Linehan 2001).

For, then as now, Spain was a land of wildly varying climates. And climate matters. Presumably it mattered to the settlers from northern Europe who came in such considerable numbers before about 1200, when the area to be settled was the area to the north of somewhere near Madrid, and to those who after about 1200, and especially after 1250, when Andalucia offered the over-populated north unrivalled opportunities, so singularly failed to follow in their predecessors' footsteps.

Maybe it was the heat that deterred the thirteenth-century descendants of those northerners who had ploughed along the pilgrim road throughout the 1100s and then (allegedly) peeled off to man (and woman) the frontier.[4] After his famous victory at Las Navas de Tolosa in July 1212, Alfonso VIII of Castile informed Pope Innocent III of the defection of the French before battle had been joined. The heat of the Spanish high summer, together with the sheer hard grind of it all, had proved too much for them. In short, the French were just not up to it (though the king left it to the pontiff to gather this for himself). There was an inwardness to this, of course, and the innate propensity of Castilians to denigrate the French to be allowed for (González 1960: iii. no. 568; Smith 1989: 14–25; Linehan 1993: 295–6) – though that was not all there was.

For northerners, whether we call them Christians or 'Christians', the frontier was the area to the south beyond which lay that part of the peninsula from which their ancestors had been forcibly ejected by gangs of trespassers. At the siege of Lisbon in 1147 the archbishop of Braga called up to the soldiery on the city's ramparts to return to the *patria Maurorum*, 'to the land of the Moors from whence you came', and from which by his reckoning it was 358 years earlier that they had come. As it happens, his reckoning was faulty, just as was that of the king of Aragón, Pedro I, in 1096, according to whose calculation the Moors had been in the peninsula since the year 656 (Linehan 1982: 188–9). But that is not the point. It was not the arithmetic of it that mattered. What mattered, and what distinguished the frontier in the vicinity of which the archbishop of Braga and the king of Aragón were active from other frontiers elsewhere and in other ages, was the elementary consideration that the cause in which they were engaged was not an adventure into the unknown. It was, as the archbishop made plain in 1147, a process of expelling intruders from territory which had been theirs all along, a process not of conquest but of reconquest. ('Incorporation', 1998's politically correct term for the reconquest of Seville in 1248, would not have cut much ice at Lisbon in 1147.) From the time of the 'invention of the Reconquest' in the ninth century until its completion in 1492, insistence on the historical continuum was an instinct deeply embedded in the collective consciousness, periodically activated by royal propaganda and social ritual (MacKay 1989: 232–41).

Here we are not concerned with the legitimacy of that conviction, with the Gothic myth which sustained it, or with the means by which successive generations were reminded of their historic mission (Maravall 1964: 249–337; Linehan 1993: 51–127), but rather with selected aspects of the social complex within which ultimately its realisation was in a certain sense achieved.

The earliest frontier between the Christian or 'Christian' area of the peninsula and the area that lay to the south of it was once believed to have been the deliberate creation of the middle years of the eighth century. A no-man's-land, a *cordon sanitaire*, according to that tradition it was established by Alfonso I, the nomadic ruler of the Asturias, in order to concentrate the peninsula's scarce human resources in the more readily defensible mountain region to the north of the Duero valley (Gil Fernández *et al*. 1985: 132, 133). Modern historians have long debated the credibility of that tradition and the plausibility of the late Claudio Sánchez-Albornoz's insistence that it was to the human desert thereby created that the proto-Castilian peasant proprietors who eventually moved into that area owed their uniquely free and unfettered condition and their natural resistance to feudal subjection (Sánchez-Albornoz 1966: 121–211).[5] And the debate continues.[6] W. P. Webb's celebrated characterisation of America's colonial frontier as 'the fifth column of liberty' (Webb 1953: 265) appears increasingly inappropriate to the Spanish case, whether in the ninth century or the thirteenth. Yet the fact remains, this at least remains unchallenged: from the very outset, one of the Spanish frontier's salient features was its lack of manpower.

Another, related to this, was the ethnic and social untidiness of the confronting hinterlands, Muslim *al-Andalus* and Christian Spain (for the Christians had appropriated the name *Hispania*), with each harbouring a substantial population of co-religionists of the other persuasion between 711 and the arrival of large numbers of Islamic fundamentalists in the eleventh century, and with Christian Mozarabs such as Alvarus vocal in Córdoba and, in those parts of the peninsula north of the line of demarcation as that line moved (oh so slowly) southward, a substantial population of Mudéjars. Not until the unassimilated Moriscos were expelled in the years after 1608 was that problem (as by then it was viewed) eradicated. Be it noted, however, that the fears which occasioned the remedy of expulsion adopted in the years after Lepanto, fears that the Moriscos were in league with Turks and Protestants, were identical in nature to those involving conspiracy on a Mediterranean-wide scale that had been entertained and had inspired the furious anti-Jewish campaign of the 680s (Gil 1977). Conversely, the catastrophic consequences for the economy which that expulsion entailed, and which came to be appreciated almost before the last Morisco had left (Elliott 1977), serve to explain why it was that over the previous several centuries the Christian rulers of Spain had stopped short of depriving themselves of that labour force whose presence, as well as constituting so mortal a danger for them, had induced northerners to seek their fortunes on the frontier in the first place and had persuaded them to venture south from Aragón and Argyll. What, indeed, was the point of attacking the Saracens at all?, Humbert de Romanis, former Master General of the Dominican Order, asked in 1274, in his *Opusculum tripartitum*. 'For when we take their lands from them none of our people come to settle them. Our people prefer to stay at home. What is the point of it therefore? What is the point, either spiritual, corporal or worldly, of all the effort?' Was there *any* point to all the exertion? (Brown 1690: 196 [trans. Linehan]; Brett 1984: 176–94). For Humbert, of course, this was a question demanding the answer Yes, and his response to subversives who reasoned otherwise he designed to prove decisive. Not all his readers in Spain, however (if any there were), would necessarily have agreed.

Although victorious, the Christians in thirteenth-century Andalucia and the Levante were hopelessly outnumbered, and their military ascendancy was challenged by the presence of a sullen, defeated and often displaced majority. The case of the kingdom of Valencia has been minutely, and repeatedly, rehearsed by Fr R. I. Burns, most recently in respect of the surrender of Játiva to Jaume I of Aragón at the conclusion of the Christian siege of that place in 1244. With the Muslims left in charge of the larger of Játiva's two fortresses, and secure in the enjoyment of their religion, their property and even the possession of their Christian captives, it appears almost a moot point who was surrendering to whom (Burns and Chevedden 1999a; Burns and Chevedden 1999b). Balkan in character though the Játiva situation was, for the Christian conquerors the thoroughgoing measures adopted in the late 1990s were not an available option. In conducting their civil war, capitulation on generous terms was the only viable policy – just as it had been for the Islamic conquerors of the cities in that same region half a millennium earlier: the Christians' dilemma in the 1240s was the mirror image of that of the 'Arabs' in the 710s. Then it had been the collaborating cousins of the (by the 1240s) reviled don Oppas who had benefited and been allowed to keep their mass (Collins 1989: 39–41). It had even been so in 1119 when, with crusading fervour in the West at its height, the Muslims of Tudela in Navarre had capitulated and those of them who were not of servile status had been allowed to retain both their landed property and their weapons (Verlinden 1955: 175–8). England's vanquished Christians in 1066, vanquished by a Christian foe, would cheerfully have settled for less.

And more. Compare and contrast these two protests, uttered by respective spokesmen of the Christian Mozarabs living under Arab domination and by the unassimilated Mudejars subject to Christian rule six centuries later:

> The Christians love to read the poems and romances of the Arabs . . . Where is the layman who now reads the Latin commentaries on the Holy Scriptures, or who studies the Gospels, Prophets or apostles? Alas! All talented young Christians read and study with enthusiasm the Arab books; . . . they despise the Christian literature as unworthy of attention. They have forgotten their language.
>
> (Paulus Alvarus, *Indiculus luminosus*: Gil 1973: i. 314;
> trans. Southern 1962: 21)

> One has to beware of the pervasive effect of their [the Christians'] way of life, their language, their dress, their objectionable habits, and influence on people living with them over long period of time, as has occurred in the case of the inhabitants of Abulla [Ávila?] and other places, for they have lost their Arabic, and when the Arabic language dies out, so does devotion in it, and there is consequential neglect of worship as expressed in words in all its richness and outstanding virtues.
>
> (Abū'l-'Abbas Aḥmad al-Wansharīshī, *Kitāb al-Mi'yār al-mugrib*:
> trans. Harvey 1990: 58. See below, chap. 4, p. 66)

The uncanny resemblance between the sentiments expressed by the biographer of Eulogius in ninth-century Córdoba and those of al-Wansharīshī at the end of the fifteenth century provides yet another expression of the social reality common to the frontier and to the two variegated communities flanking it. The frontier in medieval Spain ran through every human community, through many families, even through many individual hearts and minds, the hearts and minds of Jews as well as Christians and Muslims, and created tensions which communities learnt to transform into *convivencia* (the co-existence of peoples of different faiths) by ritualising them. In 1300 Jaume II of Aragón warned the seniors of the University of Lleida not to dress up as Muslims and Jews in order to taunt the local minorities on the feast-days of St Nicholas and St Catherine. He was perfectly prepared to allow children to do so, however (Nirenberg 1996: 224).

Christian communities and their leaders engaged in these reassuring charades (which have survived to this day) (Albert-Llorca and Albert 1995) because they had to, and they had to because there was never enough manpower available to efface the effects of those frontiers. The reason why non-Christian communities persisted in Spain until 1492 and beyond was that on neither side of that infinity of divisions which is loosely termed 'the frontier' were there sufficient resources to dispose of them. To return to the valley of the Duero. If, as there certainly appears to be (Manzano 1991; Glick 1995: 113–14), there is reason for supposing that instead of moving north in the 750s its population stayed put, then the frontier does not disappear. Rather, it acquires new contours, castles in the air constructed from the debris of old easily dismantled certainties assisting the process, and generous applications of speculative glue[7] serving to render it an area of social coagulation and social rejection, an area within which 'Mudejars' and 'Mozarabs' brushed against one another at the bakehouse and the village well, and that process of human layering got under way of which it is the historian's job to attempt to make sense.

With a view to disturbing this unsatisfactory equilibrium, as between 1936 and 1939, so between 711 and 1492 the will to prevail led both sides to bring in reinforcements from beyond the peninsula. In the case of Christian Spain, the consequences are well enough known. In order to establish a human presence in the great exposed zone which ran from Lisbon on the Atlantic to Tortosa on the Mediterranean after the reconquest of Toledo in 1085 and the ensuing Almoravid seizure of control of Andalucia, the rulers of 'Christian' (or, arguably, by this date Christian) Spain enticed the riff-raff of the West to the frontier with *al-Andalus*. These were George Duby's *jeunes*, Europe's younger sons, the extruded elements of more rational systems of estate management combined with the consequences of the Gregorian papacy's foreclosure of an easy abbacy or uneventful bishopric (Duby 1973). Students of modern empires and theories of imperialism may prefer to regard them as the beneficiaries of a 'gigantic system of outdoor relief' for the military aristocracy of Christian Europe, as the Milner's young men of their generation (cf. Robinson and Gallagher 1961) – and they may well be right. The alternative frameworks of interpretation merely set the alternative historiographical traditions, the French and the English, in starker relief. They do not account for the Spanish moment.

The *fuero* which Alfonso VI granted to Sepúlveda (not far from Segovia) in 1076 – a code subsequently adopted as far afield as Morella in Aragón (1233) and Segura de León to the south of Badajoz (1274) – provided immunity for all-comers. In this recent haunt of bears and boars, as Alfonso VI described the area in 1107, once they had crossed the Duero even murderers were guaranteed refuge (Sáez 1953: 46; Sánchez-Albornoz 1966: 388). On his way to seek monastic sanctuary at Cluny 'because there was nowhere for him to stay' in Alfonso VII's kingdoms (the usual problem in reverse), the treacherous count Gómez Núñez (Maya Sánchez 1990: 189) would have passed streams of aspiring frontiersmen travelling south for precisely the same reason.

Small wonder then that in about the year 1206 Sepúlveda witnessed the protest meeting of which so graphic an account has survived, the meeting summoned in order to plan the downfall of the bishop of Segovia for attempting to deprive the local clergy of their lady-friends. There was discussion of an appeal to the pope against this radical proposal, whereupon

> almost all the clergy of Sepúlveda, of both the town and the villages, met in a church and, joining hands, swore to assist each another against the bishop, any one of them breaking the oath to be discommuned and fined fifty *aurei*. And they then summoned the officials to their chapter and made them swear to withhold the bishop's procurations.
>
> (Linehan 1981: 485)

> The clergy of Sepúlveda drove the bishop mad . . . really unhinged him.
> (García y García 1977: 252–3).

In the period of little over a century (1085–1212) between the reconquest of Toledo and the decisive battle of Las Navas de Tolosa, Spain was a land without extradition treaties in which desperadoes were welcomed because everyone was needed. 'You were employed with arms and the sword; you were committing acts of pillage and other misdeeds of soldiers, concerning which there is no need now to speak in detail', the bishop of Porto reminded the Jerusalem-bound crusaders who stayed on to participate in the reconquest of Lisbon in 1147. Here is the authentic voice of twelfth-century Spain. 'You are (still), as is apparent, bearing arms and the insignia of war', the bishop continued, 'but with a different object'. (That was perhaps wishful thinking.) In their dealings with their co-religionists, Duby's celebrated not very gilded youth on the loose in the peninsula were hardly conspicuous for acts of selflessness (David 1936: 83; Duby 1973: 221). Indeed, those of them who stayed on to man Christendom's frontier represented a greater danger to other Christians than they did to Christendom's foe. The burning of churches full of their co-religionists was a not uncommon consequence of the generous terms of the local *fueros* whereby the arsonists had been brought in. 'We are the kings', declared Pedro Negro, leader of the *concejo* of Cordobilla in dispute with the monks of Aguilar de Campóo at about the time of the Sepúlveda affair (Pastor de Togneri 1980: 149; Linehan 1993: 264–5).

There are those who would embrace the likes of Pedro Negro as Turnerian frontiersmen *avant la lettre*, as the forebears of those 'Castilians as plainsmen', the pastoral inhabitants of the Guadiana basin whose activities were subjected to Bishko's critical scrutiny all of thirty years ago, those precursors of 'Pizarro, Valdivia, and thousands of others, whom the region early sent to the Indies and who there created New Extremaduras in Mexico and Chile' (Bishko 1963: 64). But just as the transitional significance of the Canaries experience remains to be analysed, so too does it remain the case that it was not until the 1220s that Castilians coined a word to express the concept of a territorial 'frontier'. 'It is the duty of kings to defend their frontiers', Fernando III declared in 1222 – *frontarias* constituted by series of fortresses or the course of rivers, that is (Gonzalez 1980–6: ii. nos. 154, 157; Gomes 1991: 370; Molénat 1996: 112–17).[8] The suggestion of another American medievalist, A. R. Lewis, that by the 1220s the medieval frontier was on the point of closing altogether (Lewis 1958; Linehan 1993: 207–8, 292–5), must therefore have been greeted by him with blank incomprehension.

And more than that. Lewis's suggestion would have shaken Fernando III (and with him the entire roll-call of thirteenth-century Spanish kings) to their foundations. For if the frontier was on the point of closing down, then where did that leave them? After all, was it not precisely their unique status as Christendom's frontiersmen *par excellence* that entitled them to hold to ransom both their own churches and the Roman Church itself (Linehan 1971)?

And more still. For Pedro Negro-types were by no means confined to the frontier which they patrolled, the frontier with Islam. They were as much in evidence on Christian Spain's internal frontiers, that is to say on the frontiers which separated Christian kingdoms and even Christian dioceses. In 1245, for example, while Fernando III of Castile was mustering his forces for the final push towards Seville, in the neighbouring kingdom of Aragón the bishops of Zaragoza and Huesca were clashing croziers over the nice question of which of them was entitled to the tithe of lambs and other animals conceived in one diocese and born in the other (Canellas López 1972: no. 72). And the proctor who in the 1290s pleaded for an extension of credit at the papal court on the grounds that, being 'on the frontier', the church he was representing was in a bad way, was not referring to the frontier with Islam; Tudela was in the kingdom of Navarre (Linehan 1980: 500). Nor was the habit of untidy straying peculiar to the peninsula's quadrupeds. Long before its constituent kingdoms established more or less permanent frontiers, Christian Spain was riven by frontier disputes, notably by inter-diocesan disputes concerning archdeaconries and parishes periodically reactivated by the failure of ancient ecclesiastical divisions to conform to more recent secular realities (e.g. Cañizares 1946; Duro Peña 1975). Indeed it was disputes of this nature (at every level of society) and the remedies sought for their resolution in documentary evidence and the crystal-clear memories of successive stage-armies of toothless centenarians, and the conventions adopted to mark their cessation – both physical (boundary marks protected by biblical taboo) and symbolic (crosses carved on tree or stone, libations of wine) – that prepared peninsular society for settlements such as the Treaty of Alcañices which in 1297 determined Portugal's border with its eastern neighbour forever after (Ruiz 1997; Linehan 1993: 333; Gomes 1991: 367–70; Mattoso 1995: ii.193–6). Maps came later (Gomes 1991: 374–6).

As to such conflicts themselves, it is as difficult to attribute their prevalence to the influence of Frenchmen and other northern ruffians as it is to account in such terms for the urban *hermandad* which drove the local bishop from the northerly see of Lugo in 1159 or for the succession of urban rebellions which Alfonso VI of Castile's death half a century earlier had unleashed along the whole length of the pilgrim road to Compostela (Gautier Dalché 1979: 211–30; Pastor de Togneri 1980: 147). It is also unnecessary. For not only had symptoms such as these been evident in Spain

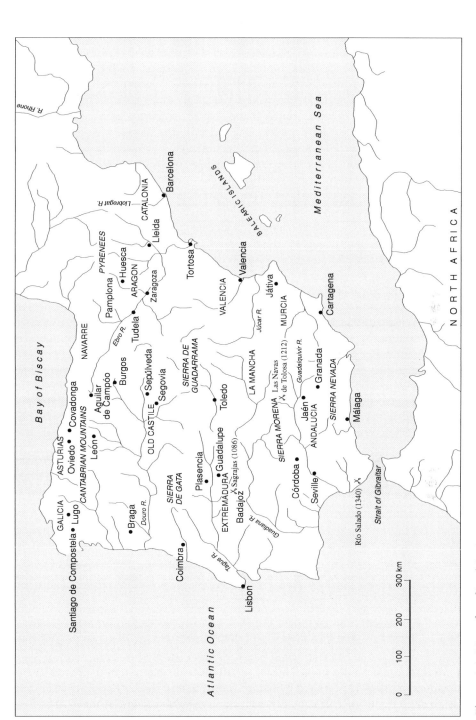

Figure 3.1 Map of medieval Spain.

well before Islam had reached the peninsula. They would also long outlast its formal extinction.

The phenomenon of urban implosion on this scale finds no place in Lewis's account of the 'Closing of the Medieval Frontier'. That is understandable inasmuch as it occurred all of a century too soon for Lewis's purposes. Not so that other element absent from his analysis, however, the fact that in the years after the decisive battle of Las Navas in 1212, just as the opportunities of Andalucia became available to the rulers of Castile, for some reason quite suddenly the human supply from north of the Pyrenees almost completely dried up – with far-reaching consequences. This deserves comment. After all, it was only recently that the confrontation with the Almohads had made Spain very much the focus of European attention (Lomax 1988). Had the pitilessly arid climate of northern Andalucia something to do with it? Was it the waterlessness of the region that deterred, just as six centuries later it would determine the course of the settlement of the American Mid-West (Webb 1931: 319–452)? May dietary fears have contributed, as in 1274 Humbert de Romanis suggested they did by deterring Westerners from travelling to the Holy Land (Brown 1690: 193)? The awesomeness for northerners of the prospect of eternal olive oil is not to be underestimated. It may well have been the effects of diarrhoea as much as the willingness of the Castilians to allow enemy strongholds to surrender on terms that caused the French contingents to defect in 1212 (Linehan 1997: 145–6). And it is certainly striking that, in selling Seville hard, Fernando III promoted the territory irrigated by the Guadalquivir as the last unspoiled preserve of fecund nature, fertile beyond all imagining. Appropriating to Seville and its environs the superlatives which in the seventh century Isidore of Seville had reserved for Spain itself, Fernando III reiterated the lavish account in the ninth-century 'Chronicle of Alfonso III' of Pelayo at Covadonga leading his people Moses-like through the Red Sea and into the Promised Land – though with the difference that in the years after 1212 it was a parched desert that barred the way (Vanderford 1984: 19–20; Linehan 1971: 106; Gil Fernández *et al*. 1985: 128–9).

And according to Fernando's contemporary, Archbishop Rodrigo of Toledo, the ruse worked – or at least it had worked when the city of Córdoba had fallen in 1236. Such was the reputation of the place that was bruited abroad that settlers (*habitatores*) flocked there from all parts of Spain 'as to a king's wedding', in such numbers indeed that more came than there was room for (Fernández Valverde 1987: 299); similarly to Jaén ten years later, attracted thither by the king's *pobladores* with their promises of 'great liberties' (González Jiménez 1994: 27). Yet from further afield still they did not come. *En masse*, Europe's younger sons continued to spurn Europe's frontier. Why this should have been so remains a mystery. There were, to all appearances, richer pickings to be had in Spain after 1212 than ever before. There were also (also more than ever before) men and families north of the Pyrenees with no means of supporting themselves. Yet demand and supply failed to make contact.

And soon the supply from south of the Pyrenees began to dry up too. As in the kingdom of Valencia as related by Father Burns, so also the 1260s and 1270s found the Christian frontier in Andalucia perilously undermanned, with many of its earliest settlers having returned home, the professional *habitatores* engaged in poaching settlers from already sparsely inhabited areas to the north, and its king seeking to make good the shortfall by conniving at clerical marriage and promoting new shrines in the south with a view to luring miracle-hungry pilgrims from Santiago where they served no practical purpose to areas where conceivably they might (González Jiménez 1988: 83–9; Linehan 1993: 510–16; Linehan 1997: 145; Linehan 1999: 676–8). In the fourteenth century such were the origins of the shrine of Guadalupe in the rocky wastes of strategically crucial Extremadura further west (Linehan 1985). And further west still, where in 1268 it was reported that 'Extrematura' was the kingdom of Portugal's most populous region, Algarve-ward migration produced the same effect as in Castile, of exacerbating deep-rooted north–south tensions (Mattoso 1995: ii.15–28; Marques 1990: 520).

But the shortfall remained, and the consequences of it determined the history of the southern part of the peninsula from that day to this. The process of colonisation failed to exploit the advantages achieved by the passage of arms. The meagre resources of a single generation were not sufficient to secure both. In the terminology adopted by Jaume Vicens Vives (1967: 144), 'la Reconquista militar' (the military reconquest) was disappointed of that supplementary 'verdadera Reconquista', 'la Reconquista lenta' (the slow reconquest). 'In a civil war', General Franco reflected in 1937, 'a systematic occupation of territory accompanied by the necessary purge (*limpieza*) is preferable to a rapid rout of the enemy armies which leaves the country still infested with enemies' (Preston 1993: 222). But though, like Franco, Spain's medieval rulers were prepared when necessary to make use of Moorish legionaries to advance their Christian cause, they shrank from the ghastly measures adopted by its twentieth-century *caudillo*. At least until the fifteenth century, ethnic cleansing was not part of their policy. And if the consequences of this were religious – to the extent that, as in the aftermath of Franco's 'crusade', the real reconquest, the 'reconquest of souls' spoken of by Chaunu (1962: 137), was postponed *sine die* – a large part of the reason for it was what historians insistent on compartmentalising body and soul would define as economic.

And another part of it, perhaps, was that those 'great liberties' which Fernando III had promised his subjects his son Alfonso X failed to deliver. After 1252 municipal government throughout Andalucia was brought increasingly under royal control, with its *alcaldes* the king's *alcaldes* and no sign in sight of Webb's famed 'fifth column of liberty' (González Jiménez 1993–4). The fifth column in the minds of the reconquerors of Andalucia was one of an altogether more sinister nature. Comprising the displaced population among whom they lived and moved, it bore all the characteristics of those Jews of Toledo who by now, according to the chronicler Lucas of Tuy, had opened the city gates to the invaders in 711 (Schottus 1608: 70). Eternal vigilance remained the rule, therefore, that vigilance in accordance with which the citizens of twelfth-century Plasencia were instructed that when there was a fire in the city their first duty was to man the city walls against invaders (Lourie 1966: 59). Reporting the return to Santiago de Compostela in the 1230s of the bells that had been carried off to Muslim Córdoba in 997, Robert Bartlett has remarked that the Galician shrine was 'now buffered by miles of Christian territory' (Bartlett 1994: 295). But oh, what folly! It was complacency of this order that undid the archbishop of Toledo, the Infante Sancho of Aragón in the 1270s. Because, as he fondly imagined, the pressure was off, because the Moors were now far away and the road north from Toledo was both safe and open, the Infante reduced the residence requirement of the canons of his church to just three months' attendance *per annum*. But D. Sancho had made the same fatal mistake as Bartlett, and after defeat in battle with the Marīnids in October 1275 he paid for it when his severed head and hand were sent back home in a casket (Linehan 1971: 179; González Jiménez 2000: 180–3).

Had he taken account of all this, Lewis would doubtless have dutifully logged it as yet another symptom of the 'Closing of the Medieval Frontier'. But he did not. Without the assistance of rear-view mirrors, on the Great Trek through History the field of vision from the covered wagon is inevitably restricted. According to Raymond Carr, 'people who wear bow ties may have an ambiguous relationship with the establishment'.[9] The same may be true of men with stetsons. 'Students of costume', Bishko has surmised (1952: 507), 'could doubtless trace back to the twelfth century regional dress of the *charros* and *serranos* of Salamanca and southern Old Castile, the cradle of the ranch cattle industry, the cowboy costume that appears with many local variations in the Indies; the low-crowned, broad-brimmed hat, the bolero jacket, the sash and tight-fitting trousers, the spurred boots.' Doubtless they could – though they had better mind their step with those spurs, for, as L. J. McCrank has counselled us (1983: 328), to 'the Americanization of a medieval episode' 'some Europeans have objected'.[10] In particular, the reservations as to the usefulness of Turnerian concepts which I had expressed in respect of the work of Father Burns, McCrank adjudges unduly narrow. 'Linehan objects to the generalization about frontier mentalities, such as Burns's notion of the "religion of the frontier",' he writes. 'Linehan's points', he continues, 'seem not to extend to the large, beyond-Turner, interpretations of frontier phenomena, and if he finds these phenomena widespread, this could mean that much of Europe was a frontier in a developmental stage and ongoing expansion. Thus the counter-argument would be that we have just begun to discover how appropriate frontier concepts and approaches are for the interpretation of medieval European history' (McCrank 1983: 329).[11] If this and the counter-argument (if that is what it is) are indeed what I meant then I can only agree with Dr McCrank's dogged exegesis of an *obiter dictum* on the subject of the proclivities of the clergy of Valencia and Segovia and of the clergy of Rouen and Lincoln contrasted (Linehan 1981: 501–2). For if *all* Europe was a frontier, where, one may ask, was the European hinterland or metropolis? Where was the other terminal of Webb's fully charged battery but for which none of those enlivening sparks would ever have moved from one pole to the other? (Webb 1953: 8–13; Barraclough 1954).

Pace McCrank, it is not a question of seeking 'to undermine the frontier interpretation of MacKay, Burns, Glick et al.' It is rather a question of measure, of proportion. As Burns himself remarked in 1989, referring to the starting point of the whole self-regarding debate, when Turner was writing and rewriting his thesis his frontier of settlement had not disappeared after all. Nor has it yet. In 1988 Turner's frontier of settlement still covered '45 percent of the land area of the United States', Burns reported, quoting a recent report in the *New York Times*. With 'fewer than six people . . . per square mile', the 1988 frontier was 'a region statistically more violent and dangerous than any urban ghetto' (Burns 1989: 308). But by a similar reckoning, when in 1965 a 13 per cent turnout for mass was 'more than usual' in a semi-rural parish in the diocese of Seville (Lannon 1987: 10) the Spanish Reconquest may be adjudged still far from complete. Though the religious sociologists were not yet out in force to advise the Mozarabs of mid-ninth-century Córdoba, it was religious indifference of precisely this order that had so alarmed Eulogius and his embattled community.

If, as may be the case, Father Burns (or, as it may be, the *New York Times* correspondent) is right on this occasion, then the distinctly downbeat account of the 1987 Edinburgh conference at which Burns's thoughts on the subject were first aired may be altogether more to the point than Dr McCrank. On that occasion, 'terminological or definitional debate about the nature of the frontier did not take up much time. . . . Most contributors were happy to pursue empirical issues and allow the frontier element in their analysis to speak for itself' (Bartlett and MacKay 1989: p. v).

As to Spain, the empirical approach is applicable even to McCrank's own particular stamping ground. There the river Llobregat marked, or was thought by some to mark, a frontier of a sort between freedom and servitude (Freedman 1991a: 111; Freedman 1991b: 135–9). And whatever may have been the case in Catalonia, on the frontier further west Cistercian monasticism did not figure at all. Further west it was hard against the Atlantic that the cloistered Cistercians made their mark, infilling the Galician hinterland. In Castile they served a different function, not on the Christian frontier with Islam, but on Castile's internal frontiers, its frontiers with its Christian neighbours. During the 1170s, at Alfonso VIII's behest, the communities of Bujedo, Herrera, Rioseco and Benavides were all relocated in order to counter the Christian king of Navarre (Pallares Méndez and Portela Silva 1971; Alvarez Palenzuela 1978; Moxó 1979: 269–75). It was their uncloistered brethren, the members of the military order of Calatrava who featured on the frontier with Islam, combining that commitment to the chastity which the Rule prescribed with an equal zeal for the shedding of Saracen blood.

Yet even in this quintessentially Christian institution, in its earlier manifestation the Aragonese Confraternity of Belchite there are identifiable indications of acculturation, with the *ribāṭ*: Islam's frontier outposts set against the other, the *dār al-ḥarb* (Lourie 1982). And so it continued in Spain's haven of *convivencia*. 'It has been the fashion to regard the war of the Reconquest . . . as a war of religion', Turner's American contemporary, H. C. Lea, remarked in 1901. 'In fact, however, the medieval history of Spain shows that in the long struggle there was little antagonism either of race or religion' (Lea 1901: 1). That is a large generalisation, of course, and the agonising over the nature of Spain's Spanishness in which Spaniards have indulged since 1898 necessitates all manner of qualifications. After all, the peninsula's Christian rulers were committed to the concept of 'a tidy kingdom' and were at pains to prevent apostates, renegades and *tornizados* from blurring ethnic and religious distinctions. Thus in 1276, after the suppression of the Muslim revolt in the kingdom of Valencia, Jaume I of Aragón decreed that those who had conveniently espoused Islam during the rebellion were either 'to go to the country of the Moors' or, if they chose to remain, 'to remain Christian', and in the *Siete Partidas*, the law-code superintended by Jaume's contemporary Alfonso X of Castile, fearsome penalties were prescribed for apostates (Burns 1972: 347, 349; Real Academia de la Historia

1807: iii. 677–80). Yet in the very next law of the relevant title of the Seventh *Partida* the safe-conduct of envoys from the 'tierra de moros' was guaranteed, whether they be 'Christian, Moor or Jew' (Real Academia de la Historia 1807: iii. 680–1). (After all, Alfonso X numbered the Nasrid king of Granada among his vassals.)

An incident noted in Angus MacKay's richly suggestive article demonstrates the extent of *convivencia* and collusion on either side of the frontier with the kingdom of Granada two hundred years later, at a time when within the Christian hinterland itself the cause of *convivencia* was already under serious strain. At the conclusion of one of those skirmishes across the lines which were so regular a feature of existence on that edge of mid-fifteenth-century Christian Europe, in this case involving the Christians of Jaén and the Moors of Colomera, on this occasion when the time came for the exchange of captives, a shepherd named Pedro made a nuisance of himself. Having converted to Islam, he now refused to return to the Christian fold. General consternation. He would not go home to mother. So his unwilling Moorish hosts found themselves constrained to ask the Christian authorities to arrange for mother to come for him and take him back, back over the frontier whose line on the map they could trace even if some historians of part of our period cannot, and haul him home to Colomera (MacKay 1976: 26; Carriazo 1971: i. 280). If only we had material of that calibre about the shepherd boys of Spain's earlier centuries we should not be so much at the mercy of scholars who lay down the law about human affairs on the strength of their lucubrations over the remains of castles and bits of pots.

The employment by both the Christian and the Moorish municipalities in the Jaén region of *rastreros*, officials whose task it was to collaborate in the settlement of trans-frontier incidents, and of *alfaqueques* responsible for organising the return of captives and 'missing persons', amply demonstrates 'that frontier authorities were fully aware of the escalating problems caused by reprisal warfare and attempted to eliminate it' (MacKay 1976: 23–5). *Alfaqueques* worked on a commission basis, even speculating in futures. This was big business: not quite such big business, admittedly, as the ransoming of French and English captives during the course of the Hundred Years War, but in its essentials governed by the same considerations, and by the same considerations that had applied in 1147 when the Jerusalem-bound crusaders from northern Europe had sold their services to the king of Portugal at the siege of Lisbon. Accordingly, the *alfaqueques* were firmly committed to the maintenance of understandings and arrangements with their opposite numbers across the line (López de Coca Castañer 1989; David 1936: 110). Such measures testify, we might say, to a shared desire to preserve (for example) the 'no-animal's land' in which Muslim and Christian flocks were pastured together, by taking the steam out of the situation (Rodríguez Molina 1997: 260–2, 272–4; Carmona Ruiz 1998: 262–5). (For the average peninsular sheep, life on the frontier with Islamic Granada in the 1470s was distinctly less fraught than it had been two hundred and more years earlier on the paternity-suits-ridden diocesan boundaries of Christian Aragón; above, p. 46.)

And yet, for all that, and scalded by that steam as they sometimes were while monitoring the press of human traffic in the direction of San Ginés de la Jara (the shrine to the Virgin near Cartagena which Alfonso X promoted in order to attract Christian settlers to the south west and to which Muslims flocked too on account of its associations with a relative of the Prophet (Linehan 1993: 513–14; MacKay 1976: 23–4)), at the time, to the proprietors of those ecumenical ruminants the proposition that actually there was *no* situation – that, despite the severed heads sent home in caskets, 'all this evidence suggests the possibility of such a degree of cultural confusion, in the broadest sense of the term, that it is almost as if a frontier, as it is normally envisaged, hardly existed' (MacKay 1989: 222; López de Coca Castañer 1989: 149) – must surely have come as a surprise.

As a surprise. But perhaps not as very much more than that. For the frontier was as much part of everyday life as the parish. Like the parish, the frontier was an institution available to be appealed to when needs must. In fact, by the 1480s the parish was no more than a venerable fiction. (It had been so ever since the years of the battle of Las Navas de Tolosa when Rome had first let the friars loose to undermine its foundations.) In theory, of course, this was untidy, just as, in theory, so were both the Crusade against Islam and the *jihād* untidy, equally and absolutely though they constituted the most sacred of obligations (Linehan 1997; Urvoy 1973).

In *theory*, the very idea of frontier *convivencia* is inconceivable. Crusade and co-existence comprise a confessional oxymoron if ever there was one. But in *fact* people aren't like that. 'In fact', as has been well observed, what 'appears increasingly strange [is] that historians [should ever] have insisted on an either/or approach towards the two modes of frontier behaviour.' 'In doing so' – the author of these remarks continues – 'they have demanded of late medieval society a degree of homogeneity they would not expect to be present in other periods. Perhaps, seeing the high premium which was placed on uniformity in the Middle Ages, they have assumed that it corresponded to reality. But in practice the inconsistencies of human behaviour and belief were probably as deep as in any age' (Housley 1996: 115).

Just so. At the Spanish frontier it was precisely those 'inconsistencies of human behaviour' that made the world go round. Despite the (intermittent) inspections of the place by 'inventive Europe', there, in Auden's fragment of hot Africa, only rarely did theory and practice, whether Islamic or Christian, ever precisely coincide, or even get on. There, all that there was to be got on with was life itself.

NOTES

1 I am indebted to María Antonia Carmona Ruiz, David Nirenberg and Margarita Torres Sevilla for their critical reading of an earlier version of this chapter.

2 Whose Turnerian characteristics were long ago stressed by the American historian of medieval Germany, J. W. Thompson (Thompson 1928: 522–4).

3 'Tocado todo morisco e bien fecho' (Carriazo 1940: 52).

4 Dillard 1984, esp. chap. 1. By contrast, women were excluded from participation in the military *jihād*, at least in theory: Khadduri 1955: 85.

5 For the view that 'of course the free proprietor was dominant in Castile in the eighth to tenth centuries: he was everywhere!' and that 'in the case of Castile . . . a more fuller [sic] feudalisation of such territories was delayed', see Glick 1995: 102.

6 And for its latest stages Glick is useful, despite factual inaccuracy (for example, it was not Alfonso II but Alfonso I who, according to Sánchez-Albornoz, took 'the remaining

population northwards and made the entire valley an empty buffer zone between the opposing blocs': Glick 1995: 113).

7 As, for example, in the fanciful description of the present writer as 'a partisan of the institutional school' (Glick 1995: 94).

8 The words 'frontera', 'frontaria' first occur in the chronicle and chancery products of Bishop Juan de Soria (or de Aza), chancellor of Castile (post-early 1220s), and (post-1236) chronicler (Linehan 1993: 263). (The question of his authorship of the later part of the *Crónica latina* has been raised by Charlo Brea 1995.) In 1239 a papal penance prescribed military service 'in frontaria regni Portugalie' (Costa 1963: 266); cf. Gomes 1991: 359.

9 Reviewing Adam Sisman, *A.J.P. Taylor: a biography: The Spectator* (London), 22 Jan. 1994, 24.

10 For a rather more nuanced treatment of McCrank's theme, viewed from a wider perspective, see Pérez-Embid Wamba 1994.

11 It is to be noted that it was not, as McCrank states, '[Burns's] "The Religion of the Frontier in Medieval Spain", *Proceedings of the Second International Colloquium in Ecclesiastical History* (Oxford 1974) which provoked Linehan's rebuttal'. The author of 'The Religion of the Frontier in Medieval Spain' was not Burns but Linehan and, so far as the latter is aware, no rebuttal has yet been issued, not even by himself – principally because, despite the bibliographical particulars helpfully provided by McCrank, the *Proceedings* of the Colloquium in question have never in fact been published.

REFERENCES

Albert-Llorca, M. and J.-P. Albert (1995) 'Mahomet, la Vierge et la frontière', *Annales HSS* 50: 855–86.

Alvarez Palenzuela, V. A. (1978) *Monasterios cistercienses en Castilla (siglos XII–XIII)*, Valladolid: Universidad de Valladolid.

Alverny, M. T. d' (1982) 'Translations and translators', in R. L. Benson and G. Constable, with C. D. Lanham (eds) *Renaissance and Renewal in the Twelfth Century*, Oxford: Clarendon Press, 421–62.

Barraclough, G. (1954) 'The metropolis and the macrocosm. Europe and the wider world, 1492–1939', *Past & Present* 5: 77–93.

Bartlett, R. (1994) *The Making of Europe. Conquest, colonisation and cultural change 950–1350*, Harmondsworth: Penguin Books.

—— and A. MacKay (eds) (1989) *Medieval Frontier Societies*, Oxford: Clarendon Press.

Bazzana, A. (1997) 'El concepto de frontera en el Mediterráneo occidental en la Edad Media', in P. Segura Artero (ed.) *Actas del Congreso 'La Frontera Oriental Nazarí como sujeto histórico (s.XIII–XVI)'. Lorca–Vera, 22 a 24 de noviembre de 1994*, Alicante: Instituto de Estudios Almerienses/Diputación de Almería, 25–46.

Bishko, C. J. (1952) 'The peninsular background of Latin American cattle ranching', *Hispanic American Historical Review* 32: 491–515.

—— (1963) 'The Castilian as plainsman: the medieval ranching frontier in La Mancha and Extremadura', in A. R. Lewis and T. F. McGann (eds) *The New World Looks at its History*, Austin, Texas: University of Texas Press, Institute of Latin American Studies, 47–69.

Boswell, J. (1977) *The Royal Treasure. Muslim communities under the Crown of Aragon in the fourteenth century*, New Haven and London: Yale University Press.

Brett, E. T. (1984?) *Humbert of Romans: his life and views on thirteenth-century society*, Toronto: Pontifical Institute of Mediaeval Studies.

Brown, E. (ed.) (1690) Humbert de Romanis. *Opus tripartitum: Fasciculus rerum expetendarum et fugiendarum*, vol. 2, London: R. Chiswell.

Burns, R. I. (1972) 'Renegades, adventurers, and sharp businessmen: the thirteenth-century Spaniard in the cause of Islam', *Catholic Historical Review* 58: 341–66.

—— (1975) *Medieval Colonialism. Postcrusade exploitation of Islamic Valencia*, Princeton NJ: Princeton University Press.

—— (1989) 'The significance of the frontier in the Middle Ages', in Bartlett and MacKay 1989: 307–30.

—— and P. E. Chevedden (1999a) *Negotiating Cultures. Bilingual surrender treaties in Muslim–Crusader Spain under James the Conqueror*, Leiden, Boston and Cologne: Brill.

—— (1999b) '"The finest castle in the world"', *History Today* 49(11): 10–20.

Canellas López, A. (ed.) (1972) *Colección diplómatica del Concejo de Zaragoza*, Zaragoza: Cátedra Zaragona en la Universidad.

—— (ed.) (1989) *Los cartularios de San Salvador de Zaragoza*, 4 vols., Zaragoza: Ibercaja.

Cañizares, B. (1946) 'Los grandes pleitos de la iglesia de Lugo: la iglesia de Lugo y la iglesia de León', *Boletín de la Comisión de Monumentos de Lugo* 2: 137–52.

Carmona Ruiz, M. A. (1998), *La ganadería en el reino de Sevilla durante la Baja Edad Media*, Seville: Diputación de Sevilla.

Carriazo, J. de M. (ed.) (1940) *Hechos del Condestable Don Miguel Lucas de Iranzo (Crónica del siglo XV)*; Colección de Crónicas Españolas, dir. J. de M. Carriazo, III, Madrid: Espasa Calpe.

—— (1971) 'Los moros de Granada en las actas del concejo de Jaén de 1479', in *Homenaje al profesor Carriazo y Arroquía*, Seville: Universidad de Sevilla, i. 265–310.

Charlo Brea, L. (1995) 'Un segundo autor para la última parte de la *Crónica latina de los reyes de Castilla?*', in M. Pérez González (ed.) *Actas I Congreso Nacional de Latín Medieval (León, 1–4 de diciembre de 1993)*, León: Universidad de León, 251–6.

Chaunu, P. (1962) 'Jansenisme et frontière de catholicité (XVIIe et XVIIIe siècles): à propos du Jansenisme lorrain', *Revue historique* 227: 115–38.

Chazan, R. (1992) *Barcelona and Beyond. The disputation of 1263 and its aftermath*, Berkeley, Los Angeles and Oxford: University of California Press.

Collins, R. (1989) *The Arab Conquest of Spain 710–797*, Oxford: Basil Blackwell.

Costa, A. Domingues de Sousa (1963) *Mestre Silvestre e Mestre Vicente, juristas da contenda entre D. Afonso II e suas irmãs*, Braga: Editorial Franciscana.

David, C. W. (ed.) (1936) *'De Expugnatione Lyxbonensi': the Conquest of Lisbon*, New York: Columbia University Press.

Defourneaux, M. (1949) *Les Français en Espagne aux XIe et XIIe siècles*, Paris: Presses Universitaires de France.

Díaz y Díaz, M. C. (1969) 'La circulation des manuscrits dans la Péninsule Ibérique du VIIIe au XIe siècle', *Cahiers de Civilisation Médiévale* 12: 219–41, 383–92.

Dillard, H. (1984) *Daughters of the Reconquest. Women in Castilian town society, 1100–1300*, Cambridge: Cambridge University Press.

Duby, G. (1973) 'Les "jeunes" dans la société aristocratique dans la France du Nord-ouest au XIIe siècle', in *Hommes et structures du Moyen Age*, Paris: Flammarion, 213–25.

Duro Peña, E. (1975) 'Diferencias sobre límites entre Braga y Orense en el siglo XII', *Archivos Leoneses* 29: 147–75.

Elliott, J. H. (1977) 'Self-perception and decline in early seventeenth-century Spain', *Past & Present* 74: 41–61.

Fernández Valverde, J. (ed.) (1987) Roderici Ximenii de Rada, *Historia de rebvs Hispanie sive Historia Gothica*, Corpus Christianorum Continuatio Mediaeualis, vol. 72, Turnhout: Brepols.

Freedman, P. (1991a) 'The Llobregat as a frontier in the thirteenth century', in *Miscellània en Homenatge al P. Agustí Altisent*, Tarragona: Diputació de Tarragona, 109–17.

—— (1991b) *The Origins of Peasant Servitude in Medieval Catalonia*, Cambridge: Cambridge University Press.

Gaibrois de Ballesteros, M. (1922–8) *Historia del reinado de Sancho IV de Castilla*, 3 vols, Madrid: Tipografía de la 'Revista de Archivos, Bibliotecas y Museos'.

García y García, A. (1977) 'Primeros reflejos del Concilio IV Lateranense en Castilla', in I. Vázquez (ed.) *Studia historico-ecclesiastica. Festgabe für prof. Luchesius G. Spätling OFM*, Rome: Pontificium Athenaeum Antonianum, 249–82.

García de Valdeavellano, L. (1968) *Historia de España, I. De los orígenes a la baja Edad Media*, 2 vols (4th edn), Madrid: Revista de Occidente.

Gautier Dalché, J. (1979) *Historia urbana de León y Castilla en la Edad Media (siglos IX–XIII)*, Madrid: Siglo Veintiuno.

Gil, J. (ed.) (1973) *Corpus scriptorum muzarabicorum*, 2 vols, Madrid: C.S.I.C.

—— (1977) 'Judíos y cristianos en la Hispania del s.VII', *Hispania Sacra* 30: 9–110.

Gil Fernández, J., J. L. Moralejo, and J. I. Ruiz de la Peña (eds) (1985) *Crónicas asturianas*, Oviedo: Universidad de Oviedo.

Glick, T. F. (1995) *From Muslim fortress to Christian castle. Social and cultural change in medieval Spain*, Manchester: Manchester University Press.

Gomes, R. Costa (1991) 'A construção das fronteiras', in F. Bethencourt and D. Ramada Curto (eds) *A memória da nação*, Lisbon: Livraria Sá da Costa, 357–82.

González, Julio (1960) *El reino de Castilla en la época de Alfonso VIII*, 3 vols, Madrid: C.S.I.C.

—— (1980–6) *Reinado y diplomas de Fernando III*, 3 vols, Córdoba: Monte de Piedad y Caja de Ahorros de Córdoba.

González Jiménez, M. (1984) *Andalucía a debate y otros estudios*, Seville: Universidad de Sevilla.

—— (1988) *En torno a los orígenes de Andalucia. La repoblación del siglo XIII*, Seville: Universidad de Sevilla.

—— (1993–4) 'Alfonso X y las oligarquías urbanas de caballeros', *Glossae* 5–6: 195–214.

—— (ed.) (2000) *Crónica de Alfonso X según el MS. II/2777 de la Biblioteca del Palacio Real (Madrid)*, Murcia: Real Academia Alfonso X el Sabio.

Harvey, L. P. (1990) *Islamic Spain 1250 to 1500*, Chicago and London: University of Chicago Press.

Housley, N. (1996) 'Frontier societies and crusading in the late Middle Ages', in B. Arbel (ed.) *Intercultural Contacts in the Medieval Mediterranean*, London and Portland OR.: Frank Cass, 104–19.

Jordan, E. (ed.) (1893–1945) *Les Registres de Clément IV. Recueil des bulles de ce Pape publiées ou analysées d'après les manuscrits originaux des Archives du Vatican*, Paris: Thorin & Fils.

Khadduri, M. (1955) *War and Peace in the Law of Islam*, Baltimore: The Johns Hopkins University Press.

Lannon, F. (1987) *Privilege, Persecution, and Prophecy. The Catholic Church in Spain 1875–1975*, Oxford: Clarendon Press.

Lea, H. C. (1901) *The Moriscos of Spain, their Conversion and Expulsion*, London: Bernard Quaritch.

Lewis, A. R. (1958) 'The closing of the mediaeval frontier', *Speculum* 32: 475–83.

Linehan, Peter (1970) 'The gravamina of the Castilian Church in 1262–3', *English Historical Review* 85: 730–54 [repr. Linehan (1983)].

—— (1971) *The Spanish Church and the Papacy in the Thirteenth Century*, Cambridge: Cambridge University Press.

—— (1980) 'Spanish litigants and their agents at the thirteenth-century papal curia', in S. Kuttner and K. Pennington (eds) *Proceedings of the Fifth International Congress of Medieval*

Canon Law, Vatican City: Biblioteca Apostolica Vaticana, 487–501 [repr. Linehan (1992)].

—— (1981) 'Segovia: a "frontier" diocese in the thirteenth century', *English Historical Review* 96: 481–508 [repr. Linehan (1983)].

—— (1982) 'Religion, nationalism and national identity in medieval Spain and Portugal', in S. Mews (ed.) *Religion and National Identity* [*Studies in Church History* 18] Oxford: 161–99 [repr. Linehan (1983)].

—— (1983) *Spanish Church and Society 1150–1300*, London: Variorum Reprints.

—— (1985) 'The beginnings of Santa María de Guadalupe and the direction of fourteenth-century Castile', *Journal of Ecclesiastical History* 36: 284–304 [repr. Linehan (1992)].

—— (1992) *Past and Present in Medieval Spain*, Aldershot: Variorum.

—— (1993) *History and the Historians of Medieval Spain*, Oxford: Clarendon Press.

—— (1997) *The Ladies of Zamora*, Manchester: Manchester University Press.

—— (1999) 'Castile, Portugal and Navarre', in D. Abulafia (ed.) *The New Cambridge Medieval History*, V, Cambridge: Cambridge University Press, 668–99.

—— (2001) ' Dates and doubts about D. Lucas', *Cahiers de linguistique hispanique médiévale* 24 (in press).

Lomax, D. W. (1988) 'La conquista de Andalucía a través de la historiografía europea de la época', in E. Cabrera (ed.) *Andalucía entre Oriente y Occidente (1236–1492). Actas del V Coloquio Internacional de Historia Medieval de Andalucía*, Córdoba: Diputación Provincial de Córdoba, 37–49.

López de Coca Castañer, J. E. (1989) 'Institutions on the Castilian–Granadan frontier 1369–1482', in Bartlett and MacKay 1989: 137–49.

Lourie, E. (1966) 'A society organized for war. Medieval Spain', *Past & Present* 35: 54–76.

—— (1982) 'The Confraternity of Belchite, the ribāt, and the Temple', *Viator* 13: 159–76.

McCrank, L. (1983) 'The Cistercians of Poblet as medieval frontiersmen. An historiographic essay and case study', in *Estudios en homenaje a D. Claudio Sánchez-Albornoz en sus 90 años*, ii, Buenos Aires: Universidad de Buenos Aires, Instituto de Historia de España, 313–60.

MacKay, A. (1976) 'The ballad and the frontier in late mediaeval Spain', *Bulletin of Hispanic Studies* 53: 15–33.

—— (1989) 'Religion, culture, and ideology on the late medieval Castilian–Granadan frontier', in Bartlett and MacKay 1989: 217–43.

Manzano, E. (1991) *La frontera de al-Andalus en época de los omeyas*, Madrid.

Maravall, J. A. (1964) *El concepto de España en la Edad Media* (2nd edn), Madrid: Instituto de Estudios Políticos.

Marques, M. A. Fernandes (1990) *O Papado e Portugal no tempo de D. Afonso III (1245–1279)*, unpublished Ph.D. diss., Coimbra: Universidade de Coimbra, Faculdade de Letras.

Mattoso, J. (1995) *Identificação de um país. Ensaio sobre as origens de Portugal 1096–1325*, 2 vols, (5th edn), Lisbon: Estampa.

Maya Sánchez, A. (ed.) (1990) *Chronica Adefonsi Imperatoris*, Corpus Christianorum Continuatio Mediaeualis, vol. 71.i, Turnhout: Brepols, 109–296.

Menéndez Pidal. R. (ed.) (1977) *Alfonso X, Primera Crónica General de España*, 2 vols (3rd impr.), Madrid: Gredos.

Molénat, J. P. (1996) 'Les diverses notions de "frontière" dans la région de Castilla–La Mancha au temps des Almoravides et des Almohades', in R. Izquierdo Benito and F. Ruiz Gómez (eds) *Alarcos 1195. Actas del Congreso Internacional Conmemorativo del VIII Centenario de la batalla de Alarcos (1995, Ciudad Real)*, Cuenca: Ediciones de la Universidad de Castilla–La Mancha, 105–23.

Morel Fatio, A., and A. Rodríguez Villa (eds) (1876) *Relación del viaje hecho por Felipe II, en*

1585, á Zaragoza, Barcelona y Valencia escrita por Henrique Cock, Madrid: Estereotipia y Galva de Aribau y Ca.

Moxó, S. de (1979) *Repoblación y sociedad en la España cristiana medieval*, Madrid: Rialp.

Nirenberg, D. (1996) *Communities of Violence. Persecution of minorities in the Middle Ages*, Princeton NJ: Princeton University Press.

Pallares Méndez, M. del C. and E. Portela Silva (1971) *El bajo valle del Miño en los siglos XII y XIII. Economia agraria y estructura social*, Santiago de Compostela: Universidad de Santiago de Compostela.

Pastor de Togneri, R. (1980) *Resistencias y luchas campesinas en la época del crecimiento y consolidación de la formación feudal. Castilla y León, siglos X–XIII*, Madrid: Siglo veintiuno.

Pérez-Embid Wamba, J. (1994) 'Le modèle domanial cistercien dans la Péninsule Ibérique', in L. Pressouyre (ed.) *L'Espace cistercien*, Paris: Comité des travaux historiques et scientifiques, 115–52.

Pérez de Urbel, J. (ed.) (1952) *Sampiro. Su crónica y la monarquía leonesa en el siglo X*, Madrid: C.S.I.C.

Powers, J. F. (1979) 'Frontier municipal baths and social interaction in thirteenth-century Spain', *American Historical Review* 84: 649–67.

Preston, P. (1993) *Franco. A Biography*, London: Fontana Press.

Real Academia de la Historia (ed.) (1807) *Las Siete Partidas del rey don Alfonso el Sabio*, 3 vols, Madrid: Real Academia de la Historia [repr. Madrid 1972].

Ricard, R. (1956) 'La dualité de la civilisation hispanique et l'histoire religieuse du Portugal', *Revue historique* 216: 1–17.

Robinson, R. and Gallagher J., with Alice Denny (1961) *Africa and the Victorians. The official mind of imperialism*, London and New York: Macmillan.

Rodríguez Fernández, J. (1987) *Sancho I y Ordoño IV, reyes de León*, León: Centro de Estudios de Investigación 'San Isidoro' (CSIC-CECEL)/Archivo Histórico Diocesano.

Rodríguez Molina, J. (1997) 'Relaciones pacíficas en la frontera con el reino de Granada', in P. Segura Artero (ed.) *Actas del Congreso 'La Frontera Oriental Nazarí como sujeto histórico (s.XIII–XVI)'. Lorca–Vera, 22 a 24 de noviembre de 1994*, Alicante: Instituto de Estudios Almerienses/Diputación de Almería, 257–90.

Ruiz, T. F. (1997) 'Fronteras: de la comunidad a la nación en la Castilla bajomedieval', *Anuario de Estudios Medievales* 27/1: 23–41.

Sáez, E. (ed.) (1953) *Los Fueros de Sepúlveda*, Segovia: Diputación Provincial de Segovia.

Sánchez-Albornoz, C. (1966) *Despoblación y repoblación del Valle del Duero*, Buenos Aires: Universidad de Buenos Aires, Instituto de Historia de España.

Schottus, A. (ed.) (1608) *Hispaniae illustratae, seu rerum urbiumque Hispaniae, Lusitaniae, Aethiopiae et Indiae scriptores varii*, vol. IV, Frankfurt: apud Claudium Marnium et heredes Ioan. Aubrii.

Smith, Colin (1989) *Christians and Moors in Spain*, II. *1195–1614*, Warminster: Aris & Phillips Ltd.

Southern, R. W. (1962) *Western Views of Islam in the Middle Ages*, Cambridge, Mass.: Harvard University Press.

Tanner, N. P. (1990) *Decrees of the Ecumenical Councils, I (Nicaea I – Lateran V)*, London and Washington DC: Sheed & Ward/Georgetown University Press.

Thompson, J. W. (1928) *Feudal Germany*, Chicago: University of Chicago Press.

Truyol y Serra, A. (1957) 'Las fronteras y las marcas. Factores geográfico-políticos de las relaciones internacionales', *Revista Española de Derecho Internacional* 10: 105–23.

Turner, F. J. (1921) 'The significance of the frontier in American history', in *The Frontier in American History*, New York: Henry Holt & Co., 1–38.

Urvoy, D. (1973) 'Sur l'évolution de la notion de *gihad* dans l'Espagne musulmane', *Mélanges de la Casa de Velázquez* 9: 335–71.

Vanderford, K. H. (ed.) (1984) *Alfonso el Sabio. Setenario* (2nd edn), Barcelona: Crítica.

Verlinden, C. (1955) *L'Esclavage dans l'Europe médiévale*: I. *Péninsule ibérique–France*, Bruges: 'De Tempel'.

Vicens Vives, J. (1967) *Manual de historia económica de España* (5th edn), Barcelona: Editorial Vicens-Vives.

Villar García, L.-M. (ed.) (1990) *Documentación medieval de la catedral de Segovia (1115–1300)*, Salamanca: Universidad de Salamanca/Universidad de Deusto.

Wasserstein, D. (1985) *The Rise and Fall of the Party-kings: politics and society in Islamic Spain, 1002–1086*, Princeton, NJ: Princeton University Press.

Webb, W. P. (1931) *The Great Plains*, Boston, Mass.: Ginn and Co.

——(1953) *The Great Frontier. An interpretation of world history since Columbus*, London: Secker and Warburg.

CHAPTER FOUR

MUSLIMS IN CHRISTIAN IBERIA, 1000–1526: VARIETIES OF MUDEJAR EXPERIENCE[1]

David Nirenberg

How does one begin to adumbrate a history as long, as complex, and as marvelous as that of the Mudejars? An eminent medievalist's strategy in introducing a more famously vanished world seems appropriate. 'What is a hobbit?' asked J. R. R. Tolkien. Hobbits are short, like dwarves, but have no beards, and there is little or no magic about them. Thus by juxtaposition with the known a new identity is ushered into the imagination. A similar process is at work in the creation of Mudejars. Mudejars are, or were, a Muslim people. But they merit a specialization and a name because, unlike Muslims *tout court*, they are subject to Christian rule.

The classification of Mudejars is therefore strictly a jurisdictional matter. Mudejars are Iberian Muslims with Christian lords. The existence of such a classification highlights a novel and important phenomenon: the birth of 'diaspora' communities of Muslims. The Mudejar experience of being a Muslim minority in a non-Muslim polity, of willingly living out one's days in the 'house of war', was exceptional for the Middle Ages. Today millions of Muslims live in non-Muslim countries. Some of these, like the Mudejars of old, live in areas 'reconquered' by Christians from their ancestors (e.g. the Muslims of the former Yugoslavia or the former Soviet Union). Others (e.g. Lebanese, Turk, African, Pakistani) are emigrants to more prosperous lands. These are all very different historical contexts from that of medieval Iberia. Nevertheless, the questions of acculturation, assimilation, and the maintenance of group identity that these Muslim populations face today bear more than a passing resemblance to those confronted by the Mudejars (Carmona González 1995; Fierro 1995). From this point of view, the 'Mudejar' category of identity is one whose relevance to contemporary issues is increasingly apparent.

MUDEJAR IDENTITY: IS JURISDICTION ENOUGH?

Like any category, however, this one obscures tremendous diversity. This is true even if we confine ourselves to the question of jurisdictional status. By strict definition, the young kingdom of Granada under Muḥammad I was by treaty a dependent state of Fernando III. But how much sense does it make to treat Granadan Muslims as

Mudejar? The Muslims of Crevillente submitted to Castilian overlordship in 1243, but they were ruled by their own *ra'is*, or lord, until they passed under the direct rule of Jaume II, king of Catalonia–Aragon, in 1318. At what point should we speak of them as Mudejars? We must not forget that Mudejar identity was a contractual identity, entered into through myriad treaties between conquerors and conquered, each different from the other, and each subject to constant renegotiation, reinterpretation, and change depending on circumstance. From a strictly jurisdictional point of view, there were probably as many Mudejar identities as there were Muslim communities.

Despite these caveats (and more to come below), it remains true that, for Mudejars and their contemporaries, all aspects of Mudejar identity flowed from their legal status, which therefore deserves attention. Mudejars were Muslims *de pacis*, that is, Muslims who had agreed, or more usually whose ancestors had so agreed, to be at peace with Christians and subject to them. In this fundamental way they differed from Muslims *de guerra*, who remained at war with Christians and could therefore legally be killed or enslaved by them. In principle, the rights of Mudejars were stipulated by treaty signed at the time of conquest. Given that the reconquest spanned half a millennium and a number of realms, it is not surprising that these treaties varied. The most important concessions, however, were fairly standard across time and are easily listed. In exchange for their labor and their taxes, Mudejars were to receive: 1) safety and confirmation of property rights; 2) guarantee of the free practice of religion, including the right to pray in their mosques, to teach Islam to their children, and to go on pilgrimage; 3) the right to rule themselves according to Muslim law (*Sharī'a*), to be judged under it in any case involving only Muslims, and to name their own religious and judicial officials; 4) the confirmation of existing pious endowments in perpetuity; 5) a limitation on taxes, which were to be roughly similar to those paid under Muslim rule. (See, e.g., treaty of Xivert (1234) in Febrer Romaguera 1991: 10–16; treaty of Granada (1491) summarized in Harvey 1990: 314–23.)

These privileges are the foundation stones of Mudejar existence, which is not to say that they could not be violated or ignored. The last treaty of this sort, that signed with Granada in 1491–2, was irreparably broken within a few years of its signing. Less dramatically, all of the privileges contained in the earlier treaties were subject to gradual erosion or circumscription. The public call to prayer was often proscribed (Ferrer i Mallol 1987: 87–94), royal and seigneurial officials interfered in the appointment of judges (*qāḍīs*) and officials (García-Arenal 1984: 41), old taxes were raised and new ones imposed (e.g. the *servicio* and *medio servicio* of 1388: Torres Fontes 1962: 166). Occasionally, as happened in parts of Huesca (Aragon) in the thirteenth century (Utrilla Utrilla 1986: 202) and at Quart (Valencia) in the early fourteenth, a Mudejar community might even be expelled, and its lands confiscated. Mudejars were not naive on this score. One fourteenth-century Andalusi *imām*, Ibn Rabī', warned that Christian kings were fickle, and that even when they kept their word they could not always enforce upon their violent subjects the provisions of treaties they had signed (Koningsveld and Wiegers 1996: 27–8). Nevertheless, these treaties articulated the contractual basis for the continued existence of Muslims in Christian Iberia in formal legal terms that were remarkably stable. The treaty of Granada would have been completely intelligible to those Muslims of Toledo who had surrendered their similarly magnificent city to the Christians nearly 500 years before.

THE SOURCES FOR MUDEJAR HISTORY

Treaties and jurisdiction alone cannot put flesh on the bones of Mudejarism. Fortunately many and diverse other sources exist from which to study how Mudejarism was experienced economically, socially, and culturally. Archaeology, for example, has yielded a vast amount of data about patterns of settlement (Glick 1995). The study of surviving pottery has underpinned arguments about the Mudejars' economic importance, as well as theses about Mudejar cultural decline based on the impoverishment of their stylistic practice (López del Alamo 1995). Here, however, I will confine myself to textual sources, which can roughly be divided into two types: those produced by Christians and Christian institutions, whether in romance or in Latin; and those produced by Mudejars and Mudejar institutions, whether in romance, in Aljamiado, or in Arabic. (Aljamiado is romance written in Arabic characters, though it often includes a good deal of Arabic vocabulary as well.)

By far the most abundant of these are Christian archival sources (by which I mean court cases, records of royal, municipal, seigneurial and ecclesiastical bureaucracies, and the records of notaries). Since the 1970s, these have served as the foundation for a body of work which established our understanding of the political, legal, and institutional underpinnings of Mudejar status. Even more recently, as scholars have become concerned about viewing the Mudejars through an excessively Christian optic, attention has shifted to Aljamiado and Arabic texts produced by Mudejar communities. Unfortunately the Mudejars themselves left little direct evidence of how they perceived their own identity, which in any case they themselves did not label as 'Mudejar'. Unlike their Granadan and North African co-religionists, Mudejars wrote no chronicles, no local histories. Perhaps for this very reason, few Mudejar scholars passed into biographical dictionaries of the type that Islamists have elsewhere put to such good use. For explicit Muslim representations of Mudejar cultural identity we need to turn to writers living elsewhere in the Islamic world, although, as we shall see, their claims have to be handled with care. But the Mudejars and their Morisco successors did leave behind a considerable number of contracts (Hoenerbach 1965), tax records (Barceló Torres 1984), polemical and religious works (Wiegers 1996; López-Morillas 1995), magical recipes (Harvey 1996; Kontzi 1984) and the like, documents which can be used to reconstruct their material and cultural world.

DEMOGRAPHY, LORDSHIP, AND ECONOMY

Perhaps the most important variable in analyzing this Mudejar world is demographic: different Iberian kingdoms had dramatically different numbers of Mudejar residents. Some 1,000 Muslims lived among 100,000 Christians in long-reconquered Navarre, while the approximately 175,000 Mudejars living in the rural villages of fourteenth-century Valencia vastly outnumbered their Christians neighbors. Within kingdoms distribution was similarly uneven. Nearly all Navarrese Muslims, for example, lived in only one of the five provinces of that kingdom. Within Catalonia, more recently reconquered south-western regions such as Tortosa or Lleida had significant Muslim populations, whereas only one Mudejar family lived in Girona, a city in the shadow of the Pyrenees and the old Frankish March. The same gradation, albeit slightly more complicated by Muslim migration, could be drawn in Castilian lands from Andalucia to Asturias (Ladero Quesada 1989).

Even within one province of a specific kingdom vast demographic differences existed. In the Aragonese region of Huesca, for example, Mudejars might live in entirely Muslim villages, in places where the population and the town government were evenly divided between Christian and Muslim, or in towns and cities where Muslims were a tiny minority (Utrilla Utrilla 1986: 199). These differences had a significant effect on how individual Mudejars experienced diaspora. We will return to this issue below, but here it is worth noting that Muslim jurists were perfectly well aware of this effect. The same Ibn Rabī' cited above went so far as to divide Mudejars into three categories: those who lived as a minority dispersed among Christians, those who lived as a minority but separated from Christians in their own quarter or village, and those who outnumbered their conquerors. Each of these groups, according to him, experienced very different conditions. The first of them, for example, was particularly at risk of violence and assimilation, while the third was the most at liberty to follow Islam and therefore, somewhat paradoxically, had the greatest obligation to end its Mudejar status by emigrating to Muslim lands (Koningsveld and Wiegers 1996: 34–5).

Another variable, almost as important as population density in understanding the varieties of Mudejar experience, is lordship. Ibn Rabī''s third category probably alluded to one singular type of lordship in which Mudejars were ruled indirectly by Christians through Muslim lords. This type of lordship, which existed in places such as Murcia until around 1300 and Crevillente until 1318, was rare and generally represented a transition stage (Guichard 1973). More common was direct Christian rule, which could take as many forms as there were types of lords: kings, secular and ecclesiastical magnates, municipalities, and even burgesses or lesser nobles owning lands with no more than seven or eight Muslim vassals, all could be lords of Mudejars. Analytically, these types of lordship are generally divided into two overlapping but significantly different categories: royal and non-royal.

These categories overlapped because legally the king was lord of all Mudejars (as of all Jews) in the sense that he reserved the right to jurisdiction over them and generally collected some tax from them. Throughout the peninsula Muslims were the 'treasure' of kings and under royal protection (Boswell 1977). In a number of these regions, however, that jurisdiction became increasingly theoretical. Aragón again provides a good example. In the immediate wake of the reconquest, Aragonese monarchs found themselves in direct control of extensive lands populated with Mudejars as well as Christians. Over the course of the thirteenth and fourteenth centuries, however, kings in need of ever greater revenues alienated more and more of their rights over these lands. By the fifteenth century the only Muslim populations still under the direct lordship of the Crown were those in the large towns (Daroca,

Calatayud, Zaragoza, etc.), while most rural Mudejars, who constituted the majority of Muslims, had slipped under the control of noble houses such as the Luna and the Urrea (García Marco 1993: 113).

This shift, coupled with the largely rural distribution of Muslim populations in Christian Iberia, gave Mudejars a proverbial importance in the seigneurial economies of regions such as Aragon, Valencia, and Murcia: 'huerta que cava un moro vale un tesoro'; 'El que tiene moro tiene oro' ('a field dug by a Muslim is worth a treasure'; 'he who has Muslims has gold'). Muslim came to represent the ideal peasant, an industrious tenant-farmer who could be relied upon to fulfill his obligations uncomplainingly. In this sense the Mudejar was not 'marginal': he was fully integrated into the seigneurial system, even to the extent of fighting alongside Christians in feuds and skirmishes with the forces of rival lords (Nirenberg 1996: 34–5). In exchange, lords tended to safeguard the religious rights of their Muslim subjects. Some even commissioned translations of Muslim law codes so as to judge Mudejars under the *Sharī'a* (e.g. Barcelò Torres 1989). More effectively than kings were able to do with their urban Mudejars, lords protected their rural Muslims from ecclesiastical initiatives of segregation (such as the wearing of distinctive badges or hair styles) and of religious repression (such as bans on the call to prayer). Later, in the Morisco period, some of these lords would be so fierce in their defense of their formerly Mudejar labor force as to attract the attention of the Inquisition. The point here is simply that the Mudejars' importance in the seigneurial agrarian economy helped to ensure that their religious rights were respected, and lent them a broader base of support than that enjoyed by that other Iberian religious minority, the Jews.

Most Mudejars were farmers on a small to medium scale (Ledesma Rubio 1981). A significant number were artisans and craftsmen. As such, Mudejars tended to specialize in particular trades, though exactly what these were varied according to region. In Valencia, for example, Mudejars dominated the pottery trade (Amigues 1992), in Murcia they played a vital role in transport, while in Aragón Muslims were particularly prominent in metalwork and construction. It has often been argued that in areas where it occurred, this specialization encouraged toleration by reducing competition between members of religious groups while preserving a vital economic role for minorities. The importance of this economic basis for *convivencia* is real, though it can be overstated. There were regions, such as Castile, where Mudejars never dominated any particular niche (Molénat 1994). Where they did, their preponderance was seldom such as to preclude significant competition from Christians: witness the conflicts between Muslim and Christian potters in Valencia. When Muslims did achieve a *de facto* monopoly, as among the blacksmiths of Daroca (Aragón), that monopoly itself could become the occasion for very significant friction.

It remains true, however, that Mudejar prosperity was very much rooted in these trades, from which many of the most prominent Muslim families emerged. The history of the Bellvís clan, a Castilian Mudejar family that moved to the Crown of Aragón, provides an excellent example. Faraig, the founder of the dynasty, was a veterinarian. Medieval veterinary medicine was primarily concerned with the care of horses and was so closely related to blacksmithing that at times the two professions shared a common guild. Not surprisingly then, Mudejars achieved some prominence within the field. Faraig was one of these, becoming veterinarian to the royal household in the fourteenth century. Through such service, Faraig and his descendants became rich and gained important offices, such as *qāḍī* general (chief judge) of all Muslims in the Crown of Aragon. But such examples tell us more about the role of the royal household in creating minority elites than they do about monopoly and the economics of *convivencia*. There were a number of important Muslim veterinarians in medieval Iberia, but they never constituted a monopoly or even a majority of the profession. Faraig's success owed as much to the king's tendency to treat minorities in his household as representatives of their communities (as occasionally he treated his Jewish physicians) as it did to a Mudejar tradition of veterinary practice (Cifuentes 1998: 12).

The Bellvís example of economic and political prominence achieved through trades points to an important characteristic of Mudejar society: its relative lack of stratification. In general, the aristocracy of surrendering Muslim kingdoms had rejected Mudejarism. Some, like Ibn Maḥfūz, the ruler of Niebla, emigrated to Marrakesh after a brief period of vassalage under Alfonso X of Castile. Others converted to Christianity, the son of the Muslim king of Mallorca, for example, adopting the name Jaime de Gotor and marrying into the Aragonese noble house of Luna. Whatever the reason, few members of the Muslim military, religious, and cultural elite remained behind in lands conquered by the Christians. The result was a society that was remarkably flat. The precipices of privilege that separated a Faraig de Bellvís from the poorest Mudejar were far less dizzying than the corresponding differences in Christian or Jewish society. This does not mean that Mudejar society was any the less conflictual than these others: the clan-based factional conflict that was endemic to Mudejar society was if anything more violent than the 'class' struggle so evident among Iberian Jews (Meyerson 1991: 247). It does mean that Mudejar society lacked the economic and political resources to generate the types of literary and artistic cultures which tend to spring up around the patronage of the powerful.

MUDEJAR CULTURE: A HISTORY OF DECLINE?

It is against this background of a largely agricultural and artisanal population, often living scattered among Christians and subjected to pressures of acculturation, dependent on Christian lords for the maintenance of the privileges necessary to follow their own religion, that we must read the judgments on mudejarism pronounced by Muslims living in Islamic lands, for whom submission to Christian jurisdiction was associated with cultural vulnerability, corruption, and decline. The most often cited of these writers is the fifteenth-century North African jurist al-Wansharīsī, whose opinion of the Mudejar was not ambivalent: 'his residence is manifest proof of his vile and base spirit'. 'To exalt Christian and diminish Muslim authority is a great and disastrous ruination . . . and he who does this is on the border of infidelity.' The late fourteenth-century mufti (and emigrant from Christian Iberia?) Ibn Miqlash illustrated this cultural vulnerability in an unusual passage which depicts the fate of Islam under Christian rule in sexual terms. The Mudejar, he claimed, mingled with worshipers of idols and lost his zeal. His wife depended upon (and was therefore sexually vulnerable to) his Christian lord. What fate could be worse, he asked, than that of one without zeal, either for his religion or for his wife! (Buzineb 1988: 59, 63).

Most jurists were less vivid. They stressed, not the debasement of the Mudejar's wife, but that of his religious and legal culture. By demonstrating that Mudejars were deficient in legal culture as defined by the Maliki scholars, these jurists argued that they were less than full Muslims. As early as the twelfth century no less an authority than Ibn Rushd (Averroes) ruled that Mudejars were of 'suspect credibility, their testimony in court cannot be accepted and they cannot be allowed to lead prayer'. The legal authority of the Mudejar scholars was doubtful, they asserted, because Mudejar judges were appointed by infidels and because they were ignorant, an ignorance which became something of a topos in the writings of North African and Granadan jurists.

There were, of course, among Maliki jurists less extreme opinions on the Mudejar question than those I have quoted (and it is to borne in mind that the Maliki school was the most uncompromising on the issue of Muslim minorities living in non-Islamic polities) (Abou el-Fadl 1994). I have dwelt on these more rigorous expressions because they provide a clear example of how a jurisdictional classification could translate into a cultural identity. The problem of Muslims who willingly and permanently resided in the lands of Christian enemies, and who by their labors directly supported these enemies in their long and successful war against Islamic polities, forced jurists to confront the question of what constituted a Muslim, and to use the ensuing characteristics, which they presented as normative, to distinguish the particular, corrupt nature of Mudejar Islam.

These jurists approached the corrupting effects of mudejarism through two quite different logics. The first was strictly jurisdictional: the Islamic life could not be fulfilled under Christian rule. How could one follow Muslim law if the scholars, judges, and officials were appointed by Christian authorities? How, without a Muslim head of state to pay it to, could one fulfill the obligation to pay *zakāt*? The second approach was more explicitly cultural. Al-Wansharīsī again, echoing Ibn Rabī':

> One has to beware of the pervasive effect of their [the Christians'] way of life, their language, their dress, their objectionable habits, and influence on people living with them over a long period of time, as has occurred in the case of the inhabitants of 'Abulla' and other places, for they have lost their Arabic, and when the Arabic language dies out, so does devotion to it, and there is a consequential neglect of worship as expressed in words in all its richness and outstanding virtues.
>
> (Harvey 1990: 58)

According to this model, the vital Islamic nature of Mudejar culture could be evaluated by measuring it against certain cultural markers drawn from the normative Islam of more central Muslim lands: language, legal procedure, dress, ritual, and custom. Ridicule of Mudejar Arabic was one very common strategy within this framework. Criticism of Mudejar legal knowledge was another, as when a Mudejar emigrant to Oran claimed, toward the end of the fourteenth century, that among

Mudejars innovation (*al-bid'a*) has 'extinguished the light of Muslim law' (Buzineb 1988: 65, lines 1–2).

MODERN APPROACHES TO MUDEJAR CULTURE: THE CONSERVATIONISTS

Modern approaches to Mudejar culture are in some ways strikingly similar to those of these medieval Muslim commentators. Like them, historians and philologists have tended to think of mudejarism as an impoverished culture in decline (Galán Sánchez 1991: 81–8). Indeed the first generation of modern scholars interested in Mudejar culture was composed of liberals who turned to the study of Mudejars expressly to show the corrupting cultural effects of intolerance, and who therefore embraced a historiography of decline. They differed from medieval Islamic commentators in that they positively valorized Mudejar culture: scholars such as Ticknor and Gayangos pointed to Aljamiado literature like the *Poema de Yusuf* in order to stress the persistence of lyrical sensibility and literary genius among the Mudejars. But like their distant predecessors, they presented their story of the weakening of Arabic as a teleological narrative of cultural destruction in which the creation of Aljamiado was a desperate effort on the part of a community under ever-increasing assimilative pressure to maintain access, no matter how impoverished, to its religious traditions.

Most later scholars have adhered to this paradigm. On the one hand they have sought to measure Mudejar culture against what they consider to be normative Islamic practice, a methodology that almost always finds the former wanting. On the other they have stressed that, to whatever extent that Mudejar practice conforms to the normative, it represents a 'courageous and stubborn defense' of Islamic identity (Harvey 1990: xi). Replication of a normative standard is here the ideal, and the Mudejar achievement consists in preserving from cultural encroachment as much of that original practice as possible: what I term the conservationist approach.

The contributions of this approach to the study of mudejarism have been enormous. Consider the question alluded to above: just how much Arabic did Mudejars know, and to what extent can their knowledge of the language serve as an index of acculturation? Until recently there was common agreement that by the fourteenth century only Mudejars in the most densely Islamic areas such as Valencia preserved a knowledge of spoken and written Arabic. In the rest of the peninsula, it was supposed, a shrinking religious elite struggled to retain Arabic as a written language, while the rest of the community became monolingual in the local romance dialect. Finally, in the late fourteenth century according to some, in the mid-fifteenth according to most, the exhaustion of Mudejar Arabic even among the elite led to the rise of Aljamiado as a replacement, its alphabet a superficial remnant of the holy language of the *Qur'ān*.

The past two decades of scholarship suggest that such a narrative does not do justice to the complexities of Mudejar bilingualism. Increasing attention to distinctions between spoken and written language, to class difference, to local and jurisdictional variation, and to genre, has made clear that Mudejars conserved a great deal more Arabic than was previously suspected. The evidence, of course, is haphazard. For example, an Aragonese student's letter (in Arabic) to his former teacher complaining that a Navarrese Mudejar had failed to send him copies of some Arabic sermons suggests that Navarrese Muslims still heard sermons in that language. (Whether they understood them or not is a different question.) That same student also told his teacher that he was up day and night studying the *Qanūn* of Avicenna, a devilishly difficult text to find 'highly acculturated' Muslims of Zaragoza reading in 1495 (Hoenerbach 1965: 345–8). Even in Ávila, which may be the city identified by al-Wansharīsī and Ibn Rabī' as a place where Arabic had been utterly lost, we find *faqīhs* (Tapia Sánchez 1991: 55). One fifteenth-century scholar from the town issued a *fatwa* in Arabic about the legitimacy of praying upon animal skins. The document was also signed in Arabic by the *faqīhs* of Burgos and Valladolid, both Castilian towns with Muslim communities considered highly acculturated (Harvey 1990: 62–3).

Given the conservatism of legal culture, it is perhaps not surprising that notarial practice is one of the best preserved domains of Mudejar Arabic. To draw again upon the example of long reconquered Navarre, there is continuous evidence into the sixteenth century of Mudejar scribes there producing legal documents in Arabic (García Arenal 1984: 36). This was a privilege Mudejars were willing to pay for, as when the Muslims of Fraga in the late fourteenth century bought a royal charter declaring Arabic their exclusive legal language. Notarial practice also makes it clear that when Muslim notaries turned to Aljamiado, it was not necessarily because they lacked a solid knowledge of written Arabic. Notaries might draw up a contract in Aljamiado rather than in Arabic because the local lord required it. Sometimes *faqīhs* tell us that they provided a document in Arabic, with a copy in Aljamiado at the request of and for the personal (i.e. non-legal) use of the client. And we can even see that some itinerant notaries would provide only Arabic documents in one village, and only Aljamiado ones in another (Miller, personal communication). Was this the result of the relative Arabic literacy of the communities? Of local seigneurial demands or customs? Or of rights specific to a given population?

It has become possible to ask these and many other questions only as recent scholarship has created what can justly be called a field of Mudejar Arabic. Its practitioners, moved by the pathos of what they perceive to be a nearly extinct Mudejar textual culture, have recovered precious examples of a vanishing species. Much the same is true of work in jurisprudence, and here too the result is a renewed respect for Mudejar conservation of textual competence. A considerable number of Mudejar legal documents survive, both in Arabic and in Aljamiado: inheritance stipulations, marriage arrangements, apprenticeship agreements, designations of procurators; in short, the entire formal apparatus of contract. These contracts were carefully regulated by Muslim law, and a number of influential formularies, called *wathā'iq* manuals, stipulated the form they should take if they were to comply with that law. That same student whose letter was quoted earlier apologized to his teacher for not being able to forward him a copy of one such manual, by al-Djazīrī, because he had left the manuscript behind in his home town. Reading Mudejar documents against such formularies thus seems to offer a good diagnostic of Mudejar knowledge. To the extent that Mudejar documents differed from the norm, whether in formal structure, in the language they employed (i.e., Aljamiado rather than Arabic), or even in handwriting quality, one could posit a loss of notarial expertise indicative of cultural decline or mixture.

This philological methodology continues to offer fascinating results. For example, discussing an Arabic document from 1451 in which an Aragonese Mudejar community designates a procurator, Alfonso Carmona shows that the redactor of the document adheres quite strictly to classical tenth- and eleventh-century manuals, and also has access to later and more detailed manuals from the twelfth and thirteenth centuries. At the same time, Carmona marks the several deviations and omissions of the document, not so much as signs of cultural decline, but as adaptations to the Christian institutional and juridical systems within which Mudejar communities functioned. The scribe, for example, inserted some Aljamiado lines into the Arabic document, not because he did not know Arabic but because these were clauses drawn from and necessary within the Aragonese notarial tradition, though alien to the Andalusi one. In a more complicated case, Carmona shows how the desire of some Mudejars to follow Castilian rather than Andalusi dowry custom resulted in notarial attempts to adapt the Arabic formulaic tradition in ways which did not explicitly violate Muslim law (Carmona González 1993; Carmona González 1992).

These contributions, and others like them, provide us with a new sense of the vibrancy and creativity of Mudejar textual production. Nevertheless throughout Mudejar studies, the emphasis remains less on how or why Mudejars wrote what they wrote and more on the rudimentary, impoverished, and mimetic nature of Mudejar manuscript production. Put more abstractly, many mudejarists, and especially those dealing with the Arabic sources, measure Mudejar culture against an imagined normative Islam. Replication is here the ideal, and difference or adaptation is seen as symptomatic of acculturation and decline.

ALTERNATIVE STRATEGIES: MUDEJARISM AS A LOCAL ISLAM

The same types of sources can be exploited to quite different effect, in part by exchanging the 'normative' optic for a more 'local' one. Put crudely, scholars of Islam have tended to divide into two camps. On the one hand there were those interested in local forms of religion, primarily anthropologists, who focussed on religious practices that they believed made a particular local group distinctive, rather than on those which that group shared with other Muslims. Islamists, on the other hand, tended to focus on texts and their interpretation, not on local religious practice. With their text-critical and philological approach, the latter ask 'where does this text come from? how do its terms and ideas relate to the canonical Islamic textual tradition?' The ethnographers' questions are somewhat different: 'how do (or did, in the case of a historical ethnographer) people understand, debate, or apply the text?' Islamists generally presume a 'conceptual and normative core to Islam (containing, of course, several different schools and positions) that, adequately understood, could stand for the religion as a whole'. Ethnographers, on the other hand, while they have often been willing to grant the existence of such a normative core, tend to ignore it in their own work, preferring to focus on the distinctively local (Bowen 1993: 5–8).

Since its rise in the 1960s under the able stewardship of Clifford Geertz, the study of 'local Islams' has become tremendously influential in Islamic anthropology, but has not made much of an impact on the treatment of historical Islam. There are at least two reasons for this. First, it was not primarily concerned with questions about the social production of texts, questions which are central to historians, whose primary sources are largely textual. And second, the insistence on a 'multiplicity' of local Islams ignored the sense of many Muslims across diverse cultures and historical periods that there was indeed an 'external, normative, reference point for their ideas and practices'. In other words, fleeing from the universalism of the Islamists (who in turn are adopting the universalist claims of the texts they study), these ethnographers tended excessively toward particularism (Miller 1998: 12).

Increasingly, however, students of modern Islams have begun to focus on the tension between local practice and prescriptive textual norms as a central part of Muslim experience, and explored this tension through studies of how texts and traditions are produced, read, and debated. In particular, they focus on the role of 'culture brokers' within local institutions and on the religious discourse produced by these intermediaries. In the Mudejar field Kathryn Miller's recent work makes clear the value of such an approach. It draws heavily upon a cache of Arabic and Aljamiado documents discovered in the nineteenth century in the walls of a house in the Aragonese village of Almonacid in order to reconstruct the role of the Mudejar *faqīh* in the creation of an identity that is simultaneously resolutely Islamic and yet also aware of its deviations from the normative. In addressing this documentation, Miller invokes an admonition of the Comaroffs: 'if texts are to be more than literary topoi, scattered shards from which we preserve worlds, they have to be anchored in the processes of their production, in the orbits of connections and influences that give them life and force' (Comaroff and Comaroff 1992: 34). She focuses, first, on a reconstruction of the textual world created by the Mudejar *faqīhs*. What texts did they have available? How, in a society predating inter-library loan and far from traditional centers of Arabic manuscript production, did the *faqīhs* set about gathering the textual infrastructure necessary to their legal practice? Thus far the project is not very dissimilar to that of the 'conservationists' (cf. e.g., Carmona González 1993 or Albarracín Navarro 1994). The difference lies in Miller's goal, which is not so much the description or evaluation of the surviving corpus of Mudejar Arabic material as an understanding of the practices of the little-studied group that produced it, the Mudejar scholarly community (the phrase is not an oxymoron).

There can be no doubt that most of these Mudejar scholars felt that theirs was a culture in decline, one whose standards were failing. 'Because of the distance of our dwelling places and our separation from our coreligionists, no one is studying or writing. . . . ' Such laments were common coin among Mudejar scholars, and marked an awareness of the gap they perceived between their practice and what they took to be normative. Nevertheless, Mudejar *faqīhs* and notaries continued to produce Arabic legal materials, including collections of *fatwas*, notarial manuals, and contracts of all sorts (Konigsveld 1992). And while they frequently deferred to North African jurists and submitted legal questions to them, they were also perfectly capable of insisting on their own abilities. In one letter, for example, Miller presents us with a Mudejar *faqīh* named Aḥmad al-Zawārī, who complains that he has been slandered as ignorant by some Muslim captives returning to the House of Islam. Al-Zawārī insists that this is a case of mistaken identity, and that he is 'a learned faqíh and a knowledgeable one, clinging to the book of God'.

Miller's point is that when we combine these traces of Mudejar bibliophilia with some of their surviving notarial production, we begin to have a sense of how the Mudejar learned classes authorized their scribal practice through constant reference to what they considered to be normative Islamic legal and textual traditions. Further, this scribal production can be contextualized within the particular structures of Christian domination experienced by Mudejars, both by studying the treatment of Arabic documents ('cartas moriscas') in Christian courts, and by following the careers of Mudejar officials through Christian archival documentation. In Calatayud (Aragón), for example, fifteenth-century notarial records can supply a wealth of information about the networks of patronage, kinship, and power within which Mudejar *faqíhs* functioned. When she has finished joining these notarial sources, recently studied by F. García Marco, to the surviving products of Mudejar scribes, Miller will have brought us a great deal closer to an understanding of how the Mudejars maintained a textual practice which they recognized as Islamic (Miller 1998).

DEFENDING ISLAM IN THE HOUSE OF WAR

Textual practice was not the only marker of Islamic identity that required defense and translation in a Mudejar world. We have already seen how the Maliki *faqíhs* insisted that Christian domination led to the degradation of a number of specific and indispensable markers of Muslim identity: Arabic, adherence to Qur'anic punishments (*ḥudūd*), inaccessibility of Muslim women to non-Muslim men. To these we might add, as North African muftis did, the inability to identify the start of *Ramaḍān*, to leave Christian lands on pilgrimage, or to fulfill the obligation of paying *zakāt*, all crucial obligations of the believer according to Muslim law. Given that many of these practices did in fact decline, how did the Mudejars mark new boundaries that they found adequate to a Muslim identity and imbue them with Islamic significance?

For some of these obligations the process is fairly straightforward. Mudejars, for example, tended to replace *zakāt* (which required a Muslim polity) with *ṣadaqa*, charity, and specifically with alms for the redemption of enslaved or captive Muslims. By the Morisco period we even find some North African muftis advocating this solution (Buzineb 1988: 60; Cantineau 1923). Other boundaries required more than reclassification to remain recognizable. Perhaps the one whose defense exacted the heaviest toll was that between Muslim women and non-Muslim men. Recall the words of Ibn Miqlash about Mudejars, whom he claimed cared neither for their religion nor for the sexual inviolability of their wives. The argument that under Christian lords Mudejars could not protect Muslim women from sexual advances by non-Muslims was often made by Granadan and North African jurists. Al-Wansharīsī even mentions the princess Zayda, who converted to Christianity and married Alfonso VI after the fall of Toledo. Without the power to enforce Islamic legal prohibitions on intercourse between Muslim women and non-Muslim men, or to punish transgression with Koranic (*ḥudūd*) punishments, how could Mudejars maintain this essential boundary?

This was not a theoretical issue. Christian archives contain references to thousands of Mudejar women engaged in sexual relations with Christians and Jews. But these references are the result, less of cultural erosion than of new ways of maintaining boundaries deemed essential. Again and again Mudejar communities purchased privileges allowing them to put to death Muslim women accused of adultery or interfaith sex, though the *ḥudūd* punishment was necessarily commuted to the social death of enslavement to the Crown. Again and again Mudejar fathers accused their own and their neighbors' wives and daughters of transgressing these boundaries, and delivered them up for punishment. The Christian nature of the records that document the legal consequences of these actions should not obscure the fact that behind them lie Muslim communities and Muslim individuals translating Islamic legal prescriptions into Mudejar idioms (cf. Nirenberg 1996: 139).

Just as the risk to Muslim women in the House of War stimulated a heightened awareness of the boundary-marking role of women on the part of Mudejars, so the possibility of conversion prompted a heightened sensitivity to markers of religious identity. Consider the case of Juan de Granada. He was born a Mudejar, Mahoma Joffre, in Aragón in the mid-fifteenth century. An orphan at the age of twelve or thirteen, he left his village and went to Valencia, where he converted to Christianity and joined a military troop on its way to fight on the Granadan frontier. But he soon abandoned the troop and settled in Granada, where he lived for two years begging alms. In Granada he behaved as a Muslim, fasting during *Ramaḍān*, etc. (though he told inquisitors that he would break his fast secretly outside the walls, since his heart remained Christian). After some time he left Granada and tried to re-enter Christian lands, but was turned away from the frontier by Muslim guards who suspected that he was a *tornadiz*, a convert to Christianity. Finally he managed to find a Christian troop on the frontier, asked for baptism, and became a Christian once more, serving the captain of the troop for four years. After that time, he decided to return to his village in Aragón as a Muslim, where he lived for several years before a traveller recognized him and denounced him to the Inquisition. Every stage of this itinerary offers evidence of the acts of discrimination and discernment by which Muslims (and Christians) established religious identity in a society where the stability of that identity could not be taken for granted. For our purposes the most interesting example comes from Juan/Mahoma's Mudejar relatives. Because Mahoma's long absence made him suspect, his cousins repeatedly interrogated him about his religion. Over the years that followed they observed his behavior closely: dress, attendance at mosque, form of prayer, and fasting during *Ramaḍān*, in particular. And they suspected him, because he drank too much wine (Ledesma Rubio 1994: 63–103).

Here, as in the previous example about Muslim women, we see the responsibility for recognizing Islam and maintaining its boundaries devolving upon the individual Mudejar. If we cannot speak broadly of a late Mudejar shift of focus from *farḍ kifāya*, collective duties, to *farḍ 'ayn*, individual obligations, we can at least suggest a process of devolution by which the individual took increasing responsibility for patrolling the boundaries of Islam. This process was, I believe, one of the most characteristic aspects of Mudejar Islam, and crucial to the production of an identity that simultaneously recognized its 'decline' yet resolutely insisted on its Muslim identity. From this perspective, much of what the North African jurists bemoaned as decline can instead be interpreted as dynamism. Consider as an example the rise of Aljamiado. From the point of view of 'class', it could equally well be studied as an example of the expansion of Islamic learning among Mudejars as of its contraction. The fact that the particular conditions in Iberia made it possible to justify an extensive practice of glossing and translation may have meant that knowledge which in more central Islamic lands was increasingly restricted to the 'learned class', the *ulamā*, in Iberia penetrated further into the 'popular' or 'ignorant' classes.

The unusually fertile field of Mudejar religious polemic may constitute evidence for this process. Beginning with Ibn Ḥazm (994–1064), Iberian Muslims seem more concerned with polemic against Christianity and Judaism than Muslims in more central lands, and this becomes increasingly true as the so-called reconquest continues. One may even speak of a tradition of polemical texts produced in Christian Spain by captives from Granada and North Africa, and circulated, glossed, and translated among Mudejars for hundreds of years. A particularly fascinating example by Muḥammad al-Qaysī, a captive in the Crown of Aragon in the early fourteenth century, has recently been published from MS. 1557 of the National Library of Algiers (Koningsveld and Wiegers 1994). Al-Qaysī offers a moving description of the cultural effects of captivity, including the claim that his soul had betrayed him and his interior and exterior had become un-Arabic. But what is relevant to my point here is that al-Qaysī also provides the text of what he claims was his disputation with a priest in the presence of the king of Aragón. Entitled 'the Key of Religion [*Kitāb Miftāḥ al-Dīn*], or the Disputation between Christians and Muslims', the text was promptly translated in the first half of the fourteenth century into versions which survive in some four Aljamiado manuscripts. Al-Qaysī is not unique, nor is the Muslim–Christian frontier the only one polemically policed. We have, for example, a mid-fourteenth-century Arabic polemic written by a Mudejar against the Jews, the *Ta'yīd al-millah*, or Defense of the Faith, which exists in multiple Arabic manuscripts. What is more, some manuscripts of this polemic contain extensive inter-linear glosses in Aljamiado, and a number of complete translations into that language, as well as several adaptations, survive (Nirenberg 1996: 196–8).

The multiple survivals of these polemics are very unusual for so fragmentary a record, and attest to their popularity. Moreover, of all genres, these were among the first to be glossed and translated, a process that was well under way already in the early fourteenth century. These translations were not for the *faqíhs*, who did not need them at this early date. It seems more likely that they were intended for the broader audience of Mudejars, to enable each to become, in this 'land of polytheism', a defender of his own faith.

It was partly through such a devolution, I would argue, that Mudejars managed to maintain a sense of the dynamism of their faith while at the same time presenting themselves as a community falling away from ideal Islam. We are oppressed and our knowledge is declining, we can imagine the Mudejars thinking, but at the local level we are heroically Islamic, we who must strive constantly to maintain our individual identities as Muslims. This productive tension between local and 'normative' is beautifully illustrated in a *fatwa* newly discovered by Kathryn Miller. It is written by al-Muwwāq, who was chief *qāḍī* of Granada in its final years. Responding to a question about how a Muslim should behave in the House of War, he replied by fusing, rather than opposing, the status of one learned in authoritative Islamic tradition with that of the individual struggling to make the discriminations necessary to maintain a Muslim identity among infidels. The individual Mudejar, he wrote, should 'be a faqīh of himself' (*faqīh al-nafs*). 'He teaches himself, and he should distinguish the good deed which presents itself from the bad one which befalls.' These words are a useful antidote to al-Wansharīsī's model of cultural corruption and to the modern historiography of decline, and a fitting characterization of the varieties of Mudejar experience (Miller 1998: 51, 57).

NOTE

1   I would like to thank Paula Sanders for her insightful readings of successive drafts; David Abulafia and Tarif Khalidi for their invitation to a symposium on Islam and the History of Europe, which provided a critical forum at an early stage; and the editors, for their thoughtful suggestions. Above all, my thanks are due to Kathryn Miller, who reintroduced me to the Mudejars as I had never known them, and whose work inspired these reflections.

GLOSSARY

Aljamiado	romance written in Arabic characters
ḥudūd	Qur'anicly prescribed punishments for which there could be no mitigation
farḍ ʿayn	religious obligations incumbent upon each person individually
farḍ kifāya	religious obligations incumbent upon the community as a whole, but performable by a few on behalf of all
fatwa	a formal juridical opinion on a question of Muslim law
faqīh	a legal officer of Mudejar society, a scholar of Islamic law
imam	a leader of prayer, or more generally a respected and learned member of a Muslim community
Maliki scholars	followers of the legal school established by Imam Mālik b. Anas, whose doctrines were prevalent in Muslim Spain
Morisco	used, in later periods, to describe Muslims who had converted, or who had been converted, to Christianity
Mudejars	Iberian Muslims who by choice submitted themselves to Christian overlordship
mufti	a legal scholar who gives a fatwa
ṣadaqa	voluntary donation of alms; charity
sharīʿa	Islamic law
qāḍī	judge

ulama   collective designation for Muslim scholars

zakāt   an obligatory charitable tax incumbent upon all Muslims and payable to the Muslim chief of state

REFERENCES

Abou el Fadl, K. (1994) 'Islamic law and Muslim minorities', *Islamic Law and Society* 1.2: 141–87.

Albarracín Navarro, J. (1994) 'Actividades de un faqíh mudéjar', in *Actas del VI Simposio internacional de Mudejarismo*, Teruel: Centro de Estudios Mudéjares del Instituto de Estudios Turolenses, 437–44.

Amigues, F. (1992) 'Potiers mudéjares et chrétiens de la région de Valence: de la convivialité à l'antagonisme', *Archéologie islamique* 3: 129–67.

Barcelò Torres, M. del C. (1989) *Un tratado catalán de derecho islámico: el llibre de la çuna e xara dels moros*, Córdoba: Universidad de Córdoba.

—— (1984) *Minorías islámicas en el país valenciano: historia y dialecto*, Valencia: Universidad de Valencia.

Boswell, J. (1977) *The Royal Treasure: Muslim communities under the Crown of Aragon in the fourteenth century*, New Haven: Yale University Press.

Bowen, J (1993) *Muslims through Discourse: religion and ritual in Gayo society*, Princeton: Princeton University Press.

Buzineb, H. (1988) 'Respuestas de jurisconsultos maghrebies en torno a la inmigración de musulmanes hispánicos', *Hespéris Tamuda* 26–7: 53–65.

Cantineau, J. (1923) 'Lettre du Moufti d'Oran aux musulmans d'andalousie', *Journal Asiatique* 210: 1–17.

Carmona González, A. (1992) 'Textos jurídico-religiosos islámicos de las épocas mudéjar y morisca', *Areas* 14: 15–26.

—— (1993) 'Consideraciones sobre la pervivencia de la jurisprudencia andalusi en las épocas mudéjar y morisca', in *Actes du Vᵉ Symposium International d'Études morisques*, vol. 1, Zaghouan: Ceromdi, 209–22.

—— (1995) 'Los nuevos mudéjares: la shari'a y los musulmanes en sociedades no-islámicas', in M. Abumalham (ed.) *Comunidades islámicas en Europa*, Madrid: Editorial Trotta, 49–59.

Cifuentes, Ll., *et al.* (1998) 'Els menescals i l'art de la menescalia a la Corona d'Aragó durant la Baixa Edat Mitjana', in *Historia de la ramaderia i la veterinária agrária*, Barcelona: University of Barcelona.

Comaroff, J. and J. Comaroff (1992) *Ethnography and the Historical Imagination*, Boulder: Westview Press.

Febrer Romaguera, M. V. (ed.) (1991) *Cartas Pueblas de las Morerias Valencianas y documentación complementaria*, vol. 1, Zaragoza: Anubar.

Ferrer i Mallol, M. T. (1987) *Els sarraïns de la Corona Catalano–Aragonesa en el segle XIV: segregació i discriminació*, Barcelona: C.S.I.C.

Fierro, M. I. (1991): 'La emigración en el Islam: conceptos antiguos, nuevos problemas', in M. Abumalham (ed.) *Comunidades islámicas en Europa*, Madrid: Editorial Trotta.

Galán Sánchez, A. (1991) *Una visión de la 'decadencia española': la historiografía anglosajona sobre mudéjares y moriscos (siglos xviii–xx)*, Málaga: Diputación Provincial.

García-Arenal, M. (1984) 'Los moros de Navarra en la baja edad media', in *eadem* and B. Leroy, *Moros y judíos en Navarra en la Baja Edad Media*, Madrid: Hiperíon, 11–139.

García Marco, F. J. (1993) *Las comunidades mudéjares de la comarca de Calatayud en el siglo XV*, Calatayud: Institución Fernando el Católico.

Glick, T. (1995) *From Muslim fortress to Christian castle: social and cultural change in medieval Spain*, Manchester: Manchester University Press.

Guichard, P. (1973) 'Un seigneur musulman dans l'Espagne chrétienne: le ra'īs de Crevillente (1248–1318)', *Mélanges de la Casa de Velázquez* 9: 282–334.

Harvey, L. P. (1990) *Islamic Spain, 1250–1500*, Chicago: University of Chicago Press.

—— (1996) 'Magic and popular medicine in an *aljamiado* manuscript, possibly of Tunisian provenance, sold in London in 1993', in J. Lüdtke (ed.) *Romania Arabica: Festschrift für Reinhold Kontzi zum 70. Geburtstag*, Tübingen: Gunter Narr Verlag, 335–44.

Hoenerbach, W. (1965) *Spanish–Islamische Urkunden aus der Zeit der Naṣriden und Moriscos*, Berkeley: University of California Press.

Koningsveld, P. S. van (1992) 'Andalusian Arabic manuscripts from Christian Spain: a comparative intercultural approach', *Israel Oriental Studies* 12: 75–110.

—— (1994) 'The polemical works of Muḥammad al-Qaysī (fl. 1309) and their circulation in Arabic and Aljamiado among the Mudejars in the fourteenth century', *Al-Qanṭara* 15: 163–99.

—— and G. A. Wiegers (1996) 'The Islamic statute of the Mudejars in the light of a new source', *Al-Qanṭara* 17: 19–58.

Kontzi, R. (1984) 'La magia en los textos aljamiados', in *Josep Maria Solà-Solé: Homage, Homenaje, Homenatge (Miscelánea de estudios de amigos y discípulos)*, vol. 1, Barcelona: Puvill, 104–26.

Ladero Quesada, M. A. (1989) *Los Mudéjares de Castilla y otros estudios de historia medieval andaluza*, Granada: Universidad de Granada.

Ledesma Rubio, M. L. (1981) 'Los mudéjares y el cultivo de la tierra en Aragón', in *Actas de las III Jornadas sobre el Estado Actual de los Estudios sobre Aragón*, Zaragoza: 905–12.

—— (1994) *Vidas mudéjares*, Zaragoza: Mira Editores.

López del Alamo, M. P. (1995) 'El proceso de mudejarización en la cerámica de al-Andalus', in *V Semana de estudios medievales*, Logroño: Gobierno de la Rioja, Instituto de Estudios Riojanos, 217–25.

López-Morillas, C. (1995) *Textos aljamiados sobre la vida de Mahoma: el profeta de los Moriscos*, Madrid: C.S.I.C.

Meyerson, M. (1991) *The Muslims of Valencia in the Age of Fernando and Isabel: between coexistence and crusade*, Berkeley: University of California Press.

Miller, K. (1998) 'Guardians of Islam: Muslim communities in medieval Aragon', unpublished Ph.D. dissertation, Yale University.

Molénat, J.-P. (1994) 'Les mudéjars de Tolède: professions et localisations urbaines', in *Actas del VI Simposio internacional de Mudejarismo*, Teruel: Centro de Estudios Mudéjares del Instituto de Estudios Turolenses, 429–35.

Nirenberg, D. (1996) *Communities of Violence: persecution of minorities in the Middle Ages*, Princeton: Princeton University Press.

Tapia Sánchez, S. (1991) *La comunidad morisca de Avila*, Salamanca: Universidad de Salamanca.

Torres Fontes, J. (1962) 'El alcalde mayor de las aljamas de moros de Castilla', *Anuario de Historia del Derecho Español* 32: 131–82.

Utrilla Utrilla, J. F. and J. C. Esco Samperiz (1986) 'La población mudéjar en la Hoya de Huesca (siglos XII y XIII)', in *Actas del III Simposio Internacional de Mudejarismo*, Teruel: Instituto de Estudios Turolenses, 187–208.

Wiegers, G. A. (1996) *Islamic Literature in Spanish and Aljamiado: Yça of Segovia (fl. 1450), his antecedents and successors*, Leiden: E. J. Brill.

CHAPTER FIVE

HOW MANY MEDIEVAL EUROPES? THE 'PAGANS' OF HUNGARY AND REGIONAL DIVERSITY IN CHRISTENDOM

Nora Berend

Central, Eastern, or East-Central Europe, as this multiplicity of possible denominations already shows, has long been searching for its identity. Leopold von Ranke, Friedrich Naumann, István Bibó, Oscar Halecki, and historians and politicians after them have invented, discussed, rejected and analysed names, geographical limits and their meaning. *Zwischeneuropa*, *Mitteleuropa* and a number of variations on the seemingly (and in this case misleadingly) straightforward geographical notions of 'eastern' and 'central' have been proposed (Schöpflin and Wood 1989; Wandycz 1992; Eberhard *et al.* 1992; Le Rider 1994). At stake is the political, economic and cultural relationship of the 'East-Central European' countries to Western Europe, indeed, to Europe. Coming to grips with the region's medieval past is part of this search. Here the example of Hungary, one of the countries of modern East-Central Europe, is used to explore this issue.

Hungary's place in the medieval world, especially its status in relation to Western Europe, has been much debated in scholarship. Without reviewing them all, the example of some of the most influential statements concerning the nature of medieval Hungary (and the entire region) suffices to show how their authors speak of two or three medieval Europes. These theories assert both the unity of 'Western Europe' and the radical difference between 'Western Europe' and 'East-Central Europe'. Thus for example Makkai has emphasized the 'original characteristics' of East-European feudalism both chronologically and structurally. He has argued that Hungarian developments differed from the West European model by a late start, and by different structures in the relations both between lords and their men, and between lords and peasants (Makkai 1970). For Jenő Szűcs, not two but three 'historical regions' existed: 'Western Europe', 'Eastern Europe' and an 'in-between' region, Central-Eastern Europe, which was sometimes drawn into the Western sphere, sometimes into the Eastern one (Szűcs 1983). In this analysis, although during the medieval period (especially after 1200) 'Western Europe' provided its model of development, the structural divergence of Central-Eastern Europe was significant enough to distinguish it as a separate region. Central-Eastern Europe was characterized, in Szűcs's view, by hybrid structures incorporating Western and Eastern elements, by undeveloped vassalage, and by incomplete urbanization. Other historians have invoked notions such as 'backwardness' or 'between East and West', in order to define the place of medieval Hungary in relation to Western Europe.

Two circumstances have distorted these comparisons: their lopsidedness, and sometimes the authors' ideological agenda. First, actual Hungarian developments are being compared with a 'Western Europe' that is an abstraction. For instance, it is regularly asserted that Hungary 'lagged behind' Western Europe in terms both of urban development and of 'feudalism'. Yet in neither respect did Western Europe itself develop in a unified way. Thus English planted towns, Italian city-states and French communes differed enormously from each other, while the securing of urban liberties followed different patterns and a different chronology even in southern and northern France. The observation that the Hungarian pattern did not conform to the 'Western' type of town development is therefore misleading. If what is being suggested is that in Hungary walled towns with urban liberties did not emerge according to the pattern of northern French communes, then neither did they in much of 'Western Europe' itself. Likewise, the notion that Hungary failed to experience full-blown 'feudalism', comprising a complex chain of vassalage and benefices granted in return for military service, has been advanced as part of the explanation of Hungarian 'backwardness'. Yet the normative model of 'feudalism' as known to Makkai or Szűcs has been increasingly challenged (Brown 1974; Reynolds 1994), and hence cannot serve as a yardstick to measure 'backwardness'. Second, in proposing that East-Central Europe (in the Middle Ages and beyond) belonged to the West, or the East, or neither, but rather followed some independent 'third road', scholars have often been influenced by ideological motivations. Modern and contemporary historical development has thus been projected onto the medieval past. The analysis of medieval Hungary's status should not turn medieval regional differences into an explanation of the country's modern backwardness and peripheral position. It still needs to be remembered that 'the explanation of the more recent by the more remote has sometimes dominated our studies to the point of hypnosis' (Bloch 1993: 85).[1]

While East-Central European scholars have been searching for definitions of the region's status in the medieval world, those working on, and in, modern Western Europe have often tended either to ignore medieval East-Central European history or to separate it from 'medieval history'.[2] As recently as 1970, the 'need for a new, less one-sided approach to European history', that is, for the integration of East-Central European history into the treatment of medieval Europe, could be announced as a novelty (Barraclough 1970: 8). True, some historians have now started to treat East-Central Europe as part of the medieval world, but much remains to be done. For example, the recent *Atlas of Medieval Europe* is in fact largely an atlas of medieval Western Europe, in which East-Central Europe makes only an occasional appearance (MacKay and Ditchburn 1997); Robert Bartlett regards Central Europe as simply copying a Western European blueprint (Bartlett 1993). All too often the region is treated according to the assumptions of modern power structures: as a periphery, and not as an integral part of Europe in the Middle Ages.

Hungary, like Bohemia and Poland, belonged to a medieval Latin Christendom, in which there were always important regional differences. But they cannot be encapsulated, in the case of its eastern region, by a mechanical recourse to characterizing differences as symptoms of 'backwardness' or stunted development. Nor should 'East-Central Europe' be contrasted with 'West' and 'East' as one of three medieval

Europes. Medieval Hungary, for example, resembled Scandinavia in some respects, and Iberia in others. A new synthesis will have to be based not on teleology but on comparative research to assess both the extent to which it is legitimate to speak of 'East-Central Europe' as an economic and social unit during the medieval period, and the role which countries that today constitute East-Central Europe played in the medieval world. This chapter addresses one aspect of regional difference: the presence and treatment of non-Christian populations. This is one indicator of Hungary's position in the medieval world.

* * *

The example of the 'pagan' Cumans in thirteenth-century Hungary provides a significant litmus test. The Cumans were not the only non-Catholic group living in medieval Hungary; there were Jews, Muslims, Armenians, Greek Orthodox, and 'heretics' as well. Yet the presence of Turkic nomads, understood to be 'pagans' by medieval Christians, most strikingly distinguished the Hungarian situation from that of France or England, and even that in Iberia or Sicily, and therefore reveals both regional diversity and similarity in Christendom the most sharply. As this case shows, Hungary was part of the Latin Christian world, but at the same time, its location on the frontier of Christendom resulted in a larger variety of influences, and the availability of a different range of choices and courses of action. Analysing the fortunes of 'pagans' in Hungary also raises the question of the applicability to medieval Hungary of the 'persecuting society' thesis (which links the emergence of persecution to the development of central lay and ecclesiastical authority, and to the exercise of power in Western Europe) (Moore 1987).

Hungary was on the frontier of Latin Christendom from the moment of its creation as a Christian kingdom in the tenth–eleventh centuries until well into the modern era. 'Frontier' is not meant to stand as a fashionable replacement for 'periphery'. It does not signify a dependent and 'underdeveloped' economy and society. Instead, it is used here to denote the meeting of different civilizations. Three spheres of influences, three worlds met here: Roman Christian, Byzantine and nomadic. The nature and relative impact of these influences on the kingdom changed over time. They ranged from acculturation to military confrontation, with Byzantine and nomadic influences fading in the later Middle Ages, the latter to be replaced by Islam and the Ottomans.

The Hungarian tribal alliance moved into the Carpathian basin in the late ninth century. Their economy and society was slowly transformed; from the late tenth century, the construction of royal power and Christianization brought the territory into the Latin Christian world, with a significant Byzantine presence of converts especially in the eastern parts and of monasteries and communities throughout the territory. From the eleventh century, the kingdom of Hungary was structurally part of Latin Christendom, and at least its intellectual elite (that is, those who produced the written sources we possess) defined it as such. Its ecclesiastical structure of dioceses, headed by two archbishoprics, the form of kingship, and a variety of institutions were those of Latin Christendom. In this, Hungary represented a regional pattern; it was one of the 'regnal communities' (Reynolds 1997: chapter 8) newly incorporated into Latin Christendom in the Scandinavian–East-Central European region in the tenth–eleventh centuries (Bartlett 1993; Gieysztor 1997; Samsonowicz 1998). Over the course of the Middle Ages an increasing number of institutions, social groups, and trends linked the kingdom to Latin Christian civilization, as demonstrated by the examples of the royal chancery, trained canon lawyers and saints' cults. Ideologies of legitimation also centered on Rome and the German Empire. Some of the ideological inventions were so powerful that to this day they continue to attract followers – as the story of St István (Stephen) of Hungary (1000/1–38) receiving his crown from the pope, for example, or the Virgin Mary as the kingdom's special protector. Some of the individuals who formulated these ideas were themselves of 'Western European' origin. Yet despite this structural conformity, Byzantine and nomad influences meant the presence of groups and trends that one would search for in vain in England or France. I shall not discuss Byzantine influence over Hungary (Moravcsik 1970), but shall instead concentrate on the impact of the nomads, and especially the Cumans.

Hungary, on the frontier of Christendom, constantly encountered and integrated groups arriving from the world of the steppe. Turkic nomads – Pechenegs, Oghuz, Cumans, and Mongols – raided the kingdom. Chronicle accounts relate many of these events, always emphasizing the suddenness of the attacks, and the looting and destruction carried out by the enemy (e.g. Szentpétery 1937: 366–71, 412–14). Other groups of Pechenegs, Oghuz and Cumans settled in the country. Narrative sources show Hungarian kings fighting against invaders, and welcoming the settlers. Thus the early twelfth-century *Life* of St István juxtaposes two stories about the king's relations with the Pechenegs. One attributes the saving of the people in a region of Transylvania to a divine vision which forewarned King István about a Pecheneg raid, so that he could alert the population to the danger and gather them in a walled city. The other tells of Pechenegs who went to Hungary attracted by István's wisdom; they were attacked and despoiled of their goods. On István's order, the guilty parties were arrested and hanged on trees along the roads, because he wished the kingdom to be open to all foreigners who entered peacefully (Szentpétery 1938: 423, 425–7).

The relationship of Hungary and the Cumans conformed to this pattern of raids and settlement. Because it is better documented, both from narrative sources and from archeological evidence, and because the Cumans gained an importance within the kingdom that far exceeded that of previous nomad groups there, it is best to focus on their example (Pálóczi-Horváth 1989).[3] The Cumans were part of a tribal confederation that became the major power on the steppe from around the mid-eleventh century (Golden 1992; 1995–7). They fought and formed alliances with Byzantium, Rus princes, and the Crusader states created in Byzantine territory after the Fourth Crusade. After Mongol victories over the Cumans, several clans, under the leadership of a chieftain named Köten, asked for and received permission to settle in Hungary.

The entry of the Cumans was fraught with tension. In the short period prior to the Mongol invasion of 1241, the Cumans clashed with the local population over land-use, and with the nobility, who (rightly) suspected the king of intending to use the newcomers in order to strengthen royal power at their expense. When the Mongol armies reached the kingdom, the local population took the recently admitted Cumans

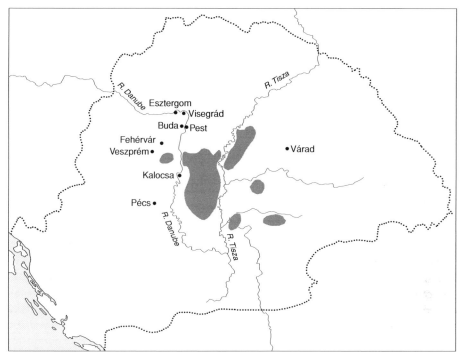

Figure 5.1 Map of medieval Hungary showing areas of Cuman settlement.

to be Mongol spies; after a massacre in which Köten and his family died, the Cumans left Hungary. After the Mongol invasion, King Béla IV (1235–70) invited the Cumans back. They returned and were settled.

The Cumans' most important function in late thirteenth-century Hungary was as light cavalry in the royal army. The king led them in numerous expeditions against neighboring countries. Most notably, they played an important part in the battle of Rudolf of Habsburg against Ottokar II of Bohemia (1278): here King László IV (1272–90) of Hungary, with a large Cuman contingent in his army, fought on Rudolf's side. This military role in foreign affairs was supplemented by the kings' reliance on them to counterbalance the growing independent power of the nobility. László IV ('the Cuman') tried to exploit this possibility to its fullest extent. In an age of growing anarchy, when the most powerful members of the nobility were carving out territorial power for themselves, László increasingly associated himself with the Cumans, creating a bodyguard from them, and adopting Cuman dress and hairstyle. He attempted to resist demands for their forcible Christianization. Prelates added their protest to that of the nobility, and papal intervention forced László to obey. Even he could not completely disengage himself from the structures imposed on a Christian king, and this finally turned the Cumans against him.

Royal policy towards the Cumans was determined by their political and military importance. The main reason for the invitation to settle and for continued royal favors was the military support the kings hoped to gain from the Cumans. Thus the most important aim was to secure Cuman loyalty by a variety of means. After the second entry of the Cumans, King Béla IV married his son István to the daughter (baptized Elizabeth) of a Cuman chieftain. When István V (1270–2) ascended the throne, Elizabeth became queen of Hungary; after István's death, she was regent during the minority of her son, László IV. Gifts of land, precious clothes and other objects were intended to ensure continued Cuman support, especially during the civil war between Béla IV and István, when both sides tried to gain Cuman backing. István took the title 'Dominus Cumanorum', certainly by 1262, and became their highest judge. Upon István's enthronement after Béla IV's death the Cumans came directly under the power of the king of Hungary. The highest official in the kingdom after the monarch, the count palatine, became the judge of the Cumans. They had recourse to the king for appeals. They were exempt from the jurisdiction of county officials, and constituted an *universitas*, with its own representatives. The legal status of the Cumans very much fitted into the pattern of privileges granted by kings to various immigrant groups and cities. The Cumans even participated in some of the early general assemblies of the kingdom, the precursors of its parliament.

From the start, the king also aimed at the conversion of the Cumans. Prior to their settlement in Hungary, missionaries had tried to convert the Cumans living in the regions to the east of the kingdom. Béla, then heir to the throne, already supported these missions, and attended the baptism of some chiefs. As King Béla IV, he continued to support the missionaries. He presented the admission of the Cumans into the kingdom as gaining new souls for Christendom, and exulted over the successes of baptism (Theiner 1859: 231, 233; Fejér 1829–44: vol. 4, pt. 3: 30–3). Having reported the complete success of Christianization, that is, the conversion of all the Cumans, King Béla found them lending support to the rebellion of his son István. Béla then described the progress of their Christianization in a much less enthusiastic manner, complaining about continuing 'pagan' customs. Although Béla's expressed views on the state of Cuman conversion were linked to his political interests, his belated awareness of the difference between baptism and conversion reflects a wider pattern repeated again and again when a large population was Christianized (Theiner 1859: 269–70; Fletcher 1997). The response to it was a hardening of ecclesiastical attitudes: less and less choice was given to the Cumans, as a 'true' conversion was to be forced on them.

During the reign of László IV, a papal legate dictated the conditions to which the Cumans had to adapt or be expelled from the kingdom. The 'Cuman law' of 1279 shows what the ecclesiastical minimum was for the acceptance of a 'pagan' population (Theiner 1859: 339–41). The law required all the Cumans to convert and accept ecclesiastical teaching and the sacraments. They were to abandon the adoration of idols and their pagan rituals. They were also to give up living in tents, and move into houses in villages, and keep Christian customs. They were to cease killing, especially Christians. The Cumans also had to relinquish every church, monastery, and ecclesiastical or lay property that they had occupied. Appointed investigators were to ensure that the Cuman clans kept these laws. If they did not conform in all the ways stipulated above, they would be subject to both ecclesiastical and temporal punishment. Finally, the Cumans had to give hostages to the king in order to ensure their obedience.

The Cuman law of 1279 set out to change a number of real or alleged characteristics of the Cumans. From a modern viewpoint, these can be divided into two main groups: those addressing strictly religious issues and those attempting to change other aspects of Cuman lifestyle. In the first category is the stipulation of baptism, obedience to the Church, and renunciation of pagan practices. In the second is the issue of permanent settlement, and the injunctions to refrain from killing and looting within the kingdom. In the text itself, however, all of these requirements were described as conforming to 'Christian' ways. To give up their tents and settle in houses is to live *Christiano more* ('according to Christian custom'); special emphasis is placed on the prohibition against killing Christians. The text itself and subsequent papal letters show that the law was not simply forced on the Cumans; negotiation preceded its promulgation. Two representatives of the Cumans (mentioned by name in the Cuman law), the king and the papal legate came to an agreement. Doubtless, the legate was unwilling to compromise on certain topics, but he did for example allow the Cumans to retain their traditional hairstyle. This resembled ecclesiastical attitudes to other newly converted peoples, or those who were thought to be open to conversion: for example Bulgarians or Mongols (Sullivan 1994; Muldoon 1979).

The Christianization and settlement of the Cumans was a lengthy process. Cuman resistance and revolt in 1280 and 1282 forced King László IV to wage war against them. The resilience of customs and beliefs, even without open resistance, meant that Christianization took over a century to accomplish; Cuman graves of the fourteenth century still contained objects associated with traditional religious practices, such as horse-teeth, certain plants, and iron knives. During the fourteenth century, the stock of Cuman names changed from the traditional Turkic to new Christian forms; Christian names outnumbered Turkic ones only in the last third of that century. Some Cuman villages had no church until the fifteenth century. Final settlement was also gradual. The Cumans had to give up nomadism upon their entry to the kingdom, as the available territories were not sufficiently extensive to allow it. The establishment of fixed permanent settlements, however, was not instantaneous. Archeological excavations attest to their development. Already in the late thirteenth century some groups established permanent settlements and cemeteries on the sites of Hungarian villages ruined during the Mongol invasions. Other groups had winter settlements but still moved around with tents within a limited territory. By the fifteenth century, all the Cumans were permanently settled in villages whose structures corresponded to those of the local population, and were Christianized.

The story of 'pagan' Cuman immigration is so singular within a medieval Christian context that it has been linked to explanations according to which Hungarian society, or its king, was more tolerant in the Middle Ages than those in Western Europe (since Deér 1934, 1938). Although individual views of tolerance or acceptance can sometimes be found in medieval texts, the Hungarian sources do not express any such notions in favor of the 'pagan' Cumans. Statements about a royal obligation to honor strangers, accept settlers, and provide protection recur in narrative sources. One of them, which recounts the first entry of the Cumans into Hungary, even connects this traditional royal attitude to the admission of the Cumans

(Szentpétery 1938: 559). This, however, did not amount to tolerance of Cuman beliefs, customs and lifestyle. Although we know more about ecclesiastical demands and papal impatience with the slow progress of Christianization, the sources that depict royal attitudes never suggest that Hungarian kings wished the Cumans to continue as nomad 'pagans'. Even László IV was more interested in building a power-base than in protecting the Cumans from the ecclesiastical policy of Christianization for the sake of preserving their traditions. When forced to choose, he submitted to papal demands. In sum, Hungarian kings were not 'tolerant' in their attitudes to the Cumans (or to other non-Christian groups). Nor can their policy be called one of 'toleration', that is, temporary acceptance of a non-Christian presence. Hungarian kings did not simply acquiesce in an already existing situation, but actively solicited the entry into their kingdom of non-Christians (Jews and Muslims as well as Cumans). They seized an opportunity, which seemed to provide a new way of strengthening royal power.

In the Hungarian case, the conflict between kings and popes over the nature of their respective powers manifested itself as a clash about immediate policies and methods, and the limits to which a Christian king can go while remaining a Christian, rather than about whether or not to integrate the Cumans. Unsurprisingly, the monarchs' opinions on those limits were invariably more elastic than the pontiffs'. King Béla IV's purpose in inviting the Cumans back, and establishing their privileged legal position, was to draw on their support to buttress his own authority, to build up strong royal power. In such an aim, Béla IV resembled his contemporaries in France or England. The means at his disposal, however, differed. Béla and his successors tried to exploit Cuman military potential as a key instrument for bolstering royal power, that is, to rely on 'pagan' nomads in support of a Christian monarchy. A fundamental tension in royal policy can be detected in this respect. The most effective way to secure their support was by subordinating the Cumans directly to royal power, while leaving their communities and internal organization intact. Yet at the same time Béla envisaged the conversion and integration of the Cumans. The pace of these processes was much slower than expected, and led to Cuman unrest and revolt. As long as the Cumans were loyal, the monarch was prepared not to insist on rapid Christianization. Ultimately, however, royal hopes of finding a power-base more dependable than the nobility were disappointed. The Cumans proved unreliable allies of the kings: during the civil war between Béla IV and his son some sided with István; and they assassinated László IV. A strong monarchy was established by the Angevin rulers of the fourteenth century on rather different foundations; although they continued to use Cuman military units in their armies, the significance of the Cumans declined and their integration accelerated.

To some extent the Christianization of the Cumans resembles medieval patterns of the conversion of 'pagans' encountered elsewhere, for example that of various Germanic peoples in the early Middle Ages, or of the Baltic peoples, but the setting was very different. In the latter cases, entire peoples converted, mainly in one of two ways: either through coercion, as a result of conquest, or because the conversion of the social and political elite, linked to new methods of strengthening their power, resulted in that of the rest of the population from the top down. The Cumans, however, constituted a minority in a Christian kingdom in which they had settled voluntarily. Such a voluntary migration of a sizeable 'pagan' minority into a Christian kingdom differed from other European encounters with 'pagans' in the thirteenth and fourteenth centuries. The main forms of such encounters were Christian conquest (as in the Baltic), and wars and negotiations (with Lithuania for example). The singularity of the Hungarian case was a result of the kingdom's geographical position and its kings' willingness to receive such immigrants. Yet the aim, conversion, the means subsequently employed, negotiations and force, and the final outcome, namely the Christianization of the Cumans, were exactly those that had characterized the encounters of Latin Christians and 'pagans' for centuries. Hungary did not conform to the steppe pattern of allowing every group to retain its own religion, nor was there a unique, specifically 'Hungarian' way of dealing with 'pagans'.

The Cumans, when they arrived in Hungary, were in every way different from the local population. Their appearance, as to both attire and hairstyle, set them apart. The traditional Cuman costume consisted of trousers and a caftan, each fastened by a belt. For the men, the top of the head was shaved, while the hair was plaited into several braids. By contrast, the local population wore tunics and the men tight trousers or hose. 'Cuman' and 'Christian' costume and hairstyle were distinguished in many contemporary sources, including papal letters. As for the Cumans' belief-system, it comprised animistic and shamanistic elements. The Cumans had their own notions of an afterlife, celebrated the cult of ancestors, and provided the dead with various objects, whose lavishness paralleled their recipients' social rank. The elite were buried with their horses. Cuman divination practices used animals, especially the wolf and the dog. Shamans communicated with the spirit world, and were consulted in order to determine the outcome of illnesses and other events. Finally, the Cumans differed fundamentally in their lifestyle: they were nomads who lived in tents as opposed to the settled local agricultural population.

Such distinctiveness, compounded by the hostility they encountered, might have marked the Cumans out to become a 'persecuted minority'. This, however, did not happen. Both royal and ecclesiastical authorities sought to incorporate, rather than exclude, the Cumans. The privileged relationship they enjoyed with Hungarian kings derived from the same mechanism that has been identified in other contexts as a reason for the emergence of persecution, namely the attempt to create a strong centralized monarchy. The extension of royal protection to different groups was as much a means of strengthening royal power as the reservation of the right of punishment and exclusion from society. In the thirteenth century, the balance of power shifted from the kings to the lay and ecclesiastical elites through the acquisition of lands and of previously exclusive royal rights, including building stone castles and settling groups of *hospites*, that is, of immigrants, but including both internal migrants and foreigners, and granting them privileges. One of the ways to counterbalance the loss of royal prerogative was the ready acceptance and even encouragement of Cuman settlement, and the effort to keep them under royal control. Royal interest and ecclesiastical views coincided on the issue of Cuman integration, even if – especially during the reign of László IV – the king clashed with prelates, supported by the popes, over immediate issues of policy considered appropriate towards the Cumans. The ecclesiastical expectation concerning 'pagans' was conversion, not exclusion. Even if expulsion was used as a threat against the Cumans,

Figure 5.2 Portrait of King László IV. The *Illuminated Chronicle* (mid-fourteenth century). Budapest, Széchényi Library, MS. Clmae 404, fo. 64v.

the ultimate aim was their Christianization. Although much more slowly than originally expected, this did in fact happen. In the long run, the Cumans lost their original language, lifestyle, attire, and beliefs, and assimilated completely to the local population. Indeed, they assimilated to such an extent that several nineteenth-century scholars maintained that the Cumans had always been Hungarians, and spoke a dialect of Hungarian; that is, that the two were 'biologically' related peoples.

Despite many similarities between the relationship of rulers to their non-Christian subjects in thirteenth-century Iberia and Hungary, the course of events relating to the Cumans in the later Middle Ages is strikingly different from the fate of Jews and Muslims in Iberia. That peninsula, on the frontier of Christendom, was, like Hungary, a meeting-place of different civilizations. Yet there was also a major difference: while Christendom was rapidly expanding in Iberia, on the eastern frontier it was on the defensive. In the mid-thirteenth century, when the Cumans arrived in Hungary, the Jews and Muslims of Iberia filled important positions in royal service and in the economic and cultural life of the peninsula. Rulers of Iberia, like those in Hungary, exploited the additional opportunities to build royal power by means that did not correspond to ecclesiastical views about the place of non-Christians. Reliance on the service of Muslims on the one hand, and fighting against Muslims reinforced by an ideology of Christian 'reconquest' on the other, did not mutually exclude each other.

At the end of the fifteenth century and the beginning of the sixteenth, by which time the Cumans of Hungary had largely been converted and assimilated, the Jews and Muslims of Iberia had to choose between baptism or expulsion. The conversion of those Iberian non-Christians who remained, instead of paving the way for a complete assimilation, served only to create new fears and suspicions. The converts were stigmatized as a special category, rather than allowed to blend in with the Christian population. *Moriscos* and *marranos* (or *conversos*) were suspect, and exposed to investigation by the Inquisition and to occasional violence; the *moriscos* were finally expelled. In the case of the Cumans, popular hostility was strongest at the beginning, at the time of the Cumans' entry, even leading to a massacre. Suspicions and fears eventually subsided. In the fifteenth century, territorial units (*sedes*) took the place of Cuman clan-organization and facilitated the survival of privileges specific to an area (Cumania) and its inhabitants (Cumans, later As-Cumans).[4] Yet this was not coupled with hostility or discrimination. Expulsion was only used as a threat very early in the conversion process, in the late thirteenth century, and was never implemented. Those Cumans who did convert were allowed to integrate and assimilate. No suspicion was harbored against them, nor were they branded as insincere Christians. One often finds the same Christian attitude with regard to other 'pagan' populations during the Middle Ages. The conversion and integration of 'pagans' was expected and usually more readily accepted than that of Jews or Muslims.

The representation of the Cumans in fourteenth-century Hungary displays an ambivalence that can be categorized as a manifestation neither of persecution nor of attraction. The Cumans did not simply become a stereotypical 'other'. The 'oriental' figure, in a costume that closely resembled that of the Cumans, became the iconographic vehicle for both a negative and a positive meaning, even in the same work. On the one hand, Cumans were depicted as enemies, sometimes in a demonized form (with fire or a devil issuing from their mouth), engaged in combat with the Hungarians or with St László I (whose legend included the description of a duel the saint fought against a Cuman attacker). László IV, in turn, was depicted in Cuman costume, in order to indicate that he was an evil, depraved king (Berend 1997: 171–2). Various nomads, including the Mongols, wore the same type of dress in the miniatures of the Hungarian *Illuminated Chronicle* (*c.*1358). On the other hand, similarly clad figures represented the ancestors of the Hungarians, the Huns and 'pagan' forefathers (Marosi 1991). Thus the 'oriental' figure stood for both the enemy and the Hungarian past.

The nomad Turkic, and especially the Cuman, presence in Hungary gave rise to explanations that sought the specificities of Hungarian development in an 'eastern', 'nomad', or 'pagan' orientation. Some authors have argued that because of nomad influence, the kingdom of Hungary was detached from Christendom in some way. This notion had its origin in medieval accusations. While Hungarian kings tried to turn Cuman military power to their advantage, their internal and external enemies complained about the use of 'pagans' against Christians. The most explicit expression of discontent came from those ecclesiastics within the kingdom who disapproved of royal reliance on the Cumans (and/or of the growth of royal power), and from Hungary's neighbors, whenever hostilities erupted in military confrontation. The sources provide detailed descriptions of atrocities (such as the looting of churches and killing not only of men, but also of women and children), attributing them to the aspiration of their 'pagan' perpetrators to harm Christians. King Béla IV himself eagerly propagated the idea of such an alleged predisposition when he was asking for help from the papacy and from kings against another 'pagan' nomad people, the Mongols. Yet because of their close association with and reliance on the Cumans, Béla, his successors, and the entire population of Hungary, were not above suspicion. They were seen as similar to the Cumans, were called 'semi-Christians', and represented as having been seduced from the Christian path (e.g. Gombos 1937–8: vol. 1: 276). The conduct of the royal army, with its Cuman contingent, during wars and invasions was in fact no different from that of medieval armies elsewhere; the cruelty was no less when the deeds were committed by 'authentic' Christians.

Modern historians of medieval Hungary have written about a thirteenth-century turn to 'paganism': László IV's attempt to set royal power free from the Christian–feudal matrix (Szűcs 1993: 310–21), and the creation of an 'ideal of deliberate barbarism' that distinguished Hungary from its Western neighbors (Klaniczay 1990). According to the first view, the king opted for a 'pagan' alternative of ruler-ship. As discussed above, this was not the case. According to the second view, the presence of the Cumans contributed to the formulation of an ideology that rejected Western norms, and offered an alternative conception of civilization. Gábor Klaniczay has claimed that the first important proponent of the 'ideal of deliberate barbarism' was Simon of Kéza in the late thirteenth century, and that he was influenced by the 'pagan' tendencies of László IV's court and the Cumans.

A court cleric of King László IV, Simon wrote (or according to some, adapted), a chronicle about the history of the Hungarians in which he fully elaborated the mythical descent of the Huns and the Hungarians from a common ancestor. Far from rejecting 'Western norms' in favor of a pagan-oriented ideology, Simon collected his sources 'through Italy, France and Germany', and developed the myth of the Hun–Hungarian relationship on the basis of Western authors (Szentpétery 1937: 141; Szűcs 1981: 263–328; Szűcs 1984: 413–555).[5] Attila and the Huns in fact fulfilled a function in placing Hungary within the structures of contemporary Latin Christendom. Simon's construction, incorporating not only a realistic 'pagan' past (that of the Hungarians prior to their conversion), but also a mythical (Hunnish) one, was an effort to create the sort of ancestry every European kingdom had been craving since the Franks (French) had appropriated the myth of Trojan descent. As the Huns and the Hungarians had already been paired off by chroniclers of Christian Europe who had experienced the Hungarian raids prior to Hungary's Christianization, this was an obvious route for a cleric trained in Bologna or Padua to follow (Szűcs 1984: 490).

Simon may have used his observations of Cuman practices to lend verisimilitude to his account of Hunnish customs, but he had nothing good to say about the Cumans themselves. In fact, only twice does he mention the Cumans living in Hungary during his own times. In the first instance, they participate in the royal army, and they loot the enemy's baggage during battle. In the second, they plot against and are defeated by the king; they are unfaithful to László IV and receive just punishment (Szentpétery 1937: 186–7). There is no sign of 'pagan' sympathies or 'deliberate barbarism' here. Moreover, in Simon's depiction Attila is generous to strangers, but also lecherous, and a tyrant. Thus Attila did not represent an alternative to 'Western norms' for Simon. This is evidenced above all by the description of the ruler's death: he choked on his own blood on his wedding night after an excess of drink and sexual exertion. The virtues lacking in Attila were to be found instead in Hungary's Christian rulers. Furthermore, Simon did not excuse the plundering raids of the pagan Hungarians, and emphasized the sanctity of various members of the Hungarian dynasty after the conversion to Christianity. In short, there is no question of a rejection of 'Western norms', especially because for Simon these norms were Christian rather than Western.

The reincorporation of a 'pagan' past that had been eradicated in the first two centuries of the new Christian kingdom was not due to a return to or the invention of 'pagan' ideals. A similar pattern is manifest, for example, in Danish historiography. Saxo Grammaticus rejected Trojan origins in favor of descent from Dan, a 'pagan' ruler, in order to demonstrate the equality of the Danes' lineage with the Roman one (Boje Mortensen 1987). Simon of Kéza elaborated the Hun–Hungarian identification not in order to advocate an ideal of barbarism, but to show that the Hungarians were descended from ancestors illustrious enough to compete with those claimed by other European communities, and that an Empire – Attila's – was at the origins of the Hungarian kingdom. Simon did not try to present Attila as a model ruler. He emphasized Attila's power, that he had been feared by the whole world, but did not condone his debauchery. In Hungary as in Denmark, a self-assured integration of the 'pagan' past was undertaken by men of ecclesiastical training, after a long period of Christianization of the kingdom, and not as part of a 'pagan' resurgence.

Christian treatment of Hungary's 'pagans' does not fit into the framework of the thesis of a 'persecuting society'. The strengthening of royal power was not envisaged through the exclusion of the Cumans, even though they differed radically from the local settled population at the time of their entry. Yet these attitudes cannot be characterized as 'tolerance', or even 'toleration', for the ultimate aim of both royal and ecclesiastical policies was the conversion and assimilation of the Cumans. Their entry and settlement, and the ways in which the monarchy and papacy dealt with their integration, highlight both significant differences between Hungary and kingdoms such as France or England, and, at the same time, certain similarities, such as papal–royal power struggles, deriving from a common structure. The distinctiveness of Hungary in the medieval period cannot be represented in terms of the peripheral 'backward' nature of the kingdom: that was due to more modern developments.

The medieval framework was that of Latin Christendom. Despite a 'pagan' presence, structurally Hungary belonged to this world. Relations with the papacy regarding policies towards the Cumans indicate how this unity was viewed at the time. Papal–royal interaction ranged from cooperation to confrontation, but never included indifference. This conforms to the way in which popes and rulers acted in other parts of Latin Christendom. The threat that Hungary would be detached from Christendom by 'pagans' without or within, deployed by Béla IV in his appeal against the Mongols, and by enemies of László IV to gain papal support, was a potent tool precisely because there was no doubt that the kingdom was part of Latin Christendom. At the same time, patterns characteristic of the interaction between the world of the steppe and sedentary societies also affected Hungary. Nomads raided and settled in the kingdom. Analogous to the relations between the Cumans and Hungary are those between the Cumans and Byzantium or Rus, comprising hostilities as well as dynastic marriages and military alliances; and especially the case of Georgia, where Cumans settled and integrated after royal initiative to call them in to assist against external and internal enemies (Golden 1984). Neither in Hungary nor in any of these other cases did steppe influences and the incorporation of the 'pagans' mean a 'pagan' orientation. Monarchs seized opportunities to strengthen their power, but they were not supplanting structures already in place. These were ecclesiastical and state structures common to Latin Christendom. The 'pagans' themselves finally assimilated into them.

There were regional differences within Christendom, which could be significant. Medieval Europe, however, did not function according to modern divisions. There was no clear or consistent East–West demarcation. On the one hand, 'Western Europe' itself was not a unified 'center' in the period. On the other, regional differences existed within a basic structural similarity, manifest in, among other things, political institutions, ecclesiastical and lay organizational forms, and the pattern of papal–royal interaction. Medieval Hungary was not 'between East and West'. Although incorporating a variety of influences in consequence of its frontier position, it was structurally part of Latin Christendom.

NOTES

1   'l'explication du plus proche par le plus lointain a parfois dominé nos études jusqu'à l'hypnose'.
2   Ranke (1874) postulated a radical division between the Slavic world and Hungary on the one hand and the West on the other.
3   I treat the position of the Cumans in detail in my book on *At the Gate of Christendom: Jews, Muslims and 'pagans' in medieval Hungary*, 2001 Cambridge University Press.
4   The As spoke an Iranian language and migrated into Hungary either together with the Cumans or separately in the thirteenth–fourteenth centuries. In the modern period, the two were treated together as one 'people'.
5   Besides the edition in Szentpétery (1937), now also see Veszprémy and Schaer (1999).

REFERENCES

Barraclough, G. (ed.) (1970) *Eastern and Western Europe in the Middle Ages*, London: Harcourt Brace Jovanovich.
Bartlett, R. (1993) *The Making of Europe*, Princeton: Princeton University Press.

Berend, N. (1997) 'Medieval patterns of social exclusion and integration: the regulation of non-Christian clothing in thirteenth-century Hungary', *Revue Mabillon* n.s. 8: 155–76.

Bloch, M. (1993) *Apologie pour l'histoire*, Paris: Armand Colin.

Boje Mortensen, L. (1987) 'Saxo Grammaticus' view of the origin of the Danes and his historiographical models', *Cahiers de l'Institut du Moyen Âge Grec et Latin* 55: 169–83.

Brown, E. A. R. (1974) 'The tyranny of a construct: feudalism and historians of medieval Europe', *American Historical Review* 79: 1063–88.

Deér, J. (1934 repr. 1969) *Heidnisches und Christliches in der altungarischen Monarchie*, Darmstadt: Wissenschaftliche Buchgesellschaft.

—— (1938, reprint 1993) *Pogány magyarság, keresztény magyarság*, Budapest: Holnap Kiadó.

Eberhard, W. *et al.* (eds) (1992) *Westmitteleuropa, Ostmitteleuropa: Vergleiche und Beziehungen. Festschrift für Ferdinand Seibt*, Munich: R. Oldenbourg Verlag.

Fejér, Gy. (1829–1844) *Codex diplomaticus Hungariae ecclesiasticus ac civilis*, 11 vols. Buda: Regiae universitatis Ungaricae.

Fletcher, R. (1997) *The Conversion of Europe*, London: HarperCollins.

Gieysztor, A. (1997) *L'Europe nouvelle autour de l'an mil. La papauté, l'Empire et les 'nouveaux venus'*, Rome: Unione Internazionale degli Istituti di Archeologia Storia e Storia dell'Arte in Roma.

Golden, P. B. (1984) 'Cumanica I: the Quipčaqs in Georgia', *Archivum Eurasiae Medii Aevi* 4: 45–87.

—— (1992) *An Introduction to the History of Turkic Peoples*, Wiesbaden: Otto Harrassowitz.

—— (1995–7) 'Cumanica IV: the tribes of the Cuman-Qipčaqs', *Archivum Eurasiae Medii Aevi* 9: 99–122.

Gombos, A. F. (1937–8) *Catalogus Fontium Historiae Hungaricae*, 3 vols. Budapest: Szent István Akadémia.

Klaniczay, G. (1990) 'Daily life and the elites in the later Middle Ages; the civilized and the barbarians', in F. Glatz (ed.) *Environment and Society in Hungary*, Budapest: MTA Történettudományi Intézet, 75–90.

Le Rider, J. (1994) *La Mitteleuropa*, Paris: Presses Universitaires de France.

MacKay, A. and Ditchburn, D. (eds) (1997) *Atlas of Medieval Europe*, London and New York: Routledge.

Makkai, L. (1970) 'Les caractères originaux de l'histoire économique et sociale de l'Europe orientale pendant le Moyen Âge', *Acta Historica Academiae Scientiarum Hungaricae* 16: 261–87.

Marosi, E. (1991) 'Zur Frage des Quellenwertes mittelalterlicher Darstellungen. "Orientalismus" in der Ungarischen Bilderchronik', in A. Kubinyi and J. Laszlovszky (eds) *Alltag und materielle Kultur im mittelalterlichen Ungarn*, Krems (Medium Aevum Quotidianum 22): 74–107.

Moore, R. I. (1987) *The Formation of a Persecuting Society*, Oxford: Basil Blackwell.

Moravcsik, Gy. (1970) *Byzantium and the Magyars*, Budapest: Akadémiai Kiadó.

Muldoon, J. (1979) *Popes, Lawyers and Infidels: the Church and the non-Christian World, 1250–1550*, Philadelphia: University of Pennsylvania Press.

Pálóczi-Horváth, A. (1989) *Pechenegs, Cumans, Iasians: Steppe peoples in medieval Hungary*, Budapest: Corvina Kiadó.

Ranke, L. von (1874) *Geschichte der romanischen und germanischen Völker von 1494 bis 1514* (2nd edn), Leipzig. Eng. tr. as *History of the Latin and Teutonic Nations (1494 to 1514)*, London: George Bell, 1909.

Reynolds, S. (1994) *Fiefs and Vassals: the medieval evidence reinterpreted*, Oxford: Oxford University Press.

—— (1997) *Kingdoms and Communities in Western Europe 900–1300* (2nd edn), Oxford: Clarendon Press.

Samsonowicz, H. (1998) 'The long 10th century, or the creation of the New Europe', *European Review* 6: 277–81.

Schöpflin, G. and Wood, N. (eds) (1989) *In Search of Central Europe*, Cambridge: Polity Press.

Sullivan, R. E. (1994) *Christian Missionary Activity in the Early Middle Ages*, Aldershot: Variorum Reprints.

Szentpétery, E. (ed.) (1937) *Scriptores Rerum Hungaricarum*, vol. 1, Budapest: Magyar Tudományos Akademia.

—— (ed.) (1938) *Scriptores Rerum Hungaricarum*, vol. 2, Budapest: Magyar Tudományos Akadémia.

Szűcs, J. (1983) 'The three historical regions of Europe: an outline', *Acta Historica Academiae Scientiarum Hungaricae* 29: 131–84; French version: *Les trois Europes*, Paris: Harmattan, 1985.

—— (1984) 'Társadalomelmélet, politikai teória és történetszemlélet Kézai *Gesta Hungarorum*–ában', in *idem*, *Nemzet és történelem* (2nd edn), Budapest: Gondolat, 413–555, German version in *idem*, *Nation und Geschichte: Studien*, Budapest: Corviana Kiadó, 1981, 263–328; short English version: 'Theoretical elements in Master Simon of Kéza's *Gesta Hungarorum* (1282–1285)' in Veszprémy, L. and Schaer, F. (eds) *Simonis de Kéza Gesta Hungarorum*, Budapest: Central European University Press, 1999, xxix–cii.

—— (1993) *Az utolsó Árpádok*, Budapest: MTA Történettudományi Intézet.

Theiner, A. (1859) *Vetera Monumenta Historica Hungariam sacram illustrantia*, vol. 1, Rome: Typis Vaticanis.

Veszprémy, L. and Schaer, F. (eds) (1999) *Simonis de Kéza Gesta Hungarorum*, Budapest: Central European University Press.

Wandycz, P. S. (1992) *The Price of Freedom: a history of East Central Europe from the Middle Ages to the present*, London and New York: Routledge.

CHAPTER SIX

CHRISTIANS, BARBARIANS AND
MONSTERS: THE EUROPEAN DISCOVERY
OF THE WORLD BEYOND ISLAM

Peter Jackson

At the dawn of the thirteenth century, and before the emergence of the Mongol empire, the horizons of Latin Christendom extended only as far as the Hungarians and Rus' in eastern Europe and the Byzantine empire and Islamic powers of the Near East (Wright 1925: 256–7; Phillips 1988: 3–25). Beyond lay a world of which educated Catholic Christians had only the haziest and most inaccurate ideas, derived from two sources. One was the Bible; the other was the lore of Classical Antiquity. To the canonical Scriptures medieval Christians were indebted for the long-lived notion of a terrestrial Paradise (Genesis, II, 8–14); the expulsion of Cain and his line (*ibid.*, IV, 9 ff.); the wanderings of Ishmael and his descendants (*ibid.*, XVI, 11–12, and XVII, 20); the centrality of Jerusalem (Ezekiel, V, 5; Psalm 73, 12); the deportation of certain tribes of Israel (the 'Ten Lost Tribes') eastwards by the Assyrians (II [IV] Kings, XVII, 6, and XVIII, 11); and the story of the Three Magi of the Nativity (Matthew, II, 1–12; subsequently metamorphosed into kings). That the Apostles had actually preached the Gospel throughout the world, in accordance with Christ's commission (Acts, I, 8), was confirmed by the apocryphal books of the New Testament, where it was claimed, notably, that St Thomas had evangelized 'India'. But the Scriptures also offered glimpses of a future that involved contact with the obscure but innumerable Gog and Magog, a nation of horsemen (Ezekiel, XXXVIII, 1–3, 14–16), whose advent would usher in the Last Things (Revelation, XX, 7–8).

Of the knowledge bequeathed by the pagan Classical world, much had been lost: Ptolemy's *Geography*, for instance, was unavailable (it was not to be translated into Latin until *c.*1400), and the West had to make do with inferior authors such as Pliny, whose *Natural History* was greatly in vogue throughout the Middle Ages (Chibnall 1975). The material found in their works was refracted, moreover, through the digest compiled by Martianus Capella (fourth century) or the encyclopedic work of Solinus (third century); and it was concerned with fantasy rather than being the fruit of direct observation. Thus the 'East' was a region of marvels and peopled by fabulous beasts and by monstrous humans – the Cynocephali (a dog-headed race) and Panotii (a race endowed with enormous ears) immortalized in the twelfth-century tympanum at Vézelay; the Parossitae, whose mouths were so small that they derived nourishment by inhaling the steam from cooking meat; the Astomi (a people with no mouth at all); the Amazons, and so on (Friedman 1981; Wittkower 1942).

Occupying the spectrum between fellow Christians and monsters were those societies whose unnatural and barbarous practices put them beyond the pale, such as the Anthropophagi (cannibals). The apocryphal account of the campaigns of Alexander the Great, dating probably from the third century AD, not only incorporated the fabulous nations referred to above, but alleged also that the Macedonian conqueror had enclosed behind an impenetrable barrier certain barbarous and unclean nations, to prevent them overrunning and contaminating the civilized lands (Anderson 1932).

We might expect that the early Christian Church would frown upon learning derived from the pagan world. But in fact certain patristic writers were ready to take on board such knowledge and to harmonize it with the history and geography that were to be gleaned from the Bible. Given the *imprimatur* of Augustine (d. 430), who seems to have accepted the existence of monstrous races, medieval Latin Christians had no reason to challenge it. The *Etymologiae* of Isidore, bishop of Seville (d. 636), which enjoyed considerable popularity in the Middle Ages, were especially indebted to Solinus for details about the fabulous races and marvels of the East. Slightly later an anonymous (probably Syrian) writer claiming to be St Methodius of Patara drew upon the prophetic material in the Bible to weave a circumstantial account of the final era of history. In his *Sermo* or *Revelations* he foresaw the irruption both of Gog and Magog, whom he equated with the unclean peoples enclosed by Alexander, and of the Ishmaelites, whose domination of the world would last for sixty years, and predicted that the latter would capture Rome (Sackur 1898: 66–75, 80–93). For Pseudo-Methodius the Ishmaelites were represented by the Midianites who had been defeated by Gideon (Judges, VI, 24) and by the Arab Muslim invaders of his own day, but the fact that the prophecy had thus largely been fulfilled was not appreciated in a later age. In the twelfth century Peter Comestor, who included a summary of the *Sermo* in his own compendium of sacred history, the *Historia Scholastica* (Smalley 1983: 178–9), substituted for Gog and Magog the Ten Lost Tribes (Anderson 1932: 65–70). Pseudo-Methodius – either directly or through the medium of Peter Comestor – was destined to wield among Western Christians an authority second only to that of Scripture itself and of the Church Fathers.

Barbarous and unclean races were to be found even within Western Europe, where by the twelfth century the Frankish aristocracy and clergy were coming to regard the Christian Celtic and Slavic peoples as representatives of an inferior culture and existing on a lower level of economic development (Jones 1971; Bartlett 1982: 158–77). Beyond the frontiers of Christendom, however, the obvious location of barbarism was the steppe zone south of the Rus' – 'Scythia', to use the designation in vogue since Classical times – through which Western Europe had suffered repeated invasions in previous centuries. The most recent invaders to penetrate Europe via this corridor were the Hungarians. Otto of Freising could still comment dismissively *c.*1150 on their primitive economy and habits (Bartlett 1982: 159), but that was before their kings had begun to encourage the immigration of substantial numbers of French knights, clerics and artisans (Fügedi 1975). And by the onset of the thirteenth century Hungarian kings and prelates were eagerly proselytizing their nomadic neighbours in the steppe, the Cumans (Polovtsy, Qipchaq). Scythia was undoubtedly alien terrain. What especially struck Western observers was the near-total absence of agriculture: Otto remarked on the fact that these regions were untouched by ploughshare or mattock (Waitz 1884: 40; Mierow 1953: 66). But the inhabitants displayed other undesirable features also. Elsewhere he alleged that the Cumans, like their predecessors the Pechenegs, ate raw flesh, including that of unclean beasts (Wilmans 1867: 233–4; Mierow 1928: 371).

* * *

Western European pilgrims had been visiting Palestine since at least the fourth century, but it was the First Crusade (1096–1101) that brought Latins into continuous contact with large numbers of Christians belonging to separated churches: Armenians and Jacobites in Syria and Palestine or representatives of other Christian communities – the Nestorians, the Ethiopians and the Georgians – on pilgrimage to the Holy Sepulchre (Hamilton 1996: 237–8, 240). Crusader conquests, however, were a mere pinprick alongside the pagan encroachments that the Islamic world suffered further east during the twelfth and thirteenth centuries. First, much of Central Asia was subjugated by a Buddhist power, the Qara-Khitan, whose ruler sealed his triumph with a victory over the Muslims of eastern Persia in 1141. Then both the Qara-Khitan empire and the territories of its Muslim neighbour and rival, the Khwārazmshāh, which embraced much of the eastern Islamic world, were overrun by the Mongols in the course of the great seven-year campaign (1218–24) led by Chinggis Khan. The Mongol attack was especially catastrophic in its scope and the scale of the devastation (Morgan 1986: 67–71).

It was natural for the beleaguered Franks of the eastern Mediterranean littoral to assume that the Muslims' enemies on each occasion were Christians. Rumours of the existence somewhere in the east of a Christian priest-king 'John', who was descended from the Magi, may already have been current for some time, and the news of the Qara-Khitan victory, reaching western Europe in 1146, was taken to signify his advance to aid his co-religionists (Nowell 1953; Beckingham 1996: 2–8). What gave especial impetus to the growth of the Prester John legend was the appearance *c.*1165 of the celebrated 'letter' of Prester John (Zarncke 1879). This document is now known to have been a forgery emanating from within the West and was possibly a device of the imperial chancery in its conflict with the Papacy (Hamilton 1985; Franco 1997). To judge from the extraordinary diffusion of manuscripts and the number of interpolations that were made, it satisfied a deep need to believe in an ideal Christian polity. The author drew upon Revelation, Isidore and Pseudo-Methodius to depict a realm that included monstrous races, Amazons and the Ten Lost Tribes; he unconsciously indicated another of his sources by referring to the palace built by St Thomas; and according to an interpolation made before 1220, Prester John numbered among his subjects the cannibalistic Gog and Magog, whom he released temporarily against his enemies before returning them once more to confinement (Slessarev 1959; Knefelkamp 1988: 339–48). John's failure to materialize did not mean that Western Christians lost hope. In 1217 Jacques de Vitry, newly arrived in Palestine as bishop of Acre, could write both that the Christians subjected to Muslim rule outnumbered their Muslim masters and that there were also many Christian kings dwelling in the east 'as far as the territory of Prester John' who might move to aid the Fifth Crusade against the Muslims (Huygens 1960: 95).

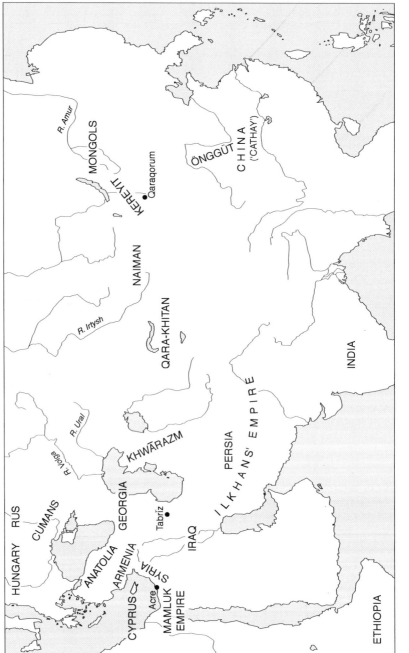

Figure 6.1 Map of Asia in the Mongol era.

When in 1221 reports of the advance of a vast Christian army under a king called David reached the army of the Fifth Crusade in Egypt, it was Jacques de Vitry who made the connection with the 'Christian' triumph eight decades before, so that King David became Prester John or his descendant (Gosman 1989; Linehan 1967). The King David story was derived in part from developments in Central Asia earlier in the century which antedated the Mongols' westward advance (Richard 1996; Jackson 1997: 428–31); but it was under this guise that the West first heard of Chinggis Khan's operations. The Mongols, a nomadic people from the steppe and forest zone that lay to the north of China, were not Christians, although Nestorianism had made some headway among certain of the neighbouring tribes they had reduced, such as the Kereyit and the Naiman. Chinggis Khan's policy, which was to be maintained by his successors, was one of toleration of all faiths and sects in return for political obedience, since the Mongols believed that Heaven had granted them a mandate to govern the whole earth (Voegelin 1941; De Rachewiltz 1973). For the eastern Christians who had lived under the constraints of Muslim rule, the Mongol conquest therefore brought deliverance; but it is also noteworthy that when Chinggis Khan's forces had invaded the Qara-Khitan territories c.1218 they were welcomed as liberators by the oppressed Muslim population (Morgan 1996: 161).

Although the Mongols undoubtedly gave priority to the reduction of China, their belief in the mandate of Heaven meant that they were bound to turn their attention westwards again. Under Chinggis Khan's son and successor, the Great Khan ('qaghan') Ögödei, Mongol forces completed the subjugation of the peoples of the Caspian and Pontic steppes, including the Cumans, devastated the Rus' principalities, and ravaged Hungary and Poland before retiring into the steppe once more in 1242 (Strakosch-Grassmann 1893). Two years later, in the course of a campaign against the Muslims of Anatolia, another Mongol army briefly menaced the Latin settlements in Syria. The West was forewarned of the renewed Mongol advance, since it was reported in 1237–8 both by the Hungarian Dominican Julian, who had visited the Ural region, and by Philip, the Dominican prior in the Holy Land (Dörrie 1956: 162–82; Luard 1876: 397–8; Scheffer-Boichorst 1874: 941–2).

It is possible that these warnings were discounted. The Mongol invasions proved all the more cataclysmic in view of the mood of optimism that had prevailed in the Latin world in recent years. In eastern Europe the conversion of some Cuman chiefs had made possible the creation in 1228 of the new episcopal see of 'Cumania' (Richard 1977a: 23–6). The Dominican Philip had assured the pope of the readiness of the Jacobite patriarch and the Nestorian catholicus to submit to Rome; only the Greeks now remained obstinately outside the Catholic fold (Scheffer-Boichorst 1874: 941–2; Luard 1876: 397–8). He referred almost incidentally to the Mongol devastation of Persia and Iraq, and it may well be that some thought the situation might be turned to the West's advantage. The pope had been in negotiations for ecclesiastical union with the Rus' since 1222, and in the wake of the Mongol attack it seems the Rus' grand prince did recognize papal primacy in 1246 (Zatko 1957). One of the aims of the parties of friars whom Pope Innocent IV sent as envoys to the Mongol world in 1245 was to make contact with the schismatic churches both of Rus' and of the Near East (Szcześniak 1956; Richard 1977a: 70–3; Jackson 1995).

The Mongol assault on eastern Europe in 1241–2 dispelled any residual illusions that the newcomers were the Christian army of Prester John, and the papal embassies of 1245–8 merely brought back ultimatums demanding the pope's submission. The Franciscan Carpini, who had taken the more northerly route through the Pontic steppe to the qaghan's headquarters, reported that the Mongols were planning a further invasion of Europe (Menestò *et al*. 1989: 294; Dawson 1955: 44; Holder-Egger 1905–13: 210). Although Carpini referred to Nestorians among the qaghan's subjects (Menestò *et al*. 1989: 255; Dawson 1955: 20), he seems to have been unaware of the fact that the qaghan Güyüg's chief advisers were Christians and does not mention Güyüg's Christian sympathies. But in 1249 word reached the West via Louis IX's crusading army in Cyprus that the qaghan had been baptized (Luard 1880: 87; D'Achéry 1723: 627a). Less credence would have been placed in this had not a letter from the Armenian king's brother Smbat, who was himself *en route* to the Mongol court, drawn attention to the great numbers of Christians in the empire and mentioned the assistance the Mongols had rendered to a Christian king in India against his Muslim enemies (Richard 1986: 690–2). Rumours of the Christian faith of various Mongol princes continued to circulate over the next few years. It was in part the report that the prince Sartaq was a Christian that served as the impulse behind the missionary journey of the Franciscan William of Rubruck in 1253. Rubruck was sceptical, and ascribed such rumours – as indeed the inflated stories about Prester John – to the excessive zeal of Nestorians (Van den Wyngaert 1929: 206; Jackson and Morgan 1990: 122). These eastern Christians had a different perspective on Mongol sovereignty, entertaining lively hopes of the conversion of their new overlords and pressing for a Mongol–Western alliance. The envoys – both Nestorians – who visited Louis IX in 1248–9 may have exceeded their brief in emphasizing the pro-Christian sentiments of the Mongol general who had sent them, and Rubruck suspected Armenian translators of misrepresenting the letter he carried from the French king as a request for Mongol assistance in his crusade (Richard 1997: 60–1; Van den Wyngaert 1929: 243; Jackson and Morgan 1990: 170–1).

But once the unitary Mongol empire disintegrated *c*.1260–1 into a number of warring khanates, and the Mongol rulers of Iran, known as the 'Ilkhans', began to court the Christian West with a view to joint action against Muslim Egypt and Syria (Boyle 1976), stories of Christian sympathies and conversion grew more persistent still. Armenian advocacy of the Mongol alliance reached its peak with the expatriate monk Hayton (Het'um). In the crusading treatise which he presented to Pope Clement V in 1307, Hayton included a sketch of Mongol history where he claimed that the qaghan had been baptized in 1254 at the instigation of the Armenian king, Hayton's own kinsman (Hayton 1906: 164–7). Polo, however, a Venetian whose home government enjoyed good commercial relations with the Ilkhan's Mamluk enemies, would be significantly less sanguine about Mongol allies (Hyde 1982–3: 130; Critchley 1992: 72–6).

The reports of the friars – in particular those of Julian, of Carpini, of Simon of Saint-Quentin, who drafted an account of the embassy of the Dominican Ascelin to the Near East, and of Rubruck – are to be numbered among our most important early sources. But the papal embassies were only the vanguard of a stream of Western visitors to the Mongol empire from the mid-thirteenth century to the mid-fourteenth. Among later missionary visitors were the Dominican Ricoldo of Montecroce, who was able to preach the Gospel in Ilkhanid Iraq, and the Franciscan John of Montecorvino, whom Pope Nicholas IV had sent to evangelize China. The rise of the Mongol empire coincided with the high water-mark of medieval Western economic development, and not far behind the friars were Latin merchants, already long active in Syria and in eastern Europe. In the 1260s we encounter Italian traders in the Black Sea ports and at Tabrīz in north-west Persia, although there is no record of a European mercantile presence in China (apart from the Polos) before 1291, when Montecorvino was accompanied by a Venetian merchant (Petech 1962; Paviot 1997).

* * *

During the crisis of 1241–2 and its immediate aftermath, the West's perception of its new neighbour can be identified at a number of different levels (Bezzola 1974: 66ff.; Klopprogge 1993: 153–236; Schmieder 1994: 73–88). In the first place, it was clearly necessary to explain what had become of the would-be Christian confederates of an earlier generation. Carpini thought that Prester John had repulsed the Mongols and that they had not ventured to attack him again (Menestò *et al.* 1989: 258–9; Dawson 1955: 22–3). But Simon of Saint-Quentin was among a series of authors to assume that the Mongols had destroyed King David, and it is evident from the details he supplies that he identified the fallen monarch with Ong Khan, the Christian ruler of the Kereyit whom Chinggis Khan had overthrown *c.*1202 (Richard 1965: 27–9 = Vincent, xxx, 69; Luard 1880: 115; Klopprogge 1993: 145–52). Subsequent visitors to the empire persisted in the search for the defunct priest-king. By dint of a bogus etymological link, Marco Polo identified Ong's people with the Turkish tribe of the Önggüt, whose territory lay on the northern borders of China and who had been among the first to submit to Chinggis Khan (Van den Wyngaert 1929: 348; Dawson 1955: 225; Latham 1958: 105–6; Morgan 1996: 165–6). But from the early fourteenth century a distinct shift occurred, and the kingdom of Prester John would come increasingly to be located in Ethiopia (Beckingham 1980: 293–4; Hamilton 1996: 251–3).

Emerging from the great wilderness that extended for hundreds of miles to the east of Latin Christendom, the Mongols belonged, as Rubruck put it, to 'another world' (Van den Wyngaert 1929: 171, 187; Jackson and Morgan 1990: 71, 97). In some measure, observers simply replicated the terminology previously applied to other pastoral nomads such as the Cumans. Thomas of Spalato, describing the devastation of Hungary, noted that the invaders abhorred bread, and believed that they drank a concoction of mare's milk and blood. Other authors echoed the Mongols' unfamiliarity with bread (Gombos 1938: 2239; Richard 1965: 32 = Vincent, xxx, 71; Waitz 1882: 522). The Mongols' atrocities, however, caused them readily to be identified as agents of Satan: the alternative name 'Tatars' under which they were known was swiftly corrupted to 'Tartars', associating them with the Hell of Classical mythology (Connell 1973: 117–18). Their savagery, of course, did not debar them from being viewed also as a scourge from God, sent to punish humanity for its sins (DeWeese 1978–9: 48–50).

As steppe horsemen the Mongols naturally evoked recollections of biblical prophecy; and elements of the Western intellectual tradition that we noticed above, particularly the *Sermo* of Pseudo-Methodius, were recruited in order to make sense of the cataclysm. Thomas claims that at the time of the Mongol invasion 'very many old men of letters' ploughed through writings and, on the basis of what Methodius had said, agreed that the Mongols were the forerunners of Antichrist (Gombos 1938: 2240). One prophecy that has come to light only in recent years referred to the 'Sons of Israel', clearly reflecting the belief that the newcomers were the Ten Lost Tribes (Lerner 1983: 15–24). Variations on the theme emerge from several writings, including Julian's report, where the Mongols are identified as Ishmaelites (Dörrie 1956: 167; Jaffé 1861: 341; Waitz 1879: 403–4; Waitz 1882: 522; Luard 1864: 118; Luard 1882: 78; Burnett and Gaultier Dalché 1991: 160). This equation was also made by the Rus' (Michell and Forbes 1914: 82), among whom we know Pseudo-Methodius had likewise been invoked from the time of the first Mongol attack in 1222–3 (*ibid.*, 64; Cross 1929). Julian had been told by a Russian cleric that the Mongols were descended from the Midianites, and the same view was communicated to the pope at Lyons in 1244 by the refugee Russian prelate Peter Akherovich (Dörrie 1956: 188; Von den Brincken 1975: 122).

A certain paranoia, linking the grim new enemy with more familiar antagonists of longer standing, is also discernible. It was part of a wider phenomenon, for the nightmare possibility of an alliance between the Muslims and Patarene heretics within the West had been in the air since the 1190s (Reeves 1974: 61). Thus, according to the Russian cleric Peter, the Mongols recruited for themselves representatives of all races and sects (Dörrie 1956: 192), and in 1241 rumours spread that they were accompanied by heretics and false Christians (Wattenbach 1851: 640; Waitz 1879: 404; Jaffé 1861: 341; Luard 1882: 82, 84; DeWeese 1978–9: 50–1). Subsequently Roger Bacon entertained the possibility that the 'Master of Hungary', the leader of the unruly 'Crusade of the Shepherds' (or Pastoureaux) who terrorized northern France in 1251, might have been an agent of the Mongols or the Muslims (Bridges 1897a: 401). A still more pernicious report, following on with remorseless logic from the belief that the Mongols were the Ten Lost Tribes, made scapegoats of the Jews, who were suspected of shipping arms to the invaders, and led to pogroms in parts of Germany (Menache 1996).

This preoccupation with the eschatological nature of current events helps to explain much of the bizarre detail about the Mongols which is to be found even in the reports of the papal envoys. It has been demonstrated that the interrogation of captured Mongols by a Hungarian bishop *c.*1239, of which an account found its way into two English chronicles, was conducted exclusively on the basis of data in Pseudo-Methodius (Bigalli 1971: 64–9; Klopprogge 1993: 162–5; Klopprogge 1997: 96–7; and cf. Fried 1986: 301). His influence is also clearly behind allusions to Rome as the Mongols' objective (Dörrie 1956: 178, 193; Luard 1877: 276). It serves to explain why Peter, Carpini and others were keen to ascertain the number of years that had elapsed since the Mongols' emergence from their homeland (Dörrie 1956: 189–90; Menestò *et al.* 1989: 264, 295; Dawson 1955: 25–6, 44–5; Luard 1882: 79; D'Achéry 1723: 627a). And stories – of which the gossipy English Benedictine Matthew Paris contributed more than his fair share – were also rife concerning their cannibalism (Luard 1876: 488; Luard 1877: 76, 273; Luard 1882: 77; Dörrie 1956: 191; Richard 1965: 38 = Vincent, xxx, 77; Waitz 1882: 522;

Figure 6.2 'Men whose heads do grow beneath their shoulders'. The *Liber de naturis rerum creatorum* ('Concerning the nature of created things'), composed in 1492 for Raphael de Mercatellis, abbot of St Bavo's, Ghent, and based on the mid-thirteenth-century work of Thomas of Cantimpré OP. On this page a selection of fantastic types in faraway places is presented, including a female cyclops, a 'sciopod' shielding himself from the sun with his enormous foot, a man with his face on his shoulders, another with six arms, another whose sole sustenance is the scent of apples; also various other exotic females reported to be dangerous when wet. (It was later, and out of consideration for the moral welfare of more modest students of the strange that the men's trousers were painted in.) Ghent, Sint-Baafskathedral, MS. 15, fo. 2r. Photo: *Circa 1492*. Exhibition catalogue, National Gallery of Art, Washington 1991 p.125 © St Baafskathedraal Gent. Photo: Paul M. R. Maevaert.

Sinor 1977: 61; Guzman 1991), since the enclosed peoples – whether or not they were called Gog and Magog – were credited with eating all animals without discrimination and even human flesh (Sackur 1898: 72–3, 92; Anderson 1932: 15–49). Although much of this lay at some distance from reality, certain of the gruesome details received support from the accounts of those who, unlike Matthew or Thomas, encountered the Mongols at first hand and found that they did appear less discriminating in their diet than Catholic Christians. Carpini listed among the items of the Mongols' diet horses, mice, lice and the afterbirth of foals; although the Mongols had been known to eat human flesh, it was only in dire military emergency (Menestò *et al.* 1989: 248, 256; Dawson 1955: 16, 21).

The view that the Mongols were the people enclosed by Alexander behind strong barriers, and of whom (Pseudo-) Methodius had written, persisted for some decades. The outbreak of the Flagellant movement in Perugia in 1260 has been persuasively linked with the Mongol attacks on eastern Europe in 1259–60 and their invasion of Syria at the beginning of the latter year and with papal appeals that were couched in apocalyptic terms (Dickson 1989). Thirty years later, the Dominican missionary Ricoldo devoted some space to this question. The identification was allegedly confirmed by the fact that the Mongols hated Alexander's name and by the close resemblance between their script and that of Chaldaea, whence the Jews originated. On the other hand, they knew nothing of the Law of Moses or of the Exodus; they had no priesthood; and they differed considerably from the Jews (not to mention every other race) both in appearance and in custom (Laurent 1873: 118). Matthew Paris had expressed similar reservations some decades earlier (Luard 1877: 78). According to Ricoldo, the Mongols themselves claimed to be descended from Gog and Magog, of which latter name 'Mogoli' was a corruption (Laurent 1873: 118–19). Marco Polo transmits a similarly strained etymology linking Magog and Mongol (Latham 1958: 106). Yet certain writers, notably Bacon and the anonymous author of a geographical treatise of *c.*1260, expressed doubts as to whether the advent of the Mongols presaged the coming of Antichrist (Bridges 1897b: 234–5; Colker 1979: 725–6).

At another level, of course, the Mongols confronted the Western Church with rival universalist claims not met with in any alien society other than Islam. Their view of international diplomacy was relatively simple: every ruler had a duty to recognize his place within the world-empire and to make peace (i.e. submit); any who neglected to do so was a rebel. It is clear that for the Mongol imperial government the papal embassies of 1245–8 betokened inadequate expressions of submission, so that the qaghan Güyüg referred to the letter brought by Carpini, for example, as a petition (Dawson 1955: 85). Ascelin and his party narrowly escaped execution for their refusal to make the triple genuflection before the qaghan's representative (Richard 1965: 101–2, 109 = Vincent, XXXII, 44, 48). Rubruck noted scornfully how the Mongols in their arrogance were unable to understand why he had come if not to make peace with them (Van den Wyngaert 1929: 244; Jackson and Morgan 1990: 172–3; Richard 1977b). To the Latins, Mongol ultimatums, with their emphasis upon the mandate of Heaven, appeared not merely ludicrous but blasphemous (Weiland 1874: 548). Direct experience of Mongol diplomacy therefore fuelled the earlier view of the newcomers as having no proper religion.

The development of friendly relations with the Ilkhans and the prospect of a Mongol alliance naturally affected the way in which the Mongols appear in the literature of the later thirteenth century. Admittedly Ricoldo of Montecroce still denounces their belief that the world had been given to them, and speaks of them in unflattering terms (Laurent 1873: 114–15). Neither was he optimistic about their potential for conversion: it was vital, in his view, to begin with the conversion of the ruler and the nobles, since the lower orders were so doltish and bestial that they would not be won for the faith unless they were offered material inducements (Dondaine 1967: 167). This was the reason why so many of the Mongols had embraced Islam, as a result of the Saracens bribing them with valuable gifts. Many of them, asserted Ricoldo, loved Christians and would have been converted to Christianity, were it not for the fact that Christians were unwilling to make them presents and that the Christian faith was extremely rigorous (Laurent 1873: 121; Dondaine 1967: 167–8). Yet it is clear that the Mongols were now seen through a different lens. Where his precursors had assumed that Chinggis Khan had killed the Christian Prester John, Marco Polo, flushed with the (doubtless overstated) patronage of the conqueror's grandson Qubilai, made of Prester John a pagan prince whose downfall had been predicted by Christian astrologers in the victor's service (Latham 1958: 95–6). Some writers observed that the Mongols had abandoned their former barbarism and become more civilized (Schmieder 1994: 132).

For some of those who travelled out to Mongol Asia, contacts with eastern Christians brought disappointment. Rubruck's report contains some particularly scathing remarks about the Nestorian clergy he encountered, although it is worth noticing that his charges – simony, clerical marriage, superfluous ordination to the priesthood – are precisely what we might expect to be levelled by a Latin Christian against an eastern clergy who largely shared the lifestyle of their Mongol masters, who had no landed endowments, who benefited only rarely from episcopal visitation, and whose church had not passed through the crucible of Gregorian Reform (Von den Brincken 1973: 304–6; Jackson 1994: 61–2). The rivalry that pitted against one another representatives of different religious communities at the qaghan's court, and which emerges so clearly from Rubruck's narrative, may well have underlain Montecorvino's complaint, four decades later, about the hostility and obstructiveness of the Nestorian clergy in China (Van den Wyngaert 1929: 346–9; Dawson 1955: 224–8). There were still those, like Burchard of Mount Sion, in whom an awareness of the great numbers of eastern Christians engendered a mood of optimism (Laurent 1873: 91–3). But Bacon concluded that the Christian population of the world was dwarfed by the vast numbers of pagans (Bridges 1900: 122).

* * *

The thirteenth century exerted a decisive influence on the development of Western ideas about the wider world. Contact with the Mongol empire greatly expanded the geographical horizons of the West. Rubruck became the first Westerner to identify 'Cathay' with the land of the Seres of Classical Antiquity, and was able to challenge Isidore's statement that the Caspian was an inland sea. Latin Christians, moreover, were introduced at this time not only to China and Central Asia but to parts of Asia that remained outside the Mongol empire, notably India. Given the vagueness of

Western geographical terminology, Montecorvino, on his way out to China by sea, is the first Latin known for certain to have set foot on the subcontinent. Marco Polo's book claimed that he visited India on behalf of the qaghan Qubilai, and when warfare between Mongol rulers towards the turn of the century rendered the land route less attractive, his party travelled back by sea as far as the Persian Gulf *c*.1292. It was not until perhaps the 1320s, however, that the West actually made contact with the genuine Indian Christians of St Thomas (Ryan 1993: 662–7).

The advent of the friars made a significant difference in terms of critical comment. True, Carpini lists the Parossitae among the peoples conquered by the Mongols (Menestò *et al.* 1989: 272, 290; Dawson 1955: 30, 41), and also describes a Mongol campaign against Isidore's Cyclopedes, who escaped by cartwheeling (Menestò *et al.* 1989: 273–4; Dawson 1955: 31). But if in some measure these visitors partook of the same misconceptions as earlier commentators, the Mongol world they described also owed a good deal to close observation and scientific judgement. This is particularly true of Rubruck's account. He emerges from his narrative as unwilling to accept anything he has not seen for himself; he expresses doubts regarding the monsters described by Isidore and Solinus, and is especially dismissive of unfounded rumours, whether about the might of Prester John or the Christian sympathies of the Mongol sovereigns (Van den Wyngaert 1929: 206, 256–7, 269; Jackson and Morgan 1990: 122, 187–8, 201; Jackson 1994: 57–8). The account of India furnished by the Franciscan John of Marignolli, who visited China as the pope's ambassador in 1342, proposed that monstrous humans and strange beasts were far thinner on the ground than had been assumed; he ingeniously attributed the stories of the monopod shading himself from the sun with an enormous foot to the Indians' practice of carrying umbrellas (Van den Wyngaert 1929: 546, 548–9; Yule 1914: 256, 258–61). Even Marco Polo's book strikes a sober note in its undertaking to differentiate between hearsay and personal observation; and although this laudable aim is not always adhered to, and although, too, the book's avowed purpose is to entertain and to edify, it is nevertheless relatively free of credulous claims and sometimes seeks to correct misapprehensions: thus the salamander, for instance, is not a living creature but a mineral (asbestos) (Jackson 1998: 89–91).

* * *

Yet it is important to recognize how limited, in some respects, was the impact on the Latin West of relations with the Mongol world. Thirteenth- and fourteenth-century Western writings reflect a considerable advance in geographical and ethnographical knowledge on the part of their authors. It is true also that the authors of imaginary travel accounts often sought to provide an accurate description of the known world, and that their work incorporated the results of genuine journeys (Richard 1981). But a century or two passed before first-hand observations were reflected in cartography (Baumgärtner 1997). And even if a more scientific spirit is discernible in the narratives of some of those who visited Asia, the same cannot always be said for those who used their work. Take, for instance, the English Franciscan Roger Bacon, who met Rubruck and read a copy of his report (Charpentier 1935). More than once, Bacon comments on the manner in which earlier authors such as Isidore and Pliny had relied on hearsay rather than upon direct experience. But he proceeds to follow not simply Rubruck, whose travels were genuine, but the eighth-century Aethicus Ister, whose voyages were certainly not, and he further shows himself ready to take Pliny and other ancient writers as authorities (Bridges 1897a: 304–5, 354, 356, 359, 361–2, 365). It was still by no means easy to ascertain which travellers were authentic and which were bogus, or which authentic travellers were gullible and which put their experiences to good use. We are left with the impression that the new knowledge was simply grafted onto the old.

The indications are, moreover, that marvels, rather than the fruits of scientific observation, were in demand among the wider reading public. For all that 'the East' enjoyed a considerable vogue in Western literature, much of what was written about it was of a fabulous nature (Richard 1966). The Franciscan Odoric of Pordenone makes no reference whatever to preaching in the account of his travels (1318–23), and no one reading it can be in any doubt that his purpose is to titillate the reader with a series of marvels (Yule 1913: 97). Even his contemporary Jordan of Séverac, who did engage in evangelistic activity, felt the need to give his own more down-to-earth work the title *Mirabilia*. One reason why Marco Polo's account may have elicited such incredulity was precisely the picture he drew of a prosperous, advanced, orderly China under Mongol government, which clashed with the earlier perceptions of the empire as primitive and barbarous (Euler 1972: 56; Gosman 1994: 83). Conversely, what enabled the discovery of the Canary Islanders to be so much more easily accommodated within the established world-picture was in part their simplicity and lack of sophistication (Hyde 1982–3: 138–40). Polo's unreceptiveness to the fabulous had no influence on many of his copyists and translators, whose illustrations often depict precisely those monstrous humans or other fantastic creatures absent from the text (Wittkower 1957). And his book was soon eclipsed by the 'Travels' of Sir John Mandeville, a collection of second-hand experiences laced with themes that dated back to the world of Antiquity. The fact that the surviving manuscripts of Mandeville's work far outnumber those of the Polo texts serves to bring home the abiding appeal of *mirabilia* (Letts 1949: 120; Bennett 1954: 219, 263–334). It took much longer for the impact of Polo's observations on academic geography or history to become visible (Hyde 1982–3: 131–2), although once it did, ironically, Polo's influence on Columbus would play a large part in concealing from the Genoese admiral his discovery of an altogether new world (Reichert 1988; Flint 1992: 45–6, 64–8).

REFERENCES

Aigle, D. (ed.) (1997) *L'Iran face à la domination mongole*, Bibliothèque Iranienne 45, Tehran: Institut Français de Recherche en Iran.

Anderson, A.R. (1932) *Alexander's Gate, Gog and Magog, and the Inclosed Nations*, Cambridge, Mass: The Mediaeval Academy of America.

Bartlett, R. (1982) *Gerald of Wales 1146–1223*, Oxford: Clarendon Press.

Baumgärtner, I. (1997) 'Weltbild und Empire. Die Erweiterung des kartographischen Weltbilds durch die Asienreisen des späten Mittelalters', *Journal of Medieval History* 23: 227–53.

Beckingham, C.F. (1980) 'The quest for Prester John', *Bulletin of the John Rylands Library* 62: 291–310; repr. in Beckingham and Hamilton (1996), 271–90.

—— (1996) 'The achievements of Prester John', in Beckingham and Hamilton (1996), 1–22.

—— and Hamilton, B. (eds) (1996) *Prester John, the Mongols and the Ten Lost Tribes*, Aldershot: Variorum.

Bennett, J.W. (1954) *The Rediscovery of Sir John Mandeville*, New York: The Modern Language Association of America.

Bezzola, G.A. (1974) *Die Mongolen in abendländischer Sicht (1220–1270). Beitrag zur Geschichte der Völkerbegegnungen*, Berne and Munich: Francke.

Bigalli, D. (1971) *I Tartari e l'Apocalisse. Ricerche sull'escatologia in Adamo Marsh e Ruggero Bacone*, Firenze: La Nuova Italia.

Boyle, J.A. (1976) 'The Ilkhans of Persia and the princes of Europe', *Central Asiatic Journal* 20: 25–40.

Bridges, J.H. (ed.) (1897a) *The Opus Maius of Roger Bacon*, vol. 1, Oxford: Oxford University Press.

—— (ed.) (1897b) *The Opus Maius of Roger Bacon*, vol. 2, Oxford: Oxford University Press.

—— (ed.) (1900) *The Opus Maius of Roger Bacon*, vol. 3, London: Williams and Norgate.

Burnett, C. and Gaultier Dalché, P. (1991) 'Attitudes towards the Mongols in medieval literature: the XXII kings of Gog and Magog from the court of Frederick II to Jean de Mandeville', *Viator* 22: 153–67.

Charpentier, J. (1935) 'William of Rubruck and Roger Bacon', in *Hyllningsskrift tillägnad Sven Hedin på hans 70-årsdag den 19 Febr. 1935*, Stockholm: Svenska Sällskapet för Antropologi och Geografi, 255–67.

Chibnall, M. (1975) 'Pliny's *Natural History* and the Middle Ages', in T.A. Dorey (ed.), *Empire and Aftermath: Silver Latin II*, London: Routledge and Kegan Paul, 57–78.

Colker, M.L. (1979) 'America rediscovered in the thirteenth century?', *Speculum* 54: 712–26.

Connell, C.W. (1973) 'Western views on the origin of the "Tartars": an example of the influence of myth in the second half of the thirteenth century', *Journal of Medieval and Renaissance Studies* 3: 115–37.

Critchley, J. (1992) *Marco Polo's Book*, Aldershot: Variorum.

Cross, S.H. (1929) 'The earliest allusion in Slavic literature to the *Revelations* of Pseudo Methodius', *Speculum* 4: 329–39.

D'Achéry, L. (ed.) (1723) *Spicilegium sive collectio veterum aliquot scriptorum qui in Galliae bibliotecis delituerant*, new edn by É. Baluze *et al.*, vol. 3, Paris: Montalant.

Dawson, C. (ed.) (1955) *The Mongol Mission: narratives and letters of the Franciscan missionaries in Mongolia and China in the thirteenth and fourteenth centuries, translated by a nun of Stanbrook Abbey*, London: Sheed and Ward.

De Rachewiltz, I. (1971) *Papal Envoys to the Great Khans*, London: Faber and Faber.

—— (1973) 'Some remarks on the ideological foundations of Chingis Khan's empire', *Papers on Far Eastern History* 7: 21–36.

DeWeese, D. (1978–9) 'The influence of the Mongols on the religious consciousness of thirteenth century Europe', *Mongolian Studies* 5: 41–78.

Dickson, G. (1989) 'The Flagellants of 1260 and the Crusades', *Journal of Medieval History* 15: 227–67.

Dondaine, A. (ed.) (1967) 'Ricoldiana: notes sur les oeuvres de Ricoldo da Montecroce', *Archivum Fratrum Praedicatorum* 37: 119–79.

Dörrie, H. (ed.) (1956) 'Drei Texte zur Geschichte der Ungarn und Mongolen. Die Missionsreisen des fr. Iulianus O.P. ins Ural-Gebiet (1234/5) und nach Rußland (1237) und der Bericht des Erzbischofs Peter über die Tartaren', *Nachrichten der Akademie der Wissenschaften zu Göttingen, phil.-hist. Klasse*, no. 6, 125–202.

Euler, H. (1972) 'Die Begegnung Europas mit den Mongolen im Spiegel abendländischer Reiseberichte', *Saeculum* 23: 47–58.

Flint, V. (1992) *The Imaginative Landscape of Christopher Columbus*, Princeton: Princeton University Press.

Franco, H., Jr (1997) 'La construction d'une utopie: l'Empire de Prêtre Jean', *Journal of Medieval History* 23: 211–25.

Fried, J. (1986) 'Auf der Suche nach der Wirklichkeit: die Mongolen und die europäische Erfahrungswissenschaft im 13. Jahrhundert', *Historische Zeitschrift* 243: 287–332.

Friedman, J.B. (1981) *The Monstrous Races in Medieval Art and Thought*, Cambridge, Mass.: Harvard University Press.

Fügedi, E. (1975) 'Das mittelalterliche Königreich Ungarn als Gastland', in Walter Schlesinger (ed.), *Die deutsche Ostsiedlung als Problem der europäischen Geschichte: Reichenau-Vorträge, 1970–72*, Vorträge und Forschungen 18, Sigmaringen: Jan Thorbecke, 471–507.

Gombos, A.F. (ed.) (1938) *Catalogus fontium historiae Hungaricae*, vol. 3, Budapest: Szent István-Akadémia.

Gosman, M. (1989) 'La légende du Prêtre Jean et la propagande auprès des croisés devant Damiette (1218–1221)', in Danielle Buschinger (ed.), *La Croisade: réalités et fictions. Actes du colloque d'Amiens 18–22 mars 1987*, Göppinger Arbeiten zur Germanistik, 503, Göppingen, 133–42.

—— (1994) 'Marco Polo's voyages: the conflict between confirmation and observation', in Von Martels (1994), 72–84.

Guzman, G.G. (1991) 'Reports of Mongol cannibalism in the thirteenth-century Latin sources: oriental fact or Western fiction?', in S.D. Westrem (ed.), *Discovering New Worlds: Essays on medieval exploration and imagination*, New York: Garland, 31–68.

Hamilton, B. (1985) 'Prester John and the Three Kings of Cologne', in H. Mayr-Harting and R.I. Moore (eds), *Studies in Medieval History presented to R.H.C. Davis*, London and Ronceverte: Hambledon, 177–91; repr. in Beckingham and Hamilton (1996), 171–85.

—— (1996) 'Continental drift: Prester John's progress through the Indies', in Beckingham and Hamilton (1996), 237–69.

Hayton (1906) 'La flor des estoires de la terre d'orient', in *Recueil des Historiens des Croisades. Documents Arméniens*, vol. 2, Paris: Imprimerie Nationale.

Holder-Egger, O. (ed.) (1905–13) 'Cronica Fratris Salimbene de Adam Ordinis Minorum', MGH, Scriptores, vol. 32, Hanover and Leipzig.

Huygens, R.B.C. (ed.) (1960) *Lettres de Jacques de Vitry*, Leiden: Brill.

Hyde, J.K. (1982–3) 'Real and imaginary journeys in the later Middle Ages', *Bulletin of the John Rylands Library* 65: 125–47.

Jackson, P. (1994) 'William of Rubruck in the Mongol empire: perception and prejudices', in Von Martels (1994), 54–71.

—— (1995) 'Early missions to the Mongols: Carpini and his contemporaries', annual lecture to the Hakluyt Society, June 1994, published with the Society's annual report for 1995.

—— (1997) 'Prester John *redivivus*: a review article', *Journal of the Royal Asiatic Society*, 3rd series, 7: 425–32.

—— (1998) 'Marco Polo and his "Travels"', *Bulletin of the School of Oriental and African Studies* 61: 82–101.

—— and Morgan, D. (trs) (1990) *The Mission of Friar William of Rubruck*, Cambridge University Press, for the Hakluyt Society, 2nd series, 173, London.

Jaffé, Ph. (ed.) (1861) 'Annales Scheftlarienses Maiores', MGH, Scriptores, vol. 17, Hanover, 335–43.

Jones, W. (1971) 'The image of the barbarian in medieval Europe', *Comparative Studies in Society and History* 13: 376–407.

Klopprogge, A. (1993) *Ursprung und Ausprägung des abendländischen Mongolenbildes im 13. Jahrhundert: ein Versuch zur Ideengeschichte des Mittelalters*, Asiatische Forschungen 122, Wiesbaden: Otto Harrassowitz.

—— (1997) 'Das Mongolenbild im Abendland', in Stephan Konermann and Jan Kusber (eds), *Die Mongolen in Asien und Europa*, Kieler Werkstücke, Reihe F, Beiträge zur osteuropäischer Geschichte 4, Frankfurt-am-Main: Peter Lang, 81–101.

Knefelkamp, U. (1988) 'Der Priesterkönig Johannes und sein Reich – Legende oder Realität?', *Journal of Medieval History* 14: 337–55.

Latham, R. (ed.) (1958) *Marco Polo. The Travels*, Harmondsworth: Penguin.

Laurent, J.C.M. (ed.) (1873) *Peregrinatores medii aevi quatuor*, 2nd edn, Leipzig: J.C. Hinrichs.

Lerner, R.E. (1983) *The Powers of Prophecy. The Cedar of Lebanon vision from the Mongol onslaught to the dawn of the Enlightenment*, Berkeley and Los Angeles: University of California Press.

Letts, M. (1949) *Sir John Mandeville: the man and his book*, London: Blatchworth.

Linehan, P. (1967) 'Documento español sobre la Quinta Cruzada', *Hispania Sacra* 20: 177–82 repr. in P. Linehan, *Past and Present in Medieval Spain*, Aldershot: Variorum (1992).

Luard, H.R. (ed.) (1864) 'Annales monasterii de Theokesberia 1066–1263', in *Annales Monastici*, vol. 1, Rolls Series, London: Longman, Green, Longman, Roberts and Green.

—— (ed.) (1876) *Matthaei Parisiensis Chronica Majora*, vol. 3, Rolls Series, London: Longman and Trubner.

—— (ed.) (1877) *Matthaei Parisiensis Chronica Majora*, vol. 4, Rolls Series, London: Longman and Trubner.

—— (ed.) (1880) *Matthaei Parisiensis Chronica Majora*, vol. 5, Rolls Series, London: Longman and Trubner.

—— (ed.) (1882) *Matthaei Parisiensis Chronica Majora*, vol. 6, Rolls Series, London: Longman and Trubner.

Menache, S. (1996) 'Tartars, Jews, Saracens and the Jewish-Mongol "Plot" of 1241', *History* 81: 319–42.

Menestò, E., Lungarotti, M.C. and Daffinà, P. (eds) (1989) *Storia dei Mongoli*, Centro italiano di studi sull'alto medioevo: Spoleto.

Michell, R., and Forbes, N. (trs) (1914) *The Chronicle of Novgorod 1016–1471*, Camden Society, 3rd series, 25, London.

Mierow, C.C. (tr.) (1928) *The Two Cities. A Chronicle of Universal History to the Year 1146 A.D. by Otto Bishop of Freising*, New York: Columbia University Press.

—— (tr.) (1953) *The Deeds of Frederick Barbarossa*, New York: Columbia University Press.

Morgan, D.O. (1986) *The Mongols*, Oxford: Blackwell.

—— (1996) 'Prester John and the Mongols', in Beckingham and Hamilton (1996), 159–70.

Nowell, C.E. (1953) 'The historical Prester John', *Speculum* 28: 435–45.

Paviot, J. (1997) 'Les marchands italiens dans l'Iran mongol', in Aigle (1997), 71–86.

Pelliot, P. (1959–73) *Notes on Marco Polo*, Paris: Imprimerie Nationale.

Petech, L. (1962) 'Les marchands italiens dans l'empire mongol', *Journal Asiatique* 250: 549–74.

Phillips, J.R.S. (1988) *The Medieval Expansion of Europe*, Oxford: Oxford University Press.

Reeves, M.E. (1974) 'History and prophecy in medieval thought', *Medievalia et Humanistica* 5: 51–75.

Reichert, F. (1988) 'Columbus und Marco Polo – Asien in Amerika', *Zeitschrift für Historische Forschung* 15: 1–63.

Richard, J. (1955–7) 'L'extrême-orient légendaire au moyen âge: Roi David et Prêtre Jean', *Annales d'Éthiopie* 2: 225–42; repr. in Richard (1976).

—— (ed.) (1965) *Simon de Saint-Quentin. Histoire des Tartares*, Documents relatifs à l'histoire des croisades 8, Paris: Paul Geuthner.

—— (1966) 'La vogue de l'Orient dans la littérature occidentale du Moyen-Age', in *Mélanges René Crozet*, Poitiers: Société d'études médiévales, 557–61; repr. in his *Les relations entre l'Orient et l'Occident au Moyen Age. Etudes et documents*, London: Variorum, 1977.

—— (1976) *Orient et Occident au Moyen Age: contacts et relations (XIIe–XVe s.)*, London: Variorum.

—— (1977a) *La Papauté et les missions d'Orient au moyen âge (XIIIe–XVe siècles)*, Rome: École Française.

—— (1977b) 'Sur les pas de Plancarpin et de Rubrouck: la lettre de saint Louis à Sartaq', *Journal des Savants*, 49–61; repr. in Richard (1983).

—— (1981) 'Voyages réels et voyages imaginaires, instruments de la connaissance géographique au Moyen-Age', in *Culture et travail intellectuel dans l'Occident médiéval*, Paris: C.N.R.S.; repr. in Richard (1983).

—— (1983) *Croisés, missionnaires et voyageurs: les perspectives orientales du monde latin médiéval*, London: Variorum.

—— (1986) 'La lettre du Connétable Smbat et les rapports entre Chrétiens et Mongols au milieu du XIIIème siècle', in Dickran Kouymjian, ed., *Armenian studies in memoriam Haïg Berbérian*, Lisbon: Calouste Gulbenkian Foundation, 683–96.

—— (1996) 'The *Relatio de Davide* as a source for Mongol history and the legend of Prester John', in Beckingham and Hamilton (1996), 139–58.

—— (1997) 'D'Älğigidäi à Gazan: la continuité d'une politique franque chez les Mongols d'Iran', in Aigle (1997), 57–69.

Ryan, J.D. (1993) 'European travelers before Columbus: the fourteenth century's discovery of India', *Catholic Historical Review* 79: 648–70.

Sackur, E. (1898) *Sibyllinische Texte und Forschungen: Pseudomethodius, Adso und die Tiburtinische Sibylle*, Halle: Max Niemeyer.

Scheffer-Boichorst, P. (ed.) (1874) 'Chronica Albrici monachi Trium Fontium', MGH, Scriptores, vol. 23, Hanover, 631–950.

Schmieder, F. (1994) *Europa und die Fremden. Die Mongolen im Urteil des Abendlandes vom 13. bis in das 15. Jahrhundert*, Beiträge zur Geschichte und Quellenkunde des Mittelalters 16, Sigmaringen: Jan Thorbecke.

Sinor, D. (1977) 'Le Mongol vu par l'Occident', in *1274 année charnière: mutations et continuités, Lyon-Paris 30 septembre–5 octobre 1974*, Paris, Centre Nationale de Recherches Scientifiques, 55–72.

Slessarev, V. (1959) *Prester John. The Letter and the Legend*, Minneapolis: University of Minnesota Press.

Smalley, B. (1983) *The Study of the Bible in the Middle Ages*, 3rd edn, Oxford: Blackwell.

Strakosch-Grassmann, G. (1893) *Der Einfall der Mongolen in Mitteleuropa in den Jahren 1241 und 1242*, Innsbruck: Verlag der Wagner'schen Universitäts-Buchhandlung.

Szcześniak, B. (1956) 'The mission of Giovanni de Plano Carpini and Benedict the Pole of Vratislavia to Halicz', *Journal of Ecclesiastical History* 7: 12–20.

Van den Wyngaert, A. (ed.) (1929) *Sinica Franciscana*, vol. 1. *Itinera et relationes Fratrum Minorum saeculi XIII et XIV*, Quaracchi-Firenze: Collegium S. Bonaventurae.

Vincent of Beauvais (1473) *Speculum Historiale*, Straßburg: Johann Mentelin.

Voegelin, E. (1940–1) 'The Mongol orders of submission to European powers, 1245–1255', *Byzantion* 15: 378–413.

Von den Brincken, A.D. (1973) *Die 'Nationes Orientalium Christianorum' im Verständnis der lateinischen Historiographie*, Kölner Historische Abhandlungen 22, Cologne: Böhlau.

—— (1975) 'Die Mongolen im Weltbild der Lateiner um die Mitte des 13. Jahrhunderts unter besonderer Berücksichtigung des "Speculum Historiale" des Vincenz von Beauvais OP', *Archiv für Kulturgeschichte* 57: 117–40.

Von Martels, Z. (ed.) (1994) *Travel Fact and Travel Fiction. Studies on fiction, literary tradition, scholarly discovery and observation in travel writing*, Leiden: Brill.

Waitz, G. (ed.) (1879) 'Gestorum Treverorum Continuatio Quarta', MGH, Scriptores, vol. 24, Hanover, 390–404.

—— (ed.) (1882) 'Ex annalibus S. Medardi Suessionensibus', MGH, Scriptores, vol. 26, Hanover, 518–22.

—— (ed.) (1884) *Ottonis et Rahewini Gesta Friderici Imperatoris*, Scriptores Rerum Germanicarum, Hanover.

Wattenbach, W. (ed.) (1851) 'Continuatio Sancrucensis secunda', MGH, Scriptores, vol. 9, Hanover, 637–46.

Weiland, L. (ed.) (1874) 'Menkonis Chronicon', MGH, Scriptores, vol. 23, Hanover, 523–61.

Wilmans, R. (ed.) (1867) 'Ottonis Episcopi Frisingensis Chronicon', MGH, Scriptores, vol. 20, Hanover, 83–301.

Wittkower, R. (1942) 'Marvels of the East: a study in the history of monsters', *Journal of the Warburg and Courtauld Institutes* 5: 159–97.

—— (1957) 'Marco Polo and the pictorial tradition of the marvels of the East', in *Oriente Poliano*, Rome: Istituto italiano per il Medio e Estemo Oriente, 155–72.

Wright, J.K. (1925) *The Geographical Lore of the Time of the Crusades*, New York: American Geographical Society, Research Series 25.

Yule, Sir H. (1913) *Cathay and the Way Thither*, 2nd edn by H. Cordier, vol. 2, London: Hakluyt Society, 2nd series, 33.

—— (1914) *Cathay and the Way Thither*, 2nd edn by H. Cordier, vol. 3, London: Hakluyt Society, 2nd series, 37.

Zarncke, F. (1879) 'Der Priester Johannes', *Abhandlungen der königlichen sächsischen Gesellschaft der Wissenschaften, phil.-hist. Klasse* 7: 872–934; repr. in Beckingham and Hamilton (1996), 40–102.

Zatko, J.J. (1957) 'The Union of Suzdal, 1222–1252', *Journal of Ecclesiastical History* 8: 33–52.

THE ESTABLISHMENT OF MEDIEVAL HERMETICISM

Charles Burnett

The mystical gnostic religion of Hermes Trismegistus was one of several cults that thrived in the late Classical period. Its roots lay in Egypt, and its sacred texts were first written in Coptic and Greek, but were soon translated or imitated in several languages of the Mediterranean basin. From the beginning they comprised both theoretical texts, concerning the bases of the Hermetic religio-philosophy, and practical (or technical) texts, giving instructions for the rituals or forms of divination. By the eleventh century a corpus of eighteen theoretical texts had been assembled in Greek. This *Corpus Hermeticum* first became available in the West through the Latin translation of its first fourteen texts by Marsilio Ficino in 1463.[1] Up to that date the only Latin theoretical Hermeticum translated directly from a Greek source was the *Asclepius*, whose earliest existence in the form known in the Middle Ages is attested by its use by St Augustine.[2] The *Asclepius* travelled with the second-century Apuleius of Madaura's 'On the god of Socrates' (*De deo Socratis*) and 'On Plato and his doctrine' (*De Platone et eius dogmate*) and his translation of the Pseudo-Aristotelian 'On the World' (*De mundo*) – works which shared the *Asclepius*' concern about gods and 'demons' (*daemones*); this combination was probably already known to Augustine. In the twelfth century this collection of texts began to be copied again in a significant number of manuscripts.[3] It is the contention of this chapter that this new interest in the *Asclepius* can be associated with a renaissance of Hermeticism, when a concerted attempt was made to supplement from Arabic sources the dearth of theoretical and technical Hermetic works in Latin.[4]

THE *ASCLEPIUS*

The language of the *Asclepius*, in common with that of the rest of the *Corpus Hermeticum*, is that of a mystery religion. Trismegistus is the initiator. Initiation takes place in a sanctuary (*adytum*). It is available only to the few. Initiation leads to knowledge; and knowledge leads to salvation. The salient points are that the universe is one and manifests perfect order; God is the creator of all things, and *is* all things; the forms of all things are already latent in matter (*hyle*) which is accompanied by spirit; matter has to be appropriately prepared before it can receive forms; generation occurs through generating (i.e. masculine) principles which come from above, and nourishing (i.e. feminine) principles which come from below; the heavens are a perceptible god which administers all bodies; growth and decline are under the control of the Sun and the Moon; the movement of the Sun and the stars determines the times of things; the thirty-six constellations of the zodiac and each of the spheres of the planets has a 'sensible god' (called an 'ousiarch') ruling it, which creates and controls the lower natures. The world of generation and corruption is created out of four elements, but man has a 'fifth part' which comes from the aether; man is a 'great wonder' (*magnum miraculum*), whose nature links the divine to the terrestrial; he can use the power of words, which are spirits declaring a person's whole wish; he can create gods by making statues (*statuae*) or 'likenesses' (*imagines*) out of plants, stones and spices (which have in them a natural power of divinity), and implanting life in them by calling up the souls of demons or angels (*daemones vel angeli*); these man-made gods have the power of looking after things and foretelling the future through lots and divination. These last points provide the rationale for technical Hermeticism. The *Asclepius* ends with a specimen of the Hermetic liturgy: a hymn to the supreme and most high god.

ARABIC TECHNICAL HERMETICISM: TALISMANS AND *NECROMANTIA*

Round about the year 1100 European thought experienced a change of climate. A new rigour was introduced in theology and spirituality, manifested especially in the Cluniac reform. But there was also a readiness to explore different ways of thinking about the world – ways in which the secular sciences achieved much greater prominence than before. In the later twelfth century, this interest is shown in the translations of the works on natural science by Aristotle, both from Greek (in Italy and Byzantium) and from Arabic (in Toledo). But at first the inspiration came mainly from the Islamic world, with which Latin scholars had contact on three fronts: in northern Spain, in Sicily, and in the Holy Land. Arabic scholars had not only brought the most important works of scholarship from Baghdad to Spain, but also developed their own scholarship there, and most significant in the early twelfth century was the valley of the Ebro, the area of influence of the last vestiges of the Moorish kingdom of Zaragoza, whose kings, the Banū Hūd, were mathematicians.[5]

The agents of the change were a few maverick scholars who travelled great distances in search of wisdom. One of these was Adelard, the son of Fastred, whose home was Bath in Somerset (*c.*1080–*c.*1152), but who travelled the length of the Mediterranean, spending time both in Syracuse (Sicily) and in the principality of Antioch. He came to know three Arabic works which included Hermetic wisdom: the *Abbreviation of the Introduction to Astrology of* Abū Ma'shar (Baghdad, 787–886), which mentions some 'lots' of Hermes, used for astrological divination (Abū Ma'shar, 1994: 130); the *Centiloquium* of Pseudo-Ptolemy, of which the ninth *verbum* gives the opinions of the 'domini prestigiorum' ('the masters of talismans'); and the *Liber prestigiorum* of Thābit [b. Qurra (Baghdad, 826–901)] following Ptolemy and Hermes'. He translated these works into Latin, as part of his study of the science of the stars, by which he and his colleagues were establishing the new profession of 'astrologer'. Adelard's choice of the term 'prestigium' implies that he thought that he had found precisely the knowledge that Isidore of Seville imputes to Mercury (i.e. Hermes), who 'is said to have been the first to invent magic (*praestigium*)' (*Etymologiae*, VIII, 9, 33). He turns the term 'praestigium' from having a negative connotation to having a positive one, and referring specifically to 'talismans'. For the text provides the instructions for summoning the aid of spirits to empower appropriately prepared inorganic matter. A common term for this procedure was also taken from Isidore: i.e. 'necromantia'. But, while Isidore etymologised the word correctly, defining 'necromantii' as those by whose incantations 'the dead, having been resuscitated, seem to divine the future and reply to questions put to them' (*Etymologiae*, VIII, 9, 11), the usual medieval sense of the word is the summoning of spirits to empower talismans, i.e. a sense much closer to the statue-making of the *Asclepius* (Kieckhefer 1989: 151–75; see also Burnett 1996: I). The main difference is that the term 'spiritus' or 'spirituale' is used instead of the 'daemones' of the *Asclepius*, which among Christians had acquired the negative sense that 'demon' still retains.

Adelard's contemporary, Petrus Alfonsi, travelled in the reverse direction. He had been born a Jew, and was educated in an Islamic milieu in Huesca, which was part of the kingdom of Zaragoza before being incorporated into Aragón in 1096. After his conversion to Christianity in 1106 he travelled in France and England, where he was closely associated with Adelard. Adelard and Petrus both knew the same version of the Arabic astronomical tables of al-Khwārizmī; it is likely that Petrus brought a copy of these tables to England where both scholars rendered them into Latin in the West Country. Petrus too, was an advocate of the new 'science of the stars', but he also wrote a book on secular education and good manners – *Disciplina clericalis* ('the education of the clerk'). Here he lists 'necromantia' as a viable alternative for one of the seven liberal arts necessary for a complete education, an alternative to be chosen by 'those who admit the possibility of prophecies' (Petrus Alfonsi, 1911: 10). Although Petrus does not name Hermes,[6] he knows of a book attributed to Plato 'on prophecies' (*ibid.*: 34–5), which describes such an expert in necromancy, named 'Marianus', who later appears in Hermetic literature as 'Morienus'.

Adelard does not use the word 'necromantia', but, in his original work, *Questions on Natural Science*, speaks of learning 'incantations from an old woman expert in prestigia (*anus prestigiosa*)' (Adelard of Bath 1998: 193).[7] In his *Liber prestigiorum* he uses precisely the term in the *Asclepius* – 'imago' – for the talismans whose manufacture he describes;[8] this term became the norm, and 'scientia imaginum' was an alternative name for 'necromantia'. As an example of how to summon spirits, we may take the invocation prescribed in the *Liber prestigiorum* for bringing about love between two people:

O shining spirits of the planets, you who descend from *al-'alām* (i.e. the macrocosm),[9] effectors of good and evil! Bind the spirit of Socrates, son of Sophroniscus, to the heart of Plato. Let their will and desire be one; let loathing and rejection be absent; but let the imagination and memory [of the other] be always present. Be present, too, spirits of the hours of the planets, not only by day, but also in the night and in their dreams. Bring the picture of Socrates' image before Plato's eyes to such an extent that, all other feelings excluded, he gives himself totally to him, by the power of God.

This invocation is pronounced as one fumigates the talisman with incense.

HERMES AND CHARTRES

Adelard and Petrus were by no means isolated figures operating on the fringes of the twelfth-century academic community. Petrus's *Disciplina clericalis* became an immediate best-seller, and Adelard's versions of Euclid's *Elements* and al-Khwārizmī's astronomical tables were introduced soon after their composition into the foremost centre of learning in France at the time: the cathedral school of Chartres. This may have been largely the work of the enterprising chancellor of the cathedral, Thierry, who apparently commissioned translations from Arabic, and incorporated some of them into his vast and ambitious 'Library of the Seven Liberal Arts' (*Heptateuchon*; early 1140s), in which he attempted to put the whole of secular learning within the covers of two massive volumes. In his original works Thierry uses the *Asclepius* as a direct source at critical points. In the culmination of his praise of man's potential in his *Glosa* on Boethius' *De Trinitate*, he states, on the authority of 'Mercurius', that in certain cases this can lead him even to becoming a god.[10] In his innovatory commentary on the first chapter of Genesis, *On the Works of the Six Days*, he quotes at length the description of God, spirit and matter (*hyle*) from 'Mercury in that book which is entitled "Trimegistus"' (Thierry of Chartres 1971: 566). Thierry claims that some people denounce him for being a 'necromancer', but his extant works do not include any references to talismans.[11]

THE COMBINATION OF THE *ASCLEPIUS* WITH ARABIC HERMETICA: HERMANN OF CARINTHIA

Hermann of Carinthia (*fl.* 1138–43) is another wandering scholar who was lured from his homeland to search for wisdom. He was first attracted, apparently, by the reputation of Chartres, for he calls Thierry his teacher, but then went on to the south of France and northern Spain to find Arabic texts on geometry and the science of the stars. In this, he collaborated with Robert of Ketton, who became an archdeacon in the church of Pamplona. At the same time Peter the Venerable, the reforming abbot of Cluny, was also travelling in search of information: this time, for reliable interpretations of the scriptures of the Muslims, in order to ward off Islam with the tools of reason. The reforming movement of the Church and the new interest in secular science met in the persons of Hermann and Robert. For, such was their reputation as interpreters of Arabic, that, in 1141, Peter the Venerable commissioned them to translate the Koran and other Islamic texts (Iogna-Prat 1998, *passim*).

Hermann knew the *Abbreviation of the Introduction to Astrology*, probably in Adelard's translation, which he replaced with a translation of Abū Maʿshar's

Introduction itself, and translated several other texts on geometry, astronomy and weather forecasting from Arabic, one of which he dedicated to Thierry. In his original work, *De essentiis*, completed in Béziers in 1143, he shows his interest in works favoured by Thierry: both the *Asclepius* and Plato's *Timaeus*, another text which became popular in the early twelfth century for its cosmological ideas.[12] The form of the *De essentiis* is based on that of the *Timaeus*, but its contents betray Hermann's intelligent use of a wide range of Latin and Arabic sources. Prominent among these are Hermetica. Hermes and 'Trimegistus' are quoted by name more than any other authority.

For Hermann, 'Trimegistus' is the author of the *Asclepius*, and 'Hermes' is a Persian philosopher 'whom the Arabic histories concerning the first authors of astronomy mention, long before Porus who was a contemporary of Alexander of Macedon' (59vA). The distinction between Trimegistus and an earlier, more divine, Hermes is already implicit in the *Asclepius* in which Trismegistus mentions 'Hermes, whose family name I bear . . . ',[13] and is made more explicit by St Augustine in his *City of God*: ' . . . the elder Hermes, whose grandson was Trismegistus.'[14] But Hermann may have known from Arabic sources of a succession of three Hermes, of which the last one passed his wisdom to Asclepius. For Abū Ma'shar relates such a story in his *Kitāb al-ulūf*, a work which Hermann cites (Pingree 1968: 14–19). The legend of the three Hermes, however, was also present in Arabic alchemical circles, from which Robert of Chester, who may be the same as Hermann's colleague Robert of Ketton,[15] took the information in the preface of his translation of the earliest attributable translation of an Arabic alchemical work into Latin, the *Liber Morieni* (this 'Morienus' is the same as the 'Marianus' known to Petrus Alfonsi). In this preface, Asclepius is not mentioned, but the third Hermes is described as 'Ter megistus' and is said to have ruled in Egypt (Burnett 1996: V).

These legends pointed out the continuity of the mystical-philosophical learning preserved and revealed by a succession of avatars of the God Hermes, and gave a rationale for medieval scholars to recover and pass on this lore. Hermann sets the scene for this learning in the preface to his *De essentiis* in which he refers to the joint studies of Robert and himself in terms of a mystery religion. The studies have taken place in 'sanctuaries' (*adyta*: Hermann uses the same word as that which occurs at the beginning of the *Asclepius*), and in writing about them for a more general public Hermann fears to incur the crime of Numenius, who dreamt that, in publicizing the Eleusinian mysteries, he had made prostitutes out of the goddesses. Religious scrupulousness (*pietas*) prevents Hermann from revealing the underclothes (*interulae*) of wisdom, which he and Robert had acquired from the innermost treasuries of the Arabs (58rD–E).

Hermann, like Thierry, quotes the *Asclepius* at climactic points in his work. For example, he ends the first of the two books of the *De essentiis* with an evocation of the harmonic make-up of the universe, as a result of which the higher parts of the world elicit the movements of the lower by sympathetic vibration: 'hence Trimegistus, too, understood that nothing is a more pleasing gift to the gods from men than the performance of music, since from time immemorial music alone has been deemed worthy for praising the deity, because those wonderful choruses of the celestial virgins chant it in perpetual harmony to preserve the peace of the whole body of the universe' (68rH–68vA; cf. *Asclepius*, 9). Hermes, on the other hand, is the venerable authority of Abū Maʿshar (63rG), whose cosmological theory, including the law of movement by sympathetic vibration, Hermann follows above that of any other source.

The authority of Hermes and Trimegistus come together in the section of the *De essentiis* devoted to 'incorporeal animals' (72rG–73vF). Here Hermann refers to Trimegistus's teaching on man-made gods and the reason why different gods are worshipped by different peoples. But he adds a detail from the *Aurea virga* ('The Golden Bough') in which 'Hermes recites the very words addressed to him by his familiar spirit (*privatus*) speaking to him' (72vD); a Hermetic work known as 'the Golden Bough' is mentioned in the *Fihrist* of the tenth-century Arabic bibliographer, al-Nadīm, but the text itself has not been identified. A more substantial quotation is taken from another Hermetic work that Hermann calls 'Aristotle's *Data neiringet*'. The quotation is long enough to make it clear that this has the same subject-matter as the group of works with names ending in *-āṭīs*, *-īṭīs*, *-ūṭās* and *-akhis*, which purport to be the words of Hermes as reported by Aristotle. Characteristic of these texts is a cosmogony in which the importance of spirits and the central position of man is emphasised; the animal, vegetable and mineral parts of the universe are inter-related, and detailed descriptions are given on how to bring together related parts in order to prepare talismans for the reception of spiritual forces. The word used for such talismans is the Persian term 'nairanjāt', which is the word that appears in the title given by Hermann (probably = *dhāt an-nairanjāt*, 'the essence of the talismans').

A Latin text is extant with the heading: 'Liber est spiritualium operum Aristotilis et est liber Antimaquis qui est liber secretorum Hermetis. Opera mira possunt operari per hunc librum et est liber antiquus septem planetarum' ('This is the book on operating spiritual forces by Aristotle, and it is the book of *Antimaquis* which is the book of the secrets of Hermes. Wonderful things can be performed by means of this book, and it is the ancient book of the seven planets').[16] This text corresponds to portions of two extant Arabic texts of this genre: one entitled 'a commentary on the book of the *Madāṭīs*', the other described as 'the book of Hermes on the spiritual forces' (*kitāb Hirmis fi'l-rūḥānīyāt*)' which is the second part of 'Hermes's *kitāb al-Ustūwaṭās*'. Both Arabic and Latin texts describe the relationship of the macrocosm to the microcosm in great detail. Man's head corresponds to the firmament, his chest to the sphere of the twelve signs, and his feet to the earth. Through the seven 'doors' of his head – two eyes, two ears, two nostrils and mouth – which are assigned to each of the seven planets – the spiritual influx passes into the chest, where it rules the seven interior organs, the heart, the stomach, the lungs, the liver, the spleen and the two kidneys. In each of these organs resides one psychological faculty, such as intelligence, anger, love, etc. Then in man, too, there are correspondences with the whole of the created world: the heart is in sympathy with two-footed animals, the liver with four-footed animals; to the lungs belong birds, to the spleen, fish; while insects are assigned to the kidneys. More obvious parallels are drawn for the blood (= water), the veins (= rivers), the sinews and nails, which are like rocks, and the bones which are like the mountains. The hair is like plants and trees, while the parts of the body without hair are like deserts. There follows a cosmogony, culminating

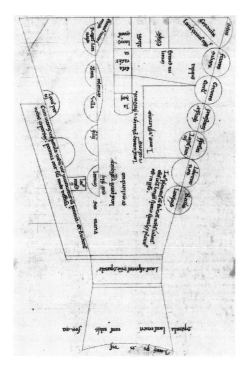

Figure 7.1 The right shoulder-blade of a sheep with places marked in Latin. © Bodleian Library, Oxford, MS. Canon. Misc. 396, fo. 112r. (see p. 120).

Figure 7.2 The right shoulder-blade of a sheep with places marked in Arabic. Istanbul, MS. Nuruosmaniye 2840. Photo: Ian Bavington Jones.

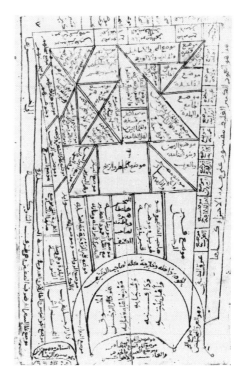

in an account of the creation of the first man and woman. The artificer God in the *Asclepius* is paralleled by the powerful spirit called Hādūs in the Arabic manuscript, and both texts have as their centrepoint the eulogy of the greatness of man. The well-known phrases of the *Asclepius* – 'a human being is a great wonder . . . everything is permitted him . . . he is everything, and he is everywhere' (*Asclepius*, 6) – are echoed in the description in the *Antimaquis* and the corresponding passages in Arabic of man as 'having power over all creatures; he knows all knowledge; he can do all things, see all things, hear all things, eat all things, drink all things. This is because he is the form of forms, embodying in himself the whole of creation, to which he is also connected by the matrix of spiritualities.'

The *Antimaquis* is not a translation by Hermann; its style is completely different, and the passage from the *Data neiringet* does not correspond verbally with the relevant passage in the *Antimaquis*. Nevertheless, Hermann's quotation of a related work suggests that this rich body of Hermetic material was available to him. In the case of another Hermetic work that he uses, however, we can be more sure that he knew the whole work. This is the *De secretis nature* attributed to Apollonius of Tyana (a contemporary of Jesus Christ). Hermann reports an episode in the discovery of the text by Apollonius underneath an altar of the Sun while he was alone in the desert (72vE–F). In another context Hermann brings together a quotation from Apollonius with one from the *Asclepius*, concerning the pre-eminent role of the Sun and the Moon in all sublunar generation.[17]

HUGO OF SANTALLA

Fortunately, Apollonius's text has survived, both in Arabic and in a Latin translation. The latter was made by Hugo of Santalla, who dedicated his translations to Michael, bishop of Tarazona from 1119 to 1151.[18] Tarazona was only a few miles from the Ebro, on whose banks Hermann and Robert had been working. The Latin translation tells the story of the discovery of the text by Apollonius underneath a statue in his home district. On the statue were some enigmatic instructions written by Hermes himself. Apollonius succeeded in interpreting these, and discovered a cave under the statue in which, after some adventures, he found an effigy of an old man with an emerald tablet in his hand and a book in front of him. The book was the *De secretis nature*, the tablet, the Emerald Tablet (*Tabula Smaragdina*), which was to become the most important text of Hermetic doctrine for Western alchemists, and of which Hugo's Latin text was apparently the earliest version (Ruska: 177–9). The last page of the *De secretis nature* finally reveals the contents of the Emerald Tablet, and here the Hermetic nature of the text, and Hugo's attitude to it, is made clear. Hugo writes:

> Having done everything that was promised, whatever Apollonius explained in this book about the secrets of nature and the recognition of things we too have poured out with a corresponding illuminating explanation, leaving out only a little. . . . At the end of his volume Apollonius says this: 'The whole teaching of the secret causes of things which the book of Hermes contained I have described in this volume for myself, my sons and any scion of philosophers, on

this condition and with the pronouncement of this anathema: that access to this treasury of wisdom should not lie open to anyone lacking in wisdom and unworthy of it. For these are the secrets of Hermes which, to guard them from less learned men, he buried, keeping them hidden in his own hands in a crypt, and raising a statue on top, so denying access to the less discerning rabble. Whoever takes pains to study them carefully will obtain the leadership in philosophy over all his contemporaries.' These are the words which Apollonius wrote at the end of his volume, leaving them to speak for themselves (*sine omni expositione*). He said: 'Entering an underground crypt, I saw a tablet of emerald between the hands of Hermes, written in this intricate truth of words (*hac verborum intricata veritate descripta*):

> Higher things from lower things, lower things from higher things,
> The operation of wonders (*prodigia*) from the One, just as all things draw
> their source from one and the same thing –
> one and the same administration of the Plan (*consilii administratione*),
> Whose father is the Sun, whose mother the Moon.
> The wind raises them in her bosom, the earth loses its bitterness.
> You, then, children of talismans (*prestigiorum filii*), workers of wonders,
> perfect in your discernment,
> generously, prudently and wisely refine what becomes earthy out of the
> subtle fire which excels all grossness and bluntness.
> It will ascend from earth to heaven, it will slip down from heaven to
> earth,
> containing the force and power of higher and lower things. Hence all
> darkness is illumined by it,
> whose power transcends whatever is subtle and penetrates every gross
> thing.
> This operation is able to subsist in accordance with the make-up of the
> macrocosm.'

This is what Hermes the philosopher calls the triple wisdom and the triple science.

This exuberant but enigmatic hymn occurs in the same position in the *De secretis naturae* as does the hymn in the *Asclepius*, and shares several of the conceits of Trismegistus, such as the unity of all things, and administration assigned to the Sun and the Moon (cf. *Asclepius*, 3). The opening and closing passages of the *De secretis naturae* express the exclusiveness of the Hermetic doctrine, which must be preserved among select wise men. They also show Hugo's personal involvement in the subject-matter. Hugo, the *magister*, uses terminology from the Latin tradition, such as 'prestigia', the Classical word re-employed by Adelard for 'talismans', and 'discretio' (in place of the Arabic 'quwwa' = 'power'), which is Adelard's favoured word for the power of discernment of the rational soul. He brings the Arabic material into the Latin Hermetic tradition.

Hugo used the same word for talismans – *praestigia* – as did Adelard, and also drew on Isidore's *Etymologies* for the names of divinatory texts that he sought to rediscover for Latin readers. He identified Arabic sand-divination with Isidore's 'geomantia', and translated a text on it, but had still to find 'aeromantia', 'piromantia' and 'idromantia'.[19] However, he made a point, above all, of translating works attributed to Hermes or depending on Hermes' authority. Among these were astrological texts: 'the hundred words' (*Centiloquium*) attributed to Ptolemy, whose 51st 'word' was Hermes' method for predicting the time of the birth of a child, and a 'book by Aristotle containing the sum of the 255 volumes of the Indians on all questions relating to nativities and the revolution of nativities' (Hugo of Santalla 1997), among whose authorities were, allegedly 'thirteen books of Hermes which they call the books of the secrets of nativities and interrogations . . . and another eight books by the same author . . . concerning what machinations the inner mind is deliberating and what issue those thoughts will have . . . '(Pro. 18–19); later in the same text we read that 'Hermes is the leader in this teaching as he is in all others' (III i 9, 22), he is 'the most skilled of the astrologers' (III ii 2, 43), and that 'people think he is the same as Buzurjmihr, the Persian sage'.[20]

A text attributed directly to Hermes and translated by Hugo is on weather forecasting: 'the book of rains produced by an ancient astrologer of the Indians called Jafar, but then abbreviated by Mercury of Cyllene'.[21] He also translated two books on divination by the shoulder-blades of sheep. One of these begins 'Incipit Liber Amblaudii et Hermetis . . . Hunc igitur librum, cuius auctor apud Caldeos Amulbarhis, apud Grecos Hermes fuisse legitur . . . ' ('Here begins the book of Amblaudius and Hermes . . . This book, whose author is said to have been Amulbarhis among the Chaldeans, but Hermes among the Greeks . . .').[22] This Latin translation closely corresponds to an Arabic text attributed to the well-known ninth-century Arab philosopher al-Kindī (whose name may lurk behind the corruption 'Amblaudius'; Baghdad, *c*. 800–870), but which in turn depends on a text attributed to 'Hermes the Philosopher' ('al-ḥakīm') of which a chapter survives. Hugo, following his Arabic source, gives the rationale for shoulder-blade divination as follows (Hugo's verbose phrases have been slightly abbreviated):

Among the many kinds of gifts of graces which God, the highest creator, wished to bestow from the treasury of his charity onto all people, the rain pours down the hidden thing of this discipline and an inner force into the very plants or grasses of the earth as the manna of His own grace and wisdom, and He marked in a marvellous way (as He wished) the shoulder-blades of those animals which feed off sustenance of this kind as if with traces and such a great secret and mystic gifts in order to instruct the ignorance of the human race. If anyone . . . wonders at the signs of the earth, the movements of the air, the reflexion of fire and flame, the flowings of waters, and what these portend [*i.e. geomancy, aeromancy, pyromancy and hydromancy*], the recognition (of the truth) of these things will not escape him. Since in these lower circles [*i.e. earth, air, fire and water*] no things exist without cause or in an otiose way, earthly things too – all of which we believe have been established for the use of men – should exhibit the effects of the same (circles). For there is in grasses, and rightly in those things that are the fuel of life, a certain force which the Creator Himself knows, inherent naturally by reason, which instils by a divine intimation the signification of superior beings, and as it were certain impressions and marks of this signification into the bodily members of grazing animals.

As far as we know, Hugo wrote no original works. However, his prefaces (such as the one just quoted), while often including material from the original Arabic prefaces, are written in the first person of the translator, and presumably express his point of view. The tone of his prefaces conjures up a secret society of mystical religio-philosophy. For example, in his preface to the *Centiloquium* of Ptolemy, Hugo exhorts his dedicatee 'not to commit the secrets of such wisdom into the hands of any unworthy individual', and in his preface to the geomancy he describes how God instils a kind of intuitive knowledge into select individuals, and the bonds which are thus established between them are parallel to the bonds which govern and preserve the universe.

This secret society, aside from recalling that of the *Asclepius*, would suit the 'adyta' in which Hermann says that Robert and he had been studying,[23] and there are evident connections between the three scholars. While the *Centiloquium* of Pseudo-Ptolemy which Hermann quotes was available in several Latin translations, the Latin translation of Apollonius's *De secretis nature* was little known. Moreover, Hermann's biological account of cosmos, in which the elements are 'seeds', generation is caused by the 'marrying' of masculine and feminine elements, and everything is connected through bonds of love, corresponds to the philosophy of the *De secretis nature*.[24]

Hermann, Robert and Hugo were active at the same time and in the same area, and Hugo and Hermann's technical terminology is remarkably similar. But there is more tangible evidence that the three scholars collaborated. For Hermann, Robert and Hugo all seem to have been involved in an elaborate project which was to replace the superstitious astrology of their Latin contemporaries with an exalted science of the stars which had as its principal authorities Hermes and Ptolemy. The plan is described by Robert, who, in a letter to Peter the Venerable, promises 'a celestial gift which embraces within itself the whole of science, revealing according to number, proportion and measure, all the celestial circles and their quantities, orders and conditions, and, finally, all the various movements of the stars and their effects and natures and everything else of this kind' (Hermann of Carinthia, 1982: 6).

The project evidently involved translating the most authoritative Arabic texts on judicial astrology[25] and arranging the chapters from each of these translations according to subject. Robert contributed by translating on Hermann's request a text on the subject by al-Kindī, 'the most authoritative of the masters in this science', and the earliest form of the project included only three Arabic astrologers, al-Kindī, Sahl ibn Bishr and 'Umar ibn al-Farrukhān.[26] The manuscripts of this 'Book of the Three Judges' (*Liber trium iudicum*) give two dedicatees, Michael, Hugo's patron, and 'mi karissime R.' ('my dearest R.'), who can hardly be anyone other than Hermann's dearest friend, Robert of Ketton, but the style of the preface is that of Hugo.[27] The full version – the 'Book of the Nine Judges' (*Liber novem iudicum*) – consists of the three judges plus four more, and a long section ('introitus') introducing the concepts and terms of astrology, drawn from a different selection of four Arabic authors (making nine different authorities altogether). Between the *introitus* and the judgements is an elaborate essay which bears indications of the hands of both Hermann and Hugo.

The preface to the *Book of the Three Judges* emphasises the exalted nature of the science of the stars, and, while it does not refer to Hermes or the *Asclepius* directly, it quotes from both Apuleius' *De deo Socratis* and his *De Platone et eius dogmate*, which accompany the *Asclepius* in the twelfth-century manuscripts of the work. In the essay within the *Book of the Nine Judges*, however, the Hermetic authority for the material is made explicit. It is here that we find the Latin authors describing the exalted nature of their subject matter, and firmly situating it within the context of Hermetic knowledge. The following sentences[28] summarise certain parts of this essay, and give some feeling for the tone of the writing:

> The wonderful nature of our subject demands that we should approach it with awe and great care. We seek to understand nature by turning our attention to the movements of created things, and the variety of the movements of the planets and stars. . . . Our science is revealed only to the intelligent chosen ones. It is based on the soundest authorities: first, Hermes, the follower of Abidemon, who investigated the kinds of movement which led to effects. Then Ptolemy, who added to this knowledge the notion of a correspondence in the proportions of the substances of the lower world and those of the heavenly natures, thus setting up a cosmological system in which one part vibrates in sympathy with the movement of the other. This explains the reason why the forces of the stars are felt not only in other animate beings,[29] but also in inanimate beings. They are felt intimately by animate beings, but they are received more swiftly by inanimate ones. This movement in inanimate beings conforms to a greater or lesser degree with the movement of the stars according to the aptitude of the form of the being for taking up that movement, and the relationship of its matter to the matter of the stars . . . How, then, can the heavens seem redundant?[30] Both Trimegistus and Plato support our view. According to Plato, all mortal things, whether they are produced by the mixing of different things, or from procreation within one species, reach their perfection to the extent that they are influenced by the heavenly bodies. Man was God's last creation, but he is not in consequence the least significant of created things. For, not only did God make him of two substances – a heavenly (soul) and an earthly (body) – He also refined that earthly element by making it conform to heaven – for the heaven itself had a body and a soul. Man was only the final thing to be caused in order that he might be obliged to use his intellect to climb back up the ladder of causes and effects until he rose to the level of contemplating the First Cause itself. But as men (in the course of history) climbed this ladder of causes they reached a stage where they were looking at the movements of the heavens, which first impressed them by their beauty, then by the regularity of their laws.

The doctrines and attitudes expressed here correspond to those in Hermann's *De essentiis* and Hugo's prefaces. They amount to a self-consistent cosmology and anthropology which, on the Latin side, drew on the *Asclepius*, Apuleius's philosophical works and other Neoplatonic writings, on the Arabic, on writings attributed to Hermes and his followers Apollonius, Thābit b. Qurra and Abū Ma'shar. This

Hermetic cosmology was an alternative system to Aristotelian cosmology. Unlike their contemporaries in Italy and Byzantium, and later translators in Toledo, Hermann, Robert and Hugo played no part in the recovery of Aristotle's natural science and metaphysics. They were drawn in another direction. They wished to establish a science which led to a virtuous life, and therefore embraced a practical as well as a theoretical dimension. The theoretical dimension focused on the wonderful nature of man and his unique relation to the creator God, and, as such, contemplated in particular the highest element in God's creation, i.e. the heavens. This science therefore was most appropriately linked with astronomy, which, in the words of the preface to the *Book of the Three Judges*, 'not only had obtained the ultimate position in mathematics, but also, being the most sublime, had merited the highest dignity' (Burnett 1977: 78). One form that the practical dimension took was that of the work of alchemy and the pursuit of the philosopher's stone. As we have seen, an early translation of an Arabic work on alchemy was made by Robert of Chester, but research on the rich and complicated Arabic–Latin tradition of alchemy is at such an early stage that it would be premature to make any further comments on this here (Halleux 1996). Another form of practice was astrology and the concomitant divinatory arts. The underlying Hermetic cosmology elevated these practices onto a spiritual level and endowed their practitioners with the reputation of sages.

To what extent these Latin scholars were influenced by mystical–philosophical sects already established in Jewish and Arabic circles in Spain is difficult to assess, and needs further research.[31] The one slender testimony we have concerning the original Arabic texts of Hugo's translations strengthens the impression that the Arabic texts too were transmitted in the context of secrecy and mystery. For he writes that he found an astronomical work 'among the more secret depths of the library' (*inter secretiora bibliotece penetralia*) of Rueda de Jalón, the stronghold to which the Banū Hūd escaped after the fall of their kingdom of Zaragoza in 1110 (Haskins 1927: 73).

But there is a contradiction in the work of Hermann, Robert and Hugo. Although Hugo might repeat the words of his original texts about the necessity for secrecy and selective initiation into the mysteries, he dedicated his translations to a public figure, Michael, bishop of Tarazona. Hermann goes further in admitting, in the *De essentiis*, that he is revealing the mysteries to a general public, and he and Robert promote their works among two of the leading churchmen and educators of their day, Peter the Venerable and Thierry of Chartres. The authority of Hermes, the alleged contemporary of Moses and supposed prophet of the birth of Christ,[32] may have been thought to be sufficient to make his writings acceptable by Christians; an anonymous twelfth-century author of a work on medical astrology could assume that the trinity associated with Hermes was the Christian Trinity.[33]

How much support this new Hermeticism enjoyed is unclear. Two English works written within the twelfth century betray a sympathetic knowledge of the new Hermetica: the *Philosophia* of Daniel of Morley, who quotes the *Asclepius* (as 'Trimegistus') and 'Magnus Hermes', and knows a 'Book of Venus' by 'Thoz the Greek'; and the *Liber Hermetis de sex rerum principiis*, which mentions the *Virga aurea* and the book on alchemy by Morienus, and also attributes a text by Adelard of Bath (his *Ezich*, or translation of the astronomical tables of al-Khwārizmī) to Hermes.[34]

Both authors are clearly indebted to the work of Adelard and Hermann. On the other hand, Bernardus Silvestris of Tours, who dedicated his *Cosmographia* to Thierry in 1148–9, adopted elements from the *Asclepius* and from Apuleius's philosophical works with enthusiasm (Dronke 1978: 17, 72–5), but his knowledge of any of the Arabic Hermetica has yet to be proved.[35]

HERMETICISM IN THE THIRTEENTH CENTURY

Where a continuation of interest in Hermetica can be demonstrated is at a less literary and more pragmatic level, namely among some thirty titles of books on the practice of the science of talismans ('imaginum scientia') in the *Speculum astronomiae*, usually attributed to Albertus Magnus, and written in 1255–65. The author classifies these books according to their attribution to Hermes (with whom Apollonius is associated) and Thoz the Greek, to Solomon, to Muhammad, and to Raziel; the first category is by far the largest.[36] What is striking is that, when we leave aside the translations of Adelard, Hermann, Robert and Hugo, the great majority of these texts are anonymous translations.[37] This might suggest that the Latin translator was afraid of revealing his identity because he feared criticism from the Church. But a likelier explanation lies in a change of translation style in the second half of the twelfth century.

It is at this time that the Arabic–Latin translation movement became centred on the city of Toledo and the activity of Gerard of Cremona (1110–87). A characteristic of the literal translations of Gerard of Cremona and his followers was the absence of prefaces and the absence of the translators' names (Burnett 1977: 65–6). That Hermetic works were translated and studied in Toledo is indicated not only by the occurrence in some of these works of terminology found in the translations of Gerard, but also by the persistence of legends of Toledo being a centre for the study of 'necromancy', which, while obviously exaggerated, probably had a basis in fact (Ferreira Alemparte 1983). If the translations originate from Gerard's circle, it is not surprising that they are anonymous.

Nevertheless, thirteenth-century discussions of Hermetic science betray a critical attitude towards it which is not present among the scholars of the valley of the Ebro. The aim of the *Speculum astronomiae* was to sort out which books in the area of the science of the stars were licit and which illicit. Talismans which rely on the power directly drawn from a celestial figure inscribed on them are allowed. However, two other categories of talismans are to be condemned: those which use inscribed names in unknown languages and 'characters' (symbols), since these inscriptions might disguise what is against the honour of the Catholic faith ('Solomonic magic'); and those which require the burning of special herbs ('suffumigations') and the chanting of invocations ('Hermetic magic'). Both these condemned types are characterised as 'necromantic'; the necromantic element being that, in the first instance, the names of planetary (and other) angels may be inscribed, in the second instance, the angels are summoned. The author of the *Speculum* suggests that these 'angels' are not angels but 'daemones'. While using the two terms already found in the *Asclepius*, 'daemones' now has its negative connotation, which was general in the Middle Ages. In a later chapter (ch. 17), geomancy, hydromancy, aeromancy, pyromancy (the 'mancies' Hugo promised to translate texts on), as well as chiromancy, are said to be 'coterminous with necromancy' (*quorum nomina necromantiae sunt conterminalia*).

A more thorough condemnation of Hermetic science, which embraces both the Latin *Asclepius* and the Arabic Hermetica, is found in the work of William of Auvergne, bishop of Paris from 1228 to 1249. In his *De legibus* he equates the talismans made by his contemporaries with the man-made statues described in the *Asclepius*, nicely bringing together the terminology from the Latin and the Arabic traditions (*De legibus*, 23, pp. 66–7):

> The third kind of idols, or talismans (*imagines*) were, according to their opinion, a man-made God (*deus factitius*), i.e. in which a kind of splendour of divinity and power of spirit (*numen*) was poured in or impressed by celestial spirits or the heavens themselves and the stars and luminaries, and this pouring or sculpting or fabricating[38] was done according to their observations of certain hours and constellations. The survivals of this error are still with us among many Christian old women . . . They have ordained suffumigations, forms of words and incantations for these talismans (*imagines*) as if they were true Gods, although man-made. Mercury Trismegistus extolled this invention in the book which he wrote 'de hellera', i.e. about the God of Gods,[39] saying these words, that 'among all the wonderful things, the most wonderful is that man could discover the divine nature and create it (*Asclepius*, 37)'. He also says there expressly that some gods are natural, others man-made (*factitii*).

William then quotes the relevant passages of the *Asclepius* in full, to demonstrate that Trismegistus really meant what he appears to be saying, and ends with the phrase concerning the gods' enjoyment of music that Hermann quoted so enthusiastically at the conclusion of the first book of his *De essentiis*. He then proceeds:

> Whether Mercury by these words understood these two kinds of idols and execrable talismans (*imagines*), or only that kind to which he says the souls of *daemones* have been given, it can in no way be doubted that he attributed a divine virtue and nature to false statues or talismans (*imagines*) of this kind, whether made only under certain constellations, or with dreadful sacrifices and orations, inscriptions and figures added to these constellations. Others seem to have been seduced into this same error from their attitude towards the planets, the luminaries and the heavens: for just as they believed that from the favour of the constellations under which they were born, certain men acquired superiority over others, i.e. as kings, princes, prophets or wise men, so certain powers not so much of obtaining as of providing these things were credited to talismans (*imagines*), and this can be read explicitly in the books they wrote about talismans (*praestigia et imagines*) and other sacrilegious malpractices.

William then gives some examples from *libri de imaginibus*, concerning talismans for ridding one place of flies, another of scorpions, and for liberating someone from captivity, and ends the chapter with an uncompromising attack on all forms of idolatry, of which the 'cultus daemonum' is the first. His wording might be strong, but his attacks here and elsewhere[40] at least attest to the success that twelfth-century scholars had in blending the Latin Hermetica of the *Asclepius* with Arabic Hermetica. However, it is a measure of the success of both his attack and that of the author of the *Speculum astronomiae* that virtually none of the Hermetic texts mentioned by both authors, except the *Asclepius* itself, survive in manuscripts of the thirteenth or early fourteenth century. They had, as it were, been driven underground by officialdom. Only in the fifteenth century do we find the twelfth and early thirteenth-century translations of Arabic Hermetica copied again in a significant number of manuscripts (Burnett 1996: XVI). This reflects the change of intellectual atmosphere which eventually led to the rediscovery of the Greek *Corpus Hermeticum* and Marsilio Ficino's translation of it.

It is not coincidental that both the fifteenth century and the twelfth century are referred to as times of renaissance. They share an openness to new ways of thought, an enthusiasm for discovering lost ancient works. And in some ways, one could say that Marsilio Ficino, Pico della Mirandola, and other Renaissance *magi* were merely picking up the Hermetic tradition where Adelard of Bath, Robert of Ketton, Hermann of Carinthia and Hugo of Santalla had left off.[41] The innovation of Ficino was to rediscover and make available the Middle- and Neoplatonic Greek sources which provided the intellectual framework into which technical Hermetic magic could be fitted. This involved translating not only the *Corpus Hermeticum*, but also portions of the *Enneads* of Plotinus, Iamblichus's *On the Mysteries of the Egyptians, Chaldeans and Assyrians*, Proclus's *On Sacrifice and Magic*, and Synesius's *On Dreams*. If twelfth-century Latin scholars had had these available, the history of Hermeticism in the Middle Ages might have taken a different course.

NOTES

1 For a useful and up-to-date account of the contents and tradition of the Greek *Corpus Hermeticum*, see the introduction to the English translation in Copenhaver 1992; see also Kingsley 1991. I am grateful to Paolo Lucentini and David Porreca for advice.

2 The only medieval Latin translations of technical Hermetica from Greek are the *Kyranides* (translated by Paschal the Roman in 1169) the *Compendium aureum, Liber Thessali de virtutibus 19 herbarum, De 7 Herbis* and the *Liber Hermetis Trismegisti de triginta sex decanis* (in two fifteenth-century manuscripts).

3 For the manuscripts see Klibansky and Regen 1993, and Lucentini 1995. For the 'Middle Platonic' nature of these texts and their influence on twelfth-century Platonism, see Gersh 1982.

4 It is not my intention to trace the sources of Arabic Hermetica, which, with few exceptions, do not correspond verbally with any Greek Hermeticum, and are usually considered to have come into being in the context of the star-worshippers of Harran (Pingree 1980 and 1987, and Burnett 1996: III).

5 For the relations between the last of these kings and the Aragonese rulers, see Beech 1993.

6 One must note, however, that the *Disciplina clericalis* begins with a quotation from 'Enoch, the philosopher who is called Idris in Arabic': these are respectively the Jewish and Arabic sages identified with Hermes.

7 For women as purveyors of popular magic, compare Daniel 1975: 285, and see p. 125 above.

8 Early in the text Adelard transcribes the Arabic word (which in turn was a transcription from Greek) 'atalecim', but for the rest of the text he uses 'ymago' or, occasionally, 'prestigium'.

9 Al-'alām' literally means 'the world'; the word appears as 'elaalem' in the Latin manuscripts.

10 Thierry of Chartres 1971: 270 (referred to in Gregory 1988: 77); cf. *Asclepius*, 7; see also Gersh 1982.

11 Thierry of Chartres 1988: 108, cited in Dronke 1988: 363.

12 Hermann of Carinthia 1982: 4–5. The system of reference to the text of the *De essentiis* is by the divisions of the folios of its principal manuscript.

13 *Asclepius*, 37. Note that nowhere in the text of the Latin *Asclepius* are the words Hermes and Trismegistus brought together. In every case the initiator-teacher is called 'Trismegistus' (usually rendered 'Trimegistus' in the Middle Ages). Only in the title are the two names brought together in an attempted transliteration of the genitive of the Greek form of the name: 'Ermu trismegiston'.

14 Augustine, *De civitate Dei*, XVIII, 39; cf. Dronke 1990: 35.

15 The two Roberts have been assumed to be the same (see Haskins 1927: 120–3), but Richard Southern's attempt to separate them (Southern 1992: xlvii–xlix) has some justification. Nevertheless, Robert of Chester may still be associated with the authors so far mentioned, since he revised Adelard's translation of the astronomical tables of al-Khwārizmī.

16 A detailed account of the contents of the *Antimaquis* and its Arabic forebears is given in Burnett 1996: VII; see Hermes, *Antimaquis* (2001).

17 *De essentiis*, 65vC: 'His duobus [*sc. Sole et Luna*] in omnem generationem tamquam – ut Apollonius Thebanus affirmat – mundi parentibus fundatis, Trimegistus vero ex altero vitam, ex altero incrementum geniture mutuatur.'

18 Apollonius of Tyana (Balīnūs) (1997–9). I quote directly from the MS Paris, BNF, lat. 13951.

19 Cf. Haskins 1927: 78, quoting the preface to Hugo's translation of an Arabic text on 'sand-divination'; Isidore, *Etymologiae*, VIII, 9, 13.

20 III iv 2, 1: 'Ante cetera ergo omnia summi astrologorum Zarmahuz quem Hermetem fore estimant sentenciam exequemini.' Other transcriptions of the name 'Zarmahuz' suggest that it is the Buzurjmihr who wrote a commentary on Vettius Valens's astrological handbook, *The Anthologies*, in Persian in the sixth century AD. The identity with Hermes may be Hugo's own (see Hugo of Santalla 1997: 159–60), but, as we have seen, Hermann also considers Hermes to be Persian.

21 Haskins 1927: 77. The identification of Mercurius as 'Cillenius' (after the cave on Mt Cyllene in Arcadia in which Hermes is said to have been born) also occurs in Apuleius, *De mundo*, 29.

22 Burnett, 1996: XIII, p. 40 and Hermes, *De spatula* (2001). See Fig.7.

23 See p. 115 above.

24 This is demonstrated at greater length in Burnett 1988: 397–400.

25 This is the genre of astrology in which the client asks the astrologer for a 'judgement' on a wide range of secular matters, such as marriage, travel, business deals, the sex of the unborn child, etc. Such 'libri iudiciorum' were usually prefixed by a general introduction to astrological theory.

26 The last two scholars were among the astrologers who cast the horoscope for the foundation of Baghdad in 762 AD.

27 Burnett 1977: 78–97.

28 This summary has been made from my unpublished edition based on MS Oxford, Bodleian Library, Savile 15.

29 This is a natural inference from a belief, characteristic of Platonists, that the stars have souls (i.e., are animate).

30 The author is replying to the typical criticism of those who deny astrology's validity.

31 Hermetic works were known not only to Petrus Alfonsi (see above) but also to Abraham ibn Ezra (*c*.1092–*c*.1157), the Jewish scholar from Tudela, who, aside from composing a wide range of works in Hebrew, collaborated with Christian scholars to produce Latin texts on the science of the stars, and to Moses ibn Ezra (Spain, *c*.1055–after 1135; see Fenton 1976).

32 See Abelard, *Theologia 'Scholarium'*, 1.115 (ed. Mews, p. 363). Abelard's quotations from the *Asclepius* are not direct, but via Pseudo-Augustine (Quodvultdeus), *Contra quinque haereses*.

33 MSS London, British Library, Royal 12.E.XXV and Oxford, Bodleian, Digby 57 refer to 'librum quem Mercurius rex Egipti de fide Trinitatis . . . composuit' ('the book which Mercury the king of Egypt composed concerning the faith of the Trinity') – a phrase reminiscent of the Greek *Suda*'s description of Hermes [*c*.1000 AD] as being called 'Trismegistus on account of his praise of the Trinity'; see Copenhaver 1992: xli.

34 In spite of its title, this text is not written in a Hermetic style, and its main reason for its claim to Hermetic authorship may be the association of Hermes with cosmology and the causes of things. Another text that may be dated to the late twelfth century is the *Book of the 24 Philosophers* (*Liber viginti quattuor philosophorum*) which comments on a set of enigmatic definitions of the nature of God; in the earliest witnesses, however, only the first definition is attributed to Hermes ('God is a *monas* giving birth to a *monas*, reflecting one glowing heat onto himself'), and the text is neither written in a Hermetic style nor dependent on any Hermetic sources.

35 Richard Lemay's case for Bernard's indebtedness to Abū Maʿshar is not convincing: Lemay 1962: 258–84.

36 *Speculum astronomiae*, 11. For identifications of these works see Pingree 1994.

37 Exceptions are John of Seville, whose name is attached to one text on talismans (*De imaginibus*), and Stephen of Messina, who translated the *Centiloquium Hermetis* for Manfred, king of Sicily, 1258–66.

38 '(in)fundere', 'imprimere', 'sculpere' and 'fabricare' are verbs commonly used in the Latin *libri de imaginibus* for the manufacture of talismans.

39 This title comes from that found in most Latin manuscripts of the *Asclepius*: 'Incipit Ermu Trismegiston dehlera ad Asclepium allocuta feliciter', where 'dehlera' is probably a corruption of the Greek 'βίβλος ἱερά'. It is possible that William's interpretation of the title is influenced by the Latin transcription of the Muslims' Allah: 'Elle/Helle'.

40 The full range of William's discussion is described in Thorndike 1927: 338–71.

41 For Renaissance Hermeticism and related philosophical magic see Walker 1958; this excellent survey does not, however, draw sufficient attention to the continuities between Medieval and Renaissance magic.

BIBLIOGRAPHY

Abelard, Peter (1987), *Opera theologica III*, ed. E. M. Buytaerts and C. J. Mews, Turnholt: Brepols.

Abū Maʿšar (1994), *The Abbreviation of the Introduction to Astrology*, together with the medieval Latin translation of Adelard of Bath, ed. C. Burnett, Michio Yano and Keiji Yamamoto, Leiden: E. J. Brill.

Adelard of Bath (1998), *Conversations with His Nephew: On the Same and the Different, Questions on Natural Science*, and *On Birds*, eds C. Burnett, P. Mantas España, I. Ronca and B. van den Abeele, Cambridge: Cambridge University Press.

Apollonius of Tyana (Balinus) (1979), *Buch über das Geheimnis der Schöpfung und die Darstellung der Natur*, Arabic text ed. U. Weisser, Aleppo: Institute for the History of Arabic Science.

—— (1997–9), *De Secretis nature*, ed. F. Hudry, *Chrysopœia* 6, pp. 1–154

Asclepius (1991): in Apuleius, *De philosophia libri*, ed. C. Moreschini, Stuttgart: Teubner.

Beech, G. (1993), 'The Eleanor of Aquitaine vase, William IX of Aquitaine, and Muslim Spain', *Gesta* 32, pp. 3–10.

Burnett, C. (1977), 'A group of Arabic–Latin translators working in Northern Spain in the mid-twelfth century', *Journal of the Royal Asiatic Society, 1977* pp. 62–108.

—— (1988), 'Hermann of Carinthia', in Dronke 1988: 386–406.

—— (1996), *Magic and Divination in the Middle Ages: texts and techniques in the Islamic and Christian worlds*, Aldershot: Variorum (cited by article number, in roman numerals).

—— (1997), 'Translating from Arabic into Latin in the Middle Ages: theory, practice, and criticism', in S. G. Lofts and P. W. Rosemann (eds) *Éditer, traduire, interpreter: essais de methodologie philosophique*, Louvain-la-Neuve: Peeters, pp. 55–78.

Copenhaver, B. P. (1992), *Hermetica: The Greek* Corpus Hermeticum *and the Latin* Asclepius *in a new English translation, with notes and introduction*, Cambridge: Cambridge University Press, 1992.

Daniel of Morley (1979), *Philosophia*, ed. G. Maurach, *Mittellateinisches Jahrbuch*, 14, pp. 204–55.

Daniel, N. (1975), *The Arabs and Mediaeval Europe*, London: Longman.

Dronke, P. ed. (1978), Bernardus Silvestris, *Cosmographia*, Leiden: Brill.

—— (1988), *A History of Twelfth-century Western Philosophy*, Cambridge: Cambridge University Press (including Dronke, 'Thierry of Chartres', pp. 358–85).

—— (1990), *Hermes and the Sibyls*, Cambridge: Cambridge University Press.

Fenton, P. (1976), 'Gleanings from Mōšeh ibn ʿEzra's *Maqâlat al-Hadîqa*', *Sefarad*, 36, pp. 284–98.

Ferreiro Alemparte, J. (1983), 'La escuela de nigromancia de Toledo', *Anuario de estudios medievales*, 13, pp. 205–68.

Gersh, S. (1982), 'Platonism–Neoplatonism–Aristotelianism: a twelfth-century metaphysical system and its sources', in R. L. Benson and G. Constable (eds) *Renaissance and Renewal in the Twelfth Century*, Oxford: Clarendon Press, pp. 512–34.

Gregory, T. (1988), 'The Platonic inheritance', in Dronke 1988, pp. 54–80.

Halleux, R. (1996), 'The reception of Arabic alchemy in the West', in R. Rashed (ed.), *Encyclopedia of the History of Arabic Science*, 3 vols, London and New York: Routledge, 3, pp. 886–902.

Haskins, C. H. (1927), *Studies in the History of Mediaeval Science*, Second edition, Cambridge, Mass.: Harvard University Press.

Hermann of Carinthia (1982), *De essentiis*, ed. C. Burnett, Leiden: E. J. Brill.

Hermes, *Antimaquis* (2001), ed. C. Burnett in P. Lucentini and V. Perrone Compagni (eds) *Hermes Latinus. Astrologica et Divinatoria*, Corpus Christianorum Continuatio Mediaeualis, vol. 144C, Turnhout: Brepols, pp. 175–228.

Hermes, *De spatula* (2001), ed. C. Burnett in P. Lucentini and V. Perrone Compagni (eds) *Hermes Latinus. Astrologica et Divinatoria*, Corpus Christianorum Continuatio Mediaeualis, vol. 144C, Turnhout: Brepols, pp. 249–347.

Hugo of Santalla (1997), *The Liber Aristotilis of Hugo of Santalla*, eds C. Burnett and D. Pingree, Warburg Institute Surveys and Texts 26, London.

Iogna-Prat, D. (1998), *Ordonner et exclure: Cluny et la société chrétienne face à l'hérésie, au judaïsme et à l'Islam, 1000–1150*, Paris: Aubier.

Kieckhefer, R. (1989), *Magic in the Middle Ages*, Cambridge: Cambridge University Press.

Kingsley, P. (1991), 'Poimandres: the etymology of the name and the origins of the *Hermetica*', *Journal of the Warburg and Courtauld Institutes*, 56, pp. 1–24.

Klibansky, R. and Regen, F. (1993), *Die Handschriften der philosophischen Werke des Apuleius*, Goettingen: Vandenhoeck und Ruprecht.

Lemay, R. (1962), *Abu Ma'shar and Latin Aristotelianism in the Twelfth Century*, Beirut: American University.

Liber Hermetis de sex rerum principiis (1955), ed. T. Silverstein, *Archives d'histoire doctrinale et littéraire du moyen âge*, 13, pp. 217–302.

Liber Hermetis Trismegisti de triginta sex decanis (1994) ed. S. Feraboli, Torhout: Brepols.

Liber Morieni (1974), ed. L. Stavenhagen, *A Testament of Alchemy*, Hanover, New Hampshire: University Press of New England.

Liber viginti quattuor philosophorum (1997), ed. F. Hudry, Turnhout: Brepols.

Lucentini, P. (1992), 'L'*Asclepius* ermetico nel secolo XII', in *From Athens to Chartres. Studies in honour of Edouard Jeauneau*, ed. H. J. Westra, Leiden: Brill, pp. 397–420.

—— ed. (1995), '*Glosae super Trismegistum*', *Archives d'histoire littéraire et doctrinale du moyen âge*, 62, pp. 189–293.

Petrus Alfonsi (1911), *Disciplina clericalis , I: Lateinischer Text*, ed. Alfons Hilka and Werner Söderhjelm, Acta societatis scientiarum Fennicae, 38.4, Helsinki: Drukerei der Finnischen Litteraturgesellschaft.

Pingree, D. (1968), *The Thousands of Abu Ma'shar*, London: The Warburg Institute.

—— (1980), 'Some of the sources of the *Ghāyat al-Ḥakīm*', *Journal of the Warburg and Courtauld Institutes*, 43, pp. 1–15.

—— (1987), 'The diffusion of Arabic magical texts in Western Europe', in *La diffusione delle scienze islamiche nel medio evo europeo*, Convegno internazionale promosso dall'Accademia nazionale dei Lincei, Rome: Accademia nazionale dei Lincei pp. 57–102.

—— (1994), 'Learned magic in the time of Frederick II', *Micrologus*, 2, pp. 39–56.

Ruska, J. (1926), *Tabula Smaragdina*, Heidelberg: Carl Winter's Universitätsbuchhandlung.

Southern, R. W. (1992), *Robert Grosseteste*, Second edn, Oxford: Oxford University Press.

Speculum astronomiae (1977), eds S. Caroti, M. Pereira, S. Zamponi and P. Zambelli, Pisa: Casa Galilaeana.

Speculum astronomiae (1992), Paola Zambelli, *The* Speculum Astronomiae *and its Enigma*, Boston Studies in the Philosophy of Science, 135, Dordrecht: Kluwer Academic Publishers.

Thābit ibn Qurra, *Liber prestigiorum secundum Ptolemeum et Hermetem*, transl. Adelard of Bath, ed. C. Burnett (in preparation).

Thierry of Chartres (1971), *Commentaries on Boethius by Thierry of Chartres and his School*, ed. N. M. Häring, Toronto: Pontifical Institute of Mediaeval Studies.

—— (1988), *The Latin Rhetorical Commentaries by Thierry of Chartres*, ed. K. M. Fredborg, Toronto: Pontifical Institute of Mediaeval Studies.

Thorndike, L. (1927), *A History of Magic and Experimental Science*, New York: Columbia University Press, vol. 2.

Walker, D. P. (1958), *Spiritual and Demonic Magic from Ficino to Campanella*, London: The Warburg Institute.

William of Auvergne (1674), *De legibus*, in *Opera omnia*, I, Paris: E. Couterot.

WHAT THE CRUSADES MEANT TO EUROPE

Christopher Tyerman

For Edward Gibbon, the crusades concerned nothing less than 'the world's debate'. Two centuries later, it can still be argued that crusading 'was of central importance to nearly every country in Europe and the Near East until the Reformation' with profound implications for modern politics, notably anti-Semitic violence, hostility between Orthodox and Catholic Christians and the escalating tensions between Moslems and Christians in the Balkans, Near East or elsewhere (Riley-Smith 1997: 1). Although lacking medieval definition in law or language, crusading is portrayed as a 'movement', implying a degree of coherence and unity of purpose, attitude or behaviour. Western historians have subsequently read into the crusades European colonialism; racial and cultural superiority; the triumph of faith over materialism or reason; nationalist epic; the opening of Europe to eastern trade, inventions and learning; the climax of shining chivalry or bestial barbarism; even 'the central drama' of the medieval period 'to which all other incidents were in some degree subordinate' (Archer and Kingsford 1894: 450–1). Yet in many respects, the dynamism of the crusade was derived from the culture that gave it birth and sustained it for half a millennium rather than the other way round.

Just war in medieval Europe boasted a Christian pedigree as old as Constantine the Great and Augustine of Hippo in the fourth and fifth centuries, with a much older parentage in Roman public war and the scriptural battles of the Israelites from Moses to the Maccabees. As Christendom appeared increasingly threatened by pagans and Islam in the eighth and ninth centuries, wars fought in defence of the Church were perceived as being in a holy cause, attracting spiritual rewards. This association sat easily in the culture of western Europe where war and religion were inseparable and Christ Himself could be portrayed as a warrior leader of a warband, in the vernacular eighth-century Anglo-Saxon *Dream of the Rood* or the ninth-century Germano-Saxon translation of the Gospels, the *Heliand*. Acceptance of Holy War, where fighting was regarded not simply as justified by circumstance, cause or legal authority but as a holy act in itself, percolated through Western aristocratic religious culture. Remission of sins was occasionally granted to warriors by popes (eg. Leo IV, 847–55; John VIII, 872–82). From the late tenth century some churchmen and their lay neighbours and relatives combined together to maintain their political and ecclesiastical order and security by establishing what were called Truces and Peaces of God. Just as the values of the arms-bearing classes appeared to be increasingly Christianised, so, in some aspects, was the Church militarised. The vernacular *Song of Roland* affirmed a warrior ethic with a Christian gloss: 'Christians are right; pagans are wrong', while contemporary eleventh-century popes employed armies to fight their wars and Gregory VII (1073–85) planned a *militia Sancti Petri* (knighthood/ army of St Peter). The Church depended on military aristocrats for patronage and protection. In return churchmen, especially monks, tried to incline these patrons if not to godliness at least to an awareness of their relationship to God through His Final Judgement. If the sentiments expressed in numerous charters of laymen granting property to monasteries are to be believed, donors took seriously the prospect of punishment for their sins in some after-life.

This symbiosis of interests and values, encouraged by developing canon law and the beginnings of a coherent and accessible penitential system, was lent focus by the political agenda of the reformed papacy after 1050. Across Western Europe during the so-called Investiture Contest ecclesiastical interests were pursued through secular politics, issues of the legitimacy of lay behaviour being interpreted in a spiritual context. This extended beyond German civil wars or the struggle for dominance in Italy to events such as the Norman conquest of England, which received enthusiastic support from the modernisers at the Roman curia. Previously the preserve, almost perquisite of emperors or kings, religious political ideology now reached the knights who were thereby lent respectability and an identifiable place in the church-created world hierarchy to match their growing material status. While contemporaries of Urban II saw his radical extension of penitential war literally as a God-sent opportunity to channel the activities of such men towards alternative, meritorious ends, such holy war soon became the acme of knightly ambition, which it remained until the end of the Middle Ages, an ideal as lustrous for Duke Philip the Good of Burgundy in the fifteenth century as for King Richard the Lionheart in the twelfth. The heroes and legends that sustained the bright image of the Wars of the Cross were military. The glamour of much crusade story-telling, in essence based on physical, not spiritual, fighting, depended on the confluence of war memoirs and moral homilies, epic meeting hagiography, although this was not the unique preserve of the crusade.

Crusading thus emerged from an existing tradition as well as a specific context. Many apparently distinctive crusading features were hardly novel: ecclesiastical acceptance of holy war; indulgences for Christian warriors; encouragement to fight the Infidel; the concept and reality of pious knights. The symbolic use of the Holy Cross, adopted as a sign of their vow by all who wished to enjoy the indulgences, was not invented for the crusade. It had been characteristic of the devotions of Peter Damian, one of the consciences of early papal reform, and was adopted by German pilgrims to Jerusalem in 1064. Holy Land pilgrims with no intention of fighting continued to adopt the Cross in the twelfth century. The term *crucesignatus* – signed with the Cross – was shared in the thirteenth century by reformed heretics.

Yet Urban II's call to arms in 1095 to recapture Jerusalem and assist the Eastern churches, although seen by some at the papal Curia as fulfilling the programme of Gregory VII, did present unique and novel features. Those who had fought for William of Normandy at Hastings in 1066 under a papal banner in what the pope had proclaimed a just cause nonetheless were enjoined to undertake penance for their acts of violence on the battlefield. In 1095, by contrast, Urban II proposed that the campaigning itself, slaughter included, was a satisfactory penitential act that remitted at the least the entire penalties of all the crusader's confessed sins. The implications were not restricted to spiritual health. Urban 'preached a holy war and thus sanctified holy pillage' (France 1996). The opportunity was provided by appeals from the East for aid, notably from the Byzantine emperor, but the concept of the relief of Jerusalem as both a physical goal and a means of grace derived in general from papal policy to impose a new hierarchic order upon clergy and laity and in particular from Urban II's perception of the nature and progress of Christian history. Thus, from its inception, crusading was a phenomenon of the culture of Western Christendom even where its implementation was not.

Whatever else, the crusades have attracted judgement. Arguably, those who planned the Wars of the Cross invited no less: such expeditions were seen as tests of the spiritual health or, more usually the 'iniquity' or malaise of Christendom, through, as Pope Innocent III put it in 1213, a contest devised by God to try the faith of Christians 'as gold in the furnace', a 'trial of the sword', even, in the words of a Second Crusade song, a 'tournament between Hell and Paradise' (Riley-Smith and Riley-Smith 1981: 65, 119; Tyerman 1998: 18). For its promoters, the stakes could not be higher. Given the successive defeats on the eastern Mediterranean front from the mid-twelfth century, this proved awkward, the ultimate failure of the Holy Land crusades haunting the imaginations of later medieval polemicists such as Philippe de Mézières (1327–1405) as a symbol of moral decadence and spiritual as well as political weakness.

This judgementalism has by no means always been positive. Wars, holy or not, claim victims. Jews and Moslems lament their dead, massacred by the First Crusaders: the Rhineland in 1096 and Jerusalem in 1099 retain the power to chill even the strongest Catholic apologist. Many southern Frenchmen had little to celebrate and much to curse in the crusades of the early thirteenth century that destroyed the Albigensian heretics and much more. Few Greeks forgave or forgot the sack of Constantinople in 1204 and the subsequent annexation of substantial parts of Greece and the Aegean by Westerners. To some later historians, such as Joseph François Michaud in the nineteenth century or Steven Runciman in the twentieth, the rape of Byzantium allowed the later conquest of south-eastern Europe by the Ottomans. Needless to say, Moslem writers are less upset at this outcome. The pagans of the Baltic lacked literacy to articulate their response to the Teutonic Knights' 'eternal crusade' of the thirteenth and fourteenth centuries in all its tedium, viciousness and squalor (or alternatively devotion, bravery and excitement) until at the Council of Constance (1414–18) the now-Christian victims found a voice that condemned the very basis of the northern crusades. Sixteenth-century Protestants thought the whole exercise of papal power corrupt and corrupting, noting with fraternal outrage the crusades launched against critics of the medieval Church, such as the Hussites. Religious fanaticism itself prompted the disdain of the Enlightenment, David Hume famously standing for a whole world-view in describing the crusades as 'the most signal and most durable monument of human folly that has yet appeared in any age or nation'. Beside the admiration and sense of tradition crusading inspired among medieval enthusiasts and Romantics in the nineteenth century ran the appreciation of waste, of loss, never better understood than by observers in the late twentieth century.

However, most critics and champions share a sense of the importance of the subject. Yet crusading was hardly free-standing. Many of the Wars of the Cross, especially in Europe – in Italy, Spain, France, Germany, England, the Baltic or the Balkans – would have been fought whatever the precise formal justification and apparatus of recruitment and propaganda. Crusading did not make western Europe a violent place; violent Europe created crusading. However significant an ideological leap was Urban II's invention of pentitential war in 1095, the practical differences were, in many instances, minimal. As often as not, crusading reflected desires and policies to which holy wars were useful but tangential: the moral, political and ecclesiastical ambitions of popes; the devotional practices of the laity, especially the nobility and propertied classes; the development of the cult of chivalry and code of aristocratic honour; the economic expansion of parts of western Europe; the religious initiatives of Church reformers. Even in the eastern Mediterranean, the one area where Urban II's vision had a unique impact, crusading – as opposed to the sort of warfare the Greeks had been conducting for centuries – was a product not of the frontier conflict with Islam but of preoccupations in the heartlands of western Christendom. Throughout, crusading was contingent on those who saw in its associated forms, rituals, rhetoric and traditions means to fulfil widely disparate and changing needs, temporal and spiritual.

The crusades were a form of Christian Holy War originally associated with the armed pilgrimage summoned by Urban II to recover Jerusalem from Moslem rule in 1095–9. Participants, who signalled their commitment by ceremonially receiving the cross and, from the later twelfth century, contributors as well earned spiritual privileges, most importantly plenary remission of sins, as well as the Church's protection for their property, immunity from repayment of debt and delays on law suits. Legal authority for such Holy Wars ostensibly derived from the pope. Yet emotions and actions allied to fighting under the Cross were never the sole prerogative of papally sanctioned expeditions. In 1110 King Sigurd of Norway, without any papal involvement, was recruited by King Baldwin I of Jerusalem 'to the service of Christ', perhaps even receiving the Cross in Jerusalem, in order to capture Sidon (Hollander 1964: 688–97). In 1228–9, the excommunicated Emperor Frederick II recovered Jerusalem on what cannot be regarded as anything other than a crusade, if that term has any meaning. True, papal authorisation and organisation, including diplomacy, propaganda, finance, at times even military recruitment, lay at the heart of most practical crusading, which became one of the most potent weapons in the armoury of the papal monarchy of the High Middle Ages. Nonetheless, at no time was a legal theory of crusading, as distinct from other forms of just or holy war, proposed let alone established. In a period and intellectual climate fond of legal codification and academic definitions, the omission is remarkable. The great Dominican theologian Thomas Aquinas, almost two centuries after the First Crusade, was still debating with students in Paris some of the unresolved technical niceties of the operation of the crusade vow and indulgence (Spiazzi 1949: ix).

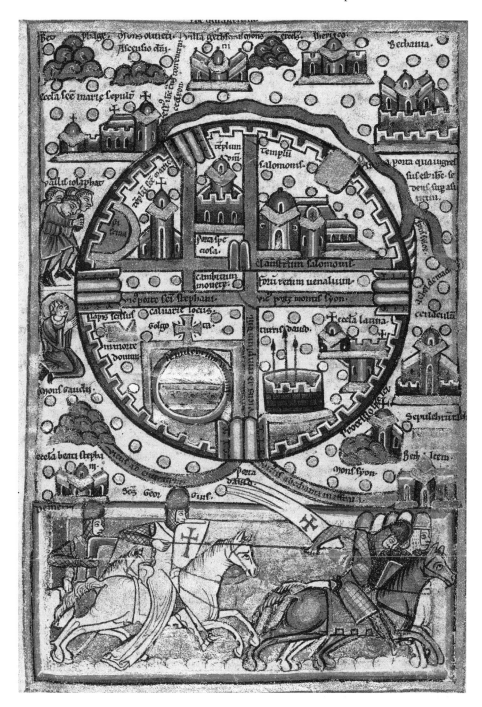

Figure 8.1 Plan of Jerusalem and its environs (*c.*1170) with, below, the Moslems getting the worst of it. Picture: The Hague, Koninklijke Bibliotheek, 76 F 5, fo. 1r.

Although a clear and lasting primacy of respect was afforded campaigns to the Holy Land, which, large and small, continued in practice to the end of the thirteenth century and in aspiration until the sixteenth, wars in defence of the Church more generally defined were understood to be legitimate on similar terms. Thus, from the early twelfth century, popes awarded privileges associated with the Jerusalem expedition to some Christian campaigns against the Moslems in Spain and, from 1147, to certain German wars against pagans in the Baltic. This form of Holy War was also employed within Christendom against Christians who presented a political threat to papal interests, such as supporters of the anti-pope Anacletus in 1135, Markward of Anweiler in Sicily in 1198 or the Hohenstaufen in Germany and Italy from the 1230s. Papal allies, such as the king of Norway in 1164 or the thirteenth-century kings John and Henry III of England, were defended by crusades which were also used to enforce political control or order, as over the *routiers* of Languedoc in 1139, or recalcitrant peasants in the Netherlands and north-west Germany in the 1220s. Crusades against Christian enemies of the Papacy became the most characteristic – and most controversial – form of crusading in the thirteenth and fourteenth centuries. The other main targets of crusades in Europe were heretics, notably the Cathars (or Albigensians) between 1208 and 1229, although charges of heresy could be employed by unscrupulous rulers, such as the kings of Hungary against the Bosnians in the 1230s, driven by zeal to acquire more land and power, a motive not far from the thoughts of King Louis VIII of France when campaigning against the Cathars in 1226. As the anti-Hussite crusades in Bohemia in the fifteenth century show, the combination of religious outrage and political ambition retained its potency. In the thirteenth century, the need to defend the Latin Empire of Constantinople and the western conquests in Greece and the Aegean established after the Fourth Crusade in 1204 led, especially after the 1230s, to regular appeals for crusades against the Byzantines. The flexible nature of the crusade as a political device is further revealed in its use from the fourteenth century in the conquest and conversion of pagan lands in Africa, the Atlantic and the Americas where the underlying justification of defence and reconquest was expanded to include the extension of Christendom.

Static neither in application nor in administration, the range of the wars of the Cross, from Russia to Spain, from England to Egypt, the involvement of so many diverse communities and the longevity of at least some associated ideals, reflected crusading's part in three powerful social and cultural forces: the expansion of western Christendom beyond its early medieval frontiers; the development of internal structures of authority and order in Church and State; and the religious reformation of the laity, spearheaded by the crusader pope Innocent III and the Fourth Lateran Council of 1215.

Nevertheless, while it may have been a characteristic feature of western European politics and Church, crusading was not a monolithic movement. Many modern historians have regarded the crusades as an autonomous force, exerting profound influence on medieval culture of which crusading was a 'defining characteristic' (Lloyd 1995: 36). When likened to a 'cancer inside the body of medieval Christendom . . . carried to every part of the organism', crusading's discrete existence is still acknowledged (Morris 1998: 201). However, the crusade was not defined in law, canon or secular. The names used to describe the activity had little consistency, there being no accepted word for crusade beyond euphemisms (holy business, cross etc.) or banalities (holy passage, voyage, journey, expedition etc.). The one technical word that retained currency and force, both in literary works and the records of law courts, was pilgrimage, an association that crusading never cast off and from which it was often hard put to distinguish itself. Charters drawn up on behalf of those departing on crusade illustrate this clearly. Even in the thirteenth century, in such diverse settings as secular law courts, eye-witness accounts by crusaders such as the Frenchman Jean de Joinville or illustrated manuscripts of crusade texts, pilgrimage and crusading continued to be inseparably, at times indistinguishably, woven together. The institutions of crusading remained firmly attached to their cultural setting, reflecting rather than illuminating their surroundings. The changing and disparate needs of society drove crusading, not the other way round. When the value-systems that sustained it changed, so it ceased to be relevant. It was not military defeat by Islam but the Reformation that brought crusading to an end. It proved to have been less a cancer than a parasite.

Equally, for all its importance in papal policy throughout the three centuries after 1100 and for many rulers during the same period, crusading was not universal. Its distinctive institutions – indulgence, penitential warfare, martial Christ-centred rhetoric, the Cross, legal immunities, etc. – did not touch every member of society or every region of Christendom evenly or at all. On the spiritual level, crusading was not a compulsory religious exercise, in the manner of oral confession after 1215. Except for Holy Land crusades, few expeditions were preached throughout Western Christendom. Crusading for most people, especially after 1200, was a local or regional affair not only in the organisation of preaching and recruitment, which was inevitably the case with all crusades, but in the nature of the declared objective: northern Frenchmen fought in Languedoc and northern Spain; Italians in Italy; Germans in Germany, the Baltic and, later, Bohemia; Hungarians in the Balkans. There were obvious exceptions, notably Charles of Anjou in Italy in the 1260s. Not all wars of cultural, religious or political aggression attracted crusading features; there were crusades in Bosnia but not in Ireland. The story of the First Crusade, which dominated the subsequent highly self-referential literature on later expeditions, was transmitted in significantly different regional versions. The picture of medieval crusading – as of medieval Europe in general – is one of fragmentation and disparity of regional interests dictating to the Curia as much as papal directives inspiring uniformity of reaction; of local perceptions, traditions and responses.

Active crusading was a minority activity. To become a *crucesignatus* implied both legal freedom and economic substance, either personal or derived from a profitable dependent relationship. As enquiries into defaulting crusaders show, for example in England in the 1190s, paupers could not go on crusade; neither could serfs. The social composition of crusade armies was little or no different from any other of the period, even if, at times, their objectives were unique. As with all secular armies, and, indeed, political society in general, recruitment was based upon the military households, affinities, employees, kindreds and geographical networks of the dominant arms-bearing class and urban elites. Crusader armies, like any others, were held together by a mixture of loyalty and cash, assembled and disciplined not by religious enthusiasm alone, but by traditional bonds of lordship, kinship, shared locality, sworn association and, from the late twelfth century, formal and specific contracts between leader and led. Written lists of such recruits survive from Italy in the early 1220s; contracts in England from 1240. With expeditions to the Holy Land, the increasing awareness, at least from the later twelfth century, of the requirement for more effective soldiers and the necessity of transport by sea, accelerated a narrowing of recruitment to the exclusion of non-combatants and hangers-on. Crusaders had to have access to money, whether theirs, their patrons' or their masters': no money, no crusade. The point was well taken by Innocent III after the Fourth Crusade had become the victim of its own indebtedness.

The evidence of chronicles, land transactions, financial deals, lawsuits, vernacular songs, sermons and poems reveals crusading as sustained by magnates and knights, landed aristocrats trained in arms, surrounded by their dependents: tenants, servants, relatives and foot-sloggers. With them were those who could ply their skills on crusade, wage earners and artisans. The sources reveal merchants, goldsmiths, dyers, bowmen, carpenters, drapers, farriers, blacksmiths, laundresses, prostitutes, millers, cobblers, tailors, fowlers, doghandlers, butchers, barbers, vintners, cooks, masons and fishmongers. Perhaps a characteristic non-aristocratic rural crusader was the sort of man who, in the different circumstances of the fourteenth century, might have fought in the Hundred Years War as an English archer, known then as a yeoman, a substantial freeman. Crusading was attractive to criminals seeking legal protection or escape. Beneficed clergy were prominent in praying, diplomacy, writing letters, composing chronicles, organising poor relief, burying the dead and even fighting. Wives took the Cross in their own right but, according to numerous widely ignored crusade ordinances, unattached women were forbidden, except for older women of good repute who acted as menials, laundresses and de-lousers. They all, however, shared the same requirement for funds, their own or somebody else's.

Many chroniclers and not a few modern historians have noted the importance of the poor on crusade, the *pauperes*, the *plebs*. However, the evidence of charters of French crusading *rustici*, or peasants, suggests they had property to dispose of, however modest. If free, the poor could in theory take the Cross, but they did not in fact embark. Some accounts explictly state that the so-called poor on crusade were those who had run out of money, called by Odo of Deuil on the Second Crusade 'new paupers', a common enough fate even for the most gently born crusader (Berry 1948: 137). 'Poor' was also used as a relative term in a literary convention that, for example, drew a pointed moral from describing the successful crusaders who captured Lisbon in 1147 as 'poor' in contrast to the 'rich' kings of Germany and France whose expeditions failed even though their participants were substantial landowners and merchants who had funded their own campaign. Using a similar euphemism of the Fourth Crusade, Robert of Clari described as 'poor' minor but well-to-do Flemish knights. Elsewhere, preachers as well as chroniclers were often more concerned with spiritual standing than with economic condition. This could lead to contradictions. Preaching the Cross under Innocent III (1198–1216) was often combined with calls to follow the *vita apostolica*, i.e. a renunciation of material wealth, itself suggestive of the economic standing of the desired audience, or paralleled by attacks on usury and denunciations of the sinfulness of borrowing as well as lending. Taken literally, acceptance of such preaching would render the would-be crusader impotent to fulfil his vow.

The image of hordes of impoverished peasants leaving their fields to employ their pitchforks in the service of the Cross is a myth. Despite its later title, the Peasants' Crusade of 1096 was led by magnates, possessed a central fund of treasure and laid siege to fortified towns in Hungary: hardly the work of a rabble of military novices fresh from the plough. Whatever else he was, Walter Sans Avoir, one of the leaders, was not penniless, Sans Avoir being a place not a condition. Those who did set out, in 1096 or on the Children's (1212) and Shepherds' (1250) Crusades, hoping to rely on charity alone, could not complete the journey unless taken on by those with funds. On the Third Crusade in 1189 the German emperor, Frederick Barbarossa, tried to insist that those who enrolled in the crusade host were able to support themselves. There was little or no mass involvement of whole communities or populations. When Martino da Canale recorded that 'the whole of the Venetian *popolo*' took the Cross in the papal cause in 1256, it is not necessary to take him literally (Housley 1982: 126). Collectively, some crusading armies may have been massive; perhaps as many as 70,000 to 80,000 reached Asia Minor on the First Crusade. The armies and fleets of the general expeditions east of 1147–8, 1189–92, 1202–4, 1217–21 and 1248–50 were impressive in size. However, with the possible exception of Louis IX of France who took farming equipment with him to Egypt in 1249, there was no sense or reality of a mass demographic movement.

That is not to say that the wars of the Cross were not popular nor that their home communities remained untouched, rather that much of their impact and popularity rested on indirect or non-military features. Civilians were unavoidably engaged through the material requirements of preparing armies: the shipbuilders of the Venetian Arsenale in 1202; the iron workers of the Forest of Dean or the cheese-makers of Hampshire in 1190. More generally, funds were raised for crusades by taxation which could, in theory, have affected more or less everyone: William Rufus's tax on England in 1096 to pay for his brother's crusade; the Saladin Tithe of 1188. By 1200, taxation of the Church for 'the public business of the cross' had become an established feature of crusading, a cost that could fall heavily on the extensive estates held by ecclesiastical corporations. Towns were tallaged in France for the crusades of their kings. Taxes reached out to all of society, pressing most heavily perhaps on those at the bottom of the economic system who were unable to become crusaders in their own right but equally unable to avoid contributing. The more positively engaged and comfortably off parishioner, from *c*.1200, would regularly find in the parish church a chest for voluntary donations to the cause. It also became fashionable and spiritually meritorious to bequeath money or goods to the crusade. Thus crusading caught the efforts of labourers, the imagination of the faithful and the thoughts of the dying, through the pockets of them all.

There was also a sense in which crusaders were regarded by their communities as expressing the repentance of all Christendom. They were sent off – literally – with the prayers of the local faithful, lay and religious, ringing in their ears. From this, the church authorities progressively and deliberately knitted crusading more tightly into the communal devotions of western Europe. By the mid-thirteenth century regular prayers, processions, bell-ringings and feast-days were dedicated to the cause, thus involving the ordinary parishioners through the liturgy and the communal round of church services and religious ceremonial. These observances formed only one part of a growing institutionalisation of the crusade, from the beginning of the Third Crusade in 1187 onwards, aimed by the Papacy at producing a more effective military response and more comprehensive, coherent and popular religious participation.

One of the central paradoxes that emerged during the twelfth century was that within the developing penitential system of the Western Church, the crusade indulgence was almost uniquely advantageous, promising, as it did, full remission of sin, both casualties and survivors enjoying the prospect of salvation. Despite the horrific and arduous penance of campaigning, it was, as Bernard of Clairvaux suggested, a very good bargain (James 1998: 462). However, this indulgence was limited to those who actually took the Cross and fulfilled their vow by at least having the intention of setting out. After the First Crusade the numbers of such people were limited and socially unequal. Beginning with Clement III at the time of the Third Crusade, popes began to allow the faithful to take the Cross in order to redeem their vow not by military action but by payment of money. This trend was completed in Innocent III's bull *Quia maior* (1213) summoning the Fifth Crusade which allowed *crucesignati* to commute their vows by sending proxies and encouraged 'anyone who wishes' to redeem crusade vows for money according to means, with non-*crucesignati* contributors receiving an appropriate proportion of the indulgence. Innocent was being deliberately inclusive, wishing to use the institutions of the crusade as part of a wider religious revival among the laity. Thus he instituted the monthly processions, fasting and almsgiving and the special prayers incorporated into the Mass (Riley-Smith and Riley-Smith 1981: 119–24).

Thereafter, personal contact with crusading did not depend on military service. Crusade preaching increasingly concentrated on vow redemptions and general amendment of spiritual life, as armies became more professional with fewer *crucesignati* in their ranks. Innocent and his agents saw taking the Cross as a form of religious conversion, meritorious in itself as a sign of a commitment to a new spiritual life. One prominent contemporary crusade preacher, Jacques de Vitry, described crusaders as constituting an order, a *religio*. By 1250, it appears that taking the Cross formed part of a pious layman's devotional programme, as a sign of purity almost without direct reference to fighting in the Wars of the Cross. In the words of Eudes de Châteauroux, papal crusade legate in France in the 1240s, 'by assumption of the Cross men are marked and distinguished as servants of God against the servants of the devil' (Tyerman 1998: 83). So powerful and attractive was the crusade indulgence that popular demand persuaded Innocent IV to sanction the transferability of the benefits of taking the Cross to wives and children. Even deceased relatives were regarded by some as able to share the spiritual rewards of the *crucesignatus*. Into this inclusive embrace could be admitted, for the first time in significant numbers, the less wealthy (who could not have afforded or been capable of a military excursion) and women.

Nonetheless, social elitism remained. Redemption of vows and purchase of indulgences cost money, openly disbursed. Although according to Innocent III the spiritual rewards were calculated relative to the wealth of the recipient, within a

Figure 8.2 The biter bit. Saladin triumphant. The Battle of Hattin (July 1187) as imagined by the English monk Matthew Paris about sixty years after the event. © The Master and Fellows of Corpus Christi College, Cambridge.

century of 1215 crusade indulgences were bought and sold outright, without any intervening redemption of the Cross, encouraging a parallel of spiritual advantage with social status. As with many other aspects of medieval devotion, the procedure seemingly favoured those who could afford and contribute most towards their spiritual well-being.

One of the most characteristic images of crusading is that of the inspirational preacher arousing his audience to paroxysms of emotion and enthusiasm. Yet most if not all such events were carefully stage-managed for crowds or groups who were already primed to receive the call to take the Cross or contribute to the cause: Bernard at Vézelay in 1147; Josias of Tyre at Gisors or Baldwin of Canterbury in Wales in 1188; Fulk of Neuilly before the Fourth Crusade; Oliver of Paderborn in Frisia before the Fifth. The audiences were expectant, neither indifferent nor surprised, willingly caught in a ritual which was challenging only within carefully subscribed limits. Often associated with the liturgy of the Mass, crusade sermons tended to focus devotion in a ceremonial as much as an evangelical manner. Crusading was not a spontaneous act, in recruitment or propaganda. The social bias of vow redemptions is confirmed by the audiences of the preachers who rarely even formally aimed their appeals at peasants. The very few sermons that are described in the twelfth century, the small number of sermon texts from the thirteenth, the preaching manuals and surviving regional instructions to teams of preachers, all suggest that crusade preaching was primarily urban or based at the courts of the great. Increasingly, as the thirteenth century progressed, the religious purpose was generally revivalist, the tangible result financial donations, the target a far wider community than that of potential warriors. With preaching as with the indulgence, the wider social popularity of crusading came as part of its incorporation into schemes of spiritual reform rather than solely as an aspect of Christian militarism or intolerance. It was in the thirteenth century, rather than with the sporadic outbursts of militant enthusiasm of the century before, that crusading became a secure social phenomenon of Western Christendom, ironically precisely because the links between taking the Cross and fighting for the Cross were being severed. The non-military aspects of the institutions surrounding the 'holy business' ensured its survival until the Reformation not simply as a martial ambition of the knightly classes but as a religious exercise of the faithful.

The effect of the crusades on Europe and Europeans tended to be of three sorts: direct, as with the crusaders themselves and the families they left behind; indirect, in the responses of the wider community to the material needs of the enterprises and to the ecclesiastical mechanisms that wove crusading into the pattern of popular spirituality; and destructive, in the fate of the victims of the exercise. The crusade proved inadequate in providing the firm, lasting focus of identity for Christendom as a whole which, arguably, some popes and apologists hoped for from it. By contrast, it successfully exacerbated alienation between Westerners and those outside the stockade of papal Christianity. When considering what the crusades meant to Europe, it is worth remembering that besides those who could be regarded as Christians in communion with Rome, there were Greek Christians. There were also non-Christians: European Jews in well-established communities in France, Spain, Germany and Italy; European Moslems in Spain and Sicily. There were European pagans, notably around the Baltic. There were European heretics, both Christian and non-Christian. There were Europeans for whom the claims of official religion meant little. The crusades may have been a signal demonstration of the penetration of religiosity in secular culture, but their social context was probably no more or no less an age of faith than is our own. Crusading, if anything, narrowed understanding, of Greeks, pagans, Jews, even Moslems, contact with whom perversely was encouraging ignorant notions of Islam as polytheistic, or as a Christian heresy or as a religion with Muḥammad as its god. Westerners increasingly appeared unable even to comprehend their cousins who had settled in Outremer who, within less than a century after 1099, were viewed with suspicion or contempt by many. This resulted in a failure to match military aid to the Holy Land with the need for it. As the First Crusade had been summoned in 1095 to suit internal politics within western Europe, so subsequent crusading, to the east no less than elsewhere, while opening avenues of commerce (especially to the entrepreneurs of Italy and the western Mediterranean), of travel, pilgrimage, advancement and adventure, confirmed a paradoxical narrowing and hardening of vision. Material and political expansion seemed to have provoked a sort of introspective self-sufficiency. In the eyes of Western observers, Outremer could be remade in the image of the West (which of course it could not) while the West was, at the same time, engaged in projecting onto itself all the culture and learning necessary for a comprehensive Christian polity, including relics from the east and replicas of holy shrines, as in round naves of churches in imitation of the Holy Sepulchre. Contact and conquest created a self-sustaining, self-congratulatory, yet paranoid ideology of superiority and rightness (righteousness?), suspicious, fearful, uncomprehending of outsiders, while enjoying their plunder.

It need not have worked out that way. There is evidence of genuine Christian fraternity during the First Crusade: cooperation between Greeks and Latins; an absence of bitterness against the Byzantines from returning crusaders below the level of grasping or disappointed magnates of the High Command; and a lasting sense of comradeship and support from Armenian Christians who saw the crusaders at Antioch and Jerusalem as liberators, not conquerors, much as Urban II may have intended. At least during the twelfth century there were always voices raised to defend the idea of Christian fellowship, just as in the thirteenth century, among the friars, conversion of infidels was seen by some as preferable to conquest. However, given the function assigned by the Papacy to Wars of the Cross in the twelfth and early thirteenth centuries, it is hard not to conclude that, within Christendom at least, it was inevitable that crusading took its place as a vehicle of a persecuting society.

Though Europe, like the crusade itself, was a scarcely defined medieval concept, for those Europeans within Christendom who were not seen as within the pale of orthodox Roman Christianity, the crusades were almost unremittingly disastrous, from the massacres of Jews that accompanied all the first three main expeditions to the east, in 1096, 1146 and 1190, to the carnage of the Albigensian crusades to local policing operations such as that to flush out the Italian Dolcino in the early fourteenth century to the Hussite wars over a century later. Yet crusading of itself was hardly the cause of this persecution, merely the instrument. It is not accurate to reverse this process of active intolerance. The crusades did not bring about the definition of orthodoxy or of the papal monarchy nor did they cause that elevation of discipline and authority within society and the Church which lay behind many accusations of heresy. While demonstrably inciting it, the crusades did not create anti-Semitism; there were pogroms in France and Spain that long pre-dated 1095. Crusading was a symptom of new strands in lay and clerical spirituality, of the fresh perspectives and policies of a reinvigorated papacy, of the greater order and prosperity in western Europe, of the emergent status and consequent social arrangements of the arms-bearing or knightly class, of a reinvigorated Christian aggression, the harsh side of Urban II's vision of Christian history.

The expeditions that resulted in the capture of Jerusalem in July 1099 exerted a significant influence on the cultural development of western Europe. The experiences and story of the journeys and campaigns between 1095 and 1099 provided contemporaries and their descendents with a new model of military and spiritual behaviour and an unexpected example of Christian triumph in a world long accustomed to images of defeat or defence – for Urban II a reversal of the long retreat of Christianity. Others could take more immediate encouragement, collectively from the victory in the east and individually from the indulgences. The First Crusade's fresh, although not exclusive, articulation of Christian Holy War provided a political weapon of great potential for the emergent Papacy; supplied an additional focus for pious martial ambition; offered a new opportunity to achieve and justify political and economic expansion; presented a unique process for individuals to achieve salvation; and left a series of indelible images in the minds of writers, poets, singers, artists and architects as well as propagandists, moralists and conquerors. Islam could be more precisely identified – or, rather, misidentified – as a demonic foe and Jews as enemies of Christ because of the new attention given to Jerusalem, the scene of Christ's life, Passion, death and Resurrection, its liminal status between Heaven and Earth consolidated and modified first by temporal control of the terrestrial city to which pilgrims as well as settlers and warriors travelled in unprecedented numbers, then by the efforts to recapture it after its loss to Saladin in 1187. To this central set of images could be attached all wars in defence of the Church in a process of Christian repentence masking triumphalism.

More tangibly, crusading created a new vocabulary of salvation for the military classes and brought the foundation of new religious orders, such as the Templars, Hospitallers and Teutonic Knights, some of which lasted for many centuries. Through contact with and control of areas beyond the confines of Latin Europe, individuals and communities from western Christendom found a sharper self-identity in relation to neighbours, including co-religionists, hitherto barely encountered. The crusades by no means caused, but did form a part of, a process of opening western Europe to a wider world, politically, culturally and commercially. The fate of the material legacy of the First Crusade in the eastern Mediterraneran, Europe's Outremer, was used by some to define the spiritual and political health of papal Christendom for more than ten generations after 1099. The aesthetic imprint of crusading on art and literature survived as long. While the potency of other theatres of crusading ebbed and flowed in contemporary imagination, the place of Jerusalem and the Holy Land remained stubbornly entrenched in Western medieval mentalities. Protean in name, essence and act, not a movement but rather a series of institutions that varied in time, space, detail and application, uniform neither in nature nor in support, reflecting rather than shaping cultural, political and religious trends, the wars associated with those to recover or defend Jerusalem constituted a vivid part of the life of medieval Christendom. Europe in the Middle Ages could be a very nasty place to live: the crusades made it marginally nastier.

REFERENCES

Archer, T. and C. Kingsford (1894) *The Crusades*, London: Unwin.

Berry, V. (ed.) (1948) *Odo of Deuil. De profectione Ludovici VII in orientem*, New York: Columbia University Press.

France, J. (1996) 'Les origines de la Première Croisade', in M. Balard (ed.) *Autour de la Première Croisade*, Paris: Publications de la Sorbonne, 43–56.

Hollander, L. (ed.) (1964) *Heimskringla: the history of the Kings of Norway*, Austin, TX: University of Texas Press.

Housley, N. (1982) *The Italian Crusades*, Oxford: Clarendon Press.

James, B. (trans.) (1998) *The Letters of St Bernard of Clairvaux*, 2nd edn, Stroud: Sutton.

Lloyd, S. (1995) 'The crusading movement', in J. Riley-Smith (ed.) *Oxford Illustrated History of the Crusades*, Oxford: Oxford University Press.

Morris, C. (1998) 'Picturing the crusades: the uses of visual propaganda *c.*1095–1250', in J. France and W. Zajac (eds) *Crusades and their Sources: essays presented to Bernard Hamilton*, Aldershot: Ashgate, 195–216.

Riley-Smith, J. (1997) 'Introduction', in J. Phillips (ed.) *The First Crusade: origins and impact*, Manchester: Manchester University Press, pp. 1–14.

—— and L. Riley-Smith (eds) (1981) *The Crusades: idea and reality*, London: Edward Arnold.

Spiazzi, R. (ed.) (1949) *Thomas Aquinas. Quaestiones quodlibetales*, Turin and Rome: Marietti.

Tyerman, C. (1998) *The Invention of the Crusades*, Basingstoke: Macmillan.

CHAPTER NINE

THE CRUSADES AND THE PERSECUTION OF THE JEWS

J. A. Watt

Persecution of Jews in the medieval world took many forms. One of the most threatening to the future survival of the European Jewries came with the war against Islam. The crusades brought to Jews violence of hitherto unparalleled ferocity. Holy War against one sort of unbeliever seemed reason to attack another. Why combat one set of God's enemies overseas, the argument ran, and yet leave unscathed an even worse set of enemies at home, living among us? It was a logic which at the time challenged the orthodoxies of Church and State, and which now confronts the historian of that age with a particularly significant phenomenon in the history of medieval anti-Semitism. 'A microcosm of medieval Jewish disasters' (Stow 1992: 115. Cf. Liebeschütz 1959; Abulafia 1996).

CHURCH, STATE AND THE PROTECTION OF JEWS

Even before Urban II formally launched the First Crusade in 1095, the alternative, baptism or death, had been presented to Jews by Christian warriors on campaign against Muslims. It had happened in Spain some thirty years earlier. In 1063, Pope Alexander II told the whole of the Spanish episcopate that he had been gratified to learn that they had defended Jews against those who, while waging war against the Muslim, had sought 'either through foolish ignorance or possibly blinded by greed' to kill them. For it was divine justice itself which protected Jews, Alexander asserted, God having predestined them for salvation. The pope obviously had in mind St Paul's assurance that Israel's blindness to the truth about Christ was temporary and would end when 'the fullness of the Gentiles should come in. And so all Israel should be saved' (Rom. 11: 25–6). He continued:

> So thus blessed [Pope] Gregory restrained certain men who were on fire to annihilate Jews, declaring it offensive to God to kill those whom God's mercy had preserved, dispersed though they were through all regions of the earth, having lost fatherland and liberty in lasting penance enjoined by the sentence passed on their fathers for shedding the blood of the Saviour.

The cases of Saracens and Jews were very different, he continued. The former sought to persecute Christians and drive them from their cities and estates; war against them was therefore just. But Jews 'are everywhere prepared to serve'. The letter concluded with his forbidding an individual bishop to destroy a synagogue. In other letters, Alexander II was to commend both the archbishop and the viscount of Narbonne for protecting Jews against those intent on killing them. He also reprimanded the lord of Benevento for seeking to convert Jews to Christianity by force: nowhere (he affirmed) is it recorded that Jesus Christ ever compelled anyone to his service by violence. The Saviour had persuaded by humble exhortation, respecting the free will of each individual person.[1]

The truncated nature of the texts of Alexander's letter as they have come down to us (they are obviously only summaries) makes them read somewhat cryptically and not without obscurity. But it is clear that Alexander II was condemning, as contrary to God's will, the killing of Jews, baptism by force, and denial of Jewish freedom of worship by attacks on synagogues.

What is not clear is what precisely he had in mind when he spoke of Jews 'being prepared to serve'. What it *might* mean, however, at least to Europe's rulers at the time, is apparent from another sort of response to attacks on Jews in this immediate pre-crusade period. Jews could serve Christians in a very practical, economic way. The *Hebrew Chronicle* which recorded the transfer of Mainz Jews to Speyer in 1084 explained why they had moved: 'the whole of the Jewish quarter was burned down and we stood in great fear of the townsmen'. In Speyer, by contrast, they were warmly welcomed by its ruler-bishop who, according to the chronicle attributed to Solomon bar Simson, 'pitied us as a man pities his son' (Eidelberg 1977: 71–2). But the bishop had more than paternal compassion in mind, and frankly admitted as much. He wanted to expand his settlement and build it up into a city. He thought the glory of Speyer would be 'increased a thousandfold if I were to bring in Jews'. In return for this service, he granted them what he claimed to be 'a better legal position than any other Jewish community in any city of the German kingdom'. And so he allocated to them a fortified area, with responsibility for their own defence, a cemetery over which they had autonomous jurisdiction, full trading rights within Speyer and on its Rhine wharf and a number of particular legal privileges, the most important of which was that of having disputes within their community settled by their own leader (Aronius 1902: 69–71).

Some six years later, the Speyer Jews, with the cooperation of the same bishop, successfully petitioned Henry IV for a more comprehensive charter of privileges. It proved to be more detailed than any such charter hitherto granted to any European Jewry. Jews and their properties were accorded royal protection from arbitrary violence. They were granted freedom of trade throughout the kingdom. Their position at law was safeguarded: when there was litigation between a Christian and a Jew each could swear on his own sacred book and Jews were not to be subject to the proof-tests of hot iron or water. They were at liberty to settle disputes within their own community in their own court, and – and in view of what was to come this was of especial relevance – they were protected against forced baptism. The removal of Jewish children from their parents in order to baptise them was proscribed. If a Jew expressed a wish to be baptised, three days should elapse before the administration of the sacrament in order to establish that the wish was sincere and unforced. There was even a deterrent set against conversion to Christianity: a baptised Jew forfeited his property to the royal treasury (Aronius 1902: 72–3).

Henry IV's charter was issued to only one Jewish community. But the incorporation of its substance into similar charters by Frederick I and Frederick II establishes its claim to be an authoritative formulation of Jewish rights as understood by the German monarchy. Henry IV had translated into practical juridical detail the principle of toleration and defined how Jews were to be protected in their persons, property, religion, status at law and economic activity.

There is no comparably detailed document from the Papacy in this period. Nothing from the papal registers has survived to take us beyond the letters of Alexander II. But the eleventh century had seen a notable advance in the number and quality of collections of canons, beginning with that of Burchard of Worms (*c*.1012) and reaching a notable peak on the very eve of the First Crusade with the *Decretum* of Ivo of Chartres and its summary, the *Panormia* (Gilchrist 1988; Gilchrist 1989). Ivo enjoyed particular authority in his own day, not least with the Papacy itself and his collections were to be very influential in the development of canon law. There need be little hesitation about adducing his work as representative of the orthodox ecclesiastical opinion of his day.

Ivo considered Christian–Jewish relations in two main contexts. His first book of the *Decretum* was a massive assembly of texts 'concerning faith and the sacrament of faith, baptism'. It included texts concerning the baptism of Jews and an examination of the rules concerning conversion to Christianity. Book XIII was of a more miscellaneous nature. The unifying theme of the texts concerning Jews may be put in this way: Jews, though tolerated, were nevertheless enemies of Christianity and therefore a threat to be controlled and contained. Thus safeguards must be erected against Jewish proselytism, against Jews exploiting Christians, against insult to Christianity, to all of which, traditionally, Jews were regarded as particularly prone. Broadly speaking, about one-third of the canons concerned with Jews which Ivo selected represented the teaching of Gregory I (590–604), another third that of the Visigothic Toledo councils, especially that presided over by Isidore of Seville (Toledo IV, 633). The remaining third is more varied, with the preponderance coming from Frankish councils of much the same period: all told, an authentic representation of what had become the standard canonical tradition, in somewhat fuller presentation than in any previous collection of canons.

What is of particular relevance here is that the canon law at this stage in its development reinforced the positions recently adopted by Alexander II. Indeed, Ivo reproduced all the Alexandrine letters. But he also reproduced additional authoritative texts, especially those of Gregory I, to establish that killing Jews, baptising them under coercion and interfering with the practice of their religion were all forbidden.

THE FIRST POGROMS IN EUROPEAN HISTORY

Behind such a barrier of principles and practices erected by the authorities of Church and State, it might be expected that Jews would feel safe. And indeed there is evidence to suggest that they did. For the contemporary Jewish record often entitled 'Mainz Anonymous' reported that when the Mainz Jewish community was warned from France of attacks on Jews by crusaders there, they replied that though greatly concerned about the welfare of their French co-religionists, as to themselves they felt no cause for anxiety: 'We have not heard a word of such matters, nor has it been hinted that our lives are threatened by the sword' (Eidelberg 1977: 100). They were to be speedily and bitterly disillusioned, however. As the First Crusade gathered momentum, the Mainz community was annihilated.

As crusaders began their march to the Holy Land, attacks on Jews took place in Rouen, spread to Prague and elsewhere in Bohemia, and were reported by one contemporary chronicler as falling on the Jewries along the Rhine, Main and Danube rivers. Some historians think they have detected them also in Provence. But no one doubts that they fell most heavily in the Rhineland: on the Jewries of Cologne, Worms and Mainz most severely, with another half-dozen harshly treated (Riley-Smith 1984; Chazan 1987).

One strand of modern crusade historiography attributes these outrages to the crazed fanaticism of an ignorant and undisciplined peasantry, seized and deluded by a 'messianism of the disoriented poor' (Cohn 1993: 61), with the extreme views that led to violence 'restricted to small and marginal groups of popular crusaders' (Chazan 1987: 219). In fact, on the evidence of the Hebrew sources the army most clearly to be identified with 'popular' crusading, that led by Peter the Hermit himself, can be acquitted of responsibility for the killing of Jews. According to the *Chronicle* of Solomon bar Simson, Peter looked for nothing more than material help for his journey. Once provided with that, 'he would speak kindly of Israel' (Eidelberg 1977: 62). On the other hand, Godfrey of Bouillon, for example, the future first ruler of the crusader kingdom of Jerusalem, is marked down in the same source as vowing to proceed on his journey, 'only after avenging the blood of the crucified by shedding Jewish blood and completely eradicating any trace of those bearing the name "Jew"' (Eidelberg 1977: 25).

It was not only important crusade leaders who promoted the assaults on the Rhineland Jewries. It was also the citizenry of the towns themselves. Responsibility for the murderous assaults on Jews must be attributed to an unholy alliance of elements of the crusading leadership with townsmen (sometimes aided by the peasantry of neighbouring villages). Albert of Aachen, fullest of the Christian chroniclers of the pogroms, lays responsibility for originating the attacks on the citizens of Cologne. But it is the Hebrew chroniclers who are most insistent on the major role of the townspeople and of their collusion with the crusaders. 'Because of our sins', the Mainz Anonymous reported, 'whenever the crusaders arrived at a city, the local burghers would harass us, for they were at one with them' (Eidelberg 1997: 100). Though they were not slow to acknowledge individual exceptions to this collaboration, reporting how some Gentiles sought to provide protection, they go on to specify the cities where crusaders and citizens combined to attack Jews. And among those they named were the cities whose Jewries suffered most cruelly.

The Jews did not get much sympathy from the main crusade chroniclers. Albert of Aachen even suggested that their fate was 'a judgement of the Lord' before adding that it might have been 'some mental aberration' on the part of the crusaders. He acknowledged that no one should be coerced into being a Christian. He was emphatic that those mainly responsible for the pogrom in Mainz were the Swabian Emich, count of Flonheim and the northern French lords in his company. Albert accused them of bearing off much wealth looted from the Jews (*Recueil* 1841–1906: 4.292). He passed over in silence the role of Godfrey of Bouillon who figures so prominently in the Hebrew accounts. The lords of Bouillon were Albert's local ruling family (Edgington 1997: 61). Ekkehard of Aura wrote of the crusaders' attacks on Jews as motivated by 'zeal for Christianity' without even a hint that such zeal was gravely immoral and seriously illegal. He wrote of Jews as 'the most impious ones' who were 'truly the internal enemies of the Church (Saracens being the external ones), whose return to Judaism after coerced baptism was a return "to their vomit"' (*Recueil* 1841–1906: 5.15, 20; Prov. 26.11). Albert registered strong disapproval at the action of Jewish mothers in Mainz, who killed their children, he thought, to prevent their being killed by 'the uncircumcised' (more likely it was to prevent their being taken for baptism and Christian upbringing). Bernold of St Blasien, writing of Jews in Worms choosing suicide rather than having baptism forced upon them, attributed their action to 'the persuasion of the devil and their own hardness of heart' (Aronius 1902: 464).

It is the survival of the so-called Hebrew Chronicles which brings home the horrific realities of the violence. They are less histories than books of remembrance, martyrologies. Within a framework of narratives of merciless persecution, they commemorate the noble dead who died to keep God's name holy. The narratives recount, town by town, incident by incident, often in great detail, the sorry tale of crusader–citizenry assault: desecration of synagogues and sacred books, the double-dealing to get hold of Jewish wealth, the savage ultimatum of baptism or death, the pitiless slaughter of men, women and children, the mutilation of corpses . . .

'A NEW-STYLE MARTYRDOM'

. . . and in face of it all, fidelity to Judaism, heroism unto death, and that not only by particular individuals but by whole families and indeed by whole communities. This literature of memorialisation commended especially those who chose to die at the hands of each other rather than reject the charge God had laid on them:

> Those who were slain sanctified the Name for all the world to see and exposed their throats for their heads to be severed for the glory of the Creator, also slaughtering one another – man, his friend, his kin, his wife, his children, even his sons-in-law and daughters-in-law; and compassionate women slaying their only children – all wholeheartedly accepting the judgement of Heaven upon themselves, and as they yielded up their souls to the Creator, they all cried out: 'Hear, O Israel, the Lord is our God, the Lord is One'.
>
> (Deut. 6: 4)

These were the words of Rabbi Eliezer bar Nathan, liturgical poet and Talmudic scholar whose 'Chronicle' brings out most clearly the essentially religious nature of this Hebrew literary genre: a narrative of pogroms certainly, but also a poetic commemorative lament for the martyrs of Speyer, Worms, Mainz and Cologne and more profoundly, a reading of God's unfolding purpose in permitting this suffering (Eidelberg 1997: 81). Eliezer recalled how when the Rhineland Jewries realised the extremity of the peril that threatened them as the crusade got under way, they had recourse to the appropriate penitential discipline of prayer, fasting and works of charity to avert God's wrath. But God hid himself, withholding his compassion, deaf to their appeal. For he had chosen this generation for a particular purpose of his own: in punishment for its sin, it should be put to the test, charged to demonstrate the strength of its faith and its fidelity to his word. The test passed, its exemplary conduct in face of a vicious foe dedicated to obliterating the name of Israel either by baptism or massacre would be meritorious for all future generations. Suffering then, but placed in the perspective of salvation history. In short, 'a new-style martyrdom' (Chazan 1987: 217–18).

This literature of panegyric was also one of polemic (Abulafia 1985). As the memorialising writers eulogised martyrdom to fortify the faith of their readers, so they sought to deter them from any possible seduction by Christianity. This they did in vituperative language, sometimes, for example, put in the mouths of Jews defying their oppressors with taunts against 'the name of the crucified, despicable and abominable son of harlotry'. Rabbi Eliezer wrote of how those who had been coerced into baptism returned to Judaism 'for in the end they regarded the object of the enemy's veneration as no more than slime and dung'. There was more of this contemptuous vilification of Jesus and his mother, in essence a denial of the central Christian doctrines of Incarnation and Resurrection, but phrased in language sharpened, it has been suggested, by drawing on the invective tradition of the centuries-old parody of the Gospels known as *Toledoth Yesu*.

The appearance of this genre of literature – at once history of persecution, martyrology, theology of suffering and polemic – is in itself evidence of how the pogroms had changed the ethos of the European Jewish world and made of the First Crusade a watershed in Jewish history.

THE FAILURE OF PROTECTION

When all official theory, civil and ecclesiastical, condemned violence against Jews, why were they not better defended? One reason was the absence of their most powerful protectors: Henry IV was in Italy, the duke of Bohemia in Poland. This meant that the local rulers – bishops in the case of the cities which saw the most devastating attacks – were overwhelmed by the superior force of the crusaders and citizens combined. The Jews looked to the bishops for sanctuary, and were prepared to pay handsomely for it, but their attempts at protection, fairly fully chronicled by the Jewish writers, were largely failures: in Worms where the crusader–townsmen collusion was particularly close; in Mainz where the archbishop's men deserted him and he was threatened with death for standing up for the Jews; in Cologne where the bishop's attempt to save the Jews by dispersing them to strongpoints outside the city, also proved ultimately unsuccessful. These were attacks of sustained intensity

Figure 9.1 The Jews of Norwich unflatteringly sketched on a tallage roll from the English exchequer, 1233. Isaac, the city's richest Jew, is represented with three heads, symbolising the worship of Antichrist, while the devil 'Colbif' berates his agents, 'Mosse Mokke' and 'Aveghaye'. © London, Public Record Office.

and persistence which overcame all opposition. Only in Speyer, with its history of good relations between its bishop and the Jewish community, was the bishop finally effective, but then only after some murders and suicides. He had at his disposal 'a large army', sufficient at any rate not only to save the Jewry but also to punish those guilty of attacking Jews by having their hands cut off.

Some bishops urged Jews to save themselves by accepting baptism. Egilbert, archbishop of Trier, was one such and he had a biographer to record how he went about it. He reported how as the crusaders approached the city, some Jews killed their children 'lest they be the victims of the derision of Christian madness'. Some Jewish women stuffed stones into their dresses and leapt into the river Moselle. The rest, however, fled to the refuge of the bishop's palace, tearfully to entreat his help. But he, 'taking advantage of a favourable opportunity', sought to convert them. He told them that this crisis had befallen them because of their sins in blaspheming the son of God and dishonouring his mother. He reminded them that they were bound in guilt to their ancestors who had crucified the son of God. He urged them to save themselves from death in body and soul by accepting baptism and the Catholic faith with a firm heart. Do this, he declared, and 'I will restore your possessions to you in peace and safety and then protect you from your enemies'. The biographer then has it that the Jews having listened to an exposition of the Catholic faith renounced Judaism and asked that their reception of baptism should be hastened so that they might escape the hands of those searching for them. But he went on to say that all returned to Judaism, save one, about whose sincerity he had doubts (Pertz 1848: 190–1).

All sources, Christian and Jewish alike, agree that the return to Judaism was universal. It was permitted by Henry IV. No one mentioned any episcopal opposition and the argument from silence might suggest that bishops concurred. The papacy remained silent though the antipope Clement III ordered the bishop of Bamberg to make haste to prevent baptised Jews returning to Judaism for that ran contrary to 'canonical sanction and the example of the fathers' (Simonsohn 1988: 42). If Clement had in mind those Jews who had conformed externally to the practice of Christianity, and there is mention of such in the Jewish sources, he may well have had in mind a canon of Toledo IV, included in Ivo's *Decretum*, which asserted that the relapsed of this sort 'should be forced to observe the faith into which they had been coerced by force and necessity, lest the name of the Lord should be blasphemed and the faith they had taken on be held as base and contemptible' (Linder 1997: 653–4). In Prague, it was alleged that it was through the clergy's negligence that Jews had forsaken Christianity after forced baptism, a charge taken sufficiently seriously by Hermann, bishop of Prague, on his death-bed in 1122 to accuse himself of negligence in allowing Jews to relapse.

There is no record of the Papacy responding in any way to the pogroms of 1096. In the pontificate of Calixtus II (1119–24), however, there was issued, in response to Jewish petitions, a letter of protection for Jews which has a good claim to be the most important single papal statement on this subject (Simonsohn 1988: 44, 51; Grayzel 1962). For it was to be frequently reissued by many popes, sometimes with updating, and it was to find a place in the official code of canon law. Calixtus was strongly committed to the crusade both in the Holy Land and in Spain. There is no evidence to link *Sicut iudeis* directly with crusade preaching. But it fits the context. It reiterates that Jews were not to be coerced into baptism, that their persons and their property should be protected from arbitrary violence and from punishment without due legal process. They were to be permitted to practise their religion, though forbidden to build new synagogues or to enlarge or make more ornate existing ones. These permissions were to apply only to those Jews who did not seek to subvert the Christian faith. That Jews were enemies awaiting their opportunity to strike against Christians was commonplace in Christian thought.

THE SECOND CRUSADE: RENEWED PERSECUTION IN 1145

The fall of Edessa in December 1144 sparked off a new burst of crusading zeal. It sparked off, too, a new burst of Jewish anxiety. Rabbi Ephraim of Bonn, a contemporary witness, gave voice to it:

> We called out to the Lord, saying 'Behold, O Lord our God, not yet fifty years have passed since our blood was spilled for the unity of Your revered name, at the time of the great slaughter. Will you forsake us for ever, O Lord? Will your anger last throughout the generations? Such tribulation should not recur twice.
>
> (Eidelberg 1977: 122)

But recur it did, *Sicut iudeis* notwithstanding. Persecution of Jews was preached to sympathetic ears especially by a maverick Cistercian, one Raoul. In many towns of France and Germany (including Mainz, Worms and Cologne, where the Jewries had earlier suffered so severely) he urged the death of Jews as enemies of the Christian religion. Peter the Venerable, Raoul's Cluniac contemporary, disclaimed any intention of 'sharpening Christian swords against this impious people'. But, nevertheless, he made a strong case for doing so. 'What would be the profit', he demanded of the king of France, Louis VII, 'if the Saracens, the enemy in distant lands were conquered, while the Jewish blasphemers, far worse enemies of Christians than Saracens, were allowed in our very midst, with impunity to blaspheme, despise and disfigure Christ and all the Christian sacraments?' How can zeal for God consume his sons if the Jews, the foremost enemies of Christ and Christians, are allowed to escape totally unscathed? A Christian king should heed the words of a holy king of old: 'Have I not hated them, O Lord, that hated thee: and pined away because of my enemies? I have hated them with a perfect hatred' (Ps. 138: 21) (Constable 1967: 327–30; Friedman 1978; Torrell 1987: 339–42). It was sentiments such as these, along with greed for Jewish wealth, which led again to crusaders and townsmen combining to present Jews with the choice of baptism or death, with desecration of Torah scrolls, and looting of Jewish properties. All the atrocities of 1096 were repeated in 1146 and in much the same region.

Ephraim of Bonn's *Book of Remembrance* suggests that despite the brutalities which attended the Second Crusade, the Jews were somewhat better protected. Otto of Freising credited Conrad III with protecting many Jews as also the citizens of some towns (unspecified) (Waitz 1912: 372). Ephraim of Bonn credited the archbishop of Cologne with considerable success in protecting Jews. He noted too that there were Gentiles who safeguarded their Jewish acquaintances. Judicious use of Jewish money is also a theme of Ephraim's account, buying protection, obtaining deterrent punishment of murderers.

Both Otto of Freising and Ephraim of Bonn, our main sources of information for the pogroms of 1146, gave prominence to the role of Bernard of Clairvaux in combating attacks on Jews. Both accounts make it twofold. He was able to silence the inflammatory preaching of Raoul. He constructed a theological defence of Jews which he propagated widely. That God himself had forbidden Jews to be killed as enemies of the Christian religion became an integral part of crusade preaching.

Both writers recorded that Bernard's argument was presented as an exegesis of Ps. 58: 12: 'God shall let me see over my enemies: slay them not, lest at any time my people forget. Scatter them by thy power: and bring them down, O Lord my protector.' The classic interpretation of this text, applied to the Jews, had been supplied by Augustine: it was God's will that Judaism should survive and that its survival and dispersal throughout the nations should serve to support the truth of Christianity. Bernard put his personal stamp on this reading. He commended the zeal for God of those who took up arms against the Saracen but instructed them to do so according to knowledge (cf. Rm. 12: 2). And the knowledge they were to have is that 'Jews should not be persecuted nor killed nor even expelled'. For Christ speaking through his Church in the psalm has stated, 'God has made it known to me not to kill these my enemies'. And discerning God's purpose in his decree, he argued that their dispersal among Christians was a reminder of Christ's redeeming suffering because it was at their hands that he had met his death. Dispersal as punishment for this very great crime had brought Jews to harsh captivity under Christian princes. There was a further reason for believing God wanted Jews to survive. Alexander II had used the same argument. God had promised that their conversion to Christ would eventually occur: 'If the Jews are totally destroyed, how can we hope for the salvation which has been promised for them at the end, their final conversion?' (Leclercq and Rochais 1977: 316; Dahan 1987: 59–64).

Peter the Venerable used the same psalm text to argue for Jewish survival. But he was arguing a particular course of action: 'Let their lives be preserved but let their money be taken from them so that the insolence of the infidel Saracens be subdued by the right arms of Christians, strengthened by the wealth of the blaspheming Jews.' He argued for the appropriateness of relieving Jews of wealth, illicitly acquired, to serve the great cause.

It was to Louis VII that he proposed his plan. Ephraim of Bonn noted that French Jews did lose much of their wealth through the action of the king. It would seem, however, that in this context of financial exploitation of Jews in support of the crusade, it was Pope Eugenius III who had more direct influence on Louis VII than Peter the Venerable. For the pope was offering privileges to crusaders, one of which was exemption from paying interest on past loans, with absolution from any oath binding them to a loan contract (*Quantum praedecessores*, 1146). Bernard supported this inducement in his crusade preaching. It is unclear how it was implemented but that it led to Jewish financial loss is not difficult to believe.

Another action of Louis VII may well have given greater cause for concern. He issued a decree against Jews who returned to Judaism after baptism (Luchaire 1885: 143). They were to be banished from the kingdom under sanction of death or mutilation. Coerced baptism was not specifically mentioned, but the implementation of this decree in the crusading context where forced baptism was a regular feature was a potentially very serious threat.

THE THIRD CRUSADE: ENGLAND AND GERMANY

At the foot of the mound which is crowned by Clifford's Tower in the city of York there stands a commemorative plaque. It reads:

> On the night of Friday 16 March 1190 some 150 Jews and Jewesses of York having sought protection in the royal castle on this site from a mob incited by Richard Malebisse and others chose to die at each other's hands rather than renounce their faith.

> Let them give glory to the Lord and let the people of the islands voice his praise [this in Hebrew].
>
> (Isaiah XLII 12)

The biblical text is doubly apt – both for what it states and for its echoes of the medieval Jewish poet Rabbi Menachem ben Joseph in his elegy on Jewish martyrs, including those of York, concluding as it did: 'They spurned the vanity of life . . . thus they gave glory to the Lord and declared his praise in the island.' That the plaque, erected as a gesture of reconciliation, is sited where it is, is also apt for it marks the scene of England's worst pogrom (Howlett 1884–9: i. 293–9, 308–24; Dobson 1974). But what happened in York was not just of local and national significance. It was another example of that European phenomenon, pogroms at the time of crusades.

The York atrocity of March 1190 was actually far worse than the plaque indicates. The memorial commemorates martyrs, those within the castle who accepted death, whether self-inflicted or at the hands of loved ones, rather than submit to baptism by force, the Jews who accepted the advice of the much-respected elder, Yomtob of Joigny who happened then to be visiting this furthest outpost of European Jewry. The rabbi in William of Newburgh's account presented the starkness of the threefold choice: between acceptance of baptism, which was to choose the disgrace of apostasy, refusal of baptism, which would mean death in mockery at the hands of impious enemies or, on the other hand, in the praiseworthy manner and in the tradition of their ancestors, a willing and devout surrender of life to the one who asked us to die for his law at our own hand. It was those who accepted this martyrdom that Jewish tradition has especially memorialised. There were, however, two other incidents of massacre to raise the death-toll substantially, significantly to increase the guilt of those responsible, and to exacerbate the horror of the whole event.

Some Jews, unable to reach the protection of the royal castle, were slaughtered in the streets when they refused to accept baptism. Others, inside the castle, were not persuaded to accept the suicide pact. Newburgh has them crying down to their besiegers that they were 'prepared to accept your accustomed demand of us that we be washed clean in holy baptism and our former rites abandoned, to be united to Christ's Church'. Their submission in the form of asking for acceptance as brothers in the peace of Christ was to be shamefully betrayed. Lured from the castle by promises of safety they were mercilessly butchered by Malebisse and his followers even before they could be baptised. In effect the York Jewish community, men, women and children, their properties and possessions and their business records, had been obliterated.

This York pogrom was no isolated incident. It was rather the culmination of a series of attacks on Jews through the length of eastern England over the previous six months. The first riot occurred on the day of Richard I's coronation at Westminster, 3 September 1189. The leaders of the English Jewish community had come to London at this time to seek renewal of the privileges conceded to them by the late king, Henry II. This would be standard procedure, not merely for Jews but for many different sorts of petitioners who felt they needed formal reassurance of their legal position at the beginning of a new reign. The Jews had some difficulty in gaining access to Richard and as they waited, they were first jostled and then severely attacked by a mob. As the convenient rumour spread through London that the king planned the expulsion of the Jews, the initial attacks escalated into a wholesale assault on the persons and properties of the London Jewish community, England's largest, by an out-of-control mob, 'foaming at the mouth for plunder and for the slaughter of a people by God's judgment hateful to all', in Newburgh's explanation of the ferocity of the onslaught. Many Jews were killed, as also some Christians, in squabbles over the booty from Jewish houses which had been thoroughly pillaged and set on fire. There were forced baptisms.

There followed in February and March 1190 attacks on the Jewish communities in Norwich, King's Lynn, Stamford, Lincoln, York and Bury St Edmunds. Greed, envy, bloodlust were at work in all these towns. In most of them some Jews were killed, others forcibly baptised, their properties looted. In some, notably Lincoln, if they moved quickly, Jews were able to secure protection in the royal castles near to which they habitually lived, against the days of just such emergencies. But in most, casualties were high in proportion to the relative smallness of these provincial communities, and the damage to their properties severe; royal protection proved in the event to be of uncertain and variable quality. It was the conspicuous failure of royal officials to deliver that security to Jews which it was their duty to provide, which made the London and York attacks particularly vicious.

The chroniclers, who bring us as near to contemporary informed opinion as we can get, represent these attacks as unprecedented in England. Up to this time the *pax Judeorum* had held good; London had witnessed no previous outrage, we are told. What had gone wrong? The novelty challenged the chroniclers to explanation. Sometimes they could pinpoint an immediate cause, discerning in a particular happening the spark of the explosion: the minor scuffle at the palace of Westminster which precipitated the London pogrom; an alleged attempt by the Jews in Stamford to seize by force a Jew who had become a Christian and who had taken refuge in a church. Without hesitation Newburgh attributes the York massacre to an organized plot devised by Malebisse and his associates all heavily in debt to the Jews to whom their lands were pledged. They were under pressure to repay their loans, as the Jews in their turn were pressurised by the king's demands on them. Significantly, Newburgh's account of the York massacre ends with the destruction in York Minster of all records of debts to the Jews which had been kept there.

More general explanations of the attacks were offered. The dean of St Paul's, London, Ralph of Diss was emphatic that the responsibility for the attacks on Jews throughout England lay on those who had vowed to go with Richard on crusade. And he condemned them succinctly, with the Bernardine defence of Jewish survival:

> Many men preparing to march on Jerusalem decided to rise against the Jews before they attacked the Saracens. Therefore on 6 February [1190] they killed as many Jews in Norwich as could be found in their homes; some Jews found refuge in the castle. On 7 March in Stamford on market day many Jews were killed. On 16 March almost five hundred died in York, it is said, of wounds inflicted on each other. For they preferred to have their blood let by their own people rather than perish at the hands of the uncircumcised. On 18 March, Palm Sunday, fifty-seven Jews are said to have been murdered at Bury St Edmunds. Wherever they could be found Jews perished at the hands of the crusaders (*peregrinantes*) unless they were rescued with the help of those living in the town. It must not be believed that this slaughter of Jews, so disgraceful, so wicked, was acceptable to thinking men; the words of David come frequently to our ears: 'Slay them not'.
>
> (Stubbs 1876: ii. 75–6)

Newburgh also recognised crusader involvement in the mounting of these attacks, though he viewed it rather differently and assigned to it only a secondary role. To his mind, the crusaders despoiled Jews in order to finance their crusading pilgrimage.

He related how crusaders at Stamford and York and probably at King's Lynn rationalised their robbery from Jews as a service to Christ, since they were using the proceeds to pay their crusading expenses. However, Newburgh did not consider the outbreaks of violence as essentially crusader-created. In his analysis, it was on Henry II that there lay primary responsibility for the violence. Three times in his *History of English Affairs* did he express his condemnation of that king. In his own financial interest, Henry had over-encouraged and over-protected these enemies of Christ and their usurious practices; as a result, they had become arrogant, extortionate, oppressive of Christians. Hence such a backlog of resentment had been built up that eventual disaster to the Jews inevitably followed. And so it was 'by the just judgement of Christ' that retribution followed, even if it were implemented by wrong-doers.

All the attacks on Jews in 1190 took place after King Richard had left the country on crusade. It may be that had he been in England more drastic intervention on behalf of his interests might have prevented the worst of the atrocities. However, it is relevant to note, at the time of his coronation in September 1189, he had been powerless to stop the London riot and totally ineffectual in punishing the criminals, despite his reported anger at the grave injury done to the royal authority. That injury was compounded when, immediately following the London incident, after he had affirmed his peace and protection for Jews, it was ignored in so many provincial towns.

The weakness of the English government in this crisis contrasted markedly with the success of the German monarchy in protecting its Jews in the context of crusader threats to their lives. The Emperor Frederick I who took the Cross in Mainz in March 1188 was already a veteran crusader having served under his uncle Conrad II on the Second Crusade. The Jews of Mainz, as of other Rhineland towns, were in their very different way also veterans of crusading, their community having suffered virtual obliteration at the time of the First Crusade and having been terrorised at the time of the Second by the inflammatorily hostile preaching of the Cistercian Raoul. In 1188–90 the experience of ruler and ruled combined to frustrate the savagery of some crusaders who, like some of their predecessors, thought that Jews were indistinguishable from Saracens as common enemies of Christ and ought either to be baptised or to be killed. The Jews were quick to take refuge in castles that proved safe. They organised for themselves a negotiating team to keep their plight in the forefront of the concerns of the civil authorities and to have it adequately provided with the cash necessary to ensure protection that was effectively activated. They were successful in securing the cooperation of the emperor. He forbade attacks on Jews under threat of condign punishments. According to a Jewish source, a letter of Rabbi Moses ben Eleazar, anyone who wounded a Jew was to have his hand cut off; anyone who killed a Jew would himself be killed (Chazan 1970: 84–93). And the emperor made sure that his officials understood he was in deadly earnest about ensuring the safety of his Jews. Furthermore he induced the German bishops to back up his measures. To quote Eleazar again, 'the bishops condemned anyone raising his hand against the Jews in order to harm them', their privileged crusader status notwithstanding. These early, coordinated and appropriately firm measures taken by the Jews themselves and the Christian authorities acting responsibly, alerted by memories of the unhappy experiences of earlier crusade ventures, contrast sharply with the ineffectuality of English officialdom with its complacent assumption that the hitherto unbreached *pax Judeorum* would continue to hold even in the circumstances of the crusade fever now affecting England for the first time.

The English government reacted strongly to the damage done to the royal authority and treasury by the violence of 1190. There was first an attempt at punitive action. At the beginning of May 1190, the chancellor William of Longchamp, bishop of Ely, arrived in York to seek out and punish those who had violated the king's peace given to Jews and to seek recompense for the damage caused to the royal treasury by destruction of their property and loss of their money. By this time the ringleaders of the conspiracy had fled either to Scotland or on crusade. The city authorities claimed that they had neither participated in the massacre nor had they been strong enough to prevent it. Hostages from the citizenry were taken and held until the richest citizens on behalf of the city as a whole paid fines. But the mass of the rioters, many of them from the surrounding countryside, could not be identified. Longchamp sacked the royal officials, that sheriff and constable of the castle whose inadequacies had allowed the initial attack to get out of hand and bring about the deaths of so many Jews whose safety in the castle should have been guaranteed. Malebisse himself forfeited his estates, which presumably was why in 1191 he joined John in rebellion against the king. When John became king in 1199 Malebisse made fine for all past offences, including his part in the York massacre, and his lands were restored to him. Careful attempts to identify the numerous other Yorkshire gentry who were Malebisse's associates have not been very successful; evidence, it would seem, though negative, that their punishments, if any, were of no great severity. Attempts to recoup in the king's interest what had been lost in the destruction of Jews' property were pursued for some years, as the instructions given to the itinerant justices in 1194 show. But their degree of success is difficult to establish. All in all, Newburgh was right if he meant no one paid with his own life for killing Jews when he wrote between two and four years later: 'Up to the present time, no one has been condemned for that massacre of Jews'.

There were, however, developments in the aftermath of the massacres of Jews of greater long-term significance than punitive measures and the securing of compensation for loss of Jewish resources. Richard made clear that Henry II's policy of privileging Jews would continue by renewing the charter by which the special position of Jews in England and Normandy would be guaranteed. It was a charter which also underlined the royal monopoly of control of the Jews. But he also went further than had Henry II in tightening the link between Crown and Jews.

This he did by establishing a permanent exchequer of the Jews, a sub-department of the Great Exchequer, the hub of royal government. There had already been, in the late 1180s, some movement towards setting up a distinct government department to deal with Jewish affairs. It had been found administratively convenient in 1186 to handle the collection of the tallage on Jews separately from the rest of the revenue-raising. Likewise, after the death of Aaron of Lincoln it had been found easier to reckon the amounts of the king's take-off from outstanding debts by setting up an 'exchequer of Aaron'. But in 1194 when Richard returned to England and ordered a general survey of his assets and a certain reorganisation of their management, earlier *ad hoc* arrangements of Jewish financial matters were put on a more permanent basis. It was then that the exchequer of the Jews began to take shape. The justices in the eyre of 1194 were instructed to register all Jewish properties of whatever sort, to nominate six or seven towns where all loan contracts were to be registered by officials appointed to oversee the appropriate procedures: 'from this time', the instruction ran, 'no contract is to be made with nor payment made to Jews nor any alteration in the bonds except before these officials or a majority of them'. Here is the birth of the exchequer of the Jews, with its 'keepers', its standard form of contract (the chirograph), its chests (*arcae*, which became the generic term for the repositories of loan records); a government department which had competence over Jewish affairs, both as a financial agency and a law court. We hear no more of such arrangements as had made York Minster a place of deposit for records of debts, readily open to the likes of Richard Malebisse and his fellow-criminals. Jews were now formally administered directly by the Crown and, while still having recourse to the ordinary royal courts, had now a court specialising in matters Jewish, especially those concerning loans. The development probably enhanced their security and the efficiency of their business dealings because they were the more clearly underwritten by the Crown and its law. But it also enhanced their vulnerability for they were now to be even more readily at the mercy of the ruthless vagaries of inherently unstable royal fiscal policies. And they shared too the unpopularity of those policies in the country at large (Stubbs 1868–71: iii, 262–7; Scott 1948–50: 446–55; Richardson 1960: 116–20).

The period of ruinously merciless taxation of Jews by the kings of England was as yet some way off (Stacey 1988: 135–50). Richard I, like his father before him, was reasonably moderate in his demands on his Jews. One sign that the Jews had weathered the storms of 1189–90 came in 1194 when the king taxed all the Jewish communities in the so-called 'Northampton *donum*' (Abrahams 1925: lix–lxxiv). Figures for the receipts of this levy are extant. They show that despite the attacks of a few years earlier healthy sums could still be raised without gross damage to Jewish businesses. In all, twenty Jewries contributed. York, King's Lynn and Stamford did not figure in this record. But London, Lincoln and Norwich did.

An even surer sign of Jewish recovery came in the reconstitution of the York community. The Pipe Rolls for 1195 show Jewish lenders active in Yorkshire. By the turn of the century, York was one of twenty-seven towns where *arcae* were established (Richardson 1960: 14; Dobson 1974: 41–2). By the end of the second decade of the new century, royal taxation records strongly suggest that York had become second only to London as the wealthiest Jewish community in the country. Such was the courage and resilience of the Jews, such was the continuing high demand for their credit services, such was (the exceptional circumstances of 1189–90 apart) the power of royal protection. We witness in England a recovery similar to that achieved by the continental Jewries after the massacres and lootings of the First Crusade.

This is not to say that the recovery of the northern European Jewries was the result of cessation of persecution. Far from it. Such persecution, in the thirteenth century and beyond, could and did take many forms: most notably, in the baseless accusations of ritual murder, blood libel and host desecration and in wholesale expulsions (Rubin 1999). Nor is it to say that persecution in the crusade context ceased totally. The Shepherds' Crusades of 1251 (Jordan 1979: 113–16) and 1320 (Barber 1981; Nirenberg 1996: 43–92) showed that at least for the peasants who made up the *pastoureaux*, the cause of the Holy Land demanded the killing of Jews as a preliminary. But in effect the chapter in the history of persecution of Jews which attended mainstream crusading closed in 1190[2] – and did so presumably because the ruling classes had at last come fully to appreciate that slaughtering Jews was inimical not only to their religion but also to their economic interests.

NOTES

1 Ivo of Chartres included them in his *Decretum* (Linder 1997: 671–2). The letter to all the Spanish bishops became particularly influential since the substance of it entered Gratian's *Decretum*, C. 23 q. 8 c. 11 (*Dispar*) and thus became an ordinary part of a canonistic education.
2 Although it has been suggested that crusade involvement stimulated some rulers to further tighten restrictions on Jews: Jordan 1979: 154; Stacey 1988: 146.

REFERENCES

Abrahams, I. (1925) 'The Northampton *donum* of 1194', in *Jewish Historical Society of England. Miscellanies*, 1, lix–lxxxvi.

Abulafia, A. S. (1982) 'The interrelationship between the Hebrew Chronicles on the First Crusade', *Journal of Jewish Studies* 27: 221–39.

—— (1985) 'Invectives against Christianity in the Hebrew chronicles of the First Crusade', in P. W. Edbury (ed.) *Crusade and Settlement*, Cardiff: University College Cardiff Press, 66–72.

—— (1996) 'Anti-Jewish crusading violence and the Christianization of Europe', *The Journal of Progressive Judaism* 7: 59–77.

Aronius, J. (1902) *Regesten zur Geschichte der Juden im fränkischen und deutschen Reiche bis zum Jahre 1273*, Berlin: rpt 1970, Hildesheim and New York: Olms.

Barber, M. (1981) 'The Pastoureaux of 1320', *Journal of Ecclesiastical History* 32: 143–66.

Chazan, R. (1970) 'The Emperor Frederick I, the Third Crusade and the Jews', *Viator* 8: 83–93.

—— (1987) *European Jewry and the First Crusade*, Berkeley: University of California Press.

Cohn, N. (1993) *The Pursuit of the Millennium. Revolutionary millenarians and mystical anarchists of the Middle Ages* (3rd edn), London: Paladin.

Constable, G. (ed.) (1967) *The Letters of Peter the Venerable*, 2 vols, Cambridge, Mass.: Harvard University Press.

Dahan, G. (1987) 'Bernard de Clairvaux et les juifs', *Archives Juives* 23: 59–64.

Dobson, R. B. (1974) *The Jews of Medieval York and the Massacre of March 1190*, Borthwick Papers 45, York: Borthwick Institute.

Edgington, S. (1997) 'The First Crusade: reviewing the evidence', in J. Phillips (ed.) *The First Crusade. Origins and impact*, Manchester: Manchester University Press, 57–77.

Eidelberg, S. (1977) *The Jews and the Crusaders*, Wisconsin: University of Wisconsin Press.

Friedman, Y. (1978) 'An anatomy of anti-semitism: Peter the Venerable's letter to Louis VII, king of France (1146)', in *Bar-Ilan Studies in History*, ed. P. Artzi, Ramat-Gan: Bar-Ilan University Press, 87–102.

Gilchrist, J. (1988) 'The perception of Jews in the canon law in the period of the first two crusades', *Jewish History* 3: 9–25.

—— (1989) 'The canonistic treatment of Jews in the Latin West in the eleventh and early twelfth centuries', *Zeitschrift der Savigny-Stiftung für Rechtsgeschichte. Kanonistische Abteilung* 75: 70–106.

Grayzel, S. (1962) 'The papal bull "Sicut iudeis"', in M. Ben-Horin (ed.), *Studies and Essays in Honor of A. A. Newman*, Leiden: Brill, 243–80.

Howlett, R. (ed.) (1884–9), William of Newburgh, *Historia rerum Anglicarum*, in *Chronicles and Memorials of the Reigns of Stephen, Henry II and Richard I*, vols i, ii, 416–583 London: Rolls Series: Longman.

Jordan, W. C. (1979) *Louis IX and the Challenge of the Crusade*, Princeton, NJ: Princeton University Press.

Leclercq, J. and Rochais, H. M. (1977) *Sancti Bernardi Opera*, vol. 8: Rome: Editiones Cistercienses.

Liebeschütz, H. (1959) 'The crusading movement in its bearing on the Christian attitude towards Jewry', *Journal of Jewish Studies* 10: 97–111.

Linder, A. (1997) *The Jews in the Legal Sources of the Early Middle Ages*, Detroit: Wayne State University Press.

Luchaire, A. (1885) *Études sur les actes de Louis VII*, Paris: Alphonse Picard.

Nirenberg, D. (1996) *Communities of Violence. Persecution of minorities in the Middle Ages*, Princeton, NJ: Princeton University Press.

Pertz, G. H. (ed.) (1848) *Chronica et gesta aevi Salici* (MGH, Scriptores 8), Hanover.

Recueil des Historiens des Croisades (1841–1906) Paris: Académie des Inscriptions et Belles Lettres.

Richardson, H. G. (1960) *The English Jewry under the Angevin Kings*, London: Methuen/The Jewish Historical Society.

Riley-Smith, J. (1984) 'The First Crusade and the persecution of the Jews', *Studies in Church History* 21: 51–72.

Rubin, M. (1999) *Gentile Tales. The narrative assault on late medieval Jews*, London and New Haven: Yale University Press.

Scott, K. (1948–50) 'The Jewish arcae', *Cambridge Law Journal* 10: 446–55.

Simonsohn, S. (1988) *The Apostolic See and the Jews. Documents: 492–1404*, Toronto: Pontifical Institute of Mediaeval Studies.

Stacey, R. (1988) '1240–1260: a watershed in Anglo-Jewish relations?', *Historical Research* 61: 135–50

Stow, K. R. (1992) *Alienated Minority. The Jews of Medieval Latin Europe*, Cambridge, Mass.: Harvard University Press.

Stubbs, W. (ed.) (1868–71) *Chronica Magistri Rogeri de Hovedene*, 4 vols, London: Rolls Series: Longmans, Green, Reader and Dyer.

Stubbs, W. (ed.) (1876) *The Historical Works of Master Ralph de Diceto*, 2 vols, London: Rolls Series: Longman.

Torrell, J.-P. (1987) 'Les Juifs dans l'oeuvre de Pierre le Vénérable', *Cahiers de civilisation médiévale* 30: 331–46.

Waitz, G. (ed.) (1912) *Ottonis et Rahewini Gesta Friderici I. imperatoris* (MGH, Scriptores rerum Germanicarum, 46), Hanover and Leipzig.

STRANGE EVENTFUL HISTORIES: THE MIDDLE AGES IN THE CINEMA

Stuart Airlie

Movies can be dangerous for medievalists. In *Monty Python and the Holy Grail* (1975) no sooner has a crusty tweed-jacketed professor of medieval history begun his lecture on the film's lack of historical accuracy than he is cut down by a mounted knight in armour who gallops off, leaving the professor's distraught wife to call the police to track down the villain from the age of chivalry. In *The Fisher King* (1991), the Robin Williams character finds that his obsession with the Middle Ages leads to him living rough on the streets or New York, streets filled with hallucinatory visions of medieval knights. Yet movies remain strangely seductive. No less a figure than Georges Duby hoped to see his book on the battle of Bouvines filmed, and fretted on the problems of representing the daily lived reality of the distant past on the big screen. How would he be able to answer Gerard Depardieu's questions on the horse-riding, eating and dating habits or Philip Augustus? How one relishes the prospect of the dapper professor encountering the great figure of Depardieu or the svelte Nastassia Kinski whom Duby's musings led him to see as Joan, countess of Flanders. Sadly, these encounters never took place; Bouvines remained unfilmed and Duby concluded that film did not yet possess a form or a language capable of transmitting historians' ideas of past societies (Duby 1991: 185–6).

Where the professors have managed to have some input on films the results have not always been satisfactory. The advice of Jacques Le Goff and a host of medievalist consultants together with the director's concern for authenticity could not prevent *The Name of the Rose* (1986), a film based on a novel by the medievalist Umberto Eco, from turning out to be a lumbering failure (Moliterno 1995). Authenticity need not be cinematic. The information carried via the screen is different in amount and kind from that carried by the printed page, the preferred medium for academic representation of the past. The conventions of one medium may not transfer well to the other (Rosenstone 1988). Questions of authenticity and fidelity to historical evidence can thus become less relevant than questions of what is appropriate to the medium, whether print or film. Does authenticity matter for the success of a historical film? Professor J. C. Holt is said to have abandoned the rarefied world of Magna Carta to offer advice to the makers of *Robin Hood* (1991). The result is an interesting film, more dramatically credible than *Robin Hood: Prince of Thieves* (1991), which was released simultaneously. Both these films are, however, cinematically trounced by the Errol Flynn version, *The Adventures of Robin Hood* (1938) which is untroubled by notions of the otherness of the past and which had enough life in it as a Hollywood classic to enjoy a re-release in Britain in 1998.

It is not surprising therefore that historians are often suspicious of the world of films. At a symposium held in Berlin in 1983 devoted to the reception of the Middle Ages, German medievalists reeled in horror at screened excerpts from such Hollywood monstrosities as *The Knights of the Round Table* (1953) and *Camelot* (1967), lamenting such films' concern with mere trappings such as costumes at the expense of a specific feel for period and of any sense of the otherness of the past (Wapnewski 1986: 366–7). Even outside Hollywood, such a serious and thoughtful film as *The Return of Martin Guerre* (1982), based on an intrinsically dramatic case of claims to identity, revealed that film-makers' priorities in presenting sixteenth-century France on screen inevitably cut across those of the historian Natalie Zemon Davies (Davies 1983; Toplin 1988: 1224; and Rosenstone 1988). The very medium seems suspect. Historians are necessarily concerned with problems of scrutinising evidence and using it to construct provisional analyses, considering alternative outcomes to events, stressing complexity. Historians are in the business of demystifying.

Films, on the other hand, particularly Hollywood films, try to show through linear narrative driving towards closure, concentration on individuals and 'invisible' technique that the world can be rendered unproblematically on screen (Rosenstone 1998 and 1992; but cf. Bordwell 1985 and see below on *The Adventures of Robin Hood*). The critical reader of history becomes a hypnotised voyeur. That at least is a view taken by mandarin figures of Western intellectual culture such as Theodor Adorno and Max Horkheimer who complained that films reduce spectators to passivity and rob them of their imagination and critical faculties (Adorno and Horkheimer 1979: 126). For some puritanical French thinkers, the cinema worked as an updated version of Plato's famous cave where spectators mistook projected shadows for the world itself and in their yearning for these shadows expressed their desire to abandon consciousness and return to the womb (Jay 1993: 477–9). This seems a little extreme. Early exposure to some of Hollywood's most mind-boggling versions of history such as *The Prince and the Pauper* where Errol Flynn briskly rights wrongs in Tudor England seems not to have robbed Gore Vidal of his sceptical world-view. In fact, Vidal notes that this film actually taught him a Machiavellian view of power (Vidal 1992: 26). Spectators are not entirely passive and Hollywood films, even bulky epics, are not as tightly closed and unproblematic as one might think, as is seen in Vidal's story of how he, as scriptwriter, managed to smuggle a gay sub-text into *Ben-Hur* (Vidal 1993: 1175–6).

Our fascination with films may therefore not be entirely suspect. The power of the visual is not confined to the twentieth century. Michael Camille sees the later Middle Ages as a culture that experienced an 'image explosion' (Camille 1992: 279; contrast Jay 1993). Certainly the medieval period continues to attract film-makers; the 1990s saw the release of the two Robin Hood films mentioned above as well as such varied Hollywood fare as *First Knight* (1995), *Braveheart* (1995) and Disney's *The Hunchback of Notre Dame* (1996). All three films revealed the continuing vitality of familiar thematic material of the cinematic Middle Ages: *First Knight* was a rather wooden version of the story of King Arthur (Sean Connery in grizzled wisdom-figure mode), Lancelot and Guinevere. *Braveheart* was a vision of the Middle Ages as a time of brutal savagery and grand battles that led to the birth of a nation. Its retelling of the conflict between Edward I and William Wallace was on an epic scale, as indeed was everything about this movie: the battle scenes, the trophies it won (five Academy Awards), the inaccuracies (Ewan 1995). The cartoon version of *The Hunchback of Notre Dame* took the familiar view of the Middle Ages as a time of dark oppression and narrow-minded persecution and gave it a fresh spin with a smart script, superb graphic art which wove tight threads of visual imagery through the film, and a Broadway-style score which blended pathos and humour to great, if disconcerting, effect. All three films drew on traditional cinematic views of the Middle Ages as a time of extremes (McArthur 1995; cf. Huizinga 1955): extreme idealism in the form of chivalry; extreme brutality in warfare, peasant life and the bonds of lordship; extreme rigidity in the persecuting mania of the inquisitorial Frollo in the *Hunchback*, depicted as agent and victim of ascetic drives towards unreal purity.

Cinematically, the Middle Ages often represent the wilder shores of human existence and this was also seen in two European productions of the decade: *The Hour of the Pig* (1994; US title: *The Advocate*), a British account of a trial of a pig for murder (the Middle Ages as a remote, weird and unhygienic world), and the broad but appealing French farce, *Les Visiteurs* (1993) in which two denizens of the Middle Ages travelled through time to 1990s France. Perhaps the last word in this depiction of the Middle Ages as a brutish world of dark superstition, persecution and grim horror dates from the 1950s in the form of Ingmar Bergman's *The Seventh Seal*, a film so stark in its excoriation of medieval darkness and so rosy in its idealising of humane values that it has not worn well. Such films, together with, say, Huizinga's view of the Middle Ages as a time of cultural extremes, in fact take their place in the general history of the reception of the Middle Ages, a topic of some interest to medievalists as they contemplate the origins of their discipline in nineteenth-century European Romantic culture (Huizinga 1955; Bloch and Nichols 1996; see also Wapnewski 1986; Frayling 1995). The cinematic depiction of history is also worth consideration as historians become ever more aware of the provisional nature of their own reconstructions of the past and the rhetorical conventions of such reconstructions (Evans 1997). Films do need, however, to be examined with care. The best studies of historical film focus on the films themselves and avoid simply pointing critical fingers at anachronisms or reducing films to the unproblematic expression of their own historical contexts (Harper 1994 is a model; Wyke 1997 is also useful). A film is a film is a film.

Within the confines of a single chapter such as this it is not possible to offer a general survey of how the cinema has treated the Middle Ages. Such a survey would need to be itself historical and take note that medieval subjects (themselves a various group) have experienced peaks and troughs of popularity, with the 1950s perhaps representing a peak for costume epics. Such a survey should also include non-western films such as Egyptian versions of the life of Saladin and the Crusades (Chahine 1996). It is also worth noting here that the medieval past may appear more fantastical in Hollywood than in Europe where monuments of medieval civilisation still survive. The weight of medieval history may press more heavily on European films concerned with such historical figures as Joan of Arc and Henry V, or even on films concerned with medieval legends such as Fritz Lang's *Nibelungen* (see below). After all, it is possible in Europe to see such films in 'medieval' settings as in the town of Conques in France, site not only of a famous medieval shrine but also, according to an advertisement in *Cahiers du cinéma* in 1997, site of a festival devoted to films about the Middle Ages. The juxtaposition of the remote past and the present can be more immediate in European art than in art produced in the USA. This point applies to more than films. A particularly stark juxtaposition is seen in the painting by Alfred Rethel (1816–59) of a modern factory built within the remains of a fourteenth-century castle in the Ruhr; the fact that Rethel later set out to depict the deeds of Charlemagne in a cycle of frescoes for the town hall of Aachen also provides food for thought here (Paret 1988: 80–91). It will not do, however, to draw too sharp a distinction between the medieval heritages of Europe and the United States. After all, Thomas Jefferson wanted Hengist and Horsa to be depicted on the Great Seal of the United States (Frantzen 1990: 15–17) while the impact of the novels of Walter Scott can be seen in such a small detail as the names given to the horses of the Confederate troops in William Faulkner's 1936 novel *Absalom, Absalom!* As we shall see below in our examination of *The Adventures of Robin Hood*, the claims of the old world were resonant in Hollywood. Such themes cannot be explored in detail here. What follows is merely an attempt to do two things: to suggest why such films might be worth watching and to recommend how to watch them. My focus is on the films themselves.

The figure of Joan of Arc has attracted film-makers since the very beginning of cinema. The great pioneer Méliès (who made a film of the Dreyfus affair in 1899) put Joan on screen in seven scenes featuring some 500 extras in 1899 or 1900 and since then Joan has enjoyed a long cinematic career in films made by directors as varied as the austere Dane Carl Theodor Dreyer (1928), the Hollywood veteran Victor Fleming, director of *The Wizard of Oz* and *Gone With the Wind*, and the former editor of *Cahiers du Cinéma*, Jacques Rivette, whose vast *Jeanne la pucelle* came out in 1993. It seems likely that films about Joan will continue to appear well into the twenty-first century. She has been portrayed by a formidable range of actresses in a remarkable range of styles: the opera singer Geraldine Farrar (in the silent film *Joan the Woman*, 1917), the stage actress Falconetti (*La Passion de Jeanne d'Arc*, 1928), the Hollywood star Ingrid Bergman (whose interest in Joan led her to play the part on stage as well as in two films, the lumbering *Joan of Arc* (1948) and a version of Honegger's 'oratorio', *Joan of Arc at the Stake* (1954)) (Harty 1996; appropriate entries in Katz 1994). Joan is part of cinema history, and particularly the history of star performances, and this cinematic Joan thus joins the immensely complex history of the picturing of Joan in the modern world where her representation, from labels on cheese boxes to appearances in the parades of the Front National, has been a potent means of articulating, and challenging, versions of French identity (Winock 1992).

Amidst this torrent of images, the great film of Dreyer, *La passion de Jeanne d'Arc* (1928) stands out, monumental and gaunt. In its quest for authenticity (it is based on the records of Joan's trial), its eschewal of battle scenes in favour of austere concentration on the trial itself, and in its setting that trial in a bare white world, the film permits viewers to focus on the precise situation of Joan at bay in front of her accusers. It is thus vastly different from the conventional Hollywood epic of 1948 and from the contemporary *La merveilleuse vie de Jeanne d'Arc* whose gargantuan battle scenes testify to the vigour of conventional French cinema and which can, in its stress on French military effort, be read as homage to the victory-bringing sacrifices of the First World War (Harty 1996; Hayward 1993: 97). Dreyer's film escapes such easy contextualising. In fact its potency would seem to remain undimmed; it was listed in both the critics' and the directors' top ten films in a poll for *Sight and Sound* in 1992.

Yet Dreyer's film is not a simple transcript of the trial proceedings and we should not approach it with an innocent eye (on what follows, see Margolis 1997). Following Aristotelian principles, Dreyer compressed Joan's trial into a single day and while he consulted historical experts he also drew on literary traditions ranging from Anatole France to surrealism. Further, when we watch Dreyer we have to be sure that we have access to a 'clean text' of his film in order to be sure that we are actually watching what he intended us to see. His film has suffered through censorship, material damage and heavy-handed restoration. As such, *La passion de Jeanne d'Arc* is a survivor from the heroic days of 'silent' cinema and carries its own historical freight in, for example, its preservation of performances by legendary figures of the French theatre such as Falconetti (in her only major film) and Antonin Artaud. Dreyer focused on the trial because of its dramatic structure but historical authenticity as such did not interest him (Margolis 1997: 470–4). The film is a highly wrought piece of poetic cinema in which the historical Joan serves as a point of departure for an intense focus on a suffering individual; the fact that that individual is located in the fifteenth century is not particularly relevant to the concerns of Dreyer and Falconetti (Thomson 1994: 210–11).

Perhaps the sheer greatness of Dreyer's film makes it elusive. A less successful version of Joan's story may, however surprisingly, conceal a hook to snag the medievalist's interest. Mauled by the critics and a flop at the box-office, Otto Preminger's *Saint Joan* (1957), based as it is on a version of George Bernard Shaw's play, may seem arid terrain, but trapped within it, in the performance of Jean Seberg in the title role, is a live historical element. At the time, Seberg and Preminger shared the blame for the film's failure (see, e.g., Greene 1993: 571) and Seberg's performance still strikes some as 'problematic' (Harty 1996: 253). Seberg in fact turned out to be a fascinating (anti-)star and comments on her later performances signal her disturbing screen presence: 'pity has not touched her, . . . cool, crop-haired grace' (Powell 1991: 134). Some of this quality is visible in her performance as Joan, where, in the words of a connoisseur of screen acting, 'even cropped and in armor she looked pretty and robust' (Thomson 1994: 682). Part of Seberg's appeal was her strikingly androgynous appearance and this, together with her lack of screen experience (*Saint Joan* was her first film), made the girl in armour stand out from the veteran actors on screen (John Gielgud, Anton Walbrook, Richard Widmark). Seberg's youthful appearance is striking; nineteen when the film was released, she was in fact fairly close to the age of the historical Joan. One recalls Marc Bloch on medieval princes: 'This world, . . . which considered itself very old, was in fact governed by young men' (Bloch 1962: 73). Seberg made Joan a cinematic outsider, a fresh presence, no mean feat considering the weight of cinematic tradition that muffled Joan; the oddness of Seberg points to the outsider status of Joan. It is no surprise to find Marina Warner noting that Seberg 'most corresponds to our contemporary feeling about her [Joan]'

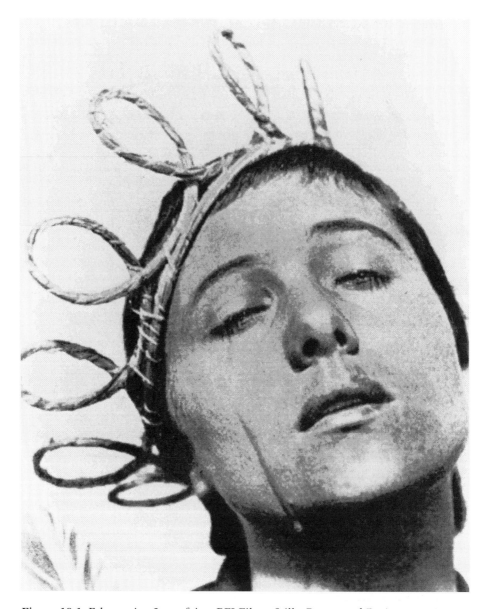

Figure 10.1 Falconetti as Joan of Arc. BFI Films: Stills, Posters and Designs.

(Warner 1981: 331). More than this, Seberg's youthful androgyny points to late medieval concerns over the seductive threat to gender roles and the established order by women who dressed in masculine clothing, whose hair was cut short like a man's (Koziol 1992: 312); the historical trial's concern with Joan's usurping of masculine status reflects this fear that gender could be abolished (Warner 1981: 139–58; Schihanoff 1996). These historical concerns are embodied in the performance of Jean Seberg.

In an extreme form, films bring home the distance between the historical Middle Ages and modern reconstructions of that period. This distance can be glimpsed through glaring anachronisms such as the wristwatches worn by extras playing the part of Huns in Fritz Lang's *Die Nibelungen* (1924). This error was spotted by a horrified Lang watching the rushes in the evening and he re-shot the scenes at great expense (Bourget 1992: 133–4). But the removal of inappropriate details such as this still leaves the film very much a product of its medium and time. Lang, and his screenwriter partner Thea von Harbou, did not want to recreate a specific historical period; their subject matter, after all, derived from the twelfth-century German poem, the *Nibelungenlied*, whose mythical characters encountered remote historical figures such as Attila the Hun from the fifth century. They were not dealing with a real historical personage such as Joan of Arc. They wished to create a world of myth (Hake 1990: 48).

The first part of the film, *Siegfried*, does indeed evoke the primitive forest, the *Urwald*, with haunting scenes of the heroic Siegfried making his way through a landscape dominated by massive tree trunks. This landscape, however, is hardly medieval. The investing of the natural landscape, particularly mountains and forests, with a spiritual meaning and the interplay between this meaning and the presence of man is a key element in German Romantic art; one need think only of the paintings of Caspar David Friedrich or Arnold Böcklin, or of the scene in Act 2 of Wagner's opera *Siegfried* (another representation of the *Nibelungenlied* material) as well as the troubling modern visions of the forest in the work of Anselm Kiefer (Hartley 1994). In fact Lang's *Siegfried*'s forest journey explicitly echoes a painting by A. Böcklin and Friedrich's work is also evoked (Eisner 1973: 155–6 and cf.106–7; Hake 1990: 44; Bourget 1992: 68).

Of course, great forests existed in the Middle Ages, but Lang was drawing on a Romantic visual tradition rather than medieval literary images such as Charles D'Orleans' fifteenth-century vision of 'la forest d'Ennuyeuse Tristesse' (Taylor 1995: 153). Furthermore, the Romantic forest could only be created on screen with the help of modern technology; the great trees through which Siegried passed were massive cement structures heroically constructed by the studio technicians on one of the stages of UFA, the German film studio, at Neubabelsberg in Berlin, just as the eerie mist that enveloped Siegfried was due to a special technical process. The *Urwald* was a triumph of cinematic artifice and the studio was distressed when the mighty trees were felled by a visiting British director, one Alfred Hitchcock, in order that he might use the stage for shooting a contemporary melodrama (Armour 1977: 76; Eisner 1973: 151–8; Eisner, 1976: 74–6; Taylor 1978: 36). Many contemporary critics realised that the forest was a set and complained about the resulting stylised appearance of the film which seemed to contradict the heroic Germanic content of the subject matter (Hake 1990: 41). In fact, the cinematic aesthetic of Lang's *Nibelungen* films places them in a very precise context of the cinema of the Weimar Republic. This means that the films' value is more than merely the sum of their seemingly Romantic parts. It also means that, in their evocation of overwhelming architectural spaces, choreographed mass movements and the cult of suicidally heroic war, they cannot be pointed to as symptomatic of Fascism, despite the famous charge levelled at them by Siegfried Kracauer (Kracauer 1947). Kracauer's analysis is flawed not only by its teleological cast, as revealed in the title of his book *From Caligari to Hitler*, but by his inability to look beyond the massive sets of the films to their specifically cinematic concerns, particularly with the power of the look, a cinematic concern par excellence (Hake 1990; Levin 1998). The medium, in other words, is the message, a point that medievalists with their strong sense of genre and the conventions of source criticism are well placed to grasp.

Film, for all its efforts to hypnotise spectators into believing that they are watching the world, does not simply open a window on a world. In seeing Fritz Lang's forests we see the technology of 1920s Germany. More extreme attempts to depict the otherness of the medieval world merely draw greater attention to the gap between that culture and ours. Eric Rohmer's film of Chrétien de Troyes, *Perceval le Gallois* (1978) deliberately opts for severe visual stylisation by attempting to reproduce the visual conventions of medieval art, eschewing perspective and so on. The result, however, does not transport the spectator to the Middle Ages but jarringly reveals the gulf between medieval conventions of representation and ours (Bourget 1992: 67, 138; De Looze 1994: 192–3). Surely it is more fitting to be aware of conventions and thus to remain aware of the essentially provisional nature of our versions of the past, in the academy as well as in Hollywood?

Such an awareness of provisionalism, of gaps, opens up various possibilities. First, there is the temptation to enjoy what one might call the camp aspect of some egregious cinematic attempts to grapple with the age of chivalry, in the sense that camp, according to the notorious analysis of Susan Sontag, is a sensibility that 'sees everything in quotation marks' and 'is alive to a double sense in which some things can be taken' (Sontag 1983: 109, 110). Thus the sonorous line, 'Yonder lies the castle of my father' never fails to raise a smile when it is uttered in the Bronx accent of Tony Curtis in *The Black Shield of Falworth* (1954). Similarly, spectators can hardly concentrate on the nonsense that is *King Richard and the Crusaders* (1954) for waiting to see whether it is true that Virginia Mayo utters the immortal line to Richard Coeur de Lion: 'War, war, war, that's all you think about, Dickie Plantagenet!' The figure-hugging dresses modelled by Janet Leigh as an Anglo-Saxon princess in *The Vikings* (1958) owe infinitely more to contemporary Hollywood ideals of feminine beauty than to evidence from medieval England or Scandinavia, a point hammered home when Tony Curtis helpfully rips the dress so that Janet Leigh can assist with the rowing. (On all this sort of thing, see Richards 1977; it is no accident that these examples are from the 1950s, when Hollywood was turning out costume films in large numbers and of varying quality: see Powell 1991: 207–8 for a fair assessment of *Ivanhoe* (1952).)

This sort of doubleness can also have a more important function. It can act as a structuring agent for an entire film. *The Lion in Winter* (1968) is a gripping version of a talky stage play which purports to tell the story of the struggle for power among the sons of Henry II as they attend the Christmas court of the old king in 1183. Henry, Richard, John, Geoffrey, their mother Eleanor of Aquitaine and Philip Augustus of France have a high old time cooking up immensely complex plots while lurking in gloomy castle corridors and hiding behind tapestries, pausing from their machinations only to swap brittle epigrams. The polished bitchiness of the script owes everything to an American tradition of snappy dialogue but the film brilliantly portrays the seething resentments of medieval dynastic politics that circle round incompatible claims to inheritance. What makes the film a classic of its kind, however, are the performances. Peter O'Toole depicts Henry II with remarkable subtlety, and he gains some authority from the fact that he had played Henry at an earlier stage in his reign four years before in *Becket* (1964). The stand-out performance, however, is by the veteran Katharine Hepburn who won an Academy Award in the role of Eleanor of Aquitaine. Already in 1968 a legendary figure in Hollywood history, Hepburn was a star associated with roles of fast-talking, independent-minded, strong women. Further, she had famously held her own in a sequence of films with two of Hollywood's most charismatic male stars, Cary Grant and Spencer Tracy, culminating in *Guess Who's Coming to Dinner* (1967), for which she had won an Academy Award. The script gives the audience all it needs to know about the history of Eleanor of Aquitaine, but without a knowledge of Hepburn's Hollywood persona the audience misses much of the impact of the film. Audiences need to grasp the importance of the persona and history of the stars in Hollywood film in order to grasp the dynamics of such films. A knowledge of the history of Hollywood is more helpful for the audience of *The Lion in Winter* than a knowledge of the twelfth century.

More broadly, films can be successfully constructed around the gap between the medieval and the modern periods. Sometimes this gap takes the form of nostalgia for a seemingly simpler, more heroic time as in *The Princess Bride* (1987), which celebrates the values of romance while simultaneously contrasting them with modern attitudes and styles. Such a balancing act is difficult and few films manage it as well as *The Princess Bride*. More often, the gap is exploited for comic effect as the archaic world of the past is forcibly juxtaposed with the breezily democratic world of the modern. (Needless to say, both worlds are presented in terms of cinematic conventions.) Here anachronism becomes the very subject of the film as in versions of Mark Twain's novel, *A Connecticut Yankee at King Arthur's Court* filmed in 1931 and 1949 with Will Rogers and Bing Crosby in the title role. The fact that Rogers' and Crosby's personae, as cowboy sage and relaxed crooner respectively, were essentially alien to the world of chivalric values was the whole point of their casting and consonant with Twain's satirical portrait of medievalism confronted by Yankee know-how. The same impulse lies behind the encounter between the heroic world of the past and the values of the Californian high school and shopping-mall in the splendidly daft *Bill and Ted's Excellent Adventure* (1989). Cinematic conventions of medieval epics of the 1950s and earlier were themselves guyed in *The Court Jester* (1956) which contrasted the stuffy medieval courtly world with the 1940s fast-talking nervy style of Danny Kaye which undercuts the plot trappings of historical drama ('The pellet with the poison's in the vessel with the pestle').

Such concerns are not confined to Hollywood. The entire plot of the hit French film *Les Visiteurs* (1993) turns on the contrast between past and present as a twelfth-century knight and his squire are catapulted into the twentieth century by black magic and meet their descendants. Much predictable farce ensues as the men from the age of chivalry ('they weren't born yesterday!') encounter such baffling paraphernalia of the bourgeois world as telephones and flasks of Chanel No. 5 to which they respond in ways that reveal the Middle Ages to be a time of coarseness, superstition and, of course, poor personal hygiene. The knight and his squire, however, are not merely the butt of the film's jokes. In their embodiment of 'chivalric' values such as loyalty, devotion to family and physical courage (and Jean Reno, as the knight, shrewdly plays his part straight) they gradually show up the shallowness of the *bon chic, bon genre* world of the present and we can thus see how this sort of juxtaposition of past and present can be used not simply as a stick to beat the past but as an effective way of satirising the present. Amidst the farce there are hints of a more delicate relationship between past and present as the knight and his descendant come to understand each other. For a fascinating depiction of such an encounter between past and present one can turn to another film of time-travellers, Vincent Ward's *The Navigator: A Medieval Odyssey* (1988). In this stark fable, a group of sufferers from the Black Death tunnel their way out of fourteenth-century northern England (filmed in black-and-white) into present-day Auckland in New Zealand (filmed in colour). The film's colour scheme thus vividly differentiates past from present but the dreams of the visionary boy from the fourteenth century turn out to resonate in the modern world. Although the film draws on conventional notions about the Middle Ages (squalor, superstition, devotion to impossibly otherworldly ideals), its intensely original presentation of these notions and its examination of them in the modern world give it a very distinctive flavour and make it a disquieting study of how individuals and communities react to destructive historical forces.

The relationship between historical films and the times that they depict is complex, as is the relationship between such films and the times that produce them. It is not easy, at any rate not for the present writer, to see how Kenneth Branagh's film of *Henry V* (1989) relates to the ideas of Margaret Thatcher, Prime Minister when the film was made, though it has been seen as doing so. Branagh's film, in itself fairly straightforward, inevitably relates to Olivier's famous 1944 version which was itself not only an epic for wartime Britain, but, like Branagh's film, a comment on the relation between stage and screen, between Shakespeare and cinema, and of course between the real battle of Agincourt and dramatic representations of it. Mapping such a film precisely onto a contemporary political context is a delicate business (Hutcheon 1994: 67–88). Even where a film can be so mapped, that does not exhaust its significance. Eisenstein proclaimed his *Alexander Nevsky* (1938) to be a 'completely contemporary picture' and so it proved, but not necessarily in ways that he could have foreseen. He took the thirteenth-century ruler Alexander Nevsky as a starting-point for a vigorous anti-German polemic in which the Teutonic Knights represent potential Nazi aggressions, an aggression that comes to grief in the face of heroic opposition from the Russian people whose ally turns out to be the landscape of Russia itself in the famous battle on the ice. Both the form and the reception of the film are directly bound up with the contemporary context of the Soviet Union. Eisenstein appears to have been unable to edit the film as he desired because an early print of it was seen and approved by Stalin with the result that no further 'improvement' was possible. By the summer of 1939 the Nazi–Soviet pact transformed the film into a political embarrassment and it was withdrawn from circulation, only for it to be re-released in the wake of the German invasion of June 1941 (Bordwell 1993: 27–8). The film bears the imprint of its context and is indeed stylistically more conventional than Eisenstein's earlier work. One does not need, however, to invoke transcendental

Figure 10.2 The bell-maker from *Andrei Rublev*. BFI Films: Stills, Posters and Designs.

or timeless values of art to argue that the film also retains a power and interest that has outlasted its context. All one needs to do is watch the film, particularly the battle on the ice sequence, which stands as one of the great attempts of cinema to depict a medieval battle, and which can be profitably compared to equally stylised depictions such as Olivier's Agincourt in *Henry V*, Orson Welles' artful carnage in his adaptation of Falstaff's career, *Chimes at Midnight* (1966) and Robert Bresson's austere self-denying account of the massacre of the Round Table in *Lancelot du lac* (1974) or indeed the seventeenth-century battle scene in the neglected *Winstanley* (1975).

I propose to conclude by examining three films in the light of our concerns: *El Cid*, *Andrei Rublev*, and *The Adventures of Robin Hood*. All three films focus on heroic individuals engaged in a struggle against overwhelming forces. The heroic individual is male. (Women certainly feature in these films but are subordinated according to cinematic, rather than feudal, laws.) The three films might loosely be defined as epic. All three place their heroically individualised protagonist in a teeming world of armoured soldiers, silkily villainous princes, formidable priests and suffering peasantry. Casts of thousands act out their grand medieval dramas in strikingly designed and photographed castles, cathedrals, hovels, etc. *El Cid* and *The Adventures of Robin Hood* glory in the great sword-fighting duels that are the hallmark of the swashbuckler movie, while *El Cid* and *Andrei Rublev*, at 184 and 185 minutes respectively, share the vast length that is the *sine qua non* of the prestigious epic production. Each film, however, was made in a very different context. *The Adventures of Robin Hood* was released in 1938 and is a product of a Hollywood studio at the peak of the success of the studio system. *El Cid* (1961) can be regarded as a Hollywood film in that it was made by a Hollywood director and features Hollywood stars but it was produced after the studio system was running into trouble, by an independent producer, Samuel Bronston, who ran his own production company in Spain where the film was made (Katz 1994: 178). *Andrei Rublev* was made in the Soviet Union in 1966 but was not released there until 1971, and while the delayed release and shelving of films happens elsewhere, *Andrei Rublev*'s fortunes were bound up with official disapproval of what the director, Andrei Tarkovsky, had created.

Tarkovsky's film is the strangest and least conventional of our trio and so we may begin with it. Its hero is the late medieval icon painter Andrei Rublev (*c.* 1370–*c.*1430). Rublev really existed but very little is known about his life and few paintings can be ascribed to him with certainty (Vzdornov 1996). Nor does the film attempt to fill in the gaps in our knowledge by simply telling the story of Rublev's life. In fact, accuracy of historical detail was not the concern of Tarkovsky, who worked on the script as well as directing the film; too much concentration on getting the fifteenth-century details right would distract, he thought, from the essence of the film (Tarkovsky 1986: 78–80). The general historical context, including Tartar invasions, rivalries between the brothers Vassily and Yuri, sons of Prince Dimitri Donskoi, and the career of the painter Theophanes the Greek, is drawn on but not in the manner of the Hollywood biopic (Strick 1991: ix–x). Instead, imagined scenes from Rublev's life are presented as a series of almost self-contained episodes and the overall narrative is generated by the juxtaposition of these episodes. This results in a fragmentary, elliptical 'story' that eschews the linear narrative and psychological development so dear to Hollywood, though one might be tempted to think that this technique of juxtaposing blocks of material is a cinematic echo of authentically medieval precedents in, for example, the parataxis of the *Song of Roland* (Auerbach 1968: 96–122.)

Given that the film's hero is a painter, we might be tempted to see Andrei Rublev as a stand-in for Andrei Tarkovsky, i.e., a maker of cinematic images transposed into the Middle Ages. Such straightforward identification is avoided, however, as the film features a variety of artists and if Tarkovsky identified himself with anyone it appears to have been with the youthful bellmaker of the film's astonishing final sequence (Strick 1991: xii). In fact the first artist that we see appears in the very first scene of the film, which sets the tone for what follows and reveals Tarkovsky's attitude to historical material. This first scene, which plunges us abruptly into the historical landscape with no preparation or context, reveals that the film, like the painters within it, is concerned with what we see. To the sound of hostile shouts and slow solemn music on the soundtrack, a man frantically launches himself into flight suspended from a hot-air balloon and the camera floats with him majestically over the earth, over rivers, churches, trees and awe-struck watchers, only to crash into the ground.

This parable of the artist's vision features none of the characters who will later appear in the film and is not referred to again. It is up to the spectator to place it beside the other views of the artist that will occur in the film, just as it is up to the spectator to try to gauge the meaning of the image of the black horse that rolls upon the ground in reaction to the balloonist's flight and fall, an image that echoes T.S. Eliot's use of images of 'symbolic value, but of what we cannot tell, for they come to represent the depths of feeling into which we cannot peer' (Eliot 1941: 53). This is no conventional epic but an intensely personal poetic vision and Tarkovsky had few qualms about introducing a hot-air balloon into the fourteenth century. As he noted wrily in his diaries, the only viewers of the film who complained about the balloon were historians (Tarkovsky 1994: 71).

While it is obvious that *Andrei Rublev* is no Hollywood epic it may not be entirely unconventional. In its view of the prevalence of savagery and superstition it draws on standard cinematic images of the Middle Ages. Further, in its presentation of wild and woolly Russians as oscillating between extremes of reverence for art and spiritual values and violent outbursts of bestial cruelty, the film seems to echo some traditional ideas of the 'Russian soul' (Billington 1966: 16–43; Davy 1967), an echo that is surely explicitly sounded in the scene where some visiting Italians, clad in Renaissance splendour, comment disparagingly on the primitive Russians only to be warned not to underestimate their spiritual resources.

And yet the film, some thirty years after its making, still retains a power to startle the spectator, not least in the climactic shift from black-and-white to colour in its final minutes. After some three hours of Tartar invasion, arbitrary acts of princely cruelty, religious persecution, all in monochrome, the icons of Rublev flood the screen with radiance and colour. In the cinema, the effect is overwhelming, though even on television or video something of that effect is caught. It may seem here that Tarkovsky is suggesting that history can be abolished and its cruelties cancelled through the beauties of art ('simple-minded schematics' according to Thomson 1994: 737), but the ending of the film is surely more open and less naively transcendental than this. The whole weight of the film and the spectator's own historical experience bear down on this final sequence. These icons remain in the world and indeed in the film's final seconds they dissolve to an enigmatic view of horses, supreme symbols of the natural world for Tarkovsky, standing in rainswept fields. The spectator has just watched a film that questions the validity of expressions of art and belief; the icons are not the 'answer' to such a bleak series of questions; they are one more element in the puzzle. Their appearance in colour gives the film a formally satisfying ending but they close the film, not an argument. The slow, incantatory art of Tarkovsky is arguably more historical than the straight linear narratives of Hollywood epics. Its closing images of angels do not lead us from darkness to light but look back into the film, into the past, and, like Walter Benjamin's famous angel of history, 'where we perceive a chain of events, he sees a single catastrophe' (Benjamin 1973: 259).

To turn from *Andrei Rublev* to *El Cid* is to see simpler, clearer pictures of the past, though not necessarily inferior ones. While we know much more of the eleventh-century Spanish warrior Rodrigo Diaz than we do of the historical Andrei Rublev, the conventional and limited nature of the surviving sources means that his own personality remains beyond our reach (Fletcher 1989). What we do possess, in the great stream of epic tradition about El Cid, is a clear picture of a noble chivalric hero and this is the picture that we see on the screen. This is not due to Hollywood indifference to history but to the fact that the historical adviser for the film was Ramón Menéndez Pidal whose intense vision of Rodrigo as a maker of Spain gives the film its coherence (and ensures its status as a cultural document of a particular twentieth-century Spain). Historians are currently much more sceptical about the existence of a 'Spanish' identity in the warring principalities of the Iberian peninsula and tend to see Rodrigo as a typical adventurer of eleventh-century Europe rather than as a selfless patriot (Fletcher 1989: 4–5, 201–5; Linehan 1993).

All this should remind us that historians' judgements are constantly subject to appeal. It is unfair to expect film-makers to 'get it right' in their depiction of the past. There is no single correct vision, though there are, of course, ways of 'getting it wrong' and film-makers can offer egregious demonstrations of this. To focus on unhistorical elements in *El Cid*, such as its Spanish patriotism, stylised costumes and schematic narrative is to miss the achievement of the film. In fact, many of the essentials of eleventh-century high politics are well caught: the jealous guarding of honour, the ideals of military prowess and largesse, the dynastic rivalries. What makes the film work is the fact that Menendez Pidal's vision, of nobility constantly challenged and constantly rising to the challenge, is not only inherently dramatic but chimed with the concerns of the film's director, Anthony Mann, who had spent the 1950s making Westerns where heroes are forced to draw on reserves of physical and moral courage in confrontations in a vast and pitiless landscape (Thomson 1994: 476–7). The result is a film that, for all its scenes of medieval splendour, never loses sight of its key themes, which are those of Mann's Westerns. The vast numbers of extras as warriors and the grand settings never overwhelm the drama, which is often played out in relatively intimate encounters between a few principals, as in the affecting sequence where Rodrigo goes into exile with only his wife Jimena and they journey on their own through an immense landscape bounded by mountains. This sequence, with its painterly evocations of the flight of the Holy Family to Egypt, moves from a quiet domestic scene between husband and wife to a screen-filling crowd of extras who call upon Rodrigo to lead them for the sake of Spain. It is a tightly controlled succession of scenes where the director unleashes the weaponry of the epic (wide screen, hosts of costumed extras) only when it can make an impact.

In his 1950s Westerns Mann's star was James Stewart who, rather surprisingly in view of his standard screen roles as the personification of small-town virtues, brought violence and neurosis to the hero-roles of films such as *The Naked Spur* (1953) and *The Man from Laramie* (1955). Stewart's performances showed how the Western genre's conventional heroes could be revitalised and surely paved the way for his disquieting appearance in Hitchcock's sombre masterpiece *Vertigo* (1958). A performance of this sort in the role of El Cid would have offered a fascinating slant on the historical epic but such a performance was not forthcoming. The title role is played by Charlton Heston, a less subtle actor than James Stewart, or rather an actor who has not been allowed to demonstrate subtlety. Charlton Heston brought to *El Cid* the aura of having played a sternly heroic Moses in *The Ten Commandments* (1956), as well as a sternly heroic *Ben-Hur* (1959); even as a modern-day Mexican cop in *Touch of Evil* (1958) he was heroic. To *El Cid*, Heston brought this well-honed persona as champion of the cinematic epic as well as his striking physical presence. In this he was matched by his screen partner, Sophia Loren, who, all curves and severe expressions, resembles some majestic Romanesque structure. Both actors look magnificent and in fact perform their roles very well, but they eschew nuance. Sophia Loren's performance acquires a weirdly stylised dimension from her refusal to be made up so as to reflect her character's aging; as the film goes on, Charlton Heston grows ever more battle-scarred and grizzled while Sophia Loren remains magnificently herself (Smith 1991: 70 and cf. Elley 1984: 157–9).

If Sophia Loren and Charlton Heston play larger-than-life figures, with little naturalism, that is not a limitation. Medieval representations of heroes and their noble ladies were governed by conventions. The fact that we know very little about the individual characteristics of Rodrigo Diaz is due not simply to the scarcity of our evidence but to its conceptual limitations (by the standards of our culture). Before the twelfth century, and in many cases long after it, writers describing great princes sought to evoke a type, not an individual. As Richard Fletcher puts it: 'Eleventh-century people are as formalised in the written sources as they are in the Bayeux Tapestry' (Fletcher 1989: 6; cf. Leyser 1982: 241–6 and Fried 1994: 92). Charlton Heston and Sophia Loren offer a modern version of the conventions of the chroniclers and epic poets and their seemingly limited portrayals are in fact supremely appropriate cinematic translations of medieval epic (cf. Bumke 1991: 275–359).

The past is always other, even the recent past. It is the past of Hollywood itself that adds an extra level of interest to films such as *The Adventures of Robin Hood* (1938). The old-style Hollywood studios were not only dream factories that possessed the personnel and skills to release a film a week (*The Adventures of Robin Hood* was only one of 52 films released by Warner Brothers in 1938 (Finler 1992: 484)); they were also mighty economic powers that distributed the films they made through the chains of cinemas that they controlled. A combination of factors, including the rise of television and government assaults on the studio ownership of cinemas meant that by the 1950s this system was finished (Schatz 1998). The era of the studios was therefore historically finite and it is to that era that *The Adventures of Robin Hood* belongs as a 'prime example of studio film-making at its best' (Finler 1992: 408; cf. Roddick 1983: 241).

There is certainly little sense of medieval 'otherness' in the film. Although its opening credits proclaim it to be 'based upon ancient Robin Hood legends' the Gothick lettering of these credits (which extends even to the Warner Brothers logo, the familiar shield of which is festooned with ivy as if it belonged to some ancestral castle of the Warners' dynasty), the soaring music and the reassuring presence of such names as Errol Flynn, Olivia de Havilland and Basil Rathbone tell us that we are in the land of the Hollywood swashbuckler. All three had already appeared in the same studio's pirate adventure *Captain Blood* (1935) and Flynn and de Havilland had also appeared in *The Charge of the Light Brigade* (1936) while Flynn had appeared in the Tudor adventure *The Prince and the Pauper* (1937). The fact that none of these films is set in the Middle Ages should not prevent us from grouping them with *The Adventures of Robin Hood*. By 1938, audiences knew what to expect of a costume drama featuring Flynn, de Havilland and Rathbone and the studio continued to mine this profitable genre with two more pictures, *The Private Lives of Elizabeth and Essex* (1939)

Figure 10.3 Errol Flynn and co. as Robin Hood and co. BFI Films: Stills, Posters and Designs.

and another fantastical pirate romp, *The Sea Hawk* (1940) (Roddick 1983: 235–48). Within this group, the fact that *The Adventures of Robin Hood* is set in the Middle Ages is less important than the fact that it featured actors and a director who could be trusted to provide swashbuckling entertainment. This was a feature of the consistency achieved by the studio system which meant that audiences acquired a formidable grasp of genre through a familiarity with even minor players in such productions. Alan Hale, for example, hardly a name to conjure with today, played the same sort of character (hearty supporter of Errol Flynn's hero) in *The Prince and the Pauper*, *The Adventures of Robin Hood*, *The Private Lives of Elizabeth and Essex* and *The Sea Hawk*; the appearance of his name on the credits of an Errol Flynn film set up expectations that would be fulfilled by the studio product.

As a product of that studio system at a particular historical moment, the film has dated. Much of the acting now seems rather crude: the merry men mug shamelessly in telegraphed response to the quips of the script; Errol Flynn, as Robin Hood, spends much screen time putting his hands on his hips, throwing back his head and laughing heartily at discomfited villains. The medieval setting mainly provides opportunities for the wearing of gorgeous costumes in great halls as well as for lusty banquets in the greenwood. The dynamics of the plot in fact owe much to Walter Scott whose novel *Ivanhoe*, published in 1819, also features Robin Hood in a tale of rivalry between grasping Norman barons and stout-hearted Saxons loyal to King Richard I. The film thus echoes nineteenth-century European interests in medieval romance, and can be profitably compared with its astoundingly dark contemporary, *The Hunchback of Notre Dame* (1939), where medievalism leads to Expressionist urban claustrophobia (Heisner 1990: 240–2).

And yet the film merits its reputation as the supreme swashbuckler and the most successful screen version of the Robin Hood stories. As such, it fully deserves our attention. I will limit my comments to three points. First, the film was the product of conscious decisions made about history and genre, decisions that cast light on the workings of the studio system. Some of the history that pressed on the film was recent Hollywood history. The original director assigned to it, William Keighley, appears to have been mesmerised by the grandiose 1922 version with Douglas Fairbanks; studio memos reveal that his labours to reproduce this were resulting in a lumbering monster without pace and coherence and he was taken off the film (Behlmer 1986, 46–51). The film therefore had to be defined against a part of Hollywood history. More interestingly, these memos reveal that the studio did not want the film to be swamped by its medieval trappings; what counted was Robin Hood himself, 'the swashbuckling, reckless . . . character . . . It is not by thoughts of knights and castles and tournaments that this character has lived . . . ' (Behlmer 1986: 47–8). Producers, director and the award-winning editor focused on character, narrative drive and, amid the spectacular sword-fights and stunts, credibility of action (by Hollywood standards); they also worried over the flavour of period dialogue and the role of women (Maid Marian was understood to be a late addition to the tales) (Behlmer 1979: 17; Behlmer 1986: 44–52; Robertson 1993: 43–4). The problems posed by the period setting and the film's genre were not only grasped but solved so successfully in cinematic terms that the film became a benchmark against which later treatments of the Robin Hood story had to be measured or against which they could creatively re-act as in the bittersweet *Robin and Marian* (1976).

Secondly, the film succeeds because it tells its story in primarily visual, cinematic terms, as seen, for example, in the love story between Robin (Errol Flynn) and Marian (Olivia de Havilland). This is a conventional enough story made more so by the limitations of Flynn's acting, the bareness of the script and the limiting of Olivia de Havilland to looking decorative in a never-ending series of beautiful gowns (this, together with other characters' comments on and reactions to her appearance establishes her part as a classic example of the 'to-be-looked-atness' of female roles, as discussed in Levin 1998). The growing closeness of the characters, however, is depicted in visual terms. When Marian encounters Robin in Sherwood Forest, long shots and medium shots of the merry men feasting are gradually replaced by shots of Robin and Marian on their own. One particular two-shot is held for some twenty seconds with Robin and Marian at extreme edges of the frame; this is followed by briefer reverse angle shots and another two-shot where the characters are closer to one another and become linked when Marian gives Robin her hand. The story is told by shooting and editing as much as by dialogue. Within the general structure of the film's narrative arc, in which the personnel and values of the forest invade and transform the castle, Marian is seen to move closer to Robin by moving from the closed world of the Norman castles to the world of the greenwood; significantly she thinks of Robin or meets him at windows which act as thresholds of and gateways to the free forest world.

Finally, the film is freighted with some of the sombre history of the 1930s. As background to the antics of Robin and company are grim sequences of Saxons being systematically robbed and beaten by black-garbed military Norman oppressors convinced of their racial superiority. Events in Europe here sound an echo in a Hollywood whose medieval romps might appear as simply self-contained worlds. In 1939 the studio released *Confessions of a Nazi Spy*, confirming the views of German-Americans that it was consistently hostile to the Nazi regime in Germany (Behlmer 1986: 188–91; Finler 1992: 404; Robertson 1993: 147; cf. also Vidal 1992). The music for *The Adventures of Robin Hood* was composed by Erich Wolfgang Korngold. A sensationally successful composer of operas in his native Vienna, Korngold had already written scores for *Captain Blood* and *The Prince and the Pauper* but did not want to write for *The Adventures of Robin Hood*, feeling out of sympathy with the project. He was eventually won over to it in February 1938 and the Nazi take-over of Austria in March of that year meant that he became an exile in Hollywood (Behlmer 1986: 52–3). Hollywood and the filmgoing public recognised Korngold's talent; his magnificent score for the film gained him an Academy Award and his work for *King's Row* (1942) generated much public interest (Behlmer 1986: 142). Yet, in serious music circles, his Hollywood success defined and limited him, and after 1945 he could not re-establish himself as a musical force in Vienna. Hollywood had saved him from Nazi persecution but the austerities of high modernism condemned him to a marginal status in music history from which he has only recently been rescued.

The Adventures of Robin Hood is thus a more complex artefact than it might at first appear. In common with many of the films discussed in this chapter it needs to be assessed on its own terms, as a film, not as an academic monograph on medieval life. As we have seen, films do not stand outside of history; they demand a knowledge of the history which they depict and the history from which they themselves come. Neither innocent nor trivial, historical films pose troubling questions about the representation of the past. Uneasily, one recalls Aristotle's view of poetry as more deserving of attention than history. Luckily for us, however, the best of the films discussed here offer as much poetry *and* history as any spectator could desire.

NOTE

I am very grateful to Anne Jenkins, Robyn Marsack and Jinty Nelson for critical comment.

REFERENCES

Adorno, T. and Horkheimer, M. (1979) *Dialectic of Enlightenment*, trans. J. Cumming, London: Verso.

Armour, R. (1976) *Fritz Lang*, Boston: Twayne.

Auerbach, E. (1968) *Mimesis: The Representation of Reality in Western Literature*, trans. W. Trask, Princeton: Princeton University Press.

Behlmer, R. (ed.) (1979) *The Adventures of Robin Hood*, Madison and London: Weidenfeld & Nicolson.

—— (ed.) (1986) *Inside Warner Bros 1935–1951*, London: Weidenfeld & Nicolson.

Benjamin, W. (1973) *Illuminations*, trans. H. Zohn, London: Fontana/Collins.

Billington, J. (1966) *The Icon and the Axe: An Interpretive History of Russian Culture*, London: Weidenfeld and Nicolson.

Bloch, M. (1962) *Feudal Society*, trans. L.A. Manyon, London: Routledge and Kegan Paul.

Bloch, R.H. and Nichols, S.G. (eds) *Medievalism and the Modernist Temper*, Baltimore and London: Johns Hopkins University Press.

Bordwell, D. (1985) *Narration in the Fiction Film*, London: Methuen.

—— (1993) *The Cinema of Eisenstein*, Cambridge, Mass. and London: Harvard University Press.

Bourget, J.-L. (1992) *L'histoire au cinéma: le passé retrouvé*, Paris: Gallimard.

Bumke, J. (1991) *Courtly Culture: Literature and Society in the High Middle Ages*, trans. T. Dunlap, Berkeley, Los Angeles and Oxford: University of California Press.

Camille, M. (1992) 'Visionary Perception and Images of the Apocalypse in the Later Middle Ages', in R.K. Emmerson and B. McGinn (eds) *The Apocalypse in the Middle Ages*, Ithaca and London: Cornell University Press.

Chahine, Y. (1996) 'Entretien avec Youssef Chahine', *Cahiers du Cinéma*, numero special, supplement au no. 506: 9–30.

Davies, N.Z. (1983) *The Return of Martin Guerre*, Cambridge, Mass. and London: Harvard University Press.

Davy, M.-M. (1967) *Nicolas Berdyaev: Man of the Eighth Day,* London: Bles.

De Looze, L. (1994) 'Modern Approaches and the "Real" Middle Ages: Bertrand Tavernier's *La Passion Béatrice*', in L.J. Workman (ed.) *Medievalism in Europe, Studies in Medievalism*, V, Cambridge: D.S. Brewer.

Duby, G. (1991) *L'histoire continue*, Paris: Editions Odile Jacob.

Eisner, L. (1973) *The Haunted Screen*, London: Secker and Warburg.

—— (1976) *Fritz Lang*, London: Secker and Warburg.

Eliot, T.S. (1941) *Points of View*, London: Faber and Faber.

Elley, D. (1984) *The Epic Film*, London: Routledge and Kegan Paul.

Evans, R.J. (1997) *In Defence of History*, London: Granta Books.

Ewan, E. (1995.) '*Braveheart*', *American Historical Review* 100, 2: 1219–21.

Finler, J.W. (1992) *The Hollywood Story*, 2nd edn, London: Mandarin.

Fletcher, R. (1989), *The Quest for El Cid*, London: Hutchinson.

Frantzen, A. (1990), *Desire for Origins*, New Brunswick and London: Rutgers University Press.

Frayling, C. (1995) *Strange Landscape: A Journey through the Middle Ages*, London: BBC Books.

Fried, J. (1994) *Der Weg in die Geschichte: die Ursprünge Deutschlands bis 1024*, Berlin: Propyläen Verlag.

Greene, G. (1993) *The Graham Greene Film Reader: Mornings in the Dark,* D. Parkinson (ed.), Manchester: Carcanet.

Hake, S. (1990) 'Architectural Hi/stories: Fritz Lang and the *Nibelungen*', *Wide Angle* 12.3: 38–57.

Harper, S. (1994) *Picturing the Past: The Rise and Fall of the British Costume Film*, London: British Film Institute.

Hartley, K. (ed.) (1994) *The Romantic Spirit in German Art 1790–1990*, Edinburgh and London: National Galleries of Scotland and London.

Harty, K. (1996 'Jeanne au Cinéma', in B. Wheeler and C. Wood (eds) *Fresh Verdicts on Joan of Arc*, New York and London: Garland.

Hayward, S. (1993) *French National Cinema*, London and New York: Routledge.

Heisner, B. (1990) *Hollywood Art: art direction in the days of the great studios*, Chicago and London: St James Press.

Huizinga, J. (1955) *The Waning of the Middle Ages*, trans. F. Hopman, Harmondsworth: Penguin Books.

Hutcheon, L. (1994) *Irony's Edge: the theory and practice of irony*, London and New York: Routledge.

Jay, M. (1993) *Downcast Eyes: the denigration of vision in twentieth-century French thought*, Berkeley, Los Angeles and London: University of California Press.

Katz, E. (1994) *The Macmillan International Film Encyclopedia*, 2nd edn, London: Macmillan.

Koziol, G. (1992) *Begging Pardon and Favor: ritual and political order in Early Medieval France*, Ithaca and London: Cornell University Press.

Kracauer, S. (1947) *From Caligari to Hitler: a psychological history of the German film*, Princeton.

Levin, D.J. (1998) *Richard Wagner, Fritz Lang and the Nibelungen*, Princeton: Princeton University Press.

Leyser, K.J. (1982) *Medieval Germany and its Neighbours 900–1250*, London: Hambledon.

Linehan, P. (1993) *History and the Historians of Medieval Spain*, Oxford: Oxford University Press.

McArthur, C. (1995) '*Braveheart*', *Sight and Sound*, no. 9: 45.

Margolis, N. (1997) 'Trial by Passion: Philology, Film and Ideology in the Portrayal of Joan of Arc (1900-1930)', *Journal of Medieval and Early Modern Studies* 27.3: 445–93.

Moliterno, G. (1995) 'Novel into Film: *The Name of the Rose*', in L. Devereaux and R. Hillman (eds) *Fields of Vision*, Berkeley, Los Angeles and London: University of California Press.

Paret, P. (1988) *Art as History: episodes in the culture and politics of nineteenth-century Germany*, Princeton, New Jersey: Princeton University Press.

Powell, D. (1991) *The Dilys Powell Film Reader*, ed. C. Cook, Manchester: Carcanet.

Richards, J. (1977) *Swordsmen of the Silver Screen*, London Routledge and Kegan Paul.

Robertson, J.C. (1993) *The Casablanca Man: the cinema of Michael Curtiz*, London and New York: Routledge.

Roddick, N. (1983) *A New Deal in Entertainment: Warner Brothers in the 1930s*, London: BFI Publishing.

Rosenstone, R. (1988) 'History in Images/History in Words' *American Historical Review* 93.2: 1173–85.

—— (1992) '*JFK*: Historical Fact/Historical Film' *American Historical Review* 97.1: 506–11.

Schatz, T. (1998) *The Genius of the System: Hollywood film-making in the studio era*, London: Faber and Faber.

Schihanoff, S. (1996) 'True Lies: transvestism and idolatry in the trial of Joan of Arc', in B. Wheeler and C. Wood (eds) *Fresh Verdicts on Joan of Arc*, New York and London: Garland.

Smith, G. (1991) *Epic Films*, Jefferson, N.C. and London.

Sontag, S. (1993) *A Susan Sontag Reader*, Harmondsworth: Penguin Books.

Strick, P. (1991) 'Introduction', in A. Tarkovsky, *Andrei Rublev*, London: Faber and Faber.

Tarkovsky, A. (1986) *Sculpting in Time*, London: Bodley Head.

—— (1994) *Time within Time: the diaries 1970–1986*, trans. K. Hunter Blair, London: Faber and Faber.

Taylor, J. (1995) 'Charles d'Orléans', in P. France (ed.) *The New Oxford Companion to Literature in French*, Oxford: Oxford University Press.

Taylor, J.R. (1978) *Hitch: the life and work of Alfred Hitchcock*, London.

Thomson, D. (1994) *A Biographical Dictionary of Film*, London: André Deutsch.

Toplin, R. (1988) 'The film maker as historian', *American Historical Review* 93.2: 1210–27.

Vidal, G. (1992) *Screening History*, London: André Deutsch.

—— (1993) *United States: Essays 1952–1992*, London: André Deutsch.

Vzdornov, G.I. (1996) 'Andrey Rublov', in J. Turner (ed.) *The Dictionary of Art* vol. 27, London: Macmillan.

Wapnewski, P. (ed.) (1986) *Mittelalter-Rezeption: Ein Symposium*, Stuttgart: Weidenfeld & Nicolson.

Warner, M. (1981) *Joan of Arc*, London: Weidenfeld & Nicolson.

Winock, M. (1992) 'Jeanne d'Arc', in P. Nora (ed.) *Les Lieux de mémoire iii: Les France*, Paris: Gallimard.

Wyke, M. (1997) *Projecting the Past: Ancient Rome, cinema and history*, London and New York: Routledge.

PART II

BELIEFS, SOCIAL VALUES
AND SYMBOLIC ORDER

INTRODUCTION

Renaissance scholars invented the notion of the 'medieval' world in order to set their own age off against it. Theirs, they believed, was a new age of enlightenment, the Middle Ages an age of barbarism. Some modern people represent the Middle Ages in a similar way, for this is the popular understanding of 'medieval' (cf. 'feudal') nowadays: the word denotes the primitive, violent, ignorant, benighted. You would steer clear of someone (it would tend to be a man rather than a woman) whose values or conduct were described as 'positively medieval'! The medieval past is a foreign country. On the other hand, since the nineteenth century at least, there has been an alternative, positive, view of the Middle Ages, as a world of domestic production in which the craftsman was not alienated from his product, an age of faith, an age of chivalry, aesthetically and morally attractive. In Part II of this book, some contributions explicitly engage in critical inspection of such stereotypes, while others do so implicitly. The object in every case is to understand the medieval world on its own terms, sympathetically but never condescendingly. We should have made little progress if after renouncing myths of medieval chivalry and piety, we derided the settlement of disputes by means of trial by battle or the execution of animals for crime, or cringed at the excesses of inquisitors as if these could safely be confined to a dark past (all these, incidentally, are reactions to the Middle Ages invited by recent films . . .), still worse, perhaps, if we failed to recognise that chivalry and piety were not merely myths.

Anthropologists and sociologists have long known the importance of rituals and formalities in oiling social relationships, but also in acting as safety-valves for tensions, in saving face when confrontation ended in a climb-down, in mystifying contradictions or leaving meanings ambiguous. Medievalists have arguably been speedier than their modernist colleagues in taking on board such insights and reading the evidence for religious belief and social values more subtly in the light of them. It was not that medieval people could not distinguish between shame and sin, or between public and private: they made and used those distinctions in their own ways and contexts. It was not that medieval understandings of gender, or of the body, were simpler, more 'primitive', than those of modern people: they were different – but the differences are not beyond our grasp provided we broaden the range of what counts as admissible evidence. Rites and representations, literary jokes, medical treatises and inquisitorial records are among the many types of historical material discussed in Part II.

These chapters don't only make medieval beliefs and practices intelligible, they reveal the extent of change, reaction and adaptation across the thousand-year span of history which they cover. The central medieval period emerges, again, as the fulcrum. The sacraments were defined with a new sharpness, for example in reference to penance and marriage, as priesthood and laity interacted in new ways. Models hypothesising the Church's self-interested imposition of its rules on lay people against their will have been subjected to increasingly sharp critique, as have assumptions of some medieval norm of opposition between secular and spiritual spheres, between kingdom (*regnum*) and priesthood (*sacerdotium*). That broad division of 'orders' and spheres of action was certainly made, but it was cross-cut by lines of mutual interest and alliance. Lay people wanted authoritative rules on prohibited degrees of marriage and on sexual offences – provided they could bend them when necessary. The lay faithful collaborated with priests in ostracising sinners and heretics. If the papacy, from the eleventh century onwards, presented itself as the supreme arbiter of Christendom's morals, it did so with the laity's active – and material – support. In the late Middle Ages, religion and its symbols became so thoroughly politicised that the alignment of Church (or particular churches) and State became closer than ever. If the ecclesiastical authorities worried about outbursts of religious enthusiasm that were potentially subversive, so too did the secular authorities. Yet that was the very period in which such outbursts were especially marked. Secularisation was emphatically not the sign of the late Middle Ages.

Part II includes chapters on gender and sexuality and attitudes to the body. This editorial decision reflects the way in which historical scholarship on these themes, though only quite recent, has already become key to our understanding of social values and practices in the past. Gender, sexuality, and attitudes to the body, all the more surprisingly given some modern writers' assertions of the natural, essential, character of these categories, and a still widespread notion of the Middle Ages as static, have turned out to reveal some important dimensions of medieval change. Gender roles are about power relations, but they also provide ways in which people make sense of, and bring meaning into, their lives. Patriarchy is not the whole story; and in any case it varied quite significantly over time, while its weight varied with social rank, and with women's stage in their life-cycle. There was misogyny in the Middle Ages, but it was neither universal nor homogenous. Medieval understandings of sexual behaviour and sexual difference were varied, and often subtle. Beliefs about what happened to a person after death affected the treatment of dead bodies, but here again, within the matrix of Christianity, not only were there changes in the central and later Middle Ages as compared with earlier, there were also notable divergences between practice in various parts of Latin Christendom, and between the views of medical practitioners and theologians, and – influenced but not wholly determined by the professionals of either of those groups – lay people.

CHAPTER ELEVEN

POLITICAL RITUALS AND POLITICAL IMAGINATION IN THE MEDIEVAL WEST FROM THE FOURTH CENTURY TO THE ELEVENTH[1]

Philippe Buc

'Medieval political rituals' is a problematic topic. For one thing, the category of the 'political' is fundamentally a creation of modernity; for another, the wide concept of 'ritual' is not only even more recent than 'politics' but also extremely vague. What warrants, then, the inclusion, in a single ensemble, of such practices as coronations and crown-wearings, princely funerals, ordeals, entries, civic games, banquets, the hunt, relic-translations and elevations, oath-takings, acclamations or *laudes*, knightings, and acts of submission or commendation (though this chapter deals with only some of these) (Le Goff 1980: 237–87; Keller 1993: 51–86; articles in *Byzantion* 61 (1991); Nelson 1999; and especially McCormick 1986, with superb bibliography)? From the point of view of the medieval observer, they were all concerned with power, order, community and hierarchy. Many of them, ideally, involved a vertical dimension, a connectedness with heavenly matters through the liturgy or through solemnities recognizably related to liturgical forms. The hunt, performed *more solemni*, in solemn fashion (*Annales regni Francorum* ad. an. 819: 152; Nelson 1987: 166–9, and in general Gorevich 1987: 562–99), and – when references to Christ's Last Supper are lacking – banquets (Hauck 1950: 611–21; Fichtenau 1984: 82–91; Althoff 1987), could belong to another group of practices. The culture which invented the dichotomy between 'sacred' and 'profane' later routinized by Durkheimian anthropology was able to conceive of 'secular rituals'. But the distinction sacred–profane implied a superiority; as a result, in eras of tension between *regnum* and *sacerdotium*, or in moments of dispute between lay and clerical entities, ecclesiastical sources could demonize as 'bad rituals' both the hunt and the banquet (Alpert of Metz, *De diversitate temporum* 2.20: 719, on Thiel merchant-guildsmen feasting *quasi solemniter ebrietati inserviunt*, Buc 1994: 225–30; cf. Buc 1989: 697–9). Conversely, authors more interested in seeing their ruler as a minister in the *ecclesia* could write them up in the same breath as solemnities of religious origin – and bridge the sacred–profane dichotomy (Thegan, *Gesta Hludowici* c. 19: 202–4; Nelson 1999: 167–8; Barthélemy 1997: 201, 207 (on Ermold, *Poème sur Louis le Pieux*, ll. 2164–2529); cf. Aymar 1951: 503–13, 527–9; Grabar 1936 (1971): 57–62; 133–44).[2] Similarly, clerics in the service of rulers had a tendency to liturgify a key pursuit of the lay aristocracy, war, and, in writing at least, deny any liturgical character to their opponents' own warfare (Koeniger 1918; Prinz 1971; McCormick 1986: 342ff.; McCormick 1992; Barthélemy 1997: 207–8; Buc 1995: 215; Buc 1996: 5).

To write of 'rituals' over time is fraught with dangers, since the functionalist baggage with which anthropology is still loaded renders the historian only too ready to seek an excessively rigid correlation between changes in ritual practice and changes in social or political structure. Many a study ends with, or hinges on, the end of (or crisis in) a system of rituals, or its transmutation through institutionalization (Kelly and Kaplan 1990; Buc forthcoming (a)). A second problem lies in the nature of the medieval evidence: authors were prone to invent rituals, which clearly were, next to miracles, the strongest keystone to a narrative. But given a culture which, like imperial Rome, took solemnities seriously, the issue of their recycling or transformation in moments of historical transition remains, despite this danger, worth exploring. All the more so as we can expect a certain degree of self-consciousness on the part of Christian authors. They thought of the relationship between an old order – that of the Old Law of Moses – and a new order – the New Dispensation inaugurated by Christ – in terms of the abrogation of earlier ceremonies; they also read into the history of Ancient Israel a series of purifying reforms inaugurated with the invention or restoration of religious practices.[3] In the following pages, I will therefore risk a diachronic approach, while well aware that clerical circles had their own sense of the relationship between ritual and history.[4]

The barbarian rulers of sub-Roman political communities clearly believed that imperial solemnities belonged to the trappings of legitimate rule – hence had to be imitated. The tenth-century Byzantine treatise, *On the Governance of the Empire*, warned against the appetite of the Franks for Roman insignia, such as the purple. Consequently, it recommended a careful control of the export of objects associated with imperial power – elements of 'the imperial vesture or diadems or state robes' (Constantine VII, *de Administrando Imperio* c. 13: 66–7; cf. Shepard, ch. 2 in this volume). But control could not forestall imitation (McCormick 1986: 330–4); and imitation of 'the sole exemplar of *imperium*' was openly the policy of the Western kings – even if the Byzantines did not always consider it flattering (Cassiodorus, *Variae* 1.1.3: 9, ll. 18–20). Already in the sixth century Procopius could find no better way to illustrate the scandalous independence of Frankish kings than to report in a single breath that they had stuck gold coins in their own image and that they were giving circus-games in Arles (Procopius, *History of the Wars* 7.33: 438, 6). Hippodrome and theatre, however, soon disappeared in the Latin West – though *venationes* (hunts) may have survived with an aristocratic, as opposed to civic, audience (Notker, *Gesta Karoli* 2.15: 79, l. 11). Perhaps more than Christian critique (Markus 1990; Weismann 1972), it may have been the decline in the vitality of towns, as well as the absence of a stable capital, which doomed the arena. It seems to have disappeared fairly late in the lands dominated by East Rome, where cities could still provide the audience and the incentives that authorities needed. Yet even a shrunken urban stage did not prevent Western kings from adapting to their uses the Late Roman ceremonies of departure for, and triumphal return from, war (McCormick 1986; cf. Julian of Toledo, *Historiae Wambae*: 500–35, and de Jong 2000). The case of the arena aside, the 'Christianization' of the imperial office entailed an influence of Christian tropes on ceremonial (since the ruler had to display his religious identity) as well as the possibility for leaders of the Church to borrow Roman forms (since they now belonged to the official elite) (Brennan 1984). The Romans considered their battle-insignia to be among the *sacra*, and could bring along in combat the statues of the gods. With Constantine's conversion, the cross and the sign in whose name the emperor had conquered his rival Maxentius took the place of the older signs (McCormick 1986: 106–7; Heim 1991: 98–105). Soon Christian armies carried relics of the saints into battle – a behaviour attested in the West by the sixth century (Gregory, *Libri Historiarum* 7.31: 350), and like so many other practices standing at the intersection between cult and politics, emerging in full light thanks to Carolingian legislative activity. Thus Carloman in a capitulary of 742 forbade all priests to accompany the Frankish armies

> with the exception of those who have been designated for the sake of performing the divine ministry, that is, the solemnities of the mass, and to carry the protective relics (*patrocinia*) of the saints. That is, let the prince take along one or two bishops with the priests of the chapel, and each prefect one priest, so that they can judge the men who confess their sins and inflict penance upon them.
>
> *(Concilium Germanicum* c. 2: 25)

Relics for victory, mass for victory, penance for victory as well. Bloodshed, even with pagans as victims, may have been polluting, but to be triumphant, the Franks had to be pure (Erdmann 1935: 14): the royal abbey of St Denis preserved in its formulary Charlemagne's 791 letter to his wife Fastrada recounting how, before initiating an expedition and combat with the enemy, he had ordered a three-day fast; the king advised that this rite be imitated, an admonition which the monks of St Denis took seriously (Zeumer, *Formulae*: 510–11; cf. McCormick 1986: 352–3). Rewriting after rewriting of Carolingian annals had increasingly transmuted the civil wars waged by the king's ancestors into regular 'holy wars'. So, for example, shortly after Charlemagne's imperial coronation, the *Annales Mettenses priores* retroactively transformed the battle of Tertry (687) between Pippin II and the Neustrians into a *iudicium Dei* (Judgement of God) meant to rectify injustice and the despoliations of churches. Before the battle, the Austrasian mayor of the palace had exhorted his great men 'to commend themselves through vows and prayers to God's omnipotence, He who gives honour and victory to all those who fear Him and keep His precepts' (*Annales Mettenses Priores*, ad an. 689: 8–12). By the eleventh century, prayer before battle had become a para-liturgical custom the lay aristocracy employed against its – Christian – enemies (Dudo of St Quentin, *De moribus* cc. 107–9: 270–2; Christiansen 1998: 144–7).

For public *potestas*, conversion meant not only tinting the old rites in Christian colours but innovation as well. For instance, in 403/4, Honorius I took off his diadem and confessed his sins before Peter's *memoria* in Rome (Augustine, Sermon Dolbeau 25.26 (Mainz 61): 76). The biblical model implicit here, that of David, which Ambrose had preached to Theodosius I, was fast becoming an actual pattern for royal rites of self-humiliation (Schieffer 1972; de Jong 1992; de Jong 1997; cf. Graboïs 1992). Barely thirty years after Honorius' visit to Rome, Theodosius II institutionalized his predecessor's pious act in an edict binding the ruler to lay down his arms and crown before entering a basilica (Treitinger 1938: 9, 150). In a more local context, bishops, in a constant struggle to impose their authority over fractious civic communities, adopted and transformed solemnities associated with Roman official-dom. Thus, the translation of relics into a *civitas*, as first fully described in Victricius of Rouen's sermon of 396, patterned itself loosely on the imperial *adventus* (Brown 1982; but see Jussen 1995; Jussen 1998). It is well known that the borrowings between Church and kingdom were a two-way street throughout the Middle Ages (Schramm 1970). Very soon, emperors, barbarian kings, and their nobles imitated bishops in caring for the poor, and Venantius Fortunatus could sing the praises of Count Sigoald, 'who fed the poor for the king's sake' so that God would grant young Childebert II a long life and the heights of royal rule. This Sigoald represented Childebert at 'sacred festivals' and provided there for thousands of sick and needy people (Venantius Fortunatus, *Carmen* 10, ll. 19–26, 31–3: 250; and Venantius Fortunatus, *Vita sancti Germani* c. 13: 381–2; Gregory, *Libri Historiarum* 8.29: 391, 393; Tinnefeld 1991: 109–13; cf. Boshof 1976).

But for Fortunatus, we might know little concerning early Frankish royal rituals. Our main sixth-century informant, Bishop Gregory of Tours, was unwilling to hallow his kings, in whom he saw at best (but rarely) devoted instruments of the episcopate, at worst (and more commonly) competitors for taxes and power. The Merovingians' Carolingian successors also contributed to this obfuscation (Hauck 1967: 72; Schneider 1972; Nelson 1987: 140–1; cf. Enright 1985). Yet incidental details in Gregory's works, combined with Fortunatus' poems praising Merovingian royalty and evidence from neighbouring kingdoms, betray the continuing importance of the *imitatio imperii*. Circus games lasted into the seventh century (Gregory, *Libri Historiarum* 5.17: 216; cf. Procopius, *History* 7.33). To accompany *laudes* and acclamations, rulers imported musical instruments from Byzantium or its western outposts (*Annales regni Francorum* ad. ann. 757: 14; cf. *Annales Petaviani*: 11; Ermold, *Poème* ll. 2520–5: 192; Cassiorodorus, *Variae* 2.41.4 (508): 92. See Zak 1991: 481–7; Schneider 1972: 234–5). Entries (*adventus*) into cities seem to have continued, both at the royal and comital level; some may have involved trains of relics; care seems to have been paid to place the *adventus* at the high dates of the liturgical calendar (Gregory, *Libri Historiarum* 6.27: 295; cf. Hauck 1967: 34–7; Schaller 1974). Kings took pains to be present at the festivals of the saints. Gregory accused the Arian king of the Visigoths of deception in honouring relics, but this worship no doubt was rendered in a public fashion (Gregory, *Libri Historiarum* 6.18: 287). Merovingian royalty might address their people during mass. We even have the trace of kings' liturgical authorship: Chilperic composed hymns, one of which, honouring St Médard, the saint of the Frankish capital city of Soissons, has survived (Gregory, *Libri Historiarum* 8.44: 410, 9.3: 416; cf. 5.44: 254 and 6.46: 320; cf. Strecker 1923: 457–9; Norberg 1954: 31–40). Well before our first surviving evidence of a Carolingian king's participation in relic translations, Lombard sources depict the role of the *princeps* Arichis in receiving the bones of twelve martyrs as well as the relics of the warrior-saint Mercurius into his capital of Benevento, 'having put off his [princely] ornaments . . . and clothed in a hair-shirt and prostrate to the ground' (*Translatio sancti Mercurii*: 580; *Translatio duodecim martyrum*: 575; Belting 1962: 156–60; with Binon 1937: 43–50). Merovingian rulers also imitated the Constantinian and Theodosian exemplar by presiding at synods. The mimesis of Constantine and

Theodosius II involved the festive ratification of orthodox councils and the condemnation of heresy – as in Visigothic Spain after Reccared's conversion (589) (Stocking 1997; Stocking 2000), or under Cunipert in Lombardy (698) (*Carmen de synodo Ticinensi*: 189–91). Through solemnities affirming the (re)foundation of a national Church purged of religious deviance, kings claimed a place in providential history (Zeddies 1995). When they condemned the Byzantines' stance on icon-worship at the Frankfurt synod of 794, the Carolingians, then, followed an established tradition. The elevation of Louis to co-emperorship in 813 not coincidentally followed immediately – at least in some contemporary sources – upon a reform council (*Annales regni Francorum* ad ann. 813: 138; *Chronicon Moissiacense* ad. ann. 813: 311).

Conciliar records themselves offer an indirect glimpse into what we may call the 'native anthropology' of early medieval assemblies. Gerd Althoff has dissected in masterly fashion the functioning of lay *colloquia*, and confirmed Hincmar of Rheims' normative description: a frank, consensus-building 'private' discussion ideally prepared and delineated the subsequent 'public' debate and its decisions (Althoff 1997(a)). But if we allow ourselves to draw in the clergy's self-reflective pronouncements, we can bring some emotional texture to Althoff's 'rules of the political game'. Early medieval political culture treasured the display of personal interaction in public settings. Here too, it stood heir to Ancient Rome, where it had been a mark of the *civilis princeps* to allow himself to be seen by all and to see all citizens (Pliny the Younger, *Panegyricus Traiani*: 140; Buc 1997: 67–70). For the fathers of the Visigothic councils, whose way of proceeding became normative for Carolingian Europe, corrective legislation was not the sole justification for their assemblies. They also served 'to stabilize concord and brotherly charity, when gathered together in the Lord's name, bishops through a salutary conversation (*conlatio*) seek among themselves those things which, according to the Apostle's teaching, foster a unity of mind and the bond of peace' (Braga I (561): 65; cf. Toledo XVI (693): 482; also Arles (813), prologue: 248, and Coulaines (843), prologue: 254). Next to *conlatio*, the visual availability of each to each also demonstrated the presence of charity (Toledo XV (688), prologue: 449; cf. Arles (813): 248). The circle provided the best vector – and spatial metaphor – for this equality, and consequently councils favoured seats placed in a crown (*corona*) (Reynolds 1987; Fichtenau 1984: 1.30, n. 106; 32 and nn.) Seating (as opposed to standing) signalled participation in authority (Alföldi 1970: 42, 44–5; cf. Jerome, *In Eph.* 5.3–4, PL 26, 552, but cf. Bede, *In Apoc.* 4.4., PL 93, 143). At councils, bishops sat, but their priests stood behind them. A throne placed in the centre marked, tautologically, the centrality of the person there seated. But centrality did not necessarily mean autocracy. In Ambrosius Autpertus' exegesis (758/767) of the heavenly ceremonial in *Revelations*, both the one seated on the central throne and the various figures placed in circles around it – notably the twenty-four *seniores* and the four animals – shared in an essentially identical judicial power (*In Apoc.* 4.4, 4.6, 7.9, 7.11, 11.15: 211, 216–17, 306–7, 312–13, 436–7; cf. Haymo of Auxerre, *in eodem*, esp. PL 117: 1006, 1023, 1039).[5] This meshes with a strand in Carolingian ecclesiology which Olivier Guillot has analysed on the basis of two capitularies: the participation by the king, the lay magnates, and the bishops in a single *honor* and power, which bound them to a common work of reform of kingdom and Church under the king's leadership (Guillot 1990: 466–7, 485; Guillot 1983: 92–5, with ref. to Coulaines (843): 254, and Ansegis, *Collectio capitularium*, 2.3: 523). In typical early medieval fashion, the disposition at assemblies could convey simultaneously equality and superiority (Buc 1994: 45–7; cf. Fichtenau 1984: 1.33–5). Positioned at the top of a *corona* (the top being identified through proximity to a cardinal direction or to the holier part of a church in which the assembly took place, as well as, more simply, through a higher throne), a person became central – as if the circle had shifted from a horizontal plane to an oblique plane, thus introducing verticality. The presentation image in the so-called Bible of Charles the Bald (MS Paris BN Latin 1, fo. 423r) – one of whose other miniatures Dominique Alibert has already related to the Carolingian ideology of participation – manages in this way to combine circularity and eminence, participation and the summit of rule (Alibert 1994: 75–91, esp. 85–6, 89–90). In fact, with the king on the throne, the twelve clerics disposed in a circle (including the non-tonsured lay abbot Vivian), the four lay figures closer to the king's seat, and the presentation of a book, it replicates the structure of the heavenly ceremonial of *Revelations*, or rather of its exegesis – since it is biblical commentaries which inform us that the twenty-four elders are in fact a double twelve, owing to the duality of Old and New Testaments. When one brings together the exegesis by Angelomus and the miniature, one finds in the latter the iconographic equivalent of the programme discovered by Guillot: king, magnates, and clergy belong as limbs to a single body – the Carolingian Church-Commonwealth – and rectify it together under royal leadership. Here iconography and exegesis offer the historian a tentative lead into the political meaning of the spatial organization at Carolingian assemblies.

The Carolingian and Ottonian centuries raise the vexing question of a seeming increase in 'rituals'. The surviving documents suggest a higher frequency of such solemnized acts – higher both between the Carolingian and Merovingian eras and between the Ottonian and Carolingian dispensations. Karl Leyser underlined this second increase, starting in the 960s and 970s with the production of Liudprand's *Antapodosis*, the Continuation of Regino of Prüm, and Widukind of Corvey's *Deeds of the Saxons*, and related it to the needs of a less literate tenth-century German kingdom. Rituals, in his opinion, fulfilled the function of the quill as a means of communication (Leyser 1994 (i): 192–6, 211). Yet, as suggested above, the first increase, from Merovingian to Carolingian, may be partly an optical illusion related to the Carolingian desire to obscure the Merovingian past. Further, the correlation ritual: orality is not an obvious one. In the Carolingian era itself, starting in the 830s, descriptions of ritual increase in the putatively more literate circles around Louis the Pious and his sons. The Carolingian educational reforms were bearing full fruits; denser narrative texts were produced, which supply more information on rituals than the more laconic sources Carolingian historiography produced before the 830s. Were Leyser's hypothesis valid, it should also apply to the early, less literate Carolingian era. There seems, rather, to be a straightforward (and unsurprising) correlation between literary productivity and the presence of rituals in writing. But the change in the type of sources is significant. For in itself the heightened loquacity about rituals points to a transformation in their functioning *vis-à-vis* the eighth century.

Figure 11.1 Charles the Bald in the structural position of *Revelations'* royal Elder of Days, surrounded by twelve *seniores*, from Bibliothèque Nationale de France, Ms. Latin 1 (*Première Bible de Charles le Chauve*), F. 423r.

With the appearance of an imperial aristocracy whose members, being spread over a far-flung territory, could not all witness each ceremony, descriptions of rituals became as important as their performance (Buc forthcoming (b)).

Furthermore, regardless of this phenomenon, qualitative changes in solemnities are clear. Most obviously, coronation, in progressively tighter conjunction with the anointing (introduced by the Visigoths in the seventh century but rediscovered for good by the Franks from 751–4), became constitutive of royal power (Klewitz 1939; Brühl 1962; Jäschke 1970; Brühl 1982). Prior to that, sub-Roman kings wore crowns, but ceremonies centred on this object – the coronation proper and various forms of crown-wearing – did not exist (Jäschke 1970: 586).[6] Still *c.* 800, a Carolingian court cleric commenting on the accession of the first king of Israel did not specifically highlight the crown, and insisted rather on the subjects' gestures of self-abasement: 'They made Saul king in that place, that is, they prepared for him a very high throne, and clothed him in royal vestments, and then they reverenced him as their king, and humbled [i.e., prostrated] themselves before him' (MS Paris BN N.a.l. 762, fos. 110v–11r, Wigbod *in 1 Reg.* 11.15: 'Et fecerunt ibi regem Saul, id est paraverunt sibi optimam sedem . et vestierunt Saul regalibus vestimentis . et tunc adoraverunt eum pro rege . et humiliati sunt coram illo.'). We owe, then, to the Carolingians' need to legitimize their coup d'état against the Merovingian 'long-haired kings,' the fact that the crown has become the sign par excellence of the monarch (Jäschke 1970: 582–5). Under the Carolingians, the crown became closely associated with Christian kingship. With Ottonian iconography, Christ himself began to be depicted with a crown (Deshman 1976: 374–7, 388–90). Kings had always worn crowns, but starting in the late eighth century, the coronation acquired a constitutive meaning, and coronations were reiterated through *coronamenta*. These crown-wearings could be occasions for hierarchical display. In his highly imaginative *Gesta Karoli*, Notker of St Gall told his audience how Louis the Pious distributed gifts 'to each and every one who served in the palace or was a member of the royal household'. Their quality varied in proportion with the recipient's status; thus sword-belts, associated with honour and office since Late Antiquity, went to 'the more noble' (Notker, *Gesta Karoli* 2.21: 91–2). According to Thietmar of Merseburg, the king walked in procession from one church to another, or from his palace to a church, surrounded by clergy, and preceded by censers and saints' relics. There he heard divine service. While the procession into the church was fully clerical, the return procession also included the lay aristocracy – dukes and counts (Thietmar, *Chronicon*: 2.30: 76 (on Otto I), but not specifically mentioning a crown-wearing). It may be that, as in neighbouring West Francia, these magnates carried tapers before the king (cf. Thietmar, *Chron.*: 76, and Eudes de St Maur, *Vie de Bouchard* 11: 29). Several sources indicate that, by custom, the Carolingian ruler bore full regalian ornaments on the occasion of church festivals (especially the great three, Christmas, Easter, and Pentecost) and only then. And even then, restraint in pomp was strongly advised (Thegan, *Gesta Hludowici* 19: 202–4). The rule obtained in Byzantium as well, justified by a legend: an angel had given Constantine I the imperial regalia, with the provision that they could be worn only on the high feast days of the Church, and otherwise kept in Hagia Sophia (Constantine VII, *De Administrando imperio* 13: 66–7). Self-restraint in ornaments had been an attribute of the good ruler since

Antiquity. Consequently, critics could brand a ruler as tyrannical by reporting (or imagining) transgressions of this customary norm – 'bad rituals' in which a prince dressed up excessively. Misguided pomp also provided material for stereotypical scenes of wise priestly advice to excess-prone lay rulers – a way to underline the superiority of the saint at the expense of another figure of power (Alföldi 1955: 33; Alföldi 1970: 8, 10–11; Tinnefeld 1971: 162; cf. *Annales Fuldenses* ad an. 876: 86). For instance, Milo Crispin's *Life of Lanfranc* recycled the story of Herod Agrippa's death, based on the *Acts of the Apostles* and on Flavius Josephus' *Antiquities*, in favour of the holy archbishop of Canterbury. The Late Antique sources had recounted how, owing to an arrogant display of regal splendour, which had provoked acclamations (*voces*) reserved 'to a god and not to a human being', the Jewish hierarch had been struck by the Lord and died 'eaten by worms' (cf. also the same episode transmitted from Josephus by Freculph of Lisieux, *Chronicon* 2.1.14, PL 106, 1129–30, and Haymo, *Historiae sacrae epitoma* 2.18, PL 118, 828). In Milo's version, during the banquet following a crown-wearing, a jester had praised King William I's splendid vestments with a sycophantic acclamation (*voce*) – 'Behold, I see a god!' – prompting Lanfranc to demand of the king that he forbid such adulation. The narrative, then, did not (as has been suggested) point to the political relationship between the ruler and his aristocracy, and encapsulate the Normans' tense unease with a duke who was now also a king with autocratic leanings, but simply to the relative wisdom of archbishop and king, the former the *Vita*'s hero, the latter a worthy straw-man (Milo, *Vita Lanfranci* 13.33, PL 150, 53–4; cf. Nelson 1986: 400–1; Koziol 1992: 290–1; Koziol 1995: 137, 145).[7]

Genetics similar to those of the coronation apply to royal anointing, a liturgical form related to post-baptismal unction. According to received wisdom, it was introduced to parallel the new Carolingian rulers with the anointed kings of the Old Testament; the usurpers badly needed some kind of aura to offset the blood-charisma of the Merovingians (Kern 1954: 66; Schramm 1954: 127; Affeldt 1980; but cf. Enright 1985: 120–3, 137). But the anointing may also have served a plurality of further purposes: to mark off Pippin's narrow family (as opposed to his Arnulfing relatives) as throne-worthy (Kern 1954: 77–9; cf. *Clausula de unctione Pippini*, and Stoclet 1980; also Ewig 1982: 46–7); when applied to a queen, to secure the fertility of the dynasty (and possibly hint at the spiritual fertility of kings) (Kantorowizc 1965; Alibert 1998: 28–32); to signal (in conformity with early medieval exegesis and the meaning then attached to baptism) the unity of the Franks with a king at its centre (Angenendt 1982; Nelson 1987: 146–7, 153; cf. (possibly inauthentic) Gregory the Great, *In primum librum Regum expositiones* 6.95, *in 1 Reg.* 16.13: 603).

Speculation regarding the exact intentions of the impresarios of the first Carolingian anointings and coronations, however intelligent and informed, remains speculation. The far from loquacious eighth-century texts which report coronations or anointings do not state *expressis verbis* anything resembling these hypotheses. Nor, for that matter, any other. One thing is, however, clear, given the survival, in a number of ninth-century cases, of a plurality of sources depicting the same ritual event: a ritual was often the object of a struggle for interpretation, a struggle whose details, in turn, inform us on the burning issues of the day. The author of the Chronicle of Moissac interrupted his writing in 818 or 819, leaving behind a narrative unadulterated by the knowledge of the crisis which struck Louis the Pious' realm in the 820s and 830s, but influenced by already existing controversies on the role of the pope in emperor-making (Kern 1954: 90–2; Ganshof 1949: 23–6; Folz 1964: 169–208). Attested to by the plural narratives of Charlemagne's 800 accession to the imperial office, as well as by the variant versions of the first meeting between a pope and a Carolingian, in 754 at Ponthion, the divergences between the Frankish and Roman understandings play themselves out in the Moissac Chronicle for the years 813, 816, and 817. Whereas the accounts of the 813 and 817 elevations of the ruler's son to co-emperorship are highly detailed, with rich biblical references to Old Testament (and especially Davidic) monarchy, the 816 visit of Pope Stephen to Rheims receives much sparser treatment (Buc 2000). For the Moissac Chronicler, then, the act constitutive of emperorship is not the papal benediction but the paternal transmission of power on the model of David to Salomon, not Stephen's gift of a crown to Louis but the imperial father's transmission of the empire 'through a crown' (likewise downplaying the papal visit, *Annales Sithienses* (St-Amand) ad an. 816: 37, written by 823; cf. slightly later *Annales regni Francorum* ad an. 813, 816, 817: 138, 144, 146). And in fact this was the meaning of the 817 ceremony for the document closest to the event, the famous *Ordinatio imperii* (prologue: 270–1). As Mariëlle Hageman has argued, it was only after the inception of the civil wars opposing Louis and his sons that the emperor's panegyrists – Ermold, the Astronomer, and Thegan – developed the 816 visit and emphasized its rituality in an attempt to strengthen Louis' position (Hageman 1997; cf. Flodoard, *Historia Remensis Ecclesiae* 2.19: 175–83). But half a generation before, the Moissac Chronicle had squarely placed sacrality – if by this term we understand references to Sacred History – in a solemnity led by the emperor, and in which the priesthood merely acquiesced alongside the lay aristocracy. In 818, it was still possible to write up the central solemnities of emperorship without granting authority to the Papacy or the episcopate. Charlemagne played David, and Louis Solomon. By the time of Thegan and Ermold, the Davidic accents had been displaced to the 816 papal visit, and Zadok the priest granted a role he lacked in the *Book of Kings* (Ermold, *Poème*, ll. 918–20: 72; Thegan, *Gesta Hluodwici* cc. 16–7: 196; cf. Buc 2000].

Why are sources emanating from Saxon Germany so rich in royal rituals? In analysing the narratives recounting Henry I's accession produced under his son, Johannes Fried has spoken of *ritualgeleitete Vergangenheitskonstruktion* (a ritual-led reconstruction of the past) – the Ottonian writers projected into the past their own issues and crystallized them around imagined rituals (Fried 1995: 311). Widukind and Liudprand wrote for aristocratic circles close to the Saxon dynasty, when not for the Liudolfings themselves. Widukind punctuated Saxon history with the solemnities of royal funerals and accessions, implicitly putting them on a par with the 'origins of the tribe' which open his work (Widukind, *Rerum gestarum Saxonicarum* 1. 2, 1.51, 2.1–2, 2.41, 3.1, 3.35–6. See Warner 1995; Althoff 1997(e): 190–9; Althoff 1997(f); Görich 1997: esp. 142–61). In this sense, tribal history and Liudolfing dynastic history became one – not an evident thesis in the light of Saxon opposition to a strengthened Ottonian rule. As for Liudprand, he intended to convince his audience of the legitimacy of Otto I's direct rule over Italy, against both Italian princes' and Byzantine emperors' own claims, as well as against the German aristocracy's recent negotiation on Berengar II's behalf of a real, if subordinate, kingship over the peninsula. To serve this argument, the *Antapodosis* mustered stories about rituals – solemnities manipulated by Otto's rivals, but sanctifying when they pertained to the German dynasty (Buc 1995; Buc 1996). Other sources contain rituals involving royalty for reasons less concerned with high power-politics, and were produced at a great distance in time from the events they purport to recount. Ekkehard IV's *Casus sancti Galli* and Arnold of St Emmeram in Regensburg's *Miracles of the blessed Emmeram* come to mind. Like the Aquitanian foundation legends so well studied by Amy Remensnyder, these texts stage past kings in relation to the monastery, in order both to heighten the institution's prestige by tying it to royal patrons or by showing its superiority even *vis-à-vis* monarchs, and to defend or advance claims to specific rights and properties (Remensnyder 1996(a); Remensnyder 1996(b)). Descriptions of rituals anchor the argument; when they are 'good rituals' they emphasize the fraternity between monks and kings, especially through shared meals in the honour of the saints (*caritates*) (Ekkehard IV, *Casus Sancti Galli* 7, 16, 38: 28, 44, 86; Arnold, *De miraculis beati Emmerammi* 1.17: 552; see Geary 1995: 165, 168–75). But the paraliturgical eating and drinking also designates monastic property – either a domain given by the king and earmarked specifically for the *caritates* or the land from whose produce the banquet is provided (both can stand metonymically for the abbey's whole endowment) (Buc 1997: 111–13; cf. *Cartulaire de Beaulieu* (en Limousin) +166: 232). In these monastic texts as well, the king may participate in the liturgy, more passively as the recipient of 'freshly dictated *laudes*' sung to welcome his arrival, more actively (like Chilperic the composer of hymns and contemporary Byzantine emperors who preached homilies) as an author of antiphonaries (Ekkehard, *Casus* 14: 40; 46: 104; cf. for Byzantium, Grosdidier de Matons 1973: 181–206). We find this clerical strategy – to solemnize claims through princely rites – in miniature with a forged diploma of Pippin King of Aquitaine. Its heavy narrative component provides one of the nicest examples of royal entries into a monastery:

> [The monks] beseeched that we [Pippin] should not in any way desist from our advent [to St Maixent]. Thus, rendering thanks to God Almighty, at the third hour on the Sunday before the Lord's Easter [Palm Sunday], they performed an *occursus* (welcoming ritual) and received us with crosses and tapers, as is customary for kings (*regio more*), but in silence, without the ringing of bells and the usual chants. And they led us to pray to the tombs of the aforesaid saints. After we had returned from this church, we washed our body as befits a man (*humano more*) and dressed up in a regal way (*regio nutu* – read *regio cultu*?). When the hour came, we waited with the greatest devotion in the church, and then we rose up in the night for this office in order to complete it as religiously as we could (. . .)
>
> (*Recueil des chartes de Pépin I*: 262)

But this wonderful text is here to ground St Maixent claims. For when Pippin leaves the church after Easter mass, he finds prostrate monks. These supplicants recount the abbey's woes, and obtain from the king's piety a diploma. Read aloud during the following mass and placed on the saint's shrine, it guarantees St Maixent

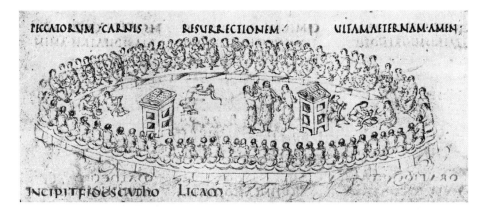

Figure 11.2 An assembly of bishops, from The Utrecht Psalter. Universiteitsbibliotheek, Utrecht, MS. 32, fo. 90v.

rights to free abbatial election, immunity from public officials, their jurisdiction and requisitions, as well as free transit without tolls and full judicial authority over one of the abbey's markets.

All this was not merely 'phantoms of remembrance', however. St Gall, for instance, boasted a rich collection of hymns composed, between the ninth and the eleventh century, to receive actual kings (Bulst 1941; Willmes 1976). Yet while these texts document the efforts of the monastery to honour visiting rulers, the actual details of the royal stays remain clouded in 'imaginative memory'.

How exclusively 'royal' were royal rituals? The question has been broached by Janet Nelson, who rightly insists that under the Carolingians at least some rituals foregrounded the community of the Frankish leadership and its God-willed consensus. Ritual was 'hierarchical' in the full sense of the term – underlining the delegation of, and sharing in authority, between ruler and leading group. In Byzantium as in the West, acclamations to officials involved acclamations to the monarch, and vice versa (Treitinger 1938 (1956): 71; Kantorowicz 1946). Under the Capetians, after the king had elevated himself above the aristocracy, the participation of the peers in the coronation still maintained the notion of a sharing in royal power (Schramm 1960 (i): 163–76). In his groundbreaking *Begging Pardon and Favor*, G. Koziol has sought to prove the progressive diffusion in West Francia, paralleling (where and when it happened) the devolution of political authority, of rituals of subordination, specifically those staged when the grant of a charter was demanded: the party demanding a favour will recognize the grantor's authority through stereotypical gestures of self-humiliation, supplication or prostration (cf. for the Carolingian period, Ermold, *Ad Pippinum Regem*, ll. 53–64: 206). Once the exclusive preserve of kings and bishops,[8] the privilege of being the target of such a 'ritual' spread (in certain zones) to lesser strata of the lay aristocracy. In the Loire valley, in particular, by the eleventh and early twelfth century, all levels, including the 'new' *milites*, simultaneously supplicated and received supplications – admittedly not the full prostration once monopolized by kings (Koziol 1992: 241–67). But here again the sources – both in the ideal interests they express and in the early medieval models which structure them as literary artefacts – are more subtle than the anthropological theories the historian employs to read them (at least as he or she employs them). Do charters document actual prostrations or the fictions of their redactors? Are these fictions penned by the monastic recipients or by notaries in the pay of the donor? Finally, what kind of gestures of respect are actually documented or fictionalized through expressions such as *supplex* or *humiliter*? We should not lump together a series of gestures that ninth-century monastic authors, in particular commentators on the *Rule of St Benedict*, differentiated, and attributed as marks of respect specific to different status groups. Both Hildemar of Corbie (d. *c.*850) and Smaragdus legislated on the reception of visitors to the monastery. For the former, the monks were to greet only kings, bishops, and abbots with prostration on the ground; for lesser visitors, 'counts, priests, monks and others' to bow one's head in salutation was enough.[9] For Smaragdus, writing perhaps shortly after 816, it seems that the first category comprised 'kings, bishops, or any powerful person belonging to the summits of rule' – possibly a wider ensemble than Hildemar's (Smaragdus, *Expositio in Regulam Benedicti* 53: 280–1; cf. Willmes 1976: 61–5). Already in the first half of the ninth century, then, different monasteries may have had different understandings as to which public figures were owed prostration, and took care to honour lesser nobility as well. Not all clerics found prostration before the king palatable: some even felt it was tantamount to idolatry. Andrew of Bergamo, writing some time after 877, could thus recall or imagine that Archbishop Agilbert of Milan had refused to fall at the Emperor Lothar's feet. Angilbert had merely 'bowed his head and uttered words of salutation, owing to the honour and reverence of the churches' he represented. When Lothar rebuked him, suggesting that he was deluded to think that he was St Ambrose himself, the archbishop retorted, 'Neither are you the Lord God Himself' (Andrew of Bergamo, *Historia* 7: 225).[10] Reformist circles would echo this distaste. A charter of 927/50 granting immunity to Sauxillanges made Christ in his *maiestas* the minster's one and only Lord (in implicit contrast to the Charles the Simple, whom the unfaithful Franks had stripped of his royal *honor*), 'so that they would live, be governed, and secured under the protection of His name. . . . ' Correspondingly, this Lord alone would receive the highest marks of honour: ' . . . and the clerics there established will bend the knee to Him alone, adore [only] Him, and invoke Him as their sole ruler (*rector*)'. Far from being a symptom in a 'ritual' of the devolution of power, then, the putative spread of lesser marks of honour may have been in fact the product of a reformist desire to deny greater lords authority and its signs, a denial which, by contrast, highlighted the less extravagant marks of respect that the *Rule* had granted to all laymen (Duke Acfred's charter for Sauxillanges (927), in *Recueil Cluny* no. 286: i: 283, 286–7; Buc 1998). In other words, in this case as well, the correlation between 'ritual' and 'social change' appears far from obvious, since we may be dealing here simply with the ideological reflexes, in text, of a number of ecclesiastical communities (cf. Koziol 1992: 237–8, 267; and for a preferable view, Barthélemy 1995: 18–9, 35; Barthélemy 1993: 17–128).[11]

Even if we were to trust that medieval narratives convey solemnities *wie eigentlich gewesen*, we should realise, first, that rituals' effectiveness may not always lie in some wondrous pull, and second, that the assumption that they strengthened social order is open to debate. Some solemnities functioned as a direct consequence of their relation to legal norms and not necessarily owing to their inscription in a liturgical frame of reference. Gerd Althoff has unearthed for tenth- and eleventh-century Germany a fairly fixed scenario for the surrender (*deditio*) of rebels to the king. Coerced through a campaign of often limited but highly demonstrative violence, and after secret negotiations handled through intermediaries, the rebel would throw himself at the king's feet or otherwise humble himself publicly. The ruler would – equally solemnly – receive him back into grace, as a general rule after only a short period of honourable imprisonment, and almost always with a full restitution of confiscated property. Althoff believes that when well negotiated, these rituals generally allowed all parties to the conflict to save face and their honour; *deditio*, then, contributed to the equilibrium of an Ottonian polity where the king, while powerful, could not elevate himself too far above the aristocracy (Althoff 1997(b); Althoff 1997(c)). According to the same author, the first testimony to this 'ritual' in its full form would be the surrender of Lothar, Hugh and Matfrid before Louis the Pious in 834 (Althoff 1997(c): 116–21; but cf. Gregory of Tours, *Libri Historiarum* 5.38: 245, and 6.32: 302–4). Here comparison between genres is fruitful, for a Carolingian capitulary explains one of the legal consequences of a *deditio*. In offering to reconsider confiscations of property effected by Pippin the Short (d. 768) after his capture of fortresses, Louis the Pious proposed to distinguish between those men 'who had resisted as long as they could and came against their will into the power of our grandfather', and those who 'while their associates resisted with pertinacity, and even though the fortress may have been taken by force (*per vim*), gave themselves up (*se dediderunt*)'. Property forfeited by men in the former category would remain the property of the royal fisc; but those who (like Lothar's cohorts in 834) had performed a *deditio* were spared confiscation (MGH Capit. I: 296). Public and manifest surrender, then, could help a claim to the full retention of property which might, otherwise, have been completely lost to one's triumphant lord.

Other practices, far from fostering peace, were meant to publicize strife. Insults and blows belonged to the repertory of stereotypical actions with a public import. Councils, supposedly havens of peace, should have been devoid of what we can identify as violence. But, to quote Heinrich Fichtenau, order and disorder are partisan concepts. 'Angered and burning with zeal, . . . all' the participants of the Roman council of 769 ceremonially slapped the papal usurper Constantine, and threw him out of the church (*Vita Stephani III* c. 19, *Liber Pontificalis* 1: 475; MGH Concilia II: 79). There existed set signs of hostility. John VIII assured empress Angilberga that he would retaliate in kind against Charles the Bald, who had maltreated his envoys:

> Whosoever comes as an envoy from Charles, the church will not be opened to him, nor communion be given to him, nor a kiss offered to him, nor any seat be prepared for him as is customary (*iuxta morem*). And according to the apostolic precept, let 'Ave' ('Greetings!') not be said to him [cf. 2 John 1.10]. Nevertheless, we shall receive him and hear him, and if he bears a letter, let him come in (the church?), but then he shall be handed a document containing admonitions and rebukes.
>
> (*Fragmentum Registri Iohannis VIII* 47 (874–early 875),
> MGH Epp. VII: 302; cf. White 1998)

Generally speaking, early medieval men and women were quite ready to stage a row using the oppositional vocabulary bequeathed by hagiography (a rich repertory of bad emperors browbeaten by the saints) (Buc 1997(a)) or employing the elements of established political rituals (Althoff 1982; cf. Leyser 1994(i): 199). But it is not simply these contentious practices which call into doubt the socially stabilizing function attributed generically to 'ritual'. Even the great 'theophanic' solemnities with their references to heavenly order could be read *mala parte* and mistrusted. Many historians attribute to political rituals the function of maintaining social groups, from the kindred to society. Rituals can perform this role, however, only if their being manipulated constitutes a rare exception rather than a frequent fact (or fear), and only if the participants are, to a great degree, sincere. The underpinning sociology sees in the Middle Ages a culture which did not differentiate between the public and private spheres, a model put forward by, among others, Jürgen Habermas in the 1960s, but related to the pre-war Neo-Catholic 'political theology' of the jurist Carl Schmitt and the historical sociology of the medievalist Otto Brunner (Habermas 1962: 58ff with references to Schmitt and Brunner). It also assumes that the fracture in human beings between interior feelings and outward demeanour – a key characteristic of modernity and the precondition of the hypocrisy attributed to the world of Castiglione's *Courtier* – hadn't yet appeared (Althoff 1997(d), criticizing J. Huizinga and N. Elias; cf. Koziol 1992: 291; and Klaniczay below). Thus Arno Borst: 'There exists no gap between the form and the intention of ceremonial behaviour; everyone means what he does, and whoever does not want to do keeps away. Thus ceremony is the foundation of community' (Borst 1973: 474–88, at 485; Fichtenau 1984, i: 76; Buc forthcoming(b)). Here medieval agents resemble the anthropologists' primitives.[12] Anthropology's primitive political being ignores the modern chasm between a private self categorized as 'individual' and a public self categorized as 'social' because he is so totally embraced in the collective that he constitutes a collective in miniature (Augé 1992: 64–5). Or, to relate this social scientific equation to a famous historiographical distinction (Kantorowicz 1957), the king is almost wholly absorbed by the one of his two bodies which represents society and the public good.

Yet medieval texts are far from ignoring hypocrisy. They often highlight it to darken a figure or make a narrative more dramatic, as a few examples will show (Buc 1996). In his *Life of Wenzel* (Venceslav) of Bohemia, written *c*.968/78, Gumpold of Mantua recounts the assassination of the saintly duke (935). His brother Boleslav organizes a banquet to which he convokes his allies 'under a mask of cheerfulness' (*sub hylaritatis specie*), then goes to Wenzel's palace and supplicates him to be his guest. *Supplex ingressus palatium . . . corrogavit . . .* – the formula would denote for Koziol a 'theophanic' prostration and petition before the ruler, which simultaneously recognizes the world-order in which the duke is an icon of the cosmic king. But here, as when he takes his brother by the hand to lead him into the hall, Boleslav, *infelix ille fraudis amicus*, intends to deceive, and the story ends with the duke's martyrdom (Gumpold, *Vita Venceslavi* c. 18: 219). Medieval authors play with the potential for deception inherent in all the forms which twentieth-century historiography has identified as political rituals. In Widukind's *Deeds of the Saxons*, a nobleman named Agina 'comes into the presence of the king (Otto I), and salutes him with humble words', announcing the 'advent' of the German ruler's brother, Henry. But the *adventus* is a hostile one, for Henry, in rebellion, is coming to meet his royal brother at the head of an army, battle-flags unfurled (Widukind, *Rerum gestarum Saxonicarum* 2.17: 81–2). Such stories of manipulated rituals do serve to dramatize the narrative. But this role is no reason to dismiss them, for why should transgression on the one hand belong to the category of the dramatic ornament, and consensual rituals on the other to the hard substance of politics?

The student of medieval political culture deals with a Christian universe whose myth of origins recounts the fateful betrayal of God, woman and man by the ambitious prince of darkness, Satan. In the 'theatre state' of Bali dear to Clifford Geertz, there may have existed a seamless correspondence between heavenly exemplar and earthly rulership. In the medieval West, satanic deceit perturbed smooth exemplarity.

Deceit, angelic as well as human, was on the minds of thinkers great and small. Tertullian had described, *c.*200 CE, how the Roman upper classes performed rites (*religio*) honouring the ruling emperor: they decorated their doors with laurel, lit their vestibules, and pulled their couches onto the street to feast in public. But the performance was wholly hypocritical:

> They performed sacred rites for the emperor's prosperity and swore by his Genius . . . , yet not in order to celebrate public rejoicings, but rather, changing the name of the ruler in their heart, to learn to perform public vows for themselves within another's ceremonial, and to consecrate an exemplar and an icon of their own hope (to rule).
>
> (Tertullian, *Apologeticum* 35.10–12: 76–7)

Eight hundred years later, squarely in the world of 'begging pardon and favour', Ralph Glaber re-imagined the betrayal of King Charles the Simple (923). His councillors, the Cluniac monk tells us, had warned him against Herbert II of Vermandois – rightly, for the man was to betray him and imprison him. Charles, however, was swayed to blind and fateful trust when the count came to his palace and bent low before him, then slapped his son on the neck to force him to bow as well: the lad, still raw and uncultured in the arts of deception, had at first been reluctant to humble himself before a lord he knew his father despised (Radulphus Glaber, *Historiarum libri quinque* 1.5: 12). The 'iconic kingship' and the 'discourse' of ritual reverence dear to Koziol could be perceived as manipulative hypocrisy.

The above remarks can be met with a set retort: any manipulation does not call in question the greater framework of ritual; thus, in the last analysis, ritual maintains order or belief in order. But the refutation of the refutation refutes only so far. Granted, just as stories of specific false saints do not invalidate belief in the existence of saints in general, the widespread presence of manipulated rituals in medieval sources might go hand in hand with unwavering belief in the order that rituals generically pointed to. Still, like so many 'in the last analysis' propositions, this one elides too easily the anxiety which must have attended many a solemnity, and even all of them. Whatever 'political ritual' may be, in a Christian political culture, it meant danger as much as communication, perversion as much as exemplarity.

NOTES

1 My thanks for discussions on the topic and/or the examples here employed to Dominique Alibert, Dominique Barthélemy, Patrick Geary, Igor Gorevich, Olivier Guillot, Dominique Iogna-Prat, Mayke de Jong, Kathryn Miller, Barbara Rosenwein, and Stephen D. White. Special thanks to Gerd Althoff for attempting to mediate in conflicts with fellow historians, as well as to the Netherlands Institute for Advanced Studies, under whose generous auspices this chapter was conceived and written. A number of the theoretical issues alluded to here (especially medievalists' problematic recourse to social science models) are developed in my forthcoming *The Dangers of Ritual* (Princeton University Press).

2 For later medieval banquets, see Olivier de la Marche's attempt to underline the parallels between the Duke of Burgundy's meals and the Eucharist, 'L'estat de la maison du Duc Charles de Bourgoingne', in *Mémoires*, ed. Henri Beaune, vol. 4, Paris, 1888, pp. 1–94 at pp. 20 and 31. Steve White (personal discussion) suggests that the vertical dimension in a number of public acts could be established through oath-swearing.

3 There is a danger in too quickly identifying rites and rituals: Buc forthcoming (b): chapter 5. Did the Christian valuation of a break with Old Testament rites transfer itself to all ceremonial forms? Cf. Buc 1997.

4 This understanding has deceived some historians into seeing the early Middle Ages as an age dominated by ritual, superseded by an age of action or of the spirit: hence Duby 1980: 226, on 'le passage d'une religion rituelle et liturgique . . . à une religion d'action et qui s'incarne'; Stock 1983: 91, 141, 472; Morghen 1971: 19. This is merely to reproduce the Christian normative opposition between Old Testament and New Testament, between ceremonies and spirit, on the basis of the polemical writings of the new monastic orders against the older Benedictines.

5 In Ambrosius Autpertus, specifically, the Lord judges the whole Church, but so do the twenty-four elders (*seniores*) who represent the 'whole body of rulers (*praepositi*)' and judge each subjected people. Simultaneously, both the Lord and the *seniores* represent, generically, the Church in its totality. The plurality of figures in the 'throne scenes' mustered in these chapters allow the 'various powers of a single body of offices' to be signified.

6 A history of crown-wearings and coronations, however, calls for a minimalist analysis taking into account only strictly contemporary sources, for, as Fried 1995 has shown for Henry I of Saxony's accession, authors are only too ready to read into the past ritual forms existing in their own era.

7 Koziol treats this scene as a symptom of the Norman aristocracy's unease with its duke having become king.

8 Monopolized, but in which domain: practice or diplomatic documents? For the eighth century, Koziol 1992: 33 sees a political culture in which all lords can be begged through gestures of humiliation but where these gestures appear in charters only for the topmost level [confirmed by Caesarius of Arles, *Sermo* 77.3: 320]. If the practice of prostration or supplication could exist without leaving traces in the prime sources used by the historian, the equivalence Koziol posits between documents and ritual (and especially the ritual's distribution in time and space) is cast into doubt.

9 Hildemar, *Expositio in Regulam Benedicti* 53, ed. Martène, p. 677: 'Aliter salutare debemus reges et episcopos et abbates, et aliter alios. Reges etiam et episcopos et abbates prostrati in terra debemus salutare propter exemplum Nathan prophetae, qui prostratus salutavit David regem [cf. III Reg. 1. 23]. Reginam vero cum videt monachus, non debet monachus prostratus salutare, sed unum genu in terram ponere, aut humiliari debet capite

suo. Abbatem vero nostrum, si rarius videmus, in terra salutare debemus. Ceteros tamen, id est comites, presbyteros, monachos et reliquos inclinato capite salutare debemus.' The description of the queen's intermediate treatment shows, against Koziol, that the term *humiliter* met in charters may not always mean 'prostrate to the ground' (*humus*) but more generically 'humbly' (as here, bowing one's head).

10 Later in the story (*Historia*: 225–6) the Emperor Louis the Pious himself, bested in debate, 'put his hand on the ground and asked mercy' (*imperator vero manum in terra ponens, veniam petivit*) – perhaps a gesture of prostration which Andrew thought the ruler owed an archbishop?

11 The 'simplification' of rituals of submission in the eleventh and twelfth centuries may be owed to new (or revivified) formulaic conventions as well as to the rewriting of original charters for their inclusion in cartularies. What is, in Koziol's analysis, a finely tuned correlation between the geography of power and that of rituals may be nothing more, then, than the idiosyncratic self-consistency of individual monastic scriptoria producing or reworking charters for the geographical areas in which the monasteries held rights and properties. The test is whether one finds the greater degree of consistency within individual areas (regardless of the scriptoria drawing up the charters for the grantors) or within individual scriptoria (regardless of the geographical origins of the grantors). For example, in the first half of the eleventh century the Cartulary of St Père de Chartres uses the same sober formula (*per deprecationem, deprecatione, deprecans*) for documents whose official grantors come from regions Koziol identifies as farther along the road of decentralization. What causes what?

12 Cf. Asad 1993, who despite his post-colonial bent swallows whole the Renaissance scholars' belief in the invention of interiority – and hypocrisy – in the early modern era. The other alternative, illustrated by White 1995, is to assimilate these agents into Pierre Bourdieu's simultaneously wily and alienated Frenchmen – a sophisticated Marxist approach, but ultimately too close to the rational choice theory of modern liberalism to take full account of medieval beliefs.

BIBLIOGRAPHY

Primary sources

Alpert of Metz, *De diversitate temporum*, ed. G.H. Pertz, MGH SS IV, Hannover, 1841, pp. 700–24.

Ambrosius Autpertus, *In Apocalypsim*, ed. R. Weber, CCCM 27, Turnhout, 1975.

Andrew of Bergamo, *Historia*, ed. L. Bethmann and G. Waitz, MGH SS rerum Langobardorum, Hannover 1878, pp. 220–30.

Annales Fuldenses, ed. F. Kurze, MGH SS rerum germanicarum in usum scholarum 7, Hannover, 1895.

Annales Mettenses priores, ed. C.G. Bernhard von Simson, MGH SS rerum Germanicarum 10, Leipzig, 1908.

Annales Petaviani, ed. G.H. Pertz, MGH SS I, Hannover, 1826, pp. 7–18.

Annales Regni Francorum, ed. F. Kurze, MGH Scriptores in usum scholarum 6, Hannover, 1895.

Annales Sithienses, ed. G. Waitz, MGH SS XIII, Hannover, 1881, pp. 34–8.

Ansegisus, *Collectivo capitularium*, ed. G. Schmitz, MGH Capitularia N.S. 1, Munich, 1996.

Arnold of St Emmeram, *De miraculis beati Emmerammi*, ed. G. Waitz, MGH SS IV, Hannover, 1841, pp. 543–74.

Augustine, *Sermons*, ed. F. Dolbeau, *26 sermons au peuple d'Afrique*, Etudes Augustiniennes série Antiquité 147, Paris, 1996.

Bede, *in Apocalypsim*, PL 93, cols. 129–206.

Caesarius of Arles, *Sermones*, ed. G. Morin, CCSL 103, Turnhout, 1953.

Carmen de synodo Ticinensi (*c.*698), ed. L. Bethmann and G. Waitz, MGH SS Rerum Langobardicarum, Hannover, 1878, pp. 189–91.

Cartulaire de Beaulieu (en Limousin), ed. M. Deloche, Paris, 1859.

Cassiodorus, *Variae*, ed. A.J. Fridh, CCSL 96, Turnhout, 1973.

Clausula de unctione Pippini, ed. G. Waitz, MGH SS XV, Hannover, 1887, p. 1.

Chronicon Moissiacense, MS Paris BN Latin 4886, edited as one text with the twelfth-century Chronicle of Aniane (BN Latin 5941) by G.H. Pertz, MGH SS I, Hannover, 1826, pp. 280–313, with revisions in MGH SS II, Hannover, 1829, p. 257.

Concilium Germanicum (742), ed. A.Boretius, MGH Capitularia regum Francorum, I, Hannover, 1883 pp. 24–6.

Constantine VII, *De administrando imperio*, ed. G. Moravcsik and R.H.J. Jenkins, Budapest, 1949; Corpus Fontium Historiae Byzantinae 1, Washington, 1967.

Dudo of St Quentin, *De moribus et actis primorum Normanniae ducum*, ed. J. Lair, *Mémoires de la Société des antiquaires de Normandie* 23, Caen, 1865; English trans. by E. Christiansen, *Dudo of St Quentin, History of the Normans, Translation with Introduction and Notes*, Boydell and Brewer, Woodbridge, 1998.

Ekkehard IV, *Casus Sancti Galli*, ed. H. F. Haefele, Darmstadt, 1980.

Ermold the Black (Ermoldus Nigellus), *Ad Pippinum Regem*, ed. E. Faral, Paris, 1932, pp. 218–33.

Ermold the Black (Ermoldus Nigellus), *Poème sur Louis le Pieux*, ed. E. Faral, Paris, 1932, pp. 2–217.

Etudes de Saint-Maur, *Vie de Bouchard le Vénérable*, ed. C. Bourel de la Roncière, Paris, 1892.

Flodoard, *Historia Remensis Ecclesiae*, ed. M. Stratmann, MGH SS XXXVI, Hannover, 1998.

Fragmentum Registri Iohannis VIII, ed. Erich Caspar, MGH Epp VII, Berlin, 1928, pp. 273–312.

Freculph of Lisieux, *Chronicon*, PL 106, cols 919–1258 .

Gregory of Tours, *Libri Historiarum*, ed. B. Krusch and W. Levison, MGH Scriptores rerum Merovingicarum I:1, Hannover, 1951.

Gregory the Great, *In primum librum Regum expositiones*, ed. P. Verbraken, CCSL 144, Turnhout, 1963.

Gumpold of Mantua, *Vita Venceslavi ducis*, ed. G.H. Pertz, MGH SS IV, Hannover, 1841, pp. 211–23.

Haymo of Auxerre, *Historiae sacrae epitoma*, PL 118, cols 817–74.

Haymo of Auxerre, *In Apoc.*, PL 117, cols 937–1220.

Hildemar of Corbie, *Expositio in Regulam Benedicti*, in E. Martène, *Commentarius in Regulam*, Paris, 1690, also in R. Mittermüller (ed.), *Expositio Regulae ab Hildemaro tradita*, = Vita et Regula SS. P. Benedicti [a Gregorio Papa] una cum expositione Regulae, 3 vols, Regensburg, 1880, vol. 3.

Jerome, *in Eph.*, PL 26, cols 467–590.

Julian of Toledo, *Historia Wambae*, ed. W. Levison, MGH SS Rerum Merovingicarum V, Hannover, 1910, pp. 486–536.

Liber Pontificalis, ed. L. Duchesne, Paris, 1955.

MGH Capitularia II, ed. A. Boretius and V. Krause, Hannover, 1897.

MGH Concilia II, ed. A. Werminghoff, Hannover, 1904.

MGH Poetae Latini IV, ed. K. Strecker, Berlin, 1923.

Milo, *Vita Lanfranci*, PL 150, cols 29–58.

Notker, *Gesta Karoli*, ed. Hans F. Haefele, MGH SS rerum Germanicarum n.s. 12, Berlin, 1959.

Ordinatio imperii, MGH Capitularia I, ed. A. Boretius, Hannover, 1883, pp. 270–1.

Pliny the Younger, *Panegyricus Traiani*, ed. M. Durry, *Lettres de Pline*, Paris, 1947.

Procopius, *History of the Wars*, tr. H.B. Dewing, 7 vols., London, 1914–1940.

Radulphus Glaber, *Historiarum libri quinque*, ed. J. France, Oxford, 1989.

Recueil des chartes de l'abbaye de Cluny, eds. A. Bernard and A. Bruel, 6 vols, Paris, 1876–1903.

Recueil des actes de Pépin Ier et de Pépin II rois d'Aquitaine, ed. L. Levillain, Paris, 1926.

Smaragdus, *Expositio in Regulam Benedicti*, eds. A. Spannagel and P. Engelbert, *Smaragdi abbatis expositio in Regulam*, Corpus Consuetudinum Monasticarum 8, Siegburg, 1974.

Tertullian, *Apologeticum*, ed. J.-P. Waltzing, Paris, 1929.

Thegan, *Gesta Hludowici Imperatoris*, ed. E. Tremp, MGH SS rerum germanicarum in usum scholarum 64, Hannover, 1995 pp. 166–277.

Thietmar, *Chronicon*, ed. R. Holtzmann, MGH SS rerum Germanicarum n.s. 9, Berlin, 1935.

Translatio duodecim martyrum (BHL 2300), ed. L. Bethmann and G. Waitz, MGH SS Rerum Langobardicarum, Hannover, 1878, pp. 574–5.

Translatio sancti Mercurii (BHL 5936), ed. L. Bethmann and G. Waitz, MGH SS Rerum Langobardicarum, Hannover, 1878, pp. 576–80.

Venantius Fortunatus, *Carmina*, ed. F. Leo, MGH Auctores Antiquissimi 4, Berlin, 1881.

Venantius Fortunatus, *Vita sancti Germani*, ed. Bruno Krusch, MGH SS rerum Merovingicarum VII, Hannover, 1920, pp. 372–418.

Vives, J. ed., *Concilios visigóticos e hispano-romanos*, Barcelona, 1963.

Widukind of Corvey, *Rerum gestarum Saxonicarum*, ed. H. Hirsch and H.-E. Lohmann, MGH SS rerum germanicarum in usum scholarum 60, Hannover, 1935.

Zeumer, K. ed., *Formulae Merovingici et Karolini aevi*, MGH Leges V, Hannover, 1882.

Secondary works

Affeldt, W. 1980 'Untersuchungen zur Königserhebung Pippins', *Frühmittelalterliche Studien* 14, pp. 95–187.

Alföldi, A. 1955 'Gewaltherrscher und Theaterkönig', in *Late Classical and Medieval Studies in Honor of A.M. Friend*, Princeton, Princeton University Press, pp. 15–44.

Alföldi, A. 1970 *Die monarchische Repräsentation im römischen Kaiserreiche*, repr. Darmstadt.

Alibert, D. 1994 'Les carolingiens et leurs images. Iconographie et idéologie', unpublished PhD dissertation, Paris IV.

Alibert, D. 1998 'Sacre royal et onction royale à l'époque carolingienne', in J. Hoareau-Dodineau and P. Texier, eds, *Anthropologies juridiques: mélanges Pierre Braun*, Limoges Presses universitaires de Limoges, pp. 19–44.

Altenburg, D., Jarnut, J. and Steinhoff, H.-H., eds, 1991 *Feste und Feiern im Mittelalter*, Sigmaringen, Thorbecke.

Althoff, G. 1982 'Das Bett des Königs in Magdeburg', in H. Maurer and H. Patze, eds, *Festschrift für Berent Schwineköper*, Sigmaringen, Thorbecke, pp. 141–53,.

Althoff, G. 1987 'Der frieden-, bündnis- und gemeinschaftstiftenden Charakter des Mahles im früheren Mittelalter', in I. Bitsch, T. Ehlert, X. von Ertzdorff *et al.*, eds, *Essen und Trinken in Mittelalter und Neuzeit*, Sigmaringen, Thorbecke, pp. 12–25.

Althoff, G. 1997(a) 'Colloquium familiare – colloquium secretum – colloquium publicum. Beratung im politischen Leben des früheren Mittelalters', repr. in his *Spielregeln der Politik im Mittelalter. Kommunikation in Frieden und Fehde*, Darmstadt, Primus Verlag, pp. 157–84.

Althoff, G. 1997(b) 'Königsherrschaft und Konfliktbewältigung', repr. in Althoff, *Spielregeln*, pp. 21–56.

Althoff, G. 1997(c) 'Das Privileg der *deditio*', repr. in Althoff, *Spielregeln*, pp. 99–125.

Althoff, G 1997(d) *Spielregeln der Politik im Mittelalter. Kommunikation in Frieden und Fehde*, Darmstadt, Primus Verlag .

Althoff, G. 1997(e) *Otto III*, Darmstadt, Primus Verlag.

Althoff, G. 1997(f) 'Otto III. und Heinrich II. in Konflikten', in B. Schneidmüller and S. Weinfurter, eds, *Otto III.-Heinrich II. Eine Wende?* (Mittelalter-Forschungen 1), Sigmaringen, Thorbecke, pp. 77–94.

Angenendt, A. 1982 'Rex et sacerdos. Zur Genese des Königssalbung', in N. Kamp and J. Wollasch, eds, *Tradition als historische Kraft*, Berlin, W. de Gruyter, pp. 100–18.

Asad, T. 1993 'Towards a genealogy of the concept of ritual', repr. in his *Genealogies of Religion*, Baltimore Johns Hopkins University Press, pp. 55–79.

Augé, M. 1992 *Non Lieux*, Paris, Le Seuil.

Aymar, J. 1951 *Essai sur les chasses romaines des origines à la fin du siècle des Antonins*, BEFAR 171, Paris.

Barthélemy, D. 1993 *La société dans le comté de Vendôme de l'an mil au quatorzième siècle*, Paris Fayard .

Barthélemy, D. 1997 *La mutation de l'an mil a-t-elle eu lieu?* Paris Fayard.

Belting, H. 1962 'Studien zum beneventanischer Hof im 8. Jahrhundert', *Dumbarton Oaks Papers* 16, pp. 141–93.

Binon, S. 1937 *Essai sur le cycle de Saint Mercure*, Paris, E. Leroux.

Borst, A. 1973 *Lebensformen im Mittelalter*, Frankfurt, Propyläen.

Boshof, E. 1976 'Untersuchungen zur Armenfürsorge im fränkischen Reich des 9 Jhs.', *Archiv für Kulturgeschichte* 58, pp. 265–339.

Brennan, B. 1984 'The image of the Frankish kings in the poetry of Venantius Fortunatus', *Journal of Medieval History* 10, pp. 1–11.

Brown, P. 1982 'Relics and Social Status in the Age of Gregory of Tours', repr. in his *Society and the Holy in Late Antiquity*, Berkeley, California University Press, pp. 222–50.

Brühl, C.-R. 1962 'Fränkischer Krönungsbrauch und das Problem der "Festkrönungen"', *Historische Zeitschrift* 194, pp. 265–326.

Brühl, C.-R. 1982 'Kronen- und Krönungsbrauch im frühen und hohen Mittelalter', *Historische Zeitschrift* 234, pp. 1–31.

Buc, P. 1989 'Pouvoir royal et commentaire de la Bible', *Annales* 44, pp. 691–713.

Buc, P. 1994 *L'ambiguïté du Livre. Prince, pouvoir et peuple dans les commentaires de la Bible*, Paris, Beauchesne.

Buc, P. 1995 'Italian Hussies and German Matrons. Liutprand of Cremona on dynastic legitimacy', *Frühmittelalterliche Studien* 29, pp. 207–25.

Buc, P. 1996 'Writing Ottonian hegemony: good rituals and bad rituals in Liutprand of Cremona', *Majestas* 4, pp. 3–38.

Buc, P. 1997(a) 'Martyre et ritualité dans l'Antiquité Tardive. Horizons de l'écriture médiévale des rituels', *Annales* 48, pp. 63–92.

Buc, P. 1997(b) 'Conversion of objects', *Viator* 28, pp. 99–143.

Buc, P. 1998 'Les débuts de Sauxillanges: à propos d'un acte de 927', *Bibliothèque de l'École des Chartes* 156, pp. 537–45.

Buc, P. 2000 'Ritual and interpretation: the medieval case', *Early Medieval Europe* 9, pp. 183–210.

Buc, P. forthcoming (a) 'Political rituals: medieval and modern interpretations', forthcoming in H.-W. Goetz, ed., *Die Aktualität des Mittelalters*, Bochum, D. Winkler Verlag, pp. 255–72.

Buc, P. forthcoming (b) *The Dangers of Ritual*, Princeton, Princeton University Press.

Bulst, W. 1941 'Susceptacula regum. Zur Kunde deutscher Reichsaltertümer', in *Corona Quernea, Festgabe K. Strecker*, Schriften der MGH (then Schriften des Reichsinstituts für ältere deutsche Geschichtskunde) 6, Stuttgart, Hiersemann, pp. 97–135.

de Jong, M. 1992 'Power and humility in Carolingian society: the public penance of Louis the Pious', *Early Medieval Europe* 1, pp. 29–52.

de Jong, M. 1997 'What was public about Carolingian public penance?', *La giustizia nell'alto medioevo (secoli IX–XI)*, Centro italiano di studi sull'alto medioevo, *Settimane* 44, 2 vols, ii, pp. 863–904.

de Jong, M. 2000 'Adding insult to injury: Julian of Toledo and his *Historia Wambae*', in P. Heather, ed., *The Visigoths from the Migration Period to the Seventh Century: an Ethnographic Perspective*, Centre for Interdisciplinary Research on Social Stress, San Marino (R.S.M.), Boydell and Brewer, Woodbridge.

Deshman, R. 1976 '*Christus Rex et Magi Reges*: Kingship and Christology in Ottonian and Anglo-Saxon Art', *Frühmittelalterliche Studien* 10, pp. 367–405.

Duby, G. 1980 *L'an mil*, Paris, Presses universitaires de France.

Enright, M. 1985 *Iona, Tara and Soissons. The Origins of the Royal Anointing Ritual*, Berlin W. de Gruyter.

Erdmann, C. 1935 *Die Entstehung des Kreuzzugsgedankens*, Stuttgart, V. Kohlhammer.

Ewig, E. 1982 'Die Gebetsdienst der Kirchen in den Urkunden der späteren Karolinger', in H. Maurer and H. Patze, eds, *Festschrift für Berent Schwineköper*, Sigmaringen, Thorbecke, pp. 45–86.

Fichtenau, H. 1984 *Lebensordnungen des 10. Jahrhunderts*, 2 vols., 1st edn, Stuttgart, Hiersemann.

Folz, R. 1964 *Le couronnement impérial de Charlemagne*, Paris Gallimard.

Fried, J. 1995 'Die Königserhebung Heinrichs I. Erinnerung, Mündlichkeit und Traditionsbildung im 10. Jahrhundert', in M. Borgolte, ed., *Mittelalterforschung nach der Wende 1989*, Historische Zeitschrift Beihefte NF 20, Munich, pp. 267–318.

Ganshof, F.L. 1949 *The Imperial Coronation of Charlemagne. Theories and Facts*, Glasgow, Glasgow University Press.

Geary, P. 1994 *Phantoms of Remembrance. Memory and Oblivion at the End of the First Millennium*, Princeton, Princeton University Press.

Gorevich, I. 1987 *O Kritike Antropologii Zhivotnikh* (Towards a critique of animal anthropology) III: *O kentavrah i rusalkah: raznovidnosti i granitsy*, Kabul-Kishinev, pp. 562–99.

Görich, K. 1997 'Eine Wende im Osten: Heinrich II. und Boleslaw Chrobry', in *Otto III.— Heinrich II.*, pp. 95–167.

Grabar, A. 1936 (1971) *L'empereur dans l'art byzantin*, Strasbourg, repr. London, Variorum.

Graboïs, A. 1992 'Un mythe fondamental de l'histoire de France au Moyen Age: Le roi David', *Revue Historique* 287, pp. 11–31.

Grosdidier de Matons, J. 1973 'Trois études sur Léon VI', in Centre de Recherche d'Histoire et de Civilisation de Byzance, *Travaux et Mémoires*, vol. 5, pp. 181–242.

Guillot, O. 1983 'L'exhortation au partage des responsabilités entre l'empereur, l'épiscopat, et les autres sujets vers le milieu du règne de Louis le Pieux', *Prédication et propagande au Moyen Age*, Paris, Presses universitaires de France, pp. 87–110 .

Guillot, O. 1990 'Une *ordinatio* méconnue: le Capitulaire de 823–825', in P. Godman and R. Collins, eds, *Charlemagne's Heir. New Perspectives on the Reign of Louis the Pious*, Oxford Oxford University Press, pp. 455–86.

Habermas, J. 1962 *Strukturwandel der Öffentlichkeit. Untersuchungen zu einer Kategorie der bürgerlichen Gesellschaft*, Frankfurt.

Hageman, M. 1997 'Louis the Pious Meets the Pope. Different Sources, Different Rituals', *Text and Identities Conference I*, NIAS, Wassenaar (Netherlands), 12 October.

Hauck, K. 1950 'Rituelle Speisegemeinschaft im 10. und 11. Jahrhundert', *Studium Generale* 3, pp. 611–21.

Hauck, K. 1967 'Von einer spätantiken Randkultur zum karolingischen Europa', *Frühmittelalterliche Studien* 1, pp. 1–93.

Heim, F. 1992 *Théologie de la victoire impériale*, Théologie Historique 89, Paris.

Jäschke, K.-U. 1970 'Frühmittelalterliche Festkrönungen? Überlegungen zur Terminologie und Methode', *Historische Zeitschrift* 211, pp. 556–88.

Jussen, B. 1995 'Über "Bishofsherrschaften" und die Prozeduren politisch-sozialer Umordnung in Gallien zwischen "Antike" und "Mittelalter"', *Historische Zeitschrift* 260, pp. 673–718.

Jussen, B. 1998 'Liturgie und Legitimation, oder: Wie die Gallo-Romanen das römische Reich beendeten,' in R. Blänker and B. Jussen, eds, *Institutionen und Ereignis: Über historische Praktiken und Vorstellungen gesellschaftlichen Ordnens* (Veröffentlichungen des Max-Planck-Instituts für Geschichte 138) Göttingen, pp. 75–136.

Kantorowicz, E.H. 1946 *Laudes regiae. A Study in Acclamations and Ruler-Worship*, Berkeley, California University Press.

Kantorowicz, E.H. 1957 *The King's Two Bodies. A Study in Medieval Political Theology*, Princeton, Princeton University Press.

Kantorowicz, E.H. 1965 'The Carolingian King in the Bible of San Paolo fuori le mura', repr. in *Selected Studies*, Locust Valley, J.J. Augustin, pp. 82–94.

Keller, H. 1993 'Die Investitur. Ein Beitrag zum Problem der "Staatssymbolik" im Hochmittelalter', *Frühmittelalterliche Studien* 27, pp. 51–86.

Kelly, J.D. and Kaplan, M. 1990 'History, structure, and ritual', *Annual Review of Anthropology*, vol. 19, pp. 119–50.

Kern, F. 1954 *Gottesgnadentum und Widerstandsrecht*, 1914; 2nd edn, Münster, Böhlau Verlag.

Klewitz, H.-W. 1939 'Die Festkrönungen der deutschen Könige', *Zeitschrift für Rechtsgeschichte* 28, Kan. Abt., pp. 48–96 .

Koeniger, A.M. 1918 *Die Militärseelsorge der Karolingerzeit*, Veröffentlichungen aus dem Kirchenhistorischen Seminar München 4:7, Munich.

Koziol, G. 1992 *Begging Pardon and Favor*, Ithaca NY, Cornell University Press.

Koziol, G. 1995 'England, France, and the problem of sacrality in twelfth-century ritual', in T. N. Bisson, ed., *Cultures of Power: Lordship, Status and Process in Twelfth-Century Europe*, Philadelphia PA, Pennsylvania University Press, pp. 124–48.

Le Goff, J. 1980 'The symbolic ritual of vassalage', in his *Time, Work and Culture*, Chicago, Chicago University Press, pp. 237–87.

Levison, W. and Löwe, H. 1953 *Deutschlands Geschichtsquellen im Mittelalter. Vorzeit und Karolinger*, vol. 2, Weimar, H. Böhlaus Nachfolger.

Leyser, K. 1994 'Ritual, Ceremony and Gesture: Ottonian Germany', in his *Communications and Power in Medieval Europe*, ed. T. Reuter, 2 vols, London, Hambledon, vol. 1, pp. 189–213.

Magnou-Nortier, E. 1978 'Contribution à l'étude des documents falsifiés . . . L'acte de fondation du monastère de Sauxillanges', *Cahiers de Civilisation Médiévale* 21, pp. 313–28.

Markus, R.A. 1990 *The End of Ancient Christianity*, Cambridge, Cambridge University Press.

McCormick, M. 1986 *Eternal Victory. Triumphal Rulership in Late Antiquity, Byzantium, and the Medieval West*, Cambridge and Paris, Cambridge University Press and Éditions de la Maison des Sciences de l'Homme.

McCormick M. 1992 'Liturgie et guerre des Carolingiens à la première croisade', in *'Militia Christi' e Crociata nei secoli XI–XIII*, Miscellanea del Centro di studi medievali 13, Milan, pp. 209–40.

Morghen, R. 1971 'Monastic reform and Cluniac spirituality', in N. Hunt, ed., *Cluniac Monasticism*, London, Macmillan, pp. 9–28.

Nelson, J.L. 1986 'The rites of the Conqueror', repr. in *eadem, Politics and Ritual*, London, Hambledon, pp. 374–401.

Nelson, J.L. 1987 'Carolingian royal ritual', in D. Cannadine and S. F. R. Price, eds, *Rituals of Royalty. Power and Ceremonial in Traditional Societies*, Cambridge, Cambridge University Press, pp. 137–80.

Nelson, J.L. 1999 'Carolingian royal funerals', in F. Theuws and J.L. Nelson, eds, *Rituals of Power in Early Medieval Europe*, Leiden, Brill, pp. 131–84 .

Norberg, D. 1954 *La poésie latine rythmique du Haut Moyen Age*, Studia latina Stockholmiensia 2, Stockholm.

Prinz, F. 1971 *Klerus und Krieg im früheren Mittelalter*, Monographien zur Geschichte des Mittelalters 2, Stuttgart, Hiersemann.

Remensnyder, A.G. 1996(a) *Remembering Kings Past. Monastic Foundation Legends in Medieval Southern France*, Ithaca NY, Cornell University Press.

Remensnyder, A.G. 1996(b) 'Legendary treasure: reliquaries and imaginative memory', *Speculum* 71, pp. 884–906.

Reynolds, R. 1987 'Rites and signs of conciliar decision in the early Middle Ages', *Segni e riti . . .* , 2 vols, Centro Italiano di studi sull'alto medioevo, *Settimane* 33, Spoleto, pp. 207–78.

Schaller, H.-M. 1974 'Der heilige Tag als Termin mittelalterlicher Staatsakte', *Deutsches Archiv* 30, pp. 1–24.

Schieffer, R. 1972 'Von Mailand nach Canossa. Ein Beitrag zur Geschichte der christlichen Herrscherbusse von Theodosius d. Gr. bis zu Heinrich IV.', *Deutsches Archiv* 28, pp. 333–70.

Schneider, R. 1972 *Königswahl und Königserhebung im Frühmittelalter. Untersuchungen zur Herrschaftsnachfolge bei den Langobarden und Merowingern*, Monographien zur Geschichte des Mittelalters 3, Stuttgart, Hiersemann.

Schramm, P.E. 1954–6 *Herrschaftszeichen und Staatssymbolik*, 3 vols, Stuttgart, Hiersemann.

Schramm, P.E. 1960 *Der König von Frankreich*, 2nd edn, 2 vols, Weimar, H. Böhlaus Nachfolger.

Schramm, P.E. 1970 'Sacerdotium und Regnum im Austausch ihrer Vorrechte. *Imitatio imperii* und *imitatio sacerdotii*', repr. in his *Kaiser, Könige und Päpste. Gesammelte Aufsätze* 4:1, Stuttgart, Hiersemann, pp. 57–102.

Stock, B. 1983 *Implications of Literacy. Written Language and Models of Interpretation in the Eleventh and Twelfth Centuries*, Princeton NJ, Princeton University Press.

Stocking, R. 1993 'Visions of community: religious diversity, conciliar authority, and political power in Visigothic Spain, 589–633', Ph.D. diss., Stanford University.

Stocking, R. 1997 'Aventius, Martianus, and Isidore: provincial councils in seventh-century Spain', *Early Medieval Europe* 6, pp. 169–88.

Stocking, R. 2000 *Bishops, Councils, and Consensus in the Visigothic Kingdom, 589–633*, Ann Arbor, University of Michigan Press.

Stoclet, A. 1980 *'La clausula de unctione Pippinis regis*: Mises au point et nouvelles hypothèses', *Francia* 8, pp. 1–42.

Tinnefeld, F. 1971 *Kategorien der Kaiserkritik in der byzantinischen Historiographie von Prokop bis Niketas Choniates*, Munich, Wilhelm Fink Verlag.

Tinnefeld, F. 1991 'Die Rolle der Armen bei Festfeiern im byzantinischen Hofzeremoniell', in D. Altenburg, J. Jarnut and H.-H. Steinhoff, eds, *Feste und Feiern im Mittelalter*, Sigmaringen, Thorbecke, pp. 109–13.

Treitinger, O. 1938 (1956) *Die Oströmische Kaiser- und Reichsidee nach ihrer Gestaltung im höfischen Zeremoniell*, Jena, repr. Darmstadt, H. Gentner.

Warner, D. 1995 'Thietmar of Merseburg on rituals of kingship', *Viator* 26, pp. 53–76.

Weismann, W. 1972 *Kirche und Schauspiele. Die Schauspiele im Urteil der lateinischen Kirchenväter*, Würzburg, Augustinus–Verlag.

White, S.D. 1995 'Proposing the ordeal and avoiding it: Strategy and power in western French litigation, 1050–1110', in T.N. Bisson, ed., *Cultures of Power: Lordship, Status and Process in Twelfth-Century Europe*, Philadelphia PA, Pennsylvania University Press, pp. 89–123.

White, S.D. 1998 'The politics of anger', in B.A. Rosenwein, ed., *Anger's Past. The Social Uses of an Emotion in the Middle Ages*, Ithaca, NY, Cornell University Press, pp. 127–52.

Willmes, P. 1976 *Der Herrscher-'Adventus' im Kloster des Frühmittelalters*, Münstersche Mittelalter-Schriften 22, Munich, Wilhelm Fink Verlag.

Zak, S. 1991 'Imitatio vorbildlicher Höfe bei der zeremoniellen Festmusik in Spätantike und Frühmittelalter', in Altenburg *et al.*, eds, *Feste und Feiern*, pp. 481–7.

Zeddies, N. 1995 'Bonifatius und zwei nützliche Rebellen', in M.-T. Fögen, ed., *Ordnung und Aufruhr im Mittelalter*, Frankfurt, V. Klostermann, pp. 217–63.

MODERN MYTHOLOGIES OF MEDIEVAL CHIVALRY

—————◆•◆————

Dominique Barthélemy

Our history-books tell the reassuring and happy story of civilisation's progress in the twelfth century. That period saw the rough habits of a warrior class becoming gentler and more courtly: if they still resorted to fighting, they did so for causes that were just, in crusades or in royal service, or as a game or sport in tournaments. They became knights, that is, members of an 'order', and they entered this through the ritual of dubbing which was at once a great celebration and almost a sacrament. Plenty of noble families still pride themselves on being descended from these people. And even a bourgeoisie as confident and proud of itself as that of the nineteenth century liked to say that it had recovered the model conduct of the chivalrous society that had come before it. Even today, western man yearns to have the courage of the knight, while western woman dreams of the knight as an ideal lover! And the ideal *chevalier* is of course a Frenchman by definition.

All that is fine – but it has little to do with the medieval world. These dreams and myths can even become a barrier to understanding the social classes and collective behaviour of the past. They have actually invented features of twelfth-century history that never existed: for instance, the social ascent of warriors of humble origin, the belated Christianisation by the Church of noble values, and for those nobles a rapid training-course in good conduct. And these dreams and myths have another draw-back: they make us lump together under the single term 'knighthood' everything that constituted the noble class of the twelfth century, or at least everything it could pride itself on. But the difficulty is that it never had a single model of conduct: tournaments were disapproved of by the Church, crusading was no game, and when men defended their honour and their class-interests, they didn't always succeed in bringing about the rule of justice!

At the risk of pitting themselves against some of those dreamers of both sexes, medieval historians have to demystify 'chivalry'. First of all, they must demystify its medieval form. True, the word 'chivalry' does appear in thirteenth-century texts to denote the conduct of those who have been dubbed knights. Some authors of that period conceive the *ordene de chevalerie* on the model of the priesthood, as a rank and a function conferred on individuals in the hope that they would keep as closely as possible to an ideal of justice and piety. Otherwise, such texts may use the phrase 'perform deeds of chivalry' (*faire chevaleries*) for the activities undertaken at tournaments and in noble battles. Mind you, these authors do not imply by this expression a code that was very explicit, or clearly defined or coherent. Instead, they used the word 'chivalry' to translate various underlying moral norms which till then had remained unarticulated, but they didn't take sufficient account of the fact that these norms sometimes contradicted each other, and that in the end you had a pious chivalry and a worldly chivalry, a bold and heedless chivalry and a judicious chivalry, an aesthetic chivalry and an ethical one, a chivalry that could not be tamed, and one that had indeed been tamed by Church or by State.

Many modern historians, instead of highlighting these contradictions, and making them the subject of their writing and thinking, have stuck with the idea of some kind of coherence. They've examined what medieval knighthood was, when and how it took shape, adjusting the sources to their own concerns and especially to their own vision of a progressive civilising of behaviour. For the most part, they have chosen literary sources: the *Tales of the Round Table* and the songs of the troubadours have been alleged to reflect the conduct of the nobility of the twelfth and thirteenth centuries; and in still later periods, court poetry and the new romances have been taken as evidence of innovations or of traditions of actual chivalric life. A whole historiography, mostly following in the footsteps of Don Quixote, has muddled dream and reality, in France, in anglophone countries, in Germany, from the eighteenth century onwards. The same thread links Sidney Painter (USA, 1940) to Léon Gautier (France, 1884) and through him to an entire old school of thought which in the years around 1830 canonised the views of Lacurne de Sainte-Palaye (1749). Of course, historians have never wholly neglected the nuances, nor wholly failed to confront dreams with realities. But measuring the size of the gap is something historians have only begun to attempt in the past half-century or so. Even now, they haven't always got free of the old paradigms that still litter the medieval history textbooks.

All too often, for instance, a historical origin is ascribed to 'chivalry', meaning by that, a military technique, a social class, and a set of values. It's certainly true that there were some developments in medieval technology: spurs appeared sometime in the eighth century; stone keeps became common atop mottes around the year 1000; there was a new tactic towards the end of the eleventh century, with the use of the couched lance by cavalry charging *en masse*. But all these innovations are hard either to date precisely or to set in any clear historical context. Above all, there is nothing to show that any of these 'revolutions' suddenly gave a new importance to warfare, or to a group of men, still less had a huge impact on a system of values. Military equipment, and the splendour of display weapons, evolved in various ways and in various stages: every time, it was the already established aristocracy that owned these things, and carefully controlled their distribution.

We can distinguish three sorts of historiographical myth, all of them created from medieval sources whose bias, legendary and ideological character, and even deliberate falsehoods, have not been sufficiently taken into account. There are myths of social ascent; myths about the Christianisation of war; myths of the civilising of social conduct. I want now to discuss each of these in turn.

MYTHOLOGIES OF SOCIAL ASCENT

Modern historians are happy to believe in a 'feudal nobility' born of the social ascent of knights through their military action, and military service. The myth takes several forms. There are stories of individuals who rose in the social scale, often accepted in the nineteenth century on the basis of family legends. Today, such tales are rightly criticised, yet historians continue to imagine a collective ascent of a sub-class, at first inferior to the nobility, then becoming part of it and mixing its values with 'noble' ones. Take for instance the French knights at the time of the alleged 'feudal mutation', or the German *ministeriales* around 1200. Are today's historical constructs any less mythical than yesterday's?

From the tenth century onwards, imaginations were excited by the exploits of the brave little soldier of humble origin. Richer of Rheims, writing about the days when defence was needed against the Vikings, inserted in his *History* a real legend: that of the stableman Ingo who in the midst of a battle made himself into an impromptu standard-bearer and so won from the king the castle of Blois and the hand of the previous castellan's widow:

> They talked about who should be chosen to carry the king's standard, because all the warriors in the ranks of the nobility were already wounded and so shirked the task. At that moment Ingo emerged from the troops, offering his services for this duty, and boldly declaring: 'I am only a royal groom of ordinary condition; but if this doesn't mean impugning the honour of the great men, I'll carry the king's standard amid the enemy ranks. I'm not afraid of the dangers of combat, because I know I can only die once!'

Later, in the twelfth century, a chronicler in Anjou claimed that Charles the Bald (840–77) had granted social advancement to many non-nobles, to reward their military prowess, indeed their chivalry. The example given is that of a forester from whom were descended the counts of Anjou, who became the Plantagenet kings of England. This man's son Tertullus 'abandoned his father's lands because they weren't big enough. Trusting in his own strength, he wanted to raise himself. So he left the borderlands of the West, came to France and served in chivalrous fashion in the royal retinue.'

Such texts were enough to convince French historians of the nineteenth century, still bedazzled by the soldiers of Year II (1793) and by the nobility of Napoleon's empire, that the knights of the Middle Ages had similar careers. Scholarly research has taken the poetry out of all that! It shows that the noble families of the twelfth century, or at any rate the highest of them, those for whom proper genealogies can be reconstructed, descended directly from those of the ninth century, which themselves were already ancient. The possibility that a few men did rise in the social scale can't be totally excluded, yet ancestors of high rank are in fact the only ones we can really discover in the sources.

Anyway, if you look at them closely, most family legends of the twelfth century don't actually describe social promotion. Rather, they tell of the geographical displacement of a man who was noble by birth and chivalric by deeds, or of his change of ethnic identity. The lords of Ardres, near Calais, claimed descent from a Viking chief. The Gérés of St-Céneri descended from an ancestor 'of great nobility, both Frankish and Breton', who did great exploits in Normandy and became Norman through the fine marriage he attained in return. . . . It's the modern gaze which, rather carelessly, transforms that into social ascent.

Was social ascent then impossible in western Europe before the twelfth century? Not entirely. Otherwise, why would we have the protests of hostile and resentful traditionalists, such as Thegan, Ratherius of Verona and a number of chroniclers? But these cases of rising in society, mostly thanks to careers in the royal palace, could only have been small ascents, a notch upwards in the Nomenklatura, exaggerated by polemical writing. Chivalric exploits were not what drove them, either. In reality, counts were only created very exceptionally on grounds of martial valour, and they were well-born to start with. The same goes for the Norman conquests of the eleventh century in Italy and in England, and for the lordships created in the East in the wake of the First Crusade. Prowess alone, unsupported by noble birth, was not enough.

The early Middle Ages never stopped using the old Roman yardstick for the high-born: weapons and wisdom, in other words merit, and the sort of drive valued in chivalry, confirmed their blue blood. To hereditary nobility, training and youthful reputation, above all, added a magic nobility: this was chivalry, consecrated by investiture with arms, that is, by a ritual celebration of entry into the group of adult males. Thereafter, the noble and chivalrous man had to maintain its external trappings and appropriate conduct.

From the twelfth and thirteenth centuries onwards, European society started to experience some clearer cases of social advance: merchants, lawyers, administrative personnel. These were based on forms of social labour that were generally anything but chivalric. Yet the rites of chivalry were at hand to consecrate them. The French king in 1328 dubbed Ysalguier of Toulouse, a man who had become rich on property confiscated from Jews while he was a royal official. Unsurprisingly, the ancient noble and knightly families protested, and tried to take action against such new men. Sometimes, the protesters got affirmations of principle from kings and princes, and won some defensive victories. . . . But the border was never hermetically sealed. Various kinds of non-chivalrous, or half-chivalrous (with the mere title of esquire) nobility tended to get established in the late Middle Ages: in France, for instance, there was the *noblesse de robe*.

From 1250 on, chivalry was less and less a *métier* genuinely concerned with military and judicial functions, and more and more a badge of status. There was a whole chivalric code, with its towered and moated castle-houses, its increasingly elaborate dubbing ceremonies, its closely linked relationships that tended to become, under royal and princely leadership, the 'orders of chivalry'. There were as many varieties of chivalry as there are today of gentlemen's clubs (the Rotary Clubs, for instance) in every country or region.

In the late Middle Ages, when chivalry remained the supreme reference-point for elites of every kind, however diversified, it became, understandably, more and more a matter of ancestry. The important thing was to tell of one's ancestor at Hastings or on the crusades. From the fifteenth century, there were Italian *condottieri*, soldiers

Figure 12.1 The knight prepares to leave on crusade, MS. Royal 2A XXII, fo. 220.
© The British Library, London.

of fortune (the captains of Charles VII, for instance), and German *Ritter* (notably in the Wars of Religion) whose careers could be projected back into times long past, the days of the Crusades or the Norman Conquest. Like the poet Ronsard in the sixteenth century, many people invented heroic ancestors for themselves, far enough back for verification to be impossible and for no-one to be too surprised at their rather unheroic descendants – but these descendants were polite, well-educated and civilised by time.

The teeming of imaginary ancestors, often forged by nothing more than pure invention, nevertheless influenced the strict, critical historians of the nineteenth century. Only gradually has research established, for example, that lordly French castellans were no military adventurers or self-made men, but heirs working hard to maintain their social rank by adapting to new conditions: local power, deeply rooted and up to a point autonomous, took the place of a career at the Carolingian court. Marc Bloch acknowledged a certain timelessness and density in this 'feudal class', and the work of Karl-Ferdinand Werner on the Loire valley region and Georges Duby on the Mâconnais clinched the argument.

Duby could not resist the rising tide of a new myth in the great postwar period (1945–80) of *marxisant* historiography: the bringing together of a knightly sub-class. The new narrative was of a 'mutation of the year 1000', characterised in France by the unleashing of barbaric violence, and raising up the knights (*milites*) who proceeded to terrorise the countryside under the command of the 'nobles'. Here one mythology, that of social ascent, was attached to another, that of unchecked violence, in tenth- and eleventh-century France, a time when there was no strong king. Again, the poetry of twelfth-century troubadours, in a state of permanent passionate and anxious expectation, is the expression of the social malaise of knights looked down on as a group by the 'nobility'. A careful reading of the texts was overwhelmed by theory. The discovery of the reality of social complexity, and even a rejection of the self-celebration of elites, were set aside. The theme of ancestors achieving promotion or being re-classed by knighthood was never anything but a deception designed to flatter those same elites.

MYTHOLOGIES OF CHRISTIANISATION

In the textbooks, the theme of the Christianisation of the knights is omnipresent. Like the other two themes, it covers a variety of arguments. The first is that of the baptism of the dubbing ceremony, that old sacral 'Germanic' rite that was more the stuff of nineteenth-century dreams than anything that left traces to be discovered in the medieval evidence. What can we really see of the 'purely Germanic' in the early Middle Ages? The etymology of the word 'dub' (*dubban* in Old High German) is entirely open to debate. The word itself is not as common as *chevalerie*, or the expression *entrée en chevalerie* (knighting), and it signifies 'arming a man as a knight', or 'investing as a knight' rather than striking with a symbolic cuff. This cuff is what modern historians have been so struck by! It is recorded late (in the twelfth century) and it appears quite seldom, usually as something of an accessory. The crucial element in the social ritual of knighthood is the giving of a sword to a young man, along with a whole set of equipment, the entire knightly costume, including the horse, and the reception of the youth, thus armed and equipped, into the society of adult males. Here is how a *chanson de geste*, *c*.1200, imagined the giving of such arms by Charlemagne:

He summoned Renaud, son of Aymon: 'The time has come to arm you as a knight, young man.' He had them bring him a coat of mail, glittering in its splendour, which the noble Renaud put on. Then Charlemagne placed on Renaud's head a most valuable helmet, while Ogier girded him with a sword, and Naime fixed on his spurs. Finally King Salomon administered the tap on the shoulder with the flat of his sword: 'Hold fast', he said, 'and may Jesus protect you! May Almighty God, master of the world, give you counsel! Take care always to remain faithful to your lord.'

In this ceremony, the religious element remains of minor importance. When it occurs, it is in the speeches of laymen. Further, the giving of arms is one of the benefits for which the vassal must thank his lord or his king. There is no question of entering a special 'order' of feudal society.

From the ninth century on, though, bishops and priests might bless swords – whether those of kings, counts, defenders of churches in general. Banners of the saints were also ritually conferred. That was something more widespread, I think, than is usually realised. But it was not related to a coherent conception of knighthood as a Christian way of life. From the ninth century to the twelfth, what was done in the most Christian manner was the renunciation of knighthood, the farewell to the arms 'of this world' in favour of penance or entry into a monastery to wage 'spiritual combat'. In 1066, the knight Morvan decided to become a monk at the monastery of Redon: 'he came, armed, up to the altar; there he laid down the arms of his knighthood, abandoning the "old man" to put on the "new"; he gave his horse, which was worth £10, and also his lands at Trefhidic [to the monastery].'

On the other hand, the attempt to sacralise the knighting ritual found success *c.*1200: now there appeared in some of the liturgies the night of prayer beforehand, and the episcopal girding on of the sword. The Pontifical of William Durand (1293–5), shows the benediction of the new knight occurring within the Mass, immediately before the Gospel:

> The bishop blesses the sword, saying, 'We pray, O God, that you will hear our prayers and deign to bless with the hand of your Majesty this sword with which your servant desires to be girded, that he may be empowered to be the defender of churches, widows and orphans and of all the servants of God against the cruelty of the pagans, and that he may inspire terror and fright in the other enemies of God, and that this sword may enable him to undertake fair pursuits of criminals and to make just defences. In Christ's name. Amen.'

Then follows another prayer, to God the Father:

> 'Thou who allowest to men the use of the sword on earth, by thy healthful disposition, to repress evil and protect justice, and who hast willed the institution of the order of knighthood for the protection of the people. . . . '

Did the people, for its part, want such protection? Of course it is easy to say that people need protection when you forbid them to bear arms: that is where ideological deceit comes in. And what guarantee was there that those who bore the sword thus consecrated would never abuse it? Institutionally, there was none: only some fine

Figure 12.2 Knights going to a tournament. London, The British Library, MS. Royal 19.C.1, fo. 204. © The British Library, London.

words, some beautiful gestures, particularly well suited to making any subsequent misdeeds difficult to prove or even believe.

> 'Dispose all things rightly in him, so that he may never wound anyone unjustly with this sword or with any other . . . '

Here again, according to St Paul's saying, the initiate 'puts off the old man to put on the new'. But this time, unlike the eleventh-century situation just cited, it's a matter of entering into knighthood, not leaving it.

After this, the bishop takes the unsheathed sword from the altar and places it in the knight's hand, with new injunctions about the service due to the Church and the king. Later, the bishop gives the knight the kiss of peace, telling him to be a peace-maker:

> And he gives him a light cuff, saying: 'wake yourself from the torpor of evil, and keep watch in the Faith of Christ and in honour's renown. Amen.' Then the nobles present put on his spurs, in the place where custom requires. . . . Finally, the bishop hands him the banner, in the place where custom requires.

Christian civilisation indeed allowed diversity of regional custom in its very heart. The above citations are of edifying liturgy. But were these rites often performed? One has the impression that, still in the fourteenth century, dubbing ceremonies were largely profane, most often done at tournaments or on the battlefield.

The second aspect of historical debate on the Christianisation of knighthood involves forms of argument even more ideological and questionable than the first. There is talk of a softening, by Christian moral teachings, of a proto-chivalric brutality which could have been that of the non-noble – those rough fellows of modern mythology, raised up by their strength and courage alone – or perhaps that of a whole period, that feudal age of 'second barbarism' which, in France, allegedly covered the entire tenth and eleventh centuries, from the Vikings to the First Crusade. An outburst of violence, a continual boiling-over which the Church at first tried to limit by bringing against it the legislation of the Peace of God (989) and the Truce of God (1027–41), then, from the First Crusade onwards (1095) tried to channel by suggesting that only non-Christians be attacked in holy wars. Nineteenth-century historians drew from all this sometimes rather self-seeking conclusions about the benefits bestowed by the Church on our societies and also the benefits of the modern State for which ecclesiastical action prepared the ground.

But what exactly is this 'second barbarism' but a modern myth? It's true that Europe in general, and France in particular, was covered in castles, that power became regionalised nearly everywhere, and that local wars proliferated, wars between neighbours, pitting counts and castellans against their opposite numbers. All that is exactly what the modern State claims to set itself up against: it purports to have delivered society from continuous warfare perpetrated by ruffians, knights by virtue of their military activity but not by adherence to any moral code. We should note, all the same, that this sort of argument is upheld in favour of colonialism as well: around 1900, France pacified the Moroccan South and Black Africa by taking possession of them. It seems to be modernist prejudice that makes us see as violent and crude both non-European societies and also certain societies of the European past.

If you read the texts without preconceptions and reflect on them in a commonsense way, 'feudal' barbarism does not seem so obvious. The wars of the tenth and eleventh centuries were institutions with their own implicit rules. Those knights regarded as so unchivalric had their own code of honour. Certainly they were brutal, but they also had a type of legalistic culture, and some skill in making agreements: witness their acts of homage, and the more or less 'feudal' and 'vassallic' deals they made with each other. It is not a matter of stark alternatives: either an entirely Christian morality, decreed by the clergy alone, or no morality at all. Besides, a certain Christian spirit seems to blend, without too much difficulty, with the ethics of a traditional society – via the Old Testament, for instance, which offers so many interesting models, from Gideon to the Maccabees. Like David and Solomon, the Carolingian kings claimed to bear the sword of justice, to defend their honour and their country, and the hereditary nobles, 'knights' by virtue of their function, took up the royal mission on their own account. What is often termed 'the chivalric ethic', the defence of the Church and the fatherland, of the widow and the orphan and of all the weak, was already Charlemagne's ethic, and that of his leading nobles. It was what was offered to the dukes, counts and lesser lords and castellans whose authority struck such deep roots in tenth- and eleventh-century France. In other words, this is really an ethic and an illusion that are timeless, constructs of civilisation.

Chivalric morality, to be sure, was an ideal seldom realised. Abbot Odo of Cluny credits Gerald of Aurillac (d. 909) with a Christian career beyond reproach, but Odo's biography of this count, written *c.*943, seems less a historical description than the blueprint of a model. Bearer of a sword, this nobleman trained in chivalric exercises wanted to make only symbolic use of it later on; and he rejected all display of wealth, all comforts of good living, and all sexual comfort too, since he refused marriage. He disarmed his enemies by his sheer desire for peace: a forerunner of Ghandi? In fact, most lords in the tenth and eleventh centuries exerted the roughest kind of military pressure on their 'neighbours' from the castles where they had their power-bases. The Council of Limoges, in November 1031, ended its first sitting with an impressive threat:

> We the bishops here assembled in the name of God excommunicate the knights of the diocese of Limoges who refuse, or have refused, to guarantee to their bishop, as he requires, peace and justice. Accursed may they be, and those who aid them in evildoing; accursed their weapons, accursed their horses. They shall be like Cain the fratricide, like the traitor Judas, like Dathan and Abiron whom Hell swallowed up alive . . .

Dathan and Abiron, yes, were prototypes of rebellion against the power of the clergy. Peace-oaths entailed respect for the privileged enclosures of churches, their rights to offer asylum, which meant that vagrants and criminals could find refuge there. Equally the oaths meant commitment not to pillage another man's lands, unless he were an enemy. Why trouble ourselves over the role of the knights in society: did they do that sort of thing every day?

Lordship in the France of the year 1000, however, even when exercised from castles, was not purely and simply a military occupation, it also rested on a kind of legitimacy. Noble knights and their escorts passed for true defenders of the law in their courts of justice, just as in their wars, they were defenders of churches on friendly terms with them, and of the countryside. Sometimes they really did act those parts. But an ideology that was already old pretends that those were the only parts they played. In the so-called Peace of God Councils, the Church of Aquitaine (989–1031) appealed to the 'princes of knighthood' to defend it against other knights.

The bad reputation of the knights of the year 1000, great lords and small, stems from the fact that the monks of the period demanded from them many gifts and restitutions of land. The monks exerted over the knights a strong moral and social pressure, by their excommunications (often likened to sword-strokes) and by their polemics. Many charters and chronicles record, often in vague terms, but sometimes more precisely, deeds of 'violence' and 'tyranny'. There must have been many bad knights, then, and the Latin play of words, '*militia* (knighthood) means *malitia* (evildoing)', applies to them. . . . All the same, comparison of the harshness of the vocabulary ('tyranny') with the actual deeds of violence makes a reduction of scale seem necessary. Furthermore, there was a striking ambivalence in the relationship of monks and clergy around the year 1000 and the knights as a collectivity. Churchmen never challenged the knights' leading role in society. Thus the monk Abbo of Fleury and Bishop Adalbero of Laon, like the Anglo-Saxons Ælfric and Wulfstan, acknowledged two dominant 'orders' in society, those who prayed and those who fought, and a third 'order' who laboured – the silent and hardworked majority. Moreover these monks only denounced the tyranny of their neighbours in the name of a shared ethic and, once peace was made between them, they were capable of passing on the very next minute to ecstatic praise for 'a nobleness of family whose

Figure 12.3 A knight overcomes a Saracen. London, The British Library, MS. Add. 42130, fo. 82. © The British Library.

knightly zeal is its chief ornament'. With 'tyrants', everything could be resolved by a gentleman's agreement.

That is why the modern argument about the Christianisation of knighthood from the eleventh and twelfth centuries contains a deep contradiction. It forgets that the early Middle Ages were Christian too. It misrepresents the complexity and ambivalence of the relations between clergy and lay lords. It neglects any decoding of the sources. Finally, the term Christianisation itself is ambiguous: does it mean a change in social practice, or does it refer to an enhanced role ascribed to the clergy as judge and consecrator of knighthood? That role increased, in any case, only very marginally, in certain thirteenth-century liturgies. From the ninth century, bishops had never stopped imposing penance on knights for murders, despoilings of churches, sexual offences; and monks had never stopped praying for knights' sins. The Council of Narbonne (1054) forbade Christians to kill each other, and enjoined them to kill only infidels. It has often been said that this paved the way for the crusades. The rest of the canon needs to be read carefully, however: 'but if there has been a murder between Christians, a judicial composition must be preferred to vengeance'. Isn't that the spirit of all early medieval law, and the very letter of Charlemagne's capitularies of 789 and 802?

The idea that there are just wars, for the Christian fatherland, and just causes in which you need the prayers of monks and the relics of saints to sustain the combatants, does not begin with the Crusade and 1095. It is a lot older – it is, indeed, another fact of civilisation. There was much in the Bible that could be cited in its support. The crusades of the twelfth and thirteenth centuries only gave old ideas a new currency and specified a certain kind of jurisdiction: for the duration of their 'pilgrimage', crusaders were at the command and under the protection, in principle, of the clergy. There are Carolingian foundations there: the ambiguity of penance goes a long way back. In practice, crusaders were often men doing penance for their own unjust quarrels, and they often began to sin again once they'd returned from Jerusalem or the Albigeois. Their relationship with the Church was no more straightforward than that of the knights of the year 1000: it continued to ask much of them, and to say many bad things about their high living, their feasts, their tournaments. When *c.*1128 St Bernard began to offer praises of 'the new knighthood' of the Templars, who were armed monks, at once ascetics and bound to physical combat, this was in no way a re-evaluation of the old knighthood, that is, of the knighthood practised, still, by everyone except the Templars. On the contrary, all the faults of the 'old' knights were highlighted by the contrast. It could be said of the Templar:

> Here is a knight without fear, protected on every side against danger. His body is covered by armour of iron, his soul by the armour of faith. Thus protected, he need never fear either evil spirits or men. And how could the man who aspires to death, fear death?

The ideal of the martyr is thus linked by Bernard with that of the just war, in order to free this new sort of knight from all blame:

> When he puts a malefactor to death, he is not a homicide but, if I may say so, a malicide. He avenges Christ against those who do evil; he defends Christians. If he himself is killed, he does not perish, he reaches his goal. The death he inflicts is for Christ's advantage: that which he receives is for his own.

On the other hand,

> why then does this *militia*, or rather this *malitia*, of the profane world exist? What purpose does it serve? It commits mortal sin when it kills; it perishes in eternal death when it gets killed.

For this reason, or from fear of the terrible cycle of reprisals involved in feud, men were perhaps in the habit of limiting themselves to a few acts of pillaging on another man's lands, but avoiding full-scale battle. Men weren't going to get themselves killed, in war between fellows of good breeding (gentlemen). The *chevauchée* did not always seem very different from a tournament. It was a game, a parade: that was what attracted the monks' vitriol. St Bernard continued his line of thought:

> You cover your horses in silk; you cover your own backs, underneath your body-armour, with I don't know what flowing gowns. You decorate with paint your lances, your shields, your saddles; you embellish with gold and silver and precious stones your bridles and your spurs. And, with all that pomp, you go into combat with shameful fury and shameless folly. Are those the emblems suitable for knights, or aren't they rather ornaments fitting for women?

MYTHOLOGIES OF COURTLY CONDUCT

The twelfth century was the time when modern coats of arms were invented. Now the great age of the tournament and of courtly literature had arrived, punctually. There was a flowering of lyric poetry and chivalric romances (Chrétien de Troyes, the authors of *Tristan*). The nineteenth century thought, rather naively, that this literature genuinely reflected life in the courts of love, and the attempts of knights to put women on a pedestal, and to play a fair game in tournaments. But didn't all that really involve a certain conventionality? When the Lancelot or the Gawain of Chrétien (1160–90) joust for honour alone and, in full view of the ladies, for the beauty of their body-blows, they are ideal models, fictional beings. Instead, the historical frequenters of tournaments, such as the Englishman William the Marshal, whose biography was written up, with a certain roughness of style, *c.*1220, fought in the 1180s to acquire ransoms in a cloud of dust:

> At this time, a knight of the Young King's retinue, whom they called Roger of Gaugi, asked him to be his companion. He was a valiant man, bold, enterprising, skilful, but a little bit too keen for profits. The Marshal, knowing he was a good knight, agreed to give his companionship. For two years, they competed in tournaments and made twice as much profit at them as six or eight of the others.

These young entrepreneurs certainly had their own accountants! But William did not deny himself generous giving: such largesse gave him prestige, to the chagrin of certain French knights, all humiliated to see an Englishman raise himself above them.

As for the troubadours' lady, object of their anxious and immature adulation, was she not the product of ambiguous male desire? Bernard de Ventadour gazes at himself rather than at his lady:

> I've no longer had any control over myself since the day when she allowed me to look into her eyes, in this mirror that pleases me so much. Mirror, since I admired myself in you, my deep sighs kill me, and I'm lost, just as the lovely Narcissus lost himself in the fountain.
>   Of all ladies, I despair . . .

Yes, they were better off among the men, among troubadours, in those 'male Middle Ages' that Georges Duby demystified so well. Because at that very time of the troubadours, in the twelfth and thirteenth centuries, the renaissance of Roman Law reduced the rights of women in Occitania, at least in theory. The real courts were those of kings and princes, in which knights were ostentatiously received yet at the same time more or less enslaved by princely power, not to mention the rivalry of clerks, financiers and lawyers, who competed with them for princely favour. These courts were the Courts of Justice, centres of political rivalry where the only women who counted were aging dowagers. These were the places of high living, showing off a world made rich, in which dubbing ceremonies proceeded to get more elaborate than ever before, whether or not they were augmented by the symbolic cuff and by Christian rites. But these knighting ceremonies were above all political gestures which assembled the nobility and various *parvenus* around princes. Knighthood was in the process of losing in consistency what it gained in splendid display.

Now, in the thirteenth century, people talked more and more about chivalry, loading it with interpretations that were sometimes in conflict (allegorising of

Figure 12.4 Knights perform for the ladies. © Bodleian Library, Oxford, MS. Bodl. 264, fo. 101v.

weapons), enlarging it, too, with elaborate rituals (masses and feasts, jousts and round tables). Hence the sheaf of principles and the series of sometimes contradictory images which I evoked at the beginning of this chapter. Among these, especially since the eighteenth century, the modern enquirer has been able to borrow, select, adapt, in order to construct his or her knighthood, his or her history of chivalry, and at the same time mask some contradictions. François Guizot, for instance, described in 1830 the shift from a kind of tenth- and eleventh-century French pre-chivalry, pre-eminently 'vassalic' and military, to the chivalry of the twelfth century 'through the work of the Church and of poetry'. But did these two sorts of work tend in the same direction? Courtly chivalry was an aesthetic dream of pleasure and social distinction, while knighthood on crusade was summoned to asceticism by St Bernard. The twelfth-century Church, assembled in councils, denounced tournaments. It refused Christian burial, in theory, to those who died accidentally, for nothing, in senseless playing at war, glorifying their own physical prowess. Furthermore, the Church could give no consent to the passionate frolics of the adulterous vassal: it contented itself with borrowing some courtly rhetoric to talk about divine love.

But let's not deceive ourselves. The contradiction between an ethical chivalry and an aesthetic one is far from complete. Between these, some compromise is possible, as in the *Livre des Manières* of Bishop Stephen de Fougères, written *c.*1175 for the Angevin court. In the thirteenth century, when fewer monastic criticisms were being voiced, men behaved once again, rather as in Charlemagne's time, but in a more sophisticated way, as if the ideal of justice and honour offered to knights was quite often realised in practice, so that lordly power could be justified, and legitimised. As if the fine talkers and fine physical specimens were also fine and noble souls!

There certainly were, in reality, brave men among the medieval elite: men who were noble, Christian and chivalric at the same time, just as kings were meant to be. But chivalric qualities, and chivalric displays, involved a certain collective illusion, a suspension of disbelief. Few people brought out the consequences of all the many hitches, and of knights' frequent unworthiness – except for a quite radical and increasingly anticlerical current of thinking that started with Jean de Meun's *Roman de la Rose*. And no-one really protested against all that the idealisation of knights entailed by contrast, in terms of the devaluing of peasants, and contempt for serfs. Declared ugly and cowardly in all the *chansons de geste*, peasants were dirty, ridiculous, or simply absent, in all later medieval literature. One group was consecrated, the other was despised. Only in modern mythologising is the medieval world beautiful because of its chivalry. A critical history must take on board the full extent of medieval complacency with regard to the powerful, and a corresponding unfair disdain for the weak. Christian morality brought some shading of these extremes of injustice, but it never seriously attempted to blow the whistle.

REFERENCES

Barbero, A. 1987 *L'aristocrazia nelle società francese del medioevo*, Bologna: Cappelli.

Barthélemy, D. 1997 'La chevalerie carolingienne', and 'Chevalerie et noblesse autour de l'an mil', in Barthélemy, *La Mutation de l'an mil à-t-elle eu lieu?*, Paris: Fayard.

Bloch, M. 1961 *Feudal Society*, trans. L.A. Manyon, London: Routledge.

Bouchard, C. 1998 *Strong of Body, Brave and Noble. Chivalric society in Medieval France*, Ithaca and London: Cornell University Press.

Contamine, P. 1992 *La guerre au moyen âge*, Paris: Presses Universitaires de France, 2nd edn.

Demurger, A. 1985 *Vie et mort de l'ordre du Temple*, Paris: Seuil.

Duby, G. 1985 *William Marshal: The Flower of Chivalry*, trans. R. Howard, New York.

Duby, G. 1996 *The Chivalrous Society*, trans. C. Postan, Berkeley CA: University of California Press.

Flori, J. 1986 *L'Essor de la chevalerie, XIe–XIIe siècles*, Geneva: Droz.

Gautier, L. 1884 *La chevalerie*, Paris.

Keen, M. 1984 *Chivalry*: New Haven and London: Yale University Press.

Martindale, J. 1997 'The French Aristocracy in the early Middle Ages: a Reappraisal', *Past and Present* 75 (1977), pp. 5–45, repr. in Martindale, *Status, Authority and Regional Power*, London: Variorum, ch. IV.

Nelson, Janet L. 1996 'Ninth-century knighthood: the evidence of Nithard', in C. Harper-Bill, C. Holdsworth and J.L. Nelson eds., *Studies in Medieval History presented to R. Allen Brown*, Woodbridge: Boydell and Brewer, 1989, repr. in Nelson, *The Medieval World*, London: Hambledon, pp. 75–88.

Painter, S. 1940 *French Chivalry*, Baltimore: The Johns Hopkins University Press.

Strickland, M. 1996 *War and Chivalry: the Conduct and Perception of War in England and Normandy, 1066–1217*, Cambridge: Cambridge University Press.

Werner, K.-F. 1998 *Naissance de la noblesse*, Paris: Fayard.

CHAPTER THIRTEEN

THE UNIQUE FAVOUR OF PENANCE: THE CHURCH AND THE PEOPLE *c.*800–*c.*1100

———•◦•———

Sarah Hamilton

I

In his mid-eleventh-century account of some previous members of his community Ekkehard IV of St Gall described in some detail how one monk, a certain Iso (*c.*830–71), was conceived on Holy Saturday, that is, the day before Easter Sunday.[1] According to Ekkehard, after Iso's mother had taken a bath in preparation for Easter her husband entered the room unexpectedly and they were both overcome by desire. But Lent was, according to the Church law of the time, a penitential period not only of fasting but also of sexual abstinence. Iso's parents knew this too and almost as soon as they had finished they realised they had sinned and reproached themselves so loudly that other members of the household rushed to the scene; the couple themselves then went and prostrated themselves, weeping, barefoot, in sackcloth and ashes, before the local priest and the entire community. The priest accepted their repentance, granted them forgiveness and gave them a penance, which was to stand by the doors of the church for a day and a night and to be excluded from communion. But they were very anxious to communicate the following day because it was the most important feast in the Church's year and so they hurried to the priest of the neighbouring village where they again confessed their sin before the priest and his parishioners and asked the priest's permission to communicate on Easter Sunday, which was refused. So they spent the Easter vigil fasting and crying. And during the Mass of Easter they stood at the back of the church and did not attempt to communicate. But after everyone had communicated the priest from the neighbouring village hurried into the church and led them by the hand to the altar and opened the pyx and gave them communion, followed by his blessing and the kiss of peace; before leaving he ordered them to dispense with their penitential garb and dress in their best clothes which were more appropriate for the feast of Easter. But when the couple sent a servant with gifts to the neighbouring priest to thank him for giving them communion, they learnt that this priest had spent the entire day in his parish, and that it had been one of God's angels who had acted in his place. And nine months later Iso was born and went on to become a monk renowned among other things for his holiness.

Ekkehard was writing with a purpose for his fellow monks at the monastery of St Gall on Lake Constance in southern Germany: his story shows how through voluntary penance Iso's parents saved not only themselves but also their unborn child from the consequences of their sin. While no doubt Ekkehard obtained his tale from oral traditions circulating within his community (he was writing *c.*1050 about events which supposedly occurred over two hundred years before) it also follows the framework of an established ecclesiastical literary tradition. Children who were conceived at a period in the Church calendar when sexual intercourse was forbidden were consequently thought to be the work of the devil, but the Saxon aristocrat and bishop, Thietmar of Merseburg, in his early eleventh-century chronicle included two accounts of children so conceived whose souls were saved through baptism.[2] The link between penance and baptism was one often made by medieval writers; according to the author of an anonymous tract *On True and False Penance*, written in the late tenth or early eleventh century, just as baptism cleansed the Christian of original sin, so penance offered Christians an opportunity to wash away the consequences of their sinful actions. But modern historians of early medieval penance have been attracted to Ekkehard's tale because of the level of detail he includes about how penance was conducted. It is probable that the details of the story reflect eleventh-century reality fairly accurately, otherwise Ekkehard would not have been successful in putting across his arguments, that good can come out of bad behaviour, if suitably atoned for, and that voluntary penance was important. He described how a lay couple instigated the penitential process in the presence not only of their priest but of the whole village community, thereby prescribing their own severe and public penance, but also, by voluntarily proclaiming their guilt and submitting to penitential discipline, achieving their own and their child's salvation. In order to be effective, penance had to be voluntary; only by personally acknowledging his or her guilt was a Christian able to obtain God's forgiveness.

This emphasis on voluntary or spontaneous confession was an important theme in penitential literature and practice: thus the liturgical *ordines* (services) for administering penance included a question in which the priest asked the penitent whether he (or she) wished to repent his (or her) sins. The priest should continue with the rite only if he received an affirmative answer. Ekkehard wrote too long after the events he describes, and combines too many topoi from pastoral literature, for his version to be accepted as an accurate account of the events surrounding Iso's conception. It does not show that the laity might, on occasion, instigate penitential proceedings but rather reflects the desire of the clergy, both monastic and secular, to promote the voluntary admission of sin and entry into penance among their flock.

It thus demonstrates one of the inherent difficulties in the study of medieval penance, namely that the history of penance is always presented from the point of view of its ministers rather than its users. It is, of course, part of a wider problem facing historians of the medieval Church: how to study the interaction between the medieval clergy and the laity when almost all the sources were written by the clergy. This is an issue I will return to later. But first we need to consider why penance mattered in medieval society and why it is of significance to medieval historians.

II

What was penance? It was a preventative act, designed to protect Christians from the consequences of their sinful mortal life in their immortal life after death. They sought to acknowledge and atone for their sinful actions through first making confession and then undertaking penitential acts such as fasting, flagellation and almsgiving, which demonstrated their repentance in order to obtain their salvation at the Last Judgement. It was thus seen as a necessary part of the Christian life in the middle ages, at least in the eyes of the Church. Quite how necessary has been a matter of considerable debate among historians. Until the mid-twentieth century this debate followed confessional paths: Protestant historians sought to show how confession in particular and penance as an ecclesiastical process in general were without biblical warrant and inventions of the medieval Church, while Roman Catholic historians argued that they existed from the days of the early Church. Their attraction as a subject for more recent historians is rather different, although they too can be divided into two main camps.

Broadly, there are those who regard the institution of penance as the means by which the ecclesiastical authorities sought to impose their own agenda on secular society. Penance – and especially the evidence provided by penitentials – has been seen by Vogel, Kottje, Payer and Brundage, for example, as an important means by which the Church sought to Christianise early medieval Europe and as important evidence for the development of moral codes and attitudes to superstition in particular. These historians work mainly with the material in the penitentials – essentially lists of sinful acts and their appropriate penitential sentence intended as a guide to priests administering penance – and concentrate mainly on how the Church sought to ensure the laity's outward conformity to the tenets of the Church's teaching. The work of scholars such as Le Goff and Murray, on the other hand, has seen penance – or rather confession (the two terms are not, as we shall see, completely co-terminous) – as an important means for studying the *mentalité* of medieval Christians – of providing evidence for how far Christians had internalised the teaching of the Church.[3] There has been a parallel debate between historians who argue for an abrupt change in the practice of penance in the eleventh century from a mechanical practice concerned with punishment and the awarding of an appropriate penitential sentence, to one in which the emphasis was upon the sinners' confession and their internal state of mind, and how contrite they were. Thus penance is seen as one aspect of the wider debate about how far the period *c*.1050–1200 witnessed the 'discovery of the individual', that is whether it was only with the revival of religion and learning that occurred in the twelfth century that the emphasis for the individual moved from outward conformity to inward reflection.[4] But early medieval penance was also concerned with self-reflection and contrition – the liturgical *ordines* (services) require the penitent to prostrate himself on the ground and acknowledge his guilt:

> Both in these and all vices, in whatever ways human weakness can sin against its Creator, God – either in thought or speech or deed or love or lust – I confess I have sinned and acknowledged myself guilty above all men in the sight of God.[5]

Both approaches have in common a top-down model which reflects the bias of the source material – they assume that the Church imposed penance on its lay users; and they ignore the idealised picture put forward by stories such as that of Iso's parents which show the laity initiating their own penance. But can historians afford to do so? Such stories reveal how central the period *c*.800–*c*.1100 is for the history of penance; it will thus be the chronological focus for this chapter in which we shall look at the two related questions which arise out of these debates: in whose favour did penance work, and how far was it a unique element in the Church's relations with the laity?

III

The story of Iso's parents provides a very vivid picture of Lenten penance as practised in an eleventh-century rural community. But it is not a straightforward one, for the penance Ekkehard described combines elements from what are usually regarded as being two distinct forms of penance: the one public, the other secret.

The origins of the process known as *poenitentia publica* can be found in Late Antique 'canonical' penance which was an episcopal prerogative and which could be performed only once in the penitent's lifetime. At the beginning of Lent on Ash Wednesday the bishop imposed penance in a public ritual: sinners confessed their sins and were enrolled in a class of penitents and dressed in sackcloth before being expelled from the Church to perform their public penance. On Maundy Thursday (the Thursday before Easter Sunday) the penitents were readmitted and reconciled in a similarly public ritual. But its non-reiterative nature made it unpopular as did the fact that penitents were unable to marry, or hold public or sacerdotal office for the remainder of their life; as a practice therefore it was increasingly postponed to the end of life and became confined to the deathbed.

The practice of secret penance is often referred to by historians as private penance and is seen as the antecedent of confession. But 'private penance', as Mayke de Jong has shown, was a term hardly ever used by early medieval writers; instead they referred to it as penance 'in the usual way' or as 'hidden penance', 'secret penance', and often simply as 'penance'. It probably developed in sixth-century Ireland and spread to Anglo-Saxon England and the Continent in the seventh century, seemingly originating in the monastic practice of devotional confession. In secret penance, the penitent confessed his sins to his priest in private and the priest then prescribed his penance according to the tariff set out in the penitentials.

This process cannot always have been secret in a modern sense; eleventh-century liturgical rites from Italy describe how the priest should administer secret penance in a communal service: the penitents enter the church together, the priest takes a seat in front of the altar, the penitents then approach him one by one to make their confession and be awarded a suitable penance. The rite seems confined to Italy, however, and is unusual in being so explicit on the publicity surrounding its administration. Rites for secret penance in tenth- and eleventh-century Frankish sources, such as that in Burchard's *Decretum*, seem intended for only one penitent and contain few indications that they were administered in front of other people. But

Figure 13.1 Giving Penance, from the Fulda Sacramentary, *c*.975/80. Niedersächsische Staats- und Universitätsbibliothek Göttingen, Codex theol. 231, fo. 187r.

even if penance was imposed in secret, in the modern sense of the phrase, it could not be performed secretly: it would be very difficult to conceal a penitential fast of bread and water at a time when so much living, whether it was in a palace or a humble village house, was communal; the giving of alms, face-to-face, would be similarly public. Penance in such circumstances may not have been secret, but nor did it contain the elements associated with 'public' penance and, unlike 'canonical' penance, this process could be repeated as often as required by the penitent's lifestyle and its administration was not an episcopal prerogative. Although priests were free to award penance it is less clear that they were allowed to reconcile penitents: seemingly in the early middle ages the penitent had to wait until Maundy Thursday for absolution by the bishop but around the year 1000 we appear to see the beginnings of change, and the introduction of a one-stop procedure in which the penitent confessed, was awarded his penance and absolved on a single occasion.

Hence the increasing popularity of secret penance with both the laity and the clergy in this period. But the early ninth-century reformers of the Carolingian Church sought also to revive public penance and under their guidance it evolved into something slightly different from its Late Antique antecedents. It followed the basic procedure I have already outlined – entry into penance on Ash Wednesday, reconciliation on Maundy Thursday – and remained an episcopal prerogative. But sources vary as to whether its consequences – abstinence from sexual relations, war and public office – had to last for a lifetime or merely for the period of the penance. It was supposedly reserved for particularly heinous and notorious sins, *scandala*, such as the murder of a kinsman or a churchman, especially a bishop, which were thus atoned for in a public manner. Similar crimes as long as they had not attracted public attention could be atoned for through secret penance, for priests were supposed to distinguish between the penitent who had sinned publicly and on whom penance was imposed publicly, and the penitent who had sinned secretly and voluntarily made confession. This distinction seems to have become current *c*.800 and was repeated in several ninth- and tenth-century episcopal statutes. It is important, for it determined who administered the penitential sentence: in the words of Ruotger, archbishop of Trier (915–931), addressed to his diocesan clergy, 'Know that you may give penance for hidden sins but for public sins you should defer to us.'[6] Public penance could only be administered by the bishop, while secret penance could be administered by local priests.

The penance performed by Iso's parents includes many elements familiar in the liturgical ritual for public penance: they dressed in sackcloth and ashes, they confessed and were awarded their penance in public; it was a two-stage procedure – they were awarded their penance and excluded from the Church before being led back into communion with the Church by one they thought was a priest on Easter Sunday. At the same time it had parallels with the rite for private penance: it was administered by the local priest, not the bishop; penance lasted for only a day and a night, not the whole of Lent; the penitents were reconciled by a priest.

IV

Evidence for the practice of penance may be divided into two main categories: the prescriptive and the descriptive. To the first category belong the great collections of canon law, such as that compiled by Regino of Prüm *c*.906 as an aid to the archbishop of Trier; and that composed in the second decade of the eleventh century by Burchard of Worms which ran to twenty books, one of which, book XIX, was wholly devoted to penance. Both Regino and Burchard included rites for and descriptions of the practice of penance, as well as citing canons from Church councils and other sources governing its administration. But manuscripts of these texts suggest they remained mainly within cathedral libraries and they are thus evidence only for episcopal practice. To these can be added penitentials which achieved a much wider circulation – some three hundred manuscripts survive from the early middle ages – and recent research suggests that in the Carolingian period, at least, they were used by the rural clergy. (Evidence from the tenth and eleventh centuries, however, suggests that these books circulated mainly in an episcopal or educational context.) To these collections can be added the proceedings of Church councils held at all levels: the great councils held to reform the Frankish Church in 813 gave approval to a dictum we have already met, namely that public penance pertains to public sins, secret penance to secret sins, while the Council of Seligenstadt in 1023 ordained, among other things, that all penitents should stay in the place where they were given their penance, so that their priest could be a witness to it, although they might move in time of war. In addition to these collective prescriptions there are the statutes which individual bishops issued to their clergy, the sermons which they preached, and the liturgy which the clergy used to administer penance, both public and private. They all share to a greater or lesser extent the same characteristic: they represent the clergy's aspirations, their wish list. They are not, on their own, evidence of reality.

Actual cases of penance imposed are not totally lacking; descriptions do survive, though they are much rarer than prescriptive sources and, as Ekkehard's tale reveals, they were often recorded with a promotional purpose. These demonstrate that penance was portrayed as universal, a practice affecting everyone in society, from the highest to the lowest.

Royal penance is a commonplace in medieval history, stretching back from Henry II of England's penance at Canterbury in 1174 for his involvement in the murder of Thomas Becket via Henry IV's barefoot vigil in the snow outside the castle of Canossa before Pope Gregory VII in 1077, the penitential pilgrimage of Otto III for his involvement in the bloody suppression of a revolt in Rome in 997 and the Carolingian Emperor Louis the Pious's two penances, to the Emperor Theodosius's penance at the behest of Ambrose, archbishop of Milan, for his involvement in the massacre of the citizens of Thessaloniki by imperial troops in 390. Penance was an established part of the political dynamic which existed between the ruler and his bishops, and could be used both positively and negatively. Thus Louis the Pious at Attigny in 822 humbled himself before an assembly of the most powerful men in his kingdom, publicly confessed to having sinned and undertook a voluntary penance, following, in the words of his biographer known as the Astronomer, the example of Theodosius. It is fairly clear that Louis decided on this action to restore a political community shattered by the revolt led by his nephew Bernard of Italy in 817–18 which had led to Bernard's death in custody. Louis set such a good example at Attigny that his bishops chose to follow him, in what seems to have been a pre-arranged collective atonement, publicly confessing that they had failed to fulfil their office of episcopal *ministerium*. He was thus able to use penance positively to strengthen his position by reinforcing and representing the consensus after an initial acknowledgement of weakness. But penance could also be used negatively, as Louis found out at Soissons in 833 when his sons united and rebelled against him. Louis was forced to confess that he had failed to live up to the ideals of the royal *ministerium* by perjuring himself, and violating the public peace, and to ask for public penance as he had committed *scandala* in the face of the Church. At the behest of the bishops supporting the rebels he then assumed the penitential garb of sackcloth and entered into public penance, as a consequence of which he was excluded from all secular business. Less than a year later, the revival of his political fortunes meant that he was fully rehabilitated by loyalist bishops. As Mayke de Jong has argued, Louis the Pious's penance at Soissons seems to have been judged a step too far by all those involved, and subsequent examples of royal penance, not just in the Carolingian era but later, did not threaten the king's status as king, however much he humbled himself.

Penance was not, of course, confined to kings: the penitential sentences issued after the battle of Soissons in 922 and that of Hastings in 1066 demonstrate that penance was imposed on all those who fought. That issued after Soissons decreed that all those who took part in the battle should do penance for three years, namely fast for Lent and for fifteen days before the nativity of St John the Baptist, at Christmas and every Friday throughout the year unless they were prevented by illness or military service from observing the fast. War, while inherently sinful, was also recognised as a necessity.

And there are tales of penance by individuals lower down the social scale from a variety of sources which are much harder to verify but which, no doubt, if they were to perform their propagandistic function must have had at least some grain of verisimilitude within them. Thus a twelfth-century recension of the chronicle of Sigebert of Gembloux records for 1094 how a woman of Laon was accused of having sexual relations with her son-in-law, successfully asserted her own innocence and had her accuser killed.[7] She then confessed her crime to a priest. Sometime later she quarrelled with the priest who consequently publicised her involvement in the murder. The relations of the dead man then accused the woman again, before the episcopal court; she confessed and was condemned to be burnt alive. But on the day of her execution as she was walking towards the pyre she halted at the cathedral of Laon and recommended herself to the Virgin Mary; she was then led to the pyre but, despite the best efforts of the murdered man's relations who added additional faggots, she was not overtaken by the flames. She then returned to the cathedral where her protection by the Virgin Mary was recognised, and died soon afterwards. This tale has been used to demonstrate how important private vengeance was in the judicial system; but it makes the point that confession and acknowledgement of a sin to a priest will lead to salvation, and it also reveals penance being performed in what sounds like an authentically urban setting.

But all these different types of evidence, both descriptive and prescriptive, pose the same problem for a modern historian: they were written by the clergy from the point of view of the minister of penance rather than of the user. Most of them seem intended to promote the use of penance and so they tell us more about their clerical authors' aspirations than about reality.

V

In the face of this clerical bias, how can we recover the users' perspective on penitential practice? To do so, rather than rely on the evidence traditionally used by historians, namely the collections of canon law, penitentials, councils and episcopal statutes, I want to suggest the value of using liturgical evidence because it provides us with a record, albeit an idealised one, of the ritual interface between minister and penitent.

Although liturgical sources are probably the most numerous to survive from this period, they have been underused by historians interested in penance with the notable exception of Mary Mansfield's recent study of public penance in northern France in the thirteenth century.[8] And those people who have studied the penitential liturgy have, on the whole, adopted a teleological approach – they have been looking for the origins of the Roman Church's liturgical practice rather than looking at the penitential experience at the time when the liturgies themselves were composed and copied.

But what evidence is there that such rites were anything other than a clerical pipe dream? How do we know that they were put into effect? There is some evidence within the rites themselves that they were applied and that a reality underlies the ideal of universality. Thus one rite for secret penance has an injunction that servants, both male and female, should not be made to undergo lengthy fasts because they had no control over their diet or work. This injunction is pragmatic and realistic though it is not actual proof of use. But a detailed comparison of individual rites in individual manuscripts often reveals minor alterations between rites which suggests adaptation to local circumstances. Thus the neighbouring archdioceses of Mainz and Trier evolved different variations on the rite for the episcopal reconciliation of penitents on Maundy Thursday.

Two examples, one for public, one for secret penance, will illustrate the value of liturgical evidence for relations between the clergy and the laity. The first example is the rite for public penance recorded in the Romano-German Pontifical. The pontifical (a collection of rites for use by the *pontifex* or bishop) was composed *c*.950 in the monastery of St Alban in Mainz and went on to enjoy a substantial circulation within the archdioceses of Mainz and Salzburg, that is most of Germany, although its circulation beyond this area was more limited. The rite was administered in two stages. On Ash Wednesday those who were about to undergo public penance were supposed to present themselves, together with their priest, before the bishop at the doors of the cathedral church. Here they were examined about their sin and a penitential sentence awarded. After awarding sentence the bishop then led them into the church where he, with the clergy, chanted psalms for their absolution, followed by a mass. At the end of the mass the priest put ashes on the heads of the penitents and said, 'Remember, O man, that you are dust and you will revert to dust.' The penitents then put on their hair shirts. And the bishop with his clergy then drove the penitents out of the church with the words, 'Behold today you are ejected from the bosom of your Holy Mother Church for your sin, as Adam the first man was ejected from paradise because of his transgression.' The symbolic ejection of the penitent from the Church suggests that this was a very public banishment. The penitent is, to some extent, a scapegoat; the community as a whole is purified through the expulsion of this sinner; and at the same time, the evocation of Adam makes the penitent stand for all mankind. The penitents' involvement in the ritual ends with their expulsion but it is not the end of the service for either the priest or the rest of the participating community. The ashes are blessed and placed on the heads of the faithful, followed by a prayer asking God to aid them in fasting and continence (as Iso's parents are said to have done, albeit unsuccessfully). This final sequence echoes the previous sequence; just as the penitent has been instructed to fast, has changed into a hair shirt, and has had ashes placed on his head, so the faithful now repeat his behaviour as part of their own Lenten devotions. Penance is therefore seen as universal; but only the public penitents are expelled from the Church. This sequence emphasises that the Ash Wednesday service was a communal service, directed not only at the penitent but at the whole population.

Lent was a penitential period of abstinence for both the penitents and the remaining Christian community. The penitents may have performed their penance in a specific place, a monastery perhaps, or more probably their own villages, for they returned on Maundy Thursday accompanied by their own priest who was to testify about their conduct in the intervening period. It should be noted that the penitents' sentence might not end with their reconciliation on Maundy Thursday: someone given a seven-year penance, for example, might be reconciled at the end of the first Lent of his penance but continue it thereafter. The first part of the reconciliation took place outside the cathedral: the bishop was seated in front of the church doors. The penitents were presented to the bishop who invited them to come into the church, chanting the antiphon *Venite, venite*, 'come ye, come ye'. The penitents then

Figure 13.2 Otto III at prayer *c.*990, Munich, Bayerische Staatsbibliothek, MS. Clm 30111, fo. 20v.

approached the bishop by walking forward, prostrating themselves, and getting up – this motion was repeated three times until they arrived prostrate at the feet of the bishop. Each penitent was then presented to the bishop in a ceremony in which they were handed up the ecclesiastical hierarchy, by their priest to his immediate superior, the dean, and by the dean to the bishop. They were then absolved and formally reconciled with the Church. In the second part everyone then entered the church for the remainder of the service, in which the bishop petitioned God through intercessory prayer before absolving the penitents. Next the bishop sprinkled holy water, censed the prostrate penitents, and then commanded them, 'Rise up, you who are asleep, rise from the dead and Christ will give you light.' The service ends with the penitents getting up; they are restored to the community and given the promise of eternal life.

How did the laity both as participants and as an audience understand a ritual all of whose spoken elements were in Latin? The physical movement involved in the rite for both days communicated the basic message: on Ash Wednesday the penitents were ritually thrown out of the church, both the physical building and the metaphysical community of the faithful. On Maundy Thursday they re-entered both the building and the community. Thus the use of physical space echoed the message of the rite and communicated it to onlookers. But the onlookers themselves were participants in the service and had ashes placed on their heads at the beginning of Lent, just as Iso's parents were said to have assumed sackcloth and ashes for the season of Lent. For them Maundy Thursday also signalled the beginning of the end of the Lenten season.

To turn to the penitent's own experience: it was a ritual in which the penitent underwent a change of status, from layman to penitent. According to the rubric of several rites, the (male) penitent put down his stick or staff (*baculus*) at the beginning of the rite for entry into (public) penance on Ash Wednesday. This transition was associated with various consequences: according to repeated canon law prescriptions a public penitent should not eat meat, carry a weapon or go to war, administer any public function or marry. Thus for Louis the Pious the imposition of public penance at Soissons in 833 meant that he could no longer administer his kingdom. Evidence from the Carolingian period suggests that sticks or staffs were regarded as weapons, although they were seen as being too ineffectual for battle, and were associated with men of low status. But here the stick seems to have become a symbol for (male) lay status generally, both high and low. By putting down his stick, a man ceased to be a member of the laity and became instead a penitent, unable to participate in the norms of the lay order. Instead he adopted a new set of defining markers – sackcloth, bare feet, ashes. Although the reference to the stick is clearly gendered, the rest of this ritual was universal: prayers refer jointly to the penitents as the servants and maidservants of God. And women are portrayed as penitents alongside men in the earliest depiction of penance to survive, a miniature in a sacramentary written at Fulda *c*.975 (see Figure 13.1).

Penance must often have been a very disquieting experience for the laity. Not only were the penitents excluded and set apart from the rest of lay society, but by putting down his weapons, as in the case of public penance, a man became vulnerable because left with no means of defence; Burchard of Worms included in his *Decretum* penances for those who attack a penitent. The rite also required the prostration of the penitent, a gesture associated with Benedictine monasticism but otherwise not found much in lay life (exceptions being the king- and queen-making rites and ordination of the clergy); the performance of such an act made public penance an impressive ritual of self-annihilation. The council of Trier (*c*.927) describes the reconciliation of the penitents on Maundy Thursday in terms which are unique and suggest it was attempting to address contemporary problems: priests should ensure that the penitents appear in order to be reconciled before the doors of the church on Maundy Thursday with downcast faces, and that they pray there rather than recount *fabulae* and *ioca* to each other. Quite what was meant by *fabula ioca* is unclear; in Aquitaine *c*.1000 peasants referred to St Foy's miraculous actions as her *ioca* – jokes; so prohibition probably meant not that the penitents were making light of a serious situation by telling each other jokes but rather that they were trying to reassure themselves with popular religious tales. In any case, they were not showing due decorum nor paying sufficient attention to the bishop. This passing reference suggests an attempt to obviate the problem generated in an existing penitential system by its popularity; in the mid-920s in Trier penitents were appearing before the bishop to be reconciled in considerable numbers. It also leaves us with a record of what in other evidence can seem rather an abstract practice: for the penitents nervously awaiting episcopal reconciliation in Trier, penance was an only too real experience.

The procedure for secret penance was more intimate but not less formal. From the early ninth century onwards penitentials include a rite for the administration of secret penance and from the end of the ninth century these rites were also included in liturgical books. These rites are much less uniform than those for public penance but nevertheless follow a standard pattern. What follows is based on that in the Romano-German Pontifical. First the priest must prepare himself to receive a confession by saying a prayer in private; then he receives the penitent and prays that God may cleanse his (or her) heart, and free his or her conscience from every fetter of iniquity and forgive their sins. The priest then asks the penitent if s/he believes in the articles of orthodox faith, and if s/he wishes to have his or her sins forgiven. He then questions the penitent about what sins s/he has committed. Then he advises him or her on future conduct and awards an appropriate penance. Most lay people did not understand Latin and the Romano-German Pontifical made provision in its rite for secret penance for penitents to be questioned on their sins and make their confession in the vernacular. Various East Frankish monasteries went further. Thus the monastery of Fulda, founded in the eighth century, included a confession prayer in Old High German. It is thus likely that both the penitent and any other lay person present would have understood the nature of his or her confession.

VI

Penance could be, and often was, administered to the clergy. For bishops, therefore, it was a useful tool for clerical discipline. Monks, of course, lived their lives according to a Rule and as such were subject to the disciplinary procedure inherent in that Rule as well as to the penitential discipline of the Church as a whole. But ecclesiastical penance was often used by bishops to discipline the secular clergy of the diocese. Thus Fulbert, bishop of Chartres (1006–28) invoked public penance as a means of punishing a cleric named Guy whom he believed was responsible for the murder of the priest Evrard.[9] Guy or his brother Rodulf, bishop of Senlis, had hoped to become subdean of Chartres on the death of the incumbent in 1018 or 1019 but Fulbert disappointed their hopes by appointing Evrard instead. On 22 February in 1018 or 1019 some members of Rodulf's household murdered Evrard. Fulbert, as Evrard's bishop, rather than his family, took responsibility for seeking justice for his killers and refused to accept the compensation for the killing proffered by Rodulf and Guy. Later Fulbert refused to attend a trial, instead insisting that Rodulf and Guy should do public penance, and when they failed to appear before him, confess and perform that penance, he excommunicated Guy (Rodulf having died in the meantime). Fulbert argued that the killing of his holy cleric should be considered differently from the murder of a layman, and should not just be paid for but rather atoned for through public penance. In this instance his insistence on penance suggests that for Fulbert, at least, the involvement of clerics in the killing of a fellow cleric required a special punishment.

Penance is often seen as one way in which the clergy sought to assert their authority over the laity. But public penance also served another purpose. Atto, bishop of the north Italian diocese of Vercelli (924–60), in a set of statutes intended for his diocesan clergy described the relationship between a rural priest and his diocesan lord the bishop. If any of their parishioners committed a crime, then the priest should make a careful inquiry in the community about how the events occurred and produce a written report. The priest should accompany the penitent and appear before the bishop at the cathedral on Ash Wednesday to present his report. The bishop should then confirm the sentence imposed on the penitent. The priest should return on Maundy Thursday to give an account of each penitent's conduct. Specific provision is also made for how the priest must seek episcopal permission to alter the penance if the penitent is unable to support it. In the bishop's absence it is the cardinal priests of the diocese who are responsible for altering a penitential sentence.

Atto's prescription demonstrates that one bishop, at least, regarded the institution of penance as an important means through which he conducted his relationship with and maintained control over his rural clergy. First Atto is concerned that a mere priest should neither set the penance ('a priest should not impose the rules of penance without respect of person or case; the times of penance or of reconciliation he should leave to the bishop's decision') nor reconcile the penitent ('a priest should not reconcile a penitent without consulting the bishop'); even in the event of the penitent's imminent death the priest should obtain the bishop's consent before reconciling the penitent. This assertion of the episcopal prerogative of control over the administration of public penance is a commonplace of episcopal statutes: the ninth-century Frankish bishop, Rodulf of Bourges (d. 866), for example, included a similar reminder in his statutes as did Hincmar of Rheims (d. 882) in his. But Atto's prescription also shows that the priest played a vital role as middleman between the bishop and the laity: when a crime was committed he had to investigate the circumstances carefully, interviewing the neighbours as well as the miscreants, and make a report which he brought to the bishop at his chief seat; the bishop then determined his penitential sentence on the basis of this report. Atto seems to envisage the penitents performing their penance while remaining part of the community. But he also ordered the priest to return to the bishop in person on both Maundy Thursday and the Wednesday after the octave of Pentecost to give an account of the penitents' behaviour. For although the penitents might be reconciled at the end of the first Lent they continued to perform their penance until they had completed their sentence. Why was such an elaborate procedure necessary? The prohibition in several episcopal statutes against priests accepting money for penance, that is bribes against the imposition of penance, provides a clue. This system of upward reporting was meant to prevent such circumvention of the penitential system. One bishop went further: Hincmar, archbishop of Rheims, ordained that any priest who was too slow in bringing such cases to the bishop's attention should be suspended from office for a few days on bread and water.

While it is important to remember that statutes are records of episcopal aspirations and not of practices, Hincmar's threat nevertheless demonstrates the importance bishops attached to the rite of penance. It allowed them to demonstrate their spiritual authority over what were often a very independent rural clergy. In theory the bishop had full responsibility for, and controlled appointment of, the clergy to all the churches in his diocese. In practice his authority was much more limited: many rural churches, and their priests, were under the control of secular lords. The bishop's authority was recognised as existing only over the altar while control over the church building and its property, and the appointment of its priest, was in the hands of its lord, sometimes a layman, sometimes a monastery. The bishop thus had very little control over appointments. In many cases the office of local priest no doubt became hereditary. In such circumstances public penance filled a significant gap in the structures of authority.

The liturgy for the reconciliation of penitents on Maundy Thursday offered bishops a welcome opportunity to promote themselves as spiritual lords of their diocese in a wider sense too. It provided a re-enactment of the penitential process and demonstrated the priest's subordination to both the dean of the cathedral and the bishop. Public penance was therefore a ritual which re-enforced the bishop's links with his diocese. The rural clergy serving small and relatively isolated communities probably rarely saw their bishop but the requirement that they accompany the penitent to the cathedral on Ash Wednesday and Maundy Thursday would bring them into contact with their superior at least twice a year. Maundy Thursday was important for other reasons. The service for the reconciliation of penitents in the tenth-century Romano-German Pontifical is sandwiched between that for the blessing of the holy fire and that for the consecration of the chrism, which the clergy of the baptismal churches had to come to the cathedral to collect on Maundy Thursday (and which they had to pay for). Holy Week was also a favoured time for the holding of diocesan synods. Penance was therefore only one of several forces drawing together the scattered rural clergy into the urban diocesan centre. And its important role in diocesan cohesion may be one of the reasons underlying the attempts of bishops to retain control over the public penitential process. Both bishops and priests were in that sense users as well as administrators of penance.

VII

Historians continue to debate whether, and if so how often, the early medieval population went to confession. The story of Iso's parents with which I began reinforces the point made by the ninth- and tenth-century episcopal statutes, that penance was associated with communion; but given that the level of provision of pastoral care in the earlier medieval world is an unknown quantity, we cannot be sure how far penance was a regular practice for the majority of the population, even in the best-run dioceses such as Rheims or Vercelli probably were. What is clear from the sources is that the Church aspired to make penance a practice which unified the different sectors of medieval society. It was, in religious terms, vital in securing divine forgiveness for sins acknowledged by individual Christians, but at the same time its effects extended to the entire local Christian community which, in turn, was a microcosm of the Church itself. In the words of the archdeacon when presenting the penitents to the bishop for reconciliation on Maundy Thursday, 'Unicum itaque est poenitentiae suffragium, quod et singulis prodest et omnibus in commune succurrit' ('Unique therefore is the favour of penance which benefits them individually and aids them all in common').[10]

NOTES

1 *Ekkehardi IV Casus sancti Galli*, ed. H. F. Haefele (Ausgewählte Quellen zur deutschen Geschichte des Mittelalters 10, Darmstadt, Wissenschaftliche Buchgesellschaft, 1980), c. 30, pp. 70–2.

2 *Thietmari Merseburgensis episcopi chronicon*, ed. R. Holtzmann (MGH SRG NS 9, Berlin, Weidmannsche Buchhandlung, 1935), I. 24, 25, pp. 30, 32.

3 J. Le Goff, *La naissance du Purgatoire* (Paris, Editions Gallimard, 1981); English trans. A. Goldhammer, *The Birth of Purgatory* (London, Scolar Press, 1984); A. Murray, 'Confession before 1215', *Transactions of the Royal Historical Society*, ser. VI, 3 (1993), 51–81.

4 For the classic statement of this thesis see C. Morris, *The Discovery of the Individual, 1050–1200* (London, SPCK for the Church Historical Society, 1972), but see also the critique by C. Walker Bynum, 'Did the twelfth century discover the individual?', in her *Jesus as Mother. Studies in the spirituality of the high Middle Ages* (Berkeley, Los Angeles and London, University of California Press, 1982), 82–109 and Morris's response: 'Individualism in twelfth-century religion: some further reflections', *Journal of Ecclesiastical History* 31 (1980), 195–206.

5 Burchard of Worms, Decretum XIX. vii, J. P. Migne (ed.), *Patrologiae cursus completus, Series Latina* 140, col. 978.

6 Council of Trier (927), c. 15, *Concilia aevi Saxonici I: 916–60*, ed. E.-D. Hehl and H. Fuhrmann, *Monumenta Germaniae Historica Concilia VI* (Hannover, Hahnsche Buchhandlung, 1987), p. 84. This injunction is a commonplace and is also found in the Council of Mainz (847), c. 31, *Concilia aevi Karolini 843–59*, ed. W. Hartmann, *Monumenta Germaniae Historica Concilia III* (Hannover, Hahnsche Buchhandlung, 1984), 176 and Regino of Prüm's collection, *Libri duo de synodalibus causis et disciplinis ecclesiasticis*, ed. F. Wasserschleben (Leipzig, W. Engelmann, 1840; repr. Graz, Akademische Druck – U. Verlagsanstalt, 1958), I. 296, p. 137.

7 Sigbert of Gembloux, *Chronica auctarium Ursicampinum*, ed. D. L. C. Bethmann, *Monumenta Germaniae Historica* SS VI (Hanover, Hahn, 1843), 471.

8 M. Mansfield, *The Humiliation of Sinners. Public Penance in Thirteenth-century France* (Ithaca and London, Cornell University Press, 1995).

9 *The Letters and Poems of Fulbert of Chartres*, ed. F. Behrends (Oxford, Oxford University Press, 1976), Epistolae 29–36, pp. 52–66.

10 *Le Pontifical Romano-Germanique du dixième siècle*, eds C. Vogel and R. Elze, (Studi e Testi 226, 227, 269, Vatican City, Biblioteca Apostolica Vaticana, 1963, 1972), XCIX no. 225, II, 60.

REFERENCES

Sources

Bieler, L., ed. and trans., *The Irish Penitentials*. Scriptores Latini Hiberniae V (Dublin, The Dublin Institute for Advanced Studies, 1975).

Kottje, R. with Körntgen, L. and Spengler-Reffgen, U., *Paenitentialia minora Franciae et Italiae saeculi VIII–IX*, Corpus Christianorum Series Latina 156.1 (Turnholt, Brepols, 1994).

McNeill, J. T. and Gamer, H. M., trans., *Medieval Handbooks of Penance. A Translation of the Principal 'Libri poenitentiales' and Selections from Related Documents* (Records of Western Civilization) New York, Columbia University Press,1938).

Schmitz, H. J., ed., *Die Bussbücher und die Bussdisciplin der Kirche* (Mainz, Verlag Franz Kirchheim, 1883; repr. Graz, Akademische Druck-U. Verlagsanstalt, 1958).

—— *Die Bussbücher und das kanonische Bussverfahren* (Düsseldorf, Verlag L. Schwann, 1898; repr. Graz, Akademische Druck- U. Verlagsanstalt, 1958).

Vogel, C., *Le pécheur et la pénitence au moyen-âge* (Paris, Les Éditions du Cerf, 1969) – a collection of sources in French translation.

—— and Elze, R., eds *Le Pontifical Romano-Germanique du dixième siècle*. Studi e Testi 226, 227, 269 (Vatican City, Biblioteca Apostolica Vaticana, 1963, 1972).

Wasserschleben, F. W. H., ed., *Die Bussordnungen der abendländischen Kirche* (Halle, Verlag von Ch. Graeger, 1851).

Secondary works

Brundage, J., *Law, Sex and Christian Society in Medieval Europe* (Chicago and London, University of Chicago Press, 1987).

—— *Medieval Canon Law* (London and New York, Longman, 1996).

Frantzen, A. *The Literature of Penance in Anglo-Saxon England* (New Brunswick, New Jersey, Rutgers University Press, 1983).

de Jong, M., 'Power and humility in Carolingian society: the public penance of Louis the Pious', *Early Medieval Europe* 1 (1992), 29–52.

—— 'What was public about public penance? *Paenitentia publica* and justice in the Carolingian world', in *La Guistizia nell'alto medioevo (secoli IX–X), I 11–17 aprile 1996*. Settimane di studio del centro italiano di studi sull'alto medioevo 44 (Spoleto, Centro Italiano di Studi sull'Alto Medioevo, 1997), 863–902.

—— 'Pollution, penance and sanctity: Ekkehard's Life of Iso of St Gall', in Joyce Hill and Mary Swan, eds, The Community, the Family and the Saint: Patterns of Power in Early Medieval Europe. Selected Proceedings of the International Medieval Congress, University of Leeds 4–7 July 1994, 10–13 July 1995 (Turnhout, 1998), 145–58.

Kottje, R., *Die Bussbücher Halitgars von Cambrai und des Hrabanus Maurus: ihre Überlieferung und ihre Quellen* (Berlin and New York, Walter de Gruyter, 1980).

Payer, P. J., *Sex and the Penitentials. The development of a sexual code, 550–1150* (Toronto, University of Toronto Press, 1984).

Poschmann, B., *Penance and the Anointing of the Sick*, English trans. F. Courtney (London and Freiburg, Burns and Oates and Herder, 1964).

Meens, R., 'The frequency and nature of early medieval penance', in A. Minnis and P. Biller, eds, *Handling Sin. Confession in the Middle Ages,* York studies in medieval theology ii (Woodbridge, York Medieval Press in association with the Boydell Press, 1998), 35–61.

Murray, A., 'Confession before 1215', *Transactions of the Royal Historical Society*, ser. VI, 3 (1993), 51–81.

Vogel, C., Les *'Libri paenitentiales'*, Typologie des sources du moyen âge occidental 27 (Turnhout, Brepols, 1978), rev. A. J. Frantzen (1985).

—— *En rémission des péchés. Recherches sur les systèmes pénitentiels dans l'Eglise latine* (Aldershot and Vermont, Variorum (Ashgate Publishing Limited), 1994).

CHAPTER FOURTEEN

GENDER NEGOTIATIONS IN FRANCE DURING THE CENTRAL MIDDLE AGES: THE LITERARY EVIDENCE

———— •◆• ————

Linda Paterson

At the epicentre of the many invigorating changes marking the 'twelfth-century renaissance' in Europe – from its innovations and importations in philosophy, literature, education, science, historiography, architecture and law to the founding and expansion of new religious establishments and dissident movements, along with the burgeoning of travel, trade, urban growth and republican aspiration – France and Occitania witnessed the unprecedented eruption of a self-confident and dynamic lay culture. Its inventions which were perhaps to have the most powerful impact in geographical space and historical time were those ideals still familiar to us, for better or for worse, of chivalry and courtly love. Intimately bound up with notions of what it meant to be a (noble) man or woman, these articulated far-reaching renegotiations of gender identities and relations. The prolific new literatures in the vernacular tongues of *oïl* and *oc*, while not the only manifestations of these ideals and cultural tensions, provide a particularly rich and subtle seam of source material for the historian: an opportunity to gauge some of the impact on aristocratic lay sensibilities of differences and disputes, for example, between Church and laity over sexual and marriage practices. Although largely written by men with male interests at heart, the literature allows some space for women's voices. These may be heard directly, through a small minority of women writers. But they also reverberate through male authors' awareness of women listeners among their audiences, whom they often perceive as a problematic presence, and through the openness and ambiguities of texts which provide space for divergent readings (Krueger 1993). Though medieval historians are often inclined to avoid literary sources or sources seemingly too tainted with literariness (Gillingham 1995: 34–7), these are in one fundamental respect no different from other written records. Whether one is dealing with a romance, a medical textbook, a chronicle or a charter, there is a document to evaluate in terms of its conventions, its conditions and purposes of production and reception, and the presence or absence of corroborative evidence. Literature, however, is particularly good at providing details of daily life and contemporary sensibility, provided these are analysed in the context of tendencies to idealise or stereotype; its themes, repetitions and silences can be used to diagnose the preoccupations and unresolved social tensions of audiences and authors; and its vocabulary and representations provide valuable tools for tracing shifts in ways of thinking. Moreover, vernacular literature provides a precious counterbalance to the predominance of Latin and hence primarily ecclesiastical written material.

This chapter will not attempt a survey of the extensive and continuously growing body of criticism devoted to gender issues in Old French and Occitan literature (Kay and Rubin 1994; Gaunt 1995; Nelson 1997; McCracken 1988), but will touch on four interrelated themes: marriage; courtly love; gender options; and violence. It will range within linguistic rather than territorial or political boundaries, drawing on textual examples from Anglo-Norman England as well as France and Occitania. The chronological focus will be primarily that of the twelfth and early thirteenth centuries, when the new ideals of chivalry and courtly love are taking hold.

MARRIAGE

The first full-length Old French liturgical play, the mid-twelfth-century 'Order for the representation of Adam', opens with Adam and Eve in the presence of God. Adam, with a self-possessed air, stands closer to the divinity; Eve is placed further away, her head covered, with a more humble demeanour. God speaks first to Adam, and like an earthly father or guardian makes him the gift of Eve as wife. As if the man might think her alien, God emphasises that as the original (and only male) parturient, Adam has given birth to flesh of his flesh: 'She is thy wife and as thou art in nature . . . I have formed her from thy rib, she is a part of thee, is born of thee . . . she is no stranger to thee' (11–20). His 'law of marriage' prescribes Eve's obedience to her husband, with Adam ruling Eve 'par raison' (21): 'in reason', that is, reasonably, but also 'by reason' because Adam is the (more or only?) rational one. They are to live with each other in love, faith, mutual service, and harmony. God then addresses Eve directly, stressing her duty to love, honour and serve her divine creator, to love and obey her husband, never going 'beyond his discipline' and being a 'good helpmate' to him. Eve promises to do this, to give Adam good counsel, and to acknowledge him as both her equal (*pareille*) and master (*forzor*, the 'stronger one').

The entertaining, subtle and educated elaboration of the two Genesis creation stories (1. 27–8 and 2. 7 to 3. 24) by an Anglo-Norman cleric for the edification of a lay congregation exemplifies issues of considerable interest to the history of gender in the central Middle Ages. First, it sets forth a 'law of marriage' at a time of conflict and debate between Church and laity: a historical and cultural flashpoint provoking a major renegotiation of sexuality in the wake of the eleventh-century Gregorian Reform (Gaunt 1995: 74), and coinciding with a dazzling explosion of new multi-generic vernacular literature. Secondly, like many other vernacular texts of the period, it explores some of the dynamics of marital relations in terms which the laity would be expected to recognise in their own lives, offering the kind of nuanced and imaginative insight and commentary which one cannot hope to locate in sources such as charters, penitentials, legal codes and so forth. Thirdly, with Eve being the prime human cause of Original Sin, it provides grist to the mill of our understanding of medieval misogyny: a mixed grist for all that, because this text, like many others, remains somewhat ambiguous.

After God has married Adam and Eve he addresses Adam alone (49). Eve remains on the margins of earshot, both included and excluded, like the rib from which she was fashioned. To Adam is given dominion over the earth, and the capacity to choose between good and evil. Does Eve receive this capacity? The Divinity seems to shrug off responsibility for his secondary creation: 'I speak with thee, but wish thy wife to hear: if she be heedless, then she is not wise'. Her future heedlessness, and guilt, seem more or less inevitable, and God's admonition to Adam to 'leave not my counsel for another's word' (71) foreshadows not only Satan's temptations but Eve's failure to give good counsel.

For man and woman alike, Paradise is plenitude: 'here you will find no lack of any delight' (90; my translation). Both will be free from the fear of ageing and death. But other fears are gendered: 'Here woman need not dread man's wrath / nor he before her suffer fear or shame; / begetting, man is not a sinner here, / and, bearing children, woman feels no pain' (93–6). For women, then, postlapsarian reality will entail fear of a husband's anger, and the pains of childbirth; for men, sexual guilt, and anxiety that his wife will bring shame on him. Medieval literature as a whole makes it plain what rendered a husband particularly vulnerable: the fear of cuckoldry.

The initial temptation scenes, lively and engaging, differentiate Adam as relatively incurious, resistant to the lure of knowledge and power, a clear-headed reader of deceiving speech; and Eve as a curious listener, eager to be privy to secrets – even those from which her husband is excluded – , easily persuaded to criticise his tendency to domineer, dangerously ready to question the divine plan, and a pushover in the face of blandishments somewhat reminiscent of the courtly lover's (227–30, 253–8). Though praised by Satan for her wisdom, when offered the fruit of *saver* (knowledge) she punningly enquires as to its *savor* (taste); unaverse to the idea of being 'dame del mond' ('lady over all the world') and 'master' too (*maistre*, 258), potentially usurping both divine and gender prerogatives, her desires reflect a sensuality untroubled by awareness of sin. As she takes her first bite of the fruit the taste fills her senses with hallucinatory delight in delusions of omniscience and power. The more sober and lucid Adam, lapsing through misplaced trust in Eve's advice, immediately recognises his sinfulness, and does not hesitate to blame his wife, at length.

Authoritative by virtue of its biblical paradigm, there are nonetheless some telling shades of difference between the play and the Vulgate. In the latter Adam is, to be sure, the first created human, namer of the animals before the formation of Eve as his helpmate and companion. But Genesis does not prescribe Eve's obedience to Adam in Paradise; only after the Fall is she doomed to subservience and, implicitly, the pair to discord: 'and thy desire shall be to thy husband, and he shall rule over thee' (3. 16). In the medieval play, by contrast, marital tension surfaces during the temptation of Eve, and in her all too effective jibe of cowardice (298). Conjugal discord seems inherent in Creation itself: women are bound to cause trouble, and men to be poor at the job of controlling them.

It would be easy to interpret the play as emblematic of medieval misogyny. An ancillary creation in a masculine universe and a masculine history (God, Cain and Abel and the Prophets are all men), Eve foreshadows the stereotypical medieval woman: sensuous, of doubtful ethical capacity, vain, garrulous, ambitious, unreliable, untrustworthy, easily tempted and tempting, the downfall of the less devious male, and henceforth doomed to be 'contrary to reason' and the source of torment to mankind (553–7). Yet ambiguity complicates and enriches this literary testimony to medieval gender relations. Unlike his wife, Adam is dull, fearful and lacking in leadership; his knowledge of sin brings misery at the consequences and anger at his wife, but little immediate sign of penitence or acceptance of responsibility. Once she understands her sinfulness, Eve accepts its painful consequences for herself and her descendants, and the blame. If she sanctions the rightful 'discipline' of the man (580), that man is fallen, weak, sinful, guilt-racked and lacking in vision and love. It is Eve who has the last word: one of hope for atonement and God's grace (587–90; Muir 1973: 83).

Literary sources offer an opportunity to explore repercussions of what Georges Duby has identified as a clash between lay and ecclesiastical models of marriage, which he saw coming to a head at the time of the first troubadour, William of Aquitaine, at the end of the eleventh century (Duby 1983). Essentially Duby saw the lay model as founded on endogamy, digamy (that is, the possibility of divorce and remarriage), and the predominance of family interests over individual choice of marriage partner, and the ecclesiastical model based on exogamy, monogamy, and the consent of the conjugal pair alone. By setting forth a 'law of marriage' (even though Genesis does not in fact mention marriage at all), the *Adam* playwright enters into a process of dialogue, and a good deal of Old French and Occitan narrative literature shows keen interest in the subject. How far and in what respects do literary sources engage with the key points of the political conflict outlined by Duby?

The issue of endogamy–exogamy or consanguinity would of course be an absurd one to raise in the case of Adam and Eve, but it rarely figures in contemporary vernacular literature. Literature is also far more interested in adultery than divorce, even though the lay nobility had hardly accepted the Church's position on consanguinity and monogamy. Perhaps the Church's grip on these matters was in practice tenuous, and the literary public did not perceive them as areas of tension. Consent is another matter. A woman's right to choose her marriage partner goes to the heart of social arrangements for the transmission of property. In literary texts it proves a question of burning interest, and multi-faceted mystification.

Some scholars have seen consent as the spark which ignited renegotiations of sexuality and gender difference in twelfth-century literature, 'raising the spectre of women's choice (and thereby desire)' (Gaunt 1995: 75). Although in reality younger sons were often prevented from marrying, and in the case of others the choice was a family rather than an individual one, consent to marriage is usually a female issue in literary texts. There may be a number of reasons for this: men were regarded as more free, or male listeners could more plausibly fantasise about their freedom whereas women were always more closely guarded; literature often shows young men chasing desirable heiresses, in cases where their families would be only too pleased for them to succeed. By the thirteenth century there is some literary evidence that the woman whose father is asked for her hand in marriage needs to give her verbal consent for the engagement to be valid, but that it is difficult for her to refuse her father's wishes. In earlier literature the woman is often simply handed over as an object of exchange. The question of consent arises where the woman actively protests, with some texts implying consent in the absence of objection. Such protest is rarely the consequence of personal preference, but rather serves to bolster the masculine values of the text, for example a widow's fidelity to a good man and the protection of his heirs by her refusal to remarry (Gaunt 1990a; Paterson 1991: 431–4; Paterson 1993: 229–32; but see also Kay 1995: 25–48). The pursuit of individual choice is usually problematic at the level of not only plot but the judgement of author and implied reader. The reader or listener wants Chrétien de Troyes' heroine Fenice, for example, to marry the man she loves and not the man prescribed for her by her family: the husband officially chosen for her is unsuitable since he has broken a vow not to marry and disinherit his nephew, the object of her preference (*Cligés*: 1957). On the other hand, audience sympathy is potentially checked by her not wholly exemplary behaviour. Moreover, the romance 'solution' to the dilemma of this twelfth-century young woman faced with a dynastic marriage consists of a self-consciously ironised fantasy, involving a magic potion and tower and a contrived ending where the obstacle to her desires conveniently dies of rage. In short, while literary texts often demonstrate sympathy for the woman married to a jealous, brutal husband, and offer fantasies of personal choice of spouse, and while they reveal an awareness of the growing relevance of the bride's consent as a prerequisite to marriage, they largely reinforce a conservative lay position that marriage is a family affair serving the inheritance rights of the male line. So in this respect literature could be seen as responding to Church pressures, but hardly accepting them wholeheartedly.

The literature also shows some signs of the Church's wish to play a more important part in marriage through its presence at wedding ceremonies. In some texts, the presence of a prelate or a ceremony in Church legitimises a marriage, their absence calling it into question (*Erec*, *Daurel*; Paterson 1991: 437–41). Aspects of marriage emphasised by the *Adam* play include fidelity to spouse and God (both expressed in contemporary terms of service to an overlord), marital affection and mutual support, the wife's role as counsellor, and the relative power of man and wife. While it shows little obvious interest in Duby's three main pairs of criteria for the clash of 'models of marriage', it resembles in several respects the defence of the goodness of marriage by the twelfth-century canonist Gratian: that it leads to conjugal fidelity, a moral and religious framework for child-rearing, and mutual love and support between the couple who express their attachment through sexual union, with the proviso that 'the woman has no power, but in everything she is subject to the control of her husband' (Brundage 1987: 235 and 255). While the *Adam* play is coy about sex, it nevertheless includes it in Eden, for God announces man's freedom here from sin in begetting children – the implication remaining, however, that after the Fall sex becomes tainted.

These features of marriage are explored at greater length by Chrétien de Troyes in his romance *Erec et Enide* which charts the relationship of a young bride and groom to present its own model of marriage, love, chivalry and kingship, and which allows a more positive view of sex. The usefulness of this text as a historical source lies in its mixture of detailed exploration of contemporary issues together with a didactic exemplarity relatively uncomplicated by the playfulness and subversive ironies of Chrétien's later romances. The marriage is contracted for practical reasons whose ethical status is left open to debate: for Erec, Enide is initially little more than a convenient pretext for a fight to avenge his honour, while Enide is moved by thoughts of increased social status. However, the match is pronounced by the narrator to be exemplary, the couple equalling each other in beauty and intelligence, and it is celebrated with the legitimacy of a public church ceremony, by contrast with the unwedded, stifling and selfish cohabitation of the lovers who figure in the Joy of the Court episode at the end of the romance. Love is clearly a vital part of their marriage, as is sexual pleasure, provided that this is not over-indulged at the expense of their role in society. This ideal resembles quite closely ideas found in Gratian; indeed, the idea that sexual attraction and satisfaction are important ingredients in a marriage is present some forty years earlier in Anglo-Norman England in Gaimar's *Estoire des Engleis* (Gillingham 1997: 51–2).

The preoccupation of twelfth- and thirteenth-century literature with the subject of love, marital affection and marital disaffection is so vast that it would be idle to attempt here a synthesis of its diverse manifestations. Suffice it to suggest that new emphasis on marital affection in canonists such as Gratian may well be a response to vernacular literature and lay expectations rather than the other way round.

The wife as giver of good counsel is another recurrent literary theme developed with some subtlety in *Erec et Enide*. Perhaps the most problematic part of this romance from the interpretative point of view concerns Erec's brusque commands to his wife, once they have quarrelled and then set out on their joint quest of self-discovery, to remain silent, whatever may befall. Enide already considers herself guilty of foolish speech, having blurted out to her husband the reproaches of Erec's male companions that he has abandoned knightly pursuits. The reader is in a position to judge her with greater detachment: inept and naïve as she is, she reveals greater alertness than her uxorious spouse to his fault and threatened reputation. Erec's harsh commands to Enide are left ambiguous: does he really *want* her to be quiet? Is he asserting dominance out of piqued pride? Is he testing her? Is his anger simply evidence of the marital disharmony precipitated by their fault and quarrel? Whatever the case, she has to learn to make her own judgements on when and what it is appropriate to speak, and this is seen as an important part of her apprenticeship as a married woman with social responsibilities. Eve as giver of bad advice is not the paradigm for vernacular epic and romance, though it is not uncommon either (*Willame*: 2590–6; *Ami*: 500–5). Wives often give wise advice which goes unheeded: a device which in some *chansons de geste* serves to offer a critique of masculine ideologies (Kay 1990c; Kay 1990d).

Erec et Enide is also a locus of discussion about the issue of power in marital relations. As we have seen, the *Adam* playwright presents a tussle for power as inevitable from the beginnings of mankind. Chrétien explores conflicting models of relations between man and wife, encapsulated in the application of the feminine tags *dame*, *feme* and *amie* to Enide by the narrator and by the male protagonist. At various stages of the narrative Erec treats Enide with the respect and deference due to a *dame*, which carries the diverse overtones of a married woman with social status and responsibilities and the courtly *domna* of troubadour poetry; the affection based on equality and intimacy implied by *amie*; and the commanding attitude of a twelfth-century husband towards his *feme*. The ideal emerging from this romance is evidently a 'proper' balance of these possibilities, though in Chrétien's next romance of *Cligés*, such a concordance, overtly achieved, is subverted by textual ironies that suggest a more worldly doubt of its practical possibility.

Old French and Occitan narrative poetry not infrequently shows noblewomen in positions of power and influence. While the *Roman de Silence* raises the issue of whether women should inherit at all (see below), heiresses often surface in vernacular texts as desirable prizes and represent a regular fantasy of the knightly audience. Sometimes, like Brunissen, the heroine of the romance of *Jaufre*, they are inclined to bossiness but worth the effort of courting. At other times their power is shown to be tenuous and hedged about with ambiguity: in his romance of *Yvain*, Chrétien de Troyes depicts the heroine Laudine on one level as a domineering autocrat, on another as the victim of the real constraints placed upon a woman ruler (Krueger 1985). Intense hostility to women's power surfaces in the Old French hagiographical epic *Ami et Amile*, where Lubias, a rich heiress who is a mere object of male exchange before her marriage, subsequently uses her position as ruler of Blaye to abuse her leprous husband and attempt to coerce the bishop into sanctioning their divorce. Vernacular literature reveals contemporary anxieties over the power not only of independent female rulers, such as Melisende of Jerusalem (Huneycutt 1994: 192), but also of consorts, especially queens, to influence government through their positions as wives and mothers and, potentially, to subvert succession (McCracken 1998).

The literature privileges above all the ideal whereby women use whatever lesser powers they have to support their husbands and their just causes. Guibourc in the *Song of William* exemplifies this in her courage, initiative, affection, nurturing, administrative and troop-raising skills and her commitment to 'exalting holy Christendom'. More tellingly in the context of property transmission, Esmenjart in *Daurel et Beton* protests vociferously against forced remarriage after her husband's death. The crudity of the financial transaction between the king her brother, who has the power to dispose of her, and the man who murdered her husband, her casting away of his ring, the absence of clergy at this second 'marriage', and her declaration that it constitutes force (in other words rape), all undermine its legality and present her as a victim. But the real point is that this remarriage jeopardises the rights of her first husband's son and heir. Here, the Church's position on consent is invoked in such a way as to shore up the very system of property transmission it could otherwise be seen to undermine. The other trick is to persuade women to want what the system wants.

As in the play of Adam, comic genres such as the *fabliaux* generally portray women as difficult to control. This applies especially to their sexuality: a great many of the *fabliaux* deal with the adultery of wives, and a good proportion of these show the husbands as fools who will swallow any tale their wives tell them, even to the point of a husband, under the delusion that he has died, inertly watching the copulation of his wife and local priest. While these tales are full of misogynistic stereotypes and categorical affirmations of the manifold vices of women, their tenor remains nonetheless ambiguous: in a world of hedonism, through their superior wits and resourcefulness women are apt to come out 'on top' (Johnson 1983). Even where men gain the upper hand their victory may pose awkward questions. The *fabliau* of *Sire Hain et Dame Anuieuse* (II, 1–26) dramatises a literal battle over who wears the trousers. Wearied of his wife's nagging and perversity – when he wants peas for

Figure 14.1 Eve emerging from Adam's rib. The Pierpont Morgan Library, New York. MS. 638, fo. 1v.

dinner she gives him leeks, and vice versa – he challenges her to fisticuffs to decide once and for all who is the boss. The tale ends with the wife beaten and docile, the 'message' rubbed in by the concluding moral; but what is the value or moral basis of a subservience based on physical violence? Given that the woman puts up a vigorous fight and only loses because she trips and falls head over heels into a laundry basket, is not the man's victory the result of pure chance? Or is this simply a case of encouragement to men, in a comic vein, to use whatever violence is necessary to ensure their mastery?

COURTLY LOVE IN THE TROUBADOUR LYRIC

While much of Old French literature, with the notable exception of the Tristran stories, presents gender relations in terms of marriage, from the late eleventh century the lyric troubadours of Occitania had been celebrating extra-marital love (Paterson 1999: 26–46). Their singular invention of Courtly Love might seem to represent the opposite of misogyny. Admiration and reverence for the *domna* or courtly lady may well have its origins, partly at least, in poetry of praise encouraged by noblewomen of some power and status (Kasten 1986: 41–5; Bond 1995: 128–37; Paterson forthcoming). But women were not the only stakeholders in *fin'amor*. In the first known troubadour, Duke William IX of Aquitaine, we can glimpse negotiations between men and women: 'If my lady is willing to grant me her love, I am ready to receive and welcome it, and to conceal and express my appreciation of it, and to say and do what pleases her, and cherish her reputation and promote praise of her' (IX, 37–42).[1] Female interest in a poetry of encomium speaks indirectly here. But the code of love formulated by William focuses not so much on the *domna* as on the social cohesion and exclusivity of the court, and the worth and privilege of the individual male troubadour (Paterson 1999: 28–31). There was no single code of love in troubadour culture, any more than there was a single code of chivalry in France, but as the troubadours negotiated ideological changes through debates within the *canso* tradition, as well as between the *canso* and other poetic genres, the *domna* came more firmly to represent a mere catalyst to masculine self-enhancement in the eyes of other men: another 'transparent object of exchange'. The *canso* celebrated the privileged sentiments of the male speaker and addressed itself, more often than not, to a male addressee (Gaunt 1990c: 311). Moreover the role of the *domna* became more prescriptive and coercive, involving what Sarah Kay has termed a three-gender system: a masculine gender, positive, undivided and unproblematical, and two female genders, a negative one of the *femna* which embodied the misogynistic stereotype of female unreliability and misconduct, and a positive one of the *domna* which, however, entailed the acquisition of stereotypically 'masculine' characteristics, the sacrifice of the woman's sexuality, and the constant danger of slipping into the negative *femna* category (Kay 1990a: 86–95). When women's voices made themselves heard in the late twelfth century and the thirteenth, in the form of the minority *trobairitz* or women troubadours, the straitjacket of these gender categories and the *domna* role prescribed by the male-authored tradition were sources of anxiety for these women. The evidence of the troubadour lyric as a whole shows that women were able to contribute to Occitan courtly culture by their social presence and their minority participation in artistic production and patronage; that there were ups and downs in their visibility; that they were sometimes able to speak out with authority, and often with wit and artistic accomplishment; but that they were having to deal with powerful constraints, serving primarily male interests (Paterson 1993: 256–65). It also suggests that poetry which may have originally responded significantly to female initiative was largely taken over by men for their own purposes.

GENDERED IDENTITY

Constructions of gender through laws, marriage customs, names, linguistic categories ('man', 'woman', 'lady'), restrictive work practices, scientific and religious theories and practices, architecture, art and literature serve, among other purposes, to ground power hierarchies and contain perceived threats of unruliness. They are moveable and may, as we have seen in the case of the troubadour *canso*, involve more than two gender categories. Women such as Guibourc (*Willame*) with supposedly masculine characteristics such as courage and firmness of purpose are often praised in Old French literature, soft or effeminate men such as Cariado denigrated (*Tristran*, 811–16), even though from the twelfth century, written and iconographical sources not infrequently represent Jesus with feminine and maternal traits (Bynum 1982: 110–69; Bynum 1987: 270–3 and plates 25–30).

Gender constructions are coercive to both men and women. In his important book *Gender and Genre*, Simon Gaunt has shown how Old French and Occitan literature constantly rehearses and reworks issues and definitions of gender difference through intra- and inter-generic dialogue, and how constructions of femininity serve as an attempt not only to control women, but also to define lay masculinity restrictively as heterosexual, homosocial and militaristic. It is uncertain to what extent this may signal opposition to what John Boswell has identified as a clerical gay sub-culture thriving from *c.*1050–1150, followed by fanatical hostility and oppression in the later Middle Ages (Boswell 1980). As far as militaristic values are concerned, some of the clerical authors of vernacular literature in France seek, in fact, to moderate or subvert them with more peaceable and spiritual ideals (Paterson 1981: 32; *Raoul*: lxxi; Kay 1990c; Kay 1990d), but heroes of Old French epics and romances, by contrast with the lover of Occitan lyrics, are expected to be accomplished knights, and behind the mitigating ethos of diverse chivalries lies the archetypal dismissiveness of that militant Christian, Archbishop Turpin of the *Chanson de Roland* (1877–82): a knight who lacks strength and ferocity is not worth fourpence and should stay at home in a monastery and pray for our souls.

Men as a whole did not, however, have to contend with the ubiquitous prejudice against their sex with which women were faced, and which they risked internalising (Blamires 1992; Radice 1974: 130–1, 161; Lawson 1985: 51; Gaunt 1995: 158). Sarah Kay has memorably divided medieval misogyny between the 'feudal' (in other words, lay) and the 'ecclesiastical' (Kay 1990b: 131). According to the first model, the woman is a transparent object of exchange between men: often virtually invisible, she functions as a trophy or reward for valorous service, as a status symbol, a channel of noble blood and property, or a means by which a man may avenge himself on another man (by seducing or raping that man's wife). The fair Aude in the Oxford *Roland*, for example, surfaces in the minds of the male heroes Roland and Oliver at a crisis-point in their relations, serving primarily as a poignant reminder of their homosocial bonds which she welds together by virtue of being Oliver's sister and Roland's fiancée. She finally appears on the narrative stage after Roland's death only to refuse any substitute husband and fall down dead: a simple sign of his prestige. The ecclesiastical model of misogyny, by contrast, ascribes to women malign agency: woman is the temptress Eve, or worse, the Whore of Babylon, manipulative, devious, treacherous, lustful, mutable, venal, the ruination of man. These contrasting approaches to women are exemplified on the one hand in the *Chanson de Roland*, where men who think too much of their lands and wives at home are blamed for weakness, but where the women themselves have no agency, and certain ecclesiastical accounts of Urban II's preaching of the First Crusade which refer to the 'seductive lures' of the wives of potential crusaders: 'the most beautiful wives became as loathsome as something putrid' (Riley-Smith 1981: 52 and 56). Such clerical disgust for women is found in the troubadour satirist Marcabru, who warns men against the wiles of the whore, who 'often stinks in her whoring, like a rotting carcass in a slaughterhouse' (XLIV, 29–32).

Biological essentialism is a standard patriarchal method of dooming women to inferiority and subservience (Paterson 1993: 270–5). Despite the fluidity and range of possible sexual identities allowed for by Aristotelian understanding of the human body (Rubin 1994: 106), it seems that everyone in the Middle Ages believed in 'the nature of women'. Overtly misogynistic writers could simply hammer out *ad infinitum* the hardy clichés going back to Juvenal and St Jerome (Blamires 1992). Others, more apparently sympathetic to women, readily lapse into them as if they had universal explanatory power (*Yvain*: 1649–52). More tellingly, women writers also draw on them. Heloïse asks in anguish whether it has always been the lot of women to bring about the downfall of great men, when it is all too clear that it was Abelard who calculatingly set out to seduce his young pupil.[2] Christine de Pisan in the later Middle Ages challenges traditional misogyny but counters it partly by the valuation of feminine qualities, such as gentleness and diplomacy, which are judged to be innate.

Yet the more that male authors insist on the unshakable nature of women, the more suspect this insistence becomes. If it is universally accepted, why reiterate it? The *Roman de Silence*, which has attracted a great deal of interest in recent feminist scholarship, shows that the nature–nurture debate was a source of lively tension for its author Heldris of Cornwall and his audience. The tale begins with a king (Eban of England) decreeing, contrary to custom, that daughters will henceforth be forbidden from inheriting their fathers' estates. This results from the fault not of women but of two men who married the twin daughters of one of his vassals and quarrelled violently over the inheritance. When a deserving knight Cador marries a count's daughter he is anxious that their child should be able to inherit their lands, and on the birth of a girl, they have it brought up as a boy. This launches the narrative into a debate on the relative influence of nurture and nature on gender. By a change of clothes and grammatical appendage, the girl *Silentia* becomes the boy *Silentius* and proves to be a highly successful male, outshining all in knightly prowess. Nature and Nurture personified battle it out, and despite the narrator's declared (though not necessarily reliable) belief in the pre-eminence of Nature (2339–42, cf. 2423–4), within a year Silence 'wasn't a girl any more' (2350). Puberty brings a crisis of identity, when Silence is smitten with an urge to 'go and learn to sew' (2543), but on considering 'the pastimes of women's chambers', decides that 'a man's way of life is much better than a woman's': 'I should make a big mistake to step down when I'm on top' (2632–41). This text therefore exposes clearly the imbalance of power and advantage inherent in gender, and demonstrates that at least in the case of a girl born with outstanding noble qualities, there is nothing to prevent her from excelling at skills and pursuits traditionally defined as masculine. Yet the conclusion, which restores to women their right to inherit but sees Silence reduced to her original female condition – and to silence – appears to suppress the debate which the preceding narrative raised with such energy and focus (Gaunt 1990: 213). Was the issue too sensitive, were the implications of the challenge to conventional gender roles too difficult to take on board? Heldris's conclusion seems to show a particular awareness, if not awkwardness, in the troubling presence of female members of the audience (6705), as he concludes that 'one should think well of a good woman more than one should dislike or blame a bad one' since 'a woman has less chance of having the situation or opportunity for a good way of life rather than for a bad one. If she acts well against nature I shall rightly teach that one should take greater account of her than of the woman who does wrong' (6685–94): a curious mix of faith in nature and an acknowledgement of the power of circumstance.

Roberta Krueger rightly stresses that many romances contain ambiguities allowing a space for a female (or indeed male) response which may be at variance with the surface one, and that even purely misogynistic texts may well have been read with resistance as much as compliance (Krueger 1993). By the time it has reached its conclusion, *Silence* has systematically undermined traditional gender role allocations, whether or not the ending draws a veil of silence over the questions raised. Readers may then choose not to accept a return to received ideas. Moreover, the text opens up issues of alternatives to a binary male–female gender opposition. The transvestism of Queen Eufeme's adulterous lover, disguised as a nun, may incur disapproval, yet Silence's cross-dressing works positively in that she subverts nature in a good cause (obedience to her father) and with good results (the restoration of women's inheritance rights, the exposure of evil, his/her various beneficial acts of prowess). Homosexuality appears negatively in Eufeme's malicious slander of the 'boy' Silence who has rebuffed her seductive overtures; yet the minstrels whose life Silence temporarily shares open up the possibility of an intermediate gender: anxious that if King Eban died women might inherit again and that s/he knows nothing of women's arts, s/he decides to go abroad with the minstrels and learn skills suitable to a woman's life: 'If you are slow at knightly pursuits, minstrelsy will be of use to you. And if the king should happen to die, you will be able to use it to entertain yourself in women's chambers; you will have your harp and viele to make up for the fact that you don't know how to fashion a fringe or border' (2863–9).

Minstrels, like Heldris himself, are marginal figures at court: artists who stand outside conventional boundaries. Another such figure is Merlin: wildman, magician, seer and soothsayer. As a wildman he too escapes the confines of convention. Like a storyteller he has the ability to create illusions and transformations; at the same time he is the knower and teller of truth. Merlin's interventions at the end of the story may offer a veiled commentary on the apparent closure of the nature–nurture debate. Curiously he embodies its contradictions: his temptation by cooked food is presented as an appeal to nature rather than nurture, when cooked food is the opposite of the natural. Subject to the power of his listeners, he subjects them to the power of knowing laughter and narrative control. The theme of silence, which permeates the romance through Silence's names, the silencing of her/his gender identity, and the characters' various disguises and subterfuges, are brought to a climax as Merlin's tantalising laughter echoes round the court and he is forced on pain of death to speak out, though fearful of his audience's anger (6308–13). Merlin, who sees and knows everything (literally 'knows the whole work'), 'hints quite closely at the pure truth, but the speech is very obscure for it is spoken in a veiled way' (6408–12; 6486–90).

A straightforward reading will interpret this simply as a build-up of narrative tension as the dénouement unfolds and truths about each character come out. But Heldris may be using Merlin to laugh at his listeners' expense. A narrative closure reverting to a reassuringly familiar mindset may be subverted by irony, not a rare event in medieval romance (Chrétien 1957: 6633–61 and 1961: 6799–6808): a more astute reading might indeed disturb the conservative (6411–12) – but ironic veiling of the truth offers a safety curtain for the author.

The forms of gendered identity explored so far concern the secular life. The religious life offers others to those in a position to take advantage of them. For women outside the nobility it was difficult to enter a convent; less so for men (Lawrence 1991: 216–17; Paterson 1993: 241–3). The *Chanson de Roland* might scorn men who chose monastic life in preference to a military profession, but for intellectuals and sons of the nobility having administrative skills it offered a potentially rewarding career path. Women, too, could wield positions of some power as abbesses and prioresses, though they were always at a disadvantage in comparison with men. As far as notions of 'the feminine' were concerned, a woman might hope to cancel the stain of Eve's sin by modelling herself on the Virgin Mary, but in Marina Warner's memorable title, the Virgin was 'alone of all her sex', and virgin motherhood was not an attainable goal for daughters of Eve. However, sanctity grew to be a greater possibility in the thirteenth century, with a marked increase in the number of canonised female saints (Bynum 1982: 137). Female saints' lives in Old French and Occitan construct woman primarily in relation to her sexuality (virginity or repentant Magdalene), unlike hagiography dealing with male saints. Her virginity may enhance her value within a masculine prestige system; it may alternatively appear as a challenge to family authority, though from the perspective of a male ecclesiastical establishment. Narratives about virgin martyrs may have been empowering for some women, but as Simon Gaunt has pointed out, this would generally entail the internalisation of a negative view of the female body (Gaunt 1995: 228).

VIOLENCE

Power in gender relations has a good deal to do with the extent to which a culture sanctions the use of violence. Masculinity in vernacular literature is largely predicated upon violence. As a general rule, in this literature, men fight, women do not.[3]

Vernacular literature tells us quite a lot about violence in gender relations. First, as one might expect, comic genres such as the *fabliaux* sometimes seem to encourage wife-beating (*Sire Hain*: *fabliaux* II, 402–14), though beaten wives often end up getting the better of their husbands (*Vilain Mire, Tresces*: *fabliaux* II, 309–47; VI, 207–58). Serious genres of literature such as epic and romance overtly disapprove of violence to women (*Raoul*: 1285–1352, 6061–83; *Daurel* 1971: 760–3, 900–41; *Erec*: 4751–814). Some go further: epics such as *Raoul de Cambrai* and *Girart de Roussillon* depict warfare at enormous length, presumably to the entertainment of their listeners, yet adopt an ultimately ecclesiastical perspective and undermine the military ideologies of the masculine characters by the futility and brutality of their wars and the contrary voices of the female characters (see above). In texts with a less marked ecclesiastical bias, male violence is glorified but contained by chivalric ideals: the romance superman such as Chrétien de Troyes' Lancelot overcomes all opponents, but tempers victory with clemency, restraint and self-sacrifice.

While the idea that chivalric ideals moderated the violence of the knights in warfare and pillaging raids may be subject to scepticism (Painter 1940: 92), noblemen probably did not consider it normal to treat their wives with physical brutality. The case of Marie de Montpellier shows that verbal forms of coercion could be effective. Forced to consent to her husband Pere of Aragon's arrangements for the betrothal of her baby daughter, she documents her declaration that he 'crucified' her with his angry insistence and his threats to the city of Montpellier; but there is no suggestion of physical aggression (Paterson 1993: 238). Eleanor of Aquitaine was imprisoned by her husband for many years, but as far as we know she was not beaten up.

But if medieval aristocratic culture in France did not sanction physical brutality towards women, vernacular literature nevertheless shows a not inconsiderable interest in sexual violence by men towards women. Part of the attraction of female saints' lives lies in the voyeuristic, pornographic contemplation of violence towards the female body (Gravdal 1991: 24–5; Gaunt 1995: 197). Rape fantasies were a common theme of romance, and comic genres offer rape as an 'enjoyable' spectacle (Gravdal 1991: 104).

What we call rape fell into the much broader medieval category of *raptus* or abduction, which comprised the violation of a man's rights over a woman's sexuality and included elopement with her consent. It is true, however, that by the twelfth century the victim's consent to sex was becoming the essential factor in determining the nature of *raptus* and the severity of the punishment (Brundage 1987: index and 209–10, 249). A huge gap separated draconian legal norms, which regularly prescribed the death penalty for the *raptus* of respectable women, from legal practice which made proof almost impossible and punishment mitigated by substitute penalties such as fines or an obligation to marry the victim (Rieger 1988: 245; Gravdal 1991: 1–20).

What does the literary evidence tell us about rape? First, it suggests that it was as much, if not more, a question of one man violating the property of another man as of a man attacking a woman; secondly, that a woman was hard put to it to prove she had been violated, had not led the man on, and had not enjoyed it; and thirdly, that the woman's interests were likely to be set aside if they were inconvenient to relations between men (Paterson 1993: 240). The *Roman de Renart* is instructive in these respects. Renart the fox is arraigned at the royal court for the rape of Hersent the she-wolf. The rape clearly took place, with her husband witnessing her resistance. However, Hersent is set up textually as a lustful female who previously led Renart on to adultery, so her protestations of nun-like virtue, convincing only to the donkey, reinforce a widespread assumption that women's testimony is unreliable and that she 'asked for it'. Emphasis lies on her husband Isengrin's humiliation rather than any feelings she might have; as a sexual crime the rape is perceived primarily as adultery, hence the violation of the bonds of marriage and Isengrin's rights, and even these are secondary to issues of Renart's disturbance of the peace and defiance of the king's authority. The latter regards the affair as trivial, and Renart as excused if he committed rape out of 'love'. Arguments among the king's counsellors demonstrate the obstacles to proof, such as the ease with which a husband can make his wife say what he wishes and the need for corroborative witnesses, as well as individuals' vested interests and personal grudges. Hersent is labelled a 'damaged vessel' and the badger proposes that it would be expedient for the blame to fall on her, to avoid conflict among the barons (*Renart*: 260–72, 346–82, 42–50). The *Renart* stories, it is true, operate within a sinful as well as a comic world where all fictional characters behave badly (Simpson 1996). However, the trial scenes correspond in many respects to evidence available from elsewhere: proof is difficult, women are regarded as suspect witnesses (Gravdal 1991: 74; Rieger 1988: 263–5).

Literature could be a source of pleasurable fantasy about rape for male writers and their audiences. 'Just as the trial scenes in *Le Roman de Renart* create an imaginary space in which rape can become comic, so too does the medieval *pastourelle* constitute a discursive space in which one can laugh at the spectacle of rape' (Gravdal 1991: 104). While Occitan *pastorelas* never depict rape as condonable, the Old French *pastourelles* contain a minority of erotic encounters between knights and shepherdesses where a violated peasant girl ends up giggling with pleasure, asking the rapist to come back another time, or contentedly accepting remuneration (Paden 1989: 331–49; compare Gravdal 1991: 109–21).[4] Courtly literature, ostensibly promoting non-violent conduct towards women, has its internal contradictions on the subject. Some Old French *lais* allow the fantasy of rape in an other-worldly context: fairies turn out to be willing after all, courtly prescriptive norms of non-violence to women can be flouted with impunity (Gravdal 1991: 44–67; Rieger 1988: 257–8). Romance is often predicated on the exploitation or mystification of rape, the pleasure of saving virgins from rape, or the justification of rape on the grounds that a man had loved a woman for a long time (Krueger 1993: 34; Rieger 1988: 260).[5]

Rather than making it into an attractive spectacle, *La fille du comte de Ponthieu* offers some oblique insight into a woman's experience of rape. The laconic tale leaves many open questions, with silences and cryptic speech forming an integral part of its thematic structure. Nothing genders the impersonal narrator, or the anonymous author, who could equally be male or female.

The nameless protagonist welcomes her father's choice of his poor knight Sir Theobald as her husband. After five years the couple set out on a pilgrimage to Santiago to pray for an heir. Ambushed by armed bandits, Theobald succeeds in killing three of their eight attackers before they overpower him and tie him up. The robbers then gang-rape his wife, declaring this to be compensation for the death of their kinsmen, and leave. Her husband asks her to untie his bonds, but she seizes one of the dead robbers' swords saying 'Sir, I will set you free all right!' and goes to run him through the body. Twisting aside, Theobald manages to free himself as the sword hits his arm. He keeps quiet about the rape and attempted murder, treats his wife with complete courtesy, houses her in a convent until his return from Santiago, takes her back home with a great show of joy and honour, but no longer sleeps in her bed. Despite Theobald's initial reserve, his father-in-law the Count of Ponthieu prises the truth out of him. The Count favours instant violent retribution, but Theobald observes that if the lady were dead she could not corroborate her husband's story. Confronted by her father, she admits to attempted homicide, but is reticent about her motive: 'for a reason that makes me still regret my not having done so'. The Count vengefully seals his daughter up in a barrel and dumps it at sea, to the horror of Theobald and the lady's step-brother. About to expire, the lady is found and released by merchants, to whom she cryptically relates that 'a cruel fate and dreadful crime had brought her to this pass'. Which crime? The rape? Her attempted murder? Her father's cruel punishment?

Sold to the Sultan of Almeria, she avoids further rape by converting to Islam and marrying him so as to 'bow to love rather than duress'. His ardent love soon leads to the conception of a son and a daughter. The Count, guilt-ridden by his sin against his daughter, takes the Cross, in company with his son and Theobald. Shipwrecked on return from the Holy Land they fall into the Sultan's hands, where the lady is in a position to save their lives. Now in control, she interrogates them about their past without revealing her own. As the Count relates truthfully the story of the attack in the forest, the lady reveals her motive for attempted murder:

> '[It was] because of the terrible shame he had seen her suffer and be subjected to before his eyes.'
> These words moved Sir Theobald to tears and he said, weeping:
> 'Alas! where was her guilt therein? Madam,' he added, 'as I hope God will deliver me from my captivity, I swear I would never have looked on her less fondly on that account.'
> 'Sir,' she replied, 'that was not her belief at the time.'

As words flow more freely between the lady, her father, her husband and her step-brother, she at last begins to release her tight hold over her 'deeply felt emotion'. The dénouement sees them back in an orderly life in Ponthieu with all four receiving penance for their misdeeds, and the rewards of lands, happiness, and heirs.

Was the woman to blame for seeking permission to accompany her husband on the risky journey? Does her austere penance at the end of the tale imply that her sins are particularly bad? If so, is this a judgement on her attempted violence, or her bigamy, or her deception and abandonment of the Sultan and the theft of his son? Or is it a sign of a strict conscience? Was Theobald at fault in his travel arrangements (he could have sent his wife on ahead with the main party), or for not making more effort to communicate better with his wife, to ensure her trust, and to find out the true reasons for her attempted violence? Why did Theobald let out the secret he had taken such pains to hide? Did he continue his courtesies to his wife out of kindness, or simply from self-interest (whereby he wished to avoid shame, and to preserve a source of corroborative testimony to his own in the event of future scandal)? Why did the Count and his son not make more effort to find out the lady's reasons for her actions?

This 'exercise in non-communication' implies, first, that the shame of rape could be appalling for both a woman and her family; secondly, that a woman was likely to believe that she might be regarded as culpable, and that she might have to 'pay a second time' (*Ponthieu* 1971: 110–12);[6] and thirdly, that a great deal concerning rape was simply unsayable. The textual gaps and silences encourage reflection about a taboo subject.[7]

CONCLUSION

Literature is not a closed system of conventions that has no impact upon reality. It articulates codes which allow and encourage writers and their public to think of themselves in relation to others in certain ways, for good or ill. In the case of medieval vernacular literature this public was largely confined to an elite of aristocratic and gentry-aping men and women, and to (primarily male) urban guilds, though epic and liturgical drama may have had a wider impact. Women's access to literature, whether through reading or listening, was no doubt particularly restricted to the nobility. Given that '"literacy" is a variable term', female literacy in the Middle Ages was 'protean' (Smith and Taylor 1995b: xi) – though the general picture for medieval Europe as a whole is one of the relative paucity of women's access to books (Smith and Taylor 1995a: x–xi).

It is not always easy to know how medieval people responded to what they heard and in some cases read, though current work on literary reception through new approaches to manuscript texts and iconography are breaking fresh ground here. There is some evidence that women writers both internalised and showed various forms of resistance to the powerful tradition of medieval misogynistic discourse, and forms of inscription of women readers in literary texts suggest that male writers could find female listeners enough of a problem to take them seriously. There is also evidence that where women took to writing, they were frequently re-written (if not written out) by editor-scribes: 'women write themselves, and men rewrite women, with surprising homogeneity across the centuries and the continents' (Smith and Taylor 1995b: ix).

Recent work on the *dames* and *demoiselles d'honneur* of Isabeau de Bavière at the court of Charles VI in the early fifteenth century tellingly illustrates the power of literature to inflict real damage and promote, on the level of reality, the scapegoating of a group of women (Solterer forthcoming). The late medieval witchcraft trials amply testify to the power of misogynistic traditions, literary and otherwise, to persecute women. Medieval literature was not just a game.

NOTES

1 While William's songs are the earliest to have survived, some of them may well have been composed in response to lost songs of the 'school' of Eble of Ventadour. See Dumitrescu 1968, though his suggested identification of these songs should be treated with caution.

2 Her anguish may be partly or wholly rhetorical, to appeal to Abelard's compassion or sense of guilt. See Clanchy's complex analysis of her writing and state of mind (Clanchy 1997: 149–72).

3 One exception is, of course, the masculinised Silence. Women's role in siege warfare is acknowledged in *Crotzada*, 113.108–9; compare Christine de Pisan's advice to baronesses (Lawson 1985: 129).

4 While one may not agree with all of Gravdal's interpretations, her book has unquestionably broken new ground.

5   For the blurring of distinctions between forced and voluntary sex in twelfth-century
    canon law and in literary texts, see Gravdal 1991: 11.

6   Compare Gillingham (1997: 52) on the story in Gaimar (late 1130s) of the rape of Buern
    Butescarl's wife, who is assured by her husband that she has no need to feel shamed and
    that he will continue to love and kiss her.

7   In the late Middle Ages Christine de Pisan (Lawson 1983: 160–1) argues vehemently
    against men who claim women want to be raped, and urges the severest punishment of
    the rapist. Although she rewrites Bocaccio's version of the story of Lucretia, she is unable
    to bypass the idea that, however blameless the victim, the shame is unbearable to the
    point of suicide. For diverse medieval interpretations of the Lucretia story see Rieger
    1998: 258–60.

REFERENCES

Texts and translations

Ami et Amile, ed. P. Dembowski (1969), Paris: Champion.

La Chanson de Roland, ed. I. Short (1990), Paris: Livre de Poche.

La chançun de Willame, ed. N.V. Iseley (1966), Chapel Hill: University of North Carolina
Press.

—— transl. *William, Count of Orange: Four Old French Epics* (1975) ed. G. Price, London:
Dent, and Totowa, NJ: Rowman and Littlefield.

Chrétien de Troyes, *Erec et Enide* ed. (1955) M. Roques, Paris: Classiques Français du Moyen
Age.

—— *Cligés*, ed. A. Micha (1957), Paris: Classiques Français du Moyen Age.

—— *Le Chevalier de la charrete* ed. (1963), M. Roques, Paris: Classiques Français du Moyen
Age.

—— *Yvain*, ed. T.B.W. Reid (1961), Manchester: Manchester University Press.

—— transl. D.D.R. Owen (1993), Chrétien de Troyes, *Arthurian Romances*, London:
Everyman Dent.

Christine de Pisan, transl. E.J. Richards (1983), *Christine de Pisan, The Book of the City of
Ladies*, Harmondsworth: Penguin.

—— transl. S. Lawson (1985), *Christine de Pisan, The Treasure of the City of Ladies*,
Harmondsworth: Penguin.

Crotzada, ed. E. Martin-Chabot, *La Chanson de la croisade albigeoise* (1931-73), 3 vols, Paris:
Les Belles Lettres.

—— transl. J. Shirley, *The Song of the Cathar Wars* (1996), Aldershot: Scolar Press.

Daurel, ed. A.S. Kimmel (1971) *A critical edition of the Old Provençal epic 'Daurel et Beton'*,
Chapel Hill: University of North Carolina Press.

—— transl. J. Shirley, *Daurel et Beton* (1997), Felinfach: Llanerch publishers.

Fabliaux: Nouveau Recueil Complet des Fabliaux, ed. W. Noomen and N. van den Boogaard,
1983–98. Assen (vols I–II), Assen and Maastricht (vols III–X).

—— *Fabliaux*, transl. G. Rouger (1978), Paris: Gallimard.

La Fille du Comte de Ponthieu, nouvelle du xiiie siècle, ed. C. Brunel (1926), Paris: Classiques
Français du Moyen Age.

—— transl. P. Matarasso (1971), *Aucassin et Nicolette and other Tales*, Harmondsworth:
Penguin, pp. 109–30.

Heldris de Cornüalle, *Le Roman de Silence*, ed. L. Thorpe (1972), Cambridge: Heffer and Sons Ltd.

—— transl. R. Psaki (1990), New York: Garland.

Le jeu d'Adam, ed. W. van Emden (1996), Edinburgh: Société Rencesvals British Branch.

The Letters of Abelard and Heloise, transl. B. Radice (1974), Harmondsworth: Penguin.

Marcabru, *Marcabru: a critical edition*, ed. S. Gaunt, R. Harvey and L. Paterson (2000), Woodbridge: D. S. Brewer.

Raoul de Cambrai (1992), ed. and transl. S. Kay, Oxford: Clarendon Press.

Le Roman de Jaufre (1960), ed. R. Lavaud and R. Nelli, Bruges: Desclée De Brouwer.

Le Roman de Renart (1985), ed. and transl. J. Dufournet (2 vols), Paris: Flammarion.

Thomas, *Les fragments du roman de Tristan*, ed. B. Wind (1960), Geneva and Paris: Droz.

William IX of Aquitaine, *Guglielmo IX: Poesie*, ed. N. Pasero (1973), Modena: S.T.E.M.-Mucchi.

Secondary literature

Blamires, A. (1992) *Woman Defamed and Woman Defended*, Oxford: Clarendon Press.

Bond, G.A. (1995) *The Loving Subject. Desire, eloquence and power in Romanesque France*, Philadelphia: University of Pennsylvania Press.

Boswell, J. (1980) *Christianity, Social Tolerance, and Homosexuality. Gay people in Western Europe from the beginning of the Christian era to the fourteenth century*, Chicago and London: University of Chicago Press.

Brundage, J.A. (1987) *Law, Sex and Christian Society in Medieval Europe*, Chicago and London: University of Chicago Press.

Bynum, C.W. (1982) *Jesus as Mother: studies in the spirituality of the High Middle Ages*, Berkeley, Los Angeles and London: University of California Press.

—— (1987) *Holy Feast and Holy Fast*, Berkeley, Los Angeles and London: University of California Press.

Clanchy, M.T. (1997) *Abelard: a medieval life*, Oxford UK and Cambridge USA: Blackwell.

Duby, G. (1983) *The Knight, the Lady and the Priest*, Harmondsworth: Penguin.

Dumitrescu, M. (1968) 'Eble II de Ventadorn et Guillaume IX d'Aquitaine', *Cahiers de Civilisation Médiévale*, 11, 379–412.

Gaunt, S. (1990a) 'Le pouvoir d'achat des femmes dans *Girart de Roussillon*', *Cahiers de Civilisation Médiévale*, 33, 305–16.

—— (1990b) 'The significance of silence', *Paragraph*, 13, 202–16.

—— (1990c) 'Poetry of exclusion: a feminist reading of some troubadour lyrics', *Modern Language Review*, 85, 310–29.

—— (1995) *Gender and Genre in Medieval French Literature*, Cambridge: Cambridge University Press.

Gillingham, J. (1997) 'Kingship, chivalry and love. Political and cultural values in the earliest history written in French: Geoffrey Gaimar's *Estoire des Engleis*', in *Anglo-Norman political culture and the twelfth-century Renaissance*. ed. W. Hollister, Woodbridge: The Boydell Press, 33–58.

Gravdal, K. (1991) *Ravishing Maidens. Writing rape in medieval French literature and law*, Philadelphia: University of Pennsylvania Press.

Huneycutt, L.L. (1994) 'Female succession and the language of power in the writings of twelfth-century churchmen', *Medieval Queenship*, ed. J.C. Parsons, Stroud: Alan Sutton.

Johnson, L. (1983) 'Women on top: antifeminism in the fabliaux', *Modern Language Review*, 78, 298–307.

Kasten, I. (1986) *Frauendienst bei Trobadors und Minnesängern im 12. Jahrhundert*, Heidelberg: Carl Winter Universitätsverlag.

Kay, S. (1990a) *Subjectivity in Troubadour Poetry*, Cambridge: Cambridge University Press.

—— (1990b) 'Seduction and suppression in *Ami et Amile*', *French Studies*, 44, 129–42.

—— (1990c) 'Compagnonnage, désordre social et hétérotextualité dans *Daurel et Beton*', in *Actes du XIe congrès international de la Société Roncesvals. Memorias de la Real Academia de Buenas Letras de Barcelona*, 22, 353–67.

—— (1990d) 'Investing the wild: women's beliefs in the *chansons de geste*', *Paragraph*, 13, 147–63.

—— (1995) *The 'Chansons de geste' in the Age of Romance*, Oxford: The Clarendon Press.

—— and Rubin, M. (1994) *Framing Medieval Bodies*, Manchester: Manchester University Press.

Krueger, R.L. (1985) 'Love, honor, and the exchange of women in *Yvain*: some remarks on the female reader', *Romance Notes*, 25 302–17.

—— (1993) *Women Readers and the Ideology of Gender in Old French Verse Romance*, Cambridge: Cambridge University Press.

Lawrence, C.H. (1991) *Medieval Monasticism*, London and New York: Longman.

McCracken, P. (1998) *The Romance of Adultery. Queenship and Sexual Transgression in Old French Literature*, Philadelphia: University of Pennsylvania Press.

Muir, L.R. (1973) *Liturgy and Drama in the Anglo-Norman Adam*, Oxford: Blackwell.

Nelson, J.L. (1997) 'Family, gender and sexuality in the Middle Ages', in M. Bentley (ed.), *Companion to Historiography*, London and New York: Routledge, 153–76.

Paden, W.D. (1989) 'Rape in the pastourelle', *Romanic Review*, 80, 331–49.

Painter, S. (1940) *French Chivalry. Chivalric ideas and practices in Medieval France*, Ithaca: Cornell University Press.

Paterson, L. (1981) 'Knights and the concept of knighthood in the twelfth-century Occitan epic', in *Knighthood in Medieval Literature*, ed. W.H. Jackson, Woodbridge: D.S. Brewer, 23–38.

—— (1991) 'L'épouse et la formation du lien conjugal selon la littérature du XIe au XIIIe s.: mutations d'une institution et condition féminine', in *Mélanges de langue et de littérature occitanes en hommage à Pierre Bec*, Poitiers: Université de Poitiers, C.E.S.C.M., pp. 425–42.

—— (1993) *The World of the Troubadours: medieval Occitan society, c. 1100–c. 1300*, Cambridge: Cambridge University Press.

—— (1999) 'Fin'Amor and the development of the courtly *canso*', in *The Troubadours: an Introduction*, ed. S. Gaunt and S. Kay, Cambridge: Cambridge University Press.

—— (forthcoming) 'Women, property, and the rise of Courtly Love', *Proceedings of the Ninth Triennial Congress of the International Courtly Literature Society, Vancouver, 1998*, ed. C. Phan, Woodbridge: Boydell.

Rieger, D. (1988) 'Le motif du viol dans la littérature de la France médiévale entre norme courtoise et réalité courtoise', *Cahiers de Civilisation Médiévale*, 31, 241–67.

Riley-Smith, L. and Riley-Smith, J. (1981) *The Crusades. Idea and Reality 1095–1274*, London: Edward Arnold.

Rubin, M. (1994) 'The person in the form: medieval challenges to bodily "order"', in Kay and Rubin, 100–22.

Simpson, J.R. (1996) *Animal Body, Literary Corpus: the Old French 'Roman de Renart'*, Amsterdam: Rodopi.

Smith, L. and Taylor, J.H. (1995a) *Women, the Book and the Godly*, Cambridge: D.S. Brewer.

—— (1995b) *Women, the Book and the Worldly*, Cambridge: D.S. Brewer.

Solterer, H. (forthcoming) 'Insiders and outsiders: the seditious *Dames d'honneur* of Isabeau de Bavière', paper given at the ICLS conference in Vancouver, 1998.

SYMBOLISM AND MEDIEVAL RELIGIOUS THOUGHT

David d'Avray

An old but good introduction to Social Anthropology suggests that symbolism is an, if not the, distinguishing feature of religion (which is not here marked off sharply from magic). On the other hand, we have scientific thought, which tends to mean no more and no less than it seems to say. Apart from knowledge for its own sake, its goals are 'instrumental': it tries to bring about the results it explicitly specifies. Magic and religion work differently. Their real meaning is not what they literally say. Words and actions, and rituals combining the two, stand for things which the anthropological observer may not immediately appreciate: say, abstractions such as 'social solidarity' which the people of a traditional society cannot express in any other way. Expression may be an end in itself, or at least a crucial concomitant of the instrumental function of magical or religious activity. Thus Beattie writes that 'the chief difference between what we call practical, common-sense techniques for doing things, and ritual or "magico-religious" ways of doing them lies basically in the presence or absence of an institutionalized symbolic element in what is done . . . [A] distinction between these two kinds of activities . . . rests simply on the presence or absence in what is done of a symbolic element . . . I have intentionally not distinguished between magic and religion; both imply ritual, symbolic ideas and activities rather than practical, "scientific" ones'. Yet Beattie goes on to observe that '[m]ost modern students of religion would hold, as against Durkheim, that religious belief and practice are more than merely a system of social and moral symbolism' (Beattie 1970: 202, 203, 212, 221).

Most medievalists will find this schema relatively inapplicable to their material, and the scientific/symbolic dichotomy misleading if religion (and magic) are to be stuffed into the 'symbolic' pigeon-hole. When medieval people talked about the Trinity, they were not trying to express something else. They used symbols to understand the Trinity but it was not a symbol itself.

Medieval intellectual life was less 'scientific' than that of the past few centuries in one sense: it was relatively weak on the empirical front. There were plenty of practical innovations (Gimpel 1977), but professional intellectuals tended not to dirty their hands with experimentation. As a result, they achieved nothing like the understanding of the workings of the natural world that has come out of the past few centuries. (This should not be regarded as some kind of peculiar shortcoming of the Middle Ages. The form of scientific culture which developed in Europe between *c*.1600 and *c*.1900, before becoming generally dispersed throughout the globe, is the peculiarity in world history.) It would be arrogant and culture-bound to assume that the modern West's attempt to understand the central problems of existence – e.g., whether there is a difference in kind as well as in degree between humans and other animals, or whether personal identity continues in any way after death – is any more 'scientific' than that of medieval people. Medieval scholars devised a method for analysing these problems: philosophical reasoning based on revealed first principles (i.e. on Scripture, to oversimplify somewhat). In the thirteenth century the idea developed that this kind of theology was a 'science' (Chenu 1957). If we grant their premises and understand 'science' to include the kind of deductive reasoning still used today by mathematicians and logicians, then their academic productions can indeed be described as scientific. This side of medieval religion was developed with a degree of sophistication which anyone should find extraordinarily impressive, though the findings of scholastic theologians will be unconvincing to anyone who does not share some of their basic postulates.

A CAROLINGIAN EXAMPLE

Thus medieval religion cannot be reduced to symbolism. Still symbolism was a crucial aspect of it. The following examples (Haymo of Auxerre, *Homilia* XVIII, *Dominica II post Epiphaniam*, cols. 126–37; cf. Barre 1962: 48, 49, 51, 54, 67) represent a dominant form of thought both in the Carolingian period from which they are taken and in the medieval period as a whole. Haymo of Auxerre is explaining the gospel reading of the marriage feast of Cana in his highly successful homiliary. Symbolism enables him to bring salvation history into a synthesis. The six water jars in the narrative stand for the six ages of history: for instance, the first stands for the period from Adam to Noah, and the last is the cue for discussion of the circumcision and presentation of Christ in the Temple. Haymo gives a short history of the world in this framework (*Homilia XVIII*, cols. 131–5). In his account of the first age, for instance, we find a fairly full précis of the creation of Adam and then Eve, and their first sin. Haymo says that contemplation of the consequences will be a warning to us. God did not spare those who sinned for the first time. Perhaps he will not spare us, since we have had the experience of the sins of so many others before us to warn us. The person who thinks about this and fears to do wrong finds in the first age of history a water jar full of water ('In prima aetate mundi legimus . . . in prima aetate hydriam aqua plenam', *Homilia XVIII*, cols 131–2). But this jar full of water is turned into wine if we raise our understanding to a new level. On this level Adam is Christ, formed from immaculate earth (i.e. the Virgin Mary). Eve is the Church. Just as Eve was formed from the side of Adam, so too the Church was formed from the side of Christ when it was pierced by a lance, and blood and water flowed from it ('At vero, si aliquid altius intellexerit . . . hydria, quam plenam invenerat aqua, conversa est in vinum', *Homilia XVIII*, col. 132). Earlier in the sermon he dwells on the fact that the marriage at Cana happened, in the words of the gospel, 'on the third day'. This leads him on to the division of history into (this time) three ages: before the law, under the law, and under grace; to the Trinity; to the distinction between memory, will, and intellect, and to Faith, Hope, and Charity ('Et bene die tertia . . . major autem his est charitas', *Homilia XVIII*, col. 128). With the speed of dream associations, different elements of the belief system could be rapidly juxtaposed. It is not a linear and logical procedure, but gives free play to a psychological process of mental association that anyone can observe in themselves if they backtrack over casual sequences of thought.

A feature of these procedures was that they made it possible to keep the Old and New Testaments close together: particularly important in the Carolingian period, with its 'mentalité vétéro-testamentaire' (though the Old Testament never lost its central place in medieval religion). The train of thought which started from the marriage on the third day and led on to the Trinity, and so on, ended up with the story of Jonah in Nineveh: 'Or the number three is perfect, because we read that when the Lord said to Jonah the prophet: "Go to Nineveh the great city, and you will say to this people, forty days more, and Nineveh will be overthrown" (Jonah 3), and he preached, the king immediately came down from his throne, and ordered the people to make a three-day fast. When that was done, the people gave up their iniquity, and turned to the Lord' ('Sive ternarius numerus . . . conversus est ad Dominum', *Homilia XVIII*, col. 128).

Symbolism was a form of aesthetic and synthetic thought, helping Haymo and his listeners or readers to keep much of their world-view before their minds at any time. Probably this style of religious thought was as important as any other in the lives of Carolingian monks, though I am not aware that the question has been posed squarely or investigated systematically. Symbolism does not get much attention in the chapters dealing with education, culture, theology and the organisation of thought in the volume of the *New Cambridge Medieval History* which covers Haymo's period (Contreni 1995; Ganz 1995). Like the volume as a whole, these chapters are in general admirable. Perhaps symbolism is still regarded by most mainstream historians as a subordinate special aspect of medieval religion and culture, rather than a central part of the system. The subject can hardly be avoided in discussion of the study of the Bible in the Middle Ages (Hamilton 1986: 64–7), though the best historian to treat this theme in depth was more interested in the development of literal exegesis (Smalley 1983, esp. ch. iv; cf. de Lubac 1959–64; Contreni 1995). De Lubac, emphasising the creativity of non-literal exegesis, was a historical theologian rather than a historian, while Contreni emphasised the contributions of the Carolingian Renaissance to literal exegesis (though he notes the allegorical significance of numbers): these contributions were doubtless of great importance, but do they represent the predominant manner of understanding the Bible in the medieval period (de Lubac 1959–64; Contreni 1995: 733–4, 739)? Historians of medieval literature and art cannot avoid talking about symbolism, of course.

HISTORIOGRAPHY

One of the best analyses of the role of symbolism in medieval religion is a book by an art historian, Émile Mâle, published at the end of the nineteenth century:

very dated, no doubt, as a study of Gothic cathedrals but still valuable for an understanding of medieval thought and religion (Mâle 1898 (1961)). In the Middle Ages, says Mâle, the world is regarded as a symbol (Mâle 1961: 29). '[I]n each being is hidden a divine thought; the world is a book written by the hand of God in which every creature is a word charged with meaning. The ignorant see the forms – the mysterious letters – understanding nothing of their meaning, but the wise pass from the visible to the invisible, and in reading nature read the thoughts of God. True knowledge, then, consists not in the study of things in themselves – the outward forms – but in penetrating to the inner meaning intended by God for our instruction' (Mâle 1961: 29). For instance, a nut could be taken to symbolise Jesus Christ: '"The green and fleshy sheath is His flesh, His humanity. The wood of the shell is the wood of the Cross on which that flesh suffered. But the kernel of the nut from which men gain nourishment is His hidden divinity."' (Mâle 1961: 30, citing Adam of St Victor, *Sequentiae*, col. 1433). Mâle devotes another chapter (Book 4, ch. I) to the symbolic correspondences found between the Old Testament and the New. In the age of 'the Gothic image', as in the Carolingian period, unifying the two Testaments was an important function of symbolism.

It is possible that Mâle influenced Johann Huizinga's remarkable account of the medieval symbolist mentality, since he too refers to the nut as symbol of Christ (Huizinga 1996: 239). In memorable paragraphs, Huizinga points out that

> almost every image could find a place in the huge, all encompassing mental system of symbolism. . . . They never forgot that everything would be absurd if it exhausted its meaning in its immediate function and form of manifestation . . . That insight is still familiar to us as an inarticulate feeling in those moments when the sound of rain on leaves or the light of a lamp on a table penetrates momentarily into a deeper level of perception than that serving practical thought and action. . . . In God, nothing empty or meaningless exists . . . everything originating in Him and finding meaning in Him also crystallised into thoughts articulated into words. And thus comes into being that noble and lofty idea of the world as a great symbolic nexus – a cathedral of ideas, the highest rhythmic and polyphonic expression of all that can be thought. . . . Symbolism created an image of the world more strictly unified by stronger connections than causal-scientific thought is capable of. . . . There is ample room in symbolic thought for an immeasurable variety of relationships among things, since anything with its individual qualities can be the symbol of yet other things, and may with one and the same quality, signify quite various other things. . . . Symbolic thought . . . permeates the idea of anything with heightened aesthetic and ethical value'.
>
> (Huizinga 1996: 235–6; 238–9)

Huizinga argued that the symbolic mode of thought was played out by the late Middle Ages (Huizinga 1996: 242, 247). Here he may have been influenced by his general conception of the period as one of decline. Ernst Gombrich argued that Huizinga (and most cultural historians of his time) believed that periods of cultural history each had an inner unity, a sort of centre-point with lines going out to the

Figure 15.1 The Marriage of Adam and Eve. Munich, Bayerische Staatsbibliothek, MS. Clm 146, fo. 4r..

different aspects of art, thought, and life: a *Zeitgeist* in effect (Gombrich 1969: 29). On this view, the later Middle Ages would be the last phase of a culture's life, and the symbolist mentality would necessarily be involved in the decline, together with everything else.

Obviously these old classics are not the only concentrated analyses of the symbolist modes of thought in medieval religion. One of the most systematic is that of M-D. Chenu. His essay on 'The Symbolist Mentality' argues that the twelfth century, in which the hard-edged logical methods of scholasticism were turning theology into a progressive scientific discipline, was also a creative age of symbolic thought (Chenu 1969: 99–145). He argues that two streams of symbolic thinking were intermingled. One derived from St Augustine of Hippo. He had analysed symbolism in terms of the human mind's use of signs. The other derived from the Pseudo-Dionysius, who emphasised the real relations of analogy between different things. As Chenu himself points out, both kinds of symbolic thought can be traced back to Neoplatonic inspiration, and 'in the twelfth century and throughout the whole of the Middle Ages, the two strains were continually crossed and are difficult to distinguish' (Chenu 1968: 119–28).

For our purposes, elaborate distinctions between different varieties of symbolism and between symbolism and allegory are probably inessential (Engemann 1997; Leisch-Kiesl 1997). A simple and workable conceptual framework would be the following. Symbol and allegory bring out perceived likenesses between distinct things. The symbol is not just a conventional sign of the symbolised, but is believed to share a real similarity with what it stands for. However, there is always a conventional element. The likeness can never be complete. If it were, symbol and symbolised would be just two items in the same class, two cases of the same thing. The conventional element consists in seeing the symbol as the symbolised. In some cases the element of convention is very considerable, as when the similarity is merely numerical. When Haymo of Auxerre makes the wedding on the *third* day a symbol of the Trinity and of the trio Faith, Hope, and Charity, convention predominates over similarity. In what is called allegory the proportion of convention to similarity also tends to be high. At the other end of the scale, the similarities between symbol and symbolised (whether the latter is real or perceived) are too far-reaching to be taken in at first glance. Exploration of them can be a source of creativity.

This seems to have been the case with the analogy between human marriage and the marriage of Christ and the Church, or the soul, or between the divine and human natures in Christ. Here symbolism penetrates the hard genres of scholastic theologians and canon lawyers, as an important and neglected book by Tomás Rincón has demonstrated in detail (Rincón-Pérez 1971). It was also the inspiration of a much better-known tradition of commentary on the Song of Songs (Matter 1990, 1992). As we shall see shortly, the symbolism of marriage was also a force capable of transforming the social life of Europe.

We have moved forward in historiographical time from Mâle through Huizinga to Chenu. Analysis of medieval religious symbolism has been taken further by contemporary scholars. George Holmes has shown how it was combined with realism in a new kind of pictorial and literary narrative around the turn of the thirteenth and fourteenth centuries.

> The essence of the new narrative was the combination of several separate characteristics. First, a limited grasp of spatial perspective of a distinctly pragmatic kind, . . . intended to give both buildings and figures a fairly shallow space within which they could be placed to front or rear realistically. Second, a highly developed capacity for drawing figures with roundness and weight, especially when they were heavily clothed with folded draperies. Third, a surface design which gave paintings patterns emphasizing the main features of the action which the painting was portraying, for example the emphasis on the direction of the movement of the figures by the patterns of lines in the partially realistic landscape. Fourth, a constant awareness of the allegorical, symbolical, or figural significance of the subjects of the paintings so that, for example, the scene of *Wedding at Cana* might be placed above the *Lamentation* over the dead body of Christ, as it is in Giotto's Arena series, because Christ's miraculous conversion of water into wine foreshadowed the eucharistic conversion of bread and wine into his body and blood as a result of the passion.
>
> (Holmes 1986: 209–10)

Holmes draws a parallel between Giotto and Dante. The poet too combined 'realism and symbolic suggestion' (Holmes 1986: 262).

Some of the most interesting ideas about symbolism have come out of gender history. Caroline Walker Bynum has suggested that there was an asymmetry between the use of gender symbolism by male and female writers. The symbolism of 'gender reversal' made a powerful point for men. For instance, 'Richard Rolle underlined his conversion and his rejection of family by fashioning hermit's clothing for himself out of two of his sister's dresses' (Bynum 1991: 36). Male biographers of women use the same kind of symbolism, so that this description of women as 'virile' is a spiritual compliment (Bynum 1991: 38). On the other hand, '[w]omen either describe themselves as truly androgynous (that is, they use male and female images without a strong sense of a given set of personality characteristics going with the one or the other gender) or as female (bride, lover, mother)' (Bynum 1991: 39). This thesis may need more testing but it is undoubtedly elegant and attractive.

The role of gender reversal in symbolism has also been explored by Barbara Newman. She points out that in the tradition of bridal mysticism the monk had to play the female role: Christ is bridegroom, the monk is bride. Female mystical writers do not necessarily take on the same female role, for 'some women forged a more complicated, less stereotypical way that allowed them a wider emotional range' (Newman 1995: 138). They adopted the language of *fin'amour*, courtly love, and took on the role of the *amie*. 'Like the bride in the Song of Songs tradition, the *amie* is already part of a couple and thus to some degree fulfilled in love. But her role is more heroic and uncertain, less maternal and nurturing' (Newman 1995: 145).

These recent studies of symbolism use the language of art- or literary criticism. They give medieval religious symbolism its due: it was a complex and sophisticated form of thought. To understand it, the historian must not be afraid of sophisticated analysis.

CHRONOLOGY

How are all these individual scholarly insights to be synthesised? The foregoing discussion has been piecemeal and historiographical precisely because a convincing synthesis of the history of religious symbolism in the period is not yet possible. Nevertheless one may propose a rough and ready framework for others to improve. In the early medieval period, symbolism was all-pervasive but derivative in the intepretation of nature and scripture. It may be guessed that symbolic interpretation substantially outweighed literal interpretation in scriptural exegesis, at least in purely quantitative terms, but that most of the symbolism could be traced back to patristic writings – though we should not be surprised to find originality, especially with a writer such as Bede or in the later Carolingian Renaissance.

In the twelfth century, symbolism's prominence was relativised. The literal sense of the Bible was investigated much more seriously, most notably by Beryl Smalley's heroes, Andrew of St Victor and Herbert of Bosham, both influenced by Jewish scholarship (Smalley 1983, ch. iv; Smalley 1973: 83–5). The incipient scholastic method was deployed with startling intelligence. Greek and Arabic science began to put the understanding of the natural world on a new footing. Nevertheless symbolism did not lose out. It too entered a creative phase. It was Chenu's achievement to have brought this home. In addition to the aspects on which Chenu concentrated, particular mention should be made of the galvanisation of the bridal mysticism tradition by Bernard of Clairvaux.

In the thirteenth and fourteenth centuries, symbolism and literal understanding were in equilibrium to a remarkable degree. In the preaching of the friars it could not be said that either predominates. In a different genre, Pierre de Limoges's treatise *On the Moral Eye* may be symptomatic of its age. It is a combination of scientific analysis and moralisation (i.e. symbolic applications of the scientific exposition). Neither is perfunctory (d'Avray 1985: 279 and n. 4). The balance between realism and symbolism which Holmes found in Giotto and Dante fits this schema well.

The jury is still out on the question of whether 'symbolism was in decline' at the end of the period. As argued above, Huizinga's view may have been overinfluenced by his conviction that medieval civilisation had as it were an individual identity and that it was near the end of its time. An alternative model would be that symbolism continued to flourish until the sixteenth or seventeenth century. It may be tentatively suggested that the Protestant emphasis on the literal sense of the Bible may have penetrated Catholic attitudes also, at the expense of interest in symbolism and allegory. Furthermore, the development of serious empiricism in natural science may have crowded out symbolic moralisation. These are crude schemata, however, scaffolding to be kicked away as soon as possible by a more serious and sustained synthesis.

CAUSE AND EFFECT

Up to this point I have confined myself to interpretative description rather than analysis of causes and effects. After a generation of 'hermeneutic' anthropology, dominated by the approach of Clifford Geertz, one need not be apologetic about description. All the same, it is natural for a historian to proceed to the analysis of causes and effects.

To begin with causes: a banally obvious explanation of the prominence of symbolic thinking is its prominence in medieval Christianity's sacred book, the Bible. In Ephesians 5, for example, the union of husband and wife is a symbol of the union of Christ and the Church. In this passage the symbol (human marriage) seems to be part of the message as well as a vehicle for it. In the Old Testament, symbolic language movingly expresses feelings about the people of Israel. To give a single example: 'Go and cry in the ears of Jerusalem, saying: "Thus says the Lord: I have remembered you, pitying your youth and the love of your espousals, when you followed me in the desert, in a land that is not sown"' (Jeremiah 2: 2).

Even so, the symbolist mentality's genesis cannot be explained by the Judaeo-Christian tradition alone. The roots in pagan antiquity are deep (Doerrie 1969: 1–12). The search for meanings below the surface in Homer may have origins in the Orphic movement of the sixth century BC. The veiled meaning of the Delphic Oracle's answers or of the Eleusinian mysteries encouraged the idea that the literal

Figure 15.2 The Marriage Feast at Cana. Paris, Cathedral of Notre-Dame. Choir screen (detail) thirteenth century. Bildarchiv Foto Marburg.

surface stood for something beyond it (Doerrie 1969: 2–3). But it was in the post-Augustan period that the symbolist method came into its own, with the help of both Stoic and Neoplatonic philosophy. Analogy became the key to understanding the world. Surface manifestations were mined for hidden meaning. This is the thought-world of second- and third-century writers such as Plutarch, Gellius and Macrobius (Doerrie 1969: 4–7).

In one respect the symbolist mentality of the Middle Ages does owe more to Christian than to pagan antiquity. Historical symbolism is conspicuous by its absence from most pagan classical writers. The conception of Old Testament history as a type or foreshadowing of the New Testament cannot easily be traced back to classical pagan symbolic thought. Plutarch comes close to it with his parallel lives, but he is untypical (Doerrie 1969: 7).

The concept of the Old Testament as a type of the Christian era can be traced back to passages from the New Testament itself (Mâle 1961: 133–43), but the systematic creator of this tradition of interpretation would seem to have been Origen; from him, the train of influence has been traced via Hilary, Ambrose, Augustine, Gregory and Isidore into the mainstream medieval tradition (Mâle 1961: 134–8).

Why did patristic and medieval religious writers find the method so appealing? The symbolism of nature helped them to make sense of the world. More important, it helped them to make sense of the Bible, and especially the parts of the Old Testament that seemed otherwise irrelevant or even shocking to Christians (Hamilton

1986: 65–6). It was noted above how symbolism enabled Haymo of Auxerre to bring
the two Testaments together within an aesthetic synthesis. It provided an instrument
of great aesthetic power, whose appeal extended beyond the elite of highly educated
clergy. Sermons and vernacular literature brought the creations of symbolic thinking
to a wide public.

Did it hamper the development of a more rigorous literal exegesis? Probably
not much. It could be argued that literal exegesis did not make its breakthrough as
an intellectual discipline until the nineteenth century (if one leaves aside Bible
translation). It was then that historical exegesis on the one hand, and serious reflection
about literary forms on the other, opened up new perspectives into the meaning of
the Bible. Symbolic interpretation had been in retreat for centuries before this
happened.

Our discussion of causes has turned into speculation about effects. One effect
of symbolic thinking stands out, as different in kind from anything discussed so
far: the effect of marriage symbolism. The ultimate starting point of the story
should probably be the comparison between Christ's union with the Church and a
marriage in Ephesians chapter 5, but the proximate starting point would seem to be
St Augustine of Hippo. He left the Latin Church a strong and explicit doctine of
the indissolubility of marriage. He did not find indissolubility in Roman Law.
Symbolic reasoning seems to play a large part in his doctrine. If marriage represented
the union of Christ with the Church, it had to conform to what it symbolised. It had
to be unbreakable to perform its representative task properly (Kuiters 1959: 5–11;
also Reynolds 1994: ch. XIII; Gaudemet 1989, ch. XII, esp. 567–9). Augustine's
reasoning does not appear to have had much obvious effect for centuries. In the pre-
Carolingian period it is remarkable how little even churchmen seemed to worry about
indissolubility. In the Carolingian period and afterwards churchmen and others did
worry about it, but on the whole men still found it easy to change wives.

In the twelfth century this kind of symbolic reasoning is taken up by influential
scholastic theologians, notably Peter Lombard (Rincón-Pérez 1971: 179–89). The
crucial development was its impact on Lothario Segni, who became Pope Innocent
III at the end of the century. Innocent closed the main loophole through which men
had escaped from marriages in the preceding century: he reduced the number of
forbidden degrees of consanguinity and affinity from seven to four, and tightened
up the requirements for proof in annulment cases. He also took an unbending line
even with kings who sought an annulment: most notably with Philip Augustus of
France. One argument tried by the French king was that his marriage to Ingeborg
of Denmark had not been consummated and that Ingeborg intended to enter a
religious order. Innocent was sceptical on both counts, but he liked to tease out the
theoretical issues in concrete cases and took the trouble to explain why it was
consummation rather than consent that made marriage indissoluble:

> since, just as the mingling of the sexes denotes the union between the Word
> and human nature, since the Word was made flesh and dwelled among us, so
> too the consent of souls signifies the love between God and the just soul, since
> he who cleaves to God, is one spirit with him; and therefore just as the bond
> of union between the Word and human nature cannot be put apart, so too the

conjugal bond between husband and wife cannot be dissolved while they are alive, after they have been made one flesh through the mingling of the sexes; but just as the glue of charity between God and the soul is often dissolved, so too can a conjugal connection be put apart when only the consent of souls exists between the husband and wife.'

(Innocent, Ep. 182, PL 215, col. 1494; cf. Imkamp 1983: 224, n. 130)

Innocent was not convinced by the evidence for non-consummation and refused the annulment. The interest of the passage quoted is that it shows how much his thinking about indissolubility was bound up with symbolic reasoning.

Innocent was a politician, but he took ideas seriously. In this case (and others) convictions seem to have mattered more to him than expediency. (The unlucky queen's father was the king of Denmark, but what was Denmark compared with France?) After Innocent it was very difficult to get an annulment, and by comparison with the preceding period it seems to have been relatively uncommon to try. Probably Innocent's hard line in high-profile cases had sent a message. His changes in the marriage law had made it much harder to find a case. By this time the Church courts controlled marriage law, which certainly had a big impact on social practice. In this case at least, even though it took centuries, symbolism was a force capable not only of understanding but of changing the world.

REFERENCES

Primary sources

Adam of St Victor, *Sequentiae*, PL 196, cols. 1423–1534
Haymo of Auxerre, *Homilia XVIII, Dominica II post Epiphaniam*, PL 118, cols. 126–37
Innocent III, *Epistolae* no. 182, PL 215, cols. 1494–8

Secondary works

Barre, H. 1962, *Les Homéliaires Carolingiens de l'Ecole d'Auxerre. Authenticité – inventaire – tableaux comparatifs – initia*, Vatican City, Bibliotheca apostolica vaticana.
Beattie, J. 1964, repr 1970, *Other Cultures. Aims, Methods and Achievements in Social Anthropology*, London, Cohen and West.
Bynum, C.W. 1991, 'Women's Stories, Women's Symbols: A Critique of Victor Turner's Theory of Liminality', in *Fragmentation and Redemption. Essays on Gender and the Human Body in Medieval Religion*, New York, Zone Books, pp. 27–51.
Chenu, M.-D. 1957, *La Théologie comme science au XIIIe siècle* (third edition, Bibliothèque Thomiste, xxxiii), Paris, Librairie philosophique J. Vrin.
Chenu, M.-D. 1968, 'The Symbolist Mentality', in his collected papers, *Nature, Man, and Society in the Twelfth Century. Essays on New Theological Perspectives in the Latin West*, selected, edited and translated by J. Taylor and L.K. Little, Chicago, Chicago University Press, pp. 99–145.
Contreni, J. 1995, 'The Carolingian Renaissance: education and literary culture', in McKitterick, pp. 709–57.

d'Avray, D. 1985, *The Preaching of the Friars. Sermons diffused from Paris before 1350*, Oxford, The Clarendon Press.

de Lubac, H. 1959–64, *Exegèse médiévale. Les quatre sens de l'Écriture*, vols. i–iv, Paris, Aubier.

Doerrie, H. 1969, 'Spätantike Symbolik und Allegorese', in *Frühmittelalterliche Studien*, 3, pp. 1–12.

Engemann, J. 1997, art. 'Symbol', in *Lexikon des Mittelalters*, 8, Munich, Artemis Verlag, cols. 351–3.

Ganz, D. 1995, 'Theology and the organisation of thought', in McKitterick 1995, pp. 758–85.

Gaudemet, J. 1989, 'L'apport d'Augustin à la doctrine médiévale du mariage', reprinted in his collected papers, *Droit de l'Église et vie sociale au Moyen Âge*, Northampton, Variorum 1989, ch. XII.

Gimpel, J. 1977, *The Medieval Machine. The Industrial Revolution of the Middle Ages*, London, Wildwood House.

Gombrich, E. 1969, *In Search of Cultural History*, Oxford, The Clarendon Press.

Hamilton, B. 1986, *Religion in the Medieval West*, London, Edward Arnold.

Holmes, G. 1986, *Florence, Rome and the Origins of the Renaissance*, Oxford, The Clarendon Press.

Huizinga, J. 1996, *The Autumn of the Middle Ages*, Chicago, Chicago University Press.

Imkamp, W. 1983, *Das Kirchenbild Innocenz' III. (1198–1216)*, Päpste und Papsttum 22, Stuttgart, Hiersemann.

Kuiters, R. 1959, 'Saint Augustin et l'indissolubilité du mariage', *Augustiniana* 9, pp. 5–11.

Leisch-Kiesl, M. 1997, art. 'Symbol', Philosophy and Theology, *Lexikon des Mittelalters*, 8, Munich, Artemis Verlag, cols. 354–8.

Mâle, É. 1898, *L'Art religieux du xiiie siècle en France. Étude sur l'iconographie du moyen âge et sur ses sources d'inspiration,* Paris, trans. *The Gothic Image*, London: Fontana, 1961.

Matter, E. Ann, 1990, 1992, *The Voice of my Beloved. The Song of Songs in Western Medieval Christianity*, Philadelphia, University of Pennsylvania Press.

McKitterick, R. ed. 1995, *The New Cambridge Medieval History*, II, *c. 700–c. 900*, Cambridge, Cambridge University Press.

Newman, B. 1995, 'La mystique courtoise', in her collected papers, *From Virile Woman to Woman Christ. Studies in Medieval Religion and Literature*, Philadelphia, University of Pennsylvania Press, pp. 137–67.

Reynolds, P.L. 1994, *Marriage in the Western Church. The Christianization of Marriage during the Patristic and Early Medieval Periods*, Leiden, Brill.

Rincón-Pérez, T. 1971, *El Matrimonio, Misterio y Signo: Siglos IX–XIII*, Pamplona, Ediciones Universidad de Navarra, S.A.

Smalley, B. 1973, *The Becket Conflict and the Schools. A Study of Intellectuals in Politics*, Oxford, The Clarendon Press.

—— 1983, *The Study of the Bible in the Middle Ages*, Oxford, Basil Blackwell.

CHAPTER SIXTEEN

SEXUALITY IN THE MIDDLE AGES

Ruth Mazo Karras

'Sexuality in the Middle Ages' seems to many to be an oxymoron. Michel Foucault's influential *History of Sexuality* (1990) argued that sexuality itself was a construct of the bourgeois culture of the nineteenth century. Other scholars have taken up this theme: a book of essays on the ancient world was titled *Before Sexuality: The Construction of Erotic Experience in the Ancient Greek World* (Halperin *et al.* 1990). Medievalists too have argued that there was no such 'thing' as sexuality in the Middle Ages, in that there was no term like '*sexualitas*' that corresponded to the modern one, no unified field of discourse (Payer 1993). Medieval people, the argument goes, had sex, but they did not have sexuality, which is not just a series of sex acts but a category of human experience, a discourse about the body and what we do with it, a way of constructing meaning around behaviour. They had sex acts, but they did not have sexual identities.

But it is no oxymoron. The fact that the medieval languages did not have a single term for sexuality does not mean that they did not think about it; they certainly had discourses of the flesh and of desire. And even though medieval people did not have the same sexual identities we are familiar with in modern culture – 'homosexual' and 'heterosexual' are not classifications they used – they certainly had categories of identity based on sexual practice. The distinction between the virgin and the non-virgin, the chaste and the unchaste, the vowed celibate and the married, was as important and fundamental a distinction for medieval culture as the modern one between gay and straight. The distinction between virgin and non-virgin, inherited from patristic times, was especially difficult for women to evade; all women were defined by their sexual relation, or lack thereof, to men – even nuns were brides of Christ – and by the childbearing that would or would not result. Sexuality for medieval people was not, as it is for us, separable from procreation; even non-reproductive sex was distinguished primarily by its relation to the potential for reproduction. But that their understanding of sexuality was different does not mean that it did not exist.

It has become fashionable now to refer to the 'history of sexualities' rather than the 'history of sexuality,' in order to emphasize diversity. But the distinction between the two terms is not just the distinction between one norm and many alternatives; it is also a question of whether we are writing the history of a series of distinct identities or writing about the ways in which a given culture approached this whole area of life. This chapter will attempt the latter rather than the former: although it will discuss sexualities (sexual orientations or identities) it will focus mainly on the ways in which various individuals and groups within medieval society approached the problem of human sexual desire generally.

The study of sexuality in the Middle Ages raises some of the same problems with regard to sources as does the study of any other subject, but it also brings with it some of its own. In an area in which there were official rules and sanctions for violating them, people (especially women) might be reluctant to speak about either their feelings or their activities, and certainly not very likely to write about them. People in the Middle Ages expected the deeds of princes to be important to later generations of historians, but they would not have expected their sexual activities, and more especially their attitudes, to be important in the same way. The nature of the love of the twelfth-century English prince Richard the Lionheart for Philip Augustus of France is hotly debated by historians precisely because the medieval sources are oblique. Of course, conclusions about attitudes can be drawn from various kinds of sources. Attitudes can also be deduced from behaviour, but often the only time sexual behaviour is recorded is when it is considered to be transgressive. Social historians have found court records an extremely rich source, but a large segment of everyday life never found its way into court.

In the study of sexuality, historians have to be even more careful than in other areas not to project their own attitudes onto the period of study. Sexuality is something about which many people in the modern world care deeply. Medieval historians are accustomed to putting aside, or taking into account, their own deeply held feelings about religion, in order to recognize that medieval people may have approached the subject quite differently. We must do the same in the area of sexuality. In particular, we must beware of the modern notion that sex is ideally an act of mutual pleasure involving two active partners, a two-way street.

Two theories about medieval attitudes toward sex dominate current popular, if not academic, thinking about the subject. One is that the Church was simply opposed to sex, ruling it permissible only within marriage and even then highly suspect. Committed to celibacy but often struggling to maintain chastity themselves, churchmen denigrated any other option, and imposed their restrictive views on Christendom. The other is that people in the Middle Ages, largely ignoring the teachings of the Church, had an earthy, liberated, jolly attitude toward sex, later shattered by the Protestant Reformation and especially by Puritanism. Both of these models, as it happens, are valid descriptions of the way some medieval people thought. Neither explains medieval culture as a whole. Medieval approaches to sexuality were characterized by variety. John Baldwin (1994) has detailed five distinct, fully elaborated discourses on sexuality merely in one part of France in one short period around the year 1200: theological, classical/Ovidian, medical, romance, and bawdy *fabliau*, each with its own unique outlook. There are, however, some features that are shared among the wide range of discourses about sexuality that have survived from medieval culture, notably that when sex is sinful, it is sinful especially for women, but when it is joyous, it is joyous especially for men.

Even the body of the Church's teaching contained a variety of points of view about

Figure 16.1 Man reaches out for woman. The Bayeux Tapestry – eleventh century. Reproduced by special permission of the City of Bayeux.

sex. Many churchmen (for it was mostly men who wrote about this topic) followed the lead of the early Church Fathers St Jerome and St Ambrose, arguing that virginity was the highest calling. Although most such writers were careful not to criticize marriage directly – it was a good thing, but virginity was better – the clear implication was that procreation was a necessary evil (Brown 1988: 361–3). Some writers did, of course, criticize marriage directly. Jerome himself (1969) let fly a long diatribe against it, quoting lavishly from a (now lost) work attributed to the pagan author Theophrastus, and many medieval authors repeated Jerome's authoritative strictures. Jerome was writing in response to Jovinian, who had questioned the value of virginity; but his writings were taken out of context and used to urge men to celibacy by criticizing women in general and marriage in particular. The aggressive anti-matrimonial passages from Jerome's work had a long career within the monastery. The critique of marriage was not the same thing as the critique of sex, but because marriage was supposed to be the only permissible outlet for the sexual urges, the overlap was great.

Not only Jerome but a great many of the other writers whose discussions of sexual desire and behaviour have come down to us were writing not for lay people but for vowed celibates. Their criticism of sexual temptation as coming from the devil must be understood in that context. So must the misogyny that resulted from it. Celibate men blamed the women whom (in most cases) they held responsible for the temptation they felt, although this did not prevent some of them from having friendships with women whom they saw as transcending their gender.

Nor did negative teachings about sexual behaviour prevent monks from having deep emotional relationships with other men; whether these relationships should be called erotic, given the absence of direct evidence of physical lovemaking, is a matter of some dispute. On the one hand it is true that medieval letter-writers, poets, and other authors used linguistic conventions that are quite different from ours. Some medieval language that sounds erotic to us may well have been as formulaic as the salutations 'dear' and 'yours truly' in contemporary letter writing; other language may have expressed deeply felt but not sexual love. On the other hand, we should not demand that writing about same-sex friendships should unequivocally refer to physical consummation before it can be considered erotic, when we demand no such evidence to classify as erotic writing addressed by a man to a woman. We need to recognize, first, that a relationship can be erotic without genital contact – indeed, without either party consciously wanting to have genital contact – and, second, that it was the possibility of genital contact that was seen as threatening by medieval monks. It was possible for a man to have a chaste (which does not necessarily mean non-erotic) friendship with another man, but according to many monastic writers, not possible with a woman: the story found in many medieval sources of the man who wrapped his arm in his cloak before carrying his own mother across a river, because the touch of any woman would arouse uncontrollable lust, encapsulates this attitude (Tubach 1969: no. 3419).

The great concern, not to say obsession, celibates displayed about sexual behaviour can be seen in the early Middle Ages in the development of the penitentials, which were used by confessors in assigning penance. Sexual offences are a major focus of penitentials – more so than any other general category of offence. Though these texts have a complicated history, it is likely that they were in continuous use for centuries, and that their contents do reflect sexual practices, or at least what the confessors were realistically concerned would happen (Payer 1984). These penitentials censured all but heterosexual married sex in the missionary position (and even that was only permissible at certain times: Brundage 1987: 162).

By the high and late Middle Ages, the penitentials were replaced by a whole body of pastoral literature. This included model sermons and books of aids for preachers, collections of saints' lives and *exempla*, treatises on the Ten Commandments, on the Seven Deadly Sins and other elements of the faith, and manuals for confessors. Some of these texts were written in or translated into the vernacular and were intended for the use of the pious laity, both female and male; others were intended to instruct the clergy, especially those who preached. Even those texts intended for the laity (including some earlier penitentials translated into the vernacular) or for the use of those preaching to the laity, however, drew on ideas developed and transmitted within the monastery. Thus they placed more emphasis on sexual purity (chastity, abstinence) than they would have done had they been directed to the laity alone.

Not only material originally intended for monks but that directed at the secular clergy influenced the way the Church taught about sexuality to lay people. From the eleventh century onwards the Church had put an increasing emphasis on clerical celibacy. Prior to this time, officially or unofficially married priests had not been unusual. But with the reform movement, the Church made it clear that a priest could not be married. The Church held its representatives to a high standard of sexual purity. This meant, of course, that the priest was also not to engage in non-marital sexual relations. Pastoral literature frequently discusses the latter, mostly by illustrating the punishments awaiting the women involved. The blame for priests' sexual liaisons was often put on their concubines (perhaps 'priests' domestic partners' would be a better translation for *concubinae*, because many of them were not what we today might think of as mistresses but rather wives in all but name). In any case, *exempla* (stories intended for use in sermons) railed against the sinfulness of these women, equating them with prostitutes by calling them *meretrices sacerdotales* or 'priests' whores'. In placing the blame for the liaison on the female partner, these critiques set the tone for attitudes toward lay sexuality.

Although some writings by clerics emphasized the superiority of virginity over marriage more than did others, all would have agreed that there was a hierarchy in sexual behaviour. The only esteemed form of sexual behaviour was chastity – lifelong virginity, chaste widowhood, chastity within marriage. For those who were not called to chastity, sex within marriage was a respectable alternative; many churchmen agreed that marital sex was not sinful, even if procreation was not the goal, as long as nothing was done to impede the possibility of procreation. Outside marriage all sexual behaviour was illicit, but even here a distinction was often drawn between potentially procreative and non-procreative sex, the former less serious than the latter.

Clearly not all lay people accepted this hierarchy of sexual behaviour. The concern of pastoral literature to combat the mistaken notion that simple fornication (sexual relations between an unmarried man and an unmarried woman) was only a venial sin reflects the persistence of this notion. Illegitimacy rates, in those few cases where we can determine them, also indicate that whether considered right or wrong fornication was not an uncommon practice. A common punishment in Church courts in the late Middle Ages was 'abjuratio sub pena nubendi', forswearing on pain of marriage: a couple who fornicated were made to repeat marriage vows in the future tense. Under canon law, such vows, when followed by sexual intercourse, constituted valid and indissoluble marriage. Thus, if the fornicators were to repeat their offence, they would automatically be married. This was enforced more strictly in some places than in others. And the canon law, unlike for example the common law of England, did rule that a child born out of wedlock became legitimate upon the subsequent marriage of its parents. These examples indicate that premarital sex was not treated as seriously in practice as in theory. However, *pre-marital* and *non-marital* are not the same thing; a parish priest might be willing to look leniently on a couple who jumped the gun, as long as they had the intention of regularizing their union at some point, but that does not mean that casual sex was the rule.

If we look beyond the teachings of the Church, as expressed in sermons and pastoral literature, to other types of medieval discourse, we find less criticism and more acceptance of non-marital sex – at least acceptance of the masculine partner's behaviour. The twelfth-century lyric poetry that has given rise to the label 'courtly love' is a good example. In the poetry of the Occitan troubadours, and in Andreas Capellanus's *De arte honeste amandi* (often known in English as *The Art of Courtly Love*) the men are seeking the love of an idolized (and idealized) woman. There is some disagreement among scholars about the nature of that love: clearly it is erotic, but is there really an intent to consummate the desire? John Benton (1968) argued that there could not be, because the women involved were generally married, and adultery was so seriously frowned upon in medieval society. This situation, however, merely reveals how differently sex was treated for women and for men. An adulterous woman brought shame on her husband and his family, and a cuckolded man had to avenge it; even in the world of courtly love men did not laugh off the possibility of other men's having sex with their wives. However, the adulterer – the man, whether married or not, who had sex with a married woman – was not shamed. He could, in fact, add to his renown through the deed, if he were not killed by the wronged husband.

The example of love lyric illustrates how, when looking at sex in the Middle Ages, we must consider the different partners to the act, not just the act itself. The prevalent late-twentieth-century Western view of sex considers the two parties involved in coitus both to be doing the same thing. 'John had sex with Jane', 'Jane had sex with

Figure 16.2 Nun harvesting penises. *Le roman de la rose.* Paris. Bibliothèque Nationale de France, MS. Fr. 25526, fo. 196r.

John', and 'Jane and John had sex' are all ways of saying basically the same thing with a minor shift of emphasis, and even the terms 'screw' and 'fuck' are now used of a couple, or with a woman as subject, as well as with a man as subject. For medieval people, sexual intercourse was not something that a couple did, it was something that a man did. He did it to someone – usually a woman, sometimes another man. 'Futuo', 'foutre', and 'swiven' are all transitive verbs, used almost exclusively with a masculine subject. Medical treatises *On Coitus* dealt almost exclusively with male physiology and experience. The man, then, is the one whose action is important, and to be the actor or the acted-upon in sexual intercourse makes a big difference. Thus, when we ask whether a particular sex act – courtly adultery, for example – was socially acceptable in the Middle Ages, we need to think not of the *act* as acceptable or not, but of the behaviour of each partner in the act separately. Indeed, when assessing the morality of a sex act, medieval theologians or canonists looked to the intentions of the partners involved, so that the 'same act' could have very different ethical ramifications for the two parties. This moral teaching reinforced the tendency to treat sexual relations as unequal transactions and to apply a double standard.

In the 'courtly love' model, at least from the lyrics written by men that scholars have classified as part of this genre, the man is seeking sexual solaces from his beloved. There is little hint of sexual desire on the part of the woman. She is to grant his solaces based on the depth of his suffering and her pity for him, or on his character and moral worth, or on his prowess in battle. She may choose among several potential lovers, but she is not to choose on the basis of her individual desire, nor does she ever seek out a lover. The woman is an object to be achieved. Indeed, as such she may in fact be a stand-in for a male figure; the practice of young men at court writing love poetry to the wife of their lord may have provided a way for them to praise him through praising one of his possessions. Women wrote love lyrics too, and here they appear more active; but, though they may choose the one for whom they feel love, they do not seek him out. When Castellozza does address a poem to her 'friend' she notes: 'I know this is a fitting thing for me, / though everybody says it isn't proper / for a lady to plead her case with a knight, / or to make such long speeches to him' (Bruckner *et al*. 1995: 19). Not everyone accepted the norm of masculine activity and feminine passivity, but it remained a norm nonetheless.

The relation of the extant body of lyrics to cultural practices of love and sex is problematic. The same is true of other sorts of literature, for example the French *fabliaux* of the late twelfth and thirteenth centuries and their analogues in other European literatures. It is clear that they do not exhibit the same censorious attitude toward sex that many of the teachings of the Church present. Sex in the *fabliaux* may be fun, or it may be funny, but it is not shameful. Moreover, the *fabliaux* present women as well as men as enjoying sex: wives who do not get satisfaction from their husbands seek it elsewhere, often with priests, and girls who are so innocent they don't even know what they are doing nonetheless find themselves enjoying intercourse. Several features of the sexual world of the *fabliaux* are noteworthy. One is the focus on genitalia and lack of attention to other body parts. Compared with modern culture's eroticization of the breast (Yalom 1997), the *fabliaux*' (and other medieval literature's) concentration on the genitalia is striking. Rather than eroticize the whole female body and concentrate on foreplay, medieval texts present both men and women as getting their pleasure from the act of penetration of penis into vagina – the act that the man does to the woman. When women enjoy sex in this literature, what they enjoy is the penis. The misogyny implicit (or explicit) in many examples of the *fabliau* genre, however, makes it unlikely that the women represented there are expressing the authentic voices of medieval women.

At least the *fabliaux* show women enjoying sex. But do they do this in a spirit of rough and ready equality, or do they do it to project masculine desire onto women and make them share equally in the blame of sexual transgression? The fear of pregnancy is absent from this body of literature (as from many others), an indication that what we are seeing here are not real-life situations between women and men but rather an unreal world in which sex has no consequences other than the just punishment of a stingy or abusive husband. Similarly, other discourses which promoted sex as natural and enjoyable focus largely on men's enjoyment. Clerical fulminations against the attitude that it was all right to go to the brothel for a good time are evidence for the existence of this attitude, and also imply that the sexual good time is to be had by men. Discourses that condemned sex as sinful, however, concentrated on women more than, or at least as much as, men.

How well did the kinds of relationships depicted in imaginative literature correspond to those that existed in reality? The concern in literature about priests seducing the wives and daughters of their parishioners is certainly reflected in the records of prosecutions. Even though sexual offenses were to be tried in Church courts, for example, the City of London in the fifteenth century arrested and tried priests for adultery and fornication, perhaps less out of concern for the general level of morality than out of a sense of defending citizens from the depredations of the clergy. Not all priests, to be sure, were as randy as those of the *fabliaux*, but the literary image corresponded with (or gave rise to) an image in the minds of many medieval people as well.

The casualness with which adultery among the nobility was treated in literature also has a complicated relation to actual practice. Certainly aristocratic men
commonly had extramarital liaisons. They had more or less consensual access to many
women of lower status in the household. Long-term mistresses with families of
illegitimate children (some legitimized, like the Beaufort descendants of John
of Gaunt, from whom the Tudor dynasty derived its genealogical claim to the English
throne) were far from infrequent. In a culture and social stratum in which marriages
were commonly arranged, such men did not necessarily expect to find in a spouse a
fulfilling life companion. Women could not expect to do so either, and if they did
expect it, they were often disappointed. The double standard of adultery, however,
governed aristocratic women, and such liaisons as they had had to be much more
discreet than those of their husbands.

We have far less literature that depicts the daily lives and loves of the most typical
medieval people – the peasants – than we do for the aristocracy, or even townspeople.
However, though we have little access to their feelings, it is still possible to know
something about their behaviour. Records from English manorial courts of fines for
leyrwite (a penalty for fornication, paid to the lord of a female serf) indicate that there
was a fair amount of pre-marital or non-marital intercourse going on. Depositions
in marriage cases in the Church courts indicate that not everyone saw sex as necessarily leading to marriage, but that when a couple were planning to marry it would
not be unusual for them to anticipate by having sex. In the sixteenth and seventeenth
centuries rates of bridal pregnancy indicate that pre-marital intercourse was quite
common (Wrightson 1982: 84-6). Because the keeping of parish records had not yet
begun, we do not have this same information for the Middle Ages, but it was
probably rather common then too.

Of course, the aristocracy and the peasantry did not restrict themselves to intra-
group sexual relations. Given the nature of power in medieval society, and given the
idea of sex as something that men did to women, it can sometimes be difficult to
distinguish consensual sex between a man of higher status and a woman of lower
status from rape. Kathryn Gravdal (1991: 104-21) has shown how the literary genre
of the *pastourelle* naturalizes rape. Cross-class rape becomes the literary expression of
social dominance. The privilege of the nobleman or the knight is assumed, and the
consent of the peasant woman is irrelevant. In some poems the shepherdess consents
and in others she does not, but the outcome is the same. The twelfth-century writer
Andreas Capellanus (1941: 150) could advise his reader, 'And, if you should by some
chance fall in love with some of [the peasants'] women, be careful to puff them up
with lots of praise and then, when you find a convenient place, do not hesitate to
take what you seek and embrace them by force. For you can hardly soften their
outward inflexibility so far that they will grant you their embraces quietly or permit
you to have the solaces you desire unless you first use a little compulsion as a
convenient cure for their shyness.' Even if this was not meant to be taken seriously
as actual advice, it still reinforces the notion that sex is always something that an
active partner does to a passive partner; if that is the case the consent of the passive
partner does not matter all that much.

Perhaps because of this blurring of the line between voluntary and forced sex,
women were often suspected or accused of complicity in their own rapes. A popular

Figure 16.3 Couples feasting while bathing. Valerius Maximus, *Facta et dicta memorabilia.* Leipzig, Universitätsbibliothek, MS. 11b, Bd. 2, fo. 269r.

medieval *exemplum* tells of a woman who brought an accusation of rape before a judge. He ordered the accused rapist to pay her a bag of silver. After the woman left the court, the judge told the defendant to follow her and take the silver from her. She, however, fought tooth and nail and refused to let him take it. The judge then ruled that if she had fought as hard for her chastity as for the silver, she would not have been raped (Tubach 1969: no. 4035). However, this view was not universal. Consent and free will were important issues in medieval thought, and by the late thirteenth century canon lawyers were beginning to consider it a sexual offence to use lies and fraud, or non-violent coercion, to erode the woman's free choice (Brundage 1982: 147).

There are relatively few court cases involving rape that can shed light about medieval attitudes toward it. Even in modern society where having been raped is not as shameful for a woman as it was in medieval times, and where there are legal curbs on the humiliation of the victim, the crime of rape still goes underreported. This must have been so *a fortiori* in the Middle Ages. A case from London in 1321 involving an eleven-year-old girl who brought a rape accusation which eventually failed on technical grounds indicates something of the difficulties that women had in bringing a successful claim (Cam 1968: 87–92). The defendant, the merchant Reymund de Limoges, claimed that she had consented, but it seems more likely that he simply saw her consent as irrelevant: he desired her, didn't care whether or not she desired him, and based on their relative social standing (she was the daughter of a petty craftsman) correctly thought he could get away with rape. In Dijon, an epidemic of gang rape in the fifteenth century may indicate the use of rape as a mechanism of social control by, for example, young men who objected to the marriage of an older man with a younger woman, or it may indicate simply a desire to take their sex where they could find it with – they thought, and often they were right – impunity (Rossiaud 1988).

Earlier in the Middle Ages, indeed, there was not really any legal offence that corresponded to the modern idea of rape. It was an offence against canon law (which was not yet codified) to have sex outside marriage; it was an offence against secular law to commit an act of violence; but it did not necessarily make a difference that that violence was sexual. Laws about '*raptus*', at least in the early Middle Ages, seem to refer to the abduction of, and sexual intercourse with, a woman in order to marry her without her father's or other guardian's permission. If this is what was at issue, then the woman's consent did not matter. Literature, such as Chrétien de Troyes's romances, presents rape as a crime, and a crime against the female victim, but more important than the woman's suffering is the opportunity for the conflict between the rapist and the gallant knight who rescues or avenges her. Later legal records make it clear that forced sexual intercourse had become a crime apart from the issue of abduction and marriage. In late medieval Venice, for example, the rhetoric about rape focused on the assaulted women rather than on the wrong done to their husbands and fathers. The line between forced and voluntary sex still remained blurred, however, since the woman was taken as passive in either case. As Guido Ruggiero (1985: 90) concludes about Venice, rape may have been seen 'as merely an extension of an exploitative sexuality that was quite common and not particularly troubling'.

The attitude that sex was something that one partner did to another was also reflected in official attitudes toward prostitution. In the later Middle Ages, many towns in France, Germany, Italy, and England established municipal brothels in which prostitutes could legally work. The justification given for condoning the sex trade was usually that it would prevent greater sin by protecting respectable women. Masculine sexuality was seen as too powerful to be controlled. It was therefore a question of finding the outlet for it that would cause the least harm to the wider society. One group of women could be sacrificed to the protection of the purity of another group. This view of the male sex drive as an irresistible force which needed to find an outlet would be understandable in a Victorian context where respectable women were not thought to experience sexual desire or pleasure, but less so in a medieval context when women's desires were seen as even stronger than men's. It is explicable, however, by the situation in which men were seen as active, women as passive. The existence of prostitutes and the legal regulation of prostitution also served as a control on the sexual behaviour of all women. Although medieval legal thinkers and people generally were very well aware that prostitution was a trade and its practitioners were paid, it was not the exchange of money that was thought to be the essence of prostitution, but rather the public and indiscriminate use of sexuality. This meant that any woman who behaved in what were considered inappropriate ways (usually but not always sexual) risked being classified with the commercial prostitutes. The prostitute was simply the extreme case of a tendency in all women.

The connection of sexual lust with the feminine, which was found in pastoral literature and elsewhere, and the tendency of all women to promiscuity or prostitution if not kept under strict control, would seem to stand in contrast to the idea of the woman as the passive partner who has something done to her. Yet just because women were seen as passive does not mean that they did not have desire. One medieval discourse in which they appear both as passive and as desiring is medicine. Many medieval writers accepted to some degree the Galenic theory that both a male and a female seed were required for conception (not all, however: the thirteenth-century Dominican scientist Albertus Magnus, adhering strictly to Aristotelian doctrine, was one who did not). They did not know of the existence of the ovum (or indeed the sperm cell), nor did they clearly articulate the position that a woman had semen analogous to men's, but they did believe that there was some sort of female sperm which gave pleasure in its emission, and had some influence on conception and the development of the fetus. This view worked to the benefit of married women's sexual pleasure, since men believed that to conceive their wives had to reach orgasm, although it could also work to vindicate rape: if the woman conceived, she must have consented. (This scientific misunderstanding has resurfaced in the state legislatures of at least two states of the USA in the 1990s, as legislators argue that permitting abortion in cases of rape is not necessary, because a woman cannot conceive without an orgasm which she presumably would not have if raped.) Conversely, it might have led to an attempt to prevent (or at least not to promote) female orgasm in sexual encounters where conception was not desired.

Medieval medical thinkers, then, were far from seeing women as sexually anesthetic, as became the fashionable medical view in Victorian times. Indeed, although they concentrated mainly on the bodies of men (except with regard to pregnancy and childbirth), medical writers saw sex as a normal appetite in both women and men, and suggested that chastity in either sex might not be healthful. One of the concerns of medical writers was to determine how best to obtain pleasure. This is true of writings by scholastics, an example of how multiple discourses within the same culture could reveal a wide variety of attitudes about sex – even within the same environment, or within the same individual. Even with sexual reciprocity in many medical texts, however, one partner still appeared as passive. Women could have orgasm, but they had it as a result of penetration: they were thought to derive their pleasure from the male partner's ejaculation into the womb.

The notion of reciprocity in sexuality also appears in the notion of the 'marriage debt'. This doctrine, based on 1 Corinthians 7: 3–4, held that either spouse was obligated to have sexual intercourse with the other upon demand. It was not a sin to render the debt, even if the time or place of intercourse was otherwise forbidden, because in doing so the rendering partner kept the demanding partner from the greater sin of adultery. The theologians and canon lawyers who discussed the marriage debt did so in terms which implied gender equality. Yet it is important to recognize that this theoretical equality did not translate into the practical. Women were urged not to fast too much, and sometimes even encouraged to adorn themselves, in order to be attractive to their husbands. Men were not encouraged to do the same, and indeed, they were exempted from rendering the debt if fasting or other penitential practice had undermined their potency. Because women were thought to be shyer about demanding the debt, husbands were to render the debt to their wives when they thought they needed it, even though they did not explicitly ask. This advice could represent a sensitivity to women's needs, but as Dyan Elliott (1996: 173) argues it also represented a transferring of female initiative back to the husband. Some medieval thinkers, the fifteenth-century friar Bernardino of Siena prominent among them, acknowledged that the debt was basically demanded of the wife by the husband, and even provided strategies by which the wife could deflect the demand.

The idea that sex was something that one partner did to another greatly influenced medieval views of same-sex relations. Most of what has been said above has discussed relations between men and women, as that is what most of the medieval texts discuss. It is important to understand that when they do refer to people of the same gender having sexual relations, they are not thinking of them as 'homosexuals' or 'lesbians'. Medieval concepts of sexual identity were not usually focused on the gender of one's partner. Rather they were most often focused on whether one played the active or the passive role. A man who was the penetrator was doing basically the same thing, whether he was doing it to a man or a woman. Arnold of Verniolles, questioned by the Inquisition in Pamiers in the fourteenth century, said that he had sex with boys because he was afraid of getting leprosy if he had sex with women (Goodich 1979: 106). Even if this was a rationalization on his part, it is an indication that sexual outlets for men were considered somewhat interchangeable. A woman who by using 'instruments' or an enlarged clitoris penetrated another woman was not a 'lesbian' (a term unknown in the Middle Ages, at least in this context) but was acting the male part. Her partner, as a passive woman, transgressed neither sexual nor gender norms.

This is not to say that the authorities in the Middle Ages did not object to same-sex sexual relations. The punishment for sodomy in the later Middle Ages could be death. But what seems to have bothered some medieval people most about it was not the use of an improper or unnatural method of intercourse – after all, heterosexual anal intercourse could be called sodomy too, but people do not seem to have been punished as sodomites for practising it – but rather the gender inversion implied in making a man the passive partner, or a woman the active one. Gender inversion was not the only issue, however: Mark Jordan (1997: 155) argues that it seems not to have been a concern for Thomas Aquinas, whose writings on sodomy as unnatural have been extremely influential over the centuries. In some places, for example fifteenth-century Florence, a model somewhat like that known from classical Athens seems to have emerged, in which it was considered normal for a male to be the passive partner as long as he was under age. Passivity in a boy was not as subversive as it was in a man, and it was only the 'inveterate' sodomite who continued in his preference for passivity and allowed other men to penetrate him as an adult who came in for the worst of condemnation. The most common pattern in Florence was for a man below the normal age of marriage to be the active partner (labeled a sodomite) and a teenager the passive partner (Rocke 1996).

To say that medieval erotic relations between men cannot be considered the same as modern 'homosexuality' and that the men involved cannot be considered 'gay' does not mean that these relations involved only a series of discrete acts that had no impact on the actors' inner life. Certainly many medieval men had passionate feelings about other men that they expressed in writing and possibly also physically. They undoubtedly would have been able to articulate a preference for sex with men over sex with women. The way they experienced desire for other men may have been similar to the way gay men today do, or at least no more dissimilar than the experiences of male/female couples in the Middle Ages and today. Sometimes, as in the Middle English poem *Cleanness*, men were said to enjoy sex with other men, without reference to role differentiation (Keiser 1997). More often, however, the dominant discourses of medieval culture did not put the question in those terms. Men were said to enjoy the act of sodomy, either as the active (generally with boys) or passive partner. John Boswell (1980: 29–30) argued that 'boy' was used simply as a diminutive in the same way as grown women are still referred to as 'girls', especially in sexual contexts. However, actual court records from late medieval Florence indicate that in the place in medieval Europe where the documentation on this subject is richest, 'boy' did mean a teenager. Certainly there were relationships between men of the same age cohort, but even if it was only a stereotype, the active adult male/passive boy distinction reinforces the medieval notion of sex as not involving an egalitarian relation.

The importance of sex as something that someone does to someone else (that something being penetration) is responsible for the near total erasure of sex between women from the historical record of the Middle Ages. There is quite a range of things that two women can do to give each other erotic pleasure, but by medieval standards many of those things did not count as sex. We find, then, notably few prosecutions of women for same-sex acts and far less comment on their practices than on those of men. Once again, there are plenty of literary expressions of love from one woman to another, and these do belong in the realm of sexuality, but they were not, in the Middle Ages, necessarily thought of as connected to sex acts. Bernadette Brooten (1996) has argued that there was, in the ancient world, a category of people, both men and women, who were seen as having a long-term homoerotic orientation. The evidence that 'women-loving women' in the Middle Ages were thought of as such a category is not at all apparent.

Sexuality is more than the sum of acts; it is even more than the sum of those acts that were written about and therefore entered into discourse. It is the way in which society creates meaning for both acts and desires. If we are looking for evidence of genital contact we must conclude that the Middle Ages did not recognize a 'lesbian' sexuality. There are extant writings, however, that indicate women's love for each other, and men's love for each other, as well as the love of men for women and women for men: poetry, saints' lives and other biographies that tell of friendship and love, letters, and similar texts. These texts do not refer specifically to genital acts; they may involve people who never performed, or even contemplated actually performing, genital acts. Yet they are still part of the general field of sexuality. Sexuality is where sex acts and the discourses of love and desire meet.

If one takes this broader sense of 'sexuality' one might argue that sexuality was as important a fact of life in the Middle Ages as it was in the nineteenth century when Foucault claims there was an outpouring of discourse about it. Certainly the issue of genital sex was a troubling enough one for medieval people, and one which gave rise to extensive discussion in a variety of fora. Whether or not one engaged in sex at all was certainly a significant determinant of personal identity in the Middle Ages, and I would suggest that 'prostitute' also meets all the criteria for a sexual identity, even if 'homosexual' in the Middle Ages does not. And if one moves beyond the question of what sex acts one engaged in to the issue of what was the nature of erotic desire and what role it had to play in human life, this was a central question for medieval thinkers and writers of all sorts, who gave almost as wide a range of answers as we do today.

REFERENCES

Andreas Capellanus (1941). *The Art of Courtly Love*. Trans. John J. Parry. New York: Columbia University Press.

Baldwin, John W. (1994). *The Language of Sex: five voices from Northern France around 1200*. Chicago: University of Chicago Press.

Benton, John (1968). 'Clio and Venus: an historical view of courtly love.' In *The Meaning of Courtly Love*. F.X. Newman, ed. Albany: State University of New York Press.

Bloch, R. Howard (1991). *Medieval Misogyny and the Invention of Western Romantic Love*. Chicago: University of Chicago Press.

Boswell, John (1980). *Christianity, Social Tolerance, and Homosexuality: gay people in western Europe from the beginning of the Christian era to the fourteenth century*. Chicago: University of Chicago Press.

Brooten, Bernadette J. (1996) *Love Between Women: early christian responses to female homoeroticism*. Chicago: University of Chicago Press.

Brown, Peter (1988). *The Body and Society: men, women, and sexual renunciation in early Christianity*. New York: Columbia University Press.

Bruckner, Matilda Tomaryn, Laurie Shepard, and Sarah White, ed. and trans. (1995). *Songs of the Women Troubadours*. New York: Garland.

Brundage, James A. (1987). *Law, Sex, and Christian Society in Medieval Europe*. Chicago: University of Chicago Press.

—— (1982). 'Rape and Seduction in the Medieval Canon Law.' In *Sexual Practices and the Medieval Church*. Vern L. Bullough and James Brundage, eds. Buffalo, New York: Prometheus Books.

Bullough, Vern L., and James A. Brundage (1996). *Handbook of Medieval Sexuality*. New York: Garland.

Burns, E. Jane (1993). *Bodytalk: when women speak in old French literature*. Philadelphia: University of Pennsylvania Press, 1993.

Cadden, Joan (1993). *Meanings of Sex Difference in the Middle Ages: medicine, science, and culture*. Cambridge: Cambridge University Press.

Cam, Helen M., ed. (1968). *The Eyre of London, 14 Edward II, A.D. 1320*. Selden Society, vols. 85–86. London: Bernard Quaritch.

Carter, John Marshall (1985). *Rape in Medieval England: an historical and sociological study*. Lanham, Maryland: University Press of America.

Elliott, Dyan (1993). *Spiritual Marriage: sexual abstinence in medieval wedlock*. Princeton: Princeton University Press.

—— 'Bernardino of Siena versus the Marriage Debt.' In Murray and Eisenbichler (1996). 168–200.

Foucault, Michel (1990). *The History of Sexuality*. Harmondsworth: Penguin.

Goodich, Michael (1979). *The Unmentionable Vice: Homosexuality in the Later Medieval Period*. Santa Barbara and Oxford: ABC- Clio.

Gravdal, Kathryn (1991). *Ravishing Maidens: writing rape in medieval French literature and law*. Philadelphia: University of Pennsylvania Press.

Halperin, David M., John J. Winkler, and Froma I. Zeitlin (1990). *Before Sexuality: the construction of erotic experience in the Ancient Greek world*. Princeton: Princeton University Press.

Hanawalt, Barbara (1998). *Of Good and Ill Repute: gender and social control in Medieval England*. New York: Oxford University Press.

Helmholz, R.H. (1974). *Marriage Litigation in Medieval England*. London: Cambridge University Press.

Jacquart, Danielle, and Claude Thomasset (1988). *Sexuality and Medicine in the Middle Ages*. Trans. Matthew Adamson. Princeton: Princeton University Press.

Jerome (1969). *Adversus Jovinianum libri duo*. In *Patriologia Latina*, ed. J.-P. Migne. Vol. 23. Reprinted Turnhout: Brepols. Cols. 222–352.

Jordan, Mark D. (1997). *The Invention of Sodomy in Christian Theology*. Chicago: University of Chicago Press.

Karras, Ruth Mazo (1996). *Common Women: prostitution and sexuality in medieval England*. New York: Oxford University Press.

Keiser, Elizabeth B. (1997). *Courtly Desire and Medieval Homophobia: the legitimation of sexual pleasure in cleanness and its contexts*. New Haven: Yale University Press.

Matter, E. Ann (1986). 'My Sister, My Spouse: Woman-Identified Women in Medieval Christianity.' *Journal of Feminist Studies in Religion* 2: 81–93.

Murray, Jacqueline, and Konrad Eisenbichler, eds. (1996). *Desire and Discipline: sex and sexuality in the premodern west*. Toronto: University of Toronto Press.

Otis, Leah Lydia (1985). *Prostitution in Medieval Society: the history of an urban institution in Languedoc*. Chicago: University of Chicago Press.

Payer, Pierre J. (1993). *The Bridling of Desire: views of sex in the later Middle Ages*. Toronto: University of Toronto Press.

—— (1984). *Sex and the Penitentials: the development of a sexual code, 550–1150*. Toronto: University of Toronto Press.

Rocke, Michael (1996). *Forbidden Friendships: homosexuality and male culture in Renaissance Florence*. New York: Oxford University Press.

Rossiaud, Jacques (1988). *Medieval Prostitution*. Trans. Lydia G. Cochrane. Oxford: Basil Blackwell.

Ruggiero, Guido (1985). *The Boundaries of Eros: sex crime and sexuality in Renaissance Venice*. New York: Oxford University Press.

Tubach, Frederic C. (1969). *Index Exemplorum: a handbook of medieval religious tales*. F.F. Communications No. 204. Helsinki: Suomalainen Tiedeakatemia.

Wrightson, Keith (1982). *English Society 1580–1680*. New Brunswick: Rutgers University Press.

Yalom, Marilyn (1997). *A History of the Breast*. New York: Knopf.

CHAPTER SEVENTEEN

SIN, CRIME, AND THE PLEASURES OF THE FLESH: THE MEDIEVAL CHURCH JUDGES SEXUAL OFFENCES

———◆·■·◆———

James A. Brundage

The sexual behavior of Christians worried medieval Church authorities. Christian moralists disapproved of all types of extramarital sex, including premarital intercourse, adultery, concubinage, and prostitution. They sternly prohibited sexual contacts of any description between persons of the same gender. Church fathers agreed that masturbation was immoral and forbade Christians to indulge in the practice. They feared that even unconscious sexual arousal during sleep might be sinful. Sexual activity of any kind that involved priests, monks, nuns, and others who had taken vows of celibacy posed a perennially embarrassing problem for the Church's leaders. Even sexual activity by married couples presented moralists with a constant stream of problems. Church doctrine, to be sure, permitted married Christians to have sexual relations with one another, but only in moderation and for the proper reasons. Since they also believed that sexual passion should have no place in Christian marriage, the Fathers of the Church fretted about the frequency and timing of marital intercourse. Church authorities consequently prohibited married couples from indulging in sex during a large part of the year and even tried to prescribe the posture in which Christian couples could properly indulge their libidinous desires (Brundage 1987). This chapter will examine the ways in which medieval Church authorities tried to implement these teachings and to regulate the sexual activities of the Christian faithful.

From early in its history, leaders of the Christian Church distinguished two overlapping categories of offences against the Church's rules: sin and crime (Kuttner 1935, 13–21, 322–6). Sin was by far the larger and more comprehensive of these two categories. Any offence against the laws of God and the Church in thought, word, or deed was sinful. These rules, known collectively as canon law, comprised a vast body of teachings and moral prescriptions drawn from the Scriptures and the decisions of councils, bishops, Church Fathers, and other ecclesiastical authorities (Van Hove 1945, 48–115; Stickler 1950; Brundage 1995; Helmholz 1996, 1–32). Learned churchmen were well aware that as a practical matter it was impossible for anyone, no matter how careful and devout, to go through life (and for many people even to go through a single day) without falling foul of one or more of this forest of rules. Belief that no one, however well meaning, not even the holiest of God's saints, can avoid committing sins constituted a fundamental axiom of Christian theology (Rom. 9–18, 23, 32).

Because their sins offended God, Christians needed to make amends for their misdeeds. First and foremost they must repent their sinful behavior. Repentance was an interior act, in the sense that it took place in the mind and soul. Repentance involved feeling genuine sorrow for having offended God and, moral writers deduced, this must necessarily involve making a determined effort not to repeat the sinful action. Sinners also needed to confess their sins, for only by doing so could they hope to obtain forgiveness. In the early period of Christian history confession was a public act (Payer 1982). The repentant sinner had to acknowledge his faults openly in the presence of the Christian community. Doing so was itself a sign of repentance. During the early Middle Ages public confession of sins gradually gave way to private confession, a practice that apparently originated in Irish monastic communities (Watkins 1961, 2: 536–49, 603–31, 643–4, 688–92; Dooley 1982). In private confession, the repentant sinner acknowledged his faults in secret to a single individual, usually a priest. The confessor, according to theologians, could then forgive the penitent on God's behalf and relieve him of the guilt he had incurred through his sins.

Sinners not only had to confess, they also needed to make reparations for their misdeeds. They could do this by performing various kinds of penitential actions. In early Christian history, when public confession was the rule, penance was also public. Repentant sinners were typically excluded from church services for a period of time, during which they had to kneel at the door of the church and beg forgiveness from the faithful as they entered. Sinners might also be whipped publicly and they were almost always required to fast and to abstain from meat and wine for a lengthy period. When the sinner fulfilled all the penitential conditions imposed on him – which for very serious sins might take many years – he could then be reconciled to the church and readmitted to communion with his fellow Christians.

When private confession replaced the older practice of public acknowledgement of sins, penance was privatized as well. Many well-known confessors wrote handbooks of penance to provide guidance for priests who needed to know what penance they ought to assign for each of the transgressions that sinners reported to them (Vogel and Frantzen 1978). These manuals prescribed, often in elaborate detail, the types, varieties, and duration of the penance appropriate for every sin that the author had ever encountered or heard of from other confessors. Modern readers of this penitential literature are often astonished at the ingenuity and imagination of medieval sinners – or perhaps of the authors of penitentials. Confessors' manuals could also of course be misused as virtual guidebooks to vice and perversion. On this account church authorities warned priests to hide these books in a secure place, lest they fall into the hands of the unregenerate, who might learn from them new and even more dreadful kinds of wickedness than the ones they already practised.

The priest who heard confession sat in judgment upon the sinners who came to him. The confessor needed to determine the seriousness of the various transgressions that each penitent confessed; he had to decide whether the sinner was truly repentant or not; and he must also prescribe an appropriate penalty for the misdeeds that the penitent confessed. The confessor, in short, was a judge, but (at least once private penance had become the general rule) a judge who conducted his business confidentially, on a one-to-one basis with each sinner who approached him. Only the penitent and the priest were supposed to know what transpired between them and confessors had a grave moral and legal obligation to keep secret anything revealed to them during confession (Kurtscheid 1927; Lea 1957). The confessor exercised an exclusively spiritual jurisdiction. The aim of the penitential process was to correct the sinner's behavior in order to save his soul from eternal damnation. Confession, people believed, would relieve the penitent of the guilt that his sins occasioned and would thus restore him to God's favor. Theologians and canon lawyers accordingly came to speak of confession and penance as 'the inner court' (*forum internum*), where the priest exercised spiritual jurisdiction over the penitent and judged his sins according to 'the law of heaven' (*ius poli*).

Alongside the 'inner court' where confessors judged sins, stood the 'outer court' (*forum externum*) where canonical judges dealt with ecclesiastical crimes. The categories of sin and crime overlap: all ecclesiastical crimes were sins, but not all sins were crimes. The distinction between sins that were crimes and those that were not depended on two fundamental criteria: public awareness of the sinful action and the penalties attached to it. Sinful activities that became generally known – such as, for example, the situation in which a married man abandoned his wife and set up housekeeping with another woman – could be prosecuted and punished in the church's 'outer court,' while at the same time the erring parties might be required to perform whatever penance a confessor might impose in the 'inner court,' when and if they repented of their misdeeds and sought absolution.

Canonical judges had great latitude in the punishments they could impose on criminals. In this hypothetical adultery and desertion case, a judge would certainly order the man to abandon his mistress and return to his wife. In addition he would probably order both man and mistress to swear that they would never see or talk to each other in future and further he would very likely impose a fine on either or both of them as additional punishment for their crime. Judges in such cases might, and often did, impose some physical punishment on the parties. Adulterers were commonly sentenced, as well, to some sort of public humiliation – female adulterers often had their heads shaved, while male adulterers might be publicly whipped. Public penalties of this sort demonstrated to the community the terrible consequences of sexual crimes and this, church authorities hoped, might deter others from following their shameful example.

Both parties also had to answer to their respective confessors for the sin of adultery. Confessors, like judges, enjoyed wide discretion in determining the penance that they might prescribe. A confessor might, for example, require each of our hypothetical adulterers to fast on bread and water for a month and to abstain from eating meat and drinking wine for, perhaps, three years. In addition the confessor might very well impose further penalties, such as a pilgrimage, or, if one of the parties were sufficiently well-to-do, founding a monastery.

Imprisonment, on the other hand, although it now plays a leading role in the penal law of most modern societies, was a sanction to which medieval judges, either civil or ecclesiastical, seldom resorted. In just one situation does imprisonment

Figure 17.1 The Devil prompting lust. Woodcut from *Der Seelentrost* (Augsburg 1478).

frequently crop up as a punishment for sexual crimes: when a bishop, priest, or other cleric in major orders was convicted of a serious sexual offence, the judge very often sentenced the offender to be enclosed involuntarily in a monastery, usually for the remainder of his life. The rationale here was, apparently, that allowing the offender to resume his ministry might not only confront him with temptations that he might prove unable to resist, but would also be likely to affront the sensibilities of the faithful. Reclusion in a monastery presumably minimized opportunities for recidivism (save, perhaps, for those convicted of homosexual offences), while at the same time it allowed the penitent sinner to exercise his sacred functions in an environment where doing so would be unlikely to scandalize those to whom he ministered.

A problem that continually bedevilled those who sought to enforce the church's laws on sexual behavior was the difficulty of convicting offenders. Sinners who repented of their misdeeds and wished to make amends for their behavior were prepared to confess their guilt and to accept the punishment that the judge considered appropriate. Hardened offenders, however, were another matter. They were not only disinclined to plead guilty, but might well contest any efforts to convict them of their crimes. Many, perhaps even most, of those charged with sexual offences may have protested their innocence in good faith. One of the most frequently prosecuted sexual offences in archidiaconal courts, for example, was fornication. Defendants in these cases not infrequently protested, however, that nothing could be more natural than for unmarried men and women to have sexual relations with one another. Although theologians and canon lawyers called this simple fornication, ordinary people often rejected this idea and justified their conduct on the grounds that 'everybody does it'. Certainly medieval confessors and lawyers frequently complained that laymen simply refused to believe that simple fornication was either a sin or a crime (Brundage 1987, 380–2). Other sexual offenders likewise resisted prosecution because they believed that what they had done was no crime. Men accused of adultery, for example, sometimes claimed that their marriages were legally flawed and hence that, because they were really unmarried, they could not be guilty of adultery (Brundage 1987, 246–7, 485–9). Some of them, no doubt, actually believed the defenses that they put forward.

Sexual offences committed by clergymen raised special problems and proved particularly difficult to prosecute. Since clerics in major orders were not supposed to marry and their attempted marriages had been made illegal by the Lateran Councils of 1123 and 1139, they lacked any legitimate outlet for their sexual urges (Tanner 1990, 1: 191, 194, 198; Lea 1968; Barstow 1982; Lynch 1972; Boelens 1968). It was easier to mandate clerical celibacy than it was to turn off basic human drives and we have no reason to believe that medieval clerics lacked the usual complement of hormonal tides. Because church authorities made it impossible for them to marry, many clerics sought, and often found, outside marriage, gratification for the sexual desires with which nature had endowed them. Since they could not have wives, numerous priests kept concubines instead. Those who did not tended to frequent brothels, while some found sexual gratification with other men. As an anonymous thirteenth-century poet put it (Map 1841, 171):

> Priests who lack a girl to cherish
> Won't be mindful lest they perish.
> They will take whom'er they find
> Married, single – never mind!

The penalties that canon law prescribed for clerics who disobeyed the rules were calculated to frighten lusty clerics into thinking twice before yielding to carnal enticements. Even a casual offender might be stripped of his position and income if convicted. A persistent offender who maintained a long-term relationship with a concubine might, in addition, face degradation from his clerical rank and imprisonment in a monastery for the remainder of his life (Brundage 1987, 253–4, 297–300). A cleric who felt strong emotional ties with his lover and their children might well be even more dismayed at the thought that, should their relationship be discovered, both his companion and his children could be enslaved (Gratian 1979, D. 81 c. 30 and C. 15 q. 8 c. 3; Schmugge 1995).[1]

Realistically, however, clerics and their concubines in most places and at most times probably had little to fear. Enforcement of the laws was sporadic and often ineffective. Church authorities faced two fundamental problems when they attempted to implement the laws against clerical concubinage. The first was that the practice was so widespread. Clerical concubinage, despite all the horrendous rhetoric condemning it, remained common throughout the high and later Middle Ages. Popes, church councils, bishops, and a succession of saints thundered against the practice generation after generation, to be sure, yet priests and other clerics – including a good many bishops and even several popes – continued to keep female companions in their households. A Flemish bishop, Henry of Gelders, for example, openly bragged of his sexual prowess and claimed to have sired fourteen sons in twenty-two months. Clerical concubinage was the rule, not the exception, in England, especially in the province of York (Brooke 1956a and 1956b). It was very common in France and Spain, as well as in Norway and Sweden (Schimmelpfennig 1980). The canonist Benencasa (d. 1206) declared that in Italy and Germany, 'priests, deacons, and subdeacons keep their concubines publicly', and concluded from this that for practical purposes the laws that prohibited clerical concubinage were simply not in force (Benencasa 1605, at D. 81 c. 15; Liotta 1971, 190; Le Bras 1959, 168). The best that authorities could do was to try to limit how much a cleric could leave to his concubine in his will and to admonish parishioners not to invite their priest's 'wife' to their social gatherings.

Procedural obstacles that made it difficult to convict fornicating clergymen posed a second basic problem for conscientious prelates who wanted to enforce the rules against clerical sex. The *ordo iuris*, which defined the procedural rules that canon law courts were supposed to observe, permitted judges to commence action against a fornicating priest only when and if some individual was willing to come forward and make a formal, public accusation against him before a judge empowered to deal with such matters. For that reason, this is sometimes called the accusatory system. Bringing an accusation in this way was not something that a reasonable person was apt to do lightly. The accuser was bound to alienate at least some, possibly even most, members of his community and the consequences of that could well be excessively unpleasant. Even worse, should the accuser fail to prove his complaint, he became liable to stiff penalties for bringing a false accusation.

Once an accuser had laid his complaint before a judge, moreover, the *ordo iuris* demanded that he meet an extremely high standard of proof in order to substantiate his charge. To achieve a conviction either the accused person had to confess or else the accuser had to convince the judge of the defendant's guilt by 'full proof' (*plena probatio*), which canonists described as evidence that was 'clearer than the noon-day light' (Gratian 1979, C. 2 q. 8 c. 2; Accursius 1584, at Cod. 4.19.25). In practice this meant that, unless the defendant broke down and confessed, the accuser needed to furnish sworn testimony from two credible witnesses who would support his charge. Both witnesses must be free adult Catholic Christian men of unblemished reputation (and sufficient wealth to make it unlikely that their testimony could be easily bought) who would swear under oath that they had personally seen and heard the behavior cited in the complaint (Tancred 1965, 222–8; Durand 1975, 1: 283–304). Finding one, let alone two, witnesses who met all of these criteria and who had actually witnessed a priest engaging in the act of intercourse with his mistress, or even with a prostitute, was a formidable challenge, one that few potential accusers could surmount. The result was that successful prosecutions for breaches of the rules against sexual activity by clerics in holy orders were not often attempted and, when attempted, were rarely successful. The evidentiary hurdles were simply too high.

Popes and other church authorities found this situation galling. Their reaction was to modify the procedural system and the rules of evidence in order to make it easier to bring complaints and secure convictions. The process began with a decision handed down by Pope Innocent III (1198–1216) in a case that originated in East Anglia. Bishop Eustace of Ely (1197–1215) informed the pope that he had ordered two clerics in his diocese who were living openly with concubines to get rid of their companions. The two clerics had ignored his order. No accuser, however, was prepared to come forward to initiate a prosecution, nor could the bishop find the necessary eyewitnesses to support a criminal case against the peccant clergymen. Bishop Eustace placed the matter before the pope and asked for further instructions about dealing with this situation. Pope Innocent's response was a sweeping statement in a decretal known from its opening words as *Tua nos duxit*, that drastically modified the law concerning criminal procedure. '[I]f the crime is so public that it can properly be called notorious', the pope declared, 'then neither an accuser nor witnesses are required, since a crime of this sort cannot be concealed by any subterfuge' (Gregory IX 1979, 3.2.8). Innocent also cautioned, however, that he was using the term 'notorious' in a technical sense. A crime was notorious when it was perpetrated so openly and publicly that both the deed and its perpetrator were known – not merely suspected, but actually known – to the general public. In that situation, Innocent ruled, neither an accuser nor witnesses were necessary. Upon a showing that an individual had committed a notorious crime, a judge could forthwith punish the offender *ex officio* and without further proceedings. Innocent carefully distinguished notorious crimes from offences that most people believed from common report (*ex fama*) had taken place. Thus, for example, if most people in a community believed that their priest was sleeping with his housekeeper, that belief was simply a matter of general suspicion, but it was not a notorious crime. Common report, in other words, was not the same as notoriety. Common report might furnish adequate grounds for a judge to inquire further about the situation, but eyewitnesses to the suspected crime were still necessary for conviction. If common report created scandal in the community, however, the pope empowered judges to demand that the suspect clear his name by *canonica purgatio*, that is by publicly swearing a solemn oath that he was innocent of the offence of which he was suspected. A clerical suspect who refused to take the oath, the pope declared, effectively confessed his guilt and the judge could forthwith proceed to punish him.

Tua nos duxit was a classic example of legal and political compromise: it remedied one important problem at the cost of creating a different, but no less important, problem. Existing procedural standards, as the pope saw matters, made it difficult to penalize offenders for their crimes. It was manifestly unjust to allow criminals to get away unpunished. To remedy that, the pope changed the law by removing a procedural hurdle, namely the necessity of finding an accuser willing to take the risks involved in making a formal complaint against a wrongdoer. This made it substantially easier to prosecute and punish criminals. At the same time, however, the new procedure *per notorium* deprived defendants of the important protection against groundless or malicious accusations that the older procedural system had guaranteed them. This considerably increased the risk that innocent persons might be harassed by jealous admirers, jilted lovers, or others who for whatever reason disliked or resented them (Fraher 1984).

Pope Innocent's decision in *Tua nos duxit* represented a policy choice that it was more important to prosecute concubinous clerics than it was to safeguard defendants against unjust charges. This policy likewise undergirded another, still more radical, experiment: the introduction of inquisitorial procedure. The pope first authorized proceedings *per inquisitionem* in the decretal *Licet Heli* of 1199 and elaborated on this approach to criminal prosecution seven years later in another decretal, *Qualiter et quando* (Gregory IX 1979, 5.1.17 and 5.3.31). These decisions were subsequently ratified by the Fourth Lateran Council in 1215 (Garcia y Garcia 1981, 54–7; Tanner 1990, 1: 237–9).

Inquisitorial procedure, like *per notorium* procedure, dispensed with the accuser. The inquisitorial system transferred the traditional accuser's function of initiating judicial proceedings to the judge, who in effect became also a prosecutor. Under this system a judge could initiate a criminal investigation *ex officio* whenever he received information that a crime had probably been committed. He might thus initiate an action based on nothing more than an anonymous denunciation, a rumor (*mala fama*), or even just personal suspicion or belief. Virtually any sort of information that came to a judge's attention might form the basis for an investigation *per inquisitionem*. Although the pope originally devised inquisitorial procedure as a method to curb furtive sexual misbehavior, it soon came to be used for dealing with a broad spectrum of other canonical crimes, including heresy. While historians often associate inquisitorial procedure almost exclusively with heresy prosecutions, it was in fact an all-purpose procedural system used in a wide variety of situations, most of them having little or nothing to do with doctrinal orthodoxy (Kelly 1989 and 1992).

Inquisitorial procedure, like procedure *per notorium*, was designed to take action against sexual offenders and those guilty of other 'secret crimes' where it was often difficult or impossible to launch a prosecution under the conventional accusatory system of the *ordo iuris*. In order to achieve this goal, the Papacy was willing not only to sacrifice procedural safeguards against prosecuting the innocent, as mentioned earlier, but also to introduce radical changes in the law of evidence.

The *ordo iuris*, as we have seen, required the testimony of two credible eyewitnesses in order to convict a defendant of a crime. This was known as full proof. Modification

Figure 17.2 Copulation sur l'herbe. Miniature from the fourteenth-century 'Smithfield Decretals'. © The British Library, London, MS. Royal 10 E. iv, fo. 115r.

of the rule that full proof was essential for conviction began to appear early in the thirteenth century, at the same time and for the same reasons that led to the introduction of inquisitorial and *per notorium* procedures. The change here involved the notion that a series of partial proofs could add up to a full proof. Tancred (*c.*1185–*c.*1236), an influential law professor at Bologna, then Europe's leading law school, proposed that judges could count a delation as a half-proof (Tancred 1965, 221–2). A delation differed from testimony because it was a statement of belief, not knowledge. The person who made a delation did not claim to have seen or heard the defendant commit the alleged offence. Rather the delator simply asserted his or her belief that a crime had occurred and that the defendant had committed it. Because a delation was a sworn statement of belief, rather than of knowledge, it failed to meet the criteria of proof, but Tancred maintained that it nonetheless ought to have some evidentiary weight. Tancred asserted that a sworn delation should count as a half proof, or in other words that it ought to carry half the weight of full proof, which, as we have seen, meant the testimony of two actual witnesses to the perpetration of a criminal act.[2]

Other jurists adopted Tancred's analysis and suggested further modifications of the strict doctrine of proof that had prevailed at the beginning of the thirteenth century. By the 1280s, when Guillaume Durand (1231–96) was revising the *Judicial Mirror* (*Speculum iudiciale*), his massive treatise on procedure, he listed six varieties of partial proofs. These included, besides the sworn delation and the testimony of a single witness, such other types of evidence as household records (*scripturas domesticas*) that confirmed sworn testimony, flight by the accused, and false statements made by the accused. In addition Durand listed common report (*mala fama*) as a partial proof in civil cases, but not for criminal prosecutions. By Durand's time, in other words, a combination of partial proofs, such as, for example, the testimony of a single eyewitness plus corroborating circumstantial evidence of other types, such as household documents, added up to a full proof sufficient to convict a defendant on a criminal charge.

These developments in the law of evidence, combined with the introduction of *per notorium* and inquisitory procedure, made it much easier by the end of the thirteenth century to prosecute and convict offenders against the church's rules about sexual behavior than it had been in 1200.

At the same time the ambitious package of reform legislation adopted by the Fourth Lateran Council in 1215 made it easier for churchmen to monitor the sexual behavior of the faithful and to implement observance of the church's sexual code. One of the council's canons obliged the faithful to confess their sins to their parish priest at least once a year (Garcia y Garcia 1981, 208–9; Tanner 1990, 1: 345). This requirement not only gave the clergy for the first time a systematic mechanism to discover and punish infractions of the church's rules, but also presented them with an opportunity to instruct members of their flock privately and on an individual basis about the behavioral standards that the church required of its members. The new instructional opportunities that this canon opened up may well have been at least as important as the chance that it furnished to detect and correct deviations from the norms of sexual behavior that leaders of the church wished members of their flock to observe. The two together made it possible for the clergy (or at least for those among them who were themselves adequately informed about these matters) to bring the behavior of their rank-and-file parishioners into line with the sexual prescriptions set down by theologians, canonists, and other church leaders (Tentler 1974; Boyle 1974).

Two further canons of the Fourth Lateran Council likewise facilitated the process of informing the faithful more adequately about the church's teachings on sexual matters. Canon ten commanded each bishop to appoint well-informed preachers to circulate through his diocese and instruct the laity about their religious duties (Garcia y Garcia 1981, 58–9; Tanner 1990, 1: 239–40). This was a momentous and radical innovation in the religious life of the Western church. Preaching had previously played only a minor and very occasional role in the ordinary round of liturgical observances. Most of the sermons that survive from before 1215 were written in Latin and addressed to the clergy rather than to the laity. And just how much the rank-and-file of the clergy understood of these discourses is, like most really interesting questions, extremely difficult to answer.

The new emphasis on preaching that commenced with the Fourth Lateran Council, combined with the instructional opportunities that annual confession afforded, made it possible, indeed virtually mandatory, for churchmen to inform the laity about ecclesiastical doctrines concerning sexual conduct more widely and in greater detail than ever before. At the same time, these developments also made it essential that the clergy themselves be better informed on these issues than had been common in the past. The eleventh canon of the council therefore addressed this issue. The fathers of the Fourth Lateran Council noted that their predecessors at the Third Lateran Council, back in 1179, had ordered each cathedral church to provide a stipend to support a schoolmaster, who would be assigned the task of providing basic theological training for the clergy of the diocese. In the generation since then, however, most dioceses had done little or nothing to implement that provision. The Fourth Lateran Council, therefore, reiterated and expanded the earlier decree by adding that not only cathedral churches, but also others with sufficient resources, shared in the duty of providing systematic instruction for the clergy (Garcia y Garcia 1981, 59–60; Tanner 1990, 1: 240).

The legislation of the Fourth Lateran Council thus furnished a blueprint for more adequate dissemination and implementation of the church's teachings on sexual matters than had hitherto existed. The primary emphasis of the council's efforts was on mechanisms for instructing and counseling both the laity and the clergy on their religious duties and obligations. The same period likewise witnessed additional developments to enhance legal enforcement of church doctrines about sexual conduct, among other matters.

Prior to the beginning of the thirteenth century the church's court system was not very efficiently structured. Every bishop, to be sure, was entitled to exercise what was called ordinary jurisdiction over the faithful, clerics and laity alike, within his diocese. This empowered him to enforce the church's disciplinary rules and to resolve disputes over issues of ecclesiastical law that arose within the diocese. When faced with a particularly critical or complex case, a bishop might summon all the clergy of his diocese to meet with him as a synod and to help him to untangle the difficulties, but this happened only in unusual situations. Prior to the beginning of the thirteenth century bishops as a rule tried to deal in person with most of their legal business as part of their daily routine. By about 1200, however, many bishops had begun to feel overwhelmed by the sheer volume of cases that came to them for settlement. To make matters worse, both the procedural and the substantive complexity of the law itself were increasing at the same time.

One way out of this difficulty was for bishops, especially those in large dioceses, simply to delegate the more routine kinds of problem to one or more specially designated clergymen, usually called archdeacons, in various parts of the diocese. The archdeacon was supposed to act as the bishop's disciplinary watchdog in the particular region to which he was appointed. He was expected both to correct many kinds of common offences against canon law – fornication cases, in particular, commonly furnished archdeacons with plenty of business to keep them steadily employed – and also to bring to the bishop's attention the more serious and complicated problems that arose within his archdeaconry. The archdeacon thus lightened the bishop's load by screening out routine, petty problems, which the archdeacon could deal with on his own, passing on only the more important and difficult cases for the bishop to deal with in person. In practice this meant that archdeacons became supervisors of public morals, who handled most complaints about public offences against the church's sexual code. The archdeacon thus became a judge and his court became the usual venue for dealing with the common run of sex offences.

The development of archdeacons' courts certainly cut down the volume of litigation that bishops had to deal with. It did little or nothing, however, to solve the problems that a continuing increase in legal technicalities and in the sheer complexity that much new ecclesiastical legislation presented. To deal with these difficulties bishops increasingly found it necessary to employ advisers with formal training in the law. By around 1200 many bishops not only relied upon the legal officials in their households for advice, but were also commencing to refer cases to them for hearing and decision. This quickly became the usual way of dealing with all but the most politically sensitive cases that came to the bishop for adjudication. In most dioceses, accordingly, a court that exercised the bishop's judicial functions gradually took shape during the course of the thirteenth century. The presiding officer in these courts was one of the bishop's officials and hence the court was commonly referred to as the Official's Court (Fournier 1984; Lefebvre-Teillhard 1973).

A large fraction of the caseload in the Official's Court nearly everywhere concerned sexual behavior. Many of these cases involved troubled marriages, where one partner or the other (and occasionally both) sought a judicial decree of separation or annulment, not infrequently on grounds of what we would now call sexual incompatibility. One method of testing the credentials of an allegedly incompatible husband employed experienced women whose task it was to attempt to stimulate the quiescent male into action. Another might involve witnesses posted to ensure that the couple were exerting themselves in bed with suitable dedication to the task in hand. The wife's credentials were also liable to inspection (Brundage 1987, 322 and p. 14; Linehan 1997). In other marriage cases, petitioners asked the Official's Court to compel a straying spouse who had run off with some other partner to return to the matrimonial bed and board.

Bishops' officials also dealt with a wide variety of criminal cases, many of which involved deviations from the church's sexual norms. While many of these cases involved violations of the vows of chastity by priests, monks, and nuns, laypersons, too, frequently appeared at the bar of the Official's Court charged with serious sexual offences (Helmholz 1974, 25–6, 74–5, 166–8; Donahue 1974, 656–78; Wunderli 1981, 68–9, 81, 101–2, 108, 113, 117, 120, 123, 142–7; Finch 1993 and 1994).

By the thirteenth century, therefore, the medieval church had produced a battery of institutions to enforce its policies concerning sexual behavior. The administration through regular, annual confession of what had by this point come to be defined as the sacrament of penance provided a private, confidential mechanism through which church authorities were able to monitor the sexual behavior of the faithful, to instruct and counsel those who were uncertain about the rules in these matters, and to administer correction to those who failed to comply. Parallel to this, a system of courts was in place to deal with sexual misbehavior that took place in public or that seemed likely to subvert the morals of the community at large.

How effective these institutions may have been in enforcing the medieval church's rules about sexual conduct is not easy to determine. What is clear from the evidence, however, is that the church took its role as a guardian of sexual morality with great seriousness and strenuously attempted to implement the teachings of theologians and ecclesiastical authorities in this area of human life. Both the content of those teachings and the belief that public authorities have a legitimate right to police private sexual behavior remain part of the modern Western heritage to this day.

NOTES

1 For a key to this and subsequent legal citations, see Brundage 1995, 190–205.
2 For the unanticipated consequences of this innovation in the development of mathematical probability theory, see Franklin 1991.

REFERENCES

Accursius, F. (1584) *Glossa ordinaria*, in *Codex Dn. Iustinianus sacratissimi principis*, Lyon: Apud Iuntas.

Barstow, A. L. (1982) *Married Priests and the Reforming Papacy*, New York: Edward Mellen.

Benencasa (1605) *Casus*, in *Decretum Gratiani*, Venice: Apud Iuntas.

Boelens, M. (1968) *Die Klerikerehe in der Gesetzgebung der Kirche unter besonderer Berücksichtigung der Strafe*, Paderborn: Ferdinand Schöningh.

Boyle, L. E. (1974) 'The Summa for Confessors as a genre and its religious intent', in C. Trinkaus and H. A. Obermann, *The Pursuit of Holiness in Late Medieval and Renaissance Religion*, Leiden: Brill.

Brooke, C. N. L. (1956a) 'The Gregorian Reform in action: clerical marriage in England, 1050–1200', *Cambridge Historical Journal* 12: 1–20.

—— (1956b) 'Married men among the English higher clergy, 1066–1200', *Cambridge Historical Journal* 12: 187–8.

Brundage, J. A. (1987) *Law, Sex, and Christian Society in Medieval Europe*, Chicago: University of Chicago Press.

—— (1995) *Medieval Canon Law*, London: Longman.

Donahue, C., Jr. (1974) 'Roman Canon Law in the medieval English Church: Stubbs vs. Maitland re-examined after 75 years in the light of some records from the church courts', *Michigan Law Review* 72: 647–716.

Dooley, K. (1982) 'From penance to confession: the celtic contribution', *Bijdragen: Tijdschrift voor filosofie en theologie* 43: 390–411.

Durand, G. (1975) *Speculum iudiciale*, Aalen: Scientia.

Finch, A. (1993) '*Repulsa uxore sua*: marital difficulties and separation in the Later Middle Ages', *Continuity and Change* 8: 11–38.

—— (1994) 'Sexual morality and canon law: the evidence of the Rochester Consistory Court', *Journal of Medieval History* 20: 261–75.

Fournier, P. (1984) *Les Officialités au moyen âge: Étude sur l'organisation, la compétence et la procédure des tribunaux ecclésiastiquest ordinaires en France de 1180 à 1328*, Aalen: Scientia.

Fraher, R. M. (1984) 'The theoretical justification for the new criminal law of the High Middle Ages: "Rei publicae interest, ne crimina remaneant impunita", *University of Illinois Law Review* 577–95.

Franklin, J. (1991) 'The ancient legal sources of seventeenth-century probability', in S. Gaukroger (ed.), *The Uses of Antiquity*, Dordrecht.

Garcia y Garcia, A. (1981) *Constitutiones Concilii quarti Lateranensis una cum commentariis glossatorum*, Vatican City: Biblioteca Apostolica Vaticana.

Gratian (1979) *Decretum Gratiani*, in E. Friedberg (ed.), *Corpus iuris canonici*, vol. 1, Graz: Akademische Druck- u. Verlagsanstalt.

Gregory IX (1979) *Decretales Gregorii IX* in E. Friedberg (ed.), *Corpus iuris canonici*, vol. 2, Graz: Akademische Druck- u. Verlagsanstalt.

Helmholz, R. C. (1974) *Marriage Litigation in Medieval England*, Cambridge: Cambridge University Press.

Helmholz, R. H. (1996) *The Spirit of Classical Canon Law*, Athens: University of Georgia Press.

Kelly, H. A. (1989) 'Inquisition and the prosecution of heresy: misconceptions and abuses', *Church History* 58: 439–51.

—— (1992) 'Inquisitorial due process and the status of secret crimes', in S. Chodorow (ed.), *Proceedings of the Eighth International Congress of Medieval Canon Law*, Vatican City, Biblioteca Apostolica Vaticana.

Kurtscheid, B. (1927) *A History of the Seal of Confession*, St. Louis: Herder.

Kuttner, S. G. (1935) *Kanonistische Schuldlehre von Gratian bis auf die Dekretalen Gregors IX.*, Vatican City: Biblioteca Apostolica Vaticana.

Lea, H. C. (1957) *A History of Sacerdotal Celibacy in the Christian Church*, New York: Russell & Russell.

Lea, H. C. (1968) *A History of Auricular Confession and Indulgences*, New York: Greenwood.

Le Bras, G. (1959) *Les Institutions ecclésiastiques de la chrétienté médiévale*, Paris: Sirey.

Lefebvre-Teillhard, A. (1973) *Les Officialités à la veille du Concile de Trente*, Paris: R. Pichon et R. Durand-Auzias.

Linehan, P. (1997) 'Two marriage cases from medieval Iberia', *Zeitschrift der Savigny – Stiftung für Rechtsgeschichte* 114 (kanonistische Abteilung 83): 333–41.

Liotta, F. (1971) *La continenza dei chierici nel pensiero canonistico classico da Graziano a Gregorio IX*, Milan: A. Giuffrè.

Lynch, J. E. (1972) 'Marriage and celibacy of the clergy: the discipline of the Western Church', *The Jurist* 32: 14–38, 189–212.

Map, Walter (1841) 'De concubinis sacerdotum', in T. Wright (ed.), *The Latin Poems Commonly Attributed to Walter Mapes*, London: Camden Society.

Payer, P. J. (1982) 'Penance and penitentials', in J. R. Strayer (ed.), *Dictionary of the Middle Ages*, New York: Scribner.

Schimmelpfennig, B. (1980) '*Ex fornicatione nati*: studies on the position of priests' sons from the twelfth to the fourteenth century', *Studies in Medieval and Renaissance History* 2: 3–50.

Schmugge, L. (1995) *Kirche, Kinder, Karrieren: Päpstliche Dispense von der unehelichen Geburt im Spätmittelalter*, Zürich: Artemis & Winkler.

Stickler, A. M. (1950) *Historia iuris canonici Latini*, Turin: Libraria Pontif. Athenaei Salesiani.

Tancred (1965) *Ordo iudiciarius*, in F. C. Bergmann (ed.), *Libri de iudiciorum ordine*, Aalen: Scientia.

Tanner, N. P. (1990) *Decrees of the Ecumenical Councils*, Washington: Georgetown University Press.

Tentler, T. N. (1974) 'The Summa for confessors as an instrument of social control', in C. Trinkhaus and H. A. Obermann (eds.), *The Pursuit of Holiness in Late Medieval and Renaissance Religion*, Leiden: Brill.

Van Hove, A. (1945) *Prolegomena*, Malines: Dessain.

Vogel, C. and Frantzen, A. J. (1978) *Les 'Libri penitentiales'*, Turnhout: Brépols.

Watkins, O. D. (1961) *A History of Penance*, New York: Burt Franklin.

Wunderli, R. M. (1981) *London Church Courts and Society on the Eve of the Reformation*, Cambridge, MA: Medieval Academy of America.

CHAPTER EIGHTEEN

THROUGH A GLASS DARKLY: SEEING MEDIEVAL HERESY

————— ••◆•• —————

Peter Biller

A modern *History of Medieval Heresy*, reduced to the back of a large postage stamp, says this. Between about 1000 and 1050 there are a scatter of reports of heresy in France, north-western Italy, Germany and perhaps Hungary, followed by silence for about fifty years – a period when the reforming Gregorian papacy may have sucked into itself whatever radicalism may have been around. Reports of heresy begin again shortly after 1100 and increase in number, and heresy shows its importance by engaging the attention of the greatest churchmen of the period, Peter the Venerable and St Bernard of Clairvaux, and of a steady sequence of Church councils. From the 1160s onwards there is a lot of evidence of heretics called *Cathars*, both in Italy and in Languedoc, whose city Albi gave them one of their names, *Albigensians*, while in the 1170s a layman called Valdes started a movement which was condemned in 1184 and acquired a name from him, *Valdenses, Waldensians*. The Cathars and the Waldensians were the major heretical movements of the central Middle Ages, spreading widely and in large numbers, and repression of heresy, particularly Catharism, in Languedoc brought about the launching of a crusade in 1209 and the founding of the inquisition in the 1230s. While inquisitors had broken Italian and Languedocian Catharism by around 1320, the Waldensians were more succcessful, surviving in many areas until around 1400, and then in the mountains between Piedmont and Dauphiné until the the sixteenth century, when they were swallowed up by the Reform, although they kept their name. In the preceding century the centre stage of the story had been occupied by national heresies inspired respectively by the Oxford master John Wyclif and the Prague master Jan Hus, English Lollardy and Czech Hussitism, both of them the last significant new movements before the Reformation, and constituting together a sort of pre-reform.

I plan to concentrate on the central Middle Ages, but rather than expanding this resumé, I am going to look at the series of lenses and filters *through* which we look at Cathars and Waldensians. First there is the evidence, whose varying quantity and survival is both an opportunity and a problem; 'absence of evidence is not evidence of absence', as the early medievalist's adage goes. Its characteristics may also tell us more about the churchmen who produced it than about heresy. Secondly, there are groups who have appropriated the history of heresy to bolster their sense of identity, most importantly Protestants seeing medieval heretics as their forerunners. Thirdly there have been movements in modern scholarship, which have sharply illuminated parts of medieval heresy, sometimes at the same time obscuring other parts. In the following I intend to look at the ways lenses and filters transmit, refract or colour a view of the major heresies of the central Middle Ages, Catharism and Waldensianism, hoping to say something about these heresies themselves as well as the struggle to *see* them.

I begin with *heresy*. Whatever it was that was there, it was called *heresy* because churchmen regarded and treated individual movements or persons as *heresies* and *heretics*. As we survey *heresy* through the central Middle Ages a hand is twiddling the zoom on the lens through which we look. The Church's notion of what was heretical fluctuated to some degree through time, and as a consequence what we are looking at fluctuates. And after the Middle Ages, beginning with Protestant and Catholic writers, historians of heresy came to concentrate mainly on such major religious movements as Catharism, Waldensianism, Lollardy and Hussitism. As the domination of confessional historiography declined, attitudes to these labels have altered. In 1935 the German historian of heresy Herbert Grundmann pointed out how much there was in common between those movements of the twelfth and early thirteenth centuries which ended up as religious Orders and those movements which ended up as heresies. They all drew something from a general impulse towards the apostolic life, embraced by people who took evangelical counsels as precepts and as a consequence renounced marriage and money, embarking on a form of life in which they wandered without fixed abode, living off casual charity, preaching and, in some cases, healing the sick. This meant a historiographical shift, away from the two separate compartments of the *history of religious Orders* and the *history of heresies*, and towards the study of them together within the category which gave Grundmann's book its title, *Religious Movements in the Middle Ages*. A further historiographical shift will come with the book which is now being written by Grundmann's brilliant pupil Alexander Patschovsky, on heresy and politics. This will explore the varying conditions of politics and power which brought about the imposition of the label *heresy* or *heretic* on emperors, kings, popes, peasants, political movements, theologians, radical Franciscans, pious lay people, and Cathars and Waldensians.[1]

Consequently, as I turn to look at the Cathars and Waldensians, I am following (a) a post-medieval historiographical tradition which has decided that these *religious heresies*, as Patschovsky calls them, dominate the theme *heresy* in the central Middle Ages. I am following (b) the Church's view that these were the major religious heretical problems of that period, and I am using Church vocabulary. I still have a large and legitimate topic – since the Church's point of view was important – but I am limiting myself to one medieval angle of vision upon these past phenomena, and to a restricted post-medieval notion of what *heresy* then covered.

Keeping this in mind, I turn to looking at the Cathar and Waldensian heretics. I see them principally through inquisition records, such as the following.

Benazeit Molinier [in a confession of 1301] . . . saw Raimond del Boc and his companion, heretics, and there he and other persons adored the said heretics, genuflecting and saying 'Bless' according to the heretics' rite. . . . *Item*, he saw Bernart de la Vigaria and his companion, heretics, together with others, whom he names, around the bed where a man was lying, whom he names. The man was ill with an illness from which he died, and Benazeit believed that the said ill man was hereticated by the said heretics. . . . These heretics used to say that they were good and holy men, and that the Church of evildoers, namely the Roman Church, persecuted them unjustly, and that they used to fast three days a week on bread and water. *Item*, they condemned marriage, saying that it was always a sin. *Item*, they condemned the sacrament of the altar, saying it was just bread. *Item*, they condemned baptism of water, saying that man was saved through their imposing hands on their believers, and that all sins were remitted without confession or satisfaction. They also said that God's incarnation was impossible, because God would never have so humbled himself as to put himself in a woman's womb. *Item*, they said that there were two Gods, a good one and an evil one, and the good one had made all visible things. *Item*, they denied the resurrection of the body. *Item*, they said that souls were nothing but spirits which had fallen through sin. He heard these and other things from the heretics whenever they preached.

(Limborch 1692: 248–9)

About eight years before her confession [to the inquisitor, 1322] . . . Joana's sister-in-law, Bevenguda, told her that there were some Good Men in her husband's house who wanted to talk to her, and that she should go there. Bevenguda told her that they were some of those who are called *Waldenses*, [although] they call themselves *friars*[2] . . . she found the two Waldenses at the house, and after some general words they admonished her not to do or say evil, nor to lie or swear, because in every case swearing was a great sin . . . and she prayed with them according to the Waldenses' mode of praying, kneeling at a bench and saying the *Our Father* several times. *Item*, she confessed her sins to the aforesaid Waldensian, Joan [John] of Cerno, and received absolution and penance from him, namely fasting some Thursdays and repeating the *Our Father*, even though she thought or knew that the said Waldensian was not a priest ordained by a bishop of the Roman Church; and she believed she was absolved just as if she had confessed to her chaplain [parish priest].

(Limborch 1692: 356)

These are extracts from the sentences passed on Benazeit and Joana, who had confessed some involvement in heresy. The two come from a larger number of sentences on such people, 930 in all, which were collected by the Dominican inquisitor Bernard Gui in his *Book of Sentences* (*Liber sententiarum*) (Pales-Gobilliard 1991).[3] This *Book* is long, and in it the reader meets large numbers of named individuals from southern France, and gets a schematic account of their involvement with heretics. Inquisitors had been working in France since the 1230s, and although most of their records do not survive, what is astonishing is the quantity and colour of what we can still look at, in about a dozen large volumes extending from the 1230s to around 1320. They are mainly depositions, virtually all concerning Cathars and only a minority the Waldensians. If Languedocian Catharism is a modern tourist industry it also dominates any serious and good modern *History of Medieval Heresy*. Because of the size of the past phenomenon? Or the size of the records still extant?

While Bernard Gui's *Book of Sentences* survives intact, only a few fragments survive of the records of inquisitions carried out in southern Bohemia by a near contemporary of Gui's, Gallus of Neuhaus (1335–mid-1350s), which were discovered and edited by Alexander Patschovsky. Consider the contrasts. Patschovsky's fragments are about 10,000 words, Gui's intact *Book* about 250,000. In the fragments over 300 people are implicated, including about 180 German-speaking Waldensians, and there are references to fifteen burnings; Gui's *Book* contains 42 death-sentences. Patschovsky calculates that the lost parts of the register would have left us with 2,640 Waldensians and 220 executions, and he points to a comment in 1315 that there were 80,000 Waldensians in Austria and an 'infinite number' in Bohemia. Though these estimates were exaggerations, the suggestion is that the reality behind them was that there were heretics in much larger numbers in Austria and Bohemia than in Gui's Languedoc (Patschovsky 1979: 18–24). Go back to the mid-thirteenth century. One manuscript now in Toulouse contains the depositions of about 5,000 people interrogated in the Languedoc in 1245–6, and it is about half a million words long, while inquisitors' discovery of heretical (Waldensian) infestation of 42 parishes in the diocese of Passau around 1260 is known only through a paragraph in an inquisitor's treatise: the inquisition records do not survive. If inquisition records in German-speaking areas north of the Alps had survived at anything like the rate of those from the Languedoc, how far would the Languedoc dwindle in our overall picture of medieval heresy?

The chronology as well as the geography of survival of evidence poses problems. The massive Languedocian records go back to slightly before 1240. Some people talking to an inquisitor around this time reminisce backwards in time, to 'before the coming of the crusaders', meaning before the launching of the crusade against Albigensian heresy in 1209, and a few very old people remember back to before 1190. As we go back earlier than this we are suddenly deprived of colour, detail, and names. Darkness falls. We are reduced to different sorts of evidence about Catharism, and problems in the evidence multiply, in particular about when Catharism reaches the Languedoc. The work of one modern historian of heresy, Bernard Hamilton, suggests one outline of earlier Catharism (Hamilton 1994). Northern Frenchmen in the wake of the First Crusade, around 1100, encountered dualist religion in the shape of the Bogomils in Constantinople. There they set up the first Latin Cathar Church and procured Latin translations of Bogomil rites, and then on their return to northern France they erected a Cathar bishopric in northern France, which was the start of the western mission. During the twelfth and early thirteenth century Catharism had considerable strength in north-western Europe, in milieux of wealth, nobility and high learning, while it was also spreading southwards to Provence, the Languedoc and Italy, and its strength in the south was soon to produce one of its names, *Albigensian* from the city of Albi. Assume for the moment that this picture is correct. The supporting (or contradictory) evidence is sparse. The records of the trials of the 180 Cathars who were executed in Champagne in the 1230s would tell us much about the character of northern French Catharism, had they survived, and the same applies to the earlier executions of Cathars, whether in areas where they were probably scarce, such as England, or in areas where they abounded, Rhineland Germany, the Low Countries and northern France. I find Bernard Hamilton's account persuasive, but others will have good arguments for rejecting it. Consider the consequences for a modern *History of Medieval Heresy*. Filled with the colour and quotidian detail of depositions, its chapter on the mid-thirteenth century can be a vivid counterpart of a past reality. By contrast the twelfth-century chapter has to be dominated by modern academics debating 'were they Cathars?' – I imply no criticism, for nothing else can be done – and its thinness is a very poor counterpart of a mainly lost past reality.

If we go further back in time we pass over the late eleventh-century gap and arrive at various reports of heretics, labelled in one source as *Manichaean*, said to be around between *c*.1000 and 1050. While there has been no consensus among scholars about the precise theological nature of heresy in this period, very considerable scholarship has been devoted to investigation of the deeper changes and tensions to which in some way the efflorescence of heresies corresponded, and also to the political squabbles and intrigues lying behind particular heresy accusations (Nelson 1972; Nelson 1980: 65–6; Moore 1996). Our concern so far has been quantity of evidence: in a century where evidence overall is not vast, the proportion of it which cries *heresy* in the first half of the century is quite large. In the thirteenth century a scholastic theologian labelling contemporary heretics as *Manichaeans* was aware of what he was doing, using doctrinal similarities between the ancient Manichaeans and modern heretics in his discussion of theological dualism (Biller 1999). Hamilton's is a lone voice, suggesting that the eleventh-century monk will have been thinking in the same way, and saying that modern scepticism about the heresies of this period has become excessive (Hamilton 1998: 196–8).

If the odd contours of the survival of inquisition records skew our view, nevertheless it is through the extant records that we have to look. Do these records invent heretics? Until thirty years ago histories of medieval heresy used to contain a chapter on the sect of the Free Spirit. This had been condemned in a decree of the Council of Vienne in 1311, which itemised the sect's bizarre doctrines, central to which was the notion that after achieving spiritual perfection an adept was freed from moral law. Then along came Robert Lerner (Lerner 1972). He described the general tradition of accusing heretics of libertinism, and against this he set close analysis of the depositions of Free Spirit heretics in Germany and central Europe confessing to inquisitors. Comparing what they said with the Vienne Council's list, Lerner made it clear that they were repeating this. Suspicion, inquisitorial method, theologically precise leading questions ('You do believe, do you not, that after achieving a state of perfection etc.'), the threat of torture and 'confessing personalities' all combined to conjure up these admissions. Conversely, Lerner's book dispelled the sect. The mirage vanished. There is no chapter entitled 'Sect of the Free Spirit' in the modern *History of Medieval Heresy*.

No. The Cathars and Waldensians were not invented, and the very detailed records and flexible questions of inquisitors in the Languedoc take us into a world which is very different from Lerner's trials. And it is this initial relief, the fact that the sources do relate to a reality, which constitutes the danger: by relaxing vigilance about how these sources have shaped that reality.

Joana, Benazeit and thousands of others gave statements to inquisitors. Our modern liberal concern with the injustice of the inquisition may give us tunnel-vision. 'A man takes an ox by its horn and a peasant by his tongue' (Biller and Hudson 1994: 9–10): this proverb, retailed as a caution to someone about to be questioned, encapsulates one clear possibility, that of theologically learned inquisitors over-whelming illiterate poor peasants. But many of the questioned suspects were men and women of high station in the world, used to receiving respect and ordering people about; a few were literate men, jurists and notaries. Envisaging suspects only as victims (which they certainly were), we may miss their resoucefulness and stratagems. Sometimes we are told of conversations among suspects, who are going to be questioned, agreeing to conceal everything from the inquisitors (Wakefield 1986). As the record of interrogation shows a suspect caving in, we can sometimes see that efforts at concealment are still going on. The suspect is naming people who are implicated in heresy, but they all happen to be dead: the living are still being protected. Or there is a suspicious absence of close family in the early part of the confession: loved ones are among the last to be named. When someone does decide to tell the truth, then there is still the perennial police problem: it is the truth only as one person saw and remembered it. Different suspects' memories of the same event both overlap and vary. A man remembers more the men attending a Cathar sermon, a woman the women.

The interrogating inquisitor's education was Latin in language and Catholic in content. The Occitan vernacular in which Benazeit and Joana made their replies was translated for the written record of the proceedings: colours reduced to black and white. The inquisitor and his scribe imposed a vocabulary based on their Catholic assumptions. Benazeit's heretics did not call themselves *heretics*. They were the *Good Men* or *Christians* to themselves and their followers, and only *Cathars* in Catholic writing about heresy. In the Languedoc the overwhelming strength of Catharism produced the equivalence in the mind of the inquisitor, *hereticus* = Cathar. In the trial record, therefore, *Good Man* becomes *heretic*, while their names for their rites are also overlaid, the administration of their *consolamentum*, for example, becoming *heretication*. The male Waldensians, as Joana tells us, called themselves *friars*, and *Waldensians* was a Catholic term. Find out the name of the inventor of a heresy and then use this to label it: *Montanus*, ergo *Montanists*, *Valdes*, ergo *Waldensians*. Insidious slants are given to our view while we persist in following inquisitors, referring to the *Good Men* and the *friars* as *Cathars* and *Waldensians*. Questioned by the Dominican Peter Sella around 1241–2, some people claimed not to know that the Church persecuted the Waldensians, and the Waldensian friars' own preferred nomenclature is one of the things which make this claim plausible: something we miss while using the Church's vocabulary.

One or two inquisitors presided in a particular case, men of varying ability. An inquisitor's mind could be crude, or perceptive and subtle, like the ideal put forward by the inquisitor Bernard Gui: a man who would be alert when looking at matters which were in doubt, not readily believing something just because it seemed probable, nor stubbornly refusing to accept something simply because it was not likely, for the unlikely can be true (Gui 1886: 233). They put the questions. The Languedoc inquisitors tended to be quite flexible, permitting suspects to digress in their answers. This tendency became quite marked with two Dominicans interrogating in Toulouse in the 1270s, Pons of Parnac and Renous of Plassac, and it was to reach its height with the late and famous inquisitor Jacques Fournier, whose relentless curiosity and tolerance of story-telling combined to permit the appearance of the richest of all sets of medieval depositions, which when published (Duvernoy 1965 and 1972), provided the material for Emmanuel Le Roy Ladurie's extraordinary account of a high Pyrenean village around 1300, *Montaillou*.

The majority of depositions – relating to the much larger Catharism of late twelfth- and thirteenth-century Languedoc – are narrower, and the nature of this narrowness needs attention. The problem is not the stark one of northern European inquisitors forcing out false confessions. Rather, it is the subtler one of confessions in southern Europe which, with all their problems, have a lot of truth, but are largely confined to a field whose borders are marked out by the inquisitor. One marker in this field is obvious. The inquisitors were usually more interested in police-work than anything else, especially in the period when Cathar supporters still numbered thousands. Did you see a Cathar or a Waldensian? If so, when was the first time? Where? Who else was present? Did you hear them preaching? Did you give them anything? When was the next time you saw them? Where? Who else was present? When was the next time? And so the questions go on. From a mid-thirteenth-century Joana or Benazeit inquisitors wanted to know (a) names of others, and (b) a crude arithmetic of Joana's and Benazeit's guilt, counting duration in sect, category of supporting activity (did you act as a messenger for them?), numbers of sermons attended and gifts given. The inquisitors had names for various categories or degrees among followers (*believer, supporter, receiver,* and *defender*) (Kolmer 1982). Like Weberian ideal-types, these were based on careful thought about the varying behaviour of followers, which they simplified and ordered into these categories – a subtle process which continued as inquisitors questioned people and pigeonholed them. At the same time these mid-thirteenth-century inquisitors tended not to be very interested in precisely what Joana and Benazeit thought, and what doctrines they could recall. Another marker on the edge of the field is more intangible. The questions asked were rooted not only in the demands of police-work but also in churchmen's very ecclesial conception of what a sect was: a counter-Church, with its ministers, and lay people hearing sermons and passively participating in ritual, and providing material support.

Let us stay with this for a moment, and reflect on the consequences. One seems clear. Answers to questions which are coloured by a relative lack of interest in deponents' beliefs and an ecclesial image of a sect are likely to flatten out the distinctiveness of possibly very different persecuted groups. We read the resulting depositions, and these flattened profiles fit very well with our habit of following the medieval Church in calling all these groups *heresies*, and our tendency – as modern liberals sympathising with those who were persecuted – to see various heresies as constituting a rainbow alliance. If we try going in the other direction, what do we find?

First, if we look carefully at the depositions we see individuals' statements about doctrine breaking through inquisitors' relative indifference. People heard doctrine from Cathar or Waldensian preachers, but there were so many other sources of information, heretical sympathisers among one's neighbours and family, and paradoxically, those whose preaching against heresy was so clear that one could pick up heretical doctrine through listening to them: the bishop, Franciscan and Dominican friars, and one's parish priest. And there were so many little disputations attested, many between Cathars and Waldensians – a disputation in a workshop about the licitness of killing, a casual conversation on a doorstep about the resurrection, and confabulations about marriage. Around 1229 as two women are walking back home from Toulouse one of them falls and says, 'Curse the master who made this fleshly woman!' The other says, 'And did not God make you?', which gets the reply, 'Do you want to write that down for me? Let's go!'[4] Allusiveness, joking, irony? Through the veils of distance and translation we cannot say exactly, but clear enough are the allusions to *who* created the body – the one and good God in Catholic belief and the evil God in Cathar belief. Clear also is what is implied by this woman's rapid reference to the maker of her flesh: the deep penetration of theological thought into the minds of ordinary people, brought about by the competition of rival preachers and acute popular interest. The problem lies in us: in our patronising reluctance to think of these people as more familiar with theology and more theologically sophisticated than we are.

Secondly, let us look at the two heresies in question. Joana received in her house Waldensian *friars*, who belonged to an Order, which they had entered, taking the monastic vows of poverty, chastity and obedience. They preached to Joana, telling her not to sin, and they heard her confession, providing penance and absolution for her sins. Both the content of their preaching and the fact of confession concerned morality – sin, penance, and behaving better – and there is hardly a whiff of doctrine, only the point that the friars are out of line in doing all this, since they are not ordained. The Waldensians had begun inside the Church around 1170, emerging from broadly the same religious movement as the later Franciscans, founded, like the Franciscans, by a man from a wealthy city background who started to become interested in literal obedience to the gospel counsel of poverty. Although Valdes and his followers were eventually excommunicated because of their unwillingness to obey local bishops, and although they eventually developed significant doctrinal heresies, in particular rejection of purgatory and the intercessory power of the saints, their deviance from the Catholic Church was usually limited. They did not develop different views about the nature of God, and their asceticism was a spiritual rather than a theological matter. This world was God's creation and was good; marriage was good. They remained like a proscribed and clandestine mendicant Order, rejected by the Church but themselves not entirely rejecting the Church nor eventually trying to form a Church, for they accepted the Church's sacraments. A Waldensian follower in the later Middle Ages was baptised, married and buried by the local parish priest, while secretly listening to the sermons of the Waldensians, sharing their faith and confessing sins both to them and to the parish priest. Going into a local church in the later Middle Ages, as we learn from depositions in German-speaking areas around 1400 and from the Alpine valleys between Piedmont and Dauphiné around 1500, Waldensian followers were engaged in a complex act, believing in some parts of what was going on and mentally rejecting others. Thus they sprinkled themselves with holy water from the stoup as they entered, 'in order not to be noticed', while saying to themselves that blessing conferred no holiness on this water, which was no better than rainwater.

Benazeit, on the other hand, received Cathar Good Men who constituted a Church, totally alternative and opposed to the Catholic Church. It had its hierarchy of bishops and deacons, and Good Men and Good Women whom we can roughly envisage as the counterparts to some degree of Catholic clergy and Catholic monks and nuns. It had its rites, and the most important of these was the *consolamentum – heretication*, as we have seen, to the inquisitors. They had a very radical theology, some of which Benazeit presents. There were two Gods or principles, and the evil one had created this world and its matter, including human bodies, which were evil fleshly envelopes imprisoning souls or spirits which had fallen from the heaven of the good God or principle. Until they received the *consolamentum* and became Cathars, the men and women who shared the beliefs of the Good Men and Women and supported them were not theologically members of a Cathar Church. They were outside, waiting to enter. Note that whereas the Waldensian friars concentrated entirely on morals, the Cathar Good Men spoke entirely about doctrine. Cathar withdrawal from the moral world of their followers was as radical as their rejection of the utterly evil material world. No Cathar sacraments marked their births and marriages, no Cathar system of penance intertwined with their good and bad deeds. The Cathar Good Men were doctrinal, the Waldensian friars were moral; the Cathars formed an independent Church, the Waldensian friars did not. These persecuted friars and Good Men were extraordinarily unlike each other, but the fundamental contrasts become veiled as the Church's vocabulary is overlaid on theirs and as we read responses to the similar questions which were addressed to their followers.

Where inquisition records survive richly, as we have seen they do in southern France, and as they also do in Italy, the skewing which is brought about by their very abundance also needs reflection. We have almost no administrative documents and theological treatises surviving from Cathars or Waldensians, in contrast to the mountains surviving from the medieval Church. What are the effects? In the late twelfth and early thirteenth centuries, dominant in the surviving sources about heresy are such things as these: various problematic names for heretics in a chronicle or the decree of a church council, some demonising rhetoric in a papal bull, and a polemical treatise attacking heretics for preaching although they are illiterate. If these are extant textual counterparts of a former reality, what do they conjure up? Something a bit inchoate, perhaps illiterate? Various rather vaguely defined movements? But we also have two exceptions in the evidence from this period, heretical documents, one concerning a Cathar Council at St Félix-de-Caraman (1167 or around 1175), the other a Waldensian Council at Bergamo (1218). In 1223 Cathars drew up a document based on three previous texts relating to the St Félix Council, a record of it, a sermon delivered at it, and the report of a commission set up to look at diocesan boundaries (Hamilton 1979). Some of the Waldensians present at Bergamo wrote a formal letter to confrères in Germany, reporting attempts to settle doctrinal and administrative problems, in which disagreeing parties exchanged views before the council, then chose delegates and met in Bergamo, where they articulated their positions in writing, handed the texts over, and debated, subsequently receiving both written and oral replies and debating these (Patschovsky and Selge 1973: 20–43;

Figure 18.1 'Take us the foxes, the little foxes, that spoil the vines; for our vines have tender grapes'. In medieval exegesis of the Song of Songs, the 'little foxes' were identified as the heretics who preyed on the Church's vineyard. In this illustration from the late twelfth-century *Hortus deliciarum* of Herrad, abbess of Hohenburg (fo. 225r), the little foxes have designs on the vines while Christ indicates the situation to three suitably concerned ladies led by Ecclesia, 'the Church'.
Photo: Warburg Institute, London.

Patschovsky 1994: 121–2). Suddenly we have swinging into view archives, everyday Latin literacy, formal procedures,[5] and organisation. Suddenly these movements appear in an unfamiliar way, no longer vague and inchoate. How different they would look if we had more of their administrative documents!

Theology is a subtler problem. We know that early northern Cathars were highly learned, among the earliest to cite one of Aristotle's newly translated works, and that Italian Cathars in Lombardy and Tuscany sent their brightest students to the university of Paris (Biller 1999). Aquinas knew the treatise of an Italian Cathar theologian called Tetricus, which he cited by book and chapter number, but only one such Cathar theological treatise survives, while others survive fragmentarily only when quoted in polemical treatises written by Catholic opponents (Paolini 1994). Where such a tiny proportion of written Cathar theology survives compared with written Catholic theology, the reverse is the case for Catholic laity and Cathar followers. While we know so much and in such colour and detail about the smaller number of people – even in the Languedoc – who were the Cathar 'laity', the piety of the majority, the Catholic laity, is known rather thinly, reconstructed from dry and indirect evidence. One pattern of survival of evidence (more theological treatises and less detailed knowledge about the laity) constructs Catholicism as more coherent and uniform than it was, while the opposite pattern constructs Catharism as less coherent and more multifarious than it was.

This is all now a very long time ago. Over the centuries polemical treatises and trial records have languished in archives and libraries, getting destroyed or lost or being rediscovered and finally preserved through publication. Various forms of

Christianity have risen, flourished or decayed, as well as new schools of thought and developments in scholarship, all mediating between us and these people as they recede further from us. In 1953 a young German historian devoted the first chapter of his book on the Cathars to a history of these later constructions (Borst 1953: 1–58). After running through the representation of medieval heretics by their Catholic contemporaries, he passed in review the period from the Reformation to 1950. Sixteenth- and seventeenth-century Protestant historians wrote of medieval heretics in their own image, as forerunners, establishing a line of witnesses to truth between the early Church and Luther, while Catholic historians turned the coin round, seeing modern Protestants as the heirs to this impure and erroneous tradition. Both lines were to persist well into the twentieth century. Romanticism added an association between heresy and liberty. Friedrich Engels prefaced his history of the peasant war in Germany with an account of medieval heretics as forerunners of revolution. The ideologists of the feudal social and political order were the clergy and the ideology was orthodox Christian faith. Therefore any protest against the existing social and political order was necessarily couched in the terms of resistance to this faith: heresy. Strip the theological veil from a medieval heresy and what you see underneath is political protest. Waldensian rejection of oaths might *appear* just to be literalism in following a gospel injunction (Matthew 5.34), but it was at the same time radical opposition to the fundamental bond of society, the feudal oath. Political and cultural separatists of the Languedoc presented medieval Cathars as representative of the spirit of Occitania, set against the brutal conquering spirit of northern France. A German National Socialist ideologue saw in medieval heretics an earlier Aryanism protesting against a Mediterranean priesthood.

So: medieval heretics have had an existence after the Middle Ages, and during this after-life they have been changed and reshaped. Consider the example of the late-medieval fossilised Waldensians who survived in the valleys between Piedmont and the Dauphiné into the sixteenth century (Audisio 1984; Cameron 1984; Paravy 1993). Still recognisably products of the apostolic religious movement of around 1200, Waldensian preachers took vows of chastity as well as of poverty and obedience, and they had itinerant missions. They had celibate sisters: nuns. The vast majority of the little books they carried around with them as aids in preaching and hearing confessions were adapted or distilled from the great standard vices and virtues literature written in the thirteenth century. They put great emphasis on good works. As the Swiss reformers around 1530 looked at these curious survivals, they saw much to embarrass them: in particular, so much that was theologically, spiritually and culturally *Catholic*. Letters between Oecolampadius and Bucer show all this being discussed and dealt with. Nominal change came with the adoption of new creeds, real change came over the middle decades of the sixteenth century with the dropping of celibate and itinerant preachers, sisters, and auricular confession, and the substitution of Calvinist theology and organisation. This real change had its counterpart in Protestant historical writing, in which the Waldensian past was increasingly dominated by their concern to possess scripture in the vernacular, their hostility to the Roman Church and, above all, their suffering of persecution. Other things receded into the shadows. During the sixteenth century medieval Waldensians became forerunners of Protestants, and then over the following centuries they became medieval Protestants. Only late in the twentieth century has scholarship at last succeeded in removing the dark filter of Protestant historiography, showing the profoundly medieval Catholic elements which still characterised the late medieval Waldensians.

It is necessary to look at all the other filters which have been interposed between us and medieval heretics over the intervening centuries, by modern schools of scholarship as well as ideologies, modern sociological history as well as, say, Occitan separatism and Catholicism, in order first to detect the distorting colour which is distinctive to the movement in question and then to struggle against the distortion. Doing this is clearly necessary, but at this point I would like to suggest that it helps us only so far. There is a rhetorical-logical danger in the way historians present their deconstructions of the earlier historiographical distortions. Distilled, they can be presented thus: 'medieval heretics have been represented as Manichees, Protestants, proletarian revolutionaries, Occitan separatists . . . '. Here it is style – the reduction to such brevity – which is insidiously making the case for absurdity. But there is a more serious problem with the method and metaphor of identifying and discounting filters and, as I shall explain, a more useful metaphor that we may employ.

I can take the writing in which medieval Languedocian Cathars are put forward as exponents of a distinctive spirit of the Languedoc – the philosopher and mystic Simone Weil is one spiritually elevated example, the Toulouse journalist-turned-historian Michel Roquebert is a more earth-bound contemporary example – and I simply point to the modern Occitan cultural and political separatist movements of which these are various expressions (Roach 1997). I can turn to Catholic historians of heresy and the age-old Catholic concern to establish the author and inventor of a heresy, or from where it comes, and I can point to the polemical agenda: how could it be the true Church, with *that* origin and history? Labelling these approaches Occitan–separatist and Catholic I then discount what these writers say. But I am being too quick. Polemically concerned to demonstrate alien origin, a Catholic historian is not necessarily mistaken when finding evidence for it: only mistaken in focusing solely on that. Searching in Languedocian depositions for evidence of hatred of the northern French (it was mainly northern French soldiers who were involved in the crusade which crushed heresy in the Languedoc), the Occitan separatist historian is not mistaken when finding it: only mistaken in forgetting that Cathars had not just been Occitan but also German, Flemish, northern French and Italian. And there is more to say. We have in fact been helped to see certain aspects of medieval heretics much more clearly by various post-medieval ideologies and movements in scholarship. Cathar theology and liturgy *was* imported from the east (Hamilton 1994; Paolini 1994; Hamilton and Hamilton 1998: 43–6); there *was* resentment of the northern French. We are indebted to a whole variety of outlooks for further understanding of particular areas. The spotlight is a more useful metaphor than the filter, suggesting more brilliant illumination than before of some aspects of medieval heresy, at the expense of others whose darkness deepens. Let us turn to some of the post-medieval schools – Protestants and Catholics, Marxists, and others – thinking in these terms.

There is real hatred in Protestant and Catholic historiography. In 1163 Cathars were burnt to death in Cologne, and in 1178 many in northern France and in 1183 many in Flanders. In 1201 a knight who was a Cathar follower was tried in Paris and burnt to death in Nevers. In 1210 a Cathar was burnt to death in London, as were also several Cathars somewhere (unspecified) in England in the following year. In Mont-Aimé in Champagne on Friday 13 May 1239, following a week of interrogation, 180 Cathars were burnt to death. While the geography of my selection – northern European – illustrates an earlier point about the southern skewing of our picture of Catharism, my main point is to remind the reader of the horror of repression. Heretics condemned and hated the Church that did this, and the Church condemned the heretics whose aberrant teachings, in its view, deceived people, leading those who died in heretical faith to suffer eternal damnation in hell: agents of the devil. Confessional historiography shrouded much in darkness, but it saw hatred more clearly than we do.

It is all too easy to parade the darkness brought about by Marx and Engels, the trimming of data about heresy to fit in with what Engels had written on the subject, and the encouragement, which was provided by Marx's and Engels' insistence – in itself provocatively useful – on the illusory self-consciousness of past epochs, simply to disregard what people in the past actually said. In need of statement, however obvious, is the debt we owe to these post-industrial patriarchs. In the halcyon years before the coming of the crusaders in 1209, the lords of a small town in the region of Toulouse supported the Cathars, as did many of the knights and ladies, and in the houses where they listened to Cathar sermons, 'adored' Good Men and Women, and ate ceremonially with them, they found Good Men and Women who were often their mothers, fathers, uncles, aunts and siblings. The Cathar Good Men sometimes had workshops. The Cathar Church disposed of large sums of money, augmented by legacies which often numbered several hundred shillings and occasionally a thousand. Nobles, workshops, cash: important themes in any attempt to investigate and depict Languedocian Catharism, and even though our categories are now very different, the direction of our attention to these themes ultimately comes from Marxist concern with the priority of material life.

Montaillou: a village is described in many layers. The base of the pyramid is the physical geography of the terrain, and following this are accounts of pasture and woodland, population, agriculture, the economy, family forms, cultural exchanges and social relationships, and concepts of time and space, all based on quotation from the extraordinary detail of depositions in front of the inquisitor Jacques Fournier in Pamiers around 1320. The culmination is religion and images of the other world. The dominant element in the village, the peasant house – more imposing in translation, the *domus* or *ostal* – is transposed into religion, becoming in villagers' minds their view of heaven: one enormous *domus*. Present in the village are various sorts of belief, Catholic, Cathar and deep-rooted peasant–Pyrenean, and they are not only themselves overlapping and inchoate but they also thoroughly imbue and are thoroughly imbued by everything in the village. We are being helped to see heresy and much else in these terms: 'the sacred is only the social' (Le Roy Ladurie 1978: 352). Others have traced the intellectual roots of this – a broader French historiographical tradition of looking at the 'lived religion' of ordinary people, and historians in the 1970s reading and being influenced by anthropology – and they have commented on Ladurie's intellectual enterprise in spotting the wonderful opportunity offered by Fournier's interrogations (Benad 1990). Once again, Catharism is represented by skewed evidence. There are abundant depositions but none of the no longer extant theological books used by the leader of the late Cathars, Peter Autier, on the basis of which he had preached, nor any document emanating from Cathar organisation. The depositions are from adherents who had listened to a handful of the Good Men of late Catharism, prominent among whom was one very peculiar man, Guillaume Belibaste. 'Adherents' – let us not forget what strikes every reader, their extraordinary life-likeness. They inhabit a curiously class- and rent-free village, and the personalities among them – an anarchic-minded shepherd, a free-loving countess – are curiously anticipatory of Bourvil, Stéphane Audran, and other players of such roles in the modern French cinema.

Central to *Montaillou* is localism: the deep study of a religion in a particular milieu. Among the brilliant exponents of localism have been Grado Merlo, in his study of Waldensians and other heretics in fourteenth-century Piedmont, and Pierette Paravy in her study of Catholics, Waldensians and sorcerers in fifteenth-century Dauphiné (Merlo 1977; Paravy 1993). While I look to the shadows I hope readers will take on trust my view that both these historians have achieved masterpieces in their *pointilliste* pictures of Waldensianism. Advocating the local method, Merlo has developed the theory that the term *Waldensianism* (*valdismo*) should be discarded and replaced by *Waldensianisms* (*valdismi*), which now becomes the semantic banner for studies which emphasise the local autonomy and particularism of these phenomena (Merlo 1984–91). Multiple and various realities in the past, they came to be labelled *Waldensian* by persecuting medieval churchmen and later post-medieval Waldensian and Protestant historians, all locked in unholy alliance in imposing this uniform identity. Attractive and powerful though the arguments are, there are grounds for reservation. First, the skewed survival of records (little written theology, many scattered local depositions) in itself promotes a fragmented picture of medieval heresy. Secondly, medieval heresies tended to be secret organisations. Consider the Germanophone 'Waldensians' and the 'Waldensians' of the Alps of Piedmont–Dauphiné who appear in the inquisition records of these regions – I use quotation marks to signal doubt about identity. Should they be looked at separately? Regarded as autonomous expressions of dissidence, produced by the very different societies and cultures of upper Austria and north-western Italy? By chance a few manuscripts preserve Latin copies of a short Waldensian historical text, called the *Book of the Elect* (*Liber electorum*), which circulated among the Waldensians of upper Austria in the mid-fourteenth century, while one manuscript alone preserves the Alpine-valley dialect version which circulated among Waldensians in north-western Italy. These tiny fragments suddenly illuminate a dark area. The sharing of the same Waldensian text implies unity and communication between Waldensians of different regions and languages. We have other fragments of information: suggestions from around 1260 and 1300 that Waldensians of different regions, Germany, Lombardy and France, held councils, and that those travelling over the Alps from Germanophone regions into Lombardy would avoid detection by disguising themselves as pilgrims. They tried to hide their organisation from inquisitors, and now a recent turn in modern scholarship conspires to help it stay hidden.

Their women preach; they argue that women can preach. Catholic polemicists said this about the Waldensians, citing some of their arguments. The turning of the spotlight to this theme we owe to modern feminist scholarship, building upon a fundamental work by an East German Marxist historian, Gottfried Koch, who adapted Engels' socio-political protesters to the particular case of women who were oppressed in feudal society. A consequence has been much illuminating modern work, which has concentrated on the high role of women among Cathars and Cathar appeal to women. It has preferred Cathars, possibly in part because they were more radical, and certainly because of the greater visibility of Cathar women (as also Cathar men) than of Waldensian women. We owe even more to the union in Koch's work of the Marxist tradition with early twentieth-century German sociology. In a wide-ranging sociological-historical survey, Ernst Troeltsch had tried to identify ideal-typical characteristics of churches and sects (Troeltsch 1931, translation of a work of 1911). Sects originate as reactions against churches, and in their beginnings they are radical, typically propounding a priesthood of all believers and a critical attitude to various social issues (e.g. opposing war). As they progress through time they undergo *Verkirchlichung*, 'churchification', adopting a separate ministry and becoming conservative on social issues. Adapted to women, this means some egalitarianism at an early stage, and then, at a later stage in a sect's history, conservative exclusion from ministry and confinement to family.

Troeltsch's model can be applied as a hypothesis to the Waldensians. Right at the beginning Waldensian men *and women* wandered the streets and squares, preaching. In a debate held at Narbonne, in the presence of the archbishop and many other ecclesiastics, the Waldensians put forward arguments for women preaching. In one early set of sentences, passed in 1241–2 by the inquisitor Peter Sella, we see individual instances of the Waldensian sisters preaching in Quercy in the preceding years or decades. Soon, however, there is silence, and then long interrogations of the Waldensian Raymond de la Côte, by the inquisitor Jacques Fournier in Pamiers in 1319, confirm what this silence suggests, that women were no longer accorded an important role. It is a resounding success for Troeltsch, as we see the transition from the Waldensian sect's early radicalism to its later hierarchisation and its counterpart in the transition from early egalitarianism for women to their later exclusion.

If we have here the benefit of a spotlight we also have shadows. The choice of Cathars is mistaken. The visibility of larger numbers of Cathar women is a simple consequence of the greater survival of records from the Languedoc, where Cathars were the majority heresy, as compared with records from Germanophone areas, where Waldensians were the majority heresy. Insufficient heed has been paid to the fact that Catholic authors from the late twelfth to the mid-thirteenth century consistently argued for a special place for women among the Waldensians, while being significantly silent on the Cathars and on women. This modern research has also bypassed the simple contrasts between *what was said* by the two groups: Waldensians said women should preach; Cathars preached that created flesh was evil, a tenet which could most easily be turned against women's bodies (Benazeit's deposition above; Note 4 below; Biller 1997).

From the sociologist's pattern there comes flickering light and shadow. Consider the decline and then absence of a role for Waldensian women, the evidence for which is the testimony of the Waldensian Raymond de la Côte. Here is the record of his interrogation. 'Asked if there are virgins among them and [if] virgins are received to their *status*, he replied no. He also said that in no way would they receive virgins to their *status*. Asked why, he said that [this was] because women cannot preach the word of God and because they cannot receive the orders of the priesthood, diaconate and *majorality* [= the three Waldensian Orders]. He also said that widows are not received among them, nor any other women, nor do they [the Brothers] cohabit with them: so he said' (Duvernoy 1965: i.74). We know that the impression given by these answers is misleading, for the Waldensian sisters still existed and we can name one of whom he must have known. The evidence is there: Raymond named various fellow friars, all male; their names overlap with those named by Waldensian followers sentenced by Bernard Gui; these names include a Waldensian sister, Raymonde of Castres. The point is generalised by a description of the Waldensians of this region and approximately of this date which says men *and women* were received in their order and that the women were called sisters; it goes on to describe the quiet and secret life of the sisters, living in houses in twos and threes pretending to be the wives or sisters of the friars, or as old women living on their own without men, though often visited by them (Gonnet 1998: 178, 180; Biller and Green 1994). The inquisitor Fournier knew that Raymond was trying to mislead, for the last words are the inquisitor's: *ut dixit*, 'so he said'. We do not have to look far for further enlightenment about Raymond's words. All we need to do is to remember that he was a brave man who knew he was going to his death. The record tells us of his refusal to co-operate with the inquisitor, his steadfast refusal to give Fournier any information which could help him capture other Waldensians. So, while he would name cities where he had worked, he refused to name the villages he visited from these cities, and he refused to give the names of Waldensians who were still alive and free. And in the words quoted above he was trying to give the impression that the Waldensian Order contained no women, in order to protect the few (?) and clandestine houses of Waldensian sisters. The moral: taken as a hypothesis, the sociologist's pattern is extraordinarily useful in suggesting patterns in the data to look for and themes to debate; taken as law, it spreads darkness. The Waldensian sisters' later history is a continuation in two senses – continued existence, and continued successful concealment, so that it is *almost* impossible for us still to see them. All that is left is the ceremony in which they took their vows, described in depositions from Strasbourg around 1400, and a description of their form of life in the correspondence of Waldensians and Swiss reformers around 1530.[6]

Finally, if the enterprise of this chapter – 'problematising the sources', as it is known in the trade – brings light, where is its shadow? My presentation of the problem of *seeing* medieval heretics is something which draws upon the work of many distinguished scholars, and this pedigree should be recapitulated first, before I suggest an answer. In 1935 Herbert Grundmann exposed the problem of following Protestant and Catholic historiography in pursuing separately the histories of religious orders and heresies. In 1953 Arno Borst showed how to write the history of the post-medieval constructions of medieval heresy, in religions, ideologies and schools of scholarship, and among others who have developed the historiography of medieval heresy further are Nelson (1980), Merlo (1984–91), and Hamilton (1998).[7]

In 1965 Herbert Grundmann showed the source-problems of depositions in which leading questions had been systematically employed (Grundmann 1965), preparing the ground for Robert Lerner's demolition of the sect of the Free Spirit in 1972, and also for Grado Merlo's analysis of fourteenth-century depositions from Piedmont as 'grilles' or 'filters'. Even as I write, this method is being further developed among the heresy-scholars of the University of Bologna, and in the study of the filters in the Languedoc depositions of 1237–84 which is now being prepared by Caterina Bruschi.[8]

The metaphors I have used have all suggested two things, that there is difficulty in seeing and that there is something to see, and the shadow cast by the first is its erosion of the second. More far-reaching scepticism in the historiographical modes which are current now may eventually suggest that the extant texts *create* these medieval heretics. A Cistercian historian wrote that, after the Albigensian crusaders had captured the fortress of Minerve, at least 140 of the Good Men and Women who were captured refused to convert and they were then thrown on to a huge pyre, where they burnt to death (Sibly and Sibly 1998: 85). Such events and their impact may be of decreasing interest to those historians who (like me) busy themselves 'problematising' their sources, and to those historians who (unlike me) are increasingly interested in destabilising the notion that history deals with past reality.

NOTES

1   I am grateful to Alexander Patschovsky for information about his book, *Häresie und Politik. Zur politischen Funktion von Häresie in der mittelalterlichen Gesellschaft (11.–15. Jh.).*

2   Friars translates the Latin *fratres*, which could also be translated *brothers*.

3   A new edition has been announced by Annette Pales-Gobilliard (Pales-Gobilliard 1991: 143 note 4).

4   Toulouse, Bibliothèque Municipale MS 609, fo. 106r: 'Maledictus sit magister qui fecit istam corporadam!'. Et ipsa testis dixit ei, 'Et nonne fecit vos Deus?'. Et ipsa respondit, 'Eamus! Vultis modo scribere mihi istud!'. I take *corporadam* to be *corporatam*: 'incarnated', 'fleshed', 'fleshly' or 'bodily woman'.

5   Formal legal procedure among Italian Cathars has been pointed out by Paolini 1994: 88–90.

6   This account is based on my article, 'The preaching of the Waldensian Sisters', no. VIII in Biller, P. (2001) Forthcoming from Shulamith Shahar is a book on Waldensian women. See also Shulamith Shahar (2001), *Women in a Medieval Heretical Sect*, Woodbridge: The Boydell Press.

7   See also the articles gathered in *Historiographie du Catharisme* 1979 and Merlo 1994.

8   Caterina Bruschi's forthcoming book is entitled *Tales of Travelling Cathars*.

REFERENCES

Benad, M. (1990) *Domus und Religion in Montaillou*, Tübingen: Verlag J.C.B. Mohr.

Biller, P. (1997) 'Cathars and material women' in Biller, P. and Minnis, A.J., ed., *This Body of Death. Medieval Theology and the Natural Body*, York Studies in Medieval Theology, 1, York: York Medieval Press: 61–107.

—— (1999) 'The Northern Cathars and higher learning', in *The Medieval Church: Universities, Heresy and the Religious Life. Essays in Honour of Gordon Leff*, ed. Biller, P. and Dobson, B., Studies in Church History, Subsidia, 11, Woodbridge: The Boydell Press: 25–53.

—— (2001) *The Waldenses, 1170–1530. Between a Religious Order and a Church*, Variorum Collected Studies Series, 676, Aldershot: Variorum.

Biller, P. and Green, J. (1994) 'Argent allemand et hérésie médiévale: appendice', in Aubrun, M. and others *Entre idéal et réalité: Finances et religion du moyen-âge à l'époque contemporaine*, Clermont-Ferrand: Publications de l'Institut d'Études du Massif Central: 49–56, reprinted as nos. VIII and XIII in Biller, P. (2001).

Biller, P. and Hudson, A. ed. (1994) *Heresy and Literacy, 1000–1500*, Cambridge: Cambridge University Press.

Borst, A. (1953) *Die Katharer*, Schriften der Monumenta Germaniae Historica, 12, Stuttgart: Anton Hiersemann.

Bruschi, C. and Biller, P. ed. (2002), *Texts and the Repression of Medieval Heresy*, York Studies in Medieval Theology, 4, York: York Medieval Press.

Duvernoy, J. ed. (1965) *Le registre d'inquisition de Jacques Fournier, évêque de Pamiers (1318–1325). Manuscrit no. Vat. Latin 4030 de la Bibliothèque Vaticane*, Bibliothèque Méridionale, 2nd series, 41, 3 vols., Toulouse: Edouard Privat.

—— (1972) *Le registre d'inquisition de Jacques Fournier, évêque de Pamiers (1318–1325): Corrections*, Toulouse: Edouard Privat.

—— (1976) *La religion des cathares*, Toulouse: Edouard Privat.

—— (1979) *L'histoire des cathares*, Toulouse: Edouard Privat.

Given, J.B. (1997) *Inquisition and Medieval Society: Power, Discipline and Resistance in Languedoc*, Ithaca and London: Cornell University Press.

Gonnet, G. ed. (1998) *Enchiridion fontium Valdensium*, II, Collana della Facoltà Valdese di Teologia, 22, Turin: Editrice Claudiana.

Grundmann, H. (1961) *Religiöse Bewegungen im Mittelalter*, 2nd edn, Hildesheim: Georg Olms Verlagsbuchhandlung; (1935) 1st edn, Berlin: Verlag Dr Emil Eberling; (1995) English translation, *Religious Movements in the Middle Ages*, Notre Dame, Indiana, and London: University of Notre Dame Press.

—— (1965) 'Ketzerverhöre des Spätmittelalters als quellenkritisches Problem', *Deutsches Archiv für Erforschung des Mittelalters*, 21: 519–75.

Hamilton, B. (1979) 'The Cathar Council of St Felix reconsidered' no. IX in Hamilton, B. *Monastic Reform, Catharism and the Crusades (900–1300)*, Variorum Collected Studies Series, 97, London: Variorum Reprints.

—— (1994) 'Wisdom from the East: the reception by the Cathars of Eastern dualist texts', in Biller and Hudson 1994: 38–60.

—— (1998) 'The State of Research. The legacy of Charles Schmidt to the study of Christian dualism', *Journal of Medieval History*, 24: 191–214.

Hamilton, J. and Hamilton, B. ed. (1998) *Christian Dualist Heresies in the Byzantine World c.650–c.1405*, Manchester: Manchester University Press.

Historiographie du Catharisme (1979), Cahiers du Fanjeaux, 14, Toulouse: Edouard Privat.

Koch, G. (1962) *Frauenfrage und Ketzertum im Mittelalter. Die Frauenfrage im Rahmen des Katharismus und des Waldensertums und ihre sozialen Wurzeln (12.–14. Jahrhundert)*, Forschungen zur mittelalterlichen Geschichte, 9, Berlin: Akademie-Verlag.

Kolmer, L. (1982) *Ad capiendas vulpes. Die Ketzerbekämpfung in Südfrankreich in der ersten Hälfte des 13. Jahrhunderts und die Ausbildung des Inquisitionsverfahrens*, Pariser Historische Studien, 19, Bonn: Ludwig Röhrscheid Verlag.

Lambert, M.D. (1992) *Medieval Heresy. Popular Movements from the Gregorian Movement to the Reformation*, Oxford: Blackwell.

—— (1998) *The Cathars*, Oxford: Blackwell.

Le Roy Ladurie, E. (1978) *Montaillou: Cathars and Catholics in a French Village, 1294–1324*, London: Scolar Press; translation and abridgement of (1975) *Montaillou, village occitan de 1294 à 1324*, Paris: Éditions Gallimard.

Lerner, R.E. (1972) *The Heresy of the Free Spirit in the Later Middle Ages*, Berkeley, Los Angeles and London: University of California Press.

Limborch, P. Van (1692) *Historia Inquisitionis, cui subiungitur Liber Sententiarum Inquisitionis Tholosanae Ab anno Christi mcccvii ad annum mcccxxiii*, Amsterdam: Henricus Wetstenius.

Merlo, G.G. (1977) *Eretici e inquisitori nella società piemontese del trecento*, Turin: Editrice Claudiana.

—— (1984–91) *Valdesi e valdismi medievali*, 2 vols, Turin: Editrice Claudiana.

—— (1994) ed. *Eretici ed eresie medievali nella storiografia contemporanea*, Torre Pellice: Società di Studi Valdesi.

Moore, R.I. (1977) *The Origins of European Dissent*, London: Allen Lane; revised edition (1985), Oxford: Basil Blackwell.

—— (1987) *The Formation of a Persecuting Society: Power and Deviance in Western Europe, 950–1250*, Oxford: Basil Blackwell.

——(1996) 'Heresy, repression and social change in the age of Gregorian reform', in Waugh, S.L. and Diehl, P.D., ed., *Christendom and its discontents. Exclusion, persecution and rebellion, 1000–1050*, Cambridge: Cambridge University Press: 19–46.

Nelson, J.L. (1972) 'Society, theodicy and the origins of heresy: towards a reassessment of the medieval evidence', in Baker, D., ed., *Schism, Heresy and Religious Protest*, Studies in Church History, 9, Cambridge: Cambridge University Press: 65–77.

—— (1980) 'Religion in "Histoire totale": Some recent work on medieval heresy and popular religion', *Religion*, 10: 60–85.

Pales-Gobilliard, A. (1991) 'Pénalités inquisitoriales au XIVe siècle', in *Crises et réformes dans l'église de la réforme grégorienne à la préréforme*, Actes du 115e Congrès National des Sociétés Savantes, Avignon 1990, Section d'Histoire Médiévale et de Philologie, Paris: Éditions du Comité des Travaux Historiques et Scientifiques: 143–54.

Paolini, L. (1994) 'Italian Catharism and written culture', in Biller and Hudson 1994: 83–103.

Paravy, P. (1993) *De la chrétienté romaine à la réforme en Dauphiné*, 2 vols., Collection de l'École Française de Rome, 183, Rome: École Française de Rome, Palais Farnèse.

Patschovsky, A. ed. (1979) *Quellen zur Böhmischen Inquisition im 14. Jahrhundert*, Monumenta Germaniae Historica, Quellen zur Geistesgeschichte des Mittelalters, 11, Weimar: Hermann Böhlaus Nachfolger.

—— (1994) 'The literacy of Waldensianism from Valdes to *c.* 1400', in Biller and Hudson 1994: 112–36.

Patschovsky, A. and Selge, K.-V. ed. (1973) *Quellen zur Geschichte der Waldenser*, Texte zur Kirchen- und Theologiegeschichte, 18, Gütersloh: Gütersloher Verlagshaus Gerd Mohn.

Pegg, M. G. (2001) *The Corruption of Angels: The Great Inquisition of 1245–1246*, Princeton: Princeton University Press.

Roach, A. (1997) 'Occitania past and present: southern consciousness in medieval and modern French politics', *History Workshop Journal* 43, pp. 1–22.

Sibly, W.A. and Sibly, M.D. tr. (1998) *The History of the Albigensian Crusade. Peter of Les Vaux-de-Cernay's Historia Albigensis*, Woodbridge: The Boydell Press.

Troeltsch, E. (1931) *The Social Teaching of the Christian Churches*, Halley Stewart Publications, 1, 2 vols, London and New York: George Allen and Unwin Ltd and The MacMillan Company.

Wakefield, W.L. (1986) 'Heretics and inquisitors: the case of Auriac and Cambiac', *Journal of Medieval History*, 12: 225–37.

THE CORPSE IN THE MIDDLE AGES: THE PROBLEM OF THE DIVISION OF THE BODY

————◆————

Agostino Paravicini Bagliani

BODY-PARTS

On 19 October 1216, John 'Lackland' king of England died at Newark near Nottingham. His body was dismembered by his confessor, the abbot of Crokestone, who had the king's entrails packed in salt and conveyed to his monastery. The body itself was clothed and buried with honour in Worcester Cathedral. One of John's predecessors, Henry I, had wished to be buried at Reading Abbey. He died at Rouen, and there his brain, his eyes and his entrails were interred. The body was cut into pieces, covered in salt and wrapped up in a leather bag. Despite these precautions, by the time the royal convoy reached Caen, the liquid seeping out of the body caused the men who were travelling with it to faint. Matthew Paris in his Chronicle tells the story:

> Now the king's body remained near Rouen for a long time unburied where his brain, eyes and entrails were interred. The rest of his body had had incisions made in it with small knives and had been packed in salt, because of the stench which was great and impregnated the atmosphere around it. The body was wrapped up in ox-hides. The doctor, hired for a large fee, had been so fearful for the preserving of the head that he had caused the brain to be extracted, but it was already rotting from the excessive stench, even though it had been wrapped in many linen cloths. The doctor died because of the foul odour. He had mistakenly been delighted by the promises made him about the size of his fee. This man was the last of the many victims of King Henry. From Rouen, the king's body was taken to Caen where his father had been buried. His body was set down in the church in front of his father's tomb, when a black and horrible liquid began to seep through the ox-hides. Collected in pots placed beneath the bier [....], this liquid aroused great horror in those who saw the sight. Finally the king's body was brought to England about Christmastime, to [....] the noble church which he himself had founded. He was interred as a king, in the presence of archbishops, bishops and the great men of the realm.
>
> (Matthew Paris, *Chronica* ad an. 1135: 161–2. Cf. Henry of Huntingdon, *Historia Anglorum* VIII, 2 (ed. Greenway, 256ff.); *Annales Wintonienses, Continuatio S. Augustini Cantuariensis*: 7)

In medieval Europe in the thirteenth century too, the dismemberment of a corpse was an essential procedure in cases where the bodily remains of the dead person had to be transported, as soon as possible after the demise, to a burial-place some distance from the site of death. To loosen the bones from the flesh and to make transport easier, the body was cut up into bits which were then boiled in water until they became completely disarticulated. Another, simpler, procedure was to open up the body and remove the entrails, which were the bits most likely to putrefy, and then bury those on the spot or nearby. They could, alternatively, be transported in a container of lead or some other metal, or in a stone urn, or a primary sarcophagus. The body itself was stuffed with aromatic substances, wrapped in hides, often of deerskin, which were then carefully sewn up (Duparc 1980–1: 360–72).

These procedures were already old: in fact they had been documented since the ninth century. The entrails of the deceased Emperor Charles the Bald (d. 877) were removed and the rest of his corpse was treated with wine and spices so that it could be carried to St-Denis where he had wished to be buried. The royal remains had to be interred at Nantua, however, on account of the frightful stench. Seven years afterwards, Charles appeared to a monk of St-Denis and a cleric of St-Quentin-en-Vermandois to inform them that Saint Denis was unhappy to know that Charles's body had not been interred in the place which he had honoured throughout his life. It was then that the monks set off to find the body (or rather what was left of it) so that it could be re-buried at the abbey.

The corpse of the emperor Otto I (d. 973) was also eviscerated, and his entrails buried at Memleben, while his body was interred at Magdeburg. Until the twelfth century, nearly all emperors' corpses underwent similar treatment. In 1167, when an epidemic decimated Frederick Barbarossa's army in Italy, the bodies of most of the dead knights and prelates were boiled, and their bones were sent to Germany. When Barbarossa himself died on crusade in 1190, his body was eviscerated and boiled. His bones were carried not to Germany but to Tyre where the emperor had planned to go on pilgrimage.

The sequence is clear: from the ninth century until the thirteenth, nearly all known cases of the division of corpses into parts concerned famous people – kings, emperors, prelates, members of the high nobility – who lived north of the Alps, especially in the empire. Medieval people themselves understood the situation in those terms. For Buoncompagno of Signa, the Italian master of rhetoric, the dismemberment of the corpse was a custom:

> The Romans of olden days used to empty corpses of their entrails. They took out all the intestines. The rest of the body was softened in salt water. Thus bodies could be preserved for a very long time, as you can still see today in ancient palaces and, near Naples, in certain caves. The Germans (*Teutonici*), by contrast, extracted the entrails from the corpses of men of high status who had died in foreign lands. They boiled the rest of the body for a long time in cauldrons until all the flesh, the nerves and sinews were separated from the bones, and after that, the bones were preserved in aromatic wine, and covered in spices, and taken back to their fatherland.
>
> (Buoncompagno da Signa, cited in Paravicini Bagliani 1991: 273)

According to Saba Malaspina, the evisceration of the corpse of Isabelle, wife of King Philip III of France, who died at Cosenza on 28 January 1271, was carried out 'according to the ancient French tradition'. A geography of attitudes to dismemberment thus seems to have existed in Europe between the ninth century and the thirteenth, and historians are beginning to be aware of this fact (Park 1994).

Such obviously crude and violent procedures nevertheless remind us of certain anthropological assumptions in those medieval centuries which did not entirely square with a Christian view of death that involved respect for mortal remains. Practices like those of dividing up bodies turned the corpse into something semi-animate and magical – as if the spirit would be separated from the body only after its final burial. The division of the body actually implies a kind of refusal to accept the corpse's putrefaction. To try to separate the flesh from the bones as soon as possible after death, or to eviscerate bodies and preserve only the non-putrescent parts, amounted to saying that it was the bones in particular that represented the dead person's identity. That is why in so many medieval wills the corpse is defined as *corpus sive ossa*: 'the body or the bones'.

MULTIPLE AND SELF-CHOSEN DIVISION OF THE BODY

The division of the body was not made for the sole purpose of separating the flesh from the bones to facilitate transport. The Emperor Henry III (d. 1056) did something new. He wanted his entrails to be interred at Goslar where his daughter Mathilda had been buried and where he used to say that his heart lay. When he died at Bodfeld, his body was carried to Speyer to be buried there beside his father. The division of the body in this case was something deliberate and freely chosen in advance. Henry III himself ordered the evisceration and a three-fold division of his corpse into entrails, heart and body.

With the exception of a few interesting episodes recorded in saints' *Lives* (Robert of Arbrissel was buried in 1117 at Fontevrault, but his heart was buried at Orsan where he died), Henry III's triple burial remained for a long time an isolated case. It is only towards the end of the twelfth century that examples of the practice begin to multiply, especially in England. Richard the Lionheart wanted his heart to be buried at Rouen (where the most corruptible parts of the body of his great-grandfather Henry I of England had been interred), his brain, blood and entrails at Charroux (a favoured monastery in northern Poitou), and his body at Fontevrault (where his father lay, and where his mother and sister Joan would also lie in their turn). Nearly all the members of the English royal family in the second half of the thirteenth century left similar instructions as to the final resting-place of their heart. Richard of Cornwall, brother of King Henry III, buried the heart of his son Henry (d.1271) near the tomb of Edward the Confessor at Westminster. Edward I (d.1307), himself a former crusader, ordered that his heart should be carried to the Holy Land by 140 knights. Perhaps inspired by English models, Blanche of Castile (d.1253), mother of St Louis, left instructions that her heart should be buried separately from her body. Three and a half months after her death, the abbess of Lys near Melun succeeded in obtaining the queen's heart, thereby carrying out her last wishes.

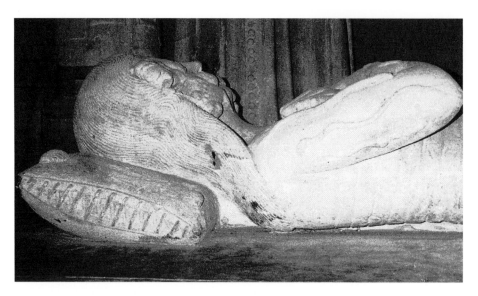

Figure 19.1 While toads feast on his eyes and face, worms burrow into the upper part of the corpse of François I de la Sarra (d. 1360). Stone effigy (detail) *c*.1400, Chapel of La Sarraz, Vaud (Switzerland). Photo: Martine Gaillard.

St Louis does not seem to have left orders about the separate burial of his heart. But when he died at Tunis in 1270, his body was taken, intact, to Sicily, where the flesh was separated from the bones by being boiled in water. The heart and the entrails were given to the king of Sicily, the dead man's brother, and buried at the abbey of Monreale near Palermo:

> The king's personal attendants, all the officials and all those whose office it was, took the king's body. They dismembered it, and had it boiled in water and wine until the bones became white and the flesh became detached and it was possible to remove it without difficulty. The entrails were removed in Sicily and taken to the Benedictine abbey of Monreale, four leagues from Palermo, to be interred there. The monks . . . received the heart and the rest of this king's entrails devotedly, as if it were a precious gift. The officials and palace servants washed the bones of the king's body with great care, and wrapped them in silken cloths with sweet-smelling spices, and placed them safely in a coffin which was to be laid in his tomb in the church of St Denis, with his ancestors and the other kings of France, when they were able to bury it there.
>
> (*Chronique de Primat*: 58G)

We have already seen that self-chosen division of the body is first documented in the Empire. At the close of the twelfth century and especially in the thirteenth, the fashion spread to England and France, then to Brabant and Castille. Evidence for Italy, however, remains extremely rare, indeed non-existent. In regard to the body and how to treat it, medieval Europe thus offers some unsuspectedly divergent attitudes.

Of course there is a great difference between dividing the body only for ease of transport, and self-chosen multiple division of the body. The latter represents the wishes of an individual who uses his or her body – for the last time – to express feelings and affections and to make plural choices. How better to express love of a dead daughter than to have one's heart buried beside her tomb? Is not the multiple and self-chosen division of the body one of the high points of what historians nowadays often call 'the discovery of the individual'? The voluntary division of the corpse implied, moreover, an extraordinary valorisation of the person's body. Certain, highly symbolic, parts of the body were assigned the task of prolonging the history of a person's identity and memory beyond death.

We can say by way of generalisation that self-chosen dismemberment of the body became an increasingly sophisticated affair. Two cases will illustrate this. On 6 December 1268, Pietro de Vico, *podestà* of Viterbo, made his will. 'Impelled by fear of God and by divine inspiration', he ordered that his body should be cut up into seven parts as a sign of his aversion to the seven deadly sins to which he acknowledged he had often succumbed:

> Terrified by heaven-sent fear and struck by divine inspiration, he humbly chose the church below-mentioned as his place of burial, asking that his body be divided into seven parts, as a sign of his detestation of the seven deadly vices of which he acknowledged he was guilty on many occasions, according to the manner and form indicated in his will and his last wishes.
>
> (Calisse 1887: 454, n. LVIII)

When the places of death and burial coincided, there was no need for dismemberment. Peter of Vico wished his body to be mutilated to purify it of its sins. Self-mutilation, a visible sign of humility and contrition, here became the instrument of salvation. But what an extraordinary wish to dispose of one's body so completely!

An administrator of church lands (*vidame*) of Anniviers (modern Swiss Valais), dictated his last wishes on 4 November 1284. After stipulating that his daughter inherit his goods, this knight gave orders that if he were to die in the ecclesiastical province of Tarentaise (to which the diocese of Sion belonged in the Middle Ages), or in the town or diocese of Lausanne, his flesh was to be separated from his bones and buried in the church of Ste-Euphémie at Anniviers. The bones thus liberated from the flesh were to be buried, half with the Cistercians of Hauterive (modern canton Fribourg, Switzerland), half with the Cistercians of Maigrauge (in the town of Fribourg). Such instructions required the boiling and dismemberment of the corpse. His fear that the separation of the bones from the flesh 'might not be sufficient' was real enough, but did not lead the testator to avoid the mutilation of his own body. On the contrary, this was just what he desired, in order to guarantee a doubling of his burial and hence even a multiplication of intercessions and prayers: these he entrusted, we may note in passing, not to the friars but to the Cistercians, in a perfect symmetry of male and female houses.

OPPOSITION AND PROHIBITION

Until the thirteenth century, evisceration and dismemberment, unusual though they were, seemed quite clearly permissible. No criticism is known to have been raised against such practices. On the level of theology, the division of the corpse posed no problem. Had not Augustine said that God's omnipotence would guarantee the reunification of all parts of the body at the Resurrection, even in cases when the body had been wholly or partly dismembered? And had not the cult of relics familiarised the West with the fragmentation of bodies?

Yet, from the mid-thirteenth century onwards, with the practice quite widespread, the division of the body provoked discussion, polemic, and resistance/opposition.[1] According to Henry of Ghent, Bishop Robert Grosseteste of Lincoln (d. 1253), chancellor of Oxford University, 'clearly and expressly forbade any such dismemberment to be performed on his body'. In many wills, there is a clear wish to avert any dismemberment of the testator's bodily remains. While some thirteenth-century cardinals, all of them French, ordered, apparently without hesitation, that their bodies were to be dismembered should they happen to die in a place far distant from that envisaged for their burials, in striking contrast, all the Italian cardinals who considered this eventually in their wills, wanted to avoid having their bodies undergo the risk of any dismemberment. Cardinal John Boccamazza (d. 1309), scion of a distinguished Roman family, even renounced burial at St Peter's if he were to die further away from the Eternal City than the distance between it and Perugia. These Italian cardinals opted for the survival intact – at least temporarily – of their mortal remains and envisaged two interments: the first at the place of death or at one or two days' distance from it, the second, after the natural process of decomposition had been completed (Paravicini Bagliani 1980).

In 1289, university circles in Paris were agitated by serious debates over the division of the corpse. The argument was provoked by Philip the Fair's decision to change the instructions left by his father, Philip III, who had died at Perpignan on 6 October 1285. In order that Philip senior's body might be carried to St Denis where he had chosen to be buried, his body was eviscerated, then boiled so as to detach the bones. The flesh and the entrails, which Philip III had wished should be interred in the Dominican church at Narbonne, ended up in the cathedral of that city. As compensation, Philip the Fair promised his confessor, the Dominican Nicholas de Gorran, that the Dominican church in Paris would receive his father's heart.

But had the king the right to alter the testamentary dispositions of his father? The masters of the Faculty of Theology who took part in the discussion, Henry of Ghent, Godfrey of Fontaines and Gervase of Mont-St-Éloi, had reservations about Philip the Fair's decision, but still did not condemn the principle of dividing the body. Even evisceration of a corpse for ease of transport alone was, they considered, legitimate. A few years later, in 1291, Olivier Tréguier, a Dominican theologian, revived the debate, no doubt with the aim of preserving the Dominicans' right to receive burials which had once been one of the key factors in their success. In favour of dismemberment and boiling of bodies Tréguier produced all the arguments about these practices not being prejudicial to the doctrine of the Resurrection, since divine power could instantly reassemble all the dismembered bodies. Godfrey of Fontaines, who re-entered the debate at this point, argued, on the contrary, that the integrity of the body must outweigh any other desire (such as wanting to be buried near the graves of close kin). Only the bodies of saints could be divided 'for the common good'.

Godfrey had a deep aversion to any dismemberment of the corpse, and the language he used to describe the horror he thought it appropriate to feel is almost identical to that to be found in the decretal *Detestande feritatis*, promulgated by Boniface VIII for the first time on 27 September 1299, to forbid the boiling and dismemberment of bodies for ease of transport:

There has come to be practised an abominable act of cruelty on the part of certain Christian people, following an atrocious custom. Justly, then, do we command that this be abolished, we who are guided by the pious aim of ensuring that this cruel practice should no longer cause human bodies to be dismembered, and should never more strike the faithful with horror nor disturb their minds.

When one of their number, whether a noble or someone bearing high office, dies, as often happens, far from his own land, and that person has chosen his burial-place in his own land or somewhere far from the place of his death, Christians subject to this perverse custom, driven by a sacrilegious concern, savagely empty the body of its entrails and, horribly dismembering it or cutting it up into bits, throw it into [a cauldron of] water to boil it up over a fire. When the fleshly covering has thus been detached from the bones, they take the bones back to the chosen site for burial. This is something which is utterly abominable if we pay regard to the Divine Majesty, but which must cause almost more horror if we pay regard to the respect we owe to man.

It is therefore our will, as is the duty of our office, that a practice so cruel, so abominable, so sacrilegious, should be completely abolished and should gain no further adherents. We decree and command by our apostolic authority that, at each person's death, whatever his birth or high office may be, in whatever place the death occurs wherever Catholic religion prevails, no-one should henceforth think of applying that practice to the body of the dead, or any other practice resembling it, and that the hand of the faithful should cease to befoul itself so monstrously.

So that the bodies of the dead should no longer be treated so cruelly, they must therefore be taken to the place which, in their lifetimes, they had chosen for their burial. If that is not possible, let them be given Christian burial at the place of their death, or near it, and let there be a period of waiting until their bodies have crumbled to dust, [so that then] they can then be carried to the place they chose for burial.

If the testamentary executors of a dead person, or those close to him or her, or anyone else whosoever, whatever their rank or birth, even if they be vested with the episcopal dignity, should dare to infringe this our edict by treating inhumanely and cruelly the body of a dead person, or causing it to be so treated, let them know that they will be struck by excommunication by the very fact of their deed – excommunication which we issue from now onwards, and from which they shall obtain no absolution, except from the Apostolic See alone, or on their deathbed. Likewise, the person whose body has been so treated in a manner so inhuman, let him be deprived of ecclesiastical burial.

(*Corpus iuris canonici* II, cols. 1271–3;
Registres de Boniface VIII, no. 3209; cf. Paravicini 1991: 269–70)

It was clearly the Paris debate which inspired the papal decision. In 1290, Benedict Gaetani, the future Boniface VIII, had stayed in Paris in his capacity as papal legate (Paravicini Bagliani 1988). Further, the papal decision of 1299 was made four days after the French cardinal Nicholas de Nonancour made his will almost certainly giving instructions for the evisceration of his corpse (Paravicini Bagliani 1980). The decretal offers not a shred of justification, theological or legal. Written in a positively impassioned tone, it reveals a profound and strongly personal aversion to the dismemberment of the body. Keenly sensitive to this problem, Boniface VIII issued the same bull a second time on 18 February 1300. Now that was just four days before the publication of indulgences for the Jubilee of that year. Was it the huge influx of pilgrims to Rome that led the pope to issue such a solemn renewal of his prohibition of the dismemberment of the bodies of the dead?

DIVISION AND ANATOMY

In an intriguing way, Boniface's decision coincided with the medieval renaissance of the study of anatomy. To be sure, William of Malmesbury, according to King Sigurd Jorsalfar of Norway (1090–1130), had given orders for the cutting open of the livers of certain members of his entourage who had died in Constantinople on the return journey from Jerusalem where they had gone on pilgrimage. Perhaps the northern ruler drew his inspiration from Byzantium where anatomy had not undergone the same eclipse that it had in the early medieval West. The first certain case, however, of the opening of a human body so that its innards could be inspected is the one recounted by the Franciscan chronicler Salimbene. In 1286, 'there was a great mortality of human beings and hens in Cremona, Piacenza, Parma, Reggio and other Italian towns and dioceses. At Cremona, one woman lost 48 hens in a very short time. A certain doctor cut open some of the hens and found . . . a bump like a blister on the top of the heart of each one. He then cut open the body of a dead man and found exactly the same thing.' Salimbene also tells a story about the Emperor Frederick II (d. 1250) ordering the stomachs of two huntsmen to be cut open and the contents inspected to see which of the two had digested his food better.[2]

A few years after the first medico-legal autopsies, in the early fourteenth century, anatomical dissection was being taught at Bologna. In 1316, Mondino de' Luzzi's *Treatise on Anatomy* offers the oldest account of a 'university' dissection. Dissections had been taking place once or twice a year. The bodies of condemned criminals, male and female, were chosen, and the *podestà* sent these to the Faculty of Medicine. The bodies were exposed for four days. Outside Italy, though, there was no parallel rapid development in anatomical studies: quite the opposite. With the exception of the University of Montpellier, the only known cases of autopsies, apart from those in

Figure 19.2 Effigy of Jean, Cardinal Lagrange (d.1402). Regardless of the canonical prohibition, the cardinal had ordered his bones to be buried at Avignon and his boiled flesh sent to Amiens. Musée du Petit Palais, Avignon.

Italy, were very rare indeed: one case each for Germany, England and France. Not until 1477–8 did the Faculty of Medicine at the University of Paris practise anatomy (Jacquart 1998). How do we reconcile the fact that Italy, where the practice of dismembering corpses for ease of transport was effectively unknown, was the one country to produce a rebirth of anatomical studies that depended on dissection? Perhaps the contradiction is more apparent than real. Corpses were dismembered in order to separate the flesh from the bones. Respect for the integrity of the body after death and acceptance of the corpse's natural dissolution meant admitting that the body was subject to the laws of nature. Lacking magical functions, the corpse could be opened up for forensic reasons, and also for scholarly ones – once the necessary cultural environment was established. And it was, precisely, in the central Italian cities during the thirteenth century that such conditions came into existence.

Medico-legal requirements exerted decisive influence here. Already at the beginning of the thirteenth century, in 1209, Pope Innocent III had demanded the examination (not an autopsy in the strict sense) by medical experts of the corpse of a homicide victim. In another case, the same pope ordered that the verdict of the surgeons and doctors who had examined (but not opened up) the corpse of a young victim should be publicly announced. These are significant episodes: they attest the fundamental role played by canon law, quite apart from other legal requirements, in the development of the intellectual and legal technologies that would later give rise to medico-legal autopsies.

DIVISION AND EMBALMMENT

The autopsies and self-chosen divisions of corpses we find so often spoken of in the thirteenth century have a further significance: they reflect a new cultural and mental desire to know about the body's internal workings. Around the year 1300, this desire to investigate the body was so strong that it affected the bodies of saints for which, until then, external marks, such as the odour of sanctity or the stigmata, had been considered sufficient.

Claire of Montefalco died on 17 August 1308 in the little Umbrian convent where she had been abbess. For five whole days, despite the intense summer heat, Claire's body remained completely incorrupt, bathed in a delightful odour of sanctity. The community then decided to embalm this precious relic. An apothecary from the town supplied 'balm and myrrh'. Four of the sisters cut open the body with their own hands, extracted the heart and placed it in a casket, then took out the entrails and burned them in the oratory. Next day, after Vespers, they took up the casket containing the heart. When they cut open the heart, they found a cross, that is, the image of Christ Risen. In the course of the following two days, they went on making incisions in the heart and found still more wondrous signs of sanctity, all of them made of flesh: the crown of thorns, the scourge and the pillar of Christ's flagellation, the rod and the sponge, and the four little nails.

A few years later, and again in Umbria, the heart of a Dominican tertiary, Margaret of Città di Castello (d. 1320) was extracted during the embalming process. In it were seen three stones on which were inscribed the images of the Holy Family. The opening of the body took place in the presence of 'a multitude of brethren' – as if they were conducting an anatomy class. Thus, in early fourteenth-century central Italy, the opening up of a woman's corpse – a holy woman's corpse – far from arousing misgivings, positively reflected a remarkable anatomical curiosity, comparable to that behind autopsies and dissections.

Finding the marks of sanctity in a body was a way of distinguishing it from the bodies of common mortals. Only a holy body could display the signs of the Passion. But the bodies of Claire and Margaret had been opened up in order to be embalmed. In fact, all embalmments were ways of registering social distinction. As Henri de Mondeville, the surgeon to Philip the Fair, put it in 1320: 'There are three procedures for preparing corpses. Some require a very simple preparation, virtually none, to preserve them from corruption: this is the case for the bodies of the poor and of some rich persons if burial can take place within three days in summer or four days in winter. A second group requires some preparation: persons of middling rank, such as knights and barons. Thirdly, there are kings and queens, popes and prelates: their bodies have to be preserved with the face uncovered.'

Kings, queens, popes and prelates represent the summit of the social hierarchy. Their corpses must be embalmed with the face uncovered, because their deaths have to be publicly authenticated, and because their bodies are objects of veneration and solemn funerals including a more or less extended period of lying in state. Embalmment and lying in state are connected. Guy de Chauliac (d.1368) wrote that embalmment should be a way of preserving the face from decay for eight days (Von Rudloff 1921: 37). Guy's pupil Pierre Argellata, who later became a distinguished professor of surgery at the University of Bologna (1397–1421), declared his satisfaction at having embalmed the body of Pope Alexander V and been able to preserve it for eight days (Paravicini Bagliani 1994: 195). Thinking, no doubt, of papal funerary rites that went on for nine days, Pierre added that he had left exposed the face, hands and feet, 'for people need to see the hands and feet as well as the face'. If every embalmment was a challenge to the body's decay, in the Middle Ages what mattered especially was the preservation of a body destined for public exposure, for the glory of the dead person, his or her family and the institution he or she had represented.

Boniface VIII's bull certainly put a brake on the custom of dismembering the corpse. Yet the practice survived long afterwards, particularly in England and France. The French kings, like other great ones of this world, whether prelates or nobles, continued to require multiple burials of their bodies and obtained the necessary dispensations from Boniface's successors. In 1350, Clement VI granted the French king John II and his wife such a dispensation, which was to hold good for all their successors as well.

The existence of a papal prohibition on the evisceration of corpses had an unexpected consequence. Although Boniface's bull had not been issued to prohibit anatomy, nearly all the great thirteenth- and fourteenth-century anatomists state that ecclesiastical authorisation is required for any dissection of a corpse. According to Henri de Mondeville, 'corpses must be preserved for more than four nights, and if you have a special privilege from the Roman Church, you can cut through the front wall of the stomach'. A few years later, the Italian surgeon Mondino de' Luzzi (*c.*1330) had made it his practice to leave aside 'the bones situated beneath the basilary bone' because these could not 'be properly examined unless they had been boiled *which is a sin*'. Curiously, Guy de Chauliac, the greatest French surgeon of his age, makes no reference whatsoever to problems of this kind. On the contrary, he described in his *Chirurgia* how he had often performed dismemberments of corpses, the very sort of operation that Boniface VIII had condemned: 'We also undertake the anatomy of corpses that have been dried in the sun, or decayed in earth, or dissolved in running or boiling water . . . ' (*La Grande Chirurgie de Guy de Chauliac*: 30; cf. Von Rudloff 1921: 34–7). Shortly after this, Guido de Vigevano (1370) recalled that 'the Church forbids the performing of anatomy on the human body':

> Since the Church forbids the performing of anatomy on the human body, and since the art of medicine cannot know everything without having first learned anatomy, . . . I wish to demonstrate the anatomy of the human body by means of pictures correctly painted, representing the parts of the human body as they are: the illustrations will show it much better than I could do, since, when we perform anatomy on a person, we are in a hurry to complete it because of [the process of] decomposition. Hence, it is enough for doctors to represent the internal parts in an enlarged way, exactly as they lie before you.
>
> (Wickersheimer 1926: 72)

Long before Boniface promulgated his bull, at the beginning of the thirteenth century, an anatomist of the school of Salerno, the doctor Nicholas, author of one of the oldest treatises on medieval anatomy (the *Anatomia*), accounted for the decline of the subject since Galen by the fact that 'the practice of anatomy has been transferred to the bodies of animals, because – especially on the part of Catholics – it was considered inhuman to treat the human body in that way' (Redeker 1917: 30).

PUTREFACTION AND REGENERATION

Fighting against the dismemberment of corpses was equivalent to defending the integrity of a body and a person in the perspective of immortality. Commenting on Boniface VIII's decision, Cardinal Jean Lemoine explained that, for the Gaetani pope, 'the human body, and the human face in consequence, was made in the likeness of God and cannot be befouled or disfigured'. In Boniface's text, the body is constructed as a memorial to the very face of man, hence must be 'protected as a temple and must not undergo any violence after death'. The pope's concern for the body is expressed in his wish for the survival of its individuality in terms of its characteristic physiognomy. In other words, the body is viewed as enjoying a continuing existence in the world beyond, in a kind of 'infinite continuity'.

Integrity and immortality are similarly at the heart of Roger Bacon's theories on the prolongation of life. Although man had fallen into sin, he could live by nature for a thousand years and more, as had been proved by the existence of the long-lived patriarchs of the Old Testament. The corruption of man derived also from the fact

Figure 19.3 Crossing the bar. Breviário Matutinal of the Cistercian monastery of Alcobaça (thirteenth century). MS. Alc.66, fo. 23lv. Photo: Lisbon, Biblioteca Nacional.

that when man left the earthly Paradise, he no longer observed the rules of a healthy way of life. Certain remedies could put brakes on the ageing process. They were to be found in alchemy, perspective, and astronomy: sciences capable of restoring the human organism to a state of harmonious equilibrium. Thus man became able not only to prolong his life but to prepare his body for the life eternal, since 'at the moment of the Resurrection the body can only obtain a state of incorruptibility and immortality through itself'. To rejuvenate and prolong life with the help of experimental science, and especially by the use of potable gold, was an essential precondition for approaching the final, perfect, ultimate state of the resuscitated body which was, in the last analysis, a rejuvenated body. For Bacon, alchemy, invoked to prepare a harmonious body, here on earth as well in the world beyond, became an instrument of salvation. Bacon's ideas on the body constituted a true theology of the body, the most exalted ever worked out in the Middle Ages. All these ideas were developed by the Oxford Franciscan in his major works, written for Pope Clement IV (1265–68) (Paravicini Bagliani 1986: 243–80).

In spite of their almost Taoist flavour (cf. Needham 1980), Bacon's theories do not contradict the idea of a necessary putrefaction. Boniface VIII, in decreeing that the corpse must undergo its natural dissolution, was also insisting on the inevitability of putrefaction. In medieval alchemic thought, putrefaction was considered the necessary source of regeneration. In his *Margarita preciosa*, Pietro Bono of Ferrara, one of the greatest Italian alchemists of the early fourteenth century, established a remarkable relationship between the philosopher's stone and the resurrection of the body: 'The body will become transfigured (*glorificatum*), incorruptible, and subtle in an almost unbelievable way, and it will pass through any solid body. Its nature will be as much spiritual as corporal. When the stone decomposes into the state of powder, just as the body does in its tomb, it will then have reinforced its substance, just as after the Resurrection a man becomes stronger and younger than he has ever been before.'

By implication, then, the body must die and decompose in order to be regenerated in glory. The alchemists termed this necessary death *negrido*, 'the black state of matter', or 'the old Adam'. This is why the processes of dissolution, calcification and separation were so often depicted symbolically by a human corpse in its black, that is, dead, state. After this putrefaction would come 'the white state', whence would emerge the final product of the alchemic process, the philosopher's stone or *lapis*. *Lapis* was often symbolised by the image of the Risen Christ. According to Nicholas Flamel (1418), the Resurrection was intimately linked to corruption: 'When the body of man presents itself at the Judgement of God, it will have the colour of putrefaction, so as to be judged and purified of all its *negrido*. Then it will become white, when it has been made spirit. The body must therefore rot before it can become immortal and incorruptible.'[3]

NOTES

1 For the sources discussed in what follows, see especially the fine article of Brown 1981, and also Bynum 1991.

2 The same story is to be found in the *Univeral Chronicle* of the German poet Jansen Enikel, Frederick's contemporary. He already embellishes the tale with legendary additions.

3 Alchemy and anatomy seem less far apart than might have been thought. See the stimulating article of Lazzerini 1999, and also Carlino 1994.

REFERENCES

Primary works

Annales Wintonienses cum continuatione S. Augustini Cantuariensis (1879), ed. F. Liebermann, *Ungedrückte anglo-normannische Geschichtsquellen*, Strassburg: K. J. Trübner, 56–83.

Chronique de Primat (1894), ed. M. Bouquet, Recueil des Historiens de la Gaule, vol. 23, Paris: H. Welter.

Corpus iuris canonici (1879; repr. 1959), ed. E. Friedberg, vol. 2, Leipzig: B. Tauchnitz.

La Grande Chirurgie de Guy de Chauliac . . . composée en l'an 1363 (1890), ed. E. Nicaise, Paris: F. Alcan.

Henry of Huntingdon, *Historia Anglorum* (1996), ed. D. Greenway, Oxford: Oxford University Press.

Matthew Paris, *Chronica* (1874), ed. H. R. Luard, vol. 2, Rolls Series, London: Longman & Trubner.

Les Registres de Boniface VIII (1294–1303) (1884–1939), eds. G. Digard *et al.*, Paris: E. de Boccard.

Secondary works

Brown, E. A. R. (1981) 'Death and the human body in the later Middle Ages: the legislation of Boniface VIII on the division of the corpse', *Viator* 12: 221–70.

Bynum, C. W. (1991) *Fragmentation and Redemption*, New York: Zone Books.

Calisse C. (1887) 'I prefetti di Vico', *Archivio della Società Romana di Storia Patria* 10: 1–136.

Carlino, A. (1994) *La fabbrica del corpo. Libri e dissezione nel Renascimento*, Turin: Einaudi.

Duparc, P. (1980–1) '"Dilaceratio corporis"', *Bulletin de la Société Nationale des Antiquaires de France 1980–1981*: 360-72.

Jacquart, D. (1998) *La médicine médiévale dans le cadre parisien: XIVe-XVe siècle*, Paris: Fayard.

Lazzerini, L. (1999) 'Il tradimento di Oporino. Anatomia e alchemia', *Micrologus* 8: 421–36.

Needham, J. (1980) *Science and Civilization in China*, vol. 5, pt 4, Cambridge: Cambridge University Press.

Paravicini Bagliani, A. (1980) *I testamenti dei cardinali del Duecento*, Rome: Società Romana di Storia Patria alla Biblioteca Vallicelliana.

—— (1986) 'Storia della scienza e storia della mentalità. Ruggero Bacone, Bonifacio VIII e la teoria della *prolongatio vitae*', in *Aspetti della letteratura latina nel secolo XIII. Atti del Primo Convegno Internazionale di Studi dell'AMUL, Perugia, 3–5 Ottobre 1983*, Perugia: Regione dell'Umbria/Florence: La Nuova Italia, 243–80.

—— (1988) 'La mobilità della Curia Romana nel Duecento: riflessi locali', in *Società e istituzioni nell'Italia comunale: l'esempio di Perugia (secoli XII-XIV), Perugia, 6–8 novembre 1985*, Perugia: Deputazione di Storia Patria per l'Umbria, 155-278.

—— (1991) *Medicina e scienze della natura alla corte dei papi nel Duecento*, Spoleto: Centro Italiano di Studi sull'Alto Medioevo.

—— (1994) *Il corpo del papa*, Turin: Einaudi [English transl. *The Pope's Body*, Chicago: Chicago University Press, 2000].

Park, K. (1994) 'The criminal and the saintly body: autopsy and dissection in Renaissance Italy', *Renaissance Quarterly* 47: 1–33.

Redeker, F. (1917) *Die* Anatomie magistri Nicolai phisici *und ihr Verhältnis zur* Anatomia Clophonis *und* Richardi, dissertation: Leipzig.

Von Rudloff, E. (1921) *Über das Konservieren von Leichen im Mittelalter. Ein Beitrag zur Geschichte der Anatomie und des Bestattungswesens*, Freiburg-im-Breisgau: K. Henn.

Wickersheimer, E. (1926) *Anatomie de Mondino dei Luzzi*, Paris: Droz.

CHAPTER TWENTY

THE CRUCIFIXION AND THE CENSORSHIP OF ART AROUND 1300

Paul Binski

For all its extraordinary diversity, the most common images in Western medieval art were of the Crucifixion and the Virgin Mary. As central representations of the Faith, around which many other concepts and images clustered in the course of the Middle Ages, both were the objects of regulation and control. Such regulations could be proactive: thus, by the thirteenth century, it was prescribed that all churches should have an image of the Virgin Mary on or near the high altar and that the celebrant at mass should have the image of Christ Crucified before him on the altar (Gardner 1994). Others – and here we introduce the subject of this chapter – were more reactive: cases where monastic or clerical authorities either openly attacked or even suppressed newfangled images.

This topic of control by the Church was once the subject of a famous (and, not coincidentally, wartime) article by Rudolph Berliner (1945) on 'The Freedom of Medieval Art': how free, how constrained, actually were medieval artists with respect to clerical authorities, patrons and a religion in which everything of importance was literally pre-scribed? (Berliner 1945; Gilbert 1985). Berliner's point was that artists were freer to innovate than one might have assumed from certain liberal Protestant critiques of the Church's attitude to art such as that by G. G. Coulton, a scholar who, incidentally, drew attention to and translated many of the more important texts cited in the debate (Coulton 1919; Gilbert 1985). This was, perhaps, one reason why canonical images of Christ's incarnation and sacrifice had a history at all: artists, and with them other discursive thinkers about religion in the Middle Ages were capable of innovation within the constraints of decorum or orthodox doctrine. As many commentators on religious art have stressed, the Crucifixion is a peculiarly sensitive barometer of aesthetic and conceptual change, that change which led, in the words of R. W. Southern, to the realisation of 'the extreme limits of human suffering: the dying figure was stripped of its garments, the arms sagged with the weight of the body, the head hung on one side, the eyes were closed, the blood ran down the Cross', the 'natural corollary' of which were changes also happening in the image of the Virgin and Child from the eleventh century onwards in the transition from the mind-set of the epic to that of the romance (Southern 1953: 226–7).

Decorum is more honoured in the breach, as they say, and changing the central symbols of a faith in the interests of greater impact, or indeed truth, is a risky business. Many of these changes may have begun in the East, in Byzantium. We know something of this from the reaction in 1054 of a papal legate and Frenchman, Cardinal Humbert of Silva Candida, to the 'image of a dying man' ('hominis morituri imago') on a Byzantine cross in Constantinople, which he perceived as being heretical (Thoby 1959–63; Belting 1990: 144, 254 n. 37). As will be seen, this association between a novel image and heresy would be resurrected by the thirteenth-century Spanish bishop, Lucas of Tuy. The particular concern of this chapter, however, is with an episode in English art. Images of Christ shown dead on the cross were also known in eleventh-century Anglo-Saxon art, though the motif was not used with consistency (O'Reilly 1987; Raw 1990: 92). By about 1300, English Gothic crucifixes generally showed the agonised dead or dying Christ, the *Christus patiens*, nailed to the cross with three nails (one only through the overlapping feet) (Figure 20.1). But, notwithstanding the existence in England of a highly developed lyrical textual tradition stressing the agonies of the cross, English crucifixion imagery itself never reached the pitch of extremes of contemporary Italian and German representations of the scene. Some English crucifixion images are cleverly innovative, but the central icon of Christ on the Cross is generally undisturbed: thus each side of an embroidered English chasuble of *c*.1300 formerly at Melk in Austria, has a Crucifixion with Mary and John at its foot, yet placed in different attitudes of reaction to the cross which were evidently exchanged as the priest turned his body while celebrating mass (Christie 1938: pl. LXXXI). But gentle conceits of animation of this type were scarcely radical. However, in 1305–6 Ralph Baldock, bishop of London, found himself in the position of actually suppressing the image of a crucifixion because, in part, it had done its job too well. Coulton and Berliner were automatically drawn to this case even though its details throw as much light on the patron and art object as on the artist's role. As will become apparent, the cross in this case was unusual – indeed, it was probably unprecedented on English soil. But the fact of its suppression is only one aspect of its interest. The case of the Conyhope Cross, in itself an entirely local affair, allows us insight into a wider range of other issues: what could happen when an image created in one context was transferred to another, and what it was that made certain images unacceptable to clerical authority but attractive to others – and this notwithstanding the fact that our story has a surprisingly banal twist at the end.

But, first, let us consider the events.

The London Annals for the year 1305 relate the following:

In that year, on April 15th, a certain terrifying Cross ['Crux horribilis'] was taken to the chapel of Conyhope, and on the following day called Good Friday was adored by many ['adorabatur a multis']; on account of which Geoffrey of Wycombe, the rector of that church, incurred considerable harm at the instigation of the canons of St Paul's [Cathedral]. On May 1st of that year, the aforesaid Cross was taken away by night to the canons of Holy Trinity [Aldgate].

(Stubbs 1882: 136; Heslop 1987: 26).

Figure 20.1 Crucifixion, Peterborough, *c.*1220. © The Society of Antiquaries of London.

A year later we read of the verdict on this event given by the bishop of London, Ralph Baldock (1303/4–1313), in a letter to the Prior of Holy Trinity, Aldgate:

August 2nd 1306. Commission to return a crucifix incorrectly made. Concerning an erroneous sculpted image of the Crucifixion ['yconia crucifixi erronee sculpta'] . . . We have heard on trustworthy authority that one Thidemann of Germany has, some time since, sold to Geoffrey, Rector of St Mildred's in the Poultry, a certain carved crucifix with a gibbet lacking a cross-beam which does not represent the true shape of the Cross ['cum patibulo sine ligno transversali veram crucis formam minime pretendente']; which Cross the said Rector had placed in his church, and whereunto the indiscreet populace flocked in crowds as if to a true image of the Cross – whereas it was no such thing; whence, as We foresaw, it could well be the case that their souls might be imperilled. By reason of which Cross We caused the said Thidemann and Geoffrey to be summoned to Our presence and, having made diligent enquiry from both, We have ordained as follows, in case persistence with this error should lead to even worse things: that the aforesaid Thidemann should take (and he has indeed so taken) his oath on the Gospels that he would never henceforth make, nor suffer to be shown for sale, within Our city or diocese of London, such a crucifix as this, or Crosses with arms contrary to the accustomed fashion, under pain of excommunication for disobedience. And because the said Thidemann claims to be a simple foreigner, who might probably and innocently have ignored the accustomed mysteries of the crucifix and the image thereunto attached, therefore We have graciously granted to him as follows: that he, having first restored to Us the letter of obligation for twenty-three pounds sterling which he has from the aforesaid Rector, shall obtain restitution of this Crucifix, which has been sequestrated and deposited in your keeping [at Aldgate], for the avoidance of peril to men's souls, by the discreet Master Richard of Newport, who was then Our Vicar and Official. Wherefore we enjoin and command you that, having received from this Thidemann the aforesaid obligation (which you will faithfully transmit to Us), you will without delay deliver to the said Thidemann his image; provided always that it be borne from your monastery to some place outside our diocese, either at early dawn or late in the evening, when it can be done most secretly and with least scandal; and that you shall set up a watch to assure the execution of this command and to intimate the same to Us . . . given at Our palace at Fulham, August 2nd 1306.

(Fowler 1911: 19; Coulton 1919: 473–4; Berliner 1945: 282 n. 69 for reading adopted here)

The events of Easter 1305 took place in a small chapel of uncertain origin, lying just to the west of the parish church of St Mildred, Poultry, so named because this was an area in the City of London where butchers, poulterers and purveyors of game worked. 'Conyhope' means 'rabbit field'. The church of St Mildred itself was replaced in the fifteenth century and the entire site cleared in the nineteenth; and nothing is known of its appearance or of that of the adjacent chapel of Conyhope. But the chapel certainly existed by 1303 and, according to later documents, was dedicated to the Virgin Mary and Corpus Christi. We shall return to the significance of this dedication later (Stow 1720: 33; Newcourt 1708: 550–1; Riley 1860: 229; Milbourn 1872: 3–5).

The first point to note about the Conyhope Cross is that it was expensive: £23 was a considerable sum for a wood sculpture in this period, exceeding the usual cost of, for example, rood-beam crucifixes of the type by now virtually mandatory for parish churches of all ranks (Duffy 1997). We could deduce from this that the cross was either extremely highly finished, with colour and gilding, or grossly overpriced as the work of a foreign craftsman in London, or simply very large – or indeed all these things. That it was removed to the chapel at Easter – and therefore presumably used in the Good Friday public procession of the Cross – indicates that it may not yet have found a permanent home. The Good Friday Veneration of the Cross entailed its procession while veiled into the church or chapel, the chanting of the *Improperia* or reproaches, the unveiling of the cross and its procession into the midst of the people. The unveiling was doubtless a moment of high drama, especially given the nature of this particular image. The overwhelming effect of suddenly exposing a large and expensively finished crucifixion of a size worthy of a great church within such a comparatively small space can readily be imagined. Circumstances as well as medium and appearance would greatly have heightened the impact of the Conyhope Cross.

But scale and relative impact aside, the cross was objectionable to Bishop Baldock – a canonist and doubtless a stickler for such formalities – because of the shape of its arms. Its lack of a proper cross-arm for the gibbet ('cum patibulo sine ligno transversali') rendered it erroneous in a commonsense way: *ipso facto* a cross requires a cross-member. Berliner was one of the first to make the logical deduction that because the sculptor concerned was German, and because his cross lacked a cross-beam, the Conyhope Cross was therefore of a type known in German as a *Gabelkreuz*, or fork-cross, otherwise a pall or plague-cross, of a type quite common by the 1300s in Italy and Germany.

What of the history of this form of cross? As a type, the rough-hewn cross seems to stem from the image of the Tree of Life, the 'Lignum vitae' of Revelation 22: 1–2, the leaves of which were for the healing of the nations (Raw 1990: 176–8, pl. x). A common method of translating this text visually was to depict the limbs of a conventional cross as bearing rough-hewn stumps or beautiful fresh buds, worthy of Aaron's rod. Examples of this are quite common in Anglo-Saxon and English Gothic art, and it is within this tradition in England that we get nearest to the Y-shaped cross (Rickert 1954: pls. 52–3, 102–3; O'Reilly 1987: 153; Raw 1990: pl. XIIb). The Y-form proper may well have had Frankish origins (Swarzenski 1974: pl. 18 fig. 40). The most celebrated early German instance is the spectacular and supposedly miraculous cross in S. Maria im Kapitol in Cologne of around 1304 (Figure 20.2). It seems likely that Thidemann was himself Rhenish in origin and that he was working in an area of London – not far from the site of the Cologne Guildhall – with strong commercial and family ties between London and Cologne of the sort recently studied by Joseph Huffman (Huffman 1998). Thidemann may also have been a goldsmith (Liebermann 1910). The type of cross he made was,

Figure 20.2 Crucifix (*Cruzifixus dolorosus*). St. Maria im Kapitol, Cologne. Bildarchiv Foto Marburg.

however, basically unknown in England and, with the exception of one related instance at Perpignan dated around 1307, was also unknown or avoided in Gothic France. The fact that such crosses were eschewed in the earliest 'homelands' of Gothic is not unimportant (Strucken 1928; Vavalà 1929: 714, figs. 25, 458; De Francovich 1938; Berliner 1945: 282 n. 70; Garrison 1949: nos. 155, 243; Thoby 1959–63: 178–9; Mühlberg 1960; Lisner 1970: figs. 6, 7, 9, 17, 20, 76; Alemann-Schwartz 1976; White 1987: 140).

Having established the basic facts of the case we need now to consider more closely what was wrong with the Conyhope Cross. That it was made by a German seems in official terms not to have been relevant, despite claims about 'natural jealousy of the foreign craftsman' made by the first commentators on the incident (Coulton 1919: 473). The ostensible case is clear: the form of the cross was an offence to Christian symbolism and an error risking men's salvation, and the honour paid to it by devotees was hence indiscreet. But the anxiety expressed was not only about the form of the cross but also about the form of the devotions which it provoked. Bishop Baldock believed by implication that mass devotion of this vigour would be appropriate to a true likeness, of the cross, but not to a false likeness. So far as we can tell, it was not part of the devotees' apprehension of the Conyhope Cross that it made any special claim to a form of authenticity over and above that of conventionally shaped crosses. Nevertheless the clerical problem was ostensibly with dangerous and misleading innovation as an end in itself, devotion being displaced, in an idolatrous fashion damaging to mens' souls, onto the outward appearance of the cross, whatever the claims for that appearance might have been (Camille 1989: 212).

In being shaped like a fork or a Y, the cognitive system of Christendom's central sign had developed a serious fault. Though sculpture tended to be the medium most subject to official disapprobation throughout the Middle Ages (e.g. Berliner 1945: 282–4), there is nothing hysterical or irrational in the official clerical case against the form of this cross. To function – and moreover to perform as an instrument of salvation – symbols should be correct and instantly recognisable.

The general thrust of Bishop Baldock's censure of innovation was not new. As is well known in the literature on the history of medieval art, it was adumbrated in the criticisms made by the Spanish bishop Lucas of Tuy, writing some time after 1227, of the cunning innovations in Christian iconography made by heretics depicting the crucified Christ attached to the cross with three (not four) nails, one nail being driven through both feet – a by then quite common thirteenth-century form of the *Christus patiens* (Coulton 1919: 474–6; Berliner 1945: 278–9). As Creighton Gilbert has noted, Lucas criticised but did not actually suppress: his views were essentially rhetorical (Gilbert 1985: 130–1). Innovation was one of the subtle means that heretics – and Lucas seems to be thinking of heretical artists rather than patrons, though the distinction in reality is unclear – used to subvert true doctrine. Lucas was not a systematic thinker, but he was capable of putting in his heretical opponents' mouths arguments of some interest to us. Heretics might claim of images of the crucifixion, as if rationally, that

somebody may state we report the Lord was crucified with one foot over the other, pierced by a single nail, and we wish to change the practice of the church, so that we may be able to excite the devotion of the people by the greater intensity of the passion of Christ and to prevent boredom by replacing the customs of long standing by something new.

(Berliner 1945: 278 n. 54; Gilbert 1985: 132–3)

Lucas seems here to have a theory of jaded sensibility or *ennui* as a precondition of radical aesthetic change that makes him almost a nineteenth-century aesthetician *avant la lettre*, in the vein of Göller or Wölfflin (Wölfflin 1964: 73–88). Indeed what is striking about these medieval accounts is how perfectly recognisable the main terms of the debate are: symbols should be correct, and innovation, even perverse and indecorous innovation, can stem from boredom. Even the sense that the artist's role is important seems modern.

A further point which also rings very true in terms of modern sensibilities is the further claim, in our first account from the London Annals, that the Conyhope Cross was a 'crux horribilis'. It was no part of Bishop Baldock's recorded censure that it was actually ugly or heretical, and clearly something could be in error without actually having those qualities. But the term 'crux horribilis' is as strong – and arguably as justified – as it is unusual in the annals of the reception of medieval art. Taking our two documentary sources together, it seems that the Conyhope Cross was evidently both erroneous and nasty, and it seems worth asking whether the improper fascination which it provoked was not related to other no less visually gripping aspects of its appearance than to its transgressive general form as a sign. Do the London Annals in fact get nearer to the truth of the problem?

To understand why this might be so we have merely to pass from the term 'crux horribilis' to look at the Cologne *Gabelkreuz* of the 1300s, cited earlier as a fair indication of what Thidemann's Cross actually looked like. Aside from the almost self-consciously Gothic form of the cross itself, so analogous to the lithe willowy intersecting ribbed forms of Gothic tracery, there is the corpus of Christ as shown on the Cologne Crucifixion. Of it one commentator has written: 'The terrible Christ on the Cross at Cologne, a flayed corpse stretched out on a scaffold of rough wood, the muscles knotted and bulging, the veins striating the limbs, the rib-cage bursting through the skin, the stomach fallen in, and the blood rolling from hands and feet and brow and side, is a "showing" for "Everyman"' which is marked by "unstinting realism" and "harsh and uncompromising realism" (Henderson 1967: 164–5). Much in this account rings true, because the formal qualities of flaying, stretching, knotting, bulging, collapsing and so on immediately bring to mind the strong vocabulary of contemporary English religious lyrics on the Passion which make extensive use of images of the stretching, ripping and forcing of Christ's limbs and flesh on the cross (Woolf 1968: 29–30: 203). Indeed this tendency to push, strain or force formal, and so one might say expressive, limits seems more generally marked in the pictorial language of the period, as in German thirteenth-century sculpture or, indeed, in the most revolutionary Italian painting and sculpture in the years around 1300. This visual and verbal culture of extremes seems to have some relation-ship to the notion of 'realism' deployed in the passage on the Cologne Cross just cited. 'Realism' here seems to be like a particularly heightened vivid sense of the immediacy or conviction of an experience, rather than ordinary mimesis or naturalism

(Camille 1998: 205). Indeed it might even be right to question whether it was a sense of something 'natural' at all.

Here we should note André Vauchez's fundamental insight that the Western Christian tradition laid such exceptional emphasis on a singular and superhuman account of sanctity that it promoted an order, moral and aesthetic, that was inherently unnatural rather than natural (Vauchez 1997). In terms of the corresponding visual order, the Viennese art historian Otto Pächt put it thus: 'If we reflect that the subject matter of Christian art consists entirely of miracles, we shall see that medieval art was constrained to create a pictorial world of its own, with a visual logic independent of what we call the laws of Nature' (Pächt 1999: 45). It seems possible that the Conyhope Cross was problematical not only because of its general form as a symbol, but also in a more fully aesthetic sense. What was at issue was its *gestalt*, i.e. its form understood as bearing a greater expressive significance than the sum of its parts. Clearly how this expressive aspect might have been regarded at the time is a relative matter, and we can scarcely guess at the quality of the emotions elicited by such objects, though their intensity can well be imagined. But the fact of difference, aesthetic, cognitive and emotional, is key: Thidemann's Cross shows every sign of having been a self-conscious and disturbing departure from the norms, employing what we would now call a tactic of defamiliarisation. The paradox of this tactic is that while apparently deploying natural forms or metaphors – the Tree of Life – the outcome is radically unnatural, in the sense of being contrary both to custom and to the phenomenal world. Thidemann emerges from this as a kind of *agent provocateur* administering a shock to his London audience by adjusting the appearance of the central icon of Christian faith to produce a heightened awareness of it. Such methods had been used by German sculptors before, both in the style and the contextual-isation of images: witness the remarkable mid-thirteenth-century rood screen of Naumburg Cathedral in which the crucifix and its emotive entourage are placed in striking proximity – perhaps both comforting and unnerving – to those entering or leaving the choir and perforce bled upon by the Redeemer (Figure 20.3). This is a form of participative theatre, and it is effects like this that have led some commen-tators to emphasise the 'expressionistic' tendencies of German art from the middle years of the thirteenth century onwards.

Realism and naturalism are not easy terms to separate, but we should remain with them for the present. It has for some time been an assumption of art history that from the mid-thirteenth century onwards naturalism was an important ploy in the new tactics of affective religious art. This view is not complete, but neither is it entirely without reason or support. In the fourteenth century, for example, we learn of a craftsman, whether lay or monastic is unclear, working – surprisingly enough – for the English Cistercians at Meaux on the manufacture of a crucifix with a real naked man before him for reference 'so that he might learn from his shapely form 'formosa imago' and carve the crucifix all the fairer': a practice which will come as no surprise to those who have pondered the mimetic triumphs – in the nominalist or Aristotelian sense – of French and German sculpture, or Italian painting, of the period (Heslop 1987: 29; Camille 1989: 212–13). In this case the good and the beautiful seem to enjoy an effortless relationship, as they did in classical art. But this was not always the case with holy images. A common method to enhance the impact

Figure 20.3 Crucifixion with Mary and John. Rood screen, Naumburg Cathedral, *c.*1250. Bildarchiv Foto Marburg.

of the cross in this period, on the contrary, was to treat the surface of Christ's body as an integument scarred and pitted with weals, a veritable inventory of suffering; and we can find instances of this tradition – which culminated in Grünewald's Isenheim altarpiece – from at least the fourteenth century in northern Europe (Hamburger 1997b; Merback 1999). The Cologne Cross has this type of integument; but its character as an image is not merely one of surfaces, as the earlier description made clear. Here the underlying form of the body itself becomes unfamiliar, for it is apparently drawn out of the same fibrous vegetal matter as the cross-stem itself (witness also the curled-leaf titulus). This is not an empirically observed human body. The head and face hang exceptionally low so that the ghastly hollow-eyed and sunken-cheeked visage disappears into shadow and is partly cancelled – and with this are cancelled or rendered ugly those sites of affective attention which made the human face a key focus for spiritual and devotional attention in this period (Ringbom 1965). Christ's sacrifice – vivid, visually gripping, and emotionally harrowing – becomes something stripped of humanity. A metaphor of life, the tree-cross, has been mingled daringly with a cadaverous Christ, the 'flayed corpse' of our earlier description.

To understand why something – art or artifice perhaps – has in this case supervened over any sense of balance and moderation between ideas and sensations, we might compare it to the serene, even sweet-toned, early thirteenth-century 'Lignum vitae' crucifixion in the Peterborough Psalter (Figure 20.1). This reminds us clearly and unambiguously, from the perspective of a 'classicising' or 'idealising' phase of English Gothic art, that the appropriate emotions due in reverence of the cross are love, grief or pity – and not revulsion; revulsion at the cross would be a sign of hard-heartedness and even closure to the message of the Redemption (Woolf 1968: 63–5). On the basis of a visual culture in England much more familiar, even by 1300, with objects like the Peterborough Psalter, we can begin to understand why a 'crux horribilis' would strain the concept of a public, or private, religious image held by those like the bishop and canons of St Paul's presumably unfamiliar with the latest subtleties of continental religious art. To assimilate such images requires a quite different sense of decorum in which, as Jeffrey Hamburger has noted, a sense of humble style or *sermo humilis* is understood as a legitimate means of conveying fundamental Christian messages (Hamburger 1997b: 19–20).

This last point about decorum – and, one might say, metaphysical wit – is important. As we have seen, Thidemann's Cross represented a type fairly new in Germany and completely unfamiliar in England; and the role of sculptors working in the years around and after 1300 in the territories between eastern France and southern Germany on new images of this type – striking, thought-provoking, paradoxical and frequently quite ugly – deserves note. It is to this period and to Germany that we attribute the invention of the so-called *Vesperbild* or *pietà*, and the *Andachtsbild* or devotional image, a category which has included the *Gabelkreuz* as well as the image of St John sleeping on Christ's breast (Passarge 1924; Panofsky 1927; Krönig 1962; Mühlberg 1960: 69). There is an undercurrent of incongruity, paradox, veiling and of visual oxymoron in some of these images, which relates well to that disconcerting mixture of life and death apparent on the Cologne Cross. Consider for example the use of fragrant roses and rose-like wounds – the rose-coloured blood of Christ alluded to by spiritual authors – on the otherwise repellent Röttgen *Pietà* (Figure 20.4) (Hamburger 1997a: 63–100; 1997b: 12); or the sense of the secret wisdom in Christ's breast imparted to John; or the 'joyful *Pietà*' (*freudvolle Vesperbild*) in which Mary's low-key but evident smile imparts her possession of private spiritual insight into events epitomised by the image itself (Reiners-Ernst 1939).

Figure 20.4 Röttgen *Pietà*. Middle Rhine, *c.*1350. Height 89cm with base. Rheinisches Landesmuseum, Bonn, Inv. Nr. 24.189.

Such new, difficult, pictures are difficult not only because they are self-reflective epitomes, but because they are bittersweet (Camille 1998: 198–9). Lacking the clarity of categories, they instead test the boundaries around human emotions and ideas, and genres of art, to the point of consciously confusing them. Emotion does not come cheaply here, for there is nothing sentimental or obvious about these new forms. Their aim is to elicit compunction, that particular and uncomfortable form of Christian catharsis. In his brilliant discussion of this sophisticated theme in the visual culture of late medieval female religious orders, Jeffrey Hamburger has drawn attention to the ugly and incongruous in the visual tactics of German wood sculpture made for such circles in the early years of the fourteenth century: for instance the *freudvolle Vesperbild* and nearby (and even more disturbing) smiling crucifix at the abbey of St Walburg at Eichstätt (Hamburger 1997b: 10–13, figs. 3, 4). These tactics mark a step away from the earlier thirteenth-century innovation in French, English and German art, and especially sculpture, of deploying the face and body together to convey a categorical Christian morality – as in the earlier Wise and Foolish Virgins at Magdeburg, or the Elect and Damned of the Last Judgement at Bamberg. In those cases extremes of bodily movement and facial expression, and clear contrasts between the sad and ugly, and happy and beautiful (though the thirteenth-century tendency to grimace does not always clearly separate the two), serve to fulfil a didactic purpose. They remind us of Thomas Bradwardine's citation in his treatise on memory of the value of extremes in image-formation to mnemonic ends, for example 'a thing of great dignity or vileness, or wounded with greatly opened wounds with a remarkably lively flowing of blood, or in another way made extremely ugly' (Carruthers 1990: 282). Yet coarse as these earlier images in some ways are, without their theatrical projection the expressivity of the later images is inconceivable. Throughout this whole development we become aware of the way in which medieval artists realised the potential of the human face and body as imaginative resources capable of expressing essentially metaphysical truths (Binski 1997). The fact that faces and bodies could eventually be ugly as well as beautiful in the service of the Christian message is not a contradiction, but a fulfilment of the dark side of the Christian mimetic tradition.

It is not difficult, as the literature on devotion to the Passion shows, to find other ways in which the striking, ugly and incongruous were eventually used as positive themes in late medieval religious discourse. Hamburger for example notes the Augustinian sentiment that Christ 'hung ugly, disfigured on the Cross, but His ugliness is our beauty' and cites Hans Robert Jauss's extremely apposite remark for the present chapter that 'the Christian concept of *humilitas passionis* shattered the canonical, classical pairings of the good with the beautiful and the ugly with the depths of evil' (Hamburger 1997b: 19–20). We find eloquent use of this type of antithesis in English medieval lyrics on the Passion such as the Good Friday *improperia* (we recall the display of the Conyhope Cross on Good Friday), and religious poems in the tradition of the *Summa praedicantium*:

You are a man and wear a wreath of flowers: and I am God and wear a crown of thorns. . . . You have gloves on your hands and I have nails through mine. You use your feet in dancing and I in toil. In the dance your arms stretch out

cross-like in empty pleasure: and mine are stretched on the Cross in shame.
Your side is slit to show your vanity: and my side is pierced for suffering.

(Woolf 1968: 41 n. 4)

This antithesis between worldy *vanitas* and the ascetic and compassionate mode – an antithesis arising exactly in this period too in the aesthetics of the macabre, as in the poems and images of the Three Living and the Three Dead – is not wholly unrelated to issues of class, always treacherous ground. For example, Vauchez's description of the character of the holy in the European Middle Ages cited earlier, entailed a distinction between the ascetic plebian tradition of Mediterranean sanctity, and the northern aristocratic tradition of the sanctified suffering leader (Vauchez 1997: 157–245, 427–43). The *Gabelkreuz*, common to Italy and Germany, indicates how problematic pan-European distinctions of this type, distinctions at once social and aesthetic, actually are. We cannot be sure that the Conyhope Cross elicited clerical disapproval because it showed the Son of God in an ugly, and hence plebeian, guise. But just enough evidence survives to suggest that in thirteenth-century England there was some sensitivity to the excessive humanising of Christ's divinity, or, conversely, the divinisation of the human. St Francis's stigmatisation had, after all, been anticipated by the actions of a certain peasant from Banbury who in 1222 inflicted the five wounds of Christ on himself before calling himself Jesus. He was duly sentenced to life imprisonment by the clerical authorities (Vauchez 1997: 440 n. 51). The path to sanctity in Assisi or Liège or the Rhineland proved to be very different (Bynum 1987; 1992; Hamburger 1997a, 1997b).

Acts of practical as opposed to verbal censorship of medieval art are not so common as to deprive the events in London in 1305–6 of interest. In what has been said so far, some effort has been made to delineate on what grounds objects such as the Conyhope Cross were held – on the face of it – to be unacceptable. As with all censorship, an element was the actual success of the image in provoking an out-of-hand, popular response, a *succès de scandale*. It is central to the argument proposed here that some consideration of aesthetic matters needs to be admitted – or re-admitted – to the discussion of this domain of objects. The notion that an unacceptable image could – as in later centuries – be excused precisely on the grounds that it was 'art' was obviously impossible, for its artfulness was clearly part of the problem.

But in admitting that the aesthetic character of this cross was one key to understanding why it was simultaneously attractive to the people and objectionable to the authorities, we can go a little further still in establishing what led to its suppression. For at heart, no matter how rational, there is something unconvincing about the official case against the Conyhope Cross. The real issue is whether what the bishop said was the whole story. What he said reveals the thinking of a lawyer intent upon establishing an unimpeachable case. But is there not also some cause for suspecting that in his estimation the offending object was a symbol of something more, something both immanent and threatening? Of particular interest is the treatment meted out to Geoffrey of Wycombe, the rector of St Mildred's and hence the patron who paid for the object. Both he and the sculptor were summoned before the bishop. Though Thidemann the sculptor may have suffered commercially, he seems otherwise to have got off quite lightly: the bishop excused him on the grounds of being a simple foreigner, ignorant of religion. It was the rector, not the artist, who suffered 'multa mala' at the hands of the cathedral clergy.

This leads us to suspect that Geoffrey and Thidemann were together responsible for introducing innovations at Conyhope of which the *Gabelkreuz* was but one, albeit an exceptionally forceful, expression. What these innovations were is unclear. One possibility is suggested by the later record of the dedication of the chapel to the Virgin Mary and Corpus Christi. Whether or not devotion to Corpus Christi had already spread to London by the 1300s is unclear: the feast of Corpus Christi was universalised in 1311–12 and was instituted in England by about 1318 (Rubin 1991: 164–212). Reference is made to it in the early fourteenth-century statutes of Bishop Baldock drawn up while he was dean, before 1303–4 (Simpson 1873: 141; Sekules 1986: 131 n. 52). The possibility exists that Geoffrey and his congregation, about which little is known, were associated with some form of Corpus Christi devotion. Such devotion had already spread to Cologne by 1279 and may well by 1300 have been associated with the *Gabelkreuz* (Mühlberg 1960: 78). As such, the politics of the Conyhope Cross went beyond the mere shape of its arms. What was at stake was the more general role of this repellent image as the focus for forms of devotion, perhaps rather energetic, hitherto more common abroad. Removing the ostensible object and expression of those devotions amounted, in effect, to a form of containment by the bishop.

Indeed a further detail suggests that what was being contained – enthusiastic local devotions focused on an obscure chapel in the City of London – was of absolutely practical consequence for the cathedral. We have still to explain quite why the canons inflicted 'multa mala' on the rector. Aesthetic discrimination, high theological principle or dislike of popular religion, are in themselves insufficient or at least undemonstrable explanations. Much more significant is the cathedral ordinance of 1300, five years before the display of the cross at Conyhope, which directed that the income from donations to a certain great cross at the north transept of St Paul's itself should be directed to the new works on that great building until they were finished (Simpson 1873: lxvi, 91). Here we get to the bottom of it: Geoffrey of Wycombe had been rash enough to set up a rival to the cathedral's own money-spinning crucifixion; and the weird form it had taken in view of its association with alien eucharistic devotion, and the compelling effect it had had on the local populace, had played straight into the bishop's hands.

Yet we are still left with the power of this image for an early fourteenth-century London congregation. That this power was in some measure a product of its terrifying appearance may go some way to shed some critical light on the notion proposed by Belting, that the late Middle Ages witnessed a crisis in the image which effectively saw a replacement of the notion of the image as 'presence' by the image as 'art'. As Belting puts it: 'The new presence *of* the work succeeds the former presence of the sacred *in* the work' (Belting 1994: 459). Censored images offer a means of assessing this generalisation. Conyhope indicates that the boundaries around image and art may in practice have been less sharply defined. In such cases, and especially in the case of those in which artists and patrons were directly held to account, images were suppressed precisely because they were effective expressions, and not just accidents, of wider phenomena of devotion. This renders it harder or impossible to separate ontologically 'image' and 'work of art'. The presences 'in' and 'of' the work were assimilated to one another – what images looked like as art was related to the way they functioned as images. As Freedberg has suggested, the fact that people might flock to a particular image of the Virgin Mary, or indeed of the cross, 'has, in profound ways, to do with how the images look' (Freedberg 1989: 120). The separation of image and art starts to look dangerously anachronistic, even modern.

The failure is of another type too. Art historians who examine the history of international aesthetic relations in a period which preceded the formation of the so-called International Gothic Style have tended to consider the evidence of the influence or actual importation of works of art from one context to another – say, in our period, the impact of Italian painting in northern Europe after 1300 – as though this were an entirely positive, progressive and smoothly uninterrupted development, a kind of predetermined teleology of style (Panofsky 1953; Meiss 1967). The possibility that alien art forms might sometimes have been disruptive is simply not considered in such accounts. As it stands, the story of the Conyhope Cross is one of controversy. Though it was no part of the case against the Conyhope Cross that it was the work of a foreigner, it has also to be said that the influence, and hence we may assume presence, of German art in England around 1300 was vastly more limited than the nature of the commercial and political relations between the two territories might at first lead us to assume. Joseph Huffman's remark in his recent study of Anglo-German relations, that 'Anglo-German relations during the Central Middle Ages were certainly not a peripheral element in western European history, although most modern accounts of this era have neglected to integrate this dimension into the more traditional preoccupation with Anglo-French and German-Italian interactions' (Huffman 1998: 240, 239, 242) cannot easily embrace the history of art. German art appears only to have become influential in England in the second half of the fourteenth century. The suppression of the Conyhope Cross may have had a terminal impact on the future of this type of image in England: for though it continued to be produced in the Rhineland well into the fourteenth century, so far as I know it disappeared almost entirely from England, with one surviving exception carved on a provincial but ambitious tomb of *c*.1340 at the Augustinian priory at Cartmel (Markus 1996: fig. 13). Coincidentally it had been to the prior of the Augustinians at Holy Trinity, Aldgate, that the bishop of London's vicar had entrusted Thidemann's Cross in 1305–6. While some images of Germanic type like Thidemann's were problematical, others, such as the *pietà*, naturalised as Our Lady of Pity, were to have a perfectly successful native history, but not until the later Middle Ages in England (Morgan 1993: 53–7). As it is, we are left wondering what happened to Thidemann's controversial cross, removed by nightfall and quietly erased from the history of English art.

REFERENCES

Alemann-Schwartz, M. von (1976) 'Cruzifixus dolorosus. Beiträge zur Polychromie und Ikonographie der rheinischen Gabelkruzifixe', unpublished Ph.D. thesis, University of Bonn.

Barasch, M. (1976) *Gestures of Despair in Medieval and Early Renaissance Art*, New York: New York University Press.

Belting, H. (1990) *The Image and its Public in the Middle Ages. Form and function of early paintings of the Passion*, transl. M. Bartusis, R. Meyer, New York: Aristide D. Caratzas.

—— (1994) *Likeness and Presence. A history of the image before the era of art*, transl. E. Jephcott, Chicago: University of Chicago Press.

Berliner, R. (1945) 'The freedom of medieval art', *Gazette des Beaux-arts* 28: 263–88.

Binski, P. (1997) 'The Angel Choir at Lincoln and the poetics of the Gothic smile', *Art History* 20/3: 350–74.

Bynum, C. W. (1987) *Holy Feast and Holy Fast. The religious significance of food to medieval women*, Berkeley: University of California Press.

—— (1992) 'Women mystics and eucharistic devotion in the thirteenth century', in C. W. Bynum (ed.) *Fragmentation and Redemption. Essays on Gender and the Human Body in Medieval Religion*, New York: Zone Books, 119–50.

Camille, M. (1989) *The Gothic Idol. Ideology and image-making in medieval art*, Cambridge: Cambridge University Press.

—— (1998) 'Mimetic identification and Passion devotion in the later Middle Ages: a double-sided panel by Meister Francke', in A. A. MacDonald, H.N.B. Ridderbos, R. M. Schlusemann (eds) *The Broken Body. Passion devotion in late-medieval Culture: Mediaevalia Groningana* 21, Groningen: Egbert Forsten, 183–210.

Carruthers, M. (1990) *The Book of Memory. A study of memory in medieval culture*, Cambridge: Cambridge University Press.

Christie, A. G. I. (1938) *English Medieval Embroidery*, Oxford: Clarendon Press.

Coulton, G.G. (1919) *Social Life in Britain from the Conquest to the Reformation*, Cambridge: Cambridge University Press.

De Francovich, G. (1938) 'L'origine e la diffusione del crocifisso gotico doloroso', *Römisches Jahrbuch für Kunstgeschichte* 2: 143–261.

Duffy, E. (1997) 'The parish, piety, and patronage in late medieval East Anglia: the evidence of rood screens', in K.L. French, G.G. Gibbs, B. A. Kümin (eds) *The Parish in English Life 1400–1600*, Manchester: Manchester University Press, 133–62.

Fowler, R.C. (ed.) (1911) *Registrum Radulphi Baldock, Gilberti Segrave, Ricardi Newport et Stephani Gravesend, episcoporum Londoniensium, A.D. MCCCIV–MCCCXXXVIII*, Canterbury and York Society, Vol. 7, London: The Canterbury and York Society.

Freedberg, D. (1989) *The Power of Images. Studies in the history and theory of response*, Chicago: University of Chicago Press.

Gardner, J. (1994) 'Altars, altarpieces, and art history: legislation and usage', in E. Borsook, F. S. Gioffredi (eds) *Italian Altarpieces 1250–1550. Function and design*, Oxford: Oxford University Press, 5–19.

Garrison, E. B. (1949) *Italian Romanesque Panel Painting*, Florence: Olschki.

Gilbert, C. (1985) 'A statement of the aesthetic attitude around 1230', *Hebrew University Studies in Literature and the Arts* 13/2: 125–52.

Hamburger, J. (1997a) *Nuns as Artists. The visual culture of a medieval convent*, Berkeley: University of California Press.

—— (1997b) "To make women weep". Ugly art as "feminine" and the origins of modern aesthetics' *Res* 31: 9–34.

Henderson, G. (1967) *Gothic*, Harmondsworth: Penguin Books.

Heslop, T. A. (1987) 'Attitudes to the visual arts: the evidence from written sources', in J. Alexander and P. Binski (eds) *Age of Chivalry. Art in Plantagenet England 1200–1400*, London: Royal Academy of Arts, 26–32.

Huffman, J. (1998) *Family, Commerce, and Religion in London and Cologne. Anglo-German emigrants, c. 1000–c. 1300*, Cambridge: Cambridge University Press.

Krönig, W. (1962) 'Rheinische Vesperbild aus Leder und ihr Umkreis', *Wallraf-Richartz-Jahrbuch* 24: 97–142.

Liebermann, F. (1910) 'Ein deutsches Bildhauer in London 1306', *Repertorium für Kunstwissenschaft* 33: 550.

Lisner, M. (1970) *Holzkruzifixie in Florenz und in der Toskana*, Munich: Bruckmann.

Markus, M. (1996) '"An attempt to discriminate the styles." The sculptors of the Harrington Tomb, Cartmel', *Church Monuments* 11: 5–24.

Meiss, M. (1967) *French Painting in the Time of Jean de Berry. The late fourteenth century and the patronage of the duke*, 2 vols, London: Phaidon.

Merback, M. B. (1999) *The Thief, the Cross and the Wheel. Pain and the spectacle of punishment in medieval and renaissance Europe*, London: Reaktion Books.

Milbourn, T. (1872) *The History of the Church of St Mildred the Virgin, Poultry, in the City of London*, London: John Russell Smith.

Morgan, N. J. (1991) 'Texts and images of Marian devotion in thirteenth-century England', in M. Ormrod (ed.) *England in the Thirteenth Century* (Harlaxton Medieval Studies 1), Stamford: Paul Watkins, 69–104.

—— (1993) 'Texts and images of Marian devotion in fourteenth-century England', in N. Rogers (ed.) *England in the Fourteenth Century* (Harlaxton Medieval Studies 3), Stamford: Paul Watkins, 34–57.

Mühlberg, F. (1960) 'Cruzifixus dolorosus. Über Bedeutung und Herkunft des gotischen Gabelkruzifixes', *Wallraf-Richartz-Jahrbuch* 24: 69–86.

Newcourt, R. (1708) *Repertorium ecclesiasticum parochiale Londiniense*, II, London: Benj. Motte, for Chr. Bateman [and others].

Newton, S. M. (1980) *Fashion in the Age of the Black Prince. A study of the years 1340–1365*, Woodbridge: Boydell Press.

O'Reilly, J. (1987), 'The rough-hewn cross in Anglo-Saxon art', in M. Ryan (ed.) *Ireland and Insular Art AD 500–1200*, Dublin: Royal Irish Academy, 153–8.

Pächt, O. (1999) *The Practice of Art History. Reflections on method*, transl. D. Britt, London: Harvey Miller.

Panofsky, E. (1927) 'Imago pietatis: ein Beitrag zur Typengeschichte des Schmerzenmanns und der Maria Mediatrix', in *Festschrift für Max J. Friedländer zum 60. Geburtstag*, Leipzig: E. A. Seemann, 261–308.

—— (1953) *Early Netherlandish Painting*, 2 vols, Cambridge, Mass.: Harvard University Press.

Passarge, W. (1924) *Das deutsche Vesperbild im Mittelalter*, Cologne: F. J. Marcan.

Raw, B. (1990) *Anglo-Saxon Crucifixion Iconography and the Art of the Monastic Revival*, Cambridge: Cambridge University Press.

Reiners-Ernst, E. (1939) *Das freudvolle Vesperbild und die Anfänge der Pietà-Vorstellung*, Munich: Neuer Filser-Verlag.

Rickert, M. (1954) *Painting in Britain: the Middle Ages*, Harmondsworth: Pelican.

Riley, H. T. (ed.) (1860) *Monumenta Gildhallae Londiniensis*, Rolls Series, London: Longman, Green, Longman, and Roberts.

Ringbom, S. (1965) *Icon to Narrative. The rise of the dramatic close-up in fifteenth-century devotional painting*, Abo: Abo Akademi.

Rubin, M. (1991) *Corpus Christi. The eucharist in late medieval culture*, Cambridge: Cambridge University Press.

Sekules, V. (1986) 'The tomb of Christ at Lincoln and the development of the sacrament shrine: Easter sepulchres reconsidered', *Medieval Art and Architecture at Lincoln Cathedral* (British Archaeological Association Conference Transactions, 8), Leeds, 118–31.

Simpson, W. Sparrow (ed.) (1873) *Registrum statutorum et consuetudinum ecclesiae cathedralis Sancti Pauli Londonensis*, London: Nichols and Sons.

Southern, R. W. (1953) *The Making of the Middle Ages*, London: Hutchinson.

Stow, J. (1720) *A Survey of the Cities of London and Westminster: containing the original, antiquity, increase, modern estate and government of those cities*. Corrected by J. Strype, Book III, London: for A. Churchill [and others].

Strucken, M. (1928) 'Literarische und künstleriche Quellen des Gabelkruzifixus', unpublished Ph.D. thesis, University of Dusseldorf.

Stubbs, W. (ed.) (1882) 'Annales Londinienses', in *Chronicles of the Reigns of Edward I and Edward II*, Rolls Series, London: Longman, Green, Longman, and Roberts.

Swarzenski, H. (1974) *Monuments of Romanesque Art*, 2nd edn, London: Faber.

Thoby, P. (1959–63) *Le Crucifix des origines au Concile de Trente*, 2 vols, Nantes: Bellanger.

Vauchez, A. (1997) *Sainthood in the Later Middle Ages*, transl. J. Birrell, Cambridge: Cambridge University Press.

Vavalà, E. (1929) *La Croce dipinta italiana*, Verona: Apollo.

White, J. (1987) *Art and Architecture in Italy 1250–1400*, Harmondsworth: Pelican.

Wölfflin, H. (1964) (1888) *Renaissance and Baroque*, transl. K. Simon, London: Fontana/Collins.

Woolf, R. (1968) *The English Religious Lyric in the Middle Ages*, Oxford: Oxford University Press.

PART III

POWER AND POWER STRUCTURES

INTRODUCTION

The chapters in this section examine varieties of medieval power in the political sense: they deal with monarchies, aristocracies and oligarchies, regimes and institutions, law and administration, but also with political actors, and with the personnel of government. Two dimensions of change and variation emerge strongly. First there is that of time: earlier medieval kingdoms were ruled extensively rather than intensively. Kings could count on widespread support from nobles whose own lands were far-flung. Solidarities within kingdoms were maintained not by administrative agencies but by broad communities of interest and shared culture. Government was a family affair, and dynasties have rightly been given pride of place in the modern historiography of medieval realms, though only recently has enough attention been paid to conflict within those dynasties, and hence to the ways the evolving shapes of ruling families helped to determine political outcomes. From the eleventh and especially the twelfth century onwards, increasingly monetised economies, the growth of literacy, and the professionalisation of law, created the possibility of more intensive government, with permanent, specialised agencies. The Church was a pioneer of these innovations; and readers keen to grasp the nature of governmental change across the medieval centuries will the more readily do so by reading the first chapter, then the last, of Part III. The Church also pioneered a new conception of power as sovereignty: theoretically and in practice, the pope's was the ultimate court of appeal. Unsurprisingly, kings followed suit, and in the fourteenth and fifteenth centuries, royal propagandists produced theories of secular sovereignty that were at once legalistic and thoroughly political.

Then there is the dimension of space: it is no coincidence that Italy looms larger in this section than in previous ones, for the political power of Italian cities, and their creation of new power-structures within urban space and also covering the surrounding countryside, are among the most striking developments of the period from the twelfth century onwards. The wealth of these cities gave them enormous political power internationally as well: the crusading activities of the twelfth century and later are unthinkable without Italian involvement. Nor could the Hundred Years War have been undertaken without the financial support of Italian bankers for both sides. Italian cities were not the only ones to emerge onto the political stage in the later medieval centuries: though the Italians remained dominant in the eastern Mediterranean, the cities of the Netherlands and northern Germany created their own spheres of commercial and political power in northern Europe, based, like that of their Italian counterparts, on *de facto* autonomous control over urban space. Cities played new roles within kingdoms too, and some, such as London and Paris, became capitals, fixed centres of government. Two new kingdoms, Portugal and Sicily, were twelfth-century creations. They could afford to be smaller than the huge amalgamated realms of the earlier Middle Ages, in part because commercial resources enabled sufficient wealth to be amassed to sustain a separate state on a smaller territorial base. Wars fought in distant theatres, and long-distance commerce, evoke the international dimension of medieval politics. In the earlier Middle Ages, exchanges of envoys had been offshoots of inter-dynastic links: later, diplomacy became a structured set of inter-state relations. But were medieval European state-structures unique to western Europe? Many explanations can be invoked to explain why it was western Europeans alone who came to dominate the globe, economically, then politically, in the early modern period, but a shift of focus to the 'medieval' African and Islamic state centred on Timbuktu allows a more critical perspective on Europe itself, and suggests that global dominance was not a foregone conclusion.

So far, the spotlight has been on change within the medieval period, yet, coexisting with change, and in some respects more important, were continuities in the ways in which power was organised, formulated and wielded. Kingship, throughout the Middle Ages, was the predominant governmental form, generalised from Uppsala to Naples, and from Lisbon to Budapest. The ideology of kingship, crystallised in the words, chants and gestures of coronation rites, though not identical, was similar throughout Latin Europe. King and Church within each realm worked closely together – which is to say that kings controlled appointments to higher ecclesiastical posts and deployed churchmen as their agents, while offering Church property and privileges protection, on royal terms. *Regnum* and *sacerdotium* might sometimes be at odds, not least when the Papacy made rare forays into the politics of kingdoms, and from the eleventh century more frequent interventions in the politics of the German Empire, but in fact the norm, like the ideal, was of harmony between them. The Church preached, and often practised, peace: when it made war, that was at the behest, or with the strong collusion, of kings (except in Central Italy where the Papacy itself was the secular as well as ecclesiastical lord). Though to varying degrees throughout Latin Europe (including England), Roman law influenced legal thought and practice, in part because the Church's law was the vehicle of that influence, in part because a professional legal training anywhere entailed close study of the Code of Justinian. In this respect, Italy presented the most Roman of faces. Italy had always been different in the extent of its persisting Roman traits: urban life never disappeared there, even in the 'Dark' Ages, and the towns always harboured some lay literacy and even a degree of legal professionalism. Another key institution that took shape in the early Middle Ages and persisted, in new guises, thereafter, was the assembly. There were local and regional assemblies, and urban assemblies, where disputes were settled by 'knowledgeable neighbours' and 'good men' according to custom. Inseparable from the habits and mentalities of those relatively frequent gatherings was the regnal assembly, or assembly of the whole kingdom. Often organised in groups of representatives of estates – churchmen, nobles, townsmen – and regional interests, and sometimes called by the informal name of parliament, or 'talking-session', the regnal assembly was the forum in which kings met with their leading subjects and power was negotiated between them in matters of law and justice on the one hand, and the raising of taxes on the other. In some kingdoms (such as France), the regnal assembly was never as important as provincial assemblies, in others (notably England) it became a regular institutional partner, sometimes (as in Aragón) a sparring-partner, of royal government. American scholars, seeking the origins of modern Western democracy, have not been wrong to insist that there really was something worthy of the name of medieval constitutionalism, and that this contributed something to modern ideas of the rule of law and representative government. At no point in the Middle Ages were such ideas and practices absent; and the underlying reason was that no medieval state could ever mobilise sufficient power to manage without consensus, achieved through talking. Power-sharing was not a choice, but a condition of political life.

Many textbooks on medieval history evade the question of the balance between change and continuity by covering only part of the Middle Ages. In many university courses, the division of medieval history into earlier ('Dark Ages', or in the English case, the Anglo-Saxons) and later (in the English case, the post-Conquest period), with the boundary somewhere around 1100, has allowed the 'earlier' brigade to evade the question, and the 'later' brigade to claim change and novelty without having to demonstrate it. Fortunately the book you are reading is no textbook, and the editors were more than happy to follow the publisher's plan of comprehensiveness! There can be no shirking the question here, therefore. In the case of earlier and later medieval government, power and power-structures, gender offers one useful axis of comparison. In the earlier Middle Ages, the women of royal dynasties could, and often did, wield ruling power alongside their menfolk through their control of royal households and convents founded by royal families and staffed by family members. Those households and convents were key agencies of government. From the twelfth century onwards, new institutions are clearly evidenced: royal courts of justice, for example, that met in or near the capital, for fixed terms, staffed by legal experts, and royal accounting and fiscal agencies staffed by financial experts. Needless to say, the experts were invariably male, since the schools and universities that trained them were for men only. In this brave new world of professionals, high-status women could no longer exercise political power as extensively or as conspicuously as before. Nevertheless, they continued to exercise it, and in the old ways, for when all was said and done, administration was not (though it was closely linked to) politics, and high-profile public talking-sessions, however much some participants enjoyed posturing, were not such central power-centres as royal and noble courts, and courts operated continuously whereas parliaments, most of the time, were not in session. It was courts, as well as parliaments, that were the key political and also social and cultural institutions of the Middle Ages. Though seldom labelled as such before the twelfth century, they existed long before. Women as well as men inhabited them − as did churchmen whose status caused some debate and many jokes; women, as well as men, formed the audience for the displays and serious entertainments, including readings of historical works, that court life turned on; women, here, were agents of as well as participants in the civilising process that helped to shape a distinctively western European culture in the course of the thousand-year span of the Middle Ages. In other words, the old forms of familial politics, at the level of the kingdom, but also of lordships where nobles aped kings and noblewomen queens, were not superseded by the new, but supplemented. Using the measure of gender, then, encourages Part III's steer towards change within continuity (or continuities), rather than the reverse.

SPACE, CULTURE AND KINGDOMS IN EARLY MEDIEVAL EUROPE

Paul Fouracre

The development of Europe from the fall of the Roman Empire to the fall of the Carolingian Empire is a subject which should be of interest to all who would seek the origins of the Europe we know today. For it is in this period that not only do we see the formation of Christendom in the broader cultural sense, but also we meet the not too distant ancestors of the languages we speak today, and first discern the territories that the major states of modern Europe would later come to occupy. The Emperor Charlemagne (d. 814) was referred to as 'the father of Europe' and it has often been remarked that in terms of territory, 'his' Europe bears a strong resemblance to the area included in the pre-1972 'common market' of Europe (EEC).

How Europe was in this sense 'made' in the early medieval period is the stuff of text books and it has what appears to be a straightforward explanation in terms of military and political history: after the decline of Rome, invasions, conquests and wars placed the peoples of Europe in the appropriate places (even if some of the names were rather different). After a frightful, even barbaric, start, these peoples, their rulers, and their political and religious institutions all became progressively better organised, the invasions stopped and European civilization began to flower from the twelfth century onwards. This outline history of the making of Europe has the advantage of hindsight. It is comprehensive and comprehensible, and to some degree it is faithful to the changing content, range and quality of the available source material. Its disadvantage lies in the way in which it treats outcome as destiny. That is to say, in describing the formation of Europe, the overview does not ask why European culture took the form it did, or why Europe should have been formed into large territorial states (like Charlemagne's) at such an early date. Why, in other words, did not the lands that had formed the Roman Empire break down rapidly into a mosaic of petty chiefdoms? Why did Europe not become a babel of languages and cultures? Conversely, why should a degree of cultural homogeneity have developed across Western Europe despite the fact that it had been divided into different states since the end of Roman rule? This chapter will address these issues of culture and space. It will first characterise the common cultural, social and economic conditions which explain why early medieval states were very large, and why there was such similarity between them that one can speak with some confidence of a common medieval culture. It will then ask how this rather conservative and stable culture could also be a vehicle for change.

The political map of modern Europe is in large part an inheritance from the Roman past, for four of the major nation states of Western Europe, that is, Britain, France, Spain and Italy, occupy territories which roughly correspond to former Roman provinces. The great exception here, Germany, was defined by its position lying outside, but also alongside, the Roman frontier. In the cases of France, Italy and Spain, it was the Roman provincial organisation which in the first instance determined the shape and size of the so-called 'successor-states', though in each case, over time these basic moulds would be broken up and reformed in the course of invasion, partition and the rise and fall of regional powers. In this way the different parts of what had been the Roman Empire in the West had their separate histories, but they also shared a common inheritance. The formation of European culture in the early middle ages lay in the accommodation of this heritage to changing local conditions, and it was the adaptation of the universal to local conditions which gave that culture its essential character of local variation upon a common theme. Let us first look at some common cultural denominators before turning to differences.

With the exception of a very few persons and places, early medieval Europe was poor by Roman standards. We have, of course, no economic statistics to prove this, but there is a consensus among historians and archaeologists that a decline in taxation, the disappearance of copper coinage, and, later, gold coinage, the decline of towns and bulk trade, the appearance of famine and plague, the reduction in the size of buildings, and the increasingly common use of wood rather than stone in their construction, are all indications that there was deep and lasting economic recession in Europe between at least the fourth and eighth centuries AD. The economy of the later Roman Empire had had a strongly fiscal basis, so that the decline of the economy and the weakening of government powers were part of the same process. In analysing the transformation of the political order which followed, the great landowning magnates who dominated the offices of the State and, increasingly, of the Church, have often been made the villains of the piece. For they are said to have withdrawn their support from the government and the army and to have kept for themselves that income from their peasant tenants which had formerly been paid in tax, and upon which the army and bureaucracy depended. This is supposed to have had the effect of 'privatising' power as these landlords came to exercise unfettered control over the countryside and its inhabitants. The key change is said to have been the transformation of taxation paid to the government into rent paid to the landlord, and with this transformation came the end of the Ancient World.

The picture is not, in fact, as clear-cut as this, for the position and power of landlords was not identical throughout Western Europe. The impression that they were selfish, short-sighted and greedy is informed on the one hand by the condemnation of abuses of power in imperial legislation which is partly formulaic and rhetorical in character, and on the other hand by writings of churchmen who used the idea of the abuse of power as a vehicle to express their particular moral agenda. In lowland Britain, the class of landed magnates of Roman or Romano-British stock seems to have disappeared in the course of the fifth century. In Spain and Italy, the wealth and power of this class were balanced by those of the cities. It is in Gaul that we find the classic examples of the magnates who did not just cling on to power and privilege, but actually reinforced their standing. Gaul, or Francia as it would soon become, is therefore often taken as a model for the development of European society as a whole. We shall return later to the question of how valid it is to use it as a model in this way.

Despite misgivings about the degree of negative influence traditionally ascribed to the great landowning aristocrats of the late Roman world, it remains true that their social and cultural predominance was passed on. Medieval Europe thus inherited, or, in some areas, came to emulate, the social hierarchy of the Roman past, and European culture developed in ways which conserved and strengthened that hierarchy. Across Europe the two leading figures in each locality were the count and the bishop, holders of offices which were Roman in origin. Their high status was in effect a benchmark against which the rest of the hierarchy was measured. In the laws of early seventh-century Kent, which had been recently converted to Christianity, we see bishops being introduced into the hierarchy, and the value put upon their honour and persons is very high indeed, being second only to that of the king.

The power of such leaders was based on a combination of landholding and officeholding, the former presupposing a stable labour force, and the latter a measure of effective public authority. In the countryside, the social structure was another element of continuity from the Roman past. Spread across the European landscape were great estates held by lords, the Church and the kings. They were worked by a dependent or unfree peasantry. There were also free peasants who worked their own lands, but the proportion of this group in the population is impossible to estimate, for by and large our evidence is concerned with the lands of the lords. We also know much more about landholding and estate organisation in some areas than in others. There are, in particular, great estate surveys (so-called 'polyptychs') from the lands of various churches between the Loire and Rhine, which were made in the ninth and tenth centuries (though evidently based on earlier, now lost, examples). Much generalisation about the nature of rural society draws upon these surveys. Although conditions could be very different in other parts of Europe, in almost every region the evidence consistently shows land described in terms of the income it could provide. The cultivators of the land were treated as a key asset, and tied to the land, along with the stock and the fixtures and fittings. Lords could expect immediate income from any land they acquired, because cultivators were already in place, both producing for direct consumption and paying rent in labour services, in cash, in kind, or even in all three. The existence of a dependent peasantry was therefore what enabled land, or, rather, estates, to be used as political reward and payment, and to circulate in other ways, through gift, purchase, exchange, partition and inheritance.

The productivity of farming seems to have been very low in the early Middle Ages, perhaps not much above subsistence level. Magnates thus needed to draw income from massive amounts of land to maintain a high status of which great wealth was a primary means of expression. The visible display of wealth came in the form of precious metals and jewellery. Stocks of precious metal, and especially gold, were declining in the post-Roman period, and continued to do so until an increasing amount of silver became available in the ninth and tenth centuries. Scarcity fuelled the demand for precious metals, and one of the hallmarks of early medieval culture is an obsession with gold and silver, or, simply, 'treasure'. The ideal lord had lots of treasure and was typically generous with it. The possibility of acquiring treasure either through gift or by political and military service was another factor which drew magnates into the entourages of kings. Access to the proceeds of taxation, tolls and tribute, that is, to the main sources of moveable wealth, all came through the king. The larger the kingdom, the more resources could be gathered and redistributed in this way, and the greater the opportunities for magnates to acquire land in different regions. It was these conditions which led to the formation of large states, and to support for an authority which might both protect widespread property holding and furnish some of the moveable wealth needed to protect status. But the magnates of early medieval Europe were not simply pathological in their greed. They faced fierce competition for their status and offices and were required to be commensurately generous to their own clients and followers. Lands could also be split up at times of inheritance, with the new generation looking for new land to add to their fractions of the patrimony.

We have seen that even if the magnates did share some of the responsibility for the decline of public authority in the later Roman Empire, in the post-Roman world they became the pillars of such authority as remained. In Francia (Gaul), Italy and Spain, barbarian kingdoms directly replaced Roman government in the fifth and sixth centuries. Each of these kingdoms was identified with the invaders who had conquered the territory and from whom its ruling families were drawn. After much initial disruption, and in the cases of Spain and Italy, some religious conflict, a social elite made up of both incomers and natives formed around the kings. It was these elites who supported the rulers and benefited from such resources as government could mobilise. It was the collective power of rulers and magnates which was the mainstay of public authority, but the royal court was also the principal focus of association between the various magnate families. As Timothy Reuter explains in Chapter 25, great assemblies of rulers and magnates were a primary organ of government, and magnates were prepared to travel hundreds of kilometres to join them. Recent work on the leading families has repeatedly shown links between them throughout these large kingdoms, and in this sense the coherence of each kingdom owed a great deal to the desire of magnates from different regions to associate with each other. Early medieval elites were, in sociological terms, highly integrated. In this way, states grew up which were larger than their capacity to tax and bigger than their ability to govern effectively. Their size was a cultural phenomenon, that is, a matter of shared habits, assumptions, practices and beliefs, rather than the product of fiscal management and bureaucratic organisation. By the later seventh century there were kingdoms in France and Spain which were actually larger than their modern counterparts. Germany developed in the same way in the tenth century. Italy was more fragmented, but even here the Lombard kingdom in the north covered roughly 175,000 square kilometres. England was a late starter in terms of state formation, beginning in the sixth century with dozens of tiny kingdoms or chieftaincies. That number was then rapidly reduced, and by the later seventh century England was dominated by one kingdom of roughly 90,000 square kilometres. The emergence of larger kingdoms in England was clearly the result of war and conquest, but it also marks the spread of Continental culture to the Anglo-Saxons, not least through the medium of bishops. Let us now turn to the interrelated areas of law, religion and political authority, for it is here that we find those cultural features which accentuated hierarchical structures throughout Europe, made magnates across Europe into mutually recognisable figures, and which encouraged association between them.

Law used to be seen as an indicator of cultural diversity, for each region had its own laws which were thought to be the codification of the customs of the different barbarian groups which had conquered the lands of Western Europe. It is now recognised that beneath the sometimes exotic customs and procedures of so-called 'barbarian law' lay a solid body of property law which was late Roman in origin. Second, the records of actual law cases show that everywhere the practice of law was pragmatic. Law courts tended to be organised as tribunals which drew upon local expertise and shared interests, as opposed to being the seats of judges who had the authority to make decisions on their own. It was the protection of property which was the focus of legal and social consensus. The similarity of the ways in which property rights were recorded, defined and protected throughout Europe is revealed by the rapid spread of *charters* throughout all regions. Charters were documents which were again of late-Roman origin. They recorded all manner of property transactions, and were increasingly used in courts as proof of ownership. Charters from the different regions of Europe may look physically very dissimilar to each other. For instance, in Croatia the first charters were written in Slavonic in the glagolitic script, and inscribed on clay tablets, whereas in England they were written in Latin on parchment in solemn uncial script, and many were copied onto the spare leaves of gospel books. It is thus striking to see how similar the contents of charters are throughout Europe, despite differences in form and even in language. They were like each other because everywhere they recorded similar property rights. Moreover, in some regions, in England or in central Germany, for instance, those rights may actually have been introduced via the dissemination of charters. The use of charters is the strongest evidence there is for the comparability of property rights across Europe, for the correspondence of the legal systems which protected those rights, and not least, for the similarity of the social structures which supported the power of elites.

The protection of property was clearly vital to those whose power was based upon it, but protection of property, and of the social order in general, was of concern to all free people. Everywhere in Western Europe a clear legal distinction between free and unfree people was fiercely maintained. This distinction was one of the most conservative features of early medieval culture, and (much to the confusion of social historians), the distinction outlived the actual social divisions in which it had had its origins. It was the desire to protect property and status which drew people to public courts, and in every region presidency of the local courts gave the representatives of the ruling authority an entry into local society. In this sense, public authority was there by demand, and that demand facilitated the building up of large territorial units. But the same demand limited the power of officials. They could not act without social support, and were typically harsh in dealing with the unfree, but often mild towards those with property. The confiscation of property was fringed with safeguards. Moreover, alongside formal legal processes, there existed an elastic body of custom and informal means of dispute settlement. Custom protected the elements of status which law could not reach, that is, honour and reputation. It was another socially conservative force in that it enshrined and protected the privileges of those with social power. The pragmatic application of law, the juxtaposition of law and custom, and the ability to work with different legal codes in a single territory, were preconditions for the existence of large states.

Throughout Europe, law and legal practice became progressively influenced by religious teachings and by the Church. The development of ordeals and oath-swearing are examples of this. The language of law-making also became more ecclesiastical in tone, and the Church's moral agenda began to be more strongly reflected in the rulers' political rhetoric. Everywhere too the Church was active in the law courts. As a major property holder without recourse to armed force, the Church became a pioneer of the protection of property rights through legal process. This activity was universal, and canon law itself was, naturally, universal in application. But the Church's part in the development of a common European culture of course went much further than this contribution to legal process and language.

From the mid-sixth century onwards the authority of the Catholic Church in Europe went virtually unchallenged, either by pagans or by dissident Christians. The simple fact that the Church was everywhere and had a common organisational structure, hierarchy, language and liturgy made it the single strongest force for cultural integration across Europe. The Church therefore had a markedly interna-tional character, despite the fact that regionally it was organised along the lines of each kingdom. It is remarkable to see how churchmen, and a few churchwomen, could move between kingdoms, and even attain positions of great influence in foreign lands. Most famous are the Irish who were prominent in Francia in the late sixth and seventh centuries, and the Anglo-Saxons who followed them into Francia and Germany in the eighth century. There were also Frankish bishops in England and Greeks in Spain and Italy, not to mention Theodore of Tarsus who became archbishop of Canterbury in 669 and his associate the abbot Hadrian, said to have been from North Africa. Mission, pilgrimage (especially to Rome) and the setting up of brotherhoods of prayer between ecclesiastical institutions in different countries all helped to reinforce the international character of early medieval Christianity.

Throughout Europe the numbers of monasteries increased steadily, and everywhere we see a pattern of local saints' cults developing within a framework of universal rules and common conventions. The cults of major international saints, such as the Apostles or prominent Roman martyrs, provided templates for the sanctification of local figures, and the writing of Saints' Lives (hagiography) was modelled upon a few highly influential texts. As in the case of charters, Saints' Lives across Europe, and indeed the Middle East, are remarkably similar to each other, even though it is possible to identify different genres of Lives and to describe significant regional variations. The common models of sanctity which developed in this period were aristocratic in inspiration and nature. Although the saintly virtues included a readiness to challenge a ruler's authority on occasion, they were, on the whole, socially conservative virtues, and those who came to be honoured as saints were over-whelmingly drawn from the nobility which now dominated the leadership of the Church. Religious prestige was another element which was added to wealth and office in the construction of high social status. If power was thus given a spiritual legitimation, it was, naturally, rulers who did most to forward this equation. The emergence of royal saints is a phenomenon so marked across Europe that many

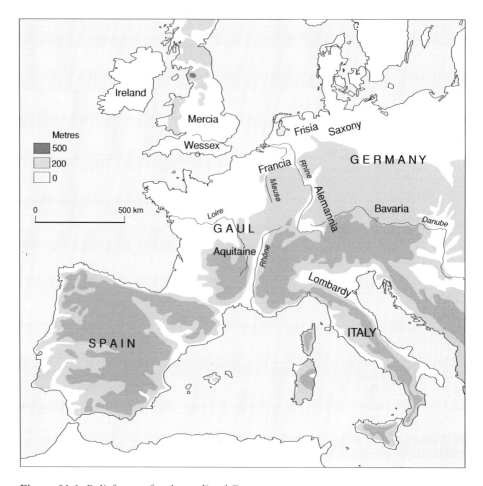

Figure 21.1 Relief map of early medieval Europe.

historians have suspected that royal sanctity was merely the clothing of pre-Christian forms of charisma, or even of magical powers, in more acceptable garb. Since we know next to nothing about any such pre-Christian charisma (or even if it existed), this is not an argument which can be proved. It is more sensible to place the phenomenon of royal saints in the context of a growing association between sanctity and power. Generosity towards, and protection of, the Church were virtuous activities in which kings, and queens, could shine. In addition, the violent death to which kings were prone, either in battle or by assassination, enabled them to be constructed as martyrs.

As we have just seen, the language of ecclesiastical concern progressively coloured law-making and was subsumed into political rhetoric. Rulers thus drew upon it to reinforce their power with moral authority. Starting in seventh-century Spain, and then, later, in Francia, England and Germany we see the Church playing an increasingly important role in the actual making of kings, leading the way in developing consecration rituals in imitation of biblical precedent, and having kings publicly state their duties towards the Church. Kings everywhere also drew on the Church for practical help in government, the clergy being the most literate element in society. Government thus acquired a theocratic aspect, and that that development was Europe-wide is shown by shockwaves moving across the whole area when in the later eleventh century the Papacy eventually called on the ecclesiastical hierarchy to stop serving rulers in this way.

Ecclesiastical participation and the presence of high-status nobles were features of royal courts everywhere. The importance of occasional kingdom-wide assemblies has already been mentioned, but royal courts were a cultural focus point at all times. It was common for young nobles to spend time at court, and it is clear that this shared experience was the chief means of integrating elites of different regional, and sometimes different ethnic, backgrounds within a single kingdom. Some members of the elite also stayed at the courts of foreign rulers, as guests, ambassadors and exiles. Courts were in this way key conduits in the dissemination of ideas across the different kingdoms, especially as they were often centres of learning which attracted a wide range of scholars. In his chapter on assemblies, Timothy Reuter draws attention to the highly ritualised nature of political interaction between people whose positions and interests were not open to negotiation. His point is that the use of ritual was a safeguard against public loss of face, and it is important to remember that what drew people to rulers' courts and assemblies was the need to maintain social status and wealth. We have seen that in the early medieval period this same need drew the elite into the formation and defence of very large territorial units. One could add that here ritual served a further purpose as a shared language between people from different regions. It was in this sense analogous to that common proced-ure in law courts which comprehended different legal traditions. The widespread use of ritual in political contexts is the reflection of an elite culture which was socially conservative. And like law and political ideas, ritual was increasingly influenced by the Church.

So far we have seen how Europe developed a degree of cultural conformity in a context of social conservatism, and in the process built up large territorial units. We now return to the question of how valid it is to characterise European culture as a whole according to a model which is based largely on Frankish history. Not all of Europe, for instance, was organised into large territorial states. In Ireland political authority was notoriously fragmented. Perhaps in Ireland wealth was more evenly distributed and the social hierarchy too diffuse to enable a small elite to dominate the whole island. Or Ireland may have been sufficiently wealthy to support nobles and their clients in a much smaller locality. In Saxony, before the Carolingian conquest of the late eighth century, there do not seem to have been paramount leaders, that is, kings and a social elite with exclusive privileges. Likewise, in Scandinavia political authority was highly unstable before the tenth century. Perhaps Saxony and Scandinavia were too poor, especially in precious metals, to support the kind of social elite which made widespread authority possible. Nor can it be coincidental that Ireland, Saxony and Scandinavia had never formed part of the Roman Empire. In Spain, the Arab conquests after 711 destroyed the single kingdom and gave a new configuration to elite culture. Italy was never reunited after the destruction of the Ostrogothic kingdom in the mid-sixth century, and subject to competing authorities in the peninsula, the Italian elite learned to live without association on a large scale. England, as we have seen, moved in the opposite direction, from fragmentation to unity. So far it looks as if Francia was in fact the exception in building up a massive and durable state in the post-Roman period, a state through which an elite whose social exclusiveness was inherited from the Romans remained culturally and politically dominant for centuries.

But there are two good reasons for judging that the general development of European culture can indeed be seen through the eyes of the Franks. First, by virtue of the fact that that Frankish state did last for so long, and since many of its ecclesiastical institutions survived into the modern period, it is one area which we can continuously document over centuries. This allows us to observe change over the longer term, and our observations can then be used to shed light on less well-documented areas. Second, the fact that it survived as a single large unit, not subject to invasion like Spain or Italy, meant that Francia became pre-eminent in Europe. We have already noted, for instance, that the Frankish king Charlemagne ruled a territory which was not far short of the old Common Market in extent. Francia thus exported its culture to neighbouring regions, including Saxony and all of Germany east of the Rhine, northern Italy, northern Spain, and, not least, England. By the end of the eleventh century, when the peoples of the Middle East came into increasing (and unwelcome) contact with West Europeans, they referred to them in general as 'Franks'. In this sense European culture had become generally 'Frankish'. Let us now turn briefly to the history of Frankish expansion, for this provides important clues about the nature of a cultural and political change in Europe which brought about the demise, albeit temporary, of the kind of large territorial units we have been looking at.

The Franks were a confederate people, and the key to Frankish history lies in their ability to assimilate other groups, beginning with the Gallo-Roman elite in the sixth century. It was because Frankish culture was based on a process of synthesis that it was able to occupy such a large space in Europe. The territory under Frankish influence was, of course, expanded by force of arms, but conquest was accompanied, and often preceded, by the acculturation of neighbours to Frankish ways. In England, elements of Frankish culture spread without conquest. Among both the Franks and their neighbours the nobility was of mixed origins, not only in terms of ethnic background, but also in terms of formation. Noble status was rarely formally defined. It could be inherited, or acquired through office and service to one of higher status, or it could simply reflect great wealth. As a consequence of this variety, the European nobility of the early middle ages was not a closed elite, especially as the dividing line between free and noble was always blurred. There were massive differences of wealth and status within this amorphous group, and, consequently, some movement within it. As we have seen, nobles struggled to maintain their wealth and status in the face of stiff competition, and it was this pressure which led them in general to cooperate in the government of large territorial units, and in particular to seek opportunities as part of an increasingly successful and powerful Frankish confederacy.

Most of those living on the periphery of Francia had always been close to the Franks in terms of language, dress and social custom. A further degree of cultural assimilation involved the adoption of Frankish religious and political organisation, in short, the acceptance of bishops and counts. With the setting-up of the Church, the strengthening of law courts, and foundation of monasteries, came charters, better defined property rights, and the restructuring of land-holding into estates based on a dependent peasantry. These were the developments which gave the emerging local nobility greater opportunities to acquire wealth, status and prestige. In the seventh and eighth centuries, right across Germany, and indeed England, we see a shift in settlement patterns which can be associated with the spread of Christianity and the development of local elites as churches were built and local leaders began to be buried in or near the church, rather than in the old communal burial areas. And sometimes the archaeological evidence can be matched with the evidence of charters to show how the local population was grouped around the central holding or hall of the leading family to provide the income needed to maintain its pre-eminence. It became increasingly common for such settlements to be called after a member of the leading family. An example would be Poapintal, modern Pfaffhofen in the Austrian Tyrol which was named after a leader called Poapo. We are fortunate to know something about this man and his family from the charters of the monastery of Scharnitz which he founded. Although important regional variations, such as the amount of money in circulation, or local dialect, or legal code, would remain, it is nevertheless true that the cultural differences between core and periphery in the Frankish world were diminishing from the seventh century onwards. Christianisation, and a shift in settlement patterns in which estates were created and the nobility's hold over the local population was strengthened, are two of the most important elements in the 'Frankification' of peripheral regions. By the time of Charlemagne (768–814) we see one massive cultural space, with plenty of local variation, but without an obvious core–periphery structure in cultural terms.

Paradoxically, developments in the peripheral regions led in the first instance to fierce resistance to Frankish influence. That is to say, the emergence of a better resourced and organised nobility in areas such as Frisia, Alemannia and Bavaria gave them the means to resist Frankish pressure. The nobles of these regions looked to their leaders (dukes) to safeguard their wealth and status, and this in turn meant that the dukes became more aggressive towards the Franks. Conflict followed. In each case the dukes were crushed and the nobility were rapidly assimilated into the Frankish polity. In central Germany, assimilation evidently took place without conflict. This pattern of resistance, conflict, conquest and assimilation used to be explained in terms of personality and political and military history. The Merovingian dynasty which ruled the Franks up to 751 was said to have become ineffective due to the degeneracy of its members, the so-called 'do-nothing kings'. Regional leaders supposedly took this opportunity to break free of Frankish influence, and it then took the more vigorous Carolingian rulers (who replaced the Merovingians in 751) to break their power and conquer their lands. But this is a Carolingian viewpoint, and one produced by a careful rewriting of history. It obscures the crucial point that Frankish culture was expanding outwards even when the kings were doing nothing, and that it was precisely because the massive Frankish state was structurally, and culturally, so stable that it was possible for it to sail on with the lightest of touches at the helm. In fact, if the later Merovingian kings did little, this was because they were often small children. Child kingship (the product of devotion to a single bloodline) is inconceivable in any other European state at this time. But if it was the same continuing process of cultural development which led the peripheral duchies into rivalry with the Franks and then resulted in their final assimilation, it was indeed the Carolingian rulers who won the vital victories and presided over the assimilation. They were, however, finishing off what the Merovingians had begun, rather than taking over where they had failed.

It was under the first Carolingian rulers that Frankish hegemony reached its maximum extent, but it was under the last Carolingians that it began to be replaced by smaller territorial units. As in the case of the change from Merovingian to Carolingian dynasties, this political fragmentation is often put down to poor leadership and military failure, but it is better described as a later phase of that same acculturation which had prepared the way for Frankish expansion in the first place. The Carolingians managed their empire by manipulating the existing tendency of the elite families to associate with each other. By rewarding favoured families with widely dispersed lands and offices, the Carolingians fostered what has been called an 'imperial aristocracy', that is, a select group of families which had branches across the empire. The cohesion of this massive territory lay very much in their hands. At the same time, success in warfare meant that the Carolingians could be generous and attractive lords. With nobles keen to serve them, and with increasing resources becoming available from plunder, tribute, rents and services, the Carolingian rulers attempted to strengthen their grip with a measure of reform, or 'renewal' as they put it. What 'renewal' (*renovatio*) amounted to in effect was the accentuation of those common cultural features which tended to reinforce the social hierarchy. There was much talk of justice, right, duty, moral behaviour, of the correct forms of liturgy and language, learning, sexual purity among the clergy, and of many other Church matters. The Carolingians sought to 'correct' society in order that the Franks might continue to be successful, and achieve salvation. But in each area of reform, the 'correct' way of doing things was by and large the traditional way of doing things with visible abuses removed. In addition there was a strong Romanising tendency (Charlemagne, for instance, famously had himself crowned as 'Roman Emperor' in the year 800), and this reinforced the Roman element in the European cultural heritage. One obvious example is in language and script, where the Carolingians insisted that the 'correct' form of language was the (Latin) language of the Vulgate Bible, and they also imitated the script of surviving Roman monuments. There has been much debate among historians about how effective the Carolingian reform programme actually was. In terms of language and script it clearly had a Europe-wide effect. It has indeed been argued that the Carolingians effectively arrested the development of written Latin into vernacular form by insisting on conformity with biblical language. This had the effect of making written Latin a fossilised language, and since relatively few women were educated in this language, it could never become a mother tongue, although it was spoken by a small and inter-nationalised intellectual elite.

Over the course of the ninth century the territorial integrity of the Carolingian empire was broken down. Partition between the grandsons of Charlemagne, and the pressure of invaders (mostly Scandinavians) have traditionally been seen as the main causes of fragmentation. In the early tenth century the eastern part of Francia became the separate kingdom of Germany. In the western part authority which had been the exclusive preserve of the kings devolved into the hands of counts and bishops, and even came to rest with lesser officials. Many historians characterise this devolution, which took place in northern Spain and Italy too, as a 'crisis of authority'. West Francia in the late tenth and eleventh centuries has even been described as a collection of 'acephalous polities'. There has recently been lively debate about the nature and extent of any such crisis. But what most commentators have failed to spell out is that they are talking about a political, not a cultural, nor an economic, crisis. Far from being the nemesis of Carolingian order, a diffusion of authority was its natural development, and far from conditions being so unstable that they inhibited cultural development, they actually ushered in a particularly dynamic phase of growth.

We have seen how the expansion of the Frankish empire was accompanied by a reorganisation of landholding into estates, and how the spread of charters reveals a stabilisation of property rights. As a consequence of these developments in the countryside, there emerged a better organised nobility which exploited peasant resources more efficiently. The drawing-up of 'polyptychs', which we have already mentioned, was part of this move to manage landed resources more effectively. The overall result was a growth in economic activity. The population grew and more precious metals became available. Lords could now begin to maintain their wealth and status by exploiting resources on a local or regional basis and there was less incentive for them to co-operate in government on a massive territorial scale. But that authority which they had exercised on behalf of the king they retained in their own hands. On one level this can be seen as usurpation, but on another it can be described as acculturation, which eventually spread the rights, and duties, of rulers to the layer of nobility below that of the old magnate families which had dominated the Carolingian empire in its heyday.

The feature of devolved power which has been a particular subject of contention is the relationship between lords and their men, so-called 'vassals'. The argument is about how institutionalised lord–vassal relations became, and whether they can be described as fundamental to the socio-political structure of Western Europe in the high Middle Ages. This is not the place to enter the debate, except in the context of this chapter it is worth drawing attention to vassalage as a good example of how relationships which were originally the preserve of those of the highest status moved down the social scale as first magnates, and then other nobles, imitated the practice of kings in having followers who had sworn a special loyalty to them in a pact of mutual support and protection. Under the Merovingians these people had been called *antrustiones*. 'Vassals' was a non-royal term which replaced *antrustiones*, the latter disappearing along with the Merovingians. Not only do we see nobles establishing special relationships in this way, we also see them having strong family ties with monasteries which supplied them with bureaucratic services, which housed their ancestors and some of their living relatives, and which provided them with spiritual prestige and opportunities to exercise patronage. Again, what a select few magnates, and kings, had been doing in the seventh and eighth centuries, was becoming much more common in the ninth and tenth centuries. Counts imitated royal practice in having courts with dignitaries, which were held in fixed places, and where they presided over meetings of local nobles. We also see the emergence of the countess figure, a consort who acquired a position and duties which emulated those of the queen. The programme of renewal which the early Carolingian kings had promoted was now voiced by the Church independently. In the late tenth and eleventh centuries Church leaders, first in Aquitaine and then more widely, called on nobles to protect Church property and the weak and the poor in society. This movement, known as the 'Peace' and 'Truce' of God, has often been interpreted as the Church coming to the aid of a peasantry oppressed by a nobility rampaging out of control. More recent thinking sees it as a continuation of Carolingian ideas, 'correction' without the king, as it were.

Because the Church and the nobility took over many of the functions once exercised by kings over an extensive area, even though the territory under the control of a single ruler might shrink drastically, the cultural space which created the early medieval states, and which they in turn reinforced, remained intact. In fact it expanded in the high Middle Ages into Scandinavia, Central Europe and Ireland, finally erasing the cultural differences between Roman and non-Roman Europe. We have seen that the fragmentation of the large kingdoms took place in a context of growing economic activity and involved a devolution of authority. The same process of growth and development paved the way for a reinvigoration of government in the central Middle Ages. Education became more widespread and rulers began to be able to rely on professional administrators and to raise the kind of revenues which would support more ambitious bureaucratic activity. The states of the early Middle Ages may have been territorially very large, but in terms of effective government they were as shallow as they were extensive. We must remember, however, that what we might term the 'large state phase' in Roman and early medieval Europe had lasted for a very long time, for nearly a millennium if we go back to Caesar's conquest of Gaul. Despite fragmentation, the memory of the spaces those states had occupied remained strong, and it was the areas under the control of the earlier kingdoms that the states of the central Middle Ages strove to recover. Later rulers might wish, like Charlemagne, to be 'fathers of Europe', but in terms of cultural and political geography Europe had already been 'made'. For West Europeans, no longer were there weaker neighbours to be assimilated and peripheral regions to be gobbled up. Government had to grow downwards in the spaces inherited from the early Middle Ages rather than outwards. It was when government began to ally with groups below the magnate class, such as urban communities and merchants, and to make use of professional administrators, that the grip of the old social hierarchy started to weaken, and the socially conservative force of European culture at last began to wane.

BIBLIOGRAPHY

Althoff, G. (1990), *Verwandte, Freunde und Getreue. Zum politischen Stellenwert der Gruppenbindungen im frühen Mittelalter*, Darmstadt: Wissenschaftliche Buchgesellschaft.
Arnold, B. (1997), *Medieval Germany 500–1300. A Political Interpretation*, London: Macmillan.

Barthélemy, D. (1996), 'Debate: The "Feudal Revolution", Comment 1', *Past and Present* 152, pp. 196–205.

Bassett, S. (1989), (ed.), *The Origins of the Anglo-Saxon Kingdoms*, Leicester: Leicester University Press.

Bisson, T. (1994), 'The "Feudal Revolution"', *Past and Present* 142, pp. 6–42.

Bisson, T. (1997), 'Debate: The "Feudal Revolution"', *Past and Present* 155, pp. 208–25.

Bonnassie, P. (1991), *From Slavery to Feudalism in South-Western Europe*, Cambridge: Cambridge University Press.

Collins, R. (1983), *Early Medieval Spain*, London: Macmillan.

Damminger, F. (1998), 'Dwellings, settlement and settlement patterns in Merovingian Southwest Germany and adjacent areas', in I. Wood (ed.), *Franks and Alemanni in the Merovingian Period. An Ethnographic Perspective*, Woodbridge: Boydell, pp. 33–89.

Davies, W., Fouracre, P. (1986), (eds.), *The Settlement of Disputes in Early Medieval Europe*, Cambridge: Cambridge University Press.

Davies, W., Fouracre, P. (1995), (eds.), *Property and Power in the Early Middle Ages*, Cambridge: Cambridge University Press.

Duby, G. (1968), *Rural Economy and Country Life*, London: Edward Arnold.

Edson, E. (1997), *Mapping Time and Space. How Medieval Mapmakers Viewed their World*, London: The British Library.

Effros, B. (1997), '*De Partibus Saxonibus* and the Regulation of Mortuary custom. A Carolingian Campaign of Christianization or the Suppression of Saxon Identity?', *Revue Belge de Philologie et d'Histoire* 75, pp. 267–86.

Esmonde Cleary, S. (1989), *The Ending of Roman Britain*, London: Batsford.

Ferreiro, A. (1998), (ed), *The Visigoths. Studies in Culture and Society*, Cologne, Leiden, Boston: Brill.

Fouracre, P. (1992), 'Cultural Conformity and Social Conservatism in Early Medieval Europe', *History Workshop Journal* 33, pp. 152–61.

Fouracre, P. (2000), *The Age of Charles Martel*, London: Longman.

Herrin, J. (1987), *The Formation of Christendom*, Princeton: Princeton University Press.

Hodges, R., Whitehouse, D. (1983), *Mohammed, Charlemagne and the Origins of Europe*, London: Duckworth.

Le Jan, R. (1995), *Famille et Pouvoir dans le Monde Franc (viie–xe siècle). Essai d'anthropologie sociale*, Paris: Publications de la Sorbonne.

McKitterick, R. (1994), (ed.), *Carolingian Culture: emulation and innovation*, Cambridge: Cambridge University Press.

Nelson, J. L. (1973), 'Royal saints and early medieval kingship', *Studies in Church History* 10, pp. 39–44.

Nelson, J. L. (1978), 'Inauguration rituals', in P. Sawyer, I. Wood eds., *Early Medieval Kingship*, Leeds: University of Leeds, pp. 50–71.

Nelson, J. L. (1994), review of Head and Landes eds., *The Peace of God: Social Violence and Religious Response in France around the Year 1000*, in *Speculum* 69, pp. 163–9.

Oexle, O. G. (1978), *Forschungen zur monastischen und geistlichen Gemeinschaften im westfränkischen Bereich*, Munich: Fink.

Prinz, F. (1974), 'Frühes Mönchtum in Südwestdeutschland und die Anfänge der Reichenau', in A. Borst (ed.), *Mönchtum, Episkopat und Adel zur Gründungszeit des Klosters Reichenau*, Sigmaringen: Thorbecke, pp. 37–76.

Reuter, T. (1991), *Germany in the Early Middle Ages*, London: Longman.

Reuter, T. (1997), 'Debate: The "Feudal Revolution"', *Past and Present* 155, pp. 177–95.

Reynolds, S. (1994), *Fiefs and Vassals. The Medieval Evidence Reinterpreted*, Oxford: Oxford University Press.

Smith, J. (1990), 'Oral and written: saints, miracles and relics in Brittany c. 850–1250', *Speculum* 65, pp. 309–43.

Theuws, F. (1991), 'Landed property and manorial organisation in Northern Austrasia. Some considerations and a case study', in N. Roymans, F. Theuws (eds.), *Images of the Past. Studies on Ancient Societies in Northwestern Europe*, Amsterdam: Institut voor Pre- und Protohistorische Archaeologie, pp. 299–407.

White, S. (1996), 'Debate: The "Feudal Revolution", Comment 2', *Past and Present* 152, pp. 205–23.

Wickham, C. (1981), *Early Medieval Italy*, London: Macmillan.

Wickham, C. (1984), 'The other transition: from the ancient world to feudalism', *Past and Present* 103, pp. 3–36.

Wickham, C. (1995), 'Rural society in Carolingian Europe', in R. McKitterick ed., *The New Cambridge Medieval History*, vol. II, Cambridge: Cambridge University Press, pp. 510–37.

Wickham, C. (1997), 'Debate: The "Feudal Revolution"', *Past and Present* 155, pp. 196–208.

Wright, R. (1982), *Late Latin and Early Romance in Spain and Carolingian France*, Liverpool: Liverpool University Press.

Wood, I. (1994), *The Merovingian Kingdoms*, London: Longman.

THE OUTWARD LOOK: BRITAIN AND BEYOND IN MEDIEVAL IRISH LITERATURE

Máire Ní Mhaonaigh

INTRODUCTION

Despite her peripheral situation, Ireland enjoyed close connections with her European neighbours throughout the Middle Ages, as has long been appreciated. Not surprisingly, the nature and extent of these contacts varied considerably over time. Evidence for trade with both Britain and the wider world is attested from earliest times (Doherty 1980: 76–85; James 1982), as is that for intercourse of a less peaceful nature. The early historic period in particular saw the Irish engaged in raiding in Britain, and the establishment of settlements in areas as far afield as western Scotland, Dyfed in Wales, and the Devon–Cornwall peninsula. It was here too, perhaps, that the Irish may first have come into contact with Christianity. In any event, it is a Briton, Patrick, who has come to be most closely associated with the Irish Christian mission, though this is due in no small measure to the success of his seventh-century biographers in presenting him as an all-converting hero (Bieler 1979: 62–167). Patrick's mission to Ireland was preceded by a Roman one, however, and in fact it was to continental Europe, as well as to Britain, that the fledgling Irish Church turned. Both areas were similarly the focus for the activities of Irish *peregrini* whose reputation as missionaries and wandering scholars in the seventh, eighth and ninth centuries is well established (Contreni 1986). Yet traffic was not all one-way; shortly after Columba laboured on Iona and Columbanus in Luxeuil, Bede informs us that Irish schools attracted English students (Colgrave and Mynors 1969: 312–13). In addition, the seventh century saw the arrival in Ireland of the writings of Isidore of Seville, together with a variety of other computistical and grammatical works, all of which had a profound influence on contemporary learning (Hillgarth 1984). Indeed, Isidore's *Etymologiae* was so revered that, according to the tale *De Fhaillsiugud Tána Bó Cúailnge*, 'Concerning the revelation of *Táin Bó Cúailnge*', it was acquired in exchange for what appears to have been the sole surviving copy of the important Irish tale, *Táin Bó Cúailnge* 'The cattle-raid of Cúailnge'. To remedy matters, two learned men were dispatched to the Continent to redeem the *Táin*; before leaving Ireland, however, one of them had a vision lasting three days and three nights, during which the complete story was revealed to him (Best, Bergin, O'Brien and O'Sullivan 1954–83: 5: 1119).

While the European journey of these two fictional characters may have been rendered unnecessary, their real-life counterparts continued to travel abroad in the Viking period and beyond. The ninth-century 'Bamberg Cryptogram' indicates that a number of Irish scholars on their way to the Continent spent time at the court of Gwynedd in Wales. These may have included Sedulius Scottus who was also attached to the court of Hartgar, bishop of Liège (Kenney 1929: 553–6). In fact, it may have been in celebration of a victory gained by Hartgar that this Irish ecclesiastic wrote his poem *De strage Normannorum* 'On the defeat of the Northmen' (Carney 1985: 54–60). His kinsmen at home faced similar turbulence. As is well known, however, contact with Scandinavian invaders brought the benefits of an extensive, international trading network in its wake. Furthermore, as Irish kings sought to gain control of Viking towns, particularly Dublin, they also attempted to dominate territories in the hands of Hiberno-Scandinavians overseas (Duffy 1992). The Irish Sea, therefore, remained in the tenth and eleventh centuries the hub of all kinds of activity. While warring factions sailed hither and thither, it also provided a haven for many a political leader seeking refuge on the other side. Thus, Gruffydd ap Cynan, son of an eleventh-century ruler of Gwynedd, came to be born in Dublin and brought up in nearby Swords. In addition, when seeking to regain his patrimony in Wales, he sought the assistance of a King Murchath who has been plausibly identified as the Munster king, Muirchertach Ua Briain (Evans 1990; Duffy 1995: 395). The latter corresponded with Archbishop Anselm of Canterbury on the state of the Irish Church, just as his father, Toirdelbach, had been engaged in debate on similar issues with Anselm's predecessor, Lanfranc (Clover and Gibson 1979). Indeed, as the interest shown by both archbishops indicates, ecclesiastical contacts with England, as well as with continental Europe, were intensified in this period as clerics came ever more into contact with the reform movement whose adherents were to bring about a gradual reorganisation of the Irish Church during the twelfth century. Increased ecclesiastical contact went hand in hand with closer co-operation in the political sphere, exemplified most clearly in the appeal by Diarmait Mac Murchada to Anglo-Norman magnates for military aid. It scarcely needs rehearsing here that it was this action which indirectly led to the addition of Ireland to the otherwise vast array of English and Angevin dominions over which Henry II held sway (Flanagan 1989).

By the time Henry made his direct intervention in Irish affairs, therefore, Ireland had behind her a long history of international relations of which no more than a brief glimpse has been afforded above. No mention has been made, for example, of a large body of evidence that bears concrete witness to interaction between Ireland and the outside world. This includes the existence in Wales and south-west England of inscriptions carved on stone in the Irish ogam script, the presence of Irish manuscripts in continental monasteries, many of them founded by the Irish themselves, and a corpus of Irish 'translation literature' freely adapted from mainly Latin exemplars. Equally significant, if somewhat less tangible, are indications of close cross-Channel cooperation in the fields of calligraphy and artwork, as well as the incorporation of outside influences into vernacular writing from an early period. In the case of the latter, biblical resonances are, not surprisingly, paramount: the Tower of Babel episode, for example, lies behind the account of the invention of the Irish language in the eighth-century poets' manual, *Auraicept na nÉces* 'The scholar's primer' (Calder 1917; Ahlqvist 1982), while scriptural law permeates the seventh- and eighth-century Old Irish law tracts (Ó Corráin 1987a). Similarly, a biblical construct informs the eleventh-century national origin-legend, *Lebor Gabála* 'The book of taking', as do the writings of Jerome, Orosius and Isidore (Carey 1994).

The likelihood is that a large number of the authors of such texts never set foot outside Ireland but gleaned their knowledge of the wider world from books, as well as from encounters with visiting foreigners and returned exiles; the same is true of their patrons, both lay and clerical. Hence, one may well question their precise acquaintance with matters of geography and query the extent to which their perception of the wider world corresponded with reality. In truth, of course, expertise in British and European affairs varied from individual to individual, or at the very least from one centre of learning to another, and fluctuated over time. Nonetheless, some understanding of the international perspective of the medieval Irish elite may be gleaned from an examination of their portrayal of all things foreign in the rich corpus of written material which has come down to us. This is, of course, an ambitious task which must proceed piecemeal. Light has already been shed, for example, on the contacts between the Irish and one specific foreign dynasty, that of Bernicia, in one particular period, the seventh century (Moisl 1982); Dauvit Broun and Máire Herbert have similarly enhanced our understanding of Scottish–Irish relations (Broun 1999; Herbert 1999). In doing so, these scholars have rightly had recourse to a range of documents, historical, hagiographical and literary, at their disposal. My purpose here is more general: with reference to a limited number of examples from narrative literature, I shall draw attention to some of the variety of guises in which foreigners appear therein. Since the texts in question are literary, we cannot claim that their depiction of the past accurately reflects reality. Yet what they do provide is a valuable insight into how their mainly anonymous and highly privileged authors perceived that past and, more importantly, how they wished their audience to view it. As tailor-made constructs, each narrative has its own particular textual and cultural history, knowledge of which is essential to any attempt to unravel its myriad layers. Nonetheless, the general backdrop of early medieval Ireland is one which is common to all. To enable us to set their portrayal of foreigners in a broader context, therefore, let us first briefly examine the categorisation of foreigners in a range of works.

OUTSIDER AND FOREIGNER

In a society such as that depicted in the seventh- and eighth-century Irish law tracts where the primary jurisdictional unit was the localised kingdom or *túath* beyond which the legal rights of the majority of the population did not extend, the concept of outsider enjoyed a wide application. Hence, compounds formed with *echtar-* 'outside, extern', such as *echtarchenél*, *echtarfine* and *echtarthúath*, occur frequently in the Laws to refer to any *cenél* 'race', *fine* 'kin' or *túath* other than one's own. Narrative literature provides further later examples: thus in *Echtra Nerai* 'The adventure of Nera', the famous Ulster warrior, Cú Chulainn, is obliged to challenge any warrior from an *echtarchenél* who ventured into his territory (Meyer 1889: 222, line 127).

Similarly, in Cuanu's death-tale, the *echtarthúatha* are specifically stated to be neighbouring Munster territories (O'Nolan 1912–13: 266, 271). In the same way, the related term *echtrann* 'strange, foreign' is used to refer to any enemy territory in the ninth-century narrative *Fled Bricrenn* 'Bricriu's feast' (Henderson 1899: 10–11, line 16). Elsewhere, however, it is used with *bélre* 'language' to designate a specifically foreign one (Stokes and Strachan 1901–3: 1: 577, Würzburg, 12c46).

Other terms prove equally ambiguous. *Loinges* 'banishment, exile', for example, is used to denote the enforced exile of Connacht of Fergus and his comrades in *Táin Bó Cúailnge* (O'Rahilly 1976: 13, 136, line 404), as well as the sojourn in Albu (Britain and later Scotland) by Naíse and his brothers in *Loinges mac nUislenn* 'The exile of the sons of Uisliu' (Hull 1949). Similarly the roughly synonymous *indarbad* can imply banishment overseas, as befalls Conaire's foster-brothers in *Togail Bruidne Da Derga* 'The destruction of Da Derga's hostel' (Knott 1936: 11, line 340), as well as dislocation within Ireland, as is the case in the later version of the narrative 'The expulsion of the Déssi' (Bergin, Best, Meyer and O'Keeffe 1907–13: 1: 15–24). In the same way, the term *deorad* 'stranger, exile', is frequently used in the Laws in opposition to the *aurrad*, the person of legal standing within a *túath* (Kelly 1988: 5); yet in later texts, he is equated with the foreign mercenary. Moreover, the term acquires a negative connotation in the phase *lám deoraid*, literally 'outlaw's hand', which is used on occasion to signify death (O'Rahilly 1976: 23, 145, line 738; Hull 1930b). In contrast with this, the exalted *deorad Dé*, the 'exile of God' or *peregrinus*, refers to one who undertakes *peregrinatio* within Ireland or without. As noted by Charles-Edwards, both types of pilgrimage are similarly within the remit of the *ailithir* 'pilgrim' as indicated by the ninth-century story of Liadain and Cuirithir where the latter is deemed a pilgrim both in the territory of the Déssi and overseas (Charles-Edwards 1976: 44, 53–4).

The use of these terms to denote outsiders in the broadest sense should not obscure the fact that elsewhere, particularly in the legal material, a clear distinction is drawn between the *ambue* or outsider from another Irish territory and the *cú glas*, literally 'grey dog or wolf', who is an exile from overseas. Furthermore, a third category, the *glasfine* 'grey kin' is used to refer to the son whom an Irish woman bears to a Briton, presumably, as Charles-Edwards notes, since the latter was the most common alien in the early period (Charles-Edwards 1976: 46–8). Moreover, a distinction is also sometimes drawn between various types of foreigner. According to the ninth-century text, *Scéla Cano meic Gartnáin* 'The tale of Cano son of Gartnán', *Saxain ocus Bretain ocus fir Alban* 'Saxons, Britons and the men of Albu' accompanied the eponymous hero on his journey to the Munster territory of Corcu Loígde (Binchy 1963: 16, line 441). The same groups are instrumental in the acquisition of the kingship of Tara by Lugaid Mac Con if the account in *Cath Maige Mucrama* 'The battle of Mag Mucrama' is to be believed (O Daly 1975: 48–9). Less plausible perhaps is the claim made by the author of 'The scholar's primer' to be able to differentiate between the seventy-two nations at Babel's tower (Calder 1917: 16–19). Finally, we must remain agnostic in the face of a reference to St Patrick's mother as a Frank (Stokes and Strachan 1901–3: 2: 309, lines 19–20); nor can we determine whether Colmán, who is described in the *Additamenta* in the Book of Armagh as having purchased a horse, was in reality a Briton (Stokes and Strachan 1901–3: 2: 240, line 2).

Assigning specific racial affiliations is one thing, understanding the precise meaning of such terms another. Nonetheless, in certain cases we can be sure that a particular term was very deliberately used. A celebrated example is found in *Críth Gablach* 'The branched purchase', a law text on status which has been dated to *c*.700 partly on historical grounds. A reference therein to a particular type of law for the expulsion of a foreign race is illustrated by reference to a specific example 'e.g. against the Saxons'. As noted by Binchy, this recalls the invasion of Brega by Egfrid, king of the Northumbrians in 684 (Binchy 1941: xiv, 20–1). Moreover, this same event probably underlies the mention of 'encircling Saxons' in the early eighth-century text, *Baile Chuinn Chétchathaig* 'The vision of Conn of the hundred battles' (Bhreathnach 1996: 81). Similarly, the ninth-century work, *Sanas Cormaic* 'Cormac's glossary', which has been attributed to the king-bishop of Munster, Cormac mac Cuilennáin, contains precise definitions of such terms as 'Gauls' and mentions Old Norse, as well as displaying some knowledge of English and considerably more of Welsh (Bergin, Best, Meyer and O'Keeffe 1907–13: 4; Charles-Edwards 1995: 710–11, 720–1). The author of this 'Irish counterpart to Isidore's *Etymologies* or *Origines*' (Sims-Williams 1985: 99) may not, of course, have been typical. Let us look more closely, therefore, at the portrayal of foreigners in the works of others writing in the early medieval period.

CONALL CORC AND BRITAIN

In view of its relative proximity, and considering the density of traffic in both directions across the Irish Sea throughout much of the period in question, it is not surprising that Britain is the most common 'abroad' in the texts, and that its inhabitants are the foreigners who feature most frequently therein. Significantly, however, Albu, the vernacular term originally used to designate the entire island of Britain, was applied from *c*.900 in a more restricted sense to refer to the northern Gaelic kingdom ruled by the descendants of Cináed mac Alpín whose ancestors had migrated from the north-east of Ireland four or five centuries previously. Later still it came to be used for the kingdom of Scotland as a whole (Broun 1994; Dumville 1996). In consequence, determining the precise meaning of Albu in texts, the dates of which are often uncertain, is not always easy. The narrative material under discussion here centring on the important figure of Conall Corc of Cashel, ancestor of the important Munster federation of dynastic groups known as the Éoganachta, proves no exception. Nonetheless, the early date of two at least of the texts in question would point to Britain as the likely meaning of Albu in this case. All the more so, since Conall's mother is named as Bolce *banbretnach*, a female satirist of the Britons (Bergin, Best, Meyer and O'Keeffe 1907–13: 3: 57; Hull 1947: 892). As an ambassador for her race, however, she is a particularly unfortunate choice. In the first place, it was Bolce who forced Conall's father to sleep with her. Furthermore, as a female satirist, she is one of a number of women deemed legally unfit to look after a child (Kelly 1988: 85). Thus, she carelessly entrusts her new-born son to the protection of one of a number of supernatural creatures whom she used to frequent. This in turn led to the burning of Conall's ear when he was hidden under a cauldron,

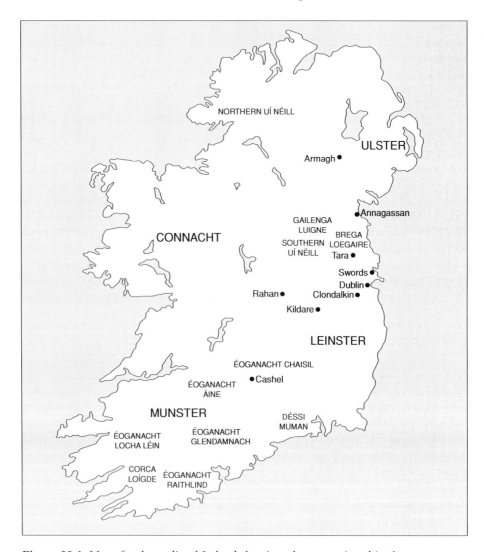

Figure 22.1 Map of early medieval Ireland showing places mentioned in the text.

as a result of which he acquired his nickname *corc* 'red' (Bergin, Best, Meyer and O'Keeffe 1907–13: 3: 57; Hull 1947: 892–3).

This account of Conall's unusual conception and birth provides him with the first essential ingredient for the creation of his standard heroic biography (Sproule 1985: 12). Mixed with this are other elements common to many a literary life, the most significant of which for our purposes is the depiction of a period spent in exile before a triumphant return to Ireland to assume the kingship. In Conall's case, it was to Albu he went to escape the unwelcome advances of the wife of King Crimthann (Bergin, Best, Meyer and O'Keeffe 1907–13: 3: 57; Hull 1947: 894, 909). Indeed such was Crimthann's jealousy of the young hero that he inscribed on Conall's shield a message in ogam script intended for Feradach, king of Albu, advising that the bearer of the shield be killed. Fortunately for Conall, however, on arrival in Albu he first encountered Gruibne, then poet and scholar to Feradach, but previously a captive of the Leinstermen whom Conall had set free. Gruibne's learning enabled him, not only to interpret the ogam, but also to alter it so that Feradach be asked to give his daughter in marriage to the man from abroad (Hull 1941: 940–1, 943–6). The record of the king's response varies: according to one version, his daughter is immediately bestowed on Conall (Bergin, Best, Meyer and O'Keeffe 1907–13, 3: 58; Hull 1947: 895), while another suggests he grudgingly consented to her becoming Conall's wife only after the birth of their son, Cairpre Lúachra (Hull 1941: 941, 948–9).

This son, Cairpre, is nicknamed *cruithnechán* 'little Pict' in the genealogical tracts (O'Brien 1962: 195, line 22). In keeping with this is the fact that his grandfather, Feradach, is deemed to be king of the Picts, as well as king of Albu in the earliest of our texts (Bergin, Best, Meyer and O'Keeffe 1907–13: 58; Hull 1947: 894–5) which dates to the beginning of the eighth century (Byrne 1994–5: 46–9). Despite his Pictish ancestry, however, Feradach is served by an Irish poet, Gruibne, and understands ogam. Yet his Gaelicisation does not extend to his readily granting his daughter to Conall, his objection being that the latter is a hired soldier from abroad (Hull 1941: 941, 947).

Conall's status as an outsider, however, is considered less relevant in the dispute concerning recognition of his son, Cairpre, who was born to Feradach's daughter out of wedlock, according to the later version of the tale (Hull 1941: 941, 947–8). As a *cú glas* or alien, Conall should not by law play any part in the upbringing of his son. On the other hand, the responsibility for the rearing of a child born to an unmarried woman of free status without her father's consent, even if she has become pregnant voluntarily, rests with the child's father (Kelly 1988: 85–6). It is the latter situation which is alluded to in our tale since the men of Albu deliberately wait a year before demanding that Conall accept his child, during which time Cairpre develops the characteristic *finechruth*, *fineguth* and *finebés* 'family appearance', 'family voice' and 'family behaviour' which are the usual markers of paternity (Kelly 1988: 103). Furthermore, by requesting that the child be bestowed on him by his grandfather, Feradach, Conall cleverly ensures that Cairpre is in fact accepted by his maternal kin. The situation is thus normalised and Conall and Feradach's daughter finally wed.

If Irish law appears to prevail even in Albu at this juncture of the tale, elsewhere the two areas are considered very different indeed. Thus, we are told that on settlement of the above dispute, Conall remained in the east until his new wife had borne him a further three sons, after which Feradach advised him to return to his own country since his family should not remain abroad (Hull 1941: 942, 949). Moreover, the earlier version suggests that Conall only remained in Albu because of druidic incantations which caused him to forget Ireland for a period of seven years. Indeed he was promised the kingship of Albu should he renounce his native land entirely; Conall's response that it is good for a man to be in his own territory further highlights his links with home (Bergin, Best, Meyer and O'Keeffe 1907–13, 3: 58–9; Hull 1947: 895–6). In addition, Conall's 'Pictish' son, Cairpre, is deemed very much the outsider (Bergin, Best, Meyer and O'Keeffe 1907–13, 3: 59–60; Hull 1947:

898–9). As ancestor of the most western branch of the Éoganachta, the Éoganacht Locha Léin, his status as interloper is graphically underlined in the account of a dream which Óebfhind, Conall's Irish wife, experienced, during which she gave birth to four puppies which she bathed in ale, wine, water and milk. A fifth came to her from outside, however; this she bathed in blood and he gnawed at her breasts (O'Brien 1962: 196, lines 33–9). The political import of the text is clear: the other four Éoganacht branches are legitimised to a greater or lesser degree while the Éoganacht Locha Léin are deemed usurpers (Ó Corráin 1980: 162). For our purposes, its significance lies in the fact that it is Cairpre's outside origins that lead to his exclusion from the inner circle.

As we might expect, therefore, Albu is certainly deemed a foreign land in the two texts concerning Conall Corc under consideration; nonetheless its social mores and structure have a somewhat Irish hue. Since this material was composed for an Irish audience, this should not surprise us. Nor should we be unduly concerned by the redactor's claim that the kingship of Albu was offered to Conall. As the founder of a powerful Munster dynasty, it was important that his power be perceived to have extended far and wide. Indeed even a less significant figure like his foster-father, Crimthann, who as we have seen became jealous of him, is said to have been king of Ireland and Albu in a narrative on Conall Corc and the kingdom of Cashel (Hull 1930a). Similarly, the ninth-century text 'Cormac's glossary' which preserves a memory of a period when 'great was the power of the Irish over the British [and] they divided Albu among them in districts', describes Crimthann as 'king of Ireland and Albu as far as the English channel' (Bergin, Best, Meyer, O'Keeffe 1907–13, 4: 75).

Vague memories of heroic conquests in Roman and sub-Roman Britain may conceivably be alluded to here. It is equally likely, however, that in some cases at least such exaggerated claims reflect the territorial ambitions of the rulers whose power the texts sought to endorse. In Crimthann's twelfth-century death-tale, for instance, the king's tour of his dominions leads him from Tara to Leinster, thence to Munster and Connacht, and finally to Ulster and Albu, used by this point in time in its more restricted sense. By having Crimthann take this circuitous route, his descendant, the ruling king of Connacht, for whom the text was written, may well have been laying claim to precedence over all other kings throughout the Gaelic-speaking world (Ó Corráin 1987b). We are reminded of the grandiose title *imperator Scottorum* assumed by an earlier king, Brian Boru, which was similarly designed to serve as a mark of his superiority (Broun 1999: 2). Moreover, according to that king's heroic biography, also of twelfth-century date and written very much in the interests of his great-grandson, Muirchertach, Brian's power was such that he levied tribute on the Saxons and Britons, as well as on the men of Albu, Lennox and Argyle (Todd 1867: 136–7; Ní Mhaonaigh 1995: 374–6).

NIALL NOÍGIALLACH, BRITAIN AND BEYOND

Though the background to Crimthann's death-tale may be twelfth-century Connacht, it is one of a nexus of texts focusing on Niall Noígiallach 'Niall of the nine hostages', eponymous ancestor of the famous Uí Néill federation, and thus, very much the northern counterpart of Munster's Conall Corc. Indeed, as David Sproule has observed, parallels between the literary presentation of the two heroes abound. Thus, both succeed Crimthann mac Fidaig in the kingship, for example; in the same way, both are only sons of women who do not bear their fathers' other children (Sproule 1985: 16, 18). We may also note that the two mothers in question are foreign. Bolce, as we have seen, is a female satirist from Britain; the origins of Niall's mother, Cairenn, on the other hand, are somewhat less clear. According to the poetic version of the eleventh-century text, *Echtra mac nEchach Mugmedóin* 'The adventure of the sons of Echaid Mugmedón', Niall's father, Echaid, carried her off from Albu 'after strife' and she is specifically identified as a 'slave-woman' elsewhere in the poem (Joynt 1908–10: 92–3, stanza 6a; 94–5, stanza 8). The prose version of the tale, however, describes her as black-haired Cairenn, daughter of Sgal *balb* 'the dumb', king of the Saxons (Stokes 1903: 190–1). Moreover, Niall's death-tale records his maternal grandfather's name as Sacheill (Meyer 1900–1: 88, 91). Cairenn's name, on the other hand, is a plausible representation of the Roman name, Carina (Byrne 1973: 76). Notwithstanding this, her Saxon ancestry is underlined in a poem by Gilla Mo Dutu ua Casaide (*fl.* 1147) where she appears as 'the daughter of the Saxon king of the treasures' (Best, Bergin, O'Brien and O'Sullivan 1954–83: 3: 548, line 16948), while a verse recounting the origin of the name of an Uí Néill citadel accords her the epithet *cruithnech* 'Pictish' (Gwynn 1903–35: 4: 118).

Cairenn is a literary character, of course, in the form in which we meet her, and while her origin may 'preserve traditions (albeit garbled) of Irish conquests in Britain', as Byrne suggested (Byrne 1973: 76), it also sheds light on the perceptions of her creators *vis-à-vis* their neighbouring island. Her multiform ancestry may indicate a certain vagueness on their part regarding distinctions between Briton, Saxon and Pict. Ultimately, however, her precise racial affiliation is less important than her presentation as a woman of foreign origin who is accorded a pivotal role in literary tradition as the mother of the man from whom the great Uí Néill claimed descent. Moreover, her begetting of Niall is depicted as an act of God (Joynt 1908–10: 92–3, stanza 6a) and this is in keeping with her positive portrayal elsewhere. Thus, Niall's first act as king is to release her from bondage, swearing that none shall henceforth lay tribute upon her (Joynt 1908–10: 98–9, stanzas 22–8). In addition, he takes her with him to Tara where she is clad in garments of royal purple as befits her status (Stokes 1903: 192–3). In this way, she is contrasted sharply with Mongfhinn, the wife of Niall's father, Echaid, who is 'skilled in every art of magic and sorcery' and who sought to poison her brother, Crimthann, in order that her son, Brian, might attain the kingship. Good is made to triumph over evil in the end, however; in the first place, Crimthann insists that Mongfhinn drink first from the poisoned cup, as a result of which both die. Furthermore her treachery proves ultimately futile since, as the author gleefully comments, it was Niall, not Brian, who assumed the kingship after Crimthann's death (Stokes 1903: 174–89).

The foreign slave-woman, Cairenn, therefore, is being deliberately exalted at the expense of her native free counterpart, Mongfhinn. Indeed, such was her eminence that Cináed ua hArtacáin (d. 975), one of the foremost poets of his day, could refer to the Uí Néill in general terms, as *cland meic Cairne* 'the dynasty of Cairenn's son'

(Best, Bergin, O'Brien and O'Sullivan 1954–83: 3: 662, line 20148). Her non-Irish ancestry would scarcely have been viewed as an impediment by that particular scholar whose work includes verse composed in honour of the Hiberno-Scandinavian king, Amlaíb *cúarán* (Óláfr *kváran*) (Gwynn 1903–35: 1: 52–3). Her literary portrayal is such, however, as to suggest that Cináed's audience and that of his eleventh- and twelfth-century successors would likewise have had no difficulty in accepting Cairenn as the founding mother of one of Ireland's leading dynasties. Nor should we expect them to have had. On an academic level, it was during this period that the doctrines brought together in 'The book of taking', tracing the origins of the Irish to another foreigner, Míl of Spain, were elaborated. Furthermore, in social terms, the enduring presence of Viking invaders turned settlers ensured that mixed marital alliances were an everyday reality.

Niall's mother may have been a foreigner but he is nonetheless depicted as engaging in military activities abroad. In fact, according to the compilation, *Cóir Anmann* 'Fitness of names', it is from his adventuring overseas that his nickname derived. Thus, one source ascribes his epithet to the five Irish hostages he had, one from every province, and the four 'he brought at will . . . out of Albu', while another has him venture further afield: 'Now Niall went to Letha [Brittany or Rome] and to Italy to seek a kingdom, as a result of which he was called "nine-hostaged", that is he had five Irish hostages and one from Albu, together with a Saxon one, and a British one, and a Frankish one' (Stokes 1897: 338–9). Similarly, his Saxon, Frankish and Roman hostages are also referred to in a poem by Cináed ua hArtacáin where it is further suggested that he divided *Muir Romuir* 'the Red Sea', while another poem by the same author has him journey *co hElpa* 'to the Alps' seven times (Gwynn 1903–35: 2: 14, 36). Elpa here as elsewhere, however, may have been confused with Albu; furthermore there is also uncertainty as to where precisely Niall met his death. According to his death-tale, he set out to march to the Alps but was halted at the Loire where he met a Roman envoy who submitted to him. Meanwhile his enemy, the Leinster king, Echu mac Énnai Chennselaig, had taken refuge with the king of Albu. It is at the latter's court that Niall is slain by Echu in one version of the tale, but another intimates that the Leinster ruler followed him to the Continent and killed him there (Meyer 1900–1: 85–92; Meyer 1907: 323–4). If Cináed ua hArtacáin is to be believed, however, Echu was aided by the Saxons and the murderous deed was carried out 'above the surf of the English channel' (Gwynn, 1903–35: 2: 36), in which location he is supported by the eleventh-century poets, Flann Mainistrech and Gilla Cóemáin (Bergin, Best, O'Brien and O'Sullivan 1954–83: 3: 489, line 15247), as well as by a number of annalistic texts (Hennessy 1866: 19).

Once again, these varying traditions scarcely suggest detailed geographical knowledge on the part of the compilers of the individual works. Nonetheless, they do indicate that for a warrior-king of Niall's stature, expeditions overseas were considered to form an important part of a successful career. Glorious victories, therefore, are vaunted: he conquered the divided world, according to one anonymous poet (Gwynn 1903–35: 4: 118), while the ninth-century poet and bishop of Kildare, Orthanach ua Cáelláma, noted that both Ireland and Albu paid tribute to him (Bergin, Best, O'Brien and O'Sullivan 1954–83: 1: 203, line 6087). For this reason, these territories will suffer after his death. A dialogue-poem lamenting Niall's downfall and put into the mouths of his foster-father and brother, for example, warns that Saxons, bringing with them hoards of Langobards from Letha, will plunder noble Irishmen and men of Albu; both Gael and Pict will henceforth be disadvantaged (Meyer 1900: 4, stanzas 8–9).

Audiences down through the ages, and in particular Niall's descendants at whom these texts were directed, would have identified readily with such sentiments. Thus, their king too, a true successor of Niall, would be equally victorious in battle and they, his subjects, would feel similarly protected. Moreover, in the post-Viking era the image of ambitious rulers attempting to extend their sway overseas was one which would certainly have rung true. Indeed if the dialogue-poem just referred to is of ninth-century date, as is perhaps indicated by its language, it is tempting to suggest that the Saxons and Langobards therein would readily have called the Viking foe to mind, particularly as the latter too reached Ireland from both Britain and the Continent.

VIKINGS

In any event, other texts contain detailed description of this particular group of outsiders whose impact on the Irish political stage was considerable. Not surprisingly, ninth-century chronicle references depict them as foreign, heathen hordes, a portrayal which is amply corroborated in literary sources. Most penetrating is the heartfelt cry of a monk of that period giving thanks to a stormy sea offering a safeguard against the 'fierce warriors from Scandinavia', and his fear is echoed in the prayer of another ecclesiastic from the monastery of Clondalkin seeking protection 'against a flood of foreigners, foes, heathens, and tribulations' (Ní Mhaonaigh 1998). Indeed such is the seriousness of the attacks that fleeing from Vikings is listed as an accepted reason for transgressing the rules of the Sabbath (O'Keeffe 1905: 208–9, §32). Help is at hand, however, in the form of heroic warriors such as Murchad, king of Leinster, whose 'wounding of idolaters' is celebrated in a number of poems (Meyer 1917: 46). In truth, however, by the time Murchad slew one of their number, Ragnall son of Ímar, towards the end of the tenth century (Mac Airt and Mac Niocaill 1983: 424–5, *s.a.* 994), the Vikings had long since settled in Ireland and become an integral part of the political scene. Already in 842, for example, Comán, abbot of Annagassan in Co. Louth, was killed by a group of Irish and Vikings working together (Mac Airt and Mac Niocaill 1983: 300–1). In addition, the Irish quickly adopted the military practices of their opponents as indicated by a reference to the midland peoples of Luigne and Gailenga plundering in 847 'in the manner of heathens' (Mac Airt and Mac Niocaill 1983: 306–7). It has been suggested that such Irishmen, easily swayed by Scandinavian customs, may in fact be implied by the term *Gall–Gaídil* 'Viking (literally 'foreign')–Irish' which is used in the Annals of Ulster to describe a group of men fighting on the side of an Ua Néill king, Máel Sechnaill, in the 850s (Mac Airt and Mac Niocaill 1983: 314–15, *s.a.* 856, 857). According to what are fanciful explanations in the eleventh-century compilation, the Fragmentary Annals of Ireland, on the other hand, these were either Irishmen who had been fostered with the Norse, or heathen converts (Radner 1978: 98–9, 104–5, §§247, 260). In reality, the term may simply indicate the existence of people of mixed Hiberno-Norse ancestry. If so, and assuming that Máel Sechnaill's *Gall–Gaídil* were young adults in the mid-ninth century, the evidence points to the formation of marital, as well as military, alliances, by the 830s.

Such alliances are reflected in the literary sources: the tenth-century poet, Cináed ua hArtacáin, composed poetry for the Hiberno-Scandinavian king, Amlaíb *cúarán*, as we have seen. Moreover, the indications are that Amlaíb was well pleased with the composition since the Irish poet received a horse in payment (Gwynn 1903–35: 1: 52–3). Other foreigners were less forthcoming, however, if an anecdote anachronistically told of the eighth-century poet, Rumann son of Colmán, is to be believed. According to this, 'Rumann' composed a great poem for the foreigners of Dublin, a phrase which can only refer to the Hiberno-Norse inhabitants of that city, who fail to reward the poet adequately for his task. In consequence, Rumann threatened to satirise anyone who refused his request for payment and cleverly ordained that every good Viking should give him two pennies, and every bad Viking one. Not surprisingly, all proffer the higher amount for, as the text says, 'none thought it right that he should be called a bad Viking'. In turn they request that he create a praise-poem in honour of the sea though we may suspect that Rumann's second offering pleased them as little as the first since he composed it when drunk (Meyer 1900–1: 79–80). There is no sense, however, that it is their foreignness which causes the Vikings to reject Rumann's wares. Indeed the relationship between poet and patron depicted in the passage is as it might have been were both parties Irish. Furthermore, our poet appears to have had frequent dealings with Vikings, encountering seven streets full of them in a place called Cell Belaig (Meyer 1900–1: 79–80) which may be as far inland as Rahan, near Tullamore, Co. Offaly. Nor was he alone in this. At any rate, by the time of the composition of *Lebor na Cert* 'The book of rights' *c.*1100, the accommodation was complete. Even if the redactor can still countenance outsiders who do not know Irish, ten of whom are included in the stipend given to one Munster king, the Scandinavians of Dublin are treated exactly like their Leinster neighbours; they too owe rent and tribute to a provincial overking (Dillon 1962: 40–1, 108–11).

Notwithstanding this, the Vikings retain something of their negative associations: the language of the *Gall–Gaídil*, for example, is termed *gic-goc* which may be onomatopoeic in origin, in the tenth-century tale, *Airec Menman Uraird meic Coisse* 'The stratagem of Urard Mac Coisse' (Bergin, Best, Meyer and O'Keeffe 1907–13: 2: 76, line 6). In addition, Guilide's daughter bemoans the poor hospitality meted out to her by King Feidlimid of Munster in the fragmentary tale, *Erchoitmed Ingine Gulidi* 'The excuse of Guilide's daughter', claiming that her miserly lot included 'Norse curds after they had been strained through the mouth of an old vessel' (Meyer 1894: 66, 69). Furthermore, St Comgall's superior piety is measured by his ability to endure a cold and hot stream better than a *gallmanach* 'foreign monk' where 'foreign' may have been equated with Scandinavian in a ninth-century context and later (Bergin, Best, Meyer and O'Keeffe 1907–13: 3: 9–10). Yet his victory was hollow when compared with that gained against the ferocious foreigners by a number of tenth-century kings, as exemplified in eleventh- and twelfth-century bombastic propaganda tracts (Todd 1867; Radner 1978). However, since the portrayal therein of a magnificent triumph over almost invincible pagan foes was designed to enhance the status of contemporary rulers who could bask in their ancestors' reflected glory, we may treat what such texts reveal of Hiberno-Scandinavian relations with caution. Even more fanciful are Vikings who resemble supernatural beings and against whom Fionn and his band of warriors regularly defend Ireland's sovereignty in the body of literature concerning him which became popular from the eleventh century onwards (Christiansen 1931). Here Lochlainn 'Scandinavia' has merged with the Otherworld and its inhabitants are awesome and mythical creatures who bear no relation to reality.

That Lochlainn could be so transformed from a concrete, albeit faraway place whence the Vikings came, to a shadowy, nebulous realm where magic and mystery prevailed, indicates a lack of precise information concerning it on the part of the Irish learned classes. A similar vagueness with regard to things foreign may be implied by the application of the term *gall*, used originally to refer to an inhabitant of Gaul, to the Scandinavians from the ninth century onwards. Moreover, a substitution of one meaning for the other can occasionally be seen at work. According to the earliest version of *Tochmarc Emere* 'The wooing of Emer', for example, Forgall Manach, Emer's father, goes to the court of King Conchobar where foreign messengers are visiting and requests golden treasures and *fín Gall* 'Gaulish wine' of the Ulster king (Meyer 1890: 442–3). In later versions of the tale, however, Forgall seeks the golden treasures of the *Finngaill* (Meyer 1901: 246), literally 'white foreigners', a term applied to the Norwegian as opposed to the Danish wave of Scandinavian invaders. In the same way, the *Dubgaill* 'dark foreigners', their Danish counterparts, make an appearance in one eleventh-century account of the origin of the Leinstermen contained in a collection of place-name lore. Here, the *Laigin* 'Leinstermen' are so called from the *laigin* 'broadheaded spears' which the *Dubgaill* brought with them out of the lands of the foreigners (Stokes 1894: 299–300). The tenth-century prose tale, *Orcun Denna Ríg* 'The destruction of Dind Ríg', on the other hand, recounts that these spears were in the hands of the many *gaill* which Labraid Móen, the ancestor of the Leinstermen, brought back with him having gained a realm which extended as far as the English Channel (Stokes 1901: 8). Significantly, the term *gall* undergoes another metamorphosis in the late twelfth century and later when it comes to be applied to the 'new foreigners', the Anglo-Normans.

CONCLUSION

The shift in meaning of this term is in a sense symptomatic of the ever-changing nature of Irish–international relations in the early medieval period. In any account of such relations, historical documents must quite rightly be accorded pride of place. Literary texts too, however, have their part to play in charting how the medieval Irish elite viewed outsiders and, in particular, how their perception evolved over time as contacts with foreign peoples changed. While scarcely to be taken at face value – any more than the often prosaic accounts provided by an annalist or genealogist should be read with an uncritical eye – these narratives provide important indicators as to how, and more especially why, external elements were cleverly accommodated in the Irish scheme of things. This process was, of course, a complex one of which the narratives chosen here for discussion provide no more than a brief glimpse. It is from an analysis of many such brief glimpses, however, that we may come to understand more fully the medieval Irish outward look.

ACKNOWLEDGEMENTS

I am greatly indebted to Professor Máire Herbert, Professor Pádraig ó Riain, Dr Colmán Etchingam and Dr Dauvit Broun for their comments on the material presented here.

REFERENCES

Ahlqvist, A. (ed. and trans.) (1982) *The Early Irish Linguist: an edition of the canonical part of the Auraicept na nÉces with Introduction, Commentary and Indices*, Helsinki: Societas Scientiarum Fennica, Commentationes Humanarum Litterarum 73.

Bergin, O., Best, R.I., Meyer, K. and O'Keeffe, J.G. (ed.) (1907–13) *Anecdota from Irish Manuscripts*, 5 vols, Halle: Max Niemeyer.

Best, R.I., Bergin, O., O'Brien, M.A. and O'Sullivan, A. (ed.) (1954–83) *The Book of Leinster formerly Lebar na Núachonghála*, 6 vols, Dublin: Dublin Institute for Advanced Studies.

Bieler, L. (1979) *The Patrician Texts in the Book of Armagh*, Dublin: Dublin Institute for Advanced Studies, Scriptores Latini Hiberniae 10.

Binchy, D.A. (ed.) (1941) *Críth Gablach*, Dublin: Dublin Institute for Advanced Studies, Mediaeval and Modern Irish Series 11.

—— (ed.) (1963) *Scéla Cano meic Gartnáin*, Dublin: Dublin Institute for Advanced Studies, Mediaeval and Modern Irish Series 18.

Bhreathnach, E. (1996) 'Temoria: caput Scotorum?', *Ériu* 47: 67–88.

Broun, D. (1994) 'The origin of Scottish identity in its European context', in B.E. Crawford (ed.), *Scotland in Dark Age Europe: the Proceedings of a day conference held on 20 February 1993*, St Andrews: University of St Andrews, St John's House Papers, No. 5, 21–31.

—— (1999) *The Irish Identity of the Kingdom of the Scots*, Woodbridge: The Boydell Press, Studies in Celtic History.

Byrne, F.J. (1973) *Irish Kings and High-Kings*, London: Batsford.

—— (1994–5) 'Dercu: the feminine of Mocu', *Éigse* 28: 42–70.

Calder, G. (ed. and trans.) (1917) *Auraicept na n-Éces: the Scholar's Primer being the texts of the Ogham Tract from the Book of Ballymote and the Yellow Book of Lecan and the text of the Trefhocul from the Book of Leinster*, Edinburgh: John Grant.

Carey, J. (1994) *The Irish National Origin-Legend: synthetic pseudohistory*, Cambridge: Department of Anglo-Saxon, Norse, and Celtic, University of Cambridge, Quiggin Pamphlets on the Sources of Mediaeval Gaelic History 1.

Carney, J. (1985) *Medieval Irish Lyrics selected and translated with the Irish Bardic Poet, a Study in the Relationship of Poet and Patron*, Portlaoise: Dolmen Press.

Charles-Edwards, T. (1976) 'The social background to Irish *peregrinatio*', *Celtica* 11: 43–59.

—— (1995) 'Language and society among the Insular Celts AD 400–1000', in M. Green (ed.), *The Celtic World*, London: Routledge, 703–36.

Christiansen, R.Th. (1931) *The Vikings and the Viking Wars in Irish and Gaelic Tradition*, Oslo: I Kommisjon Hos Jacob Dybwad, Skrifter Utgitt av det Norske Videnskaps-Akademi I Oslo II. Historisk-Filosofisk Klasse 1930, no. 1.

Clover, H. and Gibson, M. (1979) *The Letters of Lanfranc Archbishop of Canterbury*, Oxford: Clarendon Press, Oxford Medieval Texts.

Colgrave, B. and Mynors, R.A.B. (ed.) (1969) *Bede's 'Ecclesiastical History of the English People'*, Oxford: Clarendon Press, Oxford Medieval Texts.

Contreni, J. J. (1986) 'The Irish contribution to the European classroom', in D.E. Evans, J.G. Griffith and E.M. Jope (ed.), *Proceedings of the Seventh International Congress of Celtic Studies held at Oxford from 10th to 15th July, 1983*, Oxford: Cranham Press, 79–90.

Dillon, M. (ed. and trans.) (1962) *Lebor na Cert: the Book of Rights*, London and Dublin: Irish Texts Society 46.

Doherty, C. (1980) 'Exchange and trade in early medieval Ireland', *Journal of the Royal Society of Antiquaries of Ireland* 110: 67–89.

Duffy, S. (1992) 'Irishmen and Islesmen in the kingdoms of Dublin and Man, 1052–1171', *Ériu* 43: 93–133.

—— (1995) 'Ostmen, Irish and Welsh in the eleventh century', *Peritia* 9: 378–96.

Dumville, D.N. (1996) 'Ireland and Britain in *Táin Bó Fraích*', *Études Celtiques* 32: 175–85.

Evans, D.S. (ed. and trans.) (1990) *A Medieval Prince of Wales: the Life of Gruffudd ap Cynan*, Felinfach: Llanerch Press.

Flanagan, M.T. (1989) *Irish Society, Anglo-Norman Settlers, Angevin Kingship: interactions in Ireland in the late twelfth century*, Oxford: Clarendon Press.

Gwynn, E.J. (ed. and trans.) (1903–35) *The Metrical Dindshenchas*, 5 parts, Dublin: Royal Irish Academy, Todd Lecture Series 8–12.

Henderson, G. (ed. and trans.) (1899) *Fled Bricrend: the Feast of Bricriu*, London and Dublin: Irish Texts Society 2.

Hennessy, W. M. (ed. and trans.) (1866) *Chronicum Scotorum: a chronicle of Irish affairs from the earliest times to A.D. 1135 with a supplement containing the events from 1141 to 1150*, London: Longmans, Green, Reader, and Dyer.

Herbert, M. (1999) 'Sea-divided Gaels? Constructing relationships between Irish and Scots *c*.800–1169', in B. Smith (ed.), *Britain and Ireland 900–1300: Insular Responses to Medieval European Change*, Cambridge: Cambridge University Press, 87–97.

Hillgarth, J. N. (1984) 'Ireland and Spain in the seventh century', *Peritia* 3: 1–16.

Hull, V. (ed. and trans.) (1930a) 'Conall Corc and the kingdom of Cashel', *Zeitschrift für Celtische Philologie* 18: 420–1.

—— (1930b) '*Lám déoraid*' and 'A further note on *lám déoraid*', *Zeitschrift für Celtische Philologie* 18: 70–1, 286.

—— (ed. and trans.) (1941) 'The exile of Conall Corc', *Publications of the Modern Language Association of America* 56: 937–50.

—— (trans.) (1947) 'Conall Corc and the Corco Luigde', *Publications of the Modern Language Association of America* 62: 887–909.

—— (ed. and trans.) (1949) *Longes Mac n-Uislenn: the Exile of the Sons of Uisliu*, New York: Modern Language Association of America.

James, E. (1982) 'Ireland and western Gaul in the Merovingian period', in D. Whitelock, R. McKitterick and D. Dumville (eds), *Ireland in Early Mediaeval Europe: Studies in Memory of Kathleen Hughes*, Cambridge: Cambridge University Press, 362–86.

Joynt, M. (ed. and trans.) (1908–10) 'Echtra mac Echdach Mugmedóin', *Ériu* 4: 91–111.

Kelly, F. (1988) *A Guide to Early Irish Law*, Dublin: Dublin Institute for Advanced Studies, Studies in Early Irish Law 2.

Kenney, J. (1929) *The Sources for the Early History of Ireland: Ecclesiastical*, New York: Columbia University Press.

Knott, E. (ed.) (1936) *Togail Bruidne Da Derga*, Dublin: Dublin Institute for Advanced Studies, Mediaeval and Modern Irish Series 8.

Mac Airt, S. and Mac Niocaill, G. (ed. and trans.) (1983) *The Annals of Ulster (to A.D. 1131), Part I, Text and translation*, Dublin: Dublin Institute for Advanced Studies.

Meyer, K. (ed. and trans.) (1894) *Hibernica Minora being a Fragment of an Old-Irish Treatise on the Psalter with Translation, Notes and Glossary and an Appendix containing Extracts hitherto unpublished from MS. Rawlinson, B. 512 in the Bodleian Library*, Oxford: Clarendon Press.

—— (ed. and trans.) (1889) 'The adventures of Nera', *Revue Celtique* 10: 212–28.

—— (ed. and trans.) (1890) 'The oldest version of Tochmarc Emire', *Revue Celtique* 11: 433–57.

—— (ed. and trans.) (1900) 'Totenklage um König Niall Nóigiallach: ein altirisches Gedicht', in *Festschrift Whitley Stokes zum siebzigsten Geburtstage am 28. Februar 1900*, Leipzig: Otto Harrassowitz: 1–6.

—— (ed. and trans.) (1900–1) 'Stories and songs from Irish manuscripts', *Otia Merseiana* 2: 75–92.

—— (ed.) (1901) 'Mitteilungen aus Irischen Handschriften', *Zeitschrift für Celtische Philologie* 3: 226–63, 447–66.

—— (ed.) (1907) 'A medley of Irish texts', in W. Stokes and K. Meyer (ed.), *Archiv für Celtische Lexikographie*, 3, Halle: Max Niemeyer: 302–26.

—— (1917) *Miscellanea Hibernica*, Urbana, Illinois: University of Illinois, University of Illinois Studies in Language and Literature, 11, no. 4.

Moisl, H. (1982) 'The Bernician royal dynasty and the Irish in the seventh century', *Peritia* 2: 103–26.

Ní Mhaonaigh, M. (1995) '*Cogad Gáedel re Gallaib*: some dating considerations', *Peritia* 3: 354–77

—— (1998) 'Friend and foe: Vikings in ninth- and tenth-century Irish literature', in H.B. Clarke, M. Ní Mhaonaigh and R. Ó Floinn (eds), *Ireland and Scandinavia in the Early Viking Age*, Dublin: Four Courts Press: 381–402.

O'Brien, M.A. (ed.) (1962) *Corpus Genealogiarum Hiberniae*, Dublin: Dublin Institute for Advanced Studies.

Ó Corráin, D. (1980) 'Review of F.J. Byrne, *Irish Kings and High-Kings*', *Celtica* 13: 150–68.

—— (1987a) 'Irish vernacular law and the Old Testament', in P. Ní Chatháin and M. Richter (eds) *Irland und die Christenheit: Bibelstudien und Mission*, Tübingen: Klett-Cota: 284–307.

—— (1987b) 'Legend as critic', in T. Dunne (ed.), *The Writer as Witness: Literature as Historical Evidence*, Cork: Cork University Press, Historical Studies 16: 23–38.

O Daly, M. (ed. and trans.) (1975) *Cath Maige Mucrama: the Battle of Mag Mucrama*, London and Dublin: Irish Texts Society 50.

O'Keeffe, J.G. (ed. and trans.) (1905) 'Cáin Domnaig', *Ériu* 2: 189–211.

O'Nolan, T.P. (ed. and trans.) (1912–13) 'Mór of Munster and the tragic fate of Cuanu son of Cailchin', *Proceedings of the Royal Irish Academy* 30 C: 261–82.

O'Rahilly, C. (ed. and trans.) (1976) *Táin Bó Cúailnge: Recension I*, Dublin: Dublin Institute for Advanced Studies.

Radner, J.N. (ed. and trans.) (1978) *Fragmentary Annals of Ireland*, Dublin: Dublin Institute for Advanced Studies.

Sims-Williams, P. (1985) 'Some functions of origin stories in Early Medieval Wales', in T. Nyberg, I. Piø, P. Meulengracht Sørensen and A. Trommer (eds), *History and Heroic Tale: a Symposium*, Odense: University Press: 97–131.

Sproule, D. (1985) 'Politics and pure narrative in the stories about Corc of Cashel', *Ériu* 36: 11–28.

Stokes, W. (ed. and trans.) (1894) 'The prose tales in the Rennes Dindshenchas', *Revue Celtique* 15: 271–336.

—— (ed. and trans.) (1897) 'Cóir Anmann (Fitness of names)', in W. Stokes and E. Windisch (eds) *Irische Text mit Übersetzungen und Wörterbuch*, 3:2, Leipzig: Verlag von S. Hirzel: 285–444, 557.

—— (ed. and trans.) (1901) 'The destruction of Dind Ríg', *Zeitschrift für Celtische Philologie* 3: 1–14.

—— (ed. and trans.) (1903) 'The death of Crimthann son of Fidach, and the adventures of the sons of Eochaid Mugmedón', *Revue Celtique* 24: 172–207.

—— and Strachan, J. (ed. and trans.) (1901–3) *Thesaurus Palaeohibernicus: a collection of Old-Irish glosses, scholia, prose and verse*, 2 vols, Cambridge: Cambridge University Press.

Todd, J.H. (ed. and trans.) (1867) *Cogadh Gaedhel re Gallaibh: the war of the Gaedhil with the Gaill, or the invasions of Ireland by the Danes and other Norsemen*, London: Longmans, Green, Reader, and Dyer.

POWERFUL WOMEN IN THE EARLY MIDDLE AGES: QUEENS AND ABBESSES

Pauline Stafford

TENTH-CENTURY EUROPE AND SEVENTH-CENTURY ENGLAND: PARALLELS AND CONTRASTS

In 999, on the eve of the first millennium, a mother and daughter died: the dowager Empress Adelaide and her daughter Mathilda, abbess of Quedlinburg in Saxony. The chronicler of the nunnery of Quedlinburg recorded their deaths with a great panegyric praising them and their rule. The pope had died in the same year, and the emperor, stated the chronicler, was more affected by grief than could be believed. The three pillars of the Church had gone – the apostolic lord, the empress, and the imperial abbess. This celebration of powerful women is not the familiar picture of Europe at the end of the first millennium, but it is not a misleading one. A group of women played key roles in the last decades of the tenth century: Adelaide's daughter-in-law, Empress Theophano, wife and widow of Emperor Otto II and mother of his only and infant son, Otto III; Adelaide's own daughter from her first marriage, Emma queen of the West Franks, wife and widow of Adelaide's own nephew King Lothar; Beatrice, duchess of Lotharingia, Adelaide's niece; that same Beatrice's sister-in-law, Adelaide's namesake, the wife of Hugh Capet, another of Adelaide's nephews; Mathilda of Burgundy, Adelaide's sister-in-law, mother of the wife of Hugh Capet's son. In 986, much of north-western Europe was ruled by the women members of this extended family. They ruled as regents for under-age males. They and their female relatives seem even to have met together in 985 to debate and mediate the important questions of succession and dynastic interrelations which dominated the politics of the day. Adelaide, widow of Otto I and mother and grandmother of Otto II and Otto III respectively, and Mathilda, her daughter by Otto, were part of what was in every sense apparently a regiment of powerful women.

To call them powerful, however, raises problems. They certainly engaged in activities which denote the powerful in the early Middle Ages: presiding over legal cases or receiving the oaths of great men; granting land and witnessing grants of it made by others; appealed to for aid, and playing a part in the distribution of patronage, including of ecclesiastical office. But their power differed in some respects from that of their male relatives. With the exception of Mathilda, in her special position as abbess, none of these women ruled in her own right, as a female king. Nor was their position as secure as that of a male ruler, though the latter's security should not be overplayed. As regents, these women held positions which were transient by definition: as queen or empress, they lacked the uniqueness which by now marked out the king. There could be only one king; only after his death or deposition could another legitimately be chosen. Queens and empresses, on the other hand, could be duplicated. The death of king or emperor could leave a dowager to rival the new ruler's wife. These differences are important. But they should not obscure the fact that these women's activities show their ability to participate in events, with the opportunities to influence those events and to have a strategy of their own towards them – all of which amounts to power (Stafford, 1997). They do, however, signal the need for special attention to the nature and sources, including the gendered nature and sources, of that power.

The power which these women exercised was royal, noble and religious, but they acquired it through family roles and held it through offices or positions which were female if not feminine. They were widows and wives, mother and daughters, cousins, aunt and nieces: linked to each other and to the male rulers of their day in a web of kindred and affinity (Leyser, 1979). They were empresses, queens, duchesses (or, more correctly, the wives of dukes) and abbess. There were unique tenth-century circumstances which worked together to produce this extraordinary concentration of powerful women at the end of the first millennium. That very concentration became in itself significant. They reinforced each other, not just with help and contacts, but also ideologically: their very numbers normalised female power, making it thinkable and acceptable. But there are also themes and similarities which make them typical of powerful women throughout early medieval Europe, if not beyond that place and period.

In many ways later seventh-century England offers a parallel, illuminating the importance both of common factors and of distinctive circumstances. In 664 at Whitby in the kingdom of Deira (roughly equivalent to modern Yorkshire), a great meeting took place at which the future of Christianity in England was decided. In the presence of King Oswiu, ruler of Deira and Bernicia, i.e. of the Northumbrians, and overlord of much of what is now England, the rival merits and claims of Celtic and Roman Christianity were debated: the Roman champions won. Hosting that debate, and participating in it on the side of Celtic Christianity, was Abbess Hild, ruler of the religious community at Whitby. Hild was the niece of one of Oswiu's predecessors, King Edwin, and thus a cousin of Oswiu's wife, Eanflæd. The house she headed was a double house of monks and nuns. And Hild's Whitby, like Mathilda's Quedlinburg, was a dynastic centre and mausoleum. Oswiu's daughter Ælfflæd was already at Whitby under Hild's guidance; Eanflæd, Ælfflæd's mother, Oswiu's widow, Hild's cousin, would later join her. King Edwin was buried there, as Oswiu was to be later. Hild and Ælfflæd and Eanflæd had the sort of network of female relatives scattered through the kingdoms of the English which Adelaide and Mathilda could boast. Osthryth, queen of the Mercians, was Ælfflæd's sister or half-sister; Æthelthryth, abbess of Ely, was Ælfflæd's sister-in-law, and her own blood sister, Sexburh, was wife and mother of kings of Kent. Hild's sister was wife of Æthelthryth's and Sexburh's brother, king of the East Angles, and mother of his

Figure 23.1 Queen Emma and her sons Harthacnut and Edward. Frontispiece of the *Encomium of Queen Emma*, written for the queen by a Flemish monk in 1041/2. © British Library Addit. MS 32241, fo. 1v.

successor. The most intrepid genealogist would find such webs of kinship daunting, but they are the stuff out of which concentrations of women's power were woven.

In many ways seventh-century England parallels late tenth-century Europe. In the latter, Europe's emerging kingdoms were knit together by marriages which produced a network of ruling women, linked through an imperial family with pretensions to rule the whole. Seventh-century England was not a kingdom, but a series of kingdoms, also held together in an overlordship often expressed and cemented through marriage. Conversion in England was a recent phenomenon, as it was in Saxony, the heartland of the tenth-century imperial family. In both cases conversion had fostered a monasticism which came together with the family structures of the day to produce female houses, or in England double houses under female headship. Mathilda and Hild are recognisable results of similar situations. But there are differences as well as similarities. There was apparently no seventh-century English Adelaide, nor even an Emma or Beatrice: no female regents, no women ruling alongside sons or, as Adelaide did, acting as regents for them in distant territories. The power of these English women seems much less than that of their late tenth-century successors. Rather it is different women whose activity if not power is stressed: abbesses, not wives and mothers. There are occasional comments on the latter's intercession, or on their evil influence. There are events which may hint at an importance never fully described. Osthryth, queen of the Mercians, was murdered by her husband's followers. Her murder is an indication of the vulnerability of women in a political system which exchanged them in marriage, but it also raises questions about the significance of a woman who must be so brutally despatched. These are questions sharpened by the possibility that the differences between these periods are as much of sources as of substance.

The panegyric of Adelaide and Mathilda was written at Quedlinburg, in a nunnery where Mathilda had been abbess and Adelaide had often visited; it may even have been written by a woman (Althoff, 1991). Women, even the powerful women, of the early middle ages were mostly chronicled by men, often by men in all-male monastic communities. This certainly does not produce a uniformly hostile picture – Adelaide herself was the subject of an adulatory life composed by Odilo abbot of Cluny – though it does raise questions of perspective and interpretation. Almost all that we know about Hild, Eanflæd or Osthryth is what Bede, monk of Monkwearmouth and Jarrow and author of the *Ecclesiastical History of the Gens Anglorum*, chose to tell us. There may be Whitby sources behind him, but they have been lost. In the late tenth century, charters, letters and chronicles from elsewhere in Europe bear out the importance of powerful women, and add details to the picture of them. Bede stands almost alone; and, worryingly, where other sources have survived, they show his picture as partial. For Bede, Hild was a holy woman, mother of a religious community where a string of bishops were trained under her aegis. Yet Bishop Wilfrid's biographer, Eddius Stephanus, shows her deeply involved in questions of episcopal appointment, and thus in matters of secular as well as ecclesiastical politics. It is Eddius, not Bede, who reveals Ælfflæd's importance in the negotiation of the succession to the Northumbrian throne, and in the deliberations of kings and churchmen which decided the fate of Bishop Wilfrid. If the Quedlinburg chronicler raises doubts about exaggeration, Bede raises even more serious ones about studied silence. Bede's purposes did not lead him to comment on the intra-family politics which resulted from the intermarriages and serial monogamy of his kings. Such tensions and divisions had little place in the salvation history he was writing. Even his picture of abbesses is affected by his desire to paint a heroic Golden Age to contrast with his own day. His selectively remembered past had little place for the this-worldly powers of such women. Bede is a reminder that our picture of powerful women in the early Middle Ages may not simply be distorted by misogyny or stereotyping: a more serious problem is that posed by agendas which simply excluded the circumstances and politics in which women played a part.

The power of some women in seventh-century England may have been greater than we can now recover; the parallels suggest a need to allow for this. At the same time it is possible that the contrasts lie deeper than the sources. The structures which delivered power to women contained a range of possibilities which specific circumstances could variously unlock for different individuals.

STRUCTURES: KINSHIP, HOUSEHOLD AND LIFECYCLE

All these women owed their position to a greater or lesser extent to family: to birth, marriage or motherhood. They were daughters, wives and mothers. 'Family', however, is not a transhistorical constant, identical in all times and places. In the early Middle Ages kinship was among the most important social bonds. In much, though not all, of Europe, kinship was cognatic as much as agnatic: i.e. both mother's and father's kin were important for any individual, though not necessarily in the same ways. Kinship was counted not merely through a single or central male line, but through a branching and ramifying tree at whose centre stood a group of siblings who alone shared common kin. (See Stafford, 1998 for this – and also for the question of whether it changed *c*. AD 1000.) Daughters had lesser claims than sons, but they were not negligible, having claims on their family of birth which could extend to inheritance itself. A wife joined a new family, and in some ways gained a new identity, at marriage, but she did not lose these ties with and claims on her natal kin. Rather she and her children linked kingroups together, and marriage was central to many types of alliance. The exchange of women in marriage created or cemented ties, with the woman herself functioning in some ways as a gift. Like all gifts, she represented the giver to the receiver, acting as a constant reminder of friendship – or enmity. An honoured embodiment of alliance, she was also potentially a hostage or spy; her own meaning could change along with shifts in the relationship of giver and receiver. Gifts can turn to poison; indeed the two are not as clearly differentiated as at first sight appears (Bailey, 1971).

The implications of all this for women were various. It could be a source of security and power. Adelaide's Burgundian origins remained significant throughout her career, whether to husband, son or grandson. Yet the claims which secured her could also make daughters potentially threatening to their natal families. One reason for directing a king's daughter or female kin into a nunnery was to store the claims they carried in safety: hence Ælfflæd's presence at Whitby or Mathilda's at Quedlinburg. A daughter who represented her natal family was a form of human treasure and how

Figure 23.2 The Virgin Mary as ruler and intercessor. The figure of the Virgin is probably influenced by representations of Byzantine empresses, and could reflect the appearance
of the Empress Theophanu herself. Reichenau, *c.* 970–980. Bildarchiv Foto Marburg.

she was given or taken was crucial. In the sixth century, Radegund, daughter of a
Thuringian ruler, was taken as part of the booty, and the humiliation, of her family
by the Frankish king Clothar. A daughter might be freely given, as King Oswiu gave
Osthryth to the king of the Mercians, to bind peace and as a gage of future friendship;
but her marriage could later acquire new meaning, as Osthryth found when the fragile
concord between her Mercian husband and her Northumbrian kin broke.

Daughters readily appear as pawns and victims of such marriage politics, and they
can certainly be placed in danger by them. But it would be wrong to see their position
within such kinship structures and the claims this gave them as simply rendering
them passive and powerless. Early medieval abbesses, and the great nunneries over
which Hild, Ælfflæd and Mathilda ruled, owed much of their significance to the fact
that these women were royal daughters – a status which neither they nor others ever

403

forgot. Mathilda of Quedlinburg was the daughter of a king and emperor; the Quedlinburg chronicler stressed that fact. Her acceptability as regent in the 990s certainly derived from her birth. Her nieces, abbesses Sophia and Adelaide, daughters of Otto II, were among the first people whom the new emperor Henry II felt it necessary to visit. Henry's rival was unwise enough to slight them: it cost him his life. Nor was it only religious women who benefited from the daughter's continued identification with her natal family. The continued claims of a daughter on her family of birth, even after marriage, gave wives a dual identity. When a man married, he did not simply or primarily choose a bride, but a family of in-laws. The latter's attractions rather than the woman's determined his choice: and also affected her continuing importance if not survival (Strathern, 1972). The position of 'women-in-between' was fraught with danger but also full of potential. If Osthryth's was the face of victimhood, Adelaide's was that of power. Adelaide was married first to Lothar of Italy, in a double marriage in which Lothar's father Hugh married Adelaide's mother Bertha, the widow of the king of Burgundy. Adelaide's Burgundian brother Conrad remained a critical ally for Saxon kings like her second husband Otto I, especially in his rule of Italy. Conrad was a bolstering presence in the background of Adelaide's long career. Even in her long widowhood he was an ally and a refuge.

At marriage, a daughter became a wife. This role was marked first by the dual identity of an in-marrying woman who was never completely confounded with her husband and his kin. She was a foreigner or outsider, not only to his family but also to those whom he ruled: she and her followers were easily scapegoated. Osthryth's sister had married an earlier ruler in Midland England. The marriage had been part of an alliance between her Northumbrian father and his new son-in-law in which her husband also accepted Christianity. She was later suspected of involvement in his murder, which occurred during the Easter festivities. The story tells of Mercian resistance to an alliance which could be seen as domination, and to the foreign religion and woman who represented both. And it speaks of the perception of such an imperfectly assimilated outsider as dangerous, and of her vulnerability to suspicion and accusation. But once again, her dual identity could enhance a queen's position as well as place her in danger. The queen might have her own household, which could be a source of followers loyal to her. Bishop Wilfrid began his career in a queen's household. The queen and her household, however, could not be entirely separate from the king. As a comer-in, sometimes from a rival family or remote area, her presence at court helped bind other loyalties to her husband; she and her household could allow some recognition of those other allegiances while drawing them closer to her husband. She had a potential role in the network of personal ties which held early medieval kingdoms together. Seventh-century English queens, of whom Bede tells us so little, may have functioned in this way (Charles-Edwards, 1989).

The potential and expectations of the queen's position as wife were not derived solely from her ambiguous dual identity: the nature of marriage itself was one of the bedrocks on which they were built. Marriage, as distinct from other sexual relationships, was a public affair, marked by formal procedures of betrothal and by the property arrangements of dowry and dower which secured the bride's future. By the tenth century Christian marriage was the norm, at least at the social level of the royal family. Its rituals and liturgy stressed reproduction as the major aim of marriage, and called upon the wife to be faithful, chaste and blameless. This first aim was a central concern of all families in marriage and not merely a Christian one. Throughout the period, failure to produce children was the greatest threat to a queen's survival. Æthelthryth became abbess of Ely and, in Bede's view, saintly: two infertile marriages as much as religious vocation had determined her choice. The rites also emphasised that it was an indissoluble union, of two in one flesh, which marriage created. This was a more specifically Christian concern (Duby, 1984). Æthelthryth, in the earliest stages of Christian conversion, enjoyed none of the security such ideas preached. By the tenth and eleventh centuries divorce and repudiation of royal wives was still possible, but becoming more difficult. The ideology of Christian marriage might now combine with political circumstances to make individual queens more secure. The ideology, the politics and the security encouraged more formal development of another aspect of marriage, the notion of partnership. It would be foolish to translate the marriage union into equality, which it manifestly was not. But the liturgy articulated ideas of partnership, of 'consortship' in life and thus in the case of king and queen in rule. During the tenth century such ideas were developed as the earlier notion of the queen or empress as 'consors regni', sharer in rule, became a common way of thinking about the position of the queen. These ideas had their own wider basis in the queen/wife's role in the household, which was essential to her husband (Erkens, 1993).

The royal household was central to royal rule. People travelled to it from remote parts of the kingdom, and the household in turn travelled to them. It was the place where counsel was taken and patronage dispensed, where the king himself appeared in his dignified and also in his approachable faces. Its permanent or semi-permanent members shared in the process of ruling. It might be the place where young men came to serve; it was certainly where loyalties were won and confirmed. In some ways it could symbolise the kingdom itself, and its good management mirrored rule of that kingdom. Wives who were mistresses here could partake in much of this. Power through the household may have varied from time to time, but the queen's importance here was something of a constant. She might have her own household, sometimes distinct from, sometimes absorbed in, that of the larger royal one. Already, in seventh-century England, Bishop Wilfrid began his rise in the queen's household. The sources offer only infrequent glimpses of the household and its workings, and the queen's role there is often seen only in the negative form of criticism. In the tenth century, Emma of France was criticised for a too intimate relationship with a great bishop at court. The allegations echoed those hurled against Judith, wife of the Carolingian Louis the Pious, and Richardis, wife of Charles the Fat, more than a century earlier. These accusations undermined not only a queen's claims to power, but also those of her son – by casting doubt on his paternity – and of her husband, whose rule was impugned by suspicions of a feebleness at its heart. Their very form underlines the source of the queen's power here, and its vulnerability. They draw their strength precisely from the recognised and accepted roles of queen/wife in the household, from the fact that this was the place where a woman's influence could legitimately be exercised and her own alliances formed. Yet they are also fed by doubts about all power which derives from intimacy, not least sexual intimacy.

Marriage made a woman mistress of the household, and, potentially, a widow. The property arrangements which marked a marriage included provision, in the form of dower, for a woman after her husband's death. Insistence on such provision is another sign of her natal family's continuing concern for her fate, and of its precariousness. Dower also signified that a widow in some ways continued her husband's identity after death, an idea perhaps reinforced by Christian views of the indissolubility of their union; a widow's claim on her husband's lands thus extended his. Small wonder, then, that widows, who carried claims from their families of birth and marriage, could be even more desirable than virgins as marriage partners. Adelaide was not long left a widow after Lothar's death. Again, however, the situation of widowhood was one of precarious vulnerability as well as possible empowerment. A widowed queen might be at risk after her husband's death, sometimes from his male kin, even more so if there was a change of dynasty. When King Edwin of Northumbria died, Northumbria split again into Deira and Bernicia, the former passing to his cousin, the latter to a son of a former king of a rival dynasty, Æthelfrith. Neither man was a son of Eanflæd, Edwin's widow, and neither was a Christian. Eanflæd, the Kentish woman whose marriage had symbolised Edwin's conversion, had to flee with her children to her brother in Kent to find safety. The death of her first husband left even Adelaide prey to other claimants to the throne, among them her future husband Otto I. Yet Adelaide's claims as the widow of an Italian king, whether to land or loyalty, were precisely what made her an attractive match, and opened up the most successful stages of her career. They were one of the bases of her own regency.

Adelaide's acceptability was rooted also in motherhood, and most, though not all, female regents were mothers. That the widow/mother was in some sense a continuation of her husband may have helped her case, but so too did motherhood, which incorporated the wife fully as part of her son's (if not her husband's) family, and seemed to unite her interests with his. This could, of course, produce tensions between expected loyalties to husband and child. The serial marriage practices of the early Middle Ages might mean that a woman's husband was not also the father of her son, or that a queen was stepmother of her husband's older children. Adelaide was delivered from some of the difficult consequences of her stepmotherhood when Otto I's older son Liudolf died prematurely. Liudolf's earlier rebellion, sparked by the birth of Adelaide's own eldest child, indicates the sort of problem which might have festered. Judith, second wife of Louis the Pious, inevitably supported her own son's claim to a share in the inheritance: her interests here could not be identical with those of a husband who had sons by an earlier marriage. Stepmotherhood's evil face appeared particularly strongly by contrast with the overwhelmingly positive ideal of motherhood itself. That latter image was one applied to female rulers of all types, whether regents or abbesses. Its dual nature legitimated female rule: motherhood meant nurture and authority. Mothers had claims to care for their children, which could extend to their inheritance, and thus to regency itself.

Yet female regency was far from a universal phenomenon in the early Middle Ages, and cannot be taken for granted (Wolf, 1991). Regency itself is not inevitable. It springs from the fact of underage or absent kings, who may in themselves be intolerable or unnecessary. An emphasis on warrior kingship or fear of potential instability may require an adult male ruler. Norms of succession and inheritance

Figure 23.3a and 23.3b (detail). Processional cross from the Treasury of the Minster at Essen, showing Abbess Matilda and her brother Duke Otto, children of Otto I's son Liudolf. The iconography could suggest a joint gift, 973–980 Bildarchiv Foto Marburg.

might mean that brothers and uncles, if not a wider pool of male candidates, were strong contenders making the rule of an underage heir unnecessary or even difficult to argue for. Co-rule or underkingship could resolve problems of royal absence. On all of these counts, seventh-century England was unlikely to produce regency for young kings. In contrast, in tenth-century Europe there was a growing acceptance of direct succession to royal inheritance from father to son. In some cases acute fears of a rival dynasty made a desire to underline hereditary succession a family's most important aim. Even where circumstances were such as to encourage or allow regency, however, female regency might be unthinkable. Motherhood's strengths could be outweighed by female gender's incapacity. As a charter from the Imperial chancery not long after the year 1000 put it, 'there is one thing in a man, which makes him as a man strong enough to rule, another in a woman, which makes her as a woman ruled'. Children's adult male relatives shared a mother's claims to care for them, and the association of masculinity and rule strengthened them in their bid for regency: both Henry of Bavaria and Lothar of France were possible protectors of the infant Otto III in 983. But Henry, if not Lothar, was also Otto's rival for the throne. In these circumstances the child's mother and grandmother, neither of whom could claim the throne in her own right, were preferred regents.

The fact that Mathilda of Quedlinburg was the third member of the trio of women who returned to take over the protection of Otto in 983 seems to underline the extent to which it was the very restrictions on women as claimants which secured regency for them. As sister of the previous ruler and aunt of the young boy she was an unusual choice; aunts and sisters might have sons of their own to promote. It was her status as a celibate abbess which overcame any such objection. What we might choose to see as the limitation on her own life was what made her acceptable: the power of women derived paradoxically from their own restricted access to power. But this is only part of the story. The power of women was at this point peculiarly acceptable as a result of developments and traditions built up over previous decades and of their particular combination in the women candidates in the 980s. Developments in France, where wives had stood in for or beside beleaguered husbands, or in the rule of Italy, where Adelaide had been so important, were producing a tradition of female rule. Conversion in Saxony had contributed to that tradition by producing family nunneries under female heads of whom Mathilda is only the most outstanding example. Circumstances had allowed the exploitation of the positive aspects of the structures I have been outlining. Some of this tradition had been incorporated in the development of the female offices these women held.

OFFICE: QUEEN, EMPRESS AND ABBESS

Adelaide had been queen and empress, Mathilda was an abbess. Women are called 'queens' (*reginae*) or 'abbesses' throughout the period, though 'empress' is confined to the period after 800 when a Western empire had been revived. The meanings of these titles are far from clear, and may not have remained constant across time and place. They suggest offices, in the sense of highly specialised and clearly defined roles and expectations. Were these roles still family ones, writ large and formalised: 'Queen' as 'Wife' and 'Mother'? Or did they distance women from these? Supplement them? Did 'queen', 'empress' or 'abbess' make a woman 'royal' or 'religious' as much as 'wife', 'mother', 'daughter' or 'woman'? Did they make a woman the equivalent of 'king', 'emperor' or 'abbot', masculinising or even degendering her? These are important questions, on which more research is needed. To offer even provisional answers to them, it is necessary to look more closely at the period between the seventh and tenth centuries.

Throughout this period a queen had to be a king's wife. Not only was this a job description, it was the entry qualification, and sometimes 'queen' and 'wife' seem to have been synonymous. When the term *regina* was used in sixth- or seventh-century Merovingian Francia it appears to denote a king's wife. The Merovingians distinguished queens and concubines: a queen was a fully married wife, with all that that meant in terms of the formal joining of two families, property arrangements and public knowledge to protect her and her children's claims. There could, however, be wives who were not queens. In ninth-century Wessex, for example, Asser tells us that the king's wife was not called 'queen'. The explicit contrast is with contemporary Francia, where in 856 a West Saxon king had married a Frankish princess, and the latter had been raised as queen in the first known queenly consecration. But there is an implicit contrast with Wessex's northern neighbour, Mercia. Both suggest that already, in some dynasties if not all, a queen was something more than just a king's wife. It is uncertain what exactly distinguished the two, whether any formal inauguration ceremonies separate from marriage itself were involved, whether there was any developed notion of queenly office. Nor can we be sure whether seventh-century England, or sixth-century Frankia, made such distinctions, and set apart certain royal wives through them.

From the mid-eighth century the inauguration rituals of kingship become much clearer, and with them those of queenship (Elze, 1960; Nelson, 1988 and 1997). The women of the late tenth century were the beneficiaries of these rapid developments during the ninth and tenth centuries, in the Carolingian and post-Carolingian world. The supplanting of the Merovingians by the Carolingians in the 750s fostered a tradition of royal anointing. Whatever part the clergy had played in earlier royal inaugurations, their role now became more central. The political and ecclesiastical developments of the ninth century encouraged bishops such as Hincmar of Rheims to think hard about the office of kingship. The fruit of their thinking was enshrined in inauguration rituals, among them the earliest known ritual for the making of a queen, that used in 856 for Judith, granddaughter and namesake of the wife of Louis the Pious. However a queen had been made before, she had probably never been anointed as well as crowned. This became regular practice in France in the late ninth and tenth centuries. As in the 750s, dynastic changes and rivalries made pressing the need to stress the royalty of queen and king, and of their offspring. Charlemagne's revival of empire in AD 800 opened again the possibility of empresses as well as emperors in the West. Louis the Pious' first wife, Irmengard, was crowned in 816. There were women who bore imperial titles, such as 'augusta', throughout the ninth and tenth centuries, but the history of empress-making is obscure. The title of 'emperor' was sought in late ninth- and tenth-century Italy in the midst of dynastic rivalries parallel to those in contemporary France. A parallel development of empress-making rituals in this context is likely. In 962 Adelaide was probably not only crowned but anointed alongside her husband Otto I.

The rituals for the making of a queen or empress, and the circumstances in which they developed, are an important guide to ideas about these roles. The strong connection between dynastic change and the clearer definition of queenship underlines the extent to which a queen was first a wife and mother. A change of dynasty required an affirmation of the new family's right to rule; not only the new king, but also his partner and the mother of his sons had to be recognised as royal. But the rituals also developed in the context of intellectual movements deeply concerned with the definition of office and its duties. The rites themselves do not merely write 'wife' and 'mother' large. They reveal notions of queenship as office, and the relationship of that office to the king's royalty. One of the earliest rites was that for the anointing of Ermentrude in 866, which was concerned in part for her fertility. But it also stressed that she was crowned with justice, hardly necessary to the production of children. By the tenth century different rites stressed the queen's role in the promotion of the faith and the subjugation of heresy, and her partnership in rule with the king. These rituals did not grow primarily out of marriage and its rites. One central prayer, for example, was adapted from that for the making of an abbess, the one woman who could undoubtedly be said to rule. The borrowings from the king's rite to queen's and vice versa underline the extent to which both king and queen were seen to share a regality which set them apart. Above all, both king and queen were anointed, and on the head. Like priests and bishops, also anointed at their inauguration, they were going through a momentous status change. In some cases the queen prostrated herself at the beginning of the rite, a ritual which set aside the 'old' woman, and prepared her to become a new one. If the early Middle Ages saw the development of kingship as office, it also witnessed a parallel, if more faltering, definition of queenship.

Queenship was, however, fraught with ambiguity. The king remained a crowned father, warrior and judge; the queen *a fortiori* was a crowned and anointed wife if not mother, strongly gendered roles which lacked the potential to become a female king. The symbols which the queen received did not include the king's sword, sceptre or rod. She was not a warrior nor yet a judge. When Adelaide presided over judgements it is not clear whether she did so as an empress or as a regent, exercising the king's authority by proxy. The queen's partnership in rule could readily be conceived in terms of the marital partnership of husband and wife: the queen was *conlaterana regis*, 'she who is by the king's side'. There were those who argued that that was all she should be; such arguments seem to have been mounted concerning the consecration of the English queen, Ælfthryth, in 973 (Stafford, 1997). Yet the need to argue in this way suggests that 'queen' could be seen to be more. In the tenth century the description '*consors regni*' could describe the partnership of husband and wife, but it had originally been used of men who shared imperial rule. If nothing more, the growing delineation of the queen's office contained possibilities which could be capitalised on, most spectacularly by the group of ruling women of the late tenth century. Yet the differences between that office and the king's were already sufficiently clear to set boundaries to queenship.

One of those ruling women of the late tenth century was not a queen or empress, but an abbess. If the history of queenship suggests development and definition, the office of abbess was clearer from the beginning. Already by the seventh century she was a ruler of a community. If the earliest rites for the making of a queen already suggest her difference from the king, those for the making of abbot and abbess already stress their close identity. Prayers used in the making of an abbess were often identical to those used for an abbot: only the gender of the pronoun changed. In the fully fledged rituals of the tenth century, the infirmity of the female sex was stressed; but this was more than balanced by the office (*ministerium*) which the abbess was given. If the references to chastity and the castigation of the body seem redolent of

Figure 23.4 Christ adored by Emperor Otto II, his wife Theophano, and their young son Otto III. The representation of the imperial couple is characteristic of the later Ottonians. Milan, late tenth century, Museo del Castello Sforzesco. Photo: Scala

woman's frailty, they need to be compared with the parallel injunction on the abbot to remain chaste and to fast.

Abbesses were women, and some of their powers had the same gendered origins and were legitimated in the same ways as those of the queen: they ruled households and were referred to as mothers of their communities. But their position in the church hierarchy meant that they were more clearly separated from family roles than were queens or empresses. In the Carolingian period they owed military service and, like Hild, might be teachers (Nelson, 1983 and 1990). There can be no doubt that the status of their families in the world was critical to the prominence of early medieval abbesses. But their avowed celibacy, which made the nunnery, and its potential to freeze inheritance claims, so useful to family strategies, set them apart from family structures. It was as an aunt, but also as a *celibate*, that Mathilda of Quedlinburg was acceptable as a regent. Virginity was, like the roles of women in the family, double-edged. It had been a source of power as well as a rejection of the body in the early Church (Brown, 1988). But it could mean claustration, shutting off from the world women – and sometimes men. The feisty virgins who make fools of men in the plays of Hrotswitha of Hildesheim, an inmate of another German royal nunnery, show that, when combined with high birth, virginity retained some of its powerful meaning in the tenth century. When the first flush of conversion coincided with circumstances in which royal families could afford or were constrained to lock up their daughters, there was scope to develop those meanings: to produce a Hild in the seventh century or a Mathilda in the tenth.

CONCLUSION: STRUCTURES, CIRCUMSTANCES AND CONJUNCTURES

Adelaide, with whom I began, was daughter and sister of rulers of Burgundy; wife and widow of a king of Italy and a German emperor; mother and grandmother of emperors, king and queen: an embodiment of the Ottonian family ties which held their empire together. Few people could have expressed as she did a unity of kingdoms which was pre-eminently a family unity, for she exercised a female power which derived from these family sources. She was also heir to a recent tradition of active queenship and of its definition. Her power and influence did not remain uniform throughout her long career, though it culminated in regency. That regency was delivered to her by a series of accidents: the early death of her son, the fact that he and his wife had produced four daughters and only last a son who was still an infant at his father's death, and finally by a man, Henry of Bavaria, over-reaching himself.

The structures of family and household delivered power to Adelaide as to other early medieval women. That power was rooted in a series of family roles which changed across the lifecycle. In so far as it was derived from motherhood, or the role of wife, it inherited some of the contradictions and problems inherent in those roles. Even in the case of abbesses these structures were important. It was as daughters that many of them were consigned to the religious life, and as royal daughters that they became abbesses. The cycle of power and relative obscurity which can be a feature of these women's lives is related to the female lifecycle itself, which changes daughter to wife/queen to widow/dowager.

In all of these senses the roles of these women were strongly gendered – whether in the seventh or tenth century. Their power derived from the essentially female roles of daughter, wife and mother. These were not merely female but gendered 'feminine' roles, where expectations and actions were determined largely by the fact that those who played them were always women. They were gendered too in the sense that those who filled them were identified as instances of 'woman' as a type. Although in many ways it is more useful to analyse their careers in terms of 'daughter', 'wife' and 'widow', the broader and more inclusive category 'woman' remained. The established Western stereotypes of sexual temptress, of weakness and incapacity, were always available as critiques against royal women, rendering an Emma of France or an Empress Judith easy suspects of adultery. It might be as 'mother' or 'wife' that these women gained access to power and legitimated its possession and use, but it was as 'woman' that they were often judged.

Recognition of these structures is essential not only for understanding but also for effective comparison; but they are not a straitjacket. They were in themselves complex, subject to many variables and expressed in specific circumstances. The stage of a dynasty's history, or of an individual family's lifecycle; the existence of step-relationships; the size and structure of families, accidents of birth and death were, for example, all significant. The ruling women of the 980s were the product of an Ottonian family at the peak of its rise, one which had extended its control through marriage alliance and set in place a network of female relatives. The female regents of the 980s operated at a point where that family's sense of solidarity could still weigh against divergent local trends. Among those regents was Emma, Adelaide's daughter and queen of France. Like her mother-in-law Gerberga, she was a beneficiary of the Ottonian family regime which spanned Western Europe in the mid-tenth century. In the case of these French queens, however, there were other internal factors which made them crucial to their husbands and underpinned their prominent position. Established Carolingians and rising Capetians were contending for the throne. The Ottonian alliances these women cemented for their Carolingian husbands were critical, and secured their own positions. In addition both Gerberga and Emma acted as their husbands' most reliable supporters in a local situation where loyalty was not always reliable. Gerberga held fortified towns and strongpoints in her husband's name. Gerberga and Emma were among the tenth century's anointed queens. It was women like these who filled that title with its maximum meanings. In the process they, alongside an empress such as Adelaide and Ottonian abbesses such as Mathilda, created traditions of female power out of which the remarkable coincidences of female regencies in the 980s and 990s could grow.

Throughout the early Middle Ages many of the circumstances existed which could allow women's power to develop. If that power is not always at first sight obvious, that may often be because the sources to study it are inadequate. They often deal in feminine stereotypes, and, more problematically, are often uninterested in the very type of politics within which powerful women were likely to be most active. There were similarities between seventh-century England and tenth-century continental Europe which our reliance on Bede may mask. Even Bede allows us to see that Hild of Whitby and Mathilda of Quedlinburg inhabit the same world. We should feel encouraged to comb his pages carefully for signs of other parallels.

It is more difficult to be certain whether there were real differences across this period. There may have been changes in the nature of marriage, and especially shifts towards its indissolubility, which made late tenth-century royal women more secure than their seventh-century predecessors. Whatever it meant in the seventh century, queenship was acquiring clearer definition in the ninth and tenth, and perhaps with it added possibilities. Uncertainties over the succession, and norms of inheritance which opened up a pool of candidates beyond father and son, produced struggles for the throne which were areas of female political activity throughout these centuries. In seventh-century England, however, the need for warrior kings and a wide range of acceptable candidates made regency and especially female regency an unlikely outcome. In the tenth century, by contrast, the pool of candidates was often more restricted and legitimate succession of sons to fathers was, if not a rule, at least a strongly arguable case. It was precisely because Otto III's uncle threatened this that he lost much support. Warrior kings were still desirable, but the members of a more territorialised nobility were less likely to decamp during a minority. In this less volatile world it was perhaps easier for women to operate, and to be accepted as regents.

These apparent differences should, however, be viewed with caution. They may not be simple changes over time which will apply across Europe. Sixth-and seventh-century Merovingian Francia, for example, had a nobility just as prepared to accept female regency as tenth-century Germany despite apparently more open succession norms (Wood, 1994; Fouracre and Gerberding, 1996). Access to regency in particular was a result of varying political circumstances which take us far beyond the limits of the present chapter. Powerful women will only be fully understood within their wider political framework; that framework will itself only be fully comprehensible when these women are taken into account. Work on powerful women, as on all women's history, is still in its early stages. Further study may undermine any confident generalisation – but it must take as its starting-point the underlying structures of female power and the critical importance of the context in which the problems and potential of those structures were realised.

REFERENCES

Althoff, G., 1991 'Gandersheim und Quedlinburg: Ottonische Frauenklöster als Herrschafts- und Überlieferungszentren', *Frühmittelalterliche Studien*, 25, pp. 123–44.

Bailey, F.G., ed., 1971 *Gifts and Poison: the politics of reputation*, Oxford, The Clarendon Press.

Brown, P., 1988 *The Body and Society: men, women and sexual renunciation in early christianity*, New York, Columbia University Press.

Charles-Edwards, T., 1989 'Early medieval kingship in the British Isles', in S. Bassett ed., *The Origins of Anglo-Saxon Kingdoms*, London, Leicester University Press, pp. 28–39.

Duby, G., 1984 *The Knight, the Lady and the Priest: the making of modern marriage in medieval France*, London.

Elze, R., ed., 1960 *Die Ordines für die Weihe und Krönung des Kaisers und der Kaiserin*, MGH, Fontes Iuris Germanici Antiqui in usum scolarum ex Monumentis Germaniae Historicis separatim editi, vol IX, 'Ordines Coronationis Imperialis', Hanover, Hahnsche Buchhandlung.

Erkens, F-R., 1993 '*Sicut Esther Regina*. Die westfränkische Königin als *consors regni*', *Francia*, 20, pp. 15–38.

Fouracre, P. and Gerberding, R., 1996 *Late Merovingian France, History and Historiography, 640–720*, Manchester, Manchester University Press.

Leyser, K., 1979 *Rule and Conflict in an Early Medieval Society, Ottonian Saxony*, London, Edward Arnold.

Nelson, J.L., 1983 'The church's military service in the ninth century', *Studies in Church History* 20, pp. 15–30.

——, 1988 'Kingship and empire', in J.H. Burns ed., *The Cambridge History of Medieval Political Thought, c. 350–c.1450*, Cambridge, Cambridge University Press, pp. 211–51.

——, 1990 'Women and the word', *Studies in Church History* 27, pp. 53–78.

——, 1997 'Early medieval rites of queenmaking and the shaping of medieval queenship', in A. Duggan ed., *Queens and Queenship in Medieval Europe*, Woodbridge, Boydell and Brewer, pp. 301–15.

Stafford, P., 1983, repr. 1998 *Queens, Concubines and Dowagers: the king's wife in the Early Middle Ages*, Athens, Ga., University of Georgia Press, repr. London, Leicester University Press.

——, 1997 *Queen Emma and Queen Edith: queenship and women's power in eleventh-century England*, Oxford, Blackwell.

——, 1998 '"La mutation familiale": a suitable case for caution', in J. Hill and M. Swan eds, *The Community, the Family and the Saint: patterns of power in early medieval Europe*, Turnhout, Brepols, pp. 103–25.

Strathern, M., 1972 *Women in Between: Female Roles in a Male World*, London, Seminar Press.

Wolf, G., 1991 'Königinwitwe als Vormunder ihrer Söhne und Enkel in Abendland zwischen 426 und 1056', in G. Wolf ed., *Kaiserin Theophanu: Prinzessin aus der Fremde, des Westreichs grosse Kaiserin*, Cologne, pp. 39–59.

Wood, I., 1994 *The Merovingian Kingdoms, 450–751*, London, Longman.

PERCEPTIONS OF AN EARLY MEDIEVAL URBAN LANDSCAPE

Cristina La Rocca

Writing the history of settlements and landscape is necessarily a multidisci-plinary exercise. The image we have of any particular city and countryside at a point in time depends for its definition on the interpretation of archaeological data in the light (or with the support) of the terminology used in written documents. Genuine multidisciplinarity is a relatively recent phonemonenon. On the one hand, especially in Italy, but more generally too, archaeologists used to invoke written sources merely to give appropriate names to their finds (Tabacco 1967: 67–110) or to build models of different settlement patterns; on the other, historians used to cite archaeological data simply to reinforce with material evidence hypotheses based on written sources. Recently, thanks to trends in historiography, the conjunction of archaeologists and historians has produced more sophisticated interpretations of both written and material sources: no longer are these seen as simple mirrors of reality, providing historians with documents of 'what happened', and archaeologists with fixed chronological data, but as cultural products revealing a society's prejudices and projects, models and behaviours. Charters, for instance, apparently bone-dry legal documents, are no longer read as objective and impartial records of truth, and the vocabulary of settlement they present, however limited, is seen to have different meanings in different social contexts, times and spaces (Campbell 1986: 99–119; Halsall 1995) – just as a golden brooch found in a grave doesn't simply show the social rank of the individual buried there, but instead suggests the aspiration of his/her family to be associated with an aristocratic elite.

The increasingly sophisticated use of stratigraphical techniques by excavators specifically interested in early medieval phases and phenomena, and not just in the 'late phases' of Roman settlements, has encouraged some archaeologists to use their own instruments to date their finds, especially pottery, independently of written sources, and to renounce the traditional assumption that political transformations must be visible archaeologically, that is, must have resulted in sudden changes of material culture or in spatial organisation. This new methodological orientation has certainly highlighted disciplinary differences. While archaeologists still tend to present sudden changes, to underline break-points, historians nowadays, examining their sources as a mosaic of manipulated and interpreted realities, tend to stress cultural reworkings and continuities. Because the images derived from these two disciplines are contradictory, using archaeological data along with written evidence is no easy matter: any given reconstruction seems to be formed from a multiplicity of very different, even incompatible, fragments. If neither discipline can, on its own, explain the global phenomenon, history seems to have particular difficulty in explaining any individual case. In my view, then, it is impossibile to write an organic synthesis of how an urban landscape was perceived by those who inhabited it. What I shall offer, instead, are a series of contrasting perceptions, varied in chronology (from the sixth to the twelfth century), geography (a number of places in northern and central Italy), and type of evidence (archaeological and written), of a set of early medieval urban landscapes.

PEACE AND PROSPERITY: THE POLITICAL IMAGE OF THE CITY UNDER THEODERIC THE GREAT

For the twelfth-century author of the *Chronicle of Gorze*, the Italian city of Verona was (re)founded by 'Theoderic the former king of the Huns' (*Theodoricus quondam rex Hunnorum*): here the king built a 'huge palace assimilated in a wonderful way to the Romulean theatre' (*domum praegrandem quae romuleo theatro mire assimilatur*), which came to be known as the *Theodorici domus*. The description of Theoderic's building allows us to understand that it incorporated the Roman amphitheatre. Also in Rome, during the eleventh century, it was widely thought that Hadrian's mausoleum 'had been constructed by the tyrant Theoderic' (*Theoderici tyranni fuisse fabrica*), while in Ravenna in 1132 a tower of the city wall had the name of *turris quondam Theoderici regis*. This linking of Theoderic with Roman monuments is found long before the twelfth century. When Charlemagne wished to give imperial symbols to his palace in Aachen, he wrote to Pope Hadrian I for authorisation to remove from Theoderic's palace in Ravenna 'mosaics and marbles and other items located both in the streets and on walls' (*musiva atque marmora caeteraque exempla tam in stratos quamque in parietibus sitas*, Codex Carolinus 81). At the same time Charlemagne took from Ravenna to Aachen an equestrian statue of Theoderic. Paul the Deacon, in order to dignify the origins of *Modicia* (Monza) where the Lombard queen Theodelinda built a palace, stresses that Theoderic had done the same in the past, attracted by the city's good climate. All the above examples point to an aspect of Theoderic's royalty thought to be important from the eighth to the twelfth century: his reputation as a builder of imposing monuments underpinned the Carolingian tradition of connecting the name of the Ostrogothic king to public classical buildings, and this in turn had its sequel in twelfth-century imperial propaganda linking the classical buildings still standing in the Italian cities to a barbarian origin.

Theoderic as builder belonged not only to late tradition. He was celebrated during his lifetime by Ennodius and immediately after his death by an anonymous Ravenna chronicler. In the seventh century, Isidore of Seville, and in the eighth century Paul the Deacon as well as several Byzantine and Frankish sources, portrayed a common image of Theoderic as a restorer of Roman monuments and bringer-back into use of ancient buildings: palaces, amphitheatres, baths and aqueducts reflected imperial *civilitas* – 'city culture' but also 'civilisation' (Ward Perkins 1976). Theoderic's building activity was emphasised to give the king a specific identity and to define his reign as peaceful and prosperous. This positive evaluation is mirrored in recent historiography on the Ostrogothic period in Italian history: the civility of Theoderic's regime is measured by the respect it showed towards Roman institutions and structures (Moorhead 1993; Heather 1995). Still-living and long-dead historians thus share a favourable attitude towards the age of Theoderic, interpreting it as a short parenthesis of peace and prosperity, evincing at once nostalgia for a happy time, and regret for the inescapable fact that it was as transitory and illusory as an Indian summer (Costa 1977; Brown, 1984: 4).

The warmth of that summer is rapidly dissipated if we move from propaganda to material evidence. The buildings attributed by written sources to Theoderic have not yet been found by archaeologists, or else they turn out to be simply restored ancient buildings. Palaces in Ravenna, Verona and Pavia are mere adaptations of Roman structures, while in the city walls of Verona and Pavia neither radical rebuilding nor even small adaptations can be dated to the Ostrogothic period. Archaeology thus transforms Theoderic from the promoter of urban renewal into a very modest figure. The written sources seem to have covered with a golden veil a harsh reality of economic impoverishment (Johnson 1988; Righini 1986).

Is Theoderic's reputation completely false, then? It isn't that simple. Theoderic's personality is as surprisingly ambivalent in this respect as in others: *tyrannos* by name but *imperator* in fact, as Procopius wrote; a king from a military background who spent several years of his youth as a hostage at the court of Constantinople; king of the Goths but also a legitimate officer sent by Constantinople; a good and just king in the first part of his reign, but then cruel and tyrannous; a king *illitteratus*, who communicated with royal officials and the Senate of Rome through the rhetorical labyrinths of Cassiodorus. To all these contrasting elements we can add another, paradoxical ambiguity: Theoderic was praised for buildings that he never built, while the ones he really did build, for example the churches in Ravenna, are not mentioned until the ninth century in the *excursus* of Agnellus' *History of the Archbishops of Ravenna*. The Indian summer idealised by historiography seems never to have come. Yet the contrast between Theoderic's loud propaganda and his actual modest activities cannot be attributed solely to the inferiority complex that the king suffered from as a result of his long stay in Constantinople. Theoderic appears to have typified the general tendency of barbarian regimes to reinforce legitimate royal authority with external signs of power, deriving his examples not only from imperial authority but also from models offered by contemporary kings (Pferschy 1989) .

It is first of all necessary to differentiate the various sources. The official correspondence preserved in Cassiodorus's *Variae*, the inscriptions, the building materials, the types of buildings, are all direct witnesses of the regal image Theoderic wanted to give himself: they present the king as he wished to appear and at the same time are the aspects the Roman aristocracy most appreciated. Later sources reflect the effectiveness of Theoderic's propaganda. It has been said that Theoderic's building policy was merely based on a passive reappraisal of tradition and expresses a strong ambivalence towards the empire as an institution. Theoderic did homage towards Rome's past but also offered rivalry to and emulation of contemporary imperial authority in Constantinople. Did he wish to present himself simply as a conservative? Vocabulary used in Cassiodorus's *Variae* to describe the king's building projects seems to emphasise the rediscovery of ancient tradition, or rather, of a codified but chronologically unspecified civil past, but with a clear consciousness of its diversity and distance from the present age. That consciousness is registered in the difference in meaning between *antiquitas* and *vetustas*. New buildings put up by Theoderic had to restore 'ancient things to their pristine splendour' (*antiqua in nitorem pristinum*) and at the same time had to produce 'new things with similar antiquity (with a likeness of antiquity?)' (*nova simili antiquitate*) so that 'only the novelty of their constructions distinguishes [them] from the work of the men of old' (*ab opere veterum sola distet novitas fabricarum*). The *novitas* of the buildings promoted by the king is directly linked to the tradition of *antiquitas*, that is to a remote mythical past, in opposition to the *vetustas* which affected many buildings in the present. *Antiquitas* allows at the same time the renewal of 'what has been made, excluding the defects of what is old' (*facta veterum exclusis defectibus*) and their embellishment 'with a new glory of old age' (*nova vetustatis gloria*). *Vetustas*, synonymous with *senectus* (old age) is *veternosa* (worn out), *marcida* (withered), *incuriosa* (lacking in intellectual energy): it is the result of the scant attention that Theoderic's predecessors had shown towards urban *civilitas*, and represents the degradation of many ancient buildings. *Vetustas* is the material consequence of the lack of interest on the part of the aristocracy and imperial authority, in mirroring the status and dignity of the city through the quality of public buildings. It was a trend of those times which it was necessary to stop. Only the king's *diligentia* could substract monuments from 'the desiccation of age' (*vetustatis decoctione*), could avert their destruction by 'the old age that wore them down' (*senectute obrepente*).

Antiquitas is instead *provida* (armed with forethought), *beneficialis* (beneficent). It has an active role in defining the present and in this function it is associated with verbs such as *definire, nominare, praefingere, dictare* (to define, identify, shape, order), and symbolised by 'the solidity of buildings' (*soliditas edificiorum*). It is a true recovery, one that can be made only through the *novitas* legitimised by authentic ancient tradition as it restores to new buildings their original 'splendour' (*nitor*). Without this connection the new becomes an affectation of modernity (*moderna praesumptio*). Only he who is *antiquorum diligentissimus imitator* ('most diligent imitator of what is old') could truly be called *modernorum nobilissimus institutor* ('most noble establisher of what is modern'). The recovery of antiquity was the conceptual base from which to re-propose the classical image of the 'show-case city' offering a permanent exhibition of the inhabitants' benefits, and with public buildings representing the monumental transcription of the city's functions. It was a real retrieval of the nearly lost. Recent studies have clearly underlined that, from the third century onwards, urban aristocracies were uninterested in giving public buildings to their native city, and were spending their money instead on private or religious buildings. Public institutions were thus having great difficulty in maintaining already existing public buildings. The typology of monuments renewed by Theoderic – baths, amphitheatres, theatres, aqueducts, city walls – summarises in the king's person both the old private patronage and the imperial one, and it is intimately bound up with the city's role as a meeting place for citizens (*cives*).

The precise connection between *antiquitas* and *novitas* is the conceptual framework for the repair of ruined statues and buildings, celebrated in inscriptions but with radically new motives. Instead of celebrating the donation to the city of new buildings, they celebrate the restoration of already existing structures after temporary abandonment. The new buildings, inspired by antiquity, arose from the ruined monuments that public finances had not manage to repair and in which the aristocracy had shown no interest. This praise of antiquity is thus linked with criticism of Theoderic's predecessors, and of the unworthy posterity (*indigna posteritas*) which 'spurns the praises of ancient descent' (*laudes antiqui generis abnegat*). Criticism of the society of the immediate past is expressed through comments about the degradation of buildings on an objective and ostensibly neutral level, seemingly devoid of political implications, which allows the king to present his activity as a necessary restoration. This key message was promptly understood by Theoderic's panegyrist Ennodius who declared that the king's fame consisted in having averted a sunset, in having revived 'unhoped-for glory' (*insperatum decorem*) from the ashes of cities (Reydellet 1981).

Let's try now to compare Theoderic's project with what he actually achieved. It has been noted that claims for tradition are normally more intensive when tradition – as uninterrupted continuity – has already been broken or is breaking. Continuous and pointed references to the past are just masks for novelty, so that collective consciousness can insert within a known paradigm the aspects that otherwise would be considered intolerable. Genuine novelty does not appear in programmatic declarations of change but in the interstices created by declarations of fidelity to tradition. Theoderic's motto could have been: 'For everything to change it is necessary that everything continues to seem the same.' That is exactly the opposite of the conservative formula par excellence, as neatly expressed by Lampedusa's Tancredi in *The Leopard*: 'For everything to remain as it is, everything will have to change.' If the constant call to antiquity was used as clear reference to a lost civilised past, on the practical side its aim was to give an ancient and familiar veneer to the new elements, masking what was potentially least acceptable about them. The three points of Theoderic's building activity – *antiquitas*, *vetustas*, *modernitas* – are extremely clearly expressed and the building side of the king's policy was the demonstration of his fair government. We can see Theoderic's building propaganda as the ancient ideological frame in which change and novelty could be inserted.

In practice, there were many and obvious contradictions to the ancient line proposed by the king. Let's look at some examples. Theoderic allowed aristocrats *absoluta liberalitas*, to build without payment private houses on the site of public buildings, for instance in the *porticus Curvae* and on a grain-store (*horreum*) in Rome because they were 'destroyed by the oldness of long time' (*longi temporis vetustate destructa*), and a portico in Spoleto was given to Helpidius 'so that the appearance it had in its prime could be restored' (*ut facies adulta reddatur*), the only condition being the maintainance of the original structure. An aristocrat receiving such permission was formally commanded to bring new dignity to ancient structures forgotten by *incuriosa vetustas*: Cassiodorus's letters of authorisation for private building on public structures are prefaced by long rhetorical sections exalting the virtues of the showcase city.

The same ideological framework was used when the king allowed the reuse of ancient building materials in new buildings – as in the famous example of the amphitheatre of Catania whose stones he permitted to be used to fortify the city – or in his exhortations to each man to give generously 'stones of whatever kind lying about in his fields' (*cuiuslibet generis saxa in agris suis iacentia*) so that they could be used in new buildings: 'it is not right that what can increase the beauty of a city is lying on the ground'. 'We wish to increase modernity without diminishing antiquity': take to Ravenna the marbles from Ostuni because there they would have the glamour of 'antique brightness' (*antiquus nitor*). It is worth stressing at least one element of novelty proposed by the king: reusing ancient stones was considered as prestigious as building a monument with new stones. Such an attitude was very far from the classical one: a century earlier, Ammianus Marcellinus could blame an urban prefect because he was claiming to be the founder of buildings that in fact he had only restored. In spite of several imperial reminders to municipal administrations to provide for the restoration of collapsing buildings rather than to build new ones, the personal prestige and local fame of a new founder had never been the same as that of a mere *restaurator*. To be sure, expropriations of building materials, and of whole buildings, were not unknown before Theoderic: the Theodosian Code has some clauses dedicated to this subject, but they are inspired by motives quite the opposite of Theoderic's, since their aim is to restrict and regulate the use of *spolia* from public buildings, and certainly not to encourage and ennoble this practice. The novelty proposed by Theoderic, then, was to confer on the reuse of ancient buildings and building materials the ideological aura of a restoration of the classical past, even though the practical effect was simply that aristocrats continued to do what they had become used to doing in the recent past. To satisfy and enoble aristocratic ambitions and desires allowed the king to be an active element in aristocratic careers and at the same time to strengthen consent for his regime.

This firm intention to practise a 'traditional' policy, avoiding every kind of subversion, also highlights the king's lack of concern when antiquity was openly violated. Consider, for example, Theoderic's behaviour after the theft of a statue at Como: after expressing his regret, Theoderic ordered Tancila, his officer in the city, to offer a reward for the statue's return, but also to establish a special reward for confession by the offenders. 'It is for a right-thinking prince to abolish crimes rather than to want to punish them' (*Benigni quippe principis est non tam delicta velle punire quam tollere*): the important point is that nothing changes, that the statue goes back to its original place. Theoderic was extremely severe with the prefect Artemidorus, guilty of appropriating money assigned for the restoration of ancient buildings in Rome: the return of the money was considered sufficient to avoid punishment, however, because the king's *moderatrix clementia* (clemency-as-moderation) was satisfied by having discouraged someone else's cupidity (La Rocca 1993).

In response to Theoderic's compliance towards them, the aristocracy celebrated the king and his special munificence in conspicuous material forms. First of all, the ancient practice of erecting bronze statues in the *fora* to acclaim local public and private donors was re-established. It was a custom, though preserved longer in southern Italy, that Ammianus Marcellinus already considered *demodée* in the later fourth century. Statues of Theoderic, or at least thought to be of him, are mentioned in Ravenna, in Rome and in Constantinople, this last one erected by the emperor Zeno to mark Theoderic's consulship. The putting up of statues was severely regulated during Justinian's reign. The emperor forbade Theoderic's successor Theodatus to permit the erection of statues portraying himself on his own: he was always to be portrayed together with the emperor. While the more aggressive policy of Theoderic's successors made these forms of auto-celebration intolerable at Constantinople, Theoderic wisely ensured that his statues were not interpreted as symbols of political antagonism (Ward-Perkins 1984).

The king was also portrayed in mosaics at Pavia and Ravenna: according to Agnellus's description the first was an equestrian portrait, while in the second the king was flanked by the personifications of Rome and Ravenna. Rome's traditional iconography was balanced by Ravenna's new one. It was a compromise between modern and old tradition that had been seen in Theoderic's portrait on the golden coin celebrating his *tricennalia* (thirty years of rule). Here the ruler's iconography is old but mixed up with that, and partly contradicting it, are barbarian elements: the king has a moustache and quite long wavy hair, and he holds a globe in his hand. This was a portrait that, while not renouncing a timid affirmation of the king's imperial ambitions, did not exceed the permitted limits.

The king's images were widely distributed. The gift of prophecy was ascribed to some of them: the gradual disappearance of the mosaic portrait in Naples was interpreted by the Romans as a symbol of the slow dissolution of the Ostrogothic kingdom in Italy. Symmachus's daughter took revenge on Theoderic, who had had her father executed, by destroying all the king's images. The desire to celebrate the persona of the king was seen in other kingdoms too, whose rulers had dynastic links with Theoderic. Thus the Vandal king Hilderic portrayed himself with his Roman predecessors Valentinian, Theodosius and Honorius. Another form of ruler-symbolism straddling the same line between innovation and tradition was the production of stamped tiles with Theoderic's name. Theoderic's stamps are archaic (they are rectangular in form) but they are also new, especially in bearing the legend 'Regnante domino nostro Theodorico bono Roma' ('In the reign of our lord Theoderic for the Good of Rome') or 'Felix Roma', and, though very rarely, the date of emission. If this latter trait was taken from Byzantine models, it was seldom used in the eastern part of the empire and not in the age of Theoderic. Theoderic's role in renewing ancient monuments and the civil aspects of the cities is also evident in the inscription on the lead piping of Ravenna aqueduct, 'Dominus noster Theodericus civitatis [*sic*] reddidit' ('Our lord Theoderic restored this for the city'). Such symbolic enrichment of the king's prestige is also exemplified in the foundation, or perhaps just the renaming, of the city of *Thedoricopolis* in Raetia, mentioned by the Anonymous of Ravenna. To give one's own name to a city was typical imperial behaviour, as Vegetius explained in his fifth-century *Epitoma rei militaris*, but this model was widely copied by barbarian kings: *Uniricopolis*, was the old Hadrumetum, thus rebaptised in the fifth century by the Vandal king Huniric, while *Reccopolis*, founded in the later sixth century by the Visigothic king Leovigild to honour his son Reccared, was completely new (La Rocca 1993). It is worth noting that these new names or new settlements did not manage to survive in historical tradition, nor did they succeed in attracting population, being deserted, in each case, within a century. They came into being as

Figure 24.1 The mausoleum of Theoderic, Ravenna. Photo: Scala.

arbitrary decisions to celebrate rulers rather than to meet any economic need for a settlement. The chronological order of these three examples could suggest that Theoderic was imitating Huniric, not the emperor, just as the Ostrogoths imitated the Vandals in creating new multiples of their bronze coins. The Vandals may have provided a model for contemporary barbarian kingdoms in other material displays of power: for example offering equestrian and gladiatorial *ludi* in circuses and amphitheatres, or restoring residential private and public buildings. Theoderic's palace in Ravenna was a Roman *villa*, as were the small so-called palaces in Galeata and Palazzolo.

The importance of local society in defining building policy can be seen in the different forms such policies took in the old imperial capital, Rome, and in the Ostrogothic capital, Ravenna. In Rome, as already noted, the king simply restored already existing buildings, but in Ravenna he had completely new ones built. At least two more differences marked the king's self-representation in these two cities. In Rome, buildings were restored using tiles stamped with Theoderic's name, while in Ravenna this type of inscribed tile was never used. Theoderic was celebrated in Rome for buildings that gave a new imperial light to the city, while we have to await the ninth century and the relatively late source, Agnellus, to learn of the list of new churches built by Theoderic. Further, different building materials were used: in Rome, ancient stone *spolia*, in Ravenna new marbles, directly brought from the Proconnesus. In evaluating these differences, we can either emphasise them or play them down. If we take the latter option, we could observe that Ravenna's buildings are completely built with reused bricks, so that there is no real difference in the two cities. It is worth stressing, though, that if in Rome and other Italian cities Theoderic very deliberately left his mark upon the restored buildings, in Ravenna the ancient date of the building materials can only be determined after a careful analytical examination. At first sight the buildings appeared really new and this impression was enhanced by the marbles and mosaics decorating the interior of the churches. In Ravenna, where Cassiodorus's *Variae* also attest the arrival of ancient marbles from Ostuni, Rome and Faenza, as well as the activity of *marmorarii*, ancient building materials were entirely reworked, as they commonly were in Constantinople, so that their age could not immediately be detected. There clearly was a desire to build with rare materials, and when new ones could not be obtained, old ones were made new by reworking. In Rome Theoderic was underlining the *imprimatur* of antiquity, while in Ravenna he was concealing it.

Theoderic adopted an ambivalent policy which could satisfy the expectations of a society divided between Goths and Romans. He treated Rome and Ravenna as he was expected to do. Where the Roman Senate and aristocracy were concerned, he tried to recover the best classical tradition. Putting Rome at the centre of the king's attention and care meant restoring the prestige of a city that had lost its uniqueness after the rise of Constantinople, and whose benefactors now were simply local inhabitants as in any *municipium*. As for Ravenna, its position was very different – simultaneously the capital of the Gothic kingdom and the delegated seat of power of imperial authority. The palace, seat of this twofold authority, united structural and topographical elements recalling the example of Constantinople: the object was not to emulate the imperial capital but to show Ravenna's new dignity as an 'authorised branch' of the empire. The king decided to be buried in Ravenna, and the site he chose recalled Eastern imperial examples. Inscriptions with the names of the twelve Apostles on the top of the roof of Theoderic's mausoleum should be seen as imitating the Byzantine imperial funerary church. True, Theoderic was not the only barbarian king to imitate this model: Clovis was buried in a church dedicated to the twelve Apostles that he and Queen Clothild had built in Paris. Yet there is an obvious difference between Clovis's church, and the site of Theoderic's burial in an Ostrogothic cemetery and in a mausoleum built entirely out of new materials. The Anonymous of Ravenna also tells of 'a very large stone' long sought by the king for his grave. Theoderic's sarcophagus – a reused porphyry one – obviously harks back to ancient imperial practice, as used by Eastern emperors until Marcian (457), but thereafter abandoned. In this case, as in others, Theoderic chose to represent his power in a way that maintained ambiguity between new ambitions and old achievements.

Can we conclude that Theoderic adopted a specific building programme, in the sense of a homogenous sequence of activity, whether innovative or conservative? I would say no. Theoderic needed to create an ideological framework that could give a traditional veneer to the reuse of buildings and materials. He needed, therefore, to balance old and new, and this could be done by stressing the distinction between *antiquitas*, which contained within it the transcendent power of renewal, and *vetustas*, which had to be overcome. At the same time, Theoderic's equilibrium had to be a changing one, for it had to be adapted to the varying circumstances of different cities, especially Rome and Ravenna, and the varying forms in which elites sought legitimacy. Theoderic's flexible approach enabled him to satisfy the aristocracy's demands and consolidate its consent, ensuring a measure of social peace. Like every ancient political programme, Theoderic's included a building policy that gave external and visible testimony to the efficiency of the ruler's good government. Presenting himself as a benefactor of cities and especially of Rome, Theoderic was, and was remembered as, a special king, an *amator fabricarum* and *constructor civitatum*, even though in reality he did not build anything wholly new (La Rocca 1993).

PROBLEMS OF TERMINOLOGY IN THE SIXTH AND SEVENTH CENTURIES

If until the fifth century Roman society was dominated by interests, hierarchies, and an economic pattern promoted by the state, from the sixth century the relevance of state organisation underwent a sudden decline. One of the clearest signs of the impact of this decline is the change in the terminology formerly used to define and classify human settlements within the empire. Until the fifth century this vocabulary – *civitas*, *vicus*, *pagus*, *villa* – constituted the uniform expression of a settlement hierarchy formalised by the state, which reflected the different functions and characteristics of settlements in relation to the state's administration. Here, and inevitably, the payment of taxes was central (Wickham 1984). A similar uniformity of meanings simply cannot be found in the sixth century. Cassiodorus, for example, looking at the urban life, good climate, and rich monuments of Squillace, while at the same time observing that the place didn't have a proper wall, was unsure how to define its status: was it a *civitas ruralis* or a *villa urbana*? Gregory of Tours, likewise, was astonished that Dijon was not termed a *civitas*, although, for him, it had all the material and social characteristics of one. Both Cassiodorus and Gregory seem implicitly to discern and denounce a hiatus between the terms used to identify the two settlements and their ambiguous social and material characteristics. Public acknowledgement of their functions was perceived as inadequate to express and legitimate the quality of their inhabitants and their inter-relationships, and their efforts to create an urban monumental landscape. With the fading of the state, settlement hierarchies, like aristocratic hierarchies, became the object of continuous negotiation. Who, or what, could now declare a place a *civitas*?

The choice of which vocabulary was the most suitable to define the characteristics of settlements (and the ambitions of their inhabitants), even if conditioned by the limited number of terms available, was not uniform in the different *regna*. If the 'Roman' hierarchic scale was generally respected, with the *civitas* regarded as being at the top, the individual elements brought together to specify the distinctiveness of a settlement were quite varied. From the sixth century on, authors' choice of settlement words was not purely objective, nor was it always related to the material evidence: terms were chosen to indicate or to claim improved status, with buildings taken both to show the acquired status, and to anticipate it. Analysing Bede's words for places, James Campbell (Campbell 1986: 99–119) has shown that that author's choice between *villa, vicus, civitas* or *urbs* was not made simply on the basis of the existing characteristics of a settlement, but instead derived from Bede's conscious selection, and his wish to express a really new and, in his view, apposite hierarchy (Delogu 1994).

On the other hand, the decline of a settlement's status did not always have identical material consequences, nor did it necessarily imply abandonment by the inhabitants. Consider, for example, the expression 'razed to the very ground' (*ad solum usque*) used quite frequently in written sources of the seventh and eighth centuries to describe the end of some cities. The expression denotes the abolition of the dignity of a *civitas* through punitive action, including the ruin of a part of the city walls. Thus Fredegar says that when the Lombard king Rothari conquered the Ligurian coastlands, the king 'destroyed to their very foundations the walls of the listed cities, and ordered that those cities should [henceforth] be called *vici*' (*murus civitatebus supscriptis usque ad fundamento, vicus has civitates nomenare praecepit*). This destruction was in fact a symbolic act, its purpose being to disqualify the cities in an institutional sense. This did not necessarily mean that buildings were ruined or houses destroyed in the cities themselves (La Rocca 1994).

The high quality of urban buildings and the high status of the inhabitants are sometimes used to assert the rise of a settlement as a functional focus of activities of various kinds. Thus Paul the Deacon, writing his *History of the Lombards* in the later eighth century, traces the terminological transformation of Cividale: during the first phase of Lombard settlement, Cividale is simply described as a *castrum*, that is, following Isidore of Seville's *Etymologies*, 'a popular meeting-place of men' (*vulgaris hominum conventus*), but from the beginning of the seventh century Paul uses the term *civitas* to denote the qualities of this place, because the inhabitants had surrounded it with a wall during the Avar attacks, but also because the duke and 'the most noble Lombard families' lived in it. Even Callistus, patriarch of Aquileia, 'who was outstanding in nobility' (*qui erat nobilitate conspicuus*) came to live within this *civitas*, leaving the *castrum* of Cormons where he had been a refugee. In Cividale he could live 'together with the duke and the Lombards' (*cum duce et Langobardis*), whereas in Cormons his authority had been diminished because he had had to live 'only in the society of common people' (*tantum vulgis sociatus*). The high social rank of Cividale's inhabitants thus conferred dignity on Callistus, while, on the other hand, Callistus's residence there allowed Cividale to acquire an important religious function. The walls, the duke, the aristocratic elite, the patriarch, together constituted the identity of the new city. Among traits that seemed to attest the death of a *civitas*, the low social level of the inhabitants is frequently underlined. In the ninth-century *Versus de destructione Aquilegiae numquam restaurandae* ('Poem on the destruction of Aquileia, never to be restored'), the decay of Aquileia is represented in terms of social decline: the ancient 'city of nobles' (*civitas nobilium*) had become only a 'cave of rustics' (*rusticorum speleum*), the 'city of the kings' now nothing more than 'the huts of poor folk' (*pauperum tuguria*) (La Rocca 1998).

PRIVATE CHARTERS AND URBAN SPACES IN THE EIGHTH AND NINTH CENTURIES

Debate on the quality and characteristics of urban life in the early Middle Ages is, as Chris Wickham has observed, a key topic in Italian historiography (Wickham 1992). Italy's uniqueness, the political and institutional aspects of which became clear during the eleventh and twelfth centuries through the organisation of politically autonomous urban communities, has long been interpreted as the sign of a re-emergence of the old freedoms and customs that the Italians – or the Romans – enjoyed up to the fifth century, in stark contrast to the political oppression imposed on the Italians by foreign conquerors during the ensuing Lombard and Carolingian periods. Historians have made various (and very varied) attempts to find some thread of continuity which would offer an explanation, without anachronism, of Italy's peculiar trajectory. However plausible in general terms, no such explanation has really accounted for any particular case. It remains unclear how any given urban community survived underground from the sixth to the tenth century, finally to re-emerge and to assert its identity in the ensuing period. And yet, allegedly, the destiny of the individual town, as the cradle of Roman civilisation and also the ideological symbol of civilisation itself, exemplifed the general process: the city declined under barbarian, foreign, domination, but nevertheless did not die. Somehow, while its characteristic features and institutions were demolished, their memory was kept alive (though how and by whom is seldom apparent) until the eleventh century, when urban communities reappeared, free at last to show their inherent strength and dynamic energy.

This grand narrative was a construct of the nineteenth century, when Italy itself was being (re)constructed. Its main features, especially those based on assumptions about early medieval law, have long since been demolished. Nevertheless, and not only for Italian historians, the problem of the significance and of the relevance of urban life during the early Middle Ages will not go away. Nor is it merely national myth-making that has kept the problem on the agendas of Italian historians and archaeologists. No! The problem in itself is a fundamental scientific (*scientifico*, *scientifique*, *wissenschaftlich*, etc.) one in the continental sense: on its resolution, by applying appropriate methodologies, depends our knowledge of Europe's past. The sources used to construct the old narrative of the *longue durée* were always extremely various in type, quality and chronology, ranging from still-standing Roman monuments to place-names, archaeological finds, and narrative sources. Recently, however, research by both archaeologists and historians has yielded important – but apparently conflicting – evidence on the question of urban continuity.

On the archaeological side, in the past decade, with the huge increase in the quality and quantity of material data from stratigraphic digs on urban sites, the traditional two-faced image of the early medieval Italian city, with its characteristic alternation of desolate landscapes and Roman survivals, and its problematic cohabitation of barbarians and Romans, has suddenly completely disappeared. To find within the city walls wooden structures and houses, burials, vast open areas without any visible structures at all, and over everything a deep deposit of dark earth, has allowed archaeologists to set the Italian city in a northern European context, at least from the material point of view (Brogiolo and Gelichi 1998). This new picture has, paradoxically, highlighted more sharply than ever a striking difference between the early medieval urban phase and the classical one, not only accentuating all the negative motifs of the old historiographical tradition of the past, but confirming it by 'objective' material evidence. Still more paradoxically, in the new darker-than-ever archaeological account of the early medieval city, the culprits have remained the old ones: namely, the Lombards, who with their distinctive barbarian nature, their lack of familiarity with urban life and civilisation, their brutal and rather primitive social organisation, were responsible for the degradation of cities into villages. In a word, they remade cities in their own image. The archaeologists draw a correspondingly sharp contrast between Lombard Italy and Byzantine Italy. In the Byzantine area, so the argument goes, continuity of public administration maintained the identity of urban communities and their function of territorial coordination.

If that is where the archaeologists have left us, what do the historians have to say? Recently, a number of them have shown a way forward through the intensive study of private charters. Curiously, these documents had hitherto hardly ever been brought into the discussion, despite the fact that for many Italian cities they constitute a major source for the eighth, ninth and tenth centuries (La Rocca 1986). It is worth asking, first, what light charter evidence throws on the alleged contrast between the Lombard and the Byzantine territories (as if those were divided by a Maginot Line!). Many private charters contain references to urban houses. In the Lombard area private transactions centre on the land and not on the buildings, using expressions such as *terra cum casa super se habente* ('the land with a house on it') (Galetti 1994). Further, buildings are described with a very restricted terminology, most commonly the word *casa*, usually translated 'wooden hut'. In the Byzantine charters, the terminology is wider, sometimes referring to the different functions of the various parts of the house (*peristilium*, *coquina*, *cubiculum*). Moreover, it is often assumed that Byzantine houses, called *domus*, were built mainly in stone. If so, the consequence in material terms of 'the barbarisation of the urban landscape' between the sixth century and the ninth could be imagined as a contrast between stone and wood. But the archaeologists' excavations have shown that both the Lombard and the Byzantine areas had both wooden and stone buildings, and that while many Lombard *casae* were built of stone, many Byzantine *domus* were in fact wooden structures (Gelichi 1994). The evidence – or rather the interpretation – of the archaeological data does not match that of the written charters.

A more promising route, perhaps, is through examination of the charter evidence to understand which elements were perceived as significant ways of expressing the articulation of the town, and the difference between public and private spaces. This means looking for variations in the formulae used to describe and locate urban land. Variation does not directly imply material difference, and it is certainly related to the status and social level of the 'documentary authors' promoting the transaction. Yet while the image of the town provided by private charters is no straightforward mirror of reality, neither is it the mere reflection of stereotyped formulae. Take first, then, the terminology used to locate land and houses within a city. In eighth- and ninth-century Verona (La Rocca 1986), a charter will simply mention *casa mea infra civitate* ('my house within the city') without giving any further detail. This is the case in charters of the great rural landowner Engelbert of Erbé (846), of Wartus *vassus domini imperatoris* (853), and of Bishop Audo (855). But the reason for such an indefinite way of locating a house was not that the city was otherwise empty: rather, it was the high social status of the owner that was perceived as the essential element in identifying his house. In sharp contrast to this apparent topographical indifference, the lists of witnesses to the same charters show that Verona city-dwellers identified themselves not simply as *de civitate Verona*, but specifically as belonging to different parts of the city. Thus witnesses' names are always accompanied by locative references such as *de porta pontis* ('of bridge-gate'), *de fontana* ('of the fountain'), *de Arcu* ('of the Arch'), *de subtus Arena* ('from by the Arena'). None of these locations refers to any juridical or administrative division of the city: they are purely topographical indications, showing the formation of neighbourhood groups within the city, their identity defined by a physical feature in the urban landscape. Very seldom do these topographical details refer to ecclesiastical buildings, as we might have expected. Instead, they refer to various kinds of classical buildings, or to the ruins of those: the four city gates of St Firmus, St Stephen, St Zeno and St Mary in Organo, the city wall, the towers of the city wall that were still standing, new and old public palaces, the ruined theatre, were all used to define the people who lived near them. It is obviously impossible to assess how far Roman architectural remains such as the *antevoltus* (forecourt in front of an ancient vaulted building), the *murus longus non longe ab carcere* ('the long wall not far from the prison'), or the *Arcus* (triumphal arch) had in fact been preserved. The interesting point is that these buildings, even if no longer in use, were fully part of the urban landscape, and had their nicknames which were shared by the city-dwellers.

The informal topography of the town does not appear only in the charter witness-lists. Compared with the charters written for public officers or bishops, which were characterised by their brevity, the majority of urban transactions are very precise indeed. They mostly concern sales or donations of very tiny portions of land, whose location within the city is always very clearly specified. These charters also include the precise size of the piece of land, with measurements for each of the four sides, and their boundaries, that is, the names of the owners of the houses next to the land itself. This need for precision is the most evident sign of insecurity and negotiation: the listed names of the neighbours, most of whom were in fact relatives, suggest that such charters were the result of an agreement within a group of kin whose appearance in the written document underscored their final agreement to the transaction itself. Such precise indications relate especially to the long series of small donations made to the male monastery of St Mary in Organo, which was the traditional recipient of urban munificence. By an interesting contrast, the episcopal church seems only to have received pieces of public and aristocratic land, and these were, as we have seen, very vaguely described.

Turning from charters, we can look briefly at literary sources. Here the image of Verona as a city whose space is densely occupied and perceived as a multiplicity of areas inside the city walls, each area individuated by a physical feature that was quite possibly ancient, is not only confirmed but acquires an institutional prestige. The famous *Versus de civitate Verona*, composed by a member of the cathedral clergy at the beginning of the ninth century, describes Verona as a 'public city', the *regia sedes* which is the residence of Pippin, Charlemagne's son and sub-king of Italy. The city's topography is articulated as a list of the prestigious Roman public monuments: the theatre, the amphitheatre, the forum with its seven temples, the city gates, the city walls, which are the witnesses of continuous public concern for the classical past. These monuments are protected by a series of ancient churches standing outside the Roman walls, which preserve the shrines of local martyrs, giving holy guardianship to the royal town. In this poetic description, the city is not a physical image, but a juridical and public one: it is in the *civitas* that public power shows its material and monumental force, and holy protection gives to this force its special identity.

The 'empty' city of aristocratic charters with their houses and land situated *infra civitate*, the fully settled city of the monastic charters with its land divided into tiny fragments that are listed, measured, bordered by streets and houses and by land of other owners, and the imaginatively described classical city protected by churches where the Carolingian king lives: these, then, are three images and perceptions of an early medieval city during the eighth and ninth centuries. The images coexisted. They gave to the various groups of city dwellers their position and role within the city. At the same time, those images, and the boundaries they implied, were used to distinguish the people who lived inside or next to the city walls from the others who did not. Even in Lombard northern Italy, even if living in a wooden hut and walking on muddy streets, the men and women *de civitate Verona* were perfectly conscious of being part of a city.

REFERENCES

Primary Sources

Agnellus of Ravenna, *Liber Pontificalis ecclesiae Ravennatis*, ed. O. Holder-Egger, Monumenta Germaniae Historica, Scriptores rerum Langobardicarum (Hannover, 1878), pp. 265–391.

Cassiodorus, *Variae epistulae*, ed. T. Mommsen, Monumenta Germaniae Historica, Auctores Antiquissimi XII (Berlin, 1894), part-trans. S.J. Barnish (Liverpool 1992), Liverpool University Press.

Codex Carolinus, ed. W. Gundlach, Monumenta Germaniae Historica, Epistolae III (Berlin 1892).

Procopius of Caesarea, *Procopii Caesariensis Opera omnia*, eds J. Haury and G. Wirth, (Leipzig 1964), English trans. H.B. Dewing, Loeb Classical Library (London and Cambridge MA 1954).

Paul the Deacon, *Historia Langobardorum*, eds L. Bethmann and G. Waitz, Monumenta Germaniae Historica, Scriptores rerum Langobardicarum (Hannover 1878), English trans. W.D. Foulke (Philadelphia PA 1917, repr. 1974).

Secondary Works

Brogiolo, G.P. and Gelichi, S. 1998 *La città nell'alto medioevo italiano. Archeologia e storia*, Bari: Società Archeologica padana.

Brown, T.S. 1984 *Gentlemen and officers. Imperial administration and aristocratic power in Byzantine Italy, A.D. 554–800*, Rome: Publications of the British School at Rome.

Campbell, J. 1986 *Essays in Anglo-Saxon history*, London and Ronceverte: Hambledon Press.

Costa, G. 1977 *Le antichità germaniche nella cultura italiana da Machiavelli a Vico*, Naples: Istituto Benedetto Croce.

Delogu, P. 1994 'La fine del mondo antico e l'inizio del medioevo: nuovi dati per un vecchio problema', in R. Francovich, G. Noyé (ed.), *La storia dell'alto medioevo italiano alla luce dell'archeologia*, Florence: All' Insegna del Giglio, pp. 7–29.

Galetti, P. 1994 *Una campagna e la sua città. Piacenza e il suo territorio nei secoli VIII–X*, Bologna: All' Insegna del Giglio.

Gelichi, S. 1994 'Le città in Emilia Romagna tra tardo-antico e alto medioevo', in R. Francovich, G. Noyé (eds), *La storia dell'alto medioevo italiano alla luce dell'archeologia*, Florence: All' Insegna del Giglio, pp. 567–700.

Halsall, G. 1995 *Settlement and social organisation. The Merovingian region of Metz*, Cambridge: Cambridge University Press.

Heather, P. 1995 'Theoderic, King of the Goths', *Early Medieval Europe* 4, pp. 145–173.

Johnson, M.J. 1988 'Toward a history of Theoderic's building program', *Dumbarton Oaks Papers* 42, pp. 73–96.

La Rocca, C. 1986 '*Dark Ages* a Verona. Edilizia privata, aree aperte e strutture pubbliche in una città dell'Italia settentrionale', *Archeologia Medievale* 13, pp. 31–78.

—— 1993 'Una prudente maschera "antiqua". La politica edilizia di Teoderico', in *Teoderico il Grande e i Goti d'Italia. Atti del XIII Convegno internazionale di studi sull'alto medioevo*, Centro di studi, Spoleto, pp. 451–515.

—— C. 1994 '"*Castrum vel potius civitas*". Modelli di declino urbano in Italia settentrionale nell'alto medioevo', in R. Francovich, G. Noyé (eds) *La storia del'alto medioevo italiano alla luce dell'archeologia*, Florence: All' Insegna del Giglio, pp. 545–54.

—— 1998 'La trasformazione del territorio in Occidente', *Mortologie sociali e culturali in Europa fra tardo antichità e alto medioevo*, Centro di studi, Spoleto, pp. 257–290.

Moorhead, J. 1993 *Theoderic in Italy*, Oxford: Clarendon Press.

Pferschy, B. 1989 'Bauten und Baupolitik frühmittelalterlicher Könige', *Mitteilungen des Instituts für Österreichische Geschichtsforschung* 97, pp. 259–91.

Reydellet, M. 1981 *La royauté dans la littérature latine de Sidoine Apollinaire à Isidore de Seville*, Bibliothèque des Écoles françaises d'Athènes et de Rome 243, Rome.

Righini, V. 1986 '*Felix Roma, Felix Ravenna*. I bolli laterizi di Teodorico e l'attività edilizia teodericiana in Ravenna', in *Corso di cultura sull'arte ravennate e bizantina* 33, Ravenna, pp. 371–398.

Tabacco, G. 1967 'Problemi di insediamento e di popolamento nell'alto medio evo', *Rivista Storica Italiana* 79, p. 67–110.

Ward-Perkins, B. 1984 *From classical antiquity to the early Middle Ages. Urban public building in northern and central Italy (A.D.300–850)*, Oxford: Clarendon Press.

Wickham, C. 1984 'The other transition. From the ancient world to feudalism', *Past and Present* 103, pp. 5–30.

—— 1992 'Problems of comparing rural societies in early medieval western Europe', *Transactions of the Royal Historical Society* 6th series, 2, pp. 221–46.

CHAPTER TWENTY-FIVE

ASSEMBLY POLITICS IN WESTERN EUROPE FROM THE EIGHTH CENTURY TO THE TWELFTH

Timothy Reuter

The phrase 'assembly politics' in the title is deliberately ambiguous: it refers both to politics conducted *through* assemblies and to politics conducted *at* assemblies. To address this apparently narrow theme is in fact to address a much wider problem: as we shall see, it was mainly at assemblies that early and high medieval polities were able to act and indeed to exist. 'Polities' and 'politics' are here merely neutral signifiers for past human activities to which we would probably apply similar terms in our own societies; their use does not imply that prominent lay and ecclesiastical personages in this period conceived of *any* of their activities as 'politics' or of the *regna* within which they operated as 'polities'.[1] Indeed, to make that point is precisely to raise the issue of how we are to avoid anachronism in dealing with our remote pasts. The principal approaches on offer duck this difficulty. We can write conventional political history for this period by casting it as accounts of the strategies and tactics pursued by the principal actors in their attempts to acquire and retain and enhance their power and of the ways in which these attempts conflicted with each other. But if we do this we shall smooth out the lumpiness of the past. Conventional political history presents rulers and ruled as engaged *continuously* in political activity and calculation: our sources may not so present them, but the narrative strategies implicit in such writing will reframe the past to make it look like this, just as actors in a film – unless it is very experimental indeed – are assumed to be and implied as being engaged in action even when they are off camera.

To shift from political to constitutional or institutional history avoids this difficulty at the cost of introducing others. The lumpiness of the past appears to be recovered, because the rhetoric of constitutional history lies precisely in investing some past activities with more significance than others. But it is a lumpiness derived more from present reification than from past reality. The patterns of behaviour of rulers and ruled – if patterns are what they really were – are abstracted, to be reinscribed in an implicit grand narrative of ever-thickening institutionality. The result is all too often a grand narrative which does not entirely ensure suspension of disbelief. We may recall Karl Leyser's devastating critique of a century of constitutional historians' work on the Ottonian polity:

The older school assumed – with some exceptions – the state and a volume of government without asking very precise questions of how it worked from day to day. It was in its abstractions a shadow-history of institutions that did not really exist.

(Leyser 1982b: 80)

That criticism is perhaps particularly easy to make of Ottonian *Verfassungsgeschichte*; but it is arguable that even the constitutional or institutional history of a more formed and focused polity like England presents related difficulties, if not such extreme ones: the degree of abstraction and reification in recent surveys such as those by Henry Loyn and Lewis Warren on the *Governance of Medieval England* is high (Loyn 1984; Warren 1987). It would be wrong to deny altogether the existence of 'governance' in the world they are writing about, yet it is still hard to accept that this was all that the relationship between rulers and the political community was about.

Assemblies are a prominent feature of most contemporary accounts of this relationship, yet medievalists are inclined to take them more or less for granted. We are interested in their course and outcomes, but we are rather less interested in their form and function, though both were of great importance in the period selected for discussion here. The starting point is somewhat arbitrarily chosen, but although assemblies did not suddenly come into existence in the eighth century, we rarely get enough sense of their flavour and function in the preceding period to be able to say convincing and coherent things about them. The closing point, around 1200, is clearer: it is marked by the shift from assemblies to proto-parliaments and other kinds of representative institutions, which takes place from the 1180s in Spain, from the early decades of the thirteenth century in England, slightly later in France, and as usual rather differently and belatedly in Germany (Bisson 1982).[2] By around 1200 also we have clearly begun to move towards a world in which political interaction was no longer confined to assemblies; governments were increasingly governing continuously rather than in brief spurts. It is possible also that people's attitudes changed from the thirteenth century onwards: to speak one's mind at assemblies shifted from a duty to a right, perhaps even a pleasure, though this may be an illusion created by increasingly prolific source-material.

Although a constitutional historian's approach may not necessarily be the most profitable one, there are certainly questions about assemblies which can be framed in such terms and which still need satisfactory answers, in particular questions about the frequency of and the participation in assemblies. By the end of the twelfth century, rulers such as Henry II and Frederick Barbarossa were holding assemblies several times a year (Schimmelpfennig 1996: 89–90). Had this always been the case? Obviously there are problems here of evidence and definition. The terminology used for such meetings in our almost exclusively Latin sources is very variable, but it includes: *placitum* ('plea') and *curia* ('court'; both terms often imply a judicial meeting, but are not confined to such a usage); *colloquium* ('conference') and *conventus* ('gathering'); *concilium* ('council') and *synodus* ('synod'; both terms mostly used of ecclesiastical assemblies, but again not exclusively so); *magiscampum* ('Mayfield', in the eighth and early ninth centuries); *exercitus* (literally, 'army').[3] The problem is not so much that of uncertainty about whether contemporaries meant subtly differing things by their varied terminology, as that of deciding whether we should call something an assembly when we happen to know about it only from kinds of evidence which do not bother to apply a term to it at all.

The problem can be nicely illustrated by considering a related kind of meeting, church councils. Tenth-century church councils in West Francia or France hardly ever issued legislation, so we know about them largely from charters issued at them. Some of these explicitly refer to the meetings at which they were issued as synods, others do not, but there is no reason to suppose that these differences reflected a real difference in how the meetings were perceived at the time (Schröder 1980: 13–32). When we come to deal with secular assemblies the problem is still greater, because the charters issued at these were issued by kings, not by episcopal collectives. For the period before the later eleventh century, royal charters in Europe rarely had witness-lists. In theory at least, since they were their own authentication and were unchallengeable as to substance, they did not need them (Bresslau 1912: 642–6; Bresslau 1931: 202–4).[4] In consequence, royal charters may well have been issued at assemblies (and we know that they often were), but they frequently do not tell us this, nor do they normally tell us through their witness-lists about who was there. The one substantial exception to this generalisation, Anglo-Saxon England, simply presents us with a different set of problems. Not only are there uncertainties about the authenticity of royal charters on a scale long since eliminated elsewhere in Europe; Anglo-Saxon diplomata did not in any case usually bear full details of their date and place of issue, so even where we feel reasonably confident about the authenticity of a particular charter (or at least of its witness-list), we cannot necessarily convert the information it provides into information about an assembly held at a specific time and place (Keynes 1981: 126–34, 232–4). For our knowledge of assemblies and their participants across Europe we depend more and more, as we go back in time, on narrative sources and on casual survivals of legal material such as law-codes and capitularies.

By way of compensation we have some evidence of past norms from earlier periods. Both for Anglo-Saxon and early Anglo-Norman England, and for the Ottonian and Salian *Reich*, we have good reason to suppose that rulers regularly held large gatherings at the three great church feasts of Christmas, Easter and Whitsun, at which they may also have worn their crowns in state.[5] Even in the Carolingian period, the way in which annalists from the time of the Royal Frankish Annals onwards often record the places where rulers celebrated Christmas and Easter suggests that this practice was not a post-Carolingian invention. Celebrating church feasts does not in itself imply a large gathering; but crown-wearings almost certainly do – there is not much point in wearing your crown among a small circle of close friends, immediate family, and the local bishop. This is all the more true when a ruler needs what Brühl has termed a *Befestigungskrönung* ('confirmatory coronation') after his legitimacy has been impinged on (e.g. Louis II in 871 after his capture by the Beneventans, or Stephen's crown-wearing in 1146 at Lincoln, where he had been defeated and captured in 1141, or Richard I's after his return from being held for ransom in 1194). But it also holds under more normal circumstances, as can be seen from the descriptions by William of Malmesbury of the crowds at William I's assemblies (Biddle 1986: 51–2).

Also from the Carolingian period, we have Hincmar of Reims's claim – or that of his source – in his account of Carolingian royal government, *De ordine palatii*, that there would normally be two assemblies each year in Carolingian kingdoms, one a general one and one a more specialised preparatory one attended only by the most important men of the kingdom and the ruler's chief advisers (Gross and Schieffer 1980: 82–5).[6] There has been a good deal of rather inconclusive debate about this statement. The real problem is that although Carolingian assemblies are quite easy to identify, because they punctuate the accounts of the principal eighth- and ninth-century annalists, it is rarely possible to say anything much about who attended them and on what scale (Waitz 1883: 563–78; Seyfarth 1910: 78–81; Weber 1962: 75–84; Rosenthal 1964; Ganshof 1968: 21–3). However, Hincmar's statement that there was one general assembly a year in the Frankish realm lines up well with an institution of an earlier period, the Marchfield, the annual assembly of the Frankish 'nation in arms' in early March. There has been a tendency in recent years to deny that the Marchfield existed and to argue that there has been a confusion with a 'field of Mars' (i.e. of war) (Lévillain 1947/8; Wallace-Hadrill 1962: 95, n. 1; Bullough 1970: 85 and n. 3; Bachrach 1974). But to argue this is to overlook a large body of evidence which suggests that seventh- and eighth-century Franks did indeed think that there would be a major political assembly on 1 March, not least the fact that when the assembly was moved to May in the mid-eighth century it immediately changed its name to 'Mayfield'. This does not, of course, mean that this happened each and every year; early medieval polities simply did not work like that.[7] It means merely that there was a general, other-things-being-equal assumption within the political community that there would be one at that time unless there was some reason either for not holding it or for holding it at some other time. If we take this point, we can see that Hincmar's apparent belief that there would be one general assembly a year represents a continuity in the ninth century of older Frankish practice. That the origins of continental royal assemblies are to be found in a military-political gathering also ties in with the observation by Thomas Bisson and Karl Leyser among others that the boundaries between assemblies and armies were often blurred – even peacetime assemblies sitting in judgement could be called *exercitus*, while the verbs used in Latin sources for the summoning of assemblies are those used for the summoning of armies (Bisson 1966; Leyser 1994b: 62).

Already we are faced by questions about definition and participation. If in the Frankish world there was an understanding that there would be a general assembly at least once in the year, normally in the spring, but there was also an understanding that the ruler would appear 'in state' at the times of the great church feasts, then we evidently have different kinds of assembly, or at least meetings which we should call assemblies, at different times. In practice we can probably not define assemblies more closely than by saying that we are dealing with one whenever the ruler had in his presence a substantial number of people who were not permanent members of his entourage, though there is an element of circularity about that definition which is probably inescapable (Lindner 1990; Schimmelpfennig 1996). It is important to note that such meetings were not confined to *regnal* communities. Princes with quasi-regal status might also hold them, and lower down the scale the shire-meetings held regularly in late Anglo-Saxon and Anglo-Norman England, or the *mallus publicus* held regularly in Carolingian and post-Carolingian counties, might be thought of as local assemblies, at which a local or regional political community came together in much the same way as a regnal community did at a royal assembly (Fleming 1995; Schmidt-Wiegand 1984; Anstey 1947).

How such meetings were made known and called into being is largely unanswered and perhaps largely unanswerable questions. People were sometimes summoned, though this is not an activity which has left much trace in the surviving sources (Waitz 1896: 428–3). We know from Carolingian and east-Frankish/German evidence that if summoned either to a royal or to a local assembly you were indeed expected to turn up.[8] But were members of the political community entitled to turn up, even if they had not been summoned, to an assembly they knew was about to take place? At least in the Frankish and post-Frankish world there seems to have been a pragmatic distinction between general assemblies and assemblies by invitation. Hincmar refers to such a distinction, as we noted earlier; but in the eleventh and twelfth centuries meetings of all kinds, both secular and ecclesiastical, were often called *frequens*. This seems to have meant not that they were held often but rather that they were 'well-frequented'. Sometimes the word seems to imply the assembly was of a kind which anyone who wanted could attend, and that presumably implies that there were assemblies of other kinds.[9] What is clear as a basic rule of political etiquette is that those who *had* come, whether explicitly invited or not, could not depart without the ruler's leave – though it would be hard to say how far down the socio-political scale this obligation went (Reuter 2001: n. 27).[10] To depart early or without leave, as Becket did from the council of Northampton in 1164, was to make dissatisfaction and opposition clear (Reuter 2001). Equally, on the rare occasions when a ruler left an assembly early or without a formal concluding ceremony, as for example Henry IV of Germany did in the summer of 1073, or Henry II of England did at the end of the council of Westminster in October 1163, this was a means of showing displeasure (Lohmann 1937: 31–2; Reuter 2001: n. 17).

A further point about participation is that assemblies, even when 'regnal' rather than 'principal' in character, often seem to have had a regional catchment area. We can see this in the practice of West Saxon rulers in the tenth century of holding meetings very often in locations along the Thames, presumably to facilitate attendance by Mercian magnates, now notionally part of the kingdom but still in a sense not wholly of it (Hill 1981: 85–92), or in the way in which successive rulers of the east Frankish/German polity held assemblies at Regensburg for Bavarians or at Worms and the mid-Rhine region for Suabians – and in the twelfth century, when the centre of political gravity of the *Reich* had shifted southwards, of holding assemblies at places such as Fulda for Saxon magnates (Mayer 1959; Müller-Mertens 1980: 210–21; Müller-Mertens 1992: 318–22). The principle appears to have been that you summoned assemblies to an appropriate place on the edge of your own core region when encouraging attendance on a scale larger than usual from those whose power lay outside that core.

More could be said about these issues, and about venues (for larger gatherings, assemblies were often open-air meetings with accommodation in tents, but royal and ecclesiastical palaces were also used). However, to examine assemblies simply on the basis of frequency and composition would be to ignore some of their most crucial features. We need to consider the style of interaction at assemblies: to turn from who and when to how. We then need to turn to the what, in order to ask why assemblies were so important. By taking the how and the what together we can try to answer the question more holistically than can be done simply by listing their various functions. How did assemblies actually operate? One of the curious features of the subject is that for most of the period covered and most of the area covered we know surprisingly little about this. Those who are most familiar with English history would probably suppose that the richness of late-eleventh- and twelfth-century accounts of assemblies under rulers from William II to Richard I is the norm. But it is not; indeed, if this had been more widely realised there might have been more analysis than there has been of how assemblies operated, based precisely on these accounts of trials and meetings from Anglo-Norman and Angevin England. From other periods and regions there is much less: Widukind and Thietmar, for example, tell us a fair bit about the electoral assemblies of 936 and 1002, but not much about other occasions; Richer offers us a brilliant rhetorical set piece about the 987 election, but does not tell us much about the dynamics of this or other similar occasions (Leyser 1994c: 174–7; Latouche 1930–7: ii. 150–63). That does not mean that we cannot say anything – there is a great deal we can piece together from fragmentary evidence – but merely to point out that what we should think of as full accounts of assemblies are much rarer than one might think. This appears to be true also of the Carolingian era. Here, for example, is Hincmar, wearing his annalist's hat, on the 864 assembly at Pîtres, one of the defining moments of ninth-century west Frankish rulership and one with whose staging and scripting Hincmar had a good deal to do.

> On 1 June at a place called Pîtres, Charles held a general assembly, at which he received not only the annual gifts but also the tribute from Brittany . . . he ordered fortifications to be constructed there on the Seine to prevent the Northmen from coming up the river. With the advice of his faithful men and following the custom of his predecessors and forefathers he drew up *capitula* to the number of thirty-seven, and he gave orders for them to be observed as laws throughout his whole realm.
>
> (Nelson 1991: 118)[11]

This is fairly typical except in its fullness. It tells us what was done, but not how it was done. Even the more detailed accounts of assemblies which we possess in general deal with specific aspects: for example, with their functions as courts, or as electoral bodies. To get at some of the more general features of their behaviour we have to dig deeper.

Once again, there is a significant parallel for our topic in the study of church councils. Until comparatively recently these have been perceived by church historians as black boxes. We know pretty well what a council is – an assembly of prelates – and we know what the products of a council look like – a set of canons. So unless there happen to be records of debates at such councils (which are then examined primarily for their subject matter rather than for what they tell us about the way in which debates took place) we can take the details as read. Recent research, however, culminating in a comprehensive edition of the *Ordines* for celebrating a council

(Schneider 1996), has shown that councils were in form primarily liturgical occasions. The ultimate biblical basis of conciliar activity – Christ's statement that wherever two or three are gathered together in my name, there I shall also be – was given constant and staged liturgical expression at councils in this period and beyond, from small diocesan synods up to major councils of the Latin Church as a whole.[12]

Now we cannot simply equate assemblies with councils, though the boundaries between the two could be fluid across much of the area and period we are concerned with: the later Carolingians made some attempt to draw a clear line, as Charles the Great and Louis the Pious had not (Hartmann 1989: 7–10; Ganshof 1957: 27–8), but it is hard to perceive in the Ottonian Reich, and even harder in Anglo-Saxon England (Wolter 1988: 482–9; Oleson 1955: 91–100; Vollrath 1985: 10–18; Cubitt 1995: 44–59). What *is* important is that we should perceive assemblies as staged occasions. They were not simply gatherings which came together and proceeded on a pragmatic and *ad hoc* basis according to what was necessary; they were, as Thomas Bisson has pointed out, moments of celebration and persuasion (Bisson 1982). Much of this celebration will have been liturgical: no assembly, except in the most exceptional circumstances, without the Eucharist, though there is a clear distinction to be made between councils, which were in themselves complete liturgical moments, and assemblies, which included liturgical elements without being defined or wholly constrained by liturgy, though they were held frequently enough at liturgically significant points of the year (Sierck 1995; Schaller 1974). Elements such as processions, litanies, *laudes*, and the reception-ceremony known as the *adventus regis* are mentioned only rarely in narrative accounts of assemblies, and of course there were no *ordines* to lay down their place in a set of stage-directions. But these things are mentioned frequently enough to make it clear that they were a natural and standard part of such gatherings. Otto I's last assembly, spread between Magdeburg and Quedlinburg, was punctuated by processions to church in which Otto – as was his custom, we are told – was accompanied there by bishops and back (to a meal) by a great crowd of ecclesiastics, dukes and counts, while at the end of our period Becket, arriving late for the council of Northampton in 1164, found Henry II at Mass (Holtzmann 1935: 76; Reuter 2001). Where they are not mentioned, this is more probably because they were taken for granted by writers and their audiences than because they did not take place.

Of course, to point to elements of staging and of ritualised or symbolised collective behaviour is not necessarily to deny the existence of more *ad hoc* and less structured elements, and hence of ways of 'reading' these gatherings which legitimately treat the layer of staging and symbolic action as transparent and go through and beyond it. Anyone familiar with meetings of an analogous kind in our own culture (for example, meetings of political parties at all levels, parliaments and councils, boards of firms or universities or hospital trusts) will know that these too are staged occasions with their own rituals and expectations, but will also know that that does not preclude either the unpredictable, or the open and often quite unstructured debate, or even conflict. Yet our culture expects and allows for these: we accept the existence of staging and ritual in our gatherings when it is pointed out to us, but we perceive them primarily as places of functional interaction. Participants in assemblies in the period we are dealing with here probably saw the staging and ritual as primary, and were more troubled than we might be when consensus and unanimity failed to materialise. Recorded examples of open conflict suggest that these were rare and shocking events. When Otto of Wittelsbach was so provoked by Rainald of Dassel's translation of a papal letter to Frederick Barbarossa at the assembly at Besançon in 1157 as to draw his sword and threaten the papal legates (Waitz and von Simson 1912: 176–7); when Anselm and Becket found themselves facing not so much an assembly acting as a judicial body as a group of royal supporters threatening to become a lynch mob (Barlow 1983: 338–42; Barlow 1986: 111–15; Knowles 1970: 94–100; Reuter 2001); when Conrad II was so disturbed by the behaviour of his son and the bishop of Freising at an assembly in 1035 at which the fate of Duke Adalbero of Carinthia was to be decided that he broke into an uncontrollable outburst of rage (Bulst 1949: 49–52, no. 27; Heidrich 1971; Althoff 1997b: 41–3)[13] – these were not normal events. They were disruptions of the expected course of assemblies which produced powerful collective efforts to restore the harmony which had been disturbed.

What lay behind these attitudes is something which has been explored by Gerd Althoff in a number of recent studies. Althoff's conclusion, which can be extended well beyond the accounts of political action in the tenth-, eleventh- and twelfth-century *Reich* on which it is based, is that we are dealing with polities which collectively feared and shunned open expression of conflict or disagreement (Althoff 1997c). They did so because they lacked a language in which conflict or opposition could be expressed in a controllable form. To oppose, or to contradict in public, was to insult; and to insult, in a society in which the protection of one's honour was the trip-wire defending the protection of one's property and rights and hence one's power and standing, was to invite feud. The characteristic form of public political action was therefore not that of transparent mediation between divergent interests or claims openly expressed, but that of opaque ritualised behaviour symbolising closure and reaffirming an order which should if at all possible be seen not to have been threatened.

This applies to the little things as well as to the big ones. Althoff, I and others have spent some time on showing how rebellions were ended in the *Reich* by acts of ritualised submission and surrender, and these insights are certainly applicable to other regions of Europe besides the *Reich* (Reuter 1991b; Althoff 1997d; Althoff 1997e). The Becket conflict, for example, as I have shown elsewhere, was initiated by open disruptions of order and consensus at assemblies, of a kind which caused both sides to feel an almost irredeemable sense of injury: the difficulties and delays in bringing about closure in the dispute reflected the problems of agreeing on the stage-management of closure (Reuter 2001). But matters which might well be less controversial in content, from appointments to bishoprics, abbacies and high secular posts down to the granting of privileges appear also, when we have enough details to judge, to have been for preference carried out, suitably staged, at assemblies.

Staging of course implies stage managers and directors. Unlike the contemporary Byzantine and Islamic polities, and unlike more distant worlds such as imperial China, stage-management did not take the form of pre-established but nevertheless flexible and manipulable rituals governed by tradition recorded in written form and its expert and literate guardians. The relatively low level of literacy and formal education among the political elite meant that a discourse based on reference to written records of rituals – reference either as conformity or as deliberate and conscious extension, transgression, allusion – could not develop at this time, as it undoubtedly did in western Europe from the fourteenth century onwards (Reuter 1998: 369–71). Stage-management in this period meant rather the agreement of terms and forms by intermediaries. Conflict resolution in particular required *internuncii*, people who were trusted by both sides and who could arrange the precisely nuanced terms in which subsequent closure could be publicly expressed as well as guarantee with their own honour and persons the settlements so reached (Althoff 1997b: 30). If we look closely at the accounts of the most prominent political crises and discords of the period, whether we are considering the disruptions to imperial order of the 830s and 840s or the dispute between Henry IV and Gregory VII, or the Becket dispute, we find intermediaries beavering away, both before and during the assemblies at which such disputes were principally conducted.[14]

There is also evidence for a sphere of more private consultation, at which things could be said which could not possibly be said in 'public'. It is a feature of such detailed accounts of assemblies as exist that they frequently refer to demands by individual participants to break for consultations. Archbishop Conrad of Mainz, asked by Alexander III to accept Salzburg rather than be restored to Mainz as part of the settlement of the schism at Venice in 1177, requested an adjournment and 'took counsel with his friends' before agreeing, and this was a typical not an exceptional case (Arndt 1866: 455). To argue that the language in which politics was publicly expressed was one of carefully staged spontaneity does not preclude the use of the language of political calculation in other contexts: we find this at odd moments in letter-collections, and we find it also in accounts of *colloquium familiare* and *colloquium secretum*, terms which mark a contrast between private meetings and the public colloquies at which the language of political calculation would have been completely out of place.

When we move on from looking at the ways in which assemblies operated to consider what they dealt with, it becomes clear that – with the exception of military campaigns, though these were often enough a kind of assembly on the march – the major issues which concerned early and high medieval polities were treated mainly or exclusively at assemblies: legislation; diplomacy; court hearings for the political elites; military planning; any kind of consultation about the state of the realm.

Assemblies were the places for promulgating legislation or sub-legislative instructions. This is how Charles the Great and Louis the Pious and Charles the Bald behaved (Ganshof 1957: 35–40, 52–62; Hannig 1982; Nelson 1992), and their example was imitated by the hegemonic rulers of Wessex after its early-tenth-century Carolingianisation (Wormald 1978; Wormald 1999). The decline in importance of legislation across most of western Europe in the post-Carolingian era meant the decline of this aspect of assembly functionality, but it was not transferred elsewhere, and when secular legislation revived in the course of the twelfth century it was in the main at assemblies that it was proclaimed, whether in the *Landfrieden* of Henry IV, Frederick Barbarossa and Louis VII or in the assises of Roger II of Sicily and Henry II of England (Wadle 1986; Leyser 1994g: 151–3; Hudson 1995: 255 with n. 4). Even when rulers or those acting on their behalf began to promulgate legislation in a more proto-absolutist fashion, it was still in the main presented as the product of a ruler sitting amid the regnal community. The term often used in the twelfth century, 'assise' in its Latin and vernacular cognates, implies a 'session', a sitting down together (Niermeyer 1954–76: 65). It was used to clothe legislation with the authority of assembly even where it had no such origins: the earliest surviving Sicilian royal legislation purports to be the text of an assise issued by Roger II with his kingdom at Ariano in 1140, though in fact it is a learned compilation of the 1180s drawn from a variety of sources (Zecchini 1980; *Ariano* 1996; Houben 1997: 136–48; Matthew 1992: 185–8). Privileges for individual beneficiaries (churches, monasteries, major and lesser secular office-holders), which were the more normal form of 'legislation' across Europe throughout this period (Krause 1965), also seem to have been issued for preference at assemblies, though in view of their importance for our knowledge of assemblies' existence there is some danger of a circular argument here.[15] Certainly the characteristic form of the privilege, at least in the Frankish and post-Frankish world, was that of a symbolic object: large enough to be visible even in a full assembly, with elaborately decorative script and highly prominent seals. Was it something to be handed over in public with suitable ceremony, perhaps including the formal reading of its contents, not simply to be collected from a chancery clerk on payment of a fee, even if a fee might need to be paid as well (Reuter 1994: 194–6; Reuter 1998: 377).

Diplomacy was scarcely conceivable in this period without a backdrop of regnal assemblies. From the eighth through to the twelfth centuries, European rulers met face to face infrequently, though when they did so this was normally at assemblies (Voss 1987; Kolb 1998). Rather, they defined membership of their exclusive club by their repeated participation in exchanges: of brides, of gifts, of ambassadors. Like crown-wearings, such exchanges would have lacked most of their point had they taken place in private. An audience was required, and assemblies provided it. It was here that ambassadors were formally received and formally given leave to return to their masters (e.g. Reuter 1992: 67, 73, 75). If they happened to turn up when no assembly was scheduled, they might well be asked to wait until one was. If they had brought gifts, it was here, in public, that the wrapping-paper was removed (Leyser 1982c: 114–17; Leyser 1994d: 81–3). If they had come to collect a bride, it was at assemblies that she would be seen off and given a kind of preliminary reception into her new community.[16] The documentation of such practices is admittedly confined almost completely to regnal assemblies; but given the known tendency of great aristocrats to imitate rulers in their behaviour, and lesser aristocrats to imitate greater ones, it is probable that similar forms of public exchange and acknowledgement went on lower down the socio-political scale as well.

It was at assemblies also that disputes between members of the political community (including disputes between a ruler and members of his political community) were normally resolved. This is one of the best-documented and most-studied functions of assemblies. Characteristically, the ruler, though he presided over the assembly as a court, did not himself pass judgement: he would normally invite one or more of the more high-ranking persons present to utter the sentence, which was then both his sentence and that of the community in whose presence it had been uttered. This was true even when he was a party to the dispute: Henry the Lion was condemned by the sentence of the princes at Gelnhausen (Appelt 1985: 360–3, no. 795), while much of the difficulty in the final scenes at the council of Northampton lay in finding someone willing and able to promulgate the sentence on Becket which Henry II was determined to have (Knowles 1970: 97–9).

Last but not least: it was at assemblies, except in cases of dire defensive emergency, that military campaigns were normally agreed on and support was raised for them.[17] This is really only a specific instance of a more general principle. Any kind of consultation about what would later be called *status regni* (the 'state of the kingdom' or perhaps 'affairs of state') would normally and naturally take place at assemblies. Again, *regnum* does not here mean 'kingdom' alone. It is to be taken in the sense defined by Karl-Ferdinand Werner: a reasonably well-defined territorial entity with a continuing sense of political (and possibly also legal and cultural) identity (Werner 1981). As we have already noted, there is no very real difference, except in scale, between regnal assemblies and, for example, the meetings held by dukes of Normandy or Aquitaine or the counts of Flanders in the eleventh century, or the *corts* of the counts of Barcelona, or the assemblies summoned by dukes of Bavaria in 932, 933 and 990 (to name only some of the occasions we happen to know about). The distinction between regnal and princely becomes still more blurred if we take into account those assemblies held by rulers but primarily aimed at a particular regional clientele. *Any* ethnic or *regnum*-based political grouping could find itself and define itself at an assembly.

Moreover, it was in this form that it found collective action easiest, indeed found it possible at all: if we look back at the list just given of the kinds of things which were normally done at assemblies and difficult if not impossible to do elsewhere, we begin to realise that it was through embodying itself as an assembly that what has been referred to throughout this chapter as the 'political community' was empowered and enabled to practice politics. Jürgen Habermas has argued that the 'public', when thought of not as the antonym to 'private' but as a 'principle of social order implying a permanent overseeing of state power', was a product of the Enlightenment which did not exist and could not have existed before the eighteenth century (Habermas 1962: 17–21; cf. Althoff 1997d: 229). As a statement about the medieval and early modern past this is highly problematic, but, as so often when sociologists venture beyond the recent past, they frequently sharpen our own perceptions even when we find that we cannot accept theirs. For our period it would be truer to say that there was indeed a 'public', but it was a public which did not, except perhaps at moments of great crisis and heightened tension, have a permanent existence: it came into being at assemblies, and dissolved again when they ended. So indeed did politics of any kind to a great extent:

> Agriculturally and liturgically, the year moved continuously, if at varying pace, around its cycle; politically, time froze except on campaigns and at assemblies. It was here, for the most part, that movement and interaction were possible at all. Assemblies were not merely occasions when the ruler could represent himself as a ruler in the flesh; they were almost the only occasions when the polity could represent itself to itself. Outside the assembly there were the local politics of feud and *convivium*; but only at the assembly could this centreless

polity define itself, and it did so in terms of the ruler. This in the last resort was how the secular magnates within the *Reich* saw themselves.

(Reuter 1998: 378–9)

That passage refers specifically to the Ottonian *Reich*, but it might be thought to apply more generally: even smaller units such as dioceses and principalities could scarcely function except in this way, coming together at diocesan synods and local assemblies (moots, *things*, the comital *mallus*). In a world largely lacking transpersonal permanence, an ongoing public sphere, and adequate communications, virtually everything of importance had to be settled face-to-face, from conflict resolution through to the reception of ambassadors and the appointment of office-holders. Formally, it was the ruler who summoned assemblies and they were his assemblies; but if he had not existed the polity would have had to invent them. Indeed, up to about 1200 in most parts of western Europe it was precisely when the king ceased to exist that polities did have to invent their own assemblies. Unless a deceased ruler was succeeded by an adult son already confirmed in office (and often even then), an assembly had to be held to determine the succession to a kingdom or principality. By contrast, it was a sure sign that a ruler who was still alive was in serious political trouble when his leading men began to summon and meet in assemblies for themselves; such behaviour meant that he might well cease to exist, as a ruler, and, if really unlucky, as a person as well (Giese 1979: 149–54, 186–91; Holt 1992: 225–36).

Although 1200 has been chosen as a stopping point, it should be noted that even in the later twelfth century, when elements of a more modern kind of polity were clearly visible, western European kingdoms still offered such moments of celebratory or solemn coming together as much as they ever had. We can see these in the great meetings held by Henry II at Clarendon and Northampton in the 1160s, or at Westminster in 1176, when embassies from all over Europe arrived and his daughter Joanna was sent off to her husband, William II of Sicily (Warren 1973: 143), or in Louis VII's meeting at Soissons in 1155, at which a general peace was proclaimed – indeed, the increase in 'regnal' meetings under Louis VI was a sign that the Capetian kingdom was becoming a genuine kingdom once more (Bournazel 1975: 134–43, 157–61). It is visible not least in the two great assemblies held by Frederick Barbarossa in 1184 and 1188, the first to mark the knighting of his two eldest sons, the second, the 'assembly of Jesus Christ', to proclaim a new crusade following the fall of Jerusalem. With the first, much discussed by historians (Linder 1994; Fleckenstein 1972; Moraw 1988), we are evidently in the world of the great feasts marked by conspicuous consumption and competitive representation so characteristic of later medieval and early modern Europe; yet there is significant continuity here from the Carolingian era through to the eve of the new era in which such assemblies would merge imperceptibly into parliaments (while retaining much of the celebratory and consciousness-enhancing elements of the old assemblies).

The slow transformation of this assembly-dominated world needs a few words at the close. Earlier it was suggested that assemblies had begun to take on a rather different function from the late twelfth century onwards. Certainly they did not disappear; but they were now coming to be set in a context of more continuous political activity. Kingdoms and principalities in thirteenth- and fourteenth-century Europe were no longer defined solely by and at those moments when their stake-holders met together. The growth of courts (meaning permanent or semi-permanent royal entourages) and of residences, the thickening networks of homogenous judicial and administrative institutions, and last but not least the development of transpersonal conceptions of the polity, all meant that assemblies (whether 'representative' or not) were slowly transformed into functional parts of a larger whole, rather than being the occasions at which the larger whole changed from being virtual to being real.[18] But in the period we have been concerned with here, they had been precisely that.

This chapter has obviously blurred a lot of distinctions which a more extensive and detailed study would need to refine and make more explicit. It is clear, for example, that the Anglo-Saxon and Anglo-Norman polities, though showing many similarities with their continental analogues, were subtly different, in ways which still have to be properly explored. It is also clear that most of the evidence and examples for this chapter have been drawn from those parts of Europe where people cook with butter rather than olive oil, mainly because in this period the olive-oilers showed themselves much more reticent about narrative interpretation of what they were doing. It may be that Italy and the polities of Christian Spain are not quite adequately covered by the generalisations offered earlier. Elsewhere we may also assume or suspect regional differences, and again the varied survival of evidence may well have elided them for good. Not much can be said before the twelfth century about Scandinavia and Sclavinia, though some material is offered by *Sverrissaga* and the more contemporary sections of *Heimskringla*, as well as by Cosmas of Prague and Gallus Anonymus. But even if what has been said applies more strongly to transalpine Europe's Carolingian and post-Carolingian core than to other regions, this is still a great deal of Europe, and it represents a substantial and significant part of Europe's political practice in the early and high Middle Ages.

NOTES

1 On the limited degree of conceptual abstraction in political thought in this period see Nelson 1994: 65.

2 On parliaments see Moraw 1989, who stresses how long it took for the *Reichstag* to develop out of the *Hoftag*; Blockmans 1978. Fundamental on the self-realisation of political (and other) communities in this period is Reynolds 1997.

3 For the terminology see Niermeyer 1954–76: cols. 201–2, 235, 270, 288–90, 392, 801–4; *Mittellateinisches Wörterbuch* 1968–97: cols. 866–7 (*colloquium*), 1175–7 (*concilium*), 1822 (*conventus*); Latham and Howlett 1975–97: 383, 419–20, 479–80, 537. See also Waitz 1883: 563–4; Ganshof 1968: 22–3.

4 Witness-lists do not become common until the early twelfth century in Germany, rather earlier in France (cf. Lemarignier 1965: 42–78). Their function was to some extent fulfilled in earlier royal charters by the names of those who 'intervened' to further the transaction; cf. Bresslau 1931: 193–201; Faußner 1973: 388, 435–6; Gawlik 1976.

5 For the Anglo-Saxon and early Anglo-Norman rulers see Biddle 1986; for Ottonian

practice see Hüschner 1993. On the practice of crown-wearing see, besides Biddle, Brühl 1989b; Jäschke 1970; Brühl 1989c; Ott 1998.

6 On Hincmar's use of an older work by Adalhard, see *ibid.*: 11.

7 For discussions of the actual timing of assemblies in the Frankish realms see Seyfarth 1910: 62–71, 87–99; Weber 1962: 68–72; Rosenthal 1964; Sierck 1995: 276–322. The tendency to hold assemblies at particularly significant points in the liturgical year (major feasts as well as the triad of Christmas, Easter and Whitsun) has been particularly stressed by Sierck.

8 Cf. Mitteis 1927 and Reuter 1991b: 319–25, on the role of contumacy/non-appearance in 'political' trials. At a rather lower level, note the use of the verb *admallare* (to 'encourt'): Niemeyer 1954–76: 20. For participation in thirteenth-century county courts see Coss 1991: 4–5.

9 Cf. Wibald of Stavelot's letter to Anselm of Havelberg in late 1149: 'Curia futura est Bavemberch, non tamen frequens, ad quam familiariter venire iussi sumus' (Jaffé 1864, 330, no. 211).

10 For a ninth-century example see Nelson 1991: 119 (864).

11 For Hincmar's role see Nelson 1993. See also Hannig 1982 on the relationship between Frankish rulers and followers at assemblies.

12 Matthew 18: 20, cited in two of the most influential early *ordines* edited by Schneider 1996, nos. 3 and 7 (pp. 210, 311).

13 See more generally Althoff 1998 and other contributors to Rosenwein 1998 on 'demonstrative' royal anger.

14 For intermediaries see Althoff 1997a: passim; specifically on the Carolingian civil war, Lauer 1926: 68–74 (attempts at mediation before Fontenoy), and 92–4 (peace initiatives of late 841); on intermediaries at Canossa, Reuter 1991b: 322–3 and Althoff 1997d: 240–4; on their role in the Becket conflict, Reuter 2001.

15 See the discussion summarised above, at n. 4.

16 As for example Joanna of England in 1176 (Warren 1973: 143). For a very early example in Gregory of Tours, see Krusch and Levison 1937–51: 318: Chilperic invites the leading Franks to celebrate the betrothal of his daughter Rigunth to the Visigothic king.

17 See the discussion of the Mayfield above, and Leyser 1994e: 29–30.

18 I have sketched much of the background to this institutional thickening of rulership, though without specific reference to assemblies, in Reuter 1994. There is now extensive German scholarship on the development of residences. For the development of the 'modern' state in the later Middle Ages Genet 1990 should be consulted.

REFERENCES

Althoff, G. (1997a) *Spielregeln der Politik im Mittelalter: Kommunikation in Frieden und Fehde*, Darmstadt: Primus.

—— (1997b) 'Königsherrschaft und Konfliktbewältigung im 10. und 11. Jahrhundert', in Althoff 1997a: 21–56 (article first published 1989).

—— (1997c) '*Colloquium familiare – colloquium secretum – colloquium publicum.* Beratung im politischen Leben des früheren Mittelalters', in Althoff 1997a: 157–84 (article first published 1990).

—— (1997d) 'Demonstration und Inszenierung. Spielregeln der Kommunikation in mittelalterlicher Öffentlichkeit', in Althoff 1997a: 229–57 (article first published 1993).

—— (1997e) 'Das Privileg der *deditio*. Formen gütlicher Konfliktbeendigung in der mittelalterlichen Adelsgesellschaft', in Althoff 1997a: 99–125.

—— (1997f) 'Empörung, Tränen, Zerknirschung. "Emotionen" in der öffentlichen Kommunikation des Mittelalters', in Althoff 1997a: 258–81 (article first published 1996).

—— (1998) '*Ira regis*: prolegomena to a history of royal anger', in B. H. Rosenwein (ed.) *Anger's Past: the social uses of an emotion in the Middle Ages*, Ithaca, N.Y.: Cornell University Press, 59–74.

—— (1999) 'Saxony and the Elbe Slavs', in T. Reuter (ed.) *The New Cambridge Medieval History*, 3: *c.900–c.1024*, Cambridge: Cambridge University Press, 267–92.

Anstey, F. M. (1947) 'The meaning of *placitum* and *mallus* in the capitularies', *Speculum* 22: 435–9.

Appelt, H. (ed.) (1985) *Die Urkunden Friedrichs I.*, vol. III. *1168–1180*: MGH, Diplomata regum et imperatorum Germaniae, Hannover: Hahn.

Ariano (1996) *Alle origini del costituzionalismo europeo: Atti del convegno internazionale di studi sulle 'Assise di Ariano (1140)' tenuto in Ariano Irpino ad 850 anni dalla promulgazione, Ariano, 26–28 ottobre 1990* (Centro europeo di studi normanni, Fonti e Studi 1), Rome: Edizione Laterza.

Arndt, W. (ed.) (1866) Romuald of Salerno, *Annales*, MGH, Scriptores 19, Hannover: Hiersemann.

Bachrach, B. S. (1974) 'Was the Marchfield part of the Frankish constitution?', *Mediaeval Studies* 36: 178–85.

Barlow, F. (1983) *William Rufus*, London: Methuen.

—— (1986) *Thomas Becket*, London: Weidenfeld & Nicolson.

Biddle, M. (1986) 'Seasonal festivals and residence: Winchester, Westminster and Gloucester in the tenth to twelfth century', *Anglo-Norman Studies* 8: 51–72.

Bisson, T. N. (1966) 'The military origins of medieval representation', *American Historical Review* 71: 1199–1218.

—— (1982), 'Celebration and persuasion: reflections on the cultural evolution of medieval consultation', *Legislative Studies Quarterly* 7: 181–204.

Blockmans, W. P. (1978) 'A typology of representative institutions in late medieval Europe', *Journal of Medieval History* 4: 189–215.

Bournazel, E. (1975) *Le Gouvernement capétien au XII siècle*, Paris: Presses Universitaires de France.

Bresslau, H. (1912–1931), *Handbuch der Urkundenlehre für Deutschland und Italien*, 2nd edn, 2 vols, Leipzig/Berlin: Duncker & Humblot.

Brühl, C. (1989a) *Aus Mittelalter und Diplomatik. Gesammelte Aufsätze*, I: *Studien zur Verfassungsgeschichte und Stadttopographie*, Hildesheim: Weidmann.

—— (1989b) 'Fränkischer Krönungsbrauch und das Problem der Festkrönung', in Brühl 1989a: 351–412 (first published 1962).

—— (1989c) 'Kronen und Krönungsbrauch im frühen und hohen Mittelalter', in Brühl 1989a: 413–43 (first published 1982)

Brunner, Heinrich (1906, 1931) *Deutsche Rechtsgeschichte*, 2nd edn by C. von Schwerin, 2 vols, Leipzig and Munich: Duncker & Humblot.

Bullough, D. A. (1970) '*Europae Pater*: Charlemagne and his achievement in the light of recent scholarship', *English Historical Review* 84: 59–105.

Bulst, W. (ed.) (1949) *Die ältere Wormser Briefsammlung*, I, MGH, Briefe der deutschen Kaiserzeit, Munich: MGH.

Collins, R. (1996) 'Fredegar', in P. Geary (ed.) *Authors of the Middle Ages*, vol. 4 (nos 12–13), 73–138, Aldershot: Variorum.

Coss, P. R. (1991) *Lordship, Knighthood and Locality*, Cambridge: Cambridge University Press.

Cubitt, C. (1995) *Anglo-Saxon Church Councils, c. 650–c. 850*, London: Leicester University Press.

Faußner, H. C. (1973) 'Die Verfügungsgewalt des deutschen Königs über weltliches Reichsgut im Hochmittelalter', *Deutsches Archiv für Erforschung des Mittelalters* 37: 345–449.

Fleckenstein, J. (1972) 'Friedrich Barbarossa und das Rittertum. Zur Bedeutung der großen Mainzer Hoftage von 1184 und 1188', in *Festschrift für Hermann Heimpel zum 70. Geburtstag*, Göttingen: Vandenhoeck & Ruprecht, ii. 1023–41.

Fleming, R. (1995) 'Oral testimony and the Domesday Inquest', *Anglo-Norman Studies* 17: 101–22.

Fustel de Coulanges (1891) *Transformation de la royauté pendant l'époque carolingienne*, Paris: Hachette.

Ganshof, F. L. (1957) *Was waren die Kapitularien?*, Darmstadt: Wissenschaftliche Buchgesellschaft.

—— (1968) *Frankish Institutions under Charlemagne*, Providence, R.I : Brown University Press.

Gawlik, A. (1976) 'Zur Bedeutung von Intervention und Petition', *Grundwissenschaften und Geschichte. Festschrift Peter Acht*, Kallmünz Opf.: M. Lassleben, 73–7.

Giese, W. (1979) *Der Stamm der Sachsen und das Reich in ottonischer und salischer Zeit*, Wiesbaden: Steiner.

Gross, T. and R. Schieffer (ed. and trans.) (1980) *Hinkmar von Rheims, De ordine palatii*, MGH, Hannover: Hahn.

Guba, P. (1884) *Der deutsche Reichstag in den Jahren 911–1125*, Leipzig: Veit.

Habermas, J. (1962) *Strukturwandel der Offentlichkeit: Untersuchungen zu einer Kategorie der burgerlichen Gesellschaft*, Frankfurt: Suhrkamp.

Hannig, J. (1982) *Consensus fidelium*, Stuttgart: Hiersemann.

Hartmann, W. (1988) *Die Synode der Karolingerzeit im Frankreich und Italien*, Paderborn: Schöningh.

Heidrich, I. (1971), 'Die Absetzung Herzog Adalberos von Kärnten durch Kaiser Konrad II. 1035', *Historisches Jahrbuch* 91: 70–94.

Hill, D. (1981) *An Atlas of Anglo-Saxon England*, Oxford: Blackwell.

Holt, J. C. (1992) *Magna Carta*, 2nd edn, Cambridge: Cambridge University Press.

Holtzmann, R. (ed.) (1935) *Thietmari Merseburgensis episcopi Chronicon*, II, MGH, Munich: MGH.

Houben, H. (1997) *Roger II. von Sizilien*, Darmstadt: Primus.

Hudson, J. (1994) *Land, Law and Lordship in Anglo-Norman England*, Oxford: Clarendon Press.

Hüschner, W. (1993) 'Kirchenfest und Herrschaftspraxis. Die Regierungszeiten der ersten beiden Kaiser aus liudolfingischem Hause', 1: 'Otto I. (936–973)'; 2: 'Otto II. (973–983)', *Zeitschrift für Geschichtswissenschaft* 41: 24–55, 117–34.

Jaffé, P. (ed.) (1864) *Monumenta Corbeiensia*, MGH, Berlin: Weidmann.

Jäschke, K.-U. (1970) 'Frühmittelalterliche Festkrönungen? Überlegungen zur Terminologie und Methode', *Historische Zeitschrift* 211: 556–88.

Jolliffe, J. E. A. (1963) *Angevin Kingship*, 2nd edn, London: A. & C. Black.

Keynes, S. (1981) *The Diplomas of King Æthelred the Unready 978–1016: a study in their use as historical evidence*, Cambridge; Cambridge University Press.

Knowles, D. (1970) *Thomas Becket*, London: A. & C. Black.

Kolb, W. (1988) *Herrscherbegegnungen im Mittelalter*, Bern: Peter Lang.

Krause, H. (1965) 'Königtum und Rechtsordnung in der Zeit der sächsischen und salischen Herrscher', *Zeitschrift der Savigny-Stiftung für Rechtsgeschichte. Germanistische Abteilung* 82: 1–98.

Krusch, B. and W. Levison (eds) (1937–51) *Gregorii Turonensis Opera*. I. *Libri historiarum X*, MGH, Hannover: Hahn.

Latham, R. E. and D. R. Howlett (1975–97), *A Dictionary of Medieval Latin from British Sources*, 1: *A–L*, Oxford: Oxford University Press.

Latouche, R. (ed.) (1930–37) *Richer, Histoire de France (888–995)*, Paris: H. Champion.

Lauer, P. (ed.) (1926) *Nithard, Histoire des fils de Louis le Pieux*, Paris: H. Champion.

Lemarignier, J.-F. (1965) *Le Gouvernement royal aux premiers temps capétiens: 987–1108*, Paris: Picard.

Lévillain, L. (1947/8) 'Campus Martius', *Bibliothèque de l'École des Chartes* 107: 62–8.

Leyser, K. J. (1982a) *Medieval Germany and its Neighbours, 900–1250*, London: Hambledon Press.

—— (1982b) 'Ottonian Government', in Leyser 1982a: 69–101.

—— (1982c) 'The tenth century in Byzantine–Western relationships', in Leyser 1982a: 103–37.

—— (1994a) (ed. T. Reuter) *Communications and Power in Medieval Europe: the Carolingian and Ottonian centuries*, London: Hambledon.

—— (1994b) 'Early medieval canon law and the beginnings of knighthood', in Leyser 1994a: 51–71.

—— (1994c) '987: the Ottonian connection', in Leyser 1994a: 165–79.

—— (1994d) 'The Ottonians and Wessex', in Leyser 1994a: 73–104.

—— (1994e) 'Early medieval warfare', in Leyser 1994a: 29–50.

—— (1994f) (ed. T. Reuter) *Communications and Power in Medieval Europe: The Gregorian revolution and beyond*, London: Hambledon.

—— (1994g) 'Frederick Barbarossa: court and country', in Leyser 1994f, 143–55.

Lindner, M. (1990) 'Die Hoftage Friedrich Barbarossas', *Jahrbuch für die Geschichte des Feudalismus* 14: 54–74.

—— (1994) 'Fest und Herrschaft unter Kaiser Friedrich Barbarossa', in E. Engel and B. Töpfer (eds) *Kaiser Friedrich Barbarossa: Landesausbau – Aspekte seiner Politik – Wirkung*, 151–70, Weimar: Hermann Böhlaus Nachfolger.

Lintzel, M. (1924) *Die Beschlüsse der deutschen Hoftage von 911 bis 1056*, Berlin: Ebering.

Lohmann, H.-E. (ed.) (1937) *Brunos Buch vom Sachsenkrieg*, MGH, Stuttgart: Hiersemann.

Loyn, H. R. (1984) *The Governance of Anglo-Saxon England: 500–1087*, London: Edward Arnold.

Matthew, D. M. (1992) *The Norman Kingdom of Sicily*, Cambridge: Cambridge University Press.

Mayer, T. (1959) 'Das deutsche Königtum und sein Wirkungsbereich', in *idem*, *Mittelalterliche Studien*, Lindau/Konstanz: Thorbecke, 28–44 (first published 1941).

Mitteis, H. (1927) *Politische Prozesse des früheren Mittelalters in Deutschland und Frankreich*, Heidelberg: Winter.

Mittellateinisches Wörterbuch (1968–97) *Mittellateinisches Wörterbuch bis zum ausgehenden 13. Jahrhundert herausgegeben von der Bayerischen Akademie der Wissenschaften*, 2: *C*, Munich: Beck.

Moraw, P. (1988) 'Die Hoffeste Kaiser Friedrich Barbarossas von 1184 und 1188', in U. Schultz (ed.) *Das Fest. Eine Kulturgeschichte von der Antike bis zur Gegenwart*, Munich: Beck, 70–83.

—— (1989) 'Hoftag und Reichstag von den Anfängen im Mittelalter bis 1806', in H.-P. Schneider and W. Zeh (eds) *Parlamentsrecht und Parlamentspraxis in der Bundesrepublik Deutschland*, Berlin: Duncker & Humblot, 3–47.

Müller-Mertens, E. (1980) *Die Reichsstruktur im Spiegel der Herrschaftspraxis Ottos des Großen. Mit historiographischen Prolegomena zur Frage Feudalstaat auf deutschem Boden, seit wann deutscher Feudalstaat?*, Berlin: Akademie-Verlag.

—— and W. Huschner (1992) *Reichsintegration im Spiegel der Herrschafspraxis Kaiser Konrads II*, Weimar: Böhlau.

Nelson, J. L. (trans.) (1991) *The Annals of Saint-Bertin*, Manchester: Manchester University Press.

—— (1992) *Charles the Bald*, London: Longman.

—— (1994) 'Kingship and empire in the Carolingian world', in R. McKitterick (ed.) *Carolingian Culture: emulation and innovation*, Cambridge: Cambridge University Press: 52–87.

—— (1996) 'The intellectual in politics: context, content and authorship in the capitulary of Coulaines, November 843', in *idem, The Frankish World, 750–900*, London: Hambledon, 155–68 (article first published 1993).

Niermeyer, J. F. (1954–76) *Mediae Latinitatis Lexicon Minus*, Leiden: Brill.

Oleson, T. (1955) *The Witanagemot in the Reign of Edward the Confessor*, Toronto: University of Toronto Press.

Ott, J. (1998) *Krone und Krönung. Die Verheißung und Verleihung von Kronen in der Kunst von der Spätantike bis um 1200 und die geistige Auslegung der Krone*, Mainz: von Zabern.

Plassmann, A. (1998) *Die Struktur des Hofes unter Friedrich I. Barbarossa nach den deutschen Zeugen seiner Urkunden*, MGH, Hannover: Hahn.

Reuter, T. (1991a) *Germany in the Early Middle Ages, c. 800–1056*, London: Longman.

—— (1991b) 'Unruhestiftung, Fehde, Rebellion, Widerstand: Gewalt und Frieden in der Politik der Salierzeit', in S. Weinfurter (ed.) *Das Reich der Salier*, 3 vols, Sigmaringen: Thorbecke, iii: 297–325.

—— (trans.) (1992) *The Annals of Fulda*, Manchester: Manchester University Press.

—— (1994) 'The medieval German *Sonderweg*? The empire and its rulers in the high middle ages', in A. J. Duggan (ed.) *Kings and Kingship in Medieval Europe*, London: King's College London, Centre for Late Antique and Medieval Studies: 179–211.

—— (1998) '*Regemque, quem in Francia pene perdidit, in patria magnifice recepit*: Ottonian ruler-representation in synchronic and diachronic comparison', in G. Althoff and E. Schubert (eds) *Herrschaftsrepräsentation im ottonischen Sachsen*, Sigmaringen: Thorbecke, 363–80.

—— (2001) '*Velle sibi fieri in forma hac*: Symbolisches Handeln im Becketstreit', in G. Althoff (ed.) *Form und Funktion politischer Kommunikation im Mittelalter*, Sigmaringen: Thorbecke, [in press].

Reynolds, S. (1997) *Kingdoms and Communities, 900–1300*, 2nd edn, Oxford: Clarendon Press.

Rosenthal, J. T. (1964) 'The public assembly under Louis the Pious', *Traditio* 20: 25–40.

Schaller, H.-M. (1974) 'Der heilige Tag als Termin mittelalterlicher Staatsakte', *Deutsches Archiv für Erforschung des Mittelalters* 26: 1–24.

Schimmelpfennig, B. (1996) *Könige und Fürsten, Kaiser und Papst nach dem Wormser Konkordat*, Munich: R. Oldenbourg.

Schmidt-Wiegand, R. (1984) 'Mallus, mallum', in A. Erler and E. Kaufmann (eds) *Handwörterbuch der deutschen Rechtsgeschichte*, 3: *List-Protonotar*, cols. 217–18, Berlin: Erich Schmidt.

Schneider, H. (1996) *Ordines de Celebrando Concilio*, MGH, Hannover: Hahn.

Schröder, I. (1980) *Die westfränkischen Synoden von 888–987 und ihre Überlieferung*, MGH, Munich: MGH.

Seyfarth, E. (1910) *Fränkische Reichsversammlungen unter Karl dem Großen und Ludwig dem Frommen*, Borna/Leipzig: Noske.

Sierck, M. (1995) *Festtag und Politik: Studien zur Tagewahl karolingischer Herrscher* (Archiv für Kulturgeschichte, Beihefte 38), Cologne: Böhlau.

Vollrath, H. (1985) *Die Synoden Englands bis 1066*, Paderborn: Schöningh.

Voss, I. (1987) *Herrschertreffen im frühen und hohen Mittelalter*, Cologne: Böhlau.

Wacker, C. (1882) *Der Reichstag unter den Hohenstaufen*, Leipzig: Veit.

Wadle, E. (1986) 'Frühe deutsche Landfrieden', in H. Mordek (ed.) *Überlieferung und Geltung normativer Texte des frühen und hohen Mittelalters*, Sigmaringen: Thorbecke, 71–94.

Waitz, G. (1880, 1882a, 1882b, 1883, 1885, 1893, 1896, 1878a, 1878b) *Deutsche Verfassungsgeschichte*, 8 vols (vol. 2 in two parts), vols 1–6, 3rd edn (vol 5 ed. K. Zeumer, vol. 6 ed. G. Seeliger), vols 7–8, 2nd edn, Berlin: Ducker & Humblot.

—— and B. von Simson (eds) (1912) *Ottonis et Rahewini Gesta Friderici I. imperatoris*, MGH, Scriptures rerum Germanicarum in usum Scholarum, Hannover: Hahn.

Wallace-Hadrill, J. M. (1962) *The Long-haired Kings and other essays in Frankish History*, London: Methuen.

Warren, W. L. (1973) *Henry II*, London: Eyre Methuen.

—— (1987) *The Governance of Norman and Angevin England: 1086–1272*, London: Edward Arnold.

Weber, H. (1962) 'Die Reichsversammlungen im ostfränkischen Reich, 840–918. Eine entwicklungsgeschichtliche Untersuchung vom karolingischen Großreich zum deutschen Reich', unpublished Ph.D. dissertation, University of Würzburg.

Weidemann, M. (1982) 'Zur Chronologie der Merowinger im 6. Jahrhundert', *Francia* 10: 471–513.

Werner, K. F. (1981) 'La Genèse des duchés en France et en Allemagne', in *Nascità dell'Europa ed Europa Carolingia: un'equazione da verificare* (Settimane di Studio del Centro Italiano di studi sull'Alto Medioevo, 27), Spoleto: Centro Italiano di studi sull'Alto Medioevo, 175–207.

Wolter, H. (1988) *Die Synoden im Reichsgebiet und in Reichsitalien von 916 bis 1056*, Paderborn: Schöningh.

Wormald, P. (1978) 'Æthelred the lawmaker', in D. Hill (ed.) *Ethelred the Unready: Papers from the Millenary Conference*, Oxford: British Archaeological Reports, 47–80.

—— (1999), *The Making of English Law: King Alfred to the Twelfth Century, 1: legislation and its limits*, Oxford: Basil Blackwell.

Zecchini, O. (1980) *Le assise di Ruggiero II.: Problemi di storia delle fonti e di diritto penale*, Naples: Nescio.

BEYOND THE *COMUNE*: THE ITALIAN CITY-STATE AND ITS INHERITANCE[1]

Mario Ascheri

SOME ASPECTS OF ITALIAN URBAN GROWTH

Cities are at the heart of European history – or certainly were in the late Middle Ages. And in Italy in particular. In Italy, uniquely perhaps, the evidence speaks for itself. Through their buildings and their art, and the studies (many of them excellent) devoted to them by historians of art and architecture, demography and the urban economy, the cities of late medieval Italy great and small are able to appeal to us still. Not that the distinction of greater and smaller counts for much in the year 2001, when Siena, Pisa, Perugia and San Gimignano are as much suffocated by international tourism as Rome, Florence, Venice or Bologna, with all of Italy's medieval cities equally afflicted for the simple reason that they are what they are, the impotent custodians of medieval Italy's art and architecture.

Established though most of them were on ancient Roman foundations, it was in the Middle Ages, and in particular between the thirteenth century and the fifteenth, that these places assumed the appearance that they retain to this day, and on the economic vitality of those years that were based the urban achievements of the so-called Renaissance era which, while other parts of Europe lagged behind, they were to accomplish without suffering serious damage to their distinctive structures. Only since the establishment of the kingdom of Italy have such centres as Rome and Florence experienced intrinsic change. Elsewhere, late medieval Italy's essential profile has managed to survive intact, and with it the memory not only of its universities but also of Dante, Petrarch and Machiavelli, its supreme geniuses.

But these are commonplaces. There must be more to be said about both the short- and the long-term consequences of the peculiar politico-institutional organisation of these places. Certainly historians, or some historians, have thought so (Burke 1986; cf. Rossi 1987). And common sense suggests that they are right, that the architectural and artistic creativity of the thirteenth to fifteenth centuries was somehow related to the political and institutional context within which it flourished. The question is, *how*?

How was it related? Was all this cultural activity no more than an expression of politico-institutional developments? Or did it possess a rationale of its own? It could be argued that art and architecture developed in the way they did because of certain unique characteristics of the culture of the age, on account of exceptional individuals, outstanding artists, and, though quite independently, the availability of the political structures of the period. The case could be made that it was only in the fifteenth century itself that politics and culture developed that symbiotic relationship which is a distinguishing feature of the Visconti–Sforza duchy of Milan or of the kingdom of Sicily under Alfonso the Magnanimous. But by then the Italian communes were already in decline. So what of the earlier period? What of the years after 1100 when the communes and the autonomous institutions they fostered were at their most flourishing, particularly in the north and centre, that part of the peninsula which to this day remains the most politically active (Putnam 1993). As Amalfi declined, the coastal cities of Venice, Pisa and Genoa engaged in colonial activity in the eastern Mediterranean in the service of the crusading movement, with the first of these playing a significant part in the establishment of the Latin Empire of Constantinople. Meanwhile landlocked Piacenza, Modena, Lucca, Siena, and Florence in particular – banker *par excellence* to both popes and kings despite the best efforts of England's kings to bankrupt it – assumed a major role in international commerce, and Milan scandalised as much as astonished Otto of Freising when the Emperor Frederick Barbarossa's chronicler chanced there upon that unnatural thing, a city governed by consuls to whom even the neighbouring nobility paid court, a city which 'even dared incur the anger of the prince, standing in no awe of his majesty' (Mierow 1953: 129).

Extolled by the Arab chroniclers and their Christian counterparts alike, the demographic vitality of these cities between the beginning of the twelfth century and the Black Death in the mid-fourteenth is well documented. So are their beauty and their wealth. All this modern scholarship recognises and accepts. What it does not is the relationship which has been alleged (or sometimes assumed) at the institutional level between the communes and the political culture of the period of which they were part, and therefore of the civilisation which nourished and embraced them. In one way or another, historians have sometimes neglected the culture of those free cities which had established themselves as communes during this period of such remarkable growth, what for convenience might be called 'communal civilisation'. Rather than waste space on an exhaustive account of the bibliography of that lost cause, however, in what follows we shall consider, albeit very briefly, what seem to be the salient characteristics of the revisionist historiography of the more recent past.

THE REDUCTIONIST INTERPRETATION OF THE COMMUNAL EXPERIENCE

First let us scrutinise the commune's social profile. Its general physiognomy is of course already familiar to us. The Italian communes were Europe's first bourgeois societies. Formed in the social image and the political likeness of the merchants who controlled them, they stood at one end of a spectrum from whose other extreme they were glowered at by the feudal nobility which everywhere else ruled the roost. Peopled by possessive individualists, themselves the harbingers of the modern capitalist ethic, the Italian communes were political societies of equals, and thus the

Figure 26.1 The citizens of Milan return home in 1167 after the devastation of their city by the Emperor Frederick Barbarossa. Bas-relief of 1171. Milan. Civiche raccolte d'Arte antica, 767.

very antithesis of feudal society with its hierarchical structures. What more natural therefore than that, while elsewhere a courtly culture and chivalric literature flourished, the commercial and secular mentality of the democratic communes should have left as its memorial such items as the Books of the Dead (*Libri di Memorie*) of the Florentine merchants?

But in fact it is not quite as simple as that (Jones 1980; Jones 1997). On closer inspection, the descriptions provided by bourgeois historians of the nineteenth century turn out to be just that: descriptions of bourgeois society *avant la lettre*. In fact, the Italian cities which fostered communes harboured all manner of unmodern horrors, clan loyalty and the desire for ennoblement included. The case of Lombardy both points the moral and adorns the tale (Keller 1979). In the Lombard communes – and the Lombard communes were most notable of them all on account of their determined resistance to Barbarossa's imperial pretensions – society was neither bourgeois nor egalitarian. On the contrary, in common with societies everywhere else at the time, it consisted of stratified social classes, clearly differentiated from each other even in law, and with the local aristocracy very much in the ascendant. Indeed, one might even go so far as to say that the Italian cities owed their very survival to the nobility of the surrounding countryside who by deserting their castles and 'civilising' themselves reinforced the lively and multifaceted society of the cities in which they took up permanent residence.

The institutional structure generally attributed to the communes has also to be called into question. Under the guise of city-states, they have regularly been hailed as victors over emperors. But this is too facile by half. The concept of the State, a modern reality which assumed fully developed form only in the eighteenth century (if then) has been applied unthinkingly to the Middle Ages when, as a matter of fact, city-states still formed part of the Romano-Germanic Empire, the empire from which they regularly sought new privileges as well as the confirmation of ancient liberties. Furthermore, when they placed themselves under the protection of the Papacy in the general rallying of Guelf forces against the Ghibellines, the communes did so purely as a means to an end, in order to recruit local assistance against a distant imperial threat to their welfare. Autonomy was as much as they could aspire to. Independence and sovereignty in the sense in which modern states may be said to be independent and sovereign did not occur to them, and did not occur to them precisely because as yet they were inconceivable. Likewise, whatever political duties one felt oneself obliged by had nothing to do with the commune in the abstract. Such loyalty as one owed was owed to one's family, whether narrowly or more widely conceived, and to the even wider allegiance with which for the time being that family was associated. But to immediate family first and foremost.

Though universalist to an extent, therefore, the mental climate of the era was grounded in group loyalty, in a group loyalty ultimately rooted in faction and family, moreover, and to that extent was by its very nature inimical to the city-state. The 'spirit of the age' was essentially monarchical, and in Italy monarchist sensibilities were constantly refreshed by the proximity of the kingdom of Sicily and the absolutist practices of a succession of Roman pontiffs. By definition, discussion of the medieval political imagination centres on the analysis of monarchical power, the power of popes and kings (Le Goff 1997: 37–42). It was no accident that it was these figures, and above all kings, who regularly featured in millenarian prophecies as the saviours of humanity at the Last Judgement. Although paradoxically it was the city that was felt to be the seat of power, in theory as much as in practice anything resembling the later republican ideology so characteristic of the modern era, with its rooted opposition to monarchy, was at best a marginal phenomenon in the Middle Ages. Modern continental historiography has erected an unbreachable wall between these two cultures and has treated them as irreconcilable because of the absolutist development which monarchy experienced on the Continent, in contrast to England where it is perfectly legitimate to speak of a hybrid 'republican monarchy'.

Among those who have stressed both the socio-economic and the politico-institutional importance of the city in Italian history, another common failing has been a failure to appreciate the sheer institutional novelty that some cities had displayed even before the development of communes had begun (Cammarosano 1998). Indeed, their 'modernity' *vis-à-vis* their counterparts elsewhere in Europe, even before the twelfth century when they were still nominally under episcopal control, raises question of substance regarding the point in time at which communes as such began to matter.

But though it may be that for a time some cities were sufficiently powerful to rank as tiny states – and states capable of gravely embarrassing emperors and others, moreover – when we turn to the other end of our period it has also to be allowed that by and large their achievement had been but ephemeral. For although the late medieval commune continued to strive for greater internal consistency and a more robust internal structure, sooner or later it suffered crisis and mutation (Chittolini 1979). Having run the communal gamut at a precociously early stage, for example, equally early (in the thirteenth century itself) the Veneto passed under the control of individuals and families such as Ezzelino da Romano and the Estensi, the denial incarnate of communal government of the *res publica* based on popular participation, or at least on that of broad social groups. And the Veneto was not unique. The same sequence of events was enacted elsewhere. In general, indeed, the commune had not yet assumed a clear institutional structure when it was supplanted by seigneurial forms of monarchic government which emptied communal forms and procedures of all real content. In order to remedy the fratricidal internal conflicts and the endemic violence of political struggle, the councils of the communes themselves were driven ever more often to confer full powers or lifetime office on military *condottieri* or members of important local families, soon to be entitled *signori* of the city, and, as such, the holders of political power.

Hence the textbook account of the succession of typical forms of government in late medieval Italian history: the communes of the twelfth and thirteenth centuries were followed in the thirteenth and fourteenth by the *signorie*, and in the fifteenth the *signorie* were swallowed up by the principalities. By the same reckoning, there occurred simultaneously the transition from the city-state (or autonomous city if one prefers) to the regional state: a state dominated either by *signori* or by princes (fourteenth-century Lombardy under the Visconti for example) or by city-republics which had invaded large areas of the surrounding territories (Venice, Florence, Siena). According to this schema, the importance of urban institutional history is reduced to a very brief period, often of no more than a hundred years beginning in the mid-twelfth century, and by the mid-thirteenth the age of the communes is being brought to a full stop, with the future lying in an entirely different direction. From this perspective, so far as the later development of the Modern State is concerned, the city-state appears at best an irrelevance, at worst an obstacle in the path of history. To their deprecation of the factionalism which lay at the very heart of the thirteenth-century city, with its struggles between nobles and *popolo* overlapping and interwoven with conflicts between Guelfs and Ghibellines, historians thus added the further and far more serious charge that the Italian city-state failed to perform the role alloted to it in the scheme of things.

And, as though that were not sufficient, there is a further accusation more or less overt in all this. The commune is ever more frequently depicted as the locus of governmental powers wielded by an aristocracy of either land or money in the twelfth century, and thereafter as the favoured environment of a political oligarchy – an oligarchy of the rich – but now, with the abandonment of the commercial tradition which had been the cities' proper occupation, of the rich whose riches lay in land. In this scenario, the term 'oligarchy' (a term with a long tradition in the history of political ideas and deplorable throughout: the Hyde to the Jekyll of aristocratic government) is used as shorthand to allude to, if not describe, a multitude of very different situations and to make the heavy and heavily charged point that in the long run communes always fell into the hands of an extremely narrow ruling elite (Bertelli 1978). The forms of consultative assembly once apparently triumphant, and once-upon-a-time celebrated as the realisation of communal 'democracy', have now been superseded. Now oligarchic rule along these lines is presented as the cruel and naked reality of what communes were ultimately all about. There was an inevitable logic to it all, it now turns out – to the extent indeed that at last the process of dismemberment of those sometime vibrant (not to say chaotically 'democratic') communes is capable of being mapped, as though in accordance with set rules of navigation, almost by reference to a mariner's chart. And oligarchy was the lode-star.

In short, the traditional account of the honoured status of the Italian city-states has been so comprehensively rubbished as to appear at best genteely naïve and at worst the detritus of a myth lacking any basis in fact. According to today's orthodoxy, the fundamental similarity – or at least analogy – between processes of state formation in the various polities of Europe at the end of the Middle Ages has rendered the notion of the city-states' uniqueness redundant. So far as the years before 1300 are concerned,

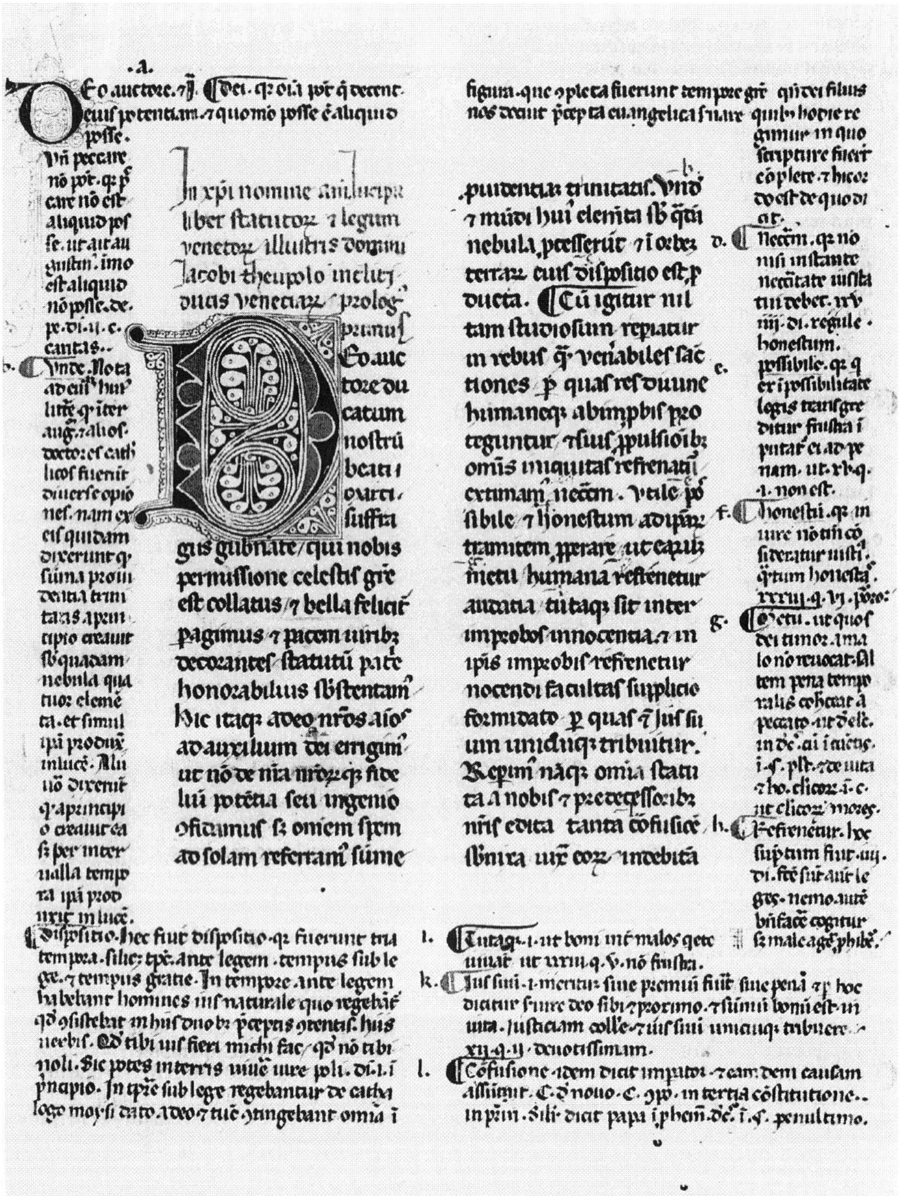

Figure 26.2 The Book of the Statutes and Laws of Venice. With its marginal glosses, this fourteenth-century codex has all the appearances of the legal or theological texts in use in universities at the time. (Compare Figure 29.1.) Venice. Biblioteca Nazionale Marciana, MS. Lat. V. 137=10453, fo. 1r.

the term 'communities' is now used to indicate societies of whatever condition, whether urban or more broadly national, in which the historian's stethoscope is able to discern so much as a murmur of assent to collective belonging. And all these communities are considered to have been very much of a muchness (Reynolds 1997). And quite possibly there is a certain coherence to this account of the matter.

But it is not the last word on the subject. Even within a European Community which has so distorted and debased the meaning of the word, it may still be permissible to disagree with the fashionable consensus on the subject of what 'communities' were in medieval Europe and to put the case for the communal city-states of medieval Italy as a peculiar and exceptional event in Europe's history. And this will be attempted in the next section of this chapter. Before embarking upon that task, however, perhaps what ought to be the obvious should be stated, namely that the greatest risk any historian runs is the risk of importing into his account of the period with which he is concerned the preoccupations of periods nearer his own. Of importing, and thereby distorting. In the present case, issues such as those of Italian political unity, Italian national identity, and such Italian peculiarities as may be thought to have survived the benevolent influence of the aforesaid European Community will need especially to be looked out for – because if to students of the subject observing it from the outside all this appears a 'problem', for those whose history it is it is very much more than that. It is live tissue.

IN SEARCH OF COMMUNAL DISTINCTIVENESS

Why do Italy's late medieval cities deserve to be regarded as remarkable, then, and not only in the Italian but also in the wider European context? After all, Europe was not short of cities brimming with interest for students of demography, economic development and art. Italy herself boasted Palermo, Naples and Rome. Take Rome, for example. Rome's history was not without its communal interludes. In the mid-twelfth century the battle-cry there was 'renovatio senatus', and in the fourteenth the place experienced the extraordinary effect of Cola di Rienzo, the tribune who strove to evoke its ancient past. Yet interludes is what these were. For the most part, the presence of the papal Curia deprived Rome of the oxygen which independent government needed. Rome was a city with a sovereign, and not the sort of city we have in mind when we speak of communal civilisation in its true sense.

Part of the problem here is terminological. In a period in which political vocabulary was consistent and unitary, the word 'commune' was employed in various situations whose politico-institutional contours had absolutely nothing in common. The rural commune, for example, whether castle or village, was one thing. Enjoying more or less complete administrative autonomy, and as often as not establishing itself at the request of the *signore* of the territory in which it was located, the rural commune developed as an administrative entity which conveyed requests to the *signore* and if necessary organised protests, thereby providing the *signore* with a licensed intermediary and agent to turn to when there was tribute to be collected or collective responsibility exercised regarding the movement and custody of wanted criminals, for example.

Altogether different was the situation of the city-states as they emerged from their communal chrysalis during their struggle against Barbarossa and Frederick II. Here the case was not just one of periodic uprisings provoked by particularly grotesque abuses of seigneurial power, or by hunger. From as early as the mid-eleventh century when, with society anyway poised on the threshold of tumultuous developments, Gregory VII had turned Milan's social turmoil to the advantage of his own reform programme, the conflict between Papacy and Empire had worked to discredit both as effective institutions for the government of urban society (Tabacco 1989: 221). As these cosmic struggles continued, the awareness dawned among particular groups of citizens – citizens of diverse social rank and standing in a variety of different relationships with the local authorities of bishop, count and marquis – that the time had come for them to take the government of their cities into their own hands even more purposefully than had been done during the tenth-century crisis of the Italian kingdom. The cultural resources were there, so was the wealth, and as conflict with the Empire continued such convictions strengthened, sustained by an urban culture firmly rooted in a laity whose growing sense of self-assurance stemmed especially from its monopoly of the provision of lawyers and notaries: the masters of the written word whose technical expertise serviced the institutions of the new rationalism and provided the mass of documentation, both legal and historical, which it depended upon for its very survival.

Thus certain cities of the north and centre, including some with no tradition of episcopal government, came to lord it over the surrounding countryside, exercise close control of the social life within the walls by means of prolific legislation, and enter into military and diplomatic agreements with other cities on an equal basis. As a demonstration of the weight of their authority they even called upon their citizens to make the supreme sacrifice. The adage *pro patria mori* became current in the thirteenth-century communal world precisely because the city was the only identifiable repository of political allegiance: a fact of city life, or rather of city-state life, which deserves emphasis.

Of course, even a city in political crisis continued to call itself a commune, whether when independent or, as was increasingly often the case as the thirteenth century advanced, when subject to a *signore* or other more powerful urban neighbour which, following the pattern set by the typical city of the first phase of communal growth, after conquering its own historical hinterland (*comitatus* or county) proceeded to prey on other free communes and their respective *comitatus*.

The 'city-state' was a particular species within the broader genus 'commune' whose right to its name, a term hallowed by long-established historiographical custom, it would be futile to challenge. In the absence of any contemporary technical term, it is hard to see why for clarity's sake a modern equivalent should not be used – particularly one whose derivation from the technical vocabulary of Greece and Rome makes it especially appropriate. If it is allowable to ascribe to the Middle Ages the anachronistic concept of civic *autonomy* (a nineteenth-century lawyer's term inconceivable in the medieval period and accordingly absent from its sources) why should we not also speak of 'state' with reference to those communes, but *only those communes*, which were masters of their own territory and sole arbiters of peace and war, justice and taxation?

It matters not that the word 'state' in today's sense of a public legal entity cropped up only very rarely in thirteenth- and fourteenth-century usage – although it is not without significance that it was in communal Italy that it did so. The fact is that at the time there was no need to invent the word. The all-purpose term *res publica* designated every type of state apparatus, from the Empire downwards. The Roman sources – which as things which people actually *read* were the objects of intense study at the time – had already spoken of the '*res publica imperii*'. In contemporary sources the word *status* was normally used in the sense of 'condition', as in 'the peaceful state of the commune' and suchlike.

Only when the military and diplomatic struggle between the commune of Florence and Visconti Milan assumed learned overtones, thanks to the writings of the humanists who employed their pens in the service of one or other antagonist, was the idea elaborated of two distinct, systematically opposed civilisations in, respectively, the state governed by the 'people' and the state governed by a single prince, in this case Giangaleazzo Visconti. A century later this opposition found expression in the opening lines of Niccolo Machiavelli's *The Prince*: 'All states, all the dominions which have held sway over men and all which still do, have been or are either republics or principalities'[2] – though Machiavelli's dyad, linked as it was specifically to the Italian situation, was unusual enough for Jean Bodin to ignore it and continue to use *res publica* in its general sense of 'state'.

There is therefore no need to apologise for speaking of 'states' and 'city-states' in a late medieval urban context, nor even for the use of inverted commas. Anglo-American historians took the conceptual plunge years ago, reflecting a less doctrinaire and more realistic approach than their Italian colleagues as well as exhibiting far greater alertness to the presence of federal features in the history of the Italian, German and Swiss polities (Clarke 1926; Waley 1988). The massive influence of Papacy and Empire between the twelfth and the fifteenth centuries should not obscure the fact that their more-or-less legitimate and historically rooted universalist aspirations were perfectly capable of coexisting with feet-on-the-ground local powers. They were not in constant collision with them, and even when they were the clash was not one of diametrically opposed principles. Indeed, it should be recognised that it was precisely the threat of an over-mighty imperial and/or papal presence in Italy which gave birth to the city-states, and determined much of their subsequent activities.

Anyway, the business of the governments of these city-states was to rule effectively and efficiently, not to theorise after the manner of university professors. Why waste effort in issuing formal denials of the imperial authority or the Church's temporal claims when the negation of both in real terms was already a *fait accompli*? The function of ruling elites was not to issue proclamations but to declare and defend their city's independence and sovereignty. Why not connive at the 'federal' aspirations of medieval universalism (Dante's *De monarchia* springs to mind) if that facilitated the stratified coexistence of more than one political power within the same territory? It is only an exaggerated as well as an anachronistic sense of deference to late-nineteenth-century theories of the state and national sovereignty that continues to prompt students to scour the past for a set of problems wholly alien to the Middle Ages – and to the *communal* Middle Ages in particular which had, after all, brought

Figure 26.3 Painted cover of the book of Finances of the City of Siena, 1385. The city's governors are represented linked by a cord – i.e. concordant – with its sovereignty symbolically personified. Siena. Museo dell'Archivio di Stato, Biccherna 19.
Photo: Fabio Lensini.

to light those Roman law texts whence the very notion of the possible coexistence of the prince's general law and local laws specific to individual cities was actually derived.

Projecting the preoccupations of the nineteenth-century state into the past means squeezing that past into a Procrustean corset wholly unsympathetic to its actual contours. Consider the direction in which the European Union is moving, or indeed the international community at large, with judges competent to sentence states for international crimes and 'allied' interventions in their internal affairs, all in accordance with a world-view for which the globalisation of ecological, military and economic issues seems to guarantee a bright future.

It is not just a question of vocabulary. The concept of 'city-state' cloaks problems of substance, the foremost of which is the need to accustom ourselves to view the commune as an entity endowed with legal personality well before the word 'state' and the university theory of legal persons had been properly formulated. Like the 'regnum', the commune operated and was the possessor of public and private rights comfortably in advance of the emergence in the thirteenth century of the idea of the '*persona ficta*' (Reynolds 1995). Much the same is true of other fundamental notions of public law which had been integral to legal and institutional terminology for centuries before the *eruditi* identified and labelled all their possible implications.

The process of identifying the Italian city-state also brings to the surface a presupposition whose normal habitat is at the murkiest depths of historical perception: namely that of the process of state-construction, and hence also human progress, towards an ever-more refined and rational statehood (itself a conglomeration of ideas and values whose validity even the most cursory consideration of the events of the past century must bring into question); that this process was a one-way operation. We are asked to subscribe to the following broad-brush scenario.

The twelfth-century commune-in-arms was a kind of sworn association with aspirations to the exercise of public power. The thirteenth century witnessed the beginnings of the realisation of these aspirations within the commune's territorial ambit by means of its imposition of monopolistic control over certain functions, especially fiscal functions. Come the fourteenth and the commune has put behind it, once and for all, its original associative nature as a coalition of factions. Courtesy of the *signore* it has begun to 'turn territorial' (the question this begs regarding its earlier supposed characteristics hardly needs drawing out). Finally, in the fifteenth – the century of the Renaissance – it transformed itself into a 'regional state': a regional state which might even go so far as to proclaim itself sovereign, as, for example, the Commune (now with a capital C, be it noted) of Florence did when claiming the right to defend itself from the crime of high treason, the '*crimen laesae maiestatis*' (save that sometimes its power in the territory was more circumscribed than before). And now, at last (and not before time) we have arrived at the Origins of the modern state, or as some would have it, of the State Full Stop: at that great Beginning whose maturity was to be marked by the momentous ejaculation of *la Grande Révolution*, and whose culture has continued to dictate historiographical categories forever after because that Event provided a break with the past, a break which the historians have consented to even though in fact it was not quite as clearcut as the less craven revolutionaries themselves could have wished.

That is one view of the matter. If, however, we were instead to acknowledge that in 1100, or at any rate by the time of the first really effective uprisings against the German Empire, the sovereign late-medieval city-states were already entities different from today's sovereign states – and which of the states represented at the United Nations in the year 2001 would we be prepared to propose as a normative state anyway? – then we would at last be in a position to historicise the state (or State) *comme soi*. In fact, we need no longer waste time calibrating, and labouring to establish just when and by what stages medieval polities either progressed towards, hovered inertially around, or actually regressed from some ontologically secure and immutable statehood, a statehood which eventually came to be considered modern but which today appears decidedly vulnerable to intrusive international intervention both public and private. The state is simply any public organisation which organises society, in one period in harmony with that society, in another in conflict with it, now cooperating with private individuals, now towering above them like a monstrous Leviathan, by turns the source of vital help and insatiable tyranny, or any one of the myriad other possibilities between those extremes.

And this approach carries an additional bonus. For it now becomes possible to examine the different permutations of the relationship between the city-state and the Church and/or Empire, those two international, supra-state entities which assumed their most concrete and tangible form in the various attempts they made to put themselves at the head of federations or confederations. (Again, it will be noted, the vocabulary used to describe those complex phenomena is not to be found in the political lexicon of the time.)

It is no argument against the statehood of the sovereign communes that they reached a *modus vivendi* with Empire and Church, nor that under certain circumstances these universal authorities might issue both general and specific privileges to local governments, and the latter answer to the name of 'vicariates', which was tantamount to an acknowledgement of their superiority. As students of modern international law well know, the existence or otherwise of the state is not determined by the fact of recognition or non-recognition on the part of an outside authority which may be no more than an expression of political opportunism. Rather, it depends upon the degree of effective control exercised by the government in question. Did England become any less of a state than it had been before when King John swore fealty to Pope Innocent III in May 1213?

When communal legislation did encounter limits, the limits it ran up against were usually those principles reckoned to constitute *Libertas ecclesiae*, the 'freedom of the Church', limits these days exclusively associated with 'the marketplace', but which in the case of the medieval Church meant the sum total of a whole complex of fiscal and jurisdictional exemptions: exemptions always fiercely defended if not always with total success – though since they certainly didn't derive either from the Empire or from the learned 'ius commune', why it was that the 'effective' defence of these principles devolved upon the Papacy and the local churches is a moot point. Regarding all social problems the communes came up with the most wide-ranging and far-reaching legislation known to the medieval West. By means of their 'statuta' and 'provisiones' they intruded without let or hindrance (that is to say, without anything remotely approximating to parliamentary consent) into society's most intimate corners, systematically encroaching in fine authoritarian style into areas which only centuries later other kinds of regime would penetrate, including such jealously defended preserves of the Church as marriage and usury (Wolf 1996: 69ff.).

This degree of interventionism leads on to the consideration of another question of the first importance to anyone interested in the structures of public life and therefore the peculiar institution of the city-state. This is the question of medieval and in particular of communal 'constitutionalism'. Here again current historiographical fashion, especially in continental Europe, is to dissociate the medieval experience from more recent and from contemporary preccupations in particular. Recent written constitutions (and particularly those protected by constitutional courts) are considered as having made a qualitative leap forward into the modern state and a clean break with all that had gone before. Presumably therefore, the proper purpose of governments and parliaments is the realisation of what certain given constitutional principles more or less explicitly demand.

This is not the place to enter into the specific merits and demerits of such politico-legal ideologies: ideologies which sanctify the present and whose high priests can only bring themselves to look the past square in the eye when the eye has been certified dead. Because the principles informing written constitutions are of such a general nature they are always susceptible to the attention of lawyers and their sophistical interpretations – all in accordance (alas) with medieval precedent. And, sure enough, even in monarchical and princely settings we find signs of precocious constitutional forces at work concerned with such issues as political participation, the fundamental articulation of public authority, and relationships between powers and between powers and those subject to them. Such were the agendas of the so-called 'pacts' or 'contracts of *signoria*' which assumed so many and such various forms during the Middle Ages, and of which Magna Carta is the most notable example only because it has proved the most durable.

In the communes too we encounter equally lively constitutional initiatives, prompted by the twin needs of organising the political and administrative authorities and providing the citizenry with protection against those authorities. It is just that these initiatives have been forgotten or minimised by comparison with what occurred in the nation-state, either because of their complexity and extreme variability, or because the process of local differentiation and fragmentation has made the identification of common characteristics virtually impossible. The fact that the communes/city-states were defeated in the long term may also help to explain why they have not enjoyed the historiographical respect which the (once) triumphant nation-state has been accorded.

Be that as it may, it deserves to be remembered that in the case of some communes constitutive and constitutional agreements of this sort served as their foundational title-deeds, no less. In the life of the communes, moreover, dispositions such as these were absolutely typical, representing as they did the most truly political norms of their statutes. In a society so deferential to the book and the written word, the imperative sense that public life should be conducted within a conventional framework of legal certitude might even result in the elevation of certain statutory norms to irreformable status, thus setting them above the usual run of legislation. In order to ensure their strict and invariable observance, these '*statuta precisa*', so-called, enjoyed immunity from legal interpretation, just as today article 139 of the Italian constitution declares the republican character of the state immutable, thus imposing an entirely exceptional restriction on future legislation. In some cases, at Genoa for example, these sacrosanct political statutes (*regulae*) were distinguished by name from the others (*capitula*) so as to indicate their unique constitutional function – though in fact they were not spared the effects of political change and ironically it tended to be the *capitula* that remained unaffected over many decades.

This is not all. The communes invariably operated within an ideology analogous to that of the eighteenth-century *Rechtsstaat*, and roughly equivalent to the English *rule of law*, insisting on the rigid separation of political powers from judicial and administrative powers and precise definition of the respective competences of the various public organs in order to protect the citizen and guarantee the impartiality of the administration. A consequence of this requirement, observable even then, was that tendency to legislative bloating which has marked the Italian experience of statehood ever since, and which is lamented on all sides today without adequate recognition of its deep historical roots.

To the theorists of communal government, posterity is indebted for the survival of the fundamental principle of the citizen's participation in the legislative process of the *polis*. From the early thirteenth century current civic practice combined with the legacy of various cultural traditions, in particular the Ciceronian and later the Aristotelian, to hammer out ideas and practices to whose novelty and importance recent students of the history of political ideas have paid proper tribute (Skinner 1978).

The widely shared conviction that the statute of the commune was a specific local pact on which the communal *universitas*[3] was based tended to promote the ideology of legality. It also helps to account for the fact that the scope of such statutes embraced the liberty of the commune as well as its constitution. It was natural therefore that whenever the political balance (*regimen*) changed the first act of the new government was to review the existing statutes. The city-state too – Venice or Florence for example – immediately it achieved dominance in a newly conquered territory would re-cast the statutes of the place in accordance with its own politico-legal prescriptions.

It follows that the sections of statutes relating to public law have every right to be treated as constitutional history, even if their wide dispersion, mutability and multiplicity make them difficult to study. Paradoxically, it is their very richness that is responsible for the comparative neglect they have suffered. Though it is certainly easier to speak of the constitutional experience of monarchies, and of the English in particular, it would be a grave mistake to forget that parliaments and councils were the source of legitimacy for communal government and communal life too, or to consign communal practices of government and assembly to oblivion. The city-states were the precursors of the majoritarian principle. In order to delimit the activities of different governmental agencies they introduced systems of checks and balances. They pioneered measures designed to depoliticise judges and the administration of justice and to moderate the excesses of their officials. The legislation they introduced confronted issues as diverse and as thorny as the conduct of elections, rotation of public office, the incompatibility of different offices, and the drawing of lots for them. And in all this activity they involved the enfranchised citizenry to a degree never previously conceived and in all likelihood never since (Ascheri 2000).

Against this, however, it has to be conceded that the situation of those beyond the walls of the city-state was one of systematic oppression. Indeed, it was the very misery of the inhabitants of the *contado* surrounding it that enabled the commune to afford its egalitarian luxury. Glaring though the contradiction is, however, it can hardly be said to provide today's more or less democratic societies with justification for mounting a moral high horse from which to sit in judgment. After all, does not our own First World, for all its assertions of international brotherhood and claims to universal solidarity, similarly depend for the maintenance of its credentials on the identical and equally deliberate exclusion of the inhabitants of the Third from the privileges it enjoys?

As to oligarchic manipulation, the charge so commonly levied against the city-states, it has to be wondered whether they were ever even capable of it. Venice apart, where a relatively stable nobility emerged, most of them were too politically rocky to allow for such a development. Though they are as profound as they are diverse, the political and cultural causes of this rockiness are all more or less related to the shared conviction that the city's inhabitants were entitled to enjoy equality of political opportunity. This was certainly the case in the thirteenth century. And, that apart, any such blanket characterisation has to be rejected if only because it lumps together and confuses the political dynamics of so many very different places. Consider, for example, the diversity of fourteenth- and fifteenth-century Florence, Milan, Venice and Siena. For that matter, consider the development of these places in modern times. Historians who pontificate on the subject of oligarchies of long ago are wont to neglect the stench beneath their own nostrils. They too readily forget the ease with which, under cover of their democratic trappings, contemporary states and would-be federations of states continue to harbour little colonies of political limpets who have grown on to their offices over decades: contemporary crustaceans whose oligarchic relationships one with another might even be described as feudal – if only the implicit oaths by which they are bound were in the public domain.

The fact is that not only did the concept of a city structured as a *universitas* conjure up visions of the commune as a political entity with its own physiognomy, distinct from its separate members, and hence the idea of the legal person as depicted in such authorised (and visible) frescoes as Ambrogio Lorenzetti's celebrated *Buon Governo* in the Palazzo Pubblico at Siena. It also implied an idea of equal participation in the government of the city by people whose relationship with each other was by very reason of such common participation best conceived as horizontal rather than vertical. Indiscriminate use of the term oligarchy tends to divert attention from the most notable feature of the entire communal experience, namely the conviction that political power derives its legitimacy from below, from every social order. And with that goes the related idea that concern for the common good, which takes precedence over the good of the individual citizens, is the affair of the *universitas* in the persons of its representatives.

In the face of a Europe by then for the most part assuming a feudal, hierarchical, vertical structure, and moulded to the monarchical requirements and habits of the governments of popes and emperors, kings and princes, the Italian cities – breaking ranks as they so obviously did with this pattern of things – were a source of scandal, each in never-ending competition with every other for the best works of art in order to affirm the *honor civitatis* to further its own prestige. Against every theory of society conceptualised as a tripartite ranking of warriors, priests and labourers, against the social reality of estates crystallised in parliaments, the city-state offered the concrete republican alternative on which the ancient Roman sources, both legal and otherwise, had discoursed. Its focus was the citizens, and in particular the members of those families which, behaving to each other within the city as the city behaved to its own neighbours, vied with each other in the building of grand palaces in celebration both of themselves and of the city. The culture of the city-state, which had to be prepared at a moment's notice to sacrifice people and wealth in order to defend itself and embark upon necessary conquests, allowed groups not traditionally called upon to join the government of the commonwealth or *res publica*, and feel as well as prove themselves more effective and more capable in power than the authorities who claimed to have been called by God. If the implications of all that the city-state represented are not understood, and the uniqueness of its contribution to Europe's collective consciousness is neglected, the sum-total of the history of European political thought and political praxis will be that much diminished.

Any account of the matter which belittles the experience of the medieval Italian city-state will necessarily finally end up by erasing this uniquely important cultural and politico-institutional element from the record altogether. To return to the question with which we began, therefore, the question of the relationship of the cultural activity of late-medieval Italy to its politico-institutional structures. The extraordinary architectural and artistic richness of the cities of northern and central Italy probably did derive cultural and material sustenance from the political and institutional exaltation they experienced in the shadow of their sovereignty. So too of course did Niccolò Machiavelli, within whose works those unaware of the bright future they were to have elsewhere suppose the medieval republican tradition to lie entombed. Towards the beginning of that tradition, however, there are the words of Dante's teacher to be considered. According to Brunetto Latini, there were three types of lordship. 'The first is that of kings, the second is where those of the better quality rule, the third is where the *communes* rule, and the third is by far the best of them.'[4]

SOME REASONS FOR AMNESIA

And yet all that the city-state stood for has largely been forgotten. Why? The reasons are not far to seek. For one thing, by the time that the Dutch, English, American and French were seeking respectable role-models for their modes of republicanism the Italian experiment had collapsed, so that apart from a brief nod in the direction of Machiavelli they all harked back to the pioneering ancients instead. Moreover, the achievements of the Swiss case of the small-scale *patria*, modelled on the Italian city-states and comparable in importance to those of the large nation-states, have remained very much on the margins of historical reflection. In modern Italy meanwhile, urban administration had degenerated to the aristocracy's advantage. Suffice it to recall Montesquieu's oft-quoted account of the sclerotic condition of eighteenth-century Venice, Genoa and Lucca, by then the only republics still surviving (Derathé 1973: i. 19–22, 170–1). These were hardly beacons of civilisation fit to serve as political or legal models.

The republican and egalitarian values of the thirteenth-century city-state which were later to become the object of universal aspiration fell victim over the next two hundred years to the ambitions of a predatory nobility. Of what followed for Italy – its conversion into a Franco-Hispanic battleground and the decay of the succeeding centuries – the results are still with us today in the shape of its 'national' question and its endemic incapacity, common to all political groupings because so deeply embedded in the country's remote past, to transcend local and sectional interests and loyalties in the service of the common good: that *bonum* of which the medieval city-states developed the first theoretical expression in the West.

Insistence on the primacy of the common good over private interest was in time transformed into a situation in which particular cities enjoyed a privileged position, political power was exercised by particular groups, and those excluded from a place in the sun were treated with contempt. All these tendencies had been latent in the city-state which even at its healthiest had imbued its ruling elites with a statist and interventionist mentality fostered by the omnipotence of political authority, an economy too frequently in public control, and naïve legislative voluntarism, and all of them were in turn passed on to unified Italy. They are with us still. The 'civic spirit' itself with its concomitant abstraction 'citizen' engendered the self-image of the city as a culturally homogeneous monolith capable of absorbing and abating its internal social conflicts, thereby encouraging a remarkable degree of social harmony, a process materially assisted by 'modern' welfare systems organised by those secular and ecclesiastical corporations which were most conspicuous in promoting the ideal of urban unity. But this same self-image also carried the seeds of the city-state's destruction. For, on the one hand, it provided the ruling classes with a refuge amenable to that state of satiated somnolence and acquiescence in their impoverishment which accounts in large part for the congenital weakness of contemporary Italian capitalism and, on the other, by eroding communal commitment to the city-state's contractual (and anyway debatable) ethos, it instilled a spirit of general resignation to the omnipotence of the public power, lay and ecclesiastical, and a stupefying willingness to accept the inefficiency and caprice of the state.

This said, however, and with due acknowledgement to the negative aspects of the communal inheritance, we must avoid the pitfall of reading history backwards. For in their own epoch, vigorous and dynamic on every level, the thirteenth- and fourteenth-century city-states provided Italy with the one true revolution in its entire history: a fact regularly ignored by modern students of the subject preoccupied with modern concerns.[5] The unwitting victims of their own teleology, these students denounce the policentric tendency evident in the cities of central and northern Italy today as the sinister agent of local particularism sworn to thwart the already problematic quest for national identity (Galli della Loggia 1998: 67ff.). In the same spirit, in their admiration for the 'culture of the state' said to have flourished in the thirteenth-century kingdom of Sicily and evinced by its secular opposition to the pretensions of the Church, they deplore the 'campanilismo' of the communes of the time.

How heavily the present weighs upon us as we labour to reconstruct the past! Is it too much to suggest that Italians over the past century and a half would have had less difficulty in imagining themselves as a nation if only they had acknowledged what is owed to the city-states: the greatest, the most original and the most historically influential creation of the Italian Middle Ages, and for that matter probably the Middle Ages' one and only genuinely 'Italian' initiative.

NOTES

1 The author and editors are indebted to Magnus Ryan for his assistance with the translation of this chapter.

2 'Tutti li Stati, tutti e' dominii che hanno avuto et hanno imperio sopra gli uomini, sono stati e sono o Repubbliche o Principati': *Il Principe*, chap. 1.

3 The closest though still inadequate English equivalent would be 'corporation'.

4 'Seignouries sont de iii manieres, l'une est des rois, la seconde est des bons, la tierce est des communes, laquelle est la trés millour entre ces autres': *Tresor*, VIII. 44 (Carmody 1948: 211).

5 See however Rosenstock-Huessy 1938: 562.

REFERENCES

Ascheri, M. (2000) *Siena nella storia*, Cinisello Balsamo: Silvana.

Bertelli, S. (1978) *Il potere oligarchico nella Stato-città medioevale*, Florence: La Nuova Italia.

Burke, P. (1986) 'City-states', in J. A. Hall (ed.), *States in History*, Oxford: Basil Blackwell, 137–53.

Cammarosano, P. (1998) *Nobili e re. L'Italia dell'alto medioevo*, Rome and Bari: Laterza.

Carmody, F. J. (ed.) (1948) *Brunetto Latini: Livres du Tresor*, Berkeley CA.: University of California Press.

Chittolini, G. (1979) *La formazione dello Stato regionale e le istituzioni del contado*, Turin: Einaudi.

Clarke, M. V. (1926) *The Medieval City-state. An Essay on Tyranny and Federation in the Later Middle Ages*, London: Methuen.

Derathé, R. (ed.) (1973) *Montesquieu. L'Esprit des lois*, 2 vols, Paris: Éds Garnier Frères.

Galli della Loggia, E. (1998) *L'identità italiana*, Bologna: Il Mulino.

Jones, P. (1980) *Economia e società nell'Italia medievale*, Turin: Einaudi.

—— (1997) *The Italian City-State. From Commune to Signoria*, Oxford: Clarendon Press.

Keller, H. (1979) *Adelsherrschaft und städtische Gesellschaft in Oberitalien. 9. bis 12. Jahrhundert*, Tübingen: Niemeyer.

Le Goff, J. (1997) 'L'immaginario medievale', in *Lo spazio letterario del Medioevo*, I: *Il Medioevo latino*, IV: *L'attualizzazione del testo*, Rome: Salerno, 11–42

Mierow, C. C. (trans.) with R. Emery (1953) *The Deeds of Frederick Barbarossa by Otto of Freising and his Continuator, Rahewin*, New York: Columbia University Press.

Putnam, R. D., with R. Leonardi and R. Y. Nanetti (1993) *Making Democracy Work: Civic Traditions in Modern Italy*, Princeton, N.J.: Princeton University Press.

Reynolds, S. (1995) 'The history of the idea of incorporation or legal personality: a case of fallacious teleology', in S. Reynolds, *Ideas and Solidarities of the Medieval Laity*, Aldershot: Variorum.

—— (1997) *Kingdoms and Communities in Western Europe 900–1300* (2nd edn), Oxford: Clarendon Press.

Rosenstock-Huessy, E. (1938) *Out of Revolution. The Autobiography of Western Man*, New York: W. Morrow & Co.

Rossi, P. (ed.) (1987) *Modelli di città. Strutture e funzioni politiche*, Turin: Einaudi.

Skinner, Q. (1978) *The Foundations of Modern Political Thought. The Renaissance*, Cambridge: Cambridge University Press.

Tabacco, G. (1989) *The Struggle for Power in Medieval Italy*, Cambridge: Cambridge University Press.

Waley, D. (1988) *The Italian City-Republics* (3rd edn), London and New York: Longman.

Wolf, A. (1996) *Die Gesetzgebung in Europa 1100–1500. Zur Entstehung der Territorialstaaten*, Munich: Beck.

TIMBUKTU AND EUROPE: TRADE, CITIES AND ISLAM IN 'MEDIEVAL' WEST AFRICA

Timothy Insoll

In the present company, demeaning the word *medieval* by encasing it in inverted commas is bound to appear bad form. But to admit the implied offence would be to beg the question of what all that follows is all about. And in justice to the subject of this chapter it has to be done. For while Western Europe was settling into its Middle Age West Africa was somewhere in its Iron stage, somewhere between its Middle and its Later stages (opinions on the matter vary). Yet it was very much more than a mere ghost at Western Europe's medieval feasts, those feasts whose tables it did so much to adorn.

So the invitation to the great states and urban centres of the Sahelian fringe to join in this medieval jamboree is warmly to be welcomed. For these regions just off the edge of medieval Europe's medieval map are all too little known about, crucial though they were for servicing the economy of Muslim North Africa by supplying it not only with gold and ivory but also with the slaves upon which its entire social structure depended. Camel caravans and slave coffles plied the trade routes across the Sahara which served to link the trade centres of the Western Sahel, the name given to the semi-desertic edge of the Sahara, with the major towns and cities of North Africa, Spain and Egypt (Figure 27.1). (The point having been made, hereafter the inverted commas will be dispensed with).

The Sahel, the main focus of discussion here, is a transitional zone between the Sahara and the more thickly wooded Sudannic savanna, and in the Sahel, rainfall, though still sparse, is more plentiful than in the Saharan zone. Cram-cram grass, acacia type thorn trees, and, alongside the River Niger, the principal watercourse in the region, Doum palms, are the characteristic vegetation of the Sahel. Below the Sahel lie the grassland and wooded or Guinea savannas, and below these the forest zone, before the Atlantic coast of West Africa is reached (Trimingham 1959: 1–3). The Sahel is home to a diverse range of peoples, nomadic pastoralists such as the Tuareg, Moors, and Fulani, sedentary farmers such as the Songhai, and Soninke, and more specialised groups such as the Bozo and Sorko who make their living from the River Niger (Rouch 1953; Nicolaisen 1963).

The history of the Sahelian trade centres and the empires to which they belonged were in part recorded by historians and geographers writing in Arabic in North Africa especially between the ninth and the fourteenth centuries of the Christian era

Figure 27.1 Map indicating the principal places mentioned and the trans-Saharan trade routes.

(Levtzion and Hopkins 1981). These sources are of great use in facilitating our understanding of many aspects of life in the medieval Western Sahel but they are not without their problems, principally because their content is frequently coloured by the world view of their authors – literate educated men who were describing societies very different from their own, predominantly black, and importantly (at least until conversions to Islam increased among the general population from the twelfth to the thirteenth century), animist. Moreover, many of these historical and geographical works were compiled with little regard to their original sources.

Incorporating and embellishing second- or third-hand accounts (Trimingham 1962: 2), they were frequently written far from the area which they purported to describe, in cities such as Cairo, Kairouan and Marrakesh for example (Insoll 1994).

To correct and supplement both these Arabic sources and the local oral traditions and chronicles for information on the societies and peoples of the Western Sahel, scholars have turned to archaeology. Archaeological research, as will become apparent in what follows, has provided information on many aspects of life given only cursory attention in the written historical sources. Furthermore, archaeological evidence has fundamentally altered our understanding of the origins of the trade centres and states in the Sahel, by revealing that these were indigenous foundations rather than colonies established by Muslim Arab or Berber traders from North Africa as was previously thought (e.g. Mauny 1961). Such approaches reflect what R.J. and S.K. McIntosh have termed the 'Arab stimulus paradigm' (1988: 146), according to which all major developments within West African complex societies are to be attributed to outside influences, arriving from the north via trans-Saharan trade, and urbanism and state development to outside 'helping hands' usually of North African or Near Eastern origin. Archaeological evidence from various sites has now largely discredited such theories. It is now recognised that urbanism, for example, was developed locally towards the beginning of the Christian era, as was trade in an inter-regional context. It was to these trade patterns that long-distance trans-Saharan commerce was attached at a later date. The events of the medieval period, the heyday of trans-Saharan trade and of flourishing cities on the very edge of the Sahara, had their origins in these pre-existing indigenous foundations.

THE MEDIEVAL EMPIRES, TRADE CENTRES, AND THE GOLD TRADE

The existence of states, empires and trade centres within this region has been referred to, but they have yet to be given an identity. The first major power of note which grew from as yet little understood origins was the Empire of Ghana, not to be confused with the modern nation of this name, a historical allusion to the same polity, situated far away in southern Mauritania and northern Mali (Figure 27.1). The origins of medieval Ghana can probably be placed in the mid-first millennium AD. It was at the height of its power between the ninth and eleventh centuries. The capital of the Empire of Ghana has never been located, though the traders' town, which, according to the Arabic historical sources, was attached to it has been identified with the site of Koumbi Saleh in southern Mauritania (Berthier 1997).

This pattern of double settlement, one for the Muslim merchants and their followers and the other for the local ruler and his people, is a common one in the 'first-contact' situation in this region, where the two groups met for the first time. At Gao, another of the major Sahelian trade centres, later to develop into the capital of the Songhai empire (discussed below), twin settlements also existed (Insoll 1996; Insoll 1997). Such settlement patterning can hardly be said to be unique to the medieval Western Sahel, and is an understandable phenomenon where two culturally and ethnically different groups enter into close proximity with one another, frequently for the purposes of trade (Dolukhanov [1996: 189] provides a similar example among the Slavs and Vikings during the medieval period). Whether Koumbi Saleh was in fact the traders' town attached to the capital of Ghana is unproved as no trace of its twin has ever been found. It is altogether more probable that the capital of Ghana shifted over time (see for example Togola 1996; R.J. McIntosh 1998), as the later capitals of the Ethiopian rulers on the other side of Africa would do, and that thus Koumbi Saleh represents no more than the remains of a trade centre without any especial political significance.

The Empire of Ghana prospered through trade, especially the gold trade. al-Idrīsī, writing in the mid-twelfth century, describes the king of Ghana tethering his horse to a 'brick of gold' (Levtzion and Hopkins 1981: 110), a brick which grew in weight from some 30 pounds in al-Idrīsī's day to a ton when Ibn Khaldūn reported its later sale in the fourteenth century (Bovill 1968: 81). Even allowing for dramatic licence, it is undeniable that large quantities of gold were available in West Africa at this time. The court of the king of Ghana was described in detail by al-Bakrī in the mid-eleventh century, and the wealth of gold available is evident in his description: the king wore a golden head-dress, the pages carried gold-hilted swords, the horses had gold trappings, and even the dogs guarding the royal pavilion wore collars with bells of silver and gold. In view of the amount of gold in circulation, steps had to be taken to ensure its continuing value and this was achieved by making all nuggets the property of the king, and only gold dust available for trade (Bovill 1968: 81–2).

Some detail of how the gold was obtained is also provided by the Arabic sources. The gold, extracted from shallow surface workings, was mined not in the Sahel but further south in the savanna regions, an area usually referred to as the Western Sudan. Two of the most important sources were at Bambuk and Bure, where gold was extracted in a process shrouded in mystery to which Yāqūt (d.1229) alludes when he records that, to quote, 'this is how their manners are reported though those people never allow a merchant to see them' (Levtzion and Hopkins 1981: 170). Once, one of the gold miners was captured by a group of traders in an attempt to discover the exact source of the gold. This was unsuccessful as Bovill (1968: 82) records. 'He pined to death without saying a word, and it was three years before the negroes would resume the trade, and then only because they had no other way of satisfying their craving for salt'. Thus the gold-miners were left largely to their own devices. As noted by Bovill, salt was one of the main commodities exchanged for gold, again according to the Arabic sources, sometimes weight for weight. The actual process of exchange was one known as 'silent trade'. This is also described in detail by al-'Umarī (d.1349) who reports that 'some of the remote peoples of the Sudan do not show themselves. When the salt merchants come they put the salt down and then withdraw. Then the Sudan put down the gold. When the merchants have taken the gold the Sudan take the salt' (Levtzion and Hopkins 1981: 273).

The importance of trade is attested archaeologically at Koumbi Saleh, a site where imported Egyptian pottery used to filter water, lustre decorated ceramics of North African origin, and blue, green, and yellow glass beads have all been found. Architecturally, Koumbi Saleh was organised on a reasonably regular plan of multi-storey houses built of stone. The remains of a large mosque and two cemeteries are also recorded (Thomassey and Mauny 1951; Thomassey and Mauny 1956;

Berthier 1997). In many respects, Koumbi Saleh resembles the neighbouring site of Tegdaoust, also an important trade centre which has been investigated archaeologically, and again a centre in all probability associated with the Empire of Ghana – the difference being that much larger quantities of imported materials were found at Tegdaoust (glass, glazed pottery, beads etc.) in a site otherwise architecturally very similar to Koumbi Saleh (D. Robert 1970; Vanacker 1979; Robert-Chaleix 1989).

Koumbi Saleh, Tegdaoust, and Gao, were towns and cities strung along the fringe of the Sahara. To these could be added Timbuktu, a famous name discussed in greater detail below, or less familiar, but equally notable sites such as Essuk/Tadmekka in the Adrar des Iforas mountains in Mali. Even closer to the Sahara than Gao, this town whose name was recorded by al-Bakrī in the second half of the eleventh century as meaning 'the Mecca-like' (Levtzion and Hopkins 1981: 85) was one of the earliest centres of Islam in West Africa. Further to the east were the great copper-working centres recorded by the Arab historians, medieval Maranda, possibly to be identified with Marendet in Niger, and medieval Takedda, possibly to be identified with Azelik, also in Niger (Lhote 1972): various settlements serving diverse functions – trade, teaching and learning, and manufacturing.

The initial caution implied by the pattern of twin settlements gradually gave way to one of mutual understanding, reflected in the amalgamation of settlements as at Gao (Insoll 1997). This process was accelerated by conversion to Islam among the local population. Frequently, initial converts to Islam were among the ruling class, sometimes for reasons of prestige, or for facilitating trade or administration through the use of Muslim officials and, importantly, through the use of Arabic writing in previously illiterate societies (Levtzion 1979: 214; Hunwick 1985a). To these factors favouring conversion must be added genuine belief in the tenets of Islam. From the ruling classes, religious conviction gradually percolated down through society. In a process taking several centuries, Islam reached the townspeople, the merchants' local partners in trade, the nomads who accompanied the caravans criss-crossing the Sahara, and the bulk of the population, the sedentary agriculturists (Trimingham 1959; Insoll 1999: 159–62).

The question when and how the conversion of the ruler and people to Islam took place in Ghana has been the subject of some controversy. On the strength of the writings of Arab historians, it was once thought that conversion was attributable to the Almoravids, a reforming puritanical movement which drew its support from the Sanhaja nomads of the Western Sahara (Levtzion 1985: 138), and was ultimately to provide a dynasty which ruled parts of the Iberian peninsula and North Africa in the late eleventh to early twelfth centuries (Lomax 1978: 68–90). It was believed that zealous hordes of Almoravid desert warriors, supported by soldiers from the Muslim kingdom of Takrur in Senegal, destroyed the pagan empire of Ghana and forcibly converted the inhabitants to Islam in 1076–7 (Trimingham 1962; Bovill 1968). However, a re-evaluation of both the Arabic and local sources, and the archaeological evidence (on the assumption that the identification of Koumbi Saleh with the merchant town is correct) showed this account of events to be erroneous (Conrad and Fisher 1982; Conrad and Fisher 1983), in particular, no evidence for the destruction thesis emerged from the archaeological record. The conquest hypothesis would therefore appear to be flawed. From this it must follow that conversion was probably a more gradual process, commencing in the late tenth–eleventh centuries and continuing thereafter. Koumbi Saleh was certainly occupied until the late fourteenth to early fifteenth centuries (Berthier 1997; R. J. McIntosh 1998: 259).

Yet Ghana did decline, though why it did remains unclear pending the outcome of further archaeological investigations. However, various causes have to be considered: a deterioration in the environment, making life more precarious in the Sahel's marginal environmental zone, dynastic infighting, unquestionably a recurring problem of the subsequent Mali and Songhai empires, a shift in trade patterns (see for example Togola 1996). Certainly by the late twelfth to early thirteenth century Ghana was no longer a force to be reckoned with. But the gap this created did not persist for long. A new state, Mali, grew to take its place (Bovill 1968; Levtzion 1973, 1985). Unfortunately, the origins of Mali are also unclear. Its centre was situated away from the Sahel (perhaps a further indication that environmental factors were in part responsible for the decline of Ghana). Mali was a product of the savanna, the vast grasslands which stretch in a broad band right across Africa from the Atlantic to the Red Sea coasts.

The early history of Mali is not well recorded in the Arabic sources, but again oral tradition helps to fill in the gaps, by means of narratives lovingly handed down through the generations by the Griots, poets charged with recording oral history. The greatest epic is perhaps *Sundiata, An Epic of Old Mali* (Niane 1986) which records the conflicts between Sumanguru, the evil-magician king and Sundiata Keita, the progenitor of the Malian dynasty in the mid-thirteenth century. Again, archaeology has been utilised in an attempt to locate the capital of Mali, with excavations undertaken within the modern Republic of Guinea at the site of Niani. Here the remains of various structures were uncovered, stone house foundations, the *miḥrāb* or prayer niche of a mosque, tombs and an audience chamber. An attempt to match the archaeological finds with the historical description of the capital of Mali provided by the famous Moroccan traveller Ibn Baṭṭuṭa in the mid-fourteenth century (Filipowiak 1978; Filipowiak 1979) has so far proved fruitless, however. Unfortunately, this identification is premature to say the least and can be questioned on various grounds. In particular, it has been convincingly argued that the capital of Mali may have shifted 'more than once during its imperial period from the twelfth century to the sixteenth century' (Conrad 1994: 377).

Niani was certainly an Islamised settlement, but it does not appear to have been associated with the Empire of Mali in its fourteenth-century heyday. The high point of Mali was without doubt the period of rule of Mansā Mūsā (1312–37). Mansā Mūsā extended the empire in all directions; north to the important salt mines in the Sahara, west to Takrur on the River Senegal, and east, encompassing Gao, as far as the frontiers of Hausaland (Levtzion 1973). He is also credited with building many of the great monuments of the Western Sahel, a palace, the Madadougou in Timbuktu (as yet undiscovered), and a mosque in Gao for example. Yet perhaps the most enduring historical memorial to Mansā Mūsā 's memory is the fabled pilgrimage he made to Mecca in and after 1324, accompanied by a vast number of retainers and huge quantities of gold (Bovill 1968). Mansā Mūsā 's prodigious spending of gold during the course of the *ḥajj* was remembered long after he had returned home to Mali. According to al-'Umarī, who was in Cairo twelve years later, the towns-people of Cairo still remembered Mansā Mūsā fondly for the gold he spent and gave away there. According to Bovill (1968: 87), 'so much gold was suddenly put into circulation in Egypt that its market value fell sharply and had not recovered in al-Umari's time'.

But Mali's days, like Ghana's, were numbered. Though remaining a powerful empire until about 1400, Mali then faced incursions by nomadic Tuareg and a revolt by Gao. The end was only a matter of time, and effective political power was finished by the mid-fifteenth century (Levtzion 1985). The final great medieval empire of West Africa was the Songhai Empire, whose origins can be placed in what is best termed the 'proto-Songhai' kingdom which had existed since at least the tenth century (Insoll 1996), though as has been noted it owed allegiance to Mali during parts of the thirteenth and fourteenth centuries (Levtzion 1985; Hunwick 1985b). The Songhai Empire was focused on Gao, the capital, a city in existence by the mid-first millennium AD, as has been shown by recent archaeological investigations described below (Insoll 1996). It also appears that by the tenth century the ruler of Gao was a Muslim, and that conversions among the population of the city proceeded rapidly in the eleventh and twelfth centuries.

In 1373 Gao recovered its independence from Mali and the era of Songhai expansion began. The first of the great Songhai rulers, comparable in his achieve-ments to Mansā Mūsā , was Sonni 'Alī, who assumed power in about 1464 and greatly expanded the Songhai domains (Hunwick 1985a and b). Sonni 'Alī, however, for all his achievements, is castigated in the local chronicles, such as the seventeenth-century, *Ta'rīkh al-Sūdān* (es-Sa'dī 1900) for not being a good Muslim. How much his 'bad press' might have been exaggerated is not certain, but we do know that on his death in 1493 he was succeeded by the first of a new line of rulers, the Askias. The assumption of power by Askiyā Muḥammad signalled a new era of Islamic revival in Gao. Muslim scholarship flourished, the Songhai empire prospered, and Askiyā Muḥammad went on pilgrimage to Mecca both to fulfil his religious duty but also to 'establish firmly' his image 'as a Muslim ruler' (Hunwick 1985a: 342).

TIMBUKTU

The paramount centre of Muslim scholarship in West Africa during the Songhai empire was Timbuktu, a city whose name is well-known in the Western world having become a metaphor for the remote and mysterious (Figure 27.1). Timbuktu served as a centre of trans-Saharan trade during the medieval period but also as a centre of Muslim learning. Alongside the city of Harar in Ethiopia, it could be classed as the pre-eminent Muslim university town in sub-Saharan Africa. Islamic texts were copied and sciences studied there, notably at the Sankore mosque complex, a building still standing today, though rebuilt, originally founded sometime during the period of Malian control between 1325 and 1433 (Mauny 1952) (Figure 27.2). Sankore was the abode of the most prominent scholars. Students were taught the Koran, ḥadīth, and Islamic law and sciences, and travelled to such other great centres of Muslim learning as Cairo and Mecca, from which scholars were likewise received. Many

Figure 27.2 The Sankore mosque, Timbuktu. Photo: R. MacLean.

private libraries were also established within the city, the noted scholar Aḥmad Bābā being reputed to have had 1,600 volumes at the time of the Moroccan conquest of Timbuktu in 1591 (Saad 1983: 79).

According to the Arabic sources, Timbuktu was a relatively late foundation (eleventh-century), which prospered through the trans-Saharan trade in salt and gold, especially during its 'high period' (c.1350–1600). Archaeological research has only just been started within the city itself, surprisingly considering its renown (Insoll 1998b). Besides the Sankore, two other mosques dating from the medieval period still stand, and have also been rebuilt over the centuries. These are the Djinguereber, possibly thirteenth-century in origin, and the Sīdī Yaḥyā, founded c.1440 (Mauny 1952: 901–11). Possible areas of early settlement in Timbuktu were suggested by evidence recorded during archaeological surveys in the vicinity of the Sankore and Djinguereber mosques. Material recovered includes a multi-coloured glass bracelet fragment similar to material dated to the fourteenth century at sites on the Red Sea coast of Egypt (Whitcomb 1983: 106–7), and resembling similar bracelets from the salt-mining site of Teghāza in the Malian Sahara (Monod 1975: 717), through which the trade caravans probably passed on leaving Timbuktu.

A further unique find made during the archaeological survey was what appears to be a sherd of southern Chinese Celadon dated to the late eleventh–early twelfth century (Insoll 1998b). This is of particular interest because of its early date, its provenance, and its location, so far removed from the West African coast, the usual area in which ceramics of Chinese porcelain have been discovered, having been brought by European traders from the late fifteenth century. Unfortunately, recent excavation in Timbuktu has not confirmed the survey evidence, with only material dating from the late eighteenth century onwards as yet recovered. However, it is probable that earlier occupation levels lie hidden since the depths of occupation deposits in Timbuktu extend as deep as 15 metres in some areas of the city. Thus, the archaeology of Timbuktu still remains something of a mystery.

Its history by contrast is fairly well established. The 'golden age' of the city occurred during the era of the Songhai Askia dynasty, established by Askyā Muḥammad (Hunwick 1985a), the Songhai ruler already referred to, a period when both scholarship and trade flourished. The population during the late sixteenth century has been estimated at a staggering 75,000, with 7,500 of this total being students (Saad 1983: 90): huge numbers to maintain on the edge of the Sahara. Inevitably, tales of fabulous wealth obviously accompanied the caravans north across the desert, and indeed the gold itself was an indicator of the riches of the Western Sahel and Sudan. Unfortunately, the consequences of this reputation were to prove profound. In 1591 a Moroccan army of conquest crossed the Sahara and routed Songhai forces at the battle of Tondibi. This defeat, the subsequent persecution of the intellectual community of Timbuktu, and the abandonment of Gao as the Songhai capital, marked the end of the last of the great medieval empires of West Africa.

But we have run ahead of ourselves. For it must be stressed that Timbuktu in its heyday did not sit in splendid isolation. To support its population, trade was essential, and it was linked through both trade and intellectual life to Djenne further to the south on the River Niger. From Djenne, Sudani gold and foodstuffs were sent north to Timbuktu in exchange for commodities such as salt, and finished items such as cloth. The salt trade was of especial significance not only between Timbuktu and Djenne but throughout the region. Salt was shipped from the Saharan sources to the major trade centres such as Gao and Timbuktu in blocks slung on camels. From here it was transported by a variety of means; riverine, and human and animal portage (Insoll 1996: 77). The scale of the demand for salt is brought home by an observation recorded by the Scottish explorer Mungo Park who travelled along part of the River Niger at the end of the eighteenth century and saw 'a child suck a piece of rock-salt, as if it were sugar' (1807: 418). Djenne was the Islamised successor of an earlier settlement, Jenne-jeno, abandoned *c.*1400, possibly because it was considered too tainted by pagan practices (S. K. and R. J. McIntosh 1980; S. K. McIntosh 1995). Jenne-jeno has been the focus of much detailed archaeological work, and can be considered the first site in the region to have benefited from examination by modern archaeological techniques.

THE APPLICATION OF ARCHAEOLOGY: GAO – A CASE STUDY

As said, archaeology has still to uncover many of the secrets of Timbuktu. By contrast, the archaeology of early Gao, the capital of the Songhai Empire, is now fairly well understood, providing a striking example of the utility of archaeology in supplementing our understanding of all aspects of the medieval period in the Western Sahel, particularly regarding settlement and architecture, religion, and trade.

Settlement and Architecture

During the initial period of contact (*c.* tenth century) between Muslim merchants and the local inhabitants settlement at Gao followed the pattern of twin centres previously described (Figure 27.3). Initially, this separation, at the sites of Gao Ancien and Gao-Saney, was probably due to religious differences, but the persistence of dual settlements after Islam had spread to the inhabitants of Gao Ancien in the late eleventh to twelfth centuries may have been attributable to security considerations, in particular the desirability of keeping nomads at a distance from Gao Ancien (Insoll 1996: 48).

Excavations in Gao Ancien have uncovered a central citadel, with elaborate fired-brick buildings being occupied in the twelfth to thirteenth centuries. This was also the peak period of the city's trans-Saharan trade and the buildings reflect the wealth created by this activity. Parts of what appears to be a mosque and a house belonging to a rich merchant have been recorded. Interestingly, these were not monochrome buildings but were decorated with coloured plaster, red on the fired-brick floors and white on the walls which were built of unfired brick, cheaper to produce in this resource-poor environment. A fragment of window glass found, along with parts of drilled alabaster frames, suggests that the walls of the principal buildings in Gao Ancien were inset with glazed panels (Insoll 1998a), perhaps similar to the palace of the king of Ghana described by al-Idrīsī as 'provided with glass windows' (Levtzion and Hopkins 1981: 110). The entire citadel appears to have been defended by a wall built of dry-stone, complete with gatehouse and well (Insoll in preparation).

Excavation in a quarter neighbouring Gao Ancien, Gadei, failed to discover evidence of such affluence. Here buildings were of a more traditional style, in mud, and rather than using rectangular plans, roundhouses were utilised, one of which was uncovered. This type of structure is still built in areas south of Gao, and its use is one of the differences evident between the two quarters, Gadei, the local quarter,

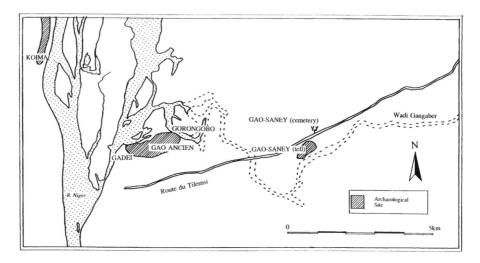

Figure 27.3 The archaeological sites at Gao.

and Gao Ancien, the mercantile centre and probable site of the rulers' settlement. A third site, Gao-Saney, some 8 km east of Gao itself, and comprising a large tell or mound and an attached cemetery (Flight 1975; Flight 1981) has proved prolific in manufacturing debris, such as slag from iron production, and fragments of carnelian from bead production (Insoll 1996). It is here that the Arab and Berber traders may have resided initially.

Religion

The inhabitants of Gao Ancien and Gao-Saney appear certainly (and those of Gadei possibly) to have been Muslim. Evidence for the presence of Muslims at Gao-Saney includes various inscribed Muslim tombstones, five of which would appear from the nature of the material and the style of epigraphy to have been imported ready-carved from the vicinity of Almería in Muslim Spain in the early twelfth century (Sauvaget 1950; Vire 1958; Moraes Farias 1990). Inscribed tombstones were not confined to Gao-Saney. Gao Ancien was also ringed with Muslim cemeteries, and the inscriptions recovered from these have also provided information on Islamisation processes within the region between the early twelfth and fourteenth centuries (Figure 27.4). At Gadei such explicit indicators of Islam were absent, though among items recovered were a large wooden bead from a set of prayer beads or Muslim 'rosary' and the remains of what appears to have been a Muslim amulet cover.

Figure 27.4 A Muslim tombstone from Gorongobo cemetery, Gao (1130). Photo: T. Insoll.

Trade

By far the most abundant evidence recovered from Gao, especially from Gao Ancien, was that indicating participation in long-distance trade. This was especially noticeable in occupation levels dated to the eleventh to twelfth centuries, and indicating a veritable boom period in trans-Saharan trade. Trade consisted largely of the export of commodities north across the desert in return for finished manufactured goods, frequently of luxury categories.

Possibly the most spectacular evidence for the export trade was a cache of over 50 hippopotamus tusks uncovered in a pit dated to the mid-ninth century in Gao Ancien (Figure 27.5). It appears that these tusks represent a consignment of ivory which was awaiting shipment to the workshops of North Africa, and for some reason was never sent (Insoll 1995). A substantial ivory trade between West and North Africa existed, but is little mentioned in the Arabic sources, possibly because the use of feathers, horns, hoofs or tusks derived from animals which were not ritually slaughtered was frowned upon by orthodox Muslims (Levtzion and Hopkins 1981: 55). Large quantities of ivory were certainly used in the workshops of the Maghreb, Islamic Spain, and Egypt, with the workshops of Islamic Spain famed for the inlaid

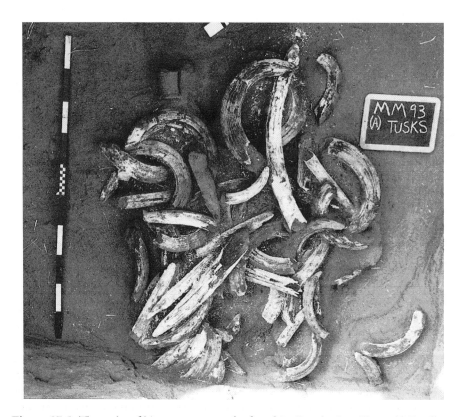

Figure 27.5 The cache of hippopotamus tusks found in Gao Ancien. Photo: T. Insoll.

and carved caskets and ivory encrusted mosque furniture which were produced in cities such as Madīnat al-Zahrā in the tenth century, and in other centres during subsequent Almoravid, Almohad and Nasrid rule. Ivory cubes, often along with blocks of ebony and other woods, were used to create inlaid patterns, and it is for this work that hippopotamus ivory would have been most suited, being whiter, denser, and less prone to splitting than elephant ivory (Penniman 1952; Krzyszkowska 1990).

It is probable that the animals from which the tusks were obtained were hunted locally, having once been common on the River Niger in the vicinity of Gao. Hippopotami were hunted by a specialist sub-group of the Songhai, the Sorko, and al-Bakrī provides us with a description of a hunt in the mid-eleventh century, without referring to the hippopotamus by name:

> In the Nil [Niger] . . . , an animal is found living in the water, which resembles the elephant in the great size of its body as well as its snout and tusks. . . . They recognize its whereabouts in the Nil by the movement of water over its back, and hasten there, armed with short javelins which have rings at the blunt end with long ropes tied to them. They throw many of these javelins at the animal which submerges and struggles at the bottom of the Nil. When it dies it floats to the surface of the water and they drag it out. They eat its flesh and from its hide make those whips called *surriyāqāt* which are carried from there to other countries.
>
> (Levtzion and Hopkins 1981: 78, 456)

Material evidence of the extensive gold trade of which the Arabic historical sources carry reports is more elusive, unsurprisingly in view of that metal's recyclability and enduring value. In Gadei a small gold bead was found, and at Gao Ancien a gold *mithqāl* coin of North African origin dating from 952–75 has been reported (Latruffe 1953), though this coin has subsequently disappeared. This meagre haul, representing the sum total of evidence for the gold trade at Gao, is matched by a similar dearth at most of the other major trade centres. Equally, evidence for the slave trade is lacking, as by its very nature it is archaeologically largely invisible.

Much more abundantly in evidence are items sourced from North Africa and elsewhere in the Muslim world, and beyond, the goods which were sent south in return for West African commodities. A large assemblage of imported glazed pottery and glass was recovered from Gao Ancien dating primarily from the eleventh to twelfth centuries (Insoll 1996: 63–6), and including products of Ifriqiyan (Tunisian) origin, and others from Egypt and Spain, along with fragments of glass from the same areas (Insoll 1996). Over a thousand glass beads have also been recovered, the majority of coloured glass and of types referred to as 'trade beads', produced in vast quantities in both India and Egypt. Semi-precious carnelian beads have also been found, again of possible Indian origin, perhaps from the coast of Gujerat in western India. These beads were then traded onwards from Gao throughout West Africa (Insoll and Shaw 1997), and testify to the extent of trade networks which linked West to North Africa and on via Egypt and the Red Sea to the Indian Ocean and even to China (Insoll 1999: 152–62).

The most active trading partner attested by the archaeological evidence, however, was Muslim Spain, especially during the period of Almoravid rule. Hippo ivory and imported tombstones of Almerian provenance apart, there are also the sherds of lustre-ware recovered from Gao Ancien which have been shown to be identical to the twelfth-century material recovered from excavations in Málaga (Gómez-Moreno 1940), and architectural parallels discernible between the fired-brick structures of Gao Ancien and those in the *alcazaba* in Almería (Insoll personal observation). Moreover, analysis of the gold bead from Gadei indicates specific Almoravid connections, though with North Africa rather than with Spain, the composition of the gold from Gao precisely matching that of Almoravid gold dinars minted at the North African city of Sijilmasa, and suggesting the use of similar West African ores, in all probability sourced via Gao (Guerra in preparation).

CONCLUSIONS

Little as is known about them, the vibrant towns of the Western Sahel, and the empires in which they were located, were an integral part of the medieval world. Though geographically peripheral, they were the source of many of the materials which helped to fuel the medieval Muslim world economy, an economic system which was, in turn, intimately related to that of Christian Western Europe. It is altogether possible that ivory or gold of West African origin via Gao and Timbuktu found its way into the workshops, treasuries and cathedrals of medieval Western Europe. 'Medieval' West Africa was truly part of the medieval world.

REFERENCES

Berthier, S. (1997) *Koumbi Saleh*, Cambridge Monographs in African Archaeology 41. BAR International Series 680, Oxford: Tempus Reparatum.

Bovill, E.W. (1968) *The Golden Trade of the Moors*, London: Oxford University Press.

Conrad, D.C. (1994) 'A town called Dakajalan: The Sunjata tradition and the question of ancient Mali's capital', *Journal of African History* 35: 355–77.

Conrad, D. C. and Fisher, H. (1982) 'The conquest that never was: Ghana and the Almoravids, 1076, Part 1: The external Arabic sources', *History in Africa* 9: 21–59.

—— (1983) 'The conquest that never was: Ghana and the Almoravids, 1076, Part 2: The local oral sources', *History in Africa* 10: 53–78.

Dolukhanov, P.M. (1996) *The Early Slavs*, Harlow: Longmans.

es-Sa'dī, A. (1900) (transl. O. Houdas), *Tarikh es-Soudan* Paris: Ernest Leroux.

Filipowiak, W. (1978) 'Results of archaeological research at Niani', *Nyame Akuma* 8: 32–3.

—— (1979) *Études archéologiques sur la capitale médiévale du Mali*, Szczecin: Muzeum Narodowe.

Flight, C. (1975) 'Gao 1972: First interim report: A preliminary investigation of the cemetery at Sané', *West African Journal of Archaeology* 5: 81–90.

—— (1981) 'The medieval cemetery at Sané. A history of the site from 1939 to 1950', in *Le sol, la parole et l'écrit. Mélanges en hommage à Raymond Mauny*, Paris: Société Française d'histoire d'Outre mer, 91–107.

Gómez-Moreno, M. (1940) 'La loza dorada primitíva de Málaga', *Al-Andalus* 5: 393–8.

Guerra, M.F. (2000), 'A report on the composition of a bead from Gao', in T. Insoll *et al.* 2000: 153–5.

Hunwick, J. O. (1985a) *Sharī'a in Songhay: The replies of al-Maghīlī to the questions of Askia al-Ḥājj Muḥammad*, London: Oxford University Press.

—— (1985b) 'Songhay, Borno and the Hausa states, 1450 – 1600', in J. F. A. Ajayi and M. Crowder (eds) *The History of West Africa*, I, Harlow: Longmans, 323–71.

Insoll, T. (1994) 'The external creation of the Western Sahel's past: The use and abuse of the Arabic sources', *Archaeological Review from Cambridge* 13: 39–49.

—— (1995) 'A cache of hippopotamus ivory at Gao, Mali; and a hypothesis of its use', *Antiquity* 69: 327–36.

—— (1996) *Islam, Archaeology and History, A Complex Relationship: The Gao Region (Mali) ca. AD 900–1250*, Cambridge Monographs in African Archaeology 39. BAR International Series 647. Oxford: Tempus Reparatum.

—— (1997) 'Iron Age Gao: An archaeological contribution', *Journal of African History* 38: 1–30.

—— (1998a) 'Islamic glass from Gao, Mali', *Journal of Glass Studies* 40: 77–88.

—— (1998b) 'Archaeological research in Timbuktu, Mali', *Antiquity* 72: 413–17.

—— (1999) *The Archaeology of Islam*, Oxford: Blackwells.

—— (2000) *et al. Urbanism, Archaeology and Trade*, BAR, S829, Oxford: British Archaeological Reports.

—— and Shaw, T. (1997), 'Gao and Igbo-Ukwu: Beads, inter-regional trade and beyond', *African Archaeological Review* 14: 9–23.

Krzyszkowska, O. (1990) *Ivory and Related Materials. An illustrated guide*, London: Institute of Classical Studies.

Latruffe, J. (1953) 'Au sujet d'une pièce d'or millénaire trouvée à Gao', *Notes Africaines* 60: 102–3.

Levtzion, N. (1973) *Ancient Ghana and Mali*, London: Methuen.

—— (1979) 'Patterns of Islamization', in N. Levtzion (ed.) *Conversion to Islam*, New York: Holmes and Meier, 207–16.

—— (1985) 'The early states of the Western Sudan to 1500', in J. F. A. Ajayi and M. Crowder (eds) *History of West Africa*. I, Harlow: Longmans, 129–66.

—— and Hopkins, J.F.P. (1981) *Corpus of Early Arabic Sources for West African History*, Cambridge: Cambridge University Press.

Lhote, H. (1972) 'Recherches sur Takedda, ville décrite par le voyageur arabe Ibn Battouta et située en Air', *Bulletin de l'Institut Fondamental d'Afrique Noire (B)* 34: 429–70.

Lomax, D. W. (1978) *The Reconquest of Spain*, London: Longmans.

Mauny, R. (1952) 'Notes d'archéologie sur Tombouctou', *Bulletin de l'Institut Français d'Afrique Noire (B)* 14: 899–918.

—— (1961) *Tableau géographique de l'Ouest Africain au Moyen Age*, Dakar: Institut Français de l'Afrique Noire.

McIntosh, R. J. (1998) *The Peoples of the Middle Niger*, Oxford: Blackwell.

—— and McIntosh, S. K. (1988) 'From *siècles obscurs* to revolutionary centuries in the Middle Niger', *World Archaeology* 20: 141–65.

McIntosh, S. K. (ed.) (1995) *Excavations at Jenne-jeno, Hambarketolo, and Kaniana (Inland Niger Delta, Mali), the 1981 Season*, Los Angeles: University of California Press.

—— and R. J. McIntosh (1980) *Prehistoric Investigations in the Region of Jenne, Mali*, Oxford: British Archaeological Reports.

Monod, T. (1975) 'À propos des bracelets de verre Sahariens', *Bulletin de l'Institut Fondamental d'Afrique Noire (B)* 37: 702–18.

Moraes Farias P.F. de (1990) 'The oldest extant writing of West Africa', *Journal des Africanistes* 602: 65–113.

Niane, D.T. (1986) *Sundiata. An Epic of Old Mali*, Harlow: Longmans.

Nicolaisen, J. (1963) *Ecology and Culture of the Pastoral Tuareg*, Copenhagen: National Museum.

Park, M. (1807) *Travels in the Interior Districts of Africa. 1795, 1796, and 1797*, London: W. Bulmer and Co.

Penniman, T.K. (1952) *Pictures of Ivory and other Animal Teeth*, Oxford: Pitt-Rivers Museum Papers on Technology 5.

Robert, D. (1970) 'Les fouilles de Tegdaoust', *Journal of African History* 11: 471–93.

Robert-Chaleix, D. (1989) *Tegdaoust V*, Paris: Éditions Recherche sur les Civilisations.

Rouch, J. (1953) *Contribution à l'histoire des Songhay*, Dakar: Institut Français de l'Afrique Noire.

Saad, E.N. (1983) *Social History of Timbuktu. The Role of Muslim Scholars and Notables 1400–1900*, Cambridge: Cambridge University Press.

Sauvaget, J. (1950) 'Les épitaphes royales de Gao', *Bulletin de l'Institut Français de l'Afrique Noire (B)* 12, 418–40.

Thomassey, P. and Mauny, R. (1951) 'Campagne de fouilles à Koumbi Saleh', *Bulletin de l'Institut Français de l'Afrique Noire (B)* 13: 438–62.

—— (1956) 'Campagne de fouilles de 1950 à Koumbi Saleh', *Bulletin de l'Institut Français de l'Afrique Noire (B)* 18: 117–40.

Togola, T. (1996) 'Iron Age occupation in the Méma region, Mali', *African Archaeological Review* 13: 91–110.

Trimingham, J.S. (1959) *Islam in West Africa*, Oxford: Clarendon Press.

—— (1962) *A History of Islam in West Africa*, London: Oxford University Press.

Vanacker, C. (1979) *Tegdaoust II. Recherches sur Aoudaghost. Fouillé d'un quartier artisanal*, Nouakchott: Institut Mauritanien de la Recherche Scientifique.

Vire, M. M. (1958) 'Notes sur trois épitaphes royales de Gao', *Bulletin de l'Institut Français de l'Afrique Noire (B)* 20: 368–76.

Whitcomb, D. S. (1983) 'Islamic glass from Al-Qadim, Egypt', *Journal of Glass Studies* 25: 101–8.

CHAPTER TWENTY-EIGHT

MEDIEVAL LAW

—•◦•—

Susan Reynolds

In 1888 F. W. Maitland, the greatest of all historians of medieval law, gave his inaugural lecture the title 'Why the history of English law is not written' (Maitland 1911). The three masterpieces he wrote in the next ten years transformed the knowledge and understanding of English law before 1272,[1] and the twentieth century has seen great advances in the history of the later medieval law both of England and of other European countries. Yet in one respect the situation has not improved. Maitland deplored the 'very complete and traditionally consecrated ignorance of French and German law' among English lawyers, since, as he put it, 'there is nothing that sets a man thinking and writing to such good effect about a system of law and its history as an acquaintance however slight with other systems and their history' (Maitland 1911: 1. 489–90). Yet, even if he was almost the only legal historian in England to be involved in it, interest in Germanic origins in his day stimulated wide-ranging work by those outside. Much of it now looks distinctly unconvincing, but during most of the twentieth century the English have not been alone in their insularity. As the history of medieval law has become more learned and specialised it has become encased in separate national traditions, transcended only in the study of medieval Roman and canon law. That has provided many valuable insights, but much of it has concentrated on academic law rather than on legal practice (Coing 1973). On practice, and on the kind of law that most affected non-lawyers, comparisons or general histories above the level of textbooks for law students have until recently been rare.[2] It is not difficult to see why, given the mass of detailed work written within different legal traditions and often making few concessions to readers unfamiliar with their respective terminologies. In the circumstances this chapter, which is primarily concerned with legal practice, will merely suggest some problems and propose a general framework within which comparisons might be made. It will concentrate on what it suggests are the bare outlines of the way in which secular law and secular jurisdictions developed, saying little about substantive law, such as rules about inheritance, family law, the rights and obligations of property, and so forth.[3] So far as ideas and doctrines are concerned it will focus more on the kind of assumptions about what is right or wrong, legal or illegal, that can be detected from the records of practice, than on the doctrines worked out by academic and professional lawyers.[4] It concentrates on Catholic Europe, and draws

485

examples from only a few countries within it. What is left out is not left out because it is not interesting or important but because a short essay has to be selective. Much of what is included should be understood as hypotheses that need to be tested.

BEFORE THE TWELFTH CENTURY

Most historians of medieval law concentrate on the later middle ages and have rather a low opinion of law before about 1100, which has traditionally been seen as based on oaths, ordeals, and 'Judgements of God' deriving from the primitive ideas and practices of barbarians, rather than on the rational arguments of classical Roman law. A good deal of this picture has been questioned in recent years as historians have looked again at the evidence surviving from the early Middle Ages in the light of what is known about societies outside Europe that have also lived by unprofessional, customary law (e.g. Clanchy 1970; Davies and Fouracre 1986; Bowman 1997; Reynolds 1997a). 'Customary law' covers a wide range. Here the expression is used to mean the kind of law that seems to have governed a good many smallish, unbureaucratic societies in different parts of the world that made little if any use of written records and are known to us chiefly through the work of anthropologists. Disputes in this kind of society are judged, and crimes punished, according to what is thought of as custom, and generally as old custom, which is declared by a person or a group thought to speak on behalf of the whole community whose custom it is. Some people speak with greater authority because of their experience and general knowledge of custom, and often too of their high social status, but there are no professional lawyers in the sense of people who have a specialised training and make their living by legal practice. According to definitions designed to suit the law of modern states, this kind of law is not law at all, but it seems to serve the purposes of what we call law in so far as it is authoritative and enforceable. It may seem unclear, variable, and poorly enforced, but then so, at times, is modern law.

Analogies prove nothing. There is no prima facie reason why societies in early medieval Europe should have managed their affairs in the way in which some early twentieth-century African societies managed theirs. What matters is the evidence. But, as Maitland indicated, looking at other systems of law may suggest new ways of looking at it. Early medieval laws, charters, and records of disputes constantly refer to what is just and right. Sometimes they equate this explicitly with what is in accord with custom (*consuetudo, mos, usus*). If they do not, it is because they assume generally accepted norms, which comes to much the same thing. Recently it has been suggested that there were no real customs in France, except within families, before the twelfth century – which presumably means no law either (Gouron 1993: XX, XXI; cf. Ourliac 1982, 1993: 271–84). This suggests both a rather culture-bound attitude to law and 'la fétichisation terminologique' into which medievalists – and not only French medievalists – have sometimes fallen (Barthélemy 1997: 10, 105). While the word *consuetudo* apparently occurs most often in eleventh-century documentary French sources to denote seigniorial dues, *mores* and *usus* are also mentioned and often convey the sense of normative custom. Irrespective of words, moreover, French documents, like those of other countries, imply assumptions about what is right or wrong, lawful or unlawful. It is hard to see how lords ruled their lordships, or local communities managed their affairs, if it was not by some kind of customary law.

The Roman law on which some groups in Italy and elsewhere in southern Europe prided themselves was also to a large extent customary law. The old obsession with defining law as Roman or Germanic has come to look more and more pointless. Roman law in the provinces had always been different from that of the classical jurists, and the collapse of Roman government in the West had changed the conditions in which it worked (Classen 1977; Bowman 1997). Some of the most apparently barbaric or Germanic features of early medieval law, such as oaths and ordeals, may have come as much from the 'vulgar law' of the provinces as from barbarian invaders. What is called 'personal law', the 'personality of law, or, even more confusingly, 'legal personality', and contrasted with 'territorial law', also looks less like a reflection of Germanic ideology than a response to the movement of people into areas with different customs (Davies and Fouracre 1986: 1–22; Amory 1993; Collins 1998; Pohl 1998). Most rulers, while allowing local variation as a matter of course, tried to apply the kind of law they cared about – that is, obedience to themselves – to everyone under their rule. The different laws inherited from their ancestors that some individuals nevertheless claimed to follow were sometimes allowed to modify procedures by which they were tried, but may sometimes have amounted to little more than rules about property and inheritance. Just at the period when historians have traditionally seen 'territorial law' replacing 'personal law', rulers started to grant collective privileges to groups, thus entrenching aspects of a new kind of 'personal law' which outlasted the Middle Ages. What collective grants emphasise above all, however, is the overriding importance of custom and its authoritative and enforceable character. From the charter secured by the Genoese in 958 on, one of the most valued privileges any local community could receive was to run its own affairs according to its own customs.

That law was thought of as custom, and preferably old custom, does not mean that kings and other rulers could not change it. They did, but when a king legislated, he did so as the supreme representative of the community of his people, correcting or clarifying their custom. Even when he did not say so, he probably consulted first – or should have consulted – with the nobles and clergy who also represented the community to him. Legislation was done most often by word of mouth, but sometimes by announcing new or amended rules in charters, and sometimes by what are misleadingly called law-codes (Wormald 1977, 1999). These did not codify law in the modern sense. How far they affected practice is much discussed and must have varied (McKitterick 1989, 1990). The collection and writing down of laws nevertheless conferred a Mosaic and Roman prestige on a king and his kingdom.

The charters and memoranda that record disputes also tell how kings and lords made their grants and adjudications with the counsel and consent of their great men. The ordeals and judicial duels that look so irrational to modern eyes seem generally to have taken place only after discussion, and if the discussion had not produced an answer (e.g. White 1995). Whether or not everyone believed in their supernatural authority – and some clearly did not, just as some people do not think judges or juries always get things right today – they had the merit of offering a final end to debates. Oath-taking did not rely only on belief in divine retribution: making someone get half a dozen or so of his neighbours to swear with him (compurgation) was like getting half a dozen public referees to his character. The character of the assemblies that met to do justice varied according to political conditions and the status of the parties: sometimes a king or other ruler, or his deputy, presided, sometimes not. Where there was no effective ruler proceedings look more like what we might call arbitrations than lawsuits. That made enforcement harder but did not necessarily affect procedures otherwise. King Alfred of Wessex (871–99) delegated the hearing of one case to an apparently ill-defined group (including 'more men than I can now name', as one of them said later) and only intervened when they asked him, while he was washing his hands, to use his authority to make one of the parties submit to their collective judgement (Keynes 1992). As this may imply, a king was the ultimate authority in secular matters. Even where there was no formal hierarchy of courts or assemblies, where the king was too remote or too weak, or some of those who felt unjustly treated by local powers were too poor and humble to get to him, his duty to protect his people and do justice to them implied some kind of right of appeal to him (Reuter 1993; Fouracre 1995; Nelson 1997).

Collective judgement in conformity with good custom was clearly what was thought normal and right (Weitzel 1985; Davies and Fouracre 1986: 214–28; Reynolds 1997a: 51–9). There was nothing democratic about this: though large assemblies were preferred for important issues, those who took the lead in them were the men (and naturally only men) of the highest status in the community, even if, in the assembly of a village or lordship, that meant only the more prosperous peasants among them. Lords could on occasion bully or overrule their subjects, which explains why in some cases it seems to have been thought right for judgements to be made by the peers of someone accused by his lord. At the lowest level, however, it is easy to see why a peasant might find it hard to get neighbours to swear to his freedom when his and their powerful and influential lord said he was a serf. At the highest level, the emperor Conrad II used emotional blackmail on his son Henry when his nobles refused to condemn a duke who was Henry's friend: the nobles were uncomfortably aware that Henry might soon have replaced his father. Conrad took to his bed and refused to speak until Henry relented (MGH *Briefe* 1949, no. 250). Henry himself, once emperor, was in a position to take a tougher line when he told the Bohemians who wanted their customs preserved that kings had long and iron hands with which to twist the wax nose of the law (Reynolds 1997a: 21). Reports of legislation and litigation nevertheless suggest that laws were supposed to embody the custom of what were thought of as communities of government and law, and that those who made judgements did so on behalf of those imagined communities. Reports of argument are rare but there are enough to suggest that it took place and that, though unsystematic, it was rational in the sense that it was conducted between human beings who were at least supposed to be thinking about what would be just and right in the case at issue. They were not just performing a ritual designed to make peace. Documentary evidence was sometimes produced, examined, and discussed, but the testimony of living witnesses, whether a sworn panel or those who had seen the grant made of the rights exercised, was often preferred. The lay defendant in a case brought by the Abbey of Prüm early in the twelfth century mocked the abbot's reliance on a charter: anyone with a pen could write anything (*Dip. H. IV*: no. 476). If witnesses took part in judgement, that did not matter: the more knowledge of facts and knowledge of law were diffused and shared, the easier it would be to achieve consensus.

Of course, rituals took place, lending authority and publicity to what was decided, but they may have been less rigidly applied than in the age of official records and courts dominated by professional lawyers and judges. Most surviving records from this period were made by churches for their own purposes and can seldom have been consulted. Custom, however supposedly old and unchanging, might therefore in practice be quite flexible. The precedents that were remembered would be those that would suit the case – or the side of the case that the dominant members of the assembly favoured. Words that would later become terms of art were used in different ways by different scribes, who in any case were nearly all writing in Latin, while the oral proceedings they described were presumably in a vernacular. The rights and obligations attached to landed property, moreover, which is what most recorded disputes were about, varied according to political and economic circumstances. Words such as *beneficium*, *feodum*, *alodis* were therefore bound to imply different rights and obligations in different places and at different times (Reynolds 1994).

None of this means that there was no place at all for professionalism or technical knowledge. Some of the commissioners (*missi*) whom Charlemagne sent out with written instructions to judge and administer his empire must have acquired expertise with time, as did the panels of *scabini* or judges, and perhaps some advocates, who served in the north Spanish kingdoms. In Catalonia the texts of Visigothic law were consulted and cited, and from the eleventh century the counts of Barcelona had an archive of charters which must have needed custodians who were at least literate. The judges and notaries of Italian cities kept official records and had a more or less professional expertise and function (Bougard 1995), while there were, of course, academic and professional lawyers in Constantinople. They, however, like the jurists of ancient Rome, may not have had much influence on provincial practice. How far the quite different and un-Roman professionals of Ireland affected practice is also uncertain (Stacey 1994: 127–9). On the evidence we have, it is in any case not easy to draw a boundary between a professionalism derived from formal training and the kind of expertise that comes from long experience and intelligence. The lawspeakers of Iceland and the *ynaid* of Wales may fall on either side of it (Miller 1990: 221–58; Davies 1986). By and large, however, what we know of law in much of Europe at this time suggests that legal knowledge was undifferentiated and widely diffused. Law was based on custom, interpreted when necessary by some kind of collective judgement or advice offered by people who carried weight in their respective communities.

THE TWELFTH CENTURY AND AFTER

Early medieval law, like most law, had some elements that to an outsider look rational and others that look irrational. What happened around the twelfth century was less that law became rational than that it began to become the business of experts, so that its rationality became at once more systematic and more esoteric. The reasons for the change were complex, but it seems clear that economic and demographic growth both encouraged rulers and lesser lords to be more demanding and made possible the spread of schools which provided them with literate and numerate servants to manage their affairs. The overlap between bureaucrats who kept records and lawyers who argued from them was large, especially at first, before jobs had multiplied and skills had become specialised. Law, however, did not become a profession only because it provided employment and profit. It was also intellectually exciting. Its study, like that of theology and philosophy, was based on texts that stimulated thought by combining high authority with length, complexity, and apparent contradictions and obscurities. Written collections of Lombard laws were being studied in north Italy by 1000, and the full text of Justinian's *Corpus* became available about 1070 (Cortese 1995: 1. 238–53, 380–8; 2. 13–27, 38–41). Canonists quickly made use of the Digest, as the study of Church law advanced under the same combination of practical and intellectual pressures (Kuttner 1982). Writers on law, both ecclesiastical and secular, began to pose problems (*quaestiones*), collect contrary authorities that bore on them, construct arguments, and make distinctions and classifications in much the same the way as came to be characteristic of medieval scholarship in general. Both kinds of law, unlike traditional law, not only relied on authoritative texts, but used written procedures. Parties submitted their claims in writing; witnesses were examined on the basis of written articles or interrogatories and their depositions were written down; and sentences or judgements were made by the presiding judge himself. If he was subject to advice it was that of academically qualified lawyers, not of the general public. It was a system well suited to the Church's need to see that decisions conformed to canon law and to allow reports and appeals to be made to Rome, but it was also used and developed in courts practising the civil law (Sayers 1971: 43–5, 78–93; cf. Collinet 1932: 9–11, 28–31, 346–7, 362–6; Fraher 1989a). The resulting records show how more structured procedures went along with more structured argument.

At Pisa the new law was enthusiastically embraced soon after the middle of the twelfth century, and not just by lawyers: the parties themselves, though they presumably took expert advice beforehand, apparently conducted their own cases using procedures and, above all, arguments drawn from Justinian's texts. Roman law evidently worked well, not only to organise witnesses' testimony effectively but to sort out its implications and relate them to explicit arguments (Wickham 1997). This was so even when it was used in the service of traditional norms. Ecclesiastical judges in a late twelfth-century Tuscan case, one of whom was a renowned canon lawyer, combined the new procedures with 'common-sense logic' and 'practical knowledge of the daily norms that governed church procedures' (Wickham 1996). Lawyers trained in the schools were meanwhile working in other Italian, Spanish, and southern French cities, and Roman procedures were widely introduced in Italy during the thirteenth century (Gouron 1993: XVI). The spread of legal expertise did not, however, please everyone. At much the same time as the Pisans – or those of them who could afford to go to law – were taking up Roman methods, complaints about ingenious and cunning arguments in Germany may suggest that law there was subject to more patchy influence from the Italian schools.

Both Catalonia and England illustrate the problem of separating the different influences, intellectual and governmental, on legal development. In Catalonia a written compilation of *Usatges* (i.e. customs) was made in the mid-twelfth century, apparently for the use of judges in the courts of the count of Barcelona. A few clauses in the earliest version possibly imply knowledge of the discussions in Lombardy that produced the *Libri Feudorum*, though probably not of its actual texts. Other clauses that, if not as early, had been included by the end of the century, certainly show knowledge of canon- and Roman-law texts.[5] A different kind of professionalism, which need not have come from the schools, is suggested by twelve documents recording disputes in the count's court between 1143 and 1162.[6] They are not charters made for the benefit of the winner of a case as one finds in many areas earlier but seem to be records which were preserved for legal and governmental use in the count's archive. They are all drawn up in the same regular and systematic way, though without betraying any particular Romanist influence. Each one separates out the different points in dispute, summarises the arguments of both sides on each point and then gives a judgement about who had to prove what and how on that point. Final judgements are rare. Although the cases were heard by panels of judges of the traditional and unprofessional sort, the documents suggest that they had access to people with expertise in legal argument and drafting.

In England the traumas of the Norman Conquest, combined with the preservation of laws issued by English kings before it, may partly explain why law there seems to have become the object of thoughtful and critical, if unsystematic, study before the middle of the twelfth century (e.g. Downer 1972; Wormald 1999: 414–15, 465–77). The real beginning of what became known as the English common law came, however, with the introduction under Henry II (1154–89) of standardised written orders (writs) which could be bought from the royal chancery with minimal trouble and expense in order to start various kinds of litigation about rights in land. The innovation seems, like Roman law in Pisa, to have been popular. The new procedures attracted a great deal of business and created a demand for judges and lawyers who understood them. In the twelfth and thirteenth centuries some English lawyers who practised in the royal courts had clearly studied Roman law and found it stimulating. Later practitioners of English common law probably had not. Their training was acquired not in universities, but by attendance in court and study of the Register of Writs, model statements of cases (pleadings, *narrationes*), and reports of arguments (yearbooks) (Baker 1990; Brand 1992). With the multiplication of writs and forms of action, the arguments of common lawyers became ever more technical and esoteric. By the end of the Middle Ages the procedures of the royal courts in which the common law was practised had become a maze of learning based on Latin writs and records but argued in a form of French that must have been impenetrable to anyone outside the charmed circle of judges, serjeants at law, and aspiring apprentices. It is not hard to see why important people had by then long retained lawyers to advise them and why poor people had long made lawyers their targets in revolts.

Peculiar as English law became, what its origins suggest, when seen alongside what was happening elsewhere, is that the biggest difference was not between Roman law and English law, or canon law and secular law, but between law interpreted by professionals trained on texts – whether the text of Justinian, Gratian, or mere writs – and law based on unwritten custom interpreted by assemblies of non-lawyers. The texts of Roman law were a great stimulus to thought but so were other texts and, above all, the arguments that clever men, trained together in shared methods of reasoning, could construct about them. The new and cunning arguments that worried some twelfth-century Germans may have come from Italy, but, if they concerned property, as they often did, they may have been derived as much from a compilation known as the *Libri Feudorum* as from Justinian (Reynolds 1994). This was soon afterwards attached to Justinian's texts and sometimes studied alongside them, but it seems to record the problems confronted by north Italian lawyers in the early and mid-twelfth century in dealing with royal and ecclesiastical property in the hands of laymen, about which Roman law was not very helpful. Eike von Repgow's *Sachsenspiegel*, written in the 1220s, suggests that German law became more systematic and expert because people like Eike, who attended courts regularly, were beginning to organise their knowledge and arguments more systematically rather than because they had learned much Roman law. The very fact that Eike had the skills to write his book and that it was then widely copied in Germany says much about what was happening to the law (Reynolds 1994: 446–56). The Italian lawyers who compiled the *Libri Feudorum* in the twelfth century, like the English lawyers who wrote *Glanvill* a little later and 'Bracton' in the thirteenth; Alfonso X (1252–84) of Castile and his collaborators on the *Siete Partidas*; Philippe de Beaumanoir, who completed his treatise on the customs of the Beauvaisis in 1283; the Suabian and other followers of Eike in Germany; the authors of the *assises* of Jerusalem in the thirteenth century and the *assises* of Romania (Frankish Greece) in the fourteenth – all display the new combination of interest in the law as practised with interest in the intellectual problems it raised. To classify any of them as 'unlearned' because doctors in law from medieval universities would have done so is to be uncritically enslaved to our sources. For all of them, hard cases made good legal arguments. The law they described, despite Roman – sometimes strong Roman – influences, was basically traditional law made more intellectual and professional and adapted to new kinds of government.

Those who acquired some degree of the new expertise covered a wide range of social status, of legal skills, and of professional commitment. Not all made their living from the law. They were variously organised in different countries and jurisdictions but, except for the canon lawyers, were predominantly laymen. Except in England, the elite who advised rulers and their richer subjects and practised in and around high courts had studied civil (i.e. Roman) or canon law at university, but the great majority of those who now earned their living, or part of it, at some kind of law were probably trained by something more like apprenticeship. As courts began to keep more regular – if maddeningly incomplete – records, and some adopted written procedures, more and more clerks must have been employed. Even more, who were often (outside England) trained as notaries, were employed in writing documents and giving advice about the everyday non-contentious business of law, such as transactions concerning land, trade, and debts. Surviving documents, as well as formularies, suggest increasing professionalism. Title deeds were becoming a normal feature of the conveyance of land and were sometimes confirmed and/or registered in a convenient court for extra security. They were drafted with increasing care, including details designed to avoid trouble in future about what was granted and on what terms. Common form was developing, with variations that should help to illustrate the way in which professional practice varied under different jurisdictions. Grants of privileges and confirmations of customs to local communities, like the collections of laws made by more or less independent communities for themselves, reflect the same need for written records and display the same increasing length, elaboration, and regularity of form, whether they were called charters or custumals in England, *Weistümer* in Germany, *fueros* in Spain, *statuti* in Italy, or *coutumiers* in France. All embodied elements of traditional customary law but were themselves products of the new, professional law, fossilising custom and adapting it to the new world of bureaucratic government. The boundary between the *pays de droit écrit* of southern France and the *pays de droit coutumier* of the north was the product of this new law, rather than a reflection of the earlier survival of provincial Roman law in the south (Krynen 1998). Much of the law of northern Europe, including English common law, the law German historians classify as German rather than Roman, and the 'customary law' of northern France, was indeed still based on custom, but it was the custom of lawyers. Perhaps, despite the tradition of contrasting Roman with customary law, there might be something to be said for considering the Roman law of the period as the custom of a different set – or different sets – of lawyers.

There is much in the new law that seems relatively familiar to modern lawyers. But much was different. Those who see the change to it primarily as from unwritten to written law may forget that the publishing and recording of legislation, for instance, like the keeping of court records, seems to have remained patchy. To some extent this may reflect the chances of survival rather than the lack of publicity at the time. By the later thirteenth century French kings, for instance, were not only legislating regularly over a wide range of matters but seem to have communicated at least some of their ordinances to local officials quite effectively (Krynen 1998). Yet even in England, where bureaucracy had developed so early, official records of legislation were kept only from the later thirteenth century, and even then with notable gaps. Lawyers who stressed the need to name defendants exactly and consistently in writs were apparently content to use books of statutes that gave only the rough gist, or worse, of the text of Magna Carta (Reynolds 1995: V, VI).

By the thirteenth century the combination of professional law and more systematic government was prompting attempts to classify jurisdictions and organise them into regular hierarchies. These were only partially successful. Kings could not yet get rid of the parallel hierarchy of church courts which culminated outside their kingdoms at the papal curia. All they could do was to circumscribe and define boundaries, which varied in different kingdoms, and then turn a blind eye to what went on in practice, provided that it did not threaten their authority too openly (Helmholz 1983; Donahue in Coing and Nörr 1985). Nor was it easy for the most powerful king to obliterate subordinate secular jurisdictions that had become entrenched in custom. The best solution was to use lawyers to classify and circumscribe, thus maintaining royal authority to supervise and adjudicate between rival jurisdictions (Reynolds 1999). Appeals to kings were now beginning to go to regular, permanent courts. The records of the Parlement at Paris show it in action as a royal court both of first instance and of appeal from 1254. Cases seem not to have come to it from all over the kingdom but royal *baillis* were increasingly active as judges in many areas. In 1235 Frederick II set up a royal court (*Reichshofgericht*) for Germany which continued to work until it was reorganised as what German historians call the *Reichskammergericht* (royal or imperial chamber court) in 1495, though the parallel development of jurisdictions within the increasingly independent principalities restricted its activity in comparison to that of royal courts elsewhere. The Italian city-states, where academic and professional law was so highly developed, had paradoxically the most complex and least unified patterns of tribunals, corresponding to their complex patterns of government. How far or when hierarchies in different kingdoms became further complicated by separate 'feudal' courts dealing only with the affairs of free or noble fiefholders is unclear: the old assumption that feudal law was normally applied in separate courts relies less on records of medieval practice than on later theories of feudalism and of the supposed need of separate courts for supposedly separate legal systems (Reynolds 1994).

Where and when experts began to dominate courts, procedures were refined and elaborated, thus inevitably restricting the participation of non-lawyers. Parties to suits needed lawyers to represent or at least advise them, while witnesses, no longer part of a general consensus of judgement, became outsiders to be examined individually according to rules. Canon law contributed a good deal to the law of evidence developed in secular courts, but what was taken from Roman law may sometimes have been little more than words and phrases that lent prestige to procedures, especially new and suspect procedures. Even when rules were derived from authoritative canon- or Roman-law texts, they tended to be amended and reinterpreted as hard cases revealed problems and practice developed (Waelkens 1985; Fraher 1989b). From the fourteenth century advancing bureaucracy brought, if not the greater centralisation and system celebrated by traditional accounts of the 'origin of the modern state', at least more records for study by late medieval and early modern historians. They have been used most for the history of crime (e.g. Gauvard 1993; Zorzi 1994; Smail 1996; Chambers and Dean 1997; Bellamy 1998), in which the beginnings of comparison between countries have been made (Kaeuper 1988; Soman 1992). Through all the changes, however, recourse to arbitration, either as an alternative to formal litigation or interposed between episodes in court, mitigated some of the rigours of law and testified to the survival of old ideas of reconciliation and justice (Powell 1983; Kuehn 1991). Negotiations and settlements out of court do not simply reflect distrust of lawyers and need not imply norms that lawyers did not share. Judges and lawyers sometimes encouraged arbitrations and took part in them. If characteristics of the old law, including the liking for consensus, and the preference for the testimony of live witnesses (even if written down) over documentary evidence, perhaps survived best in courts not dominated by the most highly trained and organised professionals, we should nevertheless not assume that professionals lost all the values of their society when they learned new rules and new methods of argument (Beckerman 1995; Smail 1997; and on thirteenth-century Poland: Górecki 1997, 1998).

There is space here to suggest only one – though an obvious one – of the ways in which the new law affected court procedures. That is its impact on the making of judgements. Collective judgement disappeared most obviously in the procedures that university-trained lawyers learnt with their Roman law. Judgements in the courts of Italian cities and in the royal court of the kingdom of Sicily were sometimes made by *iudices idiotae* – that is judges without university training – but in difficult cases they had to follow the advice of learned lawyers (*consilia sapientium*) whom they or the parties had consulted (Martines 1968). Even without Roman law, however, judgements by unlearned consensus came under threat both from government pressures and from innovations in argument and procedure that lawyers may have made on their own account. Disentangling these different causes is a problem as yet barely tackled.

Trial by one's peers, as one form of collective judgement, had been enshrined in the academic *Libri Feudorum* which some law students studied along with Roman law. One might expect that people of higher status, whose property was now classified as fiefs, were most likely to maintain their right to judgement by their peers. On the other hand, when people of really high status got into trouble they were liable to come before the kind of courts in which lawyers were most dominant and to have to confront rulers who might want them convicted. While rulers were likely to need the support of other great men in such cases, and thirteenth-century references to consultation and consent, in judgements as in legislation, still pay at least lip-service to old ideas, what happened in different kingdoms depended a good deal on political circumstances. Magna Carta's promise of trial by peers implies earlier threats against it in England. The charter no doubt helped collective judgement to survive in the rather restricted form of trial by jury, but its survival may have owed as much to the entrenchment in royal courts of various forms of jury in both civil and criminal cases before the legal profession had become well established. In 1233, when the king accused some rebellious barons of treason and they claimed trial by their peers, a royal counsellor maintained that there were no peers in England, as there were in France, and that judgements in England were made by the king's justices (Reynolds 1997a: 55). Later English kings generally managed to deal with alleged traitors by manipulating juries or bypassing them by acts of attainder passed through parliament. The peers of France meanwhile had by the fourteenth century failed in their claim to be tried only by their fellow peers. Collective judgements survived in the French royal court, but they were made by judges who were predominantly, if not yet exclusively, lawyers. Kings or emperors of Germany, on the other hand, had to treat their princes with care. As late as 1434 an electoral prince was summoned to a royal court but the judgement – if the case had come off – would have been made by the other electors (Krieger 1979: 543–6).

Outside England, the relative scarcity of records of local courts outside towns, and of modern work on their practice, makes it difficult to generalise. In the Beauvaisis during the late thirteenth century judgement of peers was reserved to fiefholders, but a surviving element of wider collective judgement is implied by Beaumanoir's suggestion that bailiffs should take counsel with the wise men in their courts when judging others (Reynolds 1994: 305). Perhaps this reflects a similar norm to that laid down in the *Sachsenspiegel*, and apparently followed generally in Germany, to the effect that people could judge those of lower, but not higher, status than themselves. The effect, as with the introduction of juries in England, was to restrict the number of judgement-makers rather than to eliminate collective judgement in principle. During the later Middle Ages most of those who presided over courts of larger lordships or provinces in France and Germany, like those who probably represented parties in an increasing number of cases before them, were expected to be more or less expert and to follow the appropriate *coutumiers* or lawbooks. It was, however, apparently only around 1500 that government officials and lawyers began to oust other judgement-makers in German provincial courts (*Landgerichte*) (Guenée 1963; Weitzel 1985: 1085).

Collective judgement by non-lawyers probably survived best in towns and villages or other local communities which had been granted the right to try their own lawsuits – except, of course, in those towns where Roman-law procedures were followed so that judgements were made by single professional judges. Charters were not always a protection against encroaching royal or seigniorial power. Many French towns came under closer royal control during the later Middle Ages. In German towns panels of town councillors (*Schöffen*) continued to make judgements and did not come to be dominated by formally trained lawyers until the sixteenth century. Well before then a habit had grown up among German towns of referring difficult cases to high courts (*Oberhöfe*) in particular towns with recognised authority though with no formal and enforceable jurisdiction. The *Schöffen* in these towns, though not trained or earning their living as lawyers, had legal advice and handbooks to consult and must have gained a good deal of expertise on the job (Diestelkamp and Funk 1994). At least some commercial courts and the less formal tribunals that arbitrated disputes between craftsmen also preserved the old ways. Senior merchants or craftsmen generally presided and judgements were generally given by a panel of colleagues, sometimes without any right of appeal beyond the craft. Some courts even tried to exclude lawyers or restrict their activities. Roman law was, however, beginning to influence some commercial courts in Italy by the fourteenth century and was taking over more of them by the sixteenth century (Thomas 1932: xix–xxiii; Ascheri 1989).

Lower courts with jurisdiction over poorer people in the countryside were probably less frequented by lawyers – except as judges – but the wide dispersal of some level of legal knowledge probably doomed to failure the recorded efforts of lords such as the thirteenth-century abbot of St Albans who tried to keep other lawyers out of his courts. Professional procedures certainly filtered down to manorial courts in England, but so did juries, which preserved an element of collective judgement even while restricting it (Maitland 1889: 135–6; Razi and Smith 1996: 26). Elsewhere lawyers presiding over courts in villages without charters or *Weistümer* may well have begun to extend their authority to make or influence judgements.

What used to be called 'the reception of Roman law' by northern Europe in the late fifteenth and early sixteenth centuries falls outside the scope of this chapter, but in so far as historians of early modern law now see it less as a new invasion of Roman ideas and practices than as an intensification of professional control over the courts, that seems consistent with the medieval background sketched here (Gorla and Moccia 1981).

CONCLUSION

There can be few changes in law as important as the change from unprofessional and largely oral customary law to professional, learned law. It is important, nevertheless, to notice that the change from one to the other in medieval Europe was slow, patchy, and incomplete (e.g. for Poland: Górecki 1997, 1998). It did not, moreover, involve a total change in principles or ideas. The Roman and canon law of the later Middle Ages is sometimes seen by its historians as embodying a new common law (*ius commune*) based on 'original and highly significant ideas on equity, human justice, and legality' that underlay and shaped the separate legal systems (*iura propria*) of states and kingdoms (Bellomo 1995: 156). It is true that academic lawyers identified *ius commune* with their sort of law, but others used the expression for the general laws or customs of kingdoms, of lordships, and for something even more vague, such as natural justice, understood in a common-sensical and moralistic, rather than a philosophical, theological, or jurisprudential way. The very idea of a *ius commune* testifies to the continuance of ideas about law and custom that lawyers, like everyone else, took for granted. There can be no doubt about the intellectual achievement of twelfth-century and later legal scholars in articulating principles and devising new methods of argument, but the new law looks more original in its methods and reasoning than in its principles. Most of its principles and values seem to have been around for centuries as unarticulated and unreasoned assumptions underlying the old customary law.

Whether the move towards professionalism made the law of Europe more uniform or more varied is debatable. There was much local variation in early medieval customary law, but the boundaries between varieties, so far as they are known, look uncertain, overlapping, and unsystematic. The effect of the new law, combined with the more systematic and bureaucratic government with which it was so closely connected, was to make boundaries firmer and differences clearer. Separate legal systems developed in separate, effectively independent jurisdictions (e.g. Blanshei 1983). Yet, at the same time, contacts between systems multiplied. The conflict between ecclesiastical law and jurisdiction had become clear by the twelfth century, but medieval people seem to have continued to be reluctant to recognise fundamental conflicts of law within Christendom: they preferred to think in terms of conflicts of jurisdictions rather than of principles. There was much mutual influence and copying, for instance in commercial law. Even English common law was not such a completely separate and total system as it later became. Scotland adapted some of the English writs to different rules, procedures, and terminology (MacQueen 1993). The procedures that were called novel disseisin in both France and England had some similar elements and some different (Reynolds 1999).

The whole subject cries out for more comparisons, not only between different jurisdictions and countries in Europe, but also with other continents – preferably without the teleological assumptions of growing rationality and European superiority that Max Weber made academically respectable. At the same time as law became more professional it changed in ways – different ways in different places – that were probably less connected with each other than tends to be assumed when they are lumped together in a supposed progress towards ever greater rationality. The different kinds of change need to be investigated. That professional law became more systematic in its reasoning is clear. Whether this means it became altogether more rational in a wider sense is harder to say. Ordeals were abandoned but torture was developed, while the trials of animals that look so ludicrous to modern eyes seem to have been a feature of learned law as much as, or more than, they were a feature of simple rustic practices (Cohen 1986). But if it is too simple to see medieval law as progressing to rationality, it is also too simple to see it regressing from happy harmony. Without taking refuge under an equally simplistic functionalism, it seems reasonable to conclude that the new system was an integral part of the new government: both surely resulted from much wider social and economic changes. People at the bottom of society came off badly under both systems, but both reflected and partly embodied aspirations to justice.

NOTES

1 The chapter on Anglo-Saxon law in Pollock and Maitland 1895 is by Pollock but *Township and Borough* and *Domesday Book and Beyond* show Maitland's work on that period. The Collected Papers and his introductions to various Selden Society volumes also contain many insights into later medieval law.
2 Some exceptions: Dawson 1960 and 1968; Berman 1983; for other work by American scholars comparing English and French government and law, see Reynolds 1997a at n. 27. The series of Comparative Studies in Continental and Anglo-American Legal History, which started with Coing and Nörr 1985, includes some volumes on the Middle Ages (e.g. vol. 5. (Baker 1989) and vols 6–7, ed. C. Donahue, on records of church courts).
3 Donahue 1986 provides a recent survey on canon law.
4 I refer generally to 'academic lawyers' rather than 'jurists', because 'jurists' can be ambiguous when used to translate Fr. *juristes* or It. *giuristi*, since these words are used of professional as well as academic lawyers.
5 Bastardas 1991, cc. 29–33, 123, and pp. 9, 170 (c. 88); Valls Taberner 1984, c. 168, and p. 66.
6 *Colección de documentos* 4: nos. 40, 67, 71, 88, 98, 99, 113, 114, 145, 146, 147; *Liber Feudorum Maior*, no. 131 (cf. vol. 2, pp. 409, 600). I am grateful to Professor Adam Kosto for drawing my attention to these documents.

REFERENCES

Amory, P. (1993) 'The meaning and purpose of ethnic terminology in the Burgundian laws', *Early Medieval Europe*, 2: 1–28.

Ascheri, M. (1989) 'La decisione nelle corti giudiziarie italiane del tre-quattrocento e il caso della Mercanzia di Siena', in Baker 1989, q.v.

Baker, J. H. (1990) *An Introduction to English Legal History*, London: Butterworth.

—— (ed.) (1989) *Judicial Records, Law Reports, and the Growth of Case Law*, Berlin: Duncker & Humblot.

Barthélemy, D. (1997) *La mutation de l'an mil a-t-elle eu lieu? Servage et chevalerie dans la France des x⁴ et xi⁴ siècles*, Paris: Fayard.

Bastardas, J. (ed.) (1991) *Usatges de Barcelona: el codi a mitjan segle XII*, Barcelona: Fundacio Noguera.

Beckerman, J. S. (1995) 'Toward a theory of medieval manorial adjudication: the nature of communal judgments in a system of customary law', *Law and History Review* 13: 1–22.

Bellamy, J. G. (1998) *The Criminal Trial in Later Medieval England*, Stroud, Sutton Publishers.

Bellomo, M.(1995) *The Common Legal Past of Europe, 1000–1800*, trans. L. G. Cochrane (of *L'Europa del diritto comune*, 2nd edn 1991), Washington: Catholic University of America Press.

Berman, H. J. (1983) *Law and Revolution*, Cambridge, Mass.: Harvard University Press.

Blanshei, S. R. (1983) 'Criminal justice in medieval Perugia and Bologna', *Law and History Review* 1: 251–75.

Bougard, F. (1995) *La justice dans le royaume d'Italie de la fin du VIIIᵉ siècle au début du XIᵉ siècle*, Rome: École Française de Rome, fasc. 291.

Bowman, J. A. (1997) 'Do neo-Romans curse? Law, land, and ritual in the Midi (900–1100)', *Viator* 28: 1–32.

Brand, P. (1992) *The Origins of the English Legal Profession*, Oxford: Blackwell.

Chambers, D. S. and Dean, T. (1997) *Clean Hands and Rough Justice: an investigating magistrate in Renaissance Italy*, Ann Arbor: University of Michigan Press.

Clanchy, M. T. (1970) 'Remembering the past and the good old law', *History* 55: 165–76.

Classen, P. (1977) 'Fortleben und Wandel spätrömischen Urkundenwesens im frühen Mittelalter', *Vorträge und Forschungen* 23: 13–54.

Cohen, E. (1986) 'Law, folklore and animal lore', *Past & Present* 110: 6–37.

Coing, H. (ed.) (1973) *Handbuch der Quellen und Literatur der neueren Europäischen Privatrechtsgeschichte, I: Mittelalter (1100–1500): Die Gelehrten Rechte und die Gesetzgebung*, Munich: C.H. Beck'sche Verlagsbuchhandlung.

Coing, H. and Nörr, K. W. (eds) (1985) *Englische und Kontinentale Rechtgeschichte/English and Continental Legal History*, Berlin: Duncker & Humblot.

Colección de Documentos inéditos del Archivo General de la Corona de Aragón (1845) ed. P. de Bofarull y Mascaró, 4: Barcelona: Archivero Mayor.

Collinet, P. (1932) *Études historiques sur le droit de Justinien*, 4: *La procédure par libelle*, Paris: Recueil Sirey.

Collins, R. (1998) 'Law and ethnic identity in the western kingdoms in the fifth and sixth centuries', in Smyth, A. P. (ed.) *Medieval Europeans*, Basingstoke: Macmillan: 1–23.

Cortese, E. (1995) *Il diritto nella storia medievale*, Rome: Cigno Galileo Galilei.

Davies, R. R. (1986) 'The administration of law in medieval Wales', in Charles-Edwards, T. and others (eds) *Lawyers and Laymen*, Cardiff: University of Wales Press.

Davies, W. and Fouracre, P. (eds) (1986) *The Settlement of Disputes in early Medieval Europe*, Cambridge: Cambridge University Press.

Dawson, J. P. (1960) *History of Lay Judges*, Cambridge, Mass., Harvard University Press.

—— (1968) *Oracles of the Law*, Ann Arbor: University of Michigan Press.

Diestelkamp, B. and Funk, K. (eds) (1994) *Der Oberhof Kleve und seine Schöffesprüche*, Kleve: Stadtarchiv Kleve.

Dip. H. IV (1941–78): *Diplomata Regum et Imperatorum Germaniae*, 6: *Heinrici IV*, Monumenta Germaniae Historica.

Donahue, C. (1986) *Why the History of Canon Law is not Written*, London: Selden Society.

Downer, L. J. (ed.) (1972) *Leges Henrici Primi*, Oxford: Clarendon Press.

Fouracre, P. (1995) 'Carolingian justice: the rhetoric of improvement and contexts of abuse', *La giustizia nell'alto medioevo (secolo v–viii) Settimane di studio del centro italiano sull'alto medioevo*, 42: 771–803.

Fraher, R. M. (1989a) 'Preventing crime in the high middle ages: the medieval lawyers' search for deterrence', in Sweeney, J. R. and Chodorow, S. (eds) *Popes, Teachers and Canon Law in the Middle Ages*, Ithaca: Cornell University Press: 212–33.

—— (1989b) 'Conviction according to conscience: the medieval jurists' debate concerning judicial discretion and the law of proof', *Law and History Review* 7: 23–88.

Gauvard, G. (1993) 'Les sources judiciaires de la fin du moyen âge peuvent-elles permettre une approche statistique?', in Contamine, P. and others (eds) *Commerce, finances et société*, Paris: Presses de l'Université de Paris-Sorbonne, 469–88.

Górecki, P. (1997) 'Rhetoric, memory, and use of the past: Abbot Peter of Henrykow as historian and advocate', *Cîteaux* 48: 261–93.

—— (1998) 'Communities of legal memory in medieval Poland, c. 1200–1240', *Journal of Medieval History* 24: 127–54.

Gorla, G. and Moccia, L. (1981) 'A "revisiting" of the comparison between "continental law" and "English law" (16th–19th century)', *Journal of Legal History* 2: 143–56.

Gouron, A. (1993) *Droit et coutumes en France aux xiiᵉ et xiiiᵉ siècles*, London: Variorum.

Guenée, B. (1963) *Tribunaux et gens de justice dans le bailliage de Senlis à la fin du moyen âge*, Paris: Faculté de Lettres de l'Université de Strasbourg.

Helmholz, R. (1983) 'Crime, compurgation and the courts of the medieval church', *Law and History Review* 1: 1–26.

Kaeuper, R. W. (1988) *War, Justice and Public Order: England and France in the later Middle Ages*, Oxford: Clarendon Press.

Keynes, S. (1992) 'The Fonthill Letter', in *Words, Texts and Manuscripts. Studies in Anglo-Saxon Culture presented to H. Gneuss*, Cambridge: D. S. Brewer, 53–97.

Krieger, K. F. (1979) *Die Lehnshoheit der deutsche König im Spätmittelalter*, Aalen, Scientia Verlag.

Krynen, J. (1998) '*Voluntas domini regis in suo regno facit ius*', in Iglesia Ferreirós, A. (ed.) *El dret comú i Catalunya: Actes del VII Simposi Internacional*, Barcelona: Fundacio Noguera.

Kuehn, T. (1991) *Law, Family and Women: Towards a Legal Anthropology of Renaissance Italy*, Chicago: University of Chicago Press.

Kuttner, S. (1982) 'The revival of jurisprudence', in Benson, R. L. and Constable, G. (eds) *Renaissance and Renewal in the Twelfth Century*, Oxford: Clarendon Press.

Liber Feudorum Maior (1945–7) ed. F. Miquel Rosell, Barcelona: Consejo Superior de Investigacio Científicas.

McKitterick, R. (1989) *The Carolingians and the Written Word*, Cambridge: Cambridge University Press.

—— (ed.) (1990) *The Uses of Literacy in Early Medieval Europe*, Cambridge: Cambridge University Press.

MacQueen, H. L. (1993) *Common Law and Feudal Society in Medieval Scotland*, Edinburgh, Edinburgh University Press.

Maitland, F. W. (1911) *Collected Papers*, Cambridge: Cambridge University Press.

—— (1898) *Township and Borough*, Cambridge: Cambridge University Press.

—— (1907) *Domesday Book and Beyond*, Cambridge: Cambridge University Press.

—— (ed.) (1889) *Select Pleas in Manorial Courts*, London: Selden Society 2.

Martines, L. (1968) *Lawyers and Statecraft in Renaissance Florence*, Princeton: Princeton University Press.

MGH Briefe (1949) *Die ältere Wormser Briefsammlung*, ed. W. Bulst, Monumenta Germaniae Historica, Briefe der deutschen Kaiserzeit, 3.

Miller, W. I. (1990) *Bloodtaking and Peacemaking: feud, law, and society in saga Iceland*, Chicago: Chicago University Press.

Nelson, J. L. (1997) 'Kings with justice, kings without justice: an early medieval paradox', *La giustizia nell'alto medioevo (secolo ix–xi) Settimane di studio del centro italiano sull'alto medioevo*, 44: 797–826.

Ourliac, P. (1982), '1210–1220: La naissance du droit français', in *Studi in onore di Arnaldo Biscardi*, Milan: Istituto Editoriale Cisalpino, 3: 489–510.

—— (1993) *Les Pays de Garonne vers l'an mil*, Toulouse: Privat.

Pohl, W. (1998) 'Telling the difference: signs of ethnic identity', in Pohl, W. (ed.) *Strategies of distinction: the construction of ethnic identities, 300–800*, Leiden: Brill: 17–69.

Pollock, F. and Maitland, F. W. (1895) *History of English Law before the Time of Edward I*, Cambridge: Cambridge University Press.

Powell, E. (1983) 'Arbitration and the law in England in the late middle ages', *Transactions of the Royal Historical Society* ser. 5, 33: 49–67.

Razi, Z. and Smith, R. M. (eds) (1996) *Medieval Society and the Manor Court*, Cambridge: Cambridge University Press.

Reuter, T. (1993) 'The medieval German *Sonderweg*? The empire and its rulers in the high middle ages', in Duggan, A. (ed.) *Kings and Kingship in Medieval Europe*, London: King's College Centre for late Antique and Medieval Studies: 179–211.

Reynolds, S. (1994) *Fiefs and Vassals: The Medieval Evidence Reinterpreted*, Oxford: Clarendon Press.

—— (1995) *Ideas and Solidarities of the Medieval Laity*, London: Variorum.

—— (1997a) *Kingdoms and Communities in Western Europe, 900–1300 (2nd edn)*, Oxford: Clarendon Press.

—— (1997b) 'The historiography of the medieval state', in Bentley, M. (ed.) *Companion to Historiography*, London: Routledge: 117–38.

—— (1999) 'How different was England?', in Prestwich, M. (ed.) *Thirteenth Century England VII*, Woodbridge: Boydell and Brewer: 1–16.

Sayers, J. (1971) *Papal Judges Delegate in the Province of Canterbury, 1198–1254*, Oxford: Oxford University Press.

Smail, D. L. (1996) 'Common violence: vengeance and inquisition in fourteenth-century Marseille', *Past & Present* 151: 28–59.

—— (1997) 'Archivos de conocimiento y la cultura legal de la publicidad en la Marsella medieval', *Hispania* 57: 1049–77.

Soman, A. (1992) *Sorcellerie et justice criminelle*, London, Variorum: IV ('Deviance and criminal justice in western Europe, 1300–1800').

Stacey, R. C. (1994) *The Road to Judgment: from custom to court in medieval Ireland and Wales*, Philadelphia: University of Pennsylvania Press.

Thomas, A. H. (ed.) (1932) *Calendar of Select Pleas and Memoranda of the City of London, 1381–1412*, Cambridge: Cambridge University Press.

Valls Taberner, F. (ed.) (1984) *Usatges de Barcelona*, Barcelona: Promociones Publicaciones Universitarias de Barcelona.

Waelkens, L. (1985) 'L'origine de l'enquête par turbe', *Revue d'histoire du droit* 53: 337–46.

Weitzel, J. (1985) *Dinggenossenschaft und Recht*, Cologne/Vienna: Böhlau.

White, S. D. (1995) 'Proposing the ordeal and avoiding it: strategy and power in western French litigation, 1050–1110', in Bisson, T. N. (ed.) *Cultures of Power*, Philadelphia: University of Pennsylvania Press: 89–123.

Wickham, C. (1996) 'Ecclesiastical dispute and lay community: Figline Valdarno in the twelfth century', *Mélanges de l'école française de Rome: moyen âge*, 108: 7–93.

—— (1997) 'Derecho y prática legal en las comunas urbanas italianas del siglo xii: el caso de Pisa', *Hispania* 197: 981–1007.

Wormald, P. (1977) '*Lex Scripta* and *Verbum Regis*: Legislation and Germanic kingship from Euric to Cnut', in Sawyer, P. H. and Wood, I. N. (eds) *Early Medieval Kingship*, Leeds: Leeds University School of History, 105–38.

—— (1999) *The Making of English Law: King Alfred to the Twelfth Century*, 1, Oxford: Blackwell.

Zorzi, A. (1994) 'The judicial system in Florence in the fourteenth and fifteenth centuries', in Dean, T. and Lowe, K. J. P. (eds) *Crime and Disorder in Renaissance Italy*, Cambridge: Cambridge University Press: 40–58.

CHAPTER TWENTY-NINE

RULERS AND JUSTICE, 1200–1500

Magnus Ryan

One of the most compact and justly famous ideal visions of late-medieval government is owed to Jean, lord of Joinville, who, in his biography of his king, fellow-crusader, and friend, Louis IX, provides a veritable idyll of kingship. It begins in the chateau of Yeres, where, in 1254, Louis IX heard a sermon preached by a Franciscan friar, who drew the lesson from scripture that 'no realm was ever lost, nor passed to the lordship of another, except by default of right'. Louis took the lesson to heart. Good and swift justice was what he owed his subjects, and delivered to them, in Joinville's opinion: 'which is why Our Lord suffered him to hold his kingdom in peace for all his life'. According to Joinville it was Louis' wont after mass to sit beneath an oak in the Bois de Vincennes, surrounded by his entourage but unencumbered by ushers or stewards, and so to make himself available to all who sought redress for their grievances. In other words, Louis held court, and Joinville describes him assigning the various pleas of his subjects to his officers and courtiers, two of whom Joinville names: Pierre de Fontaines and Geoffroi de Villette, charging them to hear a case (Jean de Joinville 1871: 199)

A great deal of later medieval kingship is in this story, and a fair portion of what is not can nevertheless be inferred from it. To begin with the obvious: there was an indissoluble link between the exercise of rule and the administration of justice. To forget that elementary connection could result in the loss of a kingdom. The Franciscan who preached before Louis would not have found it hard to illustrate the point. Had not Saul, the first king of the Chosen People, been found wanting and consequently been delivered to the Philistines along with his sons? (1 Samuel 15, 26; 1 Samuel 31). Had not David, his successor, been driven from Jerusalem by his own son Absalom, that same Absalom who, having lamented at the gates of the city that there was none to do justice in the land, had softened the people to his planned revolt by insinuating himself into David's neglected position as judge over them, innocently asking as he did so, 'Who constitutes me over the land, that all who have a suit come to me, and that I judge justly?' (2 Samuel 15). The vignette of his sylvan court is intended to show that Louis IX could never have been found wanting in the same way as David, and to warn the patroness of Joinville, Jeanne of Navarre, that her husband Philip IV might do better to show himself the king of his people and not merely of his bureaucrats.

Secondly, it should be noted that Louis delegates. The demand is not, therefore, that the king concern himself with every plea of his subjects. It is sufficient that he is accessible and equipped with the right subordinates to allow him to judge through their persons. There is, in this respect, a world of governmental assumptions in the very grammar of Louis' order to Pierre and Geoffroi: 'delivrez *moi* ceste partie'. They hear the case, but they do so for Louis. Indeed, prior to the passage in which this summary habit of dispensing justice in the open air is described, Joinville relates how Louis would drop in on two other trusted deputies, Simon de Nesle and Jean, Count of Soissons, and ask if there was any judicial business which could not be expedited without his physical presence. The bureaucrats, whose daily job it was to hear pleas and appeals according to established procedures, and in established places (rather than in woods), would on occasion want the king with them, therefore. This is why, to cite one case from dozens of possible examples, the court rolls of King John of England are occasionally annotated by his officials: 'Speak with the lord king . . . ' (Warren 1978: 143).

Who, then, were the right subordinates? By the first decade of the fourteenth century, when Joinville wrote, the administration of justice had long ceased to be the inspirational art of Solomon. It was for rulers to intervene and show clemency; it was for rulers' servants to keep the governance of the land in good order. The broad trend throughout the period is towards the professionalisation of such servants. It is typical that one of the two men to whom Louis might delegate a case beneath his oak, Pierre de Fontaines, wrote a resumé of the customs of Vermandois (where he had been royal *bailli*) for Louis' son Philip III. His treatise belongs to a well-defined genre: Philippe de Beaumanoir did the same for the customs of the Beauvaisis, and an anonymous author discussed the customs of Touraine-Anjou and Orléans in the so-called *Établissements de Saint Louis* (1272–3). Pierre's own contribution would further include a French translation of numerous passages from a text which, in many ways, underlay the professionalisation of government in France, Italy, Germany and the Hispanic kingdoms: the Roman law of Justinian, the so-called *Corpus iuris civilis*. The *Établissements* also use Roman law in some measure (Horn 1973: 279). Even in England, where the precocious Common Law deserved its name and frequently limited the application of such scholarly texts in all but the ecclesiastical courts, the author commonly referred to as Bracton still used snippets from the academic tradition to adorn his *Treatise on the Laws and Customs of England* (Brand 1996; Richardson 1965: 92–151). It is not certain (indeed, it is most unlikely) that Pierre or any of the other authors mentioned above had received a university education in Roman law. This is partly why the role of Justinian is supplementary in these texts, rather than essential: citations are made from the Roman law as examples of individual customs, or perhaps the Roman law is being used as a model for dividing the material to be discussed into clear categories and so on. The passages are in any case not quoted at random, and as the selections of practitioners who had risen high in royal and princely service, they should be taken seriously. They are testimony to the power of the great 'taught' laws of Rome outside a straightforwardly 'learned' culture.

The twelfth century had begun the age of the lawyers. The initial steps taken in Bologna were quickly emulated elsewhere in Italy and further afield, such as the Rhone valley. The first known polemic by a theologian against the venality of lawyers is dateable to around the middle of the twelfth century. By 1200 there were few areas where Roman law and the papal letters which were rapidly transforming and extending canon law were entirely unknown. The thirteenth century, however, was the age of the lawyer triumphant. The most advanced graduates bore the accolade, which was also a technical term, of 'doctor of both laws (*utriusque iuris doctor*)', meaning they had mastered both Justinian and the various collections of canon law, the law of the Church. Romanists, canonists, and doctors in both laws: these were the new force in the thirteenth century, whose influence would outlast the Middle Ages. The signs of their hegemony are to be encountered in a myriad of contexts. By the end of the century, an irate pope would declare to a French embassy, 'We have been an expert in law for forty years and *we know* that two powers have been ordained of God.' The speaker, Boniface VIII, went on to ask (rhetorically, but with the French king and his propagandists in mind) who could possibly believe the pope to be so fatuous as not to know this. The choice of words is eloquent testimony to the changes wrought in the manner in which office, responsibility and authority were regarded during the thirteenth century. Boniface is not saying that he, as pope, would hardly be so stupid as to deny the validity of God's division of powers over the Christian people. Nor is he saying that he, as a theologian, hardly needed instruction on the relationship between *regnum* and *sacerdotium*. Far from it: Boniface is a *lawyer*, and this is why the insinuations of the French are so wide of the mark. That is a very thirteenth-century progression of ideas. It is equally true to the age that when the French attempted to abduct Boniface and make him stand trial for heresy, the leader of the force sent to the papal residence at Anagni, Guillaume de Nogaret, was a Roman lawyer from the university of Montpellier (Gouron 1998). Law had become as much a part of the language and exercise of power as theology had been, and like theology was to prove more than capable of absorbing even that other great thirteenth-century vogue, Aristotelian doctrine.

There had often, if not always, been law; there had not always been lawyers, at least not in the professional and monopolistic sense now inseparable from the word in our modern vocabulary (Fried 1974; Padoa-Schioppa 1979). The one did much to bring the others into being, for the *Corpus iuris civilis* was vast, complex, and intriguing: its mastery quickly became a career, frequently involving foreign travel to a school with the authority to issue credible qualifications, a lengthy period as a resident-alien there, in many cases debt, and, as it seems, examinations of truly terrifying detail and public exposure (Bellomo 1979). Some measure of this awesome task can be gathered by reflecting on the length of the standard gloss to the Roman law, which was regularly being copied at the same time as the texts themselves by the last third of the thirteenth century. This so-called Ordinary Gloss (*Glossa ordinaria*), composed by the great teacher of law at Bologna, Accursius, amounted to over 96,000 separate annotations. Nobody knew them all, but all were potentially relevant. This, moreover, was just the beginning for many. It might have been true, as was said at the time, that 'A civilian (i.e. Roman) lawyer is worth little without the canons . . . ' but it was beyond doubt, as the same tag ran, that ' . . . a canonist without the Roman law is worth nothing whatsoever'.

Justinian was not, therefore, just the familiar of French royal servants by the end of the century. Without ever becoming the law of any given territory, the Roman law became the frequency of communication between governments across Europe, and the language in which many royal, princely, civic and ecclesiastical advisers couched their opinions. Sources everywhere reveal how inextricably administration, political advice and a knowledge of the law were linked. In 1281 the small commune of Prato, a near-neighbour of the powerful city of Florence and subservient to Florentine policies, was asked to give an oath of fealty to Rudolf of Habsburg, the emperor-elect, in the person of his Vicar General in Italy, Rudolf von Hoheneck (Kern 1911: 172). Florentine traditions and interests made it likely that Prato would eventually have to side not with the would-be emperor, but with the traditional rival of the emperors in northern Italy, the pope. Temporising until the Florentines told them what to do, the Council of Prato sent a number of embassies to the legate's court. The minutes of the council meeting of 7 August record the instructions given to the next set of ambassadors, and in so doing, refer to the outcome of a previous meeting between representatives of Prato and the imperial legate:

> [It is decided] that the ambassadors seek to discover from Rudolf, by which formula and in which way he intends and wishes that the commune of Prato should do fealty to him, receiving in the place of and in the name of the most serene lord Rudolf, King of the Romans and Perpetual Augustus, for the people of Prato are extremely puzzled by the words and response to their [previous] ambassadors by the lord Guido de Suzzara, professor of laws, insofar as the said lord Guido stated in public that the commune of Prato was not of the same condition as the other communes of Tuscany, since the commune and land of Prato had been bought, just as one buys a horse or a field. And for this reason, until they explain the foregoing, they should excuse the commune of Prato if it does not invite them [i.e. Rudolf and his court] to the aforesaid territory.

Guido de Suzzara was one of the most famous Italian lawyers of his generation (Martino 1981). Here, he is proving his worth, just as two equally august colleagues of his, Iacobus de Bellovisu and Iacobus de Butrigariis, proved their worth when they wrote a legal consultation for the commune of San Gimignano about the homage claimed by the Angevins in 1313 (Ascheri 1985). What Guido meant by saying that Prato could not give an oath because it had been bought is not clear in detail. The general point is uncontroversial, however: for legalistic reasons as obvious as the plain contract of sale, Prato was not mistress of her own destiny. The atmosphere of political interchange which this anecdote conveys is typical of the period. A court meets to welcome an embassy. The ensuing discussion of terms is for the most part a discussion between lawyers. The matters at issue are not always even mentioned in Roman law, for Justinian's men had never encountered fealty and homage (Ryan 1998). Yet the majority of the learned sources deployed in these arguments, of such importance in diplomacy, are taken from Justinian.

The Church was standard-setting in the professionalisation of political and administrative life. In the second half of the twelfth century, Gratian's *Concordance of Discordant Canons* (or, familiarly, *Decretum*), a private compilation of ancient authorities interspersed with detailed analytical passages by Gratian himself, had become the foundational text of canon law. Within a couple of decades it was being glossed, epitomised, quoted in disputations from Angevin England, through the Paris basin to the Rhineland and Italy. Little is known about Gratian. He seems to have been a Camaldolese monk working at Bologna (Cortese 1995: 200; cf. Winroth 2000: 5–8). His brilliant creation was therefore the work of a private scholar, which contemporaries occasionally even found difficult to characterise according to the broad categories of medieval library catalogues: was it theology or law? No subsequent text of any importance in the teaching of canon law would ever occasion such doubt. By 1234, in addition to the *Decretum*, which would remain the first, basic text in the education of canonists, the Church had an obviously legal text of irrefragable authority in the shape of the *Liber Extra*, containing 1,971 carefully selected and edited passages from papal letters and pre-existing collections of papal letters. Crucially, it had been commissioned and formally promulgated as law by Gregory IX. The only other legal text of comparable systematic structure to have been published by the time the *Extra* appeared was that of Frederick II for the kingdom of Sicily, the Constitutions of Melfi, subsequently called the *Liber Augustalis*, itself a landmark on the long journey to legislation in the modern sense, but for all that, not nearly as influential as Gregory IX's creation (Wolf 1973; Caravale 1997). The *Extra* was followed in 1298 by Boniface VIII's *Liber Sextus* (or simply the *Sext*). By the middle of the fourteenth century, after the addition of yet more collections of papal letters to the canonists' armoury of texts, the *Corpus iuris canonici* amounted to the largest purely medieval, collected and *edited* body of law then in existence.

The significance of all this editorial work and its diffusion is vast. The canon law could be consulted, minor variations in manuscript traditions notwithstanding, in the same form in every major library and seat of government in Europe. The great majority of popes in the period were canon-lawyers, who preferred to be surrounded by men of like mind when they did business. Most thirteenth-century cardinals, therefore, were selected for their legal expertise (Ullmann 1976). Canon law was honoured and dishonoured in different ways across Europe, such that even from one diocese – let alone country – to the next, different themes would be of practical significance. A canonist working at an ecclesiastical court in England in the late fifteenth century would find his professional time taken up by categories of litigation accounting for little if any of the practice of his French counterparts, and vice versa (Helmholz 1990; 1996). As long as we do not attribute to the canon law a territorially homogeneous field of application across Europe, then we may see it for what it actually was: an expression of a kind of universalism less concrete but no less real than architectural, musical and other artistic and devotional movements.

It will take many more years before the significance of the legal revolution in medieval government is fully appreciated. Historians of law are perforce working only slowly towards the larger questions by means of specialist studies. What effects, for example, did codifications such as the *Liber Extra* and the *Liber Augustalis* have which are not discernible in countries with vigorous, professional, non-codified legal cultures, pre-eminently England (Brand 1997)? This would be most worth answering in relation to Castile–León, where an imposing 'legislative' effort was made by Alfonso the Wise in the shape of the *Libro del Fuero de las Leyes* and its later revisions, culminating in the collection known as the *Siete Partidas* (Wolf 1973: 671–4). It is known that it took well over half a century for the collection to win much authority among the political public. How did this eventually manifest itself, and with what results? More generally, what were the results when rulers took over the function of legislation? After all, and as we have seen, the greatest descriptions of thirteenth-century legal practice such as Beaumanoir's *Coutumes* and the *Établissements* are private works. The latter were provided with a forged prologue which masqueraded as a piece of royal legislation, it is true, but even in the later Middle Ages, the actual bulk of French royal *ordonnances*, the real legislation, is very slight (Giordanengo 1988; Giordanengo 1997). The creation of law, as a more specific activity than the establishment of justice between parties, seems to have crystallised only slowly as a definitively ruling function (Gagnér 1960). We are, for example, accustomed to see the medieval papacy to a large extent as a legislative organ. How much legislation can we identify, however? True, there are the law books themselves, the decretals. Yet it appears that papal law had as much to do with the teachers of the law, that is, the canonists active at the universities, as it did with the popes themselves. In addition, the real law was much more than the contents of the decretal collections. It included the standard glosses to those collections, to name but the most prominent suppletive source. Not, of course, that the gloss itself was 'law'. Even the lawyers who maintained that it was heresy to deviate from the teachings of Accursius – and there were such people – would still have balked at calling his gloss *ius*, let alone *lex*. It is more the case that the law was mediated through the gloss and other forms of exegesis. But this summary, too, leaves something to be desired. It omits that which is perhaps most characteristic of medieval Roman-canon law, for in practice the law included that most elusive yet most influential of all forces in the alignment of powers in the Church, or in the framing of a decision in a secular court in, say, an Italian commune: the common opinion of the lawyers or *communis opinio*. Not even the most technically sophisticated, apparently modern 'codification' such as the *Liber Extra* was sufficient to itself; what was law, and what was not, was therefore by no means such a simple-minded and naïve question as it sounds today. There was little point, as lawyers themselves would occasionally point out, in having laws unless there were also people on the spot to interpret and apply them (Linehan 1971: 36 n.2). This is obvious. It is less obvious, but crucial nevertheless, that medieval lawyers created by habitual if unofficial means a great deal more of medieval law than their professional successors do in a modern state.

In the way later medieval polities functioned, the formation of a professional, administrative elite might therefore have been of equal weight to the formulation and dissemination of political doctrines. Did the deployment of these sophisticated, often highly charged written sources of law (actually, somebody else's law: either Justinian's or the pope's) by university-trained bureaucrats itself instil new habits of mind in rulers? The question is unanswerable in this form, but it can be put in other ways, which allow us at least to introduce one of the more general questions animating modern research: did the way royal, princely, papal and civic advisers worked influence the way in which assessments of legality and illegality were made at the policy-making level? Did the method, as much as the substantive learning, of these people add a significant third element to what we are accustomed to treat as a series of dialogues when we try to imagine late medieval political disputes? When, for example, Henry VII's efforts to condemn Robert of Naples for treason ran

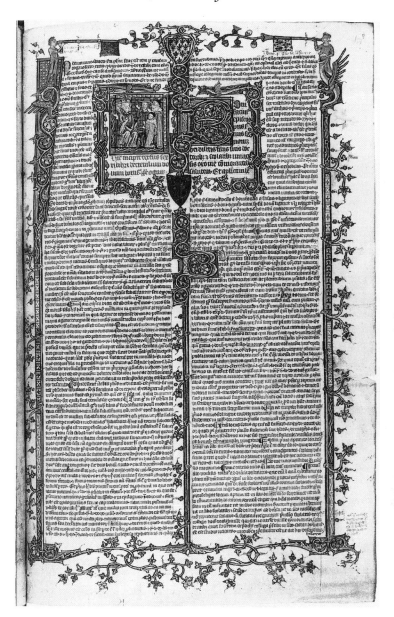

Figure 29.1 The opening of the Sext, the collection of canon law promulgated by Boniface VIII in 1298. The rectangle of text is enclosed by the gloss of Johannes Monachus which was soon adopted as its standard commentary. The disproportion of commentary to text provides a visual metaphor for the predominance of lawyers in the Church. In due course the circumambient gloss would overwhelm the text altogether. Note that, in marked contrast to the dominant figure he strikes in Figures 31.1 and 31.2, in the miniature here the seated pope is almost dwarfed by the attendant cardinals. Cambridge, St John's College, MS. 4, fo. 124r (early fourteenth century). By permission of the Master, Fellows and Scholars of St John's College, Cambridge.

foul of the papal agenda in Piedmont and Naples, the precise nature of Robert's subjection to the emperor was discussed, as it had to be, in terms of homage and fealty (Ryan 1998; Pennington 1993: 165–90). Yet the manner in which these abstract quantities of apparently impeccable medieval pedigree were weighted in the various memoranda and public declarations surviving from the three courts involved is entirely conditioned by Roman and canon law, in the form in which the respective coteries of advisers had learnt them at the universities (Schwalm 1909–11: 1312). This is in itself no different from the kind of debate between the representatives of Prato and Rudolf von Hoheneck. The question it raises, however, is subtly different. Can we be sure that Henry and Robert themselves, never mind the pope, were not thinking in terms of – the expression is ugly but expressive – *ius commune* homage and fealty when they made other decisions? In other words, the documents which tell us so much about what lawyers were capable of doing for their lords and masters when they were pitched against each other in pen-wars such as this might also imply that there was a continuity, not a disjuncture, between the way in which the advisers saw the world and the way in which their masters did. It might be seriously misconceived to imagine the lawyers, with their rebarbative and obscure authorities, translating the very stuff of medieval government, obedience and subjection (such as homage and fealty) into their own language for the purposes of explicitly legal debate. We might be better placed to understand other situations if we give at least some of these legal outpourings the benefit of the doubt, for it is possible that they are a lot closer to the mentality of the main protagonists than we are accustomed to think.

In the case at hand, for example, we should not dismiss lightly the suspiciously academic fabric of the arguments put forward on behalf of Henry VII. Emperors had, after all, been used to formulating their political objectives and prerogatives in the language of Roman law since the mid-twelfth century at least, when Frederick I (Barbarossa) redefined his imperial powers in the old Lombard kingdom with the help of the four most famous Bolognese glossators of their generation. This does not mean that Henry VII was *au fait* with the latest scholarship on the doctrine of unjust enrichment, or on the vexed relationship between right, dominion, and legal remedy (both are close contenders if we seek the medieval lawyers' version of the theological dispute about angels dancing on pin-heads). It does mean that the existence of monopolistic cliques, professional elites such as the lawyers formed wherever they were active, is not so much evidence of a gulf between their outlook and that of their clients, as a gulf between the respective levels of *expertise*. It took a lawyer to advance a well-founded case for high treason, Roman law's *crimen maiestatis*. It did not take a lawyer to sense it, give it a Roman name, and follow the outlines of any ensuing argument. Henry spoke a variety of languages to different degrees of fluency, each employed for specific purposes, evoked by specific circumstances. Who is to say whether he would first have conceived of Robert's treason as *trahison, lèse majesté* (as a noble of European standing brought up in the Francophone ethic of chivalry), or as the Latin *crimen laesae maiestatis*? (There is no German equivalent dateable to the early fourteenth century which is not an obvious translation of the Latin of Justinian.) It is precisely because so much of the evidence of professional legal activity is at the same time evidence of political consultation, evidence which opens up for us the very intimacies of medieval government, that speculations such as these are worth prosecuting. But whatever the case should turn out to be concerning secular rulers, there is no doubt whatsoever that for one government at least, the language of the university-mediated law was the language of reality: the Papacy.

Consider the following case, which exemplifies many of these themes. Sometime between 1328 and 1330, Pope John XXII asked his circle of legal advisers at the *curia* in Avignon for an opinion on the legality of a measure he was considering to combat the influence of Lewis the Bavarian, King of the Romans and would-be emperor. Lewis had succeeded in having an antipope elected in Rome, Peter of Corbara who took the name Nicholas V. Although the story of Corbara's 'pontificate' is short and depressing, the authorities in Avignon had to take the matter seriously (Partner 1972: 318–20). Could, wondered the pope, sanctions be imposed on the city of Rome to prevent the pilgrim trade enriching the enemies of the Church? We do not know how many consultations were written on the point. One has survived from the pen of one of the most celebrated practising canonists of the fourteenth century, Oldradus de Ponte (Oldradus de Ponte 1472: *consilia* no. 62). The discussion is technical, as indeed it had to be. The debate is conducted almost entirely according to the *Decretum* of Gratian, the *Liber Extra*, and the *Sext*. Roman law is also cited in plenty. As the discussion proceeds from what is allowed to what is fitting, and from what is fitting to what is the best course (*Quod licet, quod decet, quod expedit* – all in unacknowledged emulation of Innocent III's *modus operandi* in the decretal *Magnae devotionis, Extra* 3.24.7), an exquisitely nuanced, balanced and judicious analysis builds up of what papal power actually is. First, the pope has a plenitude of power, a *plenitudo potestatis*: this is beyond doubt. It means he is able to revoke judicial sentences, statutes and privileges (the last category is the relevant one in this case, for Rome is a privileged city *par excellence*, and it is precisely these privileges which, or so it is feared, will make the antipope rich). Secondly, Lewis the Bavarian and Peter of Corbara are enemies of the Church, heretics and fomenters of schism. This means there is a just cause for the exercise of the plenitude of power. On the other hand, Rome is more than just a privileged city. Her privileges stem from Christ directly, not from the pope. Canon law does not suffer an inferior to revoke the privileges conferred by his superior, therefore the pope may not tamper with Rome's special status. As for what is fitting, Oldradus has this to say:

> Most Holy Father, it seems that for as long as there are other remedies which relate directly to those damned people, the usurper and the heretic, then that which also appears to detract from the honour of the blessed apostles should be avoided. It is the business of a successor to augment the honour of his predecessors. This is why we are enjoined to complete the works initiated by a predecessor [. . .] And if injury is done to the sepulchre of a testator or his remains, then it is taken as an injury to his heir or successor [. . .] and since you are the successor of the Apostles you should augment their honour and not diminish it.

The interest of all this derives not simply from the point being made, but from the manner in which it is made. The holder of a plenitude of power, the Vicar of Christ, whose power (according to well-received, if in some quarters still-disputed papal theory) is without weight, number or measure but which itself gives weight, number and measure to all other jurisdictions, is being told that he cannot and should not do something (Giles of Rome 1929: 206–9). This, dramatic as it is, yet gives no flavour of what it was like for consultant jurists such as Oldradus to live, as it were, with a plenitude of power day by day. This is why the passage above is quoted at length. The sections omitted are actually the probative passages, references to normative sources. The first is from Roman law, more specifically *Code* 8.11.23. It prohibits incoming public officials from devoting resources to public works until those projects begun under their predecessor have been completed. The second is from canon law, *Liber Extra* 1.3.39, which establishes that when one pope has installed a cleric as a canon of a particular church by monitory letters, and the next pope sends executive letters in favour of the same person, then the act is ascribed to the first pope. Hardly the stuff of constitutional debate, one would have thought, and of course these texts were not written as such. As the very context in which Oldradus uses them shows, however, virtually every passage from the books of law could move any lawyer worth the name to a pregnant political analogy. Argument concerning central issues of politics, the government of the Church, the correct use of papal prerogative, in short, justice and injustice, frequently took this at first sight obscure, capricious form. Medieval debate about the power of popes, kings and emperors was not simply theory, as our very concrete example shows. Such debates were, on the contrary, part of the job of advising a ruler, and it was a decisively important part of the ruler's job to consider the advice tendered. Moreover, the options were not circumscribed by the clean alternatives apparently implied by vocabulary such as *potestas absoluta* (absolute power), *potestas ordinata* (ordained power) and the like. Between the polar opposites fell the shadow of *ius commune* (Pennington 1993: 38–75).

That still left some difficult matters of interpretation to the practical good sense of rulers and their lawyers alike. The way in which Oldradus broke up his discussion into the Innocentian categories of the licit, the proper and the expedient is testimony to this. However, there were some difficulties which defied such robust treatment. We note that Oldradus had no difficulty in identifying Lewis as an usurper. That was inevitable from a papal perspective. The question of legitimacy was not so easily decided in other situations, and it is to the vexed question of what, or rather *who*, constituted a just ruler that we must now turn.

Not everybody was in the enviable position of Joinville, whose king was defined as the rightful ruler by mechanisms of succession already employed for over two and a half centuries (and enhanced by the seemingly unfailing ability of the Capetians to sire sons), and the chrism of St Denis with which he was anointed at his coronation. A number of Italian cities between the Alps and the often fluid northern boundary of the Kingdom of Sicily had developed innovative means of governing themselves in the eleventh and twelfth centuries. In defiance of the emperors and occasionally of the popes, they elected their own officials, known as consuls on the Roman republican model, redacted their own statutes, laid claim to their own hinterlands and in all important respects ran themselves. By the mid-fourteenth century the surviving examples of these notoriously unstable constitutions were rare. At their best, the so-called communes (the word is inaccurately used to denote a city) were never more than oligarchies, whose power-wielding elites were mostly forced to acknowledge the claims of the richer *popolo* to rule alongside them. The result was less often the broadening of the mandate of the ruling council than the creation of a second government, with powers to legislate for the section of the populace it represented. Cities with two or more statute books were no oddity in thirteenth- and fourteenth-century northern Italy. This bewildering and violent situation prompted energetic literary activity, with the result that Italy developed its own brand within the genre known as political advice books, less accurately as 'Mirrors of princes literature' (Berges 1938).

The surviving examples repay individual analysis, but a certain formalism is unmistakeable in this tradition. The most original were written as occasional pieces by a lawyer, indeed, by *the* lawyer of the mid-fourteenth century, Bartolus of Sassoferrato (Quaglioni 1983). Bartolus' treatises *On Guelphs and Ghibellines*, *On the Governance of a City*, and *On Tyrants* are so distinctive because they represent an attempt to select for the benefit of law-students all that is important in the political advice literature composed most frequently, and most famously, by theologians. With adaptations made for an Italian context to the overwhelmingly monarchic tendencies of his main sources (Giles of Rome's *De regimine principum*, and Thomas Aquinas' work of the same name along with its continuation by Ptolemy of Lucca), Bartolus sets about analysing the strengths and weaknesses of Italian civic government, a matter which he believes (adamantly) is best left in the hands of a broadly based council, elected and replaced periodically. Bartolus combines generalisation with detail in a manner unparalleled by any other contemporary writer of political advice. For example, theologians appear to have seen nothing problematic in the notion of the common or public good, itself the main principle of organisation employed by Aristotle in his *Politics*, one of the most important authorities for such writers. Who, however, composed the collectivity in or of an Italian city, the collectivity whose good was the common one, as opposed to cliques and factions whose 'good' was only a relative one, usually inimical to the interests of the whole? What happened if a tyrant claimed to represent the whole community? There were theories at hand in the papal apologetic which, with only a little twisting, could be pressed into the service of such men in an arrant subversion of accepted values.

These questions were especially topical in the Italian cities in which Bartolus spent his life. While there is no easy answer offered in any of his writings, we might yet say that their strength lies in their weakness. Giles of Rome had listed many marks of tyranny (*De regimine principum* 3.2.10). Bartolus gives the civilian commentary on each (Quaglioni 1983: 197–202). The only ones he accepts without reservation are the encouragement of civil discord in order to prevent the formation of a common front against the tyrant, the impoverishment of the population, and, finally, the adherence to one party in disregard of all the interests of the other party or parties (although he does not insist on this final criterion). The casualties in Giles' list are important and express much about the differences in political reality across Europe, for Giles wrote for a king of France, despite his own Italian upbringing, whereas Bartolus is writing for lawyers in Perugia. The expulsion of leading citizens is not always a tyrannical act; how else should a legitimate government protect itself against insurrection by the over-mighty? The use of informers is likewise a weapon for the good as well as the bad, as is the prohibition of assemblies – even apparently legal ones, which can serve as camouflage for coups. Everything in Bartolus' vision depends upon the existence of a just cause, which excuses what otherwise appear to be heavy-handed disciplinary measures. What, however, defined the justice of the cause in a city whose claim to exist as an autonomous entity derived from an act of usurpation against the emperor? No Italian theorist ever solved this conundrum, which lost none of its ideological urgency despite the submission of the free cities (barring Florence) to the rule of one master or *signore* by the end of the fifteenth century. The comparison between Bartolus and Giles also brings out the common assumptions between the lawyers and the theologians, who formed the two broadest groups of intellectuals, opinion-makers and administrators, often portrayed as being at loggerheads with each other. What emerges in all clarity from Bartolus' treatises, barely altered in the process of transplantation from a theological to a juristic environment, is the odium in which tyrants were held. A ruler without justice was an abomination for all late-medieval authors, as he had been ever since Gregory the Great put the responsibilities of the ruler in the same category as those of the priest. Both had a pastoral care, both exercised functions which could only be understood within a Christian community (Arquillière 1934). Later-medieval thinkers took the Church not merely as a community of faith, but in some measure as a community embodying another kind of virtue as well: justice. It was, after all, a widespread and time-honoured misinterpretation that the great St Augustine had meant the visible, present-day church-militant when he declared in *The City of God* 'Justice is found where God, the one supreme God, rules an obedient City according to his grace' (Augustine of Hippo 1972: 890; Giles of Rome 1929: 70–96). This made it extremely difficult to conceive of any large section of the church militant, say a kingdom or principality, being ruled unjustly except as a deplorable deviation from the correct standard of Christian living, to be endured so long as it could not be put right. The linkage between tyranny and heresy was a natural one for many, given these theological postulates. Nonetheless, sentences of excommunication and eventual condemnation of the Italian opponents of the Papacy such as Ezzelino da Romano, lord of Verona in 1254, or the Visconti of Milan in the 1320s smacked of opportunism, and did much to discredit the orthodoxy they ostensibly defended.

The most subtle effect of legal education was to ensure that the evil that men did lived after them. Lawyers then as now relied to a great extent upon concrete examples in their teaching. Moreover, since *communis opinio* was so important in legal argument teachers often had to orientate their students in scholarly debates already decades old. In doing this, they unwittingly contributed to the collective political conscience. It is as if their frequent returns to the scene of the crime kept that crime in the public eye long after the brute facts of reality had made all amends impossible. This was the case with the kingdom of Sicily, which in 1309 descended to Robert the Wise, third son of Charles II of Anjou, when the successor should by rights have been Charles II's young grandson Carobert, the son of Charles II's dead eldest son, Charles Martel. The claims of primogeniture favoured Carobert, but the Papacy needed a vigorous protector in southern Italy, not a minor, who by virtue of his tender years might turn out a political weakling. Boniface VIII and Charles II had long ago decided the matter of the succession, therefore, in favour of Robert. At the end of the fourteenth century,

Baldus de Ubaldis, teaching law in Perugia, still felt it necessary to go over the entire argument again (Baldus de Ubaldis 1577: fo. 22ra). At least five of the most famous lawyers of the century had discussed the matter before him. It was, after all, not without educational significance to know who succeeded under such circumstances (whether the kingdom was a fief or not), and the conflicting claims of a grandson and his uncle constituted one of the oldest questions in the book. Lawyers had been alert to the issue ever since the collision of inheritance claims between Arthur of Brittany and King John of England. The subsequent case of Alfonso X of Castile and his progeny left traces in successive versions of Alfonso's legislation in the 1270s. Baldus adds one more recent example to the debate: in England, a grandson (Richard II) had just been crowned instead of his uncle. He concludes that Boniface may not have decided the issue according to justice, that the pope had, in fact, been more partial than fair in preferring Robert. A number of contemporary chroniclers relate that Robert, in advanced age, was afflicted by his conscience for taking the kingdom against the claim of his nephew Carobert. From Baldus' perspective, the dynastic turmoil which convulsed the south shortly after Robert's death in 1343 must have seemed like the intervention of Nemesis. The line of Carobert had come back to claim its own, paying in blood for its persistence, it is true, but exacting a high price in return. The Franciscan friar with whom we began would have found nothing surprising in the afflictions of the Regno. The persistent attention of the lawyers ensured, as no other mechanism could, that, even when the pope himself had been responsible for the problem, posterity would know how to evaluate it when rulers, confronted with the legal, the fitting and the expedient, made the elementary moral error of assuming they had any real choice.

REFERENCES

Arquillière, H. X. (1934) *L'Augustinisme politique*, Paris: J. Vrin.

Ascheri, M. (1985) 'Analecta manoscritta consiliare', *Bulletin of the Institute of Medieval Canon Law* 15: 61–94.

Augustine of Hippo (1972) trans. H. Bettenson, ed. J. O'Meara, *The City of God*, Harmondsworth: Penguin.

Baldus de Ubaldis (1577) *In sextum Codicis librum commentaria, Alexandri Imolensis, Andreae Barb., Celsi Philippique Decii adnotationibus illustrata . . . exornata, hac postrema editione summo studio ac diligentia ab innumeris erroribus vindicata*, Venice: Lucas Antonius Giunta.

Bellomo, M. (1979) *Saggio sull'Università nell'età del Diritto Comune*, Catania: Giannotta.

Berges, W. (1938) *Die Fürstenspiegel des hohen und späten Mittelalters*, Leipzig: K.W. Hiersmann.

Brand, P. (1996) '"The Age of Bracton"', in J. Hudson (ed.) *The History of English Law. Centenary Essays on 'Pollock and Maitland'*, Oxford: Oxford University Press for the British Academy, 65–89.

—— (1997) 'English thirteenth-century legislation', in A. Romano (ed.) *. . . colendo iustitiam et iura condendo . . . Federico II legislatore del Regno di Sicilia nell'Europa del Duecento*, Rome: Edizioni de Luca, 325–44.

Caravale, M. (1997) 'Legislazione e giustizia in Federico II. Problemi storiografici', in A. Romano (ed.) *. . . colendo iustitiam et iura condendo . . . Federico II legislatore del Regno di Sicilia nell'Europa del Duecento*, Rome: Edizioni de Luca, 109–31.

Cortese, E. (1995) *Il Diritto nella Storia Medievale*, 2 vols, Rome: Il Cigno Galileo Galilei.

Fried, J. (1974) *Die Entstehung des Juristenstandes im 12. Jahrhundert. Zur sozialen Stellung und politischen Bedeutung gelehrter Juristen in Bologna und Modena*, Cologne and Vienna: Böhlau.

Gagnér, S. (1960) *Studien zur Ideengeschichte der Gesetzgebung*, Uppsala: Almquist and Wiksell.

Giles of Rome (1498) *De regimine principum*, Venice: Simon Bevilaqua.

—— (1929) (ed. R. Scholz) *De ecclesiastica potestate*, Leipzig: Hermann Böhlau.

Giordanengo, G. (1988) 'La difficile interprétation des donées negatives: les ordonnances royales sur le droit féodal', in A. Rigaudier and A. Gouron (eds) *Renaissance du pouvoir législatif et génèse de l'État*, Montpellier: Socapress, 99–116.

—— (1997) 'Le roi de France et la loi: 1137–1285', . . . *colendo iustitiam et iura condendo . . . Federico II legislatore del Regno di Sicilia nell'Europa del Duecento*, Rome: Edizioni de Luca, 345–79.

Gouron, A. (1998) 'Comment Guillaume de Nogaret est-il entré au service de Philippe le Bel?', *Revue Historique* 289: 5–46.

Helmholz, R. (1990) *Roman Canon Law in Reformation England*, Cambridge: Cambridge University Press.

—— (1996) 'The learned laws in "Pollock and Maitland"', in J. Hudson (ed.) *The History of English Law. Centenary Essays on 'Pollock and Maitland'*, Oxford: Oxford University Press for the British Academy, 145–69.

Horn, N. (1973) 'Die legistische Literatur der Kommentatorenzeit', in H. Coing (ed.) *Handbuch der Quellen und Literatur der neueren europäischen Privatrechtsgeschichte*, Munich: C. H. Beck, 261–364.

Jean de Joinville (1871) *Histoire de Saint Louis*, in P. C. F. Daunou and J. Naudet (eds) *Recueil des Historiens des Gaules et de la France*, vol. 20, Paris: Imprimerie impériale.

Kern, F. (1911) *Acta imperii Angliae et Franciae ab anno 1267 ad annum 1313. Dokumente vornehmlich zur Geschichte der auswärtigen Beziehungen Deutschlands*, Tübingen: J. C. B. Mohr.

Linehan, P. (1971) *The Spanish Church and the Papacy in the Thirteenth Century*, Cambridge: Cambridge University Press.

Markus, R. A. (1970) *Saeculum: history and society in the theology of St Augustine*, Cambridge: Cambridge University Press.

Martino, F. (1981) *Ricerche sull'opera di Guido da Suzzara. Le 'Supleciones'*, Catania: Studi e Ricerche dei Quaderni Catanesi.

Oldradus de Ponte (1472) *Consilia et quaestiones*, Rome: Adam Rot.

Padoa-Schioppa, A. (1979) 'Le rôle du droit savant dans quelques actes judiciaires italiens des XIe et XIIe siècles', in *Actes du colloque de Montpellier . . . 1977*, Milan: Giuffrè, 343–71.

Partner, P. (1972) *The Lands of St Peter*, London: Eyre Methuen.

Pennington, K. (1993) *The Prince and the Law 1200–1600. Sovereignty and rights in the Western legal tradition*, Berkeley, CA: University of California Press.

Quaglioni, D. (1983) *Politica e diritto nel trecento italiano. Il 'De tyranno' di Bartolo da Sassoferrato*, Florence: Olschki.

Richardson, H. G. (1965) *Bracton. The problem of his text*, London: The Selden Society.

Ryan, M. (1998) 'The oath of fealty and the lawyers', in J. Canning (ed.) *Political Thought and the Realities of Power*, Göttingen: Vandenhoeck und Ruprecht, 209–26.

Schwalm, J. (1909–11) *Monumenta Germaniae Historica. Constitutiones et acta publica imperatorum et regum*, vol. IV (*1298–1313*) pt 2, Hanover and Leipzig: Hahnsche Buchhandlung.

Ullmann, W. (1976) 'Boniface VIII and his contemporary scholarship', *Journal of Theological Studies* n.s. 27: 58–87.

Warren, W. L. (1978) *King John*, London: Eyre Methuen.

Winroth, A. (2000) *The Making of Gratian's Decretum*, Cambridge: Cambridge University Press.

Wolf, A. (1973) 'Die Gesetzgebung der entstehenden Territorialstaaten', in H. Coing (ed.) *Handbuch der Quellen und Literatur der neueren europäischen Privatrechtsgeschichte*, Munich: C. H. Beck, 517–800.

THE KING'S COUNSELLORS' TWO FACES: A PORTUGUESE PERSPECTIVE

Maria João Violante Branco

How were medieval popes supposed to deal with renegade kings? Indeed what authority did they have to deal with them at all? Such questions had been latent in Christian Europe ever since 751, the year in which Pope Zacharias had authorised the deposition of the last Merovingian king of the Franks, thereby ushering in their first Carolingian ruler (Nelson 1988: 213–16). He had done so because the disposed-of, and therefore deposed, King Childeric was incompetent. That at least was how Pope Gregory VII recalled the event rather more than three centuries later ('quia non erat utilis': Wallace-Hadrill 1962: 244–5). And during the course of the following century, and especially after Gregory VII's celebrated confrontation with Henry IV of Germany, the questions were addressed ever more closely (Ullmann 1955). The debate on the matter sharpened. And above all it sharpened in the hands of lawyers. Lawyers – both Roman and canon lawyers, and above all that significant minority of twelfth-century lawyers whose competence was in both disciplines – identified the issue as *the* issue. And they were right to do so, because it was the issue that went to the heart of the question of the nature of authority in the Western Church.

It was in the last quarter of that century, the century in which the Western Church, and therefore Western society, fell into the lawyers' clutches, that the kingdom of Portugal was granted its birth certificate by Pope Alexander III. That was in 1179. In 1245 another pope, Innocent IV, declared the great-grandson of Portugal's first king 'inutilis' too, incompent like the last of the Merovingians, and therefore (again) effectively deposed him. It had taken the direct line of the kings of Portugal less than seventy years to travel full circle, from papal approval to papal rejection. By comparison with the successors of the first of the Carolingians, for whom the process took all of three hundred years, this was quick.

The purpose of this chapter is to observe this process as it developed, and in particular to scrutinise the activities of those individuals who were involved on one or other side of the barricades, and especially of those who were on both sides, as those barricades were raised.

* * *

On 16 June 1222, Pope Honorius III further prevailed upon the king of Portugal in an effort to halt his persecution of Portugal's churchmen. If Afonso II, who was already excommunicated, remained obdurate then the pontiff would absolve his subjects from their oaths of obedience and encourage other kings and princes to occupy his kingdom. Since the spiritual sanctions he had previously invoked had had no effect, the pope was now threatening other than spiritual measures in what were for him the most robust of terms (Costa 1963: 106–7).

But how was the pope's mandate to be enforced? Would the judges delegate charged with its enforcement prove equally robust? They were instructed 'not to fear the face of man more than the face of God' (Costa 1963: 108) But on reaching the king's presence would they remember this? Would they remain resolute? Judging by the example of recent peninsular history they might well not, for they would certainly come under severe pressure – pressure more effective because more immediate than the papal threats of deprivation which hung over them should they fail in their mission. Spanish kings had long been accustomed to intervene in the affairs of their churches and of their churchmen, the liberties they took with 'ecclesiastical liberties' ranging from abuse of the rights of patronage to parish churches to the intrusion of their own nominees into episcopal sees and the expoliation, even the assassination, of members of the clerical order (Fletcher 1978; Linehan 1971; Linehan 1993). It was not to be wondered at therefore if the papal delegates in 1222 hesitated regarding which 'face' they were less prepared to shun.

Nor would the pontiff himself have been greatly surprised at their hesitation. For, as he knew full well, throughout the West ecclesiastical sanctions were liable to be disregarded by laymen and clerics alike. Rather than risking the indignity of having his spiritual authority thus flouted, in the previous century Archbishop Thomas Becket had reportedly opted for monetary penalties instead (Cheney 1956: 15). But that had been in England, and had merely involved the king's subjects. What was now to be done in Portugal where it was the king himself who was proving contumacious?

It was then as now. Then as now, it was not the monarch who was first identified for censure but rather the thirteenth-century equivalent of what the modern newspaper press describes as 'members of the royal household' (meaning by that its remote hangers-on). Thus in 1222, it was not the excommunicated king whom the executors targeted but rather those 'clerics, knights and others' who had uncanonically persisted in associating with him – and three individuals in particular, all royal councillors, and named as such: Master Vicente dean of Lisbon, Master Julião dean of Coimbra, and Master Paio cantor of Oporto. The pope was well informed – and not surprisingly so, since the primate of the Portuguese Church, the archbishop of Braga, Estêvão Soares da Silva, was currently in exile at the papal court, having been hounded out of Portugal on account of a series of regalist measures for the implementation of which the trio of senior churchmen had been chiefly responsible (Mattoso 1993: 106–17).

This particular example, one among many such, serves to demonstrate the force of the conflicting pressures to which men such as Master Vicente found themselves subjected in their concurrent service to both Church and State. It was a force which constituted a powerful and permanent occupational hazard for those ecclesiastics whose *cursus honorum* involved many years of legal study and practice, with at the end of it the possibility of episcopal office – but only if the king so decreed. Assiduous in their attendance on the king though they were, however, churchmen they remained none the less, maintaining close connections with the principal cathedral churches of the kingdom, and in some cases (in that of Master Vicente, for example) establishing themselves as distinguished practitioners and theoreticians of both Roman and canon law. In view of this complex of activities and loyalties – to king and kingdom, and to the Portuguese as well as the Roman Church – the choice with which Pope Honorius's directive 'not to fear the face of man more than the face of God' had confronted them must appear as simplistic as it did stark.

In order to understand the quandary in which Master Vicente and his colleagues found themselves in the late 1220s, however, it is necessary to investigate their ecclesiastical antecedents. We must go back two or three ecclesiastical generations to the cradle from which their predecessors had emerged in the late 1130s, at the very beginnings of the kingdom of Portugal.

KING, KINGDOM AND LEGITIMACY: THE EARLIEST DIPLOMATIC CAMPAIGNS AND THE ROLE OF ARCHBISHOP JOÃO PECULIAR

Until 1128 Portugal was a county, formally dependent on the kingdom of León. But in that year Count Afonso Henriques rebelled against his widowed mother, Don Teresa, and, with the support of the territorial nobility, assumed control of the region. Thus far the story rather closely resembled that of any number of peripheral counties of the Carolingian empire in the late ninth century. In the 1120s, however, the independent county of Portugal did not remain a county. In 1139, soon after a successful encounter with the Moors, Afonso Henriques took to styling himself king (Branco 1993: 604–16; Mattoso 1993: 45–64; Buescu 1991). Then, in 1143, after his cousin the 'Emperor' Alfonso VII of León had agreed to acquiesce in his kingship in return for an oath of vassalage, he proceeded to offer himself to Pope Innocent II as a vassal of the Roman Church in return for papal recognition of his kingdom (Erdmann 1935: 44–5; Dinis 1960: 1). Thus, while the leaders of Europe's established royal dynasties were preparing to counter the Papacy's burgeoning imperialist aspirations (Kantorowicz 1965b), the *arriviste* ruler of Portugal set about exploiting those aspirations and enlisting them in the service of his own ambition to liberate himself from the ties of vassalage to others. And what better godfather could Afonso Henriques have than the earthly representative of the God of victories whose approval the details of his recent career so clearly proclaimed? *Invictus, triumphator et strenuus* were the martial and irresistible epithets regularly applied by his chancery clerks to the ruler who, as they never failed to record, ruled, moreover 'by the grace of God' (Antunes 1995: 11–17; Azevedo 1938; Mattoso 1995: 80–5).

The arguments deployed in *Claves regni*, Afonso Henriques' letter to Innocent II, were both carefully judged and revealed a shrewd awareness of recent discussions on the theme of the relationship of papal authority to royal power (Mochi Onory 1951: 11–20). They had been prepared by people who knew what they were doing and were fully informed of the advantages which had accrued to such recently established

Figure 30.1 King and Bishop brandish sword and crozier respectively. While one admonishes, the other blesses. Miniature from a thirteenth-century manuscript of the *Fuero Juzgo* (the law-code in force throughout the Spanish Peninsula prior to the 'Arab invasion' and in much of it for centuries thereafter). Lisbon, Biblioteca Nacional, MS. IL. III, fo. 21v. Reproduced by permission.

vassals of the Roman Church as Navarre, Aragon and Sicily (Kehr 1945; 1946; Feige 1991: 95; Mochi Onory 1951: 14–16). Of those responsible the most prominent, and in all likelihood the principal strategist in the lengthy campaign to secure legitimisation of the king and the kingdom, was João Peculiar, archbishop of Braga from 1138 to 1175 and the king's intimate advisor throughout those years.

When Afonso Henriques declared himself king, as well as being on the front line of the kingdom's frontier with Islam, Coimbra was home to a lively multi-cultural society which had emerged more or less unscathed from the period of Moorish domination (Mattoso *et al.* 1989: 139–41; Pradalié 1974). This was a world radically different from the seignorial north, where the Islamic threat was by now a distant memory and power was predominantly in the hands of an endogamous old nobility whose economic strength and social prestige found expression in the extensive patronage which its members were able to exercise over the religious establishments and parish churches of the region. It was with the assistance of this nobility that Afonso Henriques had prevailed over his rivals during the 1120s, and it was in order to extricate himself from their suffocating tutelage that thereafter he abandoned the north and made the city of Coimbra his centre (Mattoso 1993: 65).

João Peculiar was probably born in the vicinity of Coimbra (Costa 1984), a city which during the 1130s was fast emerging as the nascent kingdom's intellectual capital, with at its centre the recently founded monastery of Santa Cruz, a community of canons regular many of whose earliest recruits were drawn from the local cathedral chapter as part of a process in which João Peculiar, as its sometime schoolmaster, played an important part (Nascimento 1997; Nascimento 1998: 19–31). In the earliest productions of the Santa Cruz *scriptorium*, which recount the story of the convent's founder and first prior, Teotónio, and date from the mid-1150s to the early 1160s, Afonso Henriques regularly appears in the narrative, and, both before and after his assumption of the royal title, always in the guise in which he was presented to the pope in these years, as a brave and pious warrior king favoured by God in all his military endeavours. The few other chronicles of those and the next ten years – the narratives of the conquests of Lisbon and Santarém and of the foundation of the monastery of St Vincent of Lisbon, all of them composed either at Santa Cruz or at one of the houses affiliated to it – tell the same story (Herculano and Leal 1856: 93–5; David 1936: 52–185; Nascimento 1998: 54–222), exactly as did the clerks of the royal chancery in their diplomatic description of their master. Since the royal chancery was housed in Santa Cruz at this time, and since moreover the king's chancellors were as often as not canons regular themselves, it is reasonable to conclude that the contribution to the propagation of royal propaganda of the community in which Portugal's first two kings would in due course establish a pantheon for themselves and their descendants was decisive (Mattoso 1985).

In the presentation of the filtered image of the king projected by the *scriptorium* of Santa Cruz and the royal chancery alike, as well as in the overt objective that both clearly shared of legitimising his rule, the influence of João Peculiar at Coimbra was ubiquitous (Branco 1996: 127–9), and it remained effective there even after his appointment as bishop of Oporto in 1136 and archbishop of Braga in the following year. His activity between then and his death in 1175 was by no means confined to the field of public relations and royal propaganda, however. For as well as reconciling his responsibilities as both royal counsellor and ecclesiastical primate, João Peculiar was also a man of action – as he needed to be. In the course of a public career during which the kingdom's southern frontier advanced from the river Mondego almost to the Algarve, he had not only Muslims to deal with but also his royal master's Christian neighbours, the rulers of León and Castile whose own peninsular agenda posed no fewer problems for the kingdom of Portugal than did the machinations of the infidel.

As archbishop, João Peculiar was *ex professo* committed to the ongoing task of reconquest. Thus whereas on the occasion of the siege of Lisbon in 1147 Bishop Pedro of Oporto used intellectual argument to persuade the Jerusalem-bound crusaders to stay and fight there, the archbishop preferred to station himself in the front line and act the warrior. And in the front line he was regularly to be found in later military engagements, always at the side of the king. He consecrated the bishops of restored sees, as the king directed, and regardless of the rights of neighbouring metropolitans. He continued to divert both rank-and-file crusaders and members of the military orders from their Holy Land objective by means of grants of extensive benefices. Doubtless he hoped thereby to ingratiate himself with Rome. Certainly the desire to please the pope mattered as much to him as the need to attract skilled warriors and settlers to the undermanned frontier.

Central to the processes of peninsular politics during Archbishop João's life-time, and a complicating factor in all his dealings with the Papacy, was the issue of ecclesiastical primacy. Questions regarding the relationship of secular divisions to their ecclesiastical counterpart, and in particular Braga's jurisdictional conflicts with the churches of Toledo and Compostela (the metropolitan churches of the kingdoms of Castile and León respectively), were a feature of this period with which its secular complexities were inextricably entangled (Erdmann 1935: 71–4; Feige 1991: 95–9). Thus, although the ostensible purpose of the seven visits which the archbishop paid to the papal curia between 1135 and 1175 was the defence of his church's rights against the pretensions of the church of Toledo, the timing of his journeys was regularly determined by such considerations as his royal master's most recent military exploits or political developments elsewhere in the peninsula. Not that his tireless peregrinations paid significant dividends. Due as much to his own rebarbative character as to his adversaries' diplomatic exertions, it would seem, João Peculiar consistently failed to secure unequivocal papal support either for his church or for his king (Feige 1991). Yet he continued undeterred. Although suspended from the exercise of his jurisdiction between 1145 and 1148, he remained unabashed, consecrating bishops, restoring episcopal sees which although they lay within the realm of Portugal were not subject to the metropolitan jurisdiction of Portugal's primate, and even presiding over an ecclesiastical assembly in the presence of a papal legate. Like master, like servant, in short. Regardless of accusations pending against him at Rome, as for example of furiously trampling the sacred host under foot, and regardless of two other suspensions and the threat of further punishment for disobeying papal directives to submit to Toledo (Erdmann 1935: 83; Feige 1991: 114), he doggedly pursued his course. Though the paucity of evidence relating to patrimonial and pastoral activities should not necessarily be counted against him, the picture which emerges from what evidence there is is of an archbishop who was in no doubt as to where his first loyalty lay – or for that matter as to where his *only* loyalty lay. In short, here was a prelate who would have felt at home anywhere in mid-twelfth-century Europe.

But times were changing. In 1169 Afonso Henriques broke his leg at the siege of Badajoz, putting paid to his celebrated invincibility, and ten years later when the papal recognition which king and archbishop had for so long laboured was finally forthcoming, Archbishop João Peculiar was dead and the king was ruling in association with his son and heir, the future Sancho I.

ESTABLISHING THE KING IN HIS KINGDOM: THE
CHANCELLOR JULIÃO PAIS AND THE JURISTS

With jurists and the exploitation of legal science to the fore, by the late 1100s popes and kings were increasingly engaged in the process of defining and redefining their respective roles within Christian society. Developments in Portugal were part of this process.

Because it provided Afonso Henriques' *de facto* ascendancy with authoritative authentication, Pope Alexander III's privilege *Manifestis probatum* of 1179 (Dinis 1960: 9) constituted the new kingdom of Portugal's principal title deed. Hence the frequency with which it was reissued by successive popes at the behest of successive rulers and its value to their agents at the papal curia, particularly at times when (as they often did) those rulers found themselves at odds with the pontiff. Its insistence on the integrity of the kingdom, the definition it contained of the king's legitimacy in terms of his personal obligations and virtues, and its assertion of his right to enlarge his domain by waging war against the infidel, ensured for *Manifestis probatum* a uniquely privileged position in the documentary armoury of the kings of Portugal.

On Afonso Henriques' death in 1185, as well as his father's kingdom Sancho I inherited his father's chancellor, Julião Pais. The son of Paio Delgado, a warrior who had been present at the conquest of Lisbon alongside João Peculiar, Julião was a native of Coimbra, where, together with other members of his family, he acquired, by a combination of royal grant and purchase, extensive properties in the vicinity of the cathedral, as well as hosting meetings of the city council in his own home. His brother Gonçalo Dias and his son Master Julião Juliães, were successively deans of the place (from before 1195 until around 1261) and, throughout the thirty-two years of his chancellorship and beyond, other members of the clan were prominent in both Church and State. Master Julião *fils* and another son, Master Gil Juliães treasurer of Viseu and Coimbra, were intimates of Afonso II, and it may even have been that the Pedro Juliães (*alias* Pedro Hispano), the dean of Lisbon who in 1276 became Pope John XXI, was yet another of his offspring (Mattoso 1995: 105–6).

As chancellor, Julião Pais has been cast as the *éminence grise* of the Portuguese court, and, as the Bologna-educated civil lawyer responsible for secularising the ethos of the place at the turn of the twelfth century, as the man who reformulated the basis of Portugal's dealings with the Papacy, and the impresario who introduced Roman law concepts into Afonso II's general laws of 1211 (Mattoso 1995: 105). But this is no more than conjecture. In fact, there is no evidence to link him either with Bologna or with any other school of law, and not much to justify the confident description of him as 'Master' (Fleisch 1998: 71–4).

Although his innovations in the *formulae* of the *arengae* of the royal documents have been viewed as the harbingers of a new style of kingship, in reality the lay chancellor's model king was constructed very much along traditional lines: pious, principally dedicated to the administration of justice, the common good and the maintenance of social order, prodigal because prodigality was a sure sign of generosity of spirit, and dedicating himself to the cause of regnal harmony by employing written law to achieve what previously had been secured by good customs (Antunes 1995: 19; Mattoso 1995: 82–5). All of which (derived as it was from biblical models, Isidore

Figure 30.2 A Portugese king, presumably Sancho I, in a late thirteenth-century imitative copy of the foral of Penas Ruivas. Crowned and attended by the paraphernalia of Portuguese regality, the monarch was evidently meant to appear a masterful figure. Due to the draughtsman's incompetence, however, the abiding impression is less one of powerful biceps than of a weak chin and pitiful feet. Lisbon, Arquivos Nacionais, Gavetas, gav. 15, mç. 10, doc. 14. Reproduced by permission.

of Seville and the precepts of canon law) rather closely resembled the papally approved ideal of the ruler as guarantor of justice (Post 1972: 164–70). It was not fundamentally contrasting models that distinguished the Portuguese chancellor from the Roman pontiff but rather their contrasting (and distinctive) attitudes to the model they had in common – namely the blueprint of the ideal Christian king as adumbrated in *Manifestis probatum*.

The pragmatic chancellor's reputation as civilian orchestrator of royal policy is unwarranted therefore. Even so, he was closely involved at every stage of Sancho I's long-running controversy with Rome. When, for example, in connection with reports of the king's violent treatment of ecclesiastics in general and of bishop Pedro of Coimbra in particular, Innocent III had occasion to complain in 1211 that not even the heretics had thought to address him thus, and declared himself much offended by the suggestion that while the king and his warriors were starved of the means of fighting the infidel the clergy were sunk in luxurious excess, the pontiff was surely corrrect in surmising that it was not the king himself who had authorised these charges, nor even the witch whom he was reported regularly to consult, but rather Julião and his chancery colleagues (Costa and Marques 1989: nos. 154–5).

As to these chancery colleagues, and the juristic character which they had in common and which is so striking a feature of these years, it can hardly be doubted that, whatever the nature of his own juristic preparation, Julião must have been instrumental in facilitating the advancement at court of the group which after Afonso II's accession in 1211 became increasingly prominent in the conduct of the king's affairs both at home and abroad. Most of these men, of a type whose emergence was closely paralleled in many other parts of Europe in these years (Baldwin 1976; Cheney 1956: 1–17, 22–39; Cheney 1967: 1–15, 77–114; Genet 1986: 296–7, 304–6; Millet and Moret 1992: 255–76), were closely related to Julião in one way or another as well as being associated with Coimbra.

The kingdom whose chancery Julião controlled was one whose legitimacy was now no longer an issue, other of course than for his royal neighbours, even if it had still to be prepared to counter the interventionist tendencies of the likes of Innocent III (Cheney 1976: 271–4; Pennington 1994: 105–10). And since 1179 other changes had occurred in Portugal's fortunes. The last two decades of the twelfth century were years of war, famine, plague and natural disaster. Militant Islam had regained almost all the territory south of the Tagus. Soon after his father's death Sancho I found himself locked in conflict with both the nobility and the Church, Braga's contest with Compostela (with its secular dimension) reached crisis point, and relations with Rome entered a new phase in which the services of learned professionals were proving ever more necessary (Mattoso 1993: 88–9; 106–8; 119–20; Pennington 1994: 105–10; Tierney 1994: 95–9), all of which exposed the king to ever closer public scrutiny. Because in this new situation an increasingly pressing need was felt for a clearer definition of the latter's functions and attributes, Julião, the chancellor, had a very different part to play from João Peculiar. Accordingly, while the new archbishop of Braga, D. Godinho, distanced himself from his predecessor's example and was increasingly occupied with the affairs of his see and with commissions as papal judge delegate, by the time of Julião's death in 1215 a new breed of chancery servant was in the ascendant. With the exception of Master Vicente (chancellor, 1224–37: Costa 1963; Machado 1965; Ochoa Sanz 1960), we know very little about the background of Julião's successors in office (Mattoso 1995: 106–7). We do know, however, that, apart from Vicente, they were predominantly members of the middling nobility and that their careers had begun in the royal chancery rather than in the law schools.

The last years of Sancho I's reign were marked by a series of conflicts with his ecclesiastics in the resolution of which the papal curia was increasingly involved. But it was only after his death in 1211 that the impact of the new breed of royal servant became fully apparent. To his son and heir, the leprous Afonso II, Sancho bequeathed an unsettled kingdom and a state of uncertainty exacerbated by the terms of his will. By his creation of extensive hereditary appanages for three of his daughters the moribund monarch struck at the heart of his son's sovereignty (Veloso 1980). It was in these circumstances that the king's interests at Rome began to be represented by canon lawyers of the calibre of the same Master Vicente (Vincentius Hispanus), Silvestre Godinho and Lanfranco of Milan (Costa 1963: 27–8, 35, 58–61; García y García 1976: 108–12; García y García 1991: 61, 68; Maffei 1990: 18–19). With Afonso II beset by family strife, his proctors at the papal curia took their stand on the assertion that the old king's will was void by reason of his insanity (Costa 1963: 26–7) and its disregard of the principle of inalienability of the royal fisc. In the absence of any oath of inalienability akin to that later sworn by English monarchs at their coronation (Kantorowicz 1965a; Post 1964: 415–33), the new king's agents based their case on the requirement of *Manifestis probatum* and its reissues that Afonso Henriques and his successors maintain the kingdom undiminished.

In the same years two of these men, Master Vicente and Silvestre Godinho, were preparing their commentaries on Innocent III's decretal collection (*Compilatio III*), and on *Compilatio I*, and refining their glosses on such fundamental papal definitions of political theory as *Venerabilem*, *Novit* and *Per venerabilem* (Cheney 1994: 98; García y García 1976: 106–10; Post 1937: 418–19; Post 1964: 453–82; Tierney 1994: 97). Jurists such as these as well as others with peninsular and in particular Portuguese connections for whom the issue of the independence of Spanish kings from the emperor was a familiar topos (Machado 1965: 194–6; Mochi Onory 1951: 282; Post 1937; Post 1964: 482–93; Post 1972) are unlikely not to have appreciated the implications of Afonso II's struggle for the integrity of his kingdom. The emendations to the text of *Manifestis probatum* in Innocent III's reissue of the privilege in April 1212 illustrate both the difficulty of their task as the representatives of a sick king incapable of that military 'strenuousness' which had helped to justify the legitimation of his grandfather's rule and their capacity for overcoming it by stressing instead the martial qualities of Afonso's predecessors (Costa and Marques 1989: no. 176). Likewise the replacement on this same occasion of the hallowed phrase concerning the king's suitability 'to rule his people', as repeated in earlier reissues, by a reference to the 'government of his kingdom', with the change from *populi regimen* to *regni gubernatio* is probably to be understood in relation to current discussions of the theme of the autonomy of kings (and not least Spanish kings) *vis-à-vis* imperial authority (discussions in which the opinions of both Master Vicente and Silvestre Godinho were well represented) rather than as an assertion of any novel concept of territorial kingship (Mochi Onory 1951: 274–86; Post 1964: 453–82; Tierney 1994: 95–104).

In the kingdom of Portugal itself, meanwhile, Afonso II had begun his reign by summoning a curia in 1211 and, with the consent of his magnates and ecclesiastics, promulgating a series of general laws, the purpose of which was to secure his position on the throne and reassure the nobility and ecclesiastics (Branco 1997: 80–8). As an early example of a thirteenth-century European phenomenon whereby the ruler sought to define the scope of his public authority, the promulgation of the general laws of 1211 is surely to be related to the influence of those so-called 'jurists' whose activity is amply attested both in the Italian law schools and in Spain (García y García 1976; García y García 1991; Linehan 1998). Although no warrior, Afonso thus demonstrated a competence to legislate as an independent ruler, and with the advice and consent of his curia, to address his subjects and make manifest to them the reality of his legitimate authority. To that end eighteen of the twenty-eight laws are introduced by a preamble in which the characteristics of the good prince are summarised mirror-of-princes style (as bringer of justice, guarantor of equity and harmony, Christian hero), reflecting the same ideals of king and kingship as those proposed by the canonists. True, kings of Portugal cut somewhat improbable figures as

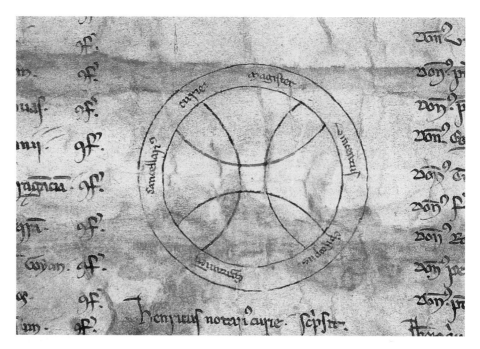

Figure 30.3 The signum of Master Vincentius 'bishop of Guarda and chancellor of the court' (Jan. 1236). Lisbon, Arquivos Nacionais/Torre do Tombo, Santa Cruz de Coimbra. Documentos régios, mç. 3, doc. 1. Reproduced by permission.

Christian heroes, at least in so far as their treatment of ecclesiastics was concerned. But this was compensated for by a prologue restating the supremacy of the laws of the Church over those of the prince – as befitted those canonists who, although in practice dualists regarding the spiritual and the temporal spheres, were in theory prepared to submit themselves to the ultimate authority of the supreme pontiff (Machado 1965: 180–9; Mochi Onory 1951: 206; Post 1937: 414–15).

The substance of the legislation contained various innovations, notably the requirement that title to property be confirmed by written record, laws of inheritance seemingly derived from Roman law, and in particular restrictions on the right of ecclesiastics to inherit property. This last, which was soon to provoke uproar and involve Afonso and his successors in the bitterest of strife, suggests that the jurists responsible for this legislation were taking their cue from the expression on the king's face, conscious though they must have been of what the pope (if not God) would think of the inevitable implications of the measures which they were advancing.

TOWARDS 1245: VICENTE HISPANO AND THE 'DEPOSITION' OF SANCHO II

This was only the earliest instance of the broadening of the jurists' range of activities. As the king's contest with his sisters developed, the jurists went from strength to strength. As early as 1214 Master Vicente, now dean of Lisbon, was instrumental in promoting the marriage of the Infanta Mafalda to King Enrique of Castile (Costa 1963: 89), and five years later the conduct of the Alcácer campaign was entrusted to the bishop of Lisbon, another of the royal proctors of 1212. A roll-call of them, as well as an indication of their importance to the king, is provided by the terms of Afonso II's grant of tithes to his bishops and to the convent of Santa Cruz of Coimbra on Good Friday 1218. His largesse was prompted, it was explained, 'by love' of a number of named individuals, among whom, apart from Master Vicente, there figure Master Paio cantor of Oporto, Master Julião dean of Coimbra, Master Silvestre archdeacon of Braga, and Master Lanfranco (Costa 1963: 48–9, 67–73, 396–7, 146–52, 509; Mattoso 1995: 106).

Churchmen in general were less favoured. Just two years later a royal inquiry into their titles to property was instituted. This provoked a furious reaction, resulting in the exile of the archbishop of Braga, Estêvão Soares da Silva, and occasioning Honorius III's letter of June 1222 which threatened the kingdom with invasion, reminded his executors where their first loyalty lay, and excoriated Master Vicente and his two colleagues for remaining in the company of their excommunicated master. Yet it was to the same Master Vicente and his colleagues that the pope had to turn in January 1224, at the beginning of a new reign, when he wrote urging them to use their best endeavours to steer the 'tender-aged and docile' Sancho II in the direction of the paths of virtue (Costa 1963: 133–4). It was the dean of Lisbon's duty to serve both his God and his king, the pontiff reminded him later that same year, while also showing himself 'benign and favourable' to churches and churchmen (Costa 1963: 136). He did not explain how those various circles were to be squared.

The multi-faceted dean of Lisbon had perforce to be a man of more than one face. As Afonso II's servant he had been aligned against Archbishop Estêvão Soares and had found himself accused of conspiracy to murder his own bishop, Soeiro Viegas (Mattoso 1993: 115; Branco 1998: 77; Costa 1963: 76–7). None the less (and surely it was no coincidence), later in his chancellorship various jurists and canonists who had been prominent during Afonso II's lifetime were appointed to Portugal's principal sees: Silvestre Godinho to Braga, Mestre Paio to Lisbon, Pedro Salvadores to Oporto – and in 1226, as Sancho II's relationship with the Portuguese Church slipped into irreversible decline – Vicente himself to Guarda. Although this was a development paralleled both elsewhere in the peninsula and also further afield in these years (García y García 1985: 46–57; Fleisch 1998; Linehan 1971; Linehan 1993), in Portugal the role recently played by such men in the kingdom's affairs gave it particular significance. No wonder Vicente was reluctant to accept episcopal office and even showed signs of resisting the pressure brought to bear in 1229 by the papal legate, Cardinal John of Abbeville (Costa 1963: 163–5). For with the kingdom threatened with the papal interdict which became a reality in 1231, how was the king's chancellor to live within the same skin as the bishop of Guarda? Needless to say the chancery records themselves are silent on the subject – though it is to be noted that when Gregory IX wrote in August 1234, forbidding the ordination of *curiales* of the king's court as both contrary to canon law and liable to bring the Church onerousness rather than honour ('*non honorem . . . sed onus*'), it was not principally to Vicente that he addressed himself but to Vicente's old teacher, Archbishop Silvestre of Braga (García y García 1976: 109; Costa 1963: 207–8).

With pressure mounting on Sancho II, Vicente as well as Silvestre cannot but have recalled their earlier adhesion to the proposition that by reason of sin (*ratione peccati*) a king was liable to deprivation of his dignity (García y García 1981: 290; Machado 1965: 182–3, 187; Mochi Onory 1951: 213–25; Post 1972: 165–8). In his *Apparatus* to the *Liber Extra* of Gregory IX, Vicente reaffirmed this doctrine, as Silvestre had done in his gloss to *Compilatio III* (Machado 1965: 185–8; Post 1937: 414–15; Post 1972: 168–70).[1]

The Portuguese bishops had been considering the question of a replacement for their king for some time already, and in 1245, when by his celebrated bull *Grandi* Innocent IV declared Sancho II to have forfeited the administration of his kingdom, only one of them, Aires Vasques of Lisbon, spoke up for the monarch (Cunha 1642: 160–3). 'What is really striking about 750/51' – where this present chapter began – is, it has been said, 'the coincidence of Frankish clerical and lay aristocratic interests and of those with the papacy's' (Nelson 1988: 214). *Mutatis mutandis*, the same goes for Portugal almost five hundred years later. It would be interesting to know Vicente's opinion of *Grandi*, enshrining as it did the fully developed canonical doctrine concerning the right of the pontiff to intervene in such a situation (Peters 1970). Unfortunately, however, though characteristically perhaps, that sedulous servant of two masters left nothing on record.

ACKNOWLEDGEMENT

My warm thanks are due to Peter Linehan for his deconstruction of successive drafts of this chapter as well as for all the time he has spent mending my English.

NOTE

1   Silvestre Godinho was in Rome from 1243 and died there in the summer of 1244. Vicente was at work on his Apparatus sometime between 1234 and 1245, the year of the Council of Lyons whose canons he does not quote (Costa 1963: 15–17; Machado 1965: 102).

REFERENCES

Primary sources

Costa, A. J. and Marques, M. A. (eds) (1989) *Bulário Português, Inocêncio III (1198–1216)*, Coimbra: Instituto Nacional de Investigação Científica.

David, C. W. (ed.) (1936) *De Expugnatione Lyxbonensi. The Conquest of Lisbon*, New York: Columbia University Press.

Dinis, A. D. (ed.) (1960), *Monumenta Henricina*, I, Coimbra: Comissão das Comemorações do Quinto Centenário da Morte do Infante D. Henrique.

Herculano, A. and Leal, J. S. (eds) (1856) *Portugaliae Monumenta Historica a saeculo octavo post Christum usque ad quintum decimum*, I. *Scriptores*, Lisbon, Academia das Ciências.

Nascimento, Aires A. (ed.) (1998), *Hagiografia de Santa Cruz de Coimbra. Vida de D. Telo, Vida de D. Teotónio, Vida de S. Martinho de Soure*, Lisbon: Cólibri.

Secondary sources

Almeida, Fortunato de (1967) *História da Igreja em Portugal*, I, Porto: Ed. Portucalense.

Antunes, J. (1995) 'A cultura erudita portuguesa nos séculos XIII e XIV (juristas e teólogos)', unpublished Ph.D. diss., University of Coimbra.

Antunes, J., Oliveira, A. R. and Monteiro, J. G. (1984) 'Conflitos políticos no reino de Portugal entre a Reconquista e a Expansão. Estado da questão', *Revista de História das Ideias* 6: 25–160.

Azevedo, R. (1938) *A chancelaria régia portuguesa nos séculos XII e XIII. Linhas gerais da sua evolução*, Coimbra: Imprensa Académica.

—— (1967) 'O livro de registo da chancelaria de Afonso II de Portugal', *Anuario de Estudios Medievales* 4: 35–62.

Baldwin, J. W. (1976) 'The penetration of university personnel into French and English administration at the turn of the twelfth and thirteenth centuries', *Revue des Études Islamiques* 46: 199–215.

Branco, M. J. V. (1993) 'Portugal no reino de Leon. Etapas de uma relação (866–1179)', in *El reino de León en la Alta Edad Media. La monarquia (1109–1230)*, León: Centro de Estudios y Investigación 'San Isidoro': 537–625.

—— (1996) 'A conquista de Lisboa revisitada: estratégias de ocupação do espaço físico, político e simbólico', in *2° Congresso histórico de Guimarães. Actas do Congresso*, II. *A política portuguesa e as suas relações exteriores*, Guimarães: Camara Municipal de Guimarães: 119–37.

—— (1997) 'The General Laws of Afonso II and his policy of "centralisation": a reassessement', in M. Gosman, A. Vanderjagt and J. Veenstra (eds) *The Propagation of Power in the Medieval West*, Groningen: Egbert Forsten: 79–95.

—— (1998) 'Bispos, reis e cabidos: a diocese de Lisboa no primeiro século da sua restauração', *Lusitania Sacra* 10: 55–94.

Buescu, A. I. (1991) 'Um mito das origens da nacionalidade: o milagre de Ourique', in F. Bethencourt and D. R. Curto (eds) *A memória da nação*, Lisbon: Sá da Costa: 49–69.

Cheney, C. R. (1956) *From Becket to Langton. English church government 1170–1213*, Manchester: Manchester University Press.

—— (1967) *Hubert Walter*, London: Nelson.

—— (1976) *Innocent III and England*, Stuttgart: A. Hiersemann.

Costa, A. D. Sousa (1963) *Mestre Silvestre e Mestre Vicente, juristas da contenda entre Afonso II e suas irmãs*, Braga: Ed. Franciscana.

Costa, A. J. da (1984) 'D. João Peculiar co-fundador do mosteiro de Santa Cruz de Coimbra, bispo do Porto e arcebispo de Braga', in *Santa Cruz de Coimbra do século XI ao século XX. Estudos*, Coimbra: 59–83.

Cunha, R. da (1742) *Cathalogo dos bispos do Porto composto pelo illustrissimo D. Rodrigo da Cunha nesta segunda impressam addicionado com suplementos de várias memórias eclesiásticas desta diocese . . .*, Porto: Officina Prototypa Episcopal.

—— (1642) *Historia Ecclesiástica da Igreja de Lisboa. Vida e acçoens dos seus prelados e varoens eminentes em santidade que nella florecerão*, Lisbon: Manoel da Sylua.

Erdmann, C. (1927) *Papsturkunden in Portugal* [*Abhandlungen der Gesellschaft der Wissenschaften zu Göttingen. Philologisch–historische Klasse*, n. F. 20/3], Berlin: Weidermannsche Buchhandlung.

—— (1935) *O Papado e Portugal no primeiro século da história portuguesa*, Coimbra: Coimbra Ed.

Feige, P. (1991) 'La primacía de Toledo y la libertad de las demás metropolis de España. El ejemplo de Braga', in *La introducción del Cister en España y Portugal*, Burgos: La Olmeda: 61–132.

Ferreira, J. A. (1923) *Memórias archeológico-históricas da Cidade do Porto (Fastos Episcopais e Políticos)* Braga: Cruz & Comp. Ed.

Fleisch, I. (1998) 'Kirche, Königtum und gelehrtes Recht im hochmittelalterlichen Portugal', unpublished M.Phil. diss., University of Bamberg.

Fletcher, R. A. (1978) *The Episcopate in the Kingdom of León in the Twelfth Century*, Oxford: Oxford University Press.

García y García, A. (1956) *Laurentius Hispanus. Datos biográficos y estudio crítico de sus obras*, Rome and Madrid: CSIC.

—— (1976) *Estudios sobre la canonística portuguesa medieval*, Madrid: Fundación Universitaria Española.

—— (ed.) (1981) *Constitutiones Concilii quarti Lateranensis una cum Comentariis glossatorum*, Vatican City: Biblioteca Apostolica Vaticana.

—— (1985) 'El *studium bononiense* y la Peninsula Iberica', in, *Iglesia, Sociedad y Derecho*, Salamanca: Universidad Pontificia de Salamanca: 45–64.

—— (1991) *Derecho común en España. Los juristas y sus obras*, Murcia: Universidad de Murcia.

Genet, J. and Vincent. B. (eds) (1986) *État et église dans la génèse de l'État Moderne*, Madrid: Casa de Velázquez.

Hageneder, O. (1963) 'Das päpstliches Recht der Fürstenabsetzung: seine kanonistische Grundlegung (1150–1250)', *Archivum Historiae Pontificiae*, 1: 53–95.

Kantorowicz, E. H. (1965a) 'Inalienability. A note on canonical practice and the English coronation oath in the thirteenth century', in *Selected Studies*, Locust Valley and New York: J. J. Augustin: 138–50.

—— (1965b) 'Kingship under the impact of scientific jurisprudence', *ibid.*: 151–66.

Kehr, P. (1945) 'Como y quando se hizo Aragón feudatario de la Santa Sede', *Estudios de Edad Media de la Corona de Aragón* 1: 286–326.

—— (1946) 'El Papado y los reinos de Navarra y Aragón hasta mediados del siglo XII', in *Estudios de Edad Media de la Corona de Aragón* 2 :74–186.

Linehan, P. (1971) *The Spanish Church and the Papacy in the Thirteenth Century*, Cambridge: Cambridge University Press.

—— (1993), *History and the Historians of Medieval Spain*, Oxford: Clarendon Press.

—— (1998) 'Some observations on Castilian scholars and the Italian schools in the age of Frederick II', in ' . . . *colendo iustitiam et iura condendo* . . . ' *Federico II legislatore del Regno di Sicilia nell'Europa del duecento. Per una storia comparata delle codificazioni europee*, Rome: Edizioni de Luca: 517–27.

Machado, A. M. B. L. (1965) *Vicente Hispano. Aspectos biográficos e doutrinais*: offprint of *Boletim do Ministério da Justiça*, 141–2.

Maffei, D. (1990) 'Fra Cremona, Montpellier e Palencia nel secolo XII. Ricerche su Ugolino da Sesso', *Rivista Internazionale di Diritto Comune* 1: 9–30.

Martins, A. A. (1996) 'O mosteiro de Santa Cruz de Coimbra séculos XII–XV. História e Instituição', unpublished PhD. diss., University of Lisbon.

Mattoso, J. (1985) 'Cluny, crúzios e Cistercienses na formação de Portugal', in *Portugal Medieval, novas interpretações*, Lisboa: Imprensa Nacional Casa da Moeda: 101–21.

—— (1993) 'Dois séculos de vicissitudes políticas', in J. Mattoso (ed.) *História de Portugal*, II. *A monarquia feudal*, Lisbon: Estampa: 11–163.

—— (1995) *Identificação de um país. Ensaio sobre as origens de Portugal 1096–1325*, 5th edn, Lisbon: Estampa.

—— with Krus, L. and Andrade. A. (1989) *O castelo e a feira. A terra de Santa Maria nos séculos XI a XIII*, Lisbon: Estampa.

Millet, H. and Mornet, E. (1992) 'Jalons pour une histoire des chanoines au service de l'état: resultats de l'exploitation de la base de données communes', in *I canonici al servizio dello stato in Europa, secoli XIII–XVI*, Ferrara: 255–90.

Mochi Onory, S. (1951) *Fonti canonistiche dell'idea moderna dello stato*, Milan: Vita e Pensiero.

Nascimento, A. A. (1997) 'Santa Cruz de Coimbra: as motivações de uma fundação particular', in *Actas do 2° Congresso histórico de Guimarães*, IV, Guimarães: CMG /Universidade do Minho: 119–27.

Nelson, J. L. (1988) 'Kingship and empire', in J. H. Burns (ed.) *The Cambridge History of Medieval Political Thought c.350–c.1450*, Cambridge: Cambridge University Press: 211–51.

Ochoa Sanz, J. (1960) *Vincentius Hispanus, canonista boloñes del siglo XIII*, Rome and Madrid: CSIC.

Pennington, K. (1994) 'Innocent III and canon law', in Powell 1994: 105–10.

—— (1993) *The Prince and the Law, 1200–1600. Sovereignty and rights in the Western legal tradition*, Berkeley, Los Angeles, Oxford: University of California Press.

Peters, E. (1970) *The Shadow King. 'Rex inutilis' in medieval law and literature, 715–1327*, New Haven and London: Yale University Press.

Post, G. (1937) 'Some unpublished glosses (*ca.* 1210–1214) on the *translatio imperii* and the two swords', *Archiv für katholisches Kirchenrecht* 117: 403–29.

—— (1964) *Studies in Medieval Legal Thought. Public law and the state (1100–1322)*, Princeton, New Jersey: Princeton University Press.

—— (1972) 'Vincentius Hispanus, *pro ratione voluntas*, and medieval and early modern theories of sovereignty', *Traditio* 28: 12–19.

Powell, J. (ed.) (1994) *Innocent III. Vicar of Christ or lord of the world*, 2nd edn, Washington: Catholic University.

Pradalié, G. (1974) 'Les faux de la cathédrale et la crise à Coïmbre au début du XII siècle', *Mélanges de la Casa de Velázquez* 10: 77–98

Santos, M. J. A. (1984) 'Fernando Peres ex-chantre da Sé de Coimbra', in *Actas do II Encontro sobre História Dominicana*, Santarém: 243–58.

Tierney, B. (1994) 'Innocent III as judge', in Powell 1994: 95–104.

Toubert, P. (1986), 'Eglise et état au XIe siècle: la signification de moment grégorien pour la genèse de l'état moderne', in *État et église dans la génèse de l'état moderne*, Madrid: Casa de Velázquez: 9–22.

Ullmann, W. (1955) *The Growth of Papal Government in the Middle Ages*, London: Methuen.

Veloso, M. T. (1980) 'A questão entre Afonso II e suas irmãs sobre a detenção dos direitos senhoriais', *Revista Portuguesa de História*, 18: 197–229.

Wallace-Hadrill, J. M. (1962) *The Long–haired Kings*, London: Methuen.

CHAPTER THIRTY-ONE

FULLNESS OF POWER? POPES, BISHOPS AND THE POLITY OF THE CHURCH 1215–1517

James Burns

I

'As we cross the threshold of the thirteenth century the dream of world dominion, which had died with an Emperor, springs to life again in the policy of a Pope' (Fisher 1936: 259). The words are those of H. A. L. Fisher, two generations ago, in his *History of Europe*. It was perhaps always an over-confident judgement on Innocent III; and the sixty years since it was pronounced have, at the very least, blunted its sharp outlines. Students of the period are now warned of 'a veritable quagmire of radically different interpretations by modern historians of Innocent's pontificate' (1198–1216) (Canning 1996: 121). In fairness to Fisher it should be pointed out that he went on to dismiss as 'false to history' the notion that Innocent's government of the Church was 'a theocracy tyrannically worked and slavishly accepted'. Yet if his reign must still be seen as crucial in the history of the Papacy, this is surely because, by consolidating and codifying the system that had developed since the mid-eleventh century, he set a coping-stone upon an edifice which is still, almost eight centuries later, by no means wholly dismantled. However circumscribed its practical scope may be, the principle of absolute monarchy remains central in the theory of the Papacy:

> The Roman Pontiff, by reason of his office as Vicar of Christ . . . and as pastor of the entire Church, has full, supreme and universal power over the whole Church, a power which he can always exercise unhindered.

That doctrine is proclaimed in the Second Vatican Council's Dogmatic Constitution on the Church (*Lumen gentium*), promulgated in 1964; but Innocent III would have had no hesitation in endorsing it.

The reference, in *Lumen gentium*, to the pope as 'pastor of the entire Church' is of particular interest because one conclusion suggested by recent scholarship is that Innocent III should be seen, not as a canon lawyer raised to the papal throne, but as, primarily, a pastoral pope (Imkamp 1983). This is connected with the question whether the young Lotario de' Conti was indeed, as has been generally supposed, a trained canonist. Whatever the answer may be, it is important to bear in mind that, since at least the time of Gregory the Great, the pope had been seen both as shepherd and as ruler. As *rector*, again, he was also *legis lator* or lawgiver; and it would be hard to deny Innocent III a critically important place in the legislative development of the Church. The first pope to promulgate an authoritative collection of decretals, he clearly conceived of his office as principally and essentially concerned with jurisdiction. Many of the familiar (not to say notorious) political events of his pontificate hinged on the papal claim to wield juridical control over temporal rulers. Yet, arguably, such episodes as Innocent's conflicts with the kings of England and France were less permanently important than matters more immediately concerned with the polity of the Church. The grounds for saying this are that Innocent III's doctrine and practice in regard to the exercise of authority in the strictly ecclesiastical sphere, continued and developed by his successors in the thirteenth and fourteenth centuries, determined the character of the dominant social structure in Europe for the rest of the Middle Ages and, in many ways, well into modern times.

What Innocent brought to fulfilment – he did not, of course, originate it – was not so much the most effective as the only effective centralised monarchy in medieval Europe. That in doing so he set up a model for aspiring temporal rulers to imitate is certainly true. It is also the case that the eventual success of temporal realms in following that example spelt the inevitable decline of the papal monarchy from its medieval grandeur. Later popes were obliged to conserve their power by compromising in practice with the kings and princes they might in principle regard as their subjects – even, in some instances, their vassals. Such considerations, however, do not lessen the magnitude of the papal achievement. Doubtless it always fell far short of Fisher's 'world dominion'; but even a superficial acquaintance with the records of papal juridical and fiscal administration as it operated throughout Latin Christendom is enough to convey the range and penetration of an astonishing bureaucracy.

In considering briefly some specific aspects of Innocent III's government of the Church, it is important to bear in mind that the pope was both *pastor* and *rector*: as shepherd he must feed the flock he ruled and guided. Sound doctrine was the wholesome food he must supply; and whether Innocent had studied law in Bologna or not, he had read theology in Paris. When we look for indications as to how papal government was affecting the lives of ordinary people, we can see at once that Innocent's rule had its roots in his theology of the Church and of the sacraments. Thus the regulation of liturgical practice in the celebration of Mass and in securing due reverence for the consecrated bread and wine reflected the clarification of the doctrine of the Eucharist. Closely related to this is the discipline of obligatory individual confession at least once a year. In the same vein, and in common with 'Sabbatarian' legislation of various kinds, the prohibition of miracle plays in church was aimed at enforcing the separation of the sacred from the profane. And, at a time when mercantile activity was growing in scale and vigour, biblical warrant could doubtless be claimed for policies which affected economic life by controlling usury and prohibiting the use of church premises as markets. Meanwhile, the Church's courts took the initiative in reforming legal procedures. The Fourth Lateran Council, in 1215, forbade the clergy to participate in trials by ordeal; and canon lawyers led the way in developing the theory and practice of 'due process' (Pennington 1984: 43–58; Pennington 1993: 132–5).

Figure 31.1 Absolute monarchy in marble. Pope Boniface VIII (1295–1303) by Arnolfo di Cambio. Florence, Museo dell' Opera del Duomo. Photo: Scala, Florence.

In these and other ways, 'the principles of a unified society under papal sovereignty were given the means of becoming a reality'(Southern 1986: 237). However, if those means were to be effective in practice, if those principles were to operate in society, there had to be a measure of what would nowadays be called 'devolution' and 'subsidiarity'. Sovereign power was doubtless vested in a centralised monarchy. The papal Curia was, to be sure, the appellate tribunal of last resort. Papal emissaries had crucial parts to play – not least in preaching the pope's message on this or that theme of urgent concern (Southern 1986: 239 n. 1). Yet much of the work 'on the ground' had to be carried out by the diocesan bishops and by those (especially the archdeacons) to whom episcopal authority was delegated. The pope's *plenitudo potestatis* was balanced by the bishop's *pars sollicitudinis*; fullness of power might often have been empty enough if the burden of implementing policy had not been shared.[1] This, of course, made it all the more important for the Papacy to maximise its control over episcopal appointments; and it is unnecessary here to do more than recall the contentious issues this raised with the kings and princes for whose government the bishops were also key figures. Up to a point, during the period when papal power reached its apogee, the interests of pope and bishops marched together. Episcopal authority could be enhanced by the bishop's assurance that he wielded the spiritual power of an organisation increasingly confident in its sovereign independence. If, however, the price of sharing in that independence proved to be undue dependence on the Papacy, there was bound to be tension within the hierarchical body of the Church.

Such tension is hardly detectable in the 'ideology' of papal power that was emerging in the writings of the canonists. Already during the pontificate of Innocent III, Laurentius Hispanus was portraying that power in what may well appear to be extravagant colours. It was he who first applied to the pope's legislative authority the phrase, borrowed from Juvenal, *sit pro ratione voluntas*. The pope's will, constituting in itself a sufficient reason for what was enacted, prevailed over any opposing positive law. The pope, Laurentius claims, 'can change the nature of things . . . he can make iniquity from justice . . . and there is no one in the world who can say to him, "Why do you do this?"' No doubt Laurentius 'meant to provoke and to teach'. And his teaching was subject to the proviso that papal power should be used 'for the public good' (Pennington 1993: 46–7). Yet such formulations of absolute power, repeated and developed by later jurists, were to reverberate down the centuries, resounding in many ears as so many harsh *leitmotive* of tyranny.

Nevertheless, as Fisher saw, the medieval Papacy was not a sheer tyrannical theocracy. The theory and practice of papal government were not those of arbitrary or merely autocratic rule. It is a striking fact that Innocent III's pontificate was finally crowned by a council in which the whole Church was intended to be associated with the pope's reforms. The Fourth Lateran Council – arguably the most important such assembly in the medieval period – was distinguished among other things by the range of its membership. The pope summoned to Rome not bishops only, but abbots, provosts of cathedral chapters, and (notably) temporal rulers. To claim that Innocent 'can be said to have paved the way for the conciliar movement' may go too far; but to describe Lateran IV as 'the first truly universal council of the Middle Ages' is a fair enough evaluation of its significance (Ullmann 1975: 156–7). Even so, Innocent's council, like every ecumenical council, was primarily a gathering of bishops presided over by the chief bishop. Like any medieval monarchy, the Church was ruled by its monarch and its magnates together, in a partnership as indispensable as it was often problematic. The papal monarch plainly had at his disposal a more sophisticated instrument of government than anything enjoyed by temporal rulers; but the stubborn problems of government itself persisted.

II

The thirteenth century was an age of notable legislators, and not the least notable were its popes. Building on the solid foundations laid by Innocent III and the Fourth Lateran Council, Gregory IX (1227–41) and Innocent IV (1243–54) – to mention the most outstanding reigns – developed still further a structure of canon law which was to have the keenest legal minds of the age as its expositors. Innocent IV, for that matter, was a distinguished jurist in his own right as well as a vigorous pontiff. He combined the two roles, commenting (for example) as a jurist on the pontifical decree whereby he had deposed the Emperor Frederick II. And in juristic doctrine his careful distinction between personal and corporate liability gives him a claim to an important place in the development of the concept of individual responsibility (Black 1988: 599, 601). A similar dual role is exemplified at the episcopal level by the leading canonist of the century, Hostiensis (Henricus de Segusio,: d. 1271). Besides teaching canon law in the universities, he 'led a life of administrative activity' as, successively, bishop of Sisteron, archbishop of Embrun, and cardinal-archbishop of Ostia (Pennington 1993: 48–75). Such a man was not likely to undervalue episcopal authority, however strenuously he upheld – as Hostiensis certainly upheld – papal supremacy. Striking the necessary balance between these two essential forces inevitably generated tension – manifested, of course, not merely in juristic doctrine and scholastic disputation but in the practical politics of Church government. The difficulties are well illustrated by the episcopal career of Robert Grosseteste (*c.*1175–1253).

Grosseteste, who became bishop of Lincoln in 1235, may seem too distinctive, too brilliant a figure to be regarded as typical. Yet however individual and original his intellectual response may have been, the problems he faced were those faced by the Church in general, and in particular by the episcopate. Grosseteste's government of his diocese, energetic and wide-ranging, exemplified the ways in which the principles of church discipline were given practical effect. His (abortive) attempt to insist that canon law should prevail over the law and custom of England in regard to legitimacy and bastardy reflected the Church's demand for a spiritual jurisdiction independent of – ultimately indeed superior to – the civil power. In such matters as these Grosseteste could look for and receive papal support. And he took an appropriately lofty view of the Papacy, addressing Gregory IX in terms of reverential obedience and dedication to devoted service in 'whatever task you may wish to impose on me' (Southern 1986: 272). Yet if Grosseteste shared 'the intense Papalism of the best men' of his day, he also believed 'that the pope was not the lord over the bishops but one of them' and that a bishop's diocesan 'authority and responsibility, like that of the pope himself, came from God' (Smith 1913: v; Southern 1986: 262–3). In practice the issue arose sharply in regard to appointment to ecclesiastical benefices.

There was, to be sure, an entirely respectable case, made out in the twelfth century, for appointments by papal 'provision'. The system might ensure, at a time when adequate clerical education could not be taken for granted throughout the Church, that offices were filled by men properly qualified for the tasks to be performed. Provision (it has been said) 'opened up, as university authorities quickly realized, opportunities for advancement to educated men whose lack of social standing would, in the eyes of . . . electors or patrons, have made them ineligible' (Oakley 1979: 51). The original purposes of the system were indeed such as Grosseteste warmly endorsed. It was, however open to abuse. When a bishop's pastoral care for his flock was under-mined by unworthy provision to benefices within his diocese (whether this was the work of the pope himself or of the 'familiars' of the Curia) the unquestioned papal fullness of power was being disastrously abused. Such alleged abuses were certainly among Grosseteste's concerns when he visited the papal Curia at Lyons in 1250; but the significance of that visit may be more complex than some accounts have suggested.

The statements (both written and oral) made to the pope and cardinals clearly express Grosseteste's impassioned condemnation of the obstacles to effective pastoral care. Those obstacles, however, were not created only by the pope and his 'familiars'. Their guilt was real; but it was shared by others – not least by the episcopate, when bishops failed to discharge their apostolic responsibilities. A recent 'diplomatic analysis' of the documents suggests that Grosseteste's main (though certainly not his sole) preoccupation in 1250 was to oppose burdensome interference by the arch-bishop of Canterbury in the sphere belonging to suffragan bishops like himself. And if Grosseteste could adopt an apocalyptic tone in his fear that the Papacy itself had 'become a source of perdition', he still looked to the pope as head of a rightly ordered hierarchy to preside over the essential remedy for what was amiss. Pope, cardinals, archbishops, and bishops must combine to ensure that the task of saving souls was 'given to those who understand the Gospel of Christ' (Goering 1997; documentation in Gieben 1971: 340–93).

Serious historians have long discounted the legendary status of this 1250 episode as a scene in the long struggle between the *ecclesia anglicana* and 'papal aggres-sion'. The analysis just summarised casts doubt even on the notion that the aged Grosseteste returned home in despair after defeat in a confrontation if not an open conflict (Southern 1986: 279–81). Yet there was still an issue here of critical importance for the polity of the Church. What, after all, *was* the status of bishops in relation to the pope? They were indeed his brethren, sharing in the apostolic succession; but he, the chief bishop, was the successor of Peter, prince of the apostles. Still more, he was, by virtue of that succession, the vicar of Christ Himself. On that basis it could be argued that episcopal authority was simply delegated by the pope, since, in the words of the Franciscan Thomas of York in 1256: 'an inferior prelate has nothing save from [his] superior, namely the supreme pontiff' (Tierney 1972: 66 n. 3). It is especially significant that Thomas was a Franciscan; for the issue in question had been greatly sharpened by the rise of the mendicant orders and the ensuing conflict with the secular clergy. Dominicans and Franciscans formed what

Figure 31.2 Boniface VIII inaugurates the Jubilee. The Lateran Palace, Rome, February 1300. Milan, Biblioteca Ambrosiana. Photo: Scala, Florence.

might be called a militia or task-force at the disposal of the pope. It was, to be sure, possible for this force to collaborate with a diocesan bishop. Grosseteste, for example, having had Franciscan support for his election, had the help of both Franciscans and Dominicans in his pastoral work (Southern 1986: 11, 258). On the other hand, there could be (and very commonly was) hostility between the mendicants and both the parish clergy and the diocesan authorities (Tierney 1972: 64–5).

The details of the controversy between mendicants and seculars lie, like the intricacies of the debate on Franciscan poverty, well beyond the limits of the present discussion. There is, however, a related issue in ecclesiastical polity which does call for comment here. It may be expressed in terms of the soldierly metaphor used above – not unsuitably, perhaps, in regard to the Church Militant. Absolute monarchy, however complex its structures, entails a single chain of command; and papal doctrine during the thirteenth century was plainly taking that direction. On that basis, bishops, secular clergy and religious orders were all forces to be disposed and directed by the pope. All other authorities were subordinate to the papal supreme command. Now such a model, even if the practical obstacles to its implementation were set aside, was inescapably problematic as a theological account of the ecclesiastical hierarchy. It was doctrinally impossible to deny to bishops and priests a sacramental authority independent of the Papacy. The pope might be *the* vicar of Christ, but every ordained priest acted in the person of Christ when he gave absolution in the confessional or celebrated Mass at the altar. This could, of course, be met by insisting on the distinction between *potestas ordinis* and *potestas iurisdictionis*; but (at least in regard to jurisdiction at the episcopal level) it was far from easy to gainsay the view that 'within his diocese it was the bishop's duty to make decisions . . . in the light of the fundamental law of the gospel, to which both he and the pope were subject' (Southern 1986: 263).

Again, even though any individual bishop was inferior to the pope in jurisdictional authority (as he manifestly was in territorial competence), this still left open the question of the authority of the pope in comparison with the bishops as a collegial body. That question would not reach its medieval point of crisis for another century and a half. No doubt the general councils held at Lyons in 1245 and 1274 were 'primarily debating assemblies presided over by the pope' (Ullmann 1975: 156). Such an assembly could serve as a forum for the contention between secular clergy and the mendicants, as proposed by the friars' most vehement adversary, William of St Amour, in the 1250s (Tierney 1982: 60–5; Linehan 1997: 16–17). A council could also provide a platform for criticism of the Papacy and opposition to papal policies; and the potent notion of an appeal against the pope to a general council was in the air. In that connection the high politics of Frederick II's appeal to the First Council of Lyons against his deposition is less significant here than the activity of the English clergy at the same period. Having failed in their protest against papal taxation at Lyons in 1245, they renewed their efforts in the following year by appealing explicitly to a future general council of the Church (Becker 1988: 47–53; Powicke and Cheney 1964: 388–401). Papal absolutism might remain unshaken, but it did not go unchallenged.

III

As Dante is led by Virgil through the third *bolgia* of Hell, he is greeted by a cry from one of the simoniac sinners:

> Se' tu già costì ritto,
> se' tu già costì ritto, Bonifazio?

The speaker is Nicholas III, supposing that Boniface VIII is 'already', in 1300, 'standing there' in the place prepared for him to occupy after his death in 1303.[2] The savage irony of this imagined case of mistaken identity may tell us more about 'the political theory of a fanatic' (Holmes 1980: 41) than about the failings of either pope. Yet it is possible to see in Boniface's pontificate, closing the thirteenth century as Innocent III's had opened it, the disastrous end to a story that had begun in triumph. His conflict with Philip the Fair of France led to humiliation soon followed by death. His ringing proclamations of papal supremacy might, within a few years, sound hollow, mocked by the 'Babylonish captivity' of the Avignon Papacy and thereafter by the forty years' scandal of the Great Schism. On the other hand, Boniface VIII was described, in his own day, as 'excelling in wisdom and providence, to guide the lofty and burdensome business of the Church' (Boase 1933: 377). In our own time, he has been reckoned as one of the popes who 'happily combined scholarship with practical statecraft' (Ullmann 1975: 168). His contribution to the codification of canon law, the *Liber Sextus decretalium*, has been called 'the lasting monument of a distinguished legislator' (Burns 1988: 663). As for what followed his reign, we shall see that the picture of the fourteenth-century Papacy as an institution in crisis and decline calls at least for questioning and qualification.

What can scarcely be questioned is that Boniface VIII's reign demonstrates the extent to which the polity of the Church was now entangled in the politics of the Papacy as a European power, and especially as a major player on the Italian political stage. When he invoked the authority of the Fourth Lateran Council in his attempt to bar the taxation of the French and English clergy to finance the war between Philip the Fair and Edward I of England, Boniface may (like another pope in the words of a lesser poet than Dante) have

> cast his arms abroad for agony and loss,
> And called the kings of Christendom for swords about the Cross.

But we may safely assume that the possibility of a new crusade was less in the forefront of his mind than the actual need to restore a united kingdom of Naples and Sicily for his Angevin ally Charles II. 'The essence of papal finance' (it has been said) 'was the imposition of taxes upon the European clergy as a whole with which to pay for armies to carry out papal policy in Italy' (Holmes 1980: 23).

The time, however, had not yet come – if come it ever did – when the Papacy would act, whether in Italy or elsewhere, simply as a 'state' engaged in the business of 'power politics'. Boniface asserted a papal supremacy which, at least in the wider perspective of Christendom at large, was primarily spiritual and which, for that very reason, ought to prevail over temporal power. His assertions were distinguished, not by any significant novelty, but rather by 'the pithy, succinct and concise formulation of mature hierocratic ideas' (Ullmann 1975: 276). The most celebrated of them, *Unam sanctam* (1302), drew on theological as well as on canon-law sources (notably on Pseudo-Dionysius, Hugh of St Victor, and Thomas Aquinas) to demonstrate that 'it is absolutely necessary for salvation that every human creature be subject to the Roman pontiff.' Whether such papal ecclesiology was undermined or fostered by the new intellectual movements produced by the full recovery of Aristotle's works, the ensuing century was to see some of the most extreme statements of medieval papalism.

What is certainly the case is that Boniface VIII had encountered and failed to overcome a new kind of opposition to the claims of the Papacy. The French monarchy under Philip the Fair had shown what a determined and highly organised temporal power could achieve by way of putting into practice the principle already acknowledged in the days of Innocent III: *Rex in regno suo est imperator*. Neither the Holy Roman Empire nor 'the Empire of the Gregories and the Innocents' (Smith 1913: 101) – to whom we may add the Bonifaces – was to prevail over the *imperium* of kings secure in their kingdoms. When we set the general principle in the context of such particular circumstances as the transfer of the papal court to Avignon in 1309 and the summoning to Vienne two years later of a general council of the Church with the posthumous condemnation of Boniface VIII for heresy on its agenda, we are bound to ask whether the Papacy itself had not indeed been captured and subdued. The answer is less straightforward than it may seem.

In the mere absence from Rome of the pope or his court there was nothing unusual: 'the papal court of audience' (it has been said, with reference to the later thirteenth century) 'was never able to remain in Rome for long' (Sayers 1980: 115). Two French popes in the 1260s never visited the city at all (Paravicini Bagliani 1995: 21). Avignon (which became papal property by purchase in 1348) offered greater security – under French protection to be sure; and now that the focus of power in Latin Christendom had moved decisively to north-west Europe there was, so to speak, a geopolitical argument for regarding Rome as a less effective centre for the government of the Church (Holmes 1975: 83–5; Oakley 1979: 38–55). Certainly papal administration lost none of its commanding efficiency during the seven decades of 'exile'. Control over appointments to benefices, and in particular to bishoprics was firmer than ever, the fiscal demands of the Curia more exacting. There is certainly a strong case for regarding the Avignon Papacy as 'the most impressive hierarchical imperialism that Europe has ever seen' (Holmes 1975: 94). Nor can it fairly be said that the popes of that period, preoccupied though they doubtless were with the grandeur of their office and the goals of nepotism, lost sight of more disinterested concerns. Benedict XII (1334–42) was active in pursuit of reunion with the Greek Church and legislated for monastic reform. Clement VI (1342–52) and Urban V (1362–70) were serious though unsuccessful in seeking to launch a new crusade. The fourteenth-century Papacy was still vigorously playing its leading role in the Church: it cannot in justice be seen as a mere instrument of temporal politics in its own or other rulers' interests.

There was of course another side to the picture. If there was nothing new in venality and ambitious corruption at the papal court, there was nothing edifying either. And if pontifical grandeur, in both its positive and its negative aspect, is one striking feature of the religious history of the fourteenth century, another is the extent to which mainstream orthodoxy was evoking dissent. Dissent as such, of course, amounting in some cases to heresy, was no novelty. Since the late eleventh century 'sect-formation' had been a recurrent phenomenon in the Latin Church.[3] Even in the fourteenth century no sect yet amounted to a threat. Some dissenting movements, however, may by then be seen as pointing to sources from which a

Figure 31.3 Andrea Bonaiuti's fresco *The Church Militant* (lower left quarter) in the Spanish Chapel, S. Maria Novella, Florence, *c.*1365. Photo: Scala, Florence.

genuinely threatening challenge would later come. In this perspective the continuing conflict with, and within, the Franciscan order over apostolic poverty is less significant than, for instance, the rise of communities of *béguines* and the less numerous male *beghards*. The *béguines* – pious women living together in the world without any formal rule or organisation – were condemned by the council of Vienne in 1311 as victims of 'a kind of madness', which led them to 'express opinions . . . contrary to the Catholic faith, deceiving many simple people' (Holmes 1975: 162). A more widespread, structured and enduring challenge to the established order came from the Waldensians. Their commitment to what Jean-Jacques Rousseau was to call 'the religion of the Gospel, pure and simple' attracted substantial followings in various regions (not least in Bohemia) and was in time to produce a separate church alongside those brought into being by the sixteenth-century Reformation.

More alarming to the ruling hierarchy was the suspicion that dissenting groups might go beyond evangelical quietism towards the anarchy of antinomianism. And here 'the complexities of deviation', compounded by the character of the evidence, pose formidable problems of interpretation (Oakley 1979: 175–212). Nowhere are these more evident than in attempts to understand 'the heresy of the Free Spirit', to whose adherents extravagance in both belief and conduct was attributed at the time and in some later historical accounts (Lerner 1972). Perhaps the most that can be said in brief is that the alarm such movements excited was as real as most of the suspicions were probably exaggerated. In any case, however deep-seated the underlying malaise may have been, the symptoms so far examined proved to be, for the most part, transitory. The Church authorities were often adept in absorbing and, as it were, domesticating what could not be suppressed. When, in the closing decades of the century, the greatest crisis of the medieval Church broke, the point of fracture lay in the ecclesiastical polity itself.

IV

On 13 June 1376 Gregory XI left Avignon for Rome. How far, if at all, his decision to do so was influenced by the urging of St Catherine of Siena may be debatable. In any case it was a decision which could, both at the time and in historical perspective, be seen as at once radical and predictable. There had always been a powerful magnetism drawing the Papacy back *ad limina apostolorum* and an enduring political (and fiscal) interest in control over the papal states in central Italy. For fourteen years the Spanish cardinal Gil de Albornoz, sent as legate by Innocent VI in 1353, directed what could almost be called a reconquest, and sought, in the *Constitutiones Egidianae*, to give the patrimony of St Peter a form of ordered government. By 1367 Urban V was able to return to Rome and, though the administrative centre did not move with him, to remain there for two years. Both then and ten years later, however, there were strong pressures and persuasive arguments against the return. Rome (as usual) was in ruinous and unhealthy decline, the populace restive when they were not rebellious, security still far from assured. And the pressures in favour of remaining in Avignon were formidable. The French monarchy, emerging under Charles V from a protracted 'time of troubles', had no inclination to surrender the leverage afforded by the location of the Papacy under its shadow if not within its territory. The college of cardinals and the greatly expanded papal bureaucracy were overwhelmingly staffed by men whose interests and instincts alike disposed them to remain north of the Alps. None of this, however, prevailed in the end over the determination of 'a serious-minded Pope . . . who hoped to unite western Europe in a crusade' (Holmes 1975: 45).

Gregory XI's determination led to a disaster even the prophetic charism of a Catherine of Siena could not foresee. He himself died only fourteen months after his solemn entry into Rome in January 1377; and the election of his successor was soon followed by the schism that split Latin Christendom into rival papal 'obediences' for almost forty years. It is tempting indeed to speculate that it might have been better for the Church if Gregory had been able to carry out his reported intention of returning to Avignon. In the event, the election of Urban VI was, from the outset, insecure. Of the twenty-three cardinals, six had remained in Avignon. Most of those who took part in the conclave were French (or at least, as we would now say, Francophone); but their divisions played into the hands of the four Italians in the college. The choice fell upon the archbishop of Bari – who, if not the 'Roman pope' for whom the mob clamoured, was 'at least an Italian'. Resentment of the new pope's austerity and harshness soon combined with doubts (both genuine and factitious) as to the validity of his election as well as with political interest to alienate the cardinals. Withdrawing to Anagni, they repudiated Urban and elected Robert of Geneva in his place as Clement VII. Clement soon made Avignon his base and secured substantial political support, with France and Castile as the pillars of his 'obedience'. The Great Schism of the West had begun (Holmes 1975: 168–95; Oakley 1979: 55–70; Thomson 1980: 3–28).

Schism as such was no new experience for the Latin Church. The eleventh century had produced four antipopes, the twelfth a further ten; and if most of these were transient figures, the schismatic succession during the pontificate of Alexander III (1159–81) showed some degree of permanence. No previous episode, however, was comparable to the all but forty years ending with the election of Martin V in November 1417. Even then, indeed, the chapter was not finally closed. To be sure, the final phase of the Avignon Papacy (latterly on the Aragonese promontory of Peñiscola) was shadowy enough (Linehan 1998); but it did not end until the adamantine Benedict XIII (1394–1422) had been succeeded by Clement VIII (1423–9). The sequel to the Council of Basel's election of Felix V in 1439 never rivalled in scale what had happened between 1378 and 1417. None the less, when that 'Little Schism' finally ended in 1449, during only one of the previous seven decades had the Church had a pope who had enjoyed totally unchallenged authority.

Plainly such a protracted crisis both reflected and prompted change in the ecclesiastical polity. Most obviously, the years of schism were the years of what historians have called the Conciliar Movement. Between 1409 and 1449 four general councils tried, with varying success, to deal with the problems facing the Church. Insofar as their concern was for 'reform in head and members' these assemblies might be regarded as continuing the work of their medieval precursors from Lateran III (1179) to Vienne. There was, however, a crucial difference. With Vienne as perhaps a partial exception, those earlier councils had worked under firm papal direction. Now, however, the most urgent problem was, precisely, a stubborn dispute as to where papal authority truly lay. The first fifteenth-century council met at Pisa when, and because, both rival popes had been deserted by their cardinals. It is especially noteworthy in the present context that, as in 1378, the initiative was again taken by the Sacred College. This draws attention to the emergence in this period of a 'cardinalist' alongside the older 'episcopalist' view of church government. The cardinals, still comparatively few in number, could claim in a special sense to embody the Roman Church and thus to have an essential role in Roman primacy – granting, when necessary, that 'Rome' was to be understood in the light of the maxim *Ubi papa ibi Roma* (Thomson 1980: 29–53). It is a not unremarkable fact that five of the most important fifteenth-century writers on ecclesiastical polity all became cardinals: Pierre d'Ailly, Franciscus Zabarella, Nicholas of Cusa, Juan de Torquemada, Juan de Segovia.

At the same time, more inclusive views of the Church did not by any means disappear or go by default. When the efforts at Pisa proved abortive – or worse, since a third papal 'obedience' emerged with the election of Alexander V and then of John XXIII – the next council, at Constance, looked to nothing less than a constitutional reform in which a broadly representative council would have an entrenched role, meeting regularly, no longer dependent on a discretionary papal summons. Such councils, moreover, were defined as holding supreme authority in the Church, with their supremacy over the pope manifested in the depositions or forced abdications which had eventually brought the schism to an end. This was not a new way of envisaging the ecclesiastical polity. A century before, at the Council of Vienne, Guillaume Durand had argued for a governmental structure in the Church very similar to what was now advocated by Pierre d'Ailly and Jean Gerson and woven by Nicholas of Cusa into his great vision of 'Catholic concordance' (Fasolt 1992; Oakley 1964; Pascoe 1973; Sigmund 1963; Sigmund 1991).

That practice in 'the real world of politics' fell short of the theory and the vision hardly needs saying. Even in its more restricted aristocratic or oligarchic form, expressed most especially perhaps by Zabarella (Canning 1996: 181), with the cardinals envisaged as acting in consistorial association with the pope, the conciliar concept made little permanent headway at a time when the current of European politics was running strongly in the direction of absolute monarchy (Burns 1992). Absolute monarchs had, it is true, powerful motives for opposing papal absolutism; but only temporary expediency was likely to attract them to the conciliar alternative. A case could even be made – and indeed was made, and vigorously made, by supporters of Eugenius IV against the Council of Basel – for the view that all monarchical authority was menaced by conciliar 'democracy' (Black 1970: 85–90). Kings, however, would see the restored papacy after 1449 as the greater threat.

On the other hand, the Council of Basel, like that of Constance before it, had as one of its concerns another, greater threat to the principle of authority. The papal schism had latterly been accompanied by a still more portentous division in Latin Christendom. Dissent and heresy had returned in the late fourteenth century in a radical form; and by the early fifteenth century the challenge reached alarming proportions. The complex heterodoxies of John Wyclif, which latterly included a sweeping attack on the papal hierocracy, incurred episcopal condemnation in England and a summons to Rome by Urban VI (with whose reforming austerity at least Wyclif certainly sympathised). That process was foreclosed only by Wyclif's death in 1384. In Bohemia, Jan Hus and his followers drew some of their inspiration from Wyclif in what has been called 'The First Reformation' (Holmes 1975: 195–213). The Hussite movement and its consequences overshadowed the Church for a century before the start of what we have been conditioned to think of as *the* Reformation (Oakley 1979: 195–209, 294–301; Ozment 1980: 165–70).

When Hus was condemned as a heretic by the Council of Constance in 1415, his treatise on the Church (*De ecclesia*, 1413) was a major ground for the sentence. Much of what he had said in that text (how much has been the subject of scholarly debate) came from Wyclif (Oberman 1981: 207–37). Hus maintains, for instance, that 'no pope is head of the catholic church': such headship belongs to Christ alone, while the Church itself is – though Hus is hesitant on this point – not so much the congregation of all believers as the community of those predestined to salvation. The hierarchy of the Church enjoyed only secondary authority; and Hus, like Wyclif, argued strongly in favour of the secular power as the instrument of Church reform. Yet he stopped short of Wyclif's more startling extremes in other aspects of theology, neither questioning the Church's essential teaching in regard to the sacraments nor endorsing Wyclif's challenge to the sacramental ministry of sinful priests. On the 'left wing' of the developing Hussite movement, to be sure, more radical views emerged. The Four Articles of Prague (1430) called not only for freedom to preach the Word and to receive communion under both kinds, but for the surrender by the

Figure 31.4 The Pope as Antichrist, *c.*1500. Jena codex. Prague, Knihovna Národního muzea, MS IV B 24.

pope and every bishop and priest of all surplus wealth and (most radical of all, no doubt) for the elimination of all public sin. The millenarian Taborites went further still, not simply in their expectation of Christ's imminent return to earth, but in their devaluing of the sacraments.

In the light of these developments, it is scarcely surprising to find that violent conflict raged in the 1420s and early 1430s both within and against the movement Hus had inspired. The settlement reached in 1435, after well over a decade of armed struggle, was the work, primarily, of the Council of Basel – arguably the greatest achievement of the entire Conciliar Movement. The terms of the settlement, however, were ominous. Peace was restored on the basis of a permanent division in Bohemia between Catholics and the moderate Hussite Utraquists, who retained communion 'under both kinds' and their separate ecclesiastical organisation. Such coexistence was predictably uneasy, even if both parties could reflect with satisfaction on the defeat of more revolutionary forces (Gill 1965: 165–91, 335–7, 338–42).

Elsewhere in Europe the pattern of religious life was undergoing diversification in less dramatic but still significant ways. Apart from lingering Lollardy in England and Scotland, Waldensian dissent (more especially in the Alpine and sub-Alpine areas of south-eastern France and north-western Italy) survived stubbornly despite intermittently violent persecution. Meanwhile, within the fold of the Church, the so-called *devotio moderna* was vigorously at work. In itself a tendency rather than a movement, this nevertheless provided the inspiration for more or less organised movements of various kinds. The common elements in these may perhaps be identified as Christ-centred asceticism and an emphasis on personal (though not necessarily individualistic) spirituality. Both elements are encapsulated in the title of the most influential text produced by the *devotio moderna*: Thomas à Kempis's *The Imitation of Christ*. Not only did these movements, often originating as lay 'confraternities', seek a way of life to be led in common, though not always, strictly speaking, monastic; more than that, they sought that life within, not in opposition to, the hierarchical and sacramental structure of the Church. The Brethren of the Common Life provide the outstanding example of such a movement, while the Augustinian canons of the Windesheim congregation serve as a reminder that the older traditions of monastic life were also being renewed and reinvigorated. The period saw the spread, across the spectrum of established religious orders, of an 'Observantine' impulse to recover the rigour of rules that had suffered inevitable relaxation over time (Oakley 1979: 100–13, 231–8; Post 1968).

If these aspects of late medieval religious history are to be properly related to the issues of authority and church government that are central here, it is important not to assume that advocates of reform and renovation were invariably cutting 'against the grain' of church policy. Bishops had an essential part to play, whether by passive allowance or by positive encouragement and leadership. Popes, likewise, could contribute to the process both by personal initiative and by means of emissaries sent out as, for example, Nicholas of Cusa was sent by Nicholas V in 1451–2 to visit and reform monastic communities in Germany and the Netherlands (Sullivan 1974). Episcopal action could be critically important: Niccolò Albergati as bishop of Bologna, Antoninus as archbishop of Florence illustrate the point (Hay 1977: 12–13, 53–7). On the other hand, local initiatives could acquire momentum independent of, and potentially on a collision course with, the authorities. An extreme and celebrated instance is provided by the activities of Girolamo Savonarola in Florence, where the confrontation ended with the reformer's execution as a heretic. That dramatic episode also serves as a reminder of the inescapable interplay of the spiritual and the temporal – of Church and State; for it was arguably Savonarola's politics rather than his religious doctrine that brought about his downfall (Weinstein 1970).

Savonarola's passionate puritanical preaching of moral and religious reform became increasingly associated with a millenarian vision of the role and destiny of the Florentine republic. In the world of political reality, the context of that vision was the invasion of Italy by Charles VIII of France in 1494: a moment once familiar as the textbook watershed between 'medieval' and 'modern' Europe. The political future (whether it was or was not by then distinctively 'modern') lay with the territorial monarchies, not with the Italian city-republics; and it is to the relationship between the Church and those monarchical states that the discussion here must finally turn – or *return*.

To say that the seamless garment of medieval Latin Christendom was, by the late fifteenth century, in tatters would be to exaggerate both in subject and in predicate. Yet to look back across the three centuries following Innocent III's death in 1216 is likely to yield the distinct impression that such seamlessness as there may once have been *was* giving way to a patchwork of increasingly 'national' allegiances. The popes might restore in Renaissance splendour the grandeur that had once been Rome. Alexander VI (1492–1503) might adjudicate on the partition of the New World (Muldoon 1979: 136–9) as well as adding new dimensions to the concept of nepotism, while Leo X (1513–21) preferred his anticipated 'enjoyment' of the Papacy to the urgencies of reform. Julius II (1503–13) certainly did much to rebuild the political and military strength of the papal state. Ultimately, however, the Papacy must now negotiate where it could no longer command. The Age of Concordats had come, and it was only in 1929 that the last concordat marked the final extinction of the pope's temporal power. When, in 1511, Pisa was again the city to which dissident cardinals, urged on by the king of France and the emperor, summoned a council, which proceeded to depose the pope, Julius II retorted by summoning the Fifth Lateran Council (1512–17). It was the belated fulfilment of an undertaking he had given when elected; and it proved to be at best a halting answer to renewed demands for 'reform in head and members' (Burns and Izbicki 1997: vii–xxii). A more significant response to the challenge of 1511 came in 1516, when a new French king and a new pope sealed the Concordat of Bologna (Knecht 1963). By then, no doubt, papalism and conciliarism in their medieval forms were both spent forces. But 'Gallican liberties' and their equivalents elsewhere, combined with and indeed dependent upon the acceptance by pope and bishops alike of substantial royal control over the Church, were to have a long future in the Europe of sovereign states.

NOTES

1 See Pennington 1988: 433–4 for the 'classic definition' of this distinction by Johannes Teutonicus, *c.*1216. The terminology derived from Pope Leo I in the mid-5th century; for early medieval development see Robinson 1988: 282–90.
2 *Inferno* xix.52–3: 'Are you already standing there, are you already standing there, Boniface?' Cf. xxvii.85, where Boniface is 'the prince of the new Pharisees'.
3 The classic account of this phenomenon is in Troeltsch 1932: i. 349ff.

REFERENCES

Becker, H.-J. (1988) *Die Appellation vom Papst an ein allgemeines Konzil*, Cologne: Böhlau.
Black, A. J. (1970) *Monarchy and Community: political ideas in the later conciliar controversy 1430–1450*, Cambridge: Cambridge University Press.
—— (1988) 'The individual and society', in Burns 1988: 588–606.
Boase, T. S. R. (1933) *Boniface the Eighth*, London: Constable.
Burns, J. H. (ed.) (1988) *The Cambridge History of Medieval Political Thought c.350–c.1450*, Cambridge: Cambridge University Press.
—— (1992) *Lordship, Kingship and Empire: the idea of monarchy 1400–1525*, Oxford: Clarendon Press.
—— and Izbicki, T. H. (eds) (1997). *Conciliarism and Papalism*, Cambridge: Cambridge University Press.
Canning, J. P. (1996) *A History of Medieval Political Thought 300–1450*, London: Routledge.
Fasolt, C. (1992). *Council and Hierarchy: the political thought of William Durand the Younger*, Cambridge: Cambridge University Press.
Fisher, H. A. L. (1936) *A History of Europe*, London: Edward Arnold.
Gieben, S. (1971) 'Robert Grosseteste at the papal court, Lyons 1250: edition of the documents', *Collectanea Franciscana* 41: 340–93.
Gill, J. (1965) *Constance et Bâle–Florence*, Paris: Éditions de l'Orante.
Goering, J. (1997) 'Robert Grosseteste at the papal court', in J. Brown and W. P. Stoneman (eds) *A Distinct Voice: medieval studies in honor of Leonard E. Boyle, O.P.*, Notre Dame, Ind.: Notre Dame University Press, 253–76.
Hay, D. (1977) *The Church in Italy in the Fifteenth Century*, Cambridge: Cambridge University Press.
Holmes, G. (1975) *Europe: hierarchy and revolt 1320–1450*, London: Fontana/Collins.
—— (1980) 'Dante and the Popes', in C. Grayson (ed.) *The World of Dante: essays on Dante and his times*, Oxford: Clarendon Press, 18–43.
Imkamp, W. (1983) *Das Kirchenbild Innocenz' III. (1198–1216)*, Stuttgart: Hiersemann.
Knecht, R. J. (1963). 'The Concordat of 1516: a reassessment', *Birmingham University Historical Journal* 9: 16–32.
Lerner, R. E. (1972) *The Heresy of the Free Spirit*, Berkeley, Los Angeles and London: University of California Press.
Linehan, P. (1997) *The Ladies of Zamora*: Manchester: Manchester University Press.
—— (1998) 'Papa Luna in 1415: a proposal by Benedict XIII for the ending of the Great Schism', *English Historical Review* 113: 91–8.
Muldoon, J. (1979) *Popes, Lawyers and Infidels*, Liverpool: Liverpool University Press.
Oakley, F. (1964) *The Political Thought of Pierre d'Ailly: the voluntarist tradition*, New Haven and London: Yale University Press.

—— (1979) *The Western Church in the Later Middle Ages*, Ithaca and London: Cornell University Press.

Oberman, H. A. (1981) *Forerunners of the Reformation. The shape of later medieval thought illustrated by key documents*, Philadelphia: Fortress Press.

Ozment, S. (1980). *The Age of Reform 1250–1550: an intellectual and religious history of late medieval and Reformation Europe*, New Haven and London: Yale University Press.

Paravicini Bagliani, A. (1995), *La cour des papes au XIIIᵉ siècle*, Paris: Hachette.

Pascoe, L. B. (1973) *Jean Gerson: principles of church reform*, Leiden: E. J. Brill.

Post, R. R. (1968) *The Modern Devotion: confrontation with Reformation and Humanism*, Leiden: E. J. Brill.

Pennington, K. (1984) *Pope and Bishops: the papal monarchy in the twelfth and thirteenth centuries*, Pennsylvania: University of Philadelphia Press.

—— (1988) 'Law, legislative authority and theories of government, 1150–1300', in Burns 1988: 424–53.

—— (1993) *The Prince and the Law 1200–1600: sovereignty and rights in the Western legal tradition*, Berkeley, Los Angeles and London: University of California Press.

Powicke, F. M. and Cheney, C. R. (eds) (1964) *Councils and Synods, with other documents relating to the English Church*, vol. ii, *A.D. 1205–1313*, Oxford: Clarendon Press.

Robinson, I. S. (1988). 'Church and papacy', in Burns 1988: 252–305.

Sayers, J. (1980) 'Centre and locality: aspects of papal administration in England in the later thirteenth century', in B. Tierney and P. Linehan (eds), *Authority and Power. Studies on medieval law and government presented to Walter Ullmann on his seventieth birthday*, Cambridge: Cambridge University Press, 115–26.

Sigmund, P. E. (1963) *Nicholas of Cusa and Medieval Political Thought*, Cambridge, Mass.: Harvard University Press.

—— (ed.) (1991) *Nicholas of Cusa: The Catholic Concordance*, Cambridge: Cambridge University Press.

Smith, A. L. (1913) *Church and State in the Middle Ages*, Oxford: Clarendon Press.

Southern, R. W. (1986) *Robert Grosseteste: the growth of an English mind in medieval Europe*, Oxford: Clarendon Press.

Sullivan, D. (1974) 'Nicholas of Cusa as reformer: the papal legation to the Germanies, 1451–1452', *Mediaeval Studies* 36: 382–428.

Thomson, J. A. F. (1980) *Popes and Princes 1417–1517: politics and polity in the late medieval Church*, London: Allen & Unwin.

Tierney, B. (1972) *Origins of Papal Infallibility: 1150–1350: a study on the concepts of infallibility, sovereignty and tradition in the Middle Ages*, Leiden: E. J. Brill.

—— (1982) *Religion, Law, and the Growth of Constitutional Thought 1150–1650*, Cambridge: Cambridge University Press.

Troeltsch, E. (1932) (trans. O. Wyon) *The Social Teaching of the Christian Churches*, 3 vols, London: Allen & Unwin.

Ullmann, W. (1975) *Law and Politics in the Middle Ages: an introduction to the sources of medieval political ideas*, London: Sources of History Ltd.

Weinstein, D. (1970) *Savonarola and Florence: prophecy and patriotism in the Renaissance*, Princeton, NJ: Princeton University Press.

PART IV

ELITES, ORGANISATIONS AND GROUPS

INTRODUCTION

Structures, mental and governmental, provided the frameworks in which medieval people thought and lived. But the best way to see them in action is to focus on groups and associations. The Middle Ages were indeed a heyday for such collectivities, whether or not they were legally labelled as privileged, meaning, literally, 'with a private law'. Some were in principle voluntary, such as a confraternity devoted to a saint's cult; but most overlapped with, or were embedded in, pre-existing groups of other kinds. Viewed horizontally, most people, whether their legal status was free or unfree, could be seen as families or kindreds, or those living in the same neighbourhood; viewed vertically, they were often men and women under a common lordship or ecclesiastical administration. Villages and parishes were simultaneously both types of association, horizontal and vertical. Many peasants lived and worked as discrete nuclear families, which is how they were listed by their lords' estate-managers; but, at the same time, as farmers of contingent areas, with important decisions, such as the leaving fallow of certain land, collectively observed and seasonal working-practices, especially harvesting, collectively allocated and timed; and also as tenants of the same, or contingent, landlords, to whom they owed dues and labour-services, and to whose court they had to come to be tried and judged if they were accused of crime. Custom ruled the lives of the legally free and unfree unlike. Yet chattel slavery, relatively unimportant in the early medieval centuries, had largely been abandoned in most of western Europe by *c.*1000. However heavy were their customary burdens, peasants, once their dues had been handed over and services done, could work on their own account, keep their surplus produce and sell in markets, in little family firms or in *consortia*, and they could form associations called *gilds* for mutual insurance and help against such scourges as fire or storm. In towns, production was carried on by family businesses, but groups, again often known as gilds, coordinated the marketing of products and services. Of course, some were more equal than others, and just as within villages richer farmers had a larger say in decisions about fallow-lands, so in towns, rich merchants dominated gilds. Nevertheless, in town and countryside alike, groups embraced richer and poorer. Consolidated by common religious practices, such as the cults of the saints of village or town (or urban quarter), and the performance of mourning-rites at each others' funerals paid for by members' dues, medieval groups formed primarily for economic purposes exuded strong social and cultural cement.

Of the professional groups that had characterised the Roman Empire, and which thrived again in the medieval world from the twelfth century onwards, lawyers left the most conspicuous evidence of their activities in the form of legal documents, and were perhaps the most successful in inserting themselves into favourable urban niches. It is no coincidence that Part IV begins and ends with chapters on, or including, lawyers. Priests can be seen as forming another kind of privileged professional group. They formed an elite of a kind: the ideology of orders and estates ranked clergy collectively top – closest to God. Yet the experience of priests on the ground could tell another story. Their livings in the ecclesiastical sense were assigned by the Church authorities in collaboration with local lay notables; but a worm's eye view would situate them within the local communities on whom they depended, in practice, for their livings in the economic sense. Again, the documentation is rich, and it throws an often kindly light, but sometimes a lurid one, on the lived realities of medieval life. Monasteries, whose origins lay in individuals' desires to escape the snares of the secular world, were thus in principle voluntary groups with strongly institutionalised internal bonds. In practice, they were mostly in very close touch with, even part of, the secular world during the medieval centuries, seldom immune from the demands of kinship and lordship, and the urgent needs of the poor. Meeting such demands and needs could be seen, though, from another angle, as fulfilling obligations to Christian service. A flourishing later-medieval vein of anti-clerical feeling was reflected in occasional violent attacks, not only by heretics, on clergy and monks, and also in humour that can still evoke a smile. Cynicism, however, would be out of order in any discussion of the medieval Church.

The Middle Ages begin with clever fourth-century lawyers trimming their skills so as to tap the rich pickings of disputes involving the newly official Christian Church, and end with nobles clustering round royal and princely courts, eagerly adopting new styles and manners, and setting the tone for *nouveaux riches* imitators. Courtly culture shaped, and was shaped by, elites with ambition and adaptability. It was international in substance and in form. It was European. It was a culture whose late-medieval manifestation contained much – not least its Latinity, its litigiousness and legalism, its elite's concern to define and legitimise itself by reference to nobility in moral, self-disciplining, as well as biological, self-reproducing, senses, its taste for the exotic, its passion for religious ceremony and symbolism, its combining of sharp gender divisions with strong forms of cultural cooperation between the sexes – that would have been quite congenial to the denizens of courts at any period from the fourth century to the fifteenth. Courts and the elites drawn to them were far from being the whole story, yet they were a key feature of the medieval world. Did the later Middle Ages see that world on the wane? Not on the showing of the final chapters of Part IV, nor indeed of the rest of this book.

A NEW LEGAL COSMOS: LATE ROMAN LAWYERS AND THE EARLY MEDIEVAL CHURCH

⸻

Caroline Humfress

On 28 October 312 the Emperor Maxentius – a polytheist and persecutor of the Christians – rode his horse into the depths of the Tiber. Still dressed in full battle armour, the body of the pagan Maxentius was hauled out of the river by the triumphal forces of the newly converted Constantine Augustus. To a Constantinian panegyrist, writing in 313, it seemed as if even the Tiber itself wished to share in Constantine's military victory that day:

> Sacred Tiber, once advisor of your guest Aeneas, next saviour of the exposed Romulus, you allowed neither the false Romulus to live for long nor the city's murderer to swim away. You who nourished Rome by conveying provisions, you who protected her by encircling walls, rightly wished to partake of Constantine's victory, to have him drive the enemy to you, and you slay him.[1]

On the following morning Constantine himself crossed the Tiber in order to assume his new role as sole emperor of the West. If we are to believe the rhetoric of Constantine's contemporary Christian apologists, he had both the eternal city of Rome and the heavenly city of the Christians firmly within his sights.[2]

Modern historians are undoubtedly right to tread cautiously when seeking to assess the impact of the conversion of Constantine. As Peter Brown warns us, a world governed by an emperor who happened to be a Christian was not yet an unambiguously Christian empire. Toleration remained the official policy from Constantine himself down to the legislation of Theodosius in 391–392, which outlawed pagan observances in public and in private. Until the 380s, the cult of the gods and the worship of the Christian God coexisted at the official level. The Christian God was actively advanced by imperial policy (the exception being the famous, although brief, reign of Julian the Apostate), but the traditional cults were still officially recognised: in Rome, the Vestal Virgins and other priesthoods still received their state subsidies. It was left to the Emperor Gratian (367–383) to advance the cause of monotheism, by sanctioning the intolerance of earthly Christian society. In 382 Gratian disestablished the Roman cult of the gods and renounced the office of 'high priest' (*pontifex maximus*), the first Christian emperor to do so. The next logical step was the official consolidation of Christianity as the only 'state' religion: that was the legacy left to the medieval world by the Emperor Theodosius I.

The transformation of a 'pagan' Roman empire into a medieval 'holy Roman empire' should not be plotted teleologically. Even after the so-called 'Theodosian settlement' the victory of Christianity over the polytheistic beliefs, practices and institutions of the past was by no means assured. In fact, modern historians increasingly reject the concept of 'the victory of Christianity' and also question the whole idea of a 'clash of cultures' between Christians and pagans in late antiquity. It is now fashionable, following Peter Brown, to play down the element of confrontation and to stress what Christianity and paganism had in common, especially among the leaders of society. Brown has argued for a shared culture or *paideia* which linked individuals throughout the Greco-Roman world, as a result of their common participation in a traditional educational system; and that *paideia*, working for unity and coexistence, was a more potent influence than religion, working for disunity and intolerance (Brown, 1992).

It is certainly true that many fourth-century pagans were both willing and anxious to maintain the mutual sphere of tolerance and shared language of cultural expression that had existed, more or less, since Constantine's conversion in 312. Polytheism did not after all entail denying all merit to Jesus Christ. It rather implied that belief in Christ was not the only route to the 'mysteries of the universe', as the pagan prefect Symmachus phrased it in his famous exchange of 384 with Ambrose, bishop of Milan. This 384 debate, which centred on the existence of a 'pagan' altar of victory in an increasingly Christianised Roman senate-house, is usually referred to as typical of the civilised discourse that prevailed between the two sides. Indeed, Ambrose's pleas to the emperor on this matter bear all the hallmarks of a *paideia* shared with his polytheist opponent – but the fact remains that he replied to Symmachus in the uncompromising and exclusive terms of Christian monotheism. There was, asserted Ambrose, only one path to heaven.

Regardless of how we view the struggle for souls between polytheism and Christianity in the fourth century, one immediate consequence of Constantine's individual conversion in 312 is indisputable. The Christian Church itself entered the imperial legal arena. In this respect, Constantine certainly did not realise the full significance of his change of religious allegiance. The Church could never be simply the religious department of the *res publica*, as the old religion had been (Liebeschuetz, 1979: 292). The conversion of Constantine ushered in nothing short of a legal revolution: the creation of a new Christian legal cosmos.

A modern historian seeking to chart the development of this new legal cosmos into the fourth and fifth centuries is straightaway confronted with a fundamental paradox. Christianity seems to have little direct effect on the existing principles of Roman private law – the branch of legal science which governed the day-to-day relations between Roman citizens. Legislation in direct conflict with Christian practice, 'such as a law of (the Emperor) Augustus which penalised celibates in order to increase the birth rate among citizens, was repealed. But in general the private law of pagan times needed little amendment to fit it for a Christian empire' (Stein, 1999: 24). In the realm of private law, the post-Constantinian empire could rightly frame itself as more or less consonant with its pagan past. In this sense legal development conformed to a more general pattern of late Roman cultural transformation: 'One of the persistent cultural features of the Roman world was its ability to reinvent itself while preserving a rhetoric of continuity. The present could be radically transformed above all by rewriting the past so that the new patterns of the present appeared as a seamless development of the past' (Elsner, 1998: 3). This continuous translation of legal sources is evident even within the most strikingly innovative aspect of post-Constantinian legislation: 'heresy law'. A focus upon the creation, and crucially the application, of anti-heretical legislation transports us to the *axis mundi* of the new Christian legal cosmos.

From the first century onwards the Christian Church developed internal ecclesiastical procedures in order to sentence baptised believers who strayed from the flock. However, wrong religious belief existed as a potential civil or criminal charge under Roman law only after Constantine incorporated Christianity into the structure of empire. Proscriptions against heretical religious practice and public prosecutions for wrong belief were legal innovations. What were the mechanisms which contributed to the development of this new branch of law?

In 414, almost exactly a century after the conversion of Constantine, St Augustine preached a sermon at Carthage (north Africa) in which he appealed to the religious legislation of the Christian emperors. Imperial legislation now prescribed civil penalties against wrong religious belief, yet the heretics against whom this legislation was directed were employing time-honoured means to circumvent the letter of the law:

> Wake up, you heretics, listen to the Shepherd's testament of peace, come to the peace. You are angry with the Christian emperors because they have decreed that your testaments shall have no validity in your families . . . How many clever legal experts (*iurisperiti*) you consult, how many loopholes you look for so that your testaments may stand against the emperor's law![3]

The use of legal experts to dodge the law was by no means a new phenomenon in late antiquity. The exercise of their ingenuity in legal cases concerning heresy was. Between the fourth and sixth centuries a vast body of anti-heretical legislation was issued by the imperial authorities, far outnumbering the surviving laws against paganism. Theology interacted with Roman law case by case, defining and categorising heretical groups and establishing penalties which covered both this life and the next. Forensic practitioners played a crucial role in the development and application of this new legal category of 'wrong belief', in both civil and ecclesiastical forums. Advocates and legal experts could transform imperial legislation by applying it to particular cases, often provoking the need for further legislation to check their forensic activities. If we wish to understand the late Roman legal cosmos, and its specific Christian context, we must thus move beyond the study of normative imperial legislation towards a detailed study of forensic activity within the late antique law courts.

Book 16.5 of the *Theodosian Code* (issued in 438) groups a series of imperial constitutions issued in the course of the fourth and early fifth centuries under the title *De Haereticis*. Taken collectively, these constitutions detail a bewildering array of heresies and their corresponding penalties. Neither the heresies condemned nor the sanctions against them remain constant. Virtually no attempt has been

Figure 32.1 Diptych of Anicius Petronius Probus, consul (Rome 406). Aosta, Tesoro del Duomo. © Fratelli Alinari, 2000.

made by historians to establish how individual prosecutions were undertaken on the basis of these laws, nor how defences were constructed in order to avoid their harsh penalties. The primary sources demonstrate that in the late Roman atmosphere of developing theological principles and shifting imperial legislation there was plenty of scope for the traditional activities of wily advocates and able *iurisperiti*. Behind the laws contained in the Theodosian Code lies the history of a skilled community of forensic practitioners, attempting to implement, extend or evade the legislation through the exercise of their forensic education. In effect, these practitioners were engaged on a day-to-day basis in the practical and piecemeal elaboration of a new legal relationship between the Church and contemporary Roman society.

The deployment of forensic techniques of argument in the service of the Church can be demonstrated from the earliest period of the Christian era in the writings of St Paul (Eger, 1918), Philo (Bentwich, 1930) and Tertullian (Beck, 1930). It has been noted, moreover, that the earliest theological writers were skilled at 'borrowing' substantive principles of Roman law and applying them metaphorically to explain principles of Christian dogma. Figures of speech from the Pauline epistles, such as 'guardianship', 'redemption', 'slavery', of being 'joint heirs with Christ' and being 'called to adoption' all drew a precise meaning from the rules and terms of Roman (and Jewish) law.[4] Here, however, the focus of attention will be the dramatic transformation in the relationship between 'law' and theology as the post-Constantinian Church of the fourth and fifth centuries sought to unravel the implications of its entry into the Roman legal arena. The advancement of the late Roman Church was won through piecemeal legal processes. In the late empire, as in the early empire, legal processes demanded the attention of practising legal professionals. The Christian Church thus increasingly required the particular forensic expertise of late Roman lawyers.

Within the late empire there were two distinct types of Roman lawyers who pleaded cases on behalf of the Church. The first type can be identified as 'theologians' who had received specific training as lawyers. As I shall demonstrate below, key fourth-century and fifth-century ecclesiastics had been trained as forensic advocates in the rhetorical schools of the late empire. Thus we can speak of a translation of forensic skills from the 'secular' sphere of traditional Roman education to the episcopal office. Their expertise in forensic rhetoric allowed ecclesiastics to participate effectively in the legal hierarchy of the imperial bureaucracy. They pleaded at the imperial court for privileges and exemptions, they argued for the extension of case-specific rescripts before praetors and proconsuls, they sought the promulgation of new imperial legislation and then transformed its content by applying it to analogous cases. The forensic skills of leading ecclesiastics thus had concrete and immediate applications, and no more so than in the field of distinguishing 'right' from 'wrong' Christian belief. Verbal disputation in a court of law was a new avenue through which orthodoxy and heresy could be defined. The dialectic of the court room also provided a singular advantage over philosophical disputation, in that it produced a legally enforceable judgement as to the winner and the loser.

The second type of Roman lawyer utilised by the late antique Church was the practising professional advocate. In fact the demand for these practising professionals was so great that it led to the creation of a new permanent legal office. This was the 'advocate for the church' (*defensor ecclesiae*).

The 'official' creation of the *defensor ecclesiae* can be traced to a single legislative act of the Emperors Honorius and Theodosius (dated 407 and included in the Theodosian Code), but the suggestion for this new office came from within the Church itself. More specifically, the establishment of this new type of Christian Roman lawyer was forced by the repeated pleadings of the North African Church for the right to have a permanent legal representative. Moreover, these pleas were framed by bishops who had received previous training as forensic advocates themselves. As we shall see, an examination of how these bishops framed their pleas to the imperial court can be followed through their deliberations in the North African Church councils of 401 and 407. Their requests were founded deliberately on Roman legal precedents: the 401 plea (which we can assume to have been unsuccessful) was framed by an analogy with the existing legal office of 'the defender of the city' (*defensor civitatis*). The successful 407 plea was framed by a startling analogy with the legal privileges traditionally accorded to the 'pagan' imperial cult. Thus the forensically skilled bishops of North Africa invoked a deliberate translation of a 'pagan' legal precedent into the Christian arena, for the benefit of the Christian Church. Of the two types of Roman lawyers employed by the Christian Church, it was the first who effectively created the second out of the institutions of the 'pagan' past.

BISHOPS AS FORENSIC ADVOCATES IN THE LATE ANTIQUE CHURCH

The fourth century is marked by increasing attempts to regulate the admission of legal practitioners into sacerdotal offices. Under the Roman Republic forensic practice had been seen as one qualification for undertaking the sacerdotal duties of the pagan priesthood and, despite the gradual eradication of the legality of pagan worship, this equation between pagan priests and legal office continued into the fourth and fifth centuries (see below). At the Council of Serdica in 343 Bishop Ossius revealed that forensic advocates were of crucial importance to the post-Constantinian Church too, by his tacit admission that they were being promoted straight to episcopal sees:

> Bishop Ossius said: 'I consider it necessary that this be gone into with all care and attention: If some rich man or forensic advocate is thought worthy of becoming a bishop, he should not be established (in this station) until he has served as lector and deacon and presbyter.'
>
> (Council of Serdica, Canon 10)

This practice of promoting forensic advocates, however, posed a certain dilemma for a late imperial church intent on a rhetoric of other-worldly separation.

Two decretals of Pope Siricius (384–398) raise the question of whether those who have distinguished themselves in forensic careers should be admitted to the priesthood at all. In one decretal Siricius forbids their ordination, basing his interdiction on the apostolic precepts of the early Church. Elsewhere, however, an elegant solution is offered, enabling imperial functionaries to be ordained after they had undertaken penance. In the early fifth century Pope Innocent I directed the attention of the bishops of Spain to one specific aspect of the ordination of individuals with pretensions to forensic practice: it had come to his attention that a number of ecclesiastics continued to plead as advocates in the court rooms of the late empire even after their ordination as priests.

A number of key bishops in the Eastern Church who had received a rhetorical education went on to practise as advocates before their episcopal appointments. From the Cappadocian Fathers we can name Basil the Great and his contemporaries Amphilocius of Iconium and Asterius of Amasea. Amphilocius became the metropolitan bishop of the new province of Lycaonia in 373 at Basil's request – having previously attended the lectures of Libanius in Antioch and practised as an advocate at Constantinople between 362 and 365. His forensic skills are clearly in evidence at the synod of Side (390), where he presided over the drafting of legal condemnations against the sects of Messalians, Euchites and Adelphians. From the beginning of his episcopacy, Amphilocius had been active in promoting legal formulae for the exclusion of named heretical sects. The church historian Theodoret mentions Amphilocius' petitions before the Emperor Theodosius against the 'Arian heretics'. Theodoret also specifies that Amphilocius' second audience before Theodosius resulted in 'an edict forbidding the congregation of heretics'. Hence Theodosius' use of Amphilocius as a touchstone for orthodoxy in a constitution issued in the year 381 and included in the *Theodosian Code* at 16.1.3.

Theodore, bishop of Mopsuestia in Cilicia, provides an unusual example of vacillation between forensic and monastic practice. Theodore studied rhetoric under Libanius and then entered a monastery near Antioch, only to leave the cloister in order to become an advocate. In two letters (addressed to 'the lapsed Theodore') John Chrysostom took it upon himself to persuade Theodore to return to monastic life. In 383 Theodore was ordained priest and in 392 was elevated to the episcopacy. His *Disputatio cum Macedoniano* dates from the same year and is worthy of examination for the light it sheds on Theodore's former practice as an advocate. The treatise is in fact the record (or a later summary) of an actual disputation held at Anazabos in which Theodore defended the divinity of Christ against named adherents of the Macedonian sect. *Theodosian Code* 16.5.11 (dated 25 July 383) had listed the Macedonian sect as heretical; moreover, it granted to all those 'who delight in the cult and the beauty of the correct observance of religion' the right to bring a legal accusation against suspected Macedonian adherents. *Theodosian Code* 16.5.12 (dated 3 December 383) charged the office staffs of the provincial judges with the duty of enforcing a proven accusation. Though presented as a theological debate, in the context of the preceding legislation Theodore's *disputatio* assumes the significance of a judicial inquiry.

Remaining within the Eastern Empire, the life of Eusebius of Dorylaeum provides a further example of a former advocate who, as a bishop, exercised his skills in the prosecution of heresy. Eusebius was an advocate at Constantinople, *c*.426–430. While practising as an advocate, he achieved notoriety by his outspoken opposition to the Marian doctrines of Nestorius, bishop of Constantinople. Following his episcopal consecration Eusebius wasted no time in bringing accusations of heresy against Eutyches, who occupied a doctrinal position at the opposite extreme to Nestorianism. Eusebius' proficiency in handling these fluid doctrinal concepts was undoubtedly advanced by his forensic career.

The example of Serapion of Thmuis suggests that the Church in Egypt also knew how to exploit the forensic training of its members. Jerome and Sozomen both refer to Serapion as having practised as an advocate and praise the power of his eloquence. His skills were equally noted by his metropolitan bishop, Athanasius. In 356 Athanasius sent Serapion, together with four Egyptian bishops and three presbyters, to the court of the Emperor Constantius in order to refute the calumnies of the Arian party. Serapion's forensic skills would have been well exercised; according to the

Figure 32.2 The San Nazaro reliquary, depicting the Judgement of Solomon. Silver gilt casket dedicated in 386 and interred beneath the main altar of St Ambrose's Basilica Apostolorum. Milan, Tesoro del Duomo. © Hirmer Verlag München.

ecclesiastical historian Theodoret, the Arian Emperor Constantius treated the Christian Church as a house of judicial business rather than the house of God.

The coincidence of forensic and ecclesiastical practice is equally evident in the Western Empire. Juvenal had famously described Africa as a 'nursemaid of advocates'. This epitaph can just as well be applied to the North Africa of the late Roman Empire, with the qualification that many of its advocates now turned their talents to the defence of the Christian Church.

North Africa's own particular late Roman ecclesiastical schism, which split the 'Donatist' from the 'Catholic' Church, was fought and won through the prosecution of legal cases. The fact that the originators of the split (*c*.312) had been the subject of judicial proceedings during the early reign of the Emperor Constantine set the entire framework for the fourth-century and fifth-century development of the controversy. From the outset both 'Catholics' and 'Donatists' employed professional advocates to argue their case. The dossiers which these professional advocates constructed were duly entered into the legal *acta* and thenceforth set out precedents that could later be claimed by each side in the dispute. These forensic dossiers (comprised of verbatim extracts from the court proceedings, imperial letters and the acts of ecclesiastical councils) were of crucial importance to both theological polemic and future concrete legal cases. The historical situation of the dissident church demanded that its bishops act before civil judges, in front of audiences held by municipal magistrates and provincial governors, and before the emperor himself. To this end, many of the leading Donatist bishops were recruited from the ranks of forensic advocates.

The forensic expertise of leading Donatist bishops can be illustrated from the *gesta* of the 411 conference of Carthage, a 'conference' between Catholics and Donatists that in fact constituted the initial proceedings of a legal case, heard according to the *mores* of Roman law and before a judge appointed by the emperor himself, as his delegate. The seven bishops mandated as *defensores* of the Donatist church at the 411 conference were Protasius of Tubanae, Gaudentius of Thamugadi, Primianus of Carthage, Montanus of Zama, Adeodatus of Mileu, Emeritus of Caesarea and Petilianus of Constantine. We have almost nothing by way of biographical information concerning the first two named bishops, and their single interventions during the 411 debate reveal little about their background or education. By contrast, Primianus (the Donatist primate) confessed that he had no forensic training and appointed Victor, bishop of Thabbora to act in his place. Victor had previously been an advocate in the secular courts. Primianus' action is significant, demonstrating as it does that forensic advocacy was regarded as an essential prerequisite for a Donatist *defensor*. Montanus and Adeodatus both reveal a forensic background in their argumentative techniques and familiarity with technical points of procedural law. Emeritus ably introduces and handles a host of pre-judicial objections against the formal lodging of the case, in a manner typical of a skilled *advocatus*. In fact we know from Augustine that Emeritus had indeed practised at the Numidian bar. Augustine also informs us that Petilianus, the most celebrated of the Donatist bishops, had also pleaded for a time as an advocate with some success. At the 411 conference Petilianus and Emeritus worked together at key stages in the development of the Donatist case. In a custom analogous to that of secular advocates, Petilianus acted as the *primus advocatus* – instructing his colleague to take over his forensic argumenation at agreed points in the debate.

Likewise, of the seven Catholic *defensores* mandated at the 411 conference five are known to have had some experience of forensic practice. Of these Augustine of Hippo is the most important. During his study of grammar and rhetoric first in his home town of Thagaste and then in the provincial capital of Carthage, Augustine had, by his own account, examined all available textbooks on eloquence with a view to distinguishing himself as an orator and one day winning distinction as an advocate in the law courts.[5] *Confessions* 4.ii.2 describes his experience teaching forensic rhetoric in a publicly appointed position at Carthage. In Augustine's account of his conversion to Christianity it is the sale of *eloquentia* and not the practice of it that assumes importance:

Lord, my helper and redeemer, I will now tell the story and confess to your name of the way in which You delivered me from the chain of sexual desire by which I was tightly bound and from the slavery of worldly affairs. I went about my usual routine in a state of mental anxiety. Every day I sighed after You. I used to frequent your church whenever I had time off from the affairs under whose weight I was groaning. With me was Alypius unemployed in his work as a *iurisconsultus* after a third period as an assessor and waiting for someone else to whom he could again sell his advice just as I was selling the art of public speaking.

In the culmination of this narrative Augustine (in parallel with Alypius), having professed the Catholic faith, announces his intention to cease trading in his profession – but not to withdraw from it altogether. Both he and Alypius were fully aware that the Catholic Church needed trained forensic practitioners. Moreover, each delayed his retirement as a vendor of forensic aid until the official end of the judicial year – a fact which was not missed by their contemporaries. Writing over a decade later, Augustine's pagan correspondent Vincentius stated that it was well known by all that after his conversion Augustine 'devoted himself to legal disputes'. As a bishop, Augustine continually employed his forensic expertise in legal prosecutions against 'Manichees', 'Arians', 'Donatists' and 'Pelagians'.

The latter years of Augustine's life were occupied with the heresy of Pelagius and more specifically the challenges posed by the 'Pelagian' Julian of Eclanum. Forensic techniques of rhetoric play an important role in Julian's own *Ad Florum* and *Ad Turbantium*. Moreover, Augustine states that, following his exile in 418, Julian made his living by teaching forensic rhetoric in Sicily. The *commonitorium* of Marius Mercator records that Julian was not the only Pelagian with a forensic background. Pelagius himself had studied law at Rome. Caelestius, one of the original exponents of 'Pelagian' doctrines, was a former advocate. Both men conducted their own defences against charges of heretical opinion laid before the ecclesiastical courts.

The forensic expertise of the key late Roman ecclesiastics discussed above was not simply gleaned from a general late Roman 'legal culture'. The biographical evidence specifies a career-orientated education: they trained as forensic practitioners and then entered the hierarchy of the Church. In the course of the late fourth century and early fifth century forensic disputes, and particularly those involving charges of heresy, increasingly required the attention of practising forensic professionals. Moreover, the specific context for the elaboration of the faculty of permanent professional advocates for the Church was the Donatist schism in North Africa. The *defensor ecclesiae* was thus originally conceived of as part of an increasingly sophisticated juridical response to the problem of heresy.

THE CREATION OF PERMANENT PROFESSIONAL ADVOCATES FOR THE CHURCH

During the period of the persecutions practising 'professional' advocates pleaded before imperial magistrates *pro causa Christianorum*. The Acts of the martyr Maximilianus record a trial held in 177–8 in which an advocate, Vettius Epagatus, pleaded in defence of his brothers who were accused of being Christians. In his

Ad Scapulam 4.3–5 Tertullian outlines the role which professional advocates could assume, even if their intervention had not been requested by the accused. He states that governors of the province could legally acquit Christians if they wished – as the proconsul Gaius Julius Asper had. The proconsuls, urges Tertullian, should consult the advocates stationed at their courts in order to advise themselves regarding the various strategies that would permit them to find the accused not guilty. Tertullian was well aware that potential martyrs might refuse forensic assistance, preferring to plead for martyrdom themselves.

Tertullian's suggestion that magistrates employ the expertise of their advocates in defence of accused Christians was not mere rhetoric. The trial of Phileas of Thmuis, before the prefect of Egypt (*c.*306–7) testifies to the presence and intervention of advocates on his behalf without his solicitation, but with the complicity of the presiding magistrate. The discovery, in 1984, of a new version of the *Acts of Phileas* gives a verbatim record of the fifth and final sitting of the process against him. The text records that the magistrate clearly wishes to arrive at a compromise solution and receives the support of the advocates present in the tribunal. These advocates attempt to modify the behaviour of the accused; they interrupt his profession of faith, exhorting him not to contradict the judge. Phileas replies: 'I have not contradicted him, I do not respond to his demands.' The magistrate urges the Christian to sacrifice and this provokes a further intervention from the advocates who state that 'he has already sacrificed in the private audience chamber'. But Phileas refutes this statement and calls the magistrate himself as witness to it, so that the proconsul has no choice but to convict him. The advocates again insist on confronting the governor: 'Phileas desires a period of reflection'. The governor would have conceded this request, but the bishop insists on refusing it: 'I have no need of a period of reflection, I have already made my choice.' At this point the advocates, the governor's staff, the curator of the city and the relatives of the bishop all jump to their feet begging Phileas to think of his wife and his children. Phileas, however, has left the governor no choice but to condemn him to death. For Phileas, forensic assistance was an obstacle to martyrdom rather than an aid to defence.

Yet the relationship between Christians and professional advocates within the pre-Constantinian Church was not always an uneasy one. The *Acts of St Sebastian* state that in 286 Pope Caius instituted a *defensor*. Some modern scholars refer to this passage as the first reference to the institution of the *defensor ecclesiae*. However, they are mistaken in dating the creation of this office as early as the late third century. Caius employed a *defensor* for a particular case, just as Vettius Epagatus had been employed as an advocate *pro causa christianorum* in 177–8. Pope Caius did not create a new permanent forensic office.

The post-Constantinian Church had more scope for legal action. Moreover, the contexts in which the Church sought forensic assistance also changed. No longer the persecuted sect, Christianity could now take its own internal disputes to 'secular' litigation and thus utilise the expertise of professional advocates. In 315 the Church in Carthage split into two factions and took its dispute to the court of the proconsul, thus instituting the first great legal process of what came to be termed the 'Donatist schism'. The acts of the 315 case reveal that *advocati*, drawn from professional corporations of advocates, were employed to argue the case for both sides.

Figure 32.3 'Christ in the Roman Forum', dating from the period of Christian 'triumphalism' after the Theodosian settlement *c*.390, with the disciples garbed as senators. Rome, Church of Santa Pudenziana. Apse mosaic. Photo: Scala.

In 368 Pope Damasus employed professional advocates in a legal case, again concerning an internal schism but this time within the Church at Rome itself. The background to the dispute is complex; here it is only necessary to note that *defensores* – acting on behalf of the faction represented by Pope Damasus against the rival faction of Pope Ursinus – petitioned the Urban Prefect for the restitution of a papal basilica. The case was referred to the Emperor Valentinian and the imperial reply was issued as a rescript.[6] Valentinian's text clearly refers to *defensores ecclesiae urbis Romae*. Accordingly modern historians have cited 368 as the first reference to the 'medieval' institution of the *defensor ecclesiae* (for example Pietri 1976: 678). Once again, however, this dating is mistaken. Valentinian's rescript also specifies that the *defensores ecclesiae urbis Romae* are charged by special procuration with the interests of Damasus himself. The *defensores* in 368 were not permanently mandated to defend the interests of the Church at Rome, but rather appointed *ad hoc* to defend the interests of a named individual in a concrete case.

The creation of permanent *defensores* mandated to act in all cases and processes in the interests of the Church is in fact datable to the early fifth century and was not a papal initiative, but was occasioned by the 'Catholic' North African Church in response to its particular circumstances *vis-à-vis* the Donatist schism. During the late fourth century the Donatist dispute was, to a large extent, played out in the courtroom. Both Catholics and Donatists litigated for the right to be regarded as the orthodox representatives of Christianity and by its very nature this litigation involved the preparation of a large number of often complex legal cases. The 'Catholic' North African Church needed permanent skilled advocates to represent all its interests, rather than repeatedly mandating individuals on an *ad hoc* basis for single cases. However, in seeking the creation of a permanent *defensor* the North African Church had to operate within a framework already established by Roman law.

The North African Church was not juridically competent to act for itself and appoint a permanent *defensor*.[7] It was a fundamental principle of Roman law that civil persons could not appoint a permanent individual to represent them in all the processes which they had to, or might, pursue. The Roman jurist Paul clearly states this principle with reference to municipal bodies (at *Digest* 3.4.6.1). Paul himself goes on to specify, however, that corporate bodies had the right to request a permanent 'actor' or 'syndic' who could be appointed to act in all cases. If the Church could present itself as a corporate body, rather than as a civil person, it could claim the rights and duties which Roman law already accorded to a 'juristic person'. In the early fifth century, however, the Church as a whole was in an ambiguous position with reference to the legal recognition of its corporate status. The North African Church was alert to this fact.

The faculty of permanent *defensores* was first requested by a Council of Carthage held on 13 September 401. The discussion earlier in the day had arrived at an unequivocal formula for viewing the universal Church as a corporate body. Moreover, this request for *defensores ecclesiae* was framed using the precedent of the *defensores* of the cities – the permanent processual representatives who acted for the municipal corporations. The North Africans thus attempted to bolster their request by an analogy with a corporate body, already unambiguously accorded the status of a juridical person in Roman law. It is to this first attempt to plead for *defensores* of the Church that we shall now turn.

PLEADING FOR DEFENSORES ECCLESIAE: THE FIRST ATTEMPT

ON SEEKING ADVOCATES FOR THE CHURCHES FROM THE EMPEROR.
Resolved, let it be requested of the universal emperors, on account of the sufferings of the poor, whose troubles burden the church without intermission, that defenders be assigned to them against the power of the rich, through the foresight of the bishops.[8]

With this canonical resolution from the September 401 Council of Carthage, the North African Church announced its intention of pleading at the imperial court for the faculty of permanent *defensores*. The canon also agreed upon the manner in which the plea was to be framed: the *defensores* were sought for the defence of the poor against the powerful rich. In 368 the Emperor Valentinian had granted the Illyrian municipalities the right to institute permanent *defensores* using exactly the same reasoning:

Emperors Valentinian and Valens to Probus, praetorian prefect. We have decreed to their benefit that all the plebians of Illyricum shall be defended by the offices of advocates against the outrages of the powerful.

(*Theodosian Code* 1.29.1)

The constitution goes on to specify that these 'defenders' are to be selected from individuals who have occupied high positions within the imperial bureaucracy or else practised as forensic advocates. The reference to the municipalities of Illyricum suggests that the imperial authorities were responding to a specific request. Over the course of the third and fourth centuries individual municipalities had in fact pleaded for the right to institute permanent defenders on the basis of their corporate status. A few months later Valentinian automatically extended this right to all cities (*Theodosian Code* 1.29.3). Through the legislative measures of 368 the imperial authorities thus created a new universal category of a permanently mandated forensic practitioner: the *defensor civitatis*.

The imperial formalization of the *defensor civitatis* in 368 provided a persuasive precedent which the North African Church could appeal to in seeking to establish its own *defensores*. If the emperors had already acknowledged the necessity of protecting the *plebs* against the outrages of the *potentes* with respect to the corporate bodies of the municipalities, how could they refuse to grant defenders to the corporate body of the Church for the same purpose? The fact that the 401 Council of Carthage appealed to the same reasoning that framed the creation of the *defensor civitatis* attests to the forensic expertise of the bishops in attendance. We have no record of the outcome of their plea. However, six years later the same bishops had occasion to appeal to the emperors once again for the faculty of permanent *defensores*. The 401 attempt seems to have failed, whereas the 407 plea succeeded (Martroye 1923: 620). In 407, however, the bishops presented the imperial authorities with a different precedent for their request.

PLEADING FOR DEFENSORES ECCLESIAE: THE SECOND ATTEMPT

Let it be resolved that the envoys Vincentius and Fortunatianus, who are about to set out to represent all the provinces, should request of the most glorious emperors that they accord the faculty for the establishment of defenders taken from the body of advocates who are employed in law cases as advocates for the defence, so that, as is the custom with provincial high-priests, those who have undertaken the defence of the Church should be empowered to enter the chambers of judges as necessity demands, so as to resist what is urged on the other side or so as to give whatever advice might be necessary.

By this canonical resolution from the Council of Carthage, 13 June 407, the bishops Vincentius and Fortunatianus were charged with a very specific mission: to plead at the imperial court for the faculty of *defensores* who would be chosen from among the corporate body of advocates (termed *scholastici*). Vincentius and Fortunatianus were to request that these defenders should have the right to represent the Church in all cases, 'as is the custom with provincial high-priests'. This phrase, *ut more sacerdotum provinciae*, was crucial to the Africans' plea. They were in fact requesting the right of permanent legal representation modelled on the permanent legal representation that the imperial cult already enjoyed, through the faculty of the provincial priesthood.[9] The Council of Carthage thus carefully framed its 407 plea to the emperors on a precedent provided by the imperial cult itself. Moreover, in seeking the faculty of a defender *ut more sacerdotum provinciae* the North African bishops were searching for much more than simply the right of a permanent legal representative.

Under the early empire the *sacerdotes provinciae* had been accorded special rights and privileges in their capacity as permanent *defensores* of the patrimony of the imperial cult. In the late empire they continued to play a key role in the provincial councils.[10]

The *sacerdotes provinciae* remained responsible for presenting the pleas of each provincial council to the imperial court. To this end the Emperor Constantius had decreed that their members should be drawn exclusively from corporations of practising advocates (*Theodosian Code* 12.1.46 [355]). As stated, the 407 council requested the same qualification for their *defensor ecclesiae*.

The *sacerdotes provinciae* were also accorded the right to collect rescripts granted in response to their pleas directly from the imperial court. This was an important privilege. Any imperial rescript had to be registered in the *acta proconsularis* before it could be cited in a legal controversy. The *sacerdotes provinciae* could thus bypass the usual (lengthy) bureaucratic channels for the transmission of documents and carry the rescript themselves to the provincial magistrates' court, thus ensuring prompt action. This privilege was particularly important to the 407 Council of Carthage, convened within the period immediately after the 'acting Emperor' Stilicho's policy of toleration towards the Donatists. In the immediate context of Stilicho's fall from power, it was imperative that the North African 'Catholic' bishops act quickly in the application of any new anti-Donatist imperial legislation, thereby frustrating Donatist appeals to Stilicho's authority. Indeed the same council instructed its legates to plead for such legislative measures at the imperial court:

> Let it be resolved that the legates sent by this glorious council to combat the Donatists and pagans and their superstitions should obtain from the most glorious emperors whatever they should perceive to be advantageous.

The legates were mandated to obtain whatever legislative measures they could against pagans and Donatists.

The 407 council also requested that its *defensores ecclesiae* should 'have the ability to enter into the private audience chamber of the judge each time they deem it necessary, so as to resist what is urged on the other side or to advise whatever might be necessary'. The free right of access to the private council chambers of magistrates had already been granted to both the *sacerdotes provinciae* and the *defensores* of the cities. This privilege of freely entering the judges' private audience chamber carried with it the more important right to be present when the judge was deliberating his sentence.[11] The *defensores* could thus directly influence the outcome of any concrete case that fell within their jurisdiction.

These requests were answered, point for point, by a constitution of the emperors Honorius and Theodosius dated 15 November 407, addressed to the Proconsul of Africa (*Theodosian Code* 16.2.38.) There is evidence to suggest that the text of the original constitution also included a forcible restatement of previous legislative measures against Donatists and pagans. The emperors Honorius and Theodosius thus provided the North African Church with a firm legislative basis on which prosecutions against the Donatists could proceed, and also supplied the faculty of permanent *defensores* who could argue the resulting cases at law.

The emperors Honorius and Theodosius can thus be said to have 'created' a new category of forensic practitioner: the *defensor ecclesiae*, a permanently mandated 'professional' advocate capable of acting for the Church in all legal cases. The elaboration of this office was, however, provoked by the meticulously phrased demands of the North African Church itself. The canonical resolutions from 401 and 407 illustrate the forensic expertise of the bishops who were responsible for their drafting. In this respect, the process lying behind the 'legislative' creation of the *defensor ecclesiae* is as important as the institution itself.

After 407 the privilege granted to the North Africans was extended to other churches on an *ad hoc* basis. The Papacy, however, was quick to exploit the potential of permanent defenders of the Church in cases involving prosecutions against heretics. Pope Innocent I offered the loan of seven *defensores*, belonging to the Roman Church, to Bishop Laurentius of Senia (Croatia) for the purpose of destroying heretics within his diocese. The Church of Rome and other metropolitan dioceses also took to permanently stationing *defensores ecclesiae* at the imperial court itself. In 438 the imperial legislation concerning the *defensor ecclesiae* was included in the *Theodosian Code* and thus, from this date, we can speak of its general application.

Between 407 and 438, however, the office of the *defensor ecclesiae* had already begun a long process of evolution. Lay *defensores* were gradually recruited into the ranks of the clergy and thereby withdrawn from their worldly responsibilities as practising lay advocates. The office of the clerical *defensor ecclesiae* was thus established. At this stage the officer himself might be a hybrid creature: witness the letter of Pope Zosimus, dated 21 February 418, stating that even though the *defensores ecclesiae* are normally taken from the laity, provisions are none the less to be made for the case 'if they desire to be in the order of the clergy' (Ep. 9.3). By the late fifth century, however, the clericalisation of the office seems to be complete.

The gradual assimilation of the *defensor ecclesiae* into the ranks of the clergy inevitably brought about an evolution in the functions of the office. Increasingly the *defensor ecclesiae* is seen assuming general responsibilities for the 'secular business' of the Church, rather than simply acting as its permanent legal representative. This development occurred as a natural consequence of the evolution of the episcopal office itself. As the bishops assumed wider civic responsibilities, relating to the day-to-day administration of early medieval society, so their need for expert clerical assistance in handling those responsibilities increased.[12]

CONCLUSION

If the transformation of the late Roman legal world can be viewed as a continuous reinvention of itself while preserving a rhetoric of continuity, the historical development of Christianity can be seen as a continuous translation of its sources. Nowhere are these intersecting paradoxes revealed to a greater extent than in the creation of 'heresy law'.

Before the conversion of Constantine prosecutions against wrong belief were not possible under Roman law. The innovative introduction of the idea of wrong belief into the Roman legislative sphere necessitated the legal categorisation and systematisation of religious belief itself. Heretics had to be grouped and named if they were to be prosecuted. Moreover, the imperial legislation had to be applied in practice and made to 'stick'. By necessity, legal definitions were elaborated case by case as new heresies were identified and classified within the ecclesiastical sphere. These definitions were then tested through their application in concrete legal cases. Forensic techniques of classification, categorisation and analogous reasoning were thus important tools, employed by both ecclesiastical and professional forensic practitioners, in seeking the application of anti-heretical legislation. In this respect, the late antique Church bequeathed a fundamental legacy to the Church of the later Middle Ages.

NOTES

1 *Panegyrici Latini* XII, 18.1 (ed. and trans. Nixon and Rodgers, 1994: 321).
2 Lactantius of Nicomedia, *On the Deaths of the Persecutors*: 44.4–5 (ed. Brandt and Laubmann, 1897) and Eusebius of Caesarea, *Life of Constantine*: 1.27 ff (ed. and trans. Richardson, 1890).
3 Augustine, *Sermon* 47.22 (ed. and trans. Hill, 1990: 317).
4 See Lyall, 1984. For an extended discussion on the use of slavery as a legal metaphor in the early Church Fathers see Garnsey, 1996: 220–35.
5 Augustine, *Confessions* 3.iii.6 (ed. and trans. Chadwick, 1991: 38).
6 The rescript is included in the *Collectio Avellana* (Guenther (ed.), 1895: 49, lines 1–17). The *Collectio Avellana* also records that Pope Damasus had previously employed 'pagan advocates' to persecute Catholic presbyters and laymen (Guenther (ed.), 1895: 30, lines 4–10).
7 *Contra* Merdinger, 1997: 105 who assumes that the 'African fathers' autonomously created the position of *defensor ecclesiae* in order to relieve themselves of 'business-related problems'.
8 Canon 11, Council of Carthage 13 September 401 (Munier (ed.), 1974: 202, lines 686–90).
9 Modern scholars agree on this interpretation of *sacerdotes provinciae* as the provincial priests of the imperial cult: Martroye, 1921: 242 and 1923: 597; Mochi Onory, 1933: 177; and Fischer, 1956: 656.
10 Chastagnol, 1994: 93–104 places the office of the provincial priesthood within the wider context of the survival of the imperial cult in North Africa, until the Vandal regime. *Theodosian Code* 16.10.20 (415), 12.1.186 (429) and *Novels of Valentinian* 13 (445) testify to the fact that the 'political' dimensions of the provincial priesthood survived well into the fifth century.

11 Clearly stated at *Theodosian Code* 6.26.16 (410).

12 Mochi Onory, 1933: 174–8 presents the *defensor ecclesiae* as 'l'uomo d'affari della chiesa'.
    Pietri, 1976: 677–9 discusses sixth-century papal elaborations of the office. He notes
    that Gregory the Great decreed that no agent of the Roman Church could take the title
    of *defensor ecclesiae* without being equipped with a special diploma – by this time the
    Roman *defensores* numbered at least fourteen and were organised into a corporate body
    with a presiding *primus defensor*. Zovatto, 1966 presents epigraphical evidence for sixth-
    century *defensores ecclesiae* in Trieste. Pergameni, 1907: 9–51 traces the office into the
    Merovingian and Carolingian epochs.

REFERENCES

Beck, A. (1930) *Römisches Recht bei Tertullian und Cyprian. Eine Studie zur frühen Kirchenrecht-
geschichte.* Schriften der Königsberger gelehrten Gesellschaft, Geisteswissenschaftliche
Klasse, 7. Jahr, Hft.2. Halle: Max Niemeyer Verlag.

Bentwich, N. (1930) 'Philo as Jurist', *Jewish Quarterly Review* 21: 151–61.

Brandt, S. and Laubmann, G. (ed.) (1897) *Lactantius. De mortibus persecutorum. Corpus scriptorum
ecclesiasticorum latinorum* 27, 2.

Brown, P. (1992) *Power and Persuasion in Late Antiquity: towards a Christian empire.* Madison:
University of Wisconsin-Madison Press.

Chadwick, H. (ed. and trans.) (1991) *Saint Augustine. Confessions.* Oxford: Oxford University
Press.

Chastagnol, A. (1994) *Aspects de l'Antiquité tardive*; Saggi di storia antica, 6. Rome:
Bretschneider.

Eger, O. (1918) 'Rechtswörter und Rechtsbilder in den Paulinischen Briefen', *Zeitschrift für
die Neutestamentliche Wissenschaft und die Kunde des Urchristentums* 18: 84–108.

Elsner, J. (1998) *Imperial Rome and Christian Triumph.* Oxford: Oxford University Press.

Fischer, B. (1956) 'Defensor Ecclesiae', in *Reallexikon für Antike und Christentum* 3:
656–8.

Garnsey, P. (1996) *Ideas of Slavery from Aristotle to Augustine.* Cambridge: Cambridge
University Press.

Guenther, O. (ed.) (1895) 'Epistulae imperatorum pontificum aliorum . . . Avellana quae
dicitur Collectio', *Corpus scriptorum ecclesiasticorum latinorum* 35, 1.

Hill, E. (1990) *The Works of Saint Augustine. A Translation for the 21st Century. Part III –
Sermons, Vol. II: Sermons 20–50.* New York: New City Press.

Liebeschuetz, J. H. W. G. (1979) *Continuity and Change in Roman Religion.* Oxford: Clarendon
Press.

Lyall, F. (1984) *Slaves, Citizens, Sons. Legal metaphors in the epistles.* Michigan: Zondervan
Publishing House.

Martroye, F. (1921) 'Les defensores ecclesiarum', *Bulletin de la Société Nationale des Antiquaires
de France*: 241–9.

Martroye, F. (1923) 'Les defensores ecclesiae aux Ve et VIe siècles', *Revue historique de droit
français et étranger* 2: 597–622.

Merdinger, J.E. (1997) *Rome and the African Church in the Time of Augustine.* New Haven and
London: Yale University Press.

Mochi Onory, S. (1933) *Vescovi e città (sec.iv–vi).* Bologna: Biblioteca della Rivista di Storia
del Diritto Italiano, n.8.

Munier, C. (ed.) (1974) *Concilia Africae a.345 – a.525. Corpus Christianorum series Latina*, 149.

Nixon, C.E.V. and Rodgers,B.S. (ed.) (1994) *In Praise of Later Roman Emperors*. Berkeley and Los Angeles, California: University of California Press.

Pergameni, C. (1907) *L'Avouerie ecclésiastique belge. Des origines a la période bourguignonne (Étude d'histoire ecclésiastique)*. Brussels: Société coopérative 'Volksdrukkerij'.

Pietri, C. (1976) *Roma Christiana. Recherches sur l'Église de Rome, son organization, sa politique, son idéologie de Miltiade à Sixte III (311–440)*, Vol. II. Rome: l'École française de Rome.

Richardson, E.C. (ed. and trans.) (1890) *Life of Constantine. A Select Library of the Nicene and Post-Nicene Fathers of the Christian Church*, ser. 2 vol. I: 481–540

Stein, P. (1999) *Roman Law in European History*. Cambridge: Cambridge University Press.

Theodosian Code and Novels and the Sirmondian Constitutions (1952) trans. C. Pharr, Princeton: Princeton University Press.

Zovatto, P.L. (1966) 'Il defensor ecclesiae e le iscrizioni musive di Trieste', *Rivista di Storia della Chiesa in Italia* 20: 1–8.

MEDIEVAL MONASTICISM

———— ∙•∙ ————

Janet L. Nelson

Whether in the physical landscape of Europe or in landscapes of the mind, monasteries have been among the most enduring signs of the Middle Ages. The earliest extant monastic buildings, still visible at St Catharine, Mount Sinai, for instance, or, thanks to archaeologists, at Whitby, on the Yorkshire coast, are telling witnesses to the unique role of monasticism in keeping alive Roman-Christian culture after the fall of the Roman Empire – while 'bare ruined choirs where late the sweet birds sang', all that survived the destructive efforts of sixteenth-century reformers, are apt markers of the break between the medieval period and the modern. The history of Christian monasticism is effectively as old as Christianity itself. Judaism in the centuries that straddled the beginning of the Christian era harboured world-renouncing sects, who lived in more or less closed small communities, practised rigorous asceticism, and were preoccupied with the imminent end of time. In the earliest centuries CE, with Christianity itself still a sect that retained its original anti-intellectualism (Weber 1965: 512) and still very largely urban, world-renouncing asceticism re-emerged as a Christian alternative, especially in the Near East. The ecology of that region provokes a sharp awareness of the otherness of the desert, the *eremos*, beyond the populated and cultivated areas surrounding cities and villages. Ascetics were men of the *eremos*. Some lived the ascetic life alone: both hermit (*eremita*) and monk (*monachos*) originated as terms referring to the solitary religious virtuoso. Others lived in groups, sharing both their daily bread, earned by small-scale artisanal production, and a common daily liturgy. By the early fourth century, there were many of these groups especially in Egypt. They were known as livers of a common life, in Greek *koinos bios*, hence collectively by the Latin term cenobites.

The world-renouncers might be spiritually detached, yet in material terms all but the most resolute survivors on honey and wild herbs depended for their sustenance on contacts with peasant cultivators and townsfolk. The earliest Lives of the desert fathers describe the hermits receiving small gifts of food from those who sought their spiritual counsel, while the cenobites sold or bartered their products, reed-baskets for example, to villagers so as to acquire the staples they needed: food, and the wine and candles required for liturgical performances. The holy men were marginal men, well-placed to provide impartial advice, to mediate disputes, to act as middlemen between rural communities and urban, even imperial, authorities (Brown 1981;

Frend 1972). But the marginal men were also integrated through precisely these links, and through economic dependence, into their social world. What remain unknown are patterns of recruitment to these ascetic networks and groups. The Lives of a few well-remembered individuals, the desert fathers, suggest that most of these, and their associates, were of peasant origin (*Sayings of the Desert Fathers*, Ward 1975). Perhaps this, and the renunciation of the little they had had, enhanced their reputations in the eyes of third-century town-dwellers.

In the course of the fourth century, Christianity was transformed from a sect to a Church – the official Church of the Roman Empire. Monasticism too became respectable. It adopted intellectualism of a sort, preoccupied with the understanding of sacred texts, with personal religious experience, and with the meanings of liturgical performance. In Cappadocia, Basil, a provincial aristocrat with connections at the imperial court, was a leading exponent of fourth-century cenobitism, and wrote a monastic Rule that has remained the most widely practised in Eastern Christendom ever since. Several of Basil's close kin were associated in his monastic enterprises, and the family's property constituted the core-endowment of these establishments (Brown 1988: 285–304). Just as Christians at large prayed regularly for the well-being of the Roman Empire, so too, and with special efficacy since the prayers of the pure were believed especially pleasing to God, did monks. Emperors in turn granted monasteries property and special legal status. To gain a vivid sense of monasticism's enduring centrality in Byzantine culture, and subsequently in Greek Orthodox culture, there is no better way than to consider the history of the cenobitic communities and hermitages on the peninsula of Mount Athos in the northern Aegean. From the tenth century onwards, a series of lavish imperial grants in mainland Greece established the economic viability of Athonite houses, and endowed them, too, with exceptional works of art. Imperial decrees supported Athonite autonomy, that is, the monasteries' exemptions from the demands of imperial officials and from normal episcopal and patriarchal jurisdiction (Morris 1995). Imperial confirmations of internal decisions allowed Athonite communities to maintain the exclusion of women and female animals from their entire territory, not just the monastic enclosures. Throughout Byzantine history, that is, till 1453, Athonite monks offered, in return, prayers for the emperors and their families and for the state as a whole. From the fifteenth century to the twentieth, similar prayers were offered for the Ottoman regime, and also, from the late eighteenth century on, for the Russian tsars whose interest in protecting Athos had a lot to do with Russian strategic interests in the Black Sea and the Near East. Athonite monks pray, to this day, for the powers that are.

In Western Christendom, on which I focus in the rest of this chapter, and where monasticism is much better documented than in Byzantium because of the plentiful survival of descriptive as well as prescriptive evidence, parallel developments can be traced in the earlier medieval centuries (Constable 1976; Lawrence 1984; de Jong 1995). Between the fourth century, when the West began to feel the impact of imperial conversion, and the eighth, when the Carolingian regime embarked on a deeper and more systematic experiment in cultural correction, the spread of various forms of monasticism was both a symptom and an important agent of Christianisation. In the East this process had to some extent worked from the bottom up: in the West, it worked unequivocally from the top down. The earliest western monasticism was aristocratic both in spirit and in terms of personnel. In the city of Rome, great ladies refused marriage (or remarriage) and set up house-convents in their own households, where they were besieged by ecclesiastics seeking their patronage (Clark 1986; Brown 1988). At the island-monastery of Lérins, off the Riviera coast near Marseilles, scions of the noblest families of Roman Gaul enjoyed (the word seems apt) a life of studious retirement from the world. Yet the retirement, in many cases, was only temporary: from Lérins, where the immigrant eastern monk John Cassian offered a programme of self-development and training in leadership, emerged a spiritual elite ready to assume episcopal office (Wallace-Hadrill 1983: 6–7; Leyser 1998).

Monasteries were founded on lands donated by kings and nobles. The donors believed in the superior efficacy of the ceaseless round of intercession offered up to the Almighty by celibate, and preferably virginal, monks and nuns on their patrons' behalf. The idea of spiritual benefits brought by vicarious devotion caused no problems for medieval benefactors. Pious gifts were believed to bring rewards in this life and the next. Through the prayers of devout monks, the souls of the dead were thought to be released from otherwordly sufferings incurred as punishments for sins committed on earth. By the mid-eighth century, most of the major monasteries of the Middle Ages were going concerns; and from that period on, large numbers of charters survive, at first from only a few monasteries, but increasingly from many, to document the vast scale of that lay piety. No less striking than its scale is the rationality of this effort. Monasteries were professional organisations, their inmates' days minutely timed to ensure the regularity of prayer, and their voices trained to produce perfect chant from musically annotated texts. In the medieval world before the thirteenth century at least, such strict time-keeping and such professionalism were distinctively monastic traits (Weber 1965: (i) 555, (ii) 1169–73).

It's sometimes suggested that monasteries that were (even when landlocked) like small islands of autonomy and self-sufficiency, were for that very reason institutions ideally suited to a decentralised world, when no other structures effectively existed. Such a view is a misreading of the Middle Ages, even at their Darkest. Kinship and patriarchy supplied durable, and flexible, bonds that embraced monasticism. This is clearest, perhaps, in the case of women's houses, which were always, as the noble ladies' house-convents suggest, liable to masculine control. Bishop Caesarius of Arles wrote the Rule for, and vigorously supervised, his sister's convent, conveniently located as it was in Arles itself; and the noble convents of tenth-century Saxony were set up, and supervised, by the inmates' kinsmen (Caesarius 1988; Leyser 1979: 63–74). Local power based on land-lordship and patronage reached out to clasp monasteries in a protective yet sometimes too-firm grip (cf. Brown ch. 39 in this volume). But throughout the Middle Ages, there existed more or less ambitious institutions and official hierarchies with claims to supervise, and exploit, monasteries. First and foremost, the Church, and specifically its bishops, wielded an authority never challenged in principle and usually ineluctable in practice. The fact that bishops were recruited from the same Roman-provincial elites as monks, and that a good many bishops were themselves former monks, meant that monasteries fitted

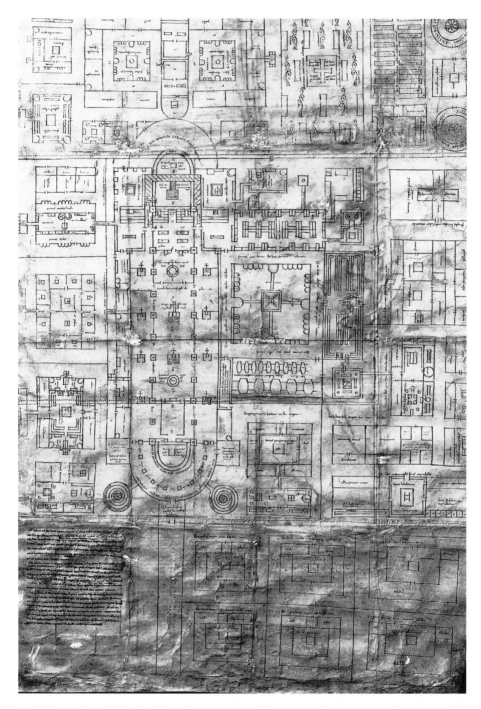

Figure 33.1a Monastic plan of St Gall. St Gallen, MS. 1092. Stiftsbibliothek, St Gallen, Switzerland.

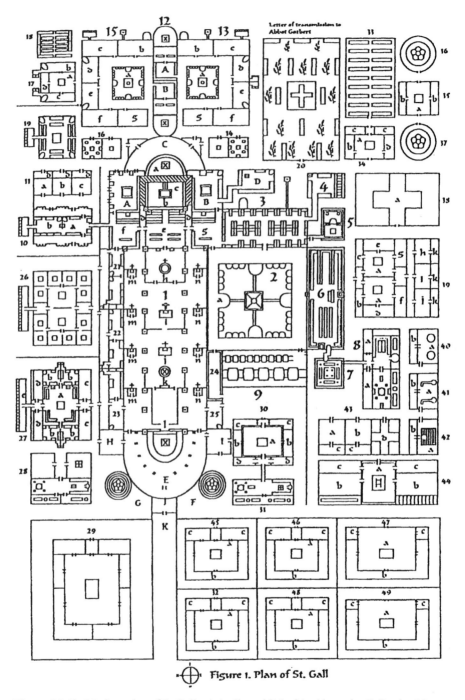

Figure 1. Plan of St. Gall

Figure 33.1b Modern plan of St Gall originally published in Alexander Callander Murray (ed.) *After Rome's Fall* (University of Toronto Press, 1998), pp. 263–5. Reprinted by courtesy of Richard E. Sullivan, Elizabeth Sullivan Hogg and with permission of the publisher.

I. MAIN CHURCH
A. Scriptorium with Library (above)
B. Sacristy with Vestry (above)
C. East Atrium (Paradise)
D. Room for Baking Communion Bread and Pressing Holy Oil
E. West Atrium (Paradise) with Roof
F. South Tower with altar to St Gabriel at top
G. North Tower with altar to St Michael at top
H. North Porch
I. South Porch
J. West Porch
K. Access Road
a. East Apse with altar to St Paul
b. Main Altar dedicated to Mary and St Gall
c. Sarcophagus
d. Entrance and Exit to Passage to Crypt (below Main Altar)
e. Choir with steps to Main Altar; altars of St Benedict and St Columban on either side; passage under steps to crypt
f. North Transept Chapel, with altar of Sts Philip and James
g. South Transept Chapel, with altar of St Andrew
h. Pulpit
i. Altar of the Holy Cross
j. Altar of John the Baptist and John the Evangelist
k. Baptismal Font
l. West Apse with Choir and Altar of St Peter
m. North Aisle with altars of St Stephen, St Martin, the Holy Innocents, and Sts Lucia and Cecilia
n. South Aisle with altars of St Lawrence. St Mauritius, St Sebastian, and Sts Agatha and Agnes
2. CLOISTER YARD with arcades
a. Gallery for meetings
3. MONKS' DORMITORY WITH WARMING-ROOM (below)
4. MONKS' PRIVY
5. MONKS' LAUNDRY AND BATH HOUSE
6. MONKS' REFECTORY WITH VESTIARY (above)
7. MONKS' KITCHEN
8. MONKS' BAKE AND BREW HOUSE, with servants quarters (a)

9. MONKS' CELLAR WITH LARDER (above)
10. ABBOT'S HOUSE
a. Sitting Room with fireplace
b. Bedroom with fireplace and privy
11. ABBOT'S KITCHEN (c), CELLAR (b), BATH (a) and SERVANTS' ROOMS (d)
12. SECOND CHURCH
A. Chapel for Novitiate
B. Chapel for Infirmary
13. NOVITIATE
a. Novices' Cloister Yard
b. Novices' Warming Room with Furnace and Smoke Stack
c. Novices' Dormitory with Privy
d. Novices' Sick Room with Fireplace and Privy
e. Quarters for Master of Novices with Fireplace and Privy
f. Novices' Refectory
g. Store Room
14. KITCHEN AND BATH FOR NOVICES
15. INFIRMARY
a. Infirmary Cloister Yard
b. Infirmary Warming Room with Furnace and Smoke Stack
c. Infirmary Dormitory with Privy
d. Sitting Room for the Ill with Fireplace and Privy
e. Quarters for Master of Infirmary with Fireplace and Privy
f. Infirmary Refectory
g. Store Room
16. KITCHEN AND BATH FOR INFIRMARY
17. PHYSICIANS' HOUSE
a. Central Chamber with Open Hearth
b. Physicians' Bedroom with Fireplace and Privy
c. Chamber for Critically Ill with Fireplace and Privy
d. Pharmacy
18. MEDICINAL HERB GARDEN
19. BLOOD-LETTING HOUSE
20. CEMETERY AND ORCHARD with graves and trees
21. LODGING FOR VISITING MONKS with Fireplaces and Privy
22. LODGING OF MASTER OF THE EXTERNAL SCHOOL with Fireplace and Privy
23. LODGING OF PORTER with Fireplace and Privy

24. PARLOUR FOR MONKS' VISITORS
25. LODGING OF MASTER OF THE HOSPICE FOR PILGRIMS AND PAUPERS with Fireplace
26. EXTERNAL SCHOOL (2 central study halls with 12 student rooms and privy)
27. HOUSE FOR DISTINGUISHED VISITORS
a. Central chamber with open hearth and dining tables
b. Bedrooms with fireplaces and privies
c. Servants' quarters
d. Horse stalk
e. Privy
28. KITCHEN, BAKE AND BREW HOUSE FOR DISTINGUISHED GUESTS
29. QUARTERS FOR RETINUE OF DISTINGUISHED GUESTS (?)
30. HOSPICE FOR PILGRIMS AND PAUPERS
a. Central chamber with open hearth
b. Dormitories
c. Servants' quarters
d. Cellar and supply room
31. KITCHEN AND BAKEHOUSE FOR HOSPICE FOR PILGRIMS AND PAUPERS
32. HOUSE FOR SERVANTS FROM OUTLYING ESTATES OR ACCOMPANYING VISITORS
a. Central chamber with open hearth
b. Stalls for animals
c. Sleeping quarters
33. MONKS' VEGETABLE GARDEN (with 18 planting beds)
34. GARDENER'S HOUSE
a. Central chamber with open hearth
b. Gardener's bedroom with fireplace
c. Servants' quarters
d. Tool and seed room
35. FOWLKEEPERS' HOUSE
a. Central chamber with open hearth
b. Keepers' bedrooms
36. GOOSE HOUSE
37. CHICKEN HOUSE
38. GRANARY with threshing floor (a)
39. COLLECTIVE WORKSHOP AND ANNEX
a. Work spaces with central hearths
b. Shoemakers
c. Saddlers
d. Sword makers

e. Shield makers
f. Wood turners
g. Leather workers
h. Fullers
i. Blacksmiths
j. Goldsmiths
k. Sleeping quarters
40. MILL HOUSE
a. Mill stones
b. Living quarters
41. MORTAR HOUSE
a. Mortars
b. Living quarters
42. DRYING KILN HOUSE
a. Furnace
b. Living quarters
43. HOUSE FOR COOPERS AND WHEELWRIGHTS
a. Coopers' workshop
b. Wheelwrights' workshop
c. Servants' quarters
d. Granary for monks brewery and bakery
44. BARN FOR HORSES AND OXEN AND THEIR KEEPERS
a. Central chamber with open hearth
b. Stalls with hayloft above
c. Keepers' sleeping quarters
45. BARN FOR SHEEP AND SHEPHERDS
a. Central chamber with open hearth
b. Sheep folds
c. Keepers' sleeping quarters
46. BARN FOR GOATS AND GOATHERDS
a. Central chamber with open hearth
b. Stables
c. Keepers' sleeping quarters
47. BARN FOR COWS AND COWHERDS
a. Central chamber with open hearth
b. Stables
c. Keepers' sleeping quarters
48. BARN FOR SWINE AND SWINEHERDS
a. Central chamber with open hearth
b. Pens
c. Keepers' sleeping quarters
49. BARN FOR BROOD MARES AND COLTS AND THEIR KEEPERS
a. Central chamber with open hearth
b. Stables
c. Keepers' sleeping quarters

Figure 33.1c Key to modern drawing of St Gall, reproduced by courtesy of Richard E. Sullivan, University of Toronto Press.

more or less snugly into the frame of diocesan government in the fifth and sixth centuries. Councils of bishops in Gaul repeated the decrees of oecumenical councils on the subordination of monasteries to episcopal authority – adding such new injunctions as that abbots must not solicit benefices, that is favours, but especially in the form of landed gifts, without their bishop's permission (Council of Orleans (511) c. 7, ed. Gaudemet and Basdevant 1989: 76–7). Bishops, who found ways to take their cut as monasteries waxed wealthy, rightly saw monastic acquisition of property as one critical point of control. Abbatial appointments were another. According to conciliar decrees and monastic Rules alike, an abbot was supposed to be elected by the members of the community, but if difficulty arose, the local bishop had the duty to intervene. Likewise, abbatial misconduct in office automatically warranted episcopal intervention and punishment. Further, priests were required in monasteries to perform the mass, and only bishops could ordain them. As lay patrons became keener to have masses said in monasteries for their own souls and the souls of their kin, more and more monk-priests were needed. Ninth-century lists show that virtually all adult inmates were priests (Schmid 1978: 592–7; de Jong 1995: 629, 647–8).

Secondly, and hardly less keen than bishops to maximise their legitimate authority, kings extended over monasteries a protection that was also a form of exploitation (Fouracre 1995). Monasteries colluded with kings to exclude episcopal intrusions and abuses of power. The seventh-century invention of monastic immunities, grants by rulers, and by bishops under royal pressure, made monasteries immune to royal agents but also to the jurisdiction of bishops. 'Let no-one think', ran one legal formula for such a grant, 'that we are decreeing new songs (*nova decernere carmina*) here, and therefore criticise us, since from ancient times, in conformity with the regulations of bishops through royal sanction, innumerable monasteries throughout the whole kingdom of the Franks clearly existed under a privilege of liberty' (Marculf 1.1: 18–24; cf. Rosenwein 1999: 103–4, 222). This liberty was evidently conditioned by the interests of Frankish kings, and worked in practice to make monasteries agents of royal government. Especially from the eleventh century onwards, exactly this mechanism operated to make a reality of papal government too (Southern 1953; cf. Boureau 2000). Throughout the Middle Ages, therefore, ecclesiastical and secular authorities jostled for influence, if not control, over monasteries and their resources. Monasteries in the countryside tended to acquire the function of pastoral care in their locality, and for that the cooperation and support of the local aristocrats were necessary. It was often monasteries that assumed responsibility for missionary activity extending beyond political frontiers, and for that the support of rulers was necessary. Fulda in northern Franconia, for example, sustained by landed patrons in its own region, was given many local churches for whose pastoral services it then became responsible (Hildebrandt 1992). At the same time, as one among the network of monasteries founded by the Anglo-Saxon monk Boniface, Fulda was in the front line of the campaign to convert the Saxons in the eighth and ninth centuries. Whenever and wherever the frontiers of Christendom expanded, monasteries were founded: in Carinthia, for instance, and on the Spanish March. Drawing on monastic traditions that favoured mobility (*peregrinatio*) rather than the stability of the Benedictine Rule, monks were in the forefront of medieval mission. Intermittently in the earlier

Middle Ages, more continuously from the eleventh century on, the Papacy protected monasteries and – the *quid pro quo* – deployed their resources in manpower and moveable wealth.

* * *

Now, as you read this at the beginning of the third millennium, a story of monasticism with contours clear since the work of the Protestant theologian Adolf Harnack in the later-nineteenth century, and of Dom David Knowles, Dom Jean Leclercq and Dom Kassius Hallinger in the twentieth (Harnack 1908; Knowles 1966, 1969; Leclercq 1979, 1982; Hallinger 1950–1, 1971, 1979) remains deeply etched in the historiography of the Middle Ages (Southern 1953; Lawrence 1984; van Engen 1986; Sullivan 1999). It belongs to the genre of ecclesiastical history, strongly tinged with the history of spirituality. This is true despite post-modernist subversion of historians' inherited paradigms, not least when those were produced from within the religious traditions they seek to explain, and despite the attractions of total history which situates religion within culture and looks to political, social and cultural conjunctures for explanations of religious change. First and foremost, the story of medieval monasticism has withstood the tests of time and revisionism because of the skilful and seductive writing of its modern narrators. Its overarching tripartite theme (and it includes many local and particular histories of rise and fall) of a heroic age, an apogee of brilliant achievement, followed by decline, has been neatly jointed into the conventional periodisation of the Middle Ages: monasticism's heroic age into the Dark Ages and the trials of Viking and Saracen attacks, its apogee into the mid-eleventh to thirteenth centuries with triumphant feudal states, new cities and newly constructed papal monarchy, its decline into the waning, warring and plague-ridden, and religiously privatised, later-medieval world.

A second and related point, though, is that the accounts of particular monastic institutions, and of monasticism in general, written by medieval monastic authors themselves already fit the paradigm – which might arouse the suspicion that the paradigm itself depends on medieval monastic histories. The great abbots are Dark Age heroes spreading the Faith to the heathen and counselling the mighty – Benedict of Monte Cassino, Pope Gregory the Great, Columbanus of Bobbio, Cuthbert of Lindisfarne, Boniface of Crediton and Fulda, Odo of Cluny – or they are reformers and remodellers of institutions, avatars of a papally centred properly Christianised world in which a new internalised spirituality replaced the ritualised formalism of Cluny as the New Testament replaced the Old – here Bernard of Clairvaux takes centre-stage, flanked by such representative figures as the monk-theologian Hugh of St Victor and the monk-bishop Hugh of Lincoln (Constable 1996). For medieval monks, all these were exemplary figures, memorable through their own often voluminous writings, or because other monks wrote memorably about them. As for the few women in the story (objects of increasing interest today), Hild of Whitby epitomises the heroic age, and Hildegard of Bingen the progressive movements of the twelfth-century renaissance (Wormald 1993; Flanagan 1989). In the later Middle Ages, the most written-about religious figures, and most widely read writings, were no longer monastic. Whereas throughout the centuries from the sixth to the twelfth monasteries had housed nearly all such learning as there was (nearly all classical texts have been transmitted through manuscripts copied in earlier medieval monasteries) and intellectuals were monks (Ganz 1995; Contreni 1995; Constable 1996; Iogna-Prat 1998), thereafter universities with their professional masters took over (Le Goff 1957). The new religious leaders, Francis and Dominic, were intimately involved with the needs of the secular world, indeed saw their primary responsibility as action in the world to save souls: hence their followers' key role in combating heresy (Southern 1970; Lambert 1992; Lawrence 1994; Biller ch. 18 in this volume). The friars lived neither as hermits nor as cenobites: in the early days, they begged their daily bread, and their establishments were always located in the towns, where they found their sustenance and their work (Le Goff 1968, 1970; Lawrence 1994). Rather than belonging in the story of medieval monasticism, therefore, they provided alternatives for it, in new social environments. Friars dominated university teaching. They took the Benedictines' and Cistercians' place in the sun of lay patronage, especially in towns (though Oxford, where the Benedictines were never quite over-shadowed by the friars, was an exception (Dobson 1997)). Histories written, as most now were, by friars or by laymen or secular clergy (that is, priests or canons), usually for consumption at royal or princely courts in urban settings, no longer privileged monastic experience, interested though their authors still were in religious events. Compare the narratives of Bede, Ralph Glaber or Orderic Vitalis, with the world evoked by Salimbene.

A third, less obvious, reason for the persisting prominence of the story of monasticism in medieval historiography is that modern sociologists of religion, from Durkheim and Weber onwards, have stressed monasticism's distinctive role in the Christian tradition and hence in the emerging distinctiveness of the West already before the modern period. For Weber, monks were religious *virtuosi* whose individual charismatic power was subsequently routinised, canalised and institutionalised in monastic communities. Monasticism typified 'the "rational restlessness" of Christianity . . . committed to improving the world' (Mann 1986: 388, quoting Weber; cf. Scharf 1970: 139, 142–6). Monks were the advance guard of ecclesiastical culture, which directly (as ideological base) or indirectly (as competitor, hence inspirer of imitation) gave rise to the medieval polities that emerged from the Carolingian period and, more permanently, the twelfth and thirteenth centuries onwards (Weber 1965: (ii) 1170–3, 1175–6). It is a curious fact that the seminal work done in the early decades of the twentieth century on the historical sociology of religion has never been revised. For their data, Weber and Wach relied on Harnack. For his, Mann relies on Weber. But the data are not inert, as you can see from a glance at more recent historiography. The sociologists (who themselves seldom if ever consult historical primary sources) are then quoted by well-intentioned social historians, who nevertheless rely (however grudgingly) on their colleagues special-ising in ecclesiastical history, who in turn tend to rely on straight readings, often, say, Knowles's readings, of medieval monastic writers.

The pitfalls for medieval historians are easier to list than to avoid (as the present writer knows all too well). The sources for monasticism are *parti pris* – chronicles written by monks, or charters produced by monastic scribes to record the gifts and 'record' the motivations of lay donors – or else they are prescriptive – monastic Rules; canons of church councils; privileges granted by bishops and popes. The chronicles,

Figure 33.2 Wall-painting of an unidentified abbot. South reliquary niche, San Vincenzo al Volturno, discovered in 1994. Reproduced by permission of Professor R. Hodges, University of East Anglia.

mostly eleventh- and twelfth-century products, were driven by apologetic and polemic priorities: that is, monks wanted to justify reform and the need for (re)endowment by offering explanations for decline and decay, either in terms of external attack (Vikings, Saracens) or in terms of the unwelcome attentions of neighbouring patrons-turned-predators. Successful reform was attributed to lay heart-searching and renewed piety, evoked by the efforts of inspirational abbots and exemplary communities. Monastic maledictions, that is, cursings of predators, were often depicted in charters, and sometimes in chronicles too (which quite often contained forged charters to clinch their central argument), as the crucial factors in softening lay hearts (Little 1993). Central Italy offers nice examples of both ways of explaining decline, the twelfth-century Chronicle of San Vincenzo invoking external pressure, the eleventh-century Chronicle of Monte Cassino greedy neighbours. The Viking card was played in Gaul at Fécamp and Aldeneik, in England at Ely; the local predators card was played in Gaul at Gembloux, in England at Abingdon. Modern historians have generally been content to reproduce monastic chronicles. Decline in the ninth and tenth centuries is still attributed, and not only in popular histories, either to Vikings and Saracens, though careful regional research on particular monasteries has generally sustained a revisionist view (Riché 1981: ch. XX; Dierkens 1985: 330–1), or to 'the church in the power of laymen', even though recent studies have shown compellingly and in detail that lay patronage was a monastery's lifeblood (Searle 1980; Rosenwein 1989; Barthélemy 1993; Bull 1993) and that particular churches had many laymen, including many creditors, in *their* power (Wickham 1988: 180–268; White 1988). The polemics of twelfth-century Cistercians are still cited to prove the spiritual deficiencies – empty formalism, vicarious piety – of Dark

Age (including Cluniac) monasticism, though such evidence is self-evidently anything but hard.

Here are some methodological rules of thumb extracted from recent work on the cultural history of the Middle Ages. (There has not been space to apply all of them in this chapter, but the point of this book is to provoke and inspire as well as inform.)

1   Start with prescriptive sources – monastic Rules, episcopal regulations, papal privileges and so forth – but always ask what *their* sources are, and what were their authors' specific contexts and agendas; be prepared for many a slip between prescription and practice, even where such slips can't be documented. Distinguish between chronicles: though each presents problems of its own, the more reliable tend to be those written nearer to events they describe, and the more plausible those that explain a monastery's ups and downs in terms of abbots and their internal policies and/or their relations with rulers. Examples would be the *Gesta* of the abbots of St Wandrille (Wood 1995), Ekkehard of St Gall (Nelson 1999a; de Jong 2000), Jocelyn of Brakelond (*Chronicle*, ed. Greenway and Sayers 1989; Carlyle 1843).

2   Handle with care the evidence of charters making grants to monasteries: beware the bias of scribes who were themselves members of those monasteries (beneficiary diplomatic); beware the use of formulae; beware historians' tendency to be deceived by what look like descriptions of substantial novelty but may only be novelties of form (Barthélemy 1993; 19–127, Stafford 1998; White 1996; Reuter 1996). Also beware inferences from varying quantities of charters: diminished volume may not mean decline in the monastery's endowment, let alone its spiritual well-being. For monasteries, like women, go through life-cycles. The generation or two following foundation often sees the amassing of large estates, first around the core endowment, then further afield. Thereafter the flow of new grants will dwindle, as the monastery digests, and manages better, what it already has (Innes 2000).

3   Take change into account but never treat its timing or tempo as foregone conclusions. Consider, in the light of the increased availability of bullion and money in the central Middle Ages, the implications of major monastic endowments, such as the Spanish royal largesse that paid for Cluny's new church (1085/8), in bullion rather than land; or the frequency with which monasteries were given local churches as profitable concerns (Bishko 1989: ch. II; Duby 1973: 61–82). At the same time, beware of exaggerating the novelty of the twelfth century in the history of monasticism. Take Cistercian polemic with a pinch of salt (Buc ch. 11 in this volume; cf. Leyser 1984): on the one hand, set it against evidence that the twelfth century was not an age of decline for Cluniac monasticism but in many ways its apogee, with new daughter houses still being founded, and the abbacy of Peter the Venerable imposing Cluny's stamp on the twelfth-century renaissance (Iogna-Prat 1998); on the other hand, reflect that the Cistercians' way with the world never, even in the early days, immunised them to materialism and political involvement (Alfonso 1989). Dip into Walter Map!

4   Read the sociologists – but read them critically. There are historical insights in Weber, Mann, Foucault, Bourdieu, to be found nowhere else. They deserve their

celebrity. Equally, their histories are only as good as the historians they read. The past is usually less tidy than their syntheses suggest. Be ready to tweak where necessary.

5   Use the evidence of aerial photography, archaeology and art history, because, though the material visible is less 'hard' than historians sometimes like to think, it offers a different take on monasticism (Knowles and St Joseph 1952; Heitz 1963; Brooke 1974; Hodges and Mitchell 1985; Gilchrist 1994; Rabe 1995; Sullivan 1999). Visualise each monastery in a landscape, which may turn out to have been, literally, and recalling the etymology of *monachos* and *eremos/eremita*, an isolated place, such as an island or a peninsula: Lérins . . . Noirmoutier . . . Lindisfarne . . . Iona . . . Skellig Michael . . . Monte Gargano Athos . . . Reichenau, but, equally and alternatively, may always have been urban/sub-urban: St Denis, Paris; St Martin, Tours; St Remi, Rheims; St Martial, Limoges; St Cybard, Angoulême; St Alban, Mainz; Sant'Ambrogio, Milan; or itself have been the nucleus of an urban centre: St Vaast, Arras; Bury St Edmunds. Never forget that medieval monasticism was always a very diverse phenomenon: despite the recurrent efforts of reformers, standardisation would always be a mirage.

6   Use gender as a category of analysis (Scott 1986; L'Hermite-Leclercq 1989). Compare monastic recruitment for women/girls and men/boys, and compare the changing tempi of recruitment in convents and male houses. Compare the sizes of male and female communities. Ask whether women's experience of monasticism meant rethinking femininity in ways similar, or different, to monastic men's rethinking of masculinity. Compare the conceptions, on the part of those outside monasteries, of women within and men within. Compare (thanks to archaeology) the scales, locations, layouts, material finds, of male and female monastic sites (Gilchrist 1994). Be willing to recognise, and explain, difference in terms of gender.

7   Finally, after all the caveats about the treacherousness of texts, read and reread some of the written evidence. Unfortunately, much that is eminently readable has never been translated from Latin. But it makes sense to start, as so many medieval people did, with the Rule of St Benedict, which has been often and sensitively translated. Once you know it well enough to appreciate some nuances, and not least its biblical quotations, you will catch its echoes in many other medieval places – and you will have gained an entrée into a number of medieval worlds. You will spot, for instance, Benedict's recommendation of the Rule of Basil, and reflect that monasticism predates and so transcends the schism between eastern and western Christendom. You may recoil from the rigours of a routine that impressed those medieval people who came from outside monasteries to witness, and, they believed, benefit from, what went on within. (Charlemagne wrote to monks throughout his empire, 'Just as whoever seeks you for the Lord's sake and for the nobility of your holy way of life (*sanctae conversationis nobilitas*) is edified, when you have been seen, by the impression you make, so may they be instructed by your wisdom, perceived in your reading and singing, and give thanks to the Lord Almighty and go away rejoicing' (*Epistola de litteris colendis*, late eighth century). You may ask yourself why the

activities of this tiny minority were credited with that capacity to benefit the vast majority: as Charlemagne declared to his people at large, 'We believe the life and chastity of monks to be the source of the greatest hope of salvation for all Christians' (MGH Cap I, no. 33 (802), c. 17: 94–5). You will smile perhaps (and wonder whether Benedict intended that) to find this Rule described as one for beginners.

* * *

Benedict saw monasteries as vulnerable to two kinds of danger, or temptation. The first was discord arising from within the community. Of the 73 chapters in Benedict's Rule, the early ones (cc. 2–5) discuss the authority of the abbot, advising how he should deal with the undisciplined and restless (c. 2), and warn monks against following 'the will of their own heart' (c. 3), against anger and treacherous thoughts (c. 4), and against slow or lukewarm obedience or 'murmuring' (c. 5). The later chapters warn against allowing the prior (the second-in-command) to become a rival focus of authority to the abbot, which led to 'grave scandals . . . envies and violent disputes' as monks 'currying favour with one side or the other run into perdition' (c. 65). Benedict's solution to the potential problem of tyrannical priors was to have them always appointed by the abbot himself, not by the bishop. Benedict warned against resistance to the abbot's commands 'even when those commands are impossible to carry out' (c. 68); against a monk's making personal protection arrangements on grounds of kinship (c. 69); against presumption and the issuing of 'private orders' (*privata imperia*, c. 71); against impatience with fellow-monks' weaknesses of body or mind (c. 72). Wilfulness and self-interest; pride in relation to the abbot; faction: these were the prime dangers. Benedict himself, according to his biographer Gregory the Great (*Dialogues*, Book II), had plenty of experience of a variety of such environments. At one stage in his career, his monks tried to poison him. For all his insistence on stability, Benedict knew when to move on. Where detailed evidence survives, it begins to look as if few medieval monasteries were without dissension, and many abbots were threatened with assassination. The authors of monastic histories offer so many examples of internal disputes on just the faultlines Benedict had foreseen that you might suspect an element of literary imitation, or even individual abbots' self-projection as imitators of Benedict. When, during his fairly brief spell as abbot of the Breton monastery of St Gildas, Peter Abelard's monks attempted to poison him, he felt fully justified in abandoning his post, just as Benedict had his (Clanchy 1998: 144–5, 246–9).

But such stories are not just literary confections. The strains of life in a monastic community were real enough, and so the temptations of monastic life were also its everyday occurrences. In one sense, enclosure bred tensions. In other senses, monasteries were anything but enclosed: they were in fact all too open to the intrusions of the world. In the early ninth century, such problems can be followed up in detail through the *Brief Account of an Earnest Request (Supplex Libellus)*, of 812 (Semmler 1963: 320–27; cf. de Jong 1995: 646–50). It describes troubles at the monastery of Fulda in the years immediately preceding its composition, and refers the monks' case against Abbot Ratgar to the judgement of Charlemagne. The document presupposes a twofold general context: on the one hand, that of monastic reform, for (as noted above), Charlemagne was concerned about standards of prayer and observance and wanted the Rule of Benedict adopted in communities throughout his empire; on the other hand, that of *raison d'état*, for the Carolingian regime established in 751 depended heavily on ecclesiastical and not least monastic resources, of prayer, gifts, hospitality, and military service performed by tenants on monastic estates, and hence abbots, recruited from the noble elite of the empire, were enrolled as senior agents of government and expected to behave as such – they were, as Weber said of the later Cluniacs and Premonstratensians, 'notables whose very moderate asceticism . . . was limited to what was compatible with their status' (Weber 1965: (ii) 1168). Part of this general context emerges from the first section of the Fulda document:

> We request Your Piety, O most merciful emperor, that permission be granted us to maintain the form of prayers, psalm-singing and vigils that our forefathers (*patres*) kept for our friends living and dead, that is:
> – daily prayer for you, Lord Augustus, and for your children and for all the Christian people, every morning when we have assembled together in one body and a chapter from the Rule is read before the brethren, and arising after the reading we chant three times the verse 'God make haste to help us', adding 'Glory to the Father', and on bended knees we sing the fiftieth psalm together with verses and a collect
> – every Monday of each week prayer for all who give us alms, that is, again, the fiftieth psalm, which the whole congregation, prostrate together, has sung by the body of the Blessed Martyr [St Boniface], with the Lord's Prayer and verses; and that commemoration of our dead brothers which we have held twice daily, that is, after morning and evening celebration [of mass], namely the antiphon 'Eternal rest' and the first part of the psalm 'A hymn is fitting for Thee, O God', a verse and a collect
> – on the first of every month, a vigil and fifty psalms
> – every year, for Abbot Sturm and the founders of this monastery, on the day of their death, a vigil and a psalter [i.e. all 150 psalms]

Preaching to the converted, in the shape of the emperor and his advisers, the monks could preface their case with a programmatic statement (giving it maximum impact) of the regime's reliance on monastic prayer. Not all monasteries proved reliable: in newly conquered Lombard Italy, the abbot of San Vincenzo had allegedly refused in 783 to chant Psalm 54 for the safety of the ruler and his children, and gone on to insult Charlemagne ('If I hadn't been so concerned about the monastery . . . , I'd have treated him as I would a dog!') and the Franks ('If only no more Franks had been left here than I could hump on my shoulder!'). The abbot was peremptorily summoned to Charlemagne's presence, accused of *infidelitas* – treason – and suspended from office (*Codex Carolinus* 66, 67, ed. Gundlach: 593–7). The monks of Fulda in 812, by contrast, were proclaiming their well-known fidelity and usefulness, not only to the emperor, but to 'our friends', that is, to the monastery's many benefactors among the Franks and the Saxons. Fulda by this time was a very large monastery: in 835/6, 602 inmates were listed by name. Some were Franks, others were Saxons. For Fulda, Boniface's foundation, and burial-place, was also a border-place, located in the frontier-zone where the Franks' lands met those of the Saxons, hence on the front line of missionary activity when the Franks conquered the Saxons in the late eighth century. Plentiful charter evidence shows how wide, and well-placed, was the circle of Fulda's friends. The best and greatest friend was of course Charlemagne himself. At his court Boniface was said to have anointed Charlemagne's father king of the Franks in 751 – the first Frankish king to be inaugurated thus. Boniface's disciple, Abbot Sturm, had been Charlemagne's keen supporter and adviser in the young king's difficult early years. The monks had the best tunes and knew how to play them attractively.

The *Brief Account*'s particular context was the monks' grievances against Abbot Ratgar. For instance in sections V, and X:

> [We request] that there be greater care of the infirm, that is, compassion for the old and sick, and that they should not be afflicted with shortage of food nor worn down by poor quality of clothing, nor vexed with any other unsuitable treatment, such as not being allowed to carry a stick to support themselves, nor, when they are still, to use a walking-stick (*inclinatorium*), or as we call it a *formula*, because a poor-sighted man or a lame man cannot walk properly without the support of a stick, nor can a frail man kneel without a *formula*. We ask this so that such men should not be thrown out of the monastery on the grounds that they are a burden, which can result in their being settled in individual cells under the charge of laymen and dying without confession or necessary deathbed rites (*viaticum*).

> [We request] that it be allowed us to have food and clothing as those who came before laid down for us, because our first abbot, Sturm, stayed at the monastery of St Benedict [on Monte Cassino] for a year and then came back here according to St Boniface's choice, and laid down that their [rules about] food and clothing be used by us. A number of men who were witnesses of this are still alive.

Here, the monks complain of the abbot's harsh treatment on sensitive points. Their appeal to their house's tradition (Sturm, Boniface, Benedict) is telling. Section XV indicates the disruptive effects of private economic interests on the life of the community, and suggests that the abbot is to blame:

> [We request] that private business and secular arrangements (*privata negotia et saecularia beneficia*) and the division of possessions and fields should not be made in the place of the monastery itself, because from such things arise disputes, 'contentions, rivalries, angers, violent quarrels', hatreds, 'dissensions, envies' [the quotes are from St Paul, Galatians 5, 20–1], furtive feastings and drinking-bouts and almost every kind of evil and things contrary to our salvation. Rather, all the lands and cells should be for all the brothers in common and all men who live in the place of the monastery should receive their clothing from the same *vestiarius* and the prior or cellarer dispenses them. Nor should any trading be carried on openly there by anyone, but all things should be common to all.

Two further sections identify forms of particularly arbitrary and burdensome behaviour on Ratgar's part. Section XII shows that his huge rebuilding programme for Fulda had laid intolerable burdens not only on the monastery's peasants, but on the brethren themselves:

[We request] that there be no place for huge and superfluous buildings and other such useless things. By these, the brethren are wearied and made anxious beyond measure, and our peasant households (*familiae*) outside our walls are destroyed. Rather, let everything be done according to moderation and good sense. Let it be permitted to the brethren, according to the Rule, to have time free for reading at certain hours, and likewise to work at other hours.

Section XVII refers to a murder for which the abbot is held indirectly responsible because of his policy of allowing 'wicked men' entry into the monastic enclosure:

[We request] that men who are wicked and inclined to violence and all too ready to perpetrate every kind of crime should not be gathered within the monastery – as occurred in the case of that homicidal cleric who killed a monk. That cleric was placed within the monastery against the will and consent of all the brethren. For we are afraid that perhaps the kinsmen of the dead monk may be inflamed, by diabolical persuasion, to avenge him, and so murder will be increased. Further, those who, on account of their crimes and wickedness, could not remain among secular men must not be gathered in droves in the neighbourhood of the monastery, because they ravage the monastic buildings by their thieving and they infest neighbouring places by their criminal acts.

The monks propose a solution in the two final sections (XIX and XX):

[We request] that that abbot himself be made to correct his actions. . . . [W]e wish above all . . . that we may have unity and peace with our abbot as we had with our former abbots, and that we may have a sense in him of kindness and warm feeling, generosity and modesty; and that he should be good to the sick, merciful to those who do wrong, affable to the brethren, a consoler of those that grieve, a helper of those who toil, a giver of aid to those who are well-disposed, and encourager of those who fight the good fight, one who re-fires those who are are tiring, who sustains those who are failing, who restores those who are falling; someone who loves all the brethren, hates none, and persecutes none of them with deceit of malice or hate, one who never becomes angered in his look nor aroused in his mind, who is not excessively harsh in judgement, nor obstinate in his own opinions, but rather a man cheerful in face, joyful in mind, discrete in deeds, ready to agree to all that is beneficial. When any one of the brethren might chance to be caught in some misdeed, [the abbot] should not immediately torment him with tyrannical revenge, but instead should hasten to correct him with kindly discipline, and when the wrong-doer has repented, should receive him kindly and not burden him any further with bad suspicions nor drive him away with ongoing hatred.

Figure 33.3 Painted bench, in shades of bright red and blue, in assembly room at San Vincenzo al Volturno. Picture supplied by University of East Anglia, Norwich.

The monks' proposed remedy is in line with Fulda's traditions, and with the Rule itself – indeed Section XX's model abbot is Benedict's – but it does not address the twin problems of the monks' individual economic interests, and the persistence of individual kin-ties and kin-obligations linking members of the community to those outside it.

Benedict had identified these problems too. Not only did the world clamour for entry to the monastery through letters and gifts sent by kin to inmates (c. 54 of the Rule prohibited the reception of those things): already in Benedict's day, child oblation, that is, the offering of a child by his kin, as a standard method of monastic recruitment gave high-status families the means to forge long-term relationships of mutual benefit with monastic communities. Chapter 59 of the Rule explains:

> If it should happen that someone from among the nobles offers or gives his son to God in a monastery, if the child is still at the age of minority, let his *parentes* (parents, kin) make a petition . . . and then at the offertory let them wrap the petition and the child's hand in the altar-cloth and so let them offer him. As regards their property, let them promise . . . that they will never give him anything or give him an opportunity of possessing anything. But if they do not want to do that, and if they wish to offer something to the monastery in alms for their own benefit (*pro mercede sua*), let them give a donation to the monastery from the property they want to give, retaining a life-interest in the income (*usufructuarium*) for themselves if they wish.

The prohibition on a monk's possessing individual property, for his own benefit, which was a fundamental requirement of the cenobitic life (Rule c. 33), is here immediately qualified by the concession that his kin may give to the monastery for their own benefit. By the ninth century, such a bond would be formalised in terms of kinsfolk's access to the community's prayers and resources as 'friends'. Their names would be inscribed in the Book of Life, containing lists, sometimes amounting to tens of thousands of names, of those individuals for whom the community offered prayers (Schmidt 1978; de Jong 1995). As for oblation, Hildemar, commenting on the Rule in *c*.850, said that Benedict 'ordered the child to be offered with an offering (*cum oblatione*) so that by this what was shown externally might signify what was actually being done, namely, that as an offering is made as a sacrifice to the Lord, so this child too is made a sacrifice to the Lord'.

Oblation was the normal form of monastic recruitment for boys in the earlier Middle Ages (Boswell 1988). The evidence for women's houses is very much thinner; and in some cases, anyway, it looks as if parents might put their daughter in a convent when she reached marriageable age as a stopgap measure, protecting her until a suitable spouse was found or an alternative decision made (Venarde 1998). The implications of all this for child-givers, for oblates, and for monasticism itself, have only recently been fully appraised by Mayke de Jong in an important book (de Jong 1996; cf. Nelson 1992). Sacrifice, and the expectation of vicarious reward for donors through the prayers of the child, lay at the heart of the system. Monasteries offered special care for their oblates, and carefully educated them to maintain liturgical tradition. Though, in the nature of things, few cases of a child's distress or resentment are documented, there is one spectacular ninth-century case of an oblate who tried to return to the world. Again, the monastery is Fulda, and the oblate was a Saxon noble named Gottschalk. His objections turned on a technicality in the ritual offering, and did not challenge the system as such. Abbot Hrabanus of Fulda nevertheless produced a spirited defence of the system, stressing biblical authority in the shape of Samuel's oblation to the temple, and affirming the religious exchange-value of gifts, whether of persons or property – and of course in oblation the two went together. For the most part, the interior tensions evoked in individuals by the monastic life, or even by exposure to its ascetic standards at one remove, as in the case of pious laymen (Nelson 1999b), are seldom even hinted at in our evidence.

While continuing parental interest in oblates is very rarely documented (though it may well have existed, especially when the chosen monastery was a local one), it is very clear that donors retained an interest in property given to monasteries. Such gifts were pledges of a social bond between the donor and the monastery which was the institutional embodiment, on earth, of a saint with power in heaven (or, though comparatively rarely, of the Blessed Virgin Mary, or of the Saviour). To give was to consort with a saint or God Himself (McLaughlin 1994). Thus to give to Cluny, for instance, was to become the neighbour of St Peter (Rosenwein 1989). The monastery gave protection, social as well as spiritual. The donor in return gave physical protection to the monastery, and also, on occasion, expected economic benefit in the form of rights of usufruct or life-interest, sometimes for several lives. But the monastery could also make grants of property it had already. Again there is a parallel with economic provisions determined by a woman's life-cycle, when a family would earmark property for the sustenance of married-in wives and widows. The woman had a life-interest only: thus such property would return, over time, to the (husband's) family to be re-assigned. Something similar could happen with precarial grants, that is, temporary grants made in response to someone's prayers (*preces*) for supernatural help. Monasteries, or rather their abbots, often found many advantages in arrangements that provided them with military and political help (Wood 1995; Wickham 1988; Rosenwein 1989; Fouracre 1995; Wood 1995). But abbatial decisions did not always meet with the community's approval. At St Wandrille, near Rouen, for instance, the early eighth-century abbot Teutsind was berated a century or so later by a monk of that house:

> What sort of a lover of God Teutsind was, what sort of supporter of churches, is shown by the works he did in this monastery . . . in the days not of his rule but of his tyranny . . . All the most noble properties were removed and this once glorious monastery fell into poverty. For he took almost a third of its property and transferred it to the possession of his relatives.
>
> (Wood 1995: 36)

Reading between the lines of the *Brief Account*, it looks as if Abbot Ratgar had done something similar at Fulda. By and large, the solution to such conflicts of interest was to earmark some of the monastery's lands for the sustenance of the community. Despite the scare stories, most abbots reached a *modus vivendi* with their monks, on the one hand, the monastery's friends, and where necessary the king, on the other. What Giles Constable recently wrote of twelfth-century monasteries could go in most respects for the rest of the Middle Ages too:

> The records . . . , especially the charters and obituaries, are filled with references to familiars, co-brothers and co-sisters, devotees, friends, adult oblates, and all sorts of people who in some way or another had attached themselves to the religious institutions. Very little is known about such relationships, but they were presumably considered mutually beneficial, like those between religious, educational, and cultural institutions today and their benefactors, patrons and friends – the same old terms – who in return for donations receive prestige, invitations to dinners and receptions, and secular immortality on a bronze plaque, bench, or bookplate or, if they give enough, a building. Medieval monasteries likewise received property and other types of help from benefactors, whose names were entered in necrologies and obituaries and who were given spiritual and sometimes material support of various kinds . . . But it was presumably a matter of opinion who got the best of the bargain.
>
> (Constable 1996: 84–5; cf Constable 1972)

It's clearly too simple to see the prioritising of 'private' relationships over collective interests as the main threat to medieval monasticism. True, both the Rule and the *Brief Account* used the term 'private' to stigmatise individual arrangements that subverted the community. Yet personal ties, such as the bonds of kinship or gift-exchange, were also what provided every monastery's support system: networks of living relationships, including both the quick and the dead. They were part of monasticism's *raison d'être* from one end of the Middle Ages to the other; and they

Figure 33.4 The chapter house and eastern claustral range, Rievaulx, Yorkshire.
© English Heritage Photo Library.

were as true of women's houses as of men's as, in their different ways, the ladies of
Zamora and the Claresses show (Linehan 1997).

Changes there nevertheless were during the twelfth and thirteenth centuries, and
they persisted thereafter. This chapter will end with an attempt to strike a balance
between change and continuity, and some reflections, in the light of that, on later
medieval 'decline'. One significant aspect of change was the appearance of criticism
of child oblation, first, and stridently, from Cistercian polemicists (for the Cistercians
recruited only adults – with significant consequences (Leclercq 1979)), and soon
after, with cool logic, from canon lawyers, who challenged the validity of any
commitment to personal *conversio* made involuntarily and vicariously, without the
rational consent of an adult (Berend 1986; cf. Brooke 1989). The gift of the child
could only be conditional: once having reached the age of consent, the oblate must
either confirm his parents' decision, or decide to leave the monastery. There is in fact
little evidence that adolescent oblates (any more than young people reaching
marriageable, or betrothable, age) were really given freedom of choice, nor that
monasteries dwindled through the haemorrhaging of oblates. Yet monastic populations certainly did diminish in the later Middle Ages. On the other hand, Jocelyn
of Brakelond's *Chronicle of Bury St Edmunds* (Greenway and Sayers 1989) provides

*c.*1200 exceptionally rich evidence of continuity in the material and social exigencies of monastic life: in short, of experiences and concerns very similar to those voiced by the author of the *Brief Account* written at Fulda four centuries earlier. It's worth recalling that Thomas Carlyle in the mid-nineteenth century used Jocelyn's text as his entrée to a medieval past which he thought (would we think otherwise?) had lessons to teach modern times (Carlyle 1843: II, pp. 115, 117, 123–4, 159–60, 160–1). Historians choose their texts for the lessons they prioritise: Abbot Ailred's Rievaulx would provide an equally vivid picture of twelfth-century monastic life and in many respects a telling contrast to Jocelyn's, but that is another story (Walter Daniel, *Vita Ailredi*).

Jocelyn's St Edmunds was, as English monasteries went, a large community, numbering some 80 monks. It had been patronised by kings since Anglo-Saxon times, and in the twelfth century, as well as possessing an extensive territorial lordship, exercised large powers of local government in Suffolk, as direct agent of the king. For Jocelyn, who seems to have been a child oblate to St Edmunds, the critical factor in the monastery's well-being was the quality of its abbot. He begins with a devastating indictment of Abbot Hugh (1157–80):

> He was a good and devout monk, but lacked ability in business matters . . . Although discipline, worship and everything connected with the Rule [of Benedict] flourished within the cloister, external affairs were badly managed . . . The abbot's villages were leased out . . . The abbot sought refuge and consolation in a single remedy: that of borrowing money.
>
> (Greenway and Sayers 1989: 3)

When Hugh died, the monks' 'free election' was in fact subjected to intensive royal interference, Henry II 'acting for the good of his kingdom' (Greenway and Sayers 1989: 15–22). The new abbot, Samson (1180–1202), understood his obligations to the king: when the papal legate (who also happened to be bishop of Ely, hence *ex officio* St Edmunds' neighbour and frequent sparring-partner) 'issued decrees against the black monks' (the Benedictines, so called from their black robes)

> and criticized the abbots, confining them to a fixed number of horses, Samson replied, 'We shall not accept any decree that is contrary to the Rule of St Benedict, which allows abbots complete control over their monks. My task is to protect the Barony [i.e. the lordship] of St Edmund and his rights: thirteen horses are sufficient for some other abbots, but not for me, as I need more in the essential administration of royal justice'.
>
> (Greenway and Sayers 1989: 49)

Samson took in hand the management of the monastery's estates, recording rents due in an account-book: 'He looked in this book every day, as if it were a mirror reflecting his own integrity' (Greenway and Sayers 1989: 27). Even for Jocelyn, who on the whole admired him, Samson could not always maintain the right balance between priorities: 'The abbot appeared to prefer the active to the contemplative life, in that he praised good obedientiaries (monastic officials) more highly than good cloister monks . . . When he chanced to hear of any Church leader resigning his pastoral work to become a hermit, he would not utter one word of commendation' (Greenway and Sayers 1989: 37). Jocelyn does not record Samson's reaction to news of monks becoming bishops. Samson's relations with the monks were chequered. Though a division between the abbot's and the community's lands had been made earlier in the twelfth century, conflicts of economic interests focused on control over the flourishing town of Bury St Edmunds (Sayers 1990; cf. White 1958). In principle, the monks owned the town, its rents, market dues and tolls. In practice, the abbot appointed not only the monastic officers, notably the prior, but also lay servants, such as the gate-keeper, who were local worthies and sometimes the abbot's relatives. In 1199, following disputes between the community and the gate-keeper, and while the abbot was away on one of his periodic visits to London, the prior took it upon himself to suspend the gate-keeper's perks. The gate-keeper complained to the abbot, who decided on a show of strength, and demanded full restitution for the gate-keeper.

> Then there was great uproar in the convent, such as I have never seen before, and it was said that the abbot's command should not be obeyed . . . Then the abbot . . . frightened some by threats, won over others by flattery, and isolated from the rest of the community the more important of the monks (who seemed to be afraid of his very cassock), so that the words of the gospel were fulfilled: 'Every kingdom divided against itself shall be brought to desolation' (Matt. 12: 25). And the abbot declared that he would not associate with us at all, because of the plots and sworn agreements which he alleged we had made, to stab him to death with our knives. . . . [A few days later] with tears streaming down, the abbot swore that he had never lamented so much as this over anything . . . and most especially because of the stain of an evil report . . . to the effect that the monks of St Edmund's wanted to murder their abbot . . . He stood up weeping, and embraced everyone with the kiss of peace. He wept: we wept too.
>
> (Greenway and Sayers 1989: 104–5)

The financial aspects of this dispute, and its urban context, were specific to the late twelfth century. But the underlying tensions were the old ones – just as kisses and tears were old solutions.

Finally: some thoughts on 'decline', demography, individual career choices, and later medieval options. 'Decline' is partly a trick of the evidential light. Just as the investigations of papal legates – investigations mounted as a consequence of political intrigues in high places – reveal the misconduct of nuns and local friars at Zamora in thirteenth-century Spain (Linehan 1997), so the detailed records of bishops' registers lift the veil on the derelictions of nuns in fourteenth- and fifteenth-century England (Power 1922). Scandal makes good copy. But we have no good reason to assume that standards of monastic conduct were higher in the less well-documented earlier medieval centuries. (Incidental references in miracle stories to the presence of prostitutes in the environs of ninth-century monasteries in Francia and Wessex give suitable grounds for caution.) Judicial inquiries are less likely than miracle stories to attest spirituality. Readers may, for that matter, be thinking that there has

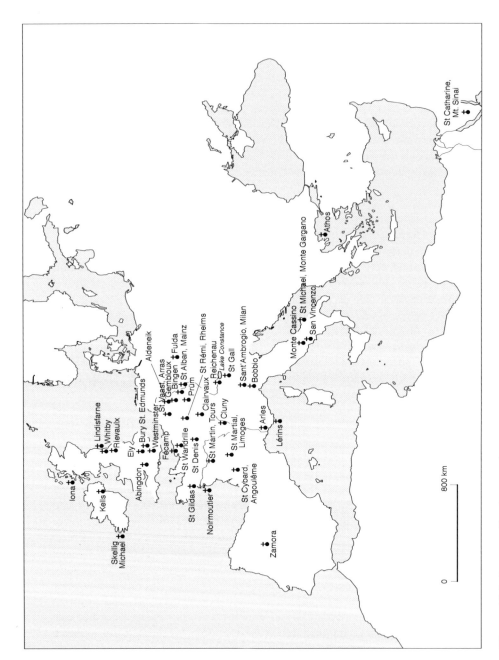

Figure 33.5 Some medieval monastic centres

been all too little evidence of spirituality in this chapter. Yet deep spiritual anxieties surely underlay Charlemagne's concerns over monastic observance ('the life and chastity of monks is the source of the greatest hope of salvation for all Christians'); and the monastic oblation of the young Samson sometime around 1140 apparently followed on a dream experienced as defining by the boy himself:

> He once told the story of how, when he was a boy of nine, he dreamt that he was standing in front of the cemetery gate of St Edmund, when the devil, with outstretched arms, tried to seize him, but St Edmund was near and rescued him, taking him in his arms. As he cried out in his dream, 'Help me, St Edmund!' . . . , he woke up. His mother was astounded . . . and when he told her his dream she took him to pray at St Edmund's shrine. As they arrived at the cemetery gate, he exclaimed, 'Mother, this is the place! Look, that is the gate I saw in my dream when the devil tried to take me.' . . . The abbot himself interpreted the dream: the devil represented worldly pleasure which would have tempted him, but St Edmund embraced him, wishing him to become a monk of his church.
>
> (Greenway and Sayers 1989: 34)

Individual spiritual experience could inspire and sustain monastic vocations through-out the medieval centuries. Yet it is the case that the numbers of monastic inmates fell dramatically, and across the board, in the later Middle Ages. The historian who suggested that demographic pressures on aristocratic inheritances powered the growth in monasticism between *c*.1050 and *c*.1150 was no materialist or cynic (Wollasch 1980). The same pressures, in other words, that drove so many young nobles to seek temporal fortunes in ventures overseas or in frontier-lands, or in chivalrous deeds that won the hands of heiresses, impelled others towards Cistercian or Templar vocations (Barthélemy, Paterson, chs. 12 and 14 in this volume). Conversely, declining numbers of monastic recruits could be seen in terms of two sorts of diminishing demand. First, from the viewpoint of potential recruits and their parents, broader options, specifically for choosers of the pen and the spoken word rather than the sword, marked the thirteenth century and after. There were more jobs, just as there were more heiresses, to be had in towns and urban businesses. At the same time, huge numbers of places – parishes, vicarages, canonries, chaplaincies and clerkships – became available in the secular church, and the growth of papal government constituted, among other things, a system for allocating these (Lawrence in this volume, ch. 37). Parental direction remained the primary determinant of career choice, but parents now saw the schools and universities as the most promising training-grounds, courts and government service the most promising openings, for likely lads. Here as in other sectors, the post-Plague conditions of the late Middle Ages strengthened the hands of sellers in the labour market.

Demand can be looked at, secondly, from the standpoint of potential patrons, for, given the cycle of gains and losses, large communities needed a steady accretion of economically viable properties and social support in managing those, to offset inevitable writing-off of the less viable or disputed. If donations to monasteries diminished, that was because donors concerned for next-worldly benefits chose to invest in other religious providers. In the case of Westminster Abbey, the high-watermark of lay patronage can be seen *c*.1200; thereafter, though personal links between certain families and the abbey continued to be renewed across the generations, contacts between the monks and the local laity on the whole diminished, whether through the monks' growing aloofness or because lay patrons preferred to endow the parish church or local charitable foundations (Rosser 1989: 255–63). The friars picked up many smaller gifts (often in cash). Still more did chantry priests, devoted to the performance of private masses for individual dead. In general the secular church benefited more than the monastic: perhaps because at least some of the secular clergy, of whom celibacy was increasingly required in practice and not just in theory, could offer the special spiritual attractions of sexual purity (Swanson 1999). For the Westminster monks by 1500, beef, eaten in a purpose-built room known, aptly, as the misericord ('mercy'), had apparently 'edged pottage off the menu'; and it is not clear that the beef was boiled (which might have discorded less with monastic custom) rather than roasted (Harvey 1993: 43, 51). Within monasticism, cycles of reform and renewal continued, but on a more restricted scale. There were simply too many alternative options. And, finally, there was the option – as there had been when upper-class monasticism began, but now no longer limited to the upper classes – of leading a life of rigorous piety at home. In that sense, it was not decline, but expansion, combining a kind of democratisation with privatisation, that was the hallmark of later medieval spirituality as of later medieval culture.

REFERENCES

Primary works

Benedict, *Rule*, ed. with French trans. by A. de Vogüe and J. Neufville, *La règle de Saint Benoît*, 7 vols., SC 181–6 (1971–2).
Benedict, *Rule*, trans. J. McCann, *The Rule of St. Benedict*, London: Sheed and Ward (1976).
'Brief Account of an Earnest Request', see *Supplex Libellus*.
Caesarius of Arles, *Regula, Oeuvres monastiques*, SC 345 (1988).
Capitularia regum Francorum, ed. A. Boretius and V. Krause, MGH Capitularia regum Francoru, vol. I, Hannover: Hahnsche Buchhandlung (1883).
Codex Carolinus nos. 66, 67, ed. W. Gundlach, MGH Epp. III, Berlin: Weidmann, pp. 593–7.
Concilia Galliae, ed. and French trans. J. Gaudemet and J. Basdevant, SC 353, 354 (1989).
Epistola de Litteris Colendis, ed. A. Boretius, MGH Capitularia regum Francorum, vol. I, Hannover: Hahnsche Buchhandlung (1883), no. 29, pp. 78–9.
Jocelyn of Brakelond, *Chronicle of Bury St Edmunds*, trans. D. Greenway and J. Sayers, Oxford: Oxford University Press (1989).
Marculfi Formularum libri duo, ed. A. Uddholm, Uppsala: Eranos Förlag (1962).
Supplex Libellus, ed. J. Semmler, *Corpus Consuetudinum Monasticarum*, ed. K. Hallinger, vol. 1, *Monumenta aevi Anianensis*, Siegburg: F. Schmitt (1963), pp. 321–7, unpublished trans. J.L. Nelson, as 'Brief Account of an Earnest Request'.
Sayings of the Desert Fathers, trans. B. Ward, London: Mowbrays (1975).
Walter Daniel, *Vita Ailredi*, ed. and trans. F.M. Powicke, Edinburgh: Nelson (1950).

Secondary works

Alfonso I. 1991 'Cistercians and Feudalism', *Past and Present* 133, pp. 3–30.

Angenendt, A. 1990 *Das Frühmittelalter: Die abendländische Christenheit von 400 bis 900*, Stuttgart, Berlin and Cologne: Kohlhammer.

Barthélemy, D. 1993 *La société dans le comté de Vendôme de l'an mil au quatorzième siècle*, Paris: CNRS.

Barthélemy, D. 1996 Debate, 'The Feudal Revolution', *Past and Present* 152, pp. 196–205.

Berend, N. 1994 'Une invisible subversion: la disparition de l'oblation irrévocable des enfants', *Médiévales* 26, pp. 123–36.

Bishko, C.J. 1989 'Fernando I and the origins of the Leonese-Castilian alliance with Cluny', in Bishko, *Studies in Medieval Frontier History*, London: Variorum, ch. II.

Boswell, J. 1991 *The Kindness of Strangers: the Abandonment of Children in Western Europe from Late Antiquity to the Renaissance*, London: Penguin.

Boureau, A. 2000 'How law came to the monks: perceptions of jurisdiction in English society at the beginning of the thirteenth century', *Past and Present* 167, pp. 29–74.

Brooke, C.N.L. 1974 *The Monastic World 1000–1300*, photography by W. Swaan, London: Elek.

—— 1989 *The Medieval Idea of Marriage*, Oxford: Oxford University Press.

Brown, P. 1971 'The holy man in Late Antiquity', *Journal of Roman Studies* 61, pp. 81–101.

—— 1987 *The Body and Society*, Oxford: Oxford University Press.

Bull, M. 1993 *Knightly Piety and the Origins of the First Crusade*, Oxford: Oxford University Press.

Carlyle, T. 1843 *Past and Present*, London: Chapman and Hall.

Clanchy, M. 1998 *Peter Abelard*, Oxford: Blackwell.

Clark, E.A. 1986 *Ascetic Piety and Women's Faith*, Lewiston NY: Edwin Mellen Press.

Constable, G. 1972 'The *Liber Memorialis* of Remiremont', *Speculum* 47, pp. 261–77.

—— 1976 *Medieval Monasticism. A Select Bibliography*, Toronto: University of Toronto Press.

—— 1996 *The Reformation of the Twelfth Century*, The Trevelyan Lectures Given at the University of Cambridge, 1985, Cambridge: Cambridge University Press.

de Jong, M. 1995 'Carolingian monasticism: the power of prayer', in R. McKitterick ed., *The New Cambridge Medieval History*, vol. II, Cambridge: Cambridge University Press, pp. 622–53.

—— 1996 *In Samuel's Image; Child Oblation in the Early Medieval West*, Leiden: Brill.

—— 2000 'Internal cloisters: the case of Ekkehard's Casus Sancti Galli', in W. Pohl and H. Reimitz ed., *Grenze und Differenzen im frühen Mittelalter*, Vienna: Verlag der österreichischen Akademie der Wissenschaften.

Dierkens, A. 1985 *Abbayes et chapîtres entre Sambre et Meuse (VIIe–XIe siècles)*, Sigmaringen: Thorbecke.

Dobson, R.B. 1997 'The Black Monks of Durham and Canterbury Colleges', in H. Wansbrough and A. Marett-Crosby eds, *Benedictines in Oxford*, London: Darton, Longman and Todd.

Duby, G. 1973 'Le budget de l'abbaye de Cluny entre 1080 et 1155: économie domaniale et économie monétaire', originally publ. 1952, repr. in Duby, *Hommes et structures du Moyen Âge*, Paris: Presses Universitaires, pp. 61–82.

Durkheim, E. 1961 *Elementary Forms of the Religious Life*, original French 1893, trans. J. Swain, New York: The Free Press.

Flanagan, S. 1989 *Hildegard of Bingen, 1098–1179: A Visionary Life*, London: Routledge.

Fouracre, P. 1995 'Eternal Light and Earthly Needs. Practical Aspects of the Development of Frankish Immunities', in W. Davies and P. Fouracre eds, *Property and Power in the Early Middle Ages*, Cambridge: Cambridge University Press, pp. 53–81.

Frend, W. 1972 'The monks and the survival of the East Roman Empire in the fifth century', *Past and Present* 54, pp. 3–24.

Gilchrist, R. 1994 *Gender and Material Culture: the Archaeology of Religious Women*, London: Routledge.

Hallinger, K. 1950–1951 *Gorze-Cluny*, 2 vols, Studia Anselmiana 22–25, Rome.

—— 1971 "The Spiritual Life at Cluny in the Early Days', in N. Hunt ed., *Cluniac Monasticism in the Central Middle Ages*, London: Macmillan, pp. 29–55.

—— 1979 'Überlieferung und Steigerung im Mönchtum des achten bis zwölften Jhdts', in *Analecta Liturgica* 1, *Studia Anselmiana* 68, Rome, pp. 125–87.

Harnack, A. von 1908 *The Mission and Expansion of Christianity*, German original 1901, trans. J. Moffatt, London: Williams and Norgate.

Harvey, B. 1993 *Living and Dying in England 1100–1540. The Monastic Experience*, Oxford: Clarendon Press.

Heitz, C. 1963 *Recherches sur les rapports entre architecture et liturgie à l'époque carolingienne*, Paris: S.E.V.P.E.N.

Hildebrandt, M.M. 1992 *The External School in Carolingian Society*, Leiden, New York and Cologne: Brill.

Hodges, R. and Mitchell, J. 1985 *San Vincenzo al Volturno: the archaeology, art and territory of an early medieval monastery*, British Archaeological Reports, International Series 252, Oxford.

Innes, M. 2000 *State and Society in the Early Middle Ages: the Middle Rhine Valley, 400–1000*, Cambridge: Cambridge University Press.

Iogna-Prat, D. 1998 *Ordonner et exclure: Cluny et la société chrétienne face à l'hérésie, au judaïsme et à l'Islam 1000–1150*, Paris: Aubier.

Knowles, D. 1940 *The Monastic Order in England*, Cambridge: Cambridge University Press.

—— 1963 *Great Historical Enterprises: Problems in Monastic History*, London: Nelson.

—— 1966 *From Pachomius to Ignatius: a Study in the Constituional History of the Religious Orders*, Oxford: Clarendon Press.

Knowles, D. and St Joseph, M. 1952 *Monastic Sites from the Air*, Cambridge: Cambridge University Press.

Lawrence, C.H. 1989 *Medieval Monasticism: Forms of Religious Life in Western Europe in the Middle Ages*, 2nd edn, London and New York: Longman.

—— 1994 *The Friars: the Impact of the Early Mendicant Movement on Western Society*, London: Longman.

Leclercq, J. 1982 *The Love of Learning and the Desire for God: a Study of Monastic Culture*, New York: Fordham University Press.

—— 1979 *Monks and Love in Twelfth-Century France*, Oxford: Clarendon Press.

Le Goff, J. 1957 *Les intellectuels au moyen âge*, Paris: Éditions du Seuil.

—— 1968 'Apostolat mendiant et fait urbain dans la France médiévale. Programme-questonnaire pour une enquête', *Annales Economies, Sociétés, Civilisations* 23, pp. 335–52.

—— 1970 'Enquête du Centre de Recherches Historiques: Ordres mendiants et urbanisation dans la France médiévale', *Annales, Economies, Sociétés, Civilisations* 25, pp. 924–65.

Leyser, C. 1998 'Monks in flux: nocturnal emission and the limits of celibacy in the early Middle Ages", in D. Hadley ed., *Masculinity in Medieval Europe*, London: Longman, pp. 103–20.

Leyser, H. 1984 *Hermits and the New Monasticism*, London: Macmillan.

Leyser, K. 1979 *Rule and Conflict in an Early Medieval Society*, London: Edward Arnold.

L'Hermite-Leclercq, P. 1989 *Le monachisme dans la société de son temps. Le monastère de La Celle (XIe – début du XVIe siècle)*, Paris: Cujas.

Little, L.K. 1993 *Benedictine Maledictions: Liturgical Cursing in Romanesque France*, Ithaca and London: Cornell University Press.

Linehan, P. 1997 *The Ladies of Zamora*, Manchester: Manchester University Press.

Mann, M. 1986 *The Sources of Social Power*, Cambridge: Cambridge University Press.

McLaughlin, M. 1994 *Consorting with Saints. Prayer for the Dead in Medieval France*, Ithaca NY: Cornell University Press.

Mitchell, J., see Hodges, R. and Mitchell J. 1985.

Morris, R. 1995 *Monks and Laymen in Tenth-Century Byzantium*, Cambridge: Cambridge University Press.

Nelson, J.L. 1992 'Parents, children and the Church in the earlier Middle Ages', *Studies in Church History* 31, pp. 81–114.

—— 1999a 'Feasts, Games and Inversions in The Ups and Downs of St-Gall', in B. Nágy and M. Sebök eds, *The Man of Many Devices, Who Wandered Full Many Ways . . . : Festschrift in Honor of Janos M. Bak*, Budapest: Central European University Press, pp. 269–76.

—— 1999b 'Monks, secular men and masculinity', in D. Hadley ed., *Masculinity in Medieval Europe*, London: Longman, pp. 121–42.

Oexle, O.G. 1993 'Les moines d'occident et la vie politique et sociale dans le haut moyen âge', *Revue Bénédictine* 103, pp. 255–72.

Power, E.E. 1922 *Medieval English Nunneries c.1275 to 1535*, Cambridge: Cambridge University Press.

Rabe, S.A. 1995 *Faith, Art and Politics at St-Riquier. The Symbolic Vision of Angilbert*, Phildelphia PA: University of Pennsylvania Press.

Reuter, T. 1997 Debate, 'The Feudal Revolution', *Past and Present* 155, pp. 177–95.

Riché, P. 1981 'Consequences des invasions normandes sur la culture monastique dans l'Occident franc', in *idem, Instruction et vie religieuse dans le haut moyen âge*, London: Variorum, ch. XX, pp. 705–21.

Rosenwein, B. 1989 *To be the Neighbor of Saint Peter: the Social Meaning of Cluny's Property*, Ithaca and London: Cornell University Press.

—— 1999 *Negotiating Space. Power, Restraint and Privileges of Immunity in Early Medieval Europe*, Ithaca and London: Cornell University Press.

Rosser, G. 1989 *Medieval Westminster 1200–1540*, Oxford: Clarendon Press.

Sayers, J. 1990 'Violence in the medieval cloister', *Journal of Ecclesiastical History* 43, pp. 533–42.

Scharf, B.R. 1970 *The Sociological Study of Religion*, London: Hutchinson.

Schmid, K. 1978 'Mönchslisten und Klosterkonvent von Fulda zur Zeit der Karolingern', in K. Schmid *et al., Die Klostergemeinschaft von Fulda im früheren Mittelalter*, 5 vols, Munich, W. Fink, vol. 2, 2, pp. 571–635.

Scott, J. 1986 'Gender: a Useful Category of Historical Analysis', *American Historical Review* 91, pp. 1053–75.

Searle, E. ed. and trans. 1980 *The Chronicle of Battle Abbey*, Oxford: Oxford University Press.

Semmler, J. 1966 'Karl der Grosse und das fränkische Mönchtum', in W. Braunfels ed., *Karl der Grosse: Lebenswerk und Nachleben*, vol. II, ed. B. Bischoff, Das geistige Leben, Düsseldorf: L. Schwann, pp. 255–89.

—— 1991 'Le souverain occidental et les communautés religieuses du IXe au début du XIe siècle', *Byzantion* 61, pp. 44–70.

—— 1993 'Le monachisme occidentale du VIIIe au XIe siècle: formation et réformation', *Revue Bénédictine* 103, pp. 68–89.

Southern, R.W. 1953 *The Making of the Middle Ages*, London: Hutchinson.

Stafford, P. 1998 'La mutation familiale? A suitable case for caution', in J. Hill and M. Swann eds., *The Community, the Family and the Saint, Patterns of Power in Early Medieval Europe*, International Medieval Research 4, Turnhout, pp. 103–26.

Sullivan, R. E. 1998 'What was Carolingian Monasticism? The Plan of St Gall and the History of Monasticism', in A. Murray ed., *After Rome's Fall. Narrators and Sources of early Medieval History. Essays presented to Walter Goffart*, Toronto: University of Toronto Press, pp. 251–87.

Swanson, R. 1999 'Angels incarnate: clergy and masculinity from Gregorian Reform to Reformation', in D. Hadley ed., *Masculinity in Medieval Europe*, London: Longman, pp. 160–77.

Troeltsch, E. 1931 *The Social Teachings of the Christian Churches*, German original 1912, trans. O. Wyon, London: Allen and Unwin.

van Engen, J. 1986 'The crisis of cenobitism reconsidered: Benedictine monasticism in the years 1050–1150', *Speculum* 61, pp. 269–304.

Venarde, B. L. 1998 *Women's Monasticism and Medieval Society. Nunneries in France and England, 890–1215*, Ithaca and London: Cornell University Press.

Wach, J. 1962 *The Sociology of Religion*, original German 1931, repr. of 1944 trans. by Wach, Chicago: Chicago University Press.

Wallace-Hadrill, J.M. 1983 *The Frankish Church*, Oxford: Oxford University Press.

Weber, M. 1965 *Economy and Society. An Outline of Interpretive Sociology*, German original 1925, trans. and ed. G. Roth and C. Wittich, New York: Bedminster Press.

White, H.V. 1958 'Pontius of Cluny, the Curia Romana and the end of Gregorianism in Rome', *Church History* 27, pp. 195–219.

White, S. 1988 *Custom, Kinship, and Gifts to Saints: the Laudatio Parentum in Western France, 1050–1150*, Chapel Hill NC: University of North Carolina Press.

—— 1996 Debate, 'The Feudal Revolution', *Past and Present* 152, pp. 205–23.

Wickham, C. 1988 *The Mountains and the City. The Tuscan Appenines in the Early Middle Ages*, Oxford: Oxford University Press.

Wollasch, J. 1972 *Mönchtum des Mittelalters zwischen Kirche und Welt*, Münster Mittelalter-Schriften 7, Munich: W. Fink.

—— 1980 'Parenté noble et monachisme réformateur. Observations sur les "conversions" à la vie monastique aux XIe et XIIe siècles', *Revue historique* 204, pp. 3–24.

Wood, I. 1995 'Teutsind, Witlaic and the history of Merovingian precaria', in W. Davies and P. Fouracre eds, *Property and Power in the Early Middle Ages*, Cambridge: Cambridge University Press, pp. 31–52.

Wormald, P. 1993 'St Hilda, Saint and Scholar (614–80)', in J. Mellanby ed., *The St Hilda's College Centenary Symposium. A Celebration of the Education of Women*, Oxford: St Hilda's College, pp. 93–103

ASPECTS OF THE EARLY MEDIEVAL PEASANT ECONOMY AS REVEALED IN THE POLYPTYCH OF PRÜM[1]

Yoshiki Morimoto

INTRODUCTION

Historians for a long time viewed the economy and society of the early Middle Ages as static. The peasantry, in particular, were thought to have been not only poor but more or less immobile. Living in a self-sufficient way, they were allegedly sedentary, handing on their plots from father to son with little change. One great achievement of the socio-economic historiography of the Middle Ages – a field where enormous progress has been made in recent years – consists in the shattering of this image. Nowadays, historians are well aware that early medieval peasants, though poor, often had to journey outside their localities, sometimes going quite long distances. Medieval historians have shown, too, that peasants were in permanent contact with a money economy, often to quite a considerable extent. True, their bonds with the land they cultivated were close, but their holdings underwent changes of size from one generation to the next as the demographic configuration of their families shifted over time (Bonnassie 1990; Devroey 1993; Verhulst 1995, with further references).

The object of this chapter is to present this new and more dynamic picture of the economic life of the early medieval peasantry. With this end in view, I shall make use of a document that has received particularly close examination during the past twenty-five years: the Polyptych of the monastery of Prüm (Kuchenbuch 1978; Schwab 1983; Nolden 1993; Devroey 1993 (1979)). It's well-known that the healthy state of research on the early Middle Ages owes a lot to archaeology. Yet the study of written sources has made a no less significant contribution thanks to progress in textual criticism. Nowadays we are much more aware of the gap between the text and historical reality, and the role of the text's producer(s), with their particular agenda, in creating that gap. Thanks to more careful and subtle interpretations of the written word, historians have become far more attentive to what writers and editors of texts intended. Modern, more rigorous, critical methods, have made it possible now to uncover the internal chronological stratigraphy of a document that on the surface seems to belong as a whole to a certain date. This chapter is one result of these recent advances in the study of written sources.

Figure 34.1 Polyptych of Prüm, Caesarius's copy of 1222: the first of three illustrations. Charlemagne and Pippin offer the church of Prüm to God. Koblenz, Germany, Landeshauptarchiv, MS. Abt. 18 – Nr. 2087, fo. 2v.

The term 'polyptych' – which means, literally, many leaves – denotes an inventory of material and human resources made on the orders of a great landed proprietor in the Carolingian period. It covers estates, the peasants living thereon, and, especially, the dues and labour-services owed by those peasants to their lord. Some thirty Carolingian polyptychs have survived, and they provide us with the best source-material for early medieval agrarian history. These documents were intensively studied in the classic works of the nineteenth and early-twentieth centuries, but in recent decades there has been a new wave of research on them. A dozen polyptychs, including that of Prüm, have been re-edited, and a number of detailed studies have been published. Thanks to all this, a new way of exploiting these texts has emerged. We are no longer content just to derive from them a transverse section of rural society, but we are beginning to use them more dynamically: that is, to focus on deciphering change. This, in a nutshell, is why Carolingian polyptychs are proving to be very effective tools for breaking with the traditionally static image of early medieval peasant life (Morimoto 1988; Morimoto 1994).

From this standpoint, the Polyptych of Prüm, whose eleventh centenary was celebrated in 1993, has been particularly well studied. Not only is it one of three really large polyptychs, along with those of St Germain-des-Prés, Paris and St Remi, Rheims, but it is the most detailed as far as burdens on the peasantry are concerned. Drawn up over a few years, around 893, and interpolated over the subsequent fifty years or so in the course of its use in estate management, the Polyptych of Prüm survives in a unique copy of 1222. The copyist was the former abbot Caesarius, and he supplied alongside his transcription a copious commentary including original information not just about his own times but also about earlier periods going right back to the early Middle Ages. The document as a whole lends itself extremely well to what I have suggested is the kind of dynamic exploitation characteristic of the genre. Using the different chronological layers visible in the original text, as well as the additional material in Caesarius's commentary, we can hope to reveal changes in socio-economic life on the monastery's estates. This is not the place to go further into the technical details of the research-methods involved. But the attentive reader will be able to see how the dynamic view developed in recent scholarship has been put to use in what follows.

While the polyptych was constructed by the monastic lord for the purposes of estate-management, it reveals a world in which life was organised under lordly control. Historians are currently debating how far the lordship, or seigneurie, structured the Carolingian agrarian regime.[2] There was certainly a lot of regional diversity. The great estate and its exploitation on behalf of its lord(s) were far more developed in the centre of the Frankish realm than at its periphery. In the Mediterranean zone, where the role of independent peasants and their communities were far larger than in the areas north of the Alps and north of the Loire, those peasants were in the process of being absorbed into lordships. This was especially true of northern and central Italy: peasants clung more tenaciously to their autonomous existence in southern France and northern Spain (Bonnassie 1991; Wickham 1994; Wickham 1995). In north-western Europe, England too saw the appearance of great estates, but these were not yet very strongly structured nor very widely diffused (Faith 1997). What Continental historians call the domanial regime

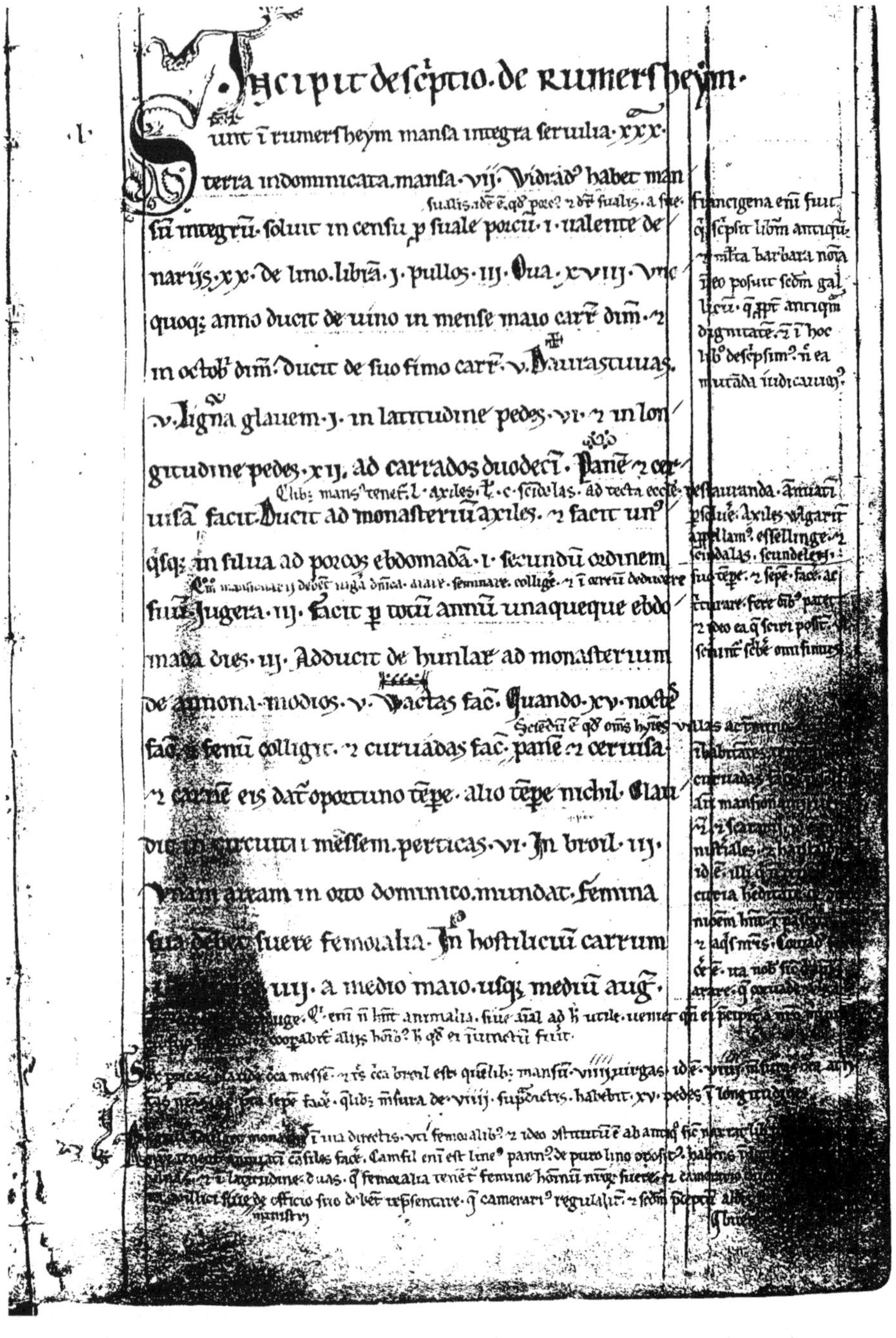

Figure 34.2 Polyptych of Prüm, transcription of ninth-century text: in larger letters 'Sunt . . .', and notes written by Caesarius in smaller letters. Koblenz, Germany, Landeshauptarchiv, MS. Abt. 18 – Nr. 2087, fo. 8r.

was best established between the Loire and the Rhine (Verhulst 1992; Devroey 1993).[3] This is the zone in which most of the places mentioned in the Polyptych of Prüm are to be found.

This chapter, using such evidence, is bound to describe peasant life already fully organised in a hierarchy under a lord's domination. This is a world we currently know much better, as far as the Carolingian period is concerned, than we know communities of more or less independent peasants. Yet the domanial regime certainly ought not to be considered virtually the only form of rural life at this time. I shall try to show in what follows that among those living on large monastic estates, there was a peasant dynamism. We can well believe that something very similar was shared by the more independent peasantry and expressed in different forms. Perhaps we should recall, at the same time, that those more independent peasants, for all their greater freedom of action, could not benefit from the protection and organisation that lordship might have offered them. I shall focus on three major aspects of peasant life about which our Polyptych is especially well suited to supply information: the manse as the fundamental peasant holding; labour services owed to the monastery; and the communications-network that put peasants in touch with the market.

THE MANSE

The Polyptych of Prüm consists of 118 chapters, each of which is essentially a description of one of the numerous estates distributed over a vast zone but most highly concentrated in some fifteen regions. The peasants were listed as tenants of some 1,750 manses spread unevenly across this collection of estates. The ninth-century manse was the normal basic unit of a peasant holding, comprising a dwelling, a cultivated area and the use of uncultivated land, the whole of which was deemed sufficient to maintain a family composed of a couple and their unmarried children and often some servants or slaves. When the Polyptych of Prüm gives the size of a manse, it ranges from between 5 and 15 hectares (approximately 12 to 37 acres). We know that the manse implied the notion of a unit that was stable over time: whoever held it from the lord would transmit tenure from father to son. But historians have often gone so far as to assert that this system imposed a rigid structure on the peasantry, and tended to limit, and even stifle, the development of the peasant economy.

On first reading, the Polyptych of Prüm presents an image of stability and rigidity, in particular, because it seems to have been drawn up on the principle of one manse held by one household. Only occasionally does the document register a manse occupied by more than one household or a fraction of a manse such as a half-manse or a quarter-manse. In line with their essentially static image of the peasant economy, modern experts have agreed that the principle of the manse as the basis of a family holding was strictly observed on the abbey's estates at the close of the ninth century. We shall show that the reality was something far more dynamic.

Chapters 45–51 of the Polyptych record a cluster of estates in the Ardennes which constituted the abbey's most westerly estates (Figure 34.3), and here we can find ample evidence of overpopulation and the splitting-up of manses.[4] In these places,

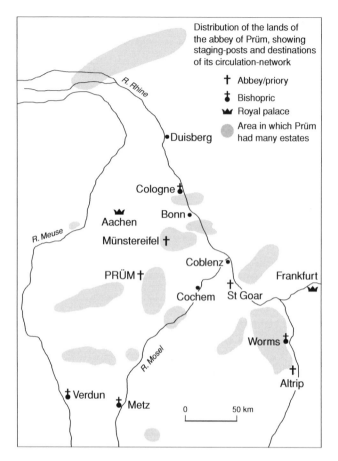

Figure 34.3 Map of estates of Prüm.

the compiler recorded the manses one by one, giving the names of the tenants on each, thus enabling us to count the number of tenants and of half- or quarter-manses in relation to the number of whole manses. Given due allowance for differences between the various estates, the statistics show that overpopulated or fractional manses comprised over 20 per cent of the total. Since the other chapters of the document are not so detailed, we have to look for fainter traces of similar conditions.

As far as overpopulation is concerned, we soon realise that its dimensions are largely concealed beneath the forms employed by the makers of the Polyptych. In most chapters, details are given only for a single manse selected as a model: the description of this model-manse, and particularly of the dues owed from it, is followed by a passage simply stating that 'x manses owed the same dues'. The compiler was mainly interested in registering the total revenue for each estate and hence had no need to trouble himself about what was going on within every manse. In cases where the model-manse was occupied by only a single family, then the rest of that entry went on to give no indication of any overpopulation of manses even when this was the actual situation on the majority of manses comprising that estate.

As far as the fractional manses were concerned, careful examination of the text reveals that this was equally, or even more, widespread on the estates outside the Ardennes than on those within that region. Here too, then, the formula conceals reality: the half- and quarter-manses that were actually recorded in the original listing could well have been 'obliterated' in the final editing of the text as it has come down to us. For instance, when an even number of half-manses existed on a particular estate, these could well have been totted up by pairs during the editing process, and so counted as whole manses. For similar reasons, we should not infer the existence of only one half-manse when the total of manses ends with a half-manse: for instance, ten-and-a-half manses could mean ten whole manses and one half-manse, but could equally well represent five whole manses and eleven halves. Taking all such technical details into account, and making use of that minority of chapters that are exceptionally revealing, we can feel fairly confident that the fractional manses accounted for over 20 per cent of peasant manses on the estates outside the Ardennes region as well. In terms of the number of holdings, one example will be enough to give an impression of the high proportion of fractional holdings: on an estate of 25 manses, there may have been more than 10 half-manses, or 20 quarters, compared with 15 whole manses.

Thus, all over Prüm's estates, a manse occupied by a single household was far from being the rule that was actually followed. Nevertheless, we ought not to think of the manse system here as already significantly 'bastardised'. Taking due account of the findings of recent research on early medieval agrarian history, my view is that the manse system was indeed fully operational, but that it could adapt to the growth of the peasant economy.

Scholars have long tended to attribute all overpopulated or fractional manses to a process known as 'the decomposition of the manse'. On this model, demographic increase within a manse originally held by a single household allegedly resulted in first the overpopulation of the holding and then its division. Recent careful study of certain polyptychs that are especially detailed, including that of Prüm, has led to the conclusion that these phenomena could have resulted not only from a process of decomposition but equally from the formation of manses. The lord might grant to new peasant units, born during the favourable demographic conditions prevailing since the seventh century, holdings that corresponded theoretically to a half of a quarter of a manse. Some of these could become sufficiently consolidated for the holding to be large enough to form a whole manse. This process could come about most readily in areas where land was being brought into cultivation, or where land was in relatively plentiful supply and holdings were therefore liable to change their shape and size. It is true that to reach such conclusions, historians generally rely on circumstantial evidence. Yet more or less direct evidence is also supplied by two features to be observed in the Polyptych of Prüm. First, the service-holding of the estate-manager or -official often appears as a half-manse. Anxious not to create a situation in which confusion could arise over the allocation of duties, the lord needed to avoid carving a half-manse as a service-holding out of a pre-existing manse. Hence the half-manses assigned to estate-officers had to be created anew on land that until then had not been organised into manses. Secondly, the term *absus*, which in the Carolingian period signified a holding on which no tenant officially resided, appears often in the Polyptych of Prüm. The term is linked with whole manses and with fractions of manses. Here we have, already, a clear indication of more or less rapid changes among tenant-farmers. Some quarter-manses classified as *absi* were held by peasants listed among the tenants of other manses. Other *mansi absi*, however, were held by peasants whose names appeared nowhere else in the document. It is reasonable to infer that quarter-manses were being created anew. Some were assigned to peasants engaged in enlarging their holdings beyond their original manses, whereas others received new tenants.

On Prüm's estates, then, small peasant-holdings were being created as half-manses and quarter-manses at just the period when economic growth and a demographic rise within the whole manses were causing overpopulation and fragmentation. It follows that the manse-system, far from being fixed in some unrealisable theory of one manse per household, was able to preserve its vitality by continually adapting to the dynamism of the peasant economy which inevitably involved variation between family fortunes. Newly created or flexibly divided, the manse could guarantee a stable base for every peasant household at any given moment of its life-cycle.

On the other hand, the vitality of the manse on Prüm's estates was ensured by the system of renders and services. The Polyptych includes much information on dues and services imposed on overpopulated or fractional manses. These details show that the burdens laid on a peasant family-unit, whether occupying a manse together with other units (overpopulation) or whether the peasant held a half-manse or quarter-manse (that is, fractions of a manse), were levied at a relatively reduced rate compared with the dues required from a whole manse. The Polyptych actually terms half-manses 'those that do half-service'. In other words, the burdens on smaller tenements were significantly lighter than those on whole manses, and this allowed their tenants the chance to intensify their input and improve the holding. In such favourable conditions, peasants could increase their holding by bringing new land into cultivation or by renting new parcels of land. The manse system, as it appears in the Polyptych, could thus favour the small tenement, and this could provide a way for a worker temporarily deprived of land to be 'rehabilitated' as an autonomous producer.

This recipe for favouring small tenements through reduced burdens did not apply to servile manses, however. In the Carolingian period, there were certain legal categories of manse, the three main ones being free manses, semi-free (*lidiles*) manses, and servile manses. Originally, the first of these had been manses granted to former free men, the second to the half-free, and the third to those whose ancestors had been slaves but who were now in the process of becoming small-scale tenant-farmers. Usually servile manses were smaller than free or half-free ones, and they were more heavily burdened with dues and especially with labour services. On Prüm's estates, some 270 out of 1,750 manses were termed 'servile', as compared with 60 'free' and 230 'half-free' manses. The fact that the great majority of manses were given no label of this kind was the outcome of a process of evolution in which differences between the categories of manse had shrunk.[5]

According to the Polyptych, servile manses were much less liable to exhibit the traits of overpopulation and fragmentation than manses in the other two categories.

Moreover, at one point, the Polyptych gives a clause which states that some half-manses owed a weekly service of three days, just as whole servile manses did. Apparently, in the case of the servile manses on the Prüm estates, the principle of demanding fewer dues for smaller tenements (as we saw with overpopulated or fractional manses) did not apply. In my view, the Polyptych of Prüm registers in the case of servile manses the factors operating at an early stage in the evolution of the manse, when smaller tenements assigned to former slaves contributed to the socio-economic improvement of such people, even though they were saddled with burdensome labour services. Proportionately reduced demands on smaller tenements, which were preferentially applied on Prüm's estates towards the end of the ninth century except in the case of servile manses, demonstrates once again the vitality of the manse: while old arrangements linked with slavery were on the way to disappearing, a new principle adapted to the growth of a more autonomous peasant economy was already well established.

LABOUR SERVICES

A peasant established more or less permanently as tenant of a manse, whether a whole manse, an overpopulated one, or a half- or quarter-section, owed the abbey of Prüm labour services and dues that were defined in terms of the manse. The Polyptych offers much information on these burdens, and makes it clear that labour services were far more important than other dues and renders. Work dues, though they varied a great deal, can be classed under three heads: weekly service, annual service, and allotment service.

The Polyptych contains frequent references to labour service of three days a week. Such service was unspecified, and could be exacted for whatever agricultural or domestic tasks the lord's management might require. The peasant who owed it might not know what s/he would be required to do until they received orders from the lord's agent, perhaps that very morning. Recent research has emphasised two aspects of weekly service. First, while it had originally been developed as the main service of former slaves, it now affected peasant tenants and in the ninth century extended across a far broader spectrum of the estate population. Second, the three-days-a-week requirement expressed the idea that nearly half the peasant's labour belonged to the lord, leaving the rest to the tenant. In reality, such service could be lengthened beyond the three days or shortened so that less was demanded.

On Prüm's estates towards the end of the ninth century, weekly labour service was most closely associated with servile manses, though other manses too were often thus burdened. The Polyptych contains a number of significant signs that these demands were closely linked with arbitrary interventions on the part of the lord. In other polyptychs, work dues are often mentioned whose duration and heaviness had always been indeterminate but which are said to depend 'on the lord's will'. In the Prüm Polyptych too, some unfree tenants have to perform 'whatever the lord requires'. Weekly service and arbitrary service are often imposed on the same manse, and in some cases they are said to alternate seasonally, while in others the requirements are simply recorded one after the other without comment. In one entry, the

Polyptych integrates the two types of labour service in a single formula: 'weekly, to do all that may have been commanded'. This curious expression symbolises the fact that the two types of service could be exacted in such a way that they amounted to more, or less, than three days a weeek. While weekly service was subject to the lord's arbitrary decision, the lord could hardly have extended such arbitrary service beyond a certain point without ruining the peasant holding.

Annual labour services form a second group. In most cases, these services are very well-defined in quantitative terms. Some are described as specific kinds of work: the marking-off and maintainance of fencing around a particular piece of land, the transport of a certain amount of wood, and other items. Other annual services are defined in terms of the duration of the work required: so many days' ploughing, harvesting, reaping, and so forth, on the lord's demesne. In the case of these major agricultural tasks, two workers per household might be required. The heaviest of these labour services was '15 nights' or '15 days', indicating that those liable had to work for two weeks consecutively, day and night, which enabled the lord to send peasants quite far from their homes. This is why such services were often associated with the transport of produce from estates.

Annual services were thus very variable and a relatively large amount of the Polyptych's details have to do with them. Quantitatively and qualitatively, though, these services were much more precisely defined than weekly services. The peasant was thus able to foresee what he would have to do in terms of annual requirements, and hence could adapt his work on his own holding to that rhythm. It was easier, in other words, for the peasant to reconcile annual service with his own economic autonomy than it was in the case of weekly service.

A third type of labour service was assessed by allotment (*lot-corvée*), that is, a peasant was required to perform the whole cycle of agricultural work on an assigned parcel of the lord's demesne. Most of the Polyptych's chapters include this simple clause: *iii. iugera*. This reference to a particular bit of land, equivalent to some two hectares (approximately five acres) in extent, is always placed in the middle of the list of the peasant's services and renders. At first it seems hard to interpret. Caesarius helpfully provided an annotation on the phrase, however: 'It is clear to almost anyone how the tenant of the manse must use his time on the lord's *iugera* in ploughing, sowing, harvesting, storing in the barn, making enclosures, and threshing. I have therefore left these well-known details out of my transcription.' It looks as if the copyist, weary of repeating a long formula specifying the nature of allotment service in terms of major agricultural tasks, took the liberty of reducing all these simply to a statement of the area of the demesne allotted to each tenant. Yet Caesarius still thought it worthwhile to add a note summarising the essential demands listed in the omitted formulae. This note can thus be read as reproducing the essential words that defined allotment service in the original polyptych.

Completely freed from direct and arbitrary interventions on the part of the lord, allotment service was thus very different from weekly service. The peasant left to organise his own work was to that extent autonomous. On the lord's demesne, three 'fields', probably farmed on a system of triennial rotation which was certainly in use in this period, were cultivated exclusively by a tenant. What that tenant owed was work. The crop was stored directly in the lord's barn. Yet the tenant could adapt his work-schedule, in its various forms, to the labour he expended on his own tenement and he could thus farm as an appendage to that tenement whatever part of the demesne he had been allocated. It seems clear that allotment service, which originated as the primary service imposed on free men who fell under a lord's domination, favoured in the longer run a reduction in the amount of labour owed, since the part of the demesne involved would tend to be integrated into a peasant holding.

The Polyptych's description of labour services laid on particular manses could be long and detailed, sometimes, as just noted, listing a variety of agricultural tasks. Such entries sometimes allow the historian to infer change over time. Allotment service, created in the first place for free peasants, had frequently come to be imposed on servile tenements, while weekly service, originally demanded of the unfree, was a burden that lay on many free or semi-free tenements in the late ninth century. In some cases, the evidence suggests that if the peasants had performed all the services required of them, they would not have had enough time left to farm their own tenements. What we should infer is that the compiler of the document was determined to list every work service that could possibly be required from each manse, but that some of those services, once a reality at some time in the past, were more or less obsolete in 893. Consequently, it looks as if each year only part of the work due actually had to be performed. The lord's demands would vary with circumstances and, not least, with what the actual power-relationship between lord and peasant at a given time and place permitted. The Polyptych needs to be interpreted, not literally, but contextually!

In any event, the details about labour services thus yield a rich harvest of insights into how the early medieval peasant economy actually operated. Certainly, the various work services constituted a heavy burden. They had been devised, after all, in the interests of lords and their estate-managers, whose demands, from the work-force's point of view, could often be fatally irregular and were often exacted in an arbitrary way. Nevertheless, there is another side to all this. A large number of these services were seasonally regular, and fixed as to quantity. Allotment work, though extensive and time-consuming, was actually carried out in ways that left the tenant a great deal of autonomy. Even when the main burden, for many unfree peasants, appeared in the Polyptych as an arbitrary service, it was nearly always exacted as three days a week. Thus while labour services were various, and certainly weighed heavily on the manses of Prüm's domain, the Polyptych shows that an autonomous peasant economy was deeply rooted in the forms and structures of estate-organisation.

COMMUNICATIONS AND MARKETS

Transport service figures conspicuously among the work services described in the Polyptych. It can be classed among annual services. It fell into two categories: the *angaria* (plural *angariae*) for the transport of heavy loads and the *scara* (plural *scarae*) for lighter ones. Recent studies of transport services on Prüm's estates reveal that the abbey's domain formed an extensive network of communication and trafficking. This research has produced two important findings: first, that the abbey's network was both internally complex and externally open to multiple contacts in the wider economy, and second that the part played by the tenants of manses in maintaining this network gave them regular contacts with the wider economy, hence with markets.

The *angaria* was a service imposed on the majority of tenants. It consisted of the duty of transporting, once or twice a year, in an ox-drawn cart or by boat, the produce of estates, usually grain or wine, but sometimes salt, flour or pigs. The amount, frequency and distance of the transport concerned varied greatly from one estate to another: in some cases, a tenant had to take a cart-load of wine more than 100 km. It was quite common for peasants to be away from home for up to a fortnight in performing such services: that is the implication of the 'fifteen nights' service mentioned so often in the Polyptych and used sometimes in reference to transport. Often, the text also specifies the destination of the *angaria*. Usually the goods were sent to the abbey of Prüm itself, or to one of its priories – Münstereifel, St Goar, or Altrip (see Figure 34.3). Occasionally, the specified destination was a place where Prüm had a house that served as a staging-post in the transport network: for instance, Cochem, Altenahr or Metz. Only two places outside Prüm's domain are mentioned as destinations: Aachen and Worms. Clearly the main purpose of the network run through *angariae* was to take agricultural surpluses from most of the abbey's estates and concentrate them at the centres of monastic life.

The geographical range of *scarae* was more limited: they were demanded above all from tenants on estates not far from Prüm, Münstereifel and Altrip. Some 30 tenants living close to the abbey were burdened with heavier *scarae* than their neighbours, and benefited from correspondingly lighter services of other kinds. These tenants were termed *scararii*, and their function shows that the monks recognised the need to be able to mobilise the transport of light goods whenever necessary. In the Polyptych, *scarae* are described in much less detail than are *angariae*. Among items transported, there are single mentions of shirts, cloth, and salmon. Performing this service often involved the carrying of messages. A tenant might perform *scara* on horseback, on foot, or by boat. As destinations of *scarae*, the Polyptych mentions, not surprisingly, Prüm and its priories. It also mentions Duisberg and Cochem, two other places where the abbey had lands. Further, by contrast with the network maintained through *angariae*, the *scarae* network included more urban sites outside the abbey's estates: Aachen, Cologne, Bonn, Coblenz, Frankfurt and Verdun.

This sketch of Prüm's economic networks and the transport services that maintained them suggests two distinct systems. The first, based on *angariae*, was designed to provision the monastic community, while the second, based on *scarae*, was designed, at least in part, to facilitate the exchange of information and less bulky goods with the world beyond the monastery. Of the two types of transport service, the abbey devoted far more attention to *angariae* than to *scarae*. Yet that should not mislead us into thinking that the distribution of goods simply constituted an autarchic system focused on the monastery. True, there are elements of autarchy: the monks can be seen principally as consumers of goods produced on their estates and brought to them through the transport services required of their peasants. Yet the monastic economy, as reflected in the Polyptych, also presents another aspect, which is both commercial and monetary.

In the first place, on certain estates around Prüm and Altrip, market service was required of tenants whose job it was to help the monks to sell wine and salt. Part of the goods carried to the abbey or its priories was thus sold on the spot, probably to a clientele consisting of the inhabitants of the surrounding area. Though the Polyptych does not specifically mention these, corn and other grains have been shown by recent research to have been among the chief items of commerce in the Carolingian period, and so it seems possible that various kinds of grain were among the things the abbey sold to people in its neighbourhood.

Secondly, the Polyptych's chapter relating to Prüm's only salt-producing estate, which was situated in Lorraine, includes an order telling estate-managers to conduct an inquiry into the price of salt. Here the compiler shows a strong interest in this subject, and also knows something about perceptible fluctuations in salt prices. It seems clear that the monks of Prüm were in the business of selling wholesale at the best, that is, the most lucrative, time, part of their estates' produce transported by means of *angariae*. The purchasers would have been merchants rather than ordinary inhabitants, and the transactions could have been made at the nodes of economic circuits which were often situated in the urban centres of the period.

The Polyptych's fragmentary information has already revealed certain commercialised aspects of Prüm's circulatory network. A different type of source-material, namely royal charters granted to Prüm, gives further information on this subject. Frankish kings imposed various taxes on traffic throughout their realms, notably on purchases and sales as well as on the transit of goods. Prüm had already benefited from a series of exemptions. Charles the Simple's charter of 919 marked the high-point of these royal grants. On the one hand, the king ordered that at no market or port anywhere in his kingdom must any toll or sales tax be levied on the monks or their agents or their tenants who travelled about the kingdom on the abbey's business in its various forms. On the other hand, the king granted the abbey the right to establish a market, and to mint coin, at any place within its seigneurie.

It is admittedly difficult to know how far the monks of Prüm were really able to exploit these economic privileges. We have no documentary record of Prüm's rights having been put to use – no toll receipts, for instance! Nor, despite the huge progress made recently in the study of early medieval numismatics, has any coin been identified which was certainly struck on Prüm's authority in the Carolingian period. At best, all we can show is that markets operated near centres of Prüm's lordship, at Rommersheim very close to Prüm itself, for instance, and also at Münstereifel, St Goar and Altrip. Two bits of data, however, support the view that the picture of a monastery involved in a trading network – the picture conveyed by the charters – is not too far from early medieval realities.

First, some ten of Caesarius's annotations to the Polyptych relate to this subject. All of these notes stress the prosperity that Prüm had derived in the past from its economic network organised on the basis of transport services. Caesarius specifically links this network with commerce. For instance, in a note on Cochem, one of Prüm's estates on the river Mosel: 'the estate and the revenue that Prüm possessed of old are now lost and in the hands of vassals. In the old days, the abbey's wine and grain were carried to this estate to be sold here, or to be transported on to Prüm by means of the *angariae* of this place. The estates of the diocese of Worms had to perform *angariae* by boat to this same place.' This is a clear description of the way the network operated, in part through a series of exchanges. In Caesarius's view, all this belonged to the lost glory of his abbey, and he continued to explain that happy past in terms of the effective royal protection of the Carolingians. It seems permissible to regard Caesarius's testimony as supporting our picture of a ninth-century monastery at the heart of an economic system that had been to some extent commercialised.

Second, the Polyptych's frequent references to renders paid in cash show that peasants on Prüm's estates had permanent contact with money. Indeed dues in cash are specified for peasant tenants on almost every estate. Even when all allowance is made for large variations in the levels of these renders as between one tenant and another and between one estate and another, it remains the case that a tenant under Prüm's authority had to make regular payments came to at least some 10d., i.e. ten silver pennies, a year each. How else could they have acquired these coins than by selling part of the surplus of their own agricultural or artisanal produce in a market? They could easily have engaged in this trafficking on their own account while performing their transport services to the abbey. If Prüm's domain as a whole was open to exchanges, it is unsurprising that those who lived thereon, that is, more or less autonomous peasants, contrived to profit from this situation.

CONCLUSION

This chapter has not tried to claim that peasants on Prüm's domain in the late ninth century were active agents in a market economy. Agricultural techniques remained relatively primitive in the Carolingian period, and peasants were poor. They lived under lordly domination, and they were heavily burdened with services. By and large, they lived off what they produced for themselves, and led a more or less autarchic life. And yet, against those negative aspects of their existence, negative, at any rate, from the standpoint of economic development, we have to set other, positive, aspects. These peasants, remember, were assured of stability of tenure, thanks to the manse system. Even those who had to begin with tiny plots were at least tenants who enjoyed some security. As producers, peasants defended a certain autonomy despite various labour services – indeed, in part, *by means of* those services. Involved in the circulation-network organised by their lord, and specifically required to transport goods to market, peasants could profit from markets on their own account.

Historians who specialise in the history of the early Middle Ages have long debated the nature of the economy and society of their chosen period. Indeed debate today remains livelier than ever. Before committing ourselves to a judgement, we ought to bear in mind that the early medieval peasant farm, the very foundation of the socio-economic structure of that period, presents two faces to the researcher. That ambivalence is precisely what I have tried to capture in writing this account of the peasants on the estates of Prüm.

NOTES

1 I am grateful to Jinty Nelson for translating this chapter from my original French.

2 Translator's note: the French word *seigneurie*, meaning a territorial lordship, is now well acclimatised in English; Davies 1988; Faith 1997.

3 'Estate' is used in this chapter to denote a substantial area of land owned by a lord in a particular locality. Its internal organisation varied. Under the domanial regime, the estate was bi-partite, that is, divided between a demesne (French: *réserve*, German: *Salland*), more or less geographically close to the residence of the lord or his agent and farmed directly by the lord using peasant labour services, and peasant tenements cultivated by tenants on their own account in return for various dues and services to the lord; Verhulst 1995: 488–9; cf. Devroey 1993, chapter 1, using the term 'manor' for what is here called an estate.

4 'Overpopulation' is used here in a technical sense, to denote the situation in which more than one nuclear family occupied a manse when the monastic inventory was made; Goetz 1995: 470–1; Verhulst 1995: 493, 496.

5 The ninth-century polyptychs show cases of peasant marriage across legal categories: e.g. free with half-free or unfree; Goetz 1995: 460. Thus we may infer that with the passage of time, intermarriage between free and half-free or unfree peasants and resultant transmissions of peasant holdings that cut across legal categories of people, together with decisions made by estate-managers and the formation of new manses, an original hypothetically tidy fit between free manses and free tenants, less free manses and less free tenants, had gradually changed into the complex varieties that confront us in the polyptychs. On Prüm's late-ninth-century estates, this mixture in status of peasant and tenement had led to a degree of indifference to legal categories: the great majority of tenants and manses appear in the Polyptych without any such qualification. A free peasant might farm (all or part of) an unfree manse, while an unfree peasant might farm (all or part of) a free one, and a peasant of any legal category might have a tenement consisting of both free and less free manses.

BIBLIOGRAPHY

Bonnassie, P. 1990 'La croissance agricole du haut moyen âge dans la Gaule du Midi et le nord-est de la péninsule ibérique', in *La croissance agricole du haut moyen âge*, Flaran 10: Auch, pp. 13–35.

—— 1991 *From Slavery to Feudalism in South-Western Europe*, Cambridge: Cambridge University Press.

Davies, W. 1988 *Small Worlds. The village community in early medieval Brittany*, London: Duckworth.

Devroey, J.-P. 1993 *Etudes sur le grand domaine carolingien*, Aldershot: Variorum.

Goetz, H.-W. 1995 'Social and military institutions', in R. McKitterick (ed.), *The New Cambridge Medieval History*, vol. II, Cambridge: Cambridge University Press, pp. 451–80.

Faith, R. 1997 *The English Peasantry and the Growth of Lordship*, London and Washington: Leicester University Press.

Kuchenbuch, L. 1978 *Bäuerliche Gesellschaft und Klosterherrschaft im 9. Jahrhundert. Studien zur Sozialstruktur der Familia der Abtei Prüm*, Wiesbaden: Franz Steiner Verlag.

Morimoto, Y. 1988 'État et perspectives de recherches sur les polyptyques carolingiens', *Annales de l'Est* 40, pp. 99–149.

——— 1994 'Autour du grand domaine carolingien: aperçu critique des recherches récentes sur l'histoire rurale du haut moyen âge (1987–1992)', in A. Verhulst and Y. Morimoto (eds), *Économie rurale et économie urbaine au moyen âge*, Publications du Centre belge d'histoire rurale 108: Ghent and Fukuoka.

Nolden, R. 1993 ed., 'anno verbi incarnati DCCCXCIII conscriptum', *Im Jahre des Herrn 893 geschrieben. 1100 Jahre Prümer Urbar*, Trier.

Schwab, I. 1983 *Das Prümer Urbar*, Rheinische Urbare 5, Düsseldorf.

Verhulst, A. 1992 *Rural and Urban Aspects of Early Medieval Northwest Europe*, Aldershot: Variorum.

Verhulst, A. 1995 'Economic organisation', in R. McKitterick (ed.), *The New Cambridge Medieval History*, vol. II, Cambridge: Cambridge University Press, pp. 481–509.

Wickham, C. 1994 *Land and Power. Studies in Italian and European social history, 400–1200*, London: British School at Rome.

——— 1995 'Rural society in Carolingian Europe', in R. McKitterick (ed.) *The New Cambridge Medieval History*, volume II, Cambridge: Cambridge University Press, pp. 510–37

PRIVILEGE IN MEDIEVAL SOCIETIES FROM THE TWELFTH TO THE FOURTEENTH CENTURIES, OR: HOW THE EXCEPTION PROVES THE RULE

Alain Boureau

The Middle Ages were a time of privilege. This statement may seem surprising, given that the idea of privilege, vague and elusive as it is, is more often associated, both in the writings of historical actors of the eighteenth century (the *Essais sur les privilèges* of the *abbé* Sieyes in 1789 having been preceded by dozens of similar such pamphlets), and in the work of modern historians with the end of the *ancien régime*. My purpose here, nevertheless, is to develop an argument that, during the period between the twelfth century and the fourteenth, the idea of privilege played a central role in social organisation and in the ways in which law was perceived.

In common parlance, privilege seems the opposite of law: whether attached to individuals or groups, it represents an exception resulting from an arbitrary decision, new or inherited. This opposition has long provided the template for an evolutionary and progressivist vision of the relationship between individuals and the law. The triumph of democracy, in Europe and in America, brought the suppression of privilege: thus, during the French Revolution, the night of 4 August 1789, when privileges were solemnly abolished, was followed soon after, on 26 August, by the Declaration of the Rights of Man.[1] This fundamental change from the inequality of privileges to a universal equality of rights was the basis on which the whole idea of an 'ancien régime' was retrospectively constructed. Societies based on a hierarchical system of order and privilege (Descimon and Guéry 1989: 325–48) were replaced by competitive (or fraternal) societies based on class and representation (Bigliadi 1993; Dölemeyer and Mohnhapt 1997, 1999). True, the early socialists of the nineteenth century were quick to denounce the camouflaged survival of ancient privilege: under the explicit forms of public, juridical rights, privileges implicitly ensured their own continuation within the substance of social domination. In modern French, where the idea of a bourgeois class has lost its sharpness, we cheerfully speak of 'the privileged classes'. The whole sociology of Pierre Bourdieu could be read, indeed, as a decoding of implicit privileges, which go under the name of 'symbolic domination'.

This disqualification of privilege, whether in the name of a philosophy of history, or of a sociology that is a-historical, has been subject to some revision, though. An important work of Émile Lousse (Lousse 1943) was devoted to a functional account of privilege, presented as a key element in the contractual construction of the social: *ancien régime* privilege was essentially a collective thing, involving the exchange of service for remuneration that could be fiscal, material (especially consisting of landed property), or symbolic. Thus society as a whole operated in an ideal sense as a federation of differentiated groups, or, to use a metaphor that appears often in eighteenth-century arguments on corporations, like a series of interlocking rings. Lousse's study was not alone in its time. Indeed, what it so vigorously propounded were the results of a vast collective enquiry pursued since the 1930s throughout Europe into the subject of the *Ständestaat*, that is, the state built up from estates, orders, corporations and so forth. Moreover, the publication of Lousse's work in 1943, and the fact that the rest of these studies betrayed a certain sympathy for contemporary neo-corporatist regimes (Germany, Italy, France) somewhat blunted their impact. But recent work on micro-history, which has been devoted to relating even such institutions as craft-guilds, institutions which once seemed as stable as they appeared archaic, to their deep historical context, has revived interest in a functional understanding of privilege within the totality of the *ancien régime* (Cerutti 1990).

So what is the relevance of the central Middle Ages to this question of the historical meaning of privilege? We can observe, first of all, that the word 'privilege' became widespread from the twelfth century onwards both in canon law and in secular writing-offices. The *Liber Extra* compiled in 1234 on the orders of Pope Gregory IX, and which formed the second pillar of Church law right down to 1917, provides good evidence of how fashionable the idea of privilege was at that time: the whole of Book V, title 33 is devoted to it. Different legal rules defined its nature and uses. On the secular side, for instance, nearly all the official documents of King Philip Augustus of France are entitled privileges. Without bothering unduly about the precise content of a papal privilege, we can follow Gerd Tellenbach in noting the swift development of papal production of privileges: the number of papal documents issued in the tenth century is only one-fifth of that of the eleventh, and the second half of the eleventh century saw a doubling of the total in the first half (Tellenbach 1993: 68).

In the second place, the content of these privileges signalled major social and political changes, for it was through grants of privileges to communes or to monasteries that local 'liberties' were constructed. Susan Reynolds has underlined the importance of horizontal elements in society which historians had long ignored in their preoccupation with vertical and hierarchical structures (Reynolds 1997). Further, liberties or privileges engendered that collaboration between the local level and the level of the sovereign power which is probably at the root of the modern state and which, in any case, clearly announces the principle of a reciprocal exchange between service and privilege. The charter of liberties granted by Philip Augustus to the town of Tournai in 1188 offers a good example: here, the judicial and fiscal privileges conferred by the king, extensive by comparison with other contemporary grants of communal liberties, were the counterpart of the particularly heavy military services owed by a key frontier-town (Delaborde 1916: 268–74).

Third and last, a paradox: particular privileges contributed to the establishment in medieval societies of the idea and practice of a generally applicable law. The study of medieval privileges is thus part of the intellectual history of the construction of norms, at a crucial moment when two institutions, the papal Church and monarchic State, both sought to monopolise control of what the norm was. During this period, indeed, the law was everywhere and nowhere: what some historians have termed 'the legal renaissance of the twelfth century' brought about both the widespread circulation of legal texts derived from Roman imperial law, and, at the same time, the assembling and systematic comparison of the canonistic texts that formed the Church's legal tradition. In the thirteenth century, large numbers of collections of customary law (*coutumiers*) were produced. Yet all this legal literature had no binding status whatsoever. All of it remained a reference tool, which judges or advocates could use. At best, it might form the basis for an agreement between disputing parties. The shift to the idea of a law that was 'common' and binding on everyone came about slowly, but it was strengthened by the tendency of centralising institutions to reinforce it, and also by the principle of an ultimate court of appeal. But struggles and arguments over privilege also played an important role, for it was through them that ideas of sovereignty, liberty and equality came to be clarified – ideas too often falsely alleged to have been unthinkable in the Middle Ages.

Debates were lively because the ambivalence of privilege – a special favour imposed by an arbitrary power? or the just reward for a task accomplished? – was something people were conscious of, not least because it was embodied in texts from the moment when charters of liberties began to be produced on a large scale. A privilege, in its very essence, is a relative idea: an abuse in the mind of whoever is deprived of it, it is perceived as a lawful right by whoever benefits. This ambivalence is clear in Gratian's *Decretum*, the great synthesis of canon law produced *c*.1140. On the one hand, Gratian reproduces Isidore of Seville's famous etymology: 'privileges are the laws of private individuals; they are so to speak private laws. For the privilege is thus called because it is issued for a private individual.' On the other, though, he includes a letter sent by Nicholas II to the Milanese in 1059, which assigns a divine origin to the general privilege of the Roman Church:

> the Roman Church has instituted the dignity of churches of every rank. God alone has established and built that Church on the Rock of a Faith that flourished so rapidly, He who confided to the holy key-bearer of eternal life the rights of the earthly empire and also of the heavenly one. The Roman Church has thus been founded not by any kind of earthly decision, but by that Word by which heaven and earth were made and by which all the elements were created. Truly the Church makes use of His privilege and exercises His authority. That is why there can be no doubt that whoever withholds from the Church that which is its due commits an injustice. Whoever tries to deny the Roman Church the privilege conferred on it by the Head of all churches falls indubitably into heresy.[2]

This strong papal statement can be readily understood in the context of what is often called the Gregorian Reform. It was from the end of the eleventh century that the four forms of clerical privilege became firmly established: canonical privilege, privilege of court, privilege of immunity and privilege of competence. Together these effectively withdrew the cleric from the secular world's jurisdiction and from its fiscal and administrative control. From the more technical point of view of documentary production, it was one of Nicholas II's predecessors, Leo IX (1049–54), who had instituted new forms for the drawing-up of privileges. At the very heart of the Roman Church, however, there remained the memory of Isidore's etymological condemnation: thus when Pope Paschal II was forced to make the Treaty of Ponte Mammolo with the Emperor Henry V in April 1111, renouncing many of the gains made during the preceding papal–imperial conflict, the bishop and abbot of Monte Cassino, Bruno of Segni, followed by numerous members of the curia, denounced this *privilegium* made by an emperor accused of heresy as a *pravilegium* – 'a grant that was an act of depravity'.

Far beyond the particular context, this ambiguous view of privilege had a long history which we need to examine more closely if we are to pick up the thread of medieval debates. The first appearance of the Latin word privilege occurs in Cicero, who refers to a lost text of the Law of the Twelve Tables: 'The sacred laws, the Twelve Tables, forbade laws to be made for the benefit of private individuals: such is a privilege' (*Pro domo* 17, 43; cf. *De legibus* III, 44). Cicero's opinion had an immediate political thrust: in the last phase of the Republic, a protest had to be made against the forms of exception forced through by whichever political clan was in charge, and also against the Senate's laws designed *ad hoc* to secure a citizen's condemnation without a prior judgement. From the origins of the Principate, however, the word privilege began to acquire the positive connotations of a decision that brought a favourable outcome for its recipient. Privilege was a benefit, an act of grace, something additional which could not be harmful. With this grace-and-favour character went the fact that the granting of such a privilege was reserved for the highest power in the state: the Senate, and later, the *princeps* or the emperor. During the imperial period, the idea of privilege grew large, and came to absorb the related ideas of 'special right' (*ius speciale*) and 'prerogative'. In Justinian's reign, they began to use a key distinction, destined to have a great future in the Middle Ages, between 'privilege of person' and 'privilege of cause'. The latter, attached to a particular reason, or particular function, could be transmitted hereditarily, and could apply to groups (Garnsey 1970). Further, a privilege, demonstrating as it did the ruler's omnipotence and beneficence, and thanks to its lofty origin, came to constitute the noblest sort of right, alongside the imperial rescript or command. This was why the royal and imperial granting of privileges continued without interruption throughout the Middle Ages, from later Roman emperors and Merovingian kings onwards: eventually the term privilege came to denote any royal or imperial act of legislation, distinguished only by its documentary form, and quite removed from the tension that had existed during the Roman Empire between rights grounded in the law and those deriving from an act of political authority.

While the multiplication of secular privileges was due in part to the twelfth-century renaissance of Roman law, the papal privilege brought in another history: that of immunities and exceptions which, from the sixth century onwards, forbade royal judges and officials access to certain religious communities. Such a grant of immunity sometimes included a declaration of the community's independence from the jurisdiction of the local bishop. Instead of stopping to consider the specific religious context of this kind of immunity, historians for a long time saw therein the effects of the weakening of central powers forced to acknowledge the *de facto* independence of certain regions. On this view, immunities looked like a prelude to feudalism. Recent research, by contrast, has shown that immunities should be understood as symptoms of new kinds of relationship between the Church and secular powers, signalled by the creation of sacred spaces (Davies and Fouracre 1995; Rosenwein 1999). Privileges were the expression of the Church's growing autonomy, but they were also a means whereby rulers conducted the politics of gift-exchange so typical of earlier medieval kingdoms. The Papacy played no more than a marginal role in the elaboration of early medieval privileges. But a turning-point came with the various foundation-charters and confirmation-privileges of the abbey of Cluny, from the early tenth century right up to Urban II's establishment in 1095 of a veritable consecrated area around the abbey-church which was declared immune to any kind of intrusion, whether lay or episcopal. The ownership of the monastery belonged to SS Peter and Paul: that gave Cluny both a papal guarantee and practical autonomy.

In the twelfth century, the general increase in attempts to get exemption-privileges on the Cluniac model went far beyond the modest and relatively infrequent immunities of the early Middle Ages. Now, and only now, did conflicts over jurisdiction become crucial, as territorial accumulations of seigneurial power, and the vigorous extension of areas under cultivation, made land a precious commodity, while bishoprics began to take shape as clearcut blocks of territorial jurisdiction.

It is hard to pin down the relationship between ecclesiastical privilege in practice and the exercise of secular liberties. To be sure, there is plenty of evidence for interactions between the secular and religious spheres. Magna Carta, which Sir James Holt called 'a privilege extended to the whole free population of England' (Holt 1992), begins with an affirmation of the liberties of the English Church; and in 1279, one of the first decisions of Archbishop John Pecham, at the Council of Reading, was to require that the text of Magna Carta be put up on the doors of all churches to proclaim loud and clear the lawfulness of the Church's liberties. Urban or corporate privileges, though, had rhythms of their own. It would be hard to exaggerate the autonomy of the authorities that issued them, especially in the case of the Italian communes whose model for exemption granted by the *princeps* for certain privileged categories derived directly from Roman law. The city-states demonstrated their sovereignty precisely by attaching their privileges to the city government. Thus, in fourteenth-century Siena, certain categories of noble were excluded from power (a negative privilege), while the Noveschi family, sprung from a merchant-banker class that had benefited from large fiscal and judicial exemptions, established an oligarchy (Bowski 1962). The very idea of citizenship had its origins in privilege, while various political changes in the cities were produced by the extension or restriction of privileges. The history of lay privilege cannot be pursued here: it includes a huge part of the social history of the central Middle Ages, and is intimately linked with the development of sworn associations, of craft-guilds, of urban governments. What we can trace in all that is a fragmentation of laws (*jura*), rights and claims associated with a particular function, rank or dignity. Yet the construction of medieval privilege cannot be reduced to some kind of prefiguration of the 'society of orders' embodied in the *ancien régime*. For one thing, a marked tension can be seen between privilege and its opposite, the common law. Further, there was hardly any way to express ideas of political contract. It was in the Church, and more specifically, around the Papacy, that these tensions were most evident, and that solutions were formulated. It is on this terrain, then, that our exploration will proceed.

The Cluniac model of direct dependence on the Holy See contributed something particularly substantial to the rise of a papal monarchy whose real power over local churches had been quite weak until the eleventh century. It is no coincidence that the same period saw the birth of systematic canon law, and the establishment of dispensations and indulgences (Paulus 1922–3). Yet it would be wrong to exaggerate the significance of whatever direct dependence privileges created: exemptions were in fact nearly always open to debate and dispute, and became subjects of compromise-settlements and divisions whose practical effects – rights of visitation, fiscal and judicial benefits, freedom of abbatial elections, and so forth – meant a lot more than institutional independence or the link with the Holy See.

It was, above all, judicial procedures that increased papal power over local churches and firmly entrenched the idea (still only incipient in Gratian's 'private enterprise' work) of a common and binding law. The growth of appellate jurisdiction, evident from the mid-twelfth century on, drew many monks and bishops to Rome. The papal Curia played the game of refereeing for all it was worth: look at the 33 chapters of the *Liber Extra*'s title on Privileges, and you find that papal decisions, selected from a very large number of decretal letters, were split more or less 50/50 between those who favoured each of the two camps, bishops and monks. It was as if Gregory IX had deliberately expressed, through Raymond of Peñafort's work of compilation, the serene impartiality of papal justice. This nice balance corresponded to the need to marry the Papacy's direct power and the Church's fundamentally episcopal structure. Moreover, the judicial practice of debate over privileges came to constitute a veritable legal apprenticeship. Papal umpiring on privileges standardised procedures and forms of proof, and objectivised them. Litigants increasingly had to master the distinction between possession and ownership, the rules on the effects of prescription, the criteria for assessing the genuineness of documents (Boureau 2000). In the course of the twelfth century, there was a notable improvement in the quality of forgers' work: vice's tribute to judicial virtue. A striking instance of this pedagogy by privilege was given by Innocent III in a decretal of 1209 incorporated in the *Liber Extra*,[3] which offered a real lesson in judicial logic and grammar where the drafting of privileges was concerned. The pope had to decide on the interpretation of a privilege granted to the monks of St Bertin, which read: 'We grant that the right to desig-nate the abbot of the monastery of St Sylvain at Auxy-le-Château shall remain in your hands according to the custom of former times.' Well, noted Innocent, 'this phrase "according to the custom of former times" may be understood in a causal sense or in a conditional one: it could refer equally well to the personal [the verb "we grant"] or to the non-personal [the Latin infinitive corresponding to the verb "remain"]'. In the former case (the causal sense), the papal judgement would acknowl-edge a right; in the latter (the conditional sense), the papal judgement would accept the privilege only on condition that the alleged cause, namely custom, could in fact be verified. The simple form of the privilege raised itself to the level of a juridical text so that it could be minutely examined according to formal legal rules.

The skilful balancing-act performed by the Papacy between episcopal rules and monastic privileges, beneficial as it was to the establishment of a common jurisdiction and a common law, and based less on grand theoretical claims than on the everyday practice of chicanery, was ruined in the thirteenth century by the growth of the mendicant orders. Like the Cluniacs, the mendicants were the beneficiaries of a direct dependence on the Papacy. But while in the Cluniacs' case, that dependence had remained quite formal, and in jurisdictional disputes constituted only one argument among others, the Dominicans and Franciscans made vigorous use of a long series of privileges allowing them not just to extract themselves from episcopal control but to open up gaps in what was properly the domain of bishops and priests, namely, the field of pastoral care (preaching, confession, the administration of the sacraments). The story of this steady process of intrusion, which continued with few interruptions from the end of Innocent IV's pontificate onwards, is a well-known one, and there is no time to re-tell it here. But it is worth pausing for a moment at a single significant episode: in 1281, Pope Martin IV published the bull *Ad fructus uberes*, which allowed mendicants the universal right to hear confessions and to grant absolutions, without needing the authorisation of either the bishop or the parish priest. This privilege provoked a lengthy dispute between the mendicants and the bishops. And the bishops were strongly supported by the masters of the University of Paris who found here the ideal grounds for picking another fight with their rivals and enemies the friars who had used papal help to defeat the masters on two previous occasions, in 1253–6, and in 1267–70 (Congar 1961–2). The dispute was long and intense because Martin IV's bull was, like so many classic privileges, equivocal: while the first paragraph established the privilege and justified it in terms of the spiritual benefits supplied by the friars' cooperation, the second paragraph added that 'nevertheless' (this *nihilominus* became the object of infinite semantic and syntactical glossing by both camps)[4] the canon 'Utriusque sexus' of the Fourth Lateran Council (1215) remained in force, according to which the parish priest had to hear annual confessions from all parishioners. The contradiction was glaring, and it caused immense difficulties especially over the question of whether or not a sacrament could be repeated. A succession of popes down to 1290 refused to clarify what *Ad fructus uberes* meant. This *dissimulatio* (a legal term denoting a judge's deliberate decision on various grounds to leave critical elements of a case in suspense) raised, quite justifiably, a lively debate on the relationship of common law to privilege. The seculars, whose cleverest spokesman was Henry of Ghent, set out a strict hierarchy of the sources of law, in which divine law, embodied in Scripture, held the top place, above the norms promulgated by the four ecumenical councils of the universal Church, the sentences of the Fathers, and the canons of synods and councils. The papal privilege thus had less force than the canons of Lateran IV. The bishops' view of what was lawful rested on tradition, for they were the successors of the Apostles and the parish priests were the successors of the Disciples. The pope's authority was simply that of the successor of the first of the Apostles. On the mendicant side, where the most active participant was the Franciscan Richard of Mediavilla, the idea of institution prevailed over both tradition and inscription in Holy Writ. Divine Providence would provide for humankind's salvation according to the urgent requirements of different times. The Franciscans, for whom the influence of Joachim of Fiore and his followers had brought a historicisation of their conception of Providence, saw the status of the Apostles no longer as the origin of a continuous transmission, but as a model long-forgotten but reactivated by the coming of St Francis. The apostolic life could be restored through the interaction of Divine Grace with the voluntary choice of a group of chosen ones. For the Franciscans, then, Martin IV's privilege in no sense represented an accommodation: rather, it expressed the institutional recognition of their own Order as one providentially established in response to urgent need.

The debate over Martin IV's privilege was a critical moment. It summoned into being a whole arsenal of political and theological concepts essential to modernity. While Henry of Ghent's arguments prepared the way for the conciliarism of the fourteenth century, those of the mendicants, which linked privilege, papal sovereignty and divine Mission, laid the foundations of papal absolutism, one of whose strongest proponents was Duns Scotus. Both sides discovered, at the same time and in rivalry with each other, the foundations of a certain individualism that was legal and also political. For Henry of Ghent, the radical rejection of the distinction between absolute power and ordained power led to the idea of subjective natural right (Tierney 1997). The Francisans' theology of divine mission, for its part, privileged the chosen over against common law and tradition alike. The Franciscan vow indeed constituted a kind of individual privilege, but one that was proclaimed by the individual himself. The Franciscans were delighted to take up again the famous papal decretal *Due sunt leges*,[5] produced by Urban II (former Cluniac and author, as noted above, of Cluny's decisive privilege), which opposed the public law, binding on all, to the 'private law' of the Holy Spirit, which he declared 'worthier' than public law because it bound only to God. This was the complete reversal of the idea of 'private law', as found in Cicero and Isidore. The possibility of an individual and universal privilege (the forerunner of a subjective natural right) meant that, in the modern period, the Dutch and American Revolutions could be brought about in the name of respect for privilege.

A few years later, theological debates over the Immaculate Conception of Mary gave the opportunity for new enquiries into the relationship of privilege and law. From the first texts expounding immaculist devotion in the twelfth century, right down to Pius IX's bull instituting the dogma in 1854, the Immaculate Conception of Mary was presented as a privilege. This privilege prevailed over the most universal of universal laws, the natural (and even genetic) law of original sin. The opposite doctrine, in the thirteenth century, allowed only a dispensation from that law: Mary was sanctified *in utero*. This dispensation was rare but not unprecedented, for there were also the cases of Jeremiah and John the Baptist. The new doctrine, by contrast, meant that at the moment of the copulation of Mary's parents, the universal law did not apply. When some Franciscans worked out the most extreme system of justification for papal absolutism, the defence of privilege against common law, and usable illustrations of privilege, mattered a great deal. Ten years after the mendicants' battle against the bishops, it was hardly a coincidence that Duns Scotus was both the chief promoter of the cause of Mary the Immaculate, and the proponent of the profound theoretical distinction between God's absolute power and His ordained power – a distinction whose political offspring were to be so significant.

But it is a less well-known English theologian, the Carmelite John Baconthorpe (*c*.1290–1348) who offers us a clearer understanding of the political implications of the definition of privilege and its relationship to the new definition of papal sovereignty, derived from divine sovereignty. Baconthorpe's case is all the more interesting in that he was responsible for producing a variant version of the doctrine of the Immaculate Conception. Around 1320, in his *Commentary on Peter Lombard* (Saggi 1955: 218–303), Baconthorpe pitched himself directly and energetically against the new doctrine. Then, around 1330, in his *Quodlibetic Questions* and in his *Commentary on Matthew*, he adopted a conciliatory position. Finally, around 1340, he opted for an immaculatist view in his *Canonical Questions on Peter Lombard*. Another kind of evolution crossed with the first: while in his early work, Baconthorpe used theological, exegetical and scientific arguments, from 1330 onwards, in the two later stages of his thinking on the Virgin, law also came into play.

Thus, when writing his *Quodlibets*, Baconthorpe seems to have taken a politico-juridical turn, even though it is impossible to say whether this shift reflected a new direction in his career and intellectual interests, or if it was related, instead, to a new ecclesiological or political context. Towards 1330, Baconthorpe found himself in the curious situation of having to defend the legitimacy of the Feast of 8 of December (*Quodlibet*, Question III, 13), while still asserting that Christ alone had been conceived without sin (the immediately preceding Question III, 12). The juridical provocation to which Baconthorpe responded was the assertion of Duns Scotus, William de Ware and Pierre Auriol that Mary had been subjected to original sin by law (*de jure*) but not by fact (*de facto*). Baconthorpe contested this distinction: 'In law, where no privilege runs *de facto*, . . . it is foolhardy and against the nature of the law to allege a privilege *de facto*. For that would be to speak of privilege as if it privatised the law.' I have used the anachronistic verb 'to privatise', to translate 'legem privans', which goes back to Isidore. What Baconthorpe presents here is a restrictive conception of privilege: it recalls the severe warnings of St Bernard to Pope Eugenius III against the growth of exemptions far more than it does papal attempts, from Innocent III onwards, to produce a juridical construction of privilege, such as we find in Gregory IX's *Liber Extra*. At this stage in his thinking, Baconthorpe never referred to this source, although he used many citations from Gratian's *Decretum*.

In reaction against the juridical monstrosity concocted by Duns Scotus, Baconthorpe, writing a century after the *Liber Extra* was produced, set out a firm and precise definition of the lawfulness of privilege. In the first place, fact could not create law, because law, which is punitive in its essential nature, arises from a cause: 'transgression is the cause of law'. Law, in the most general sense, was instituted as a substitute for natural reason, weakened by original sin. Law is therefore caused both by universal fault and by an actual fault. Hence, what is perceived as a privilege is simply a case of the absence of a cause. If Christ is exempt from original sin, that was because his parents did not sleep together. Mary was conceived by her parents' carnal act: therefore, law applies. The second condition of privilege is that it has to be established 'according to a determined form' (*in certa forma*). In Mary's case, this form is not to be found in the Bible. In the third place, a privilege must specify explicitly the category of its beneficiaries. In the Bible we find a privilege granted to Mary which observes this condition, but this privilege relates only to sanctification *in utero*, as in the cases of Jeremiah and John the Baptist. In the fourth place, a privilege of exemption must specify the personal names of the beneficiaries. Only Christ fulfils these four criteria so far as the absence of original sin is concerned.

By means of some spectacularly acrobatic juridical and theological speculation, in his *Canonical Questions on Book IV of the Sentences* Baconthorpe rejoined the immaculatist camp. The first article of Distinction II, 3 affirms that Jesus alone was exempted from 'the law instituted by God' or 'the instituted common law'. Article 2 makes clear what Mary's status is. She was exempted from the common law in respect of the fault or stain transmitted by her parents, but not in respect of the *necessity* of contracting fault. In other words, the link between necessity and its application, between the cause and the effect, has been broken. This necessity has been extinguished (*extincta*). In fact, the stain of the soul passes through the body wherein lies the cause and necessity of contamination. This solution involves nothing really surprising: it hardly differs from Duns Scotus's distinction between the situation *de jure* and the situation *de facto*.

Baconthorpe's reply is firmly set out in a statement backed by a number of different but convergent proofs: 'Speedily (*mox*) by a special privilege, at the moment of conception, the cause and the necessity of contracting original sin were extinguished in the Mother of God, in such a way that, by a private right, she did not contract that original sin which is termed fault and stain on the soul, although in other respects she remained under the common law, as I have said elsewhere.' This, then, is another invocation of privilege, but what is used now is the dossier of the *Liber Extra*, or rather in the *Liber Sextus*, which was generally favourable to the idea of a papal monopoly of authority with the force of law superior to the Law. There could be found a collection of citations, already in widespread use (so far as the *Liber Extra* went) during the disputes surrounding Martin IV's privilege, centring on the idea that the sovereign's beneficence must know no limit. A single example neutralises the juridical notion of causality established in the texts of the preceding phase. The transgression, as we recall, caused the law, made law appear; privilege could never suppress this fundamental bond. For this, Baconthorpe substituted a scenario in which the cause gets confused neither with the crime nor with the transgression. A location intended for use as a cult-site but which has not been consecrated remains profane. The lack of consecration does not in itself constitute a sin, but it is the potential cause of a sin, should a priest dare to celebrate a service in that place. There we have an instance of a cause 'of occasion', the theory of which had been developed in the thirteenth century by Roger Bacon and Henry of Ghent. Thereafter, what could slide in between cause and occasion, and neutralise the intention behind the cause, was privilege.

It was necessary to move from this possibility, which reinstalled privilege within the law, to a superior causality which located privilege above the law. We have seen that Mary enjoyed a privilege through an effect of private right (*jus privatum*). Here the 'private' loses its negative connotation. Isidorian etymology ('what privatises', 'what diminishes') is abandoned, and the private is understood, instead, as exceptional, justified by some higher reason. Baconthorpe re-used the arguments of theorists of individual inspiration, for instance, the theory of prophecy developed by Hugh of Saint-Cher, which had acquired a powerful new contemporary relevance amid the Franciscan disputes of the late thirteenth century. Baconthorpe referred to the private law of the Holy Spirit: 'As for someone who is guided by the private law of the Holy Spirit, no reason can require that he be constrained by the public law which has been established for transgressors'. In Mary's case, the superior cause justifying the grant of privilege is Providence itself: Mary was to bear God in her womb.

Baconthorpe then proceeds to a complete reversal of his earlier conception of the Law. The private law, or privilege, a distributive law, an exception by definition, directly inspired by the Holy Spirit, is superior in dignity to the common law whose general character pertains precisely to its punitive and human function. Baconthorpe's argument on the divine privilege granted to Mary in fact highlights two characteristic features of temporality (that is, existence in the world of time) which had already been sketched in the thought of Innocent IV (Melloni 1990). Baconthorpe puts the case with firmness and clarity: sovereign power is justified by a providential mission in the future and also by its continual exercise of Creation in this world of the past and the present.

Returning to the question of Mary's providential mission, and the source of her privilege, we observe that one of the many biblical texts announcing the Virgin's future role is Genesis 3: 15, where God tells the serpent: 'I will put enmity between thee and the woman and between thy seed and her seed. She shall bruise thy head.'[6] This prophecy, Baconthorpe comments, cannot relate to any woman born of the flesh, for 'such a woman would be unable to withhold from the Devil the capital right (*jus capitale*) that he wields over mankind because all human beings are conceived by semen and by copulation. The Devil's right arises from the necessity of human beings' contracting original sin'. Thus it was indeed Mary who was predestined and privileged so that she might bruise the serpent's head. The term *jus capitale* denotes precisely the right of life and death, or, to use medieval terms, high justice which was an essential preliminary to sovereignty (and we know what huge efforts late medieval and early modern monarchies devoted to the recovery of rights of high justice). By a privilege, Mary turned back against the Devil the very right he exercised over the heads of ordinary men, that is, men condemned by the Devil to spiritual death. Mary's mission, directed to redemption through Christ, also had a juridical and political meaning: it constituted a snatching of sovereignty, the power of life and death, from the Enemy of mankind. In a nutshell: the privileged woman passed on her privilege and, by using the private right that established her mission, performed a pre-eminent service for the Public Good.

The second essential feature of sovereignty shows up clearly in another argument based on Biblical exegesis. What matters here is to grasp the meaning of the word *mox*, 'speedily', which indicates the time of the process through which the cause was extinguished. Baconthorpe pondered the meaning of the opening words of Genesis (1: 2): 'The earth was without form, and void.' But how was it possible to imagine a state prior to, preliminary to, that of form, when the Creation had not yet taken place? A century earlier, Robert Grosseteste had reflected on this silence in the biblical text, and on this had based a non-Aristotelian ontology of creating light. Grosseteste's theory had considerable influence on English theologians and natural philosophers, thanks to John Pecham, and perhaps had some effect on Baconthorpe too. Before the Creation, matter and form did not exist. Nevertheless, the biblical expression, the famous *tohu-bohu* (Hebrew: *tohuwabohu*) presupposes a sort of amorphous existence in the very space where there ought to be the 'nothing' (*nihil*) implied by the concept of Creation *ex nihilo*. To talk about, or to imagine, Creation, we have to represent it as a chain of cause and effect: that is, a cause (or necessity) indicating a negative state, a lack of form, implies the positive state that is to follow, for it moves from before to after, leading to a state of unformed matter. But this 'before-and-after' unfolds 'not according to time, but according to the order of origin', for time itself must have been created by God. Even if Baconthorpe limits his exegetical justification for the ontological primacy of privilege over law to the moment of primordial Creation, it is easy to see how the argument fitted the idea of permanent sovereignty, whether God's or the prince's, through the idea of continuous creation, whether of the world or of the *regnum*.

This second feature of sovereignty takes into account both the Creation, and the ongoing movement of the world in a sequence of change. Going back to a term that played a key role in Innocent IV's doctrine, I would like to call this feature Institution. Papal absolutism, in its gradual development from Innocent III to Boniface VIII, was based on this idea of a permanent institution of the law through its definition and promulgation by a series of popes. The bishops in the great dispute of 1281–90 kept setting against this doctrine a rival one, the idea of Christ's institution of the Church and of the Truth, in other words, the designation of the Twelve Apostles and of the 72 disciples. Baconthorpe's key contribution in his discussion of Mary was to reconsider the doctrine of Institution from the point of view of the subjects (common or privileged) of a sovereign power.

This brief intellectual history of medieval privilege has pointed up the emergence of certain fundamental ideas which I have labelled, perhaps rather anachronistically, 'sovereignty', 'citizenship', 'public good'. What the arguments in favour of privilege achieved, above all, was to make the idea of *positive law* at home in Europe. This was an essentially medieval idea. Its emergence as a term in tension with that of natural law can be observed at the beginning of the twelfth century. In Roman law, such an opposition would have been virtually meaningless, for there, incontestably, 'nature' was always instituted, and never prior to law (Thomas 1991: 201–27), except in the purely theoretical time-gaps of juridical fiction. Medieval Christianity, by contrast, had to introduce divine or natural law among the sources of law. On the other hand, positive law denoted law that came from human sources, whether arbitrary or customary. Otto Brunner in his famous book *Land und Herrschaft*, published in 1939 (Brunner 1992), claimed that the distinction between positive law and natural law could never acclimatise itself in Europe nor could it get beyond the limits of purely theoretical discussion, because, in the concrete reality of disputes, the idea of law was fundamentally rooted in the land, or in the people who lived on the land. But the continual practice of legal chicanery together with debates over secular and religious privileges – privileges which rested on both human decision and providential mission – conferred on positive law, so to speak, its letters of nobility: in other words, made it thoroughly respectable. The legal norm could now be thought of as something established at a moment in time; yet this no longer implied that there had been something lacking, or something limited, before: instead, it meant that the divine Will had made a detour into history. It would be wrong, nevertheless, to impute to the Middle Ages a unanimous and fervent adherence to the doctrine of privilege. Our illustrative material has shown that from the beginnings of systematic canonistic thought, any particular privilege became a point of tension between the two senses of the word 'privilege': was it a personal favour or the selection of a worthy individual? an arbitrary act of will, or an appointment to a special mission? The slow triumph of the society of orders in modern times, something social historians have to explain, certainly weakened this tension but did not remove it completely. It reappeared when privilege, having become fossilised, could no longer be used to express or document acceptable forms of cooperation between social groups.

NOTES

1 The 'immunities and privileges' mentioned in the American Constitution of 1787 reflect, beneath the apparently different terminology, an idea quite similar to that of 'the rights of man', in the specific context of inter-state relations within the federation: 'The Citizens of each State shall be entitled to all Privileges and Immunities of Citizens in the several States', Article IV, ch.2, clause 1. Note here the defensive character of individual rights, typical of the American way of defining relations between individuals and the political community.
2 D. 22, c. 1: Friedberg 1879–81: i. 73.
3 X 5.40.25: Friedberg 1879–81: ii. 922-3.
4 Cf. Linehan 1997: 15-16.
5 C. 19 q. 2 c. 2: Friedberg 1879–81: i. 839.
6 Baconthorpe's reading of the Vulgate takes Eve to be the subject of the verb 'shall bruise'; in the Authorised Version, the serpent is the subject.

REFERENCES

Bigliadi, M. (1993) 'Contributo a una teoria del "benefici" politici e sociali', *Filosofia politica* 7/2: 251–73.
Boureau, A. (2000) 'How law came to the monks: the use of law in English society at the beginning of the thirteenth century', *Past & Present* 167: 29–74.
Bowski, W. M. (1962) 'The *Buon Governo* of Siena (1287–1355): a medieval Italian oligarchy', *Speculum* 37: 368–81.
Brunner, O. (1992), trans. H. Kaminsky and J. Van Horn Melton, *Land and Lordship: structures of governance in medieval Austria*, Philadelphia: University of Pennsylvania Press.
Cerutti, S. (1990) *La Ville et les métiers. Naissance d'un langage corporatif (Turin, XVIIe–XVIIIe siècle)*, Paris: Éditions de l'École des hautes études en sciences sociales.
Congar, Y. (1961-2) 'Aspects ecclésiologiques de la querelle entre mendiants et séculiers dans la seconde moitié du XIIIe siècle et le début du XIVe siècle', *Archives d'Histoire Doctrinale et Littéraire du Moyen Age* 36: 35–161.
Davies, W. and P. Fouracre (eds) (1995) *Property and Power in the Early Middle Ages*, Cambridge: Cambridge University Press.
Delaborde, H. (1916) *Recueil des actes de Philippe Auguste roi de France*, i, Paris: Imprimerie Nationale.

Descimon, R. and A. Guéry (1989) 'Privilèges: la législation de la société', in A. Burguière and J. Revel (eds) *Histoire de la France*, ii, Paris: Seuil.

Dölemeyer, B. and H. Mohnhapt (eds) (1997, 1999) *Das Privileg im europäischen Vergleich*, 2 vols, Frankfurt am Main: Klostermann.

Friedberg, Ae. (1879–81) *Corpus iuris canonici*, 2 vols, Leipzig: Tauchnitz.

Garnsey, P. (1970) *Social Status and Legal Privilege in the Roman Empire*, Oxford: Clarendon Press.

Holt, J. C. (1992) *Magna Carta* (2nd edn), Cambridge: Cambridge University Press.

Linehan, P. (1997) *The Ladies of Zamora*, Manchester: Manchester University Press.

Lousse, E. (1943) *La Société d'Ancien Régime*, Louvain: Bibliothèque de l'Université.

Melloni, A. (1990) *Innocenzo IV. La concezione e l'esperienza della cristianità come regimen unius personae*, Genoa: Marietti.

Paulus, N. (1922-3) *Geschichte des Ablasses im Mittelalter*, Paderborn: F. Schöningh.

Reynolds, S. (1997) *Kingdoms and Communities in Western Europe, 900–1300* (2nd edn), Oxford: Clarendon Press.

Rosenwein, B. (1999) *Negotiating Space. Power, restraint, and privileges of immunity in early medieval Europe*, Ithaca and London: Cornell University Press.

Saggi, L. (ed.) (1955) 'Ioannis Baconthorpe textus de Immaculata Conceptione', *Carmelus* 2: 218-303.

Tellenbach, G. (1993) *The Church in Western Europe from the Tenth to the early Twelfth Century*, Cambridge: Cambridge University Press.

Thomas, Y. (1991) *Théologie et droit dans la science politique de l'État moderne*, Rome: École française de Rome.

Tierney, B. (1997) *The Idea of Natural Rights. Studies on natural rights, natural law and church law, 1150–1624*, Atlanta, GA: Scholars Press.

WHAT DID THE TWELFTH-CENTURY RENAISSANCE *MEAN*?

Jacques Le Goff

The idea of renaissance, which Jacob Burckhardt's *Civilization of the Renaissance in Italy* (1860) implanted so securely in European historiography, appeared to have condemned the medieval period to languish forever in the dungeon of 'the Dark Ages' to which Petrarch, the sixteenth-century humanists and, most inexorably of all, the scholars of the Enlightenment, from Leibnitz to Voltaire, had consigned it. Against Voltaire's judgment, issued in his *Essay on Manners* (1756), no appeal seemed possible: 'The whole of Europe lay sunk in this debased state until the sixteenth century, and even then only emerged through frightful convulsions.'

Nor, despite appearances, did Romanticism succeed in rediscovering the light of the Middle Ages. In fact, all it did was to pierce these traditional shadows with a few bright shafts. Lessing put it well: 'The night of the Middle Ages, yes indeed! But it was a night shining with stars.' Michelet himself, after imagining the Middle Ages as 'beautiful', plunged them back into darkest gloom. In the first edition of his *History of France*, written between 1833 and 1844, Michelet saw three great flashes of light in the Middle Ages: the Barbarians, Gothic art, and national consciousness. 'I like this word "barbarians" – I welcome it. Yes, it means "bursting with new sap, full of life and cheerfulness".' Secondly, Michelet contrasted classical art, 'old art, which adored the physical', with 'modern art', that is, medieval art, Gothic art (barbarism had become a positive value), 'the child of soul and spirit'. And thirdly, the Middle Ages saw the realisation of 'that great progressive interior movement of the national soul' in the fourteenth and fifteenth centuries, from Jacques Bonhomme to Joan of Arc, from the peasant 'goodman', to the peasant-woman, rebels both (Le Goff 1977: 19–45).

What glimmer of light is there in the twelfth century, though? None, none at all. For in Michelet's vision, 'the beautiful Middle Ages' did not belong to the culture of the powerful but to the soul of the people: 'we other barbarians have a natural advantage – the upper classes may have culture but we have so much more of the warmth of life!' If the medieval period was one of greatness, that derived from the union of religion with the people. 'The Church at that time was the people's home . . . Religious cult was a tender dialogue between God, the Church and the people, expressing one and the same thinking.' But Michelet's 'beautiful Middle Ages' waned bit by bit. In 1855, he abandoned them, rejecting 'the bizarre and monstrous and

amazingly artificial medieval condition'. His deliverance came not through the
Renaissance but through the Reformation, and especially through Luther: 'it was
entirely salutary for me to live with that great heart who said No to the Middle
Ages'.

Yet Burckhardt's enthronement of the Renaissance did not take long to evoke
doubts in the minds of some historians. In the late nineteenth and early twentieth
centuries, there was a reaction in favour of the Middle Ages. Its chief manifestation was paradoxical, however. These new Middle Ages stole from the Renaissance
its title, its sign, its proud banner. These new Middle Ages did not invent the
Renaissance as it appeared in the fifteenth and especially the sixteenth centuries,
defined, as it had been then, in opposition to the whole preceding medieval period:
they invented a string of earlier renaissances, including one great Renaissance of
their own. It was Charles Homer Haskins who fixed its date firmly in the book
he published in 1927, *The Renaissance of the Twelfth Century*. Haskins explained in
his Preface: 'To the most important of the earlier revivals the present volume is
devoted, the Renaissance of the Twelfth Century, which is often called the Medieval
Renaissance' (Haskins 1927: viii).

This idea flourishes more strongly than ever today, and I want to devote this
chapter to a discussion of four problems it raises: (1) Were twelfth-century people,
or anyway the most distinguished twelfth-century scholars, conscious of living in
an age of renewal? (2) What was the nature of this renaissance? Was it a rediscovery
of classical Antiquity, a return to Antiquity, or was it a creative movement, a birth
rather than a re-birth? Was it, to repeat the question asked by Peter von Moos, a
Renaissance or a century of Enlightenment (von Moos 1989)? (3) Was it limited to
the realm of intellectual high culture, that is, to philosophy, theology, science and
art? Or was it associated with more general creative impulses that were also economic,
social and political? If so, was it an aspect or a consequence of those wider impulses?
(4) Accepting the idea and the label, when did this Renaissance begin and end?

First, then, were twelfth-century scholars aware of their own intellectual superiority over the great thinkers of Antiquity? Modern historians have found support
for the idea that they were, in a famous but difficult passage in John of Salisbury's
Metalogicon, written *c.*1159. Here John purported to quote a famous teacher, Bernard
of Chartres, who had been chancellor of the cathedral school from 1119 to 1126:
'We are like dwarfs sitting on the shoulders of giants. Our gaze can thus extend more
widely and reach further than theirs. It is not that we see better than they did,
of course, nor that our own height gives us any advantage. It is rather that we are
carried and raised up by the giants' lofty stature' (Webb 1929: 136). The dwarfs
were the *moderni*, the giants the *antiqui*. We have got used to thinking of 'the ancients'
as referring particularly to the writers of pagan Antiquity, hence of the twelfth-
century renaissance as consisting first and foremost of a return to Greek and Latin
philosophers, poets and grammarians, and Roman historians. True, the chapter of
the *Metalogicon* (iii. 4) in which John's comment on Bernard's metaphor appears, is
devoted to Aristotle's *Peri hermeneias*. True, M.-D. Chenu thought of the twelfth
century as an age when a variety of platonisms bloomed (Chenu 1957: 108–41).
True, Ovid's *Art of Love* so seduced twelfth-century poets and writers of romances
that the period has been termed an Ovidian age: Chrétien of Troyes plagiarised *The*

Art of Love, while the Cistercian Aelred of Rievaulx, and Peter of Blois, who was John of Salisbury's student and a member of the scholarly circle at the archiepiscopal court of Thomas Becket (the 'eruditus Sanctus Thomas'), ransacked Cicero's treatise *On Friendship* (Paré, Brunet, Tremblay 1933: 48).

Yet the term 'moderns' was applied, still more significantly, to theologians and Christian 'authorities'. The *Liber pancrisis*, an 'all-gold' anthology of citations treasured as authorities, added to the sayings of the Fathers – Augustine, Jerome, Ambrose, Gregory, Isidore and Bede – those of writers here termed 'modern masters' (*magistri moderni*), such as William of Champeaux (who taught at St-Victor near Paris from 1108 to 1113, then became bishop of Châlons-sur-Marne), Ivo of Chartres (died *c*.1116), Anselm of Laon (died 1117) and his brother Ralf. What is important here is not so much the adding on to authorities of ancient vintage other authorities of recent times, but the nature of these 'modern' ones. These recent authorities were masters (*magistri*) in the urban schools, which, at the beginning of the twelfth century, were often still episcopal schools. At the close of that century, these men were thought to be re-embodied, so to speak, above all in the masters of the budding universities. M-D. Chenu has shown very clearly how these new authorities, known as *magistralia*, gained importance during the twelfth century not in opposition to but alongside the ancient ones, the *authentica* (Chenu 1957: 351–65). The challenge posed by the moderns lay not in rejecting the ancients, or trying to prove them inferior, but in denying them a monopoly on doctrinal authority. In the ninth century, Walhfrid Strabo, one of the great men of the so-called 'Carolingian Renaissance' (the first of the medieval renaissances) spoke of his own age as 'modern times' (*saeculum modernum*). Yet where that earlier 'renaissance' had really failed, the twelfth-century philosophers and theologians succeeded in imposing a new periodisation of knowledge and of what counted as authorities. The age of the Fathers was over, no question about it: the age of the masters had arrived. Scholasticism began to hold sway.

John of Salisbury's story about Bernard of Chartres, with the metaphor of the dwarfs mounted on the shoulders of giants, was to become a commonplace among writers of the second half of the twelfth century and the early thirteenth. It has been interpreted in different ways, even in ways that are diametrically opposed: on the one hand, it has been said to convey the overwhelming superiority of the Ancients, on the other hand, to assert the superiority of the Moderns, even to imply an idea of progress. We should note at the outset that this second interpretation simply develops a view expressed in the sixth century by the great grammarian Priscian whose work was well-known to twelfth-century scholars: 'quanto juniores, tanto perspicaciores' ('the younger they are, the more perspicacious') (Ladner 1982: 8). Twelfth-century writers themselves seem to have veered between the two positions. John of Salisbury, the most eminent of them, asserted at one point elsewhere in the *Metalogicon*, 'I have not thought it worthwhile to quote the Moderns, whom I have no hesitation in preferring most of the time to the Ancients.' At another point, he asks, 'Who today is satisfied with what Aristotle teaches in the *Peri hermeneias*?' Yet John also says, 'Though as far as meaning goes, the Moderns and the Ancients are as good as each other, what is old is more worthy of veneration' ('venerabilior est vetustas') (Webb 1929: 3–4, 135–6). Among those twelfth-century writers who, implicitly or explicitly, cite the saying of Bernard of Chartres, most tend to affirm the superiority of the Ancients. This is the case, as Edouard Jeauneau rightly observed, with two of the most innovative and combative thinkers of the twelfth century: Peter Abelard and William of Conches. Abelard, whom John of Salisbury also quotes, says that it would be easy to be 'a man of his time', to write a book about logic which would not be inferior in form or content to those of the Ancients. Nevertheless he adds: 'but it would be impossible, or at least very difficult, for such a [modern] philosopher to raise himself . . . to the rank of an authority'. He goes on: 'Our age benefits from what it gains from the ages that went before it. It often knows more – yet that superiority comes not from its own talents (*ingenium*) but from the fact that it depends on another's strength and on the vast wealth of its ancestors.' According to William of Conches, one of the great masters of the School of Chartres: 'Priscian rightly said that the Moderns are more perspicacious than the Ancients, not that they are wiser. The Ancients only had their own writings at their disposal. We, however, possess all their writings and, in addition, all that has been written from the beginning right up until our own times. Furthermore, we have more perspicacity than they had, but no more wisdom. Much greater wisdom is indeed required to discover something new. That is why we are like a dwarf perched on the shoulders of a giant. . . . We see more things than the Ancients because our modest writings are added to their great ones.' The conclusion is clear: 'The Ancients were better than the Moderns' (Jeauneau 1967: 84; Jeauneau 1968: 23–6).

One last example, which brings in a further dimension. It occurs in a letter of Peter of Blois: 'How the dogs bark! How the pigs grunt! For my own part, I am always full of enthusiasm for the writings of the Ancients. . . . We are all of us like dwarfs on the shoulders of giants. Thanks to them, we see further than they could see when, attaching ourselves to the works of the Ancients, we give new life to their finest phrases' (Le Goff 1993: 14). This is not merely a claim for the superiority of the Ancients, it is, above all, a demand that they should be studied, because this is how the Moderns can surpass them.

We are now in a position to pin down just what the superiority of the Moderns over the Ancients meant, and also to see its limits. It is a quantitative superiority. It stems from a cumulative conception of learning and of thought. It shows itself in the field of accumulated knowledge that is more plentiful and more penetrating, but not in the field of wisdom. What does that mean? On the one hand, the Moderns suffer by not having the advantage of the prestige of antiquity already affirmed in the Old Testament: 'With the ancient is wisdom' (Job XII, 12). Yet is this not at the same time an incitement to the Moderns to acquire wisdom as well, on the model of biblical and pagan wisdom? Is it not an invitation to the Moderns to crown their learning, the fruit of the liberal arts and theology, with the making of a wisdom whose twin sources are biblical exegesis, that is, the perfecting of an understanding (*lectura*) of Holy Writ (the *sacra pagina*), and philosophical thought which is more or less independent of theology?

Was not the twelfth century a great age of the renewal of biblical exegesis, starting with the work of the thinkers of St-Victor, Paris, as Beryl Smalley demonstrated so well (Smalley 1968; Smalley 1983: 83–195)? Was it not also a great age of affirmation of a specifically Christian philosophy rooted in a Christian Socratism constructed in different but equally profound ways by the two great adversaries,

Abelard and St Bernard? The driving idea which inspired the use of the metaphor of the dwarfs borne on the shoulders of giants was fundamentally the discovery and powerful assertion of a sense of history. This sense was ambivalent: what comes after is, from one point of view, superior, richer and weightier, and yet what comes before also embodies a kind of superiority: it is more venerable, quite literally, more worthy of respect. This connection between authority and age in a sense bound both to the past. But twelfth-century scholars, in harmony with the increased valuation conferred by development through history, were in the process of inventing a way of transcending the contradiction between Modernity and Antiquity, Modernity and Authority. This way was embodied in a new kind of man, defined by his historical context, a new kind of intellectual: the *magister*. By means of new biblical exegesis, more authentic and more accurate as far as literal meaning went, yet at the same time new, created by Christian philosophy, the *magistri* put in place a new balance between the study of texts, scholarly research and the production of knowledge in the double form of what was spoken and what was written. Above all, the *magistri* created the authority that the Moderns lacked when they confronted the Ancients. The confusion, the contradictory attitudes, of twelfth-century thinkers confronted by a double Antiquity, pagan and Christian, were expressions of pride in a creative *renovatio* and restlessness (rather than humility) in the face of intellectual weaknesses that would not allow them to dispense with the authority of the Ancients. Medieval society, in every field, was always a brittle form of human nature.

What needs to be examined more closely is the historical context of this discussion between the relative values of Ancients and Moderns. For the context in which that discussion developed throws into relief the ambiguity of the Moderns' appeal to the Ancients. Against whom were they trying to assert themselves? They were fighting on two fronts. First they confronted the traditionalists, who were especially powerfully entrenched in the monastic world, at Cluny. More than a monastic order among other orders, Cluny was a veritable monastic *ecclesia* carrying enormous weight in the Church as a whole. Dominique Iogna Prat has recently highlighted Cluny's passionate engagement in 'ordering' Christian society on the basis of patristic doctrine and of the 'ancestral custom' worked out in Late Antiquity (Iogna Prat 1998).

The pagan Ancients were always suspect in the minds of the guarantors of the Christian order and the ancient Christian traditions to which the Modern writers and thinkers explicitly or implicitly attached themselves. Were the Moderns not closer to evangelical currents, to the evangelical renewal which the new religious movements of monks and canons, who were sometimes denounced as heretics, wanted to promote? These reformers' goal was not a literary and philosophical renaissance, but an evangelical one. From another angle, the Moderns worried about those among their own contemporaries who, far from searching for wisdom, wanted to exploit new intellectual techniques to extract worldly profit of a quite material and monetary kind. These technicians sought to establish new intellectual fashions. These were the men John of Salisbury labelled the Cornificians: they bid fair to divert modernity from the quest for wisdom (Webb 1929: 23). For modern dwarfs, ancient giants constituted a weapon that was both offensive and defensive. It was to translate this ambiguity and this embarrassment that twentieth-century historians invented the term the Twelfth-century Renaissance.

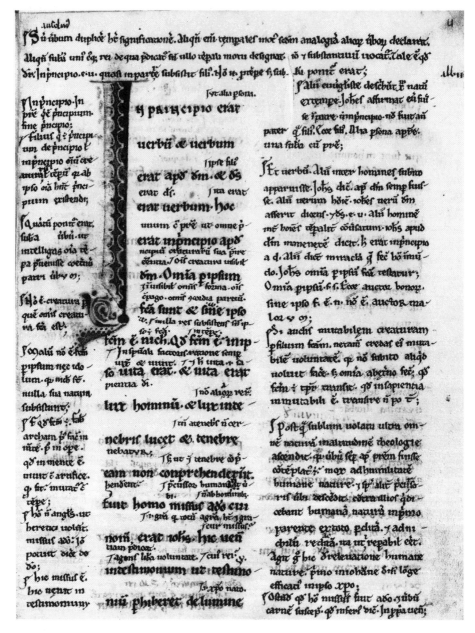

Figure 36.1 Ancient and modern. A copy of the Gloss on St John's Gospel with particular glosses attributed to 'Anselmus' (Anselm of Laon), taken from the ninth-century commentary by John the Scot. © Bodleian Library, Oxford, MS. Lyell 1, fo. 4r.

There is more to this story. The difficult discovery, or re-discovery, of History (the term *historia* itself is ambiguous) in which M.-D. Chenu discerned the heart of the twelfth century's dynamism – he saw it in Hugh of St-Victor's *Didascalion* (1130–40) 'where the term *historia* is used as often as the term *logica* and more often than *dialectica*' – was fundamentally the most important statement of those who used the metaphor of the dwarfs and the giants (Chenu 1974).We ought not to forget that in the twelfth century the dominant vision of historical evolution was that of the Ages of Man. This vision obeyed a law of decline which ended by representing the present time as that of old age: *mundus senescit* ('the world grows old'). Behind the resort to the image of the Moderns as dwarfs, in a reversal of perspective that gave the metaphor exceptional, even revolutionary, force, was a more or less veiled reference to the idea of the most extreme partisans of decline, who claimed that men were getting smaller and smaller, and that this shrinkage in size was a tangible illustration of humanity's general decadence.

What remained to the Moderns was to fight decisively against the idea of decline, by offering a new inversion of meaning in an area of fierce debate, the area of novelty. In preference to dealing with the dwarfs and giants as a pair, the Moderns threw themselves into battle against another pair of terms: *nova et vetera*, new and old. 'New' was clearer than 'modern', old age was less to be venerated than antiquity.

At the beginning of the twelfth century, one family of words was especially hateful to the Church, the monks and the clergy: these words clustered around *novus, novitas* ('new', 'novelty'). The terms evoked the *novissima*, the Last Things, the Apocalypse, the end of the world. They denoted the worst errors of mind and conduct. When in 1116, the inhabitants of the town of Laon rebelled against their bishop, who was also their lord, with shouts of '*Commune! commune!*' ('the common interest'), the Benedictine abbot Guibert of Nogent shouted back: '*Commune*: a new and detestable word!' In the field of doctrine, 'novelty', lack of respect for tradition and stability, was firmly to be condemned. There was a strong risk that it might lead to heresy. This is just what happened in the case of Abelard. At the Council of Sens (1140), Abelard was condemned as a heretic. His chief accuser was William of St-Thierry, the tool of St Bernard. William declared that Abelard had started 'to teach and write novelties' (Leclercq 1969: 377). In the course of the twelfth century mentalities changed, however. From being a negative term, the new became, first, neutral (almost the equivalent of our 'modern', or 'contemporary'), and then, positive. Alan of Lille, a distinguished university master who died *c*.1203, clothed in the Cistercian habit, balanced new things and old things, as Marie-Thérèse d'Alverny has clearly shown (d'Alverny 1968: 117–35). Walter Map, chancellor of Lincoln (1186–9) and archdeacon of Oxford (1196–1209/10), contrasted the 'novelties' of modern masters to 'the older masters', and made the twelfth century, which he defined as a period of one hundred years, a century of modernity in a positive sense. 'By our times I mean this modern period, the course of these last hundred years, at the end of which we now are, and of all of whose notable events the memory is fresh and clear enough. . . . The century which has passed I call modern times' (James 1983: 123–5). Beryl Smalley made a study of hostility to the new monastic orders during the twelfth century. She drew attention to the fact that this polemic gives us 'an overview of a change of attitudes in regard to novelty'. The Premonstratensian canon Anselm,

Bishop of Havelberg, for instance, in the first book of his *Dialogue* (*c*.1149), set out a theory of salvation-history whose object was to integrate novelties into this new perspective. St Bernard himself, in his *In Praise of the New Knighthood*, hailed the novelty of the new military orders (Leclercq and Rochais 1963: 214–15). M.-D. Chenu credited twelfth-century theology with having put the march of history on its onward path (Chenu 1957: 386–98). For Beryl Smalley, this rehabilitation of novelty relied on St Paul's appeal to 'put off the old man, and put on the new man, who has been created according to God in the justice and holiness of the truth' (Ephesians iv, 22–4); and its triumphant outcome was the foundation of the mendicant orders by St Dominic and St Francis at the beginning of the thirteenth century. Smalley shared my impression that the intellectuals of the twelfth century had 'a lively awareness of doing something new, of being new men'. M. H. Vicaire stressed that the *Life of St Dominic* in its opening pages used the terms 'new' and 'novelty' to describe the saint and his preachers; in so doing, the author of the *Life* conveyed their programme, and expressed his own admiration (Vicaire 1977: 103–5, 280–1). The first 'official' biographer of St Francis, Thomas of Celano, intended to arouse praise for the saint and his order when he exclaimed:

> *Novus ordo, nova vita*
> *Mundo surgit inaudita!*

('A new order, a new kind of religious life, has risen up, which was unknown to the world before.') And Smalley concluded (before shading the conclusion somewhat): 'An emotional change has come about in some hundred and fifty years. New has ceased to be a dirty word. It may carry the sense of "improvement", in that case it is praiseworthy. God has changed sides, he is no longer safely conservative' (Smalley 1975: 115).

This judgement of a great historian of medieval intellectual life indicates the direction in which we ought to look for a sense of the duration of the twelfth-century renaissance. It was a long twelfth century, a long renaissance. I would happily follow those modern scholars who extend Haskins's rather narrow and confined chronology, causing the century's distinctive leap forward to begin a bit earlier and reach its apogee a bit later.

As far as the beginnings go, I find it clarifies matters to see the renaissance as emerging from that great affirmative movement of Christian western Europe that we call the Gregorian Reform. Already in 1901, in volume 3 of Lavisse's *Histoire de France*, Achille Luchaire defined a change whose scope should be extended to cover the whole of the Christian Latin West:

> the period of our history that includes the last quarter of the eleventh century and the first third of the following century, saw profound changes in French society. The Church's violent effort to regenerate itself and to throw off its feudal traits; the definitive establishment of papal monarchy, whose reform and crusades ushered in its universal power; the first attempts of the great feudal powers to found states and governments; the recovery of the national monarchy in the person of Louis VI; the first attempts of the people in the towns and in

the villages to free themselves; the awakening of independent reason which gives a new character to theological studies and allowed heresy to renew its strength; the decisive progress of art manifested by the first masterpieces of vernacular literature, by the prodigious spread of Romanesque architecture and by the creation of Gothic.

(Luchaire 1901: 203–4)

Allowing for some simplifications and exaggerations, and a slightly dated vocabulary, we may say that here indeed are the essentials of a movement that involved all the structures of a society which, around the year 1100, adopted the term 'Christendom' as the sign of its cohesion and its strength.

What has not been sufficiently noticed is that, unlike modern historians such as Luchaire in the passage just quoted, not one of the intellectuals of the twelfth century, from Abelard to John of Salisbury, with the exception of Bernard of Clairvaux, made the least reference in his writings to the First Crusade and the conquest of Jerusalem. Was this military enterprise (the expedition is termed *bellum* in all the sources, even if was a war that gradually became a holy war) part of another face of Christendom, a face quite distinct from that of scholarship (*studium*)? If so, we would have to reflect on the meaning of this split, this double aspect, in the vital force of the Christian twelfth century.

I think we are now in a position to show that the twelfth century really was the century of a great take-off rather than of a renaissance: a take-off of medieval thought and knowledge, between the eleventh century's first cautious stumblings forward, and thirteenth-century scholasticism's great setting of things in order. This take-off involved every aspect of the Christian world. Christian society moved forward at the same time, if not at the same rate, in every field. And this take-off was that of a 'long twelfth century', clearly marked out in a world and at a time when the essential guidelines were bound to be religious – the Gregorian Reform and the appearance of the mendicant orders.

What were the fields and forms of thought in which this take-off was manifested most decisively and most distinctively? Haskins has already identified and described the essentials here, even though some of the nuances have been shifted to some extent by those historians who came after him. As far as intellectual centres are concerned, three emerged, one after the other, as places where the main theological innovations were made or developed: Laon, Chartres, Paris. An increase in the number of books and libraries, perhaps as a result of destruction and of inadequate stock-taking, did not emerge in the twelfth-century foreground: it was, rather, a thirteenth-century development. A significant feature, nevertheless, was the growing interest of lay aristocrats in books, their building-up of libraries, their commissioning of translations from Latin, and their enthusiasm for genealogical literature such as Lambert of Ardres' *History of the Counts of Guines* (1194), on which Georges Duby threw so much light (Duby 1977: 143–6). It was only at the turn of the twelfth/thirteenth century that there was an acceleration in the trend towards having things written down: the preservation of royal and seigneurial archives produced a great change in administrative practice 'from memory to written record' (to borrow Michael Clanchy's expressive phrase) (Clanchy 1996).

Even more than Latin poetry, what now strikes us as the great twelfth-century genre is the vernacular romance in verse, then in prose – a genre which Antiquity had barely sketched out. With the true birth of the historical romance was linked a growing sensitivity to the enduring quality and strong affirmation of the individual. History was the other genre to emerge strongly in the period. Haskins's scarce notes on this subject have crystallised in Bernard Guenée's study demonstrating the twelfth century's affirmation of a historical culture and the appearance, in terms of both method and thinking, of several works of true historians, especially in the Anglo-Norman realm with Orderic Vitalis, William of Malmesbury and, above all, Geoffrey of Monmouth (Guenée 1990).

Since Haskins, the accent has been placed, above all, on the flowering of law, on the progress of the sciences and of philosophy. These subjects had been stimulated and nurtured by translations from Greek and from Arabic, and by the activity of translators in lands bordering the Mediterranean, in Illyria, Sicily, southern Italy and above all in Spain, where Toledo was reconquered from the Moors by Alfonso VI of Castile in 1085 and became a great centre of encounters promoting the acculturation of Christian learning with the traditions, methods and achievements of Greek, Jewish and Arab science. The twelfth-century renaissance was a summons: the response was a process of reception that meant much more than the simple rediscovery of the ancient classics.

The practice of law and the forming of legal collections were responses to the demands of ecclesiastical, royal and urban institutions. Lawyers proliferated wherever officials were needed: in cathedral chapters, and in royal chanceries. The lawyers elaborated and diffused an urban legal culture. The renaissance of Roman Law has traditionally been accorded huge importance: but perhaps it was not the most important aspect of this legal explosion. Charles Radding has made a study of the changes in cognition which modified conceptions of order, law, and society (Radding 1985). A new mentality developed around the idea of community rather than that of hierarchy. Skills in discussion and debate tended to replace the mechanical rehearsal of authorities; and this opened the way to the scholastic methods of the *quaestio* and the *disputatio*. The great crucible of the transformations of law was Bologna, where a key event was the composition of the *Decretum* of the Bolognese monk Gratian, traditionally dated to *c*.1140. This gave a tremendous boost to the development of canon law, and that development in turn would reinvigorate the whole field of law and legal thinking far beyond ecclesiastical boundaries. Gratian's clearly set-out collection of authorities, with his own careful resolutions of their contradictions, not only furnished a formidable armoury of texts, but also presented a vast body of basic problems. It set going an innovative movement of critical thinking, debate and research into the theoretical and practical solutions to the problems of the new Christian society of the twelfth century. In the realm of theology where the new *magistri* ensured the development of scriptural commentary towards more 'scientific' speculation, 'theological science', likewise inspired, developed from the sacred page into sacred doctrine (*sacra doctrina*).

The School of Chartres, in particular, expanded the use of reasons, if not of reason, alongside authorities. The masters' modes of proof appealed to logic and reason. A further essential change arose from the development of a new Christian conception of nature. Tullio Gregory has defined it in the following precise and profound terms: 'One of the chief experiences of the twelfth century – in the new framework of society and culture that took shape at that period – was the gradual progressive setting-out of an idea of the natural as an ordered complex of phenomena which could be the object of rational enquiry, beyond the symbolic references that had characterised the contemplation of nature in the early Middle Ages' (Gregory 1994). The domain of the miraculous grew more limited, while that of the marvellous, the extraordinary but not the supernatural, expanded. Courtly literature did much to spread this new sense of the marvellous.

A further great change in the twelfth-century's sensibility and system of values related to work. Traditionally considered as a penance, and despised as manual activity, the concept of work preached by monastic reformers in the twelfth century and set in a place of honour in urban crafts (by contrast with the work of peasants and 'vile people') was the object of ideological promotion. Though inferior to the system of liberal arts, the system of mechanical arts brought a certain dignity to the world of the artisans. The list of unlawful or suspect *métiers*, which included the professions of merchant and lay scholar-master, grew shorter. The work these offered freed the faithful from the charge of selling either time or knowledge 'which belonged only to God'. Martha was partly rehabilitated *vis-à-vis* Mary (Constable 1995: 90–2). In Gothic art, the representation of active forms of conduct balanced that of contemplative forms. People observed that, according to Genesis (ii, 15), God had placed man in paradise 'ut operaretur et custodiret illum': 'to dress it and to keep it' (Le Goff 1977: 173). Thus, before the Fall and the imposition of work as punishment, there had been a divine calling of man to work.

The intellectual development of the twelfth century contained something hugely original in social terms: it emerged from the monastic milieu and realised itself on urban workshop floors. The new *masters* were professional men, who sought to follow the model set by others and to group themselves in corporations. Here was the birth of the universities, Bologna leading the way. By the end of the twelfth century, Paris and Oxford had begun to organise themselves. Finally, crowning this descent of values from heaven to earth, man was no longer constantly symbolised by the figure of Job, overwhelmed by God's omnipotence and the terrible trials He imposed. Men could also read in Genesis – and underline this passage too – that God had made man 'in His own image'. Romanesque art, and still more Gothic art, bore witness to this. The crowning achievement of the twelfth century was the shaping, from this material, of Christian humanism, of the Christian Socratism mentioned earlier in this chapter. It is to be seen, for instance, in those two great adversaries Abelard and Bernard.

Yet this take-off of the twelfth century also had a negative aspect: one that appeared very clearly in the century that followed. Strong in their new rights, their new dignities, increasingly enclosed in the structures of the Church and of lay powers anxious to channel and tame the often uncontrolled effervescence that had typified the twelfth century, Christian establishments were determined to defend what they had gained – and to defend their purity. As R. I. Moore (1987) and Dominique Iogna Prat (1998) have so tellingly pointed out, Christendom became an institution of persecution, marginalisation and exclusion. Behind the heretics, who were the most stubborn and most dangerous, the Jews who resisted new efforts to convert them, the homosexuals who had been relatively tolerated until then, the lepers who symbolised sinners in the impurity of their status, and right down to the poor in their ambiguous condition: all these became objects of control, of rejection, of enclosure, and, at the worst, victims of pogroms, of expulsions, of the Inquisition. This was the dark side of the 'lovely' twelfth century.

REFERENCES

Chenu, M.-D. (1957) *La Théologie au XII siècle*, Paris: J. Vrin.

—— (1974) 'Civilisation urbaine et théologie: l'École de Saint-Victor au XII siècle', *Annales-Économies-Sociétés-Civilisations* 29: 1253–63.

Clanchy, M. T. (1996) *From Memory to Written Record. England 1066–1307*, 2nd edn, London: Edward Arnold.

Classen, P. (1966) 'Die hohen Schulen und die Gessellschaft im 12. Jahrhundert', *Archiv für Kulturgeschichte* 48: 155–80.

Constable, G. (1995) *Three Studies in Medieval Religious and Social Thought. The interpretation of Mary and Martha. The ideal of the imitation of Christ. The orders of society*, Cambridge: Cambridge University Press.

d'Alverny, M.-T. (1968) 'Maître Alain – "Nova et vetera"', in Gandillac and Jeauneau: 117–45.

Duby, G. (1977), trans. C. Postan, *The Chivalrous Society*, London: Edward Arnold.

Gandillac, M. de and Jeauneau, É. (eds) (1968) *Entretiens sur la Renaissance du 12e siècle*, Paris: Mouton.

Gregory, T. (1994) 'L'ordine della natura e l'ordine del sapere', in P. Rossi and C. A. Viano, *Storia della filosofia*, II. *Il Medioevo*, Rome and Bari: Laterza, 60–77.

Guenée, B. (1980) *Histoire et culture historique dans l'Occident médiéval*, Paris: Aubier Montaigne.

Haskins, C. H. (1927) *The Renaissance of the Twelfth Century*, Cambridge, Mass.: Harvard University Press.

Iogna Prat, D. (1998) *Ordonner et exclure. Cluny et la société chrétienne face à l'hérésie, au judaïsme et à l'Islam 1000–1150*, Paris: Aubier.

James, M. R. (ed. and trans.), revised C. N. L. Brooke and R. A. B. Mynors (1983) *Walter Map. De nugis curialium. Courtiers' Trifles*, Oxford: Clarendon Press.

Jeauneau, É. (1967) '*Nani gigantum humeris insidentes*': essai d'interprétation de Bernard de Chartres', *Vivarium* 5: 79–99.

—— (1968) *Nains et géants*, in Gandillac and Jeauneau: 21–52.

Ladner, G. (1982) 'Terms and ideas of renewal', in R. L. Benson and G. Constable (eds) with C. D. Lanham, *Renaissance and Renewal in the Twelfth Century*, Oxford: Clarendon Press.

Leclercq, J. (1969) 'Les lettres de Guillaume de Saint-Thierry à Saint Bernard', *Revue Bénédictine* 79: 375–91.

Leclercq, J. and Rochais, H. (eds) (1963) *S. Bernardi Opera*, iii, Rome: Editiones Cistercienses.

Le Goff, J. (1977) *Pour un autre Moyen Âge*, Paris: Gallimard.

—— (1993) *Intellectuals in the Middle Ages*, Oxford: Basil Blackwell.

Luchaire, A. (1901) *Histoire de la France depuis les origines jusqu'à la Revolution. III. Les premiers Capetiens (987–1137)*, Paris: Hachette.

Moore, R. I. (1987) *The Formation of a Persecuting Society. Power and deviance in Western Europe, 950–1250*, Oxford: Basil Blackwell.

——(2000) *The First European Revolution (c. 970–1215)*, Oxford: Basil Blackwell.

Paré, G., Brunet, A. and Tremblay, P. (1933) *La Renaissance du XIIe siècle, les écoles et l'enseignement*, Paris: J. Vrin.

Radding, C. M. (1985) *A World Made by Men. Cognition and society 400–1200*, Chapel Hill: University of North Carolina Press.

Smalley, B. (1968) 'L'exégèse biblique du 12e siècle', in Gandillac and Jeauneau: 273–93.

—— (1975) 'Ecclesiastical attitudes to novelty *c.*1100–*c.*1250', in D. Baker (ed.) *Church Society and Politics. Studies in Church history* 12: 113–31.

—— (1983) *The Study of the Bible in the Middle Ages*, 3rd edn, Oxford: Basil Blackwell.

Southern, R. W. (1995) *Scholastic Humanism and the Unification of Europe. I. Foundations*, Oxford: Basil Blackwell.

Vicaire, M.-H. (1977) *Dominique et ses prêcheurs*, Fribourg and Paris: Éditions Universitaires Fribourg Suisse.

von Moos, P. (1988) 'Das 12. Jahrhundert – eine "Renaissance" oder ein "Aufklärungszeitalter"?', *Mittellateinisches Jahrbuch* 23: 1–10.

Webb, C. C. J. (ed.) (1929) *Ioannis Saresberiensis episcopi Carnotensis Metalogicon libri IIII*, Oxford: Clarendon Press.

THE ENGLISH PARISH AND ITS CLERGY IN THE THIRTEENTH CENTURY

C. H. Lawrence

By the thirteenth century, parishes were territories with strictly defined boundaries, and a parish church was distinguised from other churches by the exclusive right to possess a font and a graveyard for the service of its parishioners. This familiar parish structure which covered England was the outcome of a slow-working process that extended over several centuries. Some parish churches had originated in Anglo-Saxon times as official minsters or baptismal churches, which had been under episcopal supervision from the outset. Others, the greater number in fact, sprang from the initiative of landlords, monasteries and townsmen of the tenth and eleventh centuries, who built churches for themselves or their tenants on their estates and in the newly populous towns. It was through their efforts that the monk Ralph Glaber had in his lifetime seen Europe 'clothed in a white robe of churches' (France 1989: 114–17).

The lord who erected a church of this kind, whether he was a layman or the abbot of a monastery, was its proprietor. Normally he endowed it with a modicum of land to support a priest, whom he appointed or dismissed at will. If the estate was sold or passed to another by inheritance or marriage, church and priest went with it to the new owner. This was the proprietory church system that was to be found all over northern Europe. Its conversion into the nucleus of a parish organisation was one of the major achievements of the medieval canon law in the century following the pontificate of Pope Gregory VII.

Lay control over the clergy and property of the Church was unacceptable to those who had imbibed Gregorian ideas of ecclesiastical order. During the twelfth century, therefore, the canonists brought about a change in the status of the landlord in relation to his church. A decree of the Second Lateran Council of 1139 condemned the possession of tithes by the laity and bade those lay people who owned churches to hand them over – in the words of the council to 'restore' them – to the bishop (Alberigo and Tanner 1990: i. 199). Thus the laity were gradually persuaded to surrender proprietory rights over churches. It was established that the glebe land, tithes of produce within the boundaries of the parish, and altar offerings, were the property of the parish priest, who was subject to the supervision of the bishop.

Although the landlord ceased in law to be the owner of his church, he retained certain rights as its patron, and these were acknowledged by the canonists. He had the advowson, the right, that is, to present a clerk of his choice to the bishop for appointment to the living. But the clerk in question acquired a legal right to the church only when he had been formally instituted on the bishop's instructions.

The patronage or advowson of a church was an asset worth having. It enabled its possessor to present a priest of his choosing, perhaps a relative or a useful acquaintance, to a living, and in some cases it entitled him to receive an annual payment – a *pensio* – from the incumbent. The law recognised the patron's special position by permitting him to stand in the chancel – that part of the building containing the main altar and reserved to the clergy – during the celebration of divine service. All the same, he was clearly not the source of the priest's authority to dispense the sacraments; this was derived from the bishop who had instituted him and who alone could legally remove him. In this way, manorial churches, which had been founded and built by private initiative, were gradually integrated into the diocesan structure and formed the basis of the parish organisation of the Middle Ages.

The evolution of parish organisation was well advanced by the thirteenth century. But in its inconsistencies and baffling complexity it still bore the marks of its origin. The parish church existed to provide for the spiritual needs of the people living within its boundaries. But in law it was treated as a benefice, as a complex of property rights. Its rector, once instituted, acquired a legal right to the enjoyment of its endowments. He was the parson – in Latin the *persona* – who was by definition the recipient of the parish tithes. On the ground, though, the reality could be less simple. Some churches were divided into moieties (halves) or even lesser fractions, each of which constituted a separate rectory with its own incumbent. Most of these arrangements had their origin in the earlier age, when two or more landlords, whose manors lay within the parish boundaries, cooperated in building the village church, and each retained control over his portion of the endowment. This produced a church with two or more patrons, each presenting a rector of his choice to a fractional benefice.

Often such a situation arose from the subdivision of an estate, of which the church formed a part, between co-heirs or heiresses. Such was the case with the church of Penistone in the West Riding. In 1227, in the course of litigation between rival claimants to the advowson, one of them, Thomas de Burg, explained to the court that the benefice had been divided into four separate parts following the partition of the estate between two custodians of the lordship and two co-heiresses at an earlier date, and that the advowson had been similarly partitioned between the parties. Thomas based his claim on the alleged fact that a moiety of the advowson had been sold to his grandfather (Curia regis Rolls 1959: 13 no. 370).

Whatever its origin, the partition of the income and the spiritual responsibility for the parish between two or more rectors was obviously not conducive to zealous pastoral care, and in the course of the thirteenth century ecclesiastical authorities endeavoured to phase the practice out. At the Council of Oxford in 1222, Archbishop Stephen Langton forbade the division of parish churches for the future, and urged that existing churches with more than a single parson should be reintegrated as each rector died. His ruling was reiterated by the papal legate, Cardinal Otto de Monteferrato in 1237, and again by the legatine statutes of Cardinal Ottobuono in 1268 (Powicke and Cheney 1964: II.i. 111–12, 251, 762). But in each case an exception was made in favour of churches that had been divided 'from ancient times'. The claims of competing patrons were not easy to extinguish. Although the canonists maintained that advowsons – which concerned the appointment of pastors – were a matter for the ecclesiastical jurisdiction, deeply rooted social custom, ratified by the constitutions of King Henry II, treated an advowson as a piece of property enjoying the protection of English common law.

The wealth of the Church in land and tithes made it inevitable that the endowments of parish churches would be diverted into serving many and various ends in addition to those of the pastoral care. After all, in tithes the Church possessed a more comprehensive and regular form of direct taxation than was available to any medieval monarch. Out of the proceeds it had to bear the cost of a variety of services, including several that fall to the charge of the modern state. Thus richer benefices were used as a means of supporting secular administration by their conferment on royal clerks and ministers, and they provided a living for ecclesiastical lawyers and administrators, cathedral clergy, schoolmen at the universities and their pupils. Such men were necessarily non-resident in their parishes, and provided for the administration of the sacraments and the pastoral care of the people by allocating a portion of the parish endowments to a vicar or by paying a stipendiary chaplain.

The income of a parish might be diverted from the pocket of the resident priest in a variety of ways; one of the commonest was by the appropriation of the church to a monastery, cathedral or some other kind of collegiate church. A gift to a monastery was a meritorous act which might remit for the donor a long period of penance. Moreover, in return for the gift the monks would act as surrogates for the benefactor, by their lives of prayer and fasting performing penance on his behalf. Prompted by these considerations, as well as by the attitude of the post-Gregorian canonists, many lay owners or patrons donated the advowson of a parish church or a portion of its revenues to a religious house. Thus, with the consent of the bishop of Norwich, Robert Fitzwalter and his wife donated an annual rent of five marks to Binham Priory out of the endowment of the parish church of Bacton in Norfolk, while reserving the advowson of the church to themselves and their heirs (Binham Cartulary, fos 183, 184). The monks experienced some difficulty in extracting the annual rent from the rectors of Bacton and had to resort to the courts to secure payment. In the end, in the thirteenth century, during the vacancy of the benefice, the patron was persuaded to appropriate the entire church with its endowments, tithes and offerings, to Binham, initially to help pay for the rebuilding of the priory church in the style of the period, and thereafter to meet the expense of lighting it.

It was, of course, necessary to wait for the death or resignation of the rector before handing over ownership of a parish church to a monastic body. For once he had been instituted, the existing incumbent had a legal right to the endowments and offerings that could not be set aside. So it was that when one Richard of Argentein donated the church of St Peter's, Little Wymondley, in Hertfordshire, to some Austin canons for the foundation of a hospital, he wrote into his charter a clause reserving the rights of Hugh Leidet, the existing parson, and the rights of the vicars serving the church during their lifetime (Little Wymondley Cartulary, fo. 14). The canons had to wait for the church to become vacant before entering into possession.

Appropriation of parish churches by monasteries became increasingly common after the middle of the twelfth century and continued throughout the thirteenth century and beyond. In these cases, the monastery became the corporate rector of the parish and was entitled to receive its income. As monks did not as a rule perform pastoral duties – in fact, strictly speaking the canon law debarred them from doing so (Lawrence 1989: 33) – they used some portion of the income to pay a resident priest to provide for the spiritual needs of the parish. Frequently the first stage in an appropriation was the gift of an advowson to a religious body. Subsequently the monks would get the bishop's approval to appropriate the entire benefice. The reason most commonly given for the transfer was the financial need of the appropriator. For instance, in the 1220s Archbishop Langton authorised the appropriation of the Kentish churches of Appledore and Coldred by the prior and convent of St Martin's Priory, Dover, on account of 'the meagreness of their revenues and so as to make them more adequate to support the burdens of hospitality' (Major 1950: 138).

Possibly the need of the priory was genuine, for hospitality was an obligation of the Benedictine Rule that monasteries were expected to take seriously, and the location of St Martin's made it a favoured resting place for sea-sick travellers from the continent. But the plea of poverty and the demands of hospitality became legal clichés that were constantly invoked to justify the diversion of parish revenues to great and wealthy religious houses as well as to those that were small and impoverished. At St Albans, Matthew Paris listed it among the achievements of Abbot John of Hertford that he had procured the churches of Norton and Eglingham 'for the improvement of our beer' (Riley 1867: 320–1). In the course of the thirteenth century, bad management, coupled with a determination to maintain living standards in a period of steady inflation, had landed many of the Benedictine abbeys in debt, and for many of them the appropriation of a parish church offered an easy way out of their difficulties.

At an earlier stage of this development, voices had been raised against it within the monastic world itself. It was one of the reproaches with which St Bernard had lambasted Cluny:

> For what reason have you had the first fruits and tithes of parish churches conferred on you? For these things are not appropriate to monks. They have been granted to those who have the duty of baptizing and preaching and caring for souls. Why do you usurp these goods since you ought to do none of these things? As you do not carry the burden, why do you accept the rewards?
>
> (Constable 1967: i. 56)

Some of the bishops of the thirteenth century expressed similar misgivings. Robert Grosseteste in his old age delivered an excoriating address to the pope and cardinals at Lyons in 1250, in which he blamed monastic appropriation for the problem of unworthy and inadequate parish priests – 'substitutes and hirelings, who themselves receive from the property of their churches barely enough to support life' (Sieben 1971: 359). The Council of London, presided over by the legate Cardinal Ottobuono in 1268, tried to put a brake on the practice, forbidding bishops to appropriate churches to monasteries except in cases of manifest poverty (Powicke and Cheney

1964: II.ii. 770). But not all appropriators were monasteries. A lot of churches had been annexed by bishops to endow prebends for their canons in secular cathedrals. Appropriation was too deeply rooted in the economic fabric as well as in the religious assumptions of medieval society to be eradicated by simple condemnation or facile moralisation.

Where the rector of the parish was non-resident, whether the incumbent was a cathedral dignitary, a royal clerk, or a monastic corporation, arrangements had to be made for the church to be served by a paid substitute – a chaplain or vicar. The problem, which exercised conscientious bishops, was how to ensure that the priest who actually served the parish was adequately educated, and that the absentee rector paid him a decent living wage. A canon of the Lateran Council of 1215 lamented that some greedy appropriators had left priests with less than enough for subsistence, drawing a natural and well-founded conclusion that 'hence in these areas there is seldom found a parish priest who possesses even a modest knowledge of letters' (Alberigo and Tanner 1990: i. 249–50). The remedy the council proposed was that the absentee rector should be required to present a suitable vicar to the bishop for institution to the church, who was to be irremovable and who would be assigned an 'appropriate portion' of the parish endowments. The law thus demanded the establishment in all appropriated churches of a perpetual vicarage – a benefice in its own right, to which was allocated an agreed and fixed part of the parish revenues, the occupant of which would, once instituted, enjoy the same security of tenure as the rector.

It was once thought that the establishment of perpetual vicarages was a direct result of the Lateran decree. But in the Middle Ages, as in modern times, Rome had a tendency to lead its troops from the rear. More recent research has shown that English bishops were setting up vicarages long before the Lateran Council addressed itself to the problem (Cheney 1956: 131–3).[1] The more copious records of the thirteenth century show how such transactions were managed.

For a bishop with a sensitive conscience like Grosseteste, who believed that inadequate pastors were slayers of souls (Luard 1861: 151–3), the primary concern was to obtain the best possible terms for the vicarage. This could involve tough negotiation: the appropriating body usually claimed the lion's share of the endowments. On an October day in 1241, a meeting took place in the chancel of the parish church of Ashwell, in Hertfordshire, which had been appropriated to Westminster Abbey. The parish lay within the huge diocese of Lincoln, of which Grosseteste was bishop. At the meeting he was respresented by his official, the archdeacon of Hertford, and by two of his clerks; the abbey was represented by the abbot in person and a party of four monks. They had come to assess the assets of the church with a view to agreeing a division between the vicar and the abbey. As diocesan records of the period rarely, if ever, possessed the necessary financial information, it was necessary to conduct an investigation on the spot. Fourteen parishioners of Ashwell were therefore assembled, put on oath, and asked to state the income of the church from all sources other than the garb tithe – the tithe of corn – and their statements were committed to writing.

Next day the negotiators reassembled in the church. Grosseteste had made it a condition of his consent to the appropriation that the vicarage should be worth not less than forty-five marks: a good income which at that time was regarded as sufficient for a layman to maintain the state of knighthood. His clerks now pointed out that the items listed on the previous day were not enough to produce forty-five marks unless the abbot was prepared to add a portion of the garb tithe. This he at first refused to do. He was hoping to appropriate the whole of the garb tithe for the monastery, and he argued that the income from the offerings, the glebe land, and the tithe of the proceeds from the four mills in the parish were enough to endow the vicarage. But the bishop's clerks were under orders, and he had to give way. The jury of parishioners was brought back and required to value the garb tithes, which proved to be worth sixty marks. A third of this sum was therefore added to the vicarage, which raised it to a total of fifty-three marks (Davis 1913: 277–82).[2] Thus Grosseteste's firmness secured for the vicar of Ashwell more than half of the parish income.

Such a distribution between appropriator and parish priest was by no means the norm. More than fifty years later Archbishop Winchelsey, when ordering an inquiry into the value of vicarages in the diocese of Coventry–Lichfield, observed that 'we have learned that some are so meagre and wretched that the vicars of those churches cannot be supported from the income of their vicarages unless they are augmented' (Graham 1952: i. 86).

One of the consequences of treating the parish as a complex of property rights was that, once established, it tended to become fixed and indivisible in extent. Rectors and patrons resisted any attempts to carve new parishes out of their territory as these would involve the subtraction of tithes and offerings. Later needs created by population growth, new settlements and the clearance of new lands, were met not by creating new parishes but by erecting parochial chapels. Many of these were constructed by landlords or by lords and peasants acting in cooperation, to serve hamlets that had sprung up on lands newly brought under the plough. In these cases the chapel, which sometimes began life as a humble wooden structure, remained a dependency of the mother church of the parish. Its subordinate status was affirmed in a variety of ways. Usually the chaplain in charge of it was a priest appointed by the rector or vicar of the parish, who could also dismiss him if he wished. He might also be dependent upon the incumbent for his income in the form of an annual wage or stipend.

Some chapels were provided by their founders with a modest endowment of their own. An ordinance for the chapel of East Hoe in Hampshire, made after a dispute between the local people and the rector of the parish, allocated to the chaplain the lesser tithes of the village; in addition he was allowed to keep the offerings of the people, and he was provided with a house, pasturage for fifty sheep and twelve pigs on the land of the manor, and an annual gift from the patron of six cartloads of wood. The garb tithe of the manor of Hoe and all legacies and mortuary payments were reserved to the rector of the parish (Deedes 1915: 258–60). But this was a relatively lavish provision. Many dependent chapels had less than this, and the priests who served them were in general an exploited class of clerical underlings who lacked the security of a permanent benefice.

From the viewpoint of the laity who attended a parochial chapel, the outward and visible sign of their colonial status was the fact that the mother church of the parish had the exclusive right to possess a font and a graveyard. Some parishes covered a very wide area, including within their boundaries several scattered hamlets, each with its own chapel. The need to get to the mother church for baptisms and burials sometimes posed serious problems for people living in the outlying places, especially in winter when unsurfaced roads became quagmires and fords could be impassable. In face of such difficulties bishops could occasionally be persuaded to override the jealously guarded privileges of a parish church and authorise a chapel to consecrate a cemetery for its people.

The complexities and failings of the parish organisation were rooted in its long history. To understand its workings it is instructive to glance for a moment at the distribution of patronage and the recruitment of the parish clergy in a particular area during the last forty years of the thirteenth century. As a matter of fact, such an investigation is not possible much earlier than this owing to the haphazard survival of the records of institution. Let us inspect an area of Northamptonshire, which formed part of the Lincoln diocese. Here, as elsewhere, parishes were grouped into deaneries, each of which was subject to the supervision of a rural dean. The three deaneries of Rothwell, Brackley, and Preston contained in all 118 benefices.[3] The advowson of 53 of these (about 45 per cent) was in the hands of lay patrons; 61 of them (nearly 52 per cent) had monastic patrons, including six livings in the patronage of the Knights Hospitallers and one in that of the Templars. Three had other ecclesiastical patrons, including one – Brixworth – that was appropriated to a prebend in Salisbury cathedral; and the patron of one is unrecorded.

Of the 61 parishes that were in monastic patronage, 22 had been appropriated and were served by perpetual vicars. The largest single share of this property was controlled by the Cluniac priory of St Andrew's at Northampton, which had eight livings at its disposal. The abbess and convent of Delapre came a close second with seven benefices under their control. In addition to the churches it possessed in the three deaneries we are concerned with, St Andrew's priory had appropriated six of the twelve churches in the city of Northampton itself and held the patronage of four more of them. Thus in this area monasteries enjoyed a substantial quantity of parish endowments and more than half the patronage, though appropriation had not proceeded as far as it had in some other regions. Of the richer livings – those officially valued at twenty marks per annum and upwards – eight were in the gift of monastic houses and three in the gift of lay patrons.

Most of the lay patrons in this area were local landed families of the knightly class. They showed a marked tendency to present a son or some other relative to their churches. The Trussells of Marston Trussell, who were patrons of five benefices, presented two members of their own family, their own chantry chaplain, and a member of the family of Sutton, who was a relative of the bishop of Lincoln. In the same way, higher up the social scale, the earl of Gloucester presented his relative, the notorious pluralist Bogo de Clare, to the rectory of Whiston. Nor was this familial charity confined to lay patrons; Stephen Malory, who was presented to the vicarage of Draughton by the convent of Delapre in 1279, was presumably a relative of the abbess, Emma Malory.

What do the records tell us about the social origin and status of the clergy instituted to livings in this area of Northamptonshire during the years 1258 to

1299? During this period of forty years, 219 clerks were instituted. Of these, 161 have either a family name or a toponym that makes it possible to identify their place of origin. The greater number were recruited locally, a few from substantial landed families, but most of them apparently from the ranks of peasant freeholders. In all, 118 of the incumbents whose names can be located, almost three-quarters of the total, came either from Northamptonshire or from villages just over the county border. Many of them hailed from a nearby village within the same deanery. Twelve of them were apparently presented to livings in their place of birth. There were only 38 schoolmen or university graduates among the incumbents, comprising approximately 17.8 per cent of those instituted, and although some of them had local connections, the majority did not. Most of them were men in royal or episcopal service, who were clearly not going to reside in their parishes.

The picture is incomplete because over a quarter of the incumbents bear names that cannot be clearly identified with a particular place, but the pattern of clerical recruitment revealed by the rest tallies closely with findings elsewhere at this period (cf. Hilton 1966: 62; Robinson 1969). Of course, the figures only tell us about the beneficed clergy, who formed only a part, and a lesser part, of the clergy as a whole. If we had more information about the stipendiary chaplains and the great rag-tag of the unbeneficed, we should probably find that the proportion of local recruits was even higher. Certainly the proportion of graduates among the clergy as a whole was smaller than the figures suggest. If, for instance, we look at a typical ordination list of the Lincoln diocese for the period we have been examining – that of Bishop Oliver Sutton for the year 1290 – we find that out of 223 men ordained that year to the major orders of priest, deacon or subdeacon, only 29 (about 13 per cent) were described as *magistri* (Hill 1975).

'In a world full of clergy,' lamented the Franciscan Adam Marsh, the friend and counsellor of Bishop Grosseteste, 'bishops can scarcely find anyone tolerably adequate to assist in the work of salvation' (Brewer 1858: 143–4). His was not a solitary voice. In the thirteenth century we encounter a rising chorus of complaint about the abuses of the parochial system and the failings of the parish clergy. Much of this was orchestrated by the friars, whose pastoral mission to the townspeople of Europe brought them into collision with the interests of the secular clergy. Disparagement of the parish clergy was a feature of Mendicant preaching common enough to be the subject of an express prohibition by Bonaventure, the Franciscan Minister-General (Lawrence 1994: 164–5). Anecdotes illustrating the abuses of plurality, non-residence, and the ignorance, worldiness and sexual misdemeanours of the clergy were commonplace in the collections of *exempla* – the sermon-aids compiled by friars which formed part of the preacher's stock-in-trade (Polo de Beaulieu 1993).

Some of this criticism was doubtless coloured by the conflict of interests and the chronic polemic between the Mendicants and the secular clergy (Lawrence 1994: 152–65). Some of it was overstated; but much of it had a basis in reality. If it missed the mark it was because it failed to identify the economic and cultural conditions that lay at the heart of the problem. In the thirteenth century there was a growing gap between the wealth, education and status of the rectors of the better endowed churches, many of whom were non-resident, and that of the poorly paid vicars or chaplains who acted as their substitutes, who lacked security of tenure and who, for want of patrons, would in many cases never obtain a benefice.

The circumstances of parish chaplains can be gleaned from the record of a visitation of the prebendal churches appropriated to Salisbury Cathedral conducted in 1220 by the dean, William de Wanda. Some of these churches were served by vicars, others by wage-earning chaplains. The dean found that the parish church of Mere in Wiltshire was served by Geoffrey, a chaplain on an annual contract, assisted by another chaplain and a deacon who helped him run two outlying chapels, where mass was celebrated three days a week. A third chapel within the parish boundaries, belonging to the canons of Le Mans, was served by a deacon for an annual stipend of four marks. Although he did not enjoy the security of tenure he would have had as a vicar, Geoffrey, the chaplain of Mere, had a reasonable stipend consisting of income from the glebe land, offerings and tithes, other than the great tithe of corn and hay which was reserved to the cathedral chapter; but out of the proceeds he had to pay the corporate rector a rental of eight marks a year. The prebendal church of Sonning in Berkshire, unlike that of Mere, was served by a perpetual vicar named Vitalis, and had six dependent chapels within its territory. One of these was without a priest at the time of the dean's visitation. Four of them were served by chaplains on annual contract, who received a portion of the proceeds from the glebe land and the people's offerings, and paid members of the chapter an annual rental. The poorest of the group was Henry, the chaplain in charge of the chapel of Edburgfeld, who received an annual wage of only twenty shillings and was housed with the parson of Berkhampstead (Rich Jones 1883: 290).

The condition of parish chaplains attracted the solicitude of several bishops, who tried to limit their exploitation and alleviate their plight by forbidding rectors to dismiss them without just cause and by laying down minimum stipends (Powicke and Cheney 1964: II.i. 30, 84, 462–3). For the diocese of Winchester, Peter des Roches stipulated a minimum wage of fifty shillings for an annual chaplain (ibid: II.i. 129–30); in his statutes for the Worcester diocese, William de Blois decreed a minimum of three marks, unless the chaplain was provided with meals at his rector's table (ibid: II.i. 175); and in his diocese Richard of Chichester raised it to five marks (ibid: II.i. 462–3). This was, of course, only tinkering with an intractable problem.

Canonically no man was supposed to be ordained priest or deacon without a title – without, that is, a named church that he was going to serve and which would guarantee his financial support, unless he could guarantee his future subsistence from his own patrimony. But these ancient rules were widely evaded. Poor men who wanted to be ordained but had no patron to present them to a church, resorted to spurious guarantors,[4] among whom were some nunneries, which provided a title for numerous ordinands, presumably in return for payment. Once ordained these men swelled the ranks of the unbeneficed clergy, from which parish chaplains were drawn. Together with numerous clerks in minor orders, they formed an underpaid and unstable clerical proletariat. Not surprisingly, some of them drifted into crime and they figure from time to time on the rolls of the itinerant royal justices in the company of robbers and men of violence.[5] Unbeneficed clergy were the bane of the medieval Church.

Non-resident rectors who left their parishes in the hands of paid substitutes were often the butt of savage criticism. The Franciscan who compiled a Handbook of Exemplary Stories (*Tabula Exemplorum*) noted that 'many of the best people visit their churches at harvest time to collect their revenues, and at that time they reside; but at other times they never set eyes on them' (Walter 1926: 135). The abuse was more conspicuous where the absent incumbent was a foreigner. Some rich parishes in our Northamptonshire example attracted the attention of benefice hunters from abroad. We meet four cases in the years 1258 to 1299. One of them was Master William of Bouvines, a doctor of canon law, who was presented to the rectory of Towcester in 1295 by papal provision. Of the other three, two were presented by aristocratic patrons and one by Delapre Abbey. It would be a mistake to assume that the alien absentee who occupied an English benefice was necessarily an unwanted intruder. As often as not, he was presented to the living because the patron regarded him as a useful connection, especially if he was a man of status in the papal Curia. He was most likely to turn up in those livings where the patronage had fallen into the hands of the Crown. It probably did not make much difference to the rustic parishioners whether their absentee rector was a foreigner or an English clerk working in the royal bureaucracy, a bishop's secretary or a schoolman away teaching in a university. The alien was in any case a rare bird among the parish clergy.

Whether he was a native or a foreigner, the rector who was a chronic absentee was in many cases a pluralist. Pluralism was one of the most ineradicable abuses of the medieval Church. It drew its defensive tenacity from a widespread acceptance of the idea – an idea shared by pope, king and bishops alike – that government and learning, and even nobility, were a legitimate charge upon the wealth of the Church. Those preachers and moralists, including Grosseteste and Adam Marsh, who questioned this assumption were felt by many people to be dangerous revolutionaries. 'Many noble persons of our blood obtain several benefices for which they have not as yet gained a dispensation. Some of them are of an advanced age and have until now lived honourably, giving what hospitality they could and dispensing alms with open doors. It would be excessively hard for such people to be despoiled of their benefices and thrust into ignominious poverty' (Luard 1872–83: iii. 418). The speaker, though noble by birth, was not a clerical worldling, but Walter Cantilupe, a zealous and saintly bishop of Worcester, asking the cardinal legate to go easy on the pluralists. He was simply voicing the conviction of his class that the Church owed the aristocracy a living.

The canonical prohibition of plurality was clearly stated by the decree *De multa* of the Fourth Lateran Council: if anyone holding a benefice with cure of souls should receive a second such benefice, he shall *ipso facto* be deprived of the former living. If he endeavours to keep both, he shall forfeit both. But the law deliberately left yawning gaps: the holders of cathedral prebends did not come within the scope of the act; more significantly, the decree allowed the pope to dispense 'sublime and literate persons' from its operation, enabling them to hold more than a single parish living. And in fact considerable numbers of such dispensations, granted at the petition of kings and bishops, appear on the papal registers of the thirteenth century.

Who were these 'sublime and literate persons'? They were, of course, relatives of the king and nobility, and royal and papal administrators. The happy hunting ground of the pluralist was the pool of prebends in cathedrals and other collegiate churches, as these were exempt from the canonical prohibition. But parish livings were also collected. John Mansel, a leading minister of Henry III, received a papal dispensation in 1260 covering his simultaneous occupation of the treasurership of York Cathedral, the provostship of Beverley Minster, the chancellorship of St Paul's Cathedral, and numerous other benefices, ten of which were parish livings (Bliss 1893: 363).

A representative list of pluralists can be found in the register of Robert Winchelsey, archbishop of Canterbury (1294–1313). This contains the names of clerks who had rendered account at the prerogative court of Canterbury in the time of his predecessor John Pecham (1279–92) because the deceased had held property in more than one diocese. In all, fifty pluralists are listed. Some of these were small-scale aggregators with not more than two livings; but the majority held several. The most conspicuous are the king's clerks, among whom the palm is easily carried off by Adam de Stratton, Keeper of the King's Works and Chamberlain of the Exchequer, who appears as having held twenty-three churches at the same time in six different dioceses (Graham 1952: ii. 1148–9).

Denunciation of plurality was commonplace among moralists and preachers of the thirteenth century. Thomas of Cantimpré, the Dominican anecdotist, regaled his readers with a story of Philip, the Chancellor of Paris, who declined to accept the conclusion of the bishop, William of Auvergne, that no man might hold two benefices with cure of souls and be saved. He refused to repent of it even on his death-bed, saying that he intended to find out experimentally whether or not pluralism was a mortal sin. And he did. The tormented soul of the chancellor troubled the bishop in his prayers (Colverinus 1627: 73). The story was one of many cautionary tales circulated by the friars in their anthologies of *exempla*. In his *Summa of Virtues and Vices* – a popular compendium of moral theology that was widely read – William Peraldus, also a Dominican, made short work of the arguments of those who sought to justify plurality: 'some argue it is lawful because they spend the income of their benefices well, others because they are noble persons. Will it do for a barrister to spend his income well, if he misses his case in court, or for a mercenary soldier to spend his wages well, but not go to war?' The pluralists defrauded God and other poor clerks who deserved the benefices they wrongfully appropriated (Peraldus 1587, fos 59–62).

For all this, the extent of gross plurality can easily be exaggerated. It was peculiar to a limited class of clergy, most of whom were engaged in public service. It affected only a relatively small number of churches. Zealous bishops strove to control it, but they were defeated by the easy distribution of papal dispensations and by the general inertia of the social organism, as much as by the prevailing attitude of the aristocracy. It was not really capable of an isolated solution, for it was only one element in the whole system by which ecclesiastical wealth was redistributed.

Averting our eyes from the rich pluralist and the professional absentee, we come at last to the genuine parish priest, who might be a resident rector or, more often than not, a perpetual vicar or a wage-earning chaplain. He was the man entrusted with the dispensation of the sacraments and the pastoral guidance of the people of the parish. He was the occupant of the manse alongside the village church. Socially and economically he belonged to the people he served. Throughout the thirteenth century the ecclesiastical authorities multiplied instructions designed to raise his spiritual and educational level and to improve the performance of his pastoral duties, to make him in fact a man apart from the people.

The canon law required the priest to be celibate. It had been one of the cardinal aims of the Gregorian Reform to restore the ancient Western discipline of clerical celibacy, which had widely fallen into disregard. The legislation against clerical marriage culminated in a decree of the First Lateran Council (1123) declaring marriages contracted by clergy in major orders to be invalid and requiring the partners in such cases to separate (Alberigo and Tanner 1990: i.191, 194; cf. Brooke 1956). By that date, then, if not earlier, the law of clerical celibacy was complete and unequivocal. Of course, the history of its enforcement is another story altogether. Among the higher clergy, marriage or regular concubinage had been largely eliminated by the thirteenth century. But at parish level clerical marriage proved much harder to eliminate. Although the evidence does not allow us to quantify, there is enough to show that in the thirteenth century a significant number of the parish clergy still lived with women who, whatever their position under the canon law, retained the status of wives in the eyes of the local community.

The constant reiteration of the prohibitions and penalties in diocesan synods throughout the century indicates the stubbornness of the problem. 'It has come to our notice through the report of several trustworthy persons,' declared the cardinal legate in 1237, 'that many clerks, forgetful of their own salvation, after entering into clandestine marriages, are not afraid to retain their churches together with their wives. In order to deal with this malady, which is said to have grown widespread, we have made the decisions that follow' (Powicke and Cheney 1964: II.i. 252). The women themselves were brought under attack as well as their clerical spouses. They were to be denied the blessed bread, holy water, and the kiss of peace. Unless, after a third admonition, they quitted the houses of the clergy, they were to be publicly excommunicated and the secular arm was to be invoked against them (ibid: II.i. 63, 117, 132, 187, 229, 428, 440, 463, 486, 555–6; II.ii. 646, 1015, 1083). Bishop Richard le Poore of Salisbury urged that they should be either forced into a respectable marriage or dispatched to the cloister (ibid: II.i. 62). Walter Cantilupe of Worcester decreed penalties against laymen who harboured the concubines of the clergy in their houses; his archdeacons were ordered to hunt out their retreats and identify those who offered them safe lodging at the time of visitations (ibid: II.i. 312).

Despite the fulminations of authority, it is clear that some of the parish clergy remained unmoved and that their wives and children were an accepted part of village society. In 1227 a Kentish man named Allen took his wife before ecclesiastical judges to get an annulment. We do not know why he sought release from his marriage, but the basis of his claim was that his wife's father was the parish priest who had baptised him, so that a forbidden spiritual relationship (a *cognatio spiritualis*) existed between him and his wife (Bliss 1893: 118). This situation was common enough to deserve special mention in a number of diocesan statutes. No social stigma attached to being the son or daughter of a priest, and many of them seem to have lived out their lives happily in the village where their father ministered.[6]

There can be no doubt that the local community connived at the marriage of their priest and in some cases helped to conceal the facts from the ecclesiastical authorities. In 1223 the jurors of Gunthorpe in Rutland testified in a legal action that their church, which was a parochial chapel, had been served by a priest named Reginald, who had held it for life; but that in his old age his son, Henry the chaplain, had taken his place. Henry had never been instituted by the bishop and his quiet takeover at the manse had evidently escaped the notice of the archdeacon. It was only on Henry's death that litigation occurred over the status of the church and the facts, which were well known to the villagers, came to light (Curia regis Rolls 1959: no. 1044).

It must have been fairly easy for the married priest who was on good terms with his parishioners to evade the episcopal harrow. Thomas of Chobham, writing his manual for confessors shortly before the year 1216, complains that the women who co-habit with priests are never put to due penance because priests who have concubines make reciprocal arrangements with one another to hear the confessions of their womenfolk (Broomfield 1968: 386). The bishops, adds Thomas, are much to blame for allowing this kind of thing to happen. The thing that was liable to be the undoing of the married priest was litigation involving his patrons. The canons of Dunstable sought a rescript from Pope Innocent III against the rector of Marston and the vicars of their appropriated churches, alleging that they kept women publicly in fornication and adultery in their houses and refused to abandon them. We may wonder what made the canons suddenly aware of this widespread delinquency; perhaps the bishop was breathing down their necks. But more probably the answer is to be found in another papal letter which reveals that the rector of Marston and other clerks were in dispute with the canons who wanted to raise rents (Cheney and Cheney 1967: nos 1107–8). It looks rather as if the canons had not troubled themselves much about the morals of their parish clergy until their own financial interests were involved and that they then resorted to a charge of incontinence in order to get their way.

It was against the inheritance of churches, of the kind that occurred at Gunthorpe, that the reformers directed their most concentrated fire. Provincial councils and papal decretals inveighed against it, but success was hard won and for long incomplete. Social pressures were too strong. It was natural that the son of a priest should be inclined to follow his father's calling; indeed, in the tightly stratified society of the age, little alternative occupation may have been open to him unless he was to suffer social declassification. Illegitimacy was a canonical impediment to ordination which required a dispensation, but this difficulty was often evaded.[7] Many a parish chaplain who was the son of a priest must have gained all his rudimentary knowledge of Latin and the service books from the parish clerk. Having been ordained with this frail educational equipment, and perhaps with vestments lent from his father's stock,[8] he could get himself taken on as a chaplain elsewhere or even step quietly into his father's position in the village church, as the older priest grew increasingly infirm.

The struggle to prevent churches from passing from father to son was far from won at the outset of the thirteenth century. The clergy in possession put up a stiff fight, and several English bishops found it necessary to get papal mandates to deprive offenders (Powicke and Cheney 1964: II.i. 98–9). The abbot and monks of Bury complained to the pope that they were unable to recover possession of their church of Wrabness in Essex because it was occupied by a clerk and his son, who had held papal letters at bay for a long time by each pretending in turn to be the parson (Cheney and Cheney 1967: n. 11). In Wales, it was alleged in 1222 that the bishop of St Asaph allowed the bastards of priests to succeed to their fathers' churches as of right and regularised the practice by making a charge for the right of succession (Bliss 1893: 85). As late as 1235, Bishop Alexander Stavensby of Coventry obtained a mandate from Pope Gregory IX against sons of priests in his diocese, 'some of whom are married and living in concubinage, who endeavour to succeed their fathers immediately in the same churches and occupy them forcibly on the grounds of hereditary right' (Shirley 1862: 560). But the relentless pressure of authority, combined no doubt with the self-interest of patrons, gradually took its toll on clerical families. Although the Council of Lambeth in 1281 had to remind prelates of the need to prevent benefices passing from father to son, by that date the abuse seems to have become rare.

What level of education and religious knowledge did the parish clergy possess in the thirteenth century? We are not thinking of the absentee rector engaged in the administration of church or state, who might be a university product, but of the humbler priest, the peasant rector, vicar or parish chaplain, who actually occupied the manse. His illiteracy and ignorance were a favourite butt for contemporary satirists including the friars, and the object of much professed concern by the rulers of the Church. 'The ignorance of priests', observed Archbishop Pecham gloomily, 'casts the people into the ditch of error' (Powicke and Cheney 1964: II.ii. 900). Archdeacons and others who instituted clerks to parish churches were frequently reminded of their duty to examine those presented to livings and to reject those whose education was below standard. Bishops' registers record cases where the candidate was refused institution because he was 'insufficiently lettered'. Occasionally men were required to attend the schools as a condition of being accepted. Doubtless some examiners were more demanding than others, but in general these little oral tests cannot have amounted to much. And, of course, many of the unbeneficed clergy, such as parish chaplains, escaped even this perfunctory sifting.

The fact is, it is hard to discern any consistent standard in the pronouncements made by reformers and educators of the period on the one hand, and by officialdom on the other. In his *Sacerdos ad altare accessurus*, Alexander Nequam, the scholarly abbot of Cirencester, prescribes for the would-be priest a reading list that includes the Latin poets as well as the logical and scientific works of Aristotle (Haskins 1927: 356–76). 'I reckon nothing is more fitting to a clerk than to cling to the study of letters,' wrote Philip of Harvengt, 'to have a codex in his hand and to frequent lectures; and this not only in youth, but all the more graciously and with more delight in the flower of his old age' (Migne 1855: col. 159). He would have the clergy study the liberal arts to prepare themselves for studying the scriptures. But both Nequam and Philip were schoolmen writing from the cloister for a clerical elite.

The synodal statutes of English bishops constantly impress upon the parish clergy that they are bound to sing, or at least publicly to recite the divine office daily in their churches. They are told they must do so distinctly, devoutly, without making cuts in the text and without syncopating words (Powicke and Cheney 1964: II.i. 29, 79, 346, 360, 377; Martin 1884: 739). There is not much evidence to show how these requirements were observed in the thirteenth century; but authors of pastoral treatises of the time, such as Edmund of Abingdon, Thomas of Chobham, and Richard Wethershed, assume that the offices are recited daily in churches (Forshaw 1973: 57, 81).[9] Now this, if done in any meaningful way, presupposes no mean facility in reading Latin. Apart from the technical expertise necessary to find one's way through the various service books used for the office and to interpret the rubrics, it needed a fairly robust Latinist to understand many of the lessons drawn from the Fathers that formed part of matins.

At the other end of the spectrum, the Council of Oxford in 1222 instructed archdeacons on their visitations to ensure that the priest could correctly recite at least the unvarying words of the mass canon and the words of baptism, and to make sure that he understood their meaning (Powicke and Cheney 1964: II.i. 115). Here the Council was assuming, perhaps more realistically, a much lower standard of Latin literacy. A rustic priest who could scrape through this undemanding test would still be a long way from being able to recite the lectionary intelligently or to read the Vulgate text of the scriptures.

The limitations of some of the rural clergy are highlighted by the record of a visitation conducted by the dean of Salisbury in 1222. The dean, William de Wanda, whom we have already encountered, had visited the prebendal church of Sonning in Berkshire in 1220. Following this, he decided it was time to investigate the clergy serving the dependent chapels of the parish, and in the summer of 1222 the chaplains were summoned to meet him at Sonning. There, to their dismay, they were given a basic comprehension test, and six of the seven of them were found wanting. Simon, the first of them, who assisted the vicar of Sonning at the parish church, gave details of his ordination four years previously by the bishop of Lincoln. He was then tested on his ability to understand the Latin of the gospel for the first Sunday of Advent. On this he failed ignominiously. The examiners then tried him with the opening words of the eucharistic prayer in the Mass: 'Thee, therefore, most merciful father, we implore', etc. Perhaps he would be good enough to parse the sentence and explain which part of speech governed the accusative 'thee'. 'The Father,' he answered hopefully, 'for the Father governs all things.' The viva proceeded mercilessly. The candidate was unable to distinguish one antiphon from another, and he had not learned the Psalter by heart. 'He is quite illiterate', wrote the dean's clerk. The rest were set a similar test and all were failed. 'He knows nothing; he knows neither how to read nor how to sing', wrote the clerk tersely after the examination of Reginald the chaplain of Arborfield (Rich Jones 1883: 304–5). At the end, the vicar of Sonning was brusquely ordered to find himself better chaplains if he wanted to retain his benefice.

Visitation records are tricky material. An assessment in this case must make allowance for the cultural shock felt by the highly educated and well-to-do prelate, resident of the most learned chapter in England, when faced by a peasant priest who had had no more than a light brush with formal schooling. Intellectually they were denizens of different planets. There is a hint of the disdain that the new intellectual elite of the thirteenth century were inclined to express for the rustic (Murray 1978: 237–9). A man might, after all, learn the stereotype liturgical Latin texts by rote and have some understanding of their sense, yet be incapable of grammatical analysis. The chaplains of Sonning sensed that the dean was hostile, and their ruffled self-respect breaks through the record. Simon, the first victim, protested fiercely at the indecency of examining a man who had already been ordained to the priesthood; and when he emerged from the room, the rest went into a huddle and agreed they would refuse to answer any of the questions – a show of bravado none of them managed to maintain in the dean's presence. But even if the test was slightly less than fair, it revealed a serious problem: the linguistic equipment of the chaplains was so poor that they could not have done much to instruct their lay parishioners. Being themselves almost without Latin, they lacked the means of access to the written sources of religious knowledge, including the Bible.

During the twelfth and thirteenth centuries, educational opportunity expanded in England as it did elsewhere in Western Europe, but much of this improvement only touched the fringe of the parochial clergy. The spread of literacy among the urban laity, the proliferation of higher schools and the rise of the universities had, by creating a highly educated clerical elite, only served to accentuate the problems of the unlettered peasant priest living in a still largely oral society. The law permitted suitable clerks to be dispensed from the obligation of residence so that they could enjoy the emoluments of their benefices while attending the schools, and until residence was more stringently enforced by papal decree in 1274, English bishops dispensed fairly liberally (Boyle 1962). But universities did not provide elementary instruction, nor did many cathedral schools. Without fluent Latin and an agile mind, a man who was sent to the schools to find himself plunged into disputations on the logical books of Aristotle would merely drown.

Those who had the intellectual and linguistic equipment and the money that was needed to attend the schools were those clerks who, being the sons of the landed gentry, could get a benefice while still young, or the children of well-to-do merchants and professional men, who could afford to pay for their education. Most of them who emerged with the master's licence were lost to the pastoral care. They were snapped up by kings, bishops and nobility, and joined the ranks of the administrative elite and the higher clergy; for there was a buoyant market for graduates in the thirteenth century and there were tempting career prospects. Only a few of them were content to reside and work as parish priests. Besides the graduates, a number of beneficed clergy – how many we can never tell – spent a period of two or three years at the schools and returned to their livings without having attempted a degree (Dunbabin 1984: 568–9). But only a small proportion of the men who actually ministered in the parishes can ever have attended one of the higher schools.

For the annual chaplains and most of the perpetual vicars, formal education must have begun and ended at a humble song school owned by a monastery or collegiate church and conducted in the adjacent town by a hired schoolmaster. It was at such a school in the borough of Bury St Edmunds that Abbot Samson, when he was an impoverished boy clerk, had received his first lessons from Master William of Diss (Butler 1949: 44, 95). There are traces of schools like this in several English towns by the end of the twelfth century. What they provided can have been little more than elementary instruction in the Latin psalter and liturgical chant. Parish clerks, too, were expected by canon law to teach the children of their parishes, and there is evidence that some of them did so (Orme 1973: 67; Owen 1971: 106). No doubt their services were supplemented by many a village priest who taught his own or a neighbour's son to read Latin after a fashion – the same Latin that he had once acquired himself.

The gap between higher learning and the educational equipment of most of the parish clergy was widened by the activities of the schoolmen. In the course of the thirteenth century the schools fostered important developments in sacramental and moral theology and canon law. The great syntheses appearing at Paris and Bologna and the glosses of the masters were creating a new kind of theological and canonistic science, and this had important implications for the pastoral care. The practice of the confessional, for instance, was being quietly transformed by a new science of casuistry. In the hands of such early thirteenth-century masters as Robert Curzon, Thomas of Chobham and William of Auxerre, the analysis of sin and human motivation achieved a stage of refinement that was beginning to make the old penitentials look obsolete (Lottin 1949).[10]

At the same time, new and heavier demands were being made on the parish clergy. The new legislation not only reiterated the long-standing obligation of the faithful to confess at least once a year to their parish priest; it also required him to preach regularly to his people. When he attended the diocesan synod, he was constantly reminded of his duty to preach on the ten commandments, the capital sins and the articles of faith (Powicke and Cheney 1964: II.i. 268, 304, 345). These requirements, combined with the revival of popular preaching at the beginning of the century and the wider dissemination of literacy among the laity, aroused expectations that few parish chaplains would have been able to meet.

The question was how to equip the parish clergy to meet these demands in the absence of any formal institutional training. English bishops wrestled with this intractable problem in a variety of ways. They used the diocesan synod, prescribed by the General Council, as an instrument for enforcing the new legislation and training the clergy in the duties of their office. The more conscientious bishops convened a synod every year. William de Blois of Worcester showed special concern for the attendance of the annual wage-earning chaplains: their rectors were instructed to provide them with horses and victuals for the journey to and from the assembly (ibid: II.i. 175). In a number of cases they prescribed, or even themselves provided, instructional manuals containing detailed guidance on the administration of the sacraments, especially on hearing confessions and the direction of penitents. As Walter Cantilupe of Worcester explained to his clergy in 1240 at a meeting of the synod: 'Priests, some of whom are simple persons, should have the knowledge to instruct their parishioners how they ought to confess and examine their consciences, and they should know the varieties of penance that are enjoined by law. We have, in fact, composed a treatise on confession, and we have bidden all chaplains to write out a copy of it and observe it when they hear confessions, for it would have taken too long to publish it in the present synod' (ibid: II.i. 305, 320). And he meant to be read: in future, clergy were to be examined in the contents of his booklet before being instituted to livings in the diocese.

If Cantilupe needed literary models for his book, there were plenty to hand by that date. Since the end of the twelfth century a whole new genre of didactic literature had appeared, designed to instruct the parish clergy in moral theology and the rudiments of canon law and to equip them for their duties. Although they were written by schoolmen, treatises of this type were pitched at a much lower level than the scholastic literature of the university classrooms. They were essentially practical manuals, works of vulgarisation in fact, which summarised the teaching of the schools in a form digestible by a less educated readership.[11] Some of the earliest of them, such as the *Liber Poenitentialis* of Alain of Lille and the similar book by Robert of Flamborough, were designed to provide guidance on the new canon law – the *ius novum* – for those who had to hear confessions. Both writers, who were products of the Paris schools, quote extensively from the decretals. In the years before any official compilation of the decretals had been promulgated, they offered a helpful digest of ecclesiastical law on the various issues likely to arise in the confessional. Their usefulness is indicated by the many manuscripts of their works that survive both in England and on the continent.

Other manuals of this kind ranged more widely. The *Summa Confessorum* composed by Thomas of Chobham, the sub-dean of Salisbury, was the work of another schoolman who had been to Paris. He wrote his book at about the time of the Lateran Council of 1215. As he explains in his preface, his intention was severely practical: 'We shall bypass subtleties and theoretical inquiries, and deal more carefully with the working details and practical considerations that are needful to priests in hearing confessions and enjoining penances' (Broomfield 1968: 3). But within this framework he provided his readers with an extensive summary of current moral and sacramental theology. His discussion of ordination and marriage, for instance, amounts in each case to a miniature treatise on the subject.

What makes Thomas's book so interesting is not only the fact that it communicates the new thinking of the schools in a language free from jargon; it also envisages the problems faced by parish clergy in a variety of different situations. He has one foot already in the newly emerged urban societies of his time. This was the area to which the friars were about to direct their chief missionary effort. And one of the reasons for their success with the urban bourgeoisie was that they talked the language of the market-place and accepted the morality of commercial profit, even if in a limited form (Little 1978).[12] This modification of traditional teaching on the subject of commerce had been prepared at Paris in the classrooms of Peter the Chanter and his disciples; and Thomas provides a resumé of it for his clerical readers:

(The essence of) business is to buy something more cheaply, with the intention of selling it more dearly. But this is quite permissible for lay people, even if they render no compensation for the goods they have previously purchased and subsequently sold. For otherwise there would be great shortage in some areas. For merchants transport what is abundant in one area to another place where the same thing is in short supply. Therefore merchants can legitimately receive the price of their labour and carriage and their expenses over and above what they paid when they purchased the goods.

(Broomfield 1968: 301–2)

This was a reassuring message for confessors to communicate to their urban penitents, even if it was hedged about by the reservation that the seller's margin should not exceed 50 per cent of the just price of the goods.

Thomas's avowed object was to equip priests with the knowledge they needed to instruct their parishioners when they came to confession. A similar aim inspired another manual of the same period called the *Good Pastors' Summa* (*Summa qui bene presunt*) written by Master Richard of Wetheringset, who was chancellor of Cambridge. Master Richard's main concern was to help the parish clergy fulfil their obligation to preach to their people. To this end he provides a comprehensive syllabus of instruction in faith and morals. The priest should preach regularly on the articles of the creed, the seven petitions of the Pater Noster, the seven gifts of the Spirit, the seven cardinal virtues and the seven capital sins, the seven sacraments, the ten commandments, the reward of the just and the punishment of the wicked, and the duties of subordinates and their betters. For suitable authorities and illustrations 'by which untutored minds can be more easily persuaded' he refers his readers to the Bible and the commentaries of the masters, especially those of Master William de Montibus, sometime chancellor of Lincoln (London, Lambeth Palace, MS.144, fos 35v–36).

This basic syllabus of instruction was a common framework adopted by several authors of pastoral manuals writing in England in the first half of the thirteenth century. They borrow freely from one another and also from continental models including Peraldus' widely read *Summa of Virtues and Vices*. Most of them were simpler, smaller and more modest in scope than the books of Chobham and Peraldus. One of these slighter treatises that followed the plan of Wetheringset was the *Temple of the Lord* composed by Grosseteste, which resorts to elaborate schematic diagrams and cumbrous mnemonics to help memorise the virtues and vices (Goering and Mantello 1984).[13] These devices, which strike the modern eye as quaint, provide vivid testimony to the limitations of the untutored readership they were designed to help.

It was a chronic weakness of the medieval Church that it failed to solve the problem of educating the parish clergy for their task. Good intentions were defeated by the sheer dimensions of the problem. Although educational provision increased in the later Middle Ages, in the thirteenth century there were not enough schools offering the kind of instruction required, and there were not enough educated men to go round. For many city-dwellers the rise of the friars filled the gap by providing the well-trained elite that the Church needed, but their superior education and pastoral skills also accentuated the shortcomings of the secular clergy. The economic structure of the Church ensured that only a few of those who emerged from the higher schools were willing to undertake pastoral duties. The regular establishment of the diocesan seminary had to await the sixteenth century. In the absence of institutional provision, due credit must be given to the many schoolmen bishops of the thirteenth century who persevered in their efforts to improve the theological education of their parish clergy. Unfortunately we have no means of measuring the success of their programme.

NOTES

1 To the twelfth-century examples cited by Cheney can be added at least eleven vicarages ordained in the Chichester diocese by bishops John Greenford (1174–80) and Seffrid II (1180–1204) (Mayr-Harting 1964: 57–61).

2 The church was valued at 40 marks in the assessment of 1254 (Lunt 1926: 293) and at £36.13.4 in that of 1291 (Ayscough and Caley 1802: 37). A truer value (£81.16.7) was disclosed by an extent made in 1314–15 (Lunt 1926: 608).

3 The following figures are drawn from Davis and Foster 1925, and Hill 1950.

4 Robert Bingham, bishop of Salisbury, complained that many would-be ordinands deceived his official with fraudulent titles which they obtained by promising their guarantors that, once ordained, they would make no claims on them. The complaint was repeated by Fulk Basset in his London statutes of 1245–59: Powicke and Cheney 1964: II.i. 373–4, 644.

5 At the Wiltshire eyre of the judges in 1249, out of 175 persons accused of crime 21 were clerks, described as either *clerici* or *capellani*. Several of them were said to be members of gangs charged with violent robbery (Meekings 1961: 99).

6 At Great Paxton, for instance, the rector Master Peter had a son named Richard who witnessed four Paxton deeds between 1230 and 1240 as 'filius Magistri Petri' and 'filius persone' (Foster 1931: 192–4). Such attestations are not uncommon.

7 In 1228, when the chapter of Salisbury had to elect a new bishop, several members, including the dean, confessed that they were disqualified as being of illegitimate birth and lacking the necessary dispensations (Rich Jones 1883: 104–16).

8 At the visitation of Sonning in 1220 it was revealed that the vicar, Vitalis, had a son who served the church of Loddon, and that Vitalis had given him an alb belonging to the church of Sonning (Rich Jones 1883: 275).

9 Chobham gives detailed advice on the subject (Broomfield 1968: 123, 129–30). For later evidence see Bowker 1967: 112.

10 More conservative writers such as Grosseteste continued to refer to the penalties prescribed by the old penitentials, but the general trend was towards allowing the confessor wide discretion (Goering 1978).

11 For a descriptive list, to which several items could be added, see Michaud-Quantin 1962.

12 But see the critique of Little's thesis in d'Avray 1985: 204–25.

13 For other pastoral manuals of the thirteenth century, see Boyle 1977.

REFERENCES

Unpublished material

London, British Library, Add. MS. 43972 (Little Wymondley Cartulary).
London, British Library, Cotton MS. Claudius D XIII (Binham Cartulary).
London, Lambeth Palace, MS. 144.

Secondary works

Alberigo G. (ed.) and N. Tanner (trans.) (1990) *Decrees of the Ecumenical Councils*, London and Washington: Sheed and Ward and Georgetown University Press.

Bliss, W. H. (ed.) (1893) *Calendar of Entries in the Papal Registers relating to Great Britain and Ireland. Papal letters*, I. A.D. 1198–1304, London: Eyre & Spottiswoode for Her Majesty's Stationery Office.

Bowker, M. (1967) *The Secular Clergy in the Diocese of Lincoln, 1495–1520*, Cambridge: Cambridge University Press.

Boyle, L. (1962) 'The constitution *Cum ex eo* of Boniface VIII and the education of the parochial clergy', *Mediaeval Studies* 24: 263–302

—— (1977) 'Three English pastoral Summae and a Master Galienus', *Studia Gratiana* 11: 135–44.

Brewer, J. S. (ed.) (1858) *Monumenta Franciscana*, Rolls Ser., London: Longman, Brown, Green, Longmans and Roberts.

Brooke, C. N. L. (1956) 'Gregorian reform in action: clerical marriage in England, 1050–1200', *Cambridge Historical Journal* 12: 1–21.

Broomfield, F. (ed.) (1968) *Thomas of Chobham. Summa confessorum*, Louvain: Éditions Nauwelaerts

Butler, H. E. (ed.) (1949) *The Chronicle of Jocelin of Brakelond*, London: Nelson.

Cheney, C. R. (1956) *From Becket to Langton. English church government, 1170–1213*, Manchester: Manchester University Press.

—— and M. G. Cheney (eds) (1967) *The Letters of Pope Innocent III (1198–1216) concerning England and Wales. A calendar with an appendix of texts*, Oxford: Clarendon Press.

Colvenerius, G. (ed.) (1627) *Thomae Cantimprensis . . . Bonum universale de apibus . . .*, Douai.

Constable, G. (ed.) (1967) *The Letters of Peter the Venerable*, Cambridge Mass.: Harvard University Press.

Curia regis Rolls of the Reign of Henry III preserved in the Public Record Office, vols 11, 13 (1955, 1959), London: Her Majesty's Stationery Office.

d'Avray, D. L. (1985) *The Preaching of the Friars: sermons diffused from Paris before 1300*, Oxford: Clarendon Press.

David, F. W. and C. W. Foster (eds) (1925) *Rotuli Ricardi Gravesend episcopi Lincolniensis*, Lincoln: Lincoln Records Society.

Davis, F. N. (ed.) (1913) *Rotuli Roberti Grosseteste episcopi Lincolniensis*, A.D.. 1235–1253, London, issued for the Canterbury & York Society.

Deedes, C. (ed.) (1915) *Registrum Johannis de Pontissara episcopi Wyntoniensis*, A.D.. 1282–1304, vol. I, London, issued for the Canterbury & York Society.

Dunbabin, J. (1984) 'Careers and vocations', in J. Catto (ed.), *The History of the University of Oxford*, I. *The Early Oxford Schools*, Oxford: Clarendon Press, 565–605.

Forshaw, H. (ed.) (1973) *Edmund of Abingdon. Speculum religiosorum and Speculum ecclesiae*, Oxford University Press for the British Academy.

Foster, C. W. (ed.) (1931) *Registrum Antiquissimum of Lincoln*, Lincoln: Lincoln Records Society.

France, J. (ed.) (1989) *Rodulfi Glabri Historiarum libri quinque*, Oxford: Clarendon Press.

Gieben, S. (1971) 'Robert Grosseteste at the papal curia; Lyons 1250: edition of the documents', *Collectanea Franciscana* 41: 340–93.

Goering, J. (1978) 'The *Summa* of Master Serlo and thirteenth-century penitential literature', *Mediaeval Studies* 40: 290–311.

—— and F. A. C. Mantello (eds) (1984) *Robert Grosseteste. Templum Domini; edited from MS. 27 of Emmanuel College Cambridge*, Toronto: Pontifical Institute of Mediaeval Studies.

Graham, R. (ed.) (1952–6) *Registrum Roberti Winchelsey, Cantuariensis archiepiscopi*, A.D.. *1294–1313*, 2 vols, Oxford: Oxford University Press (for the Canterbury & York Society).

Haskins, C. H. (1927) *Studies in the History of Medieval Science*, Cambridge, Mass.: Harvard University Press.

Hill, R. (ed.) (1975) *The Rolls and Registers of Oliver Sutton 1280–99*, vol. 7, Lincoln: Lincoln Records Society.

Hilton, R. H. (1966) *A Medieval Society: the West Midlands at the end of the thirteenth century*, London: Weidenfeld and Nicolson.

Lawrence, C. H. (1989) *Medieval Monasticism. Forms of religious life in Western Europe in the Middle Ages* (2nd edn), London and New York: Longman.

—— (1994) *The Friars. The impact of the early mendicant movement on Western society*, London and New York: Longman.

Little, L. K. (1978) *Religious Poverty and the Profit Economy in Medieval Europe*, London: Paul Elek.

Lottin, O. (1949) *Psychologie et morale aux XIIe et XIIIe siècles*, vol. III, Louvain: Abbaye de Mont César/Gembloux: J. Duculot.

Luard, H. R. (ed.) (1861) *Roberti Grosseteste episcopi quondam Lincolniensis epistolae*, Rolls Ser., London: Longman, Green, Longman and Roberts.

—— (ed.) (1872–83) *Matthaei Parisiensis, monachi Sancti Albani, Chronica Majora*, 7 vols, Rolls Ser., London: Longman and Trübner.

Lunt, W. E. (1926) *The Valuation of Norwich*, Oxford: Clarendon Press.

Major, K (ed.) (1950) *Acta Stephani Langton Cantuariensis archiepiscopi*, A.D.. *1207–1228*, Oxford: Oxford University Press (for the Canterbury & York Society).

Martin, C. T. (ed.) (1884) *Registrum epistolarum fratris Johannis Peckham archiepiscopi Cantuariensis*, vol. II, Rolls Ser., London: Longman.

Mayr-Harting, H. (ed.) (1964) *The Acta of the Bishops of Chichester 1075–1207*, Torquay: The Devonshire Press (for the Canterbury & York Society).

Meekings, C. A. F. (ed.) (1961) *Crown Pleas of the Wiltshire Eyre, 1249*, Devizes: Wiltshire Archaeological Society Records.

Michaud-Quantin, P. (1962) *Sommes de casuistique et manuels de confession du XIIe au XIV siècles*, Louvain: Éditions Nauwelaerts.

Migne, J.-P. (ed.) (1855) *Patrologia Latina*, vol. 203, Paris: apud J.-P. Migne editorem.

Murray, A. (1978) *Reason and Society in the Middle Ages*, Oxford: Clarendon Press.

Orme, N. (1973) *English Schools in the Middle Ages*, London: Methuen.

Owen, D. M. (1971) *Church and Society in Medieval Lincolnshire*, Lincoln: Lincolnshire Local History Society.

Peraldus (1587) *Summa de Vitiis et Virtutibus*, Antwerp, vol. II.

Polo de Beaulieu, M. A. (1993) 'L'image du clergé séculier dans les recueils d'*exempla*', in *Le Clerc séculier au Moyen Age*; Actes du 22ᵉ Congrès de la S.H.M.E.S., Paris: Publications de la Sorbonne.

Powicke, F. M. and C. R. Cheney (eds) (1964) *Councils and Synods, with other Documents relating to the English Church*, II. A.D.. *1203–1313*, Oxford: Clarendon Press.

Rich Jones, W. H. (ed.) (1883) *Vetus registrum Sarisberiense alias dictum registrum S. Osmundi episcopi: the register of S. Osmund*, vol. I, Rolls Ser., London: Longman.

Riley, H. T. (ed.) (1867) *Gesta abbatum monasterii Sancti Albani a Thoma Walsingham, regnante Ricardo Secundo, ejusdem ecclesiae praecentore, compilata*, vol. I, Rolls Ser., London: Longmans, Green, Reader, and Dyer.

Robinson, D. (1969) *Beneficed Clergy in Cleveland and the East Riding 1306–1340*; York: The Borthwick Institute.

Shirley, W. W. (ed.) (1862) *Royal and Historical Letters illustrative of the reign of Henry III from the originals in the Public Records Office*, vol. I, Rolls Ser., London: Longman, Green, Longman and Roberts.

Taxatio ecclesiastica Angliae et Walliae, auctoritate P. Nicholai IV, circa A.D. *1291*, eds Ayscough, S. and J. Caley (1802) London: The Record Commission.

Walter, J. T. (ed.) (1926) *La Tabula exemplorum*, Paris.

CHAPTER THIRTY-EIGHT

EVERYDAY LIFE AND ELITES IN THE LATER MIDDLE AGES: THE CIVILISED AND THE BARBARIAN

Gábor Klaniczay

I

Historians of medieval and early modern Europe have been struggling for a long time to find the best way to characterise most appropriately the vivid variety they encounter in the documents that reveal the texture of life in those periods. If they want to go beyond nineteenth-century romanticism or antiquarianism, historians have to construct broad concepts to frame and analyse without anachronism the manifestations of originality and diversity they rightly perceive in their evidence. Since the beginning of the twentieth century, some historians have eschewed the political, legal, institutional and philological approaches that prevailed earlier, and still command allegiance in many quarters, and have turned instead to the concept of everyday life (French *la vie quotidienne*; German *Alltagsgeschichte*). With this, a whole series of scholars have set out to examine a wider and deeper sphere of experienced realities. Their aim has been to unveil the material structures defining the conditions in which life was lived during the period concerned (Schultz 1889/1965, 1892; Langlois 1926–8; Coulton 1928; Faral 1942; Delort 1972; Le Goff 1977; Brost 1983; Kühnel 1986; Jaritz 1989; *Medium Aevum Quotidianum*). Especially in recent decades, on the basis of fruitful exchanges with anthropological theory, a similar all-embracing concept has been put forward, the *histoire des mentalités* (Le Goff 1977; Martin 1996) which approaches everyday realities from the opposite side, that is, from the abstractions used by historical subjects in a given period, and the ways in which those subjects perceived time, space, nature, gender and the norms regulating behaviour in those fields. The history of material culture (German *Realienkunde*) (Braudel 1979; Krems-Veröffentlichungen 1977–98) and the various branches of historical anthropology have inherited the goals of the exponents of these two conceptual approaches, and tried to combine and nuance them in various ways by drawing on the resources of an ever-widening field of interdisciplinary methodology. All these approaches have one thing in common: the assumption that the underlying structural features – material, social, and mental – of life in a given period and place could be characterised within a single explanatory framework, which could then be subdivided further into sociological, regional and chronological categories, such as norms and modes of conduct (*Lebensformen*) (Huizinga 1924/1996; Borst 1973).

Parallel to these developments came the emergence of dualistic explanatory systems. Although histories of everyday life generally include rich material on well-documented special occasions such as feasts (Alewyn-Sälzle 1959; Heers 1971), research in this latter field has logically tended to pursue a separate line and to concentrate on the contrast between the ongoing flow of everyday life, on the one hand, and, on the other, episodic festive occasions that were ritually and ceremonially regulated or playfully exploited. There is an interesting historiography differentiating popular culture from elite culture, and exploring the interplay between them. This distinction has indeed established itself as a powerful interpretative framework capable of accounting for basic socio-cultural contrasts (ecclesiastical : secular; religious : magical; written : oral; institutional : communal; courtly/urban : secular), as well as indicating important mechanisms of historical change (vulgarisation, conflict, repression, reform) (Bakhtin 1984; Davis 1975; Burke 1978; Muchembled 1978). Similar advantages might be ascribed to the recent renewal of prosopographically orientated history of elites on the one hand (Stone and Stone 1984; Bulst and Genet 1986) and a social history 'from below' on the other (Thompson 1963). Gender has proved another fruitful binary opposition in historical analyses, not least for the periods covered in this chapter. Another contrasting pair which seems to have been quite widely used recently is public : private (Aries and Duby 1988). Finally, I would classify among dualistic explanatory systems all research that assumes an opposition between nature and culture – whether associated with the history of the body (Foucault 1977, 1990–2; Bynum 1987; Brown 1989; Feher and Nadaff 1989; Kay and Rubin 1994), childhood (Aries 1962), death (Aries 1975), or the evolution of norms, behavioural patterns, and institutions – and tries to assert the domination of culture over nature in the broader sense (Thomas 1984).

Needless to say, all these (partly overlapping and partly complementary) frameworks with their individual merits and shortcomings are relevant to the topic of this chapter. Each of them could provide a starting-point for examining the relationship of elites to everyday life at the end of the Middle Ages, and the selection of any one of them ought to be combined with the findings of rival methodologies. The starting-point I have chosen, namely Norbert Elias's theory of the civilising process, is drawn from the explanatory systems I have labelled dualistic (Elias 1939/1969, 1978).

The relevance of Elias's theory to my subject is evident, concentrating as it does on the routines, norms, forms of etiquette, and morals which regulated such manifestations of late medieval and early modern life as eating habits, dress, attitudes to bodily functions, and behaviours in public and private places. More importantly, according to Elias the changes in these areas of life were brought about by and contributed further to the distinctive ambitions of contemporary elites, whether chivalrous, urban, courtly, or intellectual. The theory of the civilising process has the advantage of taking into account the irreducible originality of the late medieval/ early modern world-views stressed by historians of mentalities and historical anthropologists, while pointing to the possible tools, agents, ideals and social conditions of the historical transformation that bridges the difference between those people and ourselves (on Elias see Aya 1978; Gleichmann, Goudsblom and Korte 1979; Chartier 1980, 1988). Other theoretically informed historical investigations have since confirmed and nuanced the outlines of the transformation: a growing self-discipline, a distancing from and repression of bodily realities, a deepening gulf between elites and popular culture, the multiplication of new techniques and cultural means for dealing with nature in all its aspects, the emergence of a set of new institutions capable of restructuring social and mental dispositions according to a new set of norms (Foucault; Ariès; Braudel; Burke).

One more thing could be added to underline the usefulness of Elias's work in the present context. Concentrating on early modern court society, which he viewed as the main historical laboratory where the new model of civilisation could be matured, Elias depicted a very special historical moment in the relationship of elites to everyday life. Within the political and sociological constraints of increasingly powerful courts, the whole of everyday life was transformed into new kinds of festive representation, blurring the boundaries between everyday and festivity, private and public. All this restructured the rules of communication, behaviour and ritual order. The emerging new norms, mediated by fashions, treatises on civility, court etiquettes and civilised eating utensils, not only brought about a growing awareness of a refined daily life in courtly elite circles, but also provided those elites with a new way of differentiating themselves from the rest of society and of criticising uncivilised aspects of the daily life of others. We have here, then, in the fifteenth and sixteenth centuries, a very complex and conflict-ridden set of relationships awaiting exploration by us.

II

I now want to examine more closely the historical transformations described by Elias; specifically, I want to reconsider his explanation of how the civilising process was intensified during the Renaissance. Elias drew attention to the increasing number and more refined character of the civility treatises of this period (Erasmus, Castiglione, Dedekind, and della Casa). That these treasties represent a turning-point in the long-term evolution of manners is beyond doubt. Yet this assertion can scarcely be accommodated within Elias's broader characterisation of the civilising process. He postulates a gradual, linear evolution from late medieval chivalry towards the elaborated hierarchical models of absolutist courts in the seventeenth and eighteenth centuries. His central argument aims to explain the 'social genesis' of the absolutist state, which deprived the nobility of their military functions and compelled them to accept new forms of social distinction by becoming courtier-prisoners of the ruler's well-isolated absolutist household, and by adapting themselves to its rigid principles.

Italy, the paradise of Renaissance courtly culture, offers the spectacle of splendid courts with no states they could control. Here, instead of a disarmed nobility, were powerful soldiers, parvenu *condottieri*, swarming from court to court together with legions of artists and humanist scholars looking for protection while, at the same time, suffering from a sense of the humiliating nature of these conditions. Respectable members of the bourgeoisie are to be found here too. As for the civility treatises of these same court milieux – Castiglione's *The Courtier*, for instance – rather than developing the original Burgundian ideal of rigid court hierarchy and strict social differentiation, they formulated a loose and playful system. An important aspect of their cultural impact lay in their openness towards the integration of various elements of popular culture, such as dances, farces, pageants, masquerades, carnivals, obscene jokes and sexual licence (Prosperi 1980; Heers 1983; Burke 1978, 1987; Trexler 1980; Lever 1983; Ginzburg 1996). All this seems at odds with Elias's emphasis on the intensification of the civilising process which repressed and sublimated basic manifestations of human nature; and it supports, instead, the thesis of Mikhail Bakhtin who regards the Renaissance as the period of the most fruitful and intensive intrusion into the sphere of high culture of what he labels popular culture (Bakhtin 1984: 15–30). It looks as if Elias's theory needs some correcting on this point, and I now want to offer some material for this correction by taking a few steps back, towards Christian attempts at civilising everyday life in the preceding medieval period.

Christianity's negative judgement on earthly bodily pleasures (Rousselle 1988; Foucault 1990–2) gave rise during the Middle Ages to various attempts to repress, sublimate and civilise them according to ascetic principles. This model, mainly elaborated in monasteries and schools (Hugh of St-Victor, *De institutione novitiorum*, PL 176: 925–52; cf. Schmitt 1990: 173–205; Pseudo-Boethius, *De disciplina scolarium*, ed. Weijers 1976; Jean de Garlande, *Morale Scolarium*, ed. Paetow 1927; Gabriel 1956), radiated from the monks and clergy towards various groups in secular society whose barbarous nature and rusticity those same ecclesiastics frequently deplored. After the emergence of court culture in the eleventh and twelfth centuries, churchmen did their best to contribute to the civilising of knightly elites. Some, including John of Salisbury and Walter Map, served as courtier clerics, criticising and scorning their surroundings; others, such as Petrus Alfonsi (Hilka and Sjöderhjelm 1911), Andreas Capellanus (Benton 1961) or Fra Bonvicino da Riva (Schirokauer and Thornton 1957; Jaeger 1985), elaborated new models of court conduct. In this context, they made the first attempts to set down the principles of a Christian pedagogy to tame and regulate the instinctive functions of human nature. Yet Erasmus, in his *De civilitate morum puerilium*, was following not so much the tradition of rudimentary prescriptions about knightly eating habits as the Christian neo-Platonist pedagogical ideal of the twelfth-century monk Hugh of St-Victor.

Besides inheriting the civilising ideals that grew out of the ascetic principles of medieval Christianity, late-medieval and Renaissance courts also borrowed and amplified the Church's symbolic capital for the ceremonial–liturgical framing of festive occasions. The secularisation of various religious and cultural forms (the cult of the saints through the veneration of relics, through legends, artistic representations, pilrimages, processions, etc.) by the chivalrous and courtly culture of the fourteenth and fifteenth centuries has been well documented (Burckhardt 1925; Huizinga 1924; Huizinga 1996; Anglo 1969). It was no concidence, therefore, that such traditional experts in prestigious ecclesiastical representation as popes and cardinals became, in fifteenth-century Italy, the leading figures in its adaptation for secular use. Paolo Cortesi's *De cardinalatu* (1510), describing the courtly activities of the *cardinale-senatore*, is the major precursor of Castiglione's *The Courtier*, dedicated to Pope Julius II, who is said to have provided its main inspiration (Prosperi 1980: 82–3). When due allowance is made for this manifold indebtedness of Renaissance court civilisation to medieval Christianity, we are better able to appreciate key elements that are new. The Renaissance witnessed a kind of rehabilitation, even a cult, of some things that had previously been condemned. With a diminished sense of sinfulness surrounding the body, sexuality, and nudity, and with a growing admiration for nature and natural behaviour, and a joyous devouring of earthly pleasures, Renaissance courts, humanists and artists extended their attention to areas that had previously been thought to constitute a menacing, hostile environment which civilisation would have to overcome (Stallybrass and White 1986). Yet, as soon as all these areas became parts of court culture and all that nourished it, civilising activity, with the taming and regulating that that entailed, had also to be extended to all the cultural manifestations of court life.

Let me give a few examples. In Renaissance representations of the naked and even erotic body, even while the transgression of earlier taboos is clear, a new canon was consolidated at the same time, in which, as Bakhtin's keen eye observed (1984: 319–22), the obscenity of the grotesque body, with its openings and meta-morphoses, was suppressed and hidden behind a façade of athletic beauty. The new canon, exemplified in *The Courtier*, introduced new distinctions, between old and young, tall and short, and prescribed a continuous effort to attain the new norms by means of diligent gymnasic exercises or refined cosmetic devices. Similarly, in the Renaissance cult of gardens, the domesticating of a piece of nature began a trend which would lead within the next century and a half to the creations of Le Nôtre which, according to Saint-Simon, 'tyrannised Nature, enslaving it with the help of money and art' (cf. Elias 1969: 338). The same applies to the passion for owning a large collection of animals in the princely zoo, tamed by a team of specialists. Renaissance ambitions to transform nature can likewise be seen in the various utopian designs described by Thomas More (Logan 1983: 148ff.). In *The Courtier*, what counts is not the quality of being natural but rather the ability to *seem* natural, an appearance created by the famous *sprezzatura* which is among those arts the courtier most needs to cultivate (cf. Loos 1955). As to real nature, Castiglione leaves readers in as little doubt as would Giovanni della Casa a few decades later: it must be domesticated by the power of reason and custom, and human manners have to be ennobled just as plants must be refined and wild animals domesticated. It is not the cult of nature that makes pastoral nostalgia reappear in Renaissance poetry (Ronsard, du Bellay), but rather, a sudden recognition of the recent loss of contact with nature (Elias 1969: 340–1, 384ff.).

A further example is that of popular culture, in Peter Burke's sense of the verbal, ritual and symbolic culture shared by everyone (1978: 23–64). It ought to be stressed again how much courtly society was indebted to the festive aspects of late medieval and Renaissance urban and rural life. Masked balls, dances, games, mock-insulting rituals, dirty jokes, impertinent fools, big carnivals where princes, courtiers, burghers and peasants rejoiced together (the Medici, for instance, were particularly keen to protect carnivals (Chastel 1946)). These were not peripheral features of Renaissance courtly life, but among the central cultural traditions on which it depended (Burke 1978: 270–80; Heers 1983: 133–40). It is obvious, though, that courtiers wanted to distinguish themselves even in these fields. Castiglione's conversations are full of recommendations as to what kind of figures a gentleman should avoid in popular dances, under what conditions he might venture to engage in competitions, games or fights with people of lower social status. Although courtly culture was just as deeply rooted in orality as popular culture in general (cf. Burke 1993), it was precisely here that it attempted to assert its distinctiveness: besides the detailed advice of Castiglione or della Casa, courtiers could also turn to the period's third extremely popular manual of civility, Stephano Guazzo's *La civile conversazione* (Quondam 1993). In the second half of the sixteenth century, an initial openness tended to yield to an increasing tendency towards aristocratic exclusivism. Courtly civilisation had by then created its elitist canon in the fields of verbal communication and colloquial genres, while popular dances were transmuted by an elaborate geometrical choreo-graphy (Lippe 1974/1988) and less and less space remained for spontaneity and popular participation in elite festivities.

The cause of this trend was not just the growing aristocratisation of court society. With the growing size and political importance of courts, it became more and more difficult to accommodate the rhythm of court life to the ritual cycles and periodic festive occasions of popular culture. As a slightly later observer noted: 'the courtiers have changed the order of nature: they make day into night and night into day. While others sleep, they stay up and make merry, and while others are awake, and work according to their duties, the courtiers sleep, to recover the strength lost in debauchery' (Alewyn and Sälzle 1959: 31). The elite lived in a permanent festive society with special highlights provided by their own micro-world: arrivals of ambassadors, princely visits, marriages, and funerals. In the long run, the daily events of the prince's life (getting up, walking, having meals, playing games, hunting) became the major regulators of court ceremony. Thus the inner logic of courtly life required the same thing as did the courtiers' mentality: namely, their withdrawal from the scene of popular culture, retaining only those elements that could be transformed, civilised and adapted to their own needs (Bakhtin 1984: 110–16; Burke 1978: 270–80).

Yet all of this must be viewed as the outcome of a series of conflicts in which at least three distinct tendencies can be observed in the fifteenth and sixteenth centuries. First, it was in the shadow of the prince's emerging secular power that the trans-gression of medieval Christian values was often carried to its utmost extreme. Writing of the courtier's morality, not only Machiavelli but Castiglione too advised hypocrisy and shrewdness: *a*morality was the necessary consequence of fierce struggles for princely favour, of power games, of the intrigues of courtly life. Hand in hand with this went loose morals, from the sacrilegious debaucheries of the Borgia courts to the refined eroticism of Fontainebleau. Court scientists did not abhor experiments with the occult and astrological speculations; hermetic and magical treatises circulated in increasing numbers (Yates 1964, 1972; Evans 1973). Courtiers found a special delight in exoticism, as shown in the famous episode from the beginning of the sixteenth century when Cardinal Ippolito Medici, bastard son of Giuliano, Prince of Nemours, gathered a crowd of barbarians – Arabian horsemen, Mongolian archers, black wrestlers, Indian divers, Turkish hunters – and enjoyed the Babel-like confusion of the many languages spoken (Burckhardt 1925: 273).

Second, the drive for regulation came to Renaissance courts not from within but from outside, that is, from humanist scholars who contemplated their lascivious surroundings with contempt, and longed to get away from the court (Bömer 1904; Smith 1966; Uhlig 1973). Most humanistic civility books, from Pier Paolo Vergerio or Aeneas Silvius Piccolomini to Erasmus or Guevara, were written with the explicit aim of educating the young prince in better conduct, counter-balancing the harmful influences of the courtly environment. The notion of *civilitas*, inherited from Antiquity, was by no means synonymous with courtliness (Ariès 1962: 388–90; Elias 1969: 91, 140). It tended, rather, to align itself with a long medieval tradition of court criticism. In a speech to the Medici in 1516, the Florentine humanist Lodovico Alamanni sharply opposed *habito civile* to *costume cortesani* (Prosperi 1980: 83–4). The impact of this humanistic trend varied. During the fifteenth century, court criticism left little mark on actual court manners. Castiglione and those who followed him were the first to try to harmonise Platonic and Stoic ideas with the realities of courtly life, to temper exaggerations and shape a 'golden middle way'. What could best and most easily be adopted from humanistic critiques were not their inner content but formal requirements for civilised everyday behaviour. Thus in della Casa's *Galateo* we hear not a word about morals or classical learned culture.

Third, even for this kind of integration into the courtly model of certain practical aspects of humanistic ideals, another, more radical, version of court criticism was needed: a version offered by preachers, whether Protestant or post-Tridentine Catholic. The German followers and translators of Erasmus, and such fiery Protestant critics as Sebastian Brandt or Geiler von Kaisersberg, disputed the superiority of the courtier as vehemently as did such Catholic moralists of the Spanish court as Antonio de Guevara, in his *Menosprezio de corte y alabanza de aldea* of 1539, or Lodovico Vives (Quondam 1980: 63–8; Burke 1995). Courtly civilisation made identical compromises with both kinds of religious sensibilities: it gave up the provocative and spectacular transgressions, and restructured courtly conduct, if not according to Christian-ascetic principles, then at least according to the rules of classical self-restraint and discipline.

To sum up the first part of my argument: the Renaissance intensification of the civilising process worked in two ways. On the one hand, there was a transgressing divergence from the road which medieval Christian and especially late-medieval Burgundian chivalrous society had been inclined to take. On the other, there was a hefty counter-reaction, as a result of which Western civilisation managed to discipline, and thus integrate within it, these broader domains of everyday life.

III

The other problem I want to discuss in connection with this late-medieval and Renaissance phase of the civilising process is the geographical diffusion of the emerging new model in Europe at large. From the moment of their birth, the ideals and everyday practices of civilisation served to define not only the social distinction of courtly milieux but equally the cultural distinction between various nations. During the Italian campaigns of the French king Charles VIII, the would-be paragons of courtliness were considered by the Italian princes as barbarians because of their slovenly appearance and the bawdy 'disorder' of the French court (Martines 1980:

234). A similar image of uncivilised Frenchmen, mouthing obscenities and reeking of cheese, haunts Castiglione's *Courtier*. In Erasmus' *Colloquia*, the typology of the inn allows the uncouth manners of the Germans to be satirised (Elias 1969: 91–2).

To avoid such an unfavourable reputation, some courts made efforts to emulate as speedily and fully as possible the most up-to-date ideals. The humanistic court of King Matthias in Hungary set out to rival contemporary Italian courts in refinement and intellectual prestige, and the dream of Hungarian humanists was to seduce the Muses themselves into the hitherto uncultivated fields of Pannonia (Schallaburg 1982). Henry VIII's courtly festivities could evoke the following comment from an Italian observer: 'the wealth and civilisation of the world are here; and those who call the English "barbarians" seem to me to render themselves such. I have perceived elegant manners, extreme decorum, and very great politeness' (Anglo 1969: 123). Elsewhere, the adoption of courtliness meant a slight change in tone and content. Norbert Elias has briefly analysed how in Germany courtly rites of civilised conduct tended to become a kind of all-embracing moral programme voiced by scholars, preachers, schoolmasters and bourgeois, all of whom urged its adoption in order to obliterate the current bad reputation of the German nation (Elias 1969: 90–6).

But all this emulation was by no means automatic. Resistance and refusal were equally natural responses. Some of the most spectacular cultural images of Renaissance transgression, whether represented by actual behaviour or expressed in mock-heroic, satirical or even deliberately exaggerated and licentious literary forms, come from countries and courts still hesitating over whether or not to adopt the new Italian–Spanish norms of civilisation. A case in point is François Rabelais, associated with the court of Francis I just at the time of the French wars against Charles V, the chief representative of Spanish courtly civilisation. Another such case is that of German Grobianistic literature. This curious genre, going back to such fourteenth-century precedents as 'The German Cato', quite deliberately attempted to shock readers by offering examples of grotesquely uncivilised behaviour. The proliferating series of depictions of Grobianic 'table manners', of the admonitions of brotherhoods of swine, of satirical guild 'regulations', and of accounts of the land of Cocaygne, began with Kobel's 1492 version and underwent successive 'improvements' at the hands of Sebastian Brandt, Hans Sachs and others (Schirokauer and Thornton 1957) until the sythesis of the Wittenberg scholar Friedrich Dedekind in 1549 (*Grobianus. De morum simplicitate*). Dedkind's work was immediately translated into German and completed by Caspar Scheidt, who taught Fischart, Rabelais' German translator (*Grobianus. Von groben Sitten und unhöflichen Gebärden*, ed. 1979), and in the course of the next century was re-translated into German and commented on no fewer than three more times (Hauffen 1889; Bömer 1904: 260–85). How are we to interpret all this enthusiasm for depicting Pantagruelian images of cheerful and aggressive barbarousness that not only violated one by one all the rules of civil decency in bodily habits, cleanliness, eating, drinking and conduct in public, but also supplied witty and revolting justifications for so doing? The sincerity of the authors' commitment to moral pedagogy need not be doubted. Nevertheless, a certain fascination with the display of barbarous *mores* cannot be excluded either. Nor should we ignore the fact that this genre enjoyed a wide audience (including some, no doubt, who were half-sympathetic to similar forms of behaviour!).

The image of popular Grobianic literature in Germany is interestingly complemented by that of Dedekind's translations. Although his excellent piece of satire inspired no Italian, Spanish or French translation or reworking, it did get translated at opposite ends of Europe: in 1592 into Hungarian by Matyas Csaktornyai, a Lutheran schoolmaster in Tirgu Mures (Marosvasarhely), Transylvania (Kiszeghy 1998), and in 1605 into English under the title *The Schoole of Slovenrie or Cato turnd wrong side outward* (Rúhl 1904). In England the book's long-lasting popularity is shown by the impact it had on Swift; and further versions were elaborated, one by Thomas Dekker (1609), another, an Oxford University drama entitled *Grobiana's Nuptials* (Rúhl 1904: 161–91). This kind of approving amplification of the image of the monstrous, uncivilised barbarian is at least as much a kind of cultural legitimation as a scornful satire. Several examples could be cited to prove that considerable numbers of the late-medieval and Renaissance elite preferred to behave like Grobianus rather than adopt the new civilised ways. (It might be instructive to compare the impact of civilised manners and the new routines of everyday life in the two Central European kingdoms of Hungary and Poland.)

From the thirteenth century onwards Hungary was being intensively influenced by chivalrous cultural models from the West. The courts of kings Bèla III, Emeric I and Andrew II received various groups of western knights and artists, for instance Peire Vidal and Gaucelm Faidit, who came in the retinues of queens. Andrew II was among the organisers of the Fifth Crusade (1217) and he seems to have absorbed something of western courtliness as far as life-styles were concerned too. He introduced the new shaving customs among his entourage, and lavished praise on one of his knights 'because of the elegance of his manners' (Kurcz 1988; Sweeney 1981). After these early influences, and thereafter with the formation in Hungarian society of a warrior-class akin to knights, Hungarian chivalrous courtly culture flourished in the thirteenth and fourteenth centuries during the reigns of the Angevin kings and of Sigismund of Luxemburg. Two orders of chivalry, the Order of St George and the Order of the Dragon, together wth several hundred newly built castles, the emergence of the chivalrously coloured cults of St Ladislaus and St George, and many other developments, testify to this belated flowering (Fügedi 1986; Marosi 1987; Klaniczay 1992).

Yet courtly and aristocratic circles in Hungary adopted an ambivalent attitude to these imported ideals. Andrew II's wife, Gertrude of Meran, was murdered in 1217 and her German relatives and retinue were expelled while the king was away on crusade (Bak 1997). The first thorough attempt to adjust social political structures to western models, by means of various royal reforms after 1241 under Bèla IV and Stephen V, was followed by a resurgence of oriental fashions under Ladislas IV 'the Cuman', who despised courtly manners and preferred to live with his Cuman soldiers and concubines. Disregarding the complaints of the Hungarian clergy and the papal legate, Ladislas in 1279 guaranteed the Cumans' legal right to stick to their traditional pointed hats, Mongolian-style clothing and traditional hairstyle (Palüczy Horvath 1989; Berend 1997). These same decades also witnessed the growing popularity of the myth of the Hunnic origin of the Hungarians, which became the central motif of the *Chronicle* of Master of Simon of Kèza, written in the 1280s (Szücs 1975).

These 'oriental' features remained in vogue in Hungary for more than a century, rivalling the attraction of western chivalrous fashions. In the first decades of the fourteenth century, some documents even reveal a kind of radiation outwards of these stylistic features towards the whole of central Europe: the *Anonymus Leobiensis* (1310) deplored the spread of these dress fashions in Styrian and German regions, and also condemned the popular practice of men's 'dividing their hair [in braids] like Hungarians or Jews' ('ut Judei vel Ungari comam dividebant . . . ') (SRA I: 947). In 1330 Peter of Zittau complained about 'strange novelties in clothing, habits and morals' in Bohemia and the surrounding regions. These novelties consisted, among other things, in men's letting their beards and moustaches grow long *more barbarorum* ('in the custom of the barbarians') (FRB IV: 404). An ambivalent response to the reception of western courtly culture was epitomised by the legend of St Ladislas, the chivalrous *athleta patriae* fighting the Cuman warrior: this hagiographic or even mythological scene was depicted on the walls of several dozen medieval Hungarian parish churches in the fourteenth and fifteenth centuries. This story directly addressed the key issue of fourteenth-century Hungarian identity: a warlike nation that had opted for Christianity and the West remained fiercely proud of its eastern marauding traditions, for the Cuman warrior fought with armour and tactics similar to those of Hungarian horsemen in pagan times and even as late as the fourteenth century. The frontispiece of the *Chronicon Pictum* shows Louis I 'the Great' (1342–82) surrounded by warriors representing the two traditions more or less equally: there are as many knights in western armour as there are orientalised figures (*Chronicon Pictum* 1986; Marosi 1991).

The 'barbarous resurgence' in late medieval Hungary in reaction to intensified western cultural influence exemplifies the precarious reception accorded in these regions to foreign models of civilisation. While the cultural impact of chivalrous manners and lifestyles remained modest throughout later centuries, similar counter-reactions occurred whenever foreign cultural or political influence was felt to be too aggressive in the royal court. The situation became further complicated after the battle of Mohács (1526), when the national kingdom was overwhelmed and one-third of the country was occupied by the Ottoman Empire, while another northwestern part went to the Habsburgs, and the eastern territories were united with the Principality of Transylvania. As for the problem of the nobility's everyday life, under the new circumstances they had to beware of oriental or Ottoman influences, but necessarily treated western-type absolutist courtly models with almost as much caution. As a possible alternative, many noble courts, as well as the princely court of Transylvania, preferred to adhere to the Italian orientation of the period of Matthias Corvinus. Even this led to various conflicts, however. A good instance of anti-Italian feeling can be cited from the end of the sixteenth century, in the words of Istvàn Szamosküzi, a critic of the Italian entourage of Prince Sigismund Bàthory (1587–99):

> This crowd of Italians was spoiling his soul with cringing adulation. . . .
> They arrived from unidentified corners of Italy in a miserable, ragged and
> dirty condition. But as soon as they joined the company of their compatriots
> here, and with their help they could get near to Sigismund, . . . they were

transformed: now they were showing off in silk clothes, having cast off their coat of dirt and misery as snakes cast off their skins. . . . Their adulatory speeches and hypocritical flattery disarmed the prince . . . who started to chase after various pleasures with them. . . . He invited singers, harpists, flute-players and other half-fools; he continually employed vegetable-growers and flower-gardeners, cooks, pastry-makers, sausage-fillers, cheese-makers, showing off in the Italian style. Then came the actors, clowns, jesters, dancers, tailors, ball-players and other experts in godless vanities. . . . Magicians and conjurers were not lacking either. . . . They kept praising the beauties of Italian cities, the splendour of the princes there, the dignity of the cardinals . . . while they scorned the customs of the Hungarians, alien as these were to gracious conversations and devoid of any seductive beauty. They contrasted their smoothness and refinements with Hungarians' alleged rusticity and coarseness. They urged [the Prince] to exchange that barbarism for Italian customs.

Szamosküzi then went on to describe at length how ridiculous he found the Italian attire adopted by Sigismund under his courtiers' influence (Szamosküzi 1876: 11–16; Klaniczay 1983). The ambiguous reputation of Italian courtiers was in any event a well-known phenomenon throughout Europe: one proverb ran: 'Inglese italianato e diavolo incarnato' (Burke 1995).

IV

Was this ambiguous situation replicated in the everyday life of the Hungarian nobility in the fifteenth and sixteenth centuries? I shall try to give a brief survey of how far these nobles adopted the new courtly conduct that came to them in such ambivalent ways. They kept up with Italian or German courts in many other fields of cultural, scholarly and political display, but where everyday life and manners were concerned, the royal court as early as the reigns of Matthias Corvinus (1458–90) and of the two Jagiellon kings Wladislas II (1490–1516) and Louis II (1516–26) tended instead to reject the exaggerations of the new ideals. When King Ferdinand of Aragon wanted to send horse-trainers to King Matthias, the latter replied in a slightly offended tone: 'We never wanted horses that jump around with curved legs in the Spanish manner, because we cannot use such horses for anything serious and not even for play. We do not need horses which prance with ankles leaning inwards. The horses we want must stand firmly and robustly on their legs' (Fraknüi 1893–95, II: 229). Galeotto Marzio reports of King Matthias that he refused to use the forks given to him as a present by the Prince of Ferrara, and instead went on eating with his fingers 'though in a very proper way' (Galeottus 1934: 17–18). Forks were still not in use in the Hungarian royal court half a century later in Louis II's time (Fügel 1913, 1917), and only after 1530 did they begin to appear regularly in noble dowries (Radvànszky 1896/1986: 139–40; cf. Braudel 1979: 174; Elias 1979: 172). As late as the early eighteenth century, the Transylvanian writer Peter Apor still mentions forks as a recent foreign import (Apor 1927). Roast meat went on being served in a single lump until the eighteenth century, in contrast to the western custom of serving meat already carved, as described by Elias; and individual spoons for diners were seldom recorded.

Somewhat unrefined eating habits did not mean a lack of interest, and even of a certain sophistication, in cooking. As far as we can judge, in late-medieval and early modern Hungary food had to be consumed among the elite in quantitites hardly imaginable for us. For a well-to-do noble family in the sixteenth century, a regular lunch consisted of ten to twenty different courses, dinners of six to fourteen. Gatherings for celebrations within the family or including the more extended kindred, such as wedding feasts, were characterised by ostentatious hospitality. Lodovico Ariosto complained that he would not come to Hungary again because 'they eat and drink too much and they consider it an offence if one does not join them!' (Elekes 1939: 296). Late sixteenth-century Transylvanian etiquette required that glasses of brandy be emptied with every toast, though foreign envoys, so Ambassador Franco Sivori recorded, could obtain a special exemption (Klaniczay 1983: 39). This Rabelaisian image could be further illustrated by examples of the court festivities of the Jagiellon kings in early sixteenth-century Hungary. On the feast of Corpus Christi 1501, a spectacular show was organised in the castle of Buda: Muhammad's coffin was ceremoniously made to explode, wine poured out of the fountains, and roast chickens, pigeons and turkeys were thrown to the spectators to be torn to pieces (all this was described in detail by the Venetian ambassador Tommaso Dainero (Szamota 1891: 497)). A rather belated flowering of chivalrous tournaments was incorporated into a series of splendid court carnivals. King Louis II himself participated, fighting in the guise of a Wild Man against the Devil personified by his friend George of Brandenburg (Radvánszky 1896/1986, I: 165–72; Fügedi 1985; cf. Bernheimer 1952). Hungarian and Polish court officials and chancellors, such as Krzysztof Szydowiecki, vainly attempted to persuade the young ruler to accept a more rational and disciplined way of life (Zombori 1987): the festivities came to a close only with the disaster of Mohács in 1526, where Louis died on the battlefield.

Looking at all this through the eyes of contemporary Hungarian scholars, we become aware of a significant imbalance. There is still much evidence of criticism of courtly vanities and immorality, like the one quoted from Transylvania, and these often echo the international commonplaces of this literary genre (Smith 1966; Uhlig 1973). Yet translations of the vast corpus of fifteenth- and sixteenth-century civility books were very scarce. Apart from a third-rate school compendium of Sebald Heyden (Bömer 1904: 262; Dèszi 1897), a medieval selection of Cato's teachings, and a catechism-like adaptation of Erasmus' *De civilitate morum puerilium*, both these last two works published by Czaktornyai in Debrecen in 1591, the only civility book translated into Hungarian was Dedekind's *Grobianus*, and, as argued earlier, its civilising value could be considered somewhat ambiguous (Kiszeghy 1999).

The absence of imports of this genre in Hungary can only partly be accounted for by the lack of a national royal court, or by the ongoing warfare against the Ottomans. If the majority of the Hungarian nobility, or even the cultivated elite, felt little attraction towards western and Mediterranean cultural models, this was more for reasons rooted in their *mentalité* than because of the conditions of their everyday life. They kept on repeating how much they despised 'great compliments'

(Turùczy-Trostler 1956: 97). Mòrton Szepsi Csombor, a Protestant savant at the end of the sixteenth century, wrote mockingly about 'courtiers who try to adjust their steps to the form of a circle, or measure each step carefully as if they were tailors of gesture, so as not to make mistakes in their ridiculous leaps. All this is unfitting for us men, who ought to move in a way that shows strength and perseverance. It is women's task to flatter others by the way they talk and dress or by variations in their hairstyles' (Szepsi Csombor 1968: 322; cf. Jankovics 1987). A few decades earlier, Johannes Cuspinianus had noted that Hungarian nobles were rather proud of the 'stiff, uncultivated multitude of their ancestors who migrated from Scythia to their present location' (*rudis illa, atque inculta Majorum nostrorum multitudo ex ipsis Scythiae . . . ad haec Loca migrasset*, Podhradzky 1842: 79). In 1581, a Polish courtier, Jan Gruszczyöski, wrote a little book on *The duties of good society* (*Powinosci dobrego towarzystva*) based on his experiences at the Transylvanian court of Prince Stehen Bàthory, where again he was met with a set of values still associated with manliness and military prowess (Kapelus 1969). It is worth mentioning that the Poles were more active at this time than the Hungarians in importing civility treatises. *The Courtier*, for instance, was translated, or rather transposed, by Lukasz Gürnicki under the title *The Polish Courtier* (*Dworzanin polski*) in 1566. Yet, on closer inspection, the impression we are left with is not so different from that of the Hungarian picture. In Gürnicki's book, the changed scenery and structure leave out women because 'in Poland ladies were not learned enough to take part in the conversation'. The sections on painting and sculpture were omitted too, on the grounds that they were less relevant for Polish courtiers. Finally, the misogynistic phrases of Gasparo Pallavicino were turned into fierce diatribes against the effeminacy of Italian courtiers (Burke 1995: 90–3).

Returning to Hungary, we find only three alternatives to the lavish immorality of the courts that aped foreign ways: the stoic isolation of the scholar, the acceptance of strict Protestant morality, and the deliberate maintenance of cheerful barbarism. The second and third of these in fact have certain features in common. In 1571, Pèter Bornemisza, one of the most acclaimed Protestant preachers of the second half of the sixteenth century, set out to bellow his religious message at the elite in a plebeian tone: 'in the manner of a villain, a peasant and a Grobianus' (Bornemisza 1955: 152). In central Europe, the ideal of ostentatious barbarism could be based on a specific historical tradition, namely, that of the Hungarians' original and oriental Scythian identity, or, in the case of the Poles, their Sarmatian ancestry. Both ideologies were rooted in the Middle Ages, and emerged in early modern times as factors of national identity or ethnic character. The earliest accounts of the Hungarians' Scythian identity came from the late-twelfth-century *Chronicle of the Anonymous*, and in the 1280s, they were further developed into a detailed identification of Huns with Hungarians by Master Simon of Kèza, mentioned above (Benda 1937; Eckhardt 1943: 11–51; Szûcs 1975, 1981). While the italianate Renaissance court of King Matthias radiated its splendour throughout Europe, the noble notary Janos Thuröczy's *Chronicle of the Hungarians* provided a lengthy amplification of the Hunnic origin-myth, and this image was equally appreciated by Matthias, whom Thuröczy sets up as the second Attila (Johannes de Thurocz 1985). All this had been elaborated by Matthias' court chronicler, Antonio Bonfini (Antonius de Bonfinis 1936/74, I:

79ff.) In 1581, the same phraseology of wild, fur-clad warrior-Scythians received further rhetorical development in *Attila*, written by the humanist bishop Miklös Olàh (Nicolaus Ohahus 1938; Pèter 1980). The Polish nobility's consciousness of their similarity to the Sarmatians became increasingly evident at this same period, when Poland was often ruled by Transylvanian princes: as early as the seventeenth century, a Polish Franciscan, Waclaw Dembolecki, advanced the hypothesis that the Scythians and Sarmatians were the same people (Michalski 1980; Petneki 1980).

This barbarian pride with its oriental tinge was also expressed in such external features as an abundance of colourful and splendidly showy costumes. The triumphal processions and entries arranged, at home or abroad, by Hungarian kings, noble ambassadors and cardinals amply illustrate all this. In 1485, Matthias's treasury was transported by 24 camels, and he also put on show large numbers of Turkish captives. In 1514, Cardinal Tamàs Baköcz entered Rome with elephants and various exotically dressed troops; and in the same year the Polish cardinal Jan Laski led a *triompho* which sought to outdo Baköcz's in mythological and oriental splendour (Petneki 1987). The Hungarian–Transylvanian nobility's colourful costumes were themselves effective vehicles of this oriental taste. They often wore the Turkish coat, the kaftàn, decorated with a special set of embroidered and ornamental motifs. The wide use of non-inverted furs is among the most exotic features of this eastern European style: the nobleman's warrior-consciousness was evoked by a piece of wolf-skin or panther-skin (*kacagàny*) worn over the shoulders and clasped at the animal's feet. Special fur-trimmed hats adorned with feathers were common to Hungarians, Poles and also Cossacks, and formed another item in this oriental repertoire (Radvònsky 1896/1986, I: 56–76). This same ideal was not only accepted but even applauded by the 'civilised' courts of fifteenth- and sixteenth-century Italy, France or Germany, keen as they were on exotic manifestations of oriental difference (Raby 1982). Hungarian and Polish noblemen, however, tended to misinterpret the exotic prestige of this style: its use seemed to spare these elites the effort of adapting to new phases of the 'civilising process' for another century or so. Thus a curious core–periphery distinction is apparent in the distribution of cultural models in early modern Europe, and this contributed to the belated spread of western cultural innovations in east-central Europe.

* * *

The result of this brief re-examination of Norbert Elias's concept of the civilising process in its fifteenth-and sixteenth-century phase has been to reveal that this evolution was not simply a cumulative process, as Elias presented it. Instead, it was interrupted by several significant deviations, like those of the deliberate cultural transgressions practised in various Italian Renaissance and Mannerist courts. The early modern intensification of the civilising process was the outcome of such conflicting tendencies, not least of the various reactions which those transgressions provoked in Renaissance court culture.

The diffusion of the model from cultural 'centres' to the 'peripheries' was accompanied by a degree of resistance, by unforeseen side-effects, and by adverse reactions. New ideals of civilisation often went hand-in-hand with attempts at political and cultural domination: hence they were received in the 'newcomer' countries with justified mistrust and ambivalence. Ostentatious barbarism and Grobianism were among the characteristic transgressive traits within Renaissance culture that could be observed all over Europe. Yet these had a special relevance, and underwent peculiarly interesting metamorphoses, in the geographical diffusion of models of civility to central Europe, where, coupled with a tradition of orientalism, they were transmuted into a special set of values, a sort of counter-hegemonic strategy, which had a major impact on the manners, the everyday life, and the material culture, of central European elites.

ACKNOWLEDGEMENTS

A version of this chapter was first presented in the framework of a stimulating conference at the Krems Institute on *Realienkunde*: Klaniczay 1990: 255–84. I am grateful to the editors of the present volume for help in producing this revised version.

REFERENCES

Alewyn, R. and K. Sälzle (1959) *Das Große Welttheater: Die Epoche der höfischen Feste in Dokument und Deutung*, Hamburg: Rowohlt.

Anglo, S. (1969) *Spectacle, Pageantry and Early Tudor Policy*, Oxford: Clarendon.

Antonio de Bonfinis (1936/74) *Rerum ungaricarum decades*, ed. I. Fógel, B. Iványi, L. Juhász, P. Kulcsár, Lipsiae-Budapest: Teubner, Egyetemi.

Apor, P. (1927) *Metamorphosis Transylvaniae*, eds. Ö. Wildner and J. Sugár, Budapest: Rzósavölgyi és Tsa.

Ariès, P. (1962) *Centuries of Childhood: a social history of family life*, tr. by Robert Baldick, New York: Random House.

—— (1975) *Western Attitudes to Death: from the middle ages to the present*, Baltimore, London: The Johns Hopkins University Press.

Ariès, P. and G. Duby, (1988) *A History of Private Life, II. Revelations of the Medieval World*, Cambridge, Mass. and London: Belknap.

Aya, R. (1978), 'Norbert Elias and the civilizing process', *Theory and Society* 5: 138–228.

Bak, J. (1997) 'Queens as scapegoats in medieval Hungary', in A. Duggan (ed.), *Queens and Queenship*, London: Boydell and Brewer, 223–33.

Bakhtin, M. (1984) *Rabelais and His World*, tr. by H. Iswolsky, Bloomington: The University of Indiana Press.

Benda, K. (1937) *A magyar nemzeti hivatástudat története* (History of the consciousness of the Hungarian 'national calling'), Budapest: Bethlen Nyomda.

Benton, J. F. (1961) 'The court of Champagne as a literary center', *Speculum* 34: 511–91.

Berend, N. (1997) 'medieval patterns of social exclusion and integration: the regulation of non-Christian clothing in thirteenth-century Hungary', *Revue Mabillon*, n.s. 8 (=60): 155–176.

Bernheimer, R. (1952) *Wild Men in the Middle Ages: a study in art, sentiment and demonology*, Cambridge, Mass.: Harvard University Press.

Berrong, R. M. (1986) *Rabelais and Bakhtin: popular culture in Gargantua and Pantagruel*, Lincoln, Nebraska, and London: University of Nebraska Press.

Bömer, A. (1904) 'Anstand und etikette in den theorien der humanisten', *Neue Jahrbücher für das klassische Altertum* 14: 223–42, 249–85, 330–55, 361–90.

Bornemisza, P. (1955) *Ördögi kisirtetekről, avagy röttenetes utálatosságáról ez megfertőzött világnak* (About devilish temptations and the loathsomeness of this wretched world), Budapest: Akadémiai.

Borst, A. (1973) *Lebensformen im Mittelalter*, Frankfurt am Main: Propiläen; Ullstein.

Borst, O. (1996) *Alltagsleben im Mittelalter*, Frankfurt am Main: Insel-Verlag.

Braudel, F. (1979) *Civilisation materielle et capitalisme. XVe-XVIIIe siècle. Les structures du quotidien. Le possible et l'impossible*, Paris, English tr. (1992) *Civilization and capitalism, 15th–18th century*, Berkeley: University of California Press.

Brown, P. (1989) *The Body and Society: men, women and sexual renunciation in early christianity*, New York: Columbia University Press.

Bulst, N. and J.-P. Genet (1986) *Medieval Lives and the Historian: studies in medieval prosopography*, Michigan: Medieval Institute Publications. Western Michigan University.

Burckhardt, J. (1925) *Die Kultur der Renaissance in Italien*, Leipzig: Alfred Kroner.

Burke, P. (1978) *Popular Culture in Early Modern Europe*, New York and London: Harper & Row.

—— (1987) *The Historical Anthropology of Early Modern Italy: essays on perception and communication*, Cambridge: Cambridge University Press.

—— (1993) *The Art of Conversation*, Cambridge: Polity Press.

—— (1995) *The Fortunes of the Courtier. the European reception of Castiglione's* Cortegiano, Cambridge: Polity Press.

Bynum, C. W. (1987) *Holy Feast and Holy Fast: the religious significance of food to Medieval Women*, Berkeley: The University of California Press.

Chartier, R. (1980) 'Norbert Elias interprète de l'histoire occidentale', *Le Débat*, 5: 138–143.

—— (1988) 'Social figuration and habitus: reading Norbert Elias', in *Cultural History*, Cambridge: Polity Press, 71–95.

Chastel, A. ed. (1946) *Laurent de Médicis-Ambre, l'altercation et les chansons de Carnaval. Lettre à Frédéric d'Aragon*, Paris: Éditions du Vieux Colombier.

Chronicon Pictum (1986) eds. comm. D. Dercsényi, K. Csapodi-Gárdonyi, I. Bellus, Gy. Kristó, Budapest: Európa.

Coulton, G. G. (1928–1930) *Life in the Middle Ages*, Cambridge: Cambridge University Press.

Csáktornyai, M. (1999) *Gróbián*, ed. P. Kőszeghy, Budapest: Balassi.

Davis, N.Z. (1975) *Society and Culture in Early Modern France*, Stanford: Stanford University Press.

Delort, R. (1972) *Le Moyen Age. Histoire illustrée de la vie quotidienne*, Lausanne: Edita.

Dézsi, L. (1897) 'Heyden Sebald "Gyermeki beszélgetései" 1531-böl' (Childish conversations by Sebald Heyden - of the year 1531) *Irodalomtörténeti Közlemények*, 7: 214–15.

Eckhardt, S. (1943) 'Sicambria, capitale légendaire des francais en Hongrie', in *idem*, *De Sicambria à Sans Souci*, Paris: PUF:11–51.

Elekes, L. (1939) 'Királyi és foúri udvar', in: *Magyar Müvelödéstörténet*, ed. S. Domanovszky, Budapest, II: Magyar Történelmi Térsulat.

Elias, N. (1939/1969) *Über den Prozeß der Zivilisation. Soziogenetische und psychogenetische Untersuchungen*, Bern, München and Baden-Baden: Suhrkamp. (1994) English tr. , *The Civilizing Process: the history of manners and state formation and civilization*, Oxford: Basil Blackwell.

—— (1978) *Die höfische Gesellschaft*, Neuwied-Berlin: Luchterhand, (1983) English tr., *The Court Society*, Oxford: Basil Blackwell.

Evans, R. J. W. (1973) *Rudolf II and His World*, Oxford: Oxford University Press.

Faral E. (1942) *La vie quotidienne au temps de Saint Louis*, Paris: Hachette.

Feher, M. ed. (1989) *Fragments for a History of the Human Body* Parts 1–2, New York: Zone Books.

Fógel, J. (1913) *II. Ulászló udvartartása* (The court of Wladislas II), Budapest: MTA.

—— (1917) *II. Lajos udvartartása* (The court of Louis II), Budapest: Hornyónszky Nyomda.

Foucault, M. (1977) *Discipline and Punish: The Birth of the Prison*, New York: Vintage Books.

—— (1990–1992) *The History of Sexuality*; 1: *An Introduction*; 2: *The Use of Pleasure*; 3: *The Care of the Self*, London: Penguin Books.

Fraknói, V. (1893–1895) *Mátyás király levelei* (The letters of King Matthias), Budapest: MTA.

Fügedi, E. (1985) 'Turniere im mittelalterlichen Ungarn', in Josef Fleckenstein (ed.), *Das ritterliche Turnier im Mittelalter. Beiträge zu einer vergleichenden Formen- und Verhaltengeschichte des Rittertums*, Göttingen: Vandenhoeck & Ruprecht: 390–400.

—— (1986) *Castle and Society in Medieval Hungary*, Budapest: Akadémiai.

Gabriel, A. (1956) *The Educational Ideas of Vincent de Beauvais*, Notre Dame, Indiana: Medieval Institute.

Galeottus Martius Narniensis (1934) *De egregie, sapienter, iocose dictis ac factis regis Mathiae, ad ducem Iohannem filium liber*, ed. L. Juhász, Lipsiae: Teubner.

Ginzburg, C. (1996) *Ritratto del buffone Gonella*, Modena: Panini.

Gleichmann, P. J. Goudsblom, and H. Korte (1979) *Materialen zu Norbert Elias' Zivilisationstheorie*, Frankfurt: Suhrkamp.

Guazzo, S. (1993) *La civil conversazione*, ed. A. Quondam, Modena: Panini.

Hauffen, A. (1889) *Caspar Scheidt, der Lehrer Fischarts. Studien zur Geschichte der Grobianischer Literatur in Deutschland*, Strassburg: Trubner.

Heers, J. (1971) *Fêtes, jeux et joutes dans les sociétés d'Occident à la fin du Moyen Age*, Paris: Vrin.

—— (1983) *Fêtes des fous et carnavals*, Paris: Fayard.

Hilka, A. and W. Sjöderhjelm (1911) *Die 'Disciplina clericalis' des Petrus Alfonsi*, Heidelberg.

Huizinga, J. (1924/1996) *The Autumn of the Middle Ages*, Chicago: The University of Chicago Press.

Jaeger, S. (1985) *The Origins of Courtliness: civilizing trends and the formation of courtly ideals*, Philadelphia: Pennsylvania University Press.

Jankovics, J. (1987) 'Udvarellenes tendenciák a 17. század eleji magyar költészetben' (Anti-courtier trends in the Hungarian poetry of the beginning of the 17th century) in Á. R. Várkonyi, ed., *Magyar reneszánsz udvari kultúra* (Hungarian Renaissance courtly culture), Budapest: Gondolat: 86–106.

Jaritz, G. (1989) *Zwischen Augenblick und Ewigkeit: Einführung in die Alltagsgeschichte des Mittelalters*, Wien and Köln: Böhlau.

Johannes de Thurocz (1985) *'Chronica Hungarorum'*, eds. E. Galántai and J. Kristó, Budapest: Akadémiai.

Kapelus, H. (1969) 'Zápolya János Zsigmond udvara Gruszczynsky epigrammáiban' (The court of John Sigismund Zápolya in the Epigrams of Gruszczynsky), in *Tanulmányok a lengyel-magyar irodalmi kapcsolatok történetéből* (Studies in Hungarian-Polish literary relations), Budapest: Akadémiai: 145–60.

Kay, S. and M. Rubin eds. (1994) *Framing Medieval Bodies*, Manchester: Manchester University Press.

Klaniczay, G. (1990) *The Uses of Supernatural Power: the transformations of popular religion in medieval and early modern Europe*, Cambridge: Polity Press.

—— (1990) 'Alltagsleben und Elite im Spätmittelalter. Zivilisierte und Barbaren', in: *Mensch und Objekt im Mittelalter und in der frühen Neuzeit. Leben – Alltag – Kultur*, Wien: Verlag der Österreichischen Akademie der Wissenschaften, 255–84.

Klaniczay, T. (1983) 'Gli antagonismi tra Corte e società in Europa centrale: la Corte transilvanica alla fine del XVI secolo', *Cheiron* 1: 31–58.

Kühnel, H. (1986) Graz – Wien – Köln: Edition Kaleidoskop.

Kurcz, A. (1988) *Lovagi kultúra Magyarországon a 13–14. században* (Chivalrous Culture in 13–14th century Hungary), Budapest: Akadémiai.

Langlois, Ch.-V. (1926–28) *La vie en France au moyen âge de la fin du XIIe au milieu du XIVe siècle*, Paris: Hachette.

Le Goff (1977) 'Les mentalités: une histoire ambiguë', in J. Le Goff and P. Nora, eds., *Faire de l'histoire*, Paris: Gallimard.

—— (1977) 'L'historien et l'homme quotidien', in *Pour un autre Moyen Age*, Paris: Gallimard.

Lever, M. (1983) *Le sceptre et la marotte*, Paris: Fayard.

Lippe, R. zur (1974/1988) *Vom Leib zum Körper: naturbeherrschung am menschen in der Renaissance*, Hamburg : Reinbek; Rowohlt.

Logan, G. M. (1983) *The Meaning of More's* Utopia, Princeton : Princeton University Press.

Loos, E. (1955) *Baldassare Castiglione's 'Libro del Cortegiano'*, Frankfurt am Main: Klostermann.

Marosi, E. (1987) 'Der heilige Ladislaus als Ungarischer Nationalheiliger. Bemerkungen zu seiner Ikonographie im 14–15. Jh.', *Acta Historiae Artium Hungariae* 33: 211–56.

—— (1991) 'Zur Frage des Quellenwertes mittelalterlicher Darstellungen. Orientalismus in der Ungarischen Bilderchronik', in *Alltag und materielle Kultur im mittelalterlichen Ungarn*, A. Kubinyi and J. Laszlovszky eds, Krems: Medium Aevum Quotidianum 22, 74–107

Martin, H. (1996) *Mentalités médiévales XIe-XVe siècle*, Paris: Presses universitaires de France.

Martines, L. (1980) *Power and Imagination: city-states in Renaissance Italy*, New York: Vintage Books.

Medium Aevum Quotidianum - series at the Krems Institute: cf. (1992) *Zwanzig Jahre Institut für Realienkunde des Mittelalters und der Frühen Neuzeit der Österreichischen Akademie der Wissenschaften*, ed. H. Kühnel, Krems.

Michalski, J. (1980) 'Le sarmatisme et le problème d'européisation de la Pologne', in: V. Zimányi, ed. *La Pologne et la Hongrie aux XVIe et XVIIe siècles*, Budapest: Akadémiai: 113–120.

Muchembled, R. (1978) *Culture populaire et culture des élites dans la France moderne*, Paris: Flammarion.

Nicolaus Olahus (1938), *Hungaria-Athila*, eds. C. Eperjessy and L. Juhász, Budapest: K. M. Egyetemi Nyomda.

Paetow, J. L. (1927) ed. *Jean de Garlande, Morale Scolarium*, in *Memoires of the University of California* 4/2: 185–257.

Pálóczy Horváth, A. (1989) *Petschenegs, Cumans, Iasians*, Budapest: Corvina.

Péter, K. (1980) 'Das skytische selbstbewüsstsein des ungarischen Adels', in V. Zimányi, ed. *La Pologne et la Hongrie aux XVIe et XVIIe siècles*, Budapest: Akadémiai: 121–133.

Petneki, A. (1980) 'Oriens in Occidente. Ungarn und Polen als exotisches Thema in der Kunst des 16. und 17. Jahrhunderts', in V. Zimányi, ed. *La Pologne et la Hongrie aux XVIe et XVIIe siècles*, Budapest: Akadémiai: 145–9.

—— (1987) 'Intrada. Az ünnepélyes bevonulás formája és szerepe a közép-kelet európai udvarokban', (Forms and functions of the intrada in Central European courts). in A. R. Várkonyi, ed. *Magyar reneszánsz udvari kultúra* (Hungarian Renaissance courtly culture), Budapest: Gondolat: 281–91.

Podhradzky, J. (1842) 'Cuspinianus János beszéde, Budának romlása emlékezetére...' (The speech of J. Cuspinianus about the fall of Buda), Buda: Gyurión-Bagá Nyomda.

Prosperi, A. (1983) 'Libri sulla corte ed esperienze curiali nel primo "500 italiano"', in *idem*, ed., *La corte e il cortegiano*, Rome: Bulzoni.

Quondam, A. (1983) 'La forma del vivere. Schede per l'analisi del discorso cortegiano', in A. Prosperi, ed., *La corte e il cortegiano*, Rome: Bulzoni: 58–63.

Raby, J. (1982) *Venice, Dürer and the Oriental Mode*, London: Islamic Art Publication.

Radvánszky, B. (1896/1986) *Magyar családélet és háztartás a XVI. és XVII században* (Hungarian family life and household in the 16th and 17th centuries), Budapest: Helikon.

Romani, M. A. (1978) *Le corti farnesiane da Parma e Piacenza*, Centro Studi 'Europa delle Corti', Roma: Bulzoni.

Rühl, E. (1904), *Grobianus in England*, Palaestra 38, Berlin: Mayer and Müller.

Schallaburg (1982) = *Matthias Corvinus und die Renaissance in Ungarn. 1458–1541*, Schallaburg: Amt der Niederösterreichischen Landesregierung.

Schirokauer, A., and T.P. Thornton (1957) *Höfische Tischzuchten*, Berlin: E. Schmidt.

—— eds (1957) *Grobianische Tischzuchten*, Berlin: E. Schmidt.

Schmitt, J.-C. (1990) *La raison des gestes dans l'Occident médiéval*, Paris: Gallimard.

Schultz, A. (1889/1965) *Das höfische Leben zur Zeit der Minnesänger* I-II, Osnabrück.

—— (1892) *Deutsches Leben im 14. und 15. Jahrhundert*, Vienna, Prague and Leipzig: S. Hirzel.

Smith, P. M. (1966) *The Anti-Courtier Trend in Sixteenth Century French Literature*, Geneva: Droz.

Stallybrass, P. and A. White (1986) *The Politics and Poetics of Transgression*, London: Cornell University Press.

Stone, L. and J.C.F. Stone (1984) *An Open Elite? England 1540–1880*, Oxford: Clarendon.

Sweeney, J. R.(1981) 'Hungary in the Crusades', *International History Review* 3: 467–81.

Szamosközi, I. (1876) *Történelmi maradványai* (Historical fragments), ed. S. Szilágyi, Budapest: MTA.

Szamota, I. (1891) *Régi utazások Magyarországon és a Balkán félszigeten, 1054–1717* (Old travel-reports about Hungary and the Balkan peninsula), Budapest: Franklin Térsulat.

Szepsi Csombor (1968) *Szepsi Csombor Márton összes müvei* (Complete works of Szepsi Csombor Márton), eds. Kovács, S. I. and Kulcsár, P. Budapest: Akadémiai.

Szűcs, J. (1975) *Theoretical Elements in Master Simon of Kéza's Gesta Hungarorum (1282–1285 A.D.)*, Budapest: Akadémiai; repr. in Simonis de Kéza, *Gesta Hungarorum. The Deeds of the Hungarians*, ed. by L. Veszprémy, tr. by F. Schaer, Central European Medieval Texts I, Budapest, Central European University Press.

Thomas, K. (1984) *Man and the Natural World, Changing Attitudes in England 1500–1800*, Harmondsworth: Penguin.

Thompson, E.P. (1963) *The Making of the English Working Class*, London: Allen Lane.

Trexler, R. C. (1980) *Public Life in Renaissance Florence*, Ithaca/London: Cornell University Press.

Turóczy-Trostler, J. (1956) *Magyar Simplicissimus* (Hungarian Simplicissimus), Budapest.

Uhlig, C. (1973) *Hofkritik im England des Mittelalters und der Renaissance*, Berlin-New York: De Gruyter.

Veröffentlichungen (1976–1991) = Veröffentlichungen des Instituts für Realienkunde Mittelalters und der frühen Neuzeit, Krems; Wien, Verlag der Österreichischen Akademie der Wissenschaften.

1 *Die Funktion der schriftlichen Quelle in der Sachkulturforschung*, 1976

2 *Das Leben in der Stadt des Spätmittelalters*, 1977

3 *Klösterliche Sachkultur des Spätmittelalters*, 1980

4 *Europäische Sachkultur. Gedenkschrift aus Anlaß des 10-jährigen Bestandes des Instituts für mittelalterliche Realienkunde*, 1980

5 *Adelige Sachkultur des Spätmittelalters*, 1982

6 *Die Erforschung von Alltag und Sachkultur des Mittelalters*, 1984

7 *Bäuerliche Sachkultur des Spätmittelalters*, 1984

8 *Alltag und Forschritt im Mittelalter*, 1986

9 *Frau und spätmittelalterlicher Alltag*, 1986

10 *Terminologie und Typologie mittelalterlicher Sachgüter*, 1987

11 *Handwerk und Sachkultur im Spätmittelalter*,1988

12 *Materielle Kultur und religiöse Stiftung im Spätmittelalter*, 1990

Weijers, O. ed. (1976) *Pseudo-Boethius, De Disciplina Scolarium*, Leiden and Köln: Brill.

Yates, F. (1964) *Giordano Bruno and the Hermetic Tradition*, London: Routledge and Kegan Paul.

—— (1972) *The Rosicrucian Enlightenment*, London: Routledge and Kegan Paul.

Zombori, I. (1987) 'II. Lajos udvara – Szydlowiecki kancellár naplója alapján', (The court of Louis II – as shown by the diaries of Chancellor Szydlowiecki), in: A.R. Várkonyi, ed., *Magyar reneszánsz udvari kultúra* (Hungarian Renaissance courtly culture), Budapest: Gondolat:107–17.

CHAPTER THIRTY-NINE

ON 1500

————•◦•◦•————

Elizabeth A. R. Brown

W hy 1500? My title might easily have featured other dates that historians have used to designate the end of what they term 'the Middle Ages'. The date itself is relatively unimportant. The subject I shall treat I consider far more significant: the barriers to understanding created by periodizing the past, and especially by dividing 'the Middle Ages' from 'the Renaissance'. Rather than confining myself to generalization, I shall deal with three specific clusters of topics: first, kingship, nobility, and lordship; second, property-holding and loyalty; and third, the development of historical-mindedness and historical perspective. I shall argue that the development of each of these phenomena has been badly distorted by the traditional separation between 'Middle Ages' and 'Renaissance'. At the end I shall propose a solution of sorts – or at least a certain solace and encouragement for the future. But first I should like to write a few words about the dates that have been assigned to the 'end of the Middle Ages' – and those assigned to the era's beginning. Then, having briefly considered some general problems raised by periodization, I shall try to explain how, in practice, periodization has affected comprehension of the three topics I have selected for scrutiny.

ENDING AND BEGINNING 'THE MIDDLE AGES'

Since in this essay I focus on France's 'Middle Ages' and 'Renaissance', I have chosen the date generally favoured there for the end of 'the Middle Ages' – 1500. Why this year is preferred is unclear to me. I suspect the influence of the conviction that 'the French Renaissance' was a sixteenth-century phenomenon and thus began in or about 1500, at which time 'the French Middle Ages' ended. The year 1500 corresponds to no particularly memorable event in the history of France, separating as it does the first two years of the reign of Louis XII from the final fifteen, and marking the inception of Italian ventures that are impossible to treat without reference to those of his distant cousin and predecessor Charles VIII (1483–98). The date does not have the obvious attraction of 1453, linked as that year is with the Ottoman Turks' capture of Constantinople and the end of the Byzantine Empire. The collapse of one empire resonates nicely with another imperial decline and fall, some thousand years earlier,

691

although the demise of the Roman Empire has proved less susceptible to precise dating than the conquest of Constantinople. The French might have been tempted to terminate their 'Middle Ages' in 1453 because their ancestors captured Bordeaux from the English in that year, but the continuing English presence on French soil until Calais was seized in 1558 doubtless diminished that date's appeal.

The dates variously assigned to the beginning of 'the Middle Ages' and the disappearance of 'Antiquity' seem to me equally arbitrary. The turning point is usually situated in the fifth century, or the sixth. The year when the Visigoth Alaric sacked Rome, 410, has dramatic appeal. But 476 (a more traditional marker) witnessed the deposition of Romulus Augustulus, the last emperor to rule in the West until in 800 Pope Leo III conferred the title on the Frankish king who came to be known as Charlemagne. Some, like Ferdinand Lot (1866–1952), opt for the split between East and West signalled by the reign of Justinian (527–65), some for the advent of what they term 'new forces' in the West in the eighth century (Lot 1927: 469–70, trans. 407; Berr 1927: xix–xxvi). These markers are for the most part politically based, linked with Empire either Roman or Byzantine. Each has the defect of excluding the centuries that saw the development of the Christian faith, arguably the single most important element in the history of the succeeding millennium – and of the millennium that followed and has just ended. But it is the termination, not the beginning, of 'the Middle Ages' that I shall examine here.

PROBLEMS OF PERIODIZATION

The predicaments entailed by splitting the past into ages have long been recognized. Marc Bloch (1886–1944) offered characteristically incisive observations on the subject. After considering how 'the Middle Ages' came to be separated from 'the Renaissance' (Bloch 1953: 178–89; Bloch 1993: 179–85; cf. Reuter 1998: 25–45; Richmond 1998: 33), he decried this partition, as he did the practice of 'counting by centuries' – centuries which never quite commence or terminate with the hundred-year divisions that order our calendar (Bloch 1953: 181–2; Bloch 1993: 92–3). Perhaps because his friend Lucien Febvre endorsed the concept, Bloch objected less strongly to the notion of 'civilizations' as an organizing principle – although he was vague as to how it could or should be used (Bloch 1953: 187–8; Bloch 1993: 96; cf. Fink 1989: 133–4, 162–3, 285, 327). He admitted that 'the Middle Ages' was a 'convenience for school curriculums', but he considered this virtue 'debatable', as he did other divisions, such as 'the Renaissance' (Bloch 1953: 181; Bloch 1993: 92). He called, rather imprecisely, for temporal categories that would reflect the variable rhythms of reality, and believed that historians should seek from the phenomena they studied 'their proper periods'. Still, like so many others, he continued to use the traditional periodizing labels in his writings – although in the books that were his masterworks, the subjects he treated determined their chronological limits (Bloch 1953: 183–4, 188–9; Bloch 1993: 93, 96–7; cf. Bloch 1931; Bloch 1913; Bloch 1924).

Bloch does not stand alone in offering mixed signals. Lord Acton (1843–1902) was no different. In the Inaugural Lecture he delivered in June 1895 as Regius

Professor of Modern History at Cambridge, he admonished historians to 'study problems in preference to periods' (Acton 1906: 26; cf. Gilmore 1952: xiii). This is similar to Bloch's advice to select temporal limits congruent with phenomena, and foreshadows the 'history focused on problems' (*histoire-problème*) that Bloch and Febvre practised, and that Fernand Braudel fervently championed (Hexter 1972: 510–12, 530–1; cf. Braudel 1950: 496). But Acton was also impressed by the continuity, the unity of history, a vision close to Braudel's conception of *histoire totale*, which J. H. Hexter suggests should be rendered 'endless history' (and which virtually excludes the possibility of *histoire-problème*) (Acton 1906: 3, 5; Hexter 1972: 511–12). In the end, however, bowing to necessity and convenience, Acton accepted the traditional compartments, declaring that Modern History began 'four hundred years ago' – thus, in 1495. Having taken this tack, he resolutely presented the modern era as 'marked off by an evident and intelligible line from the time immediately preceding, and display[ing] in its course specific and distinctive characteristics of its own'; as 'an awakening of new life'; as a 'world revolv[ing] in a different orbit, determined by influences unknown before'. 'The sixteenth century', he declared, 'went forth armed for untried experience, and ready to watch with hopefulness a prospect of incalculable change' (Acton 1906: 6; cf. Stubbs 1886, repr. 1967: 225–6).[1] To support his dramatic pronouncements, Acton invoked Columbus, Machiavelli, Erasmus, Luther, and Copernicus. Depicting them as innovative heralds of a new order, he neglected the ties that bound them to their intellectual predecessors. A brilliant tour de force of selectivity, Acton's performance calls to mind the similarly deft effort of Robert Sabatino Lopez to establish the tenth century as 'still another Renaissance' (Lopez 1951).

The division between 'the Middle Ages' and 'the Renaissance', like the names assigned to the two time-spans, has had unfortunate results. For those, like Acton, who study the later centuries, all that precedes 1500 is on the wane, in decline, and degenerate, whereas what follows is new, fresh, and full of promise, distinct and different from what came before (Kaminsky 1998: 15–22; cf. Burckhardt 1882 (1965): 61–2; Huizinga 1919). Specialists in earlier centuries, stung by such assessments, endeavour to brighten and enliven their period, discovering within it 'Renaissances', secularization and the nation state, and even a 'Reformation', as well as recognizable manifestations of individuality and skeptical rationality (Freedman and Spiegel 1998: 682–93; Spiegel 1997: 66–71; Cantor 1991: 245–86; cf. Bynum 1997: 2; Constable 1996: 1–4). Not only do they detect before 1500 traces of phenomena generally linked with later times. They are also tempted to impose closure at 1500 on whatever topic they are studying. Thus, for example, historians of historiography, anxious to date the destruction of romanticized myths of national origin before 1500, have neglected the importance of the German scholars who, in the first decades of the sixteenth century, found in Tacitus and other ancient writers the ammunition needed to dislodge the Trojans from their position of prominence (Brown 1998a; Brown 1998b; Brown 1999c).

Historians of the centuries before and after 1500 find themselves in a quandary. The terms 'Middle Ages' and 'Renaissance' are generally familiar. They are embedded in our consciousnesses. It is virtually impossible to escape them. Craig Wright wisely used musicological and liturgical criteria to set (at 500 and 1550) the chronological boundaries of his study of music and ceremony at Notre-Dame of Paris. Yet rather than considering the continuities he perceived as grounds for rejecting traditional periodization, he set Notre-Dame apart, declaring it 'astonishing to see how long medieval practices endured [there], as if the Renaissance and Counter-Reformation never occurred' (Wright 1989: 358). Consider, too, Roger Doucet's astonishment at the depth of Christian piety that Francis I (r. 1515–47) manifested on his deathbed. Convinced that among the educated in sixteenth-century, 'Renaissance' France, traditional beliefs were generally mingled with 'vaguely classical philosophical ideas', Doucet saw the king as an exception, an oddity. 'The Renaissance', Doucet concluded, 'had not affected his faith' (Doucet 1913: 314; Giesey 1960: 195 (1987: 294)). Doucet found it similarly surprising that Francis, a monarch known for his innovative administrative policies, should have delivered thoroughly traditional admonitions to his son before dying – to love God and the Catholic Church; protect, extend, and cherish the kingdom and its loyal people and nobles; preserve the Church; and maintain justice. In Doucet's judgement, his words betrayed 'a banal conception of royal power, no different from what the most mediocre of his predecessors might have had' – which was not, evidently, what Doucet expected from a king to whom he attributed a unique style of ruling, a ruler who 'had led the monarchy into new paths' (Doucet 1913: 311, 315; cf. Teall 1978: 1). In this manner obviously artificial categories vitiate the cogency with which sources are analyzed and evaluated. Events and individuals are presented as 'exceptional', 'anomalous', 'precocious', and 'curious', although, as Howard Kaminsky has observed, such judgmental terms simply reveal a 'failure of understanding' (Kaminsky 1986: 704–5).

The problem is serious. Before dealing with solutions, I should like to consider three sets of phenomena whose nature and development seem to me to have been warped by historians' acceptance of the conventional division between 'Middle Ages' and 'Renaissance'. In each case, I believe, the failure of those concentrating on the period after 1500 to appreciate the nature and significance of earlier practices and traditions has resulted in misunderstanding. Similarly, the failure of those focusing on the earlier period to pursue later developments has caused miscalculation of the strength and endurance – and even the nature – of the phenomena they study.

KINGSHIP, NOBILITY AND LORDSHIP

Roger Doucet was surprised that Francis I's religious beliefs and feelings about his and his successor's obligations as king were conventional. This judgement, however, underestimates not only the universal importance of tradition in moments of human crisis, but also the degree to which monarchical actions and pronouncements derived their force from past practices and customs. True, Francis I was raised to think of himself as another Caesar, and he doubtless relished the comparisons to antique heroes with which he was flattered (Brown 1995a; cf. Krynen 1993: 341–83; Brown 1999). On the other hand, he was, as Christian king, expected to emulate his Christian forebears, and especially St Louis (r. 1226–70), who set the standards by which all future rulers were judged. It is no accident that before Louis XVI's execution on 21 January 1793, his confessor exhorted him as 'son of Saint Louis' to rise to heaven.[2]

Francis I's dying, and the instructions he gave his son, recall and may well have been inspired by the description of St Louis' death and admonitions preserved in Joinville's Life of the king (Joinville 1867: 490–501; 1963: 346–9). They recall as well the last moments of St Louis' grandson Philip the Fair (r. 1285–1314), as Yves, monk of St-Denis, recorded them (Yves of St Denis 1858: 206-9). Francis did not, like Louis, have himself placed on a bed of ashes. He did not, like Philip the Fair, extend his arms as if he were hanging on a cross. He did not, like Louis, invoke individual saints. But like both Louis and Philip he took particular comfort from the example of Jesus Christ. And the counsel Francis bestowed on his son was markedly similar to the advice Louis and Philip gave their heirs. All emphasized love of God, the Church, and the realm, and the signal importance of justice.

This is not to say that the deathbed scenes are mirror images of one another. The differences among them shed light on the individuality of each ruler, and the milieu in which each lived. Francis I was concerned about the orthodoxy of a sermon of Origen, which was brought him instead of the homily by John Chrysostom he had requested. St Louis emphasized the personal religious duties of his son, and his heir's obligation to restore anything he wrongly possessed. Philip the Fair threatened his son with malediction if he failed to fulfil his commands, and took special pains to instruct him in the ceremony of the royal touch, the God-given power to cure scrofula which the kings were thought to possess. But the similarities and continuities are far more striking than the differences. This is true as well of the ceremonies that the rulers of France sponsored and favoured, which became increasingly elaborate, but which rarely diverged radically from those that had preceded. Indeed, the only significant innovation in the royal funeral ceremony after 1500, the service of meals (with blessing) to the royal corpse and effigy, was a Christianized revival of an antique usage, which recalls the introduction of the effigy itself many years earlier (Brown 1999b).[3] It is little wonder that a historian of fourteenth-century France, Joseph R. Strayer, should have declared how difficult it was 'to say exactly what was new' about the New Monarchies of the Renaissance (Strayer 1972: 13).

After 1500 the rulers of France employed much the same mechanisms to govern their lands as they had earlier. The extent to which they relied on the nobility, large and small, as intermediaries between themselves and their subjects recalls the similar policies that, of necessity, the Carolingians implemented. Historians of the sixteenth century are increasingly inclined to recognize the role of the nobility as executors of royal policy, in my view better termed a *noblesse de service* rather than a *noblesse seconde* (Teall 1978; Harsgor 1980: 2. 1227–324; though cf. Constant 1989: 280–4, and Bourquin 1994: 37–42, 44–7, 50–8) – more so, arguably, than scholars intent on the emergence of bureaucracy and strong centralized governments in the fourteenth and fifteenth centuries, and convinced that at that point kings controlled their realms through functional 'offices of justice, finance, and war' (Bisson 1995: 757–9). In 1500, the 'impersonal test of competence' had hardly replaced 'affective trust and fidelity' (Bisson 1995: 753) – or friendship – as a means of access to power and prestige, as those who study the nobility of sixteenth-century France know well. Indeed, the workings of contemporary government cast considerable doubt on the possibility of ever fully achieving such an ideal. The centrality of personal ties to the acquisition and exercise of power may well be a historical constant. Such bonds were pivotal in the sixteenth and seventeenth centuries.

The abundant sources that illuminate the workings of lordship in sixteenth-century France make it possible to understand its varieties far more fully than can be done for earlier times. The journals that the Norman lord of Gouberville kept between 1549 and 1562 enabled Elizabeth Teall to describe in detail his activities as landlord, royal representative, dispenser of justice both informal and formal, arbiter of morals, and sometime succourer of the poor and needy (Teall 1978; Teall 1965: 138–41). Teall examined a wealth of additional evidence in trying to comprehend the relationship between sixteenth-century French lords and their subjects. Did they oppress the peasantry or act as their advocates? Well aware of the gulf between ideal and reality, Teall sensibly concluded that much depended on the character of the individual lord. Still, there were strong moral and economic inducements to incline lords towards the good. Perhaps most potent was the commonsense realization that 'the strength and duration of [the lords'] own authority rested inevitably upon the well-being and repose of the tenantry'. The lords were unlikely to flourish if their subjects were miserable and impoverished. Further, the Christian virtues of mercy and charity were widely praised and highly valued (Teall 1965: 144).

The functional divisions of society that were elaborated in various forms by the Christian fathers and their successors in the first fifteen hundred years of the Christian era implied organic social unity and ideals of mutual obligation compatible with the activities of nobles like the lord of Gouberville and the moral values with which they were inculcated (Constable 1995: 240–350; cf. Duby 1978 (1980); Brown 1986). Such congruences explain why Teall and others have viewed as 'medieval' the loyalty of tenants and peasants towards their lords, and lords' feelings of responsibility for their subjects in the sixteenth and seventeenth centuries (Teall 1965: 150). The Christian ideals propounded from early on, the economic and social realities that, early and late, fostered the notion of mutual dependency (Brown 1992: 4–7), and the responsible attitudes of many sixteenth-century lords in turn raise questions about the likely nature of earlier lordship.

Some scholars working in the era before 1500 have painted a gloomy and depressing picture. Between the tenth and the twelfth centuries – for some three hundred years – lordship, it is said, was predominantly harsh, violent, exploitative, and cruel. In those times lords, driven by greed and violence, had little or no interest in maintaining order (Bisson 1994; Bisson 1998: 141, 143–53; but cf. Fossier 1974: 77–8, 86; Evergates 1975: 136–53; Letwin 1977: 373–5; cf. Hilton 1977: 461; and particularly useful comments in Reynolds 1984 (1997): lxii–vi). How valid is this vision? The question remains open, but the experience of sixteenth-century France, far more fully documented than that of earlier times, raises the possiblity that the earlier centuries had their share of good lords as well as bad. Then as now, the dramatic, sensational appeal of wickedness and debauchery may well have resulted in over-representation of such impulses in the surviving sources. The most successful means that were devised in earlier times to control and limit disorder were less spectacular than the famed Peace and Truce of God (whose origins await full study) (Head and Landes 1992; cf. Nelson 1994). These methods have only recently begun to be understood and appreciated (White 1978; White 1986; White 1995;

Davies and Fouracre 1986; Bongert 1949). The ingenuity that apparently inspired them is, however, reminiscent of the talents the lord of Gouberville and his peers exhibited in attempting to deal with the turmoil caused by religious warfare in sixteenth-century France. Whether or not arbitration and negotiated compromise are classed as formal governmental institutions (Baldwin 1986: 42), the norms that inspire them have often helped hold society together – as they still do. Lordship before 1500 may, in sum, have been less sinister and more varied than is generally believed.

LAND-HOLDING AND LOYALTY

Even more than historians of fourteenth- and fifteenth-century Europe, sixteenth-century specialists have neglected the importance of fiefs as a vital component of government, a means of rewarding service and reinforcing loyalty. Their attitude is doubtless affected by the assumptions of historians of the two centuries before 1500, who see feudal institutions as withering, and who in significant numbers have embraced the notion of 'bastard feudalism' (Harriss 1981: ix–xxvii; cf. McFarlane 1944 (1981): esp. 17–18; McFarlane 1945 (1981); Bean 1989: 231–4). This view is widespread. In his book on European lordship and feudalism before the twelfth century, Robert Boutruche includes texts from the fourteenth to the eighteenth centuries to illustrate 'rites of vassalage', and the later texts (including an act of homage performed on 6 July 1789) provide telling examples of what, presumably, were traditional usages. Rather than discussing the function of these practices in the later centuries, however, Boutruche identifies the fourteenth- and fifteenth-century documents as manifesting the 'first signs of decline', which he pronounces 'accentuated' in the sixteenth century, whereas the seventeenth- and eighteenth-century sources are called 'survivals' (Boutruche 1959: 332–48). The outlook these labels reveal would hardly encourage historians of the sixteenth century to pay attention to feudal tenures and ceremonies, particularly since they have more dramatic topics to consider – among many others, increasing royal power and the tensions between kings and nobles, religious strife, and the brilliant culture of the court (Jouanna 1996; Le Roy Ladurie 1987 (1994): esp. 104; Mousnier 1969: 19, 81–2; cf. Gallet 1981: 105–22; Lewis 1968: 199–201; cf. Astarita 1992).

The fourteenth and fifteenth centuries and, especially, the sixteenth thus seem strikingly different from the period from the tenth to the end of the twelfth centuries, when, for three hundred years, 'the fief' and 'vassalage' have, since the seventeenth century, figured as the chief dramatis personae of the historical narrative. The focus on the fief, the feudal law, and their accoutrements, like the invention of the constructs 'feudal system' and 'feudalism' in the eighteenth century, was in part the product of scholars' search for system and order in human society. It was also a result of the difficulty they had in finding readily comprehensible entities – whether individuals or institutions – on which to concentrate. The decline of centralized governments meant the eclipse of the empires, emperors, kings, and kingdoms that provided comfortable narrative foci. What was left was too confusingly complex and sparsely documented to permit the straightforward narration historians find most congenial. Hence constructs – feudalism, manorialism, lordship – were (as they sometimes still are) elevated to heroic status (Reynolds 1984 (1997); cf. Fossier 1974: 159–67; and still Southern 1953: 74–117). The security which these anthropomorphized constructs provide has come to be recognized as delusive, however, weakening and finally vanishing when questions are asked about the numerous individuals who populated Europe in the years when the abstractions supposedly dominated human affairs.

The attention paid to the constructs during the centuries of decentralization inevitably won them disproportionate prominence when realms and their rulers re-emerge as dominant elements, from the twelfth century on. Rather than discussing, simply, kings and kingdoms, and considering the numerous strategies rulers employed to gain, consolidate, and extend their power, historians have labelled the monarchies 'feudal', thus suggesting that the distribution and manipulation of fiefs provide the essential key to the kingdoms' newfound vitality and strength (Bisson 1978 (1989); Baldwin 1986: 259–303; cf. Giordanengo 1988; Fossier 1974: 159). To question this approach is not to deny that fiefs and ties of homage and fealty existed in twelfth-century Europe, or that rulers utilized them. Kings and their advisers, many of them lawyers, were inspired by the *Libri feudorum*, a twelfth- and thirteenth-century Lombard compilation, soon treated as an integral part of the Roman law, which set forth rules governing landed property (called *feuda* or fiefs) and their holders (called *vassi* or vassals) (Reynolds 1994: 258–9, 320–2, 483–6; Benton 1991; Evergates 1985). The issue, in my view, is one of balance, of according fiefs and the *Libri* their proper share of attention, but denying them prominence they do not merit. Historians of Europe before 1500 have erred in one direction, those of the centuries afterwards in another.

The *Libri feudorum* influenced not only twelfth- and thirteenth-century rulers, but also the seventeenth- and eighteenth-century scholars who invented the feudal constructs. These scholars were, however, also influenced by contemporary tenurial and ceremonial conventions and practices, whose origins they associated with – and proceeded to find – in the distant, 'medieval' past. Although the English finally abolished feudal tenures in 1660 (Pocock 1957: esp. 169), they and their ceremonial trappings remained vitally important in France until the Revolution. Until then the French tenurial world was fundamentally feudal and seigneurial. Those who acquired and inherited land, expanded and administered estates, and engaged in litigation involving their holdings, were enmeshed in its complexities. Much, of course, had changed since the twelfth century. Still, conflicts of loyalty similar to those that had disturbed tenants of multiple fiefs in that century and earlier troubled those who, during the religious wars, found themselves bound to superiors whose faiths were different from their own.[4] Had feudal institutions possessed as little importance after 1400 as has often been suggested, it would be hard to explain why the Assemblée nationale considered 'the feudal regime' a threat sufficient to warrant the efforts made between 1789 and 1792 to demolish it (Sagnac and Caron 1907: 1–2, 173–81; Mackrell 1973: 174–86). As it was, in 1790, inspired by the attacks on *féodalité* and the *régime féodal* in the Assemblée, Edmund Burke inveighed against 'feudality' as 'the barbarism of tyranny' (Burke 1839: 3. 255, cf. 2. 182–3).

HISTORICAL PERSPECTIVE AND THE LAW

Seventeenth- and eighteenth-century historians devised historical constructs to explain the origins of phenomena they observed around them. The feudal icons they created, which have dominated and deformed subsequent historical discourse, raise questions about the aims, standards, and methodology of those who fashioned them. The questions are particularly unsettling in view of the fact that these scholars lived long after the time when, it has been thought, those who studied the past had begun distinguishing past eras and concerns from the present and its assumptions, had developed a sense of historical perspective and awareness of anachronism, and had evolved critical techniques for evaluating evidence from the past. According to Lord Acton, historians in 'the Middle Ages' 'were careless', 'invent[ed] according to convenience, and [were] glad to welcome the forger and the cheat'. It was in 'the Renaissance', he believed, that 'History as we understand it began to be understood'. He left vague the process of development and the criteria he was employing (aside from invoking 'keen Italian minds' and their penchant for 'exposing falsehood') (Acton 1906: 6–7). Petrarch (1304–74) and Lorenzo Valla (1407–57) quickly emerged as heroes, but they, of course, lived long before 1495 (Acton's favoured date for commencing 'the Renaissance').

Whatever the shortcomings of historical scholarship in the seventeenth and eighteenth centuries, intellectuals undeniably had a keener sense of historical perspective than had been the case five centuries before. In attempting to account for the changed attitude to the past, scholars concerned with historical and political thought after 1500 have looked to the study of the Roman law, and to sixteenth-century France. By 1952 'humanist commentators on Roman law' were being credited with 'historical-mindedness' and with recognition of the pastness and unique integrity of previous civilizations (Gilmore 1952: 236; Gilmore 1941: 6–7, 70; Gilmore 1963; Maffei 1956; Mortari 1962; Pocock 1957: 10–1; Kelley 1970: 9–10, 87–106, 302–6; Kelley 1984b; Kelley 1991: 2. 123–4; Huppert 1970: 40–1, 152–4; Fumaroli 1977: 15–8, 27; Jouanna 1982: 57–9, 75–6; Barret-Kriegel 1988: 2.115).[5] Through the humanists, it is argued, lawyers in general, and especially lawyers in France, came to realize that the past could not 'speak directly to the modern world'. The lawyers recognized that whereas Roman law was a fit subject for historical study, its rules and methods were irrelevant to their work in the courts.[6] Thus, it is said, practitioners were drawn to custom and customary law, which they valued as peculiarly French. Dedicated to its codification, they accorded it preferential standing in the courtroom (Maffei 1956: 191–2; Mortari 1962: 61–2, 84–134; Kelley 1970: 260–1, 290–1).

This view of the growth of historical consciousness has distorted comprehension of, first, French attitudes to Roman law and custom before and after 1500, and, second, the arguments lawyers used and the authorities they invoked when they appeared in court. It is probably no accident that legal historians have played little part in the development and popularization of the thesis. Legal historians tend to emphasize continuity and to treat large sweeps of the past (Flach 1883: 223–4, 226; Declareuil 1925: 432–3, 829–51, 885–7; Chénon 1926–9: 1.486–9, 508–13, 2.331–3; Petot 1951: 347–51; Legendre 1988: no. VII; Kelley 1984: 44–55 (breaking with his own earlier position); Troje 1993: 71–5), whereas historians of Renaissance thought are generally more conversant with classical authors than with classical law and Justinian's codification, not to mention the arguments lawyers advanced in the courts and the treatises they wrote before and after 1500 (Giordanengo 1990: 439–40).

As legal historians have shown, from the thirteenth century on – and even before – arguments based on and derived from the Roman law were regularly used in France. They were one of the chief staples on which lawyers relied in their briefs. As students, the lawyers had immersed themselves in the Roman and canon law, which were far more accessible than the impossibly diffuse and complex customs invoked in regions of France where Roman law was not followed. The arguments that lawyers advanced before the Parlement de Paris in the sixteenth century were reported at far greater length than had been true earlier, but the authorities on which the lawyers relied and the rhetoric they employed were remarkably similar to what had been used since the thirteenth century (Brown 1995b: 326–31, 366–8). Like their predecessors, sixteenth-century lawyers (some of whom excelled at textual analysis and historical research) demonstrated their erudition and legal learning by citing the Roman law in their briefs (Brown 1995b; see further Brejon 1937: 3. 223–6, 234, 259; Thireau 1980: 30–1, 87–94; Gilmore1941: 64–71; Kelley 1970: 164–82, 189–98; Jouanna 1982: 65–6). Towards the end of the sixteenth century, after the codifiers of customary law had brought some order into French customs and published their work, the situation altered, although it is difficult to say how radically it changed. Roman law did not disappear from the courtroom or the classroom.[7] The Roman law was, of course, the customary law of southern France, and those who recorded and codified the customs of France before and after the sixteenth century were well trained in its intricacies (Thireau 1980: 31, esp. n. 84, 87–93, 209; Reulos 1963: 119–33, esp. 132). French patriots, lawyers included, sometimes inveighed against the Roman law, but they did so because they rejected the notion that France was necessarily bound by the Roman law and hence subject to the empire. The king of France, after all, had long been considered emperor in his own realm (Post 1964: 434–93, at 471–82; Krynen 1993: 384–414; also Delachenal 1885: 242–4; Chénon 1907/8: 1.195–212 at 211–12). For the Roman law itself, French lawyers and scholars had considerable admiration (Du Tillet 1606–1607: 251; Coquille 1646: 8; Le Bret 1635: 10–1; see Thireau 1980: 96–100).

The attitude of the French in the sixteenth century mirrored views that Philip the Fair expressed in 1312 in authorizing the teaching of Roman law at Orléans. The realm of France was ruled by custom, he said, not written law, and when the written law was used or studied in France it was with the express authorization of the kings of France. Why did they give their approval? Because the Roman law encouraged the development of reason and morals, and showed how justice could be implemented – as well as preparing the way for the understanding of custom. The Romans themselves had received Greek law 'pro sui eruditione' – as a source of inspiration and instruction for themselves. Similarly, owing to their excellence, the principles of Roman law were accepted in France when royal judgements and ordonnances did not resolve issues, and when custom was uncertain or lacking (Ordonnance of 17 July 1312, in Fournier 1890: no. 37: 36–9, esp. 36–7, also in de Laurière 1723:

501–4, esp. 501–2; see Chénon 1907/8: 209–10; and esp. Chénon 1926: 1.510). The legal scholars of sixteenth-century France, following Philip the Fair's lead, carefully distinguished between the use of the Roman law in the courts and admission of its binding force – and of the superiority and authority of the emperor.[8]

As to historical-mindedness, Philip the Fair, Petrarch's older contemporary, believed that the past was different from the present, and that civilizations differed in fundamental ways from one another. He thought that the Romans had adopted the Greek law. More important, at the end of his ordonnance of 1312 he declared it exceedingly beneficial for each person's education 'to know the feelings and thoughts, ceremonies, and customs of people of different places and times'.[9] This was certainly not because he believed these things were similar to what he knew in France, but because he assumed their divergence, and believed that anyone would be enlightened by learning about them. This does not mean that Philip the Fair – or Petrarch – had the same sense of anachronism and the same attitude to the historical past that would develop by the seventeenth century, but the germs are discernible in Philip's words, as they are in Petrarch's. The process of development awaits elucidation – by historians working on both sides of the divide of 1500.

CONCLUSION

My arguments here have focused on continuities between the centuries before and after the year 1500. I have concentrated on kingship and lordship, property-holding, and historical-mindedness and the law. I could have selected other topics that, equally well, would demonstrate the importance of disregarding and overstepping the barrier of 1500. As I have tried to show, this obstruction has created as many problems for historians of the centuries preceding 1500 as for those who study later times. Is there any solution to the problem? Is it possible to provide alternatives to 'the Middle Ages' and 'the Renaissance'?

The attempts at re-periodizing that have been made seem to me to create more difficulties than they resolve. The 'Middle Ages' have been extended forward by two centuries to encompass 'the Reformation'. Alternatively, an *Alteuropa* (Old Europe) is said to have developed between a starting point located somewhere between 1000 and 1300, and a terminus of *c.*1800. Neither of these approaches is satisfactory. The changes in beliefs and values linked with Luther and Calvin surely constituted more than 'a second blossoming of medieval life', whereas the phrase 'Old Europe' instantly conjures up images of a young and vibrant continent replacing one whose time has passed, and leaves unclear precisely what entity 'Old Europe' itself succeeded (Kaminsky 1988: 15–6; Kaminsky and Melton 1984: xvii; Gerhard 1981; Hassinger 1966; Brady, Oberman and Tracy 1994–5; Dickens and Tonkin 1985: 187–8; Radding 1985: 250–62).

André Ségal suggests a radical means of escaping the stifling constraints of the periodizing tradition. Focusing on 'the Middle Ages', which he denounces as 'an obstacle to understanding the origins of the West',[10] Ségal ridicules 'chronological divisions' (or, literally, 'slices' – *tranches*) as 'cold cuts' (*charcuterie*), and bemoans students' predisposition to invest periods with individual personalities and treat them as 'preexistent historical beings' (Ségal 1991: 105–14). In his teaching, Ségal deals with 'the Middle Ages' by abolishing the term from his classroom, and by requiring students to dissect alternative systems of periodizing – before, surely, discarding them. Ségal's critique is as relevant to 'the Renaissance' and 'the Reformation' as it is to 'the Middle Ages', and I heartily endorse it.

My counsel to those who study the centuries that separate Philo and Jesus Christ from Francis I and Calvin is to jettison the labels 'Middle Ages' and 'Renaissance', value-loaded as they are. I recognize the nuisance of abandoning these old, familiar tags. Constructs designating broad stretches of time are both handy and economical, far less cumbersome than more precise references to dates and centuries. As happened when I called for the abolition of 'feudalism' (Brown 1974), I have no doubt that I will be asked for constructs or schemas to replace the 'Middle Ages' and the 'Renaissance', which, like old friends, seem indispensable. But I believe that no convenient substitutes exist, and that none can or should be devised. I find thoroughly convincing the arguments that Lord Acton, Bloch, and Ségal have marshalled.

To free ourselves from the fetters of periodization will require persistence and courage. It is difficult to reject the comfort of a convenient crutch (which I myself have used), especially when doing so means recognizing the limitations of our minds, and acknowledging our inability to grasp the unity of history and envisage the past as a continuum. Having been led by our shortcomings to divide the past into easily digestible segments, we must admit the defects of this strategy, and no longer seek to justify it. We are far less confident than Vico (1668–1774) that since human beings have made the world of nations (which he calls the civil world), human beings can comprehend it. We are less ready than he to acknowledge 'the eternal and never failing light' of what he believed 'a truth beyond all question', more discouraged than he by the limitations of the human mind, whose workings we know better than he (Vico (1744) 1968: 96–7, Section III, Principles I.1–3). There is still hope for the future. Living in the age of computers, we have become familiar with and learned to tolerate new ways of looking at the world and organizing knowledge. These should make it easier for us to admit and gracefully accept the conceptual challenges posed to our digitally functioning, continually dividing, and fatally categorizing minds, by a world that operates analogically, the unbroken continuity of its evolution defying our attempts to grasp and comprehend it.[11]

NOTES

1 Stubbs 1886: 225–6, declared that the period 1500 to 1800 was dominated by 'the idea of the balance of power'. He denied that there was any 'great crash at the passing of the old things and the coming in of the new' in 1500, but, still, at that point he saw 'France emerg[ing] from tutelage and attain[ing] to such maturity of manhood as might be expressed in the later formula "The state, it is myself"'. Stubbs 1967: 13–14, termed modern historical inquiry 'the study of life' and 'the living body', and likened investigation of 'Antiquity' to the study of 'death' and 'the skeleton'.

2 On Henri-Essex Edgeworth de Firmont and his alleged admonition ('Enfant de saint

Louis, montez au ciel'), see Brosse 1968: 1–15. For the likelihood that Edgeworth actually uttered these words, see Du Fresne 1892(ii): 353–69.

3   As Giesey 1960: 205–6 (1986: 309–11) suspected might be the case, the ceremony of Anne of Brittany in 1514 seems to have been prompted by the treatise on antique funeral customs that Jean Lemaire de Belges wrote for Marguerite of Austria and revised for Claude, daughter of Anne of Brittany and Louis XII, who married Francis I. M. M.Fontaine and I will soon publish an edition of a large portion of the original treatise, which Pierre Sala included in his work on the antiquities of Lyon (Paris, Bibliothèque nationale de France, fr. 5447, fols 8v–24v).

4   Such was the situation of Jean du Tillet, dedicated Catholic and royal servant, who held land not only of the king but also of the Protestant leader Admiral Gaspard de Coligny, killed in the massacre of Saint Bartholomew Day in 1572. Jean's wife Jeanne Brinon inherited the lordships of La Bussière and Villeplate, east of Orléans, from her father Jean, master of the Chambre des comptes, who died on 6 February 1541: É. Raunié, *Épitaphier du vieux Paris . . .* , 4 vols, Histoire générale de Paris, no. 22, Paris, Imprimerie nationale, 1890–1914, vol. 1, pp. 52–53, no. 92. La Bussière was held of the king, Villeplate of Coligny (until after his death his property passed to the crown): Anselme de la Vierge Marie [Pierre Guibours], *Histoire genealogique et chronologique de la Maison Royale de France . . .* , 3rd ed., H. Caille *et al.* (ed.), 9 vols, Paris, La Compagnie des libraires, 1726–33, vol. 7, pp. 883–4. The two lordships were given to Jean du Tillet's son and namesake when he married Jeanne Nicolay, in 1567, three years before the deaths of his parents: A.-M. de Boislisle, *Histoire de la maison de Nicolay . . .* , 2 vols, Nogent-le-Rotrou: A. Gouverneur, 1873–75, vol. 1, pp. 266–69, no. 208. In September 1573 Charles IX made them a castellany: Paris, Archives nationales, X[1A] 8631, fols 44v–46v.

5   All these scholars seem to me to exaggerate the significance of the distinction between *mos italicus* and *mos gallicus*, concepts whose function in the *Dialogues* of Alberico Gentili (1552–1608), published in London in 1582, remains to be fully explored. But see Thireau 1980: 129, criticizing the tendency to present the approaches as fundamentally opposed, and for similar reservations, Kelley 1984a: nos. VI and VII.

6   Gilmore 1963: 37, attributed the response of Jacques Cujas (1522–90) to a question regarding religious conflict – 'This has nothing to do with the edict of the praetor' (*Nihil hoc ad edictum praetoris*) – to his belief that civil legislation should not govern religion, and to his antipathy, as a historian of Roman law, to commenting on current affairs. See also Pocock 1957: 10–11. Troje 1993: 95 persuasively argues that, alert to the danger of persecution, Cujas was simply avoiding compromising himself.

7   There is a crying need for systematic serial study of modes of argumentation before the Parlement de Paris from the thirteenth century to the Revolution. My own work has focused on the late fifteenth century and the first seven decades of the sixteenth, and my remarks concerning later times are based on sampling that is admittedly haphazard.

8   On 16 July 1577, Étienne Pasquier argued in a brief 'que jamais nos anciens ne furent subjectz au droict des Romains' but noted that the French used the Roman law 'en tant qu'ilz le trouvoient se conformer à une équité naturelle à faulte d'une loy françoise': see Filhol 1937: 128. Cf. Thireau 1980: 97, 99. Christofle de Thou (President of the Parlement de Paris from 1554 to 1582) has been portrayed as an opponent of the Roman law. However, although dedicated to reforming and codifying French customs, he relied on the Roman and the canon law in his arguments before the Parlement, which badly need analysis: Brown 1995b: 329–30 n. 12, 369 esp. n. 148. In 1574, dedicating to de Thou his *Mosaycarum et Romanarum Legum Collatio* (Basel, Thomas Guarinus), Pierre Pithou declared that the French utilized the laws of the Romans because of the laws' 'reason and equity, not their authority and sanction'.

9   Jean du Tillet translated this passage, 'Car scauoir les sens, meurs & coustumes des hommes de diuers tempz et lieux prouffite beaucoup a la doctrine': *Recueil*, p. 252. Philip the Fair's use of the word *sensus* is particularly noteworthy; du Tillet's 'sens' does not seem to me to capture the richness of the Latin word. Bynum 1997: 14–5, esp. n. 58, discusses the current debate over the nature of emotions and its implications for the study of feelings and sentiments in other times and places.

10 In view of the problems associated with what Bloch 1953: 29–35 (1993: 85–9) calls 'the idol of origins', I would prefer to see 'past' substituted for 'origins'. Bloch observed that the word 'origins' can be interpreted, vaguely, as 'beginnings', or, alternatively, as 'causes' – or both. He argued persuasively that 'a historical phenomenon can never be understood apart from its moment in time' and emphasized the danger of separating an event or an idea from the context in which it occurred.

11 I am grateful to Alexander S. B. Brown, Christine Brown, Lucy L. Brown, and Samuel Feldman for discussing with their minimally computer-literate relative the idea I present here. Elsewhere in this chapter, I have incurred debts to Professor Freedman for helping to locate Lopez's article, and to Professor Kaminsky for his advice, and for permitting me to see in advance of publication his study of Johan Huizinga's influence on current images of the fourteenth and fifteenth centuries, 'From lateness to waning to crisis: The burden of the later middle ages', *Journal of Early Modern History* 4 (2000), pp. 85–125.

BIBLIOGRAPHY

Primary works

Burke, Edmund, *Works*, 9 vols, Boston MA: C. C. Little and J. Brown, 1839.

Coquille, Guy, 'Institution au droit des François', in *idem*, *Les Œuvres . . .* , Paris: Anthoine de Cay, 1646 (separately paginated, following 'La Coustume du Niuernois').

Yves(Ivo), monk of St Denis, 'Vita et miracula sancti Dionysii', in *Recueil des historiens des Gaules et de la France*, ed. M. Bouquet *et al.*, 24 vols, Paris: Victor Palmé *et al.*, 1738–1904, vol. 21 1858, ed. J.-D. Guigniaut and J.-N. Natalis de Wailly.

Du Tillet, Jean, *Recueil des Roys de France, leurs Couronne et Maison. Ensemble, le rang des grands de France . . .* , Paris, Abel l'Angelier *et al.*, [1606]–1607, repr. Paris: Pierre Mettayer, 1618.

Fournier, M. ed., *Les statuts et privilèges des universités françaises depuis leur fondation jusqu'en 1789*, vol. 1, Paris: L. Larose et Forcel, 1890.

Joinville, Jean, sire de Joinville, 'Vie de Saint Louis, in Joinville, *Œuvres . . .* , ed. J.-N. Natalis de Wailly, Paris, Adrien Le Clere, 1867, trans. in Joinville and Villehardouin, *Chronicles of the Crusades*, trans. M. R. B. Shaw, Baltimore: Penguin, 1963.

Laurière, E.-J. de, *et al.*, eds, *Ordonnances des Roys de France de la Troisiéme Race*, 22 vols and Supplément, Paris: Imprimerie royale *et al.*, 1723–1849.

Le Bret, Cardin, *Les Œvvres . . .* , Paris: Toussainct du Bray, 1635.

Vico, G., *The New Science: Unabridged Translation of the Third Edition (1744) . . .* , rev. ed., trans. T. G. Bergin and M. H. Fisch, Ithaca: Cornell University Press, 1968.

Secondary works

Acton, J. E. E. D.- 1906 'Inaugural Lecture on the Study of History', in *idem, Renaissance to Revolution. The Rise of the Free State. Lectures on Modern History*, ed. H. Kohn, London: Macmillan, 1906, repr. New York: Schocken, 1961, pp. 3–30.

Astarita, T. 1992 *The Continuity of Feudal Power: The Caracciolo di Brienza in Spanish Naples*, Cambridge Studies in Early Modern History, Cambridge: Cambridge University Press.

Baldwin, J.W. 1986 *The Government of Philip Augustus: Foundations of French Royal Power in the Middle Ages*, Berkeley: University of California Press.

Barret-Kriegel, B. 1988 *Les historiens et la monarchie*, 4 vols, Les Chemins de l'histoire, Paris: Presses universitaires de France.

Bean, J.M.W. 1989 *From Lord to Patron: Lordship in Late Medieval England*, Middle Ages Series, Philadelphia: University of Pennsylvania Press.

Benton, J.F. 1991 'Written Records and the Development of Systematic Feudal Relations', a paper delivered in 1981 and published in *idem, Culture, Power and Personality in Medieval France*, ed. T. N. Bisson, London: Hambledon Press, pp. 275–90.

Berr, H. 1927 Introduction to F. Lot, *La fin du monde antique*, Paris.

Bisson, T.N. 1978 'The Problem of Feudal Monarchy: Aragon, Catalonia, and France', *Speculum* 53, pp. 460–78, repr. in *idem, Medieval France and her Pyrenean Neighbours: Studies in Early Institutional History*, Studies Presented to the International Commission for the History of Representative and Parliamentary Institutions, vol. 70, London: Hambledon Press, 1989, pp. 237–55.

—— 1994 'The "Feudal Revolution"', *Past and Present* 142, pp. 6–42.

—— 1995 'Medieval Lordship', *Speculum* 70, pp. 743–59.

—— 1998 *Tormented Voices: Power, Crisis, and Humanity in Rural Catalonia, 1140–1200*, Cambridge, MA: Harvard University Press.

Bloch, M. 1913 *L'Île-de-France (les pays autour de Paris)* (orig. pub. Paris: L. Cerf, 1913 as vol. 9 of the series 'Les régions de la France', in the Bibliothèque de synthèse historique) repr. in Bloch, *Mélanges historiques*, 2 vols, Bibliothèque générale de l'École Pratique des Hautes Études, VIe section, Paris: S.E.V.P.E.N., 1963, vol. 2, pp. 692–787; trans. J. E. Anderson, *The Ile-de-France: The Country around Paris*, Ithaca: Cornell University Press, 1971.

—— 1924 *Les rois thaumaturges: étude sur le caractère surnaturel attribué à la puissance royale, particulièrement en France et en Angleterre*, repr. 1961; trans. J. E. Anderson, *The Royal Touch: Monarchy and Miracles in France and England*, New York: Dorset, 1989.

—— 1931 *Les caractères originaux de l'histoire rurale française* trans. J. Sondheimer as *French Rural History: An Essay on its Basic Characteristics*, Berkeley: University of California Press, 1966; 2nd French edn, with a Supplement based on Bloch's work between 1931 and 1944, by R. Dauvergne, Paris: Armand Colin, 1956.

—— 1953 *The Historian's Craft*, trans. P. Putnam, New York: A. A. Knopf, 1953, from *Apologie pour l'histoire, ou Métier d'historien*, revd. ed., É. Bloch, Paris: Armand Colin, 1993.

Bongert, Y. 1949 *Recherches sur les cours laïques du Xe au XIIIe siècle*, Paris: A. et J. Picard.

Bourquin, L. 1994 *Noblesse seconde et pouvoir en Champagne aux XVIe et XVIIe siècles*, Histoire moderne, vol. 27, Université de Paris I – Panthéon Sorbonne, Paris: Publications de la Sorbonne.

Boutruche, R. 1959 *Seigneurie et féodalité: le premier âge des liens d'homme à homme*, Paris: Aubier.

Brady, T.A., Jnr, Oberman, H.A. and Tracy, J.D. 1994–5 *Handbook of European History, 1400–1600. Late Middle Ages, Renaissance and Reformation*, 2 vols, Leiden: E. J. Brill.

Braudel, F. 1950 'La Martinique', *Annales. Économies, Sociétés, Civilisations* 5, pp. 494–6.

Brejon, J. 1937 *André Tiraqueau (1488–1558)*, 3 vols, Paris: Recueil Sirey.

Brosse, J. ed 1968, *Journal de ce qui s'est passé à la Tour du Temple par Cléry suivi de Dernières*

Heures de Louis XVI par l'Abbé Edgeworth de Firmont et de Mémoire écrit par Marie-Thérèse-Charlotte de France, Le Temps retrouvé, Documents, vol. 16, Paris: Mercure de France.

Brown, E.A.R. 1974 'The Tyranny of a Construct: Feudalism and Historians of Medieval Europe', *American Historical Review* 79, pp. 1063–88.

—— 1986 'Georges Duby and the Three Orders', *Viator* 17, pp. 51–64.

—— 1992 *Customary Aids and Royal Finances in Capetian France: The Marriage Aid of Philip the Fair*, Medieval Academy Books, vol. 100, Cambridge, MA: Medieval Academy of America.

—— 1995a 'The Religion of Royalty: From Saint Louis to Henry IV (1226–1589)', in *Creating French Culture: Treasures from the Bibliothèque nationale de France*, in ed. M.-H. Tesnière and P. Gifford, New Haven: Yale University Press, pp. 130–49.

—— 1995b 'Le greffe civil du Parlement de Paris au XVIe siècle: Jean du Tillet et les registres des plaidoiries', *Bibliothèque de l'École des chartes* 153, pp. 325–72.

—— 1998a 'The Trojan Origins of the French: The Commencement of a Myth's Demise, 1450–1520', in *Medieval Europeans. Studies in Ethnic Identity and National Perspectives in Medieval Europe*, ed. A. P. Smyth, Houndmills and New York: Macmillan and St Martin's Press, pp. 135–79.

—— 1998b 'The Trojan Origins of the French and the Brothers Jean du Tillet', in A. Murray ed., *After Rome's Fall: Narrators and Sources of Early Medieval History. Essays Presented to Walter Goffart*, Toronto: University of Toronto Press, pp. 348–84.

—— 1999a 'The Dinteville Family and the Allegory of Moses and Aaron before Pharaoh', *Metropolitan Museum of Art Journal* 34, pp. 73–100.

—— 1999b 'Royal Bodies, Effigies, Funeral Meals and Office in sixteenth-century France', *Micrologus: Nature, Sciences and Medieval Societies* 7, pp. 437–508.

—— 1999c 'Myths Chasing Myths: The Legend of the Trojan Origin of the French and its Dismantling', in B. Nagy and M. Sebök eds, . . . *The Man of Many Devices, Who Wandered Full Many Ways . . . : Festschrift in Honor of János M. Bak*, Budapest: Central European University Press, pp. 613–33.

Burkhardt, J. 1882 Lecture-notes 'Zur Geschichte und Historikern', trans. H. Zohn, *On History and Historians*, Harper Torchbooks, New York: Harper and Row, 1965.

Bynum, C.W. 1997 'Wonder', *American Historical Review* 102, pp. 1–26.

Cantor, N.F. 1991 *Inventing the Middle Ages: The lives, works, and ideas of the great medievalists of the twentieth century*, New York: William Morrow.

Chénon, E. 1907/8 'Le droit romain à la *curia regis* de Philippe-Auguste à Philippe-le-Bel', in *Mélanges Fitting: LXXVe anniversaire de M. le Professeur Hermann Fitting*, 2 vols, vol. 1 Montpellier: Société anonyme de l'Imprimerie générale du Midi: pp. 195–212.

Chénon, É. 1926–9 *Histoire générale du droit français public et privé des origines à 1815*, 2 vols, Paris: Recueil Sirey.

Constable, G. 1995 *Three Studies in Medieval Religious and Social Thought: The Interpretation of Mary and Martha; The Ideal of the Imitation of Christ; The Orders of Society*, Cambridge: Cambridge University Press.

—— 1996 *The Reformation of the Twelfth Century*, The Trevelyan Lectures Given at the University of Cambridge, 1985, Cambridge: Cambridge University Press.

Constant, J.-M, 1989 'Un groupe socio-politique stratégique dans la France de la première moitié du XVIIe siècle: la noblesse seconde', in *L'État et les aristocraties: France, Angleterre, Écosse, XIIe–XVIIe siècle. Actes de la table ronde organisée par le Centre National de la Recherche Scientifique, Maison française d'Oxford, 26 et 27 septembre 1986*, ed. P. Contamine, Paris: Presses de l'École normale supérieure.

Davies, W. and Fouracre, P. eds 1986, *The Settlement of Disputes in Early Medieval Europe*, Cambridge: Cambridge University Press.

Declareuil, J. 1925 *Histoire générale du droit français des origines à 1789 à l'usage des étudiants des Facultés de Droit (Première année de licence et doctorat ès sciences politiques)*, Paris: Recueil Sirey.

Delachenal, R. 1885 *Histoire des avocats au Parlement de Paris, 1300–1600*, Paris: E. Plon, Nourrit.

Dickens, A.G. and Tonkin, J., with Powell, K. 1985 *The Reformation in Historical Thought*, Oxford: Basil Blackwell.

Doucet, R. 1913 'La mort de François Ier', *Revue historique* 113, pp. 309–16.

Duby, G. 1978 *Les trois ordres ou l'imaginaire du féodalisme*, Bibliothèque des histoires, Paris, Gallimard, trans. A. Goldhammer, as *The Three Orders: Feudal Society Imagined*, Chicago: University of Chicago Press, 1980.

Du Fresne, G., Marquis de Beaucourt ed. 1892, *Captivité et derniers moments de Louis XVI. Récits originaux & documents officiels recueillis et publiés pour la Société d'histoire contemporaine*, 2 vols, Paris: Alphonse Picard.

Durand, Y. ed. 1981, *Hommage à Roland Mousnier: clientèles et fidélités en Europe à l'époque moderne*, Paris: Presses universitaires de France.

Evergates, T. 1975 *Feudal Society in the Bailliage of Troyes under the Counts of Champagne, 1152–1284*, Baltimore: Johns Hopkins University Press.

—— 1985 'The Chancery Archives of the Counts of Champagne: Codicology and History of the Cartulary-Registers', *Viator* 16, pp. 159–79.

Filhol, R. 1937 *Le premier président Christofle de Thou et la réformation des coutumes*, Paris: Recueil Sirey.

Fink, C. 1989 *Marc Bloch: A Life in History*, Cambridge: Cambridge University Press.

Flach, J. 1883 'Cujas, les Bartolistes et les Glossateurs', *Nouvelle Revue historique de droit français et étranger* 7, pp. 205–27.

Fossier, R. 1974a *Chartes de coutume en Picardie (XIe–XIIIe siècle)*, Collection de documents inédits sur l'histoire de France, Section de philologie et d'histoire, jusqu'à 1610, Série in-8°, vol. 10, Paris: Bibliothèque nationale.

—— 1974b 'La société picarde au Moyen Âge', in *idem*, ed., *Histoire de la Picardie*, Toulouse: Privat, pp. 135–76.

Freedman, P. and G. M. Spiegel 1998 'Medievalisms Old and New: The Rediscovery of Alterity in North American Medieval Studies', *American Historical Review* 103, pp. 677–704.

Fumaroli, M. 1977 'Aux origines de la connaissance historique du Moyen Âge: humanisme, réforme et gallicanisme au XVIe siècle', *XVIIe siècle* 114/115, pp. 5–29.

Gallet, J. 1981 'Fidélité et féodalité: quelques aspects de la fidélité des vassaux en Bretagne au XVIIe siècle', in Y. Durand ed., *Hommage à Roland Mousnier. Clientèles et fidélités en Europe à l'époque moderne*, Paris: Presses universitaires de France, pp. 105–22.

Gerhard, D. 1981 *Old Europe. A Study of Continuity, 1000–1800*, Studies in Social Discontinuity, New York: Academic Press.

Giesey, R.E. 1960 *The Royal Funeral Ceremony in Renaissance France*, Travaux d'Humanisme et Renaissance, vol. 37, Geneva: E. Droz, French trans., *Le roi ne meurt jamais. Les obsèques royales dans la France de la Renaissance*, trans. Dominique Ebnöther, Paris: Flammarion, 1987.

Gilmore, M.P. 1941 *Argument from Roman Law in Political Thought, 1200–1600*, Harvard Historical Monographs, vol. 15, Cambridge, MA: Harvard University Press.

——1952 *The World of Humanism 1453–1517*, *Rise of Modern Europe*, New York: Harper.

—— 1963 'The Renaissance Conception of the Lessons of History', in *idem*, *Humanists and Jurists: Six Studies in the Renaissance*, Cambridge, MA: Belknap Press of Harvard University Press, pp. 1–37.

Giordanengo, G. 1988 *Le droit féodal dans les pays de droit écrit: l'exemple de la Provence et du*

Dauphiné, XIIe-début XIVe siècle, Bibliothèques des Écoles françaises d'Athènes et de Rome, 1st ser., vol. 266, Rome: École française de Rome.

—— 1990 'Les droits savants au Moyen Âge: textes et doctrines. La recherche en France depuis 1968', *Bibliothèque de l'École des chartes* 148, pp. 439–76.

Harriss, G.L. 1981 Introduction to K.B. McFarlane, *England in the Fifteenth Century*, London, pp. ix–xxvii.

Harsgor, M. 1980 *Recherches sur le personnel du conseil du roi sous Charles VIII et Louis XII. Thèse présentée devant l'Université de Paris le 25 novembre 1972*, 4 vols, Lille and Paris: Atelier Reproduction des thèses, Université de Lille III, and Honoré Champion.

Hassinger, E. 1959 *Das Werden des neuzeitlichen Europa, 1300–1600*, Geschichte der Neuzeit, Braunschweig: Georg Westermann, 1959, 2nd edn, 1966.

Head, T. and Landes, R. eds 1992, *The Peace of God. Social Violence and Religious Response in France around the Year 1000*, Ithaca: Cornell University Press.

Hexter, J.H. 1972 'Fernand Braudel and the *Monde Braudellien . . .* ', *Journal of Modern History* 44, pp. 480–539.

Hilton, R.H. 1977 'Feudalism and Capitalism', *Times Literary Supplement*, 15 April, p. 461.

Huizinga, J. 1919 *Herfsttij der middeleeuwen. Studie over levens- en gedachtenvormen der veertiende en vijftiende eeuw in Frankrijk en de Nederlanden*, trans. F. Hopman, *The Waning of the Middle Ages. A Study of the Forms of Life, Thought and Art in France and the Netherlands in the XIVth and XVth Centuries*, 1921, revd. trans., based on the 1921 edn but heavily influenced by the German translation, R.J. Payton and U. Mammitzsch, *The Autumn of the Middle Ages*, Chicago: University of Chicago Press, 1996.

Huppert, G. 1970 *The Idea of Perfect History: Historical Erudition and Historical Philosophy in Renaissance France*, Urbana: University of Illinois Press.

Jouanna, A. 1982 'Histoire et polémique en France dans la deuxième moitié du XVIème siècle', *Storia della storiografia / Histoire de l'historiographie / History of Historiography / Geschichte der Geschichtsschreibung* 2, pp. 57–76.

—— 1996 *La France du XVIe siècle, 1483–1598*, Collection Premier Cycle, Paris: Presses universitaires de France.

Kaminsky, H. 1986 Review of František Šmahel, *La révolution hussite. Une anomalie historique* (Paris: Presses universitaires de France, 1985), in *Speculum* 61, pp. 704–6.

—— 1998 'The Problematics of "Heresy" and "The Reformation"', in *Häresie und vorzeitige Reformation im Spätmittelalter*, ed. F. Šmahel, Schriften des Historischen Kollegs Kolloquien, vol. 39, Munich: R. Oldenbourg, pp. 1–22.

Kaminsky, H. and Van Horn Melton, J. 1984 Introduction to their translation of O. Brunner, *Land and Lordship: Structures of Governance in Medieval Austria*, Middle Ages Series, Philadelphia PA: University of Pennsylvania Press.

Kelley, D.R. 1970 *Foundations of Modern Historical Scholarship: Language, Law, and History in the French Renaissance*, New York: Columbia University Press.

—— 1984a *History, Law and the Human Sciences: Medieval and Renaissance Perspectives*, Variorum Collected Studies Series, London: Variorum.

—— 1984b 'The Rise of Legal History in the Renaissance', originally publ. 1970, repr. in *idem, History, Law and the Human Sciences: Medieval and Renaissance Perspectives*, Variorum Collected Studies Series, London: Variorum, no. V.

—— 1984c *Historians and the Law in Postrevolutionary France*, Princeton: Princeton University.

—— 1991 *Renaissance Humanism*, Twayne Studies in Intellectual and Cultural History, 2 vols, Boston: Twayne Publishers.

Krynen, J. 1993 *L'empire du roi: Idées et croyances politiques en France XIIIe–XVe siècle*, Bibliothèque des histoires, Paris: Gallimard.

Legendre, P. 1988 'La France et Bartole', originally publ. 1961, in *idem, Écrits juridiques du Moyen Âge occidental*, Collected Studies Series, London: Variorum, no. VII.

Le Roy Ladurie, E. 1987 *L'etat royal: de Louis XI à Henri IV, 1460–1610*, Histoire de France Hachette, Paris: Hachette, trans. J. Vale, *The French Royal State, 1460–1610*, Oxford: Blackwell, 1994.

Letwin, W. 1977 'The Contradictions of Serfdom', in *Times Literary Supplement*, 25 March, pp. 373–5.

Lewis, P. 1968 *Later Medieval France: The Polity*, London: Macmillan.

Lopez, R.S. 1951 'Still Another Renaissance?' *American Historical Review* 57, pp. 1–21.

Lot, F. 1927 *La fin du monde antique et le début du Moyen Âge avec quatre cartes et trois planches hors texte*, L'évolution de l'humanité, synthèse collective, vol. 31 (Deuxième section, vol. II, *L'effondrement de l'empire et l'affaiblissement de l'idée monarchique*, vol. 1), Paris: La Renaissance du Livre, trans. P. Leon and M. Leon, *The End of the Ancient World and the Beginnings of the Middle Ages*, trans. 1931, repr. with introduction by G. Downey, New York: Harper, 1961.

Mackrell, J.Q.C. 1973 *The Attack on 'Feudalism' in Eighteenth-Century France*, Studies in Social History, London and Toronto: Routledge and Kegan Paul, and the University of Toronto Press.

Maffei, D. 1956 *Gli inizi dell' Umanesimo giuridico*, Milan: A. Giuffrè.

McFarlane, K.B. 1944 (1981) 'Parliament and "Bastard Feudalism"', *Transactions of the Royal Historical Society* 4th ser., 26, pp. 53–79, repr. in *idem, England in the Fifteenth Century*, pp. 1–21.

—— 1945 (1981) '"Bastard Feudalism"', *Bulletin of the Institute for Historical Research* 20, pp. 161–80, repr. in *England in the Fifteenth Century*, pp. 23–43.

—— 1981 *England in the Fifteenth Century: Collected Essays*, London: Hambledon Press.

Mortari, V.P. 1962 *Diritto romano e diritto nazionale in Francia nel secolo XVI*, Milan: A. Giuffrè.

Mousnier, R. 1969 *Les hiérarchies sociales de 1450 à nos jours*, Collection SUP, 'L'historien', vol. 1, Paris: Presses universitaires de France.

Nelson, J.L. 1994 Review of T. Head and R. Landes eds, *The Peace of God*, 1992, in *Speculum* 69, pp. 163–9.

Petot, P. 1951 'Le droit privé français', in *Umanesimo e scienza politica. Atti del Congresso Internazionale di Studi Umanistici Roma -Firenze, 1949*, ed. Enrico Castelli, Milan: Carlo Marzorati, pp. 347–51.

Pocock, J.G.A. 1957 *The Ancient Constitution and the Feudal Law: A Study of English Historical Thought in the Seventeenth Century*, Cambridge: Cambridge University Press.

Post, G. 1964 'Public Law, the State, and Nationalism', in *idem, Studies in Medieval Legal Thought: Public Law and the State*, Princeton: Princeton University Press, pp. 434–93.

Radding, C.M. 1985 *A World Made by Men: Cognition and Society, 400–1200*, Chapel Hill NC: University of North Carolina Press.

Reulos, M. 1963 'L'importance des praticiens dans l'humanisme juridique', in *Pédagogues et juristes. Congrès du Centre d'Études Supérieures de la Renaissance de Tours. Été 1960, De Pétrarque à Descartes*, vol. 4, Paris: J. Vrin, pp. 119–33.

Reuter, T. 1998, 'Medieval: Another Tyrannous Construct', *The Medieval History Journal* 1, pp. 25–45.

Reynolds, S. 1984 *Kingdoms and Communities in Western Europe, 900–1300*, Oxford: Clarendon Press, 1984, 2nd revd edn, 1997.

—— 1994 *Fiefs and Vassals: The Medieval Evidence Reinterpreted*, Oxford: Oxford University Press.

Richmond, C. 1998 'The Not-Distant Past', in *Times Literary Supplement*, 23 October, p. 33.

Sagnac, P. and Caron, P. eds 1907, *Les Comités des droits féodaux et de législation et l'abolition du régime seigneurial (1789–1793)*, Collection de documents inédits sur l'histoire économique de la Révolution française, vol. 22, Paris: Imprimerie nationale.

Ségal, A. 1991 'Périodisation et didactique: le "moyen âge" comme obstacle à l'intelligence des origines de l'Occident', in *Périodes: la construction du temps historique. Actes du Ve Colloque d'Histoire au Présent* (Paris, 1–2 December 1989), *Sources*, vols 23–24, Paris: Éditions de l'École des Hautes Études en Sciences Sociales et Histoire au Présent, pp. 105–14.

Southern, R.W. 1953 *The Making of the Middle Ages*, New Haven: Yale University Press.

Spiegel, G.M. 1997 'In the Mirror's Eye: The Writing of Medieval History in North America', in *idem, The Past as Text: The Theory and Practice of Medieval Historiography*, Parallax: Re-Visions of Culture and Society, Baltimore: Johns Hopkins University Press, pp. 57–80.

Strayer, J.R. 1972 'The Fourth and the Fourteenth Centuries', *American Historical Review* 77, pp. 1–14.

Stubbs, W. 1867 'Inaugural' (7 February 1867), in *idem, Seventeen Lectures on the Study of Medieval and Modern History and Kindred Subjects Delivered at Oxford, under Statutory Obligation in the Years 1867–1884*, Oxford: Clarendon Press, 1886; repr. New York: Howard Fertig, 1967, pp. 1–25.

—— 1880 'On the Characteristic Differences Between Medieval and Modern History', lecture delivered on 17 April 1880, in *idem, Seventeen Lectures on the Study of Medieval and Modern History and Kindred Subjects Delivered at Oxford, under Statutory Obligation in the Years 1867–1884*, Oxford, Clarendon Press, 1886; repr. New York, Howard Fertig, 1967, pp. 224–40.

Teall, E. 1965 'The Seigneur of Renaissance France: Advocate or Oppressor?', *Journal of Modern History* 37, pp. 131–50.

—— 1978 'The Myth of Royal Centralization and the Reality of the Neighborhood: The Journals of the Sire de Gouberville, 1549–62', in *Social Groups and Religious Ideas in the Sixteenth Century*, ed. M. U. Chrisman and O. Gründler, Studies in Medieval Culture, vol. 13, Kalamazoo MI, The Medieval Institute, Western Michigan University, pp. 1–11, 139–51.

Thireau, J.-L. 1986 *Charles du Moulin (1500–1566). Étude sur les sources, la méthode, les idées politiques et économiques d'un juriste de la Renaissance*, Travaux d'Humanisme et Renaissance, vol. 176, Geneva: Droz.

Troje, H.E. 1993 'Arbeitshypothesen zum Thema "Humanistische Jurisprudenz"', orig. publ. 1970, repr. in *Humanistische Jurisprudenz: Studien zur europäischen Rechtswissenschaft unter dem Einfluss des Humanismus*, Internationale Bibliothek der Wissenschaften, Bibliotheca Eruditorum, vol. 3, Goldbach: Keip Verlag, pp. 77–123.

White, S.D. 1978 '"*Pactum . . . Legem Vincit* and *Amor Judicium*": Settlement of Disputes by Compromise in Eleventh-Century Western France', *American Journal of Legal History* 22, pp. 281–308.

—— 1986 'Feuding and Peace-Making in the Touraine around the Year 1100', *Traditio* 42, pp. 195–263.

—— 1995 'Proposing the Ordeal and Avoiding It: Strategy and Power in Western French Litigation, 1050–1110', in *Cultures of Power: Lordship, Status, and Process in Twelfth-Century Europe*, ed. T. N. Bisson, Middle Ages Series, Philadelphia PA: University of Pennsylvania Press, pp. 89–123.

Wright, C. 1998 *Music and Ceremony at Notre Dame of Paris 500–1550*, Cambridge Studies in Music, Cambridge, Cambridge University Press.

INDEX

—◆•◆•◆—

Abbreviations: abb. (abbess), abp (archbishop), abt (abbot), bp (bishop), card. (cardinal), ch. (church), conv. (convent), d. (daughter), emp. (emperor), emps (empress), histn (historian), kg (king), M. A. (Middle Ages), med. (medieval), mon. (monastery), O. Carm. (Carmelite), O. Cist. (Cistercian) OFM (Franciscan), OP (Dominican), pmh (post-med. histn), pms (post-med. scholar or writer), pr. (prior, prioress, priory).

711